COMMENTARY

ON THE

CONFLICT OF LAWS

SIXTH EDITION

By

RUSSELL J. WEINTRAUB

Professor of Law Emeritus
and
Holder of the Ben H. & Kitty King Powell Chair
in Business & Commercial Law Emeritus
University of Texas School of Law

FOUNDATION PRESS
2010

THOMSON REUTERS

© 2006 THOMSON REUTERS/FOUNDATION PRESS

© 2010 By THOMSON REUTERS/FOUNDATION PRESS
      195 Broadway, 9th Floor
      New York, NY 10007
      Phone Toll Free 1–877–888–1330
      Fax (212) 367–6799
      foundation–press.com
Printed in the United States of America

ISBN 978–1–59941–862–9

Mat # 40918085

To my best friend and dearest love, my wife Zelda

PREFACE TO THE SIXTH EDITION

This Sixth Edition increases coverage of comparative and international issues. Since the Fifth edition the European Union has amended the "Rome" Convention on the Law Applicable to Contractual Obligations and enacted it as a Regulation. The EU has also enacted a Regulation on the Law Applicable to Non–Contractual Obligations. Japan has adopted a new comprehensive choice—of-law code. The Court of Justice of the European Communities has rendered important decisions construing the "Brussels" Regulation on Jurisdiction and the Recognition of Judgments in Civil and Commercial Matters. This edition analyzes these developments and others in foreign countries.

Every course in conflict of laws should have a substantial comparative law component. Knowledge of the law of other countries is important in shaping arguments, even in cases where domestic law applies.

For example, in *Asahi Metal Industry Co. v. Superior Court*,[1] the Supreme Court of the United States unanimously held it unconstitutional for a California state court to exercise personal jurisdiction over a Japanese company whose allegedly defective tire valve caused death and personal injury in California. The opinion emphasizes the "international context" of the case and urges caution in asserting personal jurisdiction over foreign defendants to avoid damage to "foreign relations."[2] This is sensible, but it requires knowledge of comparative law. In the light of its own law, would Japan take reasonable offense if a United States court exercised personal jurisdiction over the Japanese defendant? How would other countries regard the assertion of jurisdiction? Apparently the Court was not aware that six years before it decided *Asahi*, the Japanese Supreme Court indicated that exercising jurisdiction over a foreign company under the circumstances in *Asahi* would be fair. Today the twenty-seven countries in the European Union and three countries in the European Free Trade Association would take jurisdiction on the *Asahi* facts.

Common parts of commercial contracts are agreements on forum and choice of law. Most such agreements contain ambiguities that are litigated repeatedly. This edition provides model provisions that avoid these ambiguities.

---

1. 480 U.S. 102, 107 S.Ct. 1026, 94 L.Ed.2d 92 (1997).

2. Id. at 115–116, 107 S.Ct. at 1034.

v

PREFACE TO THE SIXTH EDITION

There is discussion of choice-of-law problems in national and multi-state class actions and the effect of the federal Class Action Fairness Bill of 2005, which will move almost all such actions to federal district courts. Also much expanded is the examination of conflicts problems arising from different laws both in the U.S. and abroad concerning same-sex unions.

I am grateful to my colleague and expert on domestic relations law, Jack Sampson, for reading and commenting on a draft of chapter 5.

RUSSELL J. WEINTRAUB

January, 2010

SUMMARY OF CONTENTS

TABLE OF CONTENTS

TABLE OF CONTENTS

TABLE OF CONTENTS

COMMENTARY

ON THE

CONFLICT OF LAWS

Chapter 1

INTRODUCTION

§ 1.1 Description of the Subject

What is the subject matter of the conflict of laws? A fairly neutral definition, which attempts not to beg any of the questions considered in subsequent chapters, is that the conflict of laws is the study of whether or not and, if so, in what way, the answer to a legal question will be affected because the elements of the problem have contacts with more than one jurisdiction.[1] In a world in which interstate and international transactions take place with increasing frequency, no lawyer can ignore the subject. Knowledge of the conflict of laws is necessary not only for litigators, but also for lawyers who give advice or draft documents relating to interstate and international activities.

In interstate and international transactions, there are three major topics that lawyers must address either in the planning or dispute-resolution stage. (1) Where can the parties resolve a dispute by suit or other means, such as arbitration? (2) What law will a judge or arbitrator apply to resolve the dispute? (3) What will be the effect of any judgment or award? An example may be helpful.

A massive oil platform is situated off the coast of Scotland. The platform contains sleeping and recreational accommodations for two hundred workers. One of the platform's pumps develops a leak. The supervisor of the shift operating the platform orders the pump shut off until the leak is repaired. When the next shift takes its stations on the platform, a worker discovers that the pump is not functioning and flips a switch to turn it on. A spark ignites fumes that have accumulated because of the leak. The platform explodes in a roar of flame. Some workers are killed instantly, some die hours or weeks later from injuries resulting from the explosion, and some survive with various degrees of remaining disabilities. The platform is owned and operated by Thistle Oil, a Scottish company that is a wholly-owned subsidiary of Texas Oil, a Texas company. Ten of the deceased platform workers were Texas residents recruited in Texas by Thistle. The rest of the workers were or are residents of Scotland or England. Now let us consider the three major conflict-of-laws issues in the context of this case.[2]

---

1. See Restatement, Second, Conflict of Laws § 2 (1971) [hereinafter cited as Restatement, Second]: "Conflict of Laws is that part of the law of each state which determines what effect is given to the fact that the case may have a significant relationship to more than one state."

2. On July 6, 1988, the Piper Alpha oil platform in the North Sea exploded. The hypothetical case discussed here is suggested by that incident, but the facts stated in the hypothetical are not identical with those of the actual catastrophe.

1

§ 1.2   Where Can Plaintiffs Sue?

Section 1.3 indicates some of the tactical questions a lawyer should explore in deciding where to bring suit. Before he can decide, the lawyer must know what the possibilities are—which courts have jurisdiction over defendants. In our oil platform hypothetical, plaintiffs wish to bring personal injury, wrongful death, and survival suits against Texas Oil and, because liability of Texas Oil is doubtful, especially against Thistle. If plaintiffs sue in Texas, there is no doubt that there is personal jurisdiction over Texas Oil, but is there jurisdiction over Thistle?[3] If plaintiffs sue in Scotland, can they obtain personal jurisdiction over Texas Oil? If plaintiffs can obtain jurisdiction over Thistle in a Texas state court, will Thistle be able to remove to a federal court?[4] Will a Texas state court dismiss suits against Thistle brought on behalf of the Texas workers or the workers from Great Britain, or both, under the doctrine of forum non conveniens?[5] Will a federal court sitting in Texas apply Texas doctrines of jurisdiction and forum non conveniens?[6]

§ 1.3   What Law Will the Court Apply?

There are some tactical considerations in deciding where to sue that have little to do with the subject matter of the conflict of laws. For example, in the United States juries in one possible forum (the place where the plaintiff sues) may be likely to be more sympathetic to plaintiffs' contentions than juries in another place where there is jurisdiction over the defendant. But a key question that the lawyer should explore requires conflicts analysis—what rules will a particular court apply? What rules will that court regard as "procedural" and therefore apply the law of the forum? One would expect the applicability of some rules, such as those covering pre-trial discovery, to depend on choice of forum. How many other rules, that are likely to have a substantial effect on the outcome of the litigation, will the court in which suit is filed regard as "procedural" for the purposes of the conflict of laws so that forum law applies?[7] Will that court apply the "substantive" rules of its own state or of some other state?

In our illustrative case, at the time of the disaster there are three major differences between Texas law and Scottish law. Texas law, but not Scottish law, permits a decedent's estate to recover for pain and suffering between the times of injury and death. For the workers whose injuries were not fatal, Texas law, but not Scottish law, permits close family members to recover for loss of consortium, society, and companionship. Whether punitive damages are available will not be known until after pre-trial discovery. Pre-trial discovery in a state or federal court in Texas can be much more extensive than in a Scottish court. If the

---

3.   See Chapter 4.

4.   See § 4.33C.

5.   See §§ 4.33–4.33B, 4.33D.

6.   See §§ 4.7 n.139, 4.33C.

7.   The "procedural" concept is discussed in §§ 3.2C–3.2C4.

conduct of one or both defendants amounts to gross negligence or worse, Texas law, but not Scottish law, permits recovery of punitive damages.

If plaintiffs sue in Scotland, Scottish law will almost certainly apply to all claims for injury and death of Scottish and English workers and will very likely apply to claims for the deaths of the Texas workers.[8] If plaintiffs sue in Texas, there is a good chance that a Texas state court will apply Texas law to all claims against Texas Oil and to the claims of the Texas decedents against both defendants.[9] If suit is in Scotland, the judge is likely to rule against a trial by jury on the ground that the fact issues are complex and technical. If suit is in Texas, plaintiffs have a right to trial by jury. A Texas jury is likely to evaluate all elements of damages in a manner that produces much higher recoveries than the same damages determined by a Scottish judge, or for that matter, by a Scottish jury. Even if a Texas court rules that some claims are governed by Scottish law, that court will regard as "procedural" the quantification of the items of damages permitted under Scottish law.[10] Can plaintiffs sue in or defendants remove the case to a federal court sitting in Texas? If so, will the federal court apply the same law as would a Texas state court?[11]

A key question is, why bother with choice-of-law problems at all? It would be simpler to apply the law of the jurisdiction where the controversy is litigated and ignore any differences in law that may exist in other jurisdictions with which the facts have a connection. Always applying forum law would eliminate many difficult issues and use the law with which local lawyers and judges are most familiar.

Until the rethinking of conflicts problems that became widespread in the 1960's, the answer most often given to this question, often the only answer, was that we need choice-of-law rules to insulate the result from the selection of the forum—to avoid forum shopping.[12] But surely

---

8. On November 8, 1995, the British Parliament passed The Private International Law (Miscellaneous Provisions) Act. Part III of the Act creates a presumption that the law applicable to tort or delict is that of the place of injury (§ 11). This presumption is rebutted as to one or more issues arising in a case, only if it is "substantially more appropriate" to apply the law of another country (§ 12).

On January 11, 2009, Regulation (EC) No. 864/2007 of the European Parliament and of the Council of 11 July 2007 on the Law Applicable to Non–Contractual Obligations (Rome II) took effect. Official Journal L 199, 31/07/2007 p. 40. Article 4 of that Regulation applies the law of the country in which the damage occurs unless both the person claimed to be liable and the person sustaining damage share the same habitual residence or the tort is manifestly more closely related to another country. The United Kingdom has elected to be bound by the Regulation.

9. Cf. Perry v. Aggregate Plant Products, 786 S.W.2d 21 (Tex. App.—San Antonio, 1990, writ denied) (applying Texas law to facilitate recovery by an Indiana worker injured in Indiana while servicing a silo designed and manufactured in Texas by the Texas defendant); Trailways, Inc. v. Clark, 794 S.W.2d 479 (Tex. App.—Corpus Christi, 1990, writ denied) (applying Texas law to claims against a Mexican bus company for wrongful deaths of Texans killed in a bus crash in Mexico).

10. See § 3.2C4.

11. See Chapter 10.

12. See, e.g., Lauritzen v. Larsen, 345 U.S. 571, 591, 73 S.Ct. 921, 932, 97 L.Ed. 1254, 1272 (1953) (Jackson, J.).

there must be other reasons, probably more important reasons. If the only purpose of choice-of-law rules is to make the result independent of forum choice, not only must there be choice-of-law rules, but also those rules must be uniform in each possible forum. In the oil platform hypothetical just stated, without any choice-of-law rules, the amount of damages that plaintiffs recover depends on whether they sue in Texas or in Scotland. The same thing is true although Texas and Scotland have choice-of-law rules, because the Texas rule is likely to choose Texas law while the Scottish rule is likely to choose Scottish law. If uniformity of result were our only concern, we would need choice-of-law rules designed to guarantee simple, mechanical, uniform application, such as "apply the law of the state first in alphabetical order."[13] Such a rule, if applied generally to conflicts problems, would be ridiculous. But why? Because there are factors involved in choosing the applicable law other than insuring uniformity of result and at least equally as important as the uniformity factor. What are these other factors and how should we shape choice-of-law rules to take account of them? These are the questions that are the focus of the choice-of-law discussions in this book.

In the past, the quest to provide conflicts questions with answers that are responsive to the underlying problems has not gone well. Dean Prosser remarked that "the realm of the conflict of laws is a dismal swamp, filled with quaking quagmires, and inhabited by learned but eccentric professors who theorize about mysterious matters in a strange and incomprehensible jargon. The ordinary court, or lawyer, is quite lost when engulfed and entangled in it."[14]

There are three factors that might have led so wise and perceptive a scholar as William Prosser to make this statement. First, the problems of the conflict of laws are difficult. On the interstate level, these problems reach to the taproots of our federalism. On the international level, choice-of-law solutions are further complicated by the increased difficulty of understanding and applying foreign law and by the likelihood that differences in legal rules between countries will represent more fundamental social and political disagreements than differences in laws between sister states. One cannot restate difficult and complex problems simply without distorting them. This does not mean that the judge, lawyer, or law student who is not a conflicts specialist is unable to understand and resolve conflicts problems. It does mean that one should expect simplistic approaches to the conflict of laws to be no more satisfactory than such approaches are in other areas in which the

---

13. See B. Currie, *The Verdict of Quiescent Years: Mr. Hill and the Conflict of Laws,* 28 U. Chi. L. Rev. 258, 279 (1961). Professor Currie later referred to this suggestion as "facetious". B. Currie, *The Disinterested Third State,* 28 Law & Contemp. Problems 754, 765 (1963).

For a close approximation of Currie's "state first in alphabetical order," see Mobil Oil Exploration Co. v. Federal Energy Regulatory Commission, 814 F.2d 998 (5th Cir.1987) (when petitions for review of Commission orders are filed substantially simultaneously in two circuits, by agreement of both courts, venue would be decided by a coin toss).

14. Prosser, *Interstate Publication,* 51 Mich. L. Rev. 959, 971 (1953).

resources of the legal institution are employed to resolve varied and important social problems.

Second, Dean Prosser's remarks may have been prompted by the fact that the efforts by courts to solve conflicts problems have often been unsatisfactory. Many of the "rules" of the conflict of laws that have evolved are rigid, concept-ridden, dogma-ridden things, evidencing little insight into the real nature of the problems that they are attempting to solve.

Third, the fault lies in part with "eccentric professors." The field of conflict of laws has been blessed through the years with its share of professors of giant intellect, who were not "eccentric," who wrote lucidly and brilliantly, and who were surely not given to spouting "jargon"— men like Lorenzen and Walter Wheeler Cook and Stumberg. But much conflicts literature was written as though addressed only to other specialists. Moreover, much of the writing was metaphysical in manner, conveying the impression that there was something in the nature of the universe that made the law of the place of injury in torts or the law of the place of making in contracts, the proper governing law, whether or not this solution responded satisfactorily to the needs of real people in a real world. When this happened, the "jargon" could indeed be strange, and heaven help the uninitiated one who attempted a translation.

This state of affairs could not continue. Conflicts problems are too widespread, of too great practical importance, to be ignored. The problems must be thought out and solved in clear, understandable terms. The rules in this area must be shaped and often reshaped to yield not only solutions, but solutions that are responsive to modern social realities.

Since the early 1960's there has been a revolutionary change in choice-of-law analysis reflected not only in United States court decisions and statutes but also in foreign judgments, legislation abroad, and multinational treaties. Rules that take account of the content and purposes of the competing laws have replaced simple territorial rules, such as that selecting the law of the place of injury to apply to torts. Not all commentators applaud this change. Richard Posner, formerly professor at the University of Chicago Law School and now Judge in the Seventh Circuit, decries "the destruction of certainty in the field of conflict of laws as a result of the replacement of the mechanical common law rules by 'interest analysis.' "[15] The largely displaced territorial rules created problems. The new choice-of-law methods solve some of these problems but create others. It is a matter of judgment which set of problems is preferable, the old ones or the new ones. One of the purposes of this book is to assist the reader in making this judgment.

§ 1.4 What Is the Effect of a Judgment?

The effect of the Full Faith and Credit Clause of the United States Constitution[16] is generally to require sister states [17] to give a judgment

---

15. Richard A. Posner, The Problems of Jurisprudence 430 (1990).

16. U.S. Const. Art. IV, § 1.

17. Federal courts are required by 28 U.S.C.A. § 1738 to give full faith and credit to state judgments. A state judgment has the same preclusive effect in federal court as it had

the same claim and issue preclusion effect that it has in the state that rendered it.[18] With the exception of specialized tax treaties[19] and the occasional operation of a friendship, commerce, and navigation treaty,[20] the United States is not a party to any convention that requires recognition of judgments. Most United States jurisdictions recognize and enforce the judgments of other countries.[21] The perception that this favor is not reciprocated abroad caused the United States to propose that the Hague Conference on Private International Law[22] undertake the drafting of a multinational judgments-recognition treaty. The Hague Conference has apparently abandoned an attempt to draft a general judgment-recognition treaty. The failure resulted from disagreements between United States and European Union representatives and from opposition by human-rights litigators, trial lawyers, and e-commerce businesses. The Conference instead has promulgated a convention that enforces choice-of-forum agreements and requires enforcement of judgments rendered by the chosen forum.[23]

Returning to our oil-platform disaster, because of the difference in damages under Scottish and Texas law, it would be advantageous for the plaintiffs to sue in Texas and have Texas law applied. If a large judgment is obtained against Thistle Oil in a Texas court, does that defendant have sufficient assets in Texas or other states of the United States for

in the state where rendered. See Migra v. Warren City School District Board of Education, 465 U.S. 75, 104 S.Ct. 892, 79 L.Ed.2d 56 (1984). For discussion of the Full Faith and Credit Clause and the implementing statute see § 11.2.

18. For discussion of the effect of a judgment in the state that rendered it and full faith and credit to this effect in other states see §§ 11.3–11.5.

19. *See* Alan R, Johnson et al., *Reciprocal Enforcement of Tax Claims Through Tax Treaties*, 33 TAX LAW. 469, 472–73 (1980) (discussing "general enforcement" and "limited enforcement" treaties), 475–76 (discussing limited enforcement treaties designed to prevent abuse of treaties limiting double taxation), 484 (discussing mechanics of enforcement and desirability of a determination of liability by judgment in the taxing nation).

20. See Choi v. Kim, 50 F.3d 244, 248 (3d Cir. 1995) (stating that "[t]he Treaty of Friendship, Commerce and Navigation Between the United States of American and The Republic of Korea, 8 U.S.T. 2217, elevates a Korean judgment to the status of a sister state judgment"); Vagenas v. Continental Gin Co., 988 F.2d 104, 106 (11th Cir. 1993) (stating that the treaty between the United States and Greece, which guarantees to the citizens of each country the same access to the courts of the other country as the citizens of that country, precludes Alabama from applying a shorter statute of limitations to recognition of a Greek judgment than would be applied to a sister-state judgment).

21. See § 11.6.

22. The Hague Conference on Private International Law is an organization of 65 member countries focusing on the drafting of multilateral conventions covering choice of law and procedural problems of international litigation. The Conference first met in 1893. The United States joined in 1964. See Peter H. Pfund, *The Hague Conference Celebrates Its 100th Anniversary*, 28 TEXAS INT'L L. J. 531, 532–33 (1993). The United States ratified four of the Hague Conventions dealing with service abroad, taking evidence abroad, abolishing the requirement for legalization of foreign public documents, and international child abduction. Id. at 532–33.

23. Convention on Choice of Court Agreements, 30 June 2005, available on Hague Conference web site, convention number 37. See § 11.8 note 126 and accompanying text.

satisfaction of the judgment? If not, will a Scottish court recognize and enforce the Texas judgment?

Parties to any litigation arising out of the oil-platform disaster should carefully research the three questions discussed in this and the preceding two sections. Moreover, the parties should do the research before taking any action. Without this research, a plaintiff may make an unwise choice of forum and a defendant will not know whether to contest jurisdiction or what settlement to offer.

This illustration concerned an unintentional tort. Parties to interstate and international commercial transactions should ask and research the same basic questions before they sign a contract. In commercial agreements, the parties can, by properly drafted provisions, exercise substantial control over the place and method of dispute resolution, and the law that applies.

§ 1.5　Modern Theories

Section 1.3 referred to the revolution in approaches to choice-of-law that has occurred since the 1960's. These changes were spurred largely by the work of a small number of United States scholars. Following are brief descriptions of these seminal contributions to conflicts theory.

One of the landmark articles in conflict of laws is "Choice of the Applicable Law"[24] by *Elliott Cheatham* and *Willis Reese*. The article states nine policies that a court should use in shaping conflicts decisions, including "A Court should Seek to Effectuate the Purpose of Its Relevant Local Law Rule",[25] "Protection of Justified Expectations",[26] "Application of the Law of the State of Dominant Interest",[27] and "The Fundamental Policy Underlying the Broad Local Law Field Involved".[28] In commenting on these nine policies, Professors Cheatham and Reese articulate many useful insights into the nature of conflicts problems, including an especially eloquent statement of one possible choice-of-law criterion: "Sometimes a court is faced with a situation in which one of the possibly applicable laws is in tune with the times and the other is thought to drag on the coat tails of civilization."[29]

Professor Reese was also the Reporter for the *Second Restatement of Conflict of Laws*. A central feature of the Second Conflicts Restatement is the displacement of many standard territorially-oriented choice-of-law rules—rules that focus on one supposedly key event in an interstate transaction and direct the application of the law of the geographical location of that event. One such standard rule is to apply the law of the place of injury to tort problems.[30] The Second Restatement often substi-

---

24.　52 Colum. L. Rev. 959 (1952).

25.　Id. at 965.

26.　Id. at 970.

27.　Id. at 972.

28.　Id. at 978.

29.　Id. at 980.

30.　See Restatement, Conflict of Laws § 377 (1934).

tutes for these rigid rules a reference to the law of the state that "has the most significant relationship to the occurrence and the parties".[31] It is sometimes said that this "most significant relationship" test of the Second Restatement differs fundamentally from the "interest analysis" associated with Professor Brainerd Currie and discussed immediately below;[32] that the "most significant relationship" can be determined by the number of physical contacts with a jurisdiction without inquiring into the relationship between each contact and the purposes of the laws that seem to conflict. There are some portions of the Second Restatement that invite this interpretation.[33] It is with these portions of the Restatement that this book most often expresses disagreement. There is also adverse criticism of those Second Restatement provisions that do not signal the same departure from former concepts[34] as is evidenced in the tort and contract rules.[35]

Brainerd Currie, in a series of carefully wrought articles,[36] spear-headed the drive to focus attention on the often overlooked key to intelligent conflicts analysis—the policies underlying the domestic laws in putative conflict. He demonstrated that frequently a conflicts problem could be resolved by attention to these domestic policies. Consider, for example, a fact situation that sparked some of the early rejections of the place-of-wrong rule for choosing law to govern torts.[37] A husband and wife reside in state X. They go for a short pleasure drive into state Y. While in state Y, because of the husband's negligence, the automobile runs off the road and the wife is injured. Under the law of state X, a wife may sue her husband to recover damages that she has suffered because of his negligence. State Y, however, does not permit such suits between spouses.

In real cases, there is no substitute for determining the actual policies underlying common-law rules and statutes. Sources for these policies include judicial opinions, scholarly commentary, and legislative history. In our hypothetical husband-wife case, nevertheless, let us suppose that the rule at the place of accident, that wives cannot sue husbands for negligence, has as its purposes preserving marital harmony

---

31. See, e.g., Restatement, Second § 145(1).

32. See, e.g., Offshore Rental Co. v. Continental Oil Co., 22 Cal.3d 157, 161, 148 Cal.Rptr. 867, 869, 583 P.2d 721, 723 (1978): "Questions of choice of law are determined in California, as plaintiff correctly contends, by the 'governmental interest analysis' rather than by the trial court's 'most significant contacts theory.'"

33. See, e.g., Restatement, Second, § 145, Comment *e* ("In the case of other torts, the importance of these contacts [domicil, residence, nationality, place of incorporation, place of business] depends largely upon the extent to which they are grouped with other contacts."); § 188(3) ("If the place of negotiating the contract and the place of performance are in the same state, the local law of this state will usually be applied, except as otherwise provided in §§ 189–199 and 203.").

34. See, e.g., id. § 223 (validity and effect of conveyance of interest in land), § 260 (intestate succession to movables).

35. Id. §§ 145 (wrongs), 188 (contracts).

36. Most of them are collected in B. Currie, Selected Essays on the Conflict of Laws (1963).

37. See, e.g., Haumschild v. Continental Cas. Co., 7 Wis.2d 130, 95 N.W.2d 814 (1959).

and preventing liability insurance rates from being inflated by a possibly collusive suit. State Y, the state where the accident occurred, may legitimately wish to pursue these policies when the parties are Y spouses and the automobile is principally garaged in Y so that insurance rates in Y would be affected by a collusive recovery.[38] It would seem officious for Y to wish its domestic policies to control when the litigants are X spouses and X insurance rates are involved, if state X believes that the need for compensation outweighs the dangers of marital discord or collusion.

At his untimely death, Brainerd Currie had probably not fully articulated his approach to a conflicts problem in which two or more states have differing domestic policies and a choice of one state's law would impair the policy of another state. He did suggest that, in such a circumstance, the forum should reexamine its finding that its own domestic policy is relevant to the conflicts case "with a view to a more moderate and restrained interpretation both of the policy and of the circumstances in which it must be applied to effectuate the forum's legitimate purpose."[39]

David Cavers' "The Choice-of-Law Process"[40] is the distillation of a lifetime of research and thought. The heart of the book and the major contribution that it makes is the articulation of seven "principles of preference" for the solution of choice-of-law problems when analysis of the purposes underlying competing domestic laws indicates that there is a conflict in purposes that is not false or easily avoided. He suggests that such conflicts are best resolved by application of principles that do not turn on the specific content of the domestic laws in issue and that courts could agree on in advance as mutually acceptable, neutral bases for decision. Although stating the principles stated are "only as guides for decision,"[41] Professor Cavers believed that they "can serve as premises from which specific results can be derived in concrete cases."[42] His fifth principle, for example, is:

> Where the law of a state in which a relationship has its seat has imposed a standard of conduct or of financial protection on one party to that relationship for the benefit of the other party which was lower than the standards imposed by the state of injury, the law of the former state should determine the standard of conduct or

---

38. The premiums for liability insurance in an amount that complies with each state's financial responsibility law (e.g., $10,000 per person injured, $20,000 for personal injury per accident, $5,000 for property damage) reflect the number and cost of accidents involving cars principally garaged in that state and within a particular rating territory in the state. Loss data in excess of these basic rates is excluded in calculating rates for basic limits coverage. Rates for higher limits of coverage are generally the same in every state because they are determined from nationwide data. See R. Riegel, J. Miller, C. Williams, Jr., Insurance Principles and Practices 508–510 (6th ed. 1976); McNamara, *Automobile Liability Insurance Rates*, 35 Insurance Counsel J. 398, 401, 403–06 (1968); Stern, *Ratemaking Procedures for Automobile Liability Insurance*, 52 Proceedings Casualty Actuarial Soc'y 139, 155, 176–77, 183 (1965).

39. B. Currie, *The Disinterested Third State*, 28 Law & Contemp.Prob. 754, 757 (1963).

40. D. Cavers, The Choice-of-Law Process (1965).

41. Id. at 136.

42. Id. at 209.

financial protection applicable to the case for the benefit of the party whose liability that state's law would deny or limit.[43]

After publication of "The Choice-of-Law Process", Professor Cavers continued to develop his principles of preference. He gave the principles broader scope in determining the territorial reach of legislation and in deciding whether the different policies of two or more states are relevant or can easily be reconciled.[44] He developed a special principle for product liability that gives the claimant a choice between the law of the place of manufacture and the place where two or more of the following factors coincide: claimant's habitual residence, claimant's acquisition of the product, harm to the claimant or his property. But the claimant may not invoke the law of a state where the manufacturer could not have foreseen the presence of the product.[45]

Albert Ehrenzweig brought a thorough firsthand understanding of the civil law system to bear on his discussion of common law treatments of conflicts problems. To understand the choice-of-law discussions in his treatise,[46] one must begin with his views of judicial jurisdiction. The main thesis of his commentary on jurisdiction is that "the common law of *forum non conveniens,* with its stress on contacts and fairness, unhampered by a mythology of power and sovereignty, may yet create a new American law of jurisdiction based on the *forum conveniens.*"[47] It is upon this assumption, that the case will be tried in a convenient forum so that the forum's policies are properly and not officiously applicable to the case, that Professor Ehrenzweig advances his central suggestion for solution of choice-of-law problems. In his view, application of foreign law "must be *analytically* understood as an exception from the basic rule calling for the application of the lex fori."[48]

In conflicts cases concerning the validity of contracts, Professor Ehrenzweig would displace the basic rule pointing to forum law with the "lex validitatis."[49] Under this rule, a contract would be upheld if valid under "any law whose application the parties can reasonably be assumed to have taken into account."[50] Professor Ehrenzweig excepts "adhesion" contracts from the protection of the validating law—transactions in which the party in the inferior bargaining position is offered terms by the other party on a take-it-or-leave-it basis.[51] In torts, he returns to the theme of the lex fori as the basic rule for choice of law.[52] This, coupled

---

43. Id. at 177.

44. Cavers, Contemporary Conflicts Law in American Perspective, II Recueil de Cours of the Academy of Int'l Law 153 (1970).

45. Cavers, *The Proper Law of Producer's Liability,* 26 Int'l & Comp.L.Q. 703, 728–29 (1977).

46. A. Ehrenzweig, Conflict of Laws (1962).

47. Id. at 79.

48. Id. at 314.

49. Id. at 458.

50. Id. at 464.

51. Id. at 454–58.

52. Id. at 550.

with adoption of Professor Ehrenzweig's views on jurisdiction, would permit the plaintiff, in the field of accident law, to bring suit in and recover under the law of the forum having the rule most favorable to the plaintiff, provided that the forum is sufficiently connected to the parties and the occurrence so that the law of the forum has, for the defendant's protection, "reasonable foreseeability and calculability."[53]

Professors *Arthur von Mehren* and *Donald Trautman,* in their book, "The Law of Multistate Problems",[54] set forth "a functional approach or analysis, one that aims at solutions that are the rational elaboration and application of the policies and purposes underlying specific legal rules and the legal system as a whole."[55] They first "locate the concerned jurisdictions."[56] A concerned jurisdiction is one that "in view either of its thinking about the particular substantive issue raised or of its more general legal policies, such as concern for members of the community, can be taken to have expressed some interest in regulating an aspect of the multistate transaction in question."[57] Then Professors von Mehren and Trautman construct for each concerned jurisdiction a "regulating rule" that takes "account both of relevant policies expressed through the jurisdiction's domestic rules and policies peculiar to (or of special importance in) multistate transactions as distinguished from wholly domestic transactions."[58] Many of the "true" conflicts that remain after these steps, the authors believe can "be resolved by applying the rule of the jurisdiction predominantly concerned" when "one jurisdiction has ultimate, effective control . . . and in cases in which all concerned jurisdictions agree that one has predominant concern."[59] If this is not feasible, it may be that "the claims of one jurisdiction are so clearly superior that its rule should be recognized."[60] For conflicts that persist, resolution may be possible by applying "the more salutary rule from the standpoint of facilitating multistate activity."[61]

Professor *Robert Leflar's* "American Conflicts Law"[62] is the summary and refinement of the excellent work that he produced in the conflicts field for many years. He reviews the work of other conflicts scholars "to systematize and correlate the choice-influencing considerations"[63] that are useful in resolving choice-of-law problems. Professor Leflar finds that this survey of conflicts scholarship produces "a list of five, which seem to incorporate all that are in the longer lists:

---

53. Id. at 597.

54. A. von Mehren & D. Trautman, The Law of Multistate Problems (1965).

55. Id. at 76.

56. Id.

57. Id.

58. Id. at 77.

59. Id.

60. Id.

61. Id. at 407.

62. R. Leflar, et al. American Conflicts Law (4th ed. 1986).

63. Id. at 95.

(A) Predictability of results;

(B) Maintenance of interstate and international order;

(C) Simplification of the judicial task;

(D) Advancement of the forum's governmental interests;

(E) Application of the better rule of law."[64]

A major ingredient of this last "better rule" is whether one of the competing domestic rules, when compared with the other domestic rule, "is anachronistic, behind the times".[65]

Most *law and economics* scholars disapprove of modern approaches to choice of law.*

In the third edition of his classic work, Economic Analysis of Law,[66] Judge, formerly Professor, Richard A. Posner, inserted a one-page section on "Choice of Law."[67] He poses a case in which "a resident of State A, while driving in State B, injures a resident of B who sues."[68] He states that the law of B should apply because that state has "a comparative regulatory advantage in regard to accidents which occur in B."[69] It may be that by "comparative regulatory advantage" he is referring only to rules of the road, such as speed limits: "Presumably B's Rules are tailored to driving conditions—the state of the roads, weather, etc.—in B."[70]

He goes on to decry the fact that the place of tort rule "has given way in most states to a more complex analysis of the respective 'interests' of the states affected by the suit."[71] He then states: "The issue ought not to be interests; it ought be which state's law makes the best 'fit' with the circumstances of the suit."[72] When explaining what he means by "fit", however, he engages in the very Currie-style interest analysis that he purports to disapprove, including an inquiry into the purposes of the rule in question.[73] He concludes by changing the hypothetical with which he began to "a case where two residents of state A are involved in a collision in state B." Judge Posner then departs from

---

64. Id.

65. Id. at 298.

* Taken from Weintraub, *The Choice-of-Law Rules of the European Community Regulation on the Law Applicable to Non–Contractual Obligations: Simple and Predictable, or Consequences–Based, or Neither?*, 43 Tex. Int'l L. J. 401, 402–404, 407 (2008).

66. R. Posner, Economic Analysis of Law (3rd ed. 1986).

67. Id. § 21.15. pp. 553–54.

68. Id. at 553.

69. Id. at 554.

70. Id. But see Goldsmith & Sykes, *Lex Loci Delictus* and Global Economic Welfare, 120 Harv. L. Rev. 1137, 1147 (2007) (stating that Posner's "comparative regulatory advantage argument for *lex loci* is suspect" and preferring the reason that applying the law of the place of injury ensures "that all firms are subject to the same standard of liability for torts committed in a particular place").

71. Id.

72. Id.

73. Id.

the place-of-tort rule in a manner the devotees of interest analysis would applaud: "The tort rules of B will be better adapted to location-specific factors such as the state of the roads and climate conditions, but the tort rules of A will be better adapted to person-specific factors such as ability to take care."[74]

This short and somewhat self-contradictory statement prompted many law and economics scholars to apply their analyses to choice of law. The key difference between "traditional" and law-and-economics conflicts scholarship is the importance given to choice-of-law rules that produce easily predictable results. In *Reich v. Purcell*[75] Justice Traynor of the Supreme Court of California, a devotee of interest analysis, states: "Ease of determining applicable law and uniformity of rules of decision, however, must be subordinated to the objective of proper choice of law in conflict cases, i.e., to determine the law that most appropriately applies to the issue involved."[76] Most law and economics scholars would disagree. They prefer clear choice-of-law rules, such as the place of injury for torts and the situs of land for issues concerning real estate.[77] Clear rules, they contend, are efficient because they enable the parties to know before they act which law will apply and to conform their conduct to that law. After a claim arises, clear choice-of-law rules facilitate settlement and reduce the costs of litigation.[78] For the same efficiency reasons, law and economics scholars would permit contracting parties' complete freedom in choosing the law to apply to their transaction.[79] Some would permit no judge-made exceptions to enforcement of choice-of-law agreements and reserve to legislatures the power to indicate what mandatory rules are not subject to avoidance.[80]

Law and economics scholars find modern approaches to choice of law unpredictable, chaotic,[81] and prejudiced in favor of plaintiffs and forum

74. Id. See Solimine, *An Economic and Empirical Analysis of Choice of Law*, 24 Ga. L. Rev. 49, 65 (1989) (stating that a "criticism of Judge Posner's economic analysis of choice of law is that it utilizes the tools of interest analysis, the very theory he is criticizing").

75. 67 Cal.2d 551, 63 Cal.Rptr. 31, 432 P.2d 727 (1967).

76. Id. at 555, 63 Cal.Rptr. at 34, 432 P.2d at 730.

77. See O'Hara & Ribstein, *From Politics to Efficiency in Choice of Law*, 67 U. Chi. L. Rev. 1151, 1191 (2000); Rüle, *Methods and Approaches in Choice of Law: An Economic Perspective*, 24 Berkeley J. Int'l L. 801, 819 (2006) (stating that application of the law of the place of injury "is the most efficient way to handle the dispute"). But see Trachtman, *Economic Analysis of Prescriptive Jurisdiction*, 42 Va. J. Int'l L. 1, 77 (2001) (stating that "if clear entitlements do not match well with the distribution of effects, then under high transaction costs circumstances, another arrangement may be preferable").

78. Michaels, Two Economists, Three Opinions?, in An Economic Analysis of Private International Law 143, 156 (J. Basedow & T. Kono eds.) (2006). Professor Michaels is stating the typical position of law and economics scholars. He does not agree. See id. 168: "If only one state is interested in regulation ('false conflict') it is efficient, under both Pareto [everybody affected better off] and Kaldor–Hicks [benefits exceed costs] criteria, to give jurisdiction to that state."

79. See O'Hara & Ribstein, supra note 77, at 1152–53.

80. See Id. at 1153.

81. See R. Posner, The Problems of Jurisprudence 430 (1990) (decrying "the destruction of certainty in the field of conflict of laws as a result of the replacement of the mechanical common law rules by 'interest analysis' "); Guzman. *Choice of Law: New*

law.[82] They reject any analysis that focuses on the purposes underlying conflicting rules because of the difficulty of determining those purposes.[83]

I regard as unsound these criticisms of approaches to choice of law that focus on the consequences of selecting the applicable law. Judicial decisions that appear to be chaotic and unpredictable are the result of misunderstanding and misapplying consequence-based approaches rather than inherent defects in those approaches.[84] Determining the policies served by a common law rule or statute requires thoughtful research and analysis. Identifying those purposes, however, is essential to proper application of that rule or statute, even in a purely domestic context.[85] Often in cases confined to a single jurisdiction, the result of litigation is in doubt because there are conflicting reasonable contentions as to what rule applies or the result reached under that rule in a particular factual context.[86] I do not understand why choice-of-law rules should be singled out for reduction to mindless rigidity rather than rules of tort, contract, and other substantive areas. The answer may lie in the fact that some law-and-economics scholars do not regard choice-of-law rules as substantive, but as aspects of procedure, the simpler the better.[87] As the Louisiana Conflicts of Law Code[88] indicates, it is possible the shape

---

Foundations, 90 Geo. L. J. 883, 893 (2002); O'Hara & Ribstein, supra note 77, at 1164 ("public policy inquiries thwart certainty and predictability");

82. See Goldsmith & Sykes, supra note 70, at 1137; Rüle, supra note 77, at 828.

Both articles cite the empirical studies by professors Borchers and Solimine. See Borchers, *The Choice-of-Law Revolution: An Empirical Study*, 49 Wash. & Lee L. Rev. 357, 377 (1992) (modern approaches favor forum law, recovery, and less clearly, residents); Solimine, supra note 74, at 86–87. But cf. Thiel, *Choice of Law and the Home–Court Advantage: Evidence*, 2 Am. L. & Econ. Rev. 291 (2000) (stating that after correcting the Borchers and Solimine data to take account of differences in legal culture (id. at 307) he finds "relatively strong support for the 'pro-recovery' bias of courts, weaker support for 'pro-forum-law' bias, and reject[s] the 'pro-resident' bias"). Professor Solimine, however, noted these differences in legal culture. See Solimine, supra note 74, at 79 (stating that "state courts low on prestige or reputation, tort law innovation, and legal professionalism tend to have retained the situs approach in choice of law").

83. See Guzman, supra note 81, at 893; O'Hara & Ribstein, Conflict of Laws and Choice of Law, in 5 Encyclopedia of Law and Economics 631, 641 (B. Bouckaert & G De Geest, eds., 2000); Rüle, supra note 77, at 836.

84. See, e.g, Dym v. Gordon, 16 N.Y.2d 120, 209 N.E.2d 792, 262 N.Y.S.2d 463 (1965), overruled, Tooker v. Lopez, 24 N.Y.2d 569, 249 N.E.2d 394, 301 N.Y.S.2d 519 (1969).

85. *See, e.g.*, In re Bay Area Citizens Against Lawsuit Abuse, 982 S.W.2d 371, 380 (Tex. 1998) (citations omitted) (stating that "[c]ourts also look to legislative intent when construing a statute. To determine legislative intent, courts may consider the language of the statute, the legislative history, the nature and object to be obtained, and the consequences that would follow from alternate constructions").

86. *See, e.g.*, Peevyhouse v. Garland Coal & Mining Co., 382 P.2d 109 (Okla. 1962) (holding that land owner is only entitled to compensation in the amount of reduced market value when mining company did not performed promised restoration, but four justices dissent).

87. See O'Hara & Ribstein, supra note 77, at 639: "colleagues and higher courts are much less likely to attempt to vigilantly protect choice of law precedents than they are to protect precedents that shape forum substantive law."

88. La. C. C. arts. 3515–3549.

choice-of-law rules that take account of consequences and that also provide reasonable predictability.

Chapter 2

DOMICILE

§ 2.1 Introduction

The concept of "domicile" has many uses in the conflict of laws. It is the key word in many of the traditional territorially-oriented choice-of-law rules and designates the jurisdiction whose law applies.[1] Domicile is also used as a basis for jurisdiction over the person;[2] as a basis for divorce jurisdiction and jurisdiction in other adjudications affecting status;[3] to determine the existence of political and civil rights such as voting,[4] eligibility for office,[5] and entitlement to lower tuition rates at state universities;[6] as a jurisdictional basis for certain kinds of taxation such as an estate tax on intangible property[7] (e.g. stocks and bonds) and an income tax on income not earned in the state;[8] and as the key to diversity of citizenship jurisdiction in federal court.[9]

---

1. See, e.g., §§ 2.12 (intestate succession to movables), 2.13 (validity of a will disposing of movables).

2. See § 2.15.

3. See §§ 2.15B, 5.2A, 5.2H, 5.3A.

4. See Palla v. Suffolk County Bd. of Elections, 31 N.Y.2d 36, 334 N.Y.S.2d 860, 286 N.E.2d 247 (1972).

For rejection of an attempt by persons resident in two places in the same state to vote in local elections in both places, see Wit v. Berman, 306 F.3d 1256 (2d Cir. 2002), cert. denied, 538 U.S. 923, 123 S.Ct. 1574, 155 L.Ed.2d 313 (2003). The Second Circuit upholds the practice of voting registrars that permits persons with two or more principal residences in New York to choose one, but only one, as the voting residence. "Legal bright lines will always be under- or over-inclusive, but chaos is hardly preferable." Id. at 1262.

5. See Chimento v. Stark, 353 F.Supp. 1211 (D.N.H. 1973), aff'd mem., 414 U.S. 802, 94 S.Ct. 125, 38 L.Ed.2d 39 (1973).

6. See Vlandis v. Kline, 412 U.S. 441, 93 S.Ct. 2230, 37 L.Ed.2d 63 (1973).

7. See Curry v. McCanless, 307 U.S. 357, 59 S.Ct. 900, 83 L.Ed. 1339 (1939); Page v. Commissioner of Revenue, 389 Mass. 388, 450 N.E.2d 590 (1983) (securities are not converted from intangibles to chattels by Article 8 of the Uniform Commercial Code).

8. See Lawrence v. State Tax Comm., 286 U.S. 276, 52 S.Ct. 556, 76 L.Ed. 1102 (1932).

9. Galva Foundry Co. v. Heiden, 924 F.2d 729 (7th Cir. 1991), held that there was no diversity jurisdiction because defendant had not acquired a domicile in Florida. The court stated that the "main contemporary rationale [for diversity jurisdiction] is to protect nonresidents from the possible prejudice of local courts." The court found this purpose underlying diversity jurisdiction militated against finding that defendant had changed his domicile to Florida because defendant was a long-time resident of Illinois before acquiring a vacation home in Florida. Moreover, it was plaintiff, not defendant, that attempted to invoke diversity jurisdiction. Rodriguez–Diaz v. Sierra–Martinez, 853 F.2d 1027 (1st Cir. 1988), on the other hand, found that the plaintiff had acquired a domicile in New York and could therefore sue in federal court in Puerto Rico. Plaintiff had been domiciled in Puerto Rico before he was transferred from a Puerto Rican hospital to one in New York for medical treatment. Under Puerto Rican law, plaintiff was a minor incapable of acquiring a new domicile. Plaintiff wished to sue in federal court in order to have a right to trial by jury, which he would not have in a Puerto Rican court.

Thus scrutiny of domicile in some of its many conflicts roles will provide an excellent introduction to traditional conflict-of-laws analysis and provide useful insights into the reasons for the reanalysis of the subject, which has in part replaced the territorial approach. Before investigating various uses of domicile it is desirable to sketch the traditional understanding of the concept.

§ 2.2   The Concept

A person's domicile is the place with which that person is most closely associated—his or her "home" with all the connotations of that word.[10] A person can be domiciled in a nation, a state of the United States, a city, or a house within a city. He or she can have a domicile within a broader geographical designation without having a domicile in a narrower geographical designation. For example, a person may be domiciled in a state without being domiciled within any particular city within the state.[11] For interstate choice-of-law purposes, it is the state in which a person is domiciled that is significant.

Every person acquires a domicile by operation of law at birth. This "domicile of origin" of a legitimate child is that of the father[12] unless the child's parents are separated or divorced and the mother has been awarded custody of the child. In this latter event, the child's domicile is that of the mother,[13] as is also true of an illegitimate child or a child

---

10. One of the classic definitions of domicile is that of Judge, later Justice, Holmes in Bergner & Engel Brewing Co. v. Dreyfus, 172 Mass. 154, 157, 51 N.E. 531, 532 (1898): "[W]hat the law means by domicile is the one technically pre-eminent headquarters, which, as a result either of fact or of fiction, every person is compelled to have in order that by aid of it certain rights and duties which have been attached to it by the law may be determined."

Restatement, Second, Conflict of Laws § 11 (1971) [hereinafter cited as Restatement, Second]:

"(1) Domicil is a place, usually a person's home, to which the rules of Conflict of Laws sometimes accord determinative significance because of the person's identification with that place.

"(2) Every person has a domicil at all times and, at least for the same purpose, no person has more than one domicil at a time."

11. Winans v. Winans, 205 Mass. 388, 91 N.E. 394 (1910) (husband being sued for divorce had acquired domicile in Massachusetts although he left before selecting the particular location in Massachusetts where he intended to reside).

12. Restatement, Second § 14(2). But see Hernandez v. Baker, 936 F.2d 426 (9th Cir. 1991). Under the Covenant to Establish a Commonwealth of the Northern Mariana Islands in Political Union with the United States (48 U.S.C. § 1681), U.S. citizenship was conferred on persons continuously domiciled in the Islands from before January 1, 1974 through November 3, 1986 and on those who were their minor children on November 3, 1986. The court held that persons who were minor children on January 1, 1974, but not on November 3, 1986, did not automatically become U.S. citizens but must qualify on the basis of their own domicile. The opinion agreed with the district court "finding that the statute, by providing its own definition of domicile, did not intend to incorporate any common law rule that might set up a presumption that the domicile of a minor child is that of the father of the child." Id. at 427.

13. See Chapp v. High Sch. Dist., 118 Ariz. 25, 574 P.2d 493 (App.1978) (minor has domicile of parent to whom legal custody has been awarded despite fact that child is living in another state with aunt and uncle child is therefore a "nonresident" and must pay public school tuition); Miller v. Miller, 247 Md. 358, 364, 231 A.2d 27, 31 (1967) ("In the

born after the father's death.[14] It is doubtful that these common-law rules that discriminate based on parents' gender are still viable.[15]

During minority, the child's domicile follows that of the parent with whom the child lives.[16] If both parents are dead, or incompetent, or have abandoned the child, the child's domicile will be that of a close relative with whom the child is living.[17] When the child reaches majority, or earlier if the child is emancipated,[18] he or she may, if possessing the mental capacity to choose a home, change his or her domicile and acquire a new "domicile of choice". A person acquires a domicile of choice in a new state by being physically present in that state concurrently with an unqualified intention to make that place the new domicile.[19]

§ 2.3 Physical Presence

If, as is usually the case in United States conflict-of-laws cases, domicile within a state is in issue, presence within the state is required to satisfy one of the requirements for domicile. A person may become

---

case of a separation or divorce, the domicile of a child is that of the parent to whom legal custody has been awarded...."); Hines v. Hines, 220 Tenn. 437, 418 S.W.2d 253 (1965).

But see Elliott v. Krear, 466 F.Supp. 444 (E.D.Va.1979) (for diversity purposes, child is domiciled in state where he lives with grandparents rather than in state where his mother resides, although mother was granted custody).

14. Restatement, Second § 14(2). See Mississippi Band of Choctaw Indians v. Holyfield, 490 U.S. 30, 109 S.Ct. 1597, 104 L.Ed.2d 29 (1989) (because mother was domiciled on the reservation, an illegitimate infant born off the reservation and voluntarily surrendered for adoption was domiciled on the reservation within the meaning of the provision of the Indian Child Welfare Act giving exclusive jurisdiction over custody to a tribal court).

15. See Rosero v. Blake, 357 N.C. 193, 581 S.E.2d 41 (2003) (holding that the common-law rule that the custody of an illegitimate child presumptively vests in the mother has been abrogated by statutory and case law).

16. See Ziady v. Curley, 396 F.2d 873 (4th Cir.1968) (on death of father to whom custody had been awarded, child takes domicile of mother who assumed custody); Miller v. Miller, 247 Md. 358, 364, 231 A.2d 27, 31 (1967) ("[I]f custody has not been determined or fixed, it reposes in the parent with whom the child resides...."); Ehrich v. Ehrich, 7 Wash.App. 275, 499 P.2d 216 (1972).

But see Wilson v. Kimble, 573 F.Supp. 501 (D.Colo.1983) (in the light of the anti-bias purpose of diversity jurisdiction, an infant retains the domicile of his father though living in another state with his mother, when, although parents are estranged, there has been no divorce, separation agreement, or custody decree).

17. See Montoya v. Collier, 85 N.M. 356, 512 P.2d 684 (1973) (aunt, parents dead custody jurisdiction); In re Huck, 435 Pa. 325, 257 A.2d 522 (1969), cert. denied sub nom. Huck v. Fossleitner, 397 U.S. 1040, 90 S.Ct. 1360, 25 L.Ed.2d 651 (1970) (grandparent, mother dead and father incompetent—custody jurisdiction); Restatement, Second § 22, comment *i*. Cf. Dunlap by Wells v. Buchanan, 741 F.2d 165 (8th Cir.1984) (for diversity purposes, a child's domicile remains with his parents although an aunt residing in another state has been appointed guardian, when the child is residing, not with the aunt, but in a special care facility).

18. Restatement, Second § 22, comment *f*. But cf. Florida Bd. of Regents v. Harris, 338 So.2d 215 (Fla.App.1976) (because relevant regent's rule did not include emancipation, emancipated minor cannot become a resident for tuition purposes).

See also U.S. Const. Amend. XXVI, § 1; "The right of citizens of the United States, who are eighteen years of age or older, to vote shall not be denied or abridged by the United States or by any State on account of age."; Ownby v. Dies, 337 F.Supp. 38 (E.D.Tex.1971) (cannot determine voting residency of persons under 21 on a different basis than persons over 21); Jolicoeur v. Mihaly, 5 Cal.3d 565, 96 Cal.Rptr. 697, 488 P.2d 1 (1971) (same).

19. Restatement, Second § 15(2).

domiciled in a state although not yet decided in which town in the state to establish a home.[20] Suppose, however, that a person has selected particular town in a state for a domicile, enters the state headed for that town, but before reaching the town dies, or desists and leaves the state. Has that person acquired a domicile in the state before reaching the destination? The answer should be "yes" unless failure to reach the destination indicates that, although present within the state, the person did not have a present and unqualified intention to make a domicile in the state. Leaving the state voluntarily before reaching a destination within it may be evidence of absence of domiciliary intention,[21] but dying en route is no indication of lack of the required intent.[22]

The fact that the physical presence is illegal or is for illegal or immoral purposes should have no effect on the acquisition of domicile except as the purpose may indicate that the required domiciliary intention is not present. A South African court held that a husband, and therefore his petitioner wife, was not resident in Southern Rhodesia to give a court there jurisdiction for a declaration of nullity of marriage, because the husband was in that country in violation of immigration laws. The court said that the husband perhaps intended to remain if he could escape detection but that "a conditional ... intention of this kind cannot in law amount to the animus manendi necessary to establish a domicile of choice."[23] On the other hand, if an alien's legal status is consistent with domiciliary intention, the alien may acquire a domicile.[24]

---

20. Winans v. Winans, 205 Mass. 388, 91 N.E. 394 (1910). For the possibility of satisfying the physical presence requirement by the presence of a spouse, see § 2.15A n.154 and accompanying text.

21. Cf. Winans v. Winans, supra note 20. The court held that the husband being sued for divorce had acquired a domicile in Massachusetts although he left the state before selecting a residence, but there is a dictum that the result would have been the opposite if the husband had been on his way to some town in Massachusetts and had left the state without reaching his destination.

22. Cf. Marks v. Marks, 75 F. 321 (C.C.D.Tenn.1896). Whether a minor was a citizen of Texas for purposes of diversity jurisdiction turned on whether his widowed mother, who came to Texas from Tennessee, became a citizen of Texas before deciding upon a specific place of residence in Texas. The court held that she did, quoting with approval a passage from Dicey's treatise on Conflict of Laws [currently L. Collins et al., Dicey & Morris on The Conflict of Laws (14th ed. 2006)] stating that a Frenchman coming to England, intending to reside permanently in London, but dying before reaching London, died domiciled in England.

23. Smith v. Smith [1962] 3 S.A. 930, 936 (S.African Fed.S.Ct.). See also Puttick v. Attorney General, [1979] 3 All.E.R. 463, [1979] 3 W.L.R. 542 (Family Div.) (German fugitive did not acquire English domicile). Cf. Gasper v. Wales, 223 App.Div. 89, 91, 227 N.Y.S. 421, 424 (1928) (beneficiary of a trust living in New York with a mistress was not domiciled in Connecticut for the purpose of judicial jurisdiction to adjudicate him incompetent and appoint a conservator): "While the furtiveness of this New York home is one of the facts to be considered in deciding whether he intended it to be his legal domicile, it is not controlling." But see Plyler v. Doe, 457 U.S. 202, 102 S.Ct. 2382, 72 L.Ed.2d 786 (1982) (violation of Equal Protection Clause to deny children of undocumented aliens enrollment in public schools).

24. See Elkins v. Moreno, 435 U.S. 647, 98 S.Ct. 1338, 55 L.Ed.2d 614 (1978) (federal law does not prevent employees of international treaty organizations and their families, in the United States under "G–4" visas, from acquiring a domicile in the United States— remanded to Maryland court for determination of whether state law permits them to become domiciled for purpose of paying lower tuition at state university) (for subsequent

Sometimes it is necessary to determine the domicile of a person living in a house that is on the boundary line between two states. One approach is to make the result turn on where the entrance or some key room or rooms of the house are located.[25] When residence is on a boundary line, it is preferable to place domicile in the state with which the person is more closely associated in everyday domestic and business affairs.[26]

As is implicit in the term "domicile of choice", presence under physical or legal compulsion is usually not sufficient for the acquisition of domicile.[27] There is, however, some authority that even imprisoned convicts may be able to rebut the presumption that they have not acquired a domicile where incarcerated.[28] The requirement that presence

history, see section 2.8, note 56); Jagnandan v. Giles, 379 F.Supp. 1178 (N.D.Miss.1974), affd, 538 F.2d 1166 (5th Cir.1976), cert. denied, 432 U.S. 910, 97 S.Ct. 2959, 53 L.Ed.2d 1083 (1977) (classifying all aliens as nonresidents for tuition purposes violates Equal Protection and Due Process Clauses); Seren v. Douglas, 30 Colo.App. 110, 489 P.2d 601 (1971) (alien can become resident for tuition purposes once no longer holding a student visa); Alves v. Alves, 262 A.2d 111 (D.C.App.1970) (husband whose visa permits him to remain as long as he is employed by the International Monetary Fund is a resident for purpose of divorce jurisdiction); Abou–Issa v. Abou–Issa, 229 Ga. 77, 189 S.E.2d 443 (1972) (temporary visa does not preclude domicile for divorce jurisdiction); Gosschalk v. Gos-schalk, 28 N.J. 73, 145 A.2d 327 (1958) (an immigrant present under a temporary visa may be domiciled for divorce jurisdiction); Taubenfeld v. Taubenfeld, 276 App.Div. 873, 93 N.Y.S.2d 757 (1949) (same); cf. Williams v. Williams, 328 F.Supp. 1380 (D.Virgin Islands 1971) (nonimmigrant temporary worker may acquire divorce domicile even though the necessary domiciliary intention is a technical violation of immigration laws); In re Marriage of Pirouzkar and Pirouzkar, 51 Or.App. 519, 626 P.2d 380 (1981) (immigrant with expired visa who had applied for but not yet been granted resident status, is domiciled in the forum for purposes of divorce jurisdiction).

See also Nagaraja v. Commissioner of Revenue, 352 N.W.2d 373 (Minn.1984) (non-immigrant aliens in the state to pursue graduate education may acquire a domicile for the purpose of being entitled to a property tax refund); cf. St. Joseph's Hospital & Medical Center v. Maricopa County, 142 Ariz. 94, 688 P.2d 986 (1984) (an undocumented alien qualifies as a resident entitled to indigent medical care).

25. See Blaine v. Murphy, 265 F. 324 (D.Mass.1920) (diversity jurisdiction; location of rooms in which defendants habitually ate and slept).

26. See Aldabe v. Aldabe, 84 Nev. 392, 441 P.2d 691 (1968), cert. denied, 393 U.S. 1042, 89 S.Ct. 668, 21 L.Ed.2d 590 (1969), (divorce jurisdiction; although all buildings on boundary-line ranch were in California, parties domiciled in Nevada where their dominant interests were concentrated); Restatement, Second § 18, comment *h*.

27. Restatement, Second § 17.

28. See Sullivan v. Freeman, 944 F.2d 334 (7th Cir. 1991) (stating that "[t]he presumption is rebuttable—a prisoner might for example decide he wanted to live in another state when he was released and the federal prison authorities might therefore assign him to a prison in that state and that would be the state of his domicile," but finding the presumption not rebutted in this case and therefore the prisoner was entitled to invoke diversity jurisdiction in the state in which he was incarcerated); Stifel v. Hopkins, 477 F.2d 1116 (6th Cir.1973) (diversity, possibility of parole and manner in which personal and business transactions are conducted are relevant to corroborate the prisoner's state-ments); Dane v. Board of Registrars of Voters of Concord, 374 Mass. 152, 371 N.E.2d 1358 (1978) (presumption against acquiring a voting residence may be rebutted); Fowler v. Fowler, 191 Mich.App. 318, 477 N.W.2d 112 (1991) (presumption not rebutted and prisoner may not sue for divorce where incarcerated); McKenna v. McKenna, 282 Pa.Super. 45, 422 A.2d 668 (1980) (prisoner can acquire domicile for divorce jurisdiction); In re Marriage of Earin, 519 S.W.2d 892 (Tex. Civ.App.1975) (dictum); cf. Smith v. Cummings, 445 F.3d 1254 (10th Cir. 2006) (remanding dismissal for lack of diversity jurisdiction to afford prisoner an opportunity to rebut court's finding that he acquired new domicile in Kansas when he

be voluntary has often been applied to construction of the statutory term "residence," even when the context indicates that actual residence without full domiciliary intention will suffice. In *Neuberger v. United States*,[29] a German subject, while visiting his native Germany, was trapped by the outbreak of World War I and compelled to serve in the German army as a noncombatant. The court held that this did not interrupt the five years continuous United States residence required prior to an application for citizenship, stating: "But there is substantial unanimity that, however construed in a statute, residence involves some choice, again like domicile, and that presence elsewhere through constraint has no effect upon it."

Sometimes this insistence on voluntary presence may be carried too far. In *United States v. Stabler*,[30] venue of denaturalization proceedings was held properly laid in New Jersey even though the naturalized citizen was at the time imprisoned in Michigan and the applicable statute provided for venue where he resided. If a major purpose of this venue requirement was to insure proceedings at a place convenient for the naturalized person, this purpose was ill served by permitting venue in New Jersey.

§ 2.4 Intention and Capacity

Descriptions of the nature of the requisite intention to acquire a new domicile have differed from time to time. Courts have spoken of an intention to make a home in the new place "permanently,"[31] "for an unlimited time"[32] or, the most common form used by United States courts, "for an indefinite time".[33] In this period of rapidly shifting

---

requested transfer from Florida prison); Saienni v. Oveide, 355 A.2d 707 (Del.Super.1976) (process may not be served at defendant's former abode when he is incarcerated in another state—"usual place of abode" for purpose of service statute is not the same as "domicile") (collecting authority on both sides); State v. Lupino, 268 Minn. 344, 129 N.W.2d 294 (1964), cert. denied, 379 U.S. 978, 85 S.Ct. 681, 13 L.Ed.2d 569 (1965) (man imprisoned out of state was "not . . . an inhabitant of, or usually resident within, this state" within the meaning of a statute tolling the criminal statute of limitations). But cf. Bull v. Kistner, 257 Iowa 968, 135 N.W.2d 545 (1965) (for service of process, defendant's "usual place of abode" was at his family home in Iowa where service was made on his wife, although he was then imprisoned in Minnesota).

See also Curry v. Jackson Circuit Court, 151 Mich.App. 754, 391 N.W.2d 476 (1986), review declined, 425 Mich. 1203, 389 N.W.2d 871 (1986) (prisoner acquired domicile in county where imprisoned so as to be able to file a request there under freedom of information act). But see State ex rel. Henderson v. Blaeuer, 723 S.W.2d 589 (Mo.App. 1987) (a prisoner does not acquire a domicile for divorce in the county where he is imprisoned, but court states it has failed to find any "authority regarding the residency of incarcerated persons" (id. at 590)).

29. 13 F.2d 541, 542 (2d Cir.1926), aff'd, 270 U.S. 568, 46 S.Ct. 425, 70 L.Ed. 738 (1926).

30. 169 F.2d 995 (3d Cir.1948).

31. In re Estate of Dorrance, 115 N.J.Eq. 268, 170 A. 601 (Prerogative Ct. 1934), affd, 13 N.J.Misc. 168, 176 A. 902 (1935), aff'd, 116 N.J.Law 362, 184 A. 743 (1936), cert. denied sub nom. Dorrance v. Martin, 298 U.S. 678, 56 S.Ct. 949, 80 L.Ed. 1399 (1936).

32. In re Annesley [1926] Ch. 692.

33. White v. Tennant, 31 W.Va. 790, 8 S.E. 596 (1888).

populations, perhaps the Second Restatement's formulation of an intention "to make that place his home for the time at least"[34] is the most satisfactory. This domiciliary intent must be present rather than future and must be unqualified.[35]

The existence of an ulterior motive for wanting technical domicile found in a certain place does not preclude the requisite domiciliary intention, but may cast doubt upon the genuineness of the professed intention.[36] As for the effect of declarations of domiciliary intention, whether formal or informal, the court in *Matter of Newcomb*[37] stated it well: "While acts speak louder than words, the words are to be heard for what they are worth." In his "Reporter's Note" to section 18 of the

---

34. Restatement, Second § 18. See Lake v. Bonham, 148 Ariz. 599, 716 P.2d 56 (App. 1986) (holding that husband acquired domicile for divorce although intending to stay in state only so long as his employment required and then to move to Texas rather than return to California, his previous domicile).

Article 2(1) of the European Union Regulation on Jurisdiction and the Recognition and Enforcement of Judgments in Civil and Commercial Matters, EC No. 44/2001, provides that "persons domiciled in a Member State shall, whatever their nationality, be sued in the courts of that Member State." The United Kingdom enacted legislation to define "domiciled" in this context. Civil Jurisdiction and Judgments Act 1982 Ch. 27 § 41(2): "An individual is domiciled in the United Kingdom if and only if—(a) he is resident in the United Kingdom; and (b) the nature and circumstances of his residence indicate that he has a substantial connection with the United Kingdom."

35. See Crowley v. Glaze, 710 F.2d 676 (10th Cir.1983) (diversity, intention to return to former home if physical condition improves sufficiently to permit, does not prevent acquiring a domicile of choice in state where injured person is living with his mother); Julson v. Julson, 255 Iowa 301, 122 N.W.2d 329 (1963) (a husband who had selected a new home for his wife and family in Illinois and then learned that his wife desired a separation, did not lose his domicile in Iowa for divorce jurisdiction, because his intention to change his domicile was contingent on finding a suitable home for his family and moving the family into that home); Vickerstaff v. Vickerstaff, 392 S.W.2d 559 (Tex.Civ.App.1965) (that husband had not changed his domicile to New York so as to make property acquired while residing there his separate property was indicated by his statement that he had not sold his Texas house because something might go wrong with the business deal that had caused him to move to New York); Inland Revenue Commissioners v. Duchess of Portland, [1982] 1 All E.R. 784, [1982] 2 W.L.R. 367 (Ch.Div.1981) (visits to Canada with intention to return to major residence in England did not effect a change of domicile because the intention to change domicile was future, not present) (the case applies the Domicile and Matrimonial Proceedings Act of 1973 § 1(2), which creates a fictitious domicile of choice for women married before the effective date of the Act); Restatement, Second, § 18, comment *b*. But cf. Isaacson v. Heffernan, 189 Misc. 16, 64 N.Y.S.2d 726 (Spec.Term, 1946) (candidate for political office held to have acquired requisite residence in district while on furlough from Navy by making arrangements for a future move into premises in the district).

36. See Williamson v. Osenton, 232 U.S. 619, 625, 34 S.Ct. 442, 443, 58 L.Ed. 758, 761 (1914) (Holmes, J.) ("with possible irrelevant exceptions the motive has a bearing only when there is an issue open on the intent"); Morris v. Gilmer, 129 U.S. 315, 9 S.Ct. 289, 32 L.Ed. 690 (1889); Korn v. Korn, 398 F.2d 689 (3d Cir.1968) (self-serving declarations as to domiciliary intent by plaintiff seeking to establish domicile for divorce jurisdiction were contradicted by his entire course of conduct); Milliken v. Tri–County Elect. Co-op., 254 F.Supp. 302 (D.S.C.1966); Succession of Barnes, 490 So.2d 630, 632 (La. App. 2d Cir. 1986) (motive to acquire domicile in Texas to avoid Louisiana law giving relatives a forced share of her estate at death did not prevent decedent from acquiring a Texas domicile and "actually strengthens rather than weakens ... the other factual circumstances from which [domiciliary] intent is determined").

37. 192 N.Y. 238, 252, 84 N.E. 950, 955 (1908). For classic examples of courts making findings of domicile contrary to formal declarations of domiciliary intent, see Texas v. Florida, 306 U.S. 398, 59 S.Ct. 563, 83 L.Ed. 817 (1939); In re Dorrance's Estate, 309 Pa. 151, 163 A. 303 (1932); In re Annesley [1926] Ch. 692.

Second Restatement of Conflict of Laws, Professor Reese suggests that statements of domiciliary desires should be accorded more weight "in areas where normally the desires of the person concerned are supreme, such as in matters relating to the distribution of property upon death,"[38] but he finds "little evidence that such distinctions have been drawn by the courts".

Whether a person has capacity to acquire a domicile of choice turns on whether he or she has sufficient mental capacity to choose the place that the person regards as home.[39] A person may be incompetent for other legal purposes, but still have sufficient capacity to acquire a domicile of choice.[40] There is conflicting authority as to whether a guardian of an incompetent person can change that person's domicile.[41]

---

38. See Geier v. Mercantile–Safe Deposit & Trust Co., 273 Md. 102, 328 A.2d 311 (1974) (whether shares received in a stock split go to income or to principal beneficiaries would be controlled by the law of the state designated by the testator in his will and, in the absence of a specific designation, by the law of the state in which it was found he wished to be considered as domiciled at death). For another suggestion that the effect given to a declaration of domiciliary intention might differ with the purpose for which domicile is relevant, see Cook, The Logical and Legal Bases of the Conflict of Laws 205–06 (1942).

39. See Gosney v. Department of Public Welfare, 206 Neb. 137, 291 N.W.2d 708 (1980) (institutionalized person did not have sufficient capacity to form domiciliary intention and therefore was not entitled to medical assistance available to residents).

But see Juvelis by Juvelis v. Snider, 68 F.3d 648 (3d Cir. 1995), which holds that the Pennsylvania Department of Welfare may not require a profoundly retarded individual to form the mental intention required to establish a domicile in the state in order to qualify for welfare service. Such a requirement violated the federal Rehabilitation Act requirement that "[n]o otherwise qualified individual with a disability ... shall, solely by reason of her or his disability be excluded from participation in ... any program ... receiving Federal financial assistance." Instead, the state authorities must permit an individual who can "demonstrate good faith" to acquire a domicile and become entitled to welfare services if the individual has "substantial contacts" with the state.

40. Matter of Swertlow, 168 N.J.Super. 89, 401 A.2d 1096 (App.Div.1979) (person unable to manage his property had sufficient mental capacity to change his domicile to New Jersey and subject his estate to New Jersey inheritance tax); Restatement, Second § 23, comment *a*. But see Couyoumjian v. Anspach, 360 Mich. 371, 383, 103 N.W.2d 587, 594 (1960): A woman residing in Michigan was adjudged mentally incompetent and committed to an institution in Michigan. In July, 1953, she was paroled in the custody of a cousin and went to live in Pennsylvania until July, 1954. In July, 1954, a Michigan court declared her of sound mind and she immediately filed a divorce complaint in Michigan. Persons whose title to Michigan real estate was defeated by the divorce decree brought a deceit action against the attorney who represented the wife claiming that he knew that the wife did not have the requisite one year residence for divorce and that the decree was invalid. In reversing a judgment against the attorney, the court states that it could not "assume she [the wife] was capable of intending to relinquish her residence here even before she was adjudicated sane and judicially restored to her civil rights." Cf. In re Estate of Peck, 80 N.M. 290, 454 P.2d 772, cert. denied sub nom. Chambers v. Beauchamp, 396 U.S. 942, 90 S.Ct. 376, 24 L.Ed.2d 242 (1969) (mental patient presumed to be incapable of changing his domicile).

41. See Acridge v. Evangelical Lutheran Good Samaritan Society, 334 F.3d 444 (5th Cir. 2003) (person acting in best interests of an incompetent may change the incompetent's domicile, noting conflicting authority—diversity jurisdiction); Dakuras v. Edwards, 312 F.3d 256 (7th Cir. 2002) (citing conflicting authority and holding that a guardian had changed the domicile of an incompetent for purposes of diversity of citizenship jurisdiction but stating (at 259) "[w]e might reach a different conclusion ... if the sole or dominant reason for the change was to create federal jurisdiction").

§ 2.5 Retention of Domicile

A person retains his or her domicile until that person meets the physical presence and intention requirements for establishing a different domicile of choice.[42] A person, then, has only one domicile at a time[43] and it is this domicile to which traditional conflict-of-laws analysis has looked for a variety of purposes.

§ 2.6 Wives

In the United States, the concept of the domicile of a wife has evolved from (1) a wife may acquire a separate domicile if she has justifiably left her husband[44] to (2) she may acquire a separate domicile if in fact she is not residing with her husband,[45] to (3) a rebuttable presumption that the wife's domicile is the same as her husband's.[46] In

---

42. See White v. Tennant, 31 W.Va. 790, 792, 8 S.E. 596, 597 (1888): "The original domicile continues until it is fairly changed for another. It is a legal maxim that every person must have a domicile somewhere; and he can have but one at a time for the same purpose. From this it follows that one cannot be lost or extinguished until another is acquired."

For an especially striking example of the presumption that a domicile of origin has been retained despite absence, see Inland Revenue Comm'rs v. Bullock, [1976] 3 All E.R. 353, [1976] 1 W.L.R. 1178 (Ct. of App.), holding that a man who had resided in England for 41 years had not acquired a domicile of choice there and was therefore not subject to tax on income from non-English sources. His firm intention to return to Canada, his domicile of origin, if he survived his wife, who was unwilling to live in Canada, prevented him from having the requisite domiciliary intention toward England. See also Herzog v. Herzog, 333 F.Supp. 477 (W.D.Pa.1971) (diversity jurisdiction, need clear and convincing evidence to overcome presumption in favor of retention of domicile of origin); Walters v. Weed, 45 Cal.3d 1, 246 Cal.Rptr. 5, 752 P.2d 443 (1988) (students are permitted to vote in the precincts where they previously resided on campus because, although they have not returned to live on campus, they have not yet acquired a new domicile); Plummer v. Inland Revenue Commissioners, [1988] 1 W.L.R. 292 (Ch.1987) (for income tax purposes, the domicile of origin is not lost until the taxpayer's chief residence is established in a new place).

Cf. Kaiser v. Loomis, 391 F.2d 1007 (6th Cir.1968) (a native-born United States citizen cannot lose state citizenship for purposes of diversity jurisdiction without first acquiring a new domicile). But cf. Hardy v. Lomenzo, 349 F.Supp. 617 (S.D.N.Y.1972) (upholds refusal to register as voters United States citizens who have resided abroad for several years).

43. At least for the same purpose. See § 2.16.

44. Williamson v. Osenton, 232 U.S. 619, 34 S.Ct. 442, 58 L.Ed. 758 (1914) (federal diversity jurisdiction); Torlonia v. Torlonia, 108 Conn. 292, 142 A. 843 (1928) (divorce jurisdiction).

45. Turner v. Turner, 280 Ala. 523, 195 So.2d 900 (1967); Boardman v. Boardman, 135 Conn. 124, 62 A.2d 521 (1948) (custody jurisdiction); In re Florance's Will, 54 Hun. 328, 7 N.Y.S. 578 (S.Ct.1889), appeal dism'd, 119 N.Y. 661, 23 N.E. 1151 (1890) (law applicable to husband's forced share of wife's estate); Younger v. Gianotti, 176 Tenn. 139, 138 S.W.2d 448 (1940) (intestate distribution of personalty).

Mississippi adheres to the view that a wife's domicile is that of her husband during the time that they live together, even though she has never resided at her husband's domicile. O'Neill v. O'Neill, 515 So.2d 1208 (Miss. 1987) (life-long resident of Mississippi was not domiciled in Mississippi for divorce purposes while she was living in Germany with her husband, but acquired her husband's Minnesota domicile).

46. See Samuel v. University of Pittsburgh, 538 F.2d 991 (3d Cir.1976) (rule that for tuition purposes wife has husband's domicile is unconstitutional and university must refund excess fees charged); Mas v. Perry, 489 F.2d 1396 (5th Cir.), cert. denied, 419 U.S. 842, 95 S.Ct. 74, 42 L.Ed.2d 70 (1974) (diversity, husband is French citizen and wife never lived in France with husband); Napletana v. Hillsdale College, 385 F.2d 871 (6th Cir.1967)

the light of the status of women as equal participants in all aspects of modern society, the preferable presumption is simply that spouses have the same domicile.[47]

Recognition of a wife's right to obtain her own domicile has spread to other parts of the common-law world. The United Kingdom now[48] permits a married woman to have a domicile different from that of her husband.[49] Australia, for the purpose of application of its Family Law Act, and New Zealand, generally, have abolished the rule that a wife must have her husband's domicile.[50]

(diversity); Martin v. Hefley, 259 Ark. 484, 533 S.W.2d 521 (1976) (voting, wife retained residence in school district after marrying man resident in another district); Kirk v. Douglas, 176 Colo. 104, 489 P.2d 201 (1971) (tuition); Ashmore v. Ashmore, 251 So.2d 15 (Fla. App.1971), cert. dism'd, 256 So.2d 513 (Fla. 1972) (divorce jurisdiction); Dilsaver v. Pollard, 191 Neb. 241, 214 N.W.2d 478 (1974) (voting, county of residence); Commonwealth v. Rutherfoord, 160 Va. 524, 169 S.E. 909 (1933) (income and intangible property taxes); Restatement, Second § 21, comment b. But see Rumbel v. Schueler, 236 Md. 25, 202 A.2d 368 (1964) (eligibility for award from Unsatisfied Claim and Judgment Fund; wife's domicile is that of husband unless she has justifiably left him); Tate v. Tate, 149 W.Va. 591, 595, 142 S.E.2d 751, 754 (1965) (wife did not have requisite one year divorce residence in her domicile of origin when during the year she had lived elsewhere with her husband, a construction worker who moved from place to place: "[A] husband has the right to fix the domicile of himself and his wife, the wife's domicile merging in that of her husband, where such right is exercised in a reasonable and equitable manner and with honest intent.")

47. See Bowers v. Bowers, 287 So.2d 722 (Fla.App.1973), cert. dism'd as moot, 326 So.2d 172 (Fla.1976) (wife acquired domicile for divorce even though her serviceman husband did not); Perry v. Perry, 5 Kan.App.2d 636, 623 P.2d 513 (1981) (serviceman's wife, who had never resided at his domicile, did not acquire a domicile there and was not subject to personal jurisdiction in his divorce action filed there); Craig v. Craig, 365 So.2d 1298 (La.1978) (Louisiana statute providing that wife has husband's domicile violates Louisiana Constitution's proscription of "arbitrary [discrimination] because of . . . sex"); Green v. Commissioner of Corps. & Tax., 364 Mass. 389, 305 N.E.2d 92 (1973) (for purposes of state income tax, wife did not become a resident until she moved into the state to join her husband); Jones v. Jones, 402 N.W.2d 146 (Minn.App.1987) (wife had Minnesota domicile for divorce while married to a resident of Missouri); Keller v. Department of Revenue, 292 Or. 639, 642 P.2d 284 (1982) (example of spouses who are not estranged but are domiciled in different states).

H. Kay, Text, Cases & Materials on Sex–Based Discrimination 179 (2d Ed.1981) comments as follows on the suggestion in the text: "Why not simply provide that all competent adults, regardless of sex or marital status, may choose their own domicile?" So long, however, as it remains true that, with rare exceptions, spouses have the same domicile, the presumption suggested is efficient. It is also rebuttable. Fritzshall v. Board of Police Commissioners, 886 S.W.2d 20 (Mo.App. 1994), affirmed the discharge of a police officer on the ground that he was not, as required, domiciled in Kansas City. Although the discharge was not based on the fact that the officer's wife was domiciled in a house that the officer had purchased in the suburbs, the court stated: "While people who are legally married may have separate, fixed, permanent homes, such a state is not the norm for marriage." Id. at 25 n.1.

48. For the former view, see Garthwaite v. Garthwaite, [1964] P. 356 (jurisdiction to declare marriage subsisting, husband living abroad); Herd v. Herd [1936] P. 205 (deserted wife, divorce jurisdiction); H. v. H. [1928] P. 206 (deserted wife, divorce jurisdiction); Attorney General for Alberta v. Cook [1926] A.C. 444 (P.C.) (divorce jurisdiction).

49. U.K. Domicile & Matrimonial Proceedings Act § 1 (1973) (applicable to England, Wales, Scotland, and Northern Ireland).

50. Aust. Family Law Act 1975 § 4(3)(b); N.Z. Domicile Act § 5(l) (1976).

§ 2.7 Service Men and Women

Because of their obligation to go where they are ordered and their frequent change of station, persons serving in the armed forces rarely have the mental attitude toward their residence that is necessary to acquire a domicile of choice. This is illustrated by the many cases holding that service personnel have not obtained the domicile in the state where they are stationed that is necessary for divorce jurisdiction.[51] But it is not impossible for a service man or woman to obtain a domicile of choice.[52] A serviceperson may have been stationed in the same place for several years, have many close social and business contacts with the community, have built a home there in which there is cogent evidence that he or she plans to live after leaving the service, and separation from the service may be so near in the future that no further change of military station is likely. Under these or similar circumstances, a finding that the serviceperson has not acquired a domicile of choice in the community with which he or she has such close ties and the consequent denial of some right or privilege that depends upon domicile, would be contrary to the equal protection clause of the fourteenth amendment.[53]

The second Restatement draws a distinction between service personnel who must live on post and those who may live off post.[54] Perhaps this is a factor to be taken into account in passing on a claim of domicile, but required residence on post should not be controlling in the face of cogent evidence of domiciliary intent.[55]

---

51. See, e.g., Hammerstein v. Hammerstein, 269 S.W.2d 591 (Tex.Civ.App.1954). Cf. Jizmejian v. Jizmejian, 16 Ariz.App. 270, 492 P.2d 1208 (1972) (matrimonial domicile not established where stationed and that state's law does not determine marital property rights); Hron v. Ryan, 164 N.W.2d 815 (Iowa 1969) (serviceman's "usual place of abode" for service of process still his Iowa home when he is stationed abroad); Hart v. Queen City Coach Co., 241 N.C. 389, 85 S.E.2d 319 (1955) (service man stationed in forum was a "nonresident" within meaning of forum's nonresident motorist jurisdiction statute).

52. For cases holding service personnel have acquired a domicile where stationed, see, e.g., Codagnone v. Perrin, 351 F.Supp. 1126 (D.R.I.1972) (diversity); Smiley v. Davenport, 139 Ga.App. 753, 229 S.E.2d 489 (1976), cert. denied (personal jurisdiction not available under Georgia long-arm statute over defendant who committed tort in Georgia while domiciled there); Bannan v. Bannan, 188 So.2d 253 (Miss.1966) (divorce); Slade v. Slade, 122 N.W.2d 160 (N.D.1963) (divorce); Sasse v. Sasse, 41 Wn. 2d 363, 249 P.2d 380 (1952) (divorce). See also § 2.15B discussing service men's and women's divorce statutes; cf. Andris v. Andris, 65 N.C.App. 688, 309 S.E.2d 570 (1983) (even though not stationed there, service man acquired domicile for divorce in state where his father lived).

53. See Carrington v. Rash, 380 U.S. 89, 85 S.Ct. 775, 13 L.Ed.2d 675 (1965) (Texas constitutional provision preventing service men from acquiring a voting residence in Texas is a violation of equal protection).

54. Restatement, Second § 17, comment *d*: "A soldier or sailor, if he is ordered to a station to which he must go and live in quarters assigned to him, will probably not acquire a domicil there though he lives in the assigned quarters with his family. He must obey orders and cannot choose to go elsewhere. On the other hand, if he is allowed to live with his family where he pleases provided it is near enough to his post to enable him to perform his duties, he retains some power of choice over the place of his abode and may acquire a domicil."

55. For cases holding service personnel living on base had acquired a domicile, see Bezold v. Bezold, 95 Idaho 131, 504 P.2d 404 (1972) (divorce); Marcus v. Marcus, 3 Wash.App. 370, 475 P.2d 571 (1970) (divorce).

§ 2.8 Students

As in the case of service personnel, it is unlikely that a student will acquire a domicile of choice in the place where he or she is attending school. Usually the student's presence will be for the temporary purpose of acquiring an education and he or she will not regard the school's locality as "home". But this is not true of every student and the way should be left open for the finding of domicile if the facts in the case of a particular student warrant such a finding.[56]

---

56. See Vlandis v. Kline, 412 U.S. 441, 93 S.Ct. 2230, 37 L.Ed.2d 63 (1973) (irrebuttable presumption that student cannot meet durational domicile requirement for tuition purposes while a student violates due process). In Elkins v. Moreno, 435 U.S. 647, 98 S.Ct. 1338, 55 L.Ed.2d 614 (1978), the Court certified to the Maryland Court of Appeals the question of whether students are "incapable as a matter of state law of becoming domiciliaries" thus hoping to avoid the necessity of deciding whether to overrule Vlandis v. Kline or restrict it further than was done in Weinberger v. Salfi, 422 U.S. 749, 95 S.Ct. 2457, 45 L.Ed.2d 522 (1975). *Elkins* characterized *Weinberger* as limiting *Vlandis* "to those situations in which a state 'purport[s] to be concerned with [domicile, but] at the same time den[ies] to one seeking to meet its test of [domicile] the opportunity to show factors clearly bearing on that issue,'" 435 U.S. at 660, 98 S.Ct. at 1346, 55 L.Ed.2d at 625. (brackets in original). The Maryland Court of Appeals responded that G–4 aliens and their dependents could become Maryland domiciliaries. Toll v. Moreno, 284 Md. 425, 397 A.2d 1009 (1979). But the Board of Regents of the University of Maryland had already adopted a resolution requiring the G–4 aliens and their dependents to pay nonresident tuition whether or not they are legally domiciled in Maryland. The Supreme Court held this resolution invalid under the Supremacy Clause because it frustrated federal policies that permitted G–4 aliens to acquire domicile in the United States and that provided them with special tax exemptions. Toll v. Moreno, 458 U.S. 1, 102 S.Ct. 2977, 73 L.Ed.2d 563 (1982). Cf. Gaudin v. Remis, 379 F.3d 631, 637 (9th Cir. 2004) (for purposes of Hague Convention on the Civil Aspects of International Child Abduction, Canadian citizen present in U.S. under "nonimmigrant alien" status "is barred by law from possessing the requisite intent to establish a domicile" in the U.S). But cf. Mark v. Mark, [2005] 3 W.L.R. 111 (H.L., appeal from Eng., 2005): The Domicile and Matrimonial Proceedings Act 1973 § 5(2) provided for divorce jurisdiction if a party was habitually resident in England or Wales for one year before bringing suit. The court held that a Nigerian woman could acquire a habitual residence even though her presence was unlawful because she had overstayed the period permitted by her entry visa.

For cases upholding acquisition of domicile by students, see, e.g., Whatley v. Clark, 482 F.2d 1230 (5th Cir.1973), cert. denied sub nom. White v. Whatley, 415 U.S. 934, 94 S.Ct. 1449, 39 L.Ed.2d 492 (1974) (presumption that student has not acquired voting residence violates equal protection); Kelm v. Carlson, 473 F.2d 1267 (6th Cir. 1973) (making residence for tuition purposes dependent on proof that job available in state after graduation violates equal protection); Sloane v. Smith, 351 F.Supp. 1299 (M.D.Pa.1972) (enjoin applying different standards of voting residence to students than are applied to other registrants); Ramey v. Rockefeller, 348 F.Supp. 780 (E.D.N.Y.1972) (voting, test must be whether place is student's "home for the time at least"); Newman v. Graham, 82 Idaho 90, 349 P.2d 716 (1960) (tuition); Hershkoff v. Board of Registrars, 366 Mass. 570, 321 N.E.2d 656 (1974) (voting); Wilkins v. Bentley, 385 Mich. 670, 189 N.W.2d 423 (1971) (voting, must treat students as other registrants); Worden v. Mercer County Bd. of Elect., 61 N.J. 325, 294 A.2d 233 (1972) (even students who live in dormitories and intend to return to home towns are residents for voting purposes); Palla v. Suffolk County Bd. of Elect., 31 N.Y.2d 36, 334 N.Y.S.2d 860, 286 N.E.2d 247 (1972) (voting, students and other transients may be required to fill out special forms); Hall v. Wake Cty. Bd. of Elect., 280 N.C. 600, 187 S.E.2d 52 (1972) (voting); Kegley v. Johnson, 207 Va. 54, 147 S.E.2d 735 (1966) (student may acquire voting residence, but facts showed he had not). See also Auerbach v. Rettaliata, 765 F.2d 350 (2d Cir.1985) (the voter registration statute, as interpreted in Palla v. Suffolk County, *supra* this note, is not unconstitutional on its face); cf. Horton v. Marshall Public Schools, 769 F.2d 1323 (8th Cir. 1985) (public school district's policy of excluding from attendance minor children living in the district with relatives who are not their parents or legal guardians violates the Equal Protection Clause); Frankel v. Board of Regents of the Univ. of Maryland System, 361 Md. 298, 761 A.2d 324 (2000) (rule

§ 2.9 Government Employees

Two kinds of government employees present special domicile problems. First, there is the person who moves to the seat of government while in government service and, unlike an elected representative, may, consistently with his or her status, acquire a domicile of choice at the new residence. On the question of whether federal employees become "domiciled in the District of Columbia" for purposes of the District's income tax, the Supreme Court has said: "We hold that a man does not acquire a domicile in the District simply by coming here to live for an indefinite period while in the Government service. . . . On the other hand, we hold that persons are domiciled here who live here and have no fixed and definite intent to return and make their homes where they were formerly domiciled."[57]

Then there are the government employees who, because of the requirements of their employment, reside at a state or federal governmental institution or on a federal enclave. The courts have split as to whether such persons can acquire a domicile where they reside.[58]

§ 2.10 Durational Residence

The Privileges and Immunities Clause[59] bars discrimination against citizens of other states if there is no reason for difference in treatment

---

precluding in-state tuition status to any student whose primary monetary support comes from an out-of-state source discriminates against bona fide Maryland residents in violation of equal protection clause of state's constitution).

But cf. Hayes v. Board of Regents, 495 F.2d 1326 (6th Cir.1974) (voter registration not conclusive of residence for tuition purposes and state may require an intention to remain permanently); Cheek v. Fortune, 341 F.Supp. 729 (N.D.Miss.1972) (tuition, continued residency conditional on graduation and admission to bar insufficient); Florida Bd. of Regents v. Harris, 338 So.2d 215 (Fla.App.1976) (tuition, because statute does not include emancipation in exceptions, emancipated minor cannot acquire residence); Hancock v. Regents, 61 Wis.2d 484, 213 N.W.2d 45 (1973) (tuition, statute requires paid employment and filing of state income tax).

57. District of Columbia v. Murphy, 314 U.S. 441, 454–455, 62 S.Ct. 303, 309, 86 L.Ed. 329, 337 (1941). See also Arbaugh v. District of Columbia, 176 F.2d 28 (D.C.Cir. 1949) (applying *Murphy* and finding domicile).

58. Yes: Evans v. Cornman, 398 U.S. 419, 90 S.Ct. 1752, 26 L.Ed.2d 370 (1970) (equal protection clause requires granting of voting rights to residents of federal enclave in Maryland who are subject to state criminal and tax laws); Oakland County Taxpayers' League v. Board of Supervisors, 355 Mich. 305, 94 N.W.2d 875 (1959) (employees of an infirmary and juvenile home who, because of the nature of their employment, were required to live in the institutions, were "qualified electors" of the town ship in which they thus resided). No: Kemp v. Heebner, 77 Colo. 177, 234 P. 1068 (1925) (affirm upsetting of election result on ground of invalidity of votes of employees of a hospital operated by the United States government who resided in the hospital buildings); Langdon v. Jaramillo, 80 N.M. 255, 454 P.2d 269 (1969) (inhabitants of military installation, including a civilian, not entitled to voter registration in New Mexico because they reside on federal enclave under exclusive jurisdiction of the United States). Cf. Corr v. Westchester Cty. Dep't. of Soc. Serv., 33 N.Y.2d 111, 350 N.Y.S.2d 401, 305 N.E.2d 483 (1973) (resident of nursing home may acquire a domicile there and be entitled to state welfare payments).

59. U.S.Const. Art. IV, § 2.

except nonresidence.[60] Even with regard to the many rights and benefits that can validly be made dependent on state citizenship, there is a separate question as to whether there can be a durational residence requirement—a requirement not only that beneficiaries be residents, but also that they have maintained that residence for a prescribed period of time. In evaluating the validity of durational residence requirements under the Equal Protection Clause[61] the United States Supreme Court has distinguished between laws that substantially affect a "fundamental" or "basic" right, such as the right of inter-state travel, and those that do not. If a fundamental right is affected, the law must be necessary to promote a compelling governmental interest. If the law does not substantially affect a basic right, it is sufficient that the durational residence requirement be reasonably related to legitimate state policies.[62] As the three-judge federal court aptly said in *Chimento v. Stark*: "Semantics aside, the question is resolved judicially by determining what is more important to our form of government; the rights protected by the state law in question or the rights infringed by it."[63] Durational residence requirements have been upheld for divorce,[64] lower tuition at a

---

60. See Barnard v. Thorstenn, 489 U.S. 546, 109 S.Ct. 1294, 103 L.Ed.2d 559 (1989) (requirement that to be admitted to the Virgin Islands bar, an applicant must reside and intend to continue to reside there, violates the Privileges and Immunities Clause); Supreme Court of Virginia v. Friedman, 487 U.S. 59, 108 S.Ct. 2260, 101 L.Ed.2d 56 (1988) (same for Virginia's residency requirement for admission to state's bar without examination); cf. Frazier v. Heebe, 482 U.S. 641, 107 S.Ct. 2607, 96 L.Ed.2d 557 (1987) (the District Court was not empowered to adopt Rules requiring members of the Louisiana bar who apply for admission to district bar to live, or maintain an office, in Louisiana); Attorney General of New York v. Soto–Lopez, 476 U.S. 898, 106 S.Ct. 2317, 90 L.Ed.2d 899 (1986) (limiting civil service employment preference to veterans who were New York residents when they entered military service violates the Equal Protection Clause; four Justices also find a violation of the constitutionally protected right to travel); Hooper v. Bernalillo County Assessor, 472 U.S. 612, 105 S.Ct. 2862, 86 L.Ed.2d 487 (1985) (limiting property tax exemption to veterans who resided in New Mexico before May 8, 1976, violates the Equal Protection Clause); United Bldg. & Constr. Trades Council v. Mayor & Council, 465 U.S. 208, 104 S.Ct. 1020, 79 L.Ed.2d 249 (1984) (remand for determination of whether ordinance requiring at least 40% of employees working on city projects be city residents is carefully drafted to counteract city's unemployment and decline in population so as to avoid violation of the Privileges and Immunities Clause).

See also Supreme Court of New Hampshire v. Piper, 470 U.S. 274, 105 S.Ct. 1272, 84 L.Ed.2d 205 (1985) (New Hampshire rule limiting bar admission to state residents violates the Privileges and Immunities Clause); Hicklin v. Orbeck, 437 U.S. 518, 98 S.Ct. 2482, 57 L.Ed.2d 397 (1978) (priority to residents for employment on Alaska pipeline unconstitutional). But cf. Reeves, Inc. v. Stake, 447 U.S. 429, 100 S.Ct. 2271, 65 L.Ed.2d 244 (1980) (uphold policy allowing only residents to buy state-produced cement); Baldwin v. Fish & Game Comm'n, 436 U.S. 371, 98 S.Ct. 1852, 56 L.Ed.2d 354 (1978) (may charge nonresidents higher hunting license fees).

61. U.S. Const. Amend. XIV, § 1.

62. See cases cited in notes 64–69 this section.

63. 353 F.Supp. 1211, 1214 (D.N.H. 1973), aff'd mem., 414 U.S. 802, 94 S.Ct. 125, 38 L.Ed.2d 39 (1973).

64. Sosna v. Iowa, 419 U.S. 393, 95 S.Ct. 553, 42 L.Ed.2d 532 (1975) (uphold one-year requirement as furthering state's interest in avoiding meddling in matter in which another state has paramount interest and in minimizing susceptibility of decree to collateral attack).

state university,[65] and candidacy for office,[66] but struck down for voting,[67] receipt of welfare benefits,[68] and medical care.[69]

§ 2.11 Statutory Construction

Although there are exceptions,[70] the word "domicile" is rarely used in a statute. More commonly, a statute will contain a term such as "residence." When this occurs, in addition to the usual problems of determining domicile, there is the question of whether the statutory term is synonymous with domicile or is intended to convey a different meaning. The spectrum of possible meanings ranges through the following points: (1) technical domicile plus actual residence,[71] (2) domicile,[72] and (3) actual residence without domiciliary intention.[73] This problem of statutory construction should be approached in the light of the purposes and history of the statute.[74]

---

65. Sturgis v. Washington, 414 U.S. 1057, 94 S.Ct. 563, 38 L.Ed.2d 464 (1973) (summary affirmance). Cf. Vlandis v. Kline, § 2.8, note 56; Eastman v. University of Michigan, 30 F.3d 670 (6th Cir. 1994) (can require one-year residence before student eligible for resident tuition, but then must reduce tuition retroactively to the time that student became a domiciliary).

66. Chimento v. Stark, 353 F.Supp. 1211 (D.N.H.1973), aff'd mem., 414 U.S. 802, 94 S.Ct. 125, 38 L.Ed.2d 39 (1973) (seven-year requirement for governor); Gilbert v. State, 526 P.2d 1131 (Alaska 1974) (three years in state and one year in district for state legislature). But cf. Antonio v. Kirkpatrick, 579 F.2d 1147 (8th Cir. 1978) (ten-year requirement for auditor violates equal protection).

67. Dunn v. Blumstein, 405 U.S. 330, 92 S.Ct. 995, 31 L.Ed.2d 274 (1972) (except for a period not exceeding 30 days to complete administrative tasks needed to prevent fraud).

68. Shapiro v. Thompson, 394 U.S. 618, 89 S.Ct. 1322, 22 L.Ed.2d 600 (1969) (violates equal protection and due process).

69. Memorial Hospital v. Maricopa County, 415 U.S. 250, 94 S.Ct. 1076, 39 L.Ed.2d 306 (1974).

70. See the District of Columbia income tax act discussed in District of Columbia v. Murphy, 314 U.S. 441, 62 S.Ct. 303, 86 L.Ed. 329 (1941). Sometimes, even when "domicile" is used, it is not given its technical meaning. Roboz v. Kennedy, 219 F.Supp. 892 (D.D.C.1963); Cauble v. Gray, 604 S.W.2d 197 (Tex.Civ.App., Dallas 1979) ("domicile" in venue provision means residence even though domicile is elsewhere).

71. This is typically, though not universally, true of divorce statutes. See, e.g., Eames v. Eames, 463 S.W.2d 576 (Mo.App. 1971). But see Hagan v. Hardwick, 95 N.M. 517, 624 P.2d 26 (1981) (divorce residence requires domicile, not physical presence); Wiseman v. Wiseman, 216 Tenn. 702, 393 S.W.2d 892 (1965).

72. See, e.g., In re Estate of Gillmore, 101 N.J.Super. 77, 243 A.2d 263 (App.Div. 1968), cert. denied, 52 N.J. 175, 244 A.2d 304 (1968) (jurisdiction to levy inheritance tax on intangible assets in estate); Isaacson v. Heffernan, 189 Misc. 16, 64 N.Y.S.2d 726 (Spec. Term 1946) (candidate's "residence"); Matter of Tallmadge, 109 Misc. 696, 181 N.Y.S. 336 (Surr.Ct.1919) (construction of testamentary disposition of personalty).

73. See Edmundson v. Miley Trailer Co., 211 N.W.2d 269 (Iowa 1973) (long-arm statute limited to "resident" plaintiffs); Ortman v. Miller, 33 Mich.App. 451, 190 N.W.2d 242 (1971) (unsatisfied judgment fund, collecting authority for and against forum's interpretation); Antone v. General Motors Corp., 64 N.Y.2d 20, 484 N.Y.S.2d 514, 473 N.E.2d 742 (1984) ("resident" for purposes of exception to statute borrowing another state's shorter statute of limitations requires living in New York, but not domicile).

A point on the spectrum of meanings between domicile and simple residence is a requirement that to be entitled to free public schooling, a student living in the district for the primary purpose of attending school must be living in the district with a parent or guardian. This requirement was held constitutional in Martinez v. Bynum, 461 U.S. 321, 103 S.Ct. 1838, 75 L.Ed.2d 879 (1983).

74. See McGrath v. Kristensen, 340 U.S. 162, 175, 71 S.Ct. 224, 232, 95 L.Ed. 173, 184 (1950) ("residing"; "[t]he definition varies with the statute"); Reese & Green, *That Elusive Word, "Residence",* 6 Vand. L. Rev. 561 (1953).

With this sketch of domicile as background, it is time to scrutinize some of the typical conflicts cases in which courts have referred to domicile in solving problems. The central question is whether domicile is a useful concept that assists proper conflict-of-laws analysis.

§ 2.12   Intestate Succession to Movables

In other areas of choice of law, the second Restatement of Conflict of Laws has departed dramatically from the rules of the first Restatement. This is true, for example, in the substitution of "the state which . . . has the most significant relationship to the transaction and the parties"[75] for "the place of contracting"[76] and in the substitution of "the state which . . . has the most significant relationship to the occurrence and the parties"[77] for "law of the place of wrong."[78] These changes have had significant effects upon our courts.[79]

Insofar as intestate succession to movables[80] is concerned, however, the new Restatement is content to repeat the "law of the state of his domicile"[81] language of the first Restatement, but with a new renvoi[82] twist. The new black-letter rule reads: "The devolution of interests in movables upon intestacy is determined by the law that would be applied by the courts of the state where the decedent was domiciled at the time of his death."[83]

In the new Restatement version, the reference to the law of the domicile is to the whole law of the domicile including its conflicts rules.[84] This is to insure that all courts referring to the law of the domicile will in fact distribute the property as the courts of the domicile would under identical facts.[85]

In this age of non-music and non-books, it is probably fitting that we should have a non-rule. A purported choice-of-law rule that refers to the whole law of the indicated jurisdiction is not a choice-of-law rule at all. It

---

A similar problem of interpretation occurs when "residence" or a similar term is used in an insurance policy or other contract. See Donegal Mut. Ins. Co. v. McConnell, 562 So.2d 201 (Ala. 1990) (holding serviceman stationed in Alabama a "resident" of parents' household in Pennsylvania and therefore entitled to medical expense and underinsured motorist coverage under automobile insurance); Barker v. Iowa Mut. Ins. Co., 241 N.C. 397, 85 S.E.2d 305 (1955); Central Mfrs.' Mut. Ins. Co. v. Friedman, 213 Ark. 9, 209 S.W.2d 102, 1 A.L.R.2d 557 (1948); Clarkson v. MFA Mutual Ins. Co., 413 S.W.2d 10 (Springfield Mo.App.1967) ("actually living").

75. Restatement, Second § 188(1).

76. Restatement, § 332 (1934).

77. Restatement, Second § 145(1).

78. Restatement § 379 (1934).

79. For early cases abandoning the "place of wrong" rule under the influence of drafts of the second Restatement, see Babcock v. Jackson, 12 N.Y.2d 473, 240 N.Y.S.2d 743, 191 N.E.2d 279 (1963); Griffith v. United Air Lines, Inc., 416 Pa. 1, 203 A.2d 796 (1964).

80. "Movables" is the conflict of laws term generally equivalent to personal property; "immovables" is the term for real property. For more detailed discussion, see § 8.1.

81. Restatement § 303 (1934).

82. See § 3.3.

83. Restatement, Second § 260.

84. Id., comment *b*.

85. Id.

gives no real guidance as to which domestic law, of all those that might be applied, is in fact the most appropriate. It gives no guidance to the courts of the jurisdiction to whose law other courts are directed[86]—no guidance, that is, to the most probable forum. There is a distinction between what a forum has the power to do and what it ought to do.[87] The purpose of choice-of-law rules is to tell a court what it ought to do in selecting applicable law.

On the whole, however, the expectation of the Second Restatement, as of the first, seems to be that courts will apply the internal law of the domicile at death to intestate distribution and that this is proper.[88] Except for the insertion of the renvoi concept and the rather sensible recognition of the fact that the meaning of "domicile" may vary with the context[89] (discussed in a subsequent section)[90] the approach of the new Restatement to the problem is basically the same as that of the old. It might be well, therefore, to examine the "law of the domicile" choice-of-law rule for intestate succession and to begin by reviewing some of the classic cases applying that rule.

§ 2.12A In re Estate of Jones[91]

Evan Jones, a native of Wales, had come to America in 1883 because of proceedings to provide child support that the mother of his illegitimate daughter instituted against him. He became a naturalized citizen and married here, but his wife predeceased him. He accumulated a considerable amount of property in Iowa, where he had settled. In 1915, Jones decided to return to his native Wales to live out the rest of his days. He sold his realty, purchased a draft for about two thousand dollars, left the rest of his cash on deposit in an Iowa bank with a note and mortgage for collection, sailed on the Lusitania, and was drowned when that ship was sunk by a German submarine.

The contestants for the intestate Iowa property were, on one side, Evan's brothers and sisters and, on the other, his illegitimate daughter. Under Iowa law, because her paternity had been sufficiently proven and recognized during Evan's lifetime,[92] the daughter would inherit everything.[93] Under British law, however, it was conceded that the intestate distribution would be entirely to the decedent's brothers and sisters. It was therefore crucial to decide whether Iowa law or British law controlled the intestate distribution.

---

86. See Cook, The Logical and Legal Bases of the Conflict of Laws 264 (1942).

87. But see Baker, *In the Administration of Intangibles–Missouri's Section 466.010 in Perspective*, 19 Mo. L. Rev. 1, 15 (1954): "Not always have courts clearly distinguished between the propriety of administering at the situs, and the propriety of applying in that administration the succession law of the domicile."

88. Restatement, Second § 260, comment *b*.

89. Restatement, Second § 11, comment *o*.

90. See § 2.16.

91. 192 Iowa 78, 182 N.W. 227 (1921).

92. Iowa Code Ann. § 3385 (1897).

93. Iowa Code Ann. §§ 3362, 3378 (1897).

The court took as its guide the choice-of-law rule that the law of the decedent's domicile at death governed the intestate distribution of movables. The only issue, then, was whether Evan Jones was domiciled in Iowa or in the Britain at the time of his death. The argument for domicile in Great Britain was based on the English doctrine of reverter of the domicile of origin as soon as the domicile of choice is abandoned;[94] Evan had acquired a domicile of choice in Iowa, but as soon as he left Iowa intending to return to his domicile of origin, Wales, his domicile of origin was renewed. The court rejected this argument, viewing it as based on feelings of patriotism and ties to the mother country that might exist when a British subject went to some distant part of the Commonwealth to make his fortune, always regarding himself as an Englishman.[95] The court thought such notions inapplicable to a naturalized American citizen. Once this doctrine was rejected, it was clear that Evan was technically domiciled at death in Iowa. He had acquired a domicile of choice in Iowa and would retain it until he was physically present in another jurisdiction with a present intention to make the other jurisdiction his home. Therefore, he died domiciled in Iowa, Iowa law controlled intestate distribution of his property, and all intestate property went to the daughter.

In testing the soundness of a decision, it is often helpful to ask what reasonable arguments a lawyer representing the brothers and sisters could advance for an opposite result. First, the Iowa court misinterpreted the English rule on revival of the domicile of origin. The rule was applicable not only when a person abandoned a domicile of choice to return to the domicile of origin but also whenever a person abandoned a domicile of choice until that person acquired a new domicile of choice.[96] Further, the rule was not based solely on notions of patriotism and ties to mother England. The domicile of origin reverted because of its special nature; one acquired a domicile of origin at birth—the domicile of the child's parents at that time. When, therefore, a person had left a domicile of choice intending never to return and it seemed unrealistic to say that the person retained a domicile there, the domicile of origin, which had been originally acquired by operation of law, would renew again by operation of law, until it was once more sensible to speak of a domicile of choice elsewhere.[97] It seems very unlikely, however, that a

---

94. See Udny v. Udny, L.R. 1 H.L. 441 (1869). For a report on a proposal to abandon the rule in England, see Graveson, *Reform of the Law of Domicile*, 70 L.Q.Rev. 492, 496, 498–99 (1954). The New Zealand Domicile Act of 1976, § 11, abolishes the reverter doctrine in that country. The Australian Family Law Act 1975 § 4(3)(a) abolishes it for purposes of the use of the Act.

With regard to the intention needed for abandonment of the domicile of choice, see In re Flynn, [1968] 1 All E.R. 49, 58, [1968] 1 W.L.R. 108, 115 (Ch.Div.1967) (it is sufficient if the "intention of returning has merely withered away and [it is not necessary that there be] any positive intention never to live in the country").

95. Cf. Suglove v. Oklahoma Tax Commission, 605 P.2d 1315 (Okl.1979) (more likely that Oklahoma residence retained for tax purposes when taxpayer lives in a foreign country than when residence is in a sister state).

96. Udny v. Udny, supra note 94, at 448, 454, 460–61.

97. Id. at 452, 458–60.

correct understanding of the English rule on revival of domicile of origin would have changed the result.

Playing the domicile game with the court, one is tempted to expose the fallacy latent in the court's statement that "all will agree that the decedent did not have a domicile on the Lusitania."[98] For the purpose of the choice-of-law rule in issue, it was necessary only to decide whether Evan had died domiciled somewhere in Great Britain since Wales has no intestacy law of its own.[99] He could have died domiciled in Great Britain without having died domiciled in Wales.[100] As soon as he set foot anywhere on British territory, he would be physically present in the jurisdiction whose law was in issue with a present intention to make his home somewhere within that territory. The Lusitania was a ship of the Cunard Line flying the British flag. Because the Lusitania was a little piece of Britain and Evan Jones was on British territory with domiciliary intent before he died, he died domiciled in Britain, and the court should have applied its law, not Iowa law.[101]

Thus to play the domicile game exposes its inherent silliness. Why should the result turn on whether Evan managed to set foot on British territory again before his death or whether he retained a technical domicile in Iowa? What reasons support the rule that the law of the domicile at death governs the intestate distribution of movables; are these reasons applicable in the context of this case? Let us turn to these questions, which seem to go to the heart of the matter.

The reason most often advanced in support of the rule that the law of the domicile at death governs distribution of movables on intestacy (frequently the only reason advanced) is that it insures uniformity of distribution.[102] It is desirable, in order to avoid confusion and conflict, that the same law govern distribution of movable property everywhere; but this argument does not support any particular conflicts rule except to the extent that one choice-of-law rule lends itself more readily to uniform application than another rule. As the cases discussed in this chapter indicate, if guaranteed uniformity of application were the chief goal that choice-of-law rules seek, one would not select as the contact

---

98. 192 Iowa 78, 83, 182 N.W. 227, 229 (1921).

99. See Kaye, *The Meaning of Domicile under United Kingdom Law for the Purposes of the 1968 Brussels Convention on Jurisdiction and the Enforcement of Judgments in Civil and Commercial Matters*, 35 Netherlands Int'l L. Rev. 181, 182 (1988) ("the United Kingdom ... contains three separate legal systems, English and Welsh, Scottish, and Northern Irish").

100. Restatement, Second § 11, comments *f, g*. See also § 2.3 notes 20, 22 and accompanying text.

101. See Marshall v. Murgatroyd, 6 Q.B. 31, 33–34 (1870) involving application of a bastardy statute limited in its operation to England and Wales: "It is part of the common law and of the law of nations, that a ship on the high seas is a part of the territory of that state to which she belongs; and therefore an English ship is deemed to be part of England. The child having been born on board an English ship, the statute applies."

102. Stumberg, Conflict of Laws 374 (3d ed. 1963); Reese, *Conflict of Laws and the Restatement Second*, 28 Law & Contemp. Prob. 679, 687 (1963).

word at the heart of the rule so slippery a concept as "domicile."[103] Moreover, any choice-of-law rule for intestate distribution of movables that is uniformly interpreted and applied will assure that all movables, wherever situated, will be distributed in the same manner.

Another reason frequently given for the domiciliary rule in intestacy and stated by the court in *Jones*[104] is that the decedent is presumably more familiar with the law of his or her domicile than that of any other jurisdiction and, having left no will, wishes the estate to pass in accordance with that domiciliary law. This seems unrealistic in the extreme. An empirical study of intestate Iowans indicates that in certain circumstances a majority of them would want their property distributed in a manner different from that provided by Iowa intestacy law.[105] But, even conceding the possible validity of this presumed-intention reason as a general proposition, was it proper to presume that Evan Jones wished his bastard daughter to inherit all of his property? He seems to have made a life-long project of avoiding any responsibility for her support, and the court itself admitted that, so far as Evan's intentions were concerned, there was no basis for choosing Iowa or British law.[106]

A reason for applying the domiciliary rule in intestacy cases that is more satisfactory than either of those usually given is that the technical domicile at death is likely to be the jurisdiction that has the sole or at least the predominant interest in the application of its intestacy laws to the property of the decedent. Whatever the policies underlying a state's intestacy statute directing which of the surviving kin shall take and in what portions, the chances are that the technical domicile at death will experience the consequences if its own policies in these matters are enforced. The natural objects of the decedent's bounty, or a good portion of them, are likely to be residents of the domicile at death. If hard feelings are caused by a distribution improper in the eyes of the domicile, it is the peace and tranquility of the domicile that will suffer. If those dependent upon the decedent are not given a share the domiciliary state considers just and proper and become objects of public charity, the government and citizens of that state will pay the bill.

---

103. This is precisely the basis on which the Supreme Court rejected "last domicile of the creditor" as the test of which state has jurisdiction to take title through escheat to abandoned intangible personal property. Texas v. New Jersey, 379 U.S. 674, 681, 85 S.Ct. 626, 630, 13 L.Ed.2d 596, 601 (1965): "And by using a standard of last known address, rather than technical legal concepts of residence and domicile, administration and application of escheat laws should be simplified."

104. 192 Iowa at 95, 182 N.W. at 234.

105. Note, *A Comparison of Iowans' Dispositive Preferences with Selected Provisions of the Iowa and Uniform Probate Codes*, 63 Iowa L. Rev. 1041, 1077, 1091, 1146 (1978). And see id. at 1047: "most modern intestacy statutes are based on historical tradition rather than on empirically substantiated individual dispositive preferences." See also Trimble v. Gordon, 430 U.S. 762, 775 n. 16, 97 S.Ct. 1459, 1467 n. 16, 52 L.Ed.2d 31, 42 n.16 (1977): "Even if one assumed that a majority of the citizens of the State preferred to discriminate against their illegitimate children, the sentiment hardly would be unanimous. With respect to any individual, the argument of knowledge and approval of the state law [on intestate succession] is sheer fiction."

In a conflicts case, if the intestacy law of one state was shaped by empirical data but the law of the other was not, this might be a basis for selecting the empirically sound law as the "better law". See § 1.5, text accompanying notes 64–65.

106. 192 Iowa at 95, 182 N.W. at 234.

If the consequences of choice of law is the reason that might most plausibly be advanced for the rule selecting the law of the domicile at death to govern intestate distribution of movables, what result does this reason suggest in *Estate of Jones*? A search of the record reveals that all of the contestants, the illegitimate daughter and the brothers and sisters of the decedent, were residents of England or Wales and, with the exception of one sister who had sojourned in the United States before returning to Wales, had been so all their lives.[107] Iowa had no interest in preferring the bastard daughter over the brothers and sisters when British law would not have done so.

§ 2.12B   White v. Tennant[108]

Michael White, until less than a month before his death, had been a life-long domiciliary of West Virginia, where his wife and brothers and sisters were also domiciled. Michael owned a farm in West Virginia on which he was living with his wife. He sold the farm and reached an agreement with his mother and siblings to occupy a forty-acre tract and a house on that tract. The tract was situated in Pennsylvania, just across the state line from West Virginia. This forty-acre tract was part of a larger 240–acre family farm, the main part of which, including the mansion-house, was in West Virginia. On the morning of April 2, 1885, Michael and his wife left the West Virginia farm and house, which he had sold, and started for the house on the family farm in Pennsylvania "with the declared intent and purpose of making the Pennsylvania house his home that evening."[109] Michael and his wife arrived at the Pennsylvania house about sundown. The previous tenants had left several days before and the house was damp and uncomfortable. Michael's wife complained of feeling ill. Under the circumstances, Michael accepted the invitation of his brothers and sisters to spend the night in the mansion-house in West Virginia. He paused at the Pennsylvania house only long enough to deposit household goods and to turn loose his livestock. Michael never did return to the Pennsylvania house to live. His wife's illness was typhoid fever, and he stayed at the mansion-house to care for her. For about two weeks he went daily to the Pennsylvania tract to care for his stock, then suffered an attack of typhoid fever himself and, a short time later, died intestate in the West Virginia mansion-house.

A good deal depended upon whether West Virginia law or Pennsylvania law applied to the intestate distribution of Michael's personal property. Under West Virginia law everything would go to his widow.[110]

---

107.   The residences of the contestants are indicated in the record in the following places and are Wales unless otherwise designated. Illegitimate daughter, Margaret, appellant's abstract of record, p. 2. Brothers and sisters: William, appellees' amendment to abstract, p. 128; Rees (London), appellant's abstract of record, p. 11; Thomas, same abstract, p. 114; Sarah Williams (had lived in United States, returned to Wales), same abstract, pp. 114–15; Mary, appellees' amendment to abstract, p. 131; John, same abstract, p. 129; Elizabeth Davies, same abstract, p. 130.

108.   31 W.Va. 790, 8 S.E. 596 (1888).

109.   Id. at 794, 8 S.E. at 598.

110.   Id. at 794, 8 S.E. at 598.

The Pennsylvania statute gave half to the widow and half to the brothers and sisters.[111] Using the domicile-at-death rule, the West Virginia court ordered distribution under the Pennsylvania intestacy statute. It reasoned that Michael had been physically present at his house in Pennsylvania with a present intent to make it his home. Though he was present for only a short time, even momentary physical presence,[112] if coupled with the requisite domiciliary intention, would be sufficient. Therefore, he had acquired a domicile of choice in Pennsylvania.

Again, if one wishes to play the domiciliary game with the court and to argue for application of West Virginia law, it would first be necessary to point out the fallacy in one of the arguments the court used to establish the existence of a domicile of choice in Pennsylvania. The court reasoned[113] that Michael had to have a domicile somewhere at all times. He did not have one in the house he had sold and vacated, and he did not have one in the mansion-house in West Virginia because he did not think of it as a home. Therefore, he must have been domiciled in the Pennsylvania house. There is of course another possibility. He could have died domiciled in the State of West Virginia, though not in any house in that state.[114] This is what would necessarily have been the result had he suffered a fatal heart attack on the trip to Pennsylvania before crossing the state line but after leaving his West Virginia house and, let us assume, after it had been occupied by the new owners. The argument in support of the widow should then concentrate on the mental element part of the physical-presence-plus-domiciliary-intention combination needed to acquire a domicile of choice. The argument would be that before he had reached Pennsylvania on April 2, in view of his wife's complaints of illness, he had already decided to stay in West Virginia at the mansion-house that night and thus his domiciliary intention was but a future intention and not the required present intention. To be sure, the court specifically found that his intention to remain was a present one upon his arrival,[115] but this finding may have been changed by cogent evidence to the contrary.

Is all this, however, not beside the point? It is a common ploy for Conflicts teachers when discussing this case in class to ask whether the result would have been the same if the ultimate issue had been whether West Virginia or Pennsylvania could levy a large inheritance tax on, let us imagine, millions of dollars of intangible personalty in Michael's

---

111. Pa.P.L. 315, § 1 (1833).

112. See Perito v. Perito, 756 P.2d 895 (Alaska 1988) (wife was domiciled in Alaska when she filed for divorce one day after arrival). But see Restatement, Second § 16, comment *b*: "Courts (usually by way of dictum) and writers have sometimes said that physical presence even for a moment is enough. Such statements should not be taken literally. At least for most purposes, a person will not have a sufficient relationship to a place to warrant holding that place to be his domicil unless he has been present there for a time at least."

113. 31 W.Va. at 797, 8 S.E. at 599–600.

114. See Restatement, Second § 11, comment *f*.

115. 31 W.Va. at 796, 8 S.E. at 599.

estate.[116] The purpose of such a question may be to prepare the class for the startling revelation that "domicile" may mean different things in different contexts.

Perhaps the question indicates another reason why the result might be different. The taxation issue would focus the West Virginia court's attention on a matter that it did not seem to note in *White v. Tennant*— West Virginia's substantial interest in the outcome of the litigation. In the principal case, because all the contestants were long-time West Virginia residents, one can ask what legitimate interest Pennsylvania had in controlling the intestate distribution as between the siblings and widow of Michael White. In view of the possible policies underlying an intestate distribution statute, perhaps Pennsylvania had no interest. Michael certainly was not more familiar with the Pennsylvania law on the subject than he was with West Virginia law. West Virginia had the predominant, perhaps exclusive, interest in preventing discord among the contestants and treating them according to its own notions of fairness and their needs. Although there is no indication of where the widow settled after the death of her husband, presumably it was in West Virginia; but it would be foolish to let much turn upon that. We would not want the widow to be able to select the law to govern distribution by selecting her house.[117]

§ 2.12C   A More Useful Tool for Rational Analysis

In order to discuss the relative interests of West Virginia and Pennsylvania in the *White* case and to argue in terms of the policies underlying the statutes on intestate distribution, one might approach the problem as one of statutory construction. The statutes speak of "decedents," "intestates," "widows," and "kindred," but what decedents, what intestates, what widows and next of kin? If, as one might expect, the statutes of the two states are innocent of any answers to these questions in the interstate context of a conflicts problem, statutory construction must supply the answer. The basic technique of such construction is to inquire into the purposes of the statutes to determine which of several possible meanings would advance these purposes and which would not. Unfortunately for such an approach, the Pennsylvania legislature had succumbed to the domicile dogma and a section of its code read: "Nothing in this act contained, relative to a distribution of personal estate among kindred, shall be construed to extend to the personal estate of an intestate, whose domicile, at the time of his death, was out of this commonwealth."[118] It could be argued that the correlate of this negative statement is that the Pennsylvania statutory rules on

---

116. Cf. Reese, *Does Domicil Bear a Single Meaning?*, 55 Colum. L. Rev. 589, 593 (1955) (puts hypothetical similar to White v. Tennant with inheritance tax issue and suggests courts would fail to find requisite domiciliary intention toward new state).

117. Cf. John Hancock Mutual Life Ins. Co. v. Yates, 299 U.S. 178, 57 S.Ct. 129, 81 L.Ed. 106 (1936). But cf. Allstate Ins. Co. v. Hague, 449 U.S. 302, 101 S.Ct. 633, 66 L.Ed.2d 521 (1981). These cases are discussed in § 9.2A.

118. Pa.P.L. 315, § 20 (1833).

intestate distribution are applicable to the personalty of anyone who did die domiciled in Pennsylvania. There was no such embarrassment to rational analysis in the West Virginia code for the West Virginia forum. A code section such as the quoted Pennsylvania provision serves to buttress the argument against attempts to deal with conflict problems by statute[119] unless the statutory rules reflect the lessons learned from the many cases that have repudiated territorial rules and chosen law in the light of the consequences of that choice. A rule that provides reasonable predictability and also takes account of the consequences of choice of law might state: "An issue concerning the intestate distribution of personal property is governed by the law of the decedent's domicile at death, unless some other state has the paramount interest in the consequences of the choice of law."[120]

§ 2.13 Validity of a Will Disposing of Movables

The second Restatement adopts the same formula for determining the validity of a will of movables as it does for intestate succession:

Validity and Effect of Will of Movables

(1) Whether a will transfers an interest in movables and the nature of the interest transferred are determined by the law that would be applied by the courts of the state where the testator was domiciled at the time of his death.

(2) These courts would usually apply their own local law in determining such question.[121]

Thus is approved for continued use the supposed[122] standard choice-

---

119. For an article opposing putting choice-of-law rules in statutes see Unger, *Use and Abuse of Statutes in the Conflict of Laws*, 83 L.Q.Rev. 427 (1967).

120. But see Howard v. Reynolds, 30 Ohio St.2d 214, 283 N.E.2d 629, 59 O.O.2d 228 (1972) (applies Vermont law as that of domicile at death of intestate even though all property in Ohio, most of claimants are in Ohio, none live in Vermont, and intestate was incompetent for at least the last 15 years of his life).

121. Restatement, Second § 263.

122. There is some doubt about the universality of the rule. Alternative references are sometimes made, frequently to the situs of property, in order to uphold the will. See In re Chappell's Estate, 124 Wash. 128, 213 P. 684 (1923) (situs law applied to uphold testamentary trust as against accumulations rule of domicile); 755 Ill. Comp. Stat. Ann. 5/7–6 (nonresident testator may provide in will for application of Illinois law as to personalty having situs in Illinois); N.Y. McKinney's Est., Powers & Trusts Law § 3–5.1(h) (same effect as Illinois statute) (predecessor statute, which applied to "testamentary dispositions," was construed not to affect nonresident wife's power to elect against will of nonresident testator under law of domicile—In re Estate of Clark, 21 N.Y.2d 478, 288 N.Y.S.2d 993, 236 N.E.2d 152 (1968), but current wording that refers broadly to "disposition of ... property situated in this state" was construed to prevent a son from electing against his mother's will under the law of her domicile—In re Estate of Renard, 56 N.Y.2d 973, 453 N.Y.S.2d 625, 439 N.E.2d 341 (1982)); Yiannopoulos, *Wills of Movables in American International Conflicts Law—A Critique of the Domiciliary "Rule,"* 46 Calif. L. Rev. 185, 206 (1958): "Whenever the will does not violate superior policies of the forum essential validity is governed by the law upholding the will...." (international conflicts cases); Note, *The Testator's Intention as a Factor in Determining the Place of Probate of His Estate*, 33 Ind.L. J. 591, 599, 608 (1958); cf. Lanius v. Fletcher, 100 Tex. 550, 101 S.W. 1076 (1907) (situs law applied to prevent dissolution of trust by beneficiary under law of domicile). See also § 8.25.

of-law rule looking to the domicile of the testator at death.[123] Again, we might begin by reviewing a classic case.

§ 2.13A   An Illustrative Case: In re Annesley[124]

Mrs. Annesley died in France in 1924, having lived there since moving from England in 1866. She left two wills, a holographic will in French and a will in English form. There was also a codicil to the latter. In these wills, Mrs. Annesley purported to dispose of all of her personal property in France and in England. This was permissible under English law, but, if French law applied, she could dispose by will of only one-third of her personal property, and the rest would go to her two surviving daughters. In a contest over distribution of the personal property in England (consisting chiefly of two bank accounts) the daughters, who had received less than two-thirds of the property disposed of by the wills, contended that French law was applicable; the other legatees argued for English law.

The court, applying the domicile-at-death choice-of-law rule, began by deciding that Mrs. Annesley had acquired a domicile of choice in France, even though she had not taken the steps prescribed for obtaining a formal French domicile[125] by Article 13 of the French Civil Code and had declared in her English-form will and a codicil to it that it was not her intention to abandon her English domicile of origin. For purposes of the English choice-of-law rule, the court defined "domicile" by English standards.[126] Immediately, however, the English court ran into another difficulty. The English choice-of-law rule, domicile at death, referred to French law, but what French law—French domestic internal law only or the whole law of France including its conflicts rules? This was important because, in the case of a foreigner not legally domiciled in France, the French choice-of-law rule would select the law of that person's nationality—here, English law. Speaking for the majority of the court, Judge Russell applied the whole law of France, although he himself would have

---

With regard to formal validity, many states have statutes providing alternative references to validate the will. See Uniform Probate Code, 8 pt. 1 ULA 151, § 2–506 (validate under forum law, or law at time of execution of place of execution, or law at time of execution or death of place where testator domiciled, had place of abode, or is a national) (enacted in 19 states as of January 1, 2009); Restatement, Second § 263, comment *c*; Rees, *American Wills Statutes*, 46 Va. L. Rev. 856, 905–06 (1960) (listing thirty-two states with statutes making some alternative reference for formal validity).

123. See, e.g., Cox v. Harrison, 535 S.W.2d 78 (Ky.1975) (whether will revoked by divorce determined as to personalty by law of domicile at death, as to realty by law of situs); Memphis State Univ. v. Agee, 566 S.W.2d 283 (Tenn.App.1977), cert. denied by Tenn.S.Ct. (1978) (mortmain law of Mississippi domicile at death applies to invalidate will even though all claimants are Tennessee residents or charities). But cf. In re Estate of Garver, 135 N.J.Super. 578, 343 A.2d 817 (App.Div. 1975) (law of domicile at time of divorce, not at time of death, applied to revoke will when this accorded with intention of testator).

124. [1926] Ch. 692.

125. But see Delaume, American–French Private International Law 75 (2d ed. 1961) ("an alien residing in France with the appropriate intent could acquire a *de facto* domicile in France, a notion substantially equivalent to the general concept of domicile").

126. [1926] Ch. at 705.

preferred to apply only French internal law.[127] The method chosen for applying the whole law of France was for the English court to decide the case just as a French court would have. After hearing expert testimony on this subject, the court decided that a French court would refer to English law, including the English choice-of-law rule pointing back to France, would accept this reference back (renvoi),[128] and would apply French internal law to determine the validity of the testamentary disposition.[129] Thus Mrs. Annesley's wills were invalid insofar as they undertook to dispose of more than one-third of her personalty, and the legacies of the personalty in England, under the will in English form, could not be paid in full.

This is all wonderfully complex and interesting. The only difficulty is that it is unresponsive to the policies underlying the English and French rules on testamentary disposition and consequently the result is probably wrong.[130] The intent of the testatrix was known; it was, as expressed in her wills, to leave the bulk of her estate to persons and institutions other than her two daughters. England had no policy against giving effect to this intention. Did France have any logically applicable policy against giving effect to this intent? There was such a French policy in regard to persons "domiciled" in France in the French sense. But is not the French choice-of-law rule an indication that the French policy, as interpreted by the French courts, is inapplicable to this very testatrix? Why should an English court enforce a French limitation on the intent of the testatrix when the French courts themselves would not have enforced it but for the English reference to French law?[131]

As a first step in its conflicts analysis, the court should have determined whether there is any "real" conflict represented by the differing domestic laws—whether the contact states have applicable policies pointing to different results. If this "first step" had been taken,

---

127. Id. at 708–09.

128. See § 3.3.

129. Cf. In re Schneider's Estate, 198 Misc. 1017, 96 N.Y.S.2d 652, adhered to, 198 Misc. 1017, 100 N.Y.S.2d 371 (Surr.Ct.1950) (applying whole law of situs to determine validity of devise of realty); In re Zietz's Estate, 198 Misc. 77, 96 N.Y.S.2d 442 (Surr.Ct. 1950) (situs accepts reference by law of domicile to law of nationality); Simmons v. Simmons, 17 N.S.W.St. 419 (1917) (reference to whole law of domicile in intestacy with opposite view of that taken in principal case as to French rule on renvoi). For the very questionable use of the renvoi device to resolve an issue of will construction, see In re Duke of Wellington, [1947] Ch. 506, aff'd [1948] Ch. 118 (C.A.). This case is aptly criticized in Mann, *Succession to Immovables Abroad,* 11 Modern L. Rev. 232 (1948). For a case rejecting reference to the whole foreign law but reaching a result that should have been reached by construction alone, see Matter of Tallmadge, 109 Misc. 696, 181 N.Y.S. 336 (Surr.Ct.1919).

130. For a case fortuitously reaching the right result by the same renvoi device because the Italian conflicts rule referred back to only the internal law of the "nationality," which the court took to mean the last, but no longer continuing, American domicile, see Taormina v. Taormina Corp., 35 Del.Ch. 17, 109 A.2d 400 (1954).

131. Counsel for the parties entitled to a trust legacy made a similar argument in *Annesley.* "The origin of the rule that the law of the domicil governs the succession to movables is based on convenience and international courtesy. The rule is satisfied as soon as it is found that the law of the domicil rejects the propositus, and then both on grounds of convenience and courtesy an English court will apply English law." [1926] Ch. at 700.

it would have resulted in the application of English law and the validation of the will.

§ 2.13B A More Useful Approach

A conflicts case involving the essential validity of a will presents a problem too complex to be solved by any rigid, territorially-oriented choice-of-law rule. This is true whether we use "domicile," "nationality," "situs" or any other jurisdiction-selector as the contact word. The number of different rules under which a will might be declared invalid is great, and the policies that underlie these rules are diverse. In such a situation, when one state having a contact with the parties or the property would invalidate a will and another with such a contact would uphold it, the way to begin is by focusing on the domestic laws in apparent conflict and on the policies underlying those laws.[132] In the light of those policies and those contacts, does only one of the states have a rational interest in having its policies and its law applied? If so, the law of that state should be applied. If on the other hand, several states have legitimate reasons for having their diverse rules on validity applied, a real conflict is present. The general direction for resolution of a true conflict concerning the essential validity of a will should be toward validation.[133] It is likely, at least as between states of the United States, that the difference in the laws will be one of detail rather than basic policy. For example, one state may have a "two lives" perpetuities rule and another a "lives in being" rule. The states will share a general policy of upholding the intention of the testator, an invalidating rule being an exception carved out of this general policy.[134] If, however, the difference in laws is basic and no substantial inequity would result from invalidation, both states should agree that invalidation is the proper resolution of the conflict.

A further illustration may be helpful. Let us suppose a case in which a testator, who was a long-term resident of state X, as were all the natural objects of his bounty, dies in X bequeathing personalty located in state Y to a Y charity, which conducts its activities only in Y. If all contacts had been in Y the will would have failed, at least in part, because the will was executed closer to the time of death than is permitted by Y law for bequests to charities. If all contacts had been in X, the bequest would have failed because it gave the charity property in a greater amount than charities are permitted to take under X law.

On the surface, there appears to be no conflict, except perhaps as to the degree of invalidity, and it appears that the bequest should fail. But appearances may be deceiving. Let us assume,[135] for the purpose of

---

132. See Stumberg, Conflict of Laws 377 (3d ed. 1963): "The problem is primarily one of ascertaining the policy or purpose behind a particular prohibition and then giving it effect."

133. Cf. Yiannopoulos, *Wills of Movables in American International Conflicts Law A Critique of the Domiciliary "Rule,"* 46 Cal. L. Rev. 185, 206, 262 (1958).

134. Cf. § 7.4A (presumption in favor of validating law).

135. A limit on the amount charities can take will, to some extent, protect heirs, and protection of heirs will, to some extent, limit the amount taken by charities. In an actual

illustrative analysis, that the only policy underlying the Y time limit on bequests to charities is the protection of the decedent and next of kin from death-bed decisions prompted by solicitations or late-coming religious fervor. Let us similarly suppose that the only purpose of the X statute is to prevent local charities from becoming too powerful and to protect the local economy by limiting the amount of property that can be taken out of commercial use.[136] If so, then on these facts X has no interest in applying its invalidating rule and neither has Y. Both X and Y have a general policy of giving effect to the intention of the testator, and this general policy should be effectuated in the posited case no matter which state is the forum.

§ 2.14 Capacity of a Wife to Sue Her Husband for Negligence

§ 2.14A Illustrative Cases

(1) HAUMSCHILD V. CONTINENTAL CASUALTY CO.[137]

This case produced the rule that a wife's capacity to sue her husband for negligence is determined by the law of the marital domicile. While a husband and wife, domiciled in Wisconsin, were driving in California, the wife was injured by the husband's negligence. Under Wisconsin law, but not under California law at that time, a wife could sue her husband for negligent injury. Overruling a long line of Wisconsin cases[138] and abandoning the "place of wrong" rule in this context, the Wisconsin court permitted the wife to sue her husband and his liability insurer. The reason given was that this was a problem of family law and not tort law and therefore was governed by the law of the marital domicile rather than that of the place of wrong.

This kind of label-switching, not based on analysis of the policies underlying the apparently conflicting state laws, is arbitrary and unconvincing. Furthermore, devoid as it is of proper analysis of substantive policies, it runs the risk of creating as many spurious conflicts as did the rule it replaced. In *Haumschild* the result, fortuitously, happened to be correct. It was correct because Wisconsin had an obvious interest in permitting the wife to recover and California's rule preventing suit applied only to California husbands and wives. The reason for the California rule was that, because California is a community property state, the defendant husband would share in the fruits of his wrongdoing if the wife recovered. When the community property law was amended so

___

case a lawyer should not engage in armchair speculation about the purposes underlying a statute. He or she should seek authoritative statements of these purposes in the statute's legislative history, discussions of the statute in judicial opinions, and analysis of similar legislation in scholarly publications.

136. For an early non-conflicts case pointing out the differences in types and policies of such statutes, see Trustees of Amherst College v. Ritch, 151 N.Y. 282, 45 N.E. 876 (1897). For a masterly treatment of the problem, see Hancock, *In the Parish of St. Mary le Bow, in the Ward of Cheap*, 16 Stan. L. Rev. 561 (1964).

137. 7 Wis.2d 130, 95 N.W.2d 814 (1959).

138. E.g., Buckeye v. Buckeye, 203 Wis. 248, 234 N.W. 342 (1931).

that the husband would not share in the recovery, the Supreme Court of California terminated the disability of California wives to sue their husbands for negligence.[139] Ms. Haumschild's recovery would not be characterized as community property, even by a California court, because she was domiciled in a non-community state.[140]

(2) HAYNIE V. HANSON[141]

In a subsequent Wisconsin case applying the *Haumschild* domicile rule, however, a shift in the law-fact pattern made the result far more questionable in terms of response to underlying state policies. In *Haynie* an Illinois husband and wife were driving in Wisconsin when the wife, Mrs. Haynie, was injured in a collision with an automobile driven by Mr. Hanson. The wife sued Mr. Hanson and his liability insurer in Wisconsin. At all relevant times, Mr. Hanson was a citizen of Wisconsin and his liability insurer was a Wisconsin company.[142] The defendants attempted to implead the Illinois husband's liability insurer on the ground that the husband's negligence made him liable for contribution. The cross-complaint was dismissed on the ground that under Illinois law a wife could not sue her husband for negligence and, applying the *Haumschild* marital domicile choice-of-law rule, there was no underlying liability on which to base contribution. Unlike *Haumschild*, however, this time the place of injury, Wisconsin, had an interest in having its law applied so that the Wisconsin defendants could obtain contribution. The policies of the marital domicile, in favor of marital harmony and against collusion, might also be applicable in the light of an anti-impleader rule in a domestic case at the domicile. At the very least, however, the dangers of ill feeling between the husband and wife or that the wife and husband will invent a story to milk the husband's liability insurer, are greatly attenuated when the wife sues, not her husband, but a third party. Therefore, applying the *Haumschild* domicile choice-of-law rule to *Haynie* either resulted in the wrong answer to a false conflict or in a true conflict being resolved the wrong way. It is not surprising that the Wisconsin Supreme Court has now in effect overruled *Haynie*,[143] rejecting *Haumschild*'s "mechanical"[144] domicile rule and noting that in the

---

139. Klein v. Klein, 58 Cal.2d 692, 26 Cal.Rptr. 102, 376 P.2d 70 (1962). For a case reaching the *Haumschild* result, but on the basis of policies underlying the competing rules, see Thompson v. Thompson, 105 N.H. 86, 193 A.2d 439 (1963).

140. Bruton v. Villoria, 138 Cal.App.2d 642, 292 P.2d 638 (1956).

141. 16 Wis.2d 299, 114 N.W.2d 443 (1962).

142. Brief for Appellant, p. 11.

143. Zelinger v. State Sand & Gravel Co., 38 Wis.2d 98, 156 N.W.2d 466 (1968). See also LaChance v. Service Trucking Co., 215 F.Supp. 162 (D.Md.1963) (purposes of interspousal immunity are not relevant to a third party complaint against the husband); Restatement, Second § 169, comment *c*. Cf. B. Currie, *Justice Traynor and the Conflict of Laws*, 13 Stan. L. Rev. 719, 732 (1961); Hancock, *The Rise and Fall of Buckeye v. Buckeye*, 29 U. Chi. L. Rev. 237, 253–54 (1962).

144. 38 Wis.2d 98, 104, 156 N.W.2d 466, 468.

contribution situation "the Illinois interest of the preservation of family integrity seems hardly to be in jeopardy...."[145]

§ 2.14B   The Harm of the Domicile Concept in this Context

Aside from generating an arguably false conflict in the contribution situation, the domicile-centered rule for determining the wife's capacity to sue may disguise a real conflict and prevent its rational solution. Even if a suit against the husband is forbidden by the law of the domicile, another state may have a very significant interest in permitting recovery. This would be true, for example, if the accident happened in a state that permitted such suits, the wife was seriously injured and under intensive treatment there, there were unpaid medical creditors, and the only source of payment was the husband's liability insurance. Under such circumstances, if suit is brought at the place of injury and the main concern of the domicile is the prevention of collusive suits, the conflict should be resolved in favor of permitting recovery.[146]

Thus, once again, a domicile-centered choice-of-law rule generates false problems and interferes with the rational solution of true problems.

§ 2.15   A Constitutional Basis for Judicial Jurisdiction

Domicile within a state is a recognized constitutional basis for in personam jurisdiction,[147] provided the defendant is given such notice and opportunity to be heard as are reasonable under the circumstances.[148] But is mere technical domicile within a state always sufficient for this purpose?

§ 2.15A   Illustrative Cases

(1) ALVORD & ALVORD v. PATENOTRE[149]

In this case substituted service based on the defendant's domicile within the state was made five days after the defendant had left the state intending to establish a domicile of choice in Switzerland. At the

---

145. Id. at 113, 156 N.W.2d at 473.

In the contribution situation, there is a possibility of giving maximum effect to the laws of both states by barring the wife's suit against her husband but, if both other driver and husband are negligent, permitting the other driver to obtain contribution from the husband to the extent that the other driver pays more than his share of the judgment. This might require creating a new rule of law for this kind of conflicts case permitting contribution without underlying direct liability. See § 3.5.

146. But cf. Johnson v. Johnson, 107 N.H. 30, 216 A.2d 781 (1966) (place of injury, which permits interspousal suits, applies immunity rule of marital domicile, finding that its own interests are not seriously impaired in so doing).

147. Milliken v. Meyer, 311 U.S. 457, 61 S.Ct. 339, 85 L.Ed. 278 (1940). See § 4.11.

Domicile is the sole basis for general jurisdiction in the Brussels Regulation on Jurisdiction and Enforcement of Judgments in Civil and Commercial Matters, in force between members of the European Union. Art. 2(1). EC No. 44/2001. Article 60 states that the domicile of "a company or other legal person or association" is located at its "statutory seat, or central administration, or principal place of business."

148. McDonald v. Mabee, 243 U.S. 90, 37 S.Ct. 343, 61 L.Ed. 608 (1917).

149. 196 Misc. 524, 92 N.Y.S.2d 514 (1949).

time of service, defendant had not yet arrived in Switzerland. Therefore, lacking the necessary physical presence, he had not yet established his domicile there. Under the technical concept of domicile, he retained his former domicile in New York[150] and the court denied a motion to vacate the order for substituted service.

The core concept in satisfying the due process demands for judicial jurisdiction is one of reasonableness. In the great majority of cases, domicile within a state is likely to provide a constitutional basis for in personam jurisdiction because it is reasonable to require domiciliaries who are temporarily absent from the state to appear and defend under penalty of having their rights adjudicated by default. In the *Patenotre* case, the passage of only five days may have made the result reasonable. But suppose we extend the period of defendant's trip to his new domicile to a year or more, during which time he was undecided where to make his new home. All his property has been removed from his former home state and he has severed all other connections with it. Assuming no other basis for the forum's exercise of personal jurisdiction over the defendant, is his technical domicile there enough to answer due process objections to an attempt to assert jurisdiction over him? The answer should be "no,"[151] particularly in view of the fact that modern long-arm statutes are likely to permit jurisdiction in a forum more related to the underlying cause of action.[152]

---

150. See § 2.5.

151. See Caldas v. Zuccarello, 224 So.2d 831 (La.App.1969) (defendant no longer domiciled in forum for purpose of service of process when he had left with no intention of returning even though he had not obtained a new domicile of choice).

Cf. Amsbaugh v. Exchange Bank of Maquoketa, 33 Kan. 100, 5 P. 384 (1885) (Iowa judgment was rendered without jurisdiction over the defendant when jurisdiction was based on service on the defendant's wife in Iowa after the defendant had left Iowa intending not to return but before he had settled in a new home; Iowa was no longer his "usual place of residence" within the meaning of the Iowa service statute); Prudential Ins. Co. v. Himelfarb, 35 Del.Co. 371 (Pa.C.P.1947), aff'd, 362 Pa. 123, 66 A.2d 257 (1949) (service made after the defendant had left Pennsylvania but before he had arrived in Florida, which was to be his new domicile, was not valid, one reason being that the defendant no longer had a "residence" in Pennsylvania, but the court declared that for this purpose "residence," and "domicile" were not the same).

The Second Restatement originally took the position that domicile is a constitutional basis for jurisdiction "even though the individual's relationship to the state is slight and his domicile there is of a technical nature." Section 29, Reporter's Note. A 1988 revision changed § 29 to read: "A state has power to exercise judicial jurisdiction over an individual who is domiciled in the state, except in the highly unusual case where the individual's relationship to the state is so attenuated as to make the exercise of such jurisdiction unreasonable."

But see also Schreiber v. Schreiber, 27 Conn.Supp. 121, 231 A.2d 658 (Super.1967) (husband retains domicile at marital domicile for purposes of personal jurisdiction over him in divorce action, although he had left his Connecticut abode a few hours before service at the abode, and did not establish his domicile in New York until after the service).

152. See § 4.15. With a few exceptions, such as damage caused by motorists, it was not until 1963 that New York had a statute that conferred jurisdiction over nonresidents based on in-state acts or effects. This may explain why the focus in *Alvord* was on defendant's domicile.

(2) Lea v. Lea[153]

This case presents another example of how losing sight of the core concept of reasonableness and focusing on technical domicile may hinder rational analysis in matters of judicial jurisdiction. A woman domiciled in New Jersey was attempting to enforce an alimony award that was included in a divorce decree obtained against her former husband in New York. The former husband, now also domiciled in New Jersey, contended that the alimony award was void because the New York court did not have in personam jurisdiction over him. The New York court had based its jurisdiction on the husband's domicile in New York, although in fact, at the time of the wife's divorce in New York, the husband was living in Louisiana with another woman. He had been living and working in Louisiana for several years and had clearly established a domicile of choice there when he moved into that state with his wife and son. He had, however, sent his wife and son from Louisiana to New York to be with his mother who was dying. The husband came to New York for his mother's funeral but returned to Louisiana, leaving his wife and child in New York. Suspicious of her husband's continued insistence that she stay in New York, the wife went to Louisiana, learned that her husband had secured a purported divorce in Arkansas, and then she returned to New York to file suit for divorce. The Supreme Court of New Jersey upheld the New York alimony decree based on the husband's domicile in New York, stating: "Even conceding that the appellant has never been in the State of New York, except to pass through, since 1942, he was under a paramount duty to supply a home for his wife and child and such a home was established at his direction, insecure as it was, in New York. We therefore, conclude that the family domicile and the domicile of the appellant was in the State of New York...."[154]

New York probably had a constitutional basis for personal jurisdiction over the absent husband, because he had sent his wife and child into the state and they were there dependent on his support. He caused these consequences in New York and should be subject to the jurisdiction of a New York court in an action arising out of them.[155] Having a constitutional basis for jurisdiction, absent any outrageous surprise to the

---

153. 18 N.J. 1, 112 A.2d 540 (1955).

154. Id. at 11, 112 A.2d at 545. Cf. Bangs v. Inhabitants of Brewster, 111 Mass. 382 (1873) (domicile of choice established by wife's presence while husband at sea); Restatement, Second § 16, comment *f* (wife's presence "may, at least on occasion, serve as a substitute" for husband's to establish his domicile of choice). But cf. McIntosh v. Maricopa County, 73 Ariz. 366, 241 P.2d 801 (1952) (wife's presence while husband in armed forces did not establish husband's domicile of choice).

155. See Restatement, Second § 37. Cf. Mounts v. Mounts, 181 Neb. 542, 149 N.W.2d 435 (1967) (presume that domicile of run-away husband remained at marital domicile to provide basis for personal jurisdiction over him in support suit brought 14 years after his disappearance). But cf. Kulko v. Superior Court, 436 U.S. 84, 98 S.Ct. 1690, 56 L.Ed.2d 132 (1978) (no personal jurisdiction over husband to increase support payments when forum was never marital domicile even though husband acceded to request of child to join mother in forum). See § 4.20.

husband, the New York courts were probably free to stretch their domiciliary service statute to cover the situation[156] as other courts have stretched "doing business" statutes.[157] But we should not be so caught up in this playacting that we believe for a moment that the husband was "domiciled" in New York and that this was the basis for jurisdiction.

To test this proposition, suppose one of the husband's Louisiana creditors had moved to New York. The creditor learns of the wife's action in New York and the finding of domicile by the New York court, and sues the husband in New York using the provision for substituted service on domiciliaries. There is no constitutional basis for in personam jurisdiction over the husband in the creditor's suit.[158]

§ 2.15B   A Substitute for Domicile as a Basis for Judicial Jurisdiction

Just as technical domicile alone should not suffice as a constitutional basis for personal jurisdiction,[159] technical domicile, despite United States Supreme Court dicta to the contrary,[160] should not be a constitutional prerequisite for divorce jurisdiction.[161] What is necessary for divorce jurisdiction is some contact between the forum and the marriage to give that forum a reasonable interest in affecting the marital status. The divorce statutes for persons in the armed forces and the opinions upholding their validity seem proper by such a test.[162] The substantial period of residence in the state while stationed there, which the statutes require,[163] seems to afford the state a legitimate interest in affecting

---

156. See Stucky v. Stucky, 186 Neb. 636, 185 N.W.2d 656 (1971) (last marital domicile has personal jurisdiction for custody, support, and alimony judgments against husband who moved from forum; court notes it can reach result either under "traditional" notion that husband did not satisfy burden of showing a change of domicile or under "minimum contacts" ground that he had sufficient contacts with the forum to confer jurisdiction with regard to the matters in issue).

157. See Roy v. North Am. Newspaper Alliance, Inc., 106 N.H. 92, 205 A.2d 844 (1964); Note, *Recent Interpretations of "Doing Business" Statutes*, 44 Iowa L. Rev. 345 (1959).

158. Cf. Cook, The Logical and Legal Bases of the Conflict of Laws 199 (1942) (although the court in Winans v. Winans, 205 Mass. 388, 91 N.E. 394 (1910), found husband domiciled in Massachusetts for purpose of wife's divorce jurisdiction, Cook does not think there would be a similar finding for personal jurisdiction in a cause of action not related to the marriage).

159. See § 2.15A.

160. See, e.g., Williams v. North Carolina, 325 U.S. 226, 229, 65 S.Ct. 1092, 1095, 89 L.Ed. 1577, 1581 (1945): "Under our system of law, judicial power to grant a divorce—jurisdiction, strictly speaking—is founded on domicil."

161. See Note, *Domicile as a Constitutional Requirement for Divorce Jurisdiction*, 44 Iowa L. Rev. 765 (1959); § 5.2H.

162. See, e.g., Lauterbach v. Lauterbach, 392 P.2d 24 (Alaska 1964); Craig v. Craig, 143 Kan. 624, 56 P.2d 464 (1936); Wood v. Wood, 159 Tex. 350, 320 S.W.2d 807 (1959). Cf. English Domicile & Matrimonial Proceedings Act § 5(2)(b) (1973) conferring divorce jurisdiction if "either of the parties to the marriage ... was habitually resident in England and Wales throughout the period of one year."

163. An exception is the Alabama statute, which requires no period of residence. Ala. Code § 6–7–20(a) (1975): "Any person in any branch or service of the government of the United States of America, including those in the military, air and naval service, and the husband or wife of any such person, if he or she be living within the borders of the State of

marital status although, because of an obligation to obey orders and the nomadic nature of service life, there could not ordinarily exist the state of mind required to establish a technical domicile of choice in that state.[164]

§ 2.16 Recognizing that the Meaning of "Domicile" Changes with the Context is Not Sufficient to Make it a Useful Tool for Conflicts Analysis

In the famous debate during the proceedings of the American Law Institute concerning the adoption of the provisions on domicile of the first Restatement of the Conflict of Laws, Professor Walter Wheeler Cook advanced the following proposition concerning the meaning of that term: "There is no doubt that what you might call the core of the concept is the same in all these situations; but as you get out towards what I like to call the twilight zone of the subject, I don't believe the scope remains exactly the same for all purposes."[165] This was too much for Professor Beale, the Reporter, and his vested-rights allies to swallow, since it would upset the symmetry of the tight little syllogisms that they were fashioning and that imprisoned conflicts analysis for the better part of three decades. At least for now, however, the verdict of history has gone to Professor Cook, for the second Restatement adopts substantially his position.[166]

It cannot be otherwise. The domiciliary concept is used for too many diverse purposes; the finding of domicile is too dependent upon subjective inferences drawn from the facts, even undisputed facts,[167] for the

---

Alabama, shall be deemed to be a resident of the state of Alabama for the purpose of commencing any civil action in the courts of this State." Furthermore, the Alabama divorce statute requires a period of residence (6 months) only if the defendant is not a resident. Ala. Code § 30–2–5 (1975). The validity of the Alabama servicemen's and women's residence statute would, therefore, seem highly doubtful in divorce cases. It was, however, upheld in a case in which the plaintiff serviceman had actually lived in Alabama for almost two years. Conrad v. Conrad, 275 Ala. 202, 153 So.2d 635 (1963).

164. See § 2.7.

165. 3 Proceedings of the American Law Institute 227 (1925).

166. Restatement, Second § 11, comment *o*.

167. The classic example is the *Dorrance* litigation in which, from essentially undisputed facts, Mr. Dorrance was found domiciled in both New Jersey and Pennsylvania at death and both states levied inheritance taxes. In re Dorrance, 115 N.J.Eq. 268, 170 A. 601 (Prerogative Ct.1934), aff'd mem., 13 N.J.Misc. 168, 176 A. 902 (Sup.Ct. 1935), affd mem., 116 N.J.L. 362, 184 A. 743, cert. denied, 298 U.S. 678, 56 S.Ct. 949, 80 L.Ed. 1399 (1936); Dorrance's Estate, 309 Pa. 151, 163 A. 303 (1932), cert. denied, 288 U.S. 617, 53 S.Ct. 507, 77 L.Ed. 990. See also California v. Texas, 457 U.S. 164, 102 S.Ct. 2335, 72 L.Ed.2d 755 (1982). California was granted leave to file a complaint against Texas under the Court's original jurisdiction to determine whether Howard Hughes was domiciled in California or Texas at death. "The decision about domicile could determine which state is entitled to levy death taxes on the estate." Id. Cf. Cory v. White, 457 U.S. 85, 102 S.Ct. 2325, 72 L.Ed.2d 694 (1982) (the Eleventh Amendment prevents the administrator of the Hughes estate from interpleading the tax officials of California and Texas).

A state other than the domicile at death may have a sufficient nexus with the decedent or the property to make it reasonable to levy an estate tax on intangible property. See Curry v. McCanless, 307 U.S. 357, 59 S.Ct. 900, 83 L.Ed. 1339 (1939) (both domicile at death and situs of trust may levy death taxes on intangibles held in trust); State Tax Comm'n of Utah v. Aldrich, 316 U.S. 174, 62 S.Ct. 1008, 86 L.Ed. 1358 (1942) (Utah may

meaning of that concept not to vary with its context.[168] For this same reason, the proposition that the meaning of "domicile" shifts with the circumstances would be difficult or impossible to prove by case analysis. Articulating the same technical definition of "domicile," courts can shift its meaning subtly by shifting the emphasis to one or another element of the definition or by drawing different reasonable inferences from essentially the same fact pattern.[169]

---

impose estate tax on stock in Utah corporation even though stock's owner died domiciled in New York). Both California and Texas probably had sufficient nexus with the Hughes estate to levy a tax on its intangible property. Therefore the Supreme Court was not prudent in granting original jurisdiction to determine the domicile at death. The estate and federal and state tax authorities subsequently settled the matter. Cf. Citizen's Bk. & Trust Co. v. Glaser, 70 N.J. 72, 357 A.2d 753 (1976) (holding that New Jersey could not levy an inheritance tax on intangible personalty because the decedent had lost her domicile in New Jersey and acquired one in Virginia despite retaining a summer home in New Jersey, voting there, and listing it as her residence on federal income tax returns). The dissent rejected "the outmoded principle that no person has more than one domicile which precludes inheritance tax applications of more than one state" and pointed out that if both New Jersey and Virginia levied inheritance taxes, the estate would not be unduly burdened, but if it were, the New Jersey Tax Director was authorized to negotiate with Virginia taxing authorities. 357 A.2d at 763.

There is some dispute as to the proper standard on appeal for reviewing a finding of domicile. *Dorrance's Estate* (Pennsylvania decision supra this note) took the position that the finding of domicile was freely reviewable as a question of law. For cases in accord with this view see, e.g., Alexander v. District of Columbia, 370 A.2d 1327 (D.C.App.1977) (income tax liability); Stambaugh v. Stambaugh, 458 Pa. 147 329 A.2d 483 (1974) (collateral attack on husband's Florida divorce fails when trial court finding that husband was not domiciled there is reversed). For the opposing view that a finding of domicile should be treated as a fact and overturned only if "clearly erroneous", see, e.g., Crowley v. Glaze, 710 F.2d 676 (10th Cir.1983) (diversity); Valentin v. Hospital Bella Vista, 254 F.3d 358, 365 (1st Cir.2001) (diversity); Webb v. Nolan, 484 F.2d 1049 (4th Cir.1973), appeal dism'd for want of juris. and cert. denied, 415 U.S. 903, 94 S.Ct. 1397, 39 L.Ed.2d 461 (1974) (diversity jurisdiction); O'Hern v. Bowling, 109 Ariz. 90, 505 P.2d 550 (1973) (candidacy for office); Estate of Elson, 120 Ill.App.3d 649, 76 Ill.Dec. 237, 458 N.E.2d 637 (2d Dist.1983) (probate jurisdiction, overturn only if "against the manifest weight of the evidence"); Margani v. Sanders, 453 A.2d 501, 504 (Me.1982) (personal jurisdiction, "[a]lthough a determination of domicile is a mixed question of fact and law, the correct standard for appellate review of such a determination is the clearly erroneous test"); In re Estate of Ritter, 518 S.W.2d 453 (Mo.App.1975) (qualification of executrix); Dietz v. Medora, 333 N.W.2d 702 (N.D.1983) (eligibility for city office); Murray v. Murray, 515 S.W.2d 387 (Tex.Civ. App. Waco 1974) (personal jurisdiction); Lotz v. Atamaniuk, 172 W.Va. 116, 304 S.E.2d 20 (1983) (law applicable to husband's right to elect against will, trial court's finding treated as a finding of fact and overturned because the evidence clearly preponderated against it). See also Palazzo ex rel. Delmage v. Corio, 232 F.3d 38, 42 (2d Cir. 2000), which holds that when domicile is contested by a Fed.R.Civ.P. 12(b)(1) motion to dismiss for lack of subject matter jurisdiction, "the factual questions ... need not be submitted to a jury and may be resolved by the court."

168. See Elliott v. Krear, 466 F.Supp. 444 (E.D.Va.1979) (in the light of the purposes of diversity jurisdiction, child is domiciled in Virginia where he lives with grandparents, rather than in California where parent resides); Stumberg, Conflict of Laws 48 (3d ed. 1963); Reese, § 2.12B note 116, at 592; Yiannopoulos, § 2.13B note 133, at 259 n. 378. For a classic judicial statement of the opposing viewpoint, see Williamson v. Osenton, 232 U.S. 619, 625, 34 S.Ct. 442, 443, 58 L.Ed. 758, 761–62 (1914) (Holmes, J.): "The very meaning of domicil is the technically preeminent headquarters that every person is compelled to have in order that certain rights and duties that have been attached to it by the law may be determined.... In its nature it is one, and if in any case two are recognized for different purposes it is a doubtful anomaly." See also Mark v. Mark, [2005] 3 W.L.R. 111 (H.L., appeal from Eng., 2005): "A person must always have a domicile but can only have one domicile at a time. Hence it must be given the same meaning in whatever context it arises." Id. at 123.

169. Cf. Restatement, Second § 11, comment *o*.

Nevertheless, the common-sense recognition that the meaning of "domicile" must shift with the purpose for which we are using it, is not enough to preserve it as a viable and useful tool for conflicts analysis, especially as a contact word in choice-of-law rules. It is true that an able and enlightened court, utilizing the flexibility inherent in the term, can reach proper results in individual cases. This is not impossible, but neither is it very easy or likely. It is like retaining "place of wrong" as the basic choice-of-law rule for torts and attempting to achieve just and rational results by varying the meaning of "place of wrong"[170] or by characterization legerdemain.[171]

One of the strong points of the Second Restatement is that it has abandoned the "place of wrong" rule for torts.[172] There is no justification for retaining any rigid, territorially-oriented choice-of-law rule that utilizes contact words pointing to a place rather than focusing attention on the reasonable interests of contact states.[173] If the result in *In re Estate of Jones*[174] is wrong, the error does not lie in fixing Evan Jones' technical domicile at death in Iowa. It is wrong because Great Britain had an interest in controlling the distribution of Evan's intestate personalty as between his illegitimate daughter and his brothers and sisters; Iowa did not. If the result in *White v. Tennant*[175] is wrong, it is wrong because it fails to advance West Virginia's legitimate interests in having its own law applied, not because Michael White was domiciled at death in West Virginia. So, too, if the holding in *In re Annesley*[176] is incorrect, it is because it employs the French rule that frustrates the intention of the testatrix when the French rule is not relevant.

If it is desirable in these cases to manipulate the meaning of "domicile" so that Evan Jones will be domiciled at death in Great Britain, or Michael White in West Virginia, or Mrs. Annesley in England, it is because of reasons revealed by an analysis of the policies underlying

---

170. In cases involving harm to the incidents of marriage, the argument has some times been made that the "wrong" occurs at the marital domicile, rather than where the defendant acts. For cases rejecting the argument that the harm occurred at the marital domicile, see e.g., Sestito v. Knop, 297 F.2d 33 (7th Cir.1961) (loss of consortium); Jordan v. States Marine Corp., 257 F.2d 232 (9th Cir.1958) (loss of consortium); McVickers v. Chesapeake & O. Ry., 194 F.Supp. 848 (E.D.Mich.1961) (loss of consortium); Folk v. York–Shipley, Inc., 239 A.2d 236 (Del.1968) (loss of consortium). But see Williams v. Jeffs, 57 P.3d 232 (Utah App. 2002) (in a suit for alienation of affections, the injury occurs at the marital domicile); Lister v. McAnulty, [1944] Can.Sup.Ct. 317, [1944] 3 D.L.R. 673 (law of marital domicile applied to prevent husband's recovery for loss of consortium).

171. See, e.g., Kilberg v. Northeast Airlines, Inc., 9 N.Y.2d 34, 211 N.Y.S.2d 133 172 N.E.2d 526 (1961) ("procedural"); Haumschild v. Continental Cas. Co., 7 Wis.2d 130, 95 N.W.2d 814 (1959) ("family law"); Grant v. McAuliffe, 41 Cal.2d 859, 264 P.2d 944 (1953) ("administration of estates," "procedural").

172. Restatement, Second § 145.

173. As an indication that allowing the meaning of domicile to vary with context will not produce satisfactory results, Professor Cook, one of the champions of the flexible meaning view, cites with approval, for its awareness of the problem, In re Jones' Estate (see § 2.12A). Cook, The Logical and Legal Bases of the Conflict of Laws 196 n.3 (1942).

174. See § 2.12A.

175. See § 2.12B.

176. See § 2.13A.

the apparently conflicting domestic rules concerning intestate succession or validity of wills. Without such an analysis, manipulation of the meaning of "domicile" is unreasoned and blind and, therefore, unwise. With such an analysis, molding "domicile" to fit our needs is unnecessary. It is unnecessary because, having made the analysis, a court can base the result directly upon the relevance or irrelevance of the domestic policies in issue and explain candidly why it is not applying the law of the domicile at death.

§ 2.17   Habitual Residence

The Hague Conference on Private International Law uses "habitual residence" rather than "domicile" in its conventions.[177] For example, the Convention on the Law Applicable to Succession to the Estates of Deceased Persons[178] has the following provision covering succession in the absence of the decedent's effective designation[179] of some other law:

Article 3

(1) Succession is governed by the law of the State in which the deceased at the time of his death was habitually resident, if he was then a national of that State.

(2) Succession is also governed by the law of the State in which the deceased at the time of his death was habitually resident if he had been resident there for a period of no less than five years immediately preceding his death. However, in exceptional circumstances, if at the time of his death he was manifestly more closely connected with the State of which he was then a national, the law of that State applies.

(3) In other cases succession is governed by the law of the State of which at the time of his death the deceased was a national, unless at that time the deceased was more closely connected with another State, in which case the law of the latter State applies.

This provision is more likely to be related to the policies underlying the law of succession than a rule using technical domicile. If, for

---

177. For information on the Hague Conference, see § 1.4 n.22.

Some United States scholars have suggested substituting "habitual residence" for domicile. See Cavers, *"Habitual Residence": A Useful Concept?*, 21 Am. U. L. Rev. 475 (1972), which urges substitution of the term "habitual residence" for "domicile" in the hope that courts will find it easier to apply the newer term in a more flexible manner and reach results more in accord with common sense. Cf. L. McDougal, *Toward Application of the Best Rule of Law in Choice of Law Cases*, 35 Mercer L. Rev. 483, 500 (1984): "When identifying significantly affected states, the court should employ a broad conception of who is a resident of a state [and not] the traditional concept of domicile. . . ."

178. The text of the Convention, concluded on 1 August 1989, is available on the Internet through the home page of the Hague Conference. The site for this Convention is <http://www.hcch.net/e/conventions/text32e.html>. As of October 1, 2009, the Convention was not in force because it had not received the necessary three ratifications. The Netherlands has ratified it and Argentina, Luxembourg, and Switzerland had signed the Convention but not ratified it.

179. Article 5(1) permits the decedent to designate the law of the state that is the decedent's nationality or habitual residence at the time of designation or death.

example, *White v. Tennant*[180] were an international case to which the Convention applied, Article 3 would lead to the application of West Virginia law. This is preferable to the court's application of Pennsylvania law. Applied to *In re Estate of Jones*,[181] however, the Convention would have produced the same result that was adversely criticized in the discussion of that case. It is helpful to have general rules such as those of Article 3 that produce desirable results in most cases. Each of the paragraphs of Article 3, not just paragraph 3, should have provisions for exceptions. Moreover, the exception should designate "another state that has a more significant relationship to the effects of succession" rather than, as in Article 3(3), the decedent's connection.

A Hague Convention that is in force and that the United States has ratified is the Convention on the Civil Aspects of International Child Abduction.[182] The Convention is designed to end international snatch and run as a tactic for contesting child custody. In general, the Convention requires return of a child to the country in which the child "was habitually resident immediately before" the child was removed "in breach of custody rights."[183]

Walton v. Walton,[184] applied the Convention noting that the term "habitual residence" is more flexible than domicile. The court held that a five-year-old child who had lived in Australia for 18 months prior to being removed to the United States was habitually resident in Australia. The parents disputed whether they intended to remain in Australia for an indefinite time. The court found the child habitually resident in Australia because the family moved there with the "settled purpose" of remaining there for some significant period and not for a "mere visit."

In re J[185] is a House of Lords decision interpreting the term "habitual residence" in the Child Abduction Convention. The parents, United Kingdom citizens, emigrated to Australia where they met, cohabited, had a child, but did not wed. Over two years after the child, J, was born, the mother left Australia without notifying the father. She took the child with her to England where she intended to reside indefinitely and not return to Australia. Twenty-two days after the mother had left Australia, the father obtained an order from an Australian Family Court judge awarding the father sole custody of the child. The father's application in England for return of the child under the Convention was dismissed and this dismissal was affirmed by the Court of Appeal and by the House of Lords. The opinion in the House of Lords held that the removal of the child from Australia was not wrongful because under

---

180. See § 2.12B.

181. See § 2.12A.

182. Concluded October 25, 1980. The site for this Convention is <http://www.hcch. net/e/conventions/text28e.html>. As of 18 April 2009 this convention was in force in the United States and 80 other countries. <http://www.hcch.net/e/status/abdshte.html>.

183. Arts. 3, 12. For further discussion of the Convention see infra § 5.3B, notes 286–310 and accompanying text.

184. 925 F.Supp. 453 (S.D. Miss. 1996).

185. [1990] 2 A.C. 562 (H.L., appeal from Eng., 1990).

Australian law, until the father obtained the custody order, the sole right of custody of the illegitimate child was in the mother. The retention of the child in England after the Australian custody order was not wrongful because by that time Australia was no longer the child's "habitual residence." On this last point, the opinion stated:

> [T]here is a significant difference between a person ceasing to be habitually resident in country A, and his subsequently becoming habitually resident in country B. A person may cease to be habitually resident in country A in a single day if he or she leaves it with a settled intention not to return to it but to take up long-term residence in country B instead. Such a person cannot, however, become habitually resident in country B in a single day. An appreciable period of time and a settled intention will be necessary to enable him or her to become so. During that appreciable period of time the person will have ceased to be habitually resident in country A but not yet have become habitually resident in country B.... [W]here a child of J's age is in the sole lawful custody of the mother, his situation with regard to habitual residence will necessarily be the same as hers.[186]

---

186. Id. at 578.

Chapter 3

PERVASIVE PROBLEMS

§ 3.1 Introduction

There are certain problems that pervade attempts to resolve conflict of laws questions by traditional territorially-oriented choice-of-law rules. These problems include characterization, renvoi, dépeçage, the proper scope of the "public policy" exception, and notice and proof of foreign law. It is the purpose of this chapter to appraise the effect that change from a territorial to a functional method of choice-of-law analysis will have upon these problems.

A territorially-oriented choice-of-law rule is one that points to a geographical location as the source of the applicable law before any inquiry is made into the content of that law. The classic example of such a rule is the one selecting the law of the place of wrong[1] for application to torts conflicts problems.

On the other hand, a "functional analysis of choice-of-law problems" describes a process that first focuses on the apparently conflicting domestic rules of two or more jurisdictions having contacts with the parties and with the transaction. The analysis then identifies the policies underlying each state's rules. The key question is: "Which states are likely to experience the social consequences that their policies are attempting to avoid if a court or arbitrator does not apply their law?" It is one of the premises of functional choice-of-law analysis that at this point many conflicts problems will be resolved. Only one state will appear to have any "interest" in having its law applied, and its law, therefore, should be applied. The apparent conflict of laws is a "false" conflict.[2]

If, on the other hand, there are two or more states that will advance their policies by applying their laws, there is a "real conflict." A rational solution to this true conflict may focus on policies or trends in the development of the law that the jurisdictions share.[3] In any event, a

---

1. Restatement of Conflicts of Laws § 378 (1934): "The law of the place of wrong determines whether a person has sustained a legal injury."

2. For classic statements of this proposition see Currie, *Notes on Methods and Objectives in the Conflict of Laws,* 1959 Duke L. J. 171, 174; Traynor, *Is this Conflict Really Necessary?,* 37 Texas L. Rev. 657, 667–74 (1959). But see Leflar, *True "False Conflicts," Et Alia,* 48 Boston U. L. Rev. 164, 170–73 (1968) opposing the use of the term "false conflicts" to refer to any case in which two states have different laws on the same issue and both have contacts with the transaction in issue. Professor Leflar would limit use of the term to cases in which the two states have identical rules or different rules that would produce the same result.

3. See, e.g., § 7.4A. Perhaps, as some have suggested, a meaningful choice between truly conflicting laws may depend on the "intensity or significance of each state's interest."

court that has adopted a consequences-based approach to choice of law is likely to articulate a solution to a clash of state policies by focusing on those consequences. This chapter explores the question: what solutions does a functional method of choice-of-law analysis offer for the "pervasive problems"[4] that have puzzled conflicts scholars through the years?

§ 3.2 Characterization

"Characterization" or "classification" are fancy terms for the process of putting labels on problems. Under traditional, now largely displaced, territorially-oriented choice-of-law rules, every conflicts case requires three levels of characterization: (1) determination of the nature of the substantive problem; (2) interpretation of the choice-of-law rule chosen; and (3) a decision as to which issues are "substantive", therefore determined under the law designated by the choice-of-law rule, and which issues are "procedural", therefore determined by forum law.

§ 3.2A The Substantive Label

Affixing a label to the particular substantive problem is a crucial first step in applying territorially-oriented choice-of-law rules, for it will tell us which of the many different rules to apply. If our problem is one of "tort", we apply the law of the place of the wrong. If it is a "contract" problem, we apply another choice-of-law rule pointing to a different geographical location for the source of the governing law.[5] There is no consensus on where this place is for contract problems—perhaps the place of the making of the contract,[6] or the place of performance,[7] or the "center of gravity" of the contract.[8] The substantive label that a court

---

Horowitz, *Toward a Federal Common Law of Choice of Law,* 14 U.C.L.A. L. Rev. 1191, 1200 (1967). See also Baxter, *Choice of Law and the Federal System,* 16 Stan. L. Rev. 1, 20 (1963) ("comparative-impairment principle"). One may doubt whether a solution on the basis of "comparative impairment" will commend itself to the objective observer except, perhaps, in extreme cases that lie along the vague boundary of the "false" conflict. For a discussion of comparative impairment see infra §§ 6.24, 6.25.

4. These problems are thus referred to in E. Scoles & R. Weintraub, Cases and Materials on Conflict of Laws, ch. 3 (2d ed. 1972 with 1987 Supplement).

5. See Garza v. Greyhound Lines, Inc., 418 S.W.2d 595 (Tex.Civ.App.1967); Hudson v. Continental Bus System, Inc., 317 S.W.2d 584 (Tex.Civ.App.1958, writ ref'd n.r.e.) (both cases apply Texas law to personal injury in Mexico when the courts classify the action as breach of contract instead of tort).

For other examples of a "tort" to "Contract" characterization switch, see In re Asbestos Litigation (Bell), 517 A.2d 697 (Del.Super.1986) (the liability of a successor corporation for injuries caused by products produced by the company it acquired is a contract issue governed by the law chosen by a choice-of-law clause in the acquisition agreement); Lee v. Saliga, 179 W.Va. 762, 373 S.E.2d 345 (1988) (whether uninsured motorist coverage requires physical contact is a contract issue determined by law of state where policy was issued and not by law of state where accident occurred).

6. Restatement of Conflict of Laws § 332 (1934) ("the law of the place of contracting").

7. See Victorson v. Albert M. Green Hosiery Mills, Inc., 202 F.2d 717 (3d Cir.1953) (Pennsylvania law, as place of contracting and performance, governs action for breach of express warranty of quality).

8. Auten v. Auten, 308 N.Y. 155, 124 N.E.2d 99 (1954).

applied may be that of some other field of law, each invoking its own territorial choice-of-law rule.[9]

The importance of this first step in characterization was apparent to astute counsel. The Texas courts, following the lead of Justice Holmes in *Slater v. Mexican Nat'l R.R.*,[10] refused to enforce actions for wrongful death and personal injury based on Mexican law. This was because Texas courts considered the Mexican law in issue too "dissimilar" from Texas law. A classic type of dissimilarity occurs when the Mexican law provides for damages payable in modifiable installments similar to American alimony awards. Because territorial dogma required the court to apply the law of the place of wrong, and because the Texas court could not give the Mexican remedy, the result had been dismissal of the suit in Texas, remitting the plaintiff to whatever remedy he or she may have in Mexican courts.[11]

Plaintiffs have avoided dismissal of a suit for personal injury suffered in Mexico when the defendant is a commercial carrier and the plaintiffs' lawyers convinced the court to characterize the action as one based on a contract made in Texas, thus resulting in the application of Texas law.[12]

In two landmark conflicts wrongful death cases, *Kilberg v. Northeast Airlines, Incorporated*[13] and *Griffith v. United Air Lines, Incorporated*,[14] part of plaintiffs' tactics consisted of urging that the problem was one of "contract" rather than "tort." In these cases, this argument, if successful, would have shifted the territorial choice-of-law focus from the laws of the places of the fatal crashes, which had low ceilings on wrongful death[15] and survival[16] recovery, to the far more favorable laws of the

---

9. See, e.g., Haumschild v. Continental Casualty Co., 7 Wis.2d 130, 95 N.W.2d 814 (1959) (change from "tort" to "family law").

10. 194 U.S. 120, 24 S.Ct. 581, 48 L.Ed. 900 (1904).

11. See El Paso & Juarez Traction Co. v. Carruth, 255 S.W. 159 (Tex.Com.App.1923, holding approved) (personal injuries suffered in Mexico by Texas citizen as a result of the negligence of a Texas corporation); Carter v. Tillery, 257 S.W.2d 465 (Tex.Civ.App.1953, writ ref'd n.r.e.) (all parties Texas residents; personal injuries suffered in private plane crash in Mexico as a result of losing course while returning to Texas from New Mexico). Compare with the "dissimilarity" doctrine cases, Arabian Trading & Chem. Ind. Co. Ltd. v. B.F. Goodrich Co., 823 F.2d 60 (4th Cir. 1987) (because the forum cannot order a fine paid to Saudi Arabia or the expulsion of employees from Saudi Arabia, the only remedies available under applicable Saudi Arabian law, the case must be dismissed).

12. Garza v. Greyhound Lines, Inc., 418 S.W.2d 595 (Tex.Civ.App.1967); Hudson v. Continental Bus System, Inc., 317 S.W.2d 584 (Tex.Civ.App.1958, writ ref'd n.r.e.).

Texas has now abandoned both the place-of-wrong rule and the "dissimilarity" doctrine. Gutierrez v. Collins, 583 S.W.2d 312 (Tex.1979).

Not only have Texas courts abolished the dissimilarity doctrine, but also, without the need for switching the substantive label from "tort" to "contract," a Texas court, using the "most significant relationship" test adopted in *Gutierrez*, supra, is likely to apply Texas law to a claim for injury in Mexico. See Trailways, Inc. v. Clark, 794 S.W.2d 479 (Tex.App.—Corpus Christi 1990, writ denied) (apply Texas law to Mexican bus line in wrongful death and survival actions arising from crash in Mexico).

13. 9 N.Y.2d 34, 211 N.Y.S.2d 133, 172 N.E.2d 526 (1961).

14. 416 Pa. 1, 203 A.2d 796 (1964).

15. Kilberg v. Northeast Airlines, Inc., 9 N.Y.2d 34, 211 N.Y.S.2d 133, 172 N.E.2d 526 (1961).

forums. Forum law applied because it was the place of making of the transportation contracts, or perhaps the "center of gravity" of those contracts.[17]

The courts rejected the "contract" characterization in *Kilberg* and accepted it in *Griffith*. In *Griffith*, however, the switch to a "contract" label for the plaintiff's action did not affect the outcome. It did not affect the outcome because *Griffith* was the case in which the Supreme Court of Pennsylvania abandoned territorial conflicts analysis and adopted in its stead a functional or state-interest approach to choice-of-law problems. The court chose Pennsylvania survival law, which was far more favorable for the plaintiff than the law of the place of the crash, not because the contract of carriage was "made" in Pennsylvania, but because the court found that the domestic policies underlying Pennsylvania's survival rules were applicable despite the crash in Colorado, while the domestic policies of Colorado were either irrelevant or only tangentially relevant.

Griffith thus epitomizes the impact of a functional analysis of choice-of-law problems on first-step characterization. A method of resolving conflicts problems that focuses directly on the domestic rules in putative conflict and on their underlying policies does not require a substantive characterization of those rules, at least for the identification and elimination of "false" conflicts. If the conflict is functionally a "true" one because at least two states have domestic policies that would be substantially advanced by application of their law to the parties and the transaction in issue, it may be that once again something will turn upon the substantive identification of the problem. This will be so, for example, if a method for resolution of the true conflict is utilized that focuses on substantive policies that the two states share and on clearly discernible shared trends in the development of the substantive area in issue. It is highly unlikely, however, that substantive identification of the problem will be as determinative for functional resolution of a true conflict as it is for territorial resolution. One would hope that our legal institution has evolved with that minimum of sanity necessary to prevent policies and trends in the development of the law that are widely shared by our states from pointing in opposite directions in torts, in contracts, in property and so forth. Moreover, it is far less likely that such broadly stated policies and developments will point to different solutions of a practical problem than that two narrow domestic rules will do so.

---

16. Griffith v. United Air Lines, Inc., 416 Pa. 1, 203 A.2d 796 (1964).

17. In *Kilberg,* the plaintiff also argued for a contract measure of damages. Recovery, even under the New York wrongful death act, would be slight because the decedent was a bachelor without statutory dependents. Plaintiff sought the future earnings that decedent had been deprived of by his untimely death. After the *Kilberg* decision, the plaintiff settled the case for less than the $15,000 Massachusetts limit on recovery. See Currie, *Conflict, Crisis and Confusion in New York,* 1963 Duke L. J. 1, 7 n. 21.

§ 3.2B   Interpreting Choice-of-Law Rules

The second level of characterization problems met in applying territorially-oriented choice-of-law rules consists of interpreting the choice-of-law rules. Most often these questions of interpretation have centered on the word or words that identify the geographical location of the applicable law. Where was the decedent "domiciled" at death;[18] where is the "place of making" of the contract;[19] where is the "place of the wrong"?[20] By interpreting differently these contact or pointing words in the choice-of-law rule, two jurisdictions that appear to have identical choice-of-law rules can arrive at different solutions to the conflicts problem just as surely as if they had no choice-of-law rules, or patently different rules, or differed at the first step in substantive characterization of the problem.

Surely there will also be problems in defining and delimiting the process of functional analysis of a choice-of-law problem. What policies underlie a state's domestic law? Are we concerned with all hypothetically possible policies or only with policies that in fact have been articulated by the legislature or courts of the state involved, or at least by commentators and other legislatures and courts in dealing with similar domestic rules? May the actual facts of a case eliminate from consideration a hypothetically possible policy? For example, there is much talk of the "interest" of the place where physical injuries have occurred in providing for recovery in order to insure the payment of local medical creditors.[21] Does it matter whether in fact there are medical creditors, whether they are still unpaid, whether their payment is assured from sources independent of the plaintiff's tort recovery?

These problems are substantial when focusing simply on the actual steps in the functional analysis of a conflicts case, but they are aggravated when one seeks to state a functional choice-of-law rule that summarizes the results of the process. The Second Restatement's rule for torts illustrates the difficulties of interpretation presented by a choice-of-law rule intended to encapsulate a functional analysis. The Restatement rule refers to "the state which . . . has the most significant relationship to the occurrence and the parties . . . "[22] A functional choice-of-law rule that is

---

18. In re Estate of Jones, 192 Iowa 78, 182 N.W. 227 (1921); White v. Tennant, 31 W.Va. 790, 8 S.E. 596 (1888); Restatement, Second, Conflict of Laws § 260 (1971) (intestate succession to movables). For discussion of Estate of Jones and White v. Tennant, see §§ 2.12A, 2.12B.

19. University of Chicago v. Dater, 277 Mich. 658, 270 N.W. 175 (1936).

20. For cases interpreting "place of wrong" in actions for loss of consortium as the place where the spouse received a physical injury rather than the marital domicile see, e.g., Sestito v. Knop, 297 F.2d 33 (7th Cir.1961); Jordan v. States Marine Corp., 257 F.2d 232 (9th Cir.1958).

21. See, e.g., Currie, *The Silver Oar and All That: A Study of the Romero Case,* 27 U. Chi. L. Rev. 1, 71 (1959); Hancock, *Three Approaches to the Choice-of-Law Problem: The Classificatory, The Functional and the Result–Selective,* in XXth Century Comparative and Conflicts Law 365, 371 (1961).

22. Restatement, Second, Conflict of Laws § 145 (1971).

result-oriented rather than territorially-oriented will minimize difficulties in interpreting and applying the rule. An example of such a rule is:

> A contract is valid if valid under the law of the principal place of business or habitual residence of the party wishing to enforce the contract unless the principal place of business or habitual residence of the other party has an invalidating rule designed to protect against contracts of adhesion.[23]

Switching from a territorial analysis to a functional analysis of conflicts cases under rules like that of the Second Restatement, which use a "most significant relationship" concept, will not eliminate problems at the second level of characterization—defining the meaning of the choice-of-law rule. In fact, there is some concern that these problems may be aggravated. One argument in favor of retaining the rigid territorial choice-of-law rules is that they are simple and certain in application.[24]

This claim of simplicity and certainty for the old rules is debatable. It may well be that the new functional, state-interest conflicts analysis simplifies rather than complicates the law. It is true that on the surface nothing seemed simpler for resolving tort choice-of-law problems than the rule that had been uniformly adopted in the United States, the place-of-wrong rule.[25] Find the spot on the map where the defendant injured the plaintiff; find the tort law of that place; apply it. Yes, the old rule seemed clear and certain. But like Baron Turton,[26] a number of excellent judges, sensing on the basis of largely unarticulated premises that the result produced by the settled rule was outrageous, used their ingenuity and the play in the joints of the old system to avoid the law of the place of the wrong. Labels were switched in the best now-you-see-it-now-you-don't tradition of that most skilled of all prestidigitators, the common law judge who has decided on the correct result and is seeking a way to get there. What was a "tort" problem was changed before your eyes by the incantation "administration of decedents' estates"[27] or "family law"[28] or "contract"[29] or, most powerful conjuring word of them all,

23. See § 7.5.

24. This argument was one of the major bases for retention of the place-of-wrong rule in Dowis v. Mud Slingers, Inc., 279 Ga. 808, 816, 621 S.E.2d 413, 419 (2005).

25. See § 6.9.

26. "Let's fill the cups to Baron Turton
Who, though the law was clear and certain,
Would rather help a little foetus
Than round out Charlie Fearn's dull treatise."

The verse was written by Mr. Donald G. McNeil while a Harvard Law School student. Baron Turton, of the Court of Exchequer, defied precedent in holding that a posthumously born child could take a remainder interest in property. Reeve v. Long, 3 Lev. 408 (1695).

27. Grant v. McAuliffe, 41 Cal.2d 859, 264 P.2d 944 (1953).

28. Haumschild v. Continental Cas. Co., 7 Wis.2d 130, 95 N.W.2d 814 (1959).

29. Levy v. Daniels' U–Drive Auto Renting Co., 108 Conn. 333, 143 A. 163 (1928) (whether statute applies that imposes vicarious liability on automobile lessor); Cortes v. Ryder Truck Rental, Inc., 220 Ill.App.3d 632, 163 Ill.Dec. 50, 581 N.E.2d 1 (1991), appeal dism'd, 143 Ill.2d 637, 167 Ill.Dec. 398, 587 N.E.2d 1013 (1992) (same). Contra, Jack v.

"procedural".[30] The results, though wondrous, seemed arbitrary and unpredictable.

Although such displacements of the place-of-wrong rule were relatively rare, there is every reason to believe that these aberrations would have multiplied as dissatisfaction with the products of that rule increased. The current revolution in analysis of tort conflicts problems is unique only in that it has compressed into about a decade a process that has been repeated throughout the history of the common law, but usually over the span of a century or more. A seemingly simple, settled rule results in a growing number of adjudications that are dysfunctional responses to a social problem. Great judges, sensing the irrationality and injustice that the rule is producing, bend, avoid, evade the rule. These exceptions and evasions produce a confusing array of sub-rules. If someone says that they cannot understand the rule and sub-rules and sub-sub-rules, he or she is told that they just do not have sufficient legal aptitude. Then, after losing a sufficient number of generations of law students in the labyrinthine ways of the rule, a full functional re-analysis of the field emerges through refocusing on the underlying social problem that the rule was supposed to solve. The unarticulated becomes articulated and jargon becomes comprehensible.

In resolving contract choice-of-law problems, the old territorial rules were not as uniform, even on the surface, as the place-of-wrong rule for torts.[31] The simplistic "place of contracting"[32] rule of the first Restatement never won adherents in a majority of American jurisdictions. On further analysis, even the first Restatement formulae for solving contracts conflicts were not easy to apply. It is true that the old Restatement of Conflicts did provide for determining many important issues of contract law, including the "requirements for making a promise binding"[33] and "the nature and extent of the duty for the performance of which a party becomes bound"[34] by the law of the place that, by the technical rules of contract law, was the "place of contracting."[35] But the "law of the place of performance" determined such key issues as "the manner of performance",[36] "the sufficiency of performance"[37] and "excuse for non-performance."[38] The first Restatement itself candidly admitted that there might be some difficulty in distinguishing between the "nature and extent of the duty," to be governed by the law of the place

---

Enterprise Rent–A–Car Co. of Los Angeles, 899 P.2d 891 (Wyo. 1995) (not citing *Levy* or *Cortes*).

30. Grant v. McAuliffe, 41 Cal.2d 859, 264 P.2d 944 (1953); Kilberg v. Northeast Airlines, Inc., 9 N.Y.2d 34, 211 N.Y.S.2d 133, 172 N.E.2d 526 (1961).

31. See § 7.3.

32. Restatement, Conflict of Laws § 332 (1934).

33. Id. § 332(d).

34. Id. § 332(f).

35. Id. §§ 311–31.

36. Id. § 358(a).

37. Id. § 358(d).

38. Id. § 358(e).

of contracting, and the "sufficiency of performance", to be governed by the law of the place of performance. "A difficult problem is presented in deciding whether a question in a dispute concerning a contract is one involving the creation of an obligation or performance thereof ... The point at which initiation ceases and performance begins is not a point which can be fixed by any rule of law of universal application to all cases. Like all questions of degree, the solution must depend upon the circumstances of each case and must be governed by the exercise of judgment."[39] Furthermore, the first Restatement's invitation to debate the distinction between "initiation" and "performance" is, in the conflicts context, about as functional and therefore about as susceptible to rational conclusion as the somewhat older debate concerning the number of angels that could dance on the head of a pin.

Thus, the old territorial choice-of-law rules presented many difficulties of characterization and interpretation. The new choice-of-law rules will, in turn, present their own problems concerning their meaning and application. But the new questions will be the right questions, the questions that should have been asked in the first place. It makes functional sense to inquire into whether a state "has the most significant relationship to the occurrence and the parties" or whether "the policies underlying its rules are relevant". But it is wasted effort to agonize about the location of the "domicile at death" if applying its law will advance no policy of that jurisdiction and if such application would frustrate the policies of another jurisdiction.[40]

Moreover, the new method of conflicts analysis, which focuses on the domestic laws in putative conflict and on their underlying policies, need be no more *ad hoc* or unpredictable than adjudications that strictly applied the old territorial rules. Soon, as courts in a state decide a number of decisions applying the new methodology, new "rules" will emerge in the only sound way for rules to evolve from a case system of law—as summaries of rational and just decisions.

§ 3.2C   "Substance" and "Procedure"

The third level of characterization focuses on deciding how much of the law that the choice-of-law rule selects a court should apply. What is "substantive" to be governed by the law selected by conflict-of-laws analysis, and what is "procedural" to be determined by the law of the forum *qua* forum?

§ 3.2C1   Functional Definition of "Procedure"

Basic to any functional analysis of conflicts problems is the definition of "substance" and "procedure." Why should we label a rule as "procedural" and apply the rule of the forum without further inquiry? What factors justify such a shortcut in a functional analysis? The proper standard is one that balances the difficulty to the forum in finding and

---

39. Id. § 332, comment *c*.

40. See §§ 2.12–2.12C.

applying the foreign rule against the likelihood that the rule will affect the outcome in a manner that will invite forum shopping.[41] If it would be very difficult for local judges and lawyers to adjust to the application of the foreign rule and if it is unlikely that the outcome will be altered by application of the forum's rule, the forum's rule is properly labeled as "procedural" for conflict of laws purposes and correctly applied without further analysis. If, on the other hand, the foreign rule in issue is not especially difficult to find and apply and if the rule is likely to affect the outcome, the rule should be considered as "substantive" and subjected to further conflicts analysis. Such further analysis may result in applying the forum's rule, not *qua* forum, but because the forum's "substantive" rule provides a functionally preferable solution to the conflicts problem in issue.

Levy v. Steiger,[42] provides an illustration of this last point. The plaintiffs, Massachusetts residents, were passengers in an automobile driven by defendant, also a Massachusetts resident. The car was in an accident in Rhode Island. The guests sued their host in Massachusetts for negligence. In dispute was whether the plaintiffs had the burden of showing their freedom from contributory negligence, as required by the Rhode Island rule, or whether the defendant had to prove contributory negligence on the part of the plaintiffs, in accordance with Massachusetts law. The court labeled the problem as "procedural"[43] and applied

---

41. See Bournias v. Atlantic Maritime Co., 220 F.2d 152, 154 (2d Cir. 1955) (Harlan, J.) ("While it might be desirable, in order to eliminate 'forum-shopping,' for the forum to apply the entire foreign law, substantive and procedural—or at least as much of the procedural law as might significantly affect the choice of forum, it has been recognized that to do so involves an unreasonable burden on the judicial machinery of the forum, and perhaps more significantly, on the local lawyers involved") (citation omitted); Cook, *"Substance" and "Procedure" in the Conflict of Laws,* 42 Yale L. J. 333, 344 (1933).

42. 233 Mass. 600, 124 N.E. 477 (1919).

43. For cases holding burden of proof, presumptions, and doctrines such as res ipsa loquitur "procedural" for conflicts purposes see United Air Lines, Inc. v. Wiener, 335 F.2d 379 (9th Cir.1964), cert. dism'd 379 U.S. 951, 85 S.Ct. 452, 13 L.Ed.2d 549 (res ipsa); Marquis v. St. Louis–San Francisco Ry., 234 Cal.App.2d 335, 44 Cal.Rptr. 367 (Dist.Ct.App. 1965) (presumption of negligence); Chasse v. Albert, 147 Conn. 680, 166 A.2d 148 (1960) (res ipsa); Hutchins v. Rock Creek Ginger Ale Co., 194 A.2d 305 (D.C.App.1963) (res ipsa); Shaps v. Provident Life & Accident Ins. Co., 826 So.2d 250 (Fla. 2002) (burden of proof); Leventhal v. American Airlines, Inc., 347 Mass. 766, 196 N.E.2d 924 (1964) (res ipsa); Leebove v. Rovin, 363 Mich. 569, 111 N.W.2d 104 (1961) (whether sufficient evidence presented for submission of question of negligence to jury); Neve v. Reliance Ins. Co., 357 S.W.2d 247 (Mo.App.1962) (fire insurer defends suit on policy on ground insured set fire; presumption of innocence); Young v. Frank's Nursery & Crafts, Inc., 58 Ohio St.3d 242, 569 N.E.2d 1034 (1991) (burden of proof). Cf. B. v. O., 50 N.J. 93, 232 A.2d 401 (1967) (Pennsylvania interdiction of married woman's rebutting presumption that her child legitimate by her own testimony as to non-access is procedural and not applicable in New Jersey forum in suit by mother to obtain child support from New Jersey putative father). Contra, Fennell v. Illinois Central R.R., 383 S.W.2d 301 (Mo., St. Louis Ct.App.1964) (burden of proving contributory negligence); O'Leary v. Illinois Terminal R.R., 299 S.W.2d 873 (Mo.1957); cf. Federal Rule of Evidence 302 (effect of a presumption is determined under state law, if there is in issue an element of a claim or defense as to which state law supplies the rule of decision); Towley v. King Arthur Rings, Inc., 40 N.Y.2d 129, 386 N.Y.S.2d 80, 351 N.E.2d 728 (1976) (when applying guest statute of another state, that state's law determines whether there is sufficient evidence of "wanton negligence" to submit case to the jury); Fitzpatrick v. International Ry., 252 N.Y. 127, 169 N.E. 112, 68

A.L.R. 801 (1929) (forum's rule on burden of proof not used when applying foreign comparative negligence statute).

For other cases applying the procedural classification to a variety of matters, see Morris v. LTV Corp., 725 F.2d 1024 (5th Cir.1984) (apply forum's statute of frauds to bar recovery for services rendered in Mexico); In re Bethlehem Steel Corp., 631 F.2d 441 (6th Cir.1980), cert. denied, 450 U.S. 921, 101 S.Ct. 1370, 67 L.Ed.2d 349 (1981) (admiralty limit on liability); Chapman v. Aetna Finance Co., 615 F.2d 361 (5th Cir.1980) (compulsory counterclaim rule); Mahalsky v. Salem Tool Co., 461 F.2d 581 (6th Cir.1972) (whether a product liability action may be brought on a contract theory invoking longer statute of limitations); Short v. Grange Mut. Cas. Co., 307 F.Supp. 768 (S.D.W.Va.1969) (whether submission to arbitration is a condition precedent to suit); Sinva, Inc. v. Merrill, Lynch, Pierce, Fenner & Smith, Inc., 253 F.Supp. 359 (S.D.N.Y.1966) (same); New Empire Life Ins. Co. v. Bowling, 241 Ark. 1051, 411 S.W.2d 863 (1967) (recovery of penalty and attorney's fee for nonpayment of insurance claim); Short Line, Inc. v. Perez, 238 A.2d 341 (Del.1968) (whether defendant may implead plaintiff's wife for contribution); Talmudical Academy v. Harris, 238 So.2d 161 (Fla.App.1970) (statute of frauds for agreement to make a will); Velle Transcendental Research Ass'n., Inc. v. Esquire, Inc., 41 Ill.App.3d 799, 354 N.E.2d 622 (1976) (whether pleading must contain facts showing plaintiffs were identified in allegedly libelous article); Bologna Bros. v. Morrissey, 154 So.2d 455 (La.App.1963), writ ref'd, result correct, 245 La. 56, 156 So.2d 601 (foreign statute providing that debt for intoxicating liquor uncollectible); Kansas v. Hartford Accident & Indem. Co., 426 S.W.2d 720 (Mo.K.C.Ct.App.1968) (whether action commenced at time of filing or service); Burge v. State, 443 S.W.2d 720 (Tex.Crim.App.), cert. denied, 396 U.S. 934, 90 S.Ct. 277, 24 L.Ed.2d 233 (1969) (whether wife can consent to search); Whitworth Street Estates, Ltd. v. James Miller & Partners, Ltd., [1970] A.C. 583 (House of Lords) (whether arbitrator can decide questions of law).

For a discussion of whether statutes **permitting direct actions against liability insurers** are procedural, see § 6.12.

For a discussion of whether the **exemption of wages from garnishment** should be treated as substantive or procedural, see Lowenfeld, *In Search of the Intangible: A Comment on Shaffer v. Heitner,* 53 N.Y.U. L. Rev. 102, 115–16 (1978). See also Restatement, Second, Conflict of Laws § 132 (1971) (forum law "unless another state . . . has the dominant interest in the question of exemption"); Uniform Exemptions Act § 3(a) ("Residents of this State are entitled to the exemptions provided by this Act. Nonresidents are entitled to the exemptions provided by the laws of the jurisdiction of their residence"); Phillips v. Phillips, 159 Ga.App. 676, 285 S.E.2d 52 (1981) (law of forum and site of office from which nonresident paid); Beneficial Fin. Co. v. Yellow Transit Freight Lines, Inc., 450 S.W.2d 222 (Mo.App.1969) (law of debtor's residence). Cf. Bennett v. Arkansas, 485 U.S. 395, 108 S.Ct. 1204, 99 L.Ed.2d 455 (1988) (federal law prevents Arkansas from attaching social security payments to persons incarcerated in Arkansas prisons).

For additional examples of procedural classification, see Randall v. Arabian American Oil Co., 778 F.2d 1146 (5th Cir.1985) (provision of Saudi Arabian law reserving exclusive jurisdiction of labor disputes to which Saudi law applies); Apache Village, Inc. v. Coleman Co., 776 P.2d 1154 (Colo. App. 1989) (whether plaintiff must post bond to obtain temporary restraining order); Vanier v. Ponsoldt, 251 Kan. 88, 833 P.2d 949 (1992) (right to jury trial); Milstead v. Diamond M Offshore, Inc., 676 So.2d 89 (La. 1996) (scope of appellate review of fact determinations); In the Matter of Estate of Lingscheit, 387 N.W.2d 738 (S.D.1986) (time limit for filing election to take against will).

Courts have differed on whether the **prevailing party's right to recover attorney's fees** is substantive or procedural. Cases giving this issue a procedural characterization include Midwest Grain Products of Illinois, Inc. v. Productization, Inc., 228 F.3d 784 (7th Cir. 2000) (applying Rhode Island law, which characterizes the right to recover attorney's fees as procedural); Arno v. Club Med Boutique Inc., 134 F.3d 1424 (9th Cir. 1998); Smithco Engineering, Inc. v. International Fabricators, Inc. 775 P.2d 1011 (Wyo. 1989); cf. Mitzel v. Westinghouse Electric Corp., 72 F.3d 414 (3d Cir. 1995) (validity of contingent fee agreement). For cases treating entitlement to attorney's fees as substantive, see Ingalls Shipbuilding v. Federal Ins. Co., 410 F.3d 214 (5th Cir. 2005), rehearing granted and modified, 423 F.3d 522 (5th Cir. 2005); McMahan v. Toto, 256 F.3d 1120, 1134 (11th Cir. 2001) (characterizing as substantive the right of defendant to recover attorney's fees if plaintiff rejects defendant's settlement offer and recovers less than the offer); Aries v. Palmer Johnson, Inc., 153 Ariz. 250, 735 P.2d 1373 (App. 1987); Seattle–First Nat'l Bank v. Schriber, 51 Or.App. 441, 625 P.2d 1370 (1981); Bergstrom Air Force Base Federal Credit

the Massachusetts rule, relying on *Duggan v. Bay State Street Railway.*[44] Before 1914, Massachusetts had placed the burden of proof of freedom from contributory negligence on the plaintiff. In *Duggan,* the Supreme Judicial Court of Massachusetts held that the 1914 Massachusetts statute,[45] creating a presumption of due care on the part of injured persons and making contributory negligence an affirmative defense, was constitutional, violating neither the fourteenth amendment of the United States Constitution nor any provision of the Massachusetts Constitution. The presumption of due care was not "so unreasonable as to be purely arbitrary."[46] Moreover, the court noted that "the present statute simply affects procedure and the burden of proof. It does not work any modification of fundamental rights. The law of negligence in all its essentials remains as before."[47]

This response was proper in defending the Massachusetts statute against constitutional attack. In the different context of the conflict of laws, however, the court should have treated the burden of proof of contributory negligence as "substantive." The Rhode Island rule on burden of proof was not more difficult to find and apply at the Massachusetts forum than any other admittedly "substantive" aspect of Rhode Island negligence law. It may have been highly unlikely that, on the facts of either *Duggan* or *Levy v. Steiger,* anything in fact would turn on the burden of proof, the plaintiffs in those cases being alive and able to testify in their own behalf. Nevertheless, in view of the ease of applying foreign law on burden of proof, even a slight probability that the outcome would have been affected in a way that would have encouraged forum shopping should have resulted in a "substantive" classification.[48]

Union v. Mellon Mortgage, Inc., 674 S.W.2d 845 (Tex. App.–Tyler, 1984, writ denied, no rev. error).

There is also a split of authority as to the **requirement that plaintiff submit medical malpractice claims to a review panel before suing**. Procedural: Vest v. St. Albans Psychiatric Hospital, Inc., 182 W.Va. 228, 387 S.E.2d 282 (1989). Substantive: Bledsoe v. Crowley, 849 F.2d 639 (D.C. Cir. 1988).

Courts typically treat **prejudgment interest** as substantive. Quaker State Oil Refining Corp. v. Garrity Oil Co., 884 F.2d 1510 (1st Cir. 1989) (Massachusetts conflicts law); Thornhill v. Donnkenny Inc., 823 F.2d 782 (4th Cir. 1987) (Virginia conflicts law); AE, Inc. v. Goodyear Tire & Rubber Co., 168 P.3d 507 (Colo. 2007) (the law of the state with the most significant relationship to the occurrence and the parties applies to prejudgment interest in a tort action); Morris v. Watsco, 385 Mass. 672, 433 N.E.2d 886 (1982). But see Rhode Island Charities Trust v. Engelhard Corp., 267 F.3d 3 (1st Cir. 2001) (applying Rhode Island law, which characterizes prejudgment interest as procedural).

Courts regard **the parol evidence rule** as substantive for choice-of-law purposes. Menendez v. Perishable Distributors, Inc. 254 Ga. 300, 329 S.E.2d 149 (1985), overruled on another issue, Posey v. Medical Center–West, Inc., 257 Ga. 55, 354 S.E.2d 417 (1987); Carolina Cas. Ins. Co. v. Oregon Auto. Ins. Co., 242 Or. 407, 408 P.2d 198 (1965).

44. 230 Mass. 370, 119 N.E. 757 (1918).

45. M.G.L.A. (Mass.) ch. 553 § 1 (1914).

46. 230 Mass. at 381, 119 N.E. at 761.

47. 230 Mass. at 380, 119 N.E. at 761.

48. Article 22(1) of the European Union Regulation on the Law Applicable to Non–Contractual Obligations, [2007] Official Journal L 199/40 (Rome II), and article 18(1) of the European Union Regulation on the Law Applicable to Contractual Obligation, EC No 593/2008 (Rome I), bring burden of proof within the scope of their choice-of-law rules.

Once having fixed on a "substantive" classification for the burden of proof, a functional analysis would have produced the same result as reached by the court in *Levy*—application of Massachusetts law. Massachusetts' policies underlying the decision to shift the risk of nonproduction of evidence on the question of contributory negligence and the risk of non-persuasion of the trier of fact from the plaintiff to the defendant were as fully applicable as if the accident had occurred in Massachusetts where all parties were resident. Foreknowledge of the application of Massachusetts law rather than Rhode Island law could not have affected the primary conduct of either the defendant or, if he was insured, his liability insurer. Rhode Island could have no reason to place any impediment in the way of full recovery by the plaintiffs. The Rhode Island rule on burden of proof could not realistically be designed to make potential plaintiffs more careful for their own safety when in Rhode Island. If anything, Rhode Island, as the place of injury, would wish to ease plaintiffs' recovery to reduce the likelihood either that they would have to be cared for at public expense in Rhode Island or that Rhode Island medical creditors would go unpaid. If the Rhode Island rule was aimed at more efficient administration of justice, Massachusetts, not Rhode Island, was the forum.[49]

§ 3.2C2 Statutes of Limitations

United States courts have traditionally classified Statutes of limitations as "procedural" for conflicts purposes.[50] The chief judge-made

---

But see Shaps v. Provident Life & Accident Ins. Co., 826 So.2d 250 (Fla. 2002), which repeats all the mistakes of Levy v. Steiger. The court holds that whether the disability insurer or the insured has the burden of proof on continued disability is "procedural." Thus Florida law placing the burden on the insurer applies rather than New York law, which places the burden on the insured. New York is the state where the policy was issued and whose law the parties agree otherwise governs the dispute. As precedent that burden of proof is procedural, the court cites a case characterizing the issue for purposes of permitting retroactive application of a statute changing the burden.

49. Efficient administration of justice is an example of an interest that a forum has *qua* forum. See Elder v. Metropolitan Freight Carriers, Inc., 543 F.2d 513 (3d Cir.1976) (limit on attorneys' fees); Equitable Life Assur. Soc'y v. McKay, 306 Or. 493, 760 P.2d 871 (1988) (in the light of forum's interest in search for truth, evidence is admissible under law of forum although inadmissible under dead man's statute of state whose "substantive" law applied).

50. For cases applying the forum's shorter statute of limitation, see Namerdy v. Generalcar, 217 A.2d 109 (D.C.App.1966); Jackson v. Shuttleworth, 42 Ill.App.2d 257, 192 N.E.2d 217 (1963); McDaniel v. Mulvihill, 196 Tenn. 41, 263 S.W.2d 759 (1953); Hobbs v. Hajecate, 374 S.W.2d 351 (Tex.Civ.App.1964), writ ref'd. For cases applying the forum's longer statute of limitation see Schreiber v. Allis–Chalmers Corp., 611 F.2d 790 (10th Cir.1979); Haury v. Allstate Ins. Co., 384 F.2d 32 (10th Cir.1967) (whether arbitration of uninsured motorist insurance claim was timely; forum also place of accident); Goodwin v. Townsend, 197 F.2d 970 (3d Cir.1952); Nelson v. Browning, 391 S.W.2d 873 (Mo.1965) (also classifies as "procedural" the question of whether the plaintiff was a minor so as to suspend the running of the statute); Gordon v. Gordon, 118 N.H. 356, 387 A.2d 339 (1978); Jacques v. Jacques, 128 Vt. 140, 259 A.2d 779 (1969); cf. State v. First Nat'l Bk., 17 Ariz.App. 45, 495 P.2d 485 (1972) (Michigan statute preventing limitations from running against the state, is not applicable in Arizona); Advance Mach. Co. v. Berry, 378 So.2d 26 (Fla.App.3d Dist.1979), cert. denied, 389 So.2d 1107 (1980) (limitations period for bringing a tort action against a dissolved corporation is determined not by the law of the state of incorporation, but by the law of the forum where the defendant was doing business);

exception to this classification is the "built-in" or "specificity" test under which a statute of limitations contained in a statute creating a cause of action, or a statute of limitations specifically relating to a particular cause of action,[51] is considered substantive. The standard example of a statute of limitations that is "built-in" and therefore

---

Unnever v. Stephens, 142 Ga.App. 787, 236 S.E.2d 886 (1977), aff'd mem., 240 Ga. 313, 242 S.E.2d 478 (1977) (forum law determines whether party a minor for purpose of tolling statute of limitations); Sears, Roebuck & Co. v. Enco Associates, Inc., 43 N.Y.2d 389, 401 N.Y.S.2d 767, 372 N.E.2d 555 (1977) (choice-of-law provision in contract did not refer to statute of limitations of designated state, but even if so construed, it would also refer to that state's borrowing statute which would refer to forum law). But cf. Baron Tube Co. v. Transport Ins. Co., 365 F.2d 858 (5th Cir.1966) (forum's limitation applies, but law of state where cause accrued determines when it accrued); Oregon ex rel. Ellis v. Krause, 73 Wn.2d 688, 440 P.2d 468 (1968) (under reciprocal tax collection statute, the applicable period of limitations is that of the state making the tax claim).

Statutes are common that toll a period of limitations while an action is pending if suit is terminated without deciding the merits. There is a split of authority whether such statutes should be construed to include actions brought in another state. See Long Island Trust Co. v. Dicker, 659 F.2d 641 (5th Cir.1981) (yes); Garcia v. International Elevator Co., 358 F.3d 777 (10th Cir. 2004) (applies Kansas savings statute applies to case dismissed in Texas and also applies Kansas period to file after dismissal, which is longer than Texas period); Muzingo v. Vaught, 887 S.W.2d 693 (Mo. App. 1994) (no) (collecting authority); Howard v. Allen, 30 Ohio St.2d 130, 283 N.E.2d 167, 59 O.O.2d 148 (1972), appeal dism'd, 409 U.S. 908, 93 S.Ct. 251, 34 L.Ed.2d 169 (1972) (no); cf. Rivera v. Taylor, 61 Ill.2d 406, 336 N.E.2d 481 (1975) (forum statute extending limitations until after administrator is appointed in the forum does not apply when an administrator has been appointed in another state and is subject to personal jurisdiction in the forum); Bergeron v. Loeb, 100 Nev. 54, 675 P.2d 397 (1984) (statute barring claims against an estate not sued upon within 60 days after executor gives notice of rejection, requires that suit be brought in a court in the forum within that time, not in another state).

See also 28 U.S.C. § 1367(d): "The period of limitations for any claim asserted [under state law but over which the district court declines to exercise supplemental jurisdiction] shall be tolled while the claim is pending and for a period of 30 days after it is dismissed unless State law provides for a longer tolling period." Raygor v. Regents of the Univ. of Minnesota, 534 U.S. 533, 122 S.Ct. 999, 152 L.Ed.2d 27 (2002), held that § 1376(d) did not apply to "state law claims asserted against nonconsenting state defendants" when those claims "are dismissed on Eleventh Amendment grounds." The Court construed the section not to apply because otherwise there would be "serious doubts about the constitutionality of the provision given principles of state sovereign immunity." (The Eleventh Amendment bars suit in federal court against states by citizens of other states. Hans v. Louisiana, 134 U.S. 1, 10 S.Ct. 504, 33 L.Ed. 842 (1890), extended a state's immunity to suits brought by its own citizens.) Jinks v. Richland County, 538 U.S. 456, 123 S.Ct. 1667, 155 L.Ed.2d 631 (2003), held the federal tolling provision in § 1376(d) constitutional when applied to toll limitations against a political subdivision of a state because the Eleventh Amendment does not apply to suits against political subdivisions.

51. The classic statement of the specificity test is that of Mr. Justice Holmes in Davis v. Mills, 194 U.S. 451, 454, 24 S.Ct. 692, 694, 48 L.Ed. 1067, 1070 (1904): "But the fact that the limitation is contained in the same section or the same statute is material only as bearing on construction. It is merely a ground for saying that the limitation goes to the right created and accompanies the obligation everywhere. The same conclusion would be reached if the limitation was in a different statute, provided it was directed to the newly created liability so specifically as to warrant saying that it qualified the right."

Some courts have taken the position that whether a foreign limitation period is substantive or procedural depends on the construction the statute receives in the foreign jurisdiction. See Alabama Great Southern R.R. v. Allied Chemical Corp., 467 F.2d 679 (5th Cir.1972) (Virginia court would take view that Mississippi code makes all Mississippi limitations substantive); Ramsay v. The Boeing Co., 432 F.2d 592 (5th Cir.1970) (Belgium statute); Connecticut Valley Lumber Co. v. Maine Cent. R.R., 78 N.H. 553, 103 A. 263 (1918).

"substantive" is the special limitation period typically contained in a statute creating a cause of action for wrongful death.[52]

Statutes of repose, which many states have enacted,[53] bar an action a stated number of years after a product is sold or a service rendered, even though the injury occurred after that time. Courts have characterized these statutes as "substantive" and subjected them to choice-of-law analysis.[54]

---

52. For wrongful death cases using the "built-in" test, see Bengston v. Nesheim, 259 F.2d 566 (9th Cir.1958) (foreign shorter limitation applied); Maryland ex rel. Thompson v. Eis Automotive Corp., 145 F.Supp. 444 (D.Conn.1956) (foreign longer limitation applied); Toomes v. Continental Oil Co., 402 S.W.2d 321 (Mo.1966) (foreign shorter statute applied, forum's statute tolling period after nonsuits inapplicable); Click v. Thuron Indus., 475 S.W.2d 715 (Tex.1972) (foreign shorter limitations applied); cf. Siroonian v. Textron, Inc., 844 F.2d 289 (5th Cir. 1988) (Kentucky wrongful death limitations, now in general personal injury statute, classified as built-in because it had been transferred from the wrongful death act) (Mississippi conflicts rule). But see Chartener v. Kice, 270 F.Supp. 432 (E.D.N.Y.1967) (both New York and California death limits are procedural); Taylor v. Murray, 231 Ga. 852, 204 S.E.2d 747 (1974) (specificity rule may result in shortening forum's period, but not in extending it—forum's shorter period applies); Marshall v. George M. Brewster & Son, Inc., 37 N.J. 176, 180 A.2d 129 (1962) (applies forum's longer limitation because Pennsylvania, where death occurred, classifies its statute as procedural); Rosenzweig v. Heller, 302 Pa. 279, 153 A. 346 (1931) (forum's shorter limitation applied).

For examples of "specific" or "built-in" statutes of limitations in statutes other than wrongful death acts, see Kalmich v. Bruno, 553 F.2d 549 (7th Cir.1977), cert. denied, 434 U.S. 940, 98 S.Ct. 432, 54 L.Ed.2d 300 (1977) (Yugoslavian limitation for actions based on war crimes, specific); White v. Malone Properties, Inc. 494 So.2d 576 (Miss. 1986) (applying limitation period in Louisiana workers' compensation act); State v. Copus, 158 Tex. 196, 309 S.W.2d 227 (1958) (California liability for support of indigent mother, built in); Indon Indus., Inc. v. Charles S. Martin Distrib. Co., 234 Ga. 845, 218 S.E.2d 562 (1975) (Uniform Commercial Code § 6–111 limitation on action under Bulk Transfers article).

Sometimes a limitation period contained in a statute creating the right sued on has been held not to meet the specificity test because a number of causes of action are created by the same code. See Bournias v. Atlantic Maritime Co., 220 F.2d 152 (2d Cir.1955) (Panama Labor Code, forum's longer limitation applied); Lillegraven v. Tengs, 375 P.2d 139 (Alaska 1962) (British Columbia Motor Vehicle Act, forum's longer period applied). See also Natale v. Upjohn Co., 356 F.2d 590 (3d Cir.1966) (period in Pennsylvania Uniform Commercial Code for breach of warranty suits is "procedural" because action existed before the Code and Pennsylvania does not employ specificity test, forum's shorter period applicable). But see Gillies v. Aeronaves De Mexico, 468 F.2d 281 (5th Cir.1972), cert. denied, 410 U.S. 931, 93 S.Ct. 1375, 35 L.Ed.2d 594 (1973) ("built in" doctrine applies to limitation in Mexican Federal Labor Law).

Cf. Casselman v. Denver Tramway Corp., 195 Colo. 241, 577 P.2d 293 (1978) (**whether a corporation can be sued after dissolution and for how long** is a substantive issue governed by the law of the state of incorporation); Advance Mach. Co. v. Berry, 378 So.2d 26 (Fla.App.3d Dist.1979), cert. denied, 389 So.2d 1107 (1980) (law of forum, where corporation was doing business, determines time for suit after dissolution); Stephens v. Household Fin. Corp., 566 P.2d 1163 (Okl.1977) (can use action under Federal Consumer Protection Act as a counterclaim after Act's limitations have run).

53. See McGovern, *The Variety, Policy and Constitutionality of Product Liability Statutes of Repose,* 30 Am. U. L. Rev. 579, 580 (1981) ("ninety-eight statutes in forty-eight states"). For a federal statute of repose see P.L. 103–298, 108 Stat. 1552, as amended by P.L. 105–102, 111 Stat. 2216 (codified in 49 U.S.C. § 40101 notes), barring an action against the manufacturer of general aviation aircraft 18 year after delivery of the aircraft to the first purchaser, lessee, or a person engaged in selling or leasing.

54. See Wayne v. Tennessee Valley Authority, 730 F.2d 392 (5th Cir.1984) (a Mississippi court, using the "most significant relationship" test, would apply the Tennessee statute); Hines v. Tenneco Chemicals, Inc., 728 F.2d 729 (5th Cir.1984) (a Texas court, using the most significant relationship test, would apply the North Carolina statute); Mahne v. Ford Motor Co., 900 F.2d 83 (6th Cir.1990), cert. denied, 498 U.S. 941, 111 S.Ct. 349, 112 L.Ed.2d 313 (1990) (under Michigan conflicts rules, apply law of forum permitting

A common statutory exception to the procedural treatment of statutes of limitations is the "borrowing" statute. Such a statute borrows a shorter statute of limitations of another jurisdiction[55] and makes the foreign statute applicable at the forum. When the forum borrows a statute of limitations of another state, most courts interpret and apply the foreign limitations in the same manner as the courts in that other state.[56] Typically,[57] but not universally,[58] the statute borrowed is that of

action by Florida plaintiff because there is no good reason to displace forum law); Thornton v. Cessna Aircraft Co., 886 F.2d 85 (4th Cir. 1989) (South Carolina conflicts law); Tanges v. Heidelberg North America, Inc., 93 N.Y.2d 48, 710 N.E.2d 250, 687 N.Y.S.2d 604 (1999) (holding Connecticut statute of repose bars New York resident's claim for injury in Connecticut despite the New York borrowing statute's exception for New York residents); Crisman v. Cooper Industries, 748 S.W.2d 273 (Tex.App.—Dallas 1988, error denied) (select Florida statute of repose under most significant relationship test); cf. Beard v. J.I. Case Company, 823 F.2d 1095 (7th Cir.1987) (Wisconsin borrowing statute does not include foreign statute of repose). But see Hyde v. Hoffmann–La Roche, Inc., 511 F.3d 506 (5th Cir. 2007) (construing Texas statute to require application of Texas statute of repose to any action brought in Texas and indicating, without conducting a choice-of-law analysis, that dismissal under the repose statute would be on the merits thus barring an action in another state); Marchesani v. Pellerin–Milnor Corp., 269 F.3d 481 (5th Cir. 2001) (although Tennessee substantive law applies, under La. Civ. Code art. 3549, Tennessee's 10–year statute of repose for product liability claims does not apply to bar suit by a Tennessee domiciliary injured in Tennessee against a Louisiana manufacturer). Contra, Baxter v. Sturm, Ruger & Co., 230 Conn. 335, 644 A.2d 1297 (1994) (statutes of repose, like statutes of limitations, are procedural unless they specifically bar a statutory cause of action).

55. But see Oklahoma's backwards borrowing statute. 12 Okla.St.Ann. § 105: "The period of limitation applicable to a claim accruing outside of this state shall be that prescribed either by the law of the place where the claim accrued or by the law of this state, whichever last bars the claim."

56. See Speight v. Miller, 437 F.2d 781 (7th Cir.1971), cert. denied, 404 U.S. 827, 92 S.Ct. 60, 30 L.Ed.2d 55 (1971) (tolling provisions); Nolan v. Transocean Air Lines, 276 F.2d 280 (2d Cir.1960), remanded for reconsideration of another matter, 365 U.S. 293, 81 S.Ct. 555, 5 L.Ed.2d 571 (1961), former opinion adhered to, 290 F.2d 904 (2d Cir.1961), cert. denied, 368 U.S. 901, 82 S.Ct. 177, 7 L.Ed.2d 96 (1961) (tolling provisions); Frombach v. Gilbert Associates, Inc., 236 A.2d 363, 366 (Del.1967), cert. denied, 391 U.S. 906, 88 S.Ct. 1655, 20 L.Ed.2d 419 (1968) ("The theory is that the borrowed statute is accepted with all its accoutrements."); Bowling v. S.S. Kresge Co., 431 S.W.2d 191 (Mo.1968) (when foreign limitations began to run). See also Uniform Probate Code § 3–803(b), 8 ULA pt. 2 215 ("claim [that arose before death of decedent] which is barred by the non-claim statute at the decedent's domicile before the giving of notice to creditors in this State is barred in this State") (16 adoptions as of January 1, 2006); Drudge v. Overland Plazas Co., 670 F.2d 92 (8th Cir.1982) (forum's borrowing statute's reference to "laws . . . where the defendant has previously resided" is to the whole law of that place, including its borrowing statute, which borrows the law of the state in which the action "originated"). Contra, Hobbs v. Firestone Tire & Rubber Co., 195 F.Supp. 56 (N.D.Ind.1961) (refusal to look to borrowing statute of foreign state referred to by forum's borrowing statute, the forum's statute borrowing limitations of state where a non-resident defendant resides if the cause of action did not accrue in the forum).

See also Childs v. Brandon, 60 N.Y.2d 927, 471 N.Y.S.2d 40, 459 N.E.2d 149 (1983) (Alabama tolling provisions borrowed along with Alabama limitations); Blais v. Allied Exterminating Co., 198 W.Va. 674, 482 S.E.2d 659 (1996) (borrow doctrine of equitable estoppel along with limitations); cf. Valedon Martinez v. Hospital Presbiteriano de la Comunidad, Inc., 806 F.2d 1128 (1st Cir.1986) (apply Puerto Rican law on tolling for minority along with its limitations even though plaintiff was domiciled in a state with a lower age of majority). But see Goldsmith v. Learjet, Inc., 90 F.3d 1490 (10th Cir. 1996) (under Kansas law, do not borrow foreign savings statute); Dahlberg v. Harris, 916 F.2d 443 (8th Cir. 1990) (under Wisconsin law do not borrow foreign rule as to when action commenced); Birdsell v. Holiday Inns, 852 F.2d 1078 (8th Cir.1988) (law of Missouri forum determines when an action is commenced although borrowing limitations of another state); DeVito v. Blenc, 47 Mich.App. 524, 209 N.W.2d 728 (1973) (although borrow foreign

the state where the cause of action sued on "arose." Sometimes the borrowing statute contains an exception precluding its application against a plaintiff who has been a resident of the forum and has held the cause of action since it arose,[59] but some borrowing statutes contain no exception for forum residents.[60]

limitations, apply Michigan statute tolling action during minority); Dorris v. McClanahan, 725 S.W.2d 870 (Mo.1987) (although shorter limitations of Illinois are borrowed, Missouri law determines that the period was tolled because of the minority of the Missouri plaintiff); Tri–City Construction Co. v. A.C. Kirkwood & Associates, 738 S.W.2d 925 (Mo. App.1987) (although borrow limitations period of another state, Missouri law determines whether action was timely filed); McKinney v. Fairchild Int'l, Inc., 199 W.Va. 718, 487 S.E.2d.913 (1997) (do not borrow foreign tolling statute); Scott by Ricciardi v. First State Ins. Co., 155 Wis.2d 608, 456 N.W.2d 152 (1990) (reject majority rule that foreign tolling provision is borrowed along with foreign limitations and apply forum's law tolling limitations for minors, even though minor was injured on his family's farm in Alberta).

For discussion of borrowing statutes, see Vernon, *The Uniform Statute of Limitations on Foreign Claims Act: Tolling Problems,* 12 Vand. L. Rev. 971 (1959); Vernon, *Statutes of Limitation in the Conflict of Laws: Borrowing Statutes,* 32 Rocky Mt. L. Rev. 287 (1960).

57. See Ester, *Borrowing Statutes of Limitations and Conflict of Laws,* 15 Univ. Fla. L. Rev. 33, 81 (1962) (twenty-four states listed as having substantially this requirement). Thirty-eight states are listed as having borrowing statutes. Id. at 79. See also Sedler, *The Truly Disinterested Forum in the Conflict of Laws,* 25 S.C. L. Rev. 185, 187 n. 11 (listing 12 states and the District of Columbia that have no borrowing statute).

For cases deciding where a cause of action "arose" within the meaning of the typical borrowing statute, see, e.g., Patch v. Playboy Enterprises, Inc., 652 F.2d 754 (8th Cir.1981) (action for libel published in many states "originated" at the defendant's principal place of business where the article was printed and distributed, not at plaintiff's residence); Elmore v. Owens–Illinois, Inc., 673 S.W.2d 434 (Mo.1984) (asbestosis action "originated" where diagnosed, not where symptoms first appeared); Kansas City Star Co. v. Gunn, 627 S.W.2d 332 (Mo.App.1982) (when the defendant acts in one state causing injury in another, the action "originated" where the injury occurred); Baker v. First Nat'l Bank of Denver, 603 P.2d 397 (Wyo.1979) (action to foreclose mortgage "arose" in state where note and mortgage executed and parties resided, not where land situated); Duke v. Housen, 589 P.2d 334 (Wyo.1979), rehearing denied, 590 P.2d 1340 (1979), cert. denied, 444 U.S. 863, 100 S.Ct. 132, 62 L.Ed.2d 86 (1979) (when defendant infected plaintiff by intercourse in several states, in deciding where action "arose" court considers law of each state where intercourse occurred and whether that state's statute begins running at the time of injury or time of discovery of the injury).

58. Iowa Code Ann. § 614.7 ("any country where the defendant has previously resided" if action arose outside Iowa); Me.R.S.Ann.Tit. 14 § 866 ("barred by the laws of any state ... while all the parties have resided therein"); See Ester, supra note 57 at 81–82.

59. E.g., Idaho Code § 5–239. Cf. Miller v. Lockett, 98 Ill.2d 478, 75 Ill.Dec. 224, 457 N.E.2d 14 (1983) (exception for forum plaintiffs is inserted by construction following interest analysis). This borrowing statute exception in favor of forum residents is not a violation of the "privileges and immunities" provision of the U.S.Const. Art. IV, § 2. Canadian Northern Ry. v. Eggen, 252 U.S. 553, 40 S.Ct. 402, 64 L.Ed. 713 (1920); Pryber v. Marriott Corp., 98 Mich.App. 50, 296 N.W.2d 597 (1980), aff'd w.o. opinion, 411 Mich. 887, 307 N.W.2d 333 (1981) (uphold constitutionality of retroactive amendment to borrowing statute making an exception for a forum plaintiff).

But see Flowers v. Carville, 310 F.3d 1118 (9th Cir. 2002). The Nevada borrowing statute bars an action that is barred by the laws of the state where the action "has arisen" but has an exception "in favor of a citizen [of Nevada] who has held the cause of action from the time it accrued." The Nevada exception, unlike the exception in some other states, does not expressly state that the plaintiff must have been a citizen of the state at the time that the action accrued. The court construed the Nevada exception as permitting the plaintiff to sue. The opinion states that this avoids a constitutional issue, citing Saenz v. Roe, 526 U.S. 489, 119 S.Ct. 1518, 143 L.Ed.2d 689 (1999). *Saenz* held that California legislation limiting benefits to needy families during the recipients' first year of residency violated the Fourteenth Amendment right to travel.

60. Unif. Statute of Limitations on Foreign Claims Act § 2, withdrawn in 1978, 14 ULA 383: adopted in Oklahoma (12 Ok. St. Ann. § 105), Pennsylvania. (42 Pa. C.S.A. § 5521),

Under the twin criteria suggested above,[61] a court should always treat statutes of limitation as substantive for conflicts purposes and subject them to complete functional choice-of-law analysis.[62] A foreign

and West Va. (W.Va. Code § 55–2A–2); Rev.Stat.Mo. § 516.190; Long v. Pettinato, 394 Mich. 343, 230 N.W.2d 550 (1975) (apply statute borrowing shorter limitations in action between forum residents "although we see little value in the application of the statute to Michigan residents"); cf. Wilson v. Eubanks, 36 Mich.App. 287, 193 N.W.2d 353 (1971) (in action between residents, refuse to permit amendment when foreign limitation not pleaded in first responsive pleading). See Ester, supra note 57 at 81 (eight states have no requirement relating to residence of either plaintiff or defendant; ten require that the defendant be a non-resident).

61. See § 3.2C1.

62. Some jurisdictions that have changed to a functional conflicts analysis have adopted this approach. See Warriner v. Stanton, 475 F.3d 497 (3d Cir. 2007) (applying New Jersey's "governmental interest" test); Washburn v. Soper, 319 F.3d 338 (8th Cir. 2003), cert. denied, 540 U.S. 875, 124 S.Ct. 221, 157 L.Ed.2d 136 (2003) (predicting that Iowa would apply revised Restatement Second § 142); Estate of Darulis v. Garate, 401 F.3d 1060 (9th Cir. 2005) (California "governmental interest test"); Aalmuhammed v. Lee, 202 F.3d 1227 (9th Cir.2000) (California "comparative impairment" method); Tomlin v. Boeing Co., 650 F.2d 1065 (9th Cir.1981) (Washington conflicts rule); Gianni v. Fort Wayne Air Serv., Inc., 342 F.2d 621 (7th Cir.1965) (Indiana conflicts rule); Gore v. Debaryshe, 278 F.Supp. 883 (W.D.Ky.1968) (plaintiffs invited to amend complaint to demonstrate that some other state has a more significant relationship with the occurrence and the parties as to the limitations issue than does the forum and place of injury); Ganey v. Kawasaki Motors Corp., 366 Ark. 238, 234 S.W.3d 838 (2006); Ashland Chem. Co. v. Provence, 129 Cal.App.3d 790, 181 Cal.Rptr. 340 (4th Dist.1982) (though effect may be only to close the forum); Merkle, Jr. v. Robinson, 737 So.2d 540 (Fla. 1999) (applying longer limitations of West Virginia under "significant relationship" test); Johnson v. Pischke, 108 Idaho 397, 700 P.2d 19 (1985); Nierman v. Hyatt Corp., 441 Mass. 693, 808 N.E.2d 290 (2004); Heavner v. Uniroyal, Inc., 63 N.J. 130, 305 A.2d 412 (1973); Paris v. General Elec. Co., 54 Misc.2d 310, 282 N.Y.S.2d 348 (Sup.Ct.1967), aff'd mem., 29 A.D.2d 939, 290 N.Y.S.2d 1015 (1968) (under "grouping of contacts" analysis, statute of limitations of place where death occurred is not applicable); Air Prod. & Chem., Inc. v. Fairbanks Morse, Inc., 58 Wis.2d 193, 206 N.W.2d 414 (1973). See also, Martin, *Statutes Of Limitations And Rationality in the Conflict of Laws,* 19 Washburn L. J. 405 (1980); Note, *An Interest–Analysis Approach to the Selection of Statutes of Limitations,* 49 N.Y.U. L. Rev. 299 (1974). Cf. Hossler v. Barry, 403 A.2d 762 (Me.1979) (limitations for claim against estate characterized as procedural, but opinion justifies application of forum period on interest grounds); Myers v. Cessna Aircraft Corp., 275 Or. 501, 553 P.2d 355 (1976) (wrongful death limitation period bars right, not just remedy, so apply period of state of otherwise applicable law, selecting that state by "significant relationship" test). But for the view that functional conflicts analysis does not affect the view that statutes of limitations are "procedural", see Wright v. Fireman's Fund Ins. Co., 522 F.2d 1376 (5th Cir.1975) (La. Rule); Cuthbertson v. Uhley, 509 F.2d 225 (8th Cir.1975) (Minn. Rule); Klingebiel v. Lockheed Aircraft Corp., 372 F.Supp. 1086 (N.D.Cal.1971), aff'd, 494 F.2d 345 (9th Cir.1974); Horvath v. Davidson, 148 Ind.App. 203, 264 N.E.2d 328 (1970); Gierling v. Garner, 284 So.2d 664 (La.App.1973); Vick v. Cochran, 316 So.2d 242 (Miss.1975). For approval of choosing law for limitations on the basis of a right-remedy distinction, see Risinger, *"Substance" and "Procedure" Revisited with Some Afterthoughts on the Constitutional Problems of "Irrebuttable Presumptions,"* 30 UCLA L. Rev. 189 (1982).

Other state and federal courts have adopted or approached a functional analysis of statutes of limitations. See In re TMI, 89 F.3d 1106 (3d Cir. 1996), cert. denied, 519 U.S. 1077, 117 S.Ct. 739, 136 L.Ed.2d 678 (1997) (federal statute creating cause of action for injuries resulting from nuclear incidents directs application of "substantive rules of decision" of the State in which the incident occurs, which includes the statute of limitations of that state); Held v. Manufacturers Hanover Leasing Corp., 912 F.2d 1197 (10th Cir.1990) (apply revised Restatement approach to claim under Employee Retirement Income Security Act); Gulf Consolidated Services, Inc. v. Corinth Pipeworks, S.A., 898 F.2d 1071 (5th Cir.1990), cert. denied, 498 U.S. 900, 111 S.Ct. 256, 112 L.Ed.2d 214 (1990) (under Texas law, apply most significant relationship analysis to limitations without noting possible "procedural" characterization); Shamley v. ITT Corp., 869 F.2d 167 (2d Cir. 1989) (using New Jersey law, applies New York statute of limitations under "governmental

statute of limitations is not especially difficult to find and apply. Permitting recovery under the longer statute of limitations of the forum produces a result on the merits that may not be available in any other jurisdiction having contacts with the parties or with the transaction. This invites forum shopping for a jurisdiction that, although it has no contact with the parties or the transaction, has jurisdiction over the defendant and an unexpired statute of limitations.

The Foreign Limitation Periods Act,[63] applicable to England and Wales, takes an approach similar to the Uniform Conflict of Laws–Limitations Act, discussed infra this section. If the law of another country applies to any matter, the time limitation of that country applies to the same matter.[64] The Act does not apply a foreign tolling provision interrupting the running of limitations because of defendant's "absence."[65] There is no reference to the conflicts rules of the foreign country[66] and forum law determines when the action has been commenced.[67] A foreign ruling on limitations is regarded as on the merits.[68] There is a "public policy" exception to application of foreign limitations.[69]

---

interest test"); DeLoach v. Alfred, 192 Ariz. 28, 960 P.2d 628 (Ariz. 1998) (applies longer forum limitations under Restatement § 142 and under interest analysis); Gomez v. ITT Educational Services, Inc., 348 Ark. 69, 71 S.W.3d 542, 548 (2002) (as alternative holding applies Texas limitations to bar action because "Texas has a more significant relationship with the parties and with the issues"); New England Telephone & Telegraph Co. v. Gourdeau Constr. Co., 419 Mass. 658, 647 N.E.2d 42 (1995) (rejecting "procedural" label for statute of limitations); Sutherland v. Kennington Truck Service, Ltd., 454 Mich. 274, 562 N.W.2d 466 (1997) (applying forum's longer period in suit between nonresidents, but basing result on interest analysis); (Dabbs v. Silver Eagle Mfg. Co., Inc., 98 Or.App. 581, 779 P.2d 1104, review denied, 308 Or. 608, 784 P.2d 1101 (1989)) (apply forum's longer limitations under most significant relationship test, noting that Oregon has adopted Uniform Conflict of Laws–Limitations Act, which is not applicable here because effective date was after accrual of this action); Cribb v. Augustyn, 696 A.2d 285 (R.I. 1997) (applying forum's statute because forum "has the greater interest in determining the time period" for suit); cf. Warner v. Auberge Gray Rocks Inn, 827 F.2d 938 (3d Cir.1987) (although New Jersey would not apply its longer period when nonresidents were involved, it would do so when the plaintiff is a New Jersey domiciliary, and would not make the "most significant relationship" analysis of the issue that it would in other choice-of-law contexts); Cameron v. Hardisty, 407 N.W.2d 595 (Iowa 1987) (forum interest in protecting its courts from stale claims is reason for applying forum's shorter limitations); Keeton v. Hustler Magazine, Inc., 131 N.H. 6, 549 A.2d 1187 (1988) (application of forum's longer period is justified because some of the harm was caused in the forum—leave open question of whether will continue to treat limitations as procedural when New Hampshire's connections less substantial); Nez v. Forney, 109 N.M. 161, 783 P.2d 471 (1989) (majority applies forum's longer limitations on "procedural" grounds, but concurrence states this consistent with interest analysis on these facts).

63. 1984 L. Reports Stat. c. 16.

64. Id. § 1(1).

65. Id. § 2(3).

66. Id. § 1(5).

67. Id. § 1(3).

68. Id. § 3.

69. Id. § 2.

Uniform legislation intended for all Australian States and Territories and for New Zealand contains the same provision. It has already been enacted in New South Wales and New Zealand.[70]

Civil law countries characterize limitations as substantive for choice-of-law purposes.[71]

Article 12(1) of the Regulation on the Law Applicable to Contractual Obligations,[72] in force between members of the European Union, provides: "The law applicable to a contract by virtue of this Regulation shall govern in particular: . . . (d) the various ways of extinguishing obligations, and prescription and limitation of actions." Article 15(h) of the European Union Regulation on the Law Applicable to Non–Contractual Obligations[73] also places "rules of prescription and limitation" within the scope of the Regulation's choice-of-law rules.

The Supreme Court of Canada has held that statutes of limitations are substantive, overruling cases to the contrary.[74]

Sun Oil Co. v. Wortman,[75] discussed infra in § 9.2B, held that a state could apply its own longer statute of limitations even though limitations had expired in the states whose law it was constitutionally compelled to apply to "substantive" issues. Justice Scalia notes in his opinion for the Court that although the Constitution does not compel adopting a substantive classification for statutes of limitations, states that deem it "desirable" may do so.[76]

Treating statutes of limitations as "substantive" for choice-of-law purposes, implies some change in the standard rule that dismissal of a suit because the period of limitations has run is not on the "merits" in the sense of barring suit in another state.[77] For example, P and D, both

---

70. See New S. Wales Choice of Law (Limitation Periods) Act 1993 No. 94; N.Z. Limitations Amendment Act 1996. The New Zealand Act applies to Australia, the United Kingdom, and to any country that the Governor–General names by an order in Council.

71. See Rabel, 3 The Conflict of Laws: A Comparative Study 511–512 (2d ed. 1964 by Bernstein).

72. Regulation on the Law Applicable to Contractual Obligations (Rome I) (EC No. 593/2008).

73. Regulation on the law Applicable to Non–Contractual Obligations (Rome II) (EC No. 864/2007, [2007] Official Journal L 199/40).

74. Tolofson v. Jensen, [1994] 3 S.C.R. 1022, 1071–72 (Can. 1994).

75. 486 U.S. 717, 108 S.Ct. 2117, 100 L.Ed.2d 743 (1988).

76. Id. at 728–29, 108 S.Ct. at 2125, 100 L.Ed.2d at 756.

77. See Semtek Int'l Inc. v. Lockheed Martin Corp., 531 U.S. 497, 121 S.Ct. 1021, 149 L.Ed.2d 32 (2001) (Federal Rule of Civil Procedure 41(b) provision that dismissal "operates as an adjudication upon the merits", as applied to dismissal for running of time limitations, did not have claim-preclusive effect but simply prevented suit on the same claim in the same federal district court); Reinke v. Boden, 45 F.3d 166 (7th Cir.), cert. denied, 516 U.S. 817, 116 S.Ct. 74, 133 L.Ed.2d 34 (1995) (limitations dismissal by Minnesota court does not, under Minnesota law, bar suit in Illinois federal court); Los Angeles Airways, Inc. v. Lummis, 603 S.W.2d 246 (Tex.Civ.App.—Houston [14th Dist.], writ ref'd, no reversible error 1980), cert. denied, 455 U.S. 988, 102 S.Ct. 1610, 71 L.Ed.2d 847 (1982); Restatement of Judgments § 49, comment *a* at 194 (1942); cf. Textron, Inc. v. Whitfield, 380 So.2d 259 (Ala.1979) (amend forum limitations dismissal to recite it not with prejudice so that plaintiff can pursue the action in another state).

Even a dismissal "on the merits" may be ambiguous in the limitations context. A court may interpret such a dismissal as merely barring further litigation in the forum, not as deciding that the forum's limitations apply to the action wherever brought. See *Semtek*,

with settled residences in state X, drive together into state Y. D is driving with P as passenger when, because of D's alleged negligence, the automobile leaves the road, strikes a tree, and P is injured. P receives all his medical treatment in state X. X's statute of limitations is one year; that of Y is five years. P sues D in X four years after the accident. Treating the statute of limitations issue as substantive and subjecting it to a full functional choice-of-law analysis, X decides that the policies underlying the X short statute are fully applicable and that permitting the suit would not significantly advance any policy of Y. X therefore applies its own statute of limitations and bars suit. This decision by X should be treated as a choice on the merits between X and Y statutes of limitations and should bar suit in Y if P subsequently brings suit there before the Y five-year statute runs.[78] Assuming that X's functional analysis is correct, Y should also apply the X statute of limitations and bar suit even if plaintiff had first sued in X. A decision by the forum to apply its own shorter statute of limitations should not, however, be binding on other states if the forum purports to act only *qua* forum. This might be the case if, in the preceding hypothetical, Y, the place of injury, had the one-year statute of limitations, X, the residence of both parties, had the five-year statute and suit were originally brought in Y four years after the accident. Y might rationally decide that, because of the danger of fraud and mistake from what it considered a stale claim, Y was not willing to serve as the situs of litigation, although Y should not be concerned if X subsequently elects to permit the action to proceed in X.

Nelson v. Eckert[79] illustrates the fantastic results produced by the maze of traditional rules classifying statutes of limitations for conflicts purposes. An automobile transporting Arkansas residents back to Arkansas from Texas crashed in Texas killing all the occupants. The administrator of the deceased passengers brought a wrongful death action in Arkansas against the administrator of the deceased driver. This suit was commenced more than two years, but less than three years after the fatal crash. Both Texas and Arkansas had two-year statutes of limitations for wrongful death. Nevertheless, the court held the action timely. The Arkansas two-year statute of limitations did not apply because it

---

supra this note; Lee v. Swain Bldg. Materials Co., 529 So.2d 188 (Miss.1988) (Louisiana dismissal "with prejudice" because Louisiana limitations had run does not bar action in another state). But see Hillary v. Trans World Airlines, Inc., 123 F.3d 1041 (8th Cir. 1997), cert. denied, 522 U.S. 1090, 118 S.Ct. 881, 139 L.Ed.2d 870 (1998) (under Louisiana law, dismissal on basis of "prescription" bars subsequent suit in Missouri federal court).

78. Cf. Fender v. St. Louis Sw. Ry. Co., 73 Ill.App.3d 522, 29 Ill.Dec. 525, 392 N.E.2d 82 (5th Dist.1979), Ill. cert. denied (in FELA action in Illinois, full faith and credit must be given to Texas decision that the FELA statute of limitations has run). But see Rhoades v. Wright, 622 P.2d 343 (Utah 1980), cert. denied, 454 U.S. 897, 102 S.Ct. 397, 70 L.Ed.2d 212 (1981) (deny full faith and credit to Colorado judgment that wrongful death statute of limitations has run even if that judgment characterized the statute as substantive).

For a discussion of "substantive" and "procedural" policies underlying statutes of limitations, see Carrington, *"Substance" and "Procedure" in the Rules Enabling Act*, 1989 Duke L. J. 281, 290 (procedural policies include clearing dockets, protecting against stale and therefore "suspect" proof; substantive policies include "healing and stabilizing relationships" and to "induce economic planning and development").

79. 231 Ark. 348, 329 S.W.2d 426 (1959).

was part of the Arkansas wrongful death act and therefore substantive, applying only to wrongful death occurring in Arkansas. The Texas limitation for wrongful death actions was not part of the Texas death act and therefore it was procedural and inapplicable outside of a Texas forum.[80] This left the general Arkansas three-year statute of limitations for injury to chattels and the five-year statute for personal injuries, both procedural statutes, which the court held to be applicable.

When, as in *Nelson v. Eckert,* two states would reach the same result in a wholly domestic case and for the same reasons—to avoid stale claims, and to give peace to the defendant—there is no rational basis on which the fact that the problem has contacts with both states can change the result.[81] At least one state, here Arkansas, would advance its limitations policies by application of its statute, and the other state, Texas, having the same policies, cannot have a competing interest.

The judge-made and statutory exceptions to the procedural classification of statutes of limitation do not significantly improve the dysfunctional results flowing from that classification. *Nelson v. Eckert* illustrates the chaotic and irrational impact of the specificity exception which, indeed, in that case, aggravated rather than alleviated the problem. Nor is a borrowing statute a satisfactory solution. Borrowing statutes do not borrow a foreign statute of limitations that is longer than the one at the forum.[82] More seriously, a borrowing statute may freeze the forum's choice-of-law analysis into an undesirable territorial mold. *Girth v. Beaty Grocery Company*[83] was a suit by a Missouri resident to recover for injuries suffered in a collision in Iowa with a truck driven by another Missouri resident and owned by two Missouri corporations. Plaintiff sued more than two years but less than five years after the collision. The Iowa statute of limitations was two years. Missouri's was five years. The Missouri borrowing statute provided: "Whenever a cause of action has been fully barred by the laws of the state, territory or country in which

---

80. Perhaps the Texas statute of limitations should have been held to have met the specificity test although not part of the wrongful death act. The Texas two-year statute of limitations contained a sub-section referring specifically to wrongful death. Vernon's Tex.Rev.Civ.Stat. art. 5526.7. But cf. Franco v. Allstate Ins. Co., 505 S.W.2d 789, 793 (Tex.1974) (stating that all parts of Article 5526 "are simply subdivisions of a general limitations statute, which is procedural and may be waived if not affirmatively pleaded").

But see Gomez v. ITT Educational Services, Inc., 348 Ark. 69, 71 S.W.3d 542 (2002) (applying Texas law to bar wrongful death action on alternative ground that Texas limitations bar the right, not just the remedy).

81. See Bodnar v. Piper Aircraft Corp., 392 So.2d 1161 (Ala.1980) (reject defendant's argument that despite the fact that both Georgia and Alabama have a two year statute of limitations for wrongful death, neither applies and the Alabama general one year statute governs); cf. Braniff Airways, Inc. v. Curtiss–Wright Corp., 424 F.2d 427 (2d Cir.1970), cert. denied, 400 U.S. 829, 91 S.Ct. 59, 27 L.Ed.2d 59 (1970) (refuse to tack Florida accrual rule and New York limitation period, which would result in longer period for bringing suit than either state would permit for intrastate transactions).

82. Natale v. Upjohn Co., 356 F.2d 590 (3d Cir.1966); Keaton v. Crayton, 326 F.Supp. 1155 (W.D.Mo.1969); Conner v. Spencer, 304 F.2d 485 (9th Cir.1962). But see 12 Okl.Stat. Ann. § 105: time limitation is that "prescribed either by the law of the place where the claim accrued or by the law of this state, whichever *last* bars the claim." (emphasis added).

83. 407 S.W.2d 881 (Mo.1966).

it originated, said bar shall be a complete defense to any action thereon, brought in any of the courts of this state."[84] The plaintiff tried to dissuade the Missouri court from applying the shorter Iowa statute of limitations, arguing that, under a "center of gravity" theory, "whenever the courts are confronted with a conflict of laws problem as to which law governs, the law to be applied is that of the state of domicile of the parties if they are all residents of the same state."[85]

At least the result for which plaintiff contended was proper. Barring this suit by a Missouri resident against Missouri defendants in a Missouri forum would advance no Iowa policy. Stale claims, the danger of mistake and fraud, the desire to protect a defendant from harassment after a decent interval[86]—these were all matters in which Iowa could not properly wish its answers to the proper balancing of parties' interests substituted for those of Missouri. The plaintiff's argument was to no avail in the face of the Missouri borrowing statute. The court noted a number of cases[87] cited by the plaintiff in which other courts had rejected application of the law of the place of wrong when dealing with forum residents. But, "[i]t must be noted that in not one of them did the court go contrary to or by-pass a statute of its own state that governed the question to be decided."[88]

It is ironic that the common, seemingly chauvinistic, provision excepting forum citizens from the operation of a borrowing statute would have avoided a dysfunctional result if it had been in force in Missouri at the time of *Girth*. Such provisions are not the answer, however. The place of injury as such never has any rational purpose in having its shorter statute of limitations borrowed by another forum.[89] Shielding plaintiffs resident at the forum from the operation of the forum's borrowing statute would not prevent irrational results, for

---

84. Mo.Ann.Stat. § 516.190.

85. 407 S.W.2d at 882.

86. See Leflar, *The New Conflicts–Limitations Act,* 35 Mercer L. Rev. 461, 471 (1984), summarizing limitations policies as achieving justice, providing stability to defendants and society, and promoting efficient use of judicial resources.

87. Pearson v. Northeast Airlines, Inc., 309 F.2d 553 (2d Cir.1962), cert. denied, 372 U.S. 912, 83 S.Ct. 726, 9 L.Ed.2d 720 (1963); Fabricius v. Horgen, 257 Iowa 268, 132 N.W.2d 410 (1965); Griffith v. United Air Lines, Inc., 416 Pa. 1, 203 A.2d 796 (1964); Kilberg v. Northeast Airlines, Inc., 9 N.Y.2d 34, 211 N.Y.S.2d 133, 172 N.E.2d 526 (1961).

88. 407 S.W.2d at 883. For a similar holding that the forum's borrowing statute precludes a functional analysis, see Vaughn v. J.C. Penney Co., Inc., 822 F.2d 605 (6th Cir.1987) (Ohio law); Chartener v. Kice, 270 F.Supp. 432 (E.D.N.Y.1967); Wyatt v. United Airlines, Inc., 638 P.2d 812 (Colo.App.1981); Guertin v. Harbour Assurance Co. of Bermuda, Ltd., 141 Wis.2d 622, 415 N.W.2d 831 (1987) (statute refers to a "foreign cause of action" and, in a prior version, referred to "injuries ... received without this state"). But cf. McMahon v. Pennsylvania Life Ins. Co., 891 F.2d 1251, 1259 (7th Cir. 1989) (although "center of gravity" approach is precluded by Wisconsin borrowing statute, limitation that should be applied is that of "the only state with an interest in protecting defendants from stale claims").

89. Gianni v. Fort Wayne Air Service, Inc., 342 F.2d 621 (7th Cir.1965); Paris v. General Elec. Co., 54 Misc.2d 310, 282 N.Y.S.2d 348 (Sup.Ct.1967), aff'd mem., 29 A.D.2d 939, 290 N.Y.S.2d 1015 (1968). But cf. Fullmer v. Sloan's Sporting Goods Co., 277 F.Supp. 995 (S.D.N.Y.1967) (forum and place where defendant incorporated borrows shorter statute of limitations of state where injury occurred and plaintiff resident).

example, in the following situation. Assume that plaintiff and defendant reside in different states and that the injury occurs in a third state. It would make no sense to borrow the statute of limitations of the place of injury if the forum were the residence of the defendant, not of the plaintiff, but plaintiff's residence and defendant's residence had the same period of limitations, which was longer than that of the place of wrong.[90] Nor would the common borrowing statute exception for parties resident since the accrual of the action produce a proper result if the following events occurred. Plaintiff and defendant reside in X. Defendant injures plaintiff in Y. Defendant then moves to F. F and X have two-year limitations, but Y has a one-year period. Plaintiff sues defendant in F more than one year but less than two years after the accident.[91]

Nor did a borrowing-statute exception for forum plaintiffs help in *Global Financial Corp. v. Triarc Corp.*[92] The plaintiff was not from New York. Therefore the exception did not apply. The court held that the borrowing statute's reference to "accruing" means the state where plaintiff suffered harm, not the state indicated by a "grouping of contacts" approach that New York uses for contract choice-of-law analysis.

Perhaps the borrowing statute in *Girth* did not have the plain meaning that the court attributed to it. A court should hold that a cause of action "arises" in the state whose law, in terms of state-interest analysis, will determine the "substantive" elements of recovery. The Florida Supreme Court has adopted the view that the same "significant relationships test" used to choose law in tort actions determines the meaning of "arose" in its borrowing statute.[93] This argument, that a

---

90. But see Paganuzzi v. Steigerwald, 38 A.D.2d 631, 326 N.Y.S.2d 927 (1971) (borrow limitation of place of injury despite longer periods at residences of both parties, because plaintiff is not a forum resident, although the defendant is); cf. Strickland v. Kay, 426 S.W.2d 746 (Mo., K.C.Ct.App.1968) (forum and plaintiff's domicile borrows limitation of Oklahoma, the place of injury, to bar action against Arkansas resident).

91. See Miller v. Stauffer Chem. Co., 99 Idaho 299, 581 P.2d 345 (1978) (forum exception for resident plaintiffs not applicable to plaintiff who moved into forum after injury although plaintiff's former domicile had the same exception).

92. 93 N.Y.2d 525, 693 N.Y.S.2d 479, 715 N.E.2d 482 (1999).

93. Bates v. Cook, Inc., 509 So.2d 1112 (Fla.1987) (citing Commentary). For additional cases giving the borrowing statute reference to "arose" a functional definition, see Hamilton v. General Motors Corp., 490 F.2d 223 (7th Cir. 1973); O'Keefe v. Boeing Co., 335 F.Supp. 1104 (S.D.N.Y.1971) ("accrued"); Klondike Helicopters, Ltd. v. Fairchild Hiller Corp., 334 F.Supp. 890 (N.D.Ill.1971); Thigpen v. Greyhound Lines, Inc., 11 Ohio App.2d 179, 229 N.E.2d 107, 40 O.0.2d 335 (1967) (refuse to apply limitations of place of injury without reference to "the degree of nexus" that place has to the action, even though forum statute borrows limitation of place where action "arose"); BHP Petroleum (Americas), Inc. v. Texaco Exploration & Prod., Inc., 1 P.3d 1253, 1258 (Wyo. 2000) ("arose" refers to the state that has "the most significant relationship" to the parties). Cf. Philadelphia Housing Authority v. American Radiator & Standard Sanitary Corp., 291 F.Supp. 252 (E.D.Pa.1968) (where the claim "arose" for purposes of venue in antitrust suit is determined by the "weight of contacts" and not by a "simplistic" "where the injury occurs" test); Lumbermens Mut. Cas. Co. v. August, 530 So.2d 293 (Fla. 1988) (in contract actions, "arose" refers to the place of execution when the claim is based on contract; action against insurer for uninsured motorist benefits is characterized as contract, not tort). But see cases rejecting the argument the court should not former opinions defining "arose" after adoption of the most significant relationship test. Alberding v. Brunzell, 601 F.2d 474 (9th

cause of action "arose" in the state whose law will determine the substantive elements of recovery, is especially compelling if the place of injury would bar recovery, for example, under a guest statute, but the forum and common domicile of the parties would permit recovery for ordinary negligence. It is difficult to see how the cause of action can "arise" under the law of the place of injury if the tort law of that place grants no right of recovery.[94]

Another, less intellectually satisfying ploy, is to argue that the borrowing statute, with its dysfunctional reference to where the cause of action "arose," applies only to "procedural" statutes of limitation, and not to those that would be characterized as "substantive" under the built-in or specificity tests.[95]

A final argument to avoid the territorial imperative of a borrowing statute is to argue that when the statute refers to the "laws of the state" where the action arose, "laws" means the whole law of that state including its conflict of laws rules.[96] If that state would not regard its

Cir.1979); Antone v. General Motors Corp., 64 N.Y.2d 20, 484 N.Y.S.2d 514, 473 N.E.2d 742 (1984) (action "accrued" where the accident occurred). See also Combs v. International Ins. Co., 354 F.3d 568 (6th Cir. 2004) (predicts that Kentucky would not apply "the most significant relationship" analysis to meaning of "arisen" in its borrowing statute).

For ingenious avoidance of a dysfunctional result that would be created by a borrowing statute with no exception for forum residents, see Coan v. Cessna Aircraft, 53 Ill.2d 526, 293 N.E.2d 588 (1973). The Court reads an exception for forum parties into the statute to avoid hypothetical conflict with the tolling statute. See also Panchinsin v. Enterprise Companies, 117 Ill.App.3d 441, 72 Ill.Dec. 922, 453 N.E.2d 797 (1st Dist.1983) (*Coan* applies when only defendants are forum residents). But see Haughton v. Haughton, 76 Ill.2d 439, 31 Ill.Dec. 183, 394 N.E.2d 385 (1979), cert. denied, 444 U.S. 1102, 100 S.Ct. 1069, 62 L.Ed.2d 789 (1980) (Illinois tolling statute exception for nonresidents violates equal protection).

94. But see Trzecki v. Gruenewald, 532 S.W.2d 209 (Mo.1976) rejecting this argument. See also Global Financial Corp. v. Triarc Corp., 93 N.Y.2d 525, 693 N.Y.S.2d 479, 715 N.E.2d 482 (1999), discussed supra, text accompanying note 92.

95. See Conner v. Spencer, 304 F.2d 485, 487 (9th Cir.1962) (dictum); Pack v. Beech Aircraft, 50 Del. (11 Terry) 413, 132 A.2d 54 (1957) (borrowing statute exception for forum residents is not applicable to a foreign "built in" statute of limitations); Malone v. Jackson, 652 S.W.2d 170 (Mo.App.1983) (borrowing statute is not applicable to the special statute of limitations contained in the wrongful death statute and, under a most significant relationship test, the forum's wrongful death act applies—but the general applicability of this decision is undercut by the fact that Missouri has a statutory provision, Rev.Stat.Mo. § 516.300, which provides that the chapter of the Missouri code that includes its borrowing statute does not apply "to any action which is or shall be otherwise limited by statute"). But cf. Wenke v. Gehl Co., 274 Wis.2d 220, 682 N.W.2d 405 (2004) (borrowing statute borrows statute of repose).

For discussion of the built-in and specificity tests, see, supra, footnotes 51 and 52 and accompanying text.

96. See Drudge v. Overland Plazas Co., 670 F.2d 92 (8th Cir.1982) (holding that the Iowa borrowing statute language, "laws ... where the defendant has previously resided," referred to the whole law of that place, including its borrowing statute, which borrowed the law of the state in which the action "originated"). But see Hobbs v. Firestone Tire & Rubber Co., 195 F.Supp. 56 (N.D.Ind.1961) (rejecting a reference to the borrowing statute of the state referred to by the forum's borrowing statute); Rescildo by Rescildo v. R.H. Macy's, 187 A.D.2d 112, 594 N.Y.S.2d 139 (1st Dept.1993) (rejecting plaintiff's argument that the reference in New York's borrowing statute to the "laws" of Connecticut included Connecticut's characterization of statutes of limitations as procedural); Uniform Conflict of Laws–Limitations Act § 3, 12 U.L.A.155, 159: "If the statute of limitations of another state applies to the assertion of a claim in this State, the other state's relevant statutes and

shorter limitation as procedural and permit the action under the law of another state, then the forum may do so.[97]

But playing with the meaning of "arose" or "laws" or limiting application of a borrowing statute is not the best route. It would be preferable to repeal borrowing statutes and give the statute of limitations issue the independent functional analysis that it deserves.[98] We would not always want to apply the same law to determine the period of limitations that we apply to other issues in the same case.[99] *Schum v. Bailey*,[100] for example, decided that, since a doctor would have the same tort liability under the law of New York, where he operated, and the law of New Jersey, where the patient resided, there was no functional objection to applying New Jersey tort law. The court then held that, because it should apply the statute of limitations of the state whose tort law was applicable, there was no objection to applying the statute of the New Jersey forum. In New Jersey the limitation period had not run; it had run in New York. The court thus bootstrapped itself into application of a longer period of limitations without an independent determination of whether this was fair in the light of contacts between the forum and the defendant's course of conduct.

In 1982, the National Conference of Commissioners on Uniform State Laws approved a new uniform borrowing statute.[101] The prior uniform act had no exception for forum residents and borrowed the period of "the place where the claim accrued,"[102] if this was shorter than the forum's period. The new act ties selection of the statute of limitations to the law of the state upon which "a claim is substantively

---

other rules of law governing tolling and accrual apply in computing the limitation period, but its statutes and other rules of law governing conflict of laws do not apply"; The Foreign Limitation Periods Act 1984, L. Reports Stat. c. 16, applicable to England and Wales, § 1(5): "In this section 'law', in relation to any country, shall not include rules of private international law applicable by the courts of that country...."

97. See Ledesma v. Jack Stewart Produce, Inc., 816 F.2d 482 (9th Cir.1987), which permitted a California resident to sue Arizona and Oklahoma residents who injured the plaintiff in Arizona. The California one-year limitation had expired, but not the Arizona or Oklahoma two-year limitations. For disagreement with *Ledesma*, see Weinberg, *Choosing Law: The Limitations Debates*, 1991 U.Ill. L. Rev. 683, 720–721.

98. See Comment, 35 Albany L. Rev. 754, 766 (1971) suggesting repeal of the New York borrowing statute and enactment of a declaration that the statute of limitations be treated as substantive under a "contact-interest approach". But see Henry v. Richardson–Merrell, Inc., 508 F.2d 28, 32 n. 10 (3d Cir.1975) (trial court wrong in making interest analysis of statute of limitations as issue separate from which state's liability rule will apply).

99. See Reese, *The Second Restatement of Conflict of Laws Revisited*, 34 Mercer L. Rev. 501, 506–07 (1983).

100. 578 F.2d 493 (3d Cir.1978).

101. See Uniform Conflict of Laws–Limitations Act, 12 ULA 155; Leflar, *The New Conflicts–Limitations Act*, 35 Mercer L. Rev. 461 (1984). As of May 1, 2009 in force in Colorado, Minnesota, Montana, Nebraska, North Dakota, Oregon, and Washington. Colorado has both the Uniform Act (Col. St. §§ 13–82–101 through 13–82–106) and a statute that applies the shorter limitations period of another state or country in which the "cause of action arises" with no exception for Colorado parties (Col. St. § 13–80–110).

102. Uniform Statute of Limitations on Foreign Claims Act § 2, 14 381 ULA (withdrawn in 1978).

based."[103] The limitation period of the forum applies, however, "[i]f the court determines that the limitation period of another state ... is substantially different from the limitation period of this State and has not afforded a fair opportunity to sue upon, or imposes an unfair burden in defending against the claim...."[104]

The new act is better than the old act, which courts have interpreted to compel dysfunctional results under the law of the place of injury even though the dispute is between forum residents.[105] The current act is not as good, however, as no act at all.[106] Simple repeal of current borrowing statutes would free courts to give limitations the independent functional conflicts analysis that they require. The new act unwisely locks the limitations issue to other issues in the case, which will not always be desirable.

Cropp v. Interstate Distributor Co.[107] provides an example of the difficulties created by the Uniform Act's linking of the limitations issue to other issues. A truck owned by a Washington company and driven by a Nevada resident collided in California with a truck owned and operated by Oregon residents. Plaintiffs sued in Oregon for personal injuries and property damage. Their action was timely under the law of all of these states except California. The plaintiffs pleaded that at the time of the accident, the defendants were violating California highway regulations. Applying the Uniform Act, the court held that California's one-year period of limitations applied to bar the action because plaintiffs "claims are substantively based on California law only."

Moreover, the exception in favor of forum law if the court regards another state's limitation period as unfair is a resuscitation of the public policy[108] doctrine in its most extreme and officious form. If doing nothing is too sensible a solution to be practical, the following statute would do the least harm:

1.   Statutes of limitations should be given the same conflict-of-laws analysis as is given to other issues in transjurisdictional occurrences.

2.   A court of this state may, in the interests of efficient administration of justice, dismiss a suit without reaching a result on the merits,

---

103. § 2(a). If the claim is based "upon the law of more than one state, the limitation period of one of those states chosen by the law of conflict of laws of this State, applies." Id. § 2(a)(2).

See Perkins v. Clark Equipment Co., Melrose Division, 823 F.2d 207 (8th Cir. 1987) (apply limitations law of the state whose law is applicable to other issues, noting that the forum, North Dakota, has adopted the Uniform Act, although it was not in force at the time of the injury).

104. Uniform Act, supra note 101 § 4.

105. See Trzecki v. Gruenewald, 532 S.W.2d 209 (Mo.1976).

106. When Chaim Weizman, the first president of Israel, was a young man, he fancied himself as quite an orator and often practiced after dinner at family gatherings. After one postprandial oration, Weizman asked his grandfather, whom he greatly admired: "Well grandpa, how was that, a good speech?" His grandfather replied: "Yes Chaim, an excellent speech, but not as good as no speech at all."

107. 129 Or.App. 510, 880 P.2d 464, rev. denied, 320 Or. 407, 887 P.2d 791 (1994).

108. See, infra, § 3.6.

when this state's limitations period has expired but conflict-of-laws analysis does not indicate that the limitations law of this state should preclude suit elsewhere.[109]

A revision of the Restatement, Second, of Conflict of Laws, adopted after several drafts and extensive debate, moves a halting step closer to a functional treatment of statutes of limitations:

§ 142. Statute of Limitations

Whether a claim will be maintained against the defense of the statute of limitations is determined under the principles stated in § 6. In general, unless the exceptional circumstances of the case make such a result unreasonable:

(1) The forum will apply its own statute of limitations barring the claim.

(2) The forum will apply its own statute of limitations permitting the claim unless:

> (a) maintenance of the claim would serve no substantial interest of the forum; and

> (b) the claim would be barred under the statute of limitations of a state having a more significant relationship to the parties and the occurrence.[110]

The strong point of the provision is that subsection 2 would bring an end to forum shopping for a long statute of limitations in a state that has jurisdiction over the defendant but no other relationship to the parties or the transaction.[111] The new section is, however, far more forum-oriented than is justified if statutes of limitations receive independent functional choice-of-law analysis.

Under subsection 1, a stale claim argument will almost invariably prevail when the forum's statute of limitations is shorter. The forum should be willing to apply another state's longer statute whenever the forum is not primarily concerned with affording repose to the defendant and when, because of slight differences in forum and foreign limitation periods, staleness of the claim does not threaten to compromise the forum's administration of justice.[112]

---

109. I made it up.

110. Restatement (Second) Conflict of Laws 123 (Supp.1989) New § 142 is intended to replace §§ 142 and 143 (distinguishing a statute "which bars the right and not merely the remedy"). Huynh v. Chase Manhattan Bank, 465 F.3d 992 (9th Cir. 2006), adopts Restatement (Second) § 142 as the federal common law choice-of-law rule.

111. See Shewbrooks v. A.C. & S., Inc., 529 So.2d 557 (Miss.1988).

112. See Ledesma v. Jack Stewart Produce, Inc., 816 F.2d 482 (9th Cir. 1987). A California plaintiff was permitted to recover in a California forum after the California one-year statute of limitations had run when the injury occurred in Arizona, the defendants resided in Arizona and Oklahoma, and both Arizona and Oklahoma had two-year limitation periods. The one false note in the court's reasoning is the statement that Arizona's interest in deterring careless driving would be impaired if its longer period were not applied. The plaintiff should have prevailed because this would not significantly impair any state's policy. But see Weinberg, *Choosing Law: The Limitations Debates*, 1991 U. Ill. L. Rev. 683, 720–21 (disapproving of *Ledesma*).

Subsection 2 is also unduly favorable to forum interests, but now will affect the merits. If limitations is given the same analysis as other issues, the forum interest in recovery under its longer period will sometimes yield. This is especially likely if the forum's limitations period is substantially longer than usual.[113]

In 1991 Louisiana enacted a new Conflict of Laws Code.[114] Article 3549 of the Code begins by requiring that Louisiana limitations apply to any suit brought in Louisiana, but then provides two exceptions. Louisiana's limitations do not bar suit if the action is not "barred in the state whose law would be applicable to the merits and maintenance of the action in this state is warranted by compelling considerations of remedial justice."[115] Louisiana longer limitations do not apply if the action is "barred in the state whose law is applicable to the merits and maintenance of the action in this state is not warranted by the policies of this state and its relationship to the parties or the dispute nor by any compelling considerations of remedial justice."[116] These provisions may be sufficiently flexible to permit Louisiana courts to achieve sensible results.[117]

§ 3.2C3   Privileged Communications

Testimonial privileges were once treated as procedural.[118] Now the trend is to regard testimonial privileges as "substantive."[119] For example, although Rule 501 to Rules of Evidence for United States Courts and Magistrates governs privileges by federal common law, it provides a significant exception: "However, in civil actions and proceedings, with respect to an element of a claim or defense as to which State law supplies the rule of decision, the privilege of a witness, person, government, State, or political subdivision thereof shall be determined in

---

113. See Nierman v. Hyatt Corp., 441 Mass. 693, 808 N.E.2d 290 (2004) (construes Restatement § 142(2) and applies shorter Texas statute of limitations to bar suit by Massachusetts resident injured in Texas). But see Jackson v. Chandler, 204 Ariz. 135, 136, 61 P.3d 17, 18 (Ariz. 2003) (applying revised § 142 and choosing Arizona longer limitations for suit between California residents who collided in Arizona—"Arizona does have a substantial interest in the litigation [deterring wrongful conduct] even if it does not supersede California's").

114. La. Civ. C. Book IV (effective January 1, 1992).

115. Id. art. 3549(1).

116. Id. art. 3549(2).

117. In Smith v. ODECO (UK), Inc., 615 So.2d 407 (La.App.1993), writ denied 618 So.2d 412 (La.1993), the court found that "compelling considerations of remedial justice" permitted a resident and domiciliary of the United Kingdom to sue in Louisiana when the Louisiana period of limitations had expired but the United Kingdom period had not. Louisiana was the only forum in which jurisdiction could be obtained over all defendants. For a discussion of Art. 3549 of the Louisiana conflicts code and of cases applying it, see Symeonides, *Louisiana Conflicts Law: Two "Surprises,"* 54 La. L. Rev. 497, 530–548 (1994).

118. See, e.g., Doll v. Equitable Life Assur. Soc'y, 138 F. 705 (3d Cir. 1905) (physician-patient).

119. See, e.g., Samuelson v. Susen, 576 F.2d 546 (3d Cir. 1978) (proceedings of medical review committee); State v. Lipham, 910 A.2d 388 (Me. 2006) (applying Restatement (Second) § 139).

accordance with State law." A problem with Rule 501 is that it does not tell the federal court which state's law to apply. *Samuelson v. Susen*[120] resolved this problem by applying the conflict-of-laws rules of the state in which the federal court was sitting.

The Second Restatement places the subject of privileged communications in its Procedure chapter and, in section 139,[121] states a rule that is forum-centered with regard to exclusion and even more weighted in favor of applying the forum's rule of admission. The Restatement's rule permits the forum to exclude evidence not privileged under the law of the state that has the most significant relationship with the communication if admission "would be contrary to the strong public policy of the forum."[122] On the other hand, the forum may admit evidence privileged under the law of the state that has the most significant relationship with the communication "unless there is some special reason why the forum policy favoring admission should not be given effect."[123]

Invocation of the forum's public policy to exclude evidence even when "the state of the forum has no relationship to the transaction"[124] is likely to affect the outcome. If the forum would dismiss the case without prejudice to suit elsewhere, use of public policy would be less obnoxious than under section 139(1), which clearly contemplates proceeding with the suit.[125]

Even more undesirable is section 139(2) which, unless a "special reason" to exclude exists, admits evidence under forum law that would be excluded in the state of most significant relationship to the communication. Even the Federal Rules of Evidence defer to state law on privileged communications.[126]

---

120.   576 F.2d 546 (3d Cir. 1978).

121.   RESTATEMENT (SECOND) § 139:

"Privileged Communications"

"(1) Evidence that is not privileged under the local law of the state which has the most significant relationship with the communication will be admitted, even though it would be privileged under the local law of the forum, unless the admission of such evidence would be contrary to the strong public policy of the forum."

"(2) Evidence that is privileged under the local law of the state which has the most significant relationship with the communication but which is not privileged under the local law of the forum will be admitted unless there is some special reason why the forum policy favoring admission should not be given effect."

Section 139 was revised in 1988, but the rules quoted above were not changed. The only significant change was the addition of a new comment concerning depositions. Id. Revisions § 139, cmt. *f* (1988).

122.   Id. § 139(1). But see State v. Heaney, 689 N.W.2d 168 (Minn. 2004) (applying Restatement § 139, in criminal trial admit evidence not privileged under doctor-patient privileged of state where blood sample taken although it would be privileged under Minnesota law).

123.   Id. § 139(2).

124.   Id. cmt. *c*.

125.   Id.

126.   FED. R. EVID. 510 (stating that "in civil actions ... with respect to an element of a claim or defense as to which State law supplies the rule of decision, the privilege of a witness ... shall be determined in accordance with State law").

Section 139 works best when a court, as in *Ford Motor Co. v. Leggat*,[127] applies its provisions selectively. A Texan was killed in Texas when a Ford Bronco, which he had purchased in Texas, rolled over.[128] At issue was whether the court would admit the report of Ford's principal in-house attorney to the company's Policy and Strategy Committee.[129] The report was privileged under the law of Michigan, where Ford's general counsel delivered it, but Texas had a narrower corporate attorney-client privilege under which it was doubtful that the report could be excluded.[130] The court focused on the exception in section 139(2) finding "special reasons why Texas should defer to the broader attorney-client privilege of Michigan."[131]

The court noted that the Restatement "identifies four factors to consider when determining admissibility: number and nature of contacts of the forum with the parties or transaction, materiality of the evidence, kind of privilege, and fairness to the parties."[132] Nevertheless, the court focused only on the kind of privilege, finding that "the law of the state with the most significant relationship to the communication" should protect the old and well-established attorney-client privilege.[133]

If the court had also focused on the other three factors in section 139 comment *d*, it might have come to a different, and less desirable, conclusion. The first factor, "the number and nature of the contacts that the state of the forum has with the parties and with the transaction involved,"[134] points to admissibility under Texas law to facilitate recovery for Texas blood spilled on a Texas highway because of an allegedly defective vehicle purchased in Texas. The second factor, "materiality of the evidence,"[135] also points to admission. The fourth factor, "fairness to the parties,"[136] gives mixed signals. Ford may have relied on the broad Michigan form of the corporate attorney-client privilege,[137] but the privilege was asserted by a party and, under the Restatement, this weighs in favor of admissibility.[138]

---

127.   904 S.W.2d 643 (Tex. 1995).

128.   Id. at 645. The case does not state that Leggat was a Texan or that the vehicle was purchased in Texas. Counsel for plaintiff supplied this information. Telephone interview with J. Hadley Edgar (Sept. 20, 1996).

129.   *Leggat*, 904 S.W.2d at 645.

130.   Id. at 646.

131.   Id. at 647.

132.   Id. (citing RESTATEMENT (SECOND) § 139, cmt. *d*).

133.   Id.

134.   Restatement (Second) § 139, cmt. *d*.

135.   Id.

136.   Id.

137.   The Restatement states that "[t]he forum will be more inclined to give effect to a privilege if it was probably relied upon by the parties." Id.

138.   Id. (stating that if "the privilege belongs to a person who is not a party to the action. . . . the forum will be more inclined to recognize the privilege and to exclude the evidence than it would be in a situation where the privilege is claimed by a person who is a party").

The court chose the right law for determining admissibility of the attorney-client communication, but would have had an easier time doing so without an obligation to justify itself under the Second Restatement.

§ 3.2C4 Damages

In discussing choice of law for damages, it is helpful to distinguish between "heads" of damages and standards for quantifying recovery under those heads. Heads of damages are the categories under which the plaintiff may recover. Examples are lost wages, medical expenses, pain and suffering, and punitive damages. On the other hand, standards for quantifying recovery determine whether an award under these heads is reasonable—for example, whether an award of $500,000 for pain and suffering is excessive.

The Restatement wisely treats heads of damages as substantive and chooses the law applicable to them under the principles of section 6.[139] This reflects the long-established rule,[140] from which courts have made only aberrant departures, usually to avoid a territorial choice-of-law rule that they were about to abandon.[141] The Restatement, however, treats quantification of damages as procedural.[142] This too accords with the established rule.[143] The "established rule" is monstrous. Quantification

---

139. See Restatement (Second) §§ 178 (referring to § 175 for determining damages for wrongful death), 171 (referring to § 145 for determining damages for other torts).

140. See Slater v. Mexican Nat'l R.R., 194 U.S. 120, 126, 24 S.Ct. 581, 48 L.Ed. 900 (1904) (stating that "we may lay on one side as quite inadmissible the notion that the law of the place of the act may be resorted to so far as to show that the act was a tort, and then may be abandoned, leaving the consequences to be determined according to the accident of the place where the defendant may happen to be caught").

141. See Kilberg v. Northeast Airlines, 9 N.Y.2d 34, 211 N.Y.S.2d 133, 172 N.E.2d 526, 529 (1961) (avoiding the law the place of fatal injury by stating that damages for wrongful death are "procedural or remedial"). Two years later Babcock v. Jackson, 12 N.Y.2d 473, 240 N.Y.S.2d 743, 191 N.E.2d 279 (1963) abandoned the place-of-wrong rule for torts.

142. See Restatement (Second) § 171, cmt. *f* (stating that "[t]he forum will follow its own local practices in determining whether the damages awarded by a jury are excessive").

143. See 1 Albert Venn Dicey & J.H.C. Morris, The Conflict of Laws 192 (Lawrence Collins et al. eds., 14th ed. 2006) (stating that "[a] distinction must be drawn between remoteness and heads of damages, which are questions of substance governed by the *lex causae*, and the measure or quantification of damages, which is a question of procedure governed by the *lex fori*"). Courts have nevertheless usually treated statutory caps on damages as substantive. See, e.g., Marmon v. Mustang Aviation, 430 S.W.2d 182, 194 (Tex. 1968) (applying Colorado statutory limit on wrongful death recovery); John Pfeiffer Pty. Ltd. v. Rogerson, 172 A.L.R. 625 (Austl. 2000) (applying limit in New South Wales workers' compensation law to action brought in Australian Capital Territory, overruling Stevens v. Head, 112 A.L.R. 7 (Austl. 1993)).

For rare exceptions that treat quantification of damages as substantive, see Karim v. Finch Shipping Co., 265 F.3d 258 (5th Cir.2001) (holding that the law of Bangladesh determines the quantification of damages for pain and suffering); Bhatnagar v. Surrendra Overseas Ltd., 52 F.3d 1220, 1235 (3d Cir. 1995) (vacating award of non-pecuniary damages with instruction to "reassess those damages in accordance with Indian law"); Cunningham v. Quaker Oats Co., 107 F.R.D. 66, 73 (W.D.N.Y. 1985) (treating as substantive a statement by the Supreme Court of Canada that $100,000 should be the upper limit of non-pecuniary damages); Baird v. Bell Helicopter Textron, 491 F.Supp. 1129, 1150–52 (N.D. Tex. 1980) (same); Archuleta v. Valencia, 871 P.2d 198 (Wyo. 1994) (applying Colorado law to determine whether the jury's verdict was inadequate). Cf. Palenkas v. Beaumont Hospital, 432 Mich. 527, 443 N.W.2d 354, 358 (1989) (considering jury verdicts from other states in

of damages is the bottom line, what all the fuss at trial was about. Everything else is mere prologue. Allowing United States juries to assess what they think are proper damages for injuries abroad, even when foreign law otherwise applies, is the major reason why the United States is a magnet forum for the afflicted of the world.[144]

After years of state and federal "tort reform" in the United States, U.S. law may, in some circumstances, not provide the world's most generous recovery. For tort victims, such as retired people, who do not lose income, the law of some foreign countries provides more compensation than U.S. law. In Italy, every relative of a decedent has a claim to compensation determined by a regional table. Some regional tables provide higher compensation than others.[145] Nevertheless, if quantification of damages is procedural, in most cases foreign plaintiffs who can sue in U.S. courts will recover more than if they sued at home.

At long last a beam of sanity has pierced this darkness. In a conflict between federal circuits, some federal courts have held that *Erie R.R. v. Tompkins*[146] requires evaluating jury verdicts under the standards of the state whose law applies to heads of damages,[147] but the Seventh Circuit has disagreed.[148] Now the United States Supreme Court has resolved the controversy and held that *Erie* requires federal courts sitting in diversity

---

determining the reasonableness of a damages award); John Pfeiffer Pty. Ltd. v. Rogerson, 172 A.L.R. 625, 651 (Austl. 2000) ("*all* questions about the kinds of damage, or amount of damages that may be recovered, would likewise be treated as substantive issues governed by the lex loci delicti") (emphasis in original).

144.   See Piper Aircraft Co. v. Reyno, 454 U.S. 235, 252 n.18, 102 S.Ct. 252, 70 L.Ed.2d 419 (1981) (listing "jury trials" as one of the reasons why United States courts are attractive to foreign plaintiffs); Smith Kline & French Lab. Ltd. v. Bloch, [1983] 1 W.L.R. 730, 734 (C.A. 1982) (stating that United States juries "are prone to award fabulous damages").

145.   See Gina Passarella, *Bus Crash in Europe Gives Pa. Attorney a Taste of Italian Law*, The Legal Intelligencer, February 15, 2008, (Italian law provided twice the damages for death of retired senior citizens than U.S. law provided).

146.   304 U.S. 64, 58 S.Ct. 817, 82 L.Ed. 1188 (1938) (holding that when state law is the source of the governing rule, a federal court must apply the state common law rule and not create one of its own). See also Klaxon Co. v. Stentor Elec. Mfg. Co., 313 U.S. 487, 61 S.Ct. 1020, 85 L.Ed. 1477 (1941) (holding that the *Erie* mandate includes state choice-of-law rules).

147.   See Raucci v. Town of Rotterdam, 902 F.2d 1050, 1058–59 (2d Cir. 1990) (ordering a new trial subject to remittitur of amount in excess of awards permitted in New York state courts); Martell v. Boardwalk Enter., Inc., 748 F.2d 740, 750 (2d Cir. 1984) (stating that "[i]n determining whether an award is so excessive as to shock the judicial conscience, we look ... to other jury awards condoned by the courts of the state whose substantive law governs the rights of the parties"); Hysell v. Iowa Pub. Serv. Co., 559 F.2d 468, 472 (8th Cir. 1977) (stating that "[b]ecause this is a diversity case, we must take care that the damage award does not exceed that which could be sustained were the case before the highest court of the state whose substantive law gives rise to the claim").

148.   See Cash v. Beltmann N. Am. Co., 900 F.2d 109, 111 n.3 (7th Cir. 1990) (looking not only to forum-state decisions, but also to decisions from other circuits on the proper ratio between punitive damages and a defendant's net worth); *In re* Air Cash Disaster Near Chicago, 803 F.2d 304, 318 n.12 (7th Cir. 1986) (stating that "[i]n the case of a tort damages award in a routine diversity case, a federal court examining analogous awards is not necessarily limited to cases decided by the courts of the state whose law governs the diversity action").

to apply "the law that gives rise to the claim for relief"[149] when determining whether damages are excessive. This rule is not binding on the states,[150] but it indicates that quantification of damages is too important to be treated as procedural for conflicts purposes. This may presage a salutary change of attitude in state courts, but if reform occurs it will be without assistance from the Second Restatement.

There is an interesting development in Dominica. In order to discourage motions in U.S. courts for forum non conveniens dismissals of actions brought against U.S. defendants by citizens of Dominica who are injured in Dominica, the Commonwealth of Dominica has enacted the Transnational Causes of Action (Product Liability) Act.[151] Under the Act, if a foreign court grants the dismissal, a Dominican court hearing the case shall be guided by "damages awarded in the Courts of the country with which the defendant has a strong connection" when awarding exemplary or punitive damages.[152]

A Regulation of the European Parliament and the Council on the Law Applicable to Non–Contractual Obligations, referred to as "Rome II," includes among the issues governed by the Regulation's choice-of-law rules "the existence, the nature and the assessment of damage or the remedy claimed."[153] This language is broad enough to include quantification of damages; it constitutes a desirable reversal of the standard rule treating quantification of damages as a procedural matter to be resolved under forum standards.[154]

In 2008 the European Parliament adopted a Regulation on the Law Applicable to Contractual Obligations (Rome I), to replace the "Rome"

---

149. Gasperini v. Center for Humanities, Inc., 518 U.S. 415, 438 n.22, 116 S.Ct. 2211, 2224–25 n.22, 135 L.Ed.2d 659 (1996).

150. A state's traditional procedural characterization of a conflicts issue, though arguably wrong under modern choice-of-law analysis, is unlikely to be declared unconstitutional. *See* Sun Oil Co. v. Wortman, 486 U.S. 717, 108 S.Ct. 2117, 100 L.Ed.2d 743 (1988) (holding that Kansas may characterize time limitations as procedural and permit recovery that would be time-barred in the states whose laws apply to substantive issues).

151. Act no. 16 of 1997.

152. Id. § 12(1).

153. Regulation (EC) No. 864/2007 of 11 July 2007, OJ 2007 L199/40, art. 15 (c). Cf. art. 1(3) "This Regulation shall not apply to evidence and procedure, without prejudice to Articles 21 [choice of law for the formal validity of a unilateral act relating to a non-contractual obligation] and 22 [Regulation's choice-of-law provisions apply to 'rules which raise presumption of law or determine the burden of proof']."

154. See Maher v. Groupama Grand Est, [2009] 1 W.L.R. 1752, [2009] 1 All E.R. 1116 (Q.B. 2009) (noting, in ¶ 16, that Rome II includes assessment of damages in the scope of its choice-of-law rules, but does not apply it to this case because the injury occurred before Rome II took effect).

I urged this change from a previous draft when I was invited to address the European Parliament Committee on Legal Affairs and the Internal Market, which was working on Rome II. The draft read: "Except where otherwise provided in this Regulation or in a choice-of-law agreement, the court seised shall apply its national rules to the quantification of damages, unless the circumstance[s] of the case warrant the application of another State's rules." My comment to the Committee was: "Nothing is more likely to trigger the forum shopping that Rome II intends to discourage than permitting a forum to apply its own magnanimous view of proper compensation to a case governed by foreign law." See Weintraub, *Rome II and the Tension between Predictability and Flexibility*, 41 Rivista di Diritto Internazionale Privato e Processuale 561, 564–65 (2005) (publishing my remarks).

Convention.[155] Rome I, art. 15(c), unlike Rome II, retains the language of art. 10(c) of the Rome Convention and includes in the scope of Rome I "the assessment of damages in so far as it is governed by rules of law." Do the words "in so far as it is governed by rules of law" refer to a statute or a court decision placing a specific limit on a head of damages but treat other aspects of quantification of damages as "procedural" to be determined by forum standards? There is substantial doubt that Rome I's meaning clashes with the salutary advance of Rome II in ending the nonsense of treating quantification of damages as procedural. In their report of October 31, 1980 to the European Council on the Rome Convention, Mario Giuliano and Paul Lagarde explain the use of "in so far as it is governed by rules of law." They state:

> The assessment of damages has given rise to some difficulties. According to some delegations the assessment of the amount of damages is a question of fact and should not be covered by the Convention. To determine the amount of damages the court is obliged to take account of economic and social conditions in its country; there are some cases in which the amount of damages is fixed by a jury; some countries use methods of calculation which might not be accepted in others.

> Other delegations countered these arguments, however, by pointing out that in several legal systems there are rules for determining the amount of damages; some international conventions fix limits as to the amount of compensation (for example, conventions relating to carriage); the amount of damages in case of non-performance is often prescribed in the contract and grave difficulties would be created for the parties if these amounts had to be determined later by the court hearing the action.

> By way of compromise the Group finally decided to refer in subparagraph (c) solely to rules of law in matters of assessment of damages, given that questions of fact will always be a matter for the court hearing the action.[156]

This commentary indicates that the words "in so far as it is governed by rules of law" refer not to the procedural/substantive distinction but to the fact/law distinction. None of the objections referred to in the report to extending Rome I's scope to all aspects of quantification of damages are cogent. Thus both Rome I and Rome II sensibly treat quantification of damages as within the scope of their choice-of-law rules.

The House of Lords has taken an undesirable step in the opposite direction. One bit of sanity that survives the choice-of-law madness of characterizing quantification of damages as "procedural," is that courts regard statutory limits on recovery as "substantive." They apply those limits when their choice-of-law rules select the tort law of the jurisdic-

---

155. Regulation (EC) No. 593/2008 of The European Parliament And Of The Council Of 17 June 2008 on The Law Applicable To Contractual Obligations (Rome I).

156. OJ C 282/1 at 33.

tion where the statute is in force.[157] In *Harding v. Wealands*,[158] the House of Lords, construing the Private International Law (Miscellaneous Provisions) Act 1995, has rejected even this limit on the "procedural" label when quantifying damages.

Mr. Harding, an Englishman, and Ms. Wealands, an Australian, formed a relationship in Australia. She came to England to live with him. Ms. Wealands returned to Australia to attend a family wedding. He later joined her for a holiday and to visit her parents. While she was driving in New South Wales (NSW) with Mr. Harding as a passenger, she lost control and the vehicle turned over. He was badly injured and is tetraplegic. Ms. Wealands owned the vehicle and carried liability insurance issued by an Australian company. Both Mr. Harding and Ms. Wealands returned to England.

A NSW statute places limits on compensation for various damages including lost earnings and non-economic damages, and in other ways restricts recovery. Under NSW law the plaintiff would recover about thirty percent less than under English law. The United Kingdom Private International Law Act 1995 abolished the double actionability choice-of-law rule for torts[159] and created a presumption that that the law of the place of injury governs[160] unless it is "substantially more appropriate" to apply some other law.[161] Section 14(3)(b) states that the statute does not authorize "questions of procedure in any proceedings to be determined otherwise than in.7 accordance with the law of the forum."

Mr. Harding sued Ms. Wealands in the High Court of Justice in London. That court ruled that English law determined the damages.[162] Justice Elias gave two reasons: (1) the NSW caps on damages were "procedural";[163] (2) even if damages were substantive, it was "substantially more appropriate" to apply English law because the parties "were living together in a settled relationship and resident in England"[164] and "the costs of alleviating the consequences of the accident will be borne in" England.[165] The Court of Appeal allowed the appeal and applied

---

157. See, e.g., Marmon v. Mustang Aviation, 430 S.W.2d 182, 194 (Tex. 1968) (applying Colorado statutory limit on wrongful death recovery); John Pfeiffer Pty. Ltd. v. Rogerson, 172 A.L.R. 625 (Austl. 2000) (applying limit in New South Wales workers' compensation law to action brought in Australian Capital Territory).

158. [2007] 2 A.C. 1 (H.L. 2006) (appeal taken from Eng.). The following discussion of this case is based on Weintraub, *Choice of Law for Quantification of Damages: A Judgment of the House of Lords Makes a Bad Rule Worse*, 42 Tex. Int'l L. J. 311 (2007) © 2007 Texas International Law Journal.

159. Private International Law (Miscellaneous Provisions) Act 1995 § 10. The double actionability rule required that the tort be actionable under the laws of both the forum and of the jurisdiction where the defendant committed the tort. See Boys v. Chaplin, [1971] A.C. 356 (H.L. 1969) (appeal taken from Eng.).

160. Private International Law (Miscellaneous Provisions) Act 1995 § 11.

161. Id. § 12.

162. Harding v. Wealands, [2004] EWHC 1957 (Q.B. 2004).

163. Id. at ¶ 64.

164. Id. at ¶ 33.

165. Id. at ¶ 35.

Australian law.[166] The judges of the Court of Appeal agreed that it was not more appropriate to apply English law if the NSW statutory caps on damages were substantive,[167] but they split 2–1 on the issue of whether the caps were substantive, the majority voting for the substantive classification.[168] The House of Lords, five Law Lords participating, unanimously allowed the appeal and restored the judgment of the trial court on the ground that quantification of damages is procedural.

Lord Hoffman stated that he found no ambiguity in the meaning of "procedure" as used in section 14(3)(b) of the Private International Law Act 1995.[169] Procedure in English private international law had always included all issues relating to quantification of damages.[170] On the question of whether the NSW statutory limits on recovery are procedural, Lord Hoffman wrote that "we could not have better authority than that of the High Court of Australia in *Stevens v. Head*."[171] *Stevens v. Head*[172] held that the damage limits in an earlier version of the NSW statute were procedural and did not apply to a suit in Queensland by a New Zealand citizen against a Queensland resident. The defendant had struck the plaintiff in NSW near the Queensland border with a motor vehicle insured and registered in Queensland.[173] Lord Hoffman noted[174] that the High Court of Australia had overruled *Stevens v. Head* in *John Pfeiffer Pty. Ltd. v. Rogerson*.[175] *Pfeiffer* held that limits on non-economic damages in the NSW Workers' Compensation Act were substantive and applied to a suit in the Australian Capital Territory. Lord Hoffman dismissed this overruling as "required by constitutional imperatives of Australian federalism."[176]

Pfeiffer states:

> Within a federal nation such as Australia, the capacity of a party to legal proceedings to choose the forum within which to bring such proceedings can be one of the advantages of the interconnected polity. However, such a facility ought not to involve the capacity of one party seriously to prejudice the legal rights of an opponent....
>
> It may be reasonable to recognise the right of a litigant to choose different courts in the one nation by reason of their advantageous procedures, better facilities or greater expedition. However, it is not reasonable that such a choice, made unilaterally by the

---

166. Harding v. Wealands, [2005] 1 W.L.R. 1539 (C.A. 2004).

167. Id. at 1550 (Waller L. J.), 1557 (Arden L. J.), 1573 (Sir William Aldous).

168. Id. at 1550 (Waller L. J.) (procedural), 1560 (Arden, L. J.) (substantive); 1572 (Sir William Aldous) (substantive).

169. Harding v. Wealands, [2007] 2 A.C. 1, 16 (H.L. 2006) (appeal taken from Eng.).

170. Id.

171. Id. at 17.

172. 176 C.L.R. 433 (Austl. 1993).

173. Id. at 437–38.

174. *Harding*, [2007] 2 A.C. at 19–20.

175. 203 C.L.R. 503 (Aust. 2000).

176. *Harding*, [2007] 2 A.C. at 20.

initiating party, should materially alter that party's substantive
legal entitlements to the disadvantage of its opponents. If this could
be done, the law would no longer provide a certain and predictable
norm, neutrally applied as between the parties. Instead, it would
afford a variable rule which particular parties could manipulate to
their own advantage. Such a possibility would be obstructive to the
integrity of a federal nation, the reasonable expectations of those
living within it and the free mobility of people, goods and services
within its borders upon the assumption that such movement would
not give rise to a significant alteration of accrued legal rights.[177]

This statement expresses, not some peculiar aspect of "Australian federalism," but sound general choice-of-law principles that would mandate
the opposite result in *Harding*.

Lord Hoffman wrote that if the word "procedure" were ambiguous
in section 14(3)(b) of the Private International Law Act, "this is as clear
a case ... as anyone could hope to find"[178] where resort to legislative
history would demonstrate that Parliament intended that term to include quantification of damages:

At the Report stage in the House of Lords, Lord Howie of Troon put
down an amendment to add a further paragraph to what is now
section 14(3), so that it would read: "[nothing in this Part] (d)
authorises any court of the forum to award damages other than in
accordance with the law of the forum." Lord Howie declared an
interest on behalf of Cape Industries plc, which had a few years
earlier been sued in Texas for asbestos-related injuries and was
anxious that Part III should not import American scales of compensation into English courts. In the debate on 27 March 1995 Lord
Mackay of Clashfern LC [Lord Chancellor] made what was obviously
a carefully prepared statement: "With regard to damages, issues
relating to the quantum or measure of damages are at present and
will continue under Part III to be governed by the law of the forum;
in other words, by the law of one of the three jurisdictions in the
United Kingdom. Issues of this kind are regarded as procedural and,
as such, are covered by clause 14(3)(b). It follows from this that the
kind of awards to which the noble Lord referred of damages made in
certain states, in particular in parts of the United States, will not
become a feature of our legal system by virtue of Part III. Our
courts will continue to apply our own rules on quantum of damages
even in the context of a tort case where the court decides that the
'applicable law' should be some foreign system of law so far as
concerns the merits of the claim. Some aspects of the law of damages
are not regarded as procedural and, in accordance with the views of
the Law Commissions in their report on the subject, Part III does
not alter this. These aspects concern so-called 'heads of damages'—
the basic matter which is being compensated for—such as special

---

177. *Pfeiffer*, 203 C.L.R. at 552–553.

178. *Harding*, [2007] 2 A.C. at 16.

damage relating to direct financial loss. Whether a particular legal system permits such a head of damage is not regarded as procedural but substantive and therefore not automatically subject to the law of the forum. This seems right given the intimate connection between such a concept and the particular nature of the case in issue. But again, I foresee no significant increase in awards of damages because a particular head of damage permitted by some foreign system of law would continue, so far as the quantum allocated to it in any finding is concerned, to be regulated by our own domestic law of damages. I hope the noble Lord will feel reassured."[179]

This excerpt from the Parliamentary proceedings focuses on avoiding introducing higher "American scales of compensation into English Courts." That policy would not apply to rejecting statutory limits on damages that would reduce recovery below the English standard. Lord Roger of Earlferry recognized this distinction:

The particular problem raised by Lord Howie related to the high level of damages in the United States which he was anxious should not be replicated here. But it would be equally unacceptable if, say, United Kingdom courts had to award damages according to a statutory scale which, while adequate in another country because of the relatively low cost of services etc. there, would be wholly inadequate in this country, having regard to the cost of the corresponding items here.[180]

This is an argument, not for treating the NSW statutory limits on recovery as procedural, but for applying English substantive law on one of the grounds stated by Justice Elias in his High Court of Justice decision—it was "substantially more appropriate" to apply English law because the parties "were living together in a settled relationship and resident in England."[181]

The fact that Ms. Wealands carried liability insurance issued by an Australian company does not make it less appropriate to apply English law. Any recovery under the policy is just grist for the actuarial mill. The payment is added to costs that are used to calculate future premiums.[182]

The only viable unfair surprise argument concerning insurance focuses on unfair surprise to the insured. This may occur if the liability regimes of the place of injury and a distant forum are so different that liability insurance adequate at the place of injury is inadequate to meet forum standards for quantifying damages. If the tortfeasor cannot reasonably foresee the need for insuring at the higher level, it is unfair to impose forum law to compensate a forum resident. For example, a Texas resident vacationing in Mazatlán on the Pacific coast of Mexico is run over by a Mexican driver. The law of Sinaloa, the Mexican state where Mazatlán is located, does not permit recovery for pain and suffering and

---

179. Id. at 16–17.

180. Id. at 27.

181. *Harding*, [2004] EWCH 1957 ¶ 33.

182. See McNamara, *Automobile Liability Insurance Rates*, 35 INS. COUNSEL J. 398, 401 (1968).

has low statutory limits on recovery of economic damages.[183] Under Sinaloa law, the Texan would recover a small fraction of what he would recover under Texas law. Then a Texas court acquires personal jurisdiction over the Mexican driver in Texas by personal service while the Mexican is visiting Texas. The Mexican defendant has liability insurance adequate under Sinaloa compensation standards but wholly inadequate under Texas measurements of recovery. It would be outrageous to apply Texas law to determine either heads of damages or compensation under those heads. On the other hand, if two Texas friends vacation together in Mazatlán and one injures the other while driving in that city, the driver had better have liability insurance keyed to Texas compensation standards. A Texas court will apply Texas law as the jurisdiction that has the "most significant relationship" to the parties and the occurrence.[184] If the defendant is surprised it is because he did not heed the warning that the Supreme Court of Texas issued in 1979.[185]

There is no reasonable objection to the U.K.'s, through its Parliament or courts, declaring it against public policy to award compensation that is excessive by U.K. standards. This would not justify a court's awarding higher damages than available under the law of the place of wrong, as the House of Lords did in *Harding*. The only justification for awarding higher damages would be that substantive choice-of-law analysis pointed to English law as applicable; to use the wording of the Private International Law Act, it was "substantially more appropriate" to apply English law.

Suppose the opposite situation when English quantification of damages is lower than that of the place of wrong. A New Yorker negligently injures a fellow New Yorker in New York. The tortfeasor moves to England with all his assets. The injured party can obtain personal jurisdiction over the tortfeasor in New York under the New York long-arm statute,[186] but wisely declines to do so. Because all the tortfeasor's assets are in England, the plaintiff could not satisfy any New York judgment in the United States. The injured party would have to get the New York judgment recognized and enforced by an English court. An English court will not recognize the New York judgment. Although a tort committed in England is a basis for personal jurisdiction over the tortfeasor in an English court,[187] an English court will not recognize that basis for jurisdiction in countries with which it does not have a judgment-recognition treaty.[188] An English court is compelled by the Private

---

183. See Villaman v. Schee, 15 F.3d 1095, 1994 WL 6661, *3 (9th Cir. 1994); Vargas, *Mexican Law and Personal Injury Cases: An Increasingly Prominent Area for U.S. Legal Practitioners and Judges*, 8 San Diego Int'l L. J. 475, 503 (2007).

184. See Gutierrez v. Collins, 583 S.W.2d 312, 318–19 (Tex. 1979).

185. Id.

186. N.Y. C.P.L.R. § 302 (a)(2) (McKinney 2002).

187. See Civil Jurisdiction and Judgments Act 1982 ch. 27 (incorporating Council Regulation on Jurisdiction and the Recognition and Enforcement of Judgments in Civil and Commercial Matters, No. 44/2001, art. 5(3)).

188. See L. COLLINS ET AL., 1 DICEY & MORRIS ON THE CONFLICT OF LAWS 487–88 (14th ed. 2006).

International Law Act to quantify damages by English standards rather than New York standards. This is especially relevant for non-economic damages such as pain and suffering, for which New York standards are likely to produce a much higher award.

Is this a just result? The Act compels an English court to apply English law when proper choice-of-law analysis would not. The forum's public policy is a legitimate basis for refusing to apply a foreign rule that, to use Cardozo's classic statement, "would violate some fundamental principle of justice, some prevalent conception of good morals, some deep-rooted tradition of the common weal."[189] Cardozo assumed that a forum thus rejecting a foreign rule selected by the forum's choice-of-law rule should dismiss the case.[190] Rejecting the foreign rule does not justify the forum in applying its own substantive law. True, a number of United States courts, not prepared to replace the place-of-wrong tort choice-of-law rule, but dissatisfied with the result of applying that rule, have used public policy to substitute forum law.[191] Lord Hope of Craighead stated a better approach to using public policy to reject a foreign rule and, instead of dismissing the case, rendering a judgment on the merits under a different law. In *Kuwait Airways Corp. v. Iraqi Airways Co.*,[192] the House of Lords rejected Iraqi law that would justify the conversion of aircraft belonging to the Kuwati State. In his opinion, Lord Hope noted that the public policy under which the Lords refused to apply Iraqi law was "based on the Charter of the United Nations and the resolutions which were made under it."[193] He stated that "a principle of English public policy which was purely domestic or parochial in character would not provide clear and satisfying grounds for disapplying the primary rule which favours the lex loci delicti."[194]

In the case suggested above, of a New York tortfeasor fleeing to England with all his assets, it should not offend English public policy to apply New York law for quantification of damages. If the tortfeasor was an Englishman visiting in New York, an English court would be more justified, as Lord Howie suggested in Parliament, in refusing to "import

---

189.   Loucks v. Standard Oil Co., 224 N.Y. 99, 120 N.E. 198, 202 (1918).

190.   Id.

191.   See, e.g., Alexander v. General Motors Corp., 267 Ga. 339, 478 S.E.2d 123 (1996) (applying Georgia law of strict liability rather than Virginia law requiring proof of negligence to product liability action by Georgia resident who purchased car in Georgia and was injured by crash in Virginia, declaring Virginia law to be against Georgia's public policy); Kilberg v. Northeast Airlines, Inc., 9 N.Y.2d 34, 211 N.Y.S.2d 133, 172 N.E.2d 526 (1961) (applying New York measure of wrongful death recovery rather than statutory limits of place of wrong) (New York abandoned the place-of-wrong rule two years later in Babcock v. Jackson, 12 N.Y.2d 473, 240 N.Y.S.2d 743, 191 N.E.2d 279 (1963)); cf. Owen v. Owen, 444 N.W.2d 710 (S.D.1989) (decides to retain place-of-wrong rule, but refuses to apply guest statute of place of injury on public policy grounds; concurring opinion, joined in by a majority of the court, reaches the same result under "modern" conflicts analysis), overruled, Chambers v. Dakotah Charter, Inc., 488 N.W.2d 63 (S.D. 1992) (adopting "most significant relationship approach").

192.   [2002] 2 A.C. 883 (H.L. 2002) (appeal taken from Eng.).

193.   Id. at 1116.

194.   Id.

American scales of compensation into English courts."[195] Reasonable people may differ as to whether the Englishman should be able to injure an American in the U.S. and then draw around him the protective cloak of English law. It would make more sense to someone who has not had their mind numbed by a legal education to reach this result on the basis of public policy rather pretending that the matter is procedural. If adequately counseled, the injured American will know that if he sues in England he will get a smaller judgment than if he sued in the U.S. He would sue in England only if his choice was a partial loaf or none at all.

The Private International Law Act 1995 did not, as the House of Lords held, compel depriving the defendant of statutory limits on damages under the law of the place of wrong. If the result in *Harding* is correct it is because, in the wording of the Act, it was "substantially more appropriate" to apply English law because of the relationship between the parties and their residence in England. The real harm of the House of Lords decision is that it makes it more unlikely that courts will change the standard rule that characterizes quantification of damages as procedural and therefore determined by forum standards. That rule should change to accord with a functional view of "procedural" in the context of choice of law. This functional view would preclude the procedural label for any rule that is likely to affect the result in a manner that would invite forum shopping unless it would be unreasonably difficult for local lawyers and judges to apply foreign law to the issue. More undesirable still is that *Harding v. Wealands* extends the procedural characterization of quantification of damages to the one area where U.S. and Australian courts have had the good sense not to apply it—statutory limits on recovery.

Fortunately *Harding* may have a short life in the United Kingdom. The European Union regulation on The Law Applicable to Non–Contractual Obligations (Rome II) in Article 15(c) contains language that includes quantification of damages in the issues controlled by the regulation's choice-of-law rules.[196] The United Kingdom has agreed to be bound by Rome II.[197]

§ 3.2C5 Admiralty Proceedings: Limitation of Damages and Choice of Law

U.S. federal legislation limits the liability of a shipowner resulting from a maritime accident. Liability is limited to the "value of the vessel, and pending freight."[198] If this is insufficient to pay claims for personal

---

195. See supra text accompanying footnote 179.

196. See supra notes 153–154 and accompanying text.

197. Official Journal C 289 E, 28/11/2006 ¶ 35. Ireland has also opted in. Id. Denmark has not. Id. ¶ 36. Under the Treaty of Amsterdam, Oct. 2, 1997, 1997 O.J. (C340) 195, 197, (amending the 1992 Treaty on European Union, Feb. 7, 1992, 1992 O.J. (C191) 1, known as the "Maastricht Treaty"), the United Kingdom, Ireland, and Denmark could elect not to be bound by new Council regulations.

198. 46 U.S.C. § 30505(a).

injury and death, the statute increases the limit for these claims to "$420 times the tonnage of the vessel."[199]

Other maritime countries also permit shipowners to limit damages, but most of those countries base their limits not on the value of the ship, but on its tonnage. Under the United States limitation procedure, the value of the vessel is calculated after the accident.[200] The value of the ship before the accident is likely to exceed the amount available under foreign law.[201] Therefore United States limitations law is likely to favor the shipowner if the ship is sunk and favor the claimants if the ship emerges from the accident without serious damage.[202] The difference may be substantial, as in *The Swibon*,[203] in which one Korean ship survived a collision that sank another Korean vessel. The United States limitations were almost $9,000,000 greater than the Korean limitations. The issue of limiting damages in admiralty is therefore important, but the case law governing choice between United States and foreign limitations is inconsistent and confusing.

The difficulty begins with Justice Holmes' opinion in *The Titanic*.[204] The British ship had sunk on the high seas when it struck an iceberg, resulting in loss of lives and property. The issue was whether to apply the British or the much lower United States limitations. Justice Holmes held that the United States limitations applied declaring that the United States statute "clearly limits the remedy ... in cases where it has nothing to say about the rights."[205] Any claimant limited to the paltry recover under United States law was not likely to appreciate the Justice's distinction between "remedy" and "rights." Ironically, it is

---

199. Id. § 30506(b).

200. See Petition of Chadade Steamship Co. (*The Yarmouth Castle*), 266 F.Supp. 517, 519 (S.D. Fla. 1967) [hereinafter *Yarmouth Castle*] (following sinking of cruise ship, shipowner attempts to limit bond to $33,000, "the suggested value of the strippings of the Yarmouth Castle together with passage money" to cover claims other than injury and death); G. Gilmore & C. Black, Jr., The Law of Admiralty (1975) 940 [hereinafter Gilmore & Black].

201. For an exception, see *Yarmouth Castle*, 266 F.Supp. at 522 (stating that under Panamanian law, the value of hull and indemnity insurance is included).

202. See Gilmore & Black, supra note 200, at 940.

203. In re Complaint of K.S. Line Corp. (*The Swibon*), 596 F.Supp. 1268 (D. Alaska 1984) [hereinafter *The Swibon*].

204. Oceanic Steam Navigation Co. v. Mellor (*The Titanic*), 233 U.S. 718, 34 S.Ct. 754, 58 L.Ed. 1171 (1914) [hereinafter *The Titanic*].

205. Id. at 733. *See* Restatement of Conflict of Laws § 411 (1934) (stating that "limitation of liability in a maritime cause of action is determined by the law of the forum, irrespective of the law which created the cause of action"); cf. Maritime Code of The People's Republic of China (Adopted at the 28th Meeting of the Standing Committee of the Seventh National People's Congress on November 7, 1992, promulgated by Order No. 64 of the President of the People's Republic of China on November 7, 1992, and effective as of July 1, 1993): art. 273: "The law of the place where the infringing act is committed shall apply to claims for damages arising from collision of ships. The law of the place where the court hearing the case is located shall apply to claims for damages arising from collision of ships on the high seas. If the colliding ships belong to the same country, no matter where the collision occurs, the law of the flag State shall apply to claims against one another for damages arising from such collision."

Holmes who, in *Slater v. Mexican National R.R.*,[206] had ten years earlier eloquently rejected the argument that damages are procedural.[207]

At the time that *The Titanic* was decided, the United States limitation statute referred to "any vessel."[208] These words should not be read literally, but interpreted to mean that owners of any vessel, foreign or domestic, are entitled to the United States limitations if, under proper choice-of-law analysis, American law should apply. The subsequent 1936 amendment adding the words "whether American or foreign,"[209] does not affect this argument.[210] Other United States statutes, such as our antitrust and securities laws, contain global language,[211] and yet our courts undertake a careful analysis of the territorial reach of these statutes.[212] Moreover, Holmes' opinion in *The Titanic* does not refer to the "any vessel" language in the statute.

Justice Frankfurter further confused matters in *The Norwalk Victory*.[213] A vessel owned by the United States, while under a bareboat charter[214] to a United States company, collided with a British vessel in Belgian waters. Cargo owners sued the United States and the charterer in federal district court. Under Belgian law the limit on the shipowner's

---

206. 194 U.S. 120, 24 S.Ct. 581, 48 L.Ed. 900 (1904).

207. Id. at 126.

208. See Lauritzen v. Larsen, 345 U.S. 571, 591, 73 S.Ct. 921, 97 L.Ed. 1254 (1953).

209. 46 U.S.C. § 183(a), as amended in 1936 by 49 Stat. 1479, now 46 U.S.C. § 30505(a) ("a vessel").

210. But see *The Swibon*, 596 F.Supp. at 1271 (stating that the 1936 amendment removed "any doubt that Congress intended the domestic liability limitation to apply to all proceedings in the United States").

211. The Sherman Act begins by referring to "[e]very contract, combination in the form of trust or otherwise, or conspiracy, in restraint of trade or commerce among the several States, or with foreign nations...." 15 U.S.C. § 1. The Clayton Act defines "commerce" as "trade or commerce among the several States and with foreign nations...." 15 U.S.C. § 12. The Securities Act of 1933 refers to "trade or commerce in securities ... between any foreign country and any State, Territory, or the District of Columbia." 15 U.S.C. § 77b(7). The Securities Exchange Act of 1934 covers "trade, commerce, transportation, or communication among the several States, or between any foreign country and any State, or between any State and any place or ship outside thereof." 15 U.S.C. § 78c(a)(17). Exempted from this Act is "any person insofar as he transacts a business in securities without the jurisdiction of the United States, unless he transacts such business in contravention of such rules and regulations as the [Securities and Exchange] Commission may prescribe." Id. § 78dd(b). The Commission, however, has never implemented this exception with rules.

212. See Hartford Fire Ins. Co. v. California, 509 U.S. 764, 113 S.Ct. 2891, 125 L.Ed.2d 612 (1993) (ruling 5–4 that the Sherman Act applies to English defendants who were alleged to have conspired to restrain trade in commercial general liability insurance issued to United States policy holders); Zoelsch v. Arthur Andersen & Co., 824 F.2d 27 (D.C. Cir. 1987) (holding that the Securities Exchange Act of 1934 does not apply to activities in the United States that allegedly played a part in defrauding German investors).

213. Black Diamond S.S. Corp. v. Robert Stewart & Sons, Ltd. (*The Norwalk Victory*), 336 U.S. 386, 69 S.Ct. 622, 93 L.Ed. 754, *amended*, 69 S.Ct. 1490, 93 L.Ed. 1760 (1949) [hereinafter *The Norwalk Victory*].

214. Under a "bareboat charter," the party to whom the boat is chartered takes "full control of the ship for [the period of the charter] as though it owned it...." East River S.S. Corp. v. Transamerica Delaval, Inc., 476 U.S. 858, 860, 106 S.Ct. 2295, 90 L.Ed.2d 865 (1986).

and charterer's liability was $325,000, but under United States law it was $1,000,000. Although Frankfurter held that, in order to guard against the possibility that United States law applied, the charterer should have posted a bond of $1,000,000, the Justice considered the choice of limitations law "a knotty problem."[215] Frankfurter concluded that the Belgian limitation applied if it "attaches to the right [and] nothing in *The Titanic* stands in the way of observing that limitation."[216]

Although an admiralty text declares that "[i]t is difficult to imagine a case in which the 'limitation attaches to the right,' "[217] lower federal courts have seized on this exception to apply foreign limitation law when that law is applicable under ordinary choice-of-law principles.[218] In *The Yarmouth Castle*, Judge Mehrtens applied Panamanian limitations as attaching to the right and then wrote, "[i]f the foregoing analysis of *The Titanic* and *The Norwalk Victory* is not correct, then the Court is of the opinion that *The Titanic* should be re-examined" and the law governing limitations selected under ordinary choice-of-law principles.[219] Today conflicts principles require a most-significant-relationship analysis.[220]

---

215. *The Norwalk Victory*, 336 U.S. at 398.

216. Id. at 395 (citation omitted).

217. T. SCHOENBAUM, ADMIRALTY AND MARITIME LAW 763 (2d ed. 1994).

218. See *The Swibon*, 596 F.Supp. at 1270–73 (holding that when foreign limits are lower, a substance-procedure analysis of the foreign limits is available and that the lower Korean limits apply because they are substantive); *The Yarmouth Castle*, 266 F.Supp. at 521 (applying higher Panamanian limits); cf. In re Bethlehem Steel Corp. (The Steelton), 631 F.2d 441, 445 (6th Cir. 1980), *cert. denied*, 450 U.S. 921, 101 S.Ct. 1370, 67 L.Ed.2d 349 (1981) (finding that Canadian limitations do not apply because they are "procedural," but defending application of United States limitations as "a desirable choice-of-law decision").

219. *The Yarmouth Castle*, 266 F.Supp. at 523. For the position that admiralty limitations should be subjected to choice-of-law analysis, see Tetley, *Shipowner's Limitation of Liability and Conflicts of Law: The Properly Applicable Law*, 23 J. Mar. L. & Com. 585, 603–606 (1992) (stating a method for determining the law properly applicable to all issues, including maritime limitations); Tetley, *Division of Collision Damages: Common Law, Civil Law, Maritime Law and Conflicts of Law*, 16 Tul. Mar. L. J. 263, 287–88 (1992) (stating a method for determining "the law which has the most significant relationship" and applicable to "the right to limit liability of each shipowner" and "the law of the calculation of the limitation fund of each ship"); Comment, 31 Tex. L. Rev. 889, 895 (1953) (stating that "limitation of liability should be treated as substantive and governed by the law of the place where the tort occurred"); cf. Greenman, *Limitation of Liability: A Critical Analysis of United States Law in an International Setting*, 57 Tul. L. Rev. 1139, 1191–92 (1983) (stating that when foreign limitations are lower than United States limitations, the choice of law should be made "without slavish adherence only to the illogical attempts to differentiate substance and procedure" and suggesting Restatement (Second) § 6 for guidance); Rosenthal & Raper, *Amoco Cadiz and Limitation of Liability for Oil Spill Pollution: Domestic and International Solutions*, 5 Va. J. Nat. Resources L. 259, 286 n.230 (1985) (stating that *Lauritzen–Romero–Rhoditis*, discussed infra this section, "may signal the Supreme Court's shift away from the law of the forum and toward a consideration of contacts, interests, and expectations"); Comment, 21 Tex. Int'l L. J. 495, 515–28 (1986) (stating that, to discourage forum shopping, lower United States limits should be applied, but that if foreign limits are lower, the applicable law should be chosen by interest analysis).

220. See Restatement (Second) § 145(1) (stating the "[t]he rights and liabilities of the parties with respect to an issue in tort are determined by the local law of the state which, with respect to that issue, has the most significant relationship to the occurrence and the parties ...").

I agree with Judge Mehrtens. In *The Titanic*, Justice Holmes justified treating limitations as procedural on the ground that the limitations
imposed were not binding abroad on claimants who did not sue in the
United States.[221] This argument is not cogent because it allows claimants
to recover under United States limitations when those limitations are
higher than those of a foreign country and, under proper choice-of-law
analysis, the law of the foreign country should apply to the limitations
issue. Moreover, the argument is circular. If United States limitations
were treated as substantive and applied only when this country had the
most significant relationship to the occurrence and the parties, those
limitations would be binding abroad on all parties over whom the United
States court had personal jurisdiction. That is, the limitations would be
as binding abroad as a United States judgment can be under principles
of international comity. Unfortunately, the United States does not have
a judgment-recognition treaty with any other country. In matters concerning cargo and passengers, an arbitration award can confer on the
imposition of United States limitations substantial mandatory recognition abroad.[222] The United States is a party to multilateral conventions
requiring that signatories enforce arbitration awards of other signatories.[223]

Using a most-significant-relationship approach to choose damages
limitations would not require significant change in the methods already
used for other issues in admiralty cases. *Lauritzen v. Larsen*[224] held that
a Danish seaman injured on a Danish ship in Havana harbor could not
recover under the Jones Act.[225] The Court listed seven factors that might
affect the territorial reach of maritime law: place of the wrongful act, law
of the flag, allegiance or domicile of the injured, allegiance of the
defendant shipowner, place of contract, inaccessibility of foreign forum,
and the law of the forum.[226] *Romero v. International Terminal Operating*

---

221. *The Titanic*, 233 U.S. at 734. See Watson, *Transnational Maritime Litigation:
Selected Problems*, 8 Mar. Law. 87, 110 (1983) (stating that "[n]othing in the opinion [*The
Titanic*] indicates that the limitation decree of a United States court would not be binding
on parties who did file suit in the United States or asserted claims in the United States
limitation proceeding"). See also T. SCHOENBAUM, ADMIRALTY AND MARITIME LAW 763 (2d ed.
1994) (stating that it is "reasonable" to apply United States limitations to any actions
brought here because the limitations have "no extraterritorial effect, and claimants can
still bring suit in the courts of a foreign state").

222. See Vimar Seguros y Reaseguros, S.A. v. M/V Sky Reefer, 515 U.S. 528, 115 S.Ct.
2322, 132 L.Ed.2d 462 (1995) (enforcing against cargo owners a clause in the bill of lading
requiring arbitration in Japan); cf. Carnival Cruise Lines v. Shute, 499 U.S. 585, 111 S.Ct.
1522, 113 L.Ed.2d 622 (1991) (enforcing against passengers a clause in the cruise ticket
requiring litigation in Florida).

223. Convention on the Recognition and Enforcement of Foreign Arbitral Awards (the
"New York" Convention), June 10, 1958, 21 U.S.T 2517, 330 U.N.T.S; The Inter–American
Convention on International Commercial Arbitration (The "Panama" Convention), Janu-
ary 30, 1975, 14 I.L.M. 336.

224. 345 U.S. 571, 73 S.Ct. 921, 97 L.Ed. 1254 (1953).

225. 46 U.S.C. § 688, now § 30104.

226. *Lauritzen*, 345 U.S. at 583–90. In order to limit Jones Act recoveries under the
Lauritzen factors, Congress enacted the 1982 "brown water" amendment to the Act. 46
U.S.C. app. § 688(b). The amendment denies recovery under the Act for injury or death to
a person who was not a U.S. citizen or permanent resident alien of the U.S. and who was

Co.[227] applied the seven *Lauritzen* factors to deny coverage under the Jones Act or the general maritime law of the United States to a Spanish seaman injured in United States territorial waters off Hoboken, New Jersey. *Hellenic Line Ltd. v. Rhoditis*[228] added "base of operations"[229] to the seven *Lauritzen* factors to permit Jones Act recovery by a Greek seaman injured in United States territorial waters on a Greek ship based in the United States and operated by a Greek corporation that had its main office in New York.

Lauritzen analyzed the seven factors it enumerated in the same manner a modern court would under a most-significant-relationship approach. When the Court's analysis was complete, only three of the seven factors were considered material for Jones Act recovery—the law of the flag which "must prevail unless some heavy counterweight appears,"[230] the allegiance or domicile of the seaman, and the allegiance of the shipowner.[231] These are the same contacts that are likely to be related to some policy of compensating injured seamen. *Rhoditis* is even closer to a most-significant-relationship approach when it states that "[t]he significance of one or more factors must be considered in light of the national interest served by the assertion of Jones Act jurisdiction."[232]

State law applies in admiralty cases if there is no established admiralty rule and if there is no pressing need for a uniform federal rule governing the particular issue.[233] When federal courts use admiralty choice-of-law rules to select state law, most of them expressly utilize a most-significant-relationship approach.[234] *Lauritzen* did refer to the rule

---

employed "in the development . . . of off-shore mineral or energy resources . . . in the territorial waters or waters overlaying the continental shelf of a nation other than the United States, its territories, or possessions." See Robertson & Kelly, *Protecting U.S. Oil Companies from Lawsuits Brought by Foreign Offshore Oil and Gas Workers*, 21 Rev. Litig. 309 (2002).

227. 358 U.S. 354, 79 S.Ct. 468, 3 L.Ed.2d 368 (1959).

228. 398 U.S. 306, 90 S.Ct. 1731, 26 L.Ed.2d 252 (1970).

229. Id. at 309 (stating that "the list of seven factors in *Lauritzen* was not intended as exhaustive").

230. *Lauritzen*, 345 U.S. at 586.

231. Id. at 586–88. The court stated that "place of the wrongful act" was "of limited application to shipboard torts, because of the varieties of legal authority over waters she may navigate." Id. at 583. The court dismissed "place of contract," which was New York, as "fortuitous." Id. at 588. The Court stated that "[i]naccessibility of [the] foreign forum. . . . might be a persuasive argument for exercising a discretionary jurisdiction to adjudge a controversy; but it is not persuasive as to the law by which it shall be judged." Id. at 589–90. The Court rejected the contention that "the law of the forum" should apply, stating, "[j]urisdiction of maritime cases in all countries is so wide and the nature of its subject matter so far-flung that there would be no justification for altering the law of a controversy just because local jurisdiction of the parties is obtainable." Id. at 591.

232. *Rhoditis*, 398 U.S. at 309.

233. See Yamaha Motor Corp., U.S.A. v. Calhoun, 516 U.S. 199, 116 S.Ct. 619, 133 L.Ed.2d 578 (1996) (holding state remedies applicable to wrongful death and survival actions arising from injuries in territorial waters to persons who are not seamen); Wilburn Boat Co. v. Fireman's Fund Ins. Co., 348 U.S. 310, 314, 75 S.Ct. 368, 99 L.Ed. 337 (1955).

234. See Eli Lilly Do Brasil, Ltda. v. Federal Express Corp., 502 F.3d 78 (2d Cir. 2007) (consulting Restatement (Second)); Dresdner Bank AG v. M/V Olympia Voyager, 446 F.3d 1377, 1384 (11th Cir. 2006) (choosing law "[b]ased both on our analysis of the factors

applying United States maritime damages limitations to "foreign causes" and defended this practice on the ground that it applied "only against those who had chosen to sue in our courts on foreign transactions."[235] This passing reference to *The Titanic* should not stand in the way of applying a choice-of-law approach to damages limitations.

Neely v. Club Med Management Services, Inc.,[236] permitted a United States citizen injured in a diving accident in St. Lucia to recover under the Jones Act and United States general maritime law. The court characterized *Lauritzen* as having "adopted a form of interest analysis to cabin the sweep of the Jones Act."[237] Then, breaking new ground, a majority of the Third Circuit, sitting en banc, declared that choice of law in Jones Act cases should follow, not the Restatement (Second) of Conflict of Laws, but the Restatement (Third) of the Foreign Relations Law of the United States.[238]

This is innovative and interesting, but I think wrong. In admiralty cases, a court should choose law under the most-significant-relationship analysis of the Restatement of Conflict of Laws. The difference between the approaches of the Conflicts and Foreign Relations restatements is between a multilateral and unilateral analysis. Under the multilateral analysis of the Conflicts restatement, the court attempts to apply the law that will best accommodate the conflicting rules of different states or countries. It is not sufficient for application of forum law that this is reasonable or that forum policies will be advanced if its law applies. It is also necessary that the forum have the most significant relationship to

---

outlined in the Second Restatement of Conflicts of Law and our analysis of the competing governmental interests in this case"); Calhoun v. Yamaha Motor Corp., U.S.A., 216 F.3d 338, 346 (3d Cir.), cert. denied, 531 U.S. 1037, 121 S.Ct. 627, 148 L.Ed.2d 536 (2000) ("the *Lauritzen* factors, viewed as a whole, represented a departure from the application—in admiralty cases—of the *lex loci delicti* rule and a move toward analyzing which state had the most significant relationship to the incident and the dominant interest in having its law applied"). Albany Ins. Co. v. Anh Thi Kieu, 927 F.2d 882 (5th Cir.), cert. denied, 502 U.S. 901, 112 S.Ct. 279, 116 L.Ed.2d 230 (1991), held that state law on the effect of misrepresentations by the insured is not pre-empted by federal admiralty law and stated: "Modern choice of law analysis, whether maritime or not, generally requires the application of the law of the state with the 'most significant relationship' to the substantive issue in question." Id. at 891. See also Lien Ho Hsing Steel Enterprise Co. v. Weihtag, 738 F.2d 1455, 1458 (9th Cir. 1984) (stating that whether a maritime insurance broker is the insurer's agent is determined by "the law of the state with the greatest interest in the issue"); Edinburgh Assur. Co. v. R. L. Burns Corp., 479 F.Supp. 138, 152–53 (C.D. Cal. 1979), aff'd in part and rev'd in part on other grounds, 669 F.2d 1259 (9th Cir. 1982) (applying "the points of contact analysis of *Lauritzen* and *Romero*" and holding that English law determines the meaning of "actual total loss," because England has "the most significant relationship to the transaction," citing Restatement (Second) §§ 188, 193).

235. *Lauritzen*, 345 U.S. at 591.

236. 63 F.3d 166 (3d Cir. 1995) (en banc).

237. Id. at 181.

238. *Neely*, 63 F.3d at 185–87. The court applies Restatement (Third) of the Foreign Relations Law of the United States §§ 402, 403 (1986) [hereinafter RESTATEMENT (THIRD) FOREIGN RELATIONS]. Section 402 lists "Bases of Jurisdiction to Prescribe"—a country's legislative jurisdiction to apply its law to persons and events both inside and outside its territory. Section 403 provides standards for determining when, although a basis for jurisdiction to prescribe exists under section 402, a court may not apply United States law because "the exercise of such jurisdiction is unreasonable." RESTATEMENT (THIRD) FOREIGN RELATIONS § 403(1).

the parties and the transaction.[239] Under a unilateral approach, such as that of the Restatement of Foreign Relations, the court looks primarily at the purposes underlying forum law and applies that law if those policies will be advanced, providing this application is reasonable. It does not matter that another country, utilizing the same analysis, would apply its law and not United States law.[240] The only exception is when two countries' laws conflict so completely that a person cannot comply with the laws of both. One country orders the same person at the same time to do what the other forbids. Then "a state should defer to the other state if that state's interest is clearly greater."[241]

In *Neely*, the Third Circuit's resort to the Restatement of Foreign Relations was influenced by *Lauritzen*'s brief reference to international law.[242] *Lauritzen*, however, then indicated that choice of law in Jones Act cases should adopt the same methods used in other areas of law, such as tort and contract.[243] The Restatement of Foreign Relations law itself cautions that its focus is on the application of public law, such as antitrust and securities regulation, that advances basic United States policies and commands obedience under threat of criminal and civil penalties.[244] Moreover, although it would be feasible, though I think unwise, to apply the Foreign Relations Restatement's unilateral approach to Jones Act cases,[245] it would be outrageous to do this in other admiralty cases, such as those involving the construction of a maritime insurance policy when national laws conflict on key issues. The Third Circuit's approach would then require applying completely different choice-of-law techniques depending on the nature of the admiralty issues.

§ 3.3 Renvoi

When the forum's choice-of-law rule points to the "law" of another jurisdiction, is the reference to only the rules that jurisdiction would

---

239. See Restatement (Second) § 6, cmts. *c, d*.

240. See Restatement (Third) Foreign Relations §§ 402, 403 (1987).

241. Id. § 403(3).

242. *Neely*, 63 F.3d at 183. See *Lauritzen*, 345 U.S. at 577: "By usage as old as the Nation, such statutes [as the Jones Act] have been construed to apply only to areas and transactions in which American law would be considered operative under prevalent doctrines of international law."

243. *Lauritzen*, 345 U.S. at 582 (stating that "[m]aritime law, like our municipal law, has attempted to avoid or resolve conflicts between competing laws by ascertaining and valuing points of contact between the transaction and the states or governments whose competing laws are involved").

244. See Restatement (Third) Foreign Relations pt. IV, ch. 1 at 237: "This chapter [on jurisdiction to prescribe] concentrates on so-called public law—tax, antitrust, securities regulation, labor law, and similar legislation. The issues addressed may arise in private litigation, but the rules stated in this chapter do not necessarily apply to controversies unrelated to public law issues."

245. Workers' compensation acts are typically, but not universally, applied unilaterally. In most states the forum determines whether its own state's law applies because of the contacts of the parties and the employment relationship with that state. If forum law does not apply, the claim is dismissed. For an exception in which a court applies the workers' compensation law of a sister state, see White v. Malone Properties, Inc., 494 So.2d 576 (Miss. 1986).

apply to a purely local dispute or does the reference include choice-of-law rules? "Renvoi," meaning refer back or refer away, occurs when the forum applies a foreign choice-of-law rule that selects law different from that chosen by the forum's rule. If the foreign rule points back to the forum, there is the intriguing possibility that the court will be caught in a circle of references, from forum to foreign law to forum law, without end. Some United States courts have on this ground rejected reference to the choice-of-law rules of another state.[246] The recent Louisiana codification of conflicts law rejects renvoi but permits consideration of another state's choice-of-law rules in determining whether that failure to apply that state's law would impair that state's policies.[247]

European courts are likely to follow the conflicts rules of a country selected by the forum's choice-of-law rule. The German Civil Code accepts a reference back to German law and will follow a reference to a third country "so far as [doing so] does not contradict the meaning of the renvoi."[248] The Swiss code, on the other hand, rejects renvoi except when the code refers to a foreign conflicts rule.[249] Whether the German or Swiss code results in more frequent reference to foreign conflicts rule depends on the operation of these rules over the range of cases to which the rules apply.

Article 20 of the European Union Regulation on the Law applicable to Contractual Obligations[250] and article 24 of the Regulation on the Law Applicable to Non–Contractual Obligations (Rome II)[251] exclude renvoi.

Article 41 of the Japanese Act on the General Rules of Application of Laws[252] accepts a reference to Japanese law by the choice-of-law rule of a person's national law and applies Japanese law. The article rejects a reference to Japanese law on issues relating to the marital property regime, divorce, or the legal relationship between parents and a child when, under the Act, those issues are governed by a person's national law.[253]

To what extent, if any, should a forum committed to a functional analysis of choice-of-law problems refer to the choice-of-law rules of other states?[254] It should do so, first of all, to the extent that the choice-

---

246. See Haumschild v. Continental Cas. Co., 7 Wis.2d 130, 95 N.W.2d 814 (1959), discussed infra in this section.

247. La. Civ. C. art. 3517.

248. Germany, Intro. Law to Civil Code [EGBGB], Fed. Gaz. Part III, 400–1, Art. 4 (1986 rev.).

249. Swiss Stat. Priv. Int'l L. art. 14 (1989).

Some foreign jurisdictions reject renvoi. The Peruvian Civil Code (1984) permits reference to "only the internal law of the State that is declared competent by the Peruvian conflict rule." Art. 2048, 24 I.L.M. 997, 1002 (1985).

250. Regulation (EC) No. 593/2008 of 17 June 2008.

251. Regulation (EC) No. 864/2007 of 11 July 2007, OJ 2007 L199/40.

252. Law No. 10 of 1898 as newly titled and amended 21 June 2006.

253. Id.

254. See generally, von Mehren, *The Renvoi and its Relation to Various Approaches to the Choice-of-law Problem,* in XXth Century Comparative and Conflicts Law 380, 394

of-law decisions of another state afford information about which of several hypothetically possible domestic policies in fact underlie the foreign local law.

Haumschild v. Continental Casualty Company[255] affords a good example of what is meant. Wisconsin spouses were riding in California in a truck driven by the husband, when, because of the husband's alleged negligence, there was an accident and the wife was injured. The wife sued her husband[256] in Wisconsin, joining the liability insurer and two owners of the truck. The trial granted the defendants' motion for summary judgment on the ground that under California law a wife could not sue her husband in tort.[257] In a landmark opinion departing from the place-of-wrong rule, the Wisconsin Supreme Court reversed and applied Wisconsin law, which permitted wife-husband suits. The court reached this result by reclassifying the problem as one of "family law" rather than of "tort" and thus selecting a different territorially-oriented choice-of-law rule pointing to the marital domicile for the governing law. This method was undesirable because the label switch was made in lieu of, rather than as a result of, a functional analysis of the problem. Though the result in *Haumschild* was fortuitously functional, the new "marital domicile" rule could, in different law-fact patterns, produce results as irrational as the place-of-wrong rule.[258]

More in point for the discussion here, is that the majority rejected the plaintiff's suggestion that Wisconsin law, as that of the marital domicile, applied because California, the place of the accident, would have applied Wisconsin law. In *Emery v. Emery*,[259] the California Supreme Court had classified problems of immunity from liability due to a family relationship, child-parent, sibling-sibling, or wife-husband, as questions of "capacity to sue" rather than of "tort" and had applied the law of the family domicile. The majority in *Haumschild* elected to reach its result without reference to the freshly-coined California choice-of-law rule. The *Haumschild* court feared that it would be caught in an endless

---

(1961) ("a normal and necessary part of the analysis underlying a general functional approach").

255. 7 Wis.2d 130, 95 N.W.2d 814 (1959).

256. The marriage was annulled after the accident and before trial. The court did not rely on the annulment in reaching its decision.

257. California now permits a wife to sue her husband for negligence. Klein v. Klein, 58 Cal.2d 692, 26 Cal.Rptr. 102, 376 P.2d 70 (1962).

258. See, e.g., Haynie v. Hanson, 16 Wis.2d 299, 114 N.W.2d 443 (1962), applying the marital domicile rule to the question of whether the defendants sued by the wife may implead her husband, thus preventing Wisconsin defendants from impleading an Illinois husband. Accord, Pirc v. Kortebein, 186 F.Supp. 621 (E.D.Wis.1960). But see LaChance v. Service Trucking Co., 215 F.Supp. 162 (D.Md.1963) (policies underlying marital immunity rule are not applicable to a third-party complaint against the husband); Zelinger v. State Sand and Gravel Co., 38 Wis.2d 98, 156 N.W.2d 466 (1968) (permit Wisconsin defendants to implead Illinois wife and mother on ground that impleader does not substantially violate Illinois immunity policies and Wisconsin rule is better); Restatement, Second, Conflict of Laws § 169, comment *c* (1971); Currie, *Justice Traynor and the Conflict of Laws,* 13 Stan. L. Rev. 719, 732 n. 58 (1961); Hancock, *The Rise and Fall of Buckeye v. Buckeye,* 29 U. Chi. L. Rev. 237, 253–54 (1962). See § 2.14.

259. 45 Cal.2d 421, 289 P.2d 218 (1955).

circle of references between California and Wisconsin law if Wisconsin retained the place-of-wrong rule and interpreted it as referring to the whole law of California, including the California choice-of-law rule's reference to the whole law of the Wisconsin domicile.

As a matter of armchair speculation, three policies might have underpinned the California rule that a wife may not sue her husband in tort. California could be striving to protect marital harmony from disruptive clashes in the legal arena. Paradoxically and more realistically, California's purpose could be to protect the spouse's liability insurer from a collusive husband-wife attempt to milk the insurance policy for a maximum recovery. Further, California being a community property state, any recovery by the wife would belong to the community.[260] California might, therefore, wish to prevent the husband from sharing in the fruits of his own wrong.

California could not take any but an intolerably officious interest in the marital harmony of Wisconsin spouses when Wisconsin showed no such concern. Although many would argue that California's collusion policy is similarly inapplicable, this would be debatable if California were the forum, and perhaps the borderline of the mystical realm of the "false" conflict is not clear even with a Wisconsin forum.

A careful reading of *Emery,* however, would have revealed the California Supreme Court, as authoritative interpreter of the California immunity rule, rejecting both the family harmony and collusive suit policies.[261] Only the community property policy would remain as a viable possibility. Again, however, reference to California choice-of-law rules would end armchair speculation about whether that rule (a spouse's recovery against the other spouse is community property) is applicable to Wisconsin spouses injured in California. California did not treat as community property tort recoveries by spouses residing in non-community property states even though these recoveries were for injuries suffered in California.[262] Thus California conflicts decisions tell us in the most direct manner that no domestic purpose of California would be undermined by giving preference to Wisconsin law and compensating the Wisconsin wife for her injuries suffered as a result of her Wisconsin husband's negligence. This emerges as the sole rational result.[263]

Foreign choice-of-law decisions may assist a functional analysis even though those decisions do not, as in *Haumschild,* eliminate hypothetically possible foreign domestic policies. The foreign choice-of-law rule, fairly and reasonably interpreted, may be an indication that, although the other state has a domestic policy that might be relevant and conflict with the purposes of the forum in the interstate case in issue, in fact the

---

260. This is no longer true in California. West's Ann.Cal.Family Code § 781(c).

261. 45 Cal.2d at 430–31, 289 P.2d at 224.

262. Bruton v. Villoria, 138 Cal.App.2d 642, 292 P.2d 638 (1956).

263. Cf. Noel v. United Aircraft Corp., 202 F.Supp. 556 (D.Del.1962) (Venezuelan conflicts rules show that no Venezuelan policy will be infringed by application of United States law.).

foreign state recognizes that it would be inappropriate for it to press its policies to their logical limits and would defer to the forum's preference for the forum rule. Reference to the choice-of-law rules of another state thus removes the danger of chauvinistic blindness to the legitimate concerns of other jurisdictions from a forum determination that its own policies are clearly and strongly applicable to the conflicts case being litigated and that the policies of the foreign state are, at best, tangentially and officiously applicable.

In re Annesley[264] was probably susceptible to such an analysis and, if so, the result reached was wrong. A woman who was an English national died, according to the English definition of domicile, domiciled in France. She had not, however, taken steps required by the French code for acquiring a formal French domicile.[265] Under French domestic law, she could not bequeath, as she had, the bulk of her personal property to persons and institutions other than her two daughters. Under English domestic law, her freedom of testation in this regard was complete. England would refer the question of the validity of a will of personalty to the law of the domicile at death, France. France would decide the issue by the law of the nationality, England. The English forum was thus faced with the classic renvoi dilemma. If England applied its own choice-of-law rule without regard to what a French court would do, it risked making the result dependent upon the selection of the forum. If England took cognizance of the French choice-of-law rule, the English court would be trapped in an endless circle of references from English choice-of-law rule to the whole law of France, including the French choice-of-law rule, to the whole law of England, including the English choice-of-law rule. The court elected to refer to the French choice-of-law rule and to break the renvoi circle by placing itself in the position of a French court and deciding the case exactly as would a French court. The English court decided that a French court would refer to the English choice-of-law rule, would accept the English rule's reference back ("renvoi") to French law and would apply the domestic French law invalidating the will in part. Therefore the English court applied the French rule resulting in abatement of some of the legacies.[266]

---

264.   [1926] Ch. 692. For a fuller statement of *Annesley,* see § 2.13A.

265.   But see G. Delaume, American–French Private International Law 75 (2d ed. 1961): "an alien residing in France with the appropriate intent could acquire a *de facto* domicil in France, a notion substantially equivalent to the general concept of domicil."

266.   Cf. Taormina v. Taormina Corp., 35 Del.Ch. 17, 109 A.2d 400 (1954) (reaching result opposite that in *Annesley* because the Italian conflicts rule referred back to only the internal law of the nationality); In re Schneider, 198 Misc. 1017, 96 N.Y.S.2d 652 (1950), adhered to, 198 Misc. 1017, 1030, 100 N.Y.S.2d 371 (Sur.Ct.1950) (whole law of situs determines validity of devise); In re Zietz, 198 Misc. 77, 96 N.Y.S.2d 442 (Sur.Ct.1950) (situs accepts reference by law of domicile to law of nationality); Simmons v. Simmons, 17 N.S.W. 419 (1917) (takes view opposite to *Annesley* on content of French rule on renvoi); In re Duke of Wellington, [1947] 1 Ch. 506, aff'd [1948] 1 Ch. 118 (C.A.) (renvoi used for construction of will) (disapproved in Mann, *Succession to Immovables Abroad,* 11 Modern L. Rev. 232 (1948)). But see In re Tallmadge, 109 Misc. 696, 181 N.Y.S. 336 (Sur.Ct.1919) (refusing reference to foreign choice-of-law rule); Folk v. York–Shipley, Inc., 239 A.2d 236 (Del.1968) (same); Uniform Conflict of Laws–Limitations Act § 3, 12 ULA 159 ("If the statute of limitations of another state applies to the assertion of a claim in this State, the

This invalidation of part of the will is of doubtful wisdom. The intent of the testatrix was known. England had no domestic policy against giving effect to this intention. France's choice-of-law rule might rationally be read as a disclaimer of interest in protecting from disinheritance the children of a foreign national not formally domiciled in France.[267] Why should an English court enforce a French limitation on the intent of the testatrix when the French courts themselves would not have enforced it but for the English insistence on applying French law?

There are times when it would be wrong to attempt to derive any functional information from the foreign choice-of-law rule. This is likely to be so if the foreign choice-of-law rule is cast in a rigid territorial mold.[268] Such a territorially-oriented conflicts rule, by its nature, selects a geographical location as the source of the applicable law without first requiring inquiry into either the content of that law or that law's underlying policies. For example, if the marital domicile permits spouses to sue one another for negligence, but determines this question in conflicts cases by the law of the place of wrong, a court cannot reasonably read this choice-of-law rule as a functional decision by the domicile to defer to the superior interests of the place of wrong.

There is one situation in which a forum that would opt for a functional analysis of conflicts problems should be guided by the territorial choice-of-law rules of other states: when the forum is neutral, having

---

other state's relevant statutes and other rules of law governing tolling and accrual apply in computing the limitation period, *but its statutes and other rules of law governing conflict of laws do not apply.*") (Emphasis added); Jianfu Chen, *Australian Private International Law at the End of the 20th Century: Progress or Regress?*, in Private International Law at the End of the 20th Century: Progress or Regress? (Symeonides ed., 1998), 83, 101: (except in the area of succession, an Australian court will interpret a reference to the law of another jurisdiction as referring to the law that the courts of that place apply "in purely local situations").

See also Uniform Commercial Code § 1–105(2) (listing other U.C.C. sections whose references to law includes conflict of laws rules).

267. See Bethlehem Steel Corp. v. G.C. Zarnas & Co., Inc., 304 Md. 183, 498 A.2d 605 (1985) (decision to apply forum law confirmed because other state would also apply Maryland law, citing Commentary). Cf. Katzenbach, *Conflicts on an Unruly Horse: Reciprocal Claims and Tolerances in Interstate and International Law,* 65 Yale L. J. 1087, 1118 (1956) ("Renvoi ... may ... be a measure of the scope and intensity of the foreign domestic rule."). But see Ehrenzweig, Book Review, 8 Am.J.Comp.L. 233, 234–35 (1959) (favors rejection of renvoi doctrine).

268. See Pfau v. Trent Aluminum Co., 55 N.J. 511, 526, 263 A.2d 129, 137 (1970): "[W]e see no reason for applying Connecticut's choice-of-law rule. To do so would frustrate the very goals of governmental-interest analysis. Connecticut's choice-of-law rule does not identify that state's interest in the matter. *Lex loci delicti* was born in an effort to achieve simplicity and uniformity, and does not relate to a state's interest in having its law applied to given issues in a tort case." But see United States v. Neal, 443 F.Supp. 1307, 1315 (D.Neb.1978): "Nebraska's interest in having its guest statute apply outside of its geographical boundaries must not be very strong in light of the Nebraska Supreme Court's continued adherence to the rule of *lex loci delicti*"; Sutherland v. Kennington Truck Service, Ltd., 454 Mich. 274, 562 N.W.2d 466 (1997) (stating that Ontario did not have an interest in applying its shorter statute of limitations to protect Ontario defendants because Ontario's place-of-wrong choice-of-law rule would choose Michigan law, including Michigan time limitations); Gagne v. Berry, 112 N.H. 125, 290 A.2d 624 (1972) (same re Massachusetts); cf. Griggs v. Riley, 489 S.W.2d 469 (Mo.App.1972), application to transfer to Mo.S.Ct. denied (1973) (same re Illinois' continuing to apply place-of-wrong rule to host-guest cases after abandoning it in other contexts).

no policy of its own to advance. If all of the states that have contacts with the parties and with the transaction would reach the same solution to the choice-of-law problem, the neutral forum should mirror this result although it believes it foolishly dysfunctional, providing, of course, that the result is not so outrageous as to be unconstitutional. For a neutral forum to insist on its own solution to choice-of-law problems would invite the most aggravated form of forum shopping.[269]

The forum should inquire into what the other state would do, and then do the same thing when the foreign state has ultimate control over the result. An example of this would be a court adjudicating interests in realty in another country. Suppose that the courts in the other country would insist on determining those rights under the law of the situs and would not recognize a different determination by a non-situs court. There is no point in the non-situs court attempting to reach a different result, unless there are other assets in the forum that can be distributed to take account of the disposition in the foreign situs.[270]

A final reason to refer to the choice-of-law rule of another jurisdiction is to avoid a statutory choice-of-law rule of the forum.[271] *Richards v. United States*[272] construed the Federal Tort Claims Act's reference to "law of the place where the act or omission occurred,"[273] to mean the

---

269. Cf. Tramontana v. S. A. Empresa De Viacao Aerea Rio Grandense, 350 F.2d 468, 475 (D.C.Cir.1965) cert. denied, 383 U.S. 943, 86 S.Ct. 1195, 16 L.Ed.2d 206 (1966) ("and if a Maryland court would not disregard Brazilian law for the benefit of one of its own residents in a suit brought there, why should a court sitting in the District of Columbia do so at the expense of substantial and legitimate interests of Brazil?"); Hall v. Allied Mut. Ins. Co., 261 Iowa 1258, 158 N.W.2d 107 (1968) (in action to determine amount recoverable under uninsured motorist clause of insurance policy, apply measure of recovery that would be applied in both Oklahoma and Texas, where actions could have been brought against the uninsured motorist).

Shaffer v. Heitner, 433 U.S. 186, 97 S.Ct. 2569, 53 L.Ed.2d 683 (1977), barring the use of quasi in rem jurisdiction to adjudicate the merits of a controversy having no relationship to the forum or to the property seized, may result in narrowing the range of cases in which a forum may take jurisdiction without a reasonable nexus with the controversy. For discussion of *Shaffer*, see § 4.28.

270. In re Schneider's Estate, 198 Misc. 1017, 96 N.Y.S.2d 652 (Sur.Ct.1950), referred to the Swiss choice-of-law rule to validate the testamentary disposition of realty in Switzerland. The testator was an American citizen who died domiciled in New York. Under Swiss internal law, the testator's heirs were entitled to portions of the estate beyond the portion devised to them. The Swiss conflicts rule, however, applied the law of the domicile at death of a foreign national. Matter of Estate of Wright, 637 A.2d 106 (Me.1994) reached a similar result. The testator was an American who died domiciled in Switzerland. A Swiss statute permitted a foreigner domiciled in Switzerland to elect the law of his nationality to determine the validity of his will. The testator's will chose Maine law to govern the administration of his estate. The court held that the decedent's children were not entitled to take a forced share of the estate—a power they had under internal Swiss law.

271. See supra § 3.2C2 suggesting use of this technique in construing borrowing statutes. Cf. American Motorists Ins. Co. v. ARTRA Group, Inc., 338 Md. 560, 659 A.2d 1295 (1995) (using renvoi to avoid consideration of whether Maryland's traditional lex loci contractus test should be abandoned in favor of most significant relationship analysis).

272. 369 U.S. 1, 82 S.Ct. 585, 7 L.Ed.2d 492 (1962).

273. See Gould Elec. Inc. v. United States, 220 F.3d 169 (3d Cir. 2000) (discussing five different approaches that courts have taken to choosing law under the Federal Tort Claims Act when the defendant has committed acts and omissions in more than one state). Simon v. United States, 341 F.3d 193, 196 (3d Cir. 2003): "We synthesize the *Gould* approaches

whole law of that place, including its choice-of-law rules. The Court stated: "[T]his interpretation of the Act provides a degree of flexibility to the law to be applied in federal courts.... Recently there has been a tendency on the part of some States to depart from the general conflict rule [the law of the place of injury] in order to take into account the interests of the State having significant contact with the parties to the litigation. We can see no compelling reason to saddle the Act with an interpretation that would prevent the federal courts from implementing this policy in choice-of-law rules where the State in which the negligence occurred has adopted it."[274]

To summarize, there are four reasons why a court utilizing a functional analysis of choice-of-law would refer to the conflicts rules of another jurisdiction. (1) The forum wishes to determine whether the other jurisdiction asserts an "interest" in the application of the other jurisdiction's law. (2) The forum has no significant contacts with the parties or the issue and all states with such contacts agree on the choice of law. (3) The forum wishes to reach the same result as the other jurisdiction because the other state has ultimate control over the outcome. (4) The forum is construing a statutory choice-of-law rule that is in territorial form.

§ 3.4 Dépeçage

In its issue-by-issue approach to analysis of a conflicts problem, interest analysis has greatly increased the likelihood that a court will apply the law of one state to an aspect of the problem while applying the law of another state to a different aspect of the problem.[275] To be sure, there was some likelihood under the territorial choice-of-law rules that this splitting up of the applicable law would occur. In the first Restatement of Conflict of Laws, for example, the law of the place of contracting determined the validity of a contract,[276] but the law of the place of performance determined the sufficiency of performance.[277] The first Restatement's tort rule, place of wrong,[278] was more monolithic, but with the right chisel court could crack even that monolith. A judgment could characterize a particular issue in a "tort" case as "procedural,"[279] and apply forum law, or as a "contract"[280] claim that required use of a

---

into a single inquiry that chooses the rules of the jurisdiction containing the last significant negligent act or omission relevant to the FTCA".

274. *Richards*, 369 U.S. at 12.

275. Wilde, *Dépeçage in the Choice of Tort Law*, 41 S.Cal. L. Rev. 329, 345–46 (1968).

276. Restatement of Conflict of Laws § 332 (1934).

277. Id. § 358.

278. Id. § 378.

279. Kilberg v. Northeast Airlines, Inc., 9 N.Y.2d 34, 211 N.Y.S.2d 133, 172 N.E.2d 526 (1961) (measure of damages for wrongful death).

280. See Price v. Litton Systems, Inc., 784 F.2d 600 (5th Cir.1986) (Alabama law applies to tort claims, Mississippi law to warranty claims, Mississippi law); Handy v. Uniroyal, Inc., 327 F.Supp. 596 (D.Del.1971) (tort issues governed by law of place of injury, warranty issues by law of place where product purchased). Compare Hercules & Co. v. Shama Restaurant Corp., 566 A.2d 31 (D.C. App. 1989) (under interest analysis, different

different set of guidelines to determine where to place the pin in the map. It is true, however, that the new methodology increases the likelihood of applying different laws to different issues in the same problem, *alias dictus* "dépeçage."

The questions arise then to what extent this issue-by-issue, onion-peeling approach to conflicts problems is desirable and to what extent it is fraught with the danger of producing foolish and unjust results.

§ 3.4A Interstate Results that Differ from Intrastate Results: Dépeçage Broadly Defined

Dépeçage is defined as "applying the rules of different states to determine different issues."[281] This is a useful point of departure for

---

law applies to negligence than to breach of warranty). For other examples of application of different laws to different issues under a functional analysis, see Faloona by Fredrickson v. Hustler Magazine, Inc., 799 F.2d 1000 (5th Cir.1986) (invasion of privacy claim determined by Texas law, but validity of photographer's release by California law, Texas law); In re Air Crash Disaster at Washington, D.C., 559 F.Supp. 333 (D.D.C.1983) (D.C. law applied to liability for punitive damages, but law of defendants' places of business applied to contribution between tortfeasors); Stutsman v. Kaiser Foundation Health Plan, 546 A.2d 367 (D.C.App.1988) (Virginia law applies to loss of consortium, D.C. law to malpractice).

281. Reese, *Dépeçage: A Common Phenomenon in Choice of Law,* 73 Colum. L. Rev. 58 (1973). For illustrative cases, see, e.g., Calhoun v. Yamaha Motor Corp., U.S.A., 216 F.3d 338 (3d Cir.), cert. denied, 531 U.S. 1037, 121 S.Ct. 627, 148 L.Ed.2d 536 (2000) (applying Pennsylvania law to compensatory damages, Puerto Rican law to punitive damages, and federal admiralty law to determine liability): Corporacion Venezolana de Fomento v. Vintero Sales Corp., 629 F.2d 786 (2d Cir.1980), cert. denied, 449 U.S. 1080, 101 S.Ct. 863, 66 L.Ed.2d 804 (1981) (the validity of note guaranties by a Venezuelan government entity is determined by New York law, New York banks having purchased the notes, but Venezuelan law applies to the government entity's counterclaim against a major stockholder of a Venezuelan corporation that solicited the guaranties); Cohen v. McDonnell Douglas Corp., 389 Mass. 327, 450 N.E.2d 581 (1983) (Illinois law governs recovery for wrongful death of Illinois resident killed in Illinois, but Massachusetts law governs the claim of his Massachusetts mother for injuries she suffered in Massachusetts when she learned of his death); Erny v. Estate of Merola, 171 N.J. 86, 792 A.2d 1208 (2002) (applying New York law to determine extent of joint and several liability although New Jersey law applies to the issue of whether contributory negligence bars or diminishes recovery). But see Simon v. United States, 805 N.E.2d 798, 803 (Ind. 2004) (rejects dépeçage).

Compare the problem of **"the incidental question"**. An "incidental question" arises when, in applying the law of the state that conflict analysis has chosen, the court must conduct further choice-of-law analysis to define terms utilized in that law. For example, the traditional rule selects the law of the situs to determine succession to realty. See Restatement, Second, Conflict of Laws § 236 (1971). If the law of the situs indicates that the land is to go to the "widow" of the decedent, in determining whether a claimant was validly married to the decedent so as to qualify as the widow, the court may have to apply the law of another state where the marriage was celebrated and the decedent and the claimant were domiciled at the time. See Restatement, Second, Conflict of Laws § 283 (1971). For discussion of the incidental question, see Gotlieb, *The Incidental Question Revisited—Theory and Practice in the Conflict of Laws,* 26 Int. & Comp.L.Q. 734 (1977); cf. T. de Boer, Beyond Lex Loci Delicti 210 (1987) ("accessory choice of law ... the issue is characterized as sounding in one category, whereas the conflicts rule pertaining to another choice of law area is applied"). For illustrative cases, see, e. g., Acme Circus Operating Co., Inc. v. Kuperstock, 711 F.2d 1538 (11th Cir.1983) (law of state where defendant resides and business headquartered determines remedy for violation of right of publicity, but law of owner's domicile at death determines whether such a right of publicity survived his death); Factors, Etc., Inc. v. Pro Arts, Inc., 652 F.2d 278 (2d Cir.1981), cert. denied, 456 U.S. 927, 102 S.Ct. 1973, 72 L.Ed.2d 442 (1982) (tort conflicts rules apply to issue of conversion of property—the right of publicity, but property conflicts rules apply to whether plaintiff has title to property allegedly converted); In re Estate of O'Dea, 29 Cal.App.3d 759, 105

inquiry into the problems involved.[282] Our focus of attention in analyzing dépeçage or, to avoid offending purists, dépeçage-like issues, is whether, when the dust settles from our struggle with a conflicts problem, we have produced a result different from the result that would have been obtained in any of the states having a contact with the parties or with the transaction if this were an intrastate occurrence. If all intrastate results are thus changed, there is a good chance, but not a certainty, that the analysis has gone awry. The touchstone for reexamining the result is whether it produces a better accommodation of relevant state policies than would mirroring the intrastate results in any of the contact states and consequently is neither irrational nor unfair to the losing party.

Perhaps the easiest situation in which to justify the changing of intrastate results is when two states would reach the same result, but for different reasons, and neither of these reasons is applicable to the interstate problem being analyzed. Suppose the following case: A testator, who was a long-term resident of State X, as were all the natural objects of his bounty, dies in X devising realty located in State Y to a Y charity, which conducts its activities only in Y. If all contacts had been in Y, the devise would have failed because the will was executed closer to the time of death than is permitted by Y law for devises to charities. If all contacts had been in X, the bequest would have failed because X law forbids a charity to take realty by devise. Suppose also that thorough investigation of statutory histories and judicial constructions determines that the sole purpose of the X statute is to keep real estate out of the "dead hand" of charities—to keep it freely alienable and in the flow of commerce, and that the sole purpose of the Y statute is to protect Y testators and the natural objects of their bounty from ill-considered dispositions while in apprehension of approaching death.[283] The proper solution of this interstate problem may be to hold the devise valid, contrary to the result that would be reached in intrastate cases in either X or Y. The social evils sought to be avoided by the X statute will not occur in X, nor will failure to apply the Y statute frustrate its purpose.

Cal.Rptr. 756 (1973) (intestate succession to personalty determined by law of domicile of decedent, but the law of the place of adoption determines whether claimant had the status of an adopted child); In re Estate of Duquesne, 29 Utah 2d 94, 505 P.2d 779 (1973) (intestate succession to realty determined by law of situs, but the law of the domicile of mother and child determines whether claimant is legitimate child); Matter of Estate of Cook, 40 Wn.App. 326, 698 P.2d 1076 (1985) (do not apply law of place of birth to determine paternity when issue is intestate succession to estate of forum domiciliary).

282. In making this inquiry, we must not get sidetracked by metaphysical debate about whether a problem involves different issues or rather different rules dealing with the same issue. For example, the will problem discussed in the next paragraph of the text could be viewed either as involving two issues (the capacity of the testator to devise and the capacity of the charity to take) or as two rules concerning the same issue (the validity of the devise).

283. For an early case pointing out the differences in type and policies of statutes invalidating certain gifts to charities, see Trustees of Amherst College v. Ritch, 151 N.Y. 282, 45 N.E. 876 (1897). See also Kerr v. Dougherty, 79 N.Y. 327 (1880) (finding Pennsylvania legislation limits both the testator's right to dispose and the charity's right to take). For a thorough discussion, see Hancock, *In the Parish of St. Mary le Bow, in the Ward of Cheap,* 16 Stan. L. Rev. 561 (1964).

Therefore neither statute is applicable; the general and common policy of both states in favor of validating wills prevails.

Another situation in which the interstate result may rationally differ from common intrastate solutions is that in which two states would reach the same result for different reasons, one of which is not applicable to the interstate problem and the second, although applicable, yields to a competing policy of the other state. For example: D, who is 20 years old and resides in State X, obtains a large business loan at 9 percent interest from P, which is incorporated in and has its only office in State Y. Under X law: the maximum legal interest is 8 percent; the penalty for usury is to invalidate the obligation to repay either principal or interest; persons 18 or older have full legal capacity. Under Y law: the maximum legal interest is 10 percent; contracts made by persons under the age of 21 are void. X law should apply to determine D's contractual capacity. Although X would advance its usury policy by shielding its resident from a loan obligation involving what X considers excessive interest and by deterring the making of such contracts with its citizens, X should be willing to defer its domestic usury policy in favor of validating this interstate loan transaction which, let us assume, involves a knowledgeable borrower and no elements of adhesion.[284]

Changing of intrastate results because of the interstate nature of the facts in issue is least likely to be justifiable if the contact states would reach common results to advance the same policy. The most obvious example, and therefore one not likely to cause difficulty, is when two states have the same rules and these rules have identical underlying policies. X and Y each have guest statutes and the policy underlying both statutes is to keep down liability insurance rates. An X host, while driving his X-garaged automobile in Y, injures a Y guest. The common requirement of both statutes, that the guest cannot recover unless he shows that the host was guilty of "gross" negligence, should prevail. Consider, however, the following argument: The Y guest statute is not applicable because recovery in this case will affect insurance rates only on automobiles principally garaged in the same rating district as host's car;[285] therefore, the general Y policy of compensation for those injured by ordinary negligence is applicable. This Y compensation policy creates a "true" conflict with the X guest statute, which should be resolved in favor of the Y compensation rule. This argument is fallacious because both states have weighed the same competing social values—compensation as against keeping down insurance premiums by preventing recoveries that are likely to be collusive and in any event numerous. Each state has come to the same conclusion in resolving this social equation. There

---

284. See, e. g., Restatement (Second) of Conflict of Laws § 203 (1971), upholding a contract "against the charge of usury if it provides for a rate of interest that is permissible in a state to which the contract has a substantial relationship."

285. See McNamara, *Automobile Liability Insurance Rates,* 35 Insurance Counsel J. 398, 401, 403–06 (1968); Stern, *Ratemaking Procedures for Automobile Liability Insurance,* 52 Proceedings Casualty Actuarial Soc'y, 139, 155, 176–77, 183 (1965).

is no rational basis on which Y can claim disagreement or "conflict" with the policy underlying the X guest statute.

Although the inadvisability of changing intrastate results is obvious when both states would reach the same answer under identical domestic rules with identical policies, this folly is just as great, though less obvious and therefore more troublesome, when two states would reach the same result for the same reason, but under differently articulated domestic rules. *Maryland Casualty Co. v. Jacek*[286] is an example. An accident in New York injured a New Jersey wife while she was a passenger in an automobile driven by her husband. Under New Jersey law, a wife could not sue her husband in tort. New York law permitted interspousal suits, but would construe the husband's liability insurance as not covering this liability unless the policy expressly so provided. There was no such provision in the policy. There was a summary judgment against the insurer when it sought a declaratory judgment determining its duties under the policy. The court applied New York law to determine that the wife could sue but held that the New York insurance statute was inapplicable to a policy issued in New Jersey. On the surface this seems reasonable enough. After all, the husband's New Jersey policy did protect him against liability and New York law did impose such liability. The difficulty is that New Jersey, not New York, law should have been applied to determine the husband's liability. Both states deemed preventing possibly collusive recoveries against insurers more important than compensation to an injured spouse. New York, therefore, had no countervailing policy that could create a conflict with the New Jersey immunity rule.[287]

The most difficult dépeçage problems concern the determination of when two or more rules of the same state are so related in purpose that a court should apply them in tandem or not at all. The general answer is easy enough: apply one rule and not the other when this will produce a better accommodation of the conflicting policies of two states than will application of the entire domestic law of either state.[288] Application of this standard to individual cases, however, requires great perspicacity and common sense.

The facts of *Kilberg v. Northeast Airlines, Inc.*[289] provide an example of the improper splitting of interrelated state rules. A New York domicil-

---

286. 156 F.Supp. 43 (D.N.J.1957).

287. See Pryles, *Reflections on the False Conflict in the Choice of Law Process,* 11 Sydney L. Rev. 284, 305 (1987) ("if the domestic policies of the laws of the relevant jurisdictions are in harmony, there must be a strong argument for giving effect to these mutually shared policies by applying the law of the state which embodies these policies and which extends to the case"). But see Reese, supra note 281 at 67 (stating the result in *Maryland Casualty* is correct).

288. See Inter–American Convention on General Rules of Private International Law art. 9, reprinted in I–I F.V. Garcia–Amador, The Inter–American System: Treaties, Conventions and Other Documents 486: "The different laws that may be applicable to various aspects of one and the same juridical relationship shall be applied harmoniously in order to attain the purposes pursued by each of such laws. Any difficulties that may be caused by their simultaneous application shall be resolved in the light of the requirements of justice in each specific case."

289. 9 N.Y.2d 34, 211 N.Y.S.2d 133, 172 N.E.2d 526 (1961).

iary boarded the defendant's airplane in New York. The plane crashed at its destination in Massachusetts killing the New Yorker. The Massachusetts wrongful death act measured wrongful death recovery according to the culpability of the defendant, but had a $15,000 limit on recovery. New York had no limit on recovery, but measured compensation by the amount of pecuniary loss to the decedent's dependents. The New York Court of Appeals was probably correct in indicating that the Massachusetts recovery limit was inapplicable. It would be outrageous, however, to couple the New York rule of no statutory limit on recovery with the Massachusetts culpability measure of damages. This would produce a punitive damages recovery that would greatly exceed the amount recoverable under either New York or Massachusetts law, would accord with neither state's view of proper wrongful death compensation, and would, therefore, be grossly unfair to the defendant.[290]

On the other hand, it may be desirable to apply one of a state's rules but not a related rule when this will advance some of that state's policies and work a mutually acceptable compromise with the competing purposes of another state. Again, however, putting this fine-sounding exhortation into practice is very difficult—perhaps the most difficult task to confront adherents of "interest" or "functional" conflicts analysis. Some of the mind-boggling problems can be illustrated by *Neumeier v. Kuehner*.[291] That is the case in which the New York Court of Appeals held that the Ontario "gross negligence" standard rather than the New York ordinary negligence rule applied to a wrongful death suit brought against the estate of a New York host driver who collided with a Canadian train in Canada. The collision killed the driver and his Canadian guest.

The aspect of this case relevant to our inquiry is one not touched upon in any of the trial or appellate opinions—why did the railroad join the driver's estate in urging application of the Canadian guest statute? The answer turns upon the relationship of two Canadian statutory rules. One, of course, is the "gross negligence" barrier to passenger recovery against the driver. The other, unmentioned, Ontario rule, which explained the Canadian railroad's position, insulates the railroad from that portion of the damages attributable to the fault of the New York

290. For a different dépeçage problem drawn from *Kilberg,* see Reese, supra note 281 at 72. See also In re Air Crash Disaster Near New Orleans, La., 821 F.2d 1147 (5th Cir. 1987, en banc), judgment vac'd for reconsideration in the light of Chan v. Korean Air Lines [490 U.S. 122, 109 S.Ct. 1676, 104 L.Ed.2d 113 (1989)], 490 U.S. 1032, 109 S.Ct. 1928, 104 L.Ed.2d 400 (1989), remanded for reconsideration of damages, otherwise reinstated, 883 F.2d 17 (5th Cir.1989) (apply Louisiana law to most compensation issues, but apply Uruguayan law to permit one claimant to recover for death of aunt); LaBombard v. Peck Lumber Co., 141 Vt. 619, 451 A.2d 1093, 1096 (1982) (plaintiff cannot recover workers' compensation under Connecticut law and then apply the Vermont workers' compensation rule as to apportionment of expenses of recovery against the third party who injured plaintiff because this would "allow him to pick and choose among their terms and provisions in order to design his own compensation scheme and deny the will of both legislatures"); Neuman, *Territorial Discrimination, Equal Protection, and Self-Determination,* 135 U.Pa. L. Rev. 261, 323 (1987) (unfair disadvantage to defendants to apply law favorable to plaintiff for liability for libel and another law, unfavorable to defendant, to determine applicable privileges).

291. 31 N.Y.2d 121, 335 N.Y.S.2d 64, 286 N.E.2d 454 (1972).

driver.[292] The logic of this second rule is apparent. Given that drivers are not liable for injuries caused to passengers by ordinary negligence, this freedom from liability should not be subverted by subjecting the driver to a claim for contribution by a joint tortfeasor.[293] In fairness to the joint tortfeasor, however, it should be relieved from liability for that portion of the damages attributable to the negligence of the immune driver.

The railroad was operating on the anti-dépeçage assumption that if the Canadian guest statute were not applied, no other aspect of Canadian law would be applied, including the rule that would limit the damages recoverable from the railroad.[294] Although if New York law were applied, the railroad would have a theoretical right to contribution from the New York driver, perhaps to the full degree of the driver's contribution to the damages,[295] this might prove an empty remedy if the driver were not fully insured and could not otherwise respond to a judgment for contribution or indemnity.

Suppose now that the court reached a different conclusion than that in *Neumeier* on the applicability of the Canadian guest statute. One line of reasoning to such a different result might run as follows: The Ontario statute had as its purpose keeping down Ontario insurance rates,[296] not, as the *Neumeier* majority suggested,[297] controlling the conduct of Ontario guests so that they would not be ungrateful to their drivers. Thus, Ontario would not experience the social evil that its statute sought to prevent if the court did not apply the statute. New York's compensation rule, on the other hand, had as its purpose imposing on the New York driver the primary responsibility for providing insurance coverage so that insurance would distribute the inevitable costs of automobile injuries caused by New York drivers, no matter where, at least within the territorial coverage of policies issued in New York, or who the insured injured.[298]

---

292.   Ont.Rev.Stat. c. 296, § 2(2) (1970).

293.   Uniform Contribution Among Tortfeasors Act § 1 (1939 version) accomplished this result through its definition of "joint tortfeasors": "two or more persons jointly or severally liable in tort for the same injury to person or property." Because, under the Act's definition, the driver would be deemed not to be a "joint tortfeasor" insofar as he is not liable under the guest statute, he is not subject to a right of contribution. Id. § 2(1). For purposes of this discussion, however, the term "joint tortfeasor" will be used to signify one who jointly causes tortious injury, regardless or whether he is jointly liable for it.

294.   Letter from Courtland R. LaVallee, Counsel of Record for Canadian National Railway, to Russell J. Weintraub, Oct. 27, 1972. For an example of anti-dépeçage sentiment, see Henry v. Richardson–Merrell, Inc., 508 F.2d 28, 32 n. 10 (3d Cir.1975) (trial court wrong in making interest analysis of statute of limitations as issue separate from which state's liability rule will apply).

295.   See Dole v. Dow Chem. Co., 30 N.Y.2d 143, 282 N.E.2d 288, 331 N.Y.S.2d 382 (1972): Baade, *The Case of the Disinterested Two States: Neumeier v. Kuehner,* 1 Hofstra L. Rev. 150, 157–58 (1973) (discussion of *Dole*).

296.   See Baade, supra note 295 at 152–56.

297.   31 N.Y.2d 121, 125–26, 286 N.E.2d 454, 456, 335 N.Y.S.2d 64, 68 (1972), quoting Reese, *Chief Judge Fuld and Choice of Law,* 71 Colum. L. Rev. 548, 558 (1971).

298.   See Shapira, *"Manna for the Entire World" or "Thou Shalt Love Thy Neighbor as Thyself"—Comment on Neumeier v. Kuehner,* 1 Hofstra L. Rev. 168, 172 (1973); Note, *Choice of Law in Tort Cases: Neumeier v. Kuehner,* 37 Albany L. Rev. 173, 186 (1972).

Assuming, then, that we would not apply the Ontario guest statute, should we apply the other Ontario rule partially reducing the Canadian railroad's liability? On the surface, the answer to this question seems obvious. All of the Canadian railroad's actions and their effects in the course of this transaction were limited to Ontario. Surely the railroad is entitled to whatever benefits Ontario law would afford it. Applying the New York ordinary negligence rule and the Ontario joint tortfeasor rule would work a better accommodation of state interests than would applying the whole law of either jurisdiction, and this despite the fact that the Ontario rules are so closely related in purpose.

On closer examination, however, the answer is far more doubtful. Ironically, the two Ontario rules are so closely related in purpose that there is a substantial question whether the joint tortfeasor protecting rule has a purpose independent of the host protecting rule. Perhaps the joint tortfeasor rule exists only to alleviate unfairness to the joint tortfeasor when, because of the guest rule, contribution or indemnity is not available from the host. There is no independent Ontario policy to limit the liability of joint tortfeasors—they are jointly and severally liable for all harm done. Therefore, once it is decided not to apply the Ontario guest statute, the rule limiting liability of joint tortfeasors does not relate to any social evil that Ontario wishes to prevent and thus should fall also.

§ 3.5   Beyond Dépeçage: A "New Rule" Approach

Interest analysis of conflicts problems is most cogent when it results in advancing the policies underlying the law of one state without creating any substantial likelihood that another state will, as a consequence, feel the effects of a social evil that it has, by its different law, sought to avoid. Frequently, however, it is not possible to accomplish this. Giving effect to a policy that one state deems paramount will conflict with a purpose another state cherishes. Furthermore, there may be no mutually satisfactory basis for resolving this conflict. Both states may have a sufficient nexus with the parties and with the transaction to make it reasonable for them to assert the policies underlying their own rules. The two rules in conflict may defy analysis in terms of which is "better,"[299] at least by any standard even remotely objective. Both rules may represent widely-held views of the proper resolution of a current social issue. Neither may fairly be called "anachronistic."

When this most difficult of all conflicts problems arises, there are several tactics that may be employed: One may apply forum law on the ground that there is no cogent reason to displace it;[300] one may fall back

---

299.   See R. Leflar, American Conflicts Law 254–59 (1968). For use of the "better law" concept, see Tiernan v. Westext Transp., Inc., 295 F.Supp. 1256 (D.R.I.1969); Schneider v. Nichols, 280 Minn. 139, 158 N.W.2d 254 (1968); Mitchell v. Craft, 211 So.2d 509 (Miss. 1968); Clark v. Clark, 107 N.H. 351, 222 A.2d 205 (1966); Conklin v. Horner, 38 Wis.2d 468, 157 N.W.2d 579 (1968).

300.   See A. Ehrenzweig, Conflict of Laws 314 (1962); Currie, *Survival of Actions: Adjudication versus Automation in the Conflict of Laws,* 10 Stan. L. Rev. 205, 245 (1958).

on the security of old friends—the territorial rules that select some one event in the transaction to mark the applicable law;[301] or, as I would suggest, one may approach the conflicts problem with a result-oriented rebuttable presumption (e.g., apply the validating law to contracts)[302] that, not having been rebutted, prevails. At times, however, a more satisfactory accommodation of conflicting state policies may be available than any of these methods could achieve. It may be possible to fashion a rule for the case in issue that differs in some respects from the domestic law of either contact state but that permits the accommodation of otherwise irreconcilable policies.

In *Kearney v. Salomon Smith Barney, Inc.*[303] the Supreme Court of California shaped a new rule to better accommodate California and Georgia policies. Plaintiffs brought a class action on behalf of California clients of the defendant, a financial institution that had its principal place of business in Georgia. Without the clients' knowledge, the defendant taped telephone calls between the defendant's Georgia office and California clients. This was permitted under Georgia law but not under California law. The court held that California law applied. The taping of the calls without the clients' knowledge or consent constituted an unlawful invasion of privacy. The plaintiffs were entitled to injunctive relief barring defendant from such conduct in the future, but were not entitled to monetary damages or restitution for past conduct:

> Although we conclude that the comparative impairment analysis[304] supports the application of California law in this context, we further conclude that because one of the goals of that analysis is "the 'maximum attainment of underlying purpose by *all* governmental entities' " (Offshore Rental [Co. v. Continental Oil Co.] 22 Cal.3d 157, 166, 148 Cal.Rptr. 867, 872, 583 P.2d 721, 726 [(1978)], italics added), it is appropriate in this instance to apply California law in a restrained manner that accommodates Georgia's reasonable interest in protecting persons who in the past might have undertaken actions in Georgia in reasonable reliance on Georgia law from being subjected to monetary liability for such actions. Prior to our resolution of this case it would have been reasonable for a business entity such as SSB to be uncertain as to which state's law— Georgia's or California's—would be applicable in this context, and the denial of monetary recovery for past conduct that might have been undertaken in reliance upon another state's law is unlikely to undermine significantly the California interest embodied in the applicable invasion-of-privacy statutes. We therefore conclude that it is Georgia's, rather than California's, interest that would be more severely impaired were monetary liability to be imposed on SSB for such *past* conduct. Under these circumstances, we conclude it is

---

301. See, e.g., Restatement of Conflict of Laws § 378 (1934) ("law of the place of wrong").

302. See § 7.4A.

303. 39 Cal.4th 95, 137 P.3d 914, 45 Cal.Rptr.3d 730 (2006).

304. See § 6.26.

appropriate to decline to impose damages upon SSB (or to require it to provide restitution) on the basis of such past conduct.[305]

Thus, by fashioning a new rule of law that did not exist in either California or Georgia, the court achieved a better accommodation of state interests than it could produce by the all-or-nothing utilization of either state's law.

§ 3.6 Public Policy

One escape from the rigid syllogisms of the territorially-oriented choice-of-law rules has been the "public policy" doctrine. Invoking the concept of "public policy," a court can refuse to enforce, as contrary to its own notions of justice and fairness, a rule found in the state designated by the forum's choice-of-law rule.[306]

Mertz v. Mertz[307] is an example. Spouses domiciled in New York were traveling in Connecticut when the husband's negligent operation of his automobile injured the wife. The wife sued her husband in New York. Connecticut permitted such suits, but New York, at that time,[308] did not. Judge Lehman closed the doors of the New York forum to the wife. The New York marital immunity rule embodied New York public policy because "a state can have no public policy except what is to be found in

---

305. *Kearney*, 39 Cal.4th at 100–101, 137 P.3d at 918, 45 Cal.Rptr.3d at 734–35.

306. See, e.g., Gaillard v. Field, 381 F.2d 25 (10th Cir.1967), cert. denied, 389 U.S. 1044, 88 S.Ct. 787, 19 L.Ed.2d 836 (1968) (claim for recision based on sister state's securities law); Hartness v. Aldens, Inc., 301 F.2d 228 (7th Cir.1962) (claim under sister state's survival statute); Colyvas v. Red Hand Compositions Co., 318 F.Supp. 1376 (S.D.N.Y.1970) (fee splitting agreement); Hao Thi Popp v. Lucas, 182 Conn. 545, 438 A.2d 755 (1980) (will not enforce a Vietnamese rule under which a mother can relinquish her rights to custody); Brown & Root, Inc. v. Ring Power Corp., 450 So.2d 1245 (Fla.App. 5th Dist.1984) (refuse to apply law of the situs of sale of goods under which a good faith purchaser from a thief is entitled to be reimbursed by the true owner); Donaldson v. Fluor Eng'rs, Inc., 169 Ill.App.3d 759, 120 Ill.Dec. 202, 523 N.E.2d 1113 (1st Dist.1988) (indemnity against own negligence); J. Zeevi & Sons, Ltd. v. Grindlays Bank, Ltd., 37 N.Y.2d 220, 371 N.Y.S.2d 892, 333 N.E.2d 168 (1975), cert. denied, 423 U.S. 866, 96 S.Ct. 126, 46 L.Ed.2d 95 (1975) (contrary to public policy to recognize confiscation of funds in Uganda as defense to reimbursement); Chaudhary v. Chaudhary, [1985] 2 W.L.R. 350 (C.A.1984) (refuse to recognize talaq divorce).

For cases refusing to honor a choice-of-law clause when the law selected would validate a no-competition clause that is invalid under forum law, see Dothan Aviation Corp. v. Miller, 620 F.2d 504 (5th Cir.1980); Frame v. Merrill Lynch, Pierce, Fenner & Smith, Inc. 20 Cal.App.3d 668, 97 Cal.Rptr. 811 (1971); Nasco, Inc. v. Gimbert, 239 Ga. 675, 238 S.E.2d 368 (1977); cf. DeSantis v. Wackenhut Corp., 793 S.W.2d 670 (Tex.1990), cert. denied, 498 U.S. 1048, 111 S.Ct. 755, 112 L.Ed.2d 775 (1991) (refuse to enforce choice-of-law clause selecting Florida law to validate covenant not to compete, on ground that Florida law would "be contrary to a fundamental policy" of Texas, within the meaning of Restatement (Second) § 187(2)(b)).

For the converse position of refusing to enforce a contract between forum residents that is illegal under the law of another jurisdiction, see Wong v. Tenneco, Inc., 39 Cal.3d 126, 216 Cal.Rptr. 412, 702 P.2d 570 (1985) (marketing contract violating Mexican law against foreign ownership of land).

307. 271 N.Y. 466, 3 N.E.2d 597 (1936).

308. New York now permits wife-husband suits, but liability insurance does not cover liability to a spouse for culpable conduct unless a special provision for such liability is made. N.Y.—McKinney's Ins. Law § 3420(g); N.Y.—McKinney's Gen.Oblig.Law § 3–313(2).

its Constitution and laws."[309] The court would not permit a suit thus offending New York public policy to proceed in a New York court.

Judge Lehman's definition of public policy was so parochial that, if applied literally, it would end all conflicts analysis. The forum could not apply any foreign rule that differed from local law. Yet the result in *Mertz* may have made eminent functional sense. New York's marital immunity policies of preserving marital harmony and preventing collusive suits were as applicable as if the accident had occurred in New York. There was no showing dismissing the case would undermine any significant Connecticut policy, as might have been the case if the wife had been cared for at public expense in Connecticut or if there were private unpaid medical creditors in Connecticut who could not be paid without dipping into the wife's tort recovery. It is likely that New York husbands, if not chastened by fear for their own or their wives' safety, or by fear of Connecticut criminal law, would not drive more carefully on Connecticut highways because of knowledge that their wife-passengers could sue them for negligently inflicted injuries.[310] This is particularly so if the husband's liability insurer would in fact pay the bill.

These are the factors the New York Court of Appeals may have had in mind in *Intercontinental Hotels Corporation v. Golden*[311] when the

---

309. 271 N.Y. at 472, 3 N.E.2d at 599. Cf. Short Line, Inc. v. Perez, 238 A.2d 341 (Del.1968) (against public policy to allow defendant sued by husband and son to implead wife); Chase v. Greyhound Lines, Inc., 156 W.Va. 444, 195 S.E.2d 810 (1973) (public policy bars suit by parent against child under lex loci, but not by one sibling against another) (parental immunity overruled in Lee v. Comer, 159 W.Va. 585, 224 S.E.2d 721 (1976)). Contra, Rhee v. Combined Enterprises, Inc., 74 Md.App. 214, 536 A.2d 1197, cert. dism'd, 313 Md. 9, 542 A.2d 845 (1988) (not against Maryland public policy to permit interspousal negligence suit under law of place of injury although at time of injury Maryland law conferred immunity).

310. See Johnson v. Johnson, 107 N.H. 30, 32, 216 A.2d 781, 783 (1966): "Recognition of the Massachusetts immunity will not render Massachusetts drivers less careful on our highways since their own and their wives' safety will still be jeopardized by carelessness on their part."

311. 15 N.Y.2d 9, 254 N.Y.S.2d 527, 203 N.E.2d 210 (1964) (permitting enforcement of a gambling debt incurred at a Puerto Rican casino).

See also Kramer v. Bally's Park Place, Inc., 311 Md. 387, 535 A.2d 466 (1988) (enforce claim for debt to New Jersey gambling casino); Caribe Hilton Hotel v. Toland, 63 N.J. 301, 307 A.2d 85 (1973) (enforce Puerto Rican gambling debt); cf. Young v. Sands, Inc., 122 So.2d 618 (Fla.Dist.Ct.App.1960) (enforce claim of Nevada hotel on check on ground that evidence supported finding that the hotel's credit manager did not know that the defendant intended to use the proceeds for gambling at the hotel's casino); Kaszuba v. Zientara, 506 N.E.2d 1 (Ind.1987) (enforce contract to deliver lottery ticket in Indiana when ticket was purchased in Illinois where legal); Castilleja v. Camero, 414 S.W.2d 424 (Texas, 1967) (enforce contract between Texans to split winnings from Mexican lottery ticket). But cf. Casanova Club v. Bisharat, 189 Conn. 591, 458 A.2d 1 (1983) (refuse to enforce gambling debt incurred at English casino, but opinion states that because case came up on cross motions for summary judgment, it is a poor record on which to reconsider the public policy rule applied in similar cases in Connecticut in the past—dictum that English judgment for the debt would have been enforced). Contra, Condado Aruba Caribbean Hotel v. Tickel, 39 Colo.App. 51, 561 P.2d 23 (1977) (refuse to enforce gambling debt incurred at casino in Netherlands Antilles where legal); Dorado Beach Hotel Corp. v. Jernigan, 202 So.2d 830 (Fla.Dist.Ct.App.1967), appeal dism'd, 209 So.2d 669 (Fla.1968) (refuse to permit action by Puerto Rican casino against a Florida resident to collect gambling debts); Lauer v. Catalanotto, 522 So.2d 656 (La.App. 5th Cir.1988) (refuse to enforce agreement to split Nevada gambling winnings).

court commented thus upon *Mertz*: "As a practical matter, all the significant contacts of the case were with New York and the language of the opinion indicates that the court was in reality there making a choice-of-law decision of the kind that this court today follows under the nominal heading of the 'contacts' doctrine."[312] Perhaps, but if so, the *Mertz* result should have been on the merits for the defendant. Judge Lehman sounded as though he was merely closing the New York forum to the wife and sending her to sue elsewhere, if she could.[313]

Intercontinental Hotels does seem to repudiate the definition of "public policy" articulated in *Mertz*. The *Intercontinental Hotels* opinion states: "Public policy is not determinable by mere reference to the laws of the forum alone. Strong public policy is found in prevailing social and moral attitudes of the community."[314] There is, however, nothing wrong with Judge Lehman's definition of public policy as everything found in the laws of the forum, if the policies underlying those laws are utilized to assist in articulating a reasoned choice between the law of the forum and the law of some foreign jurisdiction. This process ought to proceed with the realization that local policies, even if applicable, should sometimes yield.

The danger of the traditional view of public policy is that its operation is likely to be haphazard and that, if utilized to avoid a result on the merits, the forum is more likely to deny enforcement to foreign law than if the forum faces the issue squarely and applies either forum

---

The plaintiff can avoid the public policy debate by using a long-arm statute to obtain personal jurisdiction over the nonresident bettor and obtaining a judgment for the gambling debt that is entitled to full faith and credit in other states. Hilton Int'l Co. v. Arace, 35 Conn.Sup. 522, 394 A.2d 739 (1977) (Puerto Rico validly exercised long-arm jurisdiction over Connecticut resident who gambled in Puerto Rico and Connecticut must give full faith and credit to the resulting default judgment for the gambling debt); Marina Associates v. Barton, 206 Ill.App.3d 122, 151 Ill.Dec. 4, 563 N.E.2d 1110 (1990) (register New Jersey judgment for recovery of casino gambling debt); MGM Desert Inn, Inc. v. Holz, 104 N.C.App. 717, 411 S.E.2d 399 (1991), rev. denied, 331 N.C. 384, 417 S.E.2d 790 (1992) (enforce Nevada default judgment for casino gambling debt); Greate Bay Hotel v. Saltzman, 415 Pa.Super. 408, 609 A.2d 817 (1992) (give full faith and credit to New Jersey judgment for casino gambling debt); Coghill v. Boardwalk Regency Corp., 240 Va. 230, 396 S.E.2d 838 (1990) (same); GNLV Corp. v. Jackson, 736 S.W.2d 893 (Tex.App.—Waco, 1987, error denied) (same re Nevada judgment for gambling debt); Conquistador Hotel Corp. v. Fortino, 99 Wis.2d 16, 298 N.W.2d 236 (App.1980) (same re Puerto Rican judgment).

For international enforcement see Desert Palace Inc. v. State of Japan, [1993] H.J. (1444) 41, [1993] H.T. (818) 56, summarized 37 Japanese Annual of Int'l L. 163 (1994). The Tokyo District Court ordered Japan to reimburse a Nevada gambling casino for money collected in Japan from Japanese who had incurred debts at the casino. The casino's Japanese agents collected the money and were arrested on charges of issuing threats and violating exchange controls. The casino's agents waived any claim to the money, which was deposited in the state treasury. The court stated, "we hold that there is no ground [on the basis of public policy] to exclude the application of the law of Nevada to the contract between the plaintiff and the Japanese tourists." The holding was limited to the facts of the case—recovery on the basis of unjust enrichment from money having reverted to the state treasury.

312. 15 N.Y.2d at 16, 254 N.Y.S.2d at 532, 203 N.E.2d at 213.

313. 271 N.Y. at 469, 3 N.E.2d at 598: "The problem presented upon this appeal is whether a wife residing here may resort to the courts of this State to enforce liability for a wrong committed outside of the State...."

314. 15 N.Y.2d at 14, 254 N.Y.S.2d at 530, 203 N.E.2d at 212–13.

law or foreign law to dispose of the case on the merits.[315] Under a functional analysis, the number of situations in which a forum with relevant policies of its own at stake could properly close its doors on the basis of "public policy" and avoid a result on the merits, would be greatly reduced, although not eliminated.[316] Cases like *Mertz* and *Kilberg v. Northeast Airlines, Incorporated,*[317] in which the New York court said it would, on "public policy" grounds, deny effect to the Massachusetts $15,000 limit on recovery for the wrongful death of a New York citizen, can be read as the half-articulated forerunners of current functional analysis.[318] But, in the words of Professor Lorenzen: "The doctrine of public policy in the Conflict of Laws ought to have been a warning that there was something the matter with the reasoning upon which the rules to which it is the exception were supposed to be based."[319]

The classic definition of public policy as a valid reason for closing the forum to suit without disposing of the merits is Judge Cardozo's in *Loucks v. Standard Oil Company*: "They do not close their doors, unless help would violate some fundamental principle of justice, some prevalent conception of good morals, some deep-rooted tradition of the common weal."[320] This standard would be proper in a functional conflicts system

---

315. See Fox v. Morrison Motor Freight, Inc., 25 Ohio St.2d 193, 267 N.E.2d 405 (1971), cert. denied, 403 U.S. 931, 91 S.Ct. 2254, 29 L.Ed.2d 710 (1971) (prefer to avoid limit on wrongful death recovery of place of injury by adopting an interest analysis rather than invoking public policy).

316. For an overstatement see Phillips v. General Motors Corp., 298 Mont. 438, 458, 995 P.2d 1002, 1015 (2000): "Considerations of public policy are expressly subsumed within the most significant relationship approach.... A 'public policy' exception to the most significant relationship test would be redundant."

For examples of arguably correct uses of "public policy", even under functional analysis, see e.g., Cerniglia v. C. & D. Farms, Inc., 203 So.2d 1 (Fla.1967) (contract not to compete is unenforceable in Florida, but may be enforceable in other states); Marchlik v. Coronet Ins. Co., 40 Ill.2d 327, 239 N.E.2d 799 (1968) (refuse to permit action against Illinois insurers under Wisconsin direct action statute). See also Simson, *The Public Policy Doctrine in Choice of Law: A Reconsideration of Older Themes,* 1974 Wash.U.L.Q. 391, 408 (1975): "Thus, a state court should countenance, in the interest of interstate or international cooperation, foreign laws incorporating economic policies quite different from its own. It should not, however, enforce a foreign law which infringes fundamental individual freedoms and human dignity."

317. 9 N.Y.2d 34, 211 N.Y.S.2d 133, 172 N.E.2d 526 (1961).

318. See also Sweeney v. Sweeney, 402 Mich. 234, 262 N.W.2d 625 (1978) (application of parental immunity doctrine of place of injury to forum residents would violate Michigan public policy—reserve question of whether lex loci should be applied in other situations).

319. Lorenzen, *Territoriality, Public Policy and the Conflict of Laws,* 33 Yale L. J. 736, 747 (1924). See also Champagnie v. W.E. O'Neil Const. Co., 77 Ill.App.3d 136, 32 Ill.Dec. 609, 395 N.E.2d 990 (1st Dist.1979) (declares that the public policy doctrine is an escape from proper choice of law—under most significant relationship test, court reaches the same result as under public policy).

320. 224 N.Y. 99, 111, 120 N.E. 198, 202 (1918). See also Wilkinson v. Manpower, Inc., 531 F.2d 712 (5th Cir.1976) (not against forum's public policy to enforce noncompetition clause against franchisee); Breslin v. Liberty Mut. Ins. Co., 69 N.J. 435, 354 A.2d 635 (1976) (permit compensation insurance company to be subrogated to employee's recovery against third parties without allowance for attorneys' fees and costs); Crair v. Brookdale Hospital Medical Center, 94 N.Y.2d 524, 728 N.E.2d 974, 707 N.Y.S.2d 375 (2000) (not against N.Y. public policy to enforce Maryland and Virginia requirements that plaintiff file a notice of claim before suing public authority); Memphis State Univ. v. Agee, 566 S.W.2d 283 (Tenn.App.1977), cert. denied, Tenn.S.Ct. (1978) (enforce mortmain law of decedent's

for a neutral forum that had no policy of its own to advance by adjudication and that was trying to decide whether relevant foreign policies were too obnoxious to be given effect at the forum. If the foreign law is this distasteful, then the forum should be closed. This will rarely if ever be justified if the foreign law is that of a sister state. In no event should a neutral forum invoke its own public policy to affect the result on the merits as it would, for example, if it denied effect to a defense based on obnoxious foreign law.

In *Loucks,* Cardozo saw as his choices either giving a remedy under the Massachusetts wrongful death act, which measured recovery within statutory limits according to the culpability of the defendant, or sending the New York plaintiff elsewhere to sue.[321] It is not strange that in 1918

domicile); Robertson v. Estate of McKnight, 609 S.W.2d 534, 537 (Tex.1980) (New Mexico rule permitting interspousal suits is not "so contrary to our public policy that our courts will refuse to enforce it"); State v. Copus, 158 Tex. 196, 309 S.W.2d 227 (1958) (enforce California claim against son for support of indigent mother for period of time that son lived in California). Compare Terenzio v. Nelson, 107 N.J.Super. 223, 258 A.2d 20 (App.Div. 1969) for a hint of the relationship between refusal to enforce the law of another jurisdiction on the ground that it is against the forum's "public policy" and refusal on the ground that the foreign law is "penal". *Terenzio* holds that the New York statute making a New Jersey domiciliary liable for the hospital care of his mother is not "penal."

The classic definition of "penal" appears in Huntington v. Attrill, 146 U.S. 657, 673–74, 13 S.Ct. 224, 230, 36 L.Ed. 1123, 1130 (1892): "The question whether a statute of one State, which in some aspects may be called penal, is a penal law in the international sense so that it cannot be enforced in the courts of another State, depends upon the question whether its purpose is to punish an offense against the public justice of the State, or to afford a private remedy to a person injured by the wrongful act." See Restatement (Second) Conflict of Laws § 120, comment *d* (1971): "The Supreme Court of the United States has never squarely decided whether a State may look through the valid money judgment of a sister State and refuse to enforce the judgment on the ground that it was based on a penal cause of action." Milwaukee County v. M.E. White Co., 296 U.S. 268, 279, 56 S.Ct. 229, 235, 80 L.Ed. 220, 235 (1935) expressly reserved this question. In Magnolia Petroleum Co. v. Hunt, 320 U.S. 430, 438, 64 S.Ct. 208, 213, 88 L.Ed. 149, 155 (1943) the Court says: "Even though we assume for present purposes that the command of the Constitution and the statute is not all-embracing, and that there may be exceptional cases in which the judgment of one state may not override the laws and policy of another [citing *Huntington*] the actual exceptions have been few and far between.... We are aware of no such exception in the case of a money judgment in a civil suit." Cf. D'Ambra v. United States, 481 F.2d 14 (1st Cir.1973), cert. denied, 414 U.S. 1075, 94 S.Ct. 592, 38 L.Ed.2d 482 (1973) (United States' immunity from punitive damages under Tort Claims Act prevents application of state law measuring wrongful death damages by economic loss to decedent rather than to survivors); Holbein v. Rigot, 245 So.2d 57 (Fla.1971) (give full faith and credit to Texas judgment for punitive damages); City of Philadelphia v. Austin, 86 N.J. 55, 429 A.2d 568 (1981) (give full faith and credit to sister-state judgment for fine for nonpayment of taxes).

For an English court's use of the penal law concept, see United States v. Inkley, [1988] 3 All E.R. 144 (C.A.) (refuse to enforce U.S. judgment for forfeiture of bail bond).

Government of the Islamic Republic of Iran v. The Barakat Galleries Ltd., [2008] 3 W.L.R. 486, [2008] 1 All E.R. 1177 (Eng. Ct. App. 2007), held that Iran's claim for return of antiquities alleged to form part of Iran's national heritage may be heard in an English court. The Court of Appeal discussed the decision in Attorney General of New Zealand v. Ortiz, [1984] A.C. 1 (H.L.), which held that English court could not enforce a claim under a similar New Zealand law, which barred export of historic artifacts without an authorizing certificate, because the claim was based on a penal law. The court noted that after *Ortiz* the U.K. ratified the UNESCO Convention of 1970 On the Means of Prohibiting and Preventing the Illicit Import, Export and Transfer of Ownership of Cultural Property.

321. *Loucks* appears to be a classic statement of the "vested rights" choice-of-law theory, which selected the law of the place of injury to apply to torts because that is where

he did not consider the third possibility of applying the New York measure of damages to this suit between the administrator of a deceased New Yorker and a New York corporation. Today a New York court would probably apply New York law.[322]

When the forum does have policies that it can fairly impose on nonresidents, the forum should make a functional analysis of the choice-of-law problem, select either forum law or foreign law, and render a decision on the merits. The problem with the opinion in *Intercontinental Hotels Corp. v. Golden*, discussed above in this section, is that neither majority nor dissent realizes the implications of the previous year's decision in *Babcock v. Jackson*,[323] which abandoned the place-of-wrong rule and adopted a functional method of conflicts analysis. The majority and dissent in *Intercontinental Hotels* participated in an unedifying debate as to whether casino gambling was significantly more immoral than betting at horse race tracks and bingo games, which were already legal in New York. The opinion began by assuming that the law of Puerto Rico must apply because that is where the defendant "validly entered into"[324] the gambling obligation. Instead the court should have used the newly adopted conflicts method to select either New York or Puerto Rican law to govern the merits. The majority might have said: "We do not want New Yorkers to feel free to incur gambling debts at foreign casinos and then scurry home to hide behind the shield of our laws." The dissent might have said: "There is no unfair surprise to the Puerto Rican casino in applying New York law under which the obligation is invalid. Intercontinental Hotels knew or should have known that they were extending credit to a New York gambler. Judgment for the defendant may prevent New Yorker's from being able to run up gambling debts in jurisdictions where such debts are legally enforceable. That is a consequence we should happily embrace."

Thus functional analysis will not provide an easy answer to the problem, but it will focus the court's attention on the policies underlying the conflicting laws and on the long-range consequences of the choice of

---

plaintiff's right "vested." In his jurisprudential writings, as might be expected, Cardozo indicated discomfort with such rigid analysis: "when I view the [conflict of laws] as a whole, I find logic to have been more remorseless here, more blind to final causes, that it has been in other fields. Very likely it has been too remorseless." B. Cardozo, The Paradoxes of Legal Science 68 (1928).

322. See Pearson v. Northeast Airlines, Inc., 309 F.2d 553 (2d Cir.1962), cert. denied, 372 U.S. 912, 83 S.Ct. 726, 9 L.Ed.2d 720 (1963) (*Kilberg,* infra this note, constitutional and that case construed as applying New York's measure of damages); Farber v. Smolack, 20 N.Y.2d 198, 282 N.Y.S.2d 248, 229 N.E.2d 36 (1967) (most significant relationship test applicable to wrongful death cases, all parties New York residents); Long v. Pan American World Airways, Inc., 16 N.Y.2d 337, 266 N.Y.S.2d 513, 213 N.E.2d 796 (1965) (same, decedents were Pennsylvania residents); Kilberg v. Northeast Airlines, Inc., 9 N.Y.2d 34, 211 N.Y.S.2d 133, 172 N.E.2d 526 (1961) (refuse to apply Massachusetts $15,000 limit on damages). But cf. McDaniel v. Petroleum Helicopters, Inc., 455 F.2d 137 (5th Cir.1972) (Columbia's limit on wrongful death recovery not against Louisiana public policy); Patch v. Stanley Works, 448 F.2d 483 (2d Cir.1971) (New Hampshire limit on wrongful death recovery not against Connecticut public policy).

323. 12 N.Y.2d 473, 240 N.Y.S.2d 743, 191 N.E.2d 279 (1963), discussed infra § 6.16.

324. *Intercontinental Hotels*, 15 N.Y.2d at 12, 203 N.E.2d at 211, 254 N.Y.S.2d at 529.

law. Under no circumstances should a forum use public policy to apply its own law on the merits. A complete choice-of-law analysis is necessary to justify choice of forum law. Nevertheless, some courts, not prepared to abandon a territorial choice-of-law rule but unsatisfied with the result, have rejected the chosen law as against public policy and applied forum law.[325]

The forum's displacement on public policy grounds of the normally applicable law may be justified if the displacement is based on international standards. In *Kuwait Airways Corp. v. Iraqi Airways Co.*,[326] the House of Lords rejected Iraqi law that would justify the conversion of aircraft belonging to the Kuwati State. In his opinion, Lord Hope of Craighead noted that the public policy under which the Lords refused to apply Iraqi law was "based on the Charter of the United Nations and the resolutions which were made under it." He stated that "a principle of English public policy which was purely domestic or parochial in character would not provide clear and satisfying grounds for disapplying the primary rule which favours the lex loci delicti."[327]

Article 21 of the European Union Regulation on the Law applicable to Contractual Obligations (Rome I)[328] and article 26 of the Regulation on the Law Applicable to Non–Contractual Obligations (Rome II)[329] state that a court may refuse to apply the law selected by those documents "only if such application is manifestly incompatible with the public policy (ordre public) of the forum." There is no indication what the court should do if it thus rejects the law selected by the provisions of Rome I and Rome II. The proper response is dismissal of the case without rendering a judgment on the merits, unless the court replaces the

---

325. See Alexander v. General Motors Corp., 267 Ga. 339, 478 S.E.2d 123 (1996) (using public policy to reject Virginia negligence rule and apply Georgia strict product liability rule); McDaniel v. Ritter, 556 So.2d 303, 317 (Miss. 1989) (using public policy to choose Mississippi comparative negligence rather than Tennessee contributory negligence and stating "[n]o extended discussion of the relevant interests ... is necessary"); Home Ins. Co. v. American Home Products Corp., 75 N.Y.2d 196, 551 N.Y.S.2d 481, 550 N.E.2d 930 (1990) (New York rule against insurance coverage of punitive damages applies to Illinois judgment when case involves a New York insured and insurer); Boone v. Boone, 345 S.C. 8, 546 S.E.2d 191 (2001) (holding interspousal immunity rule of place of wrong against public policy and applying forum law permitting suit, overruling Oshiek v. Oshiek, 244 S.C. 249, 136 S.E.2d 303 (1964)); Russell v. Bush & Burchett, Inc., 210 W.Va. 699, 559 S.E.2d 36 (2001) (holding it against public policy to apply law of place of wrong that barred tort suit against employer by employee of contractor hired by West Virginia governmental agency); cf. Owen v. Owen, 444 N.W.2d 710 (S.D.1989) (decides to retain place-of-wrong rule, but refuses to apply guest statute of place of injury on public policy grounds; concurring opinion, joined in by a majority of the court, reaches the same result under "modern" conflicts analysis).

   That the public policy doctrine has no role to play in functional conflicts analysis, see Note, *Choice of Law: A Fond Farewell to Comity and Public Policy,* 74 Cal. L. Rev. 1447, 1448, 1458 (1986). That, however, courts that have adopted a functional approach continue to employ public policy, see Corr, *Modern Choice of Law and Public Policy: The Emperor Has the Same Old Clothes,* 39 U.Miami L. Rev. 647, 649–50 (1985).

326. [2002] 2 A.C. 883 (H.L. 2002, appeal from Eng.).

327. Id. at 1116.

328. Regulation (EC) No. 593/2008 Of The European Parliament And Of The Council of 17 June 2008 on the law applicable to contractual obligations (Rome I).

329. Regulation (EC) No. 864/2007 of 11 July 2007, OJ 2007 L199/47.

indicated law with a rule based on international, not domestic, standards.

Article 42 of the Japanese Act on the General Rules of Application of Laws[330] similarly contains a public policy exception without indication what action the Japanese forum should then take. Article 22 provides special public policy limits in tort. Article 22(1) creates a double actionability rule similar to the now displaced English rule.[331] There is no recovery unless the events constitute a tort under Japanese law. Article 22(2) states that even when foreign law does apply to a tort, the plaintiff may not recover damages or any other remedy not recognized under Japanese law.

§ 3.7   Notice and Proof of Foreign Law

The problem of determining the content of foreign law in order to implement conflicts analysis has undergone dramatic changes concurrently with, but largely independently of, the emergence of functional conflicts theory. Under the classic view, law other than that of the forum, even the law of a sister state, was a fact that the parties had to plead and prove as any other fact.[332] In a few states, judicial decisions have ended the cumbersome and senseless business of dealing with foreign law as a fact and have declared sister state law a proper subject for judicial notice.[333] For the most part, the change from the old ways has been the result of statute or court rule.[334]

---

330. Law No. 10 of 1898 as newly titled and amended 21 June 2006.

331. See supra note 159.

332. See Restatement of Conflict of Laws § 621 (1934): "Except as stated in § 622 [common law of another common-law state presumed to be same as forum's], foreign law must be alleged in pleading and proved by evidence."; But cf. Rosman v. Trans World Airlines, Inc. 34 N.Y.2d 385, 358 N.Y.S.2d 97, 314 N.E.2d 848 (1974) (even though Warsaw Convention is in French, it is domestic law and its meaning is to be determined as a question of law); Byrne v. Cooper, 11 Wash.App. 549, 523 P.2d 1216 (1974) (English law a mixed question of fact and law to be determined by the trial judge).

333. Prudential Ins. Co. of America v. O'Grady, 97 Ariz. 9, 396 P.2d 246 (1964); Choate v. Ransom, 74 Nev. 100, 323 P.2d 700 (1958). Cf. Litsinger Sign Co. v. American Sign Co., 11 Ohio St.2d 1, 227 N.E.2d 609 (1967) (although forum's version of Uniform Judicial Notice of Foreign Law Act omits reference to "common law", forum may take judicial notice of cases construing sister state statutes).

334. See, e.g.:

MICH. COMP. L. ANN. ch. 600 § 2114a: "A party who intends to raise an issue concerning the law of any jurisdiction or governmental unit thereof outside this state shall give notice in his pleadings or other reasonable written notice. In determining the law of any jurisdiction or governmental unit thereof outside this state, the court may consider any relevant material or source, including testimony, whether or not submitted by a party or admissible under the rules of evidence. The court, not jury, shall determine the law of any governmental unit outside this state. Its determination is subject to review on appeal as a ruling on a question of law."

Fed.R.Civ.P. 44.1: "A party who intends to raise an issue about a foreign country's law must give notice by a pleading or other writing. In determining foreign law, the court may consider any relevant material or source, including testimony, whether or not submitted by a party or admissible under the Federal Rules of Evidence. The court's determination must be treated as a ruling on a question of law."

Ferrostaal, Inc. v. M/V Sea Phoenix, 447 F.3d 212, 216 (3d Cir. 2006): Rule 44.1 " 'provides courts with broad authority to conduct their own independent research to

These statutes and court rules facilitating determination of foreign law are improvements over the fact-proof pattern with limited appellate review[335] that previously existed. There may still be times, however, when even with the aid of the new procedures, a particular foreign law may, as a practical matter, in terms of reasonable costs of litigation, be unknowable. This was true of Saudi–Arabian law in *Walton v. Arabian American Oil Company.*[336] In *Walton* an Arkansas citizen, while temporarily in Saudi Arabia, was injured when an automobile he was driving collided with a truck owned by defendant and driven by one of defendant's employees. The defendant, incorporated in Delaware, was licensed to do business in New York, the forum, and was doing much business in Saudi Arabia. Because the court had to apply Saudi–Arabian law as the law of the place of plaintiff's injury, failure of the plaintiff to plead and prove that law resulted in a dismissal of his case on the merits.[337] Under

---

determine foreign law but imposes no duty upon them to do so.' The parties . . . carry the burden of proving foreign law; where they do not do so, we 'will ordinarily apply the forum's law.' " (quoting Bel–Ray v. Chemrite Ltd., 181 F.3d 435, 440 (3d Cir. 1999)).

With regard of adequacy of a party's notice of an issue about foreign law see Northrop Grumman Ship Systems, Inc. v. Ministry of Defense of the Republic of Venezuela, 575 F.3d 491, 497 (5th Cir. 2009) (district court abused its discretion in ruling that Venezuela failed to timely notice of intention to rely on Venezuelan law: "When the applicability of foreign law is not obvious, notice is sufficient if allows the opposing party time to research the foreign rules"); Rationis Enterprises Inc. of Panama v. Hyundai Mipo Dockyard Co.,426 F.3d 580 (2d Cir. 2005) (alternative pleading of applicability of English, Swedish, Korean, or Panamanian law satisfied obligation to provide reasonable notice under 44.1); DP Aviation v. Smiths Indus. Aerospace & Defense Systems Ltd., 268 F.3d 829 (9th Cir. 2001) (defendant did not provide reasonable notice of its contention that English law governed prejudgment interest when notice was not given until plaintiff submitted its proposed judgment).

See also Miller, *Federal Rule 44.1 and the "Fact" Approach to Determining Foreign Law,* 65 Mich. L. Rev. 615 (1967); Sass, *Foreign Law in Federal Courts,* 29 Am.J.Comp.L. 97 (1981).

M.G.L.A. (Mass.) ch. 233, § 70 ("shall take judicial notice" of the law of any United States jurisdiction or foreign country); Tex.R. Evidence 202 ("may . . . take judicial notice" of the law of United States jurisdictions on motion of party, movant to furnish judge with information and give notice to all parties); Tex.R.Evidence 203 (law of a foreign country, similar to Fed.R.C.P. 44.1).

335. See First Nat'l City Bank v. Compania de Aguaceros, S.A., 398 F.2d 779 (5th Cir.1968) (under Federal Rule of Civil Procedure 44.1, need not find that trial court determination of foreign law was "clearly erroneous" in order to reverse).

336. 233 F.2d 541 (2d Cir.), cert. denied, 352 U.S. 872, 77 S.Ct. 97, 1 L.Ed.2d 77 (1956).

337. This result does not always follow, even under traditional choice-of-law regimes. A number of courts, either directly or through various presumptions as to the content of foreign law, have applied the law of the forum when there is a default in proof of foreign law.

When party fails to give proper notice of foreign law, forum law applies: Kostelec v. State Farm Fire & Cas. Co., 64 F.3d 1220 (8th Cir. 1995) (parties having argued under forum law have waived any objection to its application); Angier v. Barton, 160 Conn. 204, 276 A.2d 782 (1970); Hogan v. Q.T. Corp., 230 Md. 69, 185 A.2d 491 (1962); Cousins v. Instrument Flyers, Inc., 44 N.Y.2d 698, 405 N.Y.S.2d 441, 376 N.E.2d 914 (1978); Gaipo v. Gaipo, 102 R.I. 28, 227 A.2d 581 (1967). But see Curley v. AMR Corp., 153 F.3d 5 (2d Cir. 1998) (Second Circuit reverses district court's application of New York law, finds Mexican law, and applies Mexican law to reach same result as trial court); James v. Powell, 19 N.Y.2d 249, 279 N.Y.S.2d 10, 225 N.E.2d 741 (1967) (reverse and remand for determination of liability for fraudulent conveyance of land under law of Puerto Rican situs, even though both parties had assumed New York law was applicable—Court makes no finding as to

a functional system of choice-of-law, however, a court would choose no law as the necessarily applicable law until the court knew the content of that law, determined its underlying policies, and made a decision as to whether or not that law's application to the parties and the transaction before the court would advance those policies. In *Walton,* the court should be free to apply forum law unless and until the court learned, with whatever techniques are available under modern procedures, that a different law exists elsewhere, that applying that law would advance its policies, and that, under all the circumstances, the court should prefer that law and those policies over those of the forum.[338]

---

content of Puerto Rican law); Frummer v. Hilton Hotels Int'l, Inc., 60 Misc.2d 840, 304 N.Y.S.2d 335 (1969) (court on own motion takes judicial notice of English law).

Absent a showing to the contrary, presume sister state's common law is the same as the forum's: Joseph E. Bennett Co. v. Trio Indus., Inc., 306 F.2d 546 (1st Cir.1962); Korn v. Tamiami Trail Tours, Inc., 108 Ga.App. 510, 133 S.E.2d 616 (1963); Otey v. Midland Valley R.R., 108 Kan. 755, 197 P. 203 (1921); Selles v. Smith, 4 N.Y.2d 412, 176 N.Y.S.2d 267, 151 N.E.2d 838 (1958), overruled on another point, Farber v. Smolack, 20 N.Y.2d 198, 282 N.Y.S.2d 248, 229 N.E.2d 36 (1967); Holcombe v. Texas, 424 S.W.2d 635 (Tex.Crim.App. 1968) (presume sister state convictions invalid because upon information and not indictment as required in Texas); Velasquez v. Greyhound Lines, Inc., 12 Utah 2d 379, 366 P.2d 989 (1961); Bailey v. Hagen, 25 Wis.2d 386, 130 N.W.2d 773 (1964).

In absence of pleading of sister state statute, the court presumes it is the same as the forum's: In re Estate of Drumheller, 252 Iowa 1378, 110 N.W.2d 833, 87 A.L.R.2d 1233 (1961). Where a sister state's statute is substantially the same as the forum's, in the absence of a showing to the contrary, presume that the judicial construction of the statute is the same as the forum's: Harper v. Hartford Acc. & Indem. Co., 14 Wis.2d 500, 111 N.W.2d 480 (1961).

Courts have applied forum law in the absence of proof of the law of a foreign country: Mutual Service Ins. Co. v. Frit Industries, Inc., 358 F.3d 1312 (11th Cir. 2004) (even though choice-of-law provision selected law of Cayman Islands, absent party presenting contrary authority, court properly presumed that Cayman law was the same as that of forum state); Alameda Films SA de CV v. Authors Rights Restoration Corp., 331 F.3d 472, 481 (5th Cir. 2003), cert. denied, 540 U.S. 1048, 124 S.Ct. 814, 157 L.Ed.2d 696 (2003) ("When there are gaps in foreign law, though, a U.S. court may use forum law to fill them") (Mexican law); Cavic v. Grand Bahama Development Co., Ltd., 701 F.2d 879 (11th Cir.1983) (Bahamas); Vishipco Line v. Chase Manhattan Bank, N.A., 660 F.2d 854 (2d Cir.1981), cert. denied, 459 U.S. 976, 103 S.Ct. 313, 74 L.Ed.2d 291 (1982) (Vietnam); 1700 Ocean Ave. Corp. v. GBR Associates, 354 F.2d 993 (9th Cir.1965) (in absence of proof to contrary, presume Canadian law same as forum's); San Rafael Compania Naviera v. American Smelting & Refining Co., 327 F.2d 581 (9th Cir.1964) (in absence of proof of Peruvian law, would assume it the same as the forum's); Tidewater Oil Co. v. Waller, 302 F.2d 638 (10th Cir.1962) (in absence of proof of Turkish law, presume on basis of "juridical principles which may be assumed to inhere in the laws of all civilized countries" that Turkish law would permit recovery on substantially the same terms as the forum law); Mastics v. Kiraly, 26 O.O.2d 266, 196 N.E.2d 172 (P.Ct.1964) (in absence of proof of Hungarian law, apply forum statute which was "so eminently fair"); Webb v. Webb, 461 S.W.2d 204 (Tex.Civ.App.1970) (assume Mexican residence requirement for divorce is the same as that of Texas).

Cf. Cal. Evidence Code § 311: "If the law of [another jurisdiction] is applicable and such law cannot be determined, the court may, as the ends of justice require, either: (a) Apply the law of this state if the court can do so consistently with the Constitution of the United States and the Constitutions of this state; or (b) Dismiss the action without prejudice or, in the case of a reviewing court, remand the case to the trial court with directions to dismiss the action without prejudice."

Cf. also White v. Borders, 104 Ga.App. 746, 123 S.E.2d 170 (1961) (common law of forum controls rather than common law of place of impact).

338. Cf. Piamba Cortes v. American Airlines, Inc., 177 F.3d 1272 (11th Cir. 1999) (holding that the difficulty of determining Colombian law "weighs heavily in favor of

Unlike common law jurisdictions, which permit a judge to apply forum law in default of a party's proof of foreign law, some civil law countries impose an obligation on the trial judge to ascertain foreign law when it is applicable.[339]

§ 3.8 Conclusion

An important test of the desirability of any proposed method of conflict of laws analysis is the degree to which it eliminates or provides satisfactory answers to the "pervasive problems" of the conflict of laws. The functional or state-interest approach to conflicts suffuses the traditional problems here surveyed with a light that reveals their real nature and permits answers that are responsive, cogent, and appeal to our common sense.

---

applying" forum law when this would advance forum policies); Gonzalez v. Volvo of America Corporation, 752 F.2d 295 (7th Cir.1985) (forum law applies when parties fail to refer to any other law); American Honda Finance Corp. v. Bennett, 232 Neb. 21, 439 N.W.2d 459 (1989) (although parties' agreement chose California law, absence of California decision on issue leads court to apply Nebraska law); Gavers v. Federal Life Ins. Co., 118 Wis.2d 113, 345 N.W.2d 900, 903 (1984) (there is a "weak" presumption "that forum law should apply unless it becomes clear that nonforum contacts are of greater significance"); Currie, *On the Displacement of the Law of the Forum,* 58 Colum. L. Rev. 964 (1958); Ehrenzweig, *The Lex Fori in the Conflict of Laws—Exception or Rule?,* 32 Rocky Mt. L. Rev. 13 (1959); Scoles, *Interstate and International Distinctions in Conflict of Laws in the United States,* 54 Cal. L. Rev. 1599, 1610–22 (1966).

But see In re Marriage of Adams, 133 Ill.2d 437, 141 Ill.Dec. 448, 551 N.E.2d 635 (1990) (reject parties' stipulation that forum law applies to liability for child support); Kramer, *Interest Analysis and the Presumption of Forum Law,* 56 U. Chi. L. Rev. 1301, 1303, 1306 (1989) (disapproving of a rebuttable presumption that forum law applies and stating that in *Walton v. Arabian Amer. Oil Co.,* discussed previously in this section, "[t]he court, quite properly, dismissed the case").

339. See Dolinger, *Application, Proof, and Interpretation of Foreign Law: A Comparative Study In Private International Law,* 12 Ariz. J. Int'l & Comp. L. 225 (1995); Sofie Geeroms, Foreign Law in Civil Litigation 43–219 (2004) (Belgium, Germany, and the Netherlands impose this duty, while France only imposes it with regard to rights that are not waivable); Mance, *Foreign and Comparative Law in the Courts,* 36 Tex. Int'l. L. J. 415, 416 (2001) (stating that unless a party pleads and establishes the effect of foreign law, "an English court will assume any applicable foreign law to be identical to English law," but noting, at id. n.4, "in some civil law systems . . . courts will, independent of any input from the parties, refer any such issue to an expert"); Siehr, *Special Courts for Conflicts Cases: A German Experiment,* 25 Am.J.Comp.L. 663, 668–69 (1977) (if parties in their pleadings reveal foreign elements in the case, court must determine and apply foreign law).

Chapter 4

JURISDICTION TO ADJUDICATE

§ 4.1 The Meaning of "Jurisdiction to Adjudicate": Scope of the Chapter

An agency of a state exercises jurisdiction to adjudicate when the agency responds to a dispute between individuals or other legally-recognized entities for the purpose of making a determination regarding the dispute that is binding within the state on the individuals or entities involved in the dispute.[1] The state agency that acts in this manner is typically a court, but there may also be adjudications by legislative, executive, or administrative agencies. A typical form of adjudication is a judgment that a sum of money is due from one or more parties to the controversy and is owed to one or more other parties. This judgment becomes a debt that, if not paid, the judgment creditor may enforce by appropriate supplementary proceedings against the debtor. If a court has jurisdiction to create this form of obligation against a person or entity, the court is said to have personal jurisdiction or jurisdiction in personam over that person or entity. Another common form of adjudication determines the interests of one or more parties in property. If a court has jurisdiction to affect the interest of a person in property but the court does not purport to create a judgment debt that is otherwise enforceable against that person, the court is said to have jurisdiction in rem or quasi in rem. Adjudications in personam and in rem are the focus of this chapter.[2]. Chapter 5 discusses judgments affecting status, such as divorces. Sections 8.2 through 8.5 focus on the special problems concerning the power of a court to affect the interest of parties in land that is not situated in the state in which the court is sitting.

On the basis of raw power, a national state may, on any terms it deems appropriate, authorize its agencies to make adjudications that are binding within that state. The term "jurisdiction to adjudicate" connotes limits on the power to adjudicate that are generally recognized and accepted between nations.[3] On the international level, these standards

---

1. See Restatement, Second, Conflict of Laws, Ch. 3, Introductory Note at 100 (1971) [hereafter cited as Restatement, Second]: "Such jurisdiction is exercised whenever action is taken in a judicial proceeding; that is, by a duly authorized state official or officials in the settlement of an individual controversy through the application of legal principles."

2. But see Cambridge Gas Transport Corp. v. Official Committee of Unsecured Creditors of Navigator Holdings Plc, [2006] 3 W.L.R. 689, 694 (Privy Council 2006) (appeal taken from Isle of Man) (adjudications in bankruptcy proceedings are neither judgments in rem or in personam).

3. See Schibsby v. Westenholz, L.R. [1870] 6 Q.B. 155 (refuse recognition of French judgment based on plaintiff's residence in France, although England had authorized similar jurisdiction in English courts); von Mehren & Trautman, The Law of Multistate

come into play most often when one nation is asked to recognize a judgment that has been rendered by the court of another nation. In *Buchanan v. Rucker,*[4] the plaintiff brought suit in England on a judgment that he had obtained against the defendant in a court on the island of Tobago. The plaintiff had served the defendant by causing a copy of the summons to be nailed on the Tobago courthouse door. There was no showing that the defendant was ever on Tobago or otherwise, according to accepted international standards, subject to the jurisdiction of the Tobago court. The English court nonsuited the plaintiff on the ground that the Tobago judgment was a nullity. In rendering his opinion, Lord Ellenborough construed the applicable Tobago statute as not authorizing the adjudication in question, but he went on to express the indignation that would greet a request to recognize a judgment that violated commonly accepted limits on the power to adjudicate:

> Supposing however that the act had said in terms, that though a person sued in the island had never been present within the jurisdiction, yet that it should bind him upon proof of nailing up the summons at the court door: how could that be obligatory upon the subjects of other countries? Can the island of *Tobago* pass a law to bind the rights of the whole world? Would the world submit to such an assumed jurisdiction?[5]

The Brussels Regulation on Jurisdiction and the Recognition and Enforcement of Judgments in Civil and Commercial Matters,[6] in force between members of the European Union (EU), except Denmark,[7] increases the risk of recognition of judgments rendered by courts with bases for jurisdiction that are generally considered improper. Article 3 exempts persons domiciled in EU countries from jurisdiction under the exorbitant bases for jurisdiction listed in Annex I. These exorbitant bases include the French rule permitting any French national[8] to acquire personal jurisdiction over any defendant,[9] and the provisions in other EU countries under which the presence of property confers personal jurisdic-

---

Problems 836 (1965) ("In Anglo–American law ... recognition of foreign judgments turns basically on the question whether in the view of the recognizing court the rendering court had adjudicatory jurisdiction in the international sense.").

4. 9 East. 192 (K.B.1808).

5. Id. at 194.

6. Council Regulation on Jurisdiction and the Recognition and Enforcement of Judgments in Civil and Commercial Matters, EC No. 44/2001, adopted by the Council of the European Union on 22 December 2000, entered into force 1 March 2002 [hereinafter Brussels Regulation].

7. The European Union Council has revised the Lugano Convention to follow the Brussels Regulation on Jurisdiction and Judgments. EU:COM (2007) 387. The parties to the revised Convention are the European Community, Iceland, Norway, Switzerland, and, because it opted out of the Brussels Regulation, Denmark. Nevertheless, pursuant to an agreement between the European Community and Denmark signed on 19 October 2005, the Brussels Regulation applies between the other European Community member states and Denmark.

8. Extended by Brussels Regulation article 2 ¶ 2 to anyone domiciled in France.

9. Articles 14 and 15 of the Code Civil.

tion over the owner.[10] Defendants not domiciled in the EU are subject to these exorbitant jurisdictional bases and the Regulation requires other EU countries to recognize and enforce the resulting judgments.[11]

In the United States, the outer limits of the power of state and federal courts to adjudicate are traced by the federal Constitution, especially by the due process clauses of the fifth and fourteenth amendments. This chapter examines these constitutional limitations on jurisdiction with particular emphasis on their effect on state courts. Sections 4.32 through 4.39 discuss some of the common limitations, narrower than the Constitution would require, that states impose on their courts and that courts, in the exercise of discretion, impose upon themselves.

Jurisdiction over persons and to affect interests in property, the focus of this chapter, should be distinguished from jurisdiction over the subject matter of the controversy. Within a state or nation there are frequently courts that, under that state or nation's scheme for distributing judicial authority, are not competent to deal with certain kinds of cases. For example, a state may have courts of limited jurisdiction that are not competent to adjudicate matters in which the amount in controversy exceeds a certain amount. Whether a court's competence to adjudicate concerning the subject matter is jurisdictional, in the sense that a judgment rendered in violation of a state or nation's internal rules of judicial competence is void and subject to collateral attack, or whether a court's exceeding its subject matter competence is merely error that may be corrected only by direct appeal, depends upon the rules of the state or nation in which the court sits. If, for example, a state would treat a court's acting in excess of its subject matter competence as an ordinary error that must be attacked directly, the erroneous judgment, once final, is entitled to full faith and credit in other states.[12] Within the United States, the subject matter jurisdiction of state courts is circumscribed not only by each state, but also, at times, by a federal statute conferring exclusive jurisdiction on federal courts.[13]

---

10. See, Austria, Jurisdiktionsnorm art. 99 (but there can be no disproportion between the value of the local assets and the amount in controversy); Greece, Code of Civil Procedure art. 40; Switzerland, Bundesgesetz Ober Das Internationale Privatrecht (IPEG) of Dec. 18, 1987, SR 291 art. 4. Germany has a similar provision (Art. 23 Zivilprozessordnung) but the German Federal Supreme Court has narrowed the scope of personal jurisdiction based on the presence of defendant's assets, requiring that in addition to the location of assets, there must be a sufficient connection between the litigation and Germany. Judgment of July 2, 1991, BGH, 1991 Neue Juristische Wochenschrift [NJW] 3092.

11. Brussels Regulation art. 35(3) provides that "[t]he test of public policy [as a basis for refusing to recognize the judgment of another EU country] may not be applied to rules relating to jurisdiction."

12. Restatement, Second, ch. 3, Introductory Note at 102. But cf. Thompson v. Whitman, 85 U.S. (18 Wall.) 457, 21 L.Ed. 897 (1874) (permits recovery of damages from New Jersey sheriff who seized boat; finding that although sheriff seized boat in New Jersey, he did not seize it within the county of which he was sheriff; no inquiry into whether New Jersey would treat court's error in condemning boat not seized in county in which it sits as jurisdictional).

13. See, e.g., 28 U.S.C.A. § 1351: ("The district courts shall have original jurisdiction, exclusive of the courts of the States, of all civil actions and proceedings against (1) consuls

In addition to subject matter competence, venue rules limit the ability of a court to adjudicate. State venue rules designate in which judicial district or division of the state a plaintiff can bring an action, even though all judicial districts of the state may have constitutional jurisdiction to adjudicate.[14] Although venue rules are not jurisdictional, limitations on the venue of federal courts may prevent difficult problems of constitutional jurisdiction to adjudicate from arising.[15]

§ 4.2   The Relationship between Jurisdiction to Adjudicate and Choice of Law

There is continuous interplay between rules determining permissible limits of jurisdiction to adjudicate a dispute arising from an interstate or international transaction and rules indicating what domestic law a court shall apply to determine the rights and duties arising from that transaction. What choice-of-law rules are desirable depends in large part on the current scope of judicial jurisdiction. The breadth of a court's jurisdiction, in turn, should be decided with reference to what law that court will apply if it adjudicates the case in issue. For example, suppose that jurisdictional rules are shaped so that the only state with jurisdiction to adjudicate is the state whose law, on the basis of a conflict of laws analysis, should apply. Under such circumstances, both the simplest and most desirable choice-of-law rule would be one designating forum law.[16] On the other hand, given the many permissible bases for judicial jurisdiction, it is imperative that choice-of-law rules take proper account of the relevant policies of states other than the forum.[17]

Chapter 9 discusses constitutional limitations on choice-of-law rules. In broad outline the constitutional standards for choice of law are similar to the standards for judicial jurisdiction.[18] Insistence on some

---

or vice consuls of foreign states; or (2) members of a mission or members of their families...."); Lemke v. Kita, 17 Mich.App. 642, 170 N.W.2d 263 (1969) (affirm granting of foreign consul's motion to quash action against him brought in state court).

14.   See Restatement, Second, ch. 3, Introductory Note at 102.

15.   See Foster, *Long–Arm Jurisdiction in Federal Courts,* 1969 Wis. L. Rev. 9, 36 n. 103 (1969).

16.   See Ehrenzweig, Conflict of Laws § 108 (1962). For the view that only the state whose law governs the issues in dispute should have jurisdiction, see Carrington, *Virtual Civil Litigation: A Visit to John Bunyan's Celestial City*, 98 Colum. L. Rev. 1516, 1535 (1998); Cox, *Razing Conflicts Facades to Build Better Jurisdiction Theory: The Foundation—There Is No Law But Forum Law*, 28 Val. U. L. Rev. 1, 8 (1993); Maier & McCoy, *A Unifying Theory for Judicial Jurisdiction and Choice of Law*, 39 Amer. J. Comp. L. 249, 256 (1991); Perdue, *Personal Jurisdiction and the Beetle in the Box*, 32 B.C. L. Rev. 529, 571 (1991).

17.   See T. de Boer, Beyond Lex Loci Delicti 393 (1987) ("Greater latitude in jurisdiction necessitates closer scrutiny of the choice of law issue"); von Mehren & Trautman, *Jurisdiction to Adjudicate: A Suggested Analysis*, 79 Harv. L. Rev. 1121, 1148–49 (1966) [hereafter in this chapter cited as von Mehren & Trautman, 79 Harv. L. Rev.]. But see Maltz, *Visions of Fairness—The Relationship Between Jurisdiction and Choice of Law,* 30 Ariz. L. Rev. 751 (1988) ("fairness is adequately vindicated through restrictions on personal jurisdiction rather than on choice of law").

18.   See Keckler v. Brookwood Country Club, 248 F.Supp. 645, 650 (N.D.Ill.1965) ("The same rationale applies in both instances."); Leflar, *The Converging Limits of State Jurisdictional Powers*, 9 J.Public L. 282 (1960).

reasonable nexus with the parties or the transaction in issue, avoidance of outrageous surprise to one whose interest is at stake—these are themes that pervade both areas. In situations that lie close to the borders of what is constitutionally permissible, whether a state can exercise judicial jurisdiction may turn upon whether that state may properly apply its own law.[19]

Perhaps another barrier to exercise of jurisdiction over defendants outside the country should be if the underlying substantive claim is frivolous. If so, it may be unfair to compel the absent defendant to appear and defend or be bound by a default judgment unilaterally obtained.[20] In the United Kingdom, a plaintiff must obtain court permission to serve process outside the jurisdiction. Supreme Court Rule 6.20 lists the bases for jurisdiction on which a court can base its permission for service. An applicant for grant of leave for such service must submit an affidavit stating, among other things, "that in the deponent's belief the plaintiff has a good cause of action."[21]. In Australia, when a party seeks leave to serve process outside the country, the party must "make out a prima facie case for relief."[22]

In cases lying within the constitutional reach of judicial jurisdiction, a court in deciding whether it should, in the exercise of a sound discretion, take jurisdiction or grant a forum non conveniens dismissal,[23] will consider such things as whether the law that should apply is that of the state in which it sits,[24] and whether, if the court should apply forum law to advance forum policies, a dismissal will sacrifice these policies.[25]

---

19. See Seymour v. Parke, Davis & Co., 294 F.Supp. 1257 (D.C.N.H.1969), aff'd, 423 F.2d 584 (1st Cir.1970) (decision that forum lacks judicial jurisdiction heavily influenced by fact that it would be inappropriate to apply forum law); von Mehren & Trautman, The Law of Multistate Problems 1342 (1965) (decision in *Hanson v. Denckla* perhaps explainable on ground that Supreme Court did not approve of Florida forum's choice of its own law); D. Currie, *The Growth of the Long Arm: Eight Years of Extended Jurisdiction in Illinois,* 1963 U.Ill.L.Forum 533, 543–44 [hereafter in this chapter cited as Currie, 1963 U.Ill.L.Forum].

20. See Carrington & Martin, *Substantive Interests and the Jurisdiction of State Courts,* 66 Mich. L. Rev. 227, 248 (1967) ("Surely, on balance, it seems reasonable to suppose that the jurisdictional decision will be much more clarified than complicated by unmasking the fact that the substantive consequences of the decision are an appropriate, if not an inevitable, concern."). But see Judas Priest v. Second Judicial Dist. Court, 104 Nev. 424, 760 P.2d 137, 139 (1988) (upholding jurisdiction over English rock band on allegation that record sold in Nevada caused suicide—"we are concerned only with the issue of jurisdiction, and we do not reach any question related to the merits of the cause of action respondents have attempted to allege").

21. *Seaconsar Far East Ltd. v. Bank Markazi Jomhouri Islami Iran,* [1994] 1 A.C. 438 (H.L.) held that when service outside the jurisdiction was based upon the predecessor of Rule 6.20, which listed as a basis for jurisdiction "a contract made within the jurisdiction or a contract made by an agent trading within the jurisdiction", it was sufficient for the applicant to establish that there was "a serious issue to be tried," without further inquiry into the merits of the case.

22. See Caterpillar Inc. v. John Deere Ltd., [1999] FCA 1503.

23. See infra §§ 4.33–4.33D.

24. See Piper Aircraft Co. v. Reyno, 454 U.S. 235, 260 n.29, 102 S.Ct. 252, 268 n. 29, 70 L.Ed.2d 419 (1981) ("Many forum non conveniens decisions have held that the need to apply foreign law favors dismissal").

25. von Mehren & Trautman, 79 Harv. L. Rev. at 1129–30, 1176–77; Wis.Stat.Ann. § 801.63(3)(c) (stating that in exercise of discretion to stay proceedings for trial outside the

Although there are these many interrelationships and similarities between standards for jurisdiction to adjudicate and choice of law, there are still differences. It is possible, though unlikely, that a state that has a sufficient nexus with the controversy to make it reasonable to apply its law to the case will not have a sufficient nexus with one of the parties to make it reasonable for it to exercise judicial jurisdiction over that party.[26] It is also possible that a state will have jurisdiction over the defendant but insufficient interest in the dispute to apply its law in determining the extent of the defendant's obligations.[27]

Transient presence in the state as a basis for jurisdiction over an individual is the chief bundling board separating jurisdiction from choice of law.[28] Other generally-affiliating[29] bases for jurisdiction, such as domicile, doing business, and incorporation, may provide situations in which the exercise of jurisdiction is reasonable, but application of forum law would violate due process.[30] For example, it may be permissible to sue the defendant at his or her domicile for a cause of action arising out of a tort in a distant state, but not reasonable to apply the law of the domicile to hold the defendant liable for conduct that the law of the other state required.

---

state a court should consider "[d]ifferences in conflict of law rules applicable in this state and in any alternative forum").

26. See Silberman, *Shaffer v. Heitner: The End of an Era,* 53 N.Y.U. L. Rev. 33, 88 (1978) ("To believe that a defendant's contacts with the forum state should be stronger under the due process clause for jurisdictional purposes than for choice of law is to believe that an accused is more concerned with where he will be hanged than whether"). But see Shaffer v. Heitner, 433 U.S. 186, 215, 97 S.Ct. 2569, 2586, 53 L.Ed.2d 683, 704 (1977) ("we have rejected the argument that if a State's law can properly be applied to a dispute, its courts necessarily have jurisdiction over the parties to that dispute"); Hanson v. Denckla, 357 U.S. 235, 254, 78 S.Ct. 1228, 1240, 2 L.Ed.2d 1283, 1298 (1958) ("It [Florida] does not acquire that jurisdiction [to adjudicate] by being the 'center of gravity' of the controversy, or the most convenient location for litigation. The issue is personal jurisdiction, not choice of law."); Southern Mach. Co. v. Mohasco Indus., Inc., 401 F.2d 374, 382 (6th Cir.1968); Agrashell, Inc. v. Bernard Sirotta Co., 344 F.2d 583, 587 (2d Cir.1965); Oliver v. American Motors Corp., 70 Wn.2d 875, 887–88, 425 P.2d 647, 655 (1967).

27. See Myers v. Brickwedel, 259 Or. 457, 486 P.2d 1286 (1971) (in a suit between California residents based on acts of alienation of affections and criminal conversation that allegedly occurred in Oregon, Oregon has sufficient interest in applying its law to make use of its long-arm statute reasonable, but leave open the question of whether Oregon law should be applied as a matter of choice of law).

28. See Burnham v. Superior Court, 495 U.S. 604, 110 S.Ct. 2105, 109 L.Ed.2d 631 (1990) (holding that service on a father while transiently present in the forum is constitutionally sufficient to confer personal jurisdiction); Restatement, Second, § 24, comment *b* (giving example in which state with jurisdiction based on temporary presence may not apply its own law).

29. A "generally-affiliating" basis for jurisdiction is one that makes it reasonable to exercise jurisdiction over the defendant as to any cause of action, not just a cause arising from acts or effects in the forum. See infra § 4.9C.

30. See Brilmayer, Haverkamp, Logan, Lynch, Neuwirth, & O'Brien, *A General Look at General Jurisdiction,* 66 Texas L. Rev. 723, 773 (1988) (some bases for general jurisdiction "justify general legislative jurisdiction" and some do not); Sedler, *Judicial Jurisdiction and Choice of Law: The Consequences of Shaffer v. Heitner,* 63 Iowa L. Rev. 1031, 1032 (1978). See also section 9.2A for discussion of due process limitations on choice of law.

§ 4.3   Due Process Limits on Jurisdiction

In the United States, the federal Constitution sets the outer limits of jurisdiction to adjudicate. The crucial constitutional provisions are the due process clauses of the Fifth and Fourteenth amendments. The Fifth Amendment controls the exercise of jurisdiction by federal courts,[31] the Fourteenth Amendment by state courts. A somewhat tautological definition of jurisdiction to adjudicate for United States courts would run as follows: a court has judicial jurisdiction if it may, without violating due process of law, make an adjudication binding parties personally or determining the rights of persons in property. If a court acts beyond the scope of its constitutionally circumscribed jurisdiction, its adjudication is a violation of due process. The judgment is invalid in the forum[32] and no court sitting in a sister state is either required or permitted[33] to give the invalid judgment full faith and credit.

If a court purports to make a judgment personally binding on a defendant over whom it does not have constitutional judicial jurisdiction, the defendant may ignore the proceedings, even if given notice of them, and then step in to make a collateral attack on the judgment as a violation of due process if the plaintiff attempts to enforce the judgment.[34] The defendant may make this attack either in the state which rendered the judgment or in a sister state. As a tactical matter, a defendant may not wish to ignore judicial proceedings of which the defendant has notice[35] and rely on collateral attack, for in doing so the defendant is likely to waive any defense to the action other than the due-

---

31.   See Horne v. Adolph Coors Co., 684 F.2d 255 (3d Cir.1982) (although state long-arm statute used in patent infringement action, the constitutional limit on personal jurisdiction is determined by the Fifth Amendment, not the Fourteenth).

32.   McDonald v. Mabee, 243 U.S. 90, 37 S.Ct. 343, 61 L.Ed. 608 (1917); Riverside & Dan River Cotton Mills, Inc. v. Menefee, 237 U.S. 189, 35 S.Ct. 579, 59 L.Ed. 910 (1915); Pennoyer v. Neff, 95 U.S. 714, 24 L.Ed. 565 (1878). See Kurland, *The Supreme Court, the Due Process Clause and the In Personam Jurisdiction of State Courts,* 25 U. Chi. L. Rev. 569, 585 (1958).

33.   Griffin v. Griffin, 327 U.S. 220, 229, 66 S.Ct. 556, 560, 90 L.Ed. 635, 640 (1946).

34.   See Baker v. Baker, Eccles & Co., 242 U.S. 394, 403, 37 S.Ct. 152, 155–56, 61 L.Ed. 386, 392–93 (1917) ("And to assume that a party resident beyond the confines of a state is required to come within its borders and submit his personal controversy to its tribunals upon receiving notice of the suit at the place of his residence is a futile attempt to extend the authority and control of a state beyond its own territory"). Cf. Mooney Aircraft, Inc. v. Donnelly, 402 F.2d 400, 406 (5th Cir.1968) ("Inaction in response to non-authorized action cannot render such action valid. The doctrine of laches has never been jurisdiction creating.") (holding based on construction of state long-arm statute, not due process); Thompson v. Whitman, 85 U.S. (18 Wall.) 457, 21 L.Ed. 897 (1874) (collateral attack on validity of seizure of property); Hughes v. Salo, 203 Mont. 52, 659 P.2d 270 (1983) (because judgment in sister state was void, plaintiff may sue on original claim) (quoting this book). But cf. Revona Realty Corp. v. Wasserman, 4 A.D.2d 444, 166 N.Y.S.2d 960 (1957), appeal dism'd, 5 N.Y.2d 931, 183 N.Y.S.2d 293, 156 N.E.2d 816 (1959) (defendant estopped to make collateral attack when he did not make the attack promptly after he appeared in a proceeding to enforce the judgment); Myers v. Mooney Aircraft, Inc., 429 Pa. 177, 240 A.2d 505 (1967) (by carelessness and inaction defendant loses right to attack judgment as not in conformity with service provisions of state statute).

35.   For discussion of special appearance for the purpose of contesting jurisdiction, see § 4.37.

process-jurisdictional defense, but the theoretical right to collateral attack is present.

Not all legal systems give a defendant this choice between a direct and a collateral attack on personal jurisdiction. Subject to a few exceptions, collateral attack is not available under the Brussels Regulation if the defendant has notice and opportunity to be heard on the jurisdictional issue in the original forum.[36] Nevertheless, the provision in article 26(1) that when an EU defendant "does not enter an appearance, the court shall declare of its own motion that is has no jurisdiction unless its jurisdiction is derived from the provisions of this Regulation," has special meaning in civil law countries. The civil law maxim, "jura novit curia," "the court knows the law," contemplates a far more active role for the judge in raising and exploring the issues than is true of the common law judge.

It is desirable to distinguish mandatory federal constitutional limitations on jurisdiction from limitations that are more restrictive than due process would require but that a jurisdiction elects to impose on its courts or that courts, in their discretion, adopt. For convenience, we might refer to those less-than-due-process limitations on judicial jurisdiction as "lesser limitations." Sections 4.32 through 4.39 of this chapter discuss a number of the more common lesser limitations on jurisdiction. If a court purports to adjudicate within the area that due process would permit, but beyond the scope of a lesser limitation on jurisdiction, the relevant forum law may treat this violation of a lesser jurisdictional limitation in two ways. First, the violation may be regarded as ordinary error permitting the adversely affected party to object and obtain a reversal on appeal. If that party does not make this direct attack on the judgment, that party loses the right to object or make a subsequent collateral attack on the judgment. Second, the flouting of the lesser jurisdictional rule may be treated in the same manner as a violation of due process limits on adjudication: error so serious as to be correctable by collateral attack. Whether a judgment, consistent with due process but violating a lesser jurisdictional limitation, is entitled to full faith and credit, depends upon whether it is subject to collateral attack in the jurisdiction in which the court sat that rendered the judgment. If a court's judgment is not subject to collateral attack, on either federal due process or lesser grounds, in the jurisdiction where the judgment was rendered, that judgment, with perhaps very rare exceptions,[37] is entitled to full faith and credit in a sister state.[38]

---

36. Brussels Regulation, supra note 6, art. 34(2). The Regulation does permit collateral attack despite notice if the exercise of jurisdiction violated the jurisdictional provisions in sections 3 (insurance), 4 (consumer contracts), or 6 (in rem, internal corporate affairs, and other matters in which jurisdiction is exclusively in a designated court). Id. art. 35(1). Even in cases involving jurisdiction under sections 3, 4, or 6, the court asked to recognize the judgment is "bound by the findings of fact on which the court of the Member State of origin based its jurisdiction." Id. art. 35(2).

37. See Restatement, Second, § 103: "Limitations on Full Faith and Credit. A judgment rendered in one State of the United States need not be recognized or enforced in a sister State if such recognition or enforcement is not required by the national policy of full faith and credit because it would involve an improper interference with important interests of the sister State." That this suggests too broad an exception, see infra § 9.3A.

38. Milliken v. Meyer, 311 U.S. 457, 61 S.Ct. 339, 85 L.Ed. 278 (1940).

Defining constitutional jurisdiction to adjudicate in terms of due process has the safety of tautology, but is not very helpful in understanding what the due process limitations are. A further step in exposition is to translate "due process" into a core concept that pervades the area of judicial jurisdiction. This core concept might be described as "reasonableness". Another such general term might be "fairness."[39] For example: a court has jurisdiction to require a person to appear and defend an action or have their rights adjudicated in their absence if it is reasonable that the court should act in this manner. Again this statement does not indicate what factors determine what is "reasonable" or "fair." To be more specific we must turn to the case law that has been built upon the due process foundation. In viewing the case law it is important to remember that we are seeing part of a continuing process of constitutional interpretation that attempts to make the answers to the basic problem of when a court has jurisdiction to adjudicate responsive to modern social realities. The current solutions are not the final ones.

As a tool for case analysis, it is useful to divide the due process jurisdictional standard into two parts: notice and nexus. First, a court can make a judgment binding a party personally or affecting the interests of a person in property only if there has been an effort that is reasonable under the circumstances to give the person affected notice of the proceedings and an opportunity to be heard.[40] Second, the adjudicating court must have some contact with the person being bound or with the property in which the court is determining rights that makes it reasonable for the court to bind the person by its decision or to affect rights in the property.

---

39. See supra note 19, Currie, 1963 U.Ill.L.Forum at 535, 577.

40. For the argument that there should be an exception to the need for notice when there are other assurances that all interests affected are adequately represented and that this applies to class actions, see Note, 56 Tex. L. Rev. 1033, 1047 (1978); cf. Mullane v. Central Hanover Bank & Trust Co., 339 U.S. 306, 70 S.Ct. 652, 94 L.Ed. 865 (1950), which held that published notice, which was not likely to result in actual notice, was sufficient as to beneficiaries of a common trust "whose interests or whereabouts could not with due diligence be ascertained." Id. at 317. The court held that service on known beneficiaries could not be made by "means less likely than the mails to apprise them of its pendency." Id. at 318. The court noted that personal service on known beneficiaries would be even more likely to give actual notice but said this was not necessary because there were a large number of beneficiaries and "notice reasonably certain to reach most of those interested in objecting is likely to safeguard the interests of all." Id. at 319. The same might be said of published notice to unknown beneficiaries, but the statement was not made in this context. The case, therefore, stands for the proposition that due process may permit giving notice in a manner not "reasonably calculated to reach the [defendant] in due time" if no method more likely to result in actual notice is reasonably available. But cf. Eisen v. Carlisle & Jacquelin, 417 U.S. 156, 94 S.Ct. 2140, 40 L.Ed.2d 732 (1974) (in class action under Federal Rule of Civ.Proc. 23, each member of the class must receive individual, not published notice, and the plaintiff must pay the cost).

Phillips Petroleum Co. v. Shutts, 472 U.S. 797, 105 S.Ct. 2965, 86 L.Ed.2d 628 (1985), held that nonresident class members, although not otherwise subject to the forum state's jurisdiction, may be bound if they receive mailed notice of the action and do not elect to opt out.

§ 4.4 Notice and Opportunity to be Heard

Under the regime of *Pennoyer v. Neff*,[41] the only way that a court could acquire personal jurisdiction over a non-resident individual who did not appear was by personal service on the defendant within the forum. Therefore it was not as necessary as it is today to draw a clear distinction between the nexus necessary to provide the constitutional basis for jurisdiction and the notice and opportunity to be heard that is equally necessary for the constitutional exercise of jurisdiction. Then the act necessary to provide a basis for jurisdiction, personal service, also assured notice and opportunity to be heard. Now that courts utilize many bases for jurisdiction other than personal presence in the forum, it is imperative to recognize notice and opportunity to be heard as a distinct and essential element in the constitutional exercise of judicial jurisdiction.[42]

Wuchter v. Pizzutti[43] illustrates the difference between a constitutional basis for jurisdiction and the constitutional exercise of that jurisdiction. While Wuchter, a Pennsylvania resident, was driving his automobile in New Jersey, he collided with a wagon driven by the plaintiff. The plaintiff brought suit against Wuchter in New Jersey utilizing a New Jersey statute that provided jurisdiction over nonresident automobile drivers as to any suit arising out of the defendant's operation of an automobile in New Jersey. The previous year, in *Hess v. Pawloski*[44] the Supreme Court had upheld this basis for personal jurisdiction. In *Wuchter,* however, the Court reversed a judgment based on the New Jersey statute. This was because the New Jersey statute, unlike the Massachusetts statute involved in *Hess,* contained no requirement that the state official, who the statute directed the plaintiff to serve, forward notice of the pending action to the nonresident defendant.

In *Washington v. Superior Court,*[45] the Court seems to have lost sight of the distinction between a constitutional basis for jurisdiction and the constitutional exercise of jurisdiction. A Delaware corporation qualified to do business in Washington and, as required by Washington statute, appointed a local agent for the service of process. The company then ceased doing business in Washington and dissolved. Its resident agent left the state. Three years later the plaintiff commenced a civil action in Washington against the corporation. The plaintiff served the Washington Secretary of State who did not give the corporation notice of

---

41. 95 U.S. 714, 24 L.Ed. 565 (1878).

42. See Peralta v. Heights Medical Center, Inc., 485 U.S. 80, 108 S.Ct. 896, 99 L.Ed.2d 75 (1988). This case invalidated as a violation of due process the Texas practice of requiring a defendant making a collateral attack on a default judgment on the grounds of absence of notice to allege and prove a meritorious defense. On remand, defendant's motion for judgment was denied and the case remanded to the trial court to permit the defendant to rebut plaintiff's allegation that in fact defendant was served. Peralta v. Heights Medical Center, Inc., unpublished, 01–85–00961–CV (Tex.App.—Houston [1st Dist.], August 11, 1988, error denied) (Unpublished case).

43. 276 U.S. 13, 48 S.Ct. 259, 72 L.Ed. 446 (1928).

44. 274 U.S. 352, 47 S.Ct. 632, 71 L.Ed. 1091 (1927).

45. 289 U.S. 361, 53 S.Ct. 624, 77 L.Ed. 1256 (1933).

the suit. The Supreme Court affirmed the Washington courts' refusal to grant the defendant's motion to quash the service. The Court indicated that if the defendant wanted to assure itself of notice, it should, as the Washington statute required, have appointed another agent when its resident agent for service of process had left the state. The Court distinguished *Wuchter* on the ground that nonresident corporations, unlike nonresident motorists, could be excluded from the state unless the corporation consented to the form of service provided in the Washington statutes. In *Wuchter,* the Court had, in similar reliance on the ability to exclude, distinguished statutes such as the Washington statute that provided for jurisdiction over foreign corporations by serving a state official but imposed no requirement that the official give notice to the corporation. The *Wuchter* court also thought it reasonable to expect the foreign corporation to make frequent inquiry of the public official to see if suit had been filed, but that "it could hardly be fair or reasonable to require a nonresident individual owner of a motor vehicle who may use the state highways to make constant inquiry of the secretary of state to learn whether he has been sued."[46]

It is difficult to see why it is more reasonable to expect the foreign corporation to make frequent inquiries as to suits filed against it after it has stopped doing business in the state than to expect inquiries by a nonresident motorist who has been involved in a collision in the state. The motorist may have more reason than the corporation to expect activities in the state to trigger a suit.[47] Nor does the distinction ring true based on the ability to exclude the defendant from the state until the defendant consents to jurisdiction conferred solely by service on a state official. In *Hess v. Pawloski,* the court upheld the Massachusetts nonresident motorist statute, in part, on the theory that Massachusetts could exclude the nonresident motorist until he or she appointed a state official as an agent for the service of process.[48] Moreover, in both cases there was ample constitutional basis for personal jurisdiction as to actions arising out of the defendant's activities within the state, whether or not the defendant "consented" to such jurisdiction. It would seem that if in *Wuchter* reasonable notice and opportunity to be heard was an additional due process requirement, this requirement was not met in *Washington v. Superior Court.*[49]

---

46. 276 U.S. at 21, 48 S.Ct. at 261, 72 L.Ed. at 450.

47. Cf. Manley v. Nelson, 50 Hawaii 524, 443 P.2d 155, 160 (1968), appeal dism'd and cert. denied, 394 U.S. 573, 89 S.Ct. 1299, 22 L.Ed.2d 555 (1969): "If a nonresident operator of a motor vehicle involved in an accident or collision sincerely desires to be informed when suit is commenced, it is a simple matter for him to leave with a person injured or suffering damages or involved in the collision or with a police officer investigating the accident his permanent address and if and when he changes his address to so notify the person or persons of the change."

48. 274 U.S. 352, 356–57, 47 S.Ct. 632, 633, 71 L.Ed. 1091, 1095 (1927).

49. See Hazard, *A General Theory of State–Court Jurisdiction,* 1965 Supreme Court Rev. 241, 274 (1965). Cf. B. Currie, *Unconstitutional Discrimination in the Conflict of Laws: Equal Protection,* 28 U. Chi. L. Rev. 1, 16–18 (1960) (violation of equal protection because Washington corporations receive notice).

The apparent failure to distinguish between a proper basis for jurisdiction and proper notice resulted in denying jurisdiction in the old Iowa case of *Raher v. Raher.*[50] In proceedings to adjudge an Iowa domiciliary incompetent and appoint a guardian of his property. the plaintiff served the alleged incompetent while the incompetent was in South Dakota. The Iowa court set aside the resulting judgment because "a state can not by providing for personal service outside of its territorial limits authorize its court to render personal judgment against a defendant thus served."[51] This is true if the state has no other nexus with the defendant, but given the constitutional nexus for personal jurisdiction, domicile, service outside the state was a reasonable method of completing the constitutional requirement by giving the defendant notice.

Absent extraordinary situations,[52] the plaintiff or a state agency must give notice and opportunity to be heard to the defendant before[53] state action[54] substantially affects the defendant's rights.[55] *Armstrong v.*

---

50. 150 Iowa 511, 129 N.W. 494 (1911), overruled in part, Edwards v. Smith, 238 Iowa 1080, 29 N.W.2d 404 (1947).

51. 150 Iowa at 532, 129 N.W. at 501.

52. For examples of such "extraordinary situations" see, e.g., Calero–Toledo v. Pearson Yacht Leasing Co., 416 U.S. 663, 94 S.Ct. 2080, 40 L.Ed.2d 452 (1974) (Puerto Rican police seize boat used to transport marihuana); Chrysler Credit Corp. v. Waegele, 29 Cal.App.3d 681, 105 Cal.Rptr. 914 (1972) (ex parte temporary restraining order to prevent debtor from disposing of collateral after moving it from Texas to California); cf. Olson v. Ische, 330 N.W.2d 710 (Minn.1983) (pre-judgment attachment of property about to be sold is unconstitutional without a hearing unless the sale is fraudulent).

For holdings permitting pre-judgment seizures of vessels without prior notice to foreclose admiralty liens, see, e.g., Amstar Corp. v. S/S Alexandros T., 664 F.2d 904 (4th Cir.1981); cf. Merchants National Bank of Mobile v. Dredge General G.L. Gillespie, 663 F.2d 1338 (5th Cir.1981), cert. dism'd, 456 U.S. 966, 102 S.Ct. 2263, 72 L.Ed.2d 865 (1982) (ship mortgages). Subsequent amendments to Admiralty Rules of Procedure B, C, and E provide pre-seizure court review of a verified complaint and affidavit, unless the plaintiff certifies exigent circumstances, and a prompt post-attachment hearing.

53. See United States v. James Daniel Good Real Property, 510 U.S. 43, 114 S.Ct. 492, 126 L.Ed.2d 490 (1993) (violation of due process to seize realty allegedly used in commission of federal drug offense without prior notice or an adversary hearing); Memphis Light, Gas & Water Division v. Craft, 436 U.S. 1, 98 S.Ct. 1554, 56 L.Ed.2d 30 (1978) (cutting off utilities supplied by governmental entity); Bell v. Burson, 402 U.S. 535, 91 S.Ct. 1586, 29 L.Ed.2d 90 (1971) (suspension of driver's license and registration of uninsured motorist); Boddie v. Connecticut, 401 U.S. 371, 378–79, 91 S.Ct. 780, 786, 28 L.Ed.2d 113, 119 (1971) (holding that persons unable to pay court costs may not be denied access to courts for divorces) ("That the hearing required by due process is subject to waiver, and is not fixed in form does not affect its root requirement that an individual be given an opportunity for a hearing *before* he is deprived of any significant property interest, except for extraordinary situations where some valid governmental interest is at stake that justifies postponing the hearing until after the event") (emphasis in original); Wisconsin v. Constantineau, 400 U.S. 433, 91 S.Ct. 507, 27 L.Ed.2d 515 (1971) (posting in liquor stores names of persons who may not purchase intoxicating beverages).

54. Most courts have found no significant state action in self-help repossession under section 9–503 (9–609 in 1999 Revision) of the Uniform Commercial Code. See, e.g., Adams v. Southern Cal. First Nat'l Bk., 492 U.S. 324 (9th Cir.1973), cert. denied, 419 U.S. 1006, 95 S.Ct. 325, 42 L.Ed.2d 282 (1974); Giglio v. Bank of Delaware, 307 A.2d 816 (Del.Ch. 1973); Northside Motors of Florida, Inc. v. Brinkley, 282 So.2d 617 (Fla.1973); Messenger v. Sandy Motors, Inc., 121 N.J.Super. 1, 295 A.2d 402 (Ch.Div.1972); Colonial Swimming Pool Co. v. Camperama of Vermont, Inc., 134 Vt. 463, 365 A.2d 262 (1976). See also, Comment, 44 Colo. L. Rev. 389 (1973) (analysis favors a finding of no state action). Contra, Boland v. Essex County Bk. & Trust Co., 361 F.Supp. 917 (D.Mass.1973). See also Yudof,

Reflections on Private Repossession, Public Policy and the Constitution, *122 U.Pa. L. Rev. 954, 963 (1974) ("the state . . . should maintain a monopoly over nonconsensual physical interference with the possessory interest of debtors in their property"). For economic analysis of outlawing self-help repossession, see, e.g., Whitford & Laufer,* The Impact of Denying Self–Help Repossession of Automobiles: A Case Study of the Wisconsin Consumer Act, *1975 Wis. L. Rev. 607 (1975) (the impact of the Wisconsin act on the availability of credit has been slight and economic benefits have resulted from the encouragement of refinancing agreements); Johnson,* Denial of Self–Help Repossession: An Economic Analysis, *47 S.Cal. L. Rev. 82 (1973) (abolition would yield few benefits to consumers but would create substantial costs for creditors that would be passed on to consumers). Cf. Lugar v. Edmondson Oil Co., 457 U.S. 922, 102 S.Ct. 2744, 73 L.Ed.2d 482 (1982) (pre-judgment judicial attachment is done "under color of state law" within meaning of 42 U.S.C.A. § 1983).*

For cases finding no substantial state involvement in various actions by private parties under authority of state law, see, e.g., Flagg Bros., Inc. v. Brooks, 436 U.S. 149, 98 S.Ct. 1729, 56 L.Ed.2d 185 (1978) (warehouseman's sale under section 7–210 of the Uniform Commercial Code); Anastasia v. Cosmopolitan Nat'l Bk. of Chicago, 527 F.2d 150 (7th Cir.1975), cert. denied, 424 U.S. 928, 96 S.Ct. 1143, 47 L.Ed.2d 338 (1976) (enforcement of hotelkeeper's lien by seizure of lodger's property); Northrip v. Federal Nat'l Mortgage Assoc., 527 F.2d 23 (6th Cir.1975) (nonjudicial mortgage foreclosure and sale); Barrera v. Security Building & Investment Corp., 519 F.2d 1166 (5th Cir.1975) (same); Bond v. Dentzer, 494 F.2d 302 (2d Cir.1974), cert. denied, 419 U.S. 837, 95 S.Ct. 65, 42 L.Ed.2d 63 (1974) (attachment of wages without court order pursuant to contractual agreement); USA I Lehndorff Vermoegensverwaltung GmbH & Cie v. Cousins Club, Inc., 64 Ill.2d 11, 348 N.E.2d 831 (1976) (landlord's seizure of tenant's property).

For cases finding state action when private parties act under authority of state law, see, e.g., Culbertson v. Leland, 528 F.2d 426 (9th Cir.1975) (hotelkeeper's seizure of lodger's property); Hernandez v. European Auto Collision, Inc., 487 F.2d 378 (2d Cir.1973) (garageman's lien with power of sale); Turner v. Blackburn, 389 F.Supp. 1250 (W.D.N.C. 1975) (foreclosure sale with substantial participation of court clerk); Adams v. Department of Motor Vehicles, 11 Cal.3d 146, 113 Cal.Rptr. 145, 520 P.2d 961 (1974) (resale under garageman's lien); Blye v. Globe–Wernicke Realty Co., 33 N.Y.2d 15, 347 N.Y.S.2d 170, 300 N.E.2d 710 (1973) (hotelkeeper's seizure of lodger's property); cf. Parks v. Ford's Speed Shop, 556 F.2d 132 (3d Cir.1977) (garageman's possessory lien does not involve state action, but foreclosure by sale does); Sharrock v. Dell Buick–Cadillac, Inc., 45 N.Y.2d 152, 408 N.Y.S.2d 39, 379 N.E.2d 1169 (1978) (foreclosure of garageman's lien by sale violates state constitution which has a more flexible test of state involvement than does the United States Constitution).

55. For holdings that the filing of mechanics' and materialmen's liens is not a taking of a significant property interest, see, e.g., Spielman–Fond, Inc. v. Hanson's Inc., 379 F.Supp. 997 (D.Ariz.1973), aff'd without opinion, 417 U.S. 901, 94 S.Ct. 2596, 41 L.Ed.2d 208 (1974); Home Building Corp. v. Ventura Corp., 568 S.W.2d 769 (Mo.1978); Bankers Trust Co. v. El Paso Pre–Cast Co., 192 Colo. 468, 560 P.2d 457 (1977). Contra, Roundhouse Constr. Corp. v. Telesco Masons Supplies Co., 168 Conn. 371, 362 A.2d 778, vacated and remanded for determination whether judgment based on federal or state grounds or both, 423 U.S. 809, 96 S.Ct. 20, 46 L.Ed.2d 29 (1975), adhered to on both federal and state grounds, 170 Conn. 155, 365 A.2d 393 (1976) cert. denied, 429 U.S. 889, 97 S.Ct. 246, 50 L.Ed.2d 172 (1976). See also Briere v. Agway, 425 F.Supp. 654 (D.Vt.1977) (non-possessory attachment constitutes sufficient taking to violate due process).

For holdings that the filing of a lis pendens is not a sufficient taking to require prior notice and opportunity to be heard, see, e.g. Chrysler Corp. v. Fedders Corp., 670 F.2d 1316 (3d Cir.1982); Williams v. Bartlett, 189 Conn. 471, 457 A.2d 290 (1983), appeal dism'd for want of substantial federal quest., 464 U.S. 801, 104 S.Ct. 46, 78 L.Ed.2d 67 (1983); Debral Realty, Inc. v. DiChiara, 383 Mass. 559, 420 N.E.2d 343 (1981); cf. O'Bannon v. Town Court Nursing Center, 447 U.S. 773, 100 S.Ct. 2467, 65 L.Ed.2d 506 (1980) (patients at nursing home not entitled to hearing before home can be decertified for receipt of Medicare and Medicaid funds).

For cases involving towing and "booting" vehicles without notice, see Miller v. City of Chicago, 774 F.2d 188 (7th Cir.1985), cert. denied, 476 U.S. 1105, 106 S.Ct. 1949, 90 L.Ed.2d 358 (1986) (constitutional to tow recovered stolen vehicles without notice and then impose towing and storage charges on owner); Sutton v. City of Milwaukee, 672 F.2d 644 (7th Cir.1982) (police may tow illegally parked cars in non-emergency situations without notice); Grant v. City of Chicago, 594 F.Supp. 1441 (N.D.Ill.1984) (constitutional to boot

Manzo,[56] held it a denial of due process to fail to notify a divorced father of adoption proceedings undertaken by the mother and her second husband.[57] A hearing afforded the father on his motion to set aside the adoption decree did not cure the constitutional infirmity because this subsequent proceeding shifted the burden of proving whether the father had properly supported the child from those seeking adoption and placed it on the father.

Sniadach v. Family Finance Corporation[58] held that it violated due process to permit garnishment of the wages of a resident defendant without affording the defendant an opportunity to be heard until a subsequent trial on the merits of the alleged obligation, thus resulting in an interim freezing of the wages.

A series of Supreme Court cases involving pre-judgment[59] garnishment and replevin played variations on the *Sniadach* theme. *Fuentes v. Shevin*[60] struck down state statutes that permitted a private party,

illegally parked vehicles and collect boot fee when prompt post-deprivation hearing is provided). But cf. Wilson v. City of New Orleans, 479 So.2d 891 (La.1985) (booting vehicles for unpaid parking tickets is unconstitutional when decision is made by private contractor who receives a commission for each vehicle booted).

56.   380 U.S. 545, 85 S.Ct. 1187, 14 L.Ed.2d 62 (1965).

57.   But cf. Lehr v. Robertson, 463 U.S. 248, 103 S.Ct. 2985, 77 L.Ed.2d 614 (1983) (putative father of child born out of wedlock need not be given notice of adoption proceedings when father did not enter his name in a registry, which would have entitled him to notice).

58.   395 U.S. 337, 89 S.Ct. 1820, 23 L.Ed.2d 349 (1969). See also Termplan Inc. v. Superior Court, 105 Ariz. 270, 463 P.2d 68 (1969) (holding *Sniadach* limited to wage garnishment); McCallop v. Carberry, 1 Cal.3d 903, 83 Cal.Rptr. 666, 464 P.2d 122 (1970); Larson v. Fetherston, 44 Wis.2d 712, 172 N.W.2d 20 (1969) (*Sniadach* not limited to wage garnishment). Cf. Goldberg v. Kelly, 397 U.S. 254, 90 S.Ct. 1011, 25 L.Ed.2d 287 (1970) (if factual issues present, evidentiary hearing must be available to welfare recipients before their benefits are terminated).

59.   But see Grupo Mexicano de Desarrollo S.A. v. Alliance Bond Fund, 527 U.S. 308, 119 S.Ct. 1961, 144 L.Ed.2d 319 (1999) (federal courts lack power to issue a pre-judgment injunction ordering defendant not to transfer assets in which no lien or equitable interest is claimed); Fed.R.Civ.Proc. 64(a) states that "every remedy is available that, under the law of the state where the court is located, provides for seizing a person or property to secure satisfaction of the potential judgment."

Since 1975 English courts have issued "Mareva" injunctions freezing assets in England pending litigation in England. Mareva Compania Naviera S.A. of Panama v. International Bulk Carriers S.A., [1980] 1 All E.R. 213 (C.A. 1975). English courts have also issued injunctions to freeze English assets pending litigation in another country, X v. Y, [1989] 3 All E.R. 689 (Q.B.); or even to freeze assets outside of England pending litigation outside of England, Derby & Co. v. Weldon, [1989] 2 W.L.R. 412 (C.A.). English Civil Procedure Rules implemented in 1999 rename a Mareva injunction as a "freezing injunction."

For conflicting holdings on whether this series of Supreme Court cases is applicable to post-judgment garnishment, see Brown v. Liberty Loan Corp. of Duval, 539 F.2d 1355 (5th Cir.1976), cert. denied, 430 U.S. 949, 97 S.Ct. 1588, 51 L.Ed.2d 797 (1977) (not applicable); City Finance Co. v. Winston, 238 Ga. 10, 231 S.E.2d 45 (1976) (applicable). See also Bittner v. Butts, 514 S.W.2d 556 (Mo.1974) (permit garnishment without new hearing on sister state judgment registered in the forum); Scott, *Constitutional Regulation of Provisional Creditor Remedies: The Cost of Procedural Due Process,* 61 Va. L. Rev. 807, 866–67 (1975) (prejudgment hearings should be limited to "brutal need debtors" and there should be "a general requirement of prompt final adjudication").

60.   407 U.S. 67, 92 S.Ct. 1983, 32 L.Ed.2d 556 (1972). See Marran v. Gorman, 116 R.I. 650, 359 A.2d 694 (1976) (*Fuentes* not applied retroactively).

without a hearing or notice to the other party, to obtain a pre-judgment writ of replevin on application to a court clerk. *Mitchell v. W.T. Grant,*[61] however, upheld the Louisiana prejudgment ex parte sequestration procedure. The Court emphasized that in *Mitchell* the party seeking sequestration had a lien on the property before the action so that the property was not exclusively the debtor's. Moreover, the Louisiana procedure required that the creditor must first obtain a judge's[62] approval of the creditor's verified affidavit setting forth the existence of a lien, debt, and delinquency. Then the debtor could immediately demand dissolution of the writ unless the creditor proved the lien, debt, and delinquency. These elements of shared title, judicial supervision from the outset, specific rather than conclusory allegations required in the application for prejudgment remedy, and prompt post-seizure hearing[63] were sufficient to meet due process requirements.

As an indication that the Court was not ready to turn back the clock to pre-*Sniadach* time, *North Georgia Finishing, Inc. v. Di–Chem, Inc.*[64] invalidated ex parte prejudgment garnishment of a merchant buyer's bank account. The writ was issued by the ministerial action of a clerk and there was no opportunity for an early post garnishment hearing on the merits of the creditor's claim. In *Connecticut v. Doehr,*[65] the plaintiff effected a prejudgment attachment of defendant's realty so that assets would be available to satisfy a tort judgment that plaintiff was seeking. The Court held that Connecticut's procedure for prejudgment seizure of realty without exigent circumstances, posting a bond, or prior hearing, violated due process. The property owner then sued the person who had attached the property under 28 U.S.C. § 1983, which provides that "[e]very person who, under color of any statute . . . of any State . . . subjects . . . any citizen . . . to the deprivation of any rights, privileges, or immunities secured by the Constitution and laws, shall be liable to the party injured." The Second Circuit held that the property owner could recover if he proved "want of probable cause, malice, and damages."[66]

---

61. 416 U.S. 600, 94 S.Ct. 1895, 40 L.Ed.2d 406 (1974).

62. But see Hood Motor Co., Inc. v. Lawrence, 320 So.2d 111 (La.1975) (Louisiana sequestration procedure valid even though clerk, not judge, approves creditor's petition, but clerk exercises "quasi-judicial power"); Persinger v. Edwin Associates, Inc., 159 W.Va. 898, 230 S.E.2d 460 (1976) (pre-judgment writ of garnishment issued by clerk is valid when based on specific factual allegations).

63. See also Carey v. Sugar, 425 U.S. 73, 96 S.Ct. 1208, 47 L.Ed.2d 587 (1976) (remand case challenging constitutionality of New York pre-judgment remedy with instructions to three-judge federal district court to abstain until parties have had an opportunity to obtain a construction of the New York law from the New York state courts, but it is clear that any hearing would be after the attachment); Connolly Development, Inc. v. Superior Ct., 17 Cal.3d 803, 132 Cal.Rptr. 477, 553 P.2d 637 (1976), appeal dism'd for want of substantial federal question, 429 U.S. 1056, 97 S.Ct. 778, 50 L.Ed.2d 773 (1977) (although filing of mechanics' liens and orders to stop payment to general contractor involve state action and constitute a significant taking, the procedure is constitutional because of the availability of a prompt post-taking hearing).

64. 419 U.S. 601, 95 S.Ct. 719, 42 L.Ed.2d 751 (1975).

65. 501 U.S. 1, 111 S.Ct. 2105, 115 L.Ed.2d 1 (1991).

66. Pinsky v. Duncan, 79 F.3d 306, 312 (2d Cir. 1996) (also discussing the standard that other circuits have imposed for recovery under § 1983).

On the question of what kind of notice is reasonable, the leading case is *Mullane v. Central Hanover Bank & Trust Company.*[67] A New York bank had pooled over one hundred small trusts into a common trust fund for administrative convenience and economy. After administering the common fund for three years, the bank petitioned a New York court to accept the bank's first accounting as trustee. The only notice of this proceeding that the bank gave to the beneficiaries of the trusts was by publication in a local newspaper, setting forth the name and address of the bank, the name and date of establishment of the common trust fund, and a list of all participating trusts. The court appointed a special guardian for all persons known or unknown not otherwise appearing who might have any interest in the income of the common fund. This guardian appeared specially and objected that the notice to beneficiaries was inadequate and violated due process. The New York Court of Appeals overruled these objections and affirmed a final decree accepting the accounting and terminating any rights the beneficiaries might have against the bank for improper management of the common trust fund during the period covered by the accounting.

The Supreme Court reversed, holding that although the published notice was sufficient as to beneficiaries "whose interests or whereabouts could not with due diligence be ascertained"[68] and as to beneficiaries with remote or contingent interests, the notice was not reasonable as to "known present beneficiaries."[69] As to these latter beneficiaries, there was a violation of due process. In order for notice to be reasonable "[t]he means employed must be such as one desirous of actually informing the absentee might reasonably adopt to accomplish it."[70] "Where the names and post office addresses of those affected by a proceeding are at hand, the reasons disappear for resort to means less likely than the mails to apprise them of its pendency."[71] The Court emphasized that what was required was a reasonable attempt to notify parties in interest, not necessarily the best possible notice. Thus mailed notice was sufficient although personal service outside the court's jurisdiction might give greater assurance of actual notice.[72]

---

67. 339 U.S. 306, 70 S.Ct. 652, 94 L.Ed. 865 (1950).

68. Id. at 317, 70 S.Ct. at 659, 94 L.Ed. at 875. See also Acevedo v. First Union National Bank, 476 F.3d 861 (11th Cir. 2007) (published notice of need to claim insured deposits in failed bank sufficient as to depositors who were not identified by name or address in failed bank's records.)

69. Id. at 318, 70 S.Ct. at 659, 94 L.Ed. at 875.

70. Id. at 315, 70 S.Ct. at 657, 94 L.Ed. at 874.

71. Id. at 318, 70 S.Ct. at 659, 94 L.Ed. at 875.

72. Id. at 319, 70 S.Ct. at 659–60, 94 L.Ed. at 876. See also Velazquez v. Thompson, 451 F.2d 202 (2d Cir.1971) (personal service is not required if the plaintiff uses other reasonable means of giving notice; requiring personal service is likely to result in fraudulent certification of service). But cf. McDonald v. Mabee, 243 U.S. 90, 92, 37 S.Ct. 343, 344, 61 L.Ed. 608, 610 (1917) (Holmes, J.): "To dispense with personal service the substitute that is most likely to reach the defendant is the least that ought to be required if substantial justice is to be done."

Dusenbery v. United States[73] held that notice to a prisoner by certified mail of a property forfeiture proceeding was sufficient even though the prisoner did not receive the notice. Four dissenters viewed the notice as constitutionally deficient, because, quoting from *Mullane*, the method used was " 'substantially less likely to bring home notice' to prison inmates than a 'feasible ... substitut[e].' "[74] A prison officer had signed for the mail. The five-justice majority found that the method used was reasonably calculated to give notice and rejected the argument that the plaintiff must use a form of mail that required the prisoner personally sign the receipt.

Dusenbery thus authorizes a U.S. version of *notification au parquet*. Under this method of service, formerly used in France, the Netherlands, Greece, Belgium, and Italy, the plaintiff can effect service on a foreign defendant by depositing documents with a local official. Failure of the official to transmit the documents to the defendant does not affect the validity of the service. A major purpose of the Convention on the Service Abroad of Judicial and Extrajudicial Documents in Civil or Commercial Matters,[75] which the U.S. has ratified, was to abolish *notification au parquet* and similar forms of service that did not "ensure that judicial and extrajudicial documents to be served abroad shall be brought to the notice of the addressee in sufficient time."[76]

Methods of notice that generally meet the reasonableness requirement are personal service outside the jurisdiction,[77] mailed notice[78] and, in the case of a domiciliary, notice left at defendant's house.[79] What is reasonable depends on the circumstances. In *Covey v. Town of Somers*,[80]

---

73. 534 U.S. 161, 122 S.Ct. 694, 151 L.Ed.2d 597 (2002).

74. Id. at 178, 122 S.Ct. at 705, 151 L.Ed.2d at 611.

75. Opened for signature Nov. 15, 1965, 20 U.S.T. 361, 658 UNTS 163.

76. Id. preamble. See Volkswagenwerk Aktiengesellschaft v. Schlunk, 486 U.S. 694, 703–04, 108 S.Ct. 2104, 2110, 100 L.Ed.2d 722, 733–34 (1988) (discussing the Convention and *notification au parquet*).

77. Allen v. Superior Court, 41 Cal.2d 306, 259 P.2d 905 (1953).

As to the ability of the defendant to make a collateral attack on a judgment on the ground that the sheriff or other server has falsely certified that the defendant was personally served see Knowles v. Logansport Gaslight & Coke Co., 86 U.S. (19 Wall.) 58, 22 L.Ed. 70 (1874) (yes, personal judgment). But cf. Miedreich v. Lauenstein, 232 U.S. 236, 34 S.Ct. 309, 58 L.Ed. 584 (1914) (no, mortgage foreclosures).

See also Ashe v. Spears, 263 Md. 622, 284 A.2d 207 (1971), cert. denied, 406 U.S. 958, 92 S.Ct. 2061, 32 L.Ed.2d 344 (1972) (defendant may impeach return of service in action to foreclose right of redemption after tax sale, but defendant has burden of proof).

78. See Note, *Service of Process by Mail,* 74 Mich. L. Rev. 381, 405 (1975) (requiring a returned receipt is unnecessary and undesirable); cf. Fed R. Civ. P. 4(d)(1)(G) (stating that by "first-class mail or other reliable means" the plaintiff may notify the defendant of the commencement of the action and request that the defendant waive service of a summons). But see Miserandino v. Resort Properties, Inc., 345 Md. 43, 691 A.2d 208, cert. denied, 522 U.S. 953, 118 S.Ct. 376, 139 L.Ed.2d 292 (1997) (refusing to give faith and credit to a Virginia judgment, holding that service by first class mail violated due process, and stating that service should be by certified or registered mail that requires a signed receipt); cf. Fed R. Civ. P. 4(f)(2)(C)(ii) (stating that a plaintiff may effect service on an individual in a foreign country by "any form of mail that the clerk addresses and sends to the individual and that requires a signed receipt" if this is not "prohibited by the foreign country's law").

79. McDonald v. Mabee, 243 U.S. 90, 92, 37 S.Ct. 343, 344, 61 L.Ed. 608, 610 (1917).

80. 351 U.S. 141, 76 S.Ct. 724, 100 L.Ed. 1021 (1956). See also Robinson v. Hanrahan, 409 U.S. 38, 93 S.Ct. 30, 34 L.Ed.2d 47 (1972) (notice is invalid when mailed to home address of person known to be in jail).

the Supreme Court held that notice of proceedings to foreclose a tax lien mailed "to a person known to be an incompetent who is without the protection of a guardian"[81] was not reasonable. In *Pierce v. Board of County Commissioners,*[82] the Kansas Supreme Court held it unreasonable to resort to published notice of tax foreclosure action after an attempt to make personal service had failed. The defendant was a resident of the state and his address was on file with the county treasurer. When service includes documents in a language other than English, a court has required at least a summary in English;[83] but a court has held service of process in English on a person who does not read English sufficient to put the defendant on inquiry notice.[84]

Courts have taken various positions on the adequacy of notice mailed to the defendant's last known address when the defendant does not receive the notice. The Supreme Court of Hawaii has held notice by publication sufficient after diligent but fruitless attempts to serve a nonresident motorist by mail.[85] *Clemens v. District Court*[86] held that notice mailed to defendant's last known address was not constitutionally sufficient when in fact the defendant did not receive the mailed notice and the plaintiff used no other method of notice. An Iowa court has gone to the extreme of refusing to take jurisdiction over a nonresident motorist who ignored two notices from the post office to call for the registered-mail notice.[87] The next year, however, the same court refused to require diligence from the plaintiff in locating a nonresident motorist, holding that, for purposes of tolling the statute of limitations by proper service, the plaintiff may rely on the address that the defendant gave to local authorities at the time of the accident until the defendant gives notice of a change of address.[88]

---

81.   351 U.S. at 146, 76 S.Ct. at 727, 100 L.Ed. at 1026.

82.   200 Kan. 74, 434 P.2d 858 (1967). See also Township of Montville v. Block 69, Lot 10, 74 N.J. 1, 376 A.2d 909 (1977) (reasonable notice of tax foreclosure is required); cf. First Sav. & Loan Assoc. v. Furnish, 174 Ind.App. 265, 367 N.E.2d 596 (1977) (reasonable notice of tax sale must be given to mortgagor, but need not be given to mortgagee). But see Marlowe v. Kingdom Hall of Jehovah's Witnesses, 541 S.W.2d 121 (Tenn.1976) (published notice is sufficient for enforcement of tax lien).

83.   Julen v. Larson, 25 Cal.App.3d 325, 101 Cal.Rptr. 796 (1972).

84.   Commonwealth v. Olivo, 369 Mass. 62, 337 N.E.2d 904 (1975).

85.   Manley v. Nelson, 50 Hawaii 524, 443 P.2d 155 (1968), appeal dism'd & cert. denied, 394 U.S. 573, 89 S.Ct. 1299, 22 L.Ed.2d 555 (1969). Accord, Evans v. Galloway, 108 Idaho 711, 701 P.2d 659 (1985); Matter of Interest of M.L.K., 13 Kan.App.2d 251, 768 P.2d 316 (1989) (published notice is sufficient when mailed notice fails, termination of parental rights); Krueger v. Williams, 410 Mich. 144, 300 N.W.2d 910, appeal dism'd for want of juris., 452 U.S. 956, 101 S.Ct. 3102, 69 L.Ed.2d 967 (1981). Contra, Graham v. Sawaya, 632 P.2d 851 (Utah 1981). With regard to how much diligence is required, see Halliman v. Stiles, 250 Ark. 249, 464 S.W.2d 573 (1971) (not sufficiently diligent to mail notice to address on defendant's driver's license when correct address had been given to police officer and entered on accident report).

86.   154 Colo. 176, 390 P.2d 83 (1964).

87.   Emery Transp. Co. v. Baker, 254 Iowa 744, 119 N.W.2d 272 (1963).

88.   Kraft v. Bahr, 256 Iowa 822, 128 N.W.2d 261 (1964).

In the absence of extraordinary circumstances that make mailed notice unreasonable,[89] a diligent attempt to notify the nonresident motorist by mail should be constitutionally adequate. It is unnecessary and unwise to require that an absconded defendant in fact receive the mailed notice.[90] Perhaps as an added precaution, a service rule should require published notice if attempts at mailed notice fail.[91]

In addition to notice, there must be an opportunity to be heard.[92] Notice that must reach the defendant so close to the time of trial that there is no adequate opportunity to defend is not reasonable.[93] Moreover, the notice must be sufficiently descriptive of the plaintiff's claim so that the defendant can make an intelligent decision as to whether to appear or to permit a default judgment.[94]

Actual notice is not necessary if the attempt to notify is reasonable, but actual notice will not suffice if the forum's statutory scheme does not require a reasonable attempt to notify. *Wuchter v. Pizzutti*[95] invalidated a nonresident motorist statute that required only service on an official of the forum state. In that case, although the New Jersey statute in issue did not require it, notice of the action was actually served personally on the defendant in Pennsylvania. With regard to this actual notice, the Court stated: "Not having been directed by the statute it cannot, therefore, supply constitutional validity to the statute or to service under

---

89. See notes 85–88 and accompanying text, supra this section.

90. Richardson v. Williams, 201 So.2d 900 (Fla. Dist. Ct. App. 1967); Swift v. Leasure, 285 A.2d 428 (Del.Super.1971). Cf. Hugel v. McNell, 886 F.2d 1 (1st Cir.1989), cert. denied, 494 U.S. 1079, 110 S.Ct. 1808, 108 L.Ed.2d 939 (1990) (published notice is sufficient when the defendants go into hiding). But cf. Miller & Crump, *Jurisdiction and Choice of Law in Multistate Class Actions After Phillips Petroleum Co. v. Shutts,* 96 Yale L. J. 1, 19 (1986) (actual notice and opportunity to opt out may be required in multi-state class actions in order to bind plaintiffs without forum contacts). The authors point out that in *Phillips Petroleum v. Shutts,* the court said "[t]he plaintiff must receive notice." 472 U.S. at 812, 105 S.Ct. at 2974, 89 L.Ed.2d at 642. In the next sentence, however, the Court says "[t]he notice must be the best practicable" and cites *Mullane,* which permitted published notice when no other notice was practicable.

91. See Ashley v. Hawkins, 293 S.W.3d 175 (Tex. 2009): "If Hawkins was unable to locate Ashley, or if Hawkins thought Ashley was evading service, other methods of service were available. In particular, no substitute service such as service by publication was attempted".

92. See Payne v. Superior Court, 17 Cal.3d 908, 132 Cal.Rptr. 405, 553 P.2d 565 (1976) (contrary to both state and federal constitutions to deny an indigent prisoner both the right of personal appearance and counsel in a civil suit).

93. Roller v. Holly, 176 U.S. 398, 20 S.Ct. 410, 44 L.Ed. 520 (1900). See Convention on the Service Abroad of Judicial and Extrajudicial Documents in Civil or Commercial Matters, Nov. 15, 1965, 20 U.S.T. 361, 658 UNTS 163, Preamble: "The States signatory to the present Convention, Desiring to create appropriate means to ensure that judicial and extrajudicial documents to be served abroad shall be brought to the notice of the addressee in sufficient time. . . ."

94. See Hansen v. Haagensen, 178 N.W.2d 325 (Iowa 1970), cert. denied, 401 U.S. 912, 91 S.Ct. 879, 27 L.Ed.2d 811 (1971) (cannot change quasi in rem to in personam proceeding without notice); Chapman v. Chapman, 284 App.Div. 504, 132 N.Y.S.2d 707 (1954) (action for separation amended to one for divorce without adequate notice); Ware v. Phillips, 77 Wn.2d 879, 468 P.2d 444 (1970) (garnishment writ invalid in not informing garnishees that a judgment might be taken against them if they failed to answer); cf. Aguchak v. Montgomery Ward Co., 520 P.2d 1352 (Alaska 1974) (violation of Alaska constitution for summons not to inform indigent defendant in remote area of right to change of venue).

95. 276 U.S. 13, 48 S.Ct. 259, 72 L.Ed. 446 (1928).

it."[96] The Court did cite, among other authorities, the following passage from *Roller v. Holly*: "The right of a citizen to due process of law must rest upon a basis more substantial than favor or discretion."[97] This doctrine, that actual notice will not suffice if the service rule does not require reasonable, has been carried to the extreme of denying recognition to a judgment under a Canadian nonresident motorist statute.[98] The Canadian statute required only published notice, but the defendant had, pursuant to an order of the Canadian court under the court's statutory discretion, received notice by mail.

It is interesting to contrast *Wuchter's* hard line on required notice with *National Equipment Rental, Ltd. v. Szukhent.*[99] *Szukhent* held that a party to a private contract may appoint an agent to receive service of process within the meaning of Federal Rule of Civil Procedure 4(d)(1)[100] even though the agent is not personally known to the party and has not expressly undertaken to transmit notice to the party, at least if the agent in fact does notify the party. The Court said: "A different case would be presented if [the agent] had not given prompt notice to the respondents, for then the claim might well be made that her failure to do so had operated to invalidate the agency."[101] The Court distinguished *Wuchter* on the ground that in *Szukhent* the defendant raised no due process objection.[102]

The requirement that notice be reasonable does not vary with the kind of judicial jurisdiction exercised, whether in personam, in rem, or quasi in rem. *Mullane* itself illustrates this in holding published notice insufficient as to known beneficiaries although the proceeding might have been classified as "in rem" since it terminated any rights that any beneficiary, known or unknown, might have against the bank for im-

---

96. Id. at 24, 48 S.Ct. at 262, 72 L.Ed. at 452. See also Sanders v. Sanders, 12 Md.App. 441, 278 A.2d 615 (1971); Ridenour v. County of Bay, 366 Mich. 225, 114 N.W.2d 172 (1962).

97. 176 U.S. 398, 409, 20 S.Ct. 410, 414, 44 L.Ed. 520, 524 (1900).

98. Boivin v. Talcott, 102 F.Supp. 979 (N.D.Ohio, 1951). But cf. Mazzoleni v. Transamerica Corp., 313 Pa. 317, 169 A. 127 (1933) (requirement for mailed notice held implied). But see Housing Authority of Atlanta v. Hudson, 250 Ga. 109, 296 S.E.2d 558 (1982) (posting and mailing notice to tenant is sufficient if tenant answers, but is insufficient if he does not) (dictum); Tripp v. Tripp, 240 S.C. 334, 126 S.E.2d 9 (1962), cert. denied, 371 U.S. 888, 83 S.Ct. 187, 9 L.Ed.2d 123 (1962) (actual notice deprives plaintiff of standing to attack constitutionality of Ohio statute that did not provide for giving to nonresidents notice of probate proceedings); City of Houston v. Parkinson, 419 S.W.2d 900 (Tex.Civ.App. 1967), writ ref'd n.r.e. (actual notice cures constitutional defect in statute requiring only published notice of assessment proceedings).

99. 375 U.S. 311, 84 S.Ct. 411, 11 L.Ed.2d 354 (1964).

100. Federal Rules of Civil Procedure 4(d): "The summons and complaint shall be served together. The plaintiff shall furnish the person making service with such copies as are necessary. Service shall be made as follows: (1) Upon an individual ... by delivering a copy of the summons and of the complaint to an agent authorized by appointment or by law to receive service of process." This was the Rule at the time of *Szukhent*. The substance of former 4(d)(1) is now in 4(e)(2) with stylistic changes.

101. 375 U.S. at 318, 84 S.Ct. at 415, 11 L.Ed.2d at 359.

102. Id. at 315, 84 S.Ct. at 414, 11 L.Ed.2d at 357.

proper management of the common trust fund during the period covered by the accounting.

Even though the plaintiff knows the defendant's location, it may be that notice other than by personal service or by mail will be reasonable. For example, in a dispute over ownership of a bank account on which the defendant is constantly drawing, attachment of the account is as likely to come to the defendant's attention as notice mailed to that party.[103] In general, however, the Supreme Court cases seem to establish that if mailed notice is feasible and the notice used is not likely to result in actual notice, the notice is constitutionally defective even though the judicial proceedings affect the party's interest in property within the court's jurisdiction and do not result in a personal judgment. *Walker v. Hutchison*[104] held that newspaper publication of condemnation proceedings against realty was not reasonable notice of those proceedings when the condemning officials knew the name of the landowner. *Schroeder v. New York*[105] also involved condemnation proceedings. In *Schroeder* the notice was by newspaper publication and by posting in the vicinity of the property, but not on it. The posting took place in January when the owners did not occupy the property, a summer home. The court held this notice insufficient to meet due process standards when the contemnors could readily ascertain the property owner's name and address from deed and tax records. The court said in *Schroeder* that "[t]he general rule that emerges from the *Mullane* case is that notice by publication is not enough with respect to a person whose name and address are known or very easily ascertainable and whose legally protected interests are directly affected by the proceedings in question."[106]

---

103. See Mullane v. Central Hanover Bank & Trust Co., 339 U.S. 306, 316, 70 S.Ct. 652, 658, 94 L.Ed. 865, 874 (1950) ("Nor is publication here reinforced by steps likely to attract the parties' attention to the proceeding. It is true that publication traditionally has been acceptable as notification supplemental to other action which in itself may reasonably be expected to convey a warning."); cf. Pennoyer v. Neff, 95 U.S. 714, 727, 24 L.Ed. 565, 570 (1878): "Substituted service by publication, or in any other authorized form, may be sufficient to inform parties of the object of proceedings taken where property is once brought under the control of the court by seizure or some equivalent act. The law assumes that property is always in the possession of its owner, in person or by agent; and it proceeds upon the theory that its seizure will inform him, not only that it is taken into the custody of the court, but that he must look to any proceedings authorized by law upon such seizure for its condemnation and sale."

104. 352 U.S. 112, 77 S.Ct. 200, 1 L.Ed.2d 178 (1956).

105. 371 U.S. 208, 83 S.Ct. 279, 9 L.Ed.2d 255 (1962).

106. Id. at 212–13, 83 S.Ct. at 282, 9 L.Ed.2d at 259. See also Mennonite Board of Missions v. Adams, 462 U.S. 791, 103 S.Ct. 2706, 77 L.Ed.2d 180 (1983) (mortgagee entitled to more notice of tax sale than given by posting in courthouse and publishing); Pierce v. Board of County Comm'rs, 200 Kan. 74, 434 P.2d 858 (1967) (tax sale); Hazard, supra note 49, at 277; cf. Greene v. Lindsey, 456 U.S. 444, 102 S.Ct. 1874, 72 L.Ed.2d 249 (1982) (forcible entry and detainer notice posted on door is not sufficient when such notices were frequently removed before seen by tenants); Womble v. Commercial Credit Corp., 231 Ga. 569, 203 S.E.2d 204 (1974) ("abode" service unconstitutional). But see Golden v. State, 373 Mich. 664, 131 N.W.2d 55 (1964) (tax sale); Tripp v. Tripp, 240 S.C. 334, 126 S.E.2d 9 (1962) cert. denied, 371 U.S. 888, 83 S.Ct. 187, 9 L.Ed.2d 123 (1962) (probate); Jenkins v. Waxahachie, 392 S.W.2d 482 (Tex.Civ.App.1965), writ ref'd n.r.e. (municipal ordinance providing for the impounding of dogs running at large and for the sale or destruction of

Tulsa Professional Collection Services, Inc. v. Pope[107]extended to probate proceedings the rule that published notice is not sufficient if better notice is feasible. *Tulsa* invalidated provisions in many probate codes, including the Uniform Probate Code,[108] requiring only published notice to creditors of the estate and cutting off claims not filed within a short time, typically four months,[109] after publication.

Many courts had assumed that the short nonclaim probate periods passed constitutional muster as statutes of limitations.[110] Justice O'Connor, however, distinguished the nonclaim probate provisions from "a self-executing statute of limitations" on the ground that "[h]ere, in contrast there is significant state action" in the form of probate court proceedings.[111] Thus "state action" again rears its head as the supposed key to due process analysis. Perhaps a more cogent basis for distinction was the unreasonably short period after which the nonclaim statute barred actions by creditors of the estate. Both Chief Justice Rehnquist, who dissented, and Justice O'Connor left open the question of whether, in any event, the shortness of the nonclaim period itself violated due process.[112] On remand, the issue would be whether the creditor's identity was "reasonably ascertainable" by "reasonably diligent efforts."[113] If not, "publication notice can suffice."[114]

Even some of the older Supreme Court opinions that seem to permit notice by publication alone in quasi in rem proceedings, do not, on careful examination, support that proposition. In *Pennington v. Fourth National Bank,*[115] a wife residing in Ohio had sued her nonresident husband in Ohio for divorce and had obtained, in addition to the divorce, an order that an Ohio bank pay to the wife as alimony the amount of a bank deposit in the name of the husband. Mr. Justice Brandeis stated that the husband was "served by publication only,"[116] yet Brandeis concluded that the proceeding was constitutional:

> Substituted service on a nonresident by publication furnishes no legal basis for a judgment in personam. Pennoyer v. Neff.... But garnishment or foreign attachment is a proceeding quasi in rem....

---

any impounded dog that is not redeemed within 72 hours is constitutional notwithstanding failure to provide for notice and judicial determination of ordinance violation).

107.   485 U.S. 478 108 S.Ct. 1340, 99 L.Ed.2d 565 (1988).

108.   8(II) U.L.A. 208, § 3–801(a). The Comment to the section warns that "if *Tulsa* ... applies to this code [publication] is useless except to bar unknown creditors." Id. at 209. § 3–801(b) provides that "[a] personal representative may give written notice by mail or other delivery to a creditor...."

109.   Id. The Oklahoma nonclaim period applicable in *Tulsa* was two months.

110.   *Tulsa*, 485 U.S. at 486, 108 S.Ct. at 1345, 99 L.Ed.2d at 576.

111.   Id.

112.   485 U.S. at 488, 108 S.Ct. at 1346, 99 L.Ed.2d at 577 (Justice O'Connor); Id. at 494, 108 S.Ct. at 1350, 99 L.Ed.2d at 581 (Chief Justice Rehnquist, dissenting).

113.   Id. at 491, 108 S.Ct. at 1348, 99 L.Ed.2d at 579.

114.   Id. at 490, 108 S.Ct. at 1347, 99 L.Ed.2d at 578.

115.   243 U.S. 269, 37 S.Ct. 282, 61 L.Ed. 713 (1917).

116.   Id. at 270, 37 S.Ct. at 282, 61 L.Ed. at 714.

The thing belonging to the absent defendant is seized and applied to the satisfaction of his obligation. The Federal Constitution presents no obstacle to the full exercise of this power.[117]

On its face, this Brandeis opinion seems solid authority that, at least formerly, notice by publication alone was sufficient if the judicial proceeding did not result in a personal judgment but affected the defendant's interest in property in the forum. It should be noted, however, that at the commencement of the wife's action, she had joined the bank in which the husband's account was deposited and had the court enjoin the bank from paying out any part of the deposit. This tying-up of the account was very likely to come to the attention of the husband. Moreover, the Ohio statute under which the wife effected service by "publication" required that, in addition to newspaper publication, the plaintiff either furnish the clerk of court copies of the publication for the clerk to mail to the defendant or must file an affidavit that the plaintiff does not know defendant's residence and cannot with reasonable diligence ascertain the address,[118] It is not surprising during the regime of *Pennoyer v. Neff,* when courts assumed that only personal service within the forum would confer judicial jurisdiction over a nonresident defendant, that the mailed notice provision of the Ohio statute did not receive special attention and was thought of as just an adjunct to service by publication.

The modern Supreme Court opinions seem to establish that, when judicial proceedings affect the interest in property of a person whose interest and whereabouts the plaintiff knows or can easily ascertain, published notice unaccompanied by other acts likely to notify the person of the proceeding does not meet due process requirements. But what of non-judicial proceedings that affect interest in property, such as assessments for improvements? The legislature may impose obligations on property owners without giving the owners any notice or opportunity to be heard, such as by passing a new property tax. But due process requires a hearing for the assessment of burdens on property when this assessment is not done by the legislature or by a body acting with delegated legislative authority.[119] Published notice alone of the hearing

---

117. Id. at 271, 37 S.Ct. at 283, 61 L.Ed. at 715. But see § 4.28 discussing Shaffer v. Heitner, 433 U.S. 186, 97 S.Ct. 2569, 53 L.Ed.2d 683 (1977), which limited the use of in rem and quasi in rem jurisdiction.

118. Ohio Gen. Code § 11294 (1910): "When in a case in which service may be made by publication, the residence of the defendant is known, it must be stated in the publication. Immediately after the first publication, the party making the service shall deliver copies thereof, with the proper postage, to the clerk of the court who shall mail a copy to each defendant, direct to his place of residence named therein, and make an entry thereof on the appearance docket. In all other cases the party who makes the service, his agent or attorney, before the hearing, must make and file an affidavit that the residence of the defendant is unknown and cannot with reasonable diligence be ascertained."

119. See Browning v. Hooper, 269 U.S. 396, 405, 46 S.Ct. 141, 143, 70 L.Ed. 330, 335 (1926): "Where a local improvement territory is selected, and the burden is spread by the legislature or by a municipality to which the State has granted full legislative powers over the subject, the owners of property in the district have no constitutional right to be heard on the question of benefits. But it is essential to due process of law that such owners be given notice and opportunity to be heard on that question where, as here, the district was

to persons that the assessors know or could easily ascertain have an interest in the property and their addresses, should be held inconsistent with due process. Perhaps in quieter times in smaller communities, notices published in the local paper proposing assessments and setting a time for the hearing of objections, were reasonable notice. But the day should be gone when the modern city dweller can be told that rights to object to an assessment on land are forfeit because the owner did not appear at a hearing, "notice" of which was buried in the mass of legal announcements in the back pages of the local paper, and many courts are coming to recognize this.[120]

§ 4.5   Waiver of Notice and Opportunity to be Heard

A party may waive notice and opportunity to be heard by agreement in advance of any litigation.[121] The classic method of making this "waiver" is the cognovit clause. This is a clause in a note or contract that empowers a creditor's attorney to confess judgment in favor of the

---

not created by the legislature, and there has been no legislative determination that their property would be benefited by the local improvement."

City of Houston v. Fore, 412 S.W.2d 35, 37 (Tex.1967): "Under the United States Constitution an owner ordinarily is not entitled to notice or hearing before assessment of the cost of public improvements in accordance with an inflexible legislative formula. The rule is otherwise, however, where the legislature, instead of prescribing an inflexible formula, authorizes an administrative determination of the lands benefited and the amount of benefits accruing to each tract."

Even if no hearing is constitutionally required, it is arguable that, as a matter of equal protection, if a hearing is in fact held, reasonable notice is necessary. Cf. Cipriano v. City of Houma, 395 U.S. 701, 89 S.Ct. 1897, 23 L.Ed.2d 647 (1969) (if a challenged state statute grants right to vote to some voters and denies it to others, the court must determine whether exclusions are necessary to promote a compelling state interest, and no less a showing that the exclusions are necessary is required merely because the question scheduled for election need not have been submitted to the voters).

120.   See International Salt Co. v. Herrick, 367 Mich. 160, 116 N.W.2d 328 (1962); Meadowbrook Manor, Inc. v. City of St. Louis Park, 258 Minn. 266, 104 N.W.2d 540 (1960); City of Houston v. Fore, 412 S.W.2d 35 (Tex.1967); Wisconsin Electric Power Co. v. Milwaukee, 275 Wis. 121, 81 N.W.2d 298 (1957) (after remand "for consideration in the light of Walker v. City of Hutchison", remanded at 352 U.S. 948, 77 S.Ct. 324, 1 L.Ed.2d 241 (1956)). But cf. City of Cedar Rapids v. Cox, 250 Iowa 457, 93 N.W.2d 216 (1958), appeal dism'd for want of sub. fed. question, 359 U.S. 498, 79 S.Ct. 1118, 3 L.Ed.2d 976 (1959) (annexation proceedings constitutional although statute provided only published notice when all but 18 of 1500 citizens in fact received mailed notice and proceedings publicized in news media); Dodson v. Ulysses, 219 Kan. 418, 549 P.2d 430 (1976) (no right to notice of proposed improvement or of meeting at which amount of assessment set so long as there is opportunity to challenge the amount later); Karpenko v. Southfield, 75 Mich.App. 188, 254 N.W.2d 839 (1977) appeal dism'd for want of substantial federal question, 435 U.S. 919, 98 S.Ct. 1479, 55 L.Ed.2d 513 (1978) (published notice to adjoining landowners of zoning change is sufficient and there is no equal protection violation in requiring mailed notice only to railroads and utilities); Jones v. Village of Farnam, 174 Neb. 704, 119 N.W.2d 157 (1963) (published notice of public hearing on resolution of necessity for improvements that will result in assessments sufficient even though objection from owners of majority of front footage that might become subject to assessment would compel defeat of resolution).

121.   See, e.g., National Equipment Rental, Ltd. v. Szukhent, 375 U.S. 311, 316, 84 S.Ct. 411, 414, 11 L.Ed.2d 354, 358 (1964) ("parties to a contract may agree in advance to submit to the jurisdiction of a given court, to permit notice to be served by the opposing party, or even to waive notice altogether"); Hazel v. Jacobs, 78 N.J.L. 459, 75 A. 903 (Ct. of Errors & App.1910); Copin v. Adamson, L.R. 9 Exch. 345 (1874).

creditor in a specific court, or sometimes in any court of record. The clause permits the creditor to obtain this confession of judgment without any notice to the debtor. States that have outlawed such agreements for domestic use grant full faith and credit to sister-state judgments obtained on the basis of cognovit clauses.[122]

The Federal Trade Commission has declared use of a cognovit clause in a consumer credit transaction "an unfair act or practice"[123] but such clauses are used in transactions between businesses. *D.H. Overmyer Co. v. Frick Co.*[124] held that cognovit clauses do not *per se* violate due process. In *Overmyer* two corporations and their counsel negotiated the cognovit clause as part of the settlement of an ongoing dispute. Moreover, under the relevant state procedure, even after entry of judgment, a debtor able to show a valid defense could reopen the judgment. The Court did note that "where the contract is one of adhesion, where there is great disparity in bargaining power, and where the debtor receives nothing for the cognovit provisions, other legal consequences may ensue."[125]

In *Swarb v. Lennox,*[126] the court refused to declare the Pennsylvania statutory cognovit procedure unconstitutional on its face. In *Swarb,* a three-judge court had declared the Pennsylvania practice unconstitutional with regard to individual debtors with incomes of less than $10,000 per year unless the creditor showed that the debtor "intentionally, understandingly and voluntarily"[127] waived notice. The three-judge court approved the Pennsylvania procedure when the cognovit clause is likely to be the product of a valid consent, such as in real estate mortgage transactions that require special warnings to the signer. The Supreme Court did not decide whether the Pennsylvania procedures were invalid to the extent decreed below because only the debtors appealed contend-

---

122. Trauger v. A.J. Spagnol Lumber Co., Inc., 442 So.2d 182 (Fla.1983); Egley v. T.B. Bennett & Co., 196 Ind. 50, 145 N.E. 830 (1924); McDade v. Moynihan, 330 Mass. 437, 115 N.E.2d 372 (1953). But cf. Hutson v. Christensen, 295 Minn. 112, 203 N.W.2d 535 (1972) (deny full faith and credit to Illinois judgment on ground it invalid in Illinois); Rogers v. Rogers, 290 So.2d 631 (Miss.), cert. denied, 419 U.S. 837, 95 S.Ct. 65, 42 L.Ed.2d 64 (1974) (deny recognition of Alabama divorce on ground that waiver of process was fraudulently obtained, but no inquiry into whether this made judgment subject to collateral attack in Alabama). But see Atlas Credit Corp. v. Ezrine, 25 N.Y.2d 219, 303 N.Y.S.2d 382, 250 N.E.2d 474 (1969) (refuse to grant full faith and credit to Pennsylvania cognovit judgment on the alternative grounds that a cognovit judgment is not a "judicial proceeding" within the meaning of Article IV, Section 1 of the U.S. Const. and that exercise of jurisdiction based on the cognovit clause's waiver of notice violated due process).

123. 16 C.F.R. § 444.2(a)(1). Previously only a few states permitted cognovit clauses in consumer transactions. See Report of the Presiding Officer on Proposed Trade Regulation Rule on Credit Practices 313 (Fed.Trade Comm. August, 1978) (use of confessions of judgment is primarily confined to Illinois, Louisiana, and Pennsylvania). Pennsylvania has also changed its law to forbid use of cognovit clauses in consumer credit transactions. Pa. R.C.P. 2950.

124. 405 U.S. 174, 92 S.Ct. 775, 31 L.Ed.2d 124 (1972).

125. Id. at 188, 92 S.Ct. at 783, 31 L.Ed.2d at 135.

126. 405 U.S. 191, 92 S.Ct. 767, 31 L.Ed.2d 138 (1972).

127. 314 F.Supp. 1091, 1103 (E.D.Pa.1970).

ing that the judgment had not gone far enough and that the Pennsylvania procedure was totally invalid.

Overmyer and *Swarb* indicate that the constitutional validity of a cognovit procedure turns on whether, in circumstances that do not indicate unconscionable overreaching, one party knowingly and voluntarily waived notice and opportunity to be heard.[128] Another factor to consider is the remedy available to the debtor after a court enters judgment. The easier it is for the debtor to open the judgment and prove a valid defense, the less prejudice and the more likely that the cognovit procedure is valid.[129] These two elements of a valid cognovit agreement, knowing and voluntary waiver and ease of opening the judgment, are closely related. One of the issues that the debtor may wish to raise in opening the judgment is whether the waiver was knowing and voluntary.[130]

§ 4.6 Continuing Jurisdiction

Once having acquired in personam jurisdiction over the parties, a court retains this jurisdiction throughout the trial and such supplementary and subsequent proceedings as are necessary to do justice between the parties with regard to the original cause of action.[131] Sometimes courts rendering support, alimony, and custody decrees retain jurisdiction for many years to modify the original decrees on application of one of the parties who alleges changed circumstances.[132] Although the court

---

128. See, e.g., the following cases upholding cognovit judgments: First Nat'l Bk. in DeKalb v. Keisman, 47 Ill.2d 364, 265 N.E.2d 662 (1970) (agreement between two knowledgeable businessmen); Billingsley v. Lincoln Nat'l Bk., 271 Md. 683, 320 A.2d 34 (1974) (defendants are endorsers and guarantors of cognovit note signed by corporation, no showing of adhesion); Huggins v. Dement, 13 N.C.App. 673, 187 S.E.2d 412 (1972), appeal dism'd for lack of substantial federal question, 281 N.C. 314, 188 S.E.2d 898 (1972), appeal dism'd for want of juris., cert. denied, 409 U.S. 1071, 93 S.Ct. 677, 34 L.Ed.2d 659 (1972) (no allegation of unequal bargaining power).

129. See Isbell v. County of Sonoma, 21 Cal.3d 61, 145 Cal.Rptr. 368, 577 P.2d 188 (1978), cert. denied, 439 U.S. 996, 99 S.Ct. 597, 58 L.Ed.2d 669 (1978) (one factor causing the court to declare unconstitutional the use of cognovit agreements against welfare recipients was that after six months the judgment could be set aside only for extrinsic fraud); Note, 34 Univ.Pitt. L. Rev. 103, 113 (1972).

130. See Billingsley v. Lincoln Nat'l Bk., 271 Md. 683, 320 A.2d 34 (1974) (no need for pre-judgment hearing on whether waiver knowing and voluntary if opportunity for the defendant to raise this issue after judgment).

131. See Ohlquist v. Nordstrom, 143 Misc. 502, 257 N.Y.S. 711 (1932), aff'd mem., 238 App.Div. 766, 261 N.Y.S. 1039, aff'd mem., 262 N.Y. 696, 188 N.E. 125 (1933) (motion for contribution from co-defendant); DiRusso v. DiRusso, 55 Misc.2d 839, 287 N.Y.S.2d 171 (1968) (jurisdiction to vacate fraudulently obtained divorce); Blumle v. Kramer, 14 Ok. 366, 79 P. 215 (1904) (jurisdiction to enter deficiency judgment after foreclosure); Fitzsimmons v. Johnson, 90 Tenn. 416, 17 S.W. 100 (1891) (petition in error filed twenty-two years after probate decree); Restatement, Second, § 26; cf. Mattel, Inc. v. Greiner & Hausser GmbH, 354 F.3d 857 (9th Cir. 2003) (party to prior suit has jurisdiction over other party to enforce that party's stipulation of dismissal made 40 years earlier). But see New York Life Ins. Co. v. Dunlevy, 241 U.S. 518, 36 S.Ct. 613, 60 L.Ed. 1140 (1916) (judgment debtor not subject to jurisdiction of court in subsequent interpleader proceedings instituted by insurer whose indebtedness to judgment debtor was attached by judgment creditor).

132. See, e.g., Opperman v. Sullivan, 330 N.W.2d 796 (Iowa 1983) (continuing jurisdiction to punish for contempt). See also Morse v. Morse, 394 So.2d 950 (Ala.1981) (recognize sister-state judgment reducing past due alimony and support to judgment, but subject to

retains jurisdiction, it is necessary to give a party notice and opportunity to be heard in such modification proceedings.[133] Even an application to enter judgment for accrued and unpaid alimony requires notice to the other spouse if, as is true in some states, the court's power of modification extends even to such accrued sums.[134]

It is not clear to what extent notice and opportunity to be heard are necessary in supplementary proceedings to obtain satisfaction of an unpaid judgment. In *Endicott–Johnson Corp. v. Encyclopedia Press, Inc.,*[135] the plaintiff had recovered a judgment against the defendant's employee, but execution thereon was returned unsatisfied. Then, without notice to the employee, the court awarded the creditor execution against the employee's wages, and directed the employer to pay over to the creditor each week ten percent of the employee's wages until the execution was satisfied. When the employer refused to make these payments, the creditor sued the employer to recover the accumulated unpaid percentages of the weekly wages. The New York courts affirmed a judgment for the creditor. The Supreme Court affirmed stating:

> [T]he established rules of our system of jurisprudence do not require that a defendant who has been granted an opportunity to be heard and has had his day in court, should, after a judgment has been rendered against him, have a further notice and hearing before supplemental proceedings are taken to reach his property in satisfaction of the judgment.[136]

---

defenses available there); Nolan v. Nolan, 488 So.2d 1260 (La.App. 4 Cir.1986), writ denied, 492 So.2d 1218 (1986) (continuing jurisdiction exercised after 17 years to divide military retirement benefits); Glading v. Furman, 282 Md. 200, 383 A.2d 398 (1978) (divorce court may order child support four years after father has left the state even though the original decree was silent on this issue). But see Veazey v. Veazey, 246 Ga. 376, 271 S.E.2d 449 (1980) (refuse to recognize Mississippi judgment exercising continuing jurisdiction to terminate alimony after wife has moved to Georgia); Frye v. Crowell, 563 S.W.2d 788 (Tenn.1978) (it would be a violation of due process to exercise jurisdiction in custody dispute after all parties have established residences in other states). For a suggestion that continuing jurisdiction not be exercised over custody when, because of a change in residence of all or some of the parties, the original court is no longer a convenient forum for determination of the child's best interests, see § 5.3B. Under 28 U.S.C.A. § 1738A(d), (f), another state may modify a custody decree if the state that rendered the original decree is no longer the residence of the child or of any contestant.

133. See, e.g., Commonwealth ex rel. Milne v. Milne, 149 Pa.Super. 100, 106, 26 A.2d 207, 210 (1942) modified, 150 Pa.Super. 606, 29 A.2d 228 (1942), allocatur ref'd ("The authorities generally hold that jurisdiction once having been obtained in domestic relation actions, subsequent proceedings require only notice and a reasonable opportunity to be heard, which notice may be sent to the party outside the State") (dictum).

134. Griffin v. Griffin, 327 U.S. 220, 66 S.Ct. 556, 90 L.Ed. 635 (1946).

135. 266 U.S. 285, 45 S.Ct. 61, 69 L.Ed. 288 (1924).

136. Id. at 288, 45 S.Ct. at 62–63, 69 L.Ed. at 292. See also Brown v. Liberty Loan Corp. of Duval, 539 F.2d 1355 (5th Cir.1976), cert. denied, 430 U.S. 949, 97 S.Ct. 1588, 51 L.Ed.2d 797 (1977) (wages may be garnished in post-judgment proceedings without prior notice); Huggins v. Deinhard, 134 Ariz. 98, 654 P.2d 32 (App., Div. I, 1982) (may garnish bank account without notice to satisfy sister-state judgment); Haas v. Haas, 282 Minn. 420, 165 N.W.2d 240 (1969) (judgment for support arrears, entered without notice, is entitled to full faith and credit); Bittner v. Butts, 514 S.W.2d 556 (Mo.1974) (sister state judgment may be levied upon before hearing on its validity). But cf. Dionne v. Bouley, 757 F.2d 1344 (1st Cir.1985) (need not notify judgment debtor before attachment, but must give notice of opportunity to challenge attachment that includes general statement that debtor may be

Knight v. DeMarcus[137] indicates some of the difficulties with the position that after judgment the defendant is not entitled to notice of supplementary proceedings. In *Knight,* the plaintiff had acted as a special master in the defendant's divorce proceedings. In that action the plaintiff was awarded a fee of slightly over $5,000 for his services. When his fee remained unpaid for four months, the plaintiff secured an execution and at the execution sale, for approximately the amount of his judgment, purchased real property belonging to the defendant. The only notice of the plaintiff's intention to execute on the property in question was by publication and public posting. The defendant claimed that, because she did not receive notice, she was unable to invoke her privilege under state law to specify which property the sheriff is to seize, was unable to demand that the sheriff first levy on personal property, and was unable to prevent the plaintiff from acquiring, for about $5,000, property that the defendant valued at $40,000. In an action by the plaintiff to quiet title to the property, an Arizona court affirmed summary judgment for the plaintiff. The Supreme Court granted certiorari[138] "to determine whether *Endicott* should be overruled."[139] Then the court dismissed the writ as improvidently granted.[140] It would seem then, that the continued viability of *Endicott Johnson* is deservedly in doubt.[141] The

---

entitled to state and federal exemptions). But see Villano v. Harper, 248 So.2d 205 (Fla.App.1971) (refuse full faith and credit to Colorado judgment for support arrears rendered without notice); City Finance Co. v. Winston, 238 Ga. 10, 231 S.E.2d 45 (1976) (post-judgment garnishment without judicial supervision or hearing violates due process).

137. 102 Ariz. 105, 425 P.2d 837 (1967), cert. dism'd sub nom. Hanner v. Demarcus, 390 U.S. 736, 88 S.Ct. 1437, 20 L.Ed.2d 270 (1968).

138. Sub nom. Hanner v. Demarcus, 389 U.S. 926, 88 S.Ct. 288, 19 L.Ed.2d 277 (1967).

139. 390 U.S. 736, 737, 88 S.Ct. 1437, 1438, 20 L.Ed.2d 270, 271 (1968) (Douglas, J., dissenting from dismissal of certiorari).

140. 390 U.S. 736, 88 S.Ct. 1437, 20 L.Ed.2d 270 (1968). In his brief on the merits, respondent argued that Arizona statutes in fact required notice to the debtor and that by failing to invoke these sections the petitioner had bypassed state grounds that entitled her to relief. Id. at 738, 88 S.Ct. at 1438, 20 L.Ed.2d at 271.

141. See Morrell v. Mock, 270 F.3d 1090 (7th Cir. 2001), cert. denied, 537 U.S. 812, 123 S.Ct. 71, 154 L.Ed.2d 14 (2002): ("*Endicott* does not entirely foreclose consideration of whether the Due Process Clause requires post-judgment notice or other procedures." Id. at 1097. Mother was entitled to notice before her child removed to another state where paternity suit pending, but because "it was not clearly established that the procedures were constitutionally infirm" [id. at 1102] mother could not recover on 42 U.S.C. § 1983 claim against law enforcement officers who took child. Section 1983 creates civil liability for depriving a person of constitutional rights under color of law).

See also Follette v. Vitanza, 658 F.Supp. 492, 514 (N.D.N.Y. 1987) (post-judgment procedures violate due process if debtors receive no notice of procedures for challenging wage garnishment); Gedeon v. Gedeon, 630 P.2d 579 (Colo.1981), appeal dism'd for want subst. fed. question, 454 U.S. 1050, 102 S.Ct. 592, 70 L.Ed.2d 585 (1981) (due process requirements for post-judgment proceedings are unclear, but notice, stay, and hearing provisions of Uniform Enforcement of Foreign Judgments Act, which permits registration of sister-state judgments, are certainly sufficient); Detamore v. Sullivan, 731 S.W.2d 122 (Tex.App.—Houston [14th Dist.], 1987, no writ) (Uniform Foreign Money–Judgments Recognition Act, which permits registering foreign country judgments, violates due process because, unlike the uniform act for registering sister-state judgments, it contains no provision for notice and hearing before execution). But cf. Beverly v. Owens, 494 So.2d 65 (Ala.1986) (cannot make collateral attack on Mississippi probate judgment for damages when plaintiff appeared but did not receive notice of additional claim).

defendant should receive notice and opportunity to be heard in supplementary execution proceedings in order to be able to assert any right under state law to limit the execution or to raise any defense, including payment of the judgment.

§ 4.7   The Contact that Makes It Reasonable to Adjudicate (Nexus): Comparison of State and Federal Courts

Turning from notice to nexus, the purpose here, before reviewing the leading United States Supreme Court cases in section 4.8 and a detailed look in sections 4.10 through 4.29 at the historical bases for judicial jurisdiction, is to take a preliminary overview of the nature of the contact with a state that is necessary to meet due process requirements for judicial jurisdiction. As the word "state" in the preceding sentence indicates, the focus of this chapter is on the judicial jurisdiction of state rather than federal courts. In diversity cases, a federal court's jurisdiction is, absent some specific federal jurisdictional provision such as 28 U.S.C.A. § 2361 (nation-wide service in interpleader), dependent on the constitutional reach of the long-arm statutes of the state in which it sits.[142]

To be sure, much of what is said of judicial jurisdiction in the state context is also applicable to federal courts. The basic concepts of reasonableness and fairness for due process are the same. It is nevertheless true that there are important differences in due process limitations on the judicial jurisdiction of state courts as compared with federal courts.

When speaking of the judicial jurisdiction of a state court, we focus on whether there is some contact between the state and the person whose rights the court is adjudicating in personam or the property in which the court is adjudicating interests in rem or quasi in rem. Unless there is some contact with the state that makes it reasonable for the state court to proceed, there is a violation of due process. Within the state there is, so far as due process is concerned, statewide jurisdiction once the required state nexus is present. On the other hand, the constitutional judicial jurisdiction of federal courts is generally assumed to be nation-wide, except perhaps in rare situations in which the inconvenience and unfairness to the defendant is so extreme as to violate due

---

In Peralta v. Heights Medical Center, Inc., 485 U.S. 80, 108 S.Ct. 896, 99 L.Ed.2d 75 (1988), holding void a judgment if obtained without notice, the judgment debtor did not receive notice of the execution sale of his realty, but this was not raised or considered as an independent due process objection.

142. See Federal Rule of Civil Procedure 4(k)(1)(A); Omni Capital Int'l v. Rudolf Wolff & Co., Ltd., 484 U.S. 97, 108 S.Ct. 404, 98 L.Ed.2d 415 (1987) (the Commodity Exchange Act does not provide for nationwide service of process, common-law service will not be devised, so federal court's jurisdiction depends on long-arm statute of the state in which it sits); Arrowsmith v. United Press Int'l, 320 F.2d 219 (2d Cir.1963); Bowman v. Curt G. Joa, Inc., 361 F.2d 706 (4th Cir.1966); Caso v. Lafayette Radio Elec. Corp., 370 F.2d 707 (1st Cir.1966); Wilshire Oil Co. v. Riffe, 409 F.2d 1277 (10th Cir.1969); Wright & Miller, Federal Practice and Proc.: Civil § 1075; Moore & Vestal, Federal Practice and Proc. §§ 6.08, 6.11 (1966); cf. Yoder v. Yamaha Int'l Corp., 331 F.Supp. 1084 (E.D.Pa.1971) (after transfer under 28 U.S.C.A. § 1404(a), transferee court looks to law of transferor state to determine jurisdictional reach).

process—a circumstance which, because of federal venue limitations, is unlikely to occur.[143]

Why is there this difference in measuring the jurisdiction of state and federal courts? Assuming a reasonable nexus between the defendant and the United States, why, when dealing with federal courts, do we ask whether, under all the circumstances, it would be reasonable to exercise in personam jurisdiction over the defendant in a particular federal district, but, when dealing with state courts, we limit this quest for reasonableness to actual physical contacts between the defendant and the forum, or to specific acts performed there, or specific consequences caused there? State lines may provide a measure of convenience to the parties, but only a very rough one. A trip of a hundred miles may cross several state boundaries or may span only a few counties in one of the larger states.

Convenience may also turn on the reach of compulsory process for the attendance of witnesses and production of documents. In state courts this process, in the absence of reciprocal legislation, runs only to the state line. But this reason for measuring state-court jurisdiction in terms of nexus with the state may be circular. If it is reasonable to adjudicate in personam against the defendant in a state court even though that state has no physical nexus with that defendant or with the acts or consequences the defendant has performed or caused, then it may also be reasonable for that state to compel attendance of witnesses and production of documents across state lines.

It may also be that requiring nexus with a state will afford some guarantee that the state will have some "interest" in adjudicating the case and applying its own law to its resolution. But this concern with a

---

143. That due process limits the nationwide jurisdiction of federal courts, see Clermont, *Restating Territorial Jurisdiction and Venue for State and Federal Courts,* 66 Cornell L. Rev. 411, 434–35 (1981); Foster, *Long–Arm Jurisdiction in Federal Courts,* 1969 Wis. L. Rev. 9, 35–36 (1969); Fullerton, *Constitutional Limits on Nationwide Personal Jurisdiction in the Federal Courts,* 79 Nw. L. Rev. 3, 4 (1984); Note, 61 B.U. L. Rev. 403, 404–05 (1981); cf. Quinones v. Pennsylvania General Ins. Co., 804 F.2d 1167 (10th Cir.1986) (Federal Rule 4(f) [now 4(k)(1)(B)], which extends service over some parties to within 100 miles of the place in which the action is pending, including adjacent states, is narrow enough to be consistent with due process); Sprow v. Hartford Ins. Co., 594 F.2d 412, 416 (5th Cir.1979) (the due process test of jurisdiction under Federal Rule of Civil Procedure 4(f) [now 4(k)(1)(B)] is "whether the party served had minimum contacts with the forum state or the bulge area so that it is fair and substantially just for the forum to impose a judgment upon the party"). But see Stafford v. Briggs, 444 U.S. 527, 554, 100 S.Ct. 774, 789, 63 L.Ed.2d 1, 21 (1980) (Stewart, J. dissenting from holding that nationwide service provisions of 28 U.S.C.A. § 1391(e) do not apply to actions for money damages brought against federal officials in their individual capacities—due process imposes no limits on nationwide jurisdiction of federal courts); Mississippi Publishing Corp. v. Murphree, 326 U.S. 438, 442, 66 S.Ct. 242, 245, 90 L.Ed. 185, 190 (1946) (dictum, "Congress could provide for service of process anywhere in the United States"); Medical Mutual of Ohio v. deSoto, 245 F.3d 561, 566–67 (6th Cir. 2001) (the nationwide service provisions of the Employee Retirement Income Security Act confer personal jurisdiction over defendant even though defendant lacked contacts with the forum state); Hogue v. Milodon Engineering, Inc., 736 F.2d 989 (4th Cir.1984) (due process does not limit the nationwide jurisdiction of bankruptcy courts); Fitzsimmons v. Barton, 589 F.2d 330 (7th Cir.1979) (jurisdiction in securities fraud action under the Securities Exchange Act is nationwide subject only to venue limits, sole remedy for action in inconvenient forum is motion for transfer under 28 U.S.C.A. § 1404(a)).

state being able to advance its own substantive policies would point toward permitting a state, which has a relevant substantive policy, to exercise judicial jurisdiction provided only that, under all the circumstances, not only nexus, it is reasonable to do so. This is probably a desirable step in the development of our law of judicial jurisdiction, but one that we have not yet taken. In large part, the insistence on thinking of state judicial jurisdiction as ending with the state boundaries and therefore requiring that the defendant have some reasonable nexus with the state is due to our history. We had sovereign states before we were a nation, our constitutional rules have developed along these lines, and we are not yet ready to break with the past and do the hard re-analysis necessary to provide a different and more flexible basis for the allocation of judicial jurisdiction in a federal nation.[144] Australia, another federal nation, has since 1992 provided nation-wide jurisdiction with transfer to another court if the defendant demonstrates inconvenience.[145] Such a re-analysis and the new constitutional standard it would produce is presented in section 4.8A(2)(D).

There have been important developments in the area of in personam jurisdiction of state courts. The changes, originally in the direction of expanding state-court jurisdiction, seem to have reversed course. The best perspective from which to view this process are the United States Supreme Court opinions that have construed the due process limitation on state-court jurisdiction.

§ 4.8 Nexus: The Supreme Court Cases

Chaos and confusion have marked attempts by conscientious state and federal judges[146] to apply the Supreme Court's prescriptions for state-court jurisdiction. Many recent decisions have thwarted reasonable attempts to obtain jurisdiction over nonresident parties.[147] The time is

---

144. See Woodward v. Keenan, 79 Mich.App. 543, 261 N.W.2d 80 (1977) (no jurisdiction over clinic in neighboring state 50 miles from plaintiff's home that misdiagnosed plaintiff's condition and forwarded its report to plaintiff's doctor in the forum); U–Anchor Advertising, Inc. v. Burt, 553 S.W.2d 760 (Tex.1977), cert. denied, 434 U.S. 1063, 98 S.Ct. 1235, 55 L.Ed.2d 763 (1978) (no jurisdiction over customer in neighboring state 150 miles away on same interstate highway); Developments in the Law, *State–Court Jurisdiction,* 73 Harv. L. Rev. 909, 917, 924–25 (1960). But see Wilkerson v. Fortuna Corp., 554 F.2d 745 (5th Cir.1977), cert. denied, 434 U.S. 939, 98 S.Ct. 430, 54 L.Ed.2d 299 (1977) (finding of jurisdiction influenced by fact defendant's business just across state line within sight of courthouse).

145. Service & Execution of Process Act 1992 §§ 12, 130; Jurisdiction of Courts (Cross–Vesting) Act 1987 § 5.

146. Federal judges decide the limits of state-court jurisdiction because in cases in which federal jurisdiction rests upon diversity of citizenship of the parties, a federal court's jurisdiction is usually dependent on the jurisdiction of the courts of the state in which it sits. See supra § 4.7 note 142.

147. See, e.g., Mountaire Feeds, Inc. v. Agro Impex, S.A., 677 F.2d 651 (8th Cir.1982) (no jurisdiction over buyer of feed manufactured to specifications in forum); Premier Corp. v. Newsom, 620 F.2d 219 (10th Cir.1980) (tax services, but contract did not require performance in the forum); Barnstone v. Congregation Am Echad, 574 F.2d 286 (5th Cir.1978) (no jurisdiction for payment for plans drafted in forum); Grobark v. Addo Mach. Co., 16 Ill.2d 426, 158 N.E.2d 73 (1959) (distributor denied jurisdiction over manufacturer in suit for manufacturer's breach of exclusive distributorship agreement); Adcock v. Surety

already late for the Court to undertake a rational reallocation of state-court jurisdictional authority.

There are two major obstacles to needed change. First, the Court has stated that due process limitations on state-court jurisdiction are shaped not only by fairness to the defendant, but also by comity to sovereign sister states.[148] Second, the Court has defined fairness to the defendant in terms of a specific contact between defendant and forum that makes it reasonable for the forum to exercise jurisdiction.[149]

Although it is too early for celebration, the first of these obstacles, the federalism incantation, may be passing from the scene.[150] The requirement of nexus between forum and defendant, however, dogs the steps of jurisdictional reform that focuses on fairness to the defendant under all the circumstances, not just contacts between forum and defendant. Justice Brennan has declared that, even applied more expansively than in recent Court decisions, the traditional standards of *"International Shoe* and its progeny . . . may already be obsolete as constitutional boundaries."[151] A number of thoughtful scholars have attempted to articulate a method of assuring fairness to nonresident defendants under which invisible state lines are not barriers to jurisdictional reform.[152]

Research & Inv. Corp., 344 So.2d 969 (La.1977) (legal drafting); Moki Mac River Expeditions v. Drugg, 221 S.W.3d 569 (Tex. 2007) (no jurisdiction over hiking-rafting company when forum resident died on hike arranged from forum).

148. See, e.g., World–Wide Volkswagen Corp. v. Woodson, 444 U.S. 286, 291–93, 100 S.Ct. 559, 564–65, 62 L.Ed.2d 490, 498–99 (1980).

149. See, e.g., id. at 291, 100 S.Ct. at 564, 62 L.Ed.2d at 497–98.

150. See Insurance Corp. of Ireland, Ltd. v. Compagnie des Bauxites de Guinee, 456 U.S. 694, 702 n. 10, 102 S.Ct. 2099, 2104 n. 10, 72 L.Ed.2d 492, 501 n. 10 (1982) (Justice White recanting his language cited, supra, note 148).

151. World–Wide Volkswagen Corp. v. Woodson, 444 U.S. 286, 299, 100 S.Ct. 559, 581, 62 L.Ed.2d 490, 503 (1980) (Brennan, J., dissenting).

152. See, e.g., Braveman, *Interstate Federalism and Personal Jurisdiction,* 33 Syracuse L. Rev. 533, 534 (1982); Clermont, *Restating Territorial Jurisdiction and Venue for State and Federal Courts,* 66 Cornell L. Rev. 411, 437, 447–48 (1981); Hazard, *Interstate Venue,* 74 Nw. L. Rev. 711 (1979); Lewis, *A Brave New World for Personal Jurisdiction: Flexible Tests Under Uniform Standards,* 37 Vand. L. Rev. 1, 5 (1984); L. McDougal III, *Judicial Jurisdiction: From a Contacts to an Interest Analysis,* 35 Vand. L. Rev. 1, 14 (1982); Redish, *Due Process, Federalism, and Personal Jurisdiction: A Theoretical Evaluation,* 75 Nw. L. Rev. 1112, 1114–15, 1133, 1137 (1981); Silberman, *Can the State of Minnesota Bind the Nation?: Federal Choice-of-Law Constraints After Allstate Insurance Co. v. Hague,* 10 Hofstra L. Rev. 103, 116 (1981); von Mehren, *Adjudicatory Jurisdiction: General Theories Compared and Evaluated,* 63 B.U. L. Rev. 279 (1983); Weinberg, *The Place of Trial and the Law Applied: Overhauling Constitutional Theory,* 59 Colo. L. Rev. 67, 102–03 (1988); Note, 69 Cornell L. Rev. 136, 163 (1983).

Not all scholars view the requirement of contacts between defendant and forum as unduly restrictive. See Brilmayer, *How Contacts Count: Due Process Limitations on State Court Jurisdiction,* 1980 S.Ct.Rev. 77, 82, which suggests limiting specifically-affiliating contacts to events that would have to be plead as part of the cause of action in a purely domestic suit. A contact that is specifically affiliating is one that makes it reasonable to exercise judicial jurisdiction only as to causes of action that are related to the contact. This contrasts with a generally-affiliating contact, which makes it reasonable to exercise judicial jurisdiction over the defendant as to any cause of action. See infra § 4.9C.

For the effect the Brilmayer test would have on the exercise of jurisdiction, see Kingsley & Keith (Canada) Ltd. v. Mercer Int'l Corp., 500 Pa. 371, 379, 456 A.2d 1333, 1338, cert.

This section and the next add to this burgeoning dialogue concerning the desirability of jurisdictional reform in the United States. The following review of the major Supreme Court opinions focuses on the development of the twin requirements of federalism and contacts that are obstacles to any attempt at reform.

A. CASES BEFORE 1977

There are four United States Supreme Court cases decided before 1977 that have had the most significant effect in shaping state-court jurisdiction. The now familiar litany is *Pennoyer v. Neff*,[153] *International Shoe Company v. Washington*,[154] *McGee v. International Life Insurance Co.*,[155] and last, but far from least, *Hanson v. Denckla*.[156] These cases sounded three themes that have been repeated to the present day and with which any scheme to reshape jurisdictional concepts must contend. These themes are the importance of federalism and comity to sovereign sister states, the requirement that the defendant have at least certain minimum contacts with the forum, and the irrelevance to jurisdictional considerations of choice of law.

Pennoyer v. Neff[157] permitted a collateral attack on an Oregon judgment that applied a nonresident defendant's interest in Oregon land to the payment of a debt. The Court held that the judgment not only was not a proper exercise of jurisdiction over the defendant's interest in property, but also was not a valid personal judgment. The Court said that a state court could render a valid personal judgment against a nonresident only if the defendant is "brought within its jurisdiction by service of process within the State, or his voluntary appearance."[158] This is the now displaced doctrine that a court must base its jurisdiction on physical power over the defendant. What has not been displaced, at least not so patently,[159] is the notion that constitutional restrictions on the

---

denied, 464 U.S. 982, 104 S.Ct. 423, 78 L.Ed.2d 358 (1983). Although an equally divided court affirmed jurisdiction over a transporter of chemicals that defendant picked up in the forum and delivered elsewhere in a contaminated condition, half of the judges voted against affirmance because the contamination did not take part in the forum, quoting from the Brilmayer article. See also Hay, *Refining Personal Jurisdiction in the United States,* 35 Int'l & Comp.L.Q. 32, 35–6 (1986); Lilly, *Jurisdiction over Domestic and Alien Defendants,* 69 Va. L. Rev. 85, 114–15 (1983) (contacts requirement should be retained, but not "confined to the deliberate, affirmative activity mandated by the Court in *Volkswagen*"); Peterson, *Jurisdiction and Choice of Law Revisited,* 59 U.Colo. L. Rev. 37, 56 (1988); Note, 61 B.U. L. Rev. 403, 421 (1981) (requiring forum contacts helps assure that the case can be conveniently tried there).

153. 95 U.S. (5 Otto) 714, 24 L.Ed. 565 (1878).

154. 326 U.S. 310, 66 S.Ct. 154, 90 L.Ed. 95 (1945).

155. 355 U.S. 220, 78 S.Ct. 199, 2 L.Ed.2d 223 (1957).

156. 357 U.S. 235, 78 S.Ct. 1228, 2 L.Ed.2d 1283 (1958).

157. 95 U.S. (5 Otto) 714, 24 L.Ed. 565 (1878). For the historical background of *Pennoyer,* see Perdue, *Sin, Scandal, and Substantive Due Process: Personal Jurisdiction and Pennoyer Reconsidered,* 62 Wash. L. Rev. 479 (1987).

158. *Pennoyer*, 95 U.S. at 733, 24 L.Ed. at 572.

159. See supra notes 148–150 and accompanying text.

personal jurisdiction of a state court serve a federalism function by preventing offense to sister states:

> [A]ny direct exertion of authority [by a state] upon [persons or property outside the state] in an attempt to give ex-territorial operation to its laws, or to enforce an ex-territorial jurisdiction by its tribunals, would be deemed an encroachment upon the independence of the State in which the persons are domiciled or the property is situated, and be resisted as usurpation.[160]

In the context of *Pennoyer*'s power theory of jurisdiction, this federalism-comity rationale has a cogency that it will lose when exercise of jurisdiction over absent defendants no longer turns on the forum's ability to compel their physical presence.

International Shoe Company v. Washington[161] marks the break with the power basis for jurisdiction. The case held that Washington could exercise jurisdiction over a foreign corporation to recover delinquent contributions to the state's unemployment compensation fund. The contributions were a percentage of wages paid to the company's salesmen who solicited orders in Washington. The opinion said, contrary to *Pennoyer*,[162] that a defendant, though not served within the state, could be subjected to personal jurisdiction if "he have certain minimum contacts with it such that the maintenance of the suit does not offend 'traditional notions of fair play and substantial justice.' "[163] The Court pointed out that defendant's activities in Washington "resulted in a large volume of interstate business, in the course of which [defendant] received the benefits and protection of the laws of the state" and "[t]he obligation which is here sued upon arose out of those very activities."[164] Thus was born a jurisdictional standard of fairness to the defendant that had to be satisfied by contacts between forum and defendant. The Court did speak of "[a]n 'estimate of the inconveniences' which would result to the corporation from a trial away from its 'home' or principal place of business,"[165] but this was in addition to, not a substitute for, the "minimum contacts" requirement.

McGee v. International Life Insurance Co.[166] is the high-water mark of personal jurisdiction. That decision permitted California to exercise jurisdiction over a Texas insurer in a suit on the only policy that the Texas defendant had ever issued or solicited in California. The Court noted "that a trend is clearly discernible toward expanding the permissi-

---

160.   *Pennoyer*, 95 U.S. at 723, 24 L.Ed. at 569.

161.   326 U.S. 310, 66 S.Ct. 154, 90 L.Ed. 95 (1945).

162.   Pennoyer v. Neff, 95 U.S. (5 Otto) 714, 24 L.Ed. 565 (1878).

163.   *International Shoe*, 326 U.S. at 316, 66 S.Ct. at 158, 90 L.Ed. at 102.

164.   Id. at 320, 66 S.Ct. at 160, 90 L.Ed. at 104.

165.   Id. at 317, 66 S.Ct. at 158, 90 L.Ed. at 102.

166.   355 U.S. 220, 78 S.Ct. 199, 2 L.Ed.2d 223 (1957). See also In Matter of All–Star Ins. Corp., 110 Wis.2d 72, 327 N.W.2d 648 (1983), appeal dism'd want subst. fed. quest., 461 U.S. 951, 103 S.Ct. 2419, 77 L.Ed.2d 1309 (1983) (jurisdiction upheld in suit by receiver of forum insurer to enforce obligation to insurer by reason of any agency or brokerage contract without other contacts—*McGee* said to have "continuing validity").

ble scope of state jurisdiction over foreign corporations and other nonresidents"[167] and traced this trend to transportation and communication
developments that "have made it much less burdensome for a party sued
to defend himself in a State where he engages in economic activity."[168]
Thus even in this most expansive of the Court's jurisdictional opinions,
the *sine qua non* is forum-defendant contacts.

Hanson v. Denckla[169] was the first of the post *International Shoe*
Supreme Court cases to invalidate a state's exercise of jurisdiction. The
Court held that Florida did not have jurisdiction over a Delaware trustee
who had received and acted on instructions mailed from Florida by the
settlor of the trust. The trustee had also remitted trust income to the
settlor in Florida. The opinion stated that "[h]owever minimal the
burden of defending in a foreign tribunal, a defendant may not be called
upon to do so unless he has had the 'minimal contacts' with that State
that are a prerequisite to its exercise of power over him."[170] The most
famous passage in the opinion, and the one that has had the most
inhibiting effect on the expansion of personal jurisdiction, is the language that defines what qualifies as "minimum contacts":

> The unilateral activity of those who claim some relationship with a
> nonresident defendant cannot satisfy the requirement of contact
> with the forum State. . . . [I]t is essential in each case that there be
> some act by which the defendant purposefully avails itself of the
> privilege of conducting activities within the forum State, thus invok-
> ing the benefits and protections of its laws.[171]

Federal and state courts struggling with the problem of constitutional
limits on personal jurisdiction have repeated many times these words,
"unilateral activity," "purposefully avails," "benefits and protections of
its laws."

Another note sounded in *Hanson* and repeated in five subsequent
Supreme Court opinions,[172] was the absence of any relationship between

---

167.   *McGee,* 355 U.S. at 222, 78 S.Ct. at 201, 2 L.Ed.2d at 226.

168.   Id. at 223, 78 S.Ct. at 201, 2 L.Ed.2d at 226. Carrington, *Virtual Civil Litigation: A
Visit to John Bunyan's Celestial City,* 98 Colum. L. Rev. 1516, 1535 (1988), states that soon
methods of distant communication over the internet will "almost" eliminate convenience of
access to court as a due process consideration. See 70 U.S. Law Week 2629, 2630 (2002)
(announcing publication for public comment of rules creating a "cybercourt" in Michigan
for commercial litigation "designed to operate without any human beings in the court-
room").

169.   357 U.S. 235, 78 S.Ct. 1228, 2 L.Ed.2d 1283 (1958).

170.   Id. at 251, 78 S.Ct. at 1238, 2 L.Ed.2d at 1296.

171.   Id. at 253, 78 S.Ct. at 1239–40, 2 L.Ed.2d at 1298.

172.   Shaffer v. Heitner, 433 U.S. 186, 215–16, 97 S.Ct. 2569, 2585–86, 53 L.Ed.2d 683,
704–05 (1977); Kulko v. Superior Court, 436 U.S. 84, 98, 98 S.Ct. 1690, 1700, 56 L.Ed.2d
132, 145 (1978); World–Wide Volkswagen Corp. v. Woodson, 444 U.S. 286, 294, 100 S.Ct.
559, 566, 62 L.Ed.2d 490, 499–500 (1980); Rush v. Savchuk, 444 U.S. 320, 325 n.8, 100
S.Ct. 571, 575 n.8, 62 L.Ed.2d 516, 523 n.8 (1980); Keeton v. Hustler Magazine, Inc., 465
U.S. 770, 778, 104 S.Ct. 1473, 1480, 79 L.Ed.2d 790, 800 (1984). See Stein, *Styles of
Argument and Interstate Federalism in the Law of Personal Jurisdiction,* 65 Texas L. Rev.
689, 753 (1987) ("when the Court has resorted to the maxim that 'the issue is jurisdiction,
not choice of law,' the result probably should have been different").

choice of forum law to decide the case and the forum's exercise of personal jurisdiction. As the majority understood it, Florida had applied its own law to determine the validity of a trust.[173] The trust instrument had been executed in Delaware and named a Delaware trustee. At that time, the settlor was domiciled in Pennsylvania. The Court addressed the relationship between choice of law and jurisdiction in three passages:

> For the purpose of applying its rule that the law of the State of its creation determines the validity of a trust, Florida ruled that the appointment amounted to a "republication" of the original trust instrument in Florida. For choice-of-law purposes such a ruling may be justified, but we think it an insubstantial connection with the trust agreement for purposes of determining the question of personal jurisdiction over a nonresident defendant.[174]
>
>   * * *
>
> As we understand [Florida] law, the trustee is an indispensable party over whom the court must acquire jurisdiction before it is empowered to enter judgment in a proceeding affecting the validity of a trust. It does not acquire that jurisdiction by being the "center of gravity" of the controversy, or the most convenient location for litigation. The issue is personal jurisdiction, not choice of law.[175]
>
>   * * *
>
> [The conclusion that Florida does not have jurisdiction over the Delaware trustee] makes unnecessary any consideration of appellants' contention that the contacts the trust agreement had with Florida were so slight that it was a denial of due process of law to determine its validity by Florida law.[176]

Thus was begun the Court's attempt to divorce jurisdiction from choice of law.

B. CASES SINCE 1977

Shaffer v. Heitner[177] held that a shareholder could not bring a derivative stockholders' suit could against nonresident corporate di-

---

173. 357 U.S. at 253, 78 S.Ct. at 1239, 2 L.Ed.2d at 1297. But see id. at 256–57 n. 1, 78 S.Ct. at 1241 n. 1, 2 L.Ed.2d at 1299 n. 1 (Black, J., dissenting): "In my judgment it is a mistake to decide this case on the assumption that the Florida courts invalidated the trust.... [A]ll they held was that an appointment made in Florida ... was ... testamentary ... and ineffective...." Although the Florida Supreme Court did label the trust as "illusory," it held the appointment invalid because of its ambulatory nature as revealed by a scrutiny of the original trust provisions. Hanson v. Denckla, 100 So.2d 378, 383 (Fla.1956), rev'd, 357 U.S. 235, 78 S.Ct. 1228, 2 L.Ed.2d 1283 (1958). For a suggestion that the result in *Hanson* is explainable on the ground that choice of Florida law was unreasonable, see A. von Mehren & D. Trautman, The Law of Multistate Problems 1342 (1965).

174. *Hanson*, 357 U.S. at 253, 78 S.Ct. at 1239, 2 L.Ed.2d at 1297–98.

175. Id. at 254, 78 S.Ct. at 1240, 2 L.Ed.2d at 1298.

176. Id. at 254, n.27, 78 S.Ct. at 1240 n.27, 2 L.Ed.2d 1298 at n.27.

177. 433 U.S. 186, 97 S.Ct. 2569, 53 L.Ed.2d 683 (1977).

rectors by exercising quasi in rem jurisdiction over their stock and other corporate rights. *Shaffer* is thus a landmark case restricting[178] the use of quasi in rem jurisdiction. Several aspects of the opinion are, however, relevant to this discussion of in personam jurisdiction.

The court again disclaimed the notion, tracing to *Pennoyer,*[179] that "territorial power is both essential to and sufficient for jurisdiction"[180] and declared that "all assertions of state-court jurisdiction must be evaluated according to the standards [of fair play and substantial justice] set forth in *International Shoe* and its progeny."[181]

Far more troublesome for development of a coherent theory of personal jurisdiction, is that portion of Justice Marshall's majority opinion that expresses doubt whether Delaware had a constitutional basis for personal jurisdiction over the directors of a Delaware corporation in a derivative stockholders' suit. Once again, the Court drew a sharp distinction between jurisdiction and choice of law, declaring that the fact that a court should apply Delaware law to determine the liability of the directors, did not mean that Delaware had a basis for personal jurisdiction over them.[182] This is untenable. It is fair to compel directors to respond to a derivative stockholders' suit in the state of incorporation. To borrow a phrase from a later case, *World–Wide Volkswagen Corp. v. Woodson,* they could "reasonably anticipate being haled into court there"[183] to account for their actions as directors. Moreover, if the state of incorporation cannot obtain jurisdiction over all directors, no other state is likely to be able to do so. Since *Shaffer,* Delaware has enacted a long-arm statute giving it personal jurisdiction over directors of Delaware corporations in actions against them for violation of their duties[184] and the Supreme Court of Delaware has held it constitutional.[185]

Kulko v. Superior Court[186] held that a father's acquiescence in his child's desire to move to California to live with the mother did not give

---

178.   There are at least four uses of in rem jurisdiction that survive *Shaffer*. See § 4.27.

179.   Pennoyer v. Neff, 95 U.S. (5 Otto) 714, 24 L.Ed. 565 (1878).

180.   *Shaffer*, 433 U.S. at 211, 97 S.Ct. at 2583, 53 L.Ed.2d at 702.

181.   Id. at 212, 97 S.Ct. at 2584–85, 53 L.Ed.2d at 703.

182.   Id. at 215–16, 97 S.Ct. at 2585–86, 53 L.Ed.2d at 704–05.

183.   444 U.S. 286, 297, 100 S.Ct. 559, 567, 62 L.Ed.2d 490, 501 (1980). The *Shaffer* opinion does state that "appellants had no reason to expect to be haled before a Delaware court." 433 U.S. at 216, 97 S.Ct. at 2586, 53 L.Ed.2d at 705. This statement is based on the fact that, at the time suit was brought, Delaware did not have a long-arm statute conferring personal jurisdiction over directors of Delaware corporations in derivative stockholders' suits. The statement is not responsive to the question of whether such a statute could constitutionally be applied to the defendants. McGee v. International Life Ins. Co., 355 U.S. 220, 78 S.Ct. 199, 2 L.Ed.2d 223 (1957), held that a California statute, which conferred jurisdiction over insurance companies that insured California residents, could be applied retroactively because the statute "was remedial, in the purest sense of that term, and neither enlarged nor impaired respondent's substantive rights or obligations under the contract." 355 U.S. at 224, 78 S.Ct. at 201–02, 2 L.Ed.2d at 226–27. In fact, the Delaware statute that was enacted after the decision in *Shaffer,* does not apply retroactively (10 Del.C. § 3114(a)), but, in the light of *McGee,* this is not a constitutional requirement.

184.   10 Del.C. § 3114.

185.   Armstrong v. Pomerance, 423 A.2d 174 (Del.1980).

186.   436 U.S. 84, 98 S.Ct. 1690, 56 L.Ed.2d 132 (1978).

California courts jurisdiction over the father in a suit to increase child-support payments. The opinion gave three reasons for this result. First, "[t]he cause of action herein asserted arises, not from the defendant's commercial transactions in interstate commerce, but rather from his personal, domestic relations."[187] Second, the only contact that the father had with California was giving his daughter a one-way ticket to there from New York, the former marital domicile. To utilize this nexus as a basis for compelling the father to litigate in California a modification of a support agreement negotiated and signed in New York "would impose an unreasonable burden on family relations, and one wholly unjustified by the 'quality and nature' of appellant's activities in or relating to the State of California."[188] Third, California's "interest in ensuring the support of children resident in California without unduly disrupting the children's lives"[189] could be protected by utilizing the procedures of the Uniform Reciprocal Enforcement of Support Act (URESA), in force in both California and New York.[190]

Kulko is a difficult case and reasonable persons might differ as to whether due process should have prevented exercise of jurisdiction over the father.[191] He did, after all, send his daughter to the forum to live with his former wife. There are several aspects of the opinion that are especially troublesome for development of sound jurisdictional theory.

The opinion's focus on the non-commercial nature of the problem[192] should not mean that reasonable long-arm concepts are not applicable to jurisdiction for child support. If, for example, a husband sends his wife and children to a distant state promising to join them, but then does not, the state of his dependents' new residence should be able to exercise

---

187. Id. at 97, 98 S.Ct. at 1699, 56 L.Ed.2d at 144.

188. Id. at 98, 98 S.Ct. at 1700, 56 L.Ed.2d at 142. For decisions after *Kulko* finding an absent parent did not have sufficient contact with the forum for personal jurisdiction in a support proceeding, see, e.g. Kumar v. Superior Ct., 32 Cal.3d 689, 186 Cal.Rptr. 772, 652 P.2d 1003 (1982) (bringing of habeas corpus proceeding to enforce visitation rights); People ex rel. Mangold v. Flieger, 106 Ill.2d 546, 88 Ill.Dec. 640, 478 N.E.2d 1366 (1985) (sending support payments to forum); Landis v. Kolsky, 81 N.J. 430, 409 A.2d 276 (1979) (paid child's fare to forum); Fox v. Fox, 103 N.M. 155, 703 P.2d 932 (App.1985) (visiting forum to see children and sending support to forum); Miller v. Kite, 313 N.C. 474, 329 S.E.2d 663 (1985) (sending support payments to forum and visiting child there). For decisions finding a sufficient contact, see, e.g., In re Marriage of Highsmith, 130 Ill.App.3d 725, 86 Ill.Dec. 1, 474 N.E.2d 915 (3d Dist. 1985) (sent child to forum with statement purporting to grant custody to forum grandparents); Howells v. McKibben, 281 N.W.2d 154 (Minn.1979) (intercourse in forum although it did not result in the pregnancy); Hann v. Hann, 175 N.J.Super. 608, 421 A.2d 607 (Ch. 1980) (threatened wife in forum and owns rental property there); Yery v. Yery, 629 P.2d 357 (Okl.1981) (entered into support agreement in forum); cf. Burrill v. Sturm, 490 So.2d 6, 8 (Ala.Civ.App.1986) (dictum distinguishing support enforcement from support modification, suggesting that a unilateral move to the forum by the dependents might be sufficient for the former).

189. *Kulko*, 436 U.S. at 98, 98 S.Ct. at 1700, 56 L.Ed.2d at 145.

190. West's Ann.Cal.Code Civ.Proc. § 1650 et seq.; N.Y.—McKinney's Dom.Rel.Law § 30 et seq. (since superseded in both states by Uniform Interstate Family Support Act).

191. See McDougal, supra note 152 at 54 (jurisdiction should have been upheld because Mr. Kulko was a dentist and would not have been subjected to an undue burden by defending in California).

192. See, supra note 187 and accompanying text.

personal jurisdiction over the husband to provide for their support.[193] Furthermore, the state where a child resides should have personal jurisdiction to determine the support obligations of a father who has there impregnated a forum resident.[194]

The statement that California's "interest in ensuring the support of children resident in California ... is already being served by"[195] the availability of proceedings under URESA, is not cogent. Although the Act was helpful in enforcing child support obligations across state lines, no mother who could obtain personal jurisdiction over the obligor and afford private counsel was likely to trust her rights and her children's' rights to the tender mercies of the Act's procedures. A public prosecutor will present the claim in a distant state.[196] Other matters are likely to come higher on that prosecutor's agenda than representation of nonresident claimants for child support.[197] Even in the initiating state, non-welfare mothers' petitions are not likely to receive as high a priority as that given to claims that will reimburse the state for support that it has provided.[198] The fact that the claimant does not appear personally in the responding state is likely to make her plight less sympathetic to the judge than that of the resident obligor, who may have acquired new family responsibilities.[199] Moreover, under URESA the law that determined the obligor's duty of support is that of the "state where the obligor was present for the period during which support is sought."[200] Only three years after *Kulko,* the Court found "persuasive" the argument "that the URESA does not provide an adequate means of enforcing the support obligations of parents who abandon their children and leave the jurisdiction."[201]

---

193. Cf. Lea v. Lea, 18 N.J. 1, 112 A.2d 540 (1955) (father who had sent his wife and children to New York was "domiciled" there for the purpose of obtaining jurisdiction over him to award alimony and support to the wife and children).

194. See, e.g., Gentry v. Davis, 512 S.W.2d 4 (Tenn.1974).

195. *Kulko,* 436 U.S. at 98, 98 S.Ct. at 1700, 56 L.Ed.2d at 145.

196. Uniform Reciprocal Enforcement of Support Act (URESA) § 18(b). The Uniform Interstate Family Support Act (UIFSA), 9 U.L.A. (pt. 1) 348 (Supp. 1999) has superseded URESA. Although the procedures under UIFSA give greater protection to the obligee, an in personam judgment entitled to full faith and credit is the only guaranty that the responding state will enforce the support order in full. See discussion of UIFSA infra § 5.2E4.

197. See Elrod, *Enforcing Child Support Using the Revised Uniform Reciprocal Enforcement of Support Act,* 36 Juvenile & Fam.Ct.J. 57 (#3 1985) (practical problems of using URESA); Note, *Interstate Enforcement of Support Obligations through Long Arm Statutes and URESA,* 18 J. Family L. 537, 541 (1980).

198. Id.

199. Id.

200. URESA § 7. Under UIFSA a responding tribunal continues to determine "the duty of support and the amount payable in accordance with the law and support guidelines of [its own] State." UIFSA § 303(2).

201. Jones v. Helms, 452 U.S. 412, 425, 101 S.Ct. 2434, 2443, 69 L.Ed.2d 118, 129 (1981). The case held that for the crime of nonsupport, a state may punish parents who leave the state more severely than resident parents. Despite the observation quoted in the text accompanying this note, the court said that the argument concerning the inadequacy of URESA procedures was not necessary to its conclusion and stated "we neither accept nor reject it." Id.

Again, the Court insists on a lack of relationship between jurisdiction and choice of law:

> But while the presence of the children and one parent in California arguably might favor application of California law in a lawsuit in New York, the fact that California may be the "center of gravity" for choice-of-law purposes does not mean that California has personal jurisdiction over the defendant.[202]

This attempt to distinguish jurisdiction and choice of law is particularly inappropriate in this context. If, because of the father's lack of contacts with California, it was unreasonable for California to exercise in personam jurisdiction over him to modify his support obligations, it would have been even more unreasonable to apply California law if that law imposed more onerous obligations on him than would be imposed under New York law. URESA carried this insight to an absurd extreme by measuring the father's obligations by the law of his residence no matter how significant his contacts with the residence of mother and children.[203]

Another unfortunate aspect of Justice Marshall's majority opinion in *Kulko* is his comment that "California has not attempted to assert any particularized interest in trying [child support] cases in its courts by, e.g., enacting a special jurisdictional statute."[204] This is a reference to the fact that California has a simple one-sentence long-arm statute stating that "[a] court of this state may exercise jurisdiction on any basis not inconsistent with the Constitution of this state or of the United States."[205]

It is not apparent why California would manifest any greater "interest" in providing jurisdiction over absent parents in child support cases by enacting a long-arm statute that listed numerous specific contacts with California. Justice Marshall's comment is likely to deter drafters from following California's example. Perhaps a long string of contacts can serve as a handy check list for bench and bar, but most states have interpreted their long-arm statutes to go to the constitutional limits[206] and cases like *Kulko* are not made any easier by detailed as distinguished from simple statutes. There is also the danger of omitting an important basis for jurisdiction from a detailed list. Perhaps a good compromise after Justice Marshall's vote against simplicity is a detailed list followed by a due process catch-all provision. But that should be a matter drafting policy. Justice Marshall's comment wrongly suggests that due process turns on such details.

The Brussels Regulation[207] provides for the European Union a basis for jurisdiction in support matters that would reach the opposite result on the *Kulko* facts. Article 5(2) provides:

---

202. *Kulko,* 436 U.S. at 98, 98 S.Ct. at 1700, 56 L.Ed.2d at 145.

203. See supra note 200 and accompanying text.

204. *Kulko,* 436 U.S. at 98, 98 S.Ct. at 1700, 56 L.Ed.2d at 145.

205. West's Ann.Cal.Code Civ.Proc. § 410.10.

206. See § 4.9A.

207. Council Regulation (EC) No. 44/2001 of 22 December 2000 on Jurisdiction and the Recognition and Enforcement of Judgments in Civil and Commercial Matters Official Journal L 012, 16/01/2001 P. 0001–0023.

A person domiciled in a Member State may, in another Member State, be sued ... in matters relating to maintenance, in the courts for the place where the maintenance creditor is domiciled or habitually resident. . . .

World–Wide Volkswagen Corp. v. Woodson[208] has had an inhibiting effect on the exercise of state-court jurisdiction. Harry and Kay Robinson, residents of New York, purchased an Audi automobile from an Audi–Volkswagen dealer in Massena, New York. The following year, the Robinsons and their two children left New York for a new home in Arizona. As they were passing through Oklahoma, their Audi was struck in the rear by another car and caught fire, severely burning Kay Robinson and the children.

The Robinsons brought a products-liability action in state court in Creek County, Oklahoma, claiming that the automobile's defective design caused injuries. They joined as defendants the New York dealer that had sold the car., the automobile's German manufacturer, the United States importer, and the regional distributor. Because of the large volume of business that the manufacturer and importer conducted in Oklahoma, there was little doubt that the Oklahoma state court had personal jurisdiction over those defendants.[209] The assertion of jurisdiction over the New York dealer and the regional distributor, however, raised difficult questions about the constitutional limits of personal jurisdiction. Despite its name, "World–Wide Volkswagen," the regional distributor limited its sales to New York, New Jersey, and Connecticut. There was no showing that either the distributor or the dealer "ships or sells any products to or in [Oklahoma], has an agent to receive process there, ... purchases advertisements in any media calculated to reach Oklahoma. . . . [or] that any automobile sold by [them] has ever entered Oklahoma with the single exception of the vehicle involved in the present case."[210]

Justice Blackmun, in his dissenting opinion, wondered why "the plaintiffs in this litigation are so insistent that the regional distributor and the retail dealer ... be named defendants."[211] The manufacturer and importer were solvent, there was jurisdiction over them, and the nature of the claim, design defect, created no danger of inconsistent findings in different forums as to which of multiple defendants was at fault. The answer to Justice Blackmun's question is a simple tactical move familiar to any litigator. "Creek County, Oklahoma ... is one of the best jurisdictions in the United States in which to try a plaintiff's lawsuit. It ranks on a par with Dade County, Florida, and Cook County

---

208. 444 U.S. 286, 100 S.Ct. 559, 62 L.Ed.2d 490 (1980).

209. The importer had entered a special appearance in the Oklahoma trial court but did not seek review when that court held that it had jurisdiction over the importer. Id. at 288 n.3, 100 S.Ct. at 562 n.3, 62 L.Ed.2d at 496 n.3.

210. Id. at 289, 100 S.Ct. at 563, 62 L.Ed.2d at 496.

211. Id. at 317, 100 S.Ct. at 570, 62 L.Ed.2d at 514. (Blackmun, J., dissenting).

Illinois. . . ."[212] Counsel for the Robinsons did not want the defendants to be able to remove the case from this plaintiffs' paradise to the Federal District Court in Tulsa, Oklahoma. His theory was that, at the time suit was brought, the Robinsons were still domiciled in New York, because they had not yet arrived in Arizona. They were, therefore, still residents of New York for the purpose of determining whether there was federal jurisdiction on the basis of diversity of citizenship. By joining the dealer and regional distributor, both New York corporations, he could prevent the complete diversity of citizenship between plaintiffs and defendants that was necessary for removal.[213]

In an opinion by Justice White, the Court held that the Oklahoma court's assertion of jurisdiction over the dealer and regional distributor violated due process. Although the result and the reasons given for it have, on balance, inhibited courts in their exercise of personal jurisdiction over nonresidents, some aspects of the opinion may expand what some courts have regarded as their permissible jurisdictional reach. The Court repudiated the notion that the reason jurisdiction over nonresident motorists is permitted is because the automobile is a "dangerous instrumentality."[214] This idea had restricted some courts' exercise of jurisdiction in cases involving products that are not inherently dangerous.[215] The opinion specifically endorses the "stream of commerce" theory, under which, in cases involving claims arising from the sale of products, a court may exercise jurisdiction over those in the chain of distribution if they expect that chain to stretch to the forum.[216] Moreover, even if the defendant's sales are not made in the forum, it is subject to jurisdiction there if it regularly sells to forum residents or solicits their business.[217]

---

212. Letter to the author, dated November 9, 1983, from Jefferson G. Greer, Esq., counsel for the plaintiffs at all levels of the litigation.

213. Id. See Strawbridge v. Curtiss, 7 U.S. (3 Cranch) 267, 2 L.Ed. 435 (1806), overruled on another point, Louisville C. & C. R.R. v. Letson, 43 U.S. (2 How.) 497, 11 L.Ed. 353 (1844), (construing statutory grant of diversity jurisdiction as requiring that no plaintiff reside in the same state as any defendant, so-called "complete diversity").

The litigator's ploy of destroying diversity to prevent removal from state court has become so prevalent that a body of authority has emerged concerning burden of proof when the nonresident defendant charges that the plaintiff has fraudulently joined local defendants to prevent removal. See, e.g., B., Inc. v. Miller Brewing Co., 663 F.2d 545, 549 (5th Cir.1981) (the nonresident defendant has the burden of showing that there is "no possibility" that the plaintiff could establish a cause of action against the local defendants).

214. *World–Wide Volkswagen*, 444 U.S. at 296–97 n.11, 100 S.Ct. at 567 n.11, 62 L.Ed.2d at 501 n.11.

215. See, e.g., Mueller v. Steelcase, Inc., 172 F.Supp. 416, 418 (D.Minn.1959).

216. *World–Wide Volkswagen*, 444 U.S. at 297–98, 100 S.Ct. at 567, 62 L.Ed.2d at 501–02. But see Asahi Metal Ind. Co. v. Superior Court, 480 U.S. 102, 107 S.Ct. 1026, 94 L.Ed.2d 92 (1987), discussion infra accompanying notes 304–309, in which four justices join in an opinion that would greatly restrict the stream-of-commerce basis for jurisdiction.

217. *World–Wide Volkswagen*, 444 U.S. at 297–98, 100 S.Ct. at 567, 62 L.Ed.2d at 501–02. See e.g., Garrett v. Key Ford, Inc., 403 So.2d 923 (Ala.Civ.App.1981) (jurisdiction over Florida car dealer who solicited Alabama customers). But see, Growden v. Ed Bowlin & Associates, Inc., 733 F.2d 1149 (5th Cir.1984) (forum buyer cannot get jurisdiction over company that sold it a used airplane and advertised in a national magazine distributed in

Two parts of the opinion have had an inhibiting effect on the exercise of jurisdiction by lower courts and are roadblocks in the way of any major reassessment of the jurisdictional power of state courts. These two aspects of the Court's reasoning are its discussions of foreseeability and federalism.

The plaintiffs argued that it was foreseeable that an automobile purchased in New York would be driven to Oklahoma and there be involved in an accident. The Court responded that foreseeability that a product would enter the forum and cause harm there was not "the criterion,"[218] and proceeded to parade the horrors to which such a notion would lead. For example, the owner of a road-side soft drink stand in Florida, who sold bottles of soda to the driver of a car with Alaska plates, would be subject to the jurisdiction of Alaska courts if one of the bottles exploded there and caused injury.[219] After all, it was "foreseeable" that the buyer would take some of the soda home. The Court made it clear that more than this was required:

> [T]he foreseeability that is critical to due process analysis is not the mere likelihood that a product will find its way into the forum State. Rather, it is that the defendant's conduct and connection with the forum State are such that he should reasonably anticipate being haled into court there. The Due Process Clause, by ensuring the "orderly administration of the laws," gives a degree of predictability to the legal system that allows potential defendants to structure their primary conduct with some minimum assurance as to where that conduct will and will not render them liable to suit.[220]

The first part of this attack on the due process sufficiency of the mere foreseeability that a product will cause harm in the forum, is unobjectionable. The hypotheticals put by the Court concern small local sellers of inexpensive items. The sales are to the ultimate user who then takes the product to a distant state. It is understandable to be sympathetic with the plight of such a defendant faced with the prospect of suit thousands of miles from the scene of localized small business operations. But the second prong of the attack, the quoted passage,[221] would protect from suit even a large, multi-state seller of high-priced goods and, perhaps more to the point, would protect that seller's liability insurer. Moreover, this protection would obtain even though the situs of the forum not only did not support a claim of unfairness to defendant, but also was convenient both for the plaintiff's appearance and for presentation of evidence concerning the nature of the events causing harm. For example, the reasoning of the opinion would have led to the same result if the Audi had been rear-ended in Pennsylvania and suit had been

---

the forum); Woodfield Ford, Inc. v. Akins Ford Corp., 77 Ill.App.3d 343, 32 Ill.Dec. 750, 395 N.E.2d 1131 (1st Dist.1979) (no jurisdiction over seller of fleet of cars to forum buyer).

218. *World–Wide Volkswagen*, 444 U.S. at 296, 100 S.Ct. at 566, 62 L.Ed.2d at 500.

219. Id.

220. Id. at 297, 100 S.Ct. at 567, 62 L.Ed.2d at 501. (Citations omitted).

221. See text accompanying supra note 220.

brought there, just across the state line from a courthouse in New York where the regional distributor was then in litigation.[222] No due process test that focused on fairness to the defendant could produce such a result.[223]

What can produce this result is a due process test that focuses on the states as individual sovereigns and views exercise of jurisdiction across state lines as inconsistent with our federal system. Under this view, jurisdiction is proper only if the defendant has contacts with the forum that make it so clearly fair to exercise jurisdiction over causes of action arising out of those contacts, that the defendant's home state could not reasonably take umbrage at exercise of power over "their boy." This is the position taken by Justice White's majority opinion:

> [A] state court may exercise personal jurisdiction over a nonresident defendant only so long as there exist "minimum contacts" between the defendant and the forum State. The concept of minimum contacts, in turn can be seen to perform two related, but distinguishable, functions. It protects the defendant against the burdens of litigating in a distant or inconvenient forum. And it acts to ensure that the States, through their courts, do not reach out beyond the limits imposed on them by their status as coequal sovereigns in a federal system.[224]
>
> . . .
>
> Even if the defendant would suffer minimal or no inconvenience from being forced to litigate before the tribunals of another State; even if the forum State has a strong interest in applying its law to the controversy; even if the forum State is the most convenient location for litigation, the Due Process Clause, acting as an instrument of interstate federalism, may sometimes act to divest the State of its power to render a valid judgment.[225]

This notion that basic concepts of federalism prevent exercise of state-court jurisdiction across state boundaries is the major obstacle to removal of the "minimum contacts" requirement. Federalism as a limit on state-court jurisdiction may have made sense in the days of *Pennoyer v. Neff*[226] when exercise of jurisdiction was thought to turn on physical power over the defendant. A sister state might object to this exercise of power within her territory. This federalism appendage to due process is now misplaced. Ironically, the exercise of personal jurisdiction by one state over another might be thought to strain our federal fabric, but

---

222. See Lilly, supra note 152, at 109–110.

223. See id. at 114–15.

224. *World–Wide Volkswagen*, 444 U.S. at 291–92, 100 S.Ct. at 564, 62 L.Ed.2d at 498. (Citations omitted). That this sovereignty limitation on jurisdiction also operates when the defendant is incorporated abroad, see Donahue v. Far Eastern Air Transport Corp., 652 F.2d 1032, 1038 (D.C.Cir.1981).

225. *World–Wide Volkswagen*, 444 U.S. at 294, 100 S.Ct. at 565–66, 62 L.Ed.2d at 499–500.

226. 95 U.S. (5 Otto) 714, 24 L.Ed. 565 (1878), discussed supra, text accompanying notes 12–15.

Nevada v. Hall[227] permitted this. The time has come to remove the federalism cloud from due process limitations on state-court jurisdiction so that the "minimum contacts" requirement can be examined in the clear light of fairness to the defendant.[228]

Justice White, as the author of the majority opinion in *Volkswagen,* gave expression to the notion that federalism is a component of jurisdictional due process. Oddly, it is he who has started the process of repudiating that concept. Two and a half years after *Volkswagen,* he wrote for the Court in *Insurance Corporation of Ireland, Ltd. v. Compagnie des Bauxites de Guinee.*[229] Plaintiffs sued foreign insurance companies in a Federal District Court in Pennsylvania. The basis for federal jurisdiction was diversity of citizenship.[230] Plaintiffs claimed recovery under a business interruption policy for damage to operations in Guinea.

The defendants appeared and made a motion under Federal Rule of Civil Procedure 12(b)(2) to dismiss for lack of personal jurisdiction over them. On plaintiff's motion, the court ordered the defendants to produce documents showing the extent of their business activities in Pennsylvania, but they refused to do so. As a sanction for refusal to obey the court's orders, the judge imposed on the defendants the burden of proving that they were not subject to personal jurisdiction in the forum. The court held that defendants waived their right to have the plaintiff bear this burden. The Supreme Court approved. Justice White realized that although a defendant could waive its own constitutional rights, it could not waive its state's or country's rights that were an incident of

---

227. 440 U.S. 410, 99 S.Ct. 1182, 59 L.Ed.2d 416 (1979). For exercise of jurisdiction over sister states or their governmental units or agencies, see, e.g., Franchise Tax Board of California v. Hyatt, 538 U.S. 488, 123 S.Ct. 1683, 155 L.Ed.2d 702 (2003) (Nevada state court need not give full faith and credit to California statute conferring complete immunity from suit on California state agencies); Struebin v. State, 322 N.W.2d 84 (Iowa 1982), cert. denied, 459 U.S. 1087, 103 S.Ct. 570, 74 L.Ed.2d 933 (1982); Head v. Platte County, Mo., 242 Kan. 442, 749 P.2d 6 (1988); Wendt v. County of Osceola, Iowa, 289 N.W.2d 67 (Minn.1979); Mianecki v. Second Judicial Dist. Ct., 99 Nev. 93, 658 P.2d 422, cert. dism'd want final j., 464 U.S. 806, 104 S.Ct. 195, 78 L.Ed.2d 171 (1983); Ehrlich–Bober & Co., Inc. v. University of Houston, 49 N.Y.2d 574, 427 N.Y.S.2d 604, 404 N.E.2d 726 (1980). But for cases declining jurisdiction on the grounds of comity, see Simmons v. State, 206 Mont. 264, 670 P.2d 1372 (1983) (also on due process grounds); Ramsden v. Illinois, 695 S.W.2d 457 (Mo.1985); Newberry v. Georgia Dept. of Ind. & Trade, 286 S.C. 574, 336 S.E.2d 464 (1985) (as a matter of comity, a non-consenting sister state may not be sued in a South Carolina court). See also Rogers, *Applying the International Law of Sovereign Immunity to the States of the Union,* 1981 Duke L. J. 449, 472 (1981) (Nevada v. Hall reached proper result under "principles of international sovereign immunity").

228. For commentary favoring the elimination of federalism from jurisdictional analysis, see Hay, *Judicial Jurisdiction and Choice of Law: Constitutional Limitations,* 59 Colo. L. Rev. 9, 22 (1988); Juenger, *Judicial Jurisdiction in the United States and in the European Communities: A Comparison,* 82 Mich. L. Rev. 1195, 1196 (1984); Redish, *Due Process, Federalism, and Personal Jurisdiction: A Theoretical Evaluation,* 75 Nw. L. Rev. 1112, 1113–14, 1129, 1132 (1981). For the opposing view, see Rosenberg, *Foreword to the Colorado Symposium,* 59 Colo. L. Rev. 1, 8 (1988); Stein, *Styles of Argument and Interstate Federalism in the Law of Personal Jurisdiction,* 65 Texas L. Rev. 689, 690 (1987).

229. 456 U.S. 694, 102 S.Ct. 2099, 72 L.Ed.2d 492 (1982).

230. See 28 U.S.C. § 1332.

sovereignty. Justice White met the point directly. First he quoted his own language in *Volkswagen*[231] and then stated:

> The restriction on state sovereign power described in World–Wide Volkswagen Corp., however, must be seen as ultimately a function of the individual liberty interest preserved by the Due Process Clause. That Clause is the only source of the personal jurisdiction requirement and the Clause itself makes no mention of federalism concerns. Furthermore, if the federal concept operated as an independent restriction on the sovereign power of the court, it would not be possible to waive the personal jurisdiction requirement: Individual actions cannot change the powers of sovereignty, although the individual can subject himself to powers from which he may otherwise be protected.[232]

He insisted that:

> [O]ur holding today does not alter the requirement that there be "minimum contacts" between the nonresident defendant and the forum State. Rather, our holding deals with how the facts needed to show those "minimum contacts" can be established when a defendant fails to comply with court-ordered discovery.[233]

But now "minimum contacts" would have to be defended as constitutionally required to ensure fairness to the defendant, not as an attribute of federalism. If this holds true, many more battles will have to be fought, but the war for a rational reallocation of jurisdictional authority has been won.

If fairness to the parties is the criterion, the result in *Volkswagen* is wrong.[234] The Oklahoma site of the accident was convenient for presenting evidence concerning the circumstances of the crash and the injuries to the plaintiffs.[235] The manufacturer and importer were already before the court. Oklahoma, as scene of the accident and where medical expenses were incurred, had an interest in providing a forum to deter-

---

231. *Insurance Corp. of Ireland*, 456 U.S. at 702 n.10, 102 S.Ct. at 2104 n.10, 72 L.Ed.2d at 501 n.10. For the language quoted, see text accompanying supra note 225.

232. *Insurance Corp. of Ireland*, 456 U.S. at 702 n.10, 102 S.Ct. at 2104 n.10, 72 L.Ed.2d at 501 n.10. But see Stroman Realty, Inc. v. Wercinski, 513 F.3d 476, 488 (5th Cir. 2008), cert. denied, 129 S.Ct. 63, 172 L.Ed.2d 25 (2008) (holding it a violation of due process to sue an Arizona official in Texas, quoting the "interstate federalism" language of World–Wide Volkswagen).

233. Id.

234. See World–Wide Volkswagen Corp. v. Woodson, 444 U.S. 286, 311, 100 S.Ct. 559, 587, 62 L.Ed.2d 490, 510 (1980): "When an action in fact causes injury in another State, the actor should be prepared to answer for it there unless defending in that State would be unfair for some reason other than that a state boundary must be crossed." (Brennan, J., dissenting). Justice Brennan wrote a combined dissent to both *Rush* and *Volkswagen*. His opinion is a seminal attack on the requirement of "minimum contacts" between defendant and forum. See Note, 94 Harv. L. Rev. 77, 112 (1980); cf. Hedrick v. Daiko Shoji Co., Ltd., 715 F.2d 1355 (9th Cir.1983) (jurisdiction over manufacturer of component part that caused injury when boat came to forum, distinguishing *Volkswagen*); Tyson v. Whitaker & Son, Inc., 407 A.2d 1 (Me.1979) (result contra *World–Wide Volkswagen* before *Volkswagen* decided).

235. See Lilly, supra note 152, at 109–110 (convenience of forum in *World–Wide Volkswagen*); cf. von Mehren, supra note 152, at 322 ("litigational advantages" of a forum where the accident occurred).

mine responsibility for that accident and those expenses. The New York dealer and distributor were part of a network of Volkswagen service facilities that stretched into Oklahoma and encouraged owners of Audis and Volkswagens to venture there.[236] A few hours air travel would bring any necessary representatives of the dealer and distributor to Oklahoma. There is no substance to the claim that fundamental fairness shields these defendants, or more likely, their liability insurers, from litigating in the Oklahoma state court.

Two cases decided on the same day in 1984, *Keeton v. Hustler Magazine, Inc.*,[237] and *Calder v. Jones*,[238] were both actions for defamation by publications in the forum, but they raised different issues.

In *Keeton,* the plaintiff brought a suit in a New Hampshire federal district court against a magazine[239] for libel. Ten to fifteen thousand copies were sold in New Hampshire, the forum state, each month. Arguments against jurisdiction centered on the facts that plaintiff was a resident of New York, had suffered most of her harm outside the forum, and was engaged in blatant forum-shopping. New Hampshire was the only state in which the statute of limitations had not run. The Court, nevertheless, held that there was jurisdiction over the magazine.

The opinion conceded that "the 'fairness' of haling [defendant] into a New Hampshire court depends to some extent on whether [defendant's] activities relating to New Hampshire are such as to give that State a legitimate interest in holding [defendant] answerable on a claim related to those activities."[240] The Court found sufficient New Hampshire interest in providing a forum because some injury had occurred in New Hampshire. "[P]laintiff's previous reputation [in New Hampshire] was, however small, at least unblemished."[241] In addition, New Hampshire readers of the libel were harmed because they were deceived.

The Court said that plaintiff's forum shopping "is no different from the litigation strategy of countless plaintiffs who seek a forum with favorable substantive or procedural rules or sympathetic local populations."[242] The Court suggested two possible rulings on remand that might mitigate the "unfairness" of applying New Hampshire's statute of

---

236. This point is made by some of the dissenters. See *World–Wide Volkswagen,* 444 U.S. at 307, 100 S.Ct. at 585, 62 L.Ed.2d at 508 (Brennan, J., dissenting); id. at 315, 100 S.Ct. at 569, 62 L.Ed.2d at 513 (Marshall, J., dissenting). See also Note, 94 Harv. L. Rev. 77, 112 (1980). But see Brilmayer, supra note 152, at 88 ("defendant's affiliation with other dealers doing business in Oklahoma was not a related contact since there was no reason to allege that fact other than to manufacture a jurisdictional connection").

237. 465 U.S. 770, 104 S.Ct. 1473, 79 L.Ed.2d 790 (1984).

238. 465 U.S. 783, 104 S.Ct. 1482, 79 L.Ed.2d 804 (1984).

239. In addition to the magazine, plaintiff joined the publisher and the magazine's holding company as defendants. Because it decided that there was no jurisdiction even over the magazine, the Court of Appeals did not reach the question of jurisdiction over the other defendants. That question was open on remand. See *Keeton,* 465 U.S. at 781 n.13, 104 S.Ct. at 1482 n.13, 79 L.Ed.2d at 802 n.13.

240. Id. at 775–76, 104 S.Ct. at 1479, 79 L.Ed.2d at 798.

241. Id. at 777, 104 S.Ct. at 1479, 79 L.Ed.2d at 799.

242. Id. at 779, 104 S.Ct. at 1480, 79 L.Ed.2d at 800.

limitations to permit a suit barred everyplace else—a change in choice-of-law rules applicable to statutes of limitations and limiting recovery of damages to those suffered in the forum. First, and most intriguing, was the Court's mention of "academic criticism"[243] of the application of the longer statute of limitations of a forum that has no interest in permitting the plaintiff to recover when all states that will experience the social consequences of the result have decided that the defendant's need for repose and protection from stale claims outweighs the desirability of compensating the plaintiff. The Court then said that "we find it unnecessary to express an opinion at this time as to whether any arguable unfairness rises to the level of a due process violation."[244]

The second possibility for mitigating the effects of plaintiff's forum shopping would be to decide on remand that, contrary to the usual result under the "single publication rule,"[245] plaintiff may recover for the harm she suffered in New Hampshire, but not elsewhere. This is especially desirable under the "peculiar circumstances of this case";[246] most of the harm was caused elsewhere and all other statutes of limitations had run. Interestingly enough, this is exactly the result that the Court of Justice of the European Communities reached in interpreting the jurisdictional provisions of the Brussels Convention.[247]

In *Keeton,* the Court repeats yet again its position that the forum's jurisdiction does not turn on the appropriateness of applying forum law:

> Strictly speaking, however, any potential unfairness in applying New Hampshire's statute of limitations to all aspects of this nationwide suit has nothing to do with the jurisdiction of the Court to adjudicate the claims. "The issue is personal jurisdiction, not choice of law." *Hanson v. Denckla,* 357 U.S. 235, 254, 78 S.Ct. 1228, 1240, 2 L.Ed.2d 1283 (1958). The question of the applicability of New Hampshire's statute of limitations to claims for out-of-state damages presents itself in the course of litigation only after jurisdiction over respondent is established, and we do not think that such choice of law concerns should complicate or distort the jurisdictional inquiry.[248]

On remand in *Keeton,* the federal court certified to the New Hampshire Supreme Court the question of whether New Hampshire's statute of limitations should be applied to permit recovery for damages caused in

---

243. Id. n.10 (citing i.a. § 9.2B infra).

244. Id. Sun Oil Co. v. Wortman, 486 U.S. 717, 108 S.Ct. 2117, 100 L.Ed.2d 743 (1988), discussed infra § 9.2B, held that a state can apply its own longer statute of limitations although it could not constitutionally apply its law to determine the interest due plaintiffs.

245. See Restatement (Second) of Torts § 577A(4)(b) (1977).

246. *Keeton,* 465 U.S. at 778 n.9, 104 S.Ct. at 1480 n.9, 79 L.Ed.2d at 799 n.9.

247. See Shevill v. Presse Alliance S.A., 1995 E.C.R. 1–415 (Ct.J.E.C., Case C–68/93) (holding that a victim of libel may sue at the publisher's domicile and recover for all harm suffered anywhere, or may sue anyplace the libel was published, but may recover only for harm caused there).

248. *Keeton,* 465 U.S. at 778, 104 S.Ct. at 1480, 79 L.Ed.2d at 800.

all states in which publication occurred. The New Hampshire Supreme Court replied that New Hampshire limitations should be applied.[249]

In *Calder*, the libel defendants contesting the jurisdiction of a California court were an editor and a reporter who lived and worked in Florida.[250] The publication occurred in California, where the plaintiff resided and in other states.

The opinion holds that a California court can exercise jurisdiction over the defendants because of the intended and foreseeable " 'effects' of their Florida conduct in California"[251] and rejects arguments based on the First Amendment[252] and on the defendant's status as employees.

The Court rejected the argument that the need for First Amendment protection of the defendants raised the jurisdictional hurdle:

> The infusion of such considerations would needlessly complicate an already imprecise inquiry.... Moreover, the potential chill on protected First Amendment activity stemming from libel and defamation actions is already taken into account in the constitutional limitations on the substantive law governing such suits. See *New York Times, Inc. v. Sullivan*, 376 U.S. 254, 84 S.Ct. 710, 11 L.Ed.2d 686 (1964); *Gertz v. Robert Welch, Inc.*, 418 U.S. 323, 94 S.Ct. 2997, 41 L.Ed.2d 789 (1974).[253]

Calder, also gave the "fiduciary shield" doctrine its deserved quietus. This is the notion, espoused in a few cases, that jurisdiction may be

---

249.   Keeton v. Hustler Magazine, Inc., 131 N.H. 6, 549 A.2d 1187 (1988).

250.   The reporter disputed the trial court's finding that he had visited California to research the article, but the Court did not base its holding on this disputed visit. *Calder*, 465 U.S. at 785–86 n.4, 104 S.Ct. at 1485 n.4, 79 L.Ed.2d at 810 n.4.

251.   Id. at 789, 104 S.Ct. at 1487, 79 L.Ed.2d at 812. See also Schwarzenegger v. Fred Martin Motor Co., 374 F.3d 797, 805 (9th Cir. 2004) (the *Calder* effects test requires that the defendant commit an intentional act expressly aimed at the forum state that causes foreseeable harm there); Burt v. Board of Regents of Univ. of Nebraska, 757 F.2d 242 (10th Cir.1985) vacated and remanded with directions to dismiss complaint as moot, 475 U.S. 1063, 106 S.Ct. 1372, 89 L.Ed.2d 599 (1986) (jurisdiction upheld in libel action based on letters sent into forum in response to inquiry concerning plaintiff's qualifications). But cf. Marten v. Godwin, 499 F.3d 290 (3d Cir. 2007) (no jurisdiction over Kansas defendants in Pennsylvania even though Pennsylvania plaintiff was taking internet course from defendants when expelled for plagiarism; plaintiff did not show that defendants expressly aimed their conduct at Pennsylvania); Demaris v. Greenspun, 712 F.2d 433 (9th Cir.1983) (jurisdiction denied in libel action by forum resident because only a small percentage of newspaper's revenue is derived from forum sales or advertisements).

252.   U.S. Const. Amend 1: "Congress shall make no law ... abridging the freedom of speech, or of the press...." In the light of the fact that the First Amendment focuses on action by the federal Congress, its limitations are made applicable to state action by the due process clause of the Fourteenth Amendment. See Frankfurter, *Memorandum on "Incorporation" of the Bill of Rights into the Due Process Clause of the Fourteenth Amendment,* 78 Harv. L. Rev. 746, 747–48 (1965).

253.   *Calder,* 465 U.S. at 790, 104 S.Ct. at 1487–88, 79 L.Ed.2d at 813. See also Philadelphia Newspapers, Inc. v. Hepps, 475 U.S. 767, 106 S.Ct. 1558, 89 L.Ed.2d 783 (1986) (when a newspaper publishes speech of public concern about a private figure, the private-figure plaintiff must have the burden of proof on the issue of falsity); Bose Corp. v. Consumers Union of United States, Inc., 466 U.S. 485, 104 S.Ct. 1949, 80 L.Ed.2d 502 (1984) (a finding of actual malice in a case governed by *New York Times v. Sullivan* is reviewed, not under the clearly-erroneous standard of Federal Rule of Civil Procedure 52(a), but by exercise of the appellate court's independent judgment).

obtained over an employer corporation but not over its employees, even though, under the law of torts, the employees are personally liable for the harm caused.[254] The ability of a particular defendant to engage in interstate litigation is a factor that will be considered in any jurisdictional test that focuses on fairness to the defendant, but the fiduciary shield doctrine is a misguided way to go about this. As the Court put it:

> [Defendants] are correct that their contacts with California are not to be judged according to their employer's activities there. On the other hand, their status as employees does not somehow insulate them from jurisdiction.[255]

Helicopteros Nacionales de Colombia, S.A. v. Hall,[256] examines the permissible scope of general jurisdiction. A helicopter crash in Peru killed four United States citizens, none of them residents of the Texas forum. A consortium composed of two Texas corporations and a Delaware corporation employed them. The consortium was constructing a pipeline in Peru. The defendant had contracted with the consortium[257] to transport personnel and equipment to Peru. The contract had been negotiated in Houston, but the formal document was signed in Peru. Payments for defendant's services were made from a Houston bank to an account in a New York bank. The Texas Supreme Court upheld jurisdiction over the defendant on the ground that although the cause of action did not arise out of defendant's Texas contacts, defendant's extensive business activities in the state[258] made it reasonable to exercise personal jurisdiction over it.[259] In an 8–1 decision, the Court reversed and held that due process did not permit the exercise of jurisdiction over Heli-

---

254. See, e.g., Marine Midland Bank, N.A. v. Miller, 664 F.2d 899 (2d Cir.1981); cf. same doctrine in contract actions, Thames v. Gunter–Dunn, Inc., 373 So.2d 640 (Ala.1979); Laufer v. Ostrow, 55 N.Y.2d 305, 449 N.Y.S.2d 456, 434 N.E.2d 692 (1982). But see Columbia Briargate Co. v. First Nat'l Bank, 713 F.2d 1052, 1059–60 (4th Cir.1983), cert. denied, 465 U.S. 1007, 104 S.Ct. 1001, 79 L.Ed.2d 233 (1984) (should have jurisdiction over a corporate agent if he is personally liable for the tort); Kreutter v. McFadden Oil Corp., 71 N.Y.2d 460, 527 N.Y.S.2d 195, 522 N.E.2d 40 (1988) (rejecting fiduciary shield doctrine as an unnecessary supplement to due process).

For adoption of a "government contacts" exception to the exercise of personal jurisdiction see Lamb v. Turbine Design, Inc., 273 Ga. 154, 538 S.E.2d 437 (2000) (a non-resident is not subject to personal jurisdiction based on his alleged improper disclosure of a trade secret to a federal agency at its office in the state when the defendant submitted an application for design modification to the agency).

255. *Calder,* 465 U.S. at 790, 104 S.Ct. at 1487, 79 L.Ed.2d at 813.

256. 466 U.S. 408, 104 S.Ct. 1868, 80 L.Ed.2d 404 (1984).

257. The contract was technically with a Peruvian company set up by the consortium to comply with Peruvian law. See opinion below, 638 S.W.2d at 877 (Pope, J., dissenting).

258. The majority recited a list of contacts that Helicopteros had with Texas: negotiated its contract with the consortium, purchased substantially all its helicopters and millions of dollars worth of spare parts and equipment, trained maintenance personnel and pilots, sent pilots there to fly purchased helicopters to Colombia, had employees in Texas on a year-round rotational basis, received payments under its contract with the consortium from a Houston bank, and directed a Houston bank to make payments to a United States helicopter company for lease of a large helicopter to be used in performing the contract for the consortium. Id. at 871–72. In its amicus brief, the Justice Department argued that exercising jurisdiction over Helicopteros would discourage foreign companies from doing business in the United States. See Brief for the United States as Amicus Curiae, pp. 1–2.

259. 638 S.W.2d at 872.

copteros Nacionales de Colombia ("Helicol") in a cause of action unrelated to the defendant's Texas activities.

The case foreshadows substantial limitations on the exercise of general jurisdiction based on a corporation's business dealings in the forum. In the seven years before the fatal crash and one year following the accident, Helicol purchased 80% of its fleet in Texas, amounting to over four million dollars in planes, spare parts, and accessories. Yet these and other commercial transactions that defendant conducted in Texas,[260] did not "constitute the kind of continuous and systematic general business contacts the Court found to exist in *Perkins v. Benguet Consolidated Mining Co.*"[261] No, and the extraordinary circumstances of *Perkins* are unlikely to occur again. In *Perkins,* the defendant had its main office in the Ohio forum, having moved there from the Philippine Islands during the Japanese occupation.[262] If that is what is necessary, the term "general jurisdiction," when based on business activity, should be changed to "Perkins."

Taking his lead from the government's amicus brief, Justice Blackmun's majority opinion resurrects *Rosenberg Bros. & Co., Inc. v. Curtis Brown Company,*[263] a case more than sixty years old, and finds it controlling. The defendant, a "small retail dealer in men's clothing and furnishings at Tulsa, Oklahoma"[264] purchased "a large part"[265] of its merchandise in New York. Defendant's officers made the purchases both by correspondence and during visits to plaintiff's New York office. While defendant's president was in New York to buy merchandise and see the sights, the plaintiff served him in a suit arising out of a contract that he had made for defendant on a previous trip to New York. The Court saw the "sole question" as "whether, at the time of the service of process, defendant was doing business within the state of New York in such manner and to such extent as to warrant the inference that it was present there."[266] The Court answered "no" and, to highlight the time warp through which has emerged this ghost of "present" past, the opinion concludes "as [defendant] was not found there, the fact that the alleged cause of action arose in New York is immaterial."[267] Yet, over six decades later, Justice Blackmun says:

---

260. See supra note 258.

261. *Helicopteros*, 466 U.S. at 416, 104 S.Ct. at 1873, 80 L.Ed.2d at 412. See Porina v. Marward Shipping Co., 521 F.3d 122 (2d Cir. 2008) (to obtain general jurisdiction over a ship owner, forum contacts must be that of the owner, not companies that chartered the ship).

262. Perkins v. Benguet Consolidated Mining Co., 342 U.S. 437, 447–48, 72 S.Ct. 413, 419, 96 L.Ed. 485, 493–94 (1952).

263. 260 U.S. 516, 43 S.Ct. 170, 67 L.Ed. 372 (1923). Brief for the United States as Amicus Curiae at pp. 5–6 relied on *Rosenberg.*

264. Id. at 518, 43 S.Ct. at 171, 67 L.Ed. at 375.

265. Id.

266. Id. at 517, 43 S.Ct. at 171, 67 L.Ed. at 375.

267. Id. at 518, 43 S.Ct. at 171, 67 L.Ed. at 375.

In accordance with *Rosenberg,* we hold that mere purchases, even if occurring at regular intervals, are not enough to warrant a State's assertion of in personam jurisdiction over a nonresident corporation in a cause of action not related to those purchase transactions.[268]

It is debatable whether *Helicopteros* should be dealt with as a "general jurisdiction" case. Justice Blackmun says that "[a]ll parties to the present case concede that respondents' claims against Helicol did not 'arise out of,' and are not related to, Helicol's activities within Texas,"[269] but that does not make it so. The deaths in Peru "arose out of" Helicol's Texas business contacts in the broadest "but for" sense. If the chief executive officer had not come to Texas and convinced the Texas-based joint venture to retain Helicol's services to transport employees, Helicol would not have carried these employees to their deaths. Moreover, the helicopter was purchased in Texas and the pilot trained in Texas.[270]

Treating *Helicopteros* as a general jurisdiction case illustrates the fallacy of drawing a sharp line between specifically and generally affiliating contacts. The more contacts the defendant has with the forum, the less the relationship between forum contacts and the cause of action that should be required.[271] The defendant in *Rosenberg* was a local Tulsa retail store. Helicol provides transportation services throughout South America and its officers travel abroad, including to Texas, to negotiate contracts for those services.

Some courts have rejected the notion that the more contacts a defendant has with the forum, the less the relationship that is required between forum contacts and the cause of action to assert jurisdiction over the defendant. Rejection has been on the ground that this "sliding scale" jurisdictional theory "blurs the distinction between general and specific jurisdiction."[272] It is real life rather than the "sliding scale" view

---

268. *Helicopteros,* 466 U.S. at 418, 104 S.Ct. at 1874, 80 L.Ed.2d at 413.

269. Id. at 415, 104 S.Ct. at 1872–73, 80 L.Ed.2d at 411.

270. Id. at 426, 104 S.Ct. at 1878, 80 L.Ed.2d at 418 (Brennan, J., dissenting).

271. See Le Manufacture Francaise Des Pneumatiques Michelin v. District Court, 620 P.2d 1040, 1047 (Colo.1980) (jurisdiction upheld over foreign manufacturer although product purchased in Germany when identical tires are sold in the forum, remarking that "although not directly arising from [defendant's] purposeful activity in Colorado, the cause of action ... is sufficiently related to that activity"); Camelback Ski Corp. v. Behning, 312 Md. 330, 338, 539 A.2d 1107, 1111 (1988) ("the proper approach is to identify the approximate position of the case on the [specific-general] continuum ... recognizing that the quantum of required contacts increases as the nexus between the contacts and the cause of action decreases"). But see Twitchell, *The Myth of General Jurisdiction,* 101 Harv. L. Rev. 610, 613 (1988) ("courts must redefine the scope of specific jurisdiction to include all exercises of jurisdiction based even remotely on the nature of the claim presented and must restrict general jurisdiction to those exercises of jurisdiction that are truly dispute-blind").

272. O'Connor v. Sandy Lane Hotel Co., 496 F.3d 312, 321 (3d Cir. 2007) (although court finds jurisdiction over Barbados hotel, it rejects an approach that varies the relatedness requirement according to the quantity and quality of the defendant's contacts, preferring to treat "general and specific jurisdiction as analytically distinct categories, not two points on a sliding scale"); Dudnikov v. Chalk & Vermilion Fine Arts, Inc., 514 F.3d 1063, 1078 (10th Cir. 2008) (although finding jurisdiction over a foreign corporation, rejects a theory under which "the relationship between the contacts and the suit can be weaker when the contacts themselves are more extensive" because it "blurs the distinction

of personal jurisdiction that "blurs the distinction between general and specific jurisdiction."

Helicopteros may have a limiting effect not only on the exercise of general jurisdiction, but also on the use of specific jurisdiction. The modern concept of specifically affiliating jurisdictional contacts was unknown at the time of *Rosenberg* and therefore that case focused on whether the purchases in New York made the defendant "present" there and subject to jurisdiction for any purpose in New York courts. The suit in *Rosenberg* was, however, to recover on a contract that the defendant's president had entered into on a previous trip to the forum. Justice Blackmun reminds us of this, thus casting *Helicopteros'* shadow over specific jurisdiction:

> This Court in *International Shoe* cited *Rosenberg* for the proposition that "the commission of some single or occasional acts of the corporate agent in a state sufficient to impose an obligation or liability on the corporation has not been thought to confer upon the state authority to enforce it." 326 U.S. at 318, 66 S.Ct. at 159. Arguably therefore, *Rosenberg* also stands for the proposition that mere purchases are not a sufficient basis for either general or specific jurisdiction. Because the case before us is one in which there has been an assertion of general jurisdiction over a foreign defendant, we need not decide the continuing validity of *Rosenberg* with respect to an assertion of specific jurisdiction, i.e., where the cause of action arises out of or relates to the purchases by the defendant in the forum State.[273]

Such a limit on specific jurisdiction no matter how active the buyer in seeking out the seller,[274] or how extensive the seller's performance of services required in the forum by the contract,[275] would make even modest uses of long-arm concepts[276] seem like lawless exercises of exorbitant jurisdiction. Moreover, the citation to *International Shoe* is misleading. Immediately after the passage quoted by Justice Black-

---

between specific and general personal jurisdiction"); Moki Mac River Expeditions v. Drugg, 221 S.W.3d 569, 583 (Tex. 2007) (rejecting a "sliding scale" approach under which "as the extent of forum contacts goes up, the degree of relatedness to the litigation necessary to establish specific jurisdiction goes down" because this test "blurs the distinction between general and specific jurisdiction").

273. *Helicopteros*, 466 U.S. at 418 n.12, 104 S.Ct. at 1874 n.12, 80 L.Ed.2d at 413 n.12.

274. Some courts in deciding whether a merchant seller can obtain jurisdiction over a merchant buyer have drawn a distinction between "passive" buyers and buyers who solicited the seller. See Mississippi Interstate Express, Inc. v. Transpo, Inc., 681 F.2d 1003, 1007–09 (5th Cir.1982) (jurisdiction upheld in suit to recover payment for transportation services when, after plaintiff had first solicited the defendant, the defendant repeatedly ordered more services); Al–Jon, Inc. v. Garden St. Iron & Metal, 301 N.W.2d 709, 714 (Iowa 1981) (no jurisdiction over buyer solicited by seller).

275. See Premier Corp. v. Newsom, 620 F.2d 219 (10th Cir.1980) (no jurisdiction in suit for tax-shelter services performed in forum for physicians when contract did not require performance there); cf. Mountaire Feeds, Inc. v. Agro Impex, S. A., 677 F.2d 651, 655 n.5 (8th Cir.1982) (leave open question of whether jurisdiction would have been found if the contract had required performance in the forum).

276. See, e.g., Mississippi Interstate Express, Inc. v. Transpo, Inc., 681 F.2d 1003 (5th Cir.1982) (upholding jurisdiction in suit for transportation services).

mun,[277] the Court adds, "other such acts, because of their nature and quality and the circumstances of their commission, may be deemed sufficient to render the corporation liable to suit."[278] *International Shoe* then cites three nonresident motorist cases, two involving tort claims[279] and one a criminal penalty for failure to register the automobile.[280] This is an echo of the dangerous-versus-not-dangerous-act distinction discarded as a test for specific jurisdiction in *World–Wide Volkswagen*.[281] But *International Shoe* itself demonstrates that the passing remark quoted by Justice Blackmun is not to be given the inflated importance that he accords it. In the same paragraph in which it cites *Rosenberg*, *International Shoe* disavows the "presence" fiction on which *Rosenberg* rested.[282] Then the Court repudiates statements, such as that in *Rosenberg*, that it is irrelevant if the suit arises out of forum contacts:

> But to the extent that a corporation exercises the privilege of conducting activities within a state, it enjoys the benefits and protection of the laws of that state. The exercise of that privilege may give rise to obligations; and, so far as those obligations arise out of or are connected with the activities within the state, a procedure which requires the corporation to respond to a suit brought to enforce them can, in most instances, hardly be said to be undue.[283]

Thus *Helicopteros* rattles *Rosenberg*'s chains so loudly that it does not hear *International Shoe*'s call for new jurisdictional theory shaped to accord with modern realities. Let us hope that *Helicopteros* does not raise the barrier to needed jurisdictional reform and that *Rosenberg* resumes its rightful place as the championship question in games of legal trivia.

Aside from insurance cases,[284] *Burger King Corp. v. Rudzewicz*[285] is the first of the modern Supreme Court decisions focusing on long-arm jurisdiction based on a contractual transaction. The result should dispel some of the cloud that Justice Blackmun's dictum in *Helicopteros*[286] cast on specifically affiliating jurisdiction related to contracts. Burger King, a

---

277. See supra text accompanying note 273.

278. International Shoe Co. v. Washington, 326 U.S. 310, 318, 66 S.Ct. 154, 159, 90 L.Ed. 95, 103 (1945).

279. Hess v. Pawloski, 274 U.S. 352, 47 S.Ct. 632, 71 L.Ed. 1091 (1927); Young v. Masci, 289 U.S. 253, 53 S.Ct. 599, 77 L.Ed. 1158 (1933).

280. Kane v. New Jersey, 242 U.S. 160, 37 S.Ct. 30, 61 L.Ed. 222 (1916).

281. See supra note 214 and accompanying text.

282. International Shoe Co. v. Washington, 326 U.S. 310, 318, 66 S.Ct. 154, 159, 90 L.Ed. 95, 103 (1945).

283. Id. at 329, 66 S.Ct. at 160, 90 L.Ed. at 104.

284. See McGee v. International Life Ins. Co., 355 U.S. 220, 78 S.Ct. 199, 2 L.Ed.2d 223 (1957) (jurisdiction over insurer to enforce claim in state in which life insurance policy issued to resident); cf. Travelers Health Ass'n v. Virginia, 339 U.S. 643, 70 S.Ct. 927, 94 L.Ed. 1154 (1950) (Virginia has jurisdiction to institute cease and desist proceedings against Nebraska corporation conducting a mail-order health insurance business in Virginia).

285. 471 U.S. 462, 105 S.Ct. 2174, 85 L.Ed.2d 528 (1985).

286. See supra note 273 and accompanying text.

Florida corporation with principal offices in Miami, conducts most of its restaurant business through franchises. Burger King licenses its franchisees to use its trademarks and leases facilities to franchisees. In exchange, the franchisees pay an initial fee and monthly royalties, fees, and rent. Franchisees make payments to Burger King's Miami headquarters.

Rudzewicz and MacShara applied to Burger King's Michigan district office for a franchise. They carried on negotiations resulting in the granting of a franchise with the district office and the Miami headquarters. MacShara attended the prescribed management courses in Miami. Burger King terminated the franchise for nonpayment of monthly fees and ordered Rudzewicz and MacShara to vacate the premises, but they refused. Burger King sued them in Florida federal District Court seeking damages and injunctive relief. *Burger King* holds that the Florida court had personal jurisdiction over the defendants.

The majority opinion by Justice Brennan holds that, although a contract with a nonresident does not "automatically establish sufficient minimum contacts,"[287] the negotiations, contract terms, contemplated consequences, and course of dealing indicated that defendants "deliberately"[288] established the required forum contacts and that it would not be unfair to subject them to personal jurisdiction at the franchiser's headquarters. Defendants chose affiliation with a national franchise, voluntarily accepted "long-term and exacting regulation of [their] business from"[289] plaintiff's headquarters, and their continued use of the premises and trade marks after termination "caused foreseeable injuries to the corporation in Florida."[290] As for foreseeability that they might be sued in Florida for breach of the agreement, defendants learned during negotiations that major policy decisions had to come from Miami headquarters, and the franchise agreement provided that it was "governed and construed under and in accordance with the laws of the State of Florida. The choice of law designation does not require that all suits concerning this Agreement be filed in Florida." Justice Brennan noted that this last sentence "should have suggested to Rudzewicz that by negative implication such suits *could* be filed there."[291]

The Court's use of the choice-of-law clause is especially interesting. As noted previously, the Court's jurisdiction opinions had repeatedly disclaimed any connection between jurisdiction and choice of law.[292] Justice Brennan had often disagreed with this position, arguing that if the law of a state was properly applicable, it would be efficient for the courts of that state to be able to adjudicate the matter, thus avoiding problems of determining and applying foreign law, and that this efficiency reason should result in resolving close cases in favor of a finding of

287. *Burger King*, 471 U.S. at 478, 105 S.Ct. at 2185, 85 L.Ed.2d at 545.

288. Id. at 479, 105 S.Ct. at 2186, 85 L.Ed.2d at 545.

289. Id. at 480, 105 S.Ct. at 2186, 85 L.Ed.2d at 545.

290. Id. at 480, 105 S.Ct. at 2186, 85 L.Ed.2d at 546.

291. Id. at 482 n.24, 105 S.Ct. at 2187 n.24, 85 L.Ed.2d at 547 n.24.

292. See supra note 172 and accompanying text.

jurisdiction.[293] Justice Brennan, now writing for the majority, notes the distinction between choice of law and jurisdiction that the court has drawn,[294] but then adds:

> Nothing in our cases, however, suggests that a choice-of-law *provision* should be ignored in considering whether a defendant has "purposefully invoked the benefits and protections of a State's law" for jurisdictional purposes.[295]

Justice Stevens, with whom Justice White joined, dissented primarily on the ground that Rudzewicz had no "reason to anticipate a Burger King suit outside of Michigan."[296] If this were the problem, the question arises why Burger King did not use its "bargaining power,"[297] to which Justice Stevens also refers, and insert in the franchise agreement a consent to the jurisdiction of Florida courts. In this regard Burger King's franchise agreement was superbly drafted. The Michigan Franchise Investment Act, as interpreted and applied by the Act's administrator,[298] forbade a consent to a jurisdiction clause. The choice-of-law clause was not forbidden, so long as it did not purport to prevent application of the Act to issues covered by the Act.[299] That clause, with the accompanying disclaimer to the effect that it did not mean that "all" suits concerning the franchise agreement had to be filed in Florida, may have tipped the balance in favor of finding sufficient Florida "minimum contacts."

Asahi Metal Industry Co. v. Superior Court,[300] has the potential of further complicating the due process test for personal jurisdiction and

---

293.   See, e.g., Shaffer v. Heitner, 433 U.S. 186, 224–26, 97 S.Ct. 2569, 2590–91, 53 L.Ed.2d 683, 710–11 (1977) (Brennan, J., concurring in part and dissenting in part).

294.   *Burger King,* 471 U.S. at 481–82, 105 S.Ct. at 2187, 85 L.Ed.2d at 547.

295.   Id. at 482, 105 S.Ct. at 2187, 85 L.Ed.2d at 547. Cf. N.Y.—McKinney's Gen. Oblig.L. §§ 5–1401, 5–1402 (parties to contracts involving not less than amount specified in sections may agree to have New York law apply even though contract does not bear a reasonable relation to New York, and, if this is done, and defendant has consented to the jurisdiction of New York courts, suit may be maintained in New York); Iowa Elec. Light & Power Co. v. Atlas Corp., 603 F.2d 1301 (8th Cir.1979), cert. denied, 445 U.S. 911, 100 S.Ct. 1090, 63 L.Ed.2d 327 (1980) (clause choosing forum law not sufficient to confer jurisdiction); United States Trust Co. v. Bohart, 197 Conn. 34, 495 A.2d 1034 (1985) (choice of forum law a factor in deciding jurisdiction exists); Dent–Air, Inc. v. Beech Mountain Air Service, 332 N.W.2d 904 (Minn.1983) (no jurisdiction despite clause choosing forum law).

296.   *Burger King,* 471 U.S. at 488, 105 S.Ct. at 2190, 85 L.Ed.2d at 551 (quoting from opinion of Court of Appeals).

297.   Id. at 489, 105 S.Ct. at 2191, 85 L.Ed.2d at 552 (quoting from opinion of Court of Appeals).

298.   The relevant statutory provision in 1979 when the franchise contract was entered into was: Mich.Comp.L.Ann. § 445.1513: "The department may summarily issue a stop order ... revoking effectiveness of any registration or suspend or revoke an exemption [from registration, to which Burger King was entitled] if it finds ... (c) The offering ... would create an unreasonable risk to prospective franchisees...." (These provisions were revised in 1984). "Unreasonable risk" was interpreted to include having to go to a foreign state to defend an action. Telephone interview with Ms. Ann Baker, administrator of Michigan Franchise Investment Act during relevant period.

299.   The following provision was so interpreted: Mich.Comp.L.Ann. § 445.1504(1): "[Michigan] act applies to all written or oral arrangements between a franchiser and franchisee in connection with the offer or sale of a franchise." Telephone interview with Ms. Ann Baker.

300.   480 U.S. 102, 107 S.Ct. 1026, 94 L.Ed.2d 92 (1987).

inviting an even greater amount of litigation on that issue. When his motorcycle's rear tire suddenly lost air and exploded, Gary Zurcher, a California resident, lost control of his motorcycle and fell in front of a truck on a California highway.[301] Zurcher was injured and his wife, a passenger, was killed. Zurcher and his children sued Cheng Shin, the Taiwanese manufacturer of the tire tube. They also sued the California retail distributor of the tire, but not Asahi, the Japanese manufacturer of the tube's valve assembly. Cheng Shin filed a cross-complaint seeking indemnity from its codefendants and from new cross-defendants, including Asahi. Asahi manufactured valve assemblies in Japan and sold them to several tube manufacturers. The valves sold to Cheng Shin were shipped from Japan to Taiwan. Cheng Shin used over 100,000 Asahi valves a year. Twenty percent of Cheng Shin's sales in the United States were in California. Asahi knew that Cheng Shin would use some of the valve assemblies in tubes sold in California. Asahi also sold valves to other tube manufacturers who sold tubes in California. Asahi had no offices, property, or agents in California, solicited no business there, and made no direct sales in California.

Asahi moved to quash the summons on the grounds of lack of personal jurisdiction and inconvenient forum.[302] The trial court denied the motion but the California intermediate appellate court reversed. After the plaintiffs filed a petition for hearing in the California Supreme Court, Zurcher and his children accepted a settlement payment from Cheng Shin and their complaint was dismissed with prejudice. The California Supreme Court found that "the dismissal has no bearing on the propriety of California's exercise of jurisdiction over Asahi" with regard to Cheng Shin's cross-complaint and affirmed the trial court's denial of the motion to quash.[303] The Supreme Court of the United States granted certiorari and reversed.

Although all nine justices joined in the result, their reasoning varied. Justice O'Connor, in an opinion joined by three other justices,[304] held that Asahi did not have sufficient "minimum contacts" with California to permit exercise of jurisdiction. She noted a split in the way in which lower courts had applied the "stream of commerce" basis for jurisdiction that the Court had approved in *World–Wide Volkswagen Corp. v. Woodson*.[305] "Some courts have understood the Due Process

---

301. Response to Petition for a Writ of Certiorari to United States Supreme Court in *Asahi*, p. 1. [Unless otherwise indicated, all references to documents are to those filed in the United States Supreme Court in *Asahi*.]

302. Motion to Quash Summons in Superior Court of California, County of Solano, Zurcher v. Dunlop Tire & Rubber Co. No. 76180 filed December 16, 1982. California procedure permits combining a motion to quash for lack of jurisdiction with a forum non conveniens motion to stay or dismiss. Cal.C.Civ.Proc. § 418.10(a).

303. Asahi Metal Indus. Co. v. Superior Court, 39 Cal.3d 35, 52 n.9 n.9, 216 Cal.Rptr. 385, 395 n.9, 702 P.2d 543, 552, n.9. (1985), reversed, 480 U.S. 102, 107 S.Ct. 1026, 94 L.Ed.2d 92 (1987).

304. Chief Justice Rehnquist and Justices Powell and Scalia.

305. 444 U.S. 286, 100 S.Ct. 559, 62 L.Ed.2d 490 (1980). [Discussed supra text accompanying notes 208–228].

Clause ... to allow an exercise of personal jurisdiction to be based on no more than the defendant's act of placing the product in the stream of commerce. Other courts have understood the Due Process Clause ... to require the action of the defendant to be more purposefully directed at the forum State than the mere act of placing a product in the stream of commerce."[306] Justice O'Connor agreed with this second position and found that this reasoning precluded jurisdiction over Asahi by a California state court[307] because "[a]ssuming ... that respondents have established Asahi's awareness that some of the valves sold to Cheng Shin would be incorporated into tire tubes sold in California, respondents have not demonstrated any action by Asahi to purposefully avail itself of the California market."[308] Asahi "did not create, control, or employ the distribution system that brought its valves to California."[309]

Then, in a part of her opinion joined in by eight Justices,[310] Justice O'Connor stated that even if Asahi had "minimum contacts" with California, under the peculiar facts of this case, exercise of jurisdiction would nevertheless be unreasonable. The original California plaintiffs had settled, so that "[a]ll that remains is a claim for indemnification asserted by Cheng Shin, a Taiwanese corporation, against Asahi."[311] Therefore, in the light of "the burden on the defendant, the interests of the forum state, and the plaintiff's interest in obtaining relief,"[312] fairness precluded jurisdiction over Asahi. The burden on the Japanese

---

306. *Asahi*, 480 U.S. at 110, 107 S.Ct. at 1031.

307. Justice O'Connor left open the question of whether Congress could authorize a federal court to exercise jurisdiction over an alien defendant "based on the aggregate of *national* contacts." Id. at 113 n.*, 107 S.Ct. at 1032 n.* (Emphasis in original).

Federal Rule of Civil Procedure 4(k)(2), which took effect on December 1, 1993, permits accumulating national contacts to obtain jurisdiction over defendants to pursue federal claims. A requirement is that "the defendant is not subject to jurisdiction in any state's courts of general jurisdiction." (As reworded in 2007). This requirement may reverse the usual tactical position of the parties. United States v. Swiss American Bank, Ltd., 191 F.3d 30 (1st Cir. 1999), rules that a plaintiff seeking to use 4(k)(2) must make a prima facie showing "(1) that the claim asserted arises under federal law, (2) that personal jurisdiction is not available under any situation-specific federal statute, and (3) that the putative defendant's contacts with the nation as a whole suffice to satisfy the applicable constitutional requirements. The plaintiff, moreover, must certify that, based on the information that is readily available to the plaintiff and his counsel, the defendant is not subject to suit in the courts of general jurisdiction of any state. If the plaintiff makes out his prima facie case, the burden shifts to the defendant to produce evidence which, if credited, would show either than one or more specific states exist in which it would be subject to suit or that its contacts with the United States are constitutionally insufficient." Id. at 41. ISI Int'l, Inc. v. Borden Ladner Gervais LLP, 256 F.3d 548 (7th Cir. 2001), suggests a different and preferable allocation of burdens. A defendant who wants to avoid the use of Rule 4(k)(2) must name some other state in which the plaintiff has jurisdiction over the defendant, thereby consenting to jurisdiction there.

308. *Asahi*, 480 U.S. at 112, 107 S.Ct. at 1032.

309. Id.

310. Only Justice Scalia did not join.

311. *Asahi*, 480 U.S. at 114, 107 S.Ct. at 1033.

312. Id. Justice O'Connor added that the court "must also weigh in its determination 'the interstate judicial system's interest in obtaining the most efficient resolution of controversies; and the shared interest of the several States in furthering fundamental substantive social policies.' World–Wide Volkswagen [v. Woodson], 444 U.S. [286], at 292 [(1980)]."

defendant, if required to defend itself "in a foreign legal system," would be "severe."[313] "California's legitimate interests in the dispute have considerably diminished"[314] because no California plaintiff is now involved. Although "[t]he possibility of being haled into a California court . . . creates an additional deterrent to the manufacture of unsafe components; . . . similar pressure will be placed on Asahi by the purchasers of its components" who sell in California products incorporating those components and who "are subject to California tort law."[315] As for plaintiff's interest, "Cheng Shin has not demonstrated that it is more convenient for it to litigate its indemnity claim against Asahi in California rather than in Taiwan or Japan."[316] Moreover, the "international context"[317] of the case was a significant weight against the exercise of jurisdiction. "[T]he Federal interest in its foreign relations policies, will be best served by a careful inquiry into the reasonableness of the assertion of jurisdiction in the particular case, and an unwillingness to find the serious burdens on an alien defendant outweighed by minimal interests on the part of the plaintiff or the forum State."[318]

The portion of the opinion of greatest importance is the holding, joined in by eight Justices, that even if Asahi had "minimum contacts" with California out of which the action arose, due process would prevent jurisdiction in California courts because of countervailing considerations of fairness in the light of the burden on the defendant, the interest of the forum in providing redress, and the interest of the plaintiff in obtaining relief in the forum. As Justice Brennan said in concurring in this part of the opinion, "[t]his is one of those rare cases in which 'minimum requirements inherent in the concept of fair play and substantial justice' . . . defeat the reasonableness of jurisdiction even [though] the defendant has purposefully engaged in forum activities."[319] Although Justice Brennan labels this effect as "rare," the requirement of "contacts-plus" has created an additional incentive for litigation on the threshold issue of jurisdiction over the defendant. Forests have already been denuded to print the case reports in which courts analyze the *Asahi* fairness factors to determine the due process limits on jurisdiction. Courts have even applied the *Asahi* factors when the defendant's contacts with the forum are so continuous and systematic as to confer general jurisdiction over the defendant.[320]

---

313. *Asahi*, 480 U.S. at 114, 107 S.Ct. at 1033.

314. Id.

315. Id.

316. Id.

317. Id. at 116, 107 S.Ct. at 1035.

318. Id.

319. Id. (Brennan, J., concurring in part and in the judgment). See TH Agriculture & Nutrition, LLC v. Ace European Group Ltd., 488 F.3d 1282 (10th Cir. 2007) (after finding minimum contacts, court holds that *Asahi* factors prevent jurisdiction over Dutch owners of insurers).

320. See Tuazon v. R.J. Reynolds Tobacco Co., 433 F.3d 1163 (9th Cir. 2006); Metropolitan Life Ins. Co. v. Robertson–Ceco Corp., 84 F.3d 560 (2d Cir.), cert. denied, 519 U.S. 1006, 117 S.Ct. 508, 136 L.Ed.2d 398 (1996). Walker, J., dissents, disagreeing with the

It is not a new concept that sometimes, despite a defendant-forum nexus out of which the claim arises, considerations of fairness may preclude jurisdiction, but *Asahi* is its most dramatic realization. The Second Restatement of Conflict of Laws, in section 37, describes the jurisdictional test in cases like *Asahi* as follows:

> A state has power to exercise judicial jurisdiction over an individual who causes effects in the state by an act done elsewhere with respect to any cause of action arising from these effects *unless the nature of the effects and of the individual's relationship to the state make the exercise of such jurisdiction unreasonable.*[321]

Comment *a* adds another reasonableness factor, "[t]he plaintiff's relationship to the state."[322] Moreover, the California Supreme Court opinion in *Asahi* echoed these concepts: "If minimum contacts exist, the due process clause also requires this court to determine whether jurisdiction is fair and reasonable."[323]

This notion, that a court must balance the defendant's minimum contacts against other factors, developed slowly in United States Supreme Court opinions and, until *Asahi,* always in dicta. In *International Shoe Co. v. Washington,*[324] the focus was on the requirement of "minimum contacts,"[325] although the Court also spoke of "the inconveniences" to the defendant resulting from a trial in the forum.[326] *McGee v. International Life Insurance Co.*[327] noted that "California has a manifest interest in providing effective means of redress for its residents"[328] and that "there may be inconvenience to the insurer ... but certainly nothing which amounts to a denial of due process."[329] *Kulko v. Superior Court*[330] quotes the Second Restatement of Conflicts, section 37[331] and notes that under it, even when the defendant's acts outside the forum have caused injury in the forum or otherwise affected forum residents, "there might be circumstances that would render 'unreasonable' the

---

cases he collects that apply *Asahi* in general jurisdiction cases and urging that in *Metropolitan Life* the court should reach the result under the discretionary doctrine of forum non conveniens. Id. at 577–78.

321.   Restatement, Second, § 37 (1971) (emphasis added).

322.   Id. comment *a*.

323.   Asahi Metal Indus. Co. v. Superior Court, 39 Cal.3d 35, 52, 216 Cal.Rptr. 385, 394, 702 P.2d 543, 552 (1985) reversed, 480 U.S. 102, 107 S.Ct. 1026, 94 L.Ed.2d 92 (1987).

324.   326 U.S. 310, 66 S.Ct. 154, 90 L.Ed. 95 (1945). [Discussed supra text accompanying notes 161–165].

325.   Id. at 316, 66 S.Ct. at 158, 90 L.Ed. at 102.

326.   Id. at 317, 66 S.Ct. at 158, 90 L.Ed. at 102.

327.   355 U.S. 220, 78 S.Ct. 199, 2 L.Ed.2d 223 (1957). [Discussed supra text accompanying notes 166–168].

328.   Id. at 223, 78 S.Ct. at 201, 2 L.Ed.2d at 226.

329.   Id. at 224, 78 S.Ct. at 201, 2 L.Ed.2d at 226.

330.   436 U.S. 84, 98 S.Ct. 1690, 56 L.Ed.2d 132 (1978). [Discussed supra text accompanying notes 186–207.]

331.   Id. at 96, 98 S.Ct. at 1699, 56 L.Ed. at 143–144. For text of Restatement, Second, § 37, see supra note 321 and accompanying text.

assertion of jurisdiction over the nonresident defendant."[332] The Court's conclusion that there was no jurisdiction over the nonresident father was based on "basic considerations of fairness."[333] *World–Wide Volkswagen Corp. v. Woodson*[334] listed a number of factors to be weighed against "the burden on the defendant":[335]

> the forum State's interest in adjudicating the dispute; the plaintiff's interest in obtaining convenient and effective relief, at least when that interest is not adequately protected by the plaintiff's power to choose the forum; the interstate judicial system's interest in obtaining the most efficient resolution of controversies; and the shared interest of the several States in furthering fundamental substantive social policies.[336]

Rush v. Savchuk[337] stated that "[i]f a defendant has certain judicially cognizable ties with a State, a variety of factors relating to the particular cause of action may be relevant to the determination whether the exercise of jurisdiction would comport with 'traditional notions of fair play and substantial justice.' "[338]

In sharp contrast with *Asahi, Keeton v. Hustler Magazine, Inc.*[339] rejected an argument based on plaintiff's lack of contacts with the forum:

> [W]e have not to date required a plaintiff to have "minimum contacts" with the forum State....

> The plaintiff's residence is not ... completely irrelevant.... [Plaintiff's residence] may ... enhance defendant's contacts with the forum.... [and] may be the focus of the activities of the defendant out of which the suit arises. But plaintiff's residence in the forum State is not a separate requirement, and lack of residence will not defeat jurisdiction established on the basis of defendant's contacts.[340]

The Court did note that "the 'fairness' of haling respondent into a New Hampshire court depends to some extent on whether respondent's activities relating to New Hampshire are such as to give that State a legitimate interest in holding respondent answerable on a claim related to those activities."[341]

---

332. Id.

333. Id. at 97, 98 S.Ct. at 1699, 56 L.Ed.2d at 144.

334. 444 U.S. 286, 100 S.Ct. 559, 62 L.Ed.2d 490 (1980). [Discussed supra text accompanying notes 208–228].

335. Id. at 292, 100 S.Ct. at 564, 62 L.Ed.2d at 498.

336. Id. (Citations omitted).

337. 444 U.S. 320, 100 S.Ct. 571, 62 L.Ed.2d 516 (1980). (Discussed in § 4.29).

338. Id. at 332, 100 S.Ct. at 579, 62 L.Ed.2d at 528.

339. 465 U.S. 770, 104 S.Ct. 1473, 79 L.Ed.2d 790 (1984). [Discussed supra text accompanying notes 239–249].

340. Id. at 779–80, 104 S.Ct. at 1480–81, 79 L.Ed.2d at 800–01.

341. Id. at 775–76, 104 S.Ct. at 1479, 79 L.Ed.2d at 798.

Calder v. Jones,[342] decided the same day as *Keeton*, said with regard to the relevance of plaintiff's relationship to the forum, "[t]he plaintiff's lack of 'contacts' will not defeat otherwise proper jurisdiction, but they may be so manifold as to permit jurisdiction when it would not exist in their absence."[343]

Finally, in *Burger King Corp. v. Rudzewicz*,[344] there appears in dicta the clearest statement before *Asahi* that minimum contacts between defendant and forum may not suffice in the face of countervailing considerations of fairness:

> Once it has been decided that a defendant purposefully established minimum contacts with the forum State, these contacts may be considered in light of other factors to determine whether the assertion of personal jurisdiction would comport with "fair play and substantial justice." . . . These considerations sometimes serve to establish the reasonableness of jurisdiction upon a lesser showing of minimum contacts than would otherwise be required. On the other hand, where a defendant who purposefully has directed his activities at forum residents seeks to defeat jurisdiction, he must present a compelling case that the presence of some other considerations would render jurisdiction unreasonable. . . . Nevertheless, *minimum requirements inherent in the concept of "fair play and substantial justice" may defeat the reasonableness of jurisdiction even if the defendant has purposefully engaged in forum activities.*[345]

> [There is jurisdiction over the defendant because of his] substantial and continuing relationship with [the forum], . . . fair notice . . . that he might be subject to suit [there], and [he] *has failed to demonstrate how jurisdiction in the forum would otherwise be fundamentally unfair. . . .* [346]

Although, therefore, there is precedent for *Asahi*'s contacts-plus rationale, the question remains whether it is wise. The success of this argument in *Asahi*, as noted above, has encouraged its use in many special appearances,[347] which are already one of the major burdens on

---

342. 465 U.S. 783, 104 S.Ct. 1482, 79 L.Ed.2d 804 (1984). [Discussed supra text accompanying notes 250–255].

343. Id. at 788, 104 S.Ct. at 1486, 79 L.Ed.2d at 811. (Citation omitted).

344. 471 U.S. 462, 105 S.Ct. 2174, 85 L.Ed.2d 528 (1985). [Discussed supra text accompanying notes 285–300].

345. Id. at 476, 105 S.Ct. at 2184, 85 L.Ed.2d at 543–44. (Emphasis added).

346. Id. at 487, 105 S.Ct. at 2190, 85 L.Ed.2d at 550. (Emphasis added).

347. See § 4.37. City of Monroe Employees Retirement System v. Bridgestone Corporation, 399 F.3d 651 (6th Cir. 2005), cert. denied, 546 U.S. 936, 126 S.Ct. 423, 163 L.Ed.2d 322 (2005), affirmed the district court's holding of no jurisdiction over a defendant solely on the *Asahi* factors without considering whether that defendant purposefully availed himself of the privilege of acting in the forum or whether the action arose from his actions in the forum. See also Benton v. Cameco Corp., 375 F.3d 1070 (10th Cir. 2004), cert. denied, 544 U.S. 974, 125 S.Ct. 1826, 161 L.Ed.2d 723 (2005) (case dismissed for lack of jurisdiction because even though defendant had sufficient forum contacts to warrant assertion of specific jurisdiction, exercise of jurisdiction would violate *Asahi* fairness factors).

our courts. The portion of the opinion joined in by eight of the Justices raises to the level of due process concepts usually associated with the discretionary dismissal doctrine of forum non conveniens.[348] Asahi's motion to the trial court to quash the summons was "for lack of jurisdiction *and inconvenient forum.*"[349] From that point on, the forum non conveniens aspects of *Asahi* seem to have been lost sight of. Asahi's trial brief discussed only whether jurisdiction was constitutionally permissible.[350] The closest the California Supreme Court opinion comes to mentioning forum non conveniens is in the last paragraph of the dissent:

> The net result of the majority decision is that a Taiwanese corporation can litigate in California against a Japanese corporation that has absolutely no connection with California in a case in which the California plaintiffs have declared themselves made whole. Surely our overburdened courts should be concerned with disputes that more directly involve California.[351]

A way in which the also "overburdened" United States Supreme Court could have been spared deciding this "rare"[352] case would have been for the California Supreme Court to have remanded the matter to the trial judge so that he might exercise his discretion on the forum non conveniens motion in the light of a circumstance he could not previously have considered—the settlement by the California plaintiffs after the petition for hearing was filed with the California Supreme Court. Instead the California high court chose to declare that the settlement "has no bearing on the propriety of California's exercise of jurisdiction over Asahi."[353]

Even granting that the interest of the forum state in hearing the case and the burden on the defendant in appearing in that forum are circumstances to be weighed against minimum contacts in determining the reasonableness of jurisdiction, it is not self-evident that the Court struck a proper balance in *Asahi*. The least cogent portion of Justice O'Connor's opinion is that which responds to the California Supreme Court's assertion that "California has a strong interest in protecting its

---

348. See § 4.33. In *Burger King* there is the statement that "a defendant claiming substantial inconvenience may seek a change of venue." 471 U.S. at 487, 105 S.Ct. at 2190, 85 L.Ed.2d at 544. There is then a reference to 28 U.S.C.A. § 1404(a) with the comment: "This provision embodies in an expanded version the common law doctrine of forum non conveniens...." Id. at 477 n.20, 105 S.Ct. at 2190 n.20, 85 L.Ed.2d at 544 n.20.

349. See supra note 301 (emphasis added).

350. Memorandum of Points and Authorities filed by attorneys for Asahi (cross-defendants) in Zurcher v. Dunlop Tire & Rubber Co., No. 76180, Superior Court of California, County of Solano, January 5, 1983.

351. Asahi Metal Indus. Co. v. Superior Court, 39 Cal.3d 35, 56, 216 Cal.Rptr. 385, 397, 702 P.2d 543, 555 (1985) (Lucas, J., dissenting), reversed, 480 U.S. 102, 107 S.Ct. 1026, 94 L.Ed.2d 92 (1987).

352. *Asahi*, 480 U.S. at 116, 107 S.Ct. at 1035 (Brennan, J. concurring in part and in the judgment).

353. Asahi Metal Indus. Co. v. Superior Court, 39 Cal.3d 35, 52 n.9 216, 216 Cal.Rptr. 385, 702 P.2d 543, 552, n.9 (1985) rev'd, 480 U.S. 102, 107 S.Ct. 1026, 94 L.Ed.2d 92 (1987).

consumers by ensuring that foreign manufacturers comply with the state's safety standards."[354] Justice O'Connor responds:

> The possibility of being haled into a California court … undoubtedly creates an additional deterrent to the manufacture of unsafe components; however, similar pressures will be placed on Asahi by the purchasers of its components as long as those who use Asahi components in their final products, and sell those products in California, are subject to the application of California tort law.[355]

Justice O'Connor also states that "it is not at all clear" that California law should govern Cheng Shin's claim against Asahi for indemnity.[356] On this choice-of-law issue, it is important to distinguish between the law that will determine whether, as a foundation for Cheng Shin's claim for indemnity, Asahi is liable to the injured users, and the law that will determine to what indemnity, if any, Cheng Shin is entitled if Asahi is liable for personal injury. California law should apply to the issue of Asahi's underlying liability, although Japanese or Taiwanese law might govern the issue of indemnity.[357] The importance of having California strict liability law apply to Asahi's liability should have Cheng Shin's answer the O'Connor's statement: "Cheng Shin has not demonstrated that it is more convenient for it to litigate its indemnification claim against Asahi in California rather than in Taiwan or Japan."[358] Even as to the law of indemnity, until Asahi demonstrates that relevant foreign law is different from that of California, considerations of judicial efficiency justify regarding foreign law as the same as forum law.[359]

The Court's description of defendant's burden reads as though Asahi would travel by canoe, had no product liability insurance, and could not, as it did, hire excellent lawyers:

> Certainly the burden on the defendant in this case is severe. Asahi has been commanded … not only to, traverse the distance between Asahi's headquarters in Japan and … California, but also to submit its dispute with Cheng Shin to a foreign nation's judicial system. The unique burdens placed upon one who must defend oneself in a foreign legal system should have significant weight in assessing the reasonableness of stretching the long arm of personal jurisdiction

---

354. Id. at 53, 216 Cal.Rptr. at 395, 702 P.2d at 553. The California high court also asserted that California was interested in providing a forum for "the orderly administration of its laws [because] most of the evidence … is within its borders" and, in the light of the multiple cross-defendants, to prevent "multiple and possibly conflicting adjudications." Id.

355. 480 U.S. at 115, 107 S.Ct. at 1033.

356. Id.

357. See Piper Aircraft Co. v. Reyno, 454 U.S. 235, 243 n.7, 102 S.Ct. 252, 259 n.7, 70 L.Ed.2d 419, 428 n.7 (1981) ("The District Court explained that inconsistent verdicts might result [if United States defendants filed indemnity or contribution suits against Scottish defendants in Scotland] if [United States defendants] were held liable on the basis of strict liability here, and then required to prove negligence in an indemnity action in Scotland").

358. *Asahi*, 480 U.S. at 114, 107 S.Ct. at 1033.

359. See § 3.7. For discussion of applying the laws of different jurisdictions to different issues in the same case, see §§ 3.4 and 3.4A.

This reference to "national borders" brings attention to the "international context"[360] of *Asahi* as emphasized in Justice O'Connor's opinion.[361] Concern to avoid offending friendly foreign nations is commendable, but is relevant only if a United States court is exercising jurisdiction that is "exorbitant"[362] under international standards. Forbidding the exercise of jurisdiction over foreign manufacturers simply because they are foreigners would give them an unwarranted advantage over United States manufacturers.[363] A good measure of commonly accepted bases for jurisdiction in cases such as *Asahi* is provided by the Brussels Regulation:

Article 5:

> A person domiciled in a Contracting State may, in another Contracting State, be sued: . . . 3. in matters relating to tort, delict or quasi-delict, in the courts for the place where the harmful event occurred or may occur.

Article 6:

> A person domiciled in a Contracting State may also be sued: . . . 2. as a third party in an action on a warranty or guarantee or in any other third party proceedings, in the court seized of the original proceedings, unless these were instituted solely with the object of removing him from the jurisdiction of the court which would be competent in his case.[364]

Thus, under the Brussels Regulation, if the injuries had occurred in the European Union, either of these two articles would confer jurisdiction over Asahi.

Perhaps even more to the point, six years before the Supreme Court of the United States decided *Asahi,* the Japanese Supreme Court took an expansive view of international jurisdiction. *Goto v. Malaysian Airline System Berhad*[365] upheld jurisdiction over the Malaysian Airline in a suit for breach of an air transportation contract resulting in the death of plaintiffs' husband and father. The crash occurred in Malaysia on a domestic Malaysian flight. The court indicated that in international cases jurisdiction is based on rules of reason for maintaining impartiality, fairness, and speediness. These requirements are met if the Japanese court has jurisdiction over the foreign party in accordance with the Japanese Code of Civil Procedure's venue provisions including the defendant's residence, the place where the defendant has a place of business

---

360. *Asahi*, 480 U.S. at 116, 107 S.Ct. at 1034.

361. Id.

362. See § 4.1 notes 3–11 and accompanying text.

363. See Asahi, Respondent's Brief in the Supreme Court of the United States, pp. 27–28; cf. Helicopteros Nacionales de Colombia, S.A. v. Hall, 466 U.S. 408, 104 S.Ct. 1868, 80 L.Ed.2d 404 (1984), Brief for the United States as Amicus Curiae at 1–2 (should not exert general jurisdiction based on purchases here because this would discourage foreign corporations from buying American products).

364. Brussels Regulation, supra § 4.1 note 6.

365. 35 Minshu 1224 (1981).

(the provision applicable in *Goto*—the defendant had an office in Tokyo although this office had no connection to the relevant transportation contract), where the defendant's property is located, and "a place of tort."[366]

The most ominous aspect of the *Asahi* opinion is that four Justices joined in the finding that Asahi did not have "minimum contacts" with California.[367] Although none of the opinions says so in plain English, this means that jurisdiction over Asahi was not available in the California courts even on behalf of the slain and mangled California residents.[368] The reasoning of this portion of the opinion was that minimum contacts did not exist because Asahi did not "purposefully avail itself of the California market.... It did not create, control, or employ the distribution system that brought its valves to California."[369] It was not sufficient that Asahi was aware "that the stream of commerce may or will sweep the product into the forum state."[370]

These terms describe the typical manufacturer of a component part. That component part makers are intended to be exempt from jurisdiction even in suits by injured consumers in the state where the finished product caused blood to flow, is indicated by the cases cited favorably[371]

---

366. Japanese C. Civ. P. art. 15. In Mukoda v. The Boeing Co. (Far Eastern Air Transport Case), 604 Hanrei Taimuzu (The Law Times Report) 138 (1986), summary and partial English translation in 31 Japanese Annual of Int'l Law 216 (1988), the Tokyo District Court dismissed a wrongful death suit against United States defendants even though, under the Japanese Civil Code, venue was proper. Suit was for wrongful deaths resulting from an airplane crash in Taiwan. The reasons for dismissal resembled the doctrine of forum non conveniens. The court found that suit in Japan was unfair because evidence and witnesses in Taiwan were important to the defense. A Japanese court could not obtain this evidence or the testimony of these witnesses by judicial assistance because Japan did not have diplomatic relations with Taiwan.

367. *Asahi*, 480 U.S. at 108–13, 107 S.Ct. at 1030–32.

368. See *Asahi*, Petitioner's Brief in the Supreme Court of the United States, p. 23 n.33: "Even if the California plaintiffs sued Asahi for their personal injuries there would still be no basis for the exercise of jurisdiction over Asahi." See also Seidelson, *A Supreme Court Conclusion and Two Rationales That Defy Comprehension: Asahi Metal Indus. Co., Ltd. v. Superior Court of California*, 53 Brooklyn L. Rev. 563, 578 (1987) (shielding Asahi from suit by the injured users when Asahi "utilizes a distributive chain that it knows will carry its products into the forum" is "without an apparent rationale").

369. *Asahi*, 480 U.S. at 112, 107 S.Ct. at 1032.

370. Id.

371. Id. at 111, 107 S.Ct. at 1032 citing and discussing Humble v. Toyota Motor Co., 727 F.2d 709 (8th Cir.1984) (injured forum resident denied jurisdiction over manufacturer of automobile seat).

Justice O'Connor indicates forum contacts that may subject the defendant to jurisdiction, some of which might apply to component part manufacturers: "Additional conduct of the defendant may indicate an intent or purpose to serve the market in the forum State, for example, designing the product for the market in the forum State, advertising in the forum State, establishing channels for providing regular advice to customers in the forum State, or marketing the product through a distributor who has agreed to serve as the sales agent in the forum State." *Asahi,* 480 U.S. at 112, 107 S.Ct. at 1032. Justice O'Connor cites Rockwell Int'l Corp. v. Costruzioni Aeronautiche Giovanni Agusta, S.P.A., 553 F.Supp. 328 (E.D.Pa. 1982) as an example of a case in which a component part manufacturer "designed its product in anticipation of sales in [the forum]." *Asahi,* 480 U.S. at 113, 107 S.Ct. at 1032. In *Rockwell,* the part was a replacement part purchased in the forum and custom designed for the product of which it was a part. It should be noted, however, that in

and with disapproval[372] by Justice O'Connor in this portion of her opinion. The headwaters of the "stream of commerce" basis for jurisdiction, *Gray v. American Radiator & Standard Sanitary Corp.,*[373] was itself a case permitting an injured forum resident to obtain jurisdiction over a component part manufacturer. *Gray* received a "cf." citation after the declaration in *World–Wide Volkswagen* that "[t]he forum State does not exceed its powers under the Due Process Clause if it asserts personal jurisdiction over a corporation that delivers its products into the stream of commerce with the expectation that they will be purchased by consumers in the forum State."[374] This did not escape the notice of counsel for Asahi who argued in their brief that "the Court had at that point not cited Gray for the purpose of embracing any more than the concept which Gray had expressed."[375] It is noteworthy that *Gray* is not cited by Justice O'Connor in finding no minimum contacts, but is cited by Justice Brennan in expressing his disagreement with that conclusion.[376]

If an injured user is not able to obtain jurisdiction over a component part manufacturer, is this of any real consequence? In many cases, perhaps in most cases, as in *Asahi,* the seller of the finished product and the local retailer will be amenable to jurisdiction, responsible under doctrines such as strict liability in tort[377] for the injury caused by the defective component, and have assets sufficient to pay the judgment. There is, however, a danger that the user's recovery may depend upon jurisdiction over the component part maker. The component part manufacturer may be a giant corporation selling its parts for inclusion in the products of many companies. The manufacturer of the finished product and the retailer, on the other hand, may not be adequately insured and may not otherwise have the resources to satisfy the judgment.

Moreover, the injury may occur under circumstances in which only the component part manufacturer is liable. *Hedrick v. Daiko Shoji Co., Ltd,*[378] one of the cases Justice O'Connor cites with disapproval in *Asahi,*[379] provides an example. An Oregon longshoreman was injured in

---

Humble, supra this note, in which jurisdiction was denied, the component part was a car seat manufactured to the automobile maker's specifications.

372. *Asahi,* 480 U.S. at 111, 107 S.Ct. at 1031, citing Bean Dredging Corp. v. Dredge Technology Corp., 744 F.2d 1081 (5th Cir.1984) (uphold jurisdiction over impleaded component part manufacturer in suit for property damage); Hedrick v. Daiko Shoji Co., Ltd., 715 F.2d 1355 (9th Cir.1983), modified, 733 F.2d 1335 (9th Cir.1984) (uphold jurisdiction over maker of defective splice in wire rope that caused injury to longshoreman working on ship in forum) (misspelled "Hendrick") [*Hedrick is* discussed infra notes 378–381 and accompanying text].

373. 22 Ill.2d 432, 176 N.E.2d 761 (1961).

374. 444 U.S. at 297–98, 100 S.Ct. at 567, 62 L.Ed.2d at 501–02.

375. *Asahi,* Petitioner's Brief in the Supreme Court of the United States, p. 20.

376. 480 U.S. at 120, 107 S.Ct. at 1036 (Brennan J. concurring in part and in the judgment).

377. See Restatement (Second) Torts § 402A (1965).

378. 715 F.2d 1355 (9th Cir.1983), modified, 733 F.2d 1335 (9th Cir.1984).

379. *Asahi,* 480 U.S. at 111, 107 S.Ct. at 1031.

an Oregon port while working on a ship owned by a Japanese company. The injury occurred when a defective splice in a wire rope parted and allowed a boom to strike the longshoreman. He sued the shipowner and another Japanese company that had manufactured the splice. The splice maker won dismissal at trial on the ground of lack of jurisdiction. The Ninth Circuit reversed, distinguishing this case from *World–Wide Volkswagen,* on the ground that the "probability that the part, sold to an ocean carrier will be used in a foreign port is not fortuitous. It is certain."[380] The court also indicated that the liability of the shipowner would depend on whether the jury found the shipowner negligent in using a poorly designed splice or in not detecting the defect.[381] Thus, depending on a finding of fact, the only defendant liable for plaintiff's injuries may be the splice manufacturer.

Not only the injured plaintiff, but also the manufacturer of the completed product may have a compelling interest in being able to sue the component part maker in the forum. If, for example, there is a factual dispute as to which of several component parts caused the malfunction, the manufacturer that used the parts must be able to implead all the makers in the same lawsuit or face the possibility of losing its claims against all component part manufacturers because of inconsistent verdicts in different forums.[382]

The finding of no minimum contacts may have implications for defendants other than component part manufacturers. The manufacturer of the finished product may utilize a tactic that predated modern long-arm statutes—sell the product at the place of manufacture to an "independent" distributor and claim that the resulting layers in the marketing process insulate the maker from suit in a forum where the product is finally sold to a user and causes injury.[383] *Hutson v. Fehr Bros., Inc.,*[384] cited with approval by Justice O'Connor,[385] is a case in which this argument prevailed. Lumberyard employees were injured in the forum

---

380. *Hedrick,* 715 F.2d at 1358.

381. Id. at 1357.

382. Cf. Uniform Commercial Code § 2–607(5): "Where the buyer is sued for breach of a warranty or other obligation for which his seller is answerable over (a) he may give his seller written notice of the litigation. If the notice states that the seller may come in and defend and that if the seller does not do so he will be bound in any action against him by his buyer by any determination of fact common to the two litigations, then unless the seller after seasonable receipt of the notice does come in and defend he is so bound."

This procedure is sometimes referred to as "vouching in" the seller. See Travelers Indem. Co. v. Evans Pipe Co., 432 F.2d 211 (6th Cir.1970) (vouched-in seller bound by prior litigation in court that did not have jurisdiction over the seller). But see Comment, *Constitutional Limitations on Vouching,* 118 U.Pa. L. Rev. 237, 268 (1969) (vouching in is "subject to the same jurisdictional due process restraints" as impleader).

383. Cf. Watson v. Employers Liability Assurance Corp., 348 U.S. 66, 72, 75 S.Ct. 166, 170, 99 L.Ed. 74, 82 (1954) (permitting injured consumer to sue manufacturer's liability insurer, which had a certificate to do business in the forum, and stating "[i]n this case efforts to serve the [manufacturer] were answered by a motion to dismiss on the ground that [the manufacturer] had no [forum] agent on whom process could be served").

384. 584 F.2d 833 (8th Cir.1978), cert. denied 439 U.S. 983, 99 S.Ct. 573, 58 L.Ed.2d 654 (1978).

385. *Asahi,* 480 U.S. at 111, 107 S.Ct. at 1032.

when a chain broke. The distribution stream that the chain traveled was from an unknown Yugoslavian manufacturer, to an Italian corporation, to a British corporation, to the British corporation's American subsidiary, to the local retailer. In a four-to-three en banc decision, the Eighth Circuit held that the injured employees could not obtain jurisdiction over the Italian corporation even though it had transferred the chain to the British company with exclusive North American resale rights. The reasoning of *Hutson* resembles that of Justice O'Connor: "The [British company] exercises control over the selection of the customers and other marketing decisions relative to the sales of the [Italian company's] products which it purchases."[386]

The contacts-plus reasoning of *Asahi* is not compelling even when applied to the unusual circumstances of that case and is likely to encourage even more challenges to personal jurisdiction. The no "minimum contacts" portion of the opinion threatens a return to the days when injured users of defective products had to hunt afar for a forum in which they could sue the manufacturers.

Federal circuits[387] and state courts[388] have split as to whether part IIA of *Asahi*, which held that Asahi did not have minimum contacts with California, is binding on lower courts. Part IIA received four votes and courts have referred to it as a "plurality" opinion.[389] It is doubtful that IIA is entitled to "plurality" status. Not only did four justices repudiate IIA's conversion of the stream of commerce to a pathetic trickle,[390] but also Justice White refused to join IIA as both unnecessary and as a misapplication of the "purposeful availment" requirement.[391] He indicated that based on "the volume, the value, and the hazardous character of the components," Asahi's contacts with California were sufficiently purposeful to constitute "minimum contacts."[392]

Burnham v. Superior Court,[393] holds that service on a defendant while transiently present in the forum is constitutionally sufficient to

---

386. *Hutson*, 584 F.2d at 837.

387. Circuits following *Asahi* part IIA: Stanton v. St. Jude Medical, Inc., 340 F.3d 690, 694 (8th Cir. 2003) ("cf." cite to part IIA to support holding no jurisdiction over component part maker); Bridgeport Music, Inc. v. Still N The Water Pub, 327 F.3d 472, 480 (6th Cir. 2003), cert. denied, 540 U.S. 948, 124 S.Ct. 399, 157 L.Ed.2d 279 (2003); Boit v. Gar–Tec Products, Inc., 967 F.2d 671 (1st Cir. 1992) (citing cases in accord from 8th and 11th circuits). Contra: Ham v. La Cienega Music Co., 4 F.3d 413 (5th Cir. 1993). Noting split but avoiding ruling on IIA: Pennzoil Products Co. v. Colelli & Associates, Inc., 149 F.3d 197 (3d Cir. 1998); Kernan v. Kurz–Hastings, Inc., 175 F.3d 236 (2d Cir. 1999).

388. Following IIA: Ex parte Alloy Wheels Int'l, Ltd., 882 So.2d 819 (Ala. 2003); Anderson v. Metropolitan Life Ins. Co., 694 A.2d 701 (R.I. 1997); CSR Ltd. v. Link, 925 S.W.2d 591 (Tex. 1996). Contra: Showa Denko K.K. v. Pangle, 202 Ga.App. 245, 414 S.E.2d 658 (1991), Ga. cert. denied (1992); Cox v. Hozelock, Ltd., 105 N.C.App. 52, 411 S.E.2d 640 (1992), review denied, 331 N.C. 116, 414 S.E.2d 752 (1992); Hill v. Showa Denko K.K., 188 W.Va. 654, 425 S.E.2d 609 (1992).

389. See, e.g., Kernan v. Kurz–Hastings, Inc., 175 F.3d 236, 244 (2d Cir. 1999).

390. *Asahi*, 480 U.S. 102, 116, 107 S.Ct. 1026, 1034, 94 L.Ed.2d 92 (1987) (Brennan, J., concurring, joined by White, Marshall, and Blackmun, JJ.)

391. Id. at 121, 107 S.Ct. at 1037 (Stevens, J., concurring).

392. Id.

393. 495 U.S. 604, 110 S.Ct. 2105, 109 L.Ed.2d 631 (1990).

confer personal jurisdiction. The defendant, an estranged husband, while in California attending a business conference and visiting his children, was served with a California court summons and his wife's divorce petition. The marital domicile had been New Jersey and the husband still lived there.

This was not a case that presented an unfair use of transient jurisdiction. Mr. Burnham had been thrown out of his residential forum, New Jersey, and told to litigate his divorce in California. The New Jersey courts found that he "had deliberately and unfairly manipulated [Mrs. Burnham] into moving to California so that he could bring his divorce action in New Jersey where it would be most convenient for him and most inconvenient for [her]."[394] Justice Stevens is right. This was one of those "easy cases" that make "bad law."[395]

Justice Scalia announced the judgment of a unanimous court, but only Chief Justice Rehnquist and Justice Kennedy concurred in his reasoning. Justice Scalia took the position that due process is satisfied "if a state adheres to jurisdictional rules that are generally applied and have always been applied in the United States."[396] Any other standard, he argues, would elevate to constitutional dignity "each Justice's subjective assessment of what is fair and just."[397] Justice Scalia characterizes as "imperious" the notion that "shifting majorities" of the Supreme Court should act "as a platonic check upon the society's greedy adherence to its traditions. . . ."[398]

I leave evaluation of Scalia's constitutional philosophy to others and focus on his argument that declaring transient jurisdiction unconstitutional would be "subjective" and "imperious." One way to rebut this argument is to identify an objective basis for casting transient jurisdiction beyond the pale of civilized procedure. An objective basis is provided by the fact that the use of the defendant's temporary presence in the forum as a basis for personal jurisdiction is contrary to the consensus of civilized nations and, if used against foreigners, may violate international law.

Civil law countries regard transient presence as an unacceptable basis for judicial jurisdiction.[399] One of the basic documents of the

---

394. Burnham v. Burnham (Superior Ct. of N.J.App.Div., July 24, 1989), Joint Appendix II at 31, *Burnham.* See Uniform Interstate Family Support Act (2001) 9 pt. IB ULA 159, 185 § 201: "(a) In a proceeding to establish or enforce a support order or determine parentage, a tribunal of this State my exercise personal jurisdiction over a nonresident individual if: . . . (5) the child resides in this State as a result of the acts or directives of the individual"; Sneed v. Sneed, 164 Ohio App.3d 496, 503, 842 N.E.2d 1095, 1101 (2005) ("when there is a pattern of abuse or harassment, the resident parent will be considered to have fled as a result of the 'acts or directives' of the nonresident parent, and, as such, personal jurisdiction is appropriate under the UIFSA statute").

395. *Burnham,* 495 U.S. at 640 & id. n.*, 110 S.Ct. at 2126 & id. n.*, 109 L.Ed.2d at 658 & id. n.* (Stevens, J., concurring in the judgment).

396. Id. at 623, 110 S.Ct. at 2117, 109 L.Ed.2d at 647.

397. Id.

398. Id. at 627 n.5, 110 S.Ct. at 2119 n.5, 109 L.Ed.2d at 650 n.5.

399. See Ginsburg, *The Competent Court in Private International Law: Some Observations on Current Views in the United States,* 20 Rutgers L. Rev. 89, 90, 98 (1965); Hay,

European Union is the Brussels Regulation.[400] Annex I of this Regulation lists all the exorbitant bases for personal jurisdiction used by any of the Union members. These grounds for jurisdiction that are not generally recognized include, in France, plaintiff's domicile[401], and, in Germany, the presence of defendant's property.[402] In other words, French courts have jurisdiction over nonresidents even though the case has no nexus with France other than the plaintiff's domicile; in Germany, the kind of quasi in rem jurisdiction rejected in *Shaffer v. Heitner*,[403] was, until reined in by the German Federal Supreme Court,[404] not only alive and well, but also expanded to afford full in personam jurisdiction.

These exorbitant jurisdictional bases are listed in Annex I of the Regulation in order to eliminate them from use against European Union (EU) domiciliaries.[405] When the United Kingdom and Ireland joined the EU, their rules that permitted obtaining jurisdiction over a defendant by

---

Transient Jurisdiction, Especially Over International Defendants. Critical Comments on Burnham v. Superior Court of California, 1990 U.Ill. L. Rev. 593, 600; Nadelmann, *Jurisdictionally Improper Fora,* in XXth Century Comparative and Conflicts Law 321, 331 (K. Nadelmann, A. von Mehren, & J. Hazard eds. 1961).

Whether civil law countries always rejected transient jurisdiction, is debatable. Ulric Huber, the seventeenth century scholar, law professor, and judge, "emphatically denies the propriety of transient jurisdiction." Weinstein, *The Dutch Influence on the Conception of Judicial Jurisdiction in 19th Century America,* 38 Am.J. Comp.L. 73, 89 (1990). According to Professor Weinstein, however, "when Huber states that transient presence is not sufficient to confer jurisdiction, he is not speaking of jurisdiction in the *international* sense, (i.e. jurisdiction that other states will recognize,) but is referring to a jurisdictional limitation imposed by Frisian *municipal* law." Id. at 90. Professor Weinstein then states that transient jurisdiction was not, in Huber's time, regarded as contrary to international law. Id. Professor Weinstein's position contradicts the views of other scholars that continental jurisdictions always followed Roman law's rejection of transient jurisdiction. See, e.g., Lorenzen, *Huber's De Conflictu Legum,* 13 Ill. L. Rev. 375, 390 (1919).

400. Brussels Regulation, supra § 4.1 note 6.

401. Id. Annex I ("in France, Articles 14 and 15 of the civil code"). See Juenger, supra note 228 (describing the French provisions).

402. Brussels Regulation, Annex I ("in the Federal Republic of Germany: Article 23 of the code of civil procedure"). See Juenger, supra note 228 (describing the German provisions).

403. 433 U.S. 186, 97 S.Ct. 2569, 53 L.Ed.2d 683 (1977) (discussed supra text accompanying notes 177–185 and §§ 4.26, 4.27, and 4.28).

404. The German Federal Supreme Court has narrowed the scope of personal jurisdiction based on the presence of defendant's assets, requiring that in addition to the location of assets, there must be a sufficient connection between the litigation and Germany. Judgment of July 2, 1991, BGH, 1991 Neue Juristische Wochenschrift [NJW] 3092. The Munich Court of Appeals has affirmed a district court's rejection of jurisdiction in a suit by a Saudi–Arabian plaintiff against a United States airline, which had assets in Germany. The court noted that the suit, based on a contract between the parties, had no connection with Germany and that Germany was not the only jurisdiction in which the plaintiff could obtain a judgment that would be enforced in Germany. Judgment of October 7, 1992, OLG München, 1993 Recht der internationalen Wirtschaft [RIW] 66.

There are other EU and EFTA countries that provide for personal jurisdiction over the owner of assets within the country. See, Austria, Jurisdiktionsnorm art. 99 (but there can be no disproportion between the value of the local assets and the amount in controversy); Greece, Code of Civil Procedure art. 40; Switzerland, Bundesgesetz Ober Das Internationale Privatrecht (IPEG) of Dec. 18, 1987, SR 291 art. 4.

405. Brussels Regulation, supra § 4.1 note 6, art. 3.

service "on the defendant during his temporary presence in the" forum were listed and banned.[406]

In *Burnham*, the defendant's brief quotes from an article by Professor Schlesinger expounding the civil law view that transient jurisdiction is exorbitant.[407] The brief, however, apparently interprets Professor Schlesinger's reference to "civilians" as a reference to persons who are not lawyers.[408] In the opinion, there is only one cryptic reference to the civil law view. In his concurrence, Justice Brennan writes: "Undeniably, Story's views are in considerable tension with English common law—a 'tradition' closer to our own and thus, I would imagine, one that in Justice Scalia's eyes is more deserving of our study than civil law practice." [409]

Although EU members promise not to use Annex I jurisdictional monstrosities against one another,[410] they remain free to use them against outsiders[411] and, if they do, other members must recognize the resulting judgments.[412] Under the Brussels Convention, which the Regulation replaced, one ray of hope for a nonmember country is to obtain a bilateral treaty with one or more EU countries. The Brussels Convention authorized an EU member to enter into a treaty with a nonmember country and therein promise not to use Annex I (in the Convention listed in Article 3) jurisdiction against domiciliaries of the nonmember and not to recognize judgments of other EU countries if those judgments are based on Annex I jurisdiction.[413] The Regulation deletes this provision.

The United States attempted to utilize this former escape from Annex I jurisdiction by negotiating a bilateral treaty with the United Kingdom (UK). Although a text was initialed,[414] the UK eventually rejected the treaty because of displeasure with huge United States verdicts and the triple damages available through extraterritorial application of United States antitrust law.[415] Nevertheless, it is significant that the initialed text of this treaty between the great champions of the common law tradition omitted transient presence from the list of jurisdictional bases that would earn the judgments of one country recognition in the other.[416]

---

406. Id. Annex I.

407. Schlesinger, *Methods of Process in Conflict of Laws. Some Comments on Ehrenzweig's Treatment of "Transient" Jurisdiction,* 9 J.Pub.L. 313, 317 (1960).

408. See Brief for Petitioner at 68: "[Transient jurisdiction] also conflicts with a lay person's intuitive sense of fairness. As Professor Schlesinger points out . . . ."

409. *Burnham,* 495 U.S. at 635 n.8, 110 S.Ct. at 2122 n.8, 109 L.Ed.2d at 654 n.8 (Brennan, J. concurring in the judgment).

410. Brussels Regulation, supra § 4.1 note 6, art. 3.

411. Id. art. 4.

412. Id. arts. 33–35.

413. Brussels Convention, art. 59.

414. United Kingdom–United States Convention on the Reciprocal Recognition and Enforcement of Judgments in Civil Matters, 16 I.L.M. 71 (1977) [hereinafter U.K.–U.S. Convention].

415. See Brand, *Enforcement of Foreign Money–Judgments in the United States: In Search of Uniformity and International Acceptance,* 67 Notre Dame L. Rev. 253, 297 (1991).

416. See U.K.–U.S. Convention art. 10.

There is authority that jurisdiction based on transient presence violates international law. The Restatement of Foreign Relations[417] carefully distinguishes between "jurisdiction to prescribe"[418] and "jurisdiction to adjudicate."[419] The least controversial basis for jurisdiction to prescribe (to apply law to persons and events) is territorial.[420] Thus, "a state has jurisdiction to prescribe law with respect to . . . conduct that, wholly or in substantial part, takes place within its territory [and with respect to] the status of persons, or interests in things, present within its territory. . . ."[421] Jurisdiction to adjudicate, however, is available only if a "person or thing is present in the . . . state, *other than transitorily.*"[422] A comment to the jurisdiction-to-adjudicate section states that "jurisdiction based on service of process on a person only transitorily in the territory of the state, is not generally acceptable under international law [and although jurisdiction may properly be based on] a less extended stay than is required to constitute residence it does not include merely transitory presence, such as while changing planes at an airport, coming on shore from a cruise ship, or a few days' sojourn unconnected with the activity giving rise to the claim."[423]

International law would not prevent a California court from exercising jurisdiction over Mr. Burnham, a New Jersey resident. How the United States allocates state-court jurisdiction over United States defendants is the business of the United States.[424] Determining whether tag jurisdiction violates due process requires a re-analysis of personal jurisdiction in the light of practical considerations of fairness and convenience.

Some of the reasons that Justice Brennan gives for concurring in the *Burnham* judgment are that modern transportation and communications make defense in a distant forum less burdensome,[425] and modern procedural devices, such as summary judgment, inexpensive discovery, federal venue transfer, and forum non conveniens dismissal,[426] are likely to ameliorate "any burdens that do arise."[427] These are reasons not for transient jurisdiction, but for nationwide jurisdiction when, as in *Burnham,* the forum has a rational interest in securing recovery for the

---

417. Restatement (Third) of the Foreign Relations Law of the United States (1987).

418. Id. § 421.

419. Id. § 402; id. 421 comment *a* ("[t]he standards of reasonableness under [§§ 421 and 402] are not the same").

420. Id. § 402 comment *c.*

421. Id. § 402(1)(a) & (b).

422. Id. § 421(2)(a) (emphasis added).

423. Id. § 421 comment *e*; id. Reporter's Notes at 310–11 (transitory presence "no longer acceptable under international law" as a basis for personal jurisdiction).

424. Id. comment *f.*

425. *Burnham,* 495 U.S. at 638, 110 S.Ct. at 2125, 109 L.Ed.2d at 657 (Brennan, J. concurring in the judgment).

426. Id. at 639 n.13, 110 S.Ct. at 2125 n.13, 109 L.Ed.2d at 657 n.13.

427. Id. at 639, 110 S.Ct. at 2125, 109 L.Ed.2d at 657.

plaintiff and the defendant cannot demonstrate any substantial unfairness.[428]

The only argument that Justice Brennan offers for transient jurisdiction that could not also be applied to nationwide jurisdiction is: "That the defendant has already journeyed at least once before to the forum—as evidenced by the fact that he was served with process there—is an indication that suit in the forum likely would not be prohibitively inconvenient."[429] This is perhaps the least cogent statement in Brennan's opinion. Much more must be known before tag jurisdiction can be justified on the basis of convenience. For example, was the defendant passing through a state thousands of miles from home for the first time, intending never to return, or does the defendant travel there hundreds of times a year on the way to work?

As Justice Scalia candidly concedes, his formula, traditional and continued use equals constitutional, is inconsistent with the "basic approach"[430] taken in *Shaffer v. Heitner.*[431] *Shaffer* declared invalid the exercise of jurisdiction to affect interests in property in the forum when the claim in litigation is unrelated to the property[432] and reached this result despite the fact that this procedure had a pedigree and continued following as impressive as that of transient jurisdiction.[433]

Justice Scalia writes, however, that he is "in no way receding from or casting doubt upon the holding of *Shaffer*...."[434] Moreover, Scalia describes *Shaffer* as standing for "the proposition that when the 'minimal contact' that is a substitute for physical presence consists of property ownership it must, like other minimum contacts, be related to the litigation."[435] This interpretation of *Shaffer* is inconsistent with Justice Scalia's view of jurisdictional due process and is unlikely to survive if the issue again reaches the court and if he can garner sufficient votes to limit *Shaffer* to intangible property that has no reasonable nexus with the forum or whose location the defendant cannot knowingly and voluntarily control.[436] There may already be sufficient votes on the Court to

---

428.   For a proposal to establish nationwide jurisdiction, see § 8A.

429.   *Burnham,* 495 U.S. at 638–39, 110 S.Ct. at 2125, 109 L.Ed.2d at 657 (Brennan, J. concurring in the judgment).

430.   Id. at 621, 110 S.Ct. at 2116, 109 L.Ed.2d at 646 (Scalia, J.).

431.   433 U.S. 186 97 S.Ct. 2569, 53 L.Ed.2d 683 (1977) [discussed supra text accompanying notes 177–185 and infra in §§ 4.28, 4.29].

432.   Id. at 208–09, 97 S.Ct. at 2581–82, 53 L.Ed.2d at 700–01.

433.   *Burnham,* 495 U.S. at 630, 110 S.Ct. at 2121, 109 L.Ed.2d at 652 (Brennan, J. concurring in the Judgment).

434.   Id. at 622, 110 S.Ct. at 2116, 109 L.Ed.2d at 647 (Scalia, J.). But see Pacific Mut. Life Ins. v. Haslip, 499 U.S. 1, 36, 111 S.Ct. 1032, 1054, 113 L.Ed.2d 1, 32 (1991) (Scalia, J., concurring in judgment) (stating that *Shaffer* was "wrongly decided" with regard to its "broad pronouncements," but indicating he might agree with the result on the ground that Delaware could not exercise quasi in rem jurisdiction over stock "when both the owner and custodian of the stock resided elsewhere").

435.   *Burnham,* 495 U.S. at 620, 110 S.Ct. at 2115, 109 L.Ed.2d at 645.

436.   In *Shaffer,* Delaware, the forum in which the case arose, was the only state that would have purported to exercise jurisdiction over interests in stock when negotiable

overrule *Shaffer* or limit it to its facts,[437] but it will take a courageous or foolhardy attorney to make the attempt because of the threat of liability under 42 U.S.C. § 1983 if the attempt fails.[438]

Republic of Argentina v. Weltover, Inc.[439] holds that two Panamanian corporations and a Swiss bank can obtain jurisdiction over Argentina in a federal district court in New York to recover repayment of bonds that Argentina issued, stating:

> Assuming, without deciding, that a foreign state is a "person" for purposes of the Due Process Clause, cf. *South Carolina v. Katzenbach*, 383 U.S. 301, 323–324, 86 S.Ct. 803, 815–816, 15 L.Ed.2d 769 (1966) (States of the Union are not "persons" for purposes of the Due Process Clause), we find that Argentina possessed "minimum contacts" that would satisfy the constitutional test. By issuing negotiable debt instruments denominated in U.S. dollars and payable in New York and by appointing a financial agent in that city, Argentina "purposefully avail[ed] itself of the privilege of conducting activities within the [United States]."[440]

In *Weltover* Justice Scalia assumes "without deciding, that a foreign state is a 'person' for purposes of the Due Process Clause." He cites *South Carolina v. Katzenbach*,[441] in which South Carolina contended that the Voting Rights Act of 1965 violated the Due Process Clause of the Fifth Amendment by employing an invalid presumption and barring judicial review of administrative findings. The cited opinion stated: " 'person' in the context of the Due Process Clause of the Fifth Amend-

---

certificates had been issued and were not in the forum. *Shaffer* 433 U.S. at 217–19, 97 S.Ct. at 2587–88, 53 L.Ed.2d at 706–07 (Stevens, J., concurring). In *Shaffer* the court disapproved of the quasi in rem basis for the decision in Harris v. Balk, 198 U.S. 215, 25 S.Ct. 625, 49 L.Ed. 1023 (1905), in which a creditor was able to attach an account receivable by serving his debtor's debtor, who was present in the creditor's state. *Shaffer,* 433 U.S. at 208, 97 S.Ct. at 2582, 53 L.Ed.2d at 700.

437. Justice Kennedy joined in Justice Scalia's opinion, which used a test for due process based on historic and continued use. Justice Steven's concurrence in *Shaffer* suggested that he would not prohibit quasi in rem jurisdiction over tangible property knowingly acquired in or placed in the forum. *Shaffer,* 433 U.S. at 218, 97 S.Ct. at 2587, 53 L.Ed.2d at 106. In *Burnham,* Justice Stevens repeats his misgivings concerning the "unnecessarily broad reach" of *Shaffer. Burnham,* 495 U.S. at 640, 110 S.Ct. at 2126, 109 L.Ed.2d at 658 (Stevens, J. concurring). Of the current justices, only Stevens was on the Court that decided *Shaffer.*

438. Cf. Pinsky v. Duncan, 79 F.3d 306, 312 (2d Cir. 1996), in which the party who had established that prejudgment attachment of his realty violated due process sues the person who had attached the property. Plaintiff asserts a claim under 28 U.S.C. § 1983 [now § 1983(a)], which provides that "[e]very person who, under color of any statute ... of any State ... subjects ... any citizen of the United States or other person within the jurisdiction thereof to the deprivation of any rights, privileges, or immunities secured by the Constitution and laws, shall be liable to the party injured." The Second Circuit held that the property owner could recover if he proved "want of probable cause, malice, and damages" and discusses the standards that other circuits have imposed for recovery of monetary damages under § 1983.

439. 504 U.S. 607, 112 S.Ct. 2160, 119 L.Ed.2d 394 (1992).

440. Id. at 619, 112 S.Ct. at 2169. The court also held that Argentina's commercial activity had a "direct effect in the United States" within the meaning of 28 U.S.C. § 1605(a)(2) to permit suit under the Foreign Sovereign Immunities Act.

441. 383 U.S. 301, 86 S.Ct. 803, 15 L.Ed.2d 769 (1966).

ment cannot ... be expanded to encompass the States of the Union...."[442]

Price v. Socialist People's Libyan Arab Jamahiriya,[443] considered a claim against Libya under 28 U.S.C. § 1605(a)(7) [now 1605A], the provision of the Foreign Sovereign Immunities Act that provides an action against foreign countries for engaging in terrorist activities. The court held that a foreign state is not a "person" within the meaning of the Due Process Clause of the Fifth Amendment and therefore is not protected by constitutional limits on personal jurisdiction. The court expressed "no view" on whether "a corporation in which a foreign state owns a majority interest" is a "person."[444]

TMR Energy Ltd. v. State Property Fund of Ukraine,[445] extended *Price* to dispose of due process protection for the Fund, which the court found to be an "agent" and therefore an "agency or instrumentality" of Ukraine because the country had plenary control over the Fund. TMR brought the suit to confirm an arbitration award that TMR had obtained against the Fund in Sweden. The court also rejected the argument that, if not due process, public international law required minimum contacts with the U.S. for the exercise of personal jurisdiction. "Never does customary international law prevail over a contrary federal statute."[446] This statement referred to the fact that the Foreign Sovereign Immunities Act conflates subject-matter jurisdiction with personal jurisdiction. Section 1330(b) provides "[p]ersonal jurisdiction over a foreign state shall exist as to every claim for relief over which the district courts have jurisdiction under [the provisions of the Act providing exceptions to sovereign immunity]."

It is true that Congress is free to pass legislation that violates international law, with the possible exception of norms so peremptory as to be classified as *jus cogens*.[447] Nevertheless, it is a matter of construction of the Foreign Sovereign Immunities Act as to whether it mandates exercise of exorbitant jurisdiction over foreign sovereigns. The Supreme Court of the United States has stated that the Act does not preclude forum non conveniens dismissal of actions over which it confers jurisdic-

---

442. Id. at 323.

443. 294 F.3d 82 (D.C. Cir. 2002).

444. Id. at 99–100. Under the Act a corporation majority owned by a foreign country is treated as a foreign state. 28 U.S.C. § 1603(a), (b)(2).

445. 411 F.3d 296 (D.C. Cir. 2005).

446. Id. at 302.

447. See Committee of United States Citizens Living in Nicaragua v. Reagan, 859 F.2d 929, 935–36 (D.C. Cir. 1988) (dismissing suit to enjoin funding of "Contras" in Nicaragua): "Here the alleged violation [of international law] is the law that Congress enacted and that the President signed, appropriating funds for the Contras. When our government's two political branches, acting together, contravene an international legal norm, does this court have any authority to remedy the violation? The answer is 'no' if the type of international obligation that Congress and the President violate is either a treaty or a rule of customary international law. If, on the other hand, Congress and the President violate a peremptory norm (or *jus cogens*), the domestic legal consequences are unclear."

tion.[448] Exercising exorbitant jurisdiction over foreign sovereign would be contrary to the basic purposes of the Act—to avoid offense to foreign countries by unifying the bases for denying them sovereign immunity and permitting defendants to remove to federal court for a trial without a jury.[449] If not due process, then international law or federal judge-made law should prevent federal courts from exercising exorbitant jurisdiction over foreign sovereigns.[450]

Moreover, it was not necessary for the court in *TMR Energy Ltd.* to decide that an "agency or instrumentality" is not protected by due process. If the arbitral tribunal had personal jurisdiction over the Fund, personal jurisdiction necessary is not necessary in the U.S. to confirm the award.[451]

§ 4.8A   Confusion Resulting from Supreme Court Jurisdictional Decisions and Proposals for Change

§ 4.8A(1)   Tripartite Test for Specific Jurisdiction

A typical distillation of the effect of the Supreme Court decisions discussed in section 4.8 produces a tri-partite test for specific jurisdiction: (1) the defendant must purposefully avail itself of the privilege of conducting activities in the forum; (2) the cause of action must arise out of or relate to these activities; (3) the exercise of jurisdiction must also be reasonable under the *Asahi* factors.[452] It is a commonplace that the results of this analysis are fact driven; minor changes in circumstances

---

448. See Verlinden B.V. v. Central Bank of Nigeria, 461 U.S. 480, 491 n. 15, 103 S.Ct. 1962, 1970 n.15, 76 L.Ed.2d 81 (1983): "The Act does not appear to affect the traditional doctrine of forum non conveniens."

449. 28 U.S.C. § 1441(d).

450. For comments on whether foreign states are entitled to due process protection, see Lee M. Caplan, The Constitution and Jurisdiction over Foreign States: The 1991 Amendment to the Foreign Sovereign Immunities Act in Perspective, 41 Va. J. Int'l L. 369. 421 (2001) (although foreign states and corporations in which a foreign state owns a majority interest are not entitled to due process protection, U.S. courts may apply minimum contacts to all but 1605(a)(7) "as a matter of judicial policy or federal common law"; for cases brought under 1605(a)(7), "international jurisdictional principles apply"); Karen Halverson, Is a Foreign State a "Person"? Does it Matter?: Personal Jurisdiction, Due Process, and the Foreign Sovereign Immunities Act, 34 J. Int'l L. & Pol. 115, 187 (2001), (even if a foreign state is not a "person," "the customary international law of personal jurisdiction is an appropriate protective filter through which to interpret and apply the FSIA"); Stephen J. Leacock, The Commercial Activity Exception Under The FSIA, Personhood Under The Fifth Amendment And Jurisdiction Over Foreign States: A Partial Roadmap For The Supreme Court In The New Millennium, 9 Willamette J. Int'l L. & Disp. Resol., 41, 55 (2001) ("The U.S. Supreme Court should grant foreign states the status of 'persons' at least for the limited purposes of constitutional due process").

451. Cf. Shaffer v. Heitner, 433 U.S. 186, 210 n.36, 97 S.Ct. 2582, 2583 n.36, 53 L.Ed.2d 683, 702 n.36 (1977): "Once it has been determined by a court of competent jurisdiction that the defendant is a debtor of the plaintiff, there would seem to be no unfairness in allowing an action to realize on that debt in a State where the defendant has property, whether or not that State would have jurisdiction to determine the existence of the debt as an original matter."

452. See, e.g., Payne v. Motorists' Mut. Ins. Co., 4 F.3d 452, 455 (6th Cir. 1993).

can change the result.[453] That alone would make prediction in a particular case difficult, but matters are even worse. Courts cannot agree on which facts matter. A court surveying decisions on a specific recurring jurisdictional issue is likely to find "the case law in a muddle."[454]

Courts do not agree on the application of the second part of the tripartite test: the cause of action arises out of or relates to the defendant's activities in the forum. Decisions have used four different tests or taken intermediate positions[455]: (1) a "but for" test—the cause of action would not have arisen but for the defendant's forum activities; (2) the defendant's forum activities must be substantively relevant or even necessary to proof of the claim;[456] (3) a "sliding scale" approach—as the number of the defendant's forum contacts increases, there is less need for the cause of action to arise out of or be related to those contacts; (4) the defendant's forum activities must have a substantial connection with the facts necessary to establish the cause of action.

Moki Mac River Expeditions v. Drugg[457] discusses these four tests and illustrates the difficulty of applying them. Defendant had its headquarters in Utah and conducted rafting-hiking trips in the Grand Canyon. A mother of a boy who took one of defendant's trips had corresponded with defendant after reading brochures that defendant had sent to a family friend and after viewing defendant's website. Defendant sent to the mother brochures and a publicity release that stated: "You don't need 'mountain man' camping skills to participate in one of our trips. . . . Moki Mac has taken reasonable steps to provide you with appropriate equipment and/or skilled guides." The plaintiffs, who reside in Texas, then sent their sixteen-year-old son on one of defendant's trips. Their son fell to his death from a narrow spot on the hiking trail. The Supreme Court of Texas held that a Texas court did not have specific jurisdiction over defendant in plaintiffs' wrongful death suit and remanded the case for determination of whether defendant had sufficient continuous and systematic contacts with Texas for general jurisdiction.[458]

---

453. See Madara v. Hall, 916 F.2d 1510, 1515 (11th Cir. 1990) (stating that satisfaction of the requirements of a long-arm statute will not necessarily satisfy due process "because each case will depend upon the facts").

454. Ticketmaster–New York, Inc. v. Alioto, 26 F.3d 201, 208 (1st Cir. 1994).

455. See Oldfield v. Pueblo De Bahia Lora, S.A., 558 F.3d 1210, 1222–23 (11th Cir. 2009) ("we have not developed or adopted a specific approach. . . . the contact must be a 'but-for' cause of the tort, yet the causal nexus between the tortious conduct and the purposeful contact must be such that the out-of-state resident will have 'fair warning that a particular activity will subject [it] to the jurisdiction of a foreign sovereign' Burger King [Corp. v. Rudzewicz], 471 U.S. at 472, 105 S.Ct. at 2182"); Nowak v. Tak How Investments, Ltd., 94 F.3d 708 (1st Cir.1996), cert. denied, 520 U.S. 1155, 117 S.Ct. 1333, 137 L.Ed.2d 493 (1997) (adopts a jurisdictional standard between a "but for" and a strict "arising out of" test).

456. See Dudnikov v. Chalk & Vermilion Fine Arts, Inc., 514 F.3d 1063, 1079 (10th Cir. 2008) (no need to chose between "but-for and proximate causation tests" because both met).

457. 221 S.W.3d 569 (Tex. 2007).

458. On remand, the Court of Appeals found that there were not sufficient contacts for general jurisdiction and dismissed the case. 270 S.W.3d 799 (Tex. App.—Dallas 2008).

The court rejected the "but for" test as "too broad and judicially unmoored to satisfy due-process concerns."[459] The court also rejected requiring "forum-related contacts to be substantively relevant, or even necessary, to proof of the claim" as "posing too narrow an inquiry."[460] The court refused to take a "sliding scale" approach because it "blurs the distinction between general and specific jurisdiction."[461] The court adopted the following test: "for a nonresident defendant's forum contacts to support an exercise of specific jurisdiction, there must be a substantial connection between those contacts and the operative facts of the litigation."[462] The court explained why, under this test, the defendant was not subject to specific jurisdiction in Texas:

> Certainly on a river rafting trip safety is a paramount concern, and we accept as true the Druggs' claim that Andy might not have gone on the trip were it not for Moki Mac's representations about safety. However, the operative facts of the Druggs' suit concern principally the guides' conduct of the hiking expedition and whether they exercised reasonable care in supervising Andy. The events on the trail and the guides' supervision of the hike will be the focus of the trial, will consume most if not all of the litigation's attention, and the overwhelming majority of the evidence will be directed to that question. Only after thoroughly considering the manner in which the hike was conducted will the jury be able to assess the Druggs' misrepresentation claim. In sum, "the [alleged misrepresentation] is not the subject matter of the case … nor is it related to the operative facts of the negligence action." *Rush* [v. Savchuk], 444 U.S. at 329. Whatever connection there may be between Moki Mac's promotional materials sent to Texas and the operative facts that led to Andy's death, we do not believe it is sufficiently direct to meet due-process concerns.[463]

Thus the court, after rejecting the substantive relevance test, applies a "substantial connection" criterion in a manner that is indistinguishable from the approach it purports the reject. With regard to the court's statement that a "sliding scale" test blurs the distinction between general and specific jurisdiction, as stated in § 4.8 while discussing *Helicopters Nacionales De Colombia, S.A. v. Hall*, the actions of real parties in a real world, not the test, blurs that distinction.

The following section illustrates this with examples of three fact patterns that frequently produce decisions concerning personal jurisdictional.

---

459. 221 S.W.3d at 581.

460. Id. at 583.

461. Id.

462. Id. at 585.

463. Id. But see O'Connor v. Sandy Lane Hotel Co., 496 F.3d 312 (3d Cir. 2007), which adopts a similar test that relates the defendant's forum contacts to the cause of action "in a jurisdictionally significant way." The court finds jurisdiction over a Barbados hotel in a suit to recover for injuries in the hotel's spa. The hotel had sent a brochure to the plaintiffs advertising the spa and advising the plaintiffs to schedule spa treatments in advance of their trip, which they did in a series of telephone calls.

§ 4.8B(1)   Examples of Confusion in Jurisdictional Decisions

§ 4.8B(1)(A)   Suits Between Merchant Buyers and Merchant Sellers

In *Lakeside Bridge & Steel Co. v. Mountain State Construction Co.,*[464] the Seventh Circuit held that the fabricator of steel structural assemblies could not obtain jurisdiction in its home state to sue the buyer for the unpaid purchase price. When the United States Supreme Court denied certiorari, Justice White, joined by Justice Powell, took the unusual step of publishing a dissent from the denial:

> [T]he question of personal jurisdiction over a nonresident corporate defendant based on contractual dealings with a resident plaintiff has deeply divided the federal and state courts. Cases arguably in conflict with the decision below include [full-page string citation omitted]. The question at issue is one of considerable importance to contractual dealings between purchasers and sellers located in different States. The disarray among federal and state courts noted above may well have a disruptive effect on commercial relations in which certainty of result is a prime objective. This disarray also strongly suggests that prior decisions of this Court offer no clear guidance on the question.[465]

Amen, and the situation has not gotten any better. A lawyer familiar with the cases in the area, if, for example, representing a seller, will ask his client a series of questions. ''Were the goods a catalogue item or custom made?''[466] ''Did a representative of the buyer come here to negotiate the contract or supervise manufacture?''[467] ''Did you solicit the sale or did the buyer contact you first?''[468] ''Did the contract required manufacture in this state''?[469] ''Has the buyer purchased from you before?''[470] Then, in the light of the conflicting treatment these elements

---

464.   597 F.2d 596 (7th Cir. 1979), cert. denied, 445 U.S. 907, 100 S.Ct. 1087, 63 L.Ed.2d 325 (1980).

465.   Id., 445 U.S. at 909–11.

466.   See Nicholstone Book Bindery, Inc. v. Chelsea House Publishers, 621 S.W.2d 560 (Tenn. 1981), cert. denied, 455 U.S. 994, 102 S.Ct. 1623, 71 L.Ed.2d 856 (1982) (jurisdiction upheld over buyer of books printed and bound in the forum). But see Hydrokinetics, Inc. v. Alaska Mechanical, Inc., 700 F.2d 1026 (5th Cir. 1983), cert. denied, 466 U.S. 962, 104 S.Ct. 2180, 80 L.Ed.2d 561 (1984) (denying jurisdiction over buyer of custom-made product).

467.   See Dahlberg Co. v. Western Hearing Aid Center, 259 Minn. 330, 107 N.W.2d 381, cert. denied, 366 U.S. 961, 81 S.Ct. 1921, 6 L.Ed.2d 1253 (1961) (jurisdiction over buyer who came to the forum to negotiate and sign the sales contract).

468.   See Michiana Easy Livin' Country, Inc. v. Holten, 168 S.W.3d 777 (Tex. 2005) (no jurisdiction over nonresident seller contacted by resident buyer); cf. Al–Jon, Inc. v. Garden St. Iron & Metal, Inc., 301 N.W.2d 709 (Iowa 1981) (no jurisdiction over buyer solicited by seller).

469.   Cf. Premier Corp. v. Newsom, 620 F.2d 219 (10th Cir. 1980) (no jurisdiction in suit for payment for tax-shelter services performed in the forum when the contract did not require performance there).

470.   See Mississippi Interstate Express v. Transpo, Inc., 681 F.2d 1003 (5th Cir. 1982) (upholding jurisdiction when there has been a sustained relationship between the parties). But see Dent–Air, Inc. v. Beech Mountain Air Service, 332 N.W.2d 904 (Minn. 1983) (denying jurisdiction in suit by lessor for breach of plane rental agreements although three

have received in the cases, the best the lawyer can do will be to give his client a rough estimate of the probability of success in obtaining jurisdiction.[471]

§ 4.8B(1)(B)   Suits against Hotels, Resorts, and Cruise Lines

Vacationer, a resident of F, attracted by local advertisements for a distant vacation paradise, makes reservations for accommodations. The reservations are either made directly by Vacationer or by Vacationer's travel agent. The holiday turns into a nightmare when Vacationer is injured because of the negligence of the company providing the accommodations. Home and mending, Vacationer's thoughts turn to compensation. Do the courts in Vacationer's home state have jurisdiction over the hotel, resort, or cruise line?

This issue is repeatedly litigated in our courts. The vacation cases illustrate as well as any other group the uncertainty and confusion that is the legacy of the Supreme Court's jurisdiction decisions. One would expect that a study of cases from different states narrowly focused on the same issue and fact pattern would yield sure guides to predicting the outcome of a jurisdictional challenge. Instead the cases reveal conflicting results and analyses.

A major issue on which the cases differ is whether the negligent injury at the distant vacation spot "arises out of" the local promotional activities that induced the victim's visit. This was one of the issues in *Carnival Cruise Lines v. Shute*[472] that the Supreme Court did not reach when it held that the tort suit in the vacationers' forum was barred by a forum selection clause.[473] Below, the Ninth Circuit found the forum selection clause "unenforceable"[474] and thus the jurisdictional issue was dispositive. The circuit court held that a Washington couple could obtain jurisdiction over the cruise line at home because "a tort can arise from prior business solicitation in the forum state"[475] and approved of decisions that "apply a 'but for' test of causality in this type of situation."[476] In other words, the plaintiffs would not have gone on the cruise, and Mrs. Shute would not have slipped on a deck mat "but for" defendant's solicitation of business from Washington residents. The court rejected

---

leases were executed between the parties and although a choice-of-law clause in the leases chose forum law).

471. Five years after the Supreme Court denied certiorari to the Seventh Circuit decision in *Lakeside Bridge*, that Circuit expressed its own frustration with the issue:

> Now, one would think that in a rational system ... experienced lawyers could simply and with conviction unanimously answer [the merchant buyer's question whether it can get jurisdiction over its merchant seller]. But alas we know, to our embarrassment, that the only honest answer the lawyer can probably give is "Gee, I can't say for sure."

Hall's Specialties, Inc. v. Schupbach, 758 F.2d 214, 216 (7th Cir. 1985).

472.   499 U.S. 585, 111 S.Ct. 1522, 113 L.Ed.2d 622 (1991).

473.   Id. at 595.

474.   Shute v. Carnival Cruise Lines, 897 F.2d 377, 389 (9th Cir. 1990), rev'd, 499 U.S. 585, 111 S.Ct. 1522, 113 L.Ed.2d 622 (1991).

475.   897 F.2d at 384.

476.   Id.

opinions from the First, Second, and Eighth Circuits that had held that negligent injuries elsewhere did not "arise out of" solicitation of forum vacationers.[477] Decisions in state courts have reflected this split in the federal circuits concerning the "but for, arising out of" argument.[478]

Some of the resort cases have based their jurisdictional findings on other issues. A Texas federal district case held that suit against a New Mexico ski resort for a fall on hotel stairs did not arise out of the defendant's Texas activities, which included solicitation of business,[479] but then found that the solicitations plus other contacts with Texas were sufficiently "continuous and systematic" to confer general jurisdiction.[480] A Seventh Circuit court upheld jurisdiction over a Cayman Island hotel without reaching the "arising out of" issue, perhaps assisted by the fact that the complaint pled not only negligence, but also breach of express and implied warranties, and breach of contract.[481]

§ 4.8B(1)(C)   Defamation over the Telephone

Soliciting information about Victim, an F resident, Reporter from a newspaper in F telephones Bigmouth, who is in X. Bigmouth makes

---

477.   Id. at 383. Recently the First Circuit retreated from its former position and upheld jurisdiction on facts similar to *Shute*. Nowak v. Tak How Investments, Ltd., 94 F.3d 708 (1st Cir.1996), cert. denied, 520 U.S. 1155, 117 S.Ct. 1333, 137 L.Ed.2d 493 (1997), adopted a jurisdictional standard between a "but for" and a strict "arising out of" test. The court upheld jurisdiction over a Hong Kong hotel in a wrongful death action resulting from the drowning in the hotel's pool of a guest from Massachusetts. The guest accompanied her husband whose Massachusetts company had negotiated special rates at the hotel. "While the nexus between [the hotel's] solicitation of [the company's] business and Mrs. Nowak's death does not constitute a proximate cause relationship, it does represent a meaningful link between [the hotel's] contact and the harm suffered." Id. at 716. See also Oldfield v. Pueblo De Bahia Lora, S.A., 558 F.3d 1210 (11th Cir. 2009): Over the internet, plaintiff made a reservation with a Costa Rican resort and made arrangements with the resort for a fishing trip on a boat that the resort did not own or operate. Plaintiff sued the resort for injuries he suffered on the boat. The Eleventh Circuit vacated the district court's order denying the defendant's motion to set aside the default judgment and remanded with directions to dismiss the case without prejudice because of lack of personal jurisdiction over the defendant. The injury on the boat was not "a foreseeable consequence of his viewing the Parrot Bay Village website, reserving a room at the resort, and arranging for a fishing trip run by someone else." Id. at 1223.

478.   See Tatro v. Manor Care, Inc., 416 Mass. 763, 625 N.E.2d 549, 554 (1994) (accept "but for" test in suit against hotel); Munley v. Second Judicial Dist. Ct., 104 Nev. 492, 761 P.2d 414, 415 (1988) (no jurisdiction over ski resort because injury there did not "arise out of" forum solicitations); State ex rel. Circus Circus Reno, Inc. v. Pope, 317 Or. 151, 854 P.2d 461, 466 (1993) (reject Ninth Circuit's "but for" test and find no jurisdiction over resort). For an argument that a "but for" test would have provided specific jurisdiction in Helicopteros Nacionales de Columbia v. Hall, 466 U.S. 408, 104 S.Ct. 1868, 80 L.Ed.2d 404 (1984), see Seidelson, *Recasting World–Wide Volkswagen As a Source of Longer Jurisdictional Reach*, 19 Tulsa L. J. 1, 27 n.105 (1983).

479.   Kervin v. Red River Ski Area, Inc., 711 F.Supp. 1383, 1389–90 (E.D. Tex. 1989).

480.   Id. at 1392. The other Texas contacts were that four of defendant's five shareholders resided in Texas, defendant was originally incorporated in Texas before dissolving and reincorporating in New Mexico, recruiting ski instructors from Texas, having its brochures printed in Texas, employing a Texas accountant, and drawing approximately 47% of its clientele from Texas. Id. at 1388. At the opposite extreme, Witbeck v. Bill Cody's Ranch Inn, 428 Mich. 659, 411 N.W.2d 439, 445 (1987) held that an advertisement in an AAA guidebook "does not by itself, constitute 'purposeful availment' of the forum state."

481.   Wilson v. Humphreys (Cayman) Ltd., 916 F.2d 1239, 1241, 1244 (7th Cir. 1990), cert. denied, 499 U.S. 947, 111 S.Ct. 1415, 113 L.Ed.2d 468 (1991).

statements that defame Victim and appear in Reporter's article published in the newspaper in F. Victim sues Bigmouth in F for defamation and
Bigmouth contests jurisdiction. What result?

Ticketmaster–New York, Inc. v. Alioto[482] surveyed the case law and
predictably found it "in a muddle."[483] The cases seemed to be reasonably
consistent in holding that when "the source of an allegedly defamatory
remark did not initiate the pivotal contact, and the in-forum injury is not
reasonably foreseeable, jurisdiction may not be asserted"[484] and that
jurisdiction was available in the converse situation, the defendant initiated the contact with the reporter and caused foreseeable injury in the
forum.[485] The case before the court, however, fell "between the stools"[486]
—the reporter made the call and the defendant's response caused foreseeable injury in the forum. In this situation the court found the results
conflicting, some courts taking jurisdiction, some not, some treating the
fact that the defendant did not initiate the contact as dispositive, some
not even discussing this element.[487] The First Circuit held that the
plaintiff could not obtain jurisdiction. The court found the *Asahi* reasonableness factors[488] controlling, stating that these factors should be used
not rarely, but frequently, to defeat jurisdiction.[489] This guarantees that
in these telephone-defamation cases in which the defendant does not
initiate the contact, the result will remain unpredictable, turning on the
circumstances of each case. In *Ticketmaster*, the court suspected that
plaintiff had sued in Massachusetts to harass Alioto, a California lawyer
who was bringing a class action there against a company affiliated with
the plaintiff.[490]

§ 4.8B(1)(D)   A Proposal for Major Changes in Jurisdictional Doctrine: Fairness Without Contacts

In suits by United States plaintiffs against United States defendants, the best way to stem the flood of litigation over the jurisdictional
issue is to regard due process as requiring only that the forum have some
rational basis for wishing to decide the case, either because the plaintiff
resides there or because the defendant acted or caused consequences
there, or both. This change should include easy transfer to a more
appropriate forum if the defendant makes a cogent showing of unfairness in plaintiff's chosen forum.[491]

---

482.   26 F.3d 201 (1st Cir. 1994).

483.   Id. at 208.

484.   Id.

485.   Id. See Acquadro v. Bergeron, 851 So.2d 665 (Fla. 2003) (phone calls made to
persons in forum were sufficient to establish jurisdiction over nonresidents in defamation
action).

486.   Id.

487.   Id.

488.   See supra note 312 and accompanying text.

489.   *Ticketmaster*, 26 F.3d. at 210.

490.   Id. at 211 (noting that the plaintiff did not sue the reporter or newspaper and that
the Massachusetts forum does not permit recovery of punitive damages).

491.   Cf. Unif. Transfer of Litigation Act § 103, 14 U.L.A. (Pocket Part) (providing for
transfer from a state court that lacks personal jurisdiction to a court of another state that
has jurisdiction).

Australia, another federal nation, has had such a system since 1992. The temporary presence of an individual in Australia is a basis for general jurisdiction over that individual if he or she is served while present.[492] Jurisdiction is nationwide. A writ issued by the High Court of Australia or the Federal Court of Australia can be served anywhere in Australia. For state and territorial courts, service under the Service and Execution of Process Act 1992 has the same effect as service effected within the territory of the court issuing the writ.[493] If the writ is issued out of a supreme court, a defendant who claims that the forum is not appropriate may seek a transfer to the appropriate court[494] or a stay to compel the plaintiff to sue in the more appropriate forum.

The two factors that are likely to make suit in an interested forum unfair to the defendant are the forum's choice-of-law rule and serious inconvenience to the defendant. If the forum's sole nexus is the plaintiff's residence, it would be unfair to the defendant to allow suit there if this would result in choosing law more unfavorable to the defendant than would be chosen in all states that have contacts with both the parties and the transaction.[495] The defendant should be protected against lunatic choice-of-law rules, such as the now abrogated Mississippi rule that regarded its tort statute of limitations, longest in the nation, as "procedural."[496] It might be thought preferable to attack fairness in choice of law directly by constitutional rules addressed to that issue, but placing more stringent constitutional limitations on conflicts rules raises issues more complex than reforming jurisdictional theory. It is probably just as well that the Supreme Court allows the states to do pretty much what they will with choice of law, so long as they do not do it in the street and scare the horses.[497] If only the Court would take the same view of jurisdiction.

---

492. Laurie v. Carroll, (1958) 98 C.L.R. 310.

493. Service and Execution of Process Act 1992 §§ 12, 130.

494. Jurisdiction of Courts (Cross–Vesting) Act 1987 § 5.

495. For the view that jurisdiction should depend upon the propriety of the forum's applying its own law, See, Cox, *Razing Conflicts Facades to Build Better Jurisdiction Theory: The Foundation—There is No Law But Forum Law*, 28 VAL. U. L. REV. 1, 8 (1993); Maier & McCoy, *A Unifying Theory for Judicial Jurisdiction and Choice of Law*, 39 AM. J. COMP. L. 249, 256 (1991). For disapproval of adding choice of law to the jurisdictional formula, see Silberman, *Reflections on Burnham v. Superior Court: Toward Presumptive Rules of Jurisdiction and Implications for Choice of Law*, 22 RUTGERS L. J. 569, 589 (1991) (stating that "the complexity of comparing the relative choice-of-law analyses of the competing courts undermines the very reason for a nationwide rule in the first place").

496. Mississippi was a target forum because it had a six-year tort limitations period and regarded limitations as "procedural" so that the Mississippi period applied to any suit brought in Mississippi, even though the injury occurred in a state with a shorter period that had run before suit in Mississippi. See Ferens v. John Deere Co., 494 U.S. 516, 110 S.Ct. 1274, 108 L.Ed.2d 443 (1990). Mississippi has shortened its tort limitations to 3 years (Miss. Code Ann. § 15–1–49 and has passed a "borrowing" statute that applies the shorter statute of limitations of the place where the cause of action "accrued" if the plaintiff is not a Mississippi resident (Miss. Code Ann. § 15–1–65)).

497. See Allstate Ins. Co. v. Hague, 449 U.S. 302, 101 S.Ct. 633, 66 L.Ed.2d 521 (1981). Chapter 9 focuses on constitutional limits on choice of law.

As for inconvenience to the defendant, this attack on jurisdiction would be reserved primarily for individuals or mom and pop operations that did not customarily engage in interstate transactions and who were the real parties in interest, not for example, nominal parties being defended and indemnified by an interstate insurer. Inconvenience might consist of the distance that the defendant must travel, difficulties of proof that defendant will not encounter in another available forum, or factors such as physical handicap or employment that make especially onerous the additional time and travel necessary to litigate at a distance from defendant's home.

With regard to all aspects of the fairness attack on jurisdiction, with the exception of individuals and small enterprises, the burden on the defendant will be heavy. Unless a compelling showing is made, jurisdiction exists in an interested forum. We must avoid a "mini-trial" on the jurisdictional issue.[498]

For defendants residing or headquartered abroad, a decent respect for foreign countries requires that the defendant have some contact with the United States, not with any individual state, that makes it reasonable under the circumstances to order the foreigner to appear and defend here. The idea of focusing on nation-wide contacts has received limited and halting recognition in Federal Rule of Civil Procedure 4(k)(2),[499] which took effect on December 1, 1993. For federal law claims, that rule permits accumulating national contacts, but does it in a bizarre manner. As a condition precedent, the defendant must "not [be] subject to jurisdiction in any state's courts of general jurisdiction."[500] Thus the plaintiff is in the position of contending that it could not get jurisdiction over the defendant in a state court, and the defendant is in the posture of saying "yes you could."[501] This apparently is a result of following the

---

498. See Posnak, *The Court Doesn't Know Its Asahi from its Wortman: A Critical View of the Constitutional Constraints on Jurisdiction and Choice of Law*, 41 SYRACUSE L. REV. 875, 896 (1990) (stating that considering such matters as the forum's interest, choice of law, and convenience to the defendant "would often consume more time and resources than the trial on the merits").

499. Fed R. Civ. P. 4(k)(2):

For a claim that arises under federal law, serving a summons or filing a waiver of service establishes personal jurisdiction over a defendant if: (A) the defendant is not subject to jurisdiction in any state's courts of general jurisdiction; and (B) exercising jurisdiction is consistent with the United States Constitution and laws.

500. Id.

501. United States v. Swiss American Bank, Ltd., 191 F.3d 30 (1st Cir. 1999), rules that a plaintiff seeking to use 4(k)(2) must make a prima facie showing that it has satisfied the requirements of 4(k)(2). If the plaintiff makes out this prima facie case, the burden shifts to the defendant to produce evidence which shows either than one or more specific states exist in which it would be subject to suit or that its contacts with the United States are constitutionally insufficient.

ISI Int'l, Inc. v. Borden Ladner Gervais LLP., 256 F.3d 548 (7th Cir. 2001), suggests a different and preferable allocation of burdens. A defendant who wants to avoid the use of Rule 4(k)(2) must name some other state in which the plaintiff has jurisdiction over the defendant, thereby consenting to jurisdiction there.

drafting advice that Justice Blackmun gave in *Omni Capital International v. Rudolf Wolff & Co.*[502]

U.S. plaintiffs suing U.S. defendants should have greatly expanded rights to sue in the plaintiffs' home forums. In order to accomplish such a thoroughgoing change in jurisdictional doctrine, we will have to reject once and for all the notion that state sovereignty and state lines are important constants in the due process analysis.[503] This will be a wrench and reasonable people differ as to whether it is desirable or feasible.[504]

Phillips Petroleum Co. v. Shutts[505] held nonresident class members that have no contacts with the forum are nevertheless bound by the court's judgment if they receive mailed notice of the action and do not elect to opt out. The Court concluded that in the light of the protection of nonresident plaintiffs' interest by the forum court and by the named plaintiffs,[506] the ability to opt out,[507] or "sit back and allow the litigation to run its course,"[508] places "fewer burdens upon absent class plaintiffs than ... upon absent defendants in nonclass suits, [and therefore] the Due Process Clause need not and does not afford the former as much protection from state-court jurisdiction as it does the latter."[509] Ah, but what about those state lines? If they can be ignored in one context in

---

502. 484 U.S. 97, 111, 108 S.Ct. 404, 98 L.Ed.2d 415 (1987) (suggesting "[a] narrowly tailored service of process provision, authorizing service on an alien in a federal-question case when the alien is not amenable to service under the applicable state long-arm statute").

503. See supra notes 224–225 and accompanying text.

504. See Kogan, *A Neo–Federalist Tale of Personal Jurisdiction*, 63 S. Cal. L. Rev. 257, 269 (1990) (stating that the key to state-court jurisdiction to adjudicate is "the meaning of interstate federalism"); Stewart, *A New Litany of Personal Jurisdiction*, 60 U. Colo. L. Rev. 5, 18–19 (1989) (stating that whether or not it is wise to permit concepts of state sovereignty to control jurisdictional doctrine, its "recognition is mandated by history and can be refused only if the concept of a nation of states is abrogated by constitutional amendment"); Weinstein, *The Federal Common Law Origins of Judicial Jurisdiction: Implications for Modern Doctrine*, 90 Va. L. Rev. 169, 300 (2004) (the territorial limitations on the jurisdiction of state courts are federal common law rules authorized by constitutional structure and are not mandated by the Due Process Clause); Weinstein, *The Early American Origins of Territoriality in Judicial Jurisdiction*, 37 St. Louis U. L. J. 1, 60 (1992) (stating that "since states are territorially defined, the measure of the legitimacy of a state's assertion of authority over an individual should reflect this territoriality").

505. 472 U.S. 797, 105 S.Ct. 2965, 86 L.Ed.2d 628 (1985).

506. Id. at 809.

507. Id. at 810.

508. Id.

509. Id. at 811. But see State v. Homeside Lending, Inc., 826 A.2d 997, 2003 Vt. 17, 175 Vt. 239 (2003): Vermont members of a national class action in an Alabama state court are not bound by the judgment of that court approving a settlement because the Alabama proceeding violated their due process rights. Notice of the opportunity to opt out of the class action did not adequately inform members of the potential burdens of the litigation. The class representatives did not adequately represent absent class members because the incentive payments to the representatives provided an economic benefit far greater than the value of the settlement. Moreover, when a class action can impose monetary burdens on class members that exceed any benefits, a state court has personal jurisdiction only over those class members who have minimum contacts with the state.

which there is a cogent argument that there is no unfairness to the affected party, can they be ignored in others?[510]

§ 4.8B(1)(E)   A Proposal for Modest Changes in Jurisdictional Doctrine

If we are not able to adopt a system of nationwide jurisdiction for interstate cases, the second-best method of stemming the flood of litigation over jurisdiction is to modify existing doctrine sufficiently to eliminate major points of contention while preserving fairness to defendants. This section makes recommendations on the three major issues that arise in any attempt at reform: stream-of-commerce theory, the place in the scheme of general jurisdiction, and the doctrine of piercing the corporate veil.

Stream of Commerce

We should discard the suggestion by four justices in *Asahi* for drastic restriction of the stream-of-commerce basis for jurisdiction over distant manufacturers.[511] That suggestion, and Justice O'Connor's citing with approval a case in which layers of independent distributors shielded the foreign defendant from jurisdiction,[512] have already produced, in jurisdictions following that part of the opinion, decisions preventing injured United States users from obtaining jurisdiction over foreign[513] and even United States[514] manufacturers. A defendant that releases a product for sale should be subject to jurisdiction in any state where the product causes harm if the product comes there either in the normal course of commercial distribution or is brought into that state by someone using the product as it is intended to be used.[515] Otherwise we turn the clock back to the days before modern long-arm statutes when a manufacturer, to avoid being haled into court where a user is injured, need only Pilate-like wash its hands of a product by having independent distributors market it.[516]

---

510. See Weber, *Purposeful Availment*, 39 S. Cal. L. Rev. 815, 864 (1988) (stating that "the *Shutts* opinion does not seem to have had much impact" on other contexts of territorial jurisdiction).

511. See supra notes 304–309 and accompanying text.

512. *Asahi*, 480 U.S. at 111–12, citing Hutson v. Fehr Bros., 584 F.2d 833 (8th Cir.), cert. denied, 439 U.S. 983, 99 S.Ct. 573, 58 L.Ed.2d 654 (1978).

513. See Wiles v. Morita Iron Works Co., Ltd., 125 Ill.2d 144, 125 Ill.Dec. 812, 530 N.E.2d 1382 (1988); Parry v. Ernst Home Center, 779 P.2d 659 (Utah 1989); Vargas v. Hong Jin Crown Corp., 247 Mich.App. 278, 636 N.W.2d 291 (2001).

514. See Lesnick v. Hollingsworth & Vose, 35 F.3d 939 (4th Cir. 1994) (component part maker, asbestos cigarette filter); Boit v. Gar–Tec Products, Inc., 967 F.2d 671 (1st Cir. 1992).

515. But see World–Wide Volkswagen Corp. v. Woodson, 444 U.S. 286, 100 S.Ct. 559, 62 L.Ed.2d 490 (1980) (no jurisdiction at crash site over automobile's seller or distributor); Kennedy, *Stretching the Long–Arm in Asahi Metal Industry Co., Ltd. v. Superior Court: Worldwide Jurisdiction after World–Wide Volkswagen?*, 4 B.U. Int'l L. J. 327, 343 (1986) (stating that a foreign manufacturer should not be subject to jurisdiction in a United States forum unless the forum state could constitutionally require the manufacturer to obtain a license to do business in the state); Stewart, supra note 504, at 37–38 (stating that even in interstate suits, state sovereignty requires the defendant's intentional affiliation with the state before jurisdiction is exercised).

516. See Watson v. Employers Liability Assurance Corp., 348 U.S. 66, 72, 75 S.Ct. 166, 99 L.Ed. 74 (1954) (stating that the inability of an injured user to get jurisdiction over the manufacturer gives the forum an interest in permitting a direct action against the manufacturer's liability insurer).

General Jurisdiction

Is it desirable to retain a concept of general jurisdiction when the action does not arise out of and is not related to anything done or caused in the forum? The Brussels Regulation limits general jurisdiction to a defendant's domicile,[517] which, in the case of a corporation, is its statutory seat, or place of central administration, or principal place of business.[518] When a plaintiff invokes general jurisdiction, the forum is less likely to be able to apply its own law.

If courts follow the suggestions in this section concerning stream of commerce, there would be little need for general jurisdiction. The argument that the plaintiff should be guaranteed a forum someplace would then ring hollow under modern long-arm theory. The case that might then tug at the heartstrings would be one in which the plaintiff is horrendously injured abroad[519] by a product manufactured by a company that has sufficient continuous and systematic contacts with plaintiff's home to confer general jurisdiction there over the defendant even after *Helicopteros*.[520] If the suggestion in section 4.8A(1)(D) concerning nationwide jurisdiction for interstate suits were followed, the issue of general jurisdiction in such cases would become moot. Then only general jurisdiction over foreign companies would be in issue and it might be well, in the interest of comity, to adjust our views to international standards, which are inconsistent with an expansive view of general jurisdiction.[521] On the other hand, travel and communications have become easy, especially for multinational enterprises. I would prefer exercising jurisdiction over them where they have continuous and systematic contacts and permitting them to object on the basis of demonstrated unfairness, particularly with regard to difficulties in obtaining evidence.[522] If, as is likely in such cases, foreign law applies, the defendant would also have to be protected against the choice-of-law doctrine that permits an American jury to assess damages in an amount that far exceeds what the foreign forum would have awarded.[523]

Piercing the Corporate Veil

Discussion of what contacts with a forum are sufficient for specific or general jurisdiction should include a focus on when a plaintiff can

---

517. Brussels Regulation, supra § 4.1 note 6, art. 2.

518. Id. art. 60.

519. See Miller v. Honda Motor Co., 779 F.2d 769 (1st Cir. 1985) (the plaintiff was made a quadriplegic by a moped accident in Bermuda, but could not obtain general jurisdiction over Honda in Massachusetts, though unable to travel to Bermuda).

520. See Roethlisberger v. Tokyo Aircraft Instrument Co. (TKK) of Japan, 1991 WL 347671 (W.D. Mich. 1991), declining to follow Bearry v. Beech Aircraft Corp., 818 F.2d 370 (5th Cir. 1987). The text accompanying notes 256–282 discusses *Helicopteros*.

521. See Brussels Regulation, supra § 4.1 note 6, art. 2 (providing the only basis for general jurisdiction, domicile of the defendant).

522. See Gonzalez v. Naviera Neptuno A.A., 832 F.2d 876, 888 (5th Cir. 1987) (reversing a denial of a forum non conveniens motion after trial and verdict because the foreign defendant had shown prejudice resulting from "difficulties associated with obtaining foreign witnesses or their deposition testimony").

523. See § 3.2C4.

ascribe actions of one member of a corporate family to another member. Analysis in this area has been confused by ignoring the differences between holding a parent company liable for its subsidiary's torts and holding that the subsidiary's forum contacts can be ascribed to the parent for jurisdictional purposes when the parent is liable for its own conduct.[524] When the issue is vicarious liability for the torts of a subsidiary, a standard is appropriate that focuses on the amount of control the parent exercises over the subsidiary.[525] When the issue is jurisdiction, we should attribute to the parent any act of the subsidiary that, but for delegation to the subsidiary, the parent itself would have to perform in the forum.[526] For specific jurisdiction, under a proper application of stream-of-commerce theory, it should be unnecessary to struggle with piercing the corporate veil.[527] If the subsidiary's acts in the forum in the process of selling the parent's product are sufficiently continuous and systematic for general jurisdiction over the subsidiary, they should also accord general jurisdiction over the parent.[528]

Conclusion

It is a disgrace that we have made what should be a matter of interstate venue a constitutional issue and then have micromanaged state-court jurisdiction to adjudicate so that this threshold issue is one of the most litigated. Worse, litigating the same situations over and over does not increase predictability. The determination is fact driven and we cannot agree on what facts are relevant.

---

524. See Miller v. Honda Motor Co., 779 F.2d 769, 772–73 (1st Cir. 1985) refusing to "pierce the corporate veil" to exercise general jurisdiction over Honda based on the continuous and systematic forum contacts of its United States wholly-owned subsidiary and quoting the applicable standard from a forum decision (My Bread Baking Co. v. Cumberland Farms, Inc., 353 Mass. 614, 233 N.E.2d 748 (1968)) in which the issue was vicarious liability for the subsidiary's conversion; PHC–Minden, L.P. v. Kimberly–Clark Corp., 235 S.W.3d 163 (Tex. 2007) ("jurisdictional veil-piercing and substantive veil-piercing involve different elements of proof"); Phillip I. Blumberg, The Multinational Challenge to Corporation Law 116–17 (1993) (stating that the justification for treating a multi-corporate enterprise as a single entity varies with the issue); Knudsen, *Jurisdiction over a Corporation Based on the Contacts of a Related Corporation: Time for a Rule of Attribution*, 92 Dick. L. Rev. 917, 919 (1988) (stating that the more exacting standard for determining vicarious liability should not determine jurisdiction over an out-of-state corporation based on the acts of an in-state corporation).

525. See My Bread Baking Co. v. Cumberland Farms, Inc., 353 Mass. 614, 233 N.E.2d 748, 752 (1968).

526. See Meier v. Sun Int'l Hotels, 288 F.3d 1264 (11th Cir. 2002) (when forum subsidiaries conduct business solely for a foreign parent there is jurisdiction over the parent); Anderson v. Dassault Aviation, 361 F.3d 449 (8th Cir. 2004), cert. denied, 543 U.S. 1015, 125 S.Ct. 606, 160 L.Ed.2d 484 (2004) (subsidiaries activities in forum sufficient for jurisdiction over French parent). But see Bauman v. DaimlerChrysler Corp., 579 F.3d 1088, 1095 (9th Cir. 2009) (requiring in addition that "the parent must exert control that is so pervasive and continual that the subsidiary may be considered an agent"). A dissent would "require a *less* stringent showing of control for the limited purpose of establishing personal jurisdiction." Id. at1099 (emphasis in original).

527. See Blumberg, supra note 524 at 117 (stating that "the 'stream of commerce' doctrine has ... made the debate over enterprise and entity essentially irrelevant").

528. For an opposing view, see Voxman, *Jurisdiction over a Parent Corporation in its Subsidiary's State of Incorporation*, 141 U. Pa. L. Rev. 327, 328 (1992).

I have suggested two paths out of the labyrinth in which we are trapped like the Minotaur,[529] devouring not human sacrifices but thousands of pages of case reports. The preferable way is to permit a plaintiff to bring suit against a United States defendant in any forum that has a reasonable interest in adjudicating the case: the plaintiff's residence, the place of injury, defendant's residence or principal place of business. A defendant without "minimum contacts" with that forum could then move for transfer to a more appropriate venue, but would have the burden of demonstrating why suit there would be unfair to the defendant. In most cases, such contentions by United States defendants that are frequently engaged in interstate transactions should be summarily dismissed. Foreign defendants would not be subject to suit here unless their cumulated national contacts made this reasonable.

The second path mapped herein is not-so-minor tinkering with the current system. We could greatly reduce litigation of the jurisdictional issue by making it clear that commercial buyers and sellers who deal with one another can bring suit in their home forums in disputes arising out of the sale; that any defendant who deals with a product in the chain of distribution is subject to suit where the product causes injury if the product has reached that forum either in the usual course of commercial distribution or is brought there by a someone using the product as it was intended to be used.

The windmills, however, show no sign of weakening. It is likely that for many more years, attorneys who are expert at operating under current doctrine can profitably fill their calendars by litigating the threshold issue of jurisdiction to adjudicate. And we wonder why folks tell such cruel lawyer jokes.

§ 4.9 Forum Contacts Sufficient for Jurisdiction In Personam: Introduction: Survey of Long–Arm Statutes

Sections 4.10 through 4.22 survey those contacts between defendant and forum that courts have held justify the exercise of in personam jurisdiction. Sections 4.11 through 4.20 discuss the bases for in personam jurisdiction over individuals rather than over corporations or over partnerships and unincorporated associations. Many of the bases for jurisdiction over individuals such as consent, appearance, doing business, an act done or consequences caused in the forum, and ownership of property in the forum, will also be bases for jurisdiction over corporations, and many of the cases cited to illustrate these bases involve corporate defendants.

Some bases for jurisdiction over individuals, such as presence and domicile, are not applicable to corporations except, perhaps, as loose circumlocutions for other bases, such as incorporation and doing business, that are applicable to corporations. After surveying the bases for jurisdiction over individuals, sections 4.21 and 4.22 discuss differences in

---

529. The myth is that Daedalus constructed a labyrinth on Crete in which the Minotaur, a creature with the body of a bull and a human head, was imprisoned. For a short account, see 8 Encyclopaedia Britannica, Minotaur 171 (15th ed. 1985).

application to corporations and unincorporated associations of what appear to be the same bases as those used for individuals, bases applicable to corporations and associations that are not applicable to individuals, and special problems concerning jurisdiction over corporations and associations that are not encountered when considering jurisdiction over individuals.

Some of the bases for jurisdiction over individuals have been recognized at common law without the need for a statute authorizing use of those bases for jurisdiction. These "common law" bases are presence, consent, and appearance.[530] Courts have utilized the other bases for jurisdiction over individuals only to the extent a statute authorizes this use. *Wuchter v. Pizzutti*[531] held that actual notice is not constitutionally sufficient if the statutory scheme does not provide for reasonable notice to the defendant. Thus, courts refusing to extend by judicial decision the "common law" bases of jurisdiction may be doing what is constitutionally required when such extension would rely on ad hoc judicial orders for giving defendants notice and opportunity to be heard.

§ 4.9A   Survey of Long–Arm Statutes

The need for a statute in order for most of the bases for jurisdiction to be available raises the issue of what sort of statute a state should enact. A survey of the kinds of so-called "long-arm" statutes in the United States reveals that states have enacted three different kinds of statutes. Some states have simple one-sentence statutes that expressly confer jurisdiction to the limits of due process.[532] Some state statutes first list various fact situations under which the courts of the state will acquire personal jurisdiction and then include a catchall provision that expressly goes to the limits of due process.[533] Some state statutes contain the laundry list without a catchall clause.[534] In this third group of

---

530. See Knowles v. Logansport Gaslight & Coke Co., 86 U.S. (19 Wall.) 58, 22 L.Ed. 70 (1874) (dictum); Restatement, Second, Ch. 3, Introductory Note at 102; cf. Lindley v. St. Louis–San Francisco Ry., 276 F.Supp. 83 (N.D.Ill.1967), rev'd on other grounds 407 F.2d 639 (7th Cir.1968) (utilizes "common law" basis for jurisdiction over corporation doing business in Illinois when the cause of action does not, as required by the applicable Illinois statute, arise out of the transaction of business in Illinois).

531. 276 U.S. 13, 48 S.Ct. 259, 72 L.Ed. 446 (1928).

532. See, e.g., Ariz.R.Civ.P. 4.2(a); West's Ann.Cal.Code Civ.Proc. § 410.10; N.J.P.R. 4:4–4(b) ("consistent with due process of law"); R.I.Gen.Laws Ann. § 9–5–33 ("in every case not contrary to the provisions of the constitution or laws of the United States").

533. See, e.g., Or. R.C.P. 4(L), which, after a long list of acts and consequences in Oregon that confer specific jurisdiction, states: "Notwithstanding a failure to satisfy the requirement of sections B through K of this rule, in any action where prosecution of the action against a defendant in this state is not inconsistent with the Constitution of this state or the Constitution of the United States."

534. An extreme example is Michigan, which has separate lists for general jurisdiction over individuals (Mi. Comp.L.Ann § 600.701), specific jurisdiction over individuals (id. § 600.705), general jurisdiction over corporations (id. § 600.711), specific jurisdiction over corporations (id. § 600.715), general jurisdiction over partnerships (id. § 600.721), specific jurisdiction over partnerships (id. § 600.725), general jurisdiction over partnership associations or unincorporated voluntary associations (id. § 600.731), and specific jurisdiction over partnership associations or unincorporated voluntary associations (id. § 600.735). The laundry list for specific jurisdiction over corporations is: "(1) The transaction of any

statutes without catchall provisions, some have been interpreted to go to the limits of due process and some have not. Courts in eight states and the District of Columbia that have detailed statutes without catchall due process provisions have not interpreted those statutes as going to the limits of due process.[535] That means that in these states and the District of Columbia a court goes through a two-step analysis of jurisdiction. First, do the facts fit within the wording of the long-arm statute? Second, will exercise of jurisdiction comport with due process? Even in some states that have interpreted statutes without catchall clauses to go to the limits of due process, courts have warned that the statutes may not reach as far as due process.[536] This is because the statute's laundry list may not include all permissible circumstances. Thus courts in these states proceed under the same two-step analysis of first statutory wording and then due process.

How should a state draft its long-arm statute if the state wishes to extend the jurisdiction of its courts to the limits of due process? The

---

business within the state. (2). The doing or causing any act to be done, or consequence to occur, in the state resulting in an action for tort. (3) The ownership, use, or possession of any real or tangible personal property situated within the state. (4) Contracting to insure any person, property, or risk located within this state at the time of contracting. (5) Entering into a contract for services to be performed or for materials to be furnished in the state by the defendant." Id. § 600.715.

535. Which jurisdictions fall into this category is somewhat uncertain because even though the highest state court has said that the state's long-arm statute does not go to due process limits, it is necessary to analyze the jurisdictional decisions in the courts of that state. These decisions may apply the long-arm statute in a manner that indicates little or no difference from due process limits. My best estimate of these jurisdictions is the following: Connecticut, U.S. Trust Co. v. Bohart, 197 Conn. 34, 495 A.2d 1034 (1985); District of Columbia, Helmer v. Doletskaya, 393 F.3d 201 (D.C. Cir. 2004) (D.C. long-arm provision for transacting business goes to due process limits, but not the provision for tortious injury); Florida, Georgia Insurers Insolvency Pool v. Brewer, 602 So.2d 1264 (Fla. 1992); Hawaii, Norris v. Six Flags Theme Parks, Inc., 102 Haw. 203, 74 P.3d 26 (2003) (no jurisdiction over defendant under long-arm statute); Iowa, Cross v. Lightolier, 395 N.W.2d 844 (Iowa 1986); Mississippi, Sorrells v. R & R Custom Coach Works, 636 So.2d 668 (Miss. 1994); Montana, Edsall Constr. Co. v. Robinson, 246 Mont. 37, 804 P.2d 1039 (1991); New Mexico, State Farm Mut. Ins. Co. v. Conyers, 109 N.M. 243, 784 P.2d 986 (1989); New York, Banco Amborsiano, S.P.A. v. Artoc Bank & Trust Ltd., 62 N.Y.2d 65, 464 N.E.2d 432, 476 N.Y.S.2d 64 (1984); West Virginia, Abbott v. Owens–Corning Fiberglass, 191 W.Va. 198, 444 S.E.2d 285 (1994).

For a different list citing cases see Utermohle, *Maryland's Diminished Long–Arm Jurisdiction in the Wake of Zavian v. Foudy*, 31 U. Balt. L. Rev. 1, 39 n.69 (2001) (listing Connecticut, Florida, Illinois, Indiana, Mississippi, New York, and Ohio); McFarland, *Dictum Run Wild: How Long–Arm Statutes Extended to the Limits of Due Process*, 84 Boston. U. L. Rev. 491, 525 (2004) (listing eighteen states that "have enumerated-acts long-arm statutes, and their courts determine long-arm jurisdiction by interpreting the language of those statutes in the first step of a two-step inquiry").

Cf. United States v. Bigford, 365 F.3d 859, 867 (10th Cir. 2004) (if jurisdiction over the defendant is proper under due process but not under the forum's jurisdictional rule, the resulting judgment is not void and the forum may place limits on the grounds for collaterally attacking the judgment) (dictum).

536. See, e.g., Green v. Wilson, 455 Mich. 342, 351, 565 N.W.2d 813, 817 (1997) (stating that "[t]he provisions enumerated [in the Michigan long-arm statute] would be superfluous if the Legislature intended that any activity that is constitutional also satisfies a long-arm statute"); Werner v. Werner, 84 Wash.2d 360, 364, 526 P.2d 370, 374 (1974) (stating that "[l]ong-arm jurisdiction in this state was intended to be operative to the full extent allowed by due process except where limited by the terms of the statute").

simple one-sentence anything-due-process-permits-our-courts-can-do has the benefit of leaving no margin for error. One of Mr. Justice Marshall's remarks in his majority opinion in *Kulko v. Superior Court*[537] may dampen enthusiasm for simple "due process" long-arm statutes. In the course of holding that California did not have jurisdiction over the nonresident father for the purpose of increasing his support obligation, Marshall states "California has not attempted to assert any particularized interest in trying such cases in its courts by, e.g., enacting a special jurisdictional statute."[538] This is a reference to the fact that California's long-arm statute does not enumerate specific fact situations in which jurisdiction may be obtained but states simply that California courts may exercise in personam jurisdiction on "any basis not inconsistent with the Constitution."[539] It is difficult to understand why a state manifests less "interest" in asserting jurisdiction by electing an anything-due-process-permits statute rather than an everything-and-the-kitchen-sink list.

If the legislature rejects a one-sentence long-arm statute either because of Justice Marshall's comment or because the legislature considers such a statute an insufficient guide to courts and lawyers, the statute should have a detailed list of contacts with the state that confer general and specific jurisdiction. Then the statute should have a catchall clause that expressly goes to due process limits and makes it clear that the preceding laundry list is merely for purposes of illustration and does not impose limits on constitutional jurisdiction.[540]

§ 4.9B   Retroactive Application of a Long–Arm Statute

McGee v. International Life Ins. Co. rejected the contention that retroactive application of the California long-arm statute "improperly impairs the obligation of the [insurance] contract."[541] This holding was based on the conclusion that the California statute was "remedial ... and neither enlarged nor impaired ... substantive rights ..."[542] Since this holding, the overwhelming majority of courts that have passed on the issue of retroactive application of a statute extending a state's judicial jurisdiction have applied the statute to events occurring before the statute's enactment.[543] A few courts have, however, refused to apply

---

537. 436 U.S. 84, 98 S.Ct. 1690, 56 L.Ed.2d 132 (1978).

538. Id. at 98, 98 S.Ct. at 1700, 56 L.Ed.2d at 145.

539. West's Ann.Cal.Civ.Proc.Code § 410.10.

540. See LinkAmerica Corp. v. Albert, 857 N.E.2d 961, 967 (Ind. 2006) ("Retention of the enumerated acts found in Rule 4.4(A) served as a handy checklist of activities that usually support personal jurisdiction but does not serve as a limitation on the exercise of personal jurisdiction by a court of this state").

541. 355 U.S. 220, 224, 78 S.Ct. 199, 201, 2 L.Ed.2d 223, 226 (1957).

542. Id., 78 S.Ct. at 201, 2 L.Ed.2d at 226–27.

543. See, e.g., Liberty Mut. Ins. Co. v. American Pecco Corp., 334 F.Supp. 522 (D.D.C.1971); deLeo v. Childs, 304 F.Supp. 593 (D.Mass.1969); Coreil v. Pearson, 242 F.Supp. 802, 806 (W.D.La.1965) ("majority rule"); Eudaily v. Harmon, 420 A.2d 1175 (Del.1980); Nelson v. Miller, 11 Ill.2d 378, 143 N.E.2d 673 (1957); Woodring v. Hall, 200 Kan. 597, 438 P.2d 135 (1968); Hunt v. Nevada State Bank, 285 Minn. 77, 172 N.W.2d 292 (1969), cert. denied, 397 U.S. 1010, 90 S.Ct. 1239, 25 L.Ed.2d 423 (1970); Property Owners

their state's statute retroactively.[544] In holding that the Iowa long-arm statute applied only prospectively, the Iowa Supreme Court drew a distinction between statutes that provide for service on the defendant out of state and those, like the Iowa statute, that provide for substituted service on a state official based on the defendant's fictional consent to this service.[545] The Iowa court said that a statute providing for direct out-of-state service is "procedural" and retroactive, but a statute based on defendant's consent to service on a state official is "substantive" and prospective. It is difficult to see why this difference in the form of the long-arm statute should affect the issue of its retroactive application.

A due process objection against retroactive application of a long-arm statute may be tenable if the defendant can show that "the acts serving as the predicate for jurisdiction under the new section ... have been carried out in justifiable reliance on the prior law."[546] In *Minichiello v. Rosenberg,*[547] the court applied a New York service rule to permit attachment of insurance policies issued by insurers doing business in New York. The attached policies were used for quasi-in-rem enforcement of claims arising from out-of-state automobile accidents. The court raised, but because the insurer did not appeal, found it unnecessary to decide whether making this construction of the rule retroactive, so as to apply before the insurer involved had an opportunity to withdraw from doing business in New York, violated due process.[548] *Rush v. Savchuk*[549] has held unconstitutional the kind of quasi-in-rem jurisdiction used in *Minichiello*, whether used retroactively or prospectively.

Although *Minichiello* may come close, it is extremely unlikely that a defendant can establish unfair surprise, which is necessary for a tenable constitutional objection to retroactive application of a long-arm statute. In the absence of such unfairness, a long-arm statute's salutary removal of artificial restrictions on the plaintiff's choice of forum should be

Ass'n v. Sholley, 111 N.H. 363, 284 A.2d 915 (1971); Singer v. Walker, 15 N.Y.2d 443, 261 N.Y.S.2d 8, 209 N.E.2d 68 (1965), cert. denied, 382 U.S. 905, 86 S.Ct. 241, 15 L.Ed.2d 158 (1965); Myers v. Mooney Aircraft, Inc., 429 Pa. 177, 240 A.2d 505 (1967); Johnson v. Kusel, 298 N.W.2d 91 (S.D.1980); Walke v. Dallas, Inc., 209 Va. 32, 161 S.E.2d 722 (1968); cf. Republic of Austria v. Altmann, 541 U.S. 677, 124 S.Ct. 2240, 159 L.Ed.2d 1 (2004) (the Foreign Sovereign Immunities Act applies to all pending cases regardless of when the underlying conduct occurred). But cf. McCully–Smith Associates, Inc. v. Armour & Co., 349 F.Supp. 694 (W.D.Pa.1972) (though long-arm statute is retroactive, it does not validate service made before the effective date of the statute).

544. See Gordon v. John Deere Co., 264 So.2d 419 (Fla.1972); Castleberry v. Gold Agency, Inc., 124 Ga.App. 694, 185 S.E.2d 557 (1971); Krueger v. Rheem Mfg. Co., 260 Iowa 678, 149 N.W.2d 142 (1967); Rauser v. Rauser, 52 Wis.2d 665, 190 N.W.2d 875 (1971); cf. Fibreboard Corp. v. Kerness, 625 So.2d 457, 458 (Fla. 1993) (refuse to apply doing business general jurisdiction statute retroactively when plaintiff's injuries incurred while he resident in another state, stating that "retroactive application of a long-arm statute would violate the requirement of fair notice").

545. Krueger v. Rheem Mfg. Co., 260 Iowa 678, 149 N.W.2d 142 (1967).

546. Simonson v. International Bank, 14 N.Y.2d 281, 290, 251 N.Y.S.2d 433, 440, 200 N.E.2d 427, 432 (1964) (dictum).

547. 410 F.2d 106 (2d Cir.1968), cert. denied, 396 U.S. 844, 90 S.Ct. 69, 24 L.Ed.2d 94.

548. Id. at 118, n.1.

549. 444 U.S. 320, 100 S.Ct. 571, 62 L.Ed.2d 516 (1980).

applied retroactively whenever the statutory wording permits this construction.

§ 4.9C   Distinction between General and Specific Jurisdiction

In the course of surveying those contacts between defendant and forum that have been held reasonable bases for judicial jurisdiction, it will be useful to keep in mind the distinction between generally-affiliating contacts and specifically-affiliating contacts. A contact that is generally-affiliating is one that makes it reasonable to exercise judicial jurisdiction over the defendant as to any cause of action. A contact that is specifically-affiliating is one that makes it reasonable to exercise judicial jurisdiction only as to causes of action that are related to the contact.[550] Although the discussion in section 4.8 of *Helicopteros Nacionales de Colombia v. Hall,*[551] indicated that these distinctions are not bright lines, they retain analytic utility.

Finally, it should be remembered that the jurisdictional contacts here surveyed are probably not the exclusive bases for judicial jurisdiction in personam in state courts. The past fifty years have seen such rapid development and expansion of the traditional concepts of judicial jurisdiction that no one should be so benighted as to think that the process of development and change has run its course. What follows is simply a listing and commentary on some of the bases for judicial jurisdiction that a number of states have already used. Other bases are likely to emerge. If anything is immutable in the subject of judicial jurisdiction, it is the core concept of reasonableness and fairness.

§ 4.10   Presence

The oldest of all the generally-affiliating bases for judicial jurisdiction over persons is personal service on the defendant while physically present in the forum.[552] In the absence of defendant's waiver of jurisdic-

---

550. See von Mehren and Trautman, The Law of Multistate Problems 656 (1965). See also, Pugh v. Oklahoma Farm Bureau Mut. Ins. Co., 159 F.Supp. 155, 158 (E.D.La.1958) ("Where, as here, the litigation arises directly from the contact with the state, considerations concerning the continuous presence of the company within the state may be irrelevant"); cf. Seiferth v. Helicopteros Atuneros, Inc., 472 F.3d 266 (5th Cir. 2006) (on an issue of first impression in the circuit, holds that if plaintiff's claims relate to different forum contacts by defendant, the plaintiff must establish specific jurisdiction for each claim; in an action to recover for death resulting from the collapse of a work platform, the court finds jurisdiction over the failure to warn and negligence claims but not over the defective design claim); Remick v. Manfredy, 238 F.3d 248 (3d Cir. 2001) (court had jurisdiction over defendant for breach-of-contract claim but not for claims of defamation and misappropriation of image). Contra, Helmer v. Doletskaya, 393 F.3d 201, 203 (D.C. Cir. 2004) (in the light of a decision that district court has specific jurisdiction over defendant for one claim but not for others, "the district court may have discretion to exercise pendent personal jurisdiction over the dismissed claims").

551. 466 U.S. 408, 104 S.Ct. 1868, 80 L.Ed.2d 404 (1984). See § 4.8 text accompanying note 271.

552. As to the standard for attacking an alleged false affidavit of service, see, e.g., Prairie Finance, Inc. v. Perry, 389 So.2d 1131 (La.App.3d Cir.1980) (clear and positive proof, uncorroborated testimony of defendant is not sufficient); Carnes v. Carnes, 668 P.2d 555 (Utah 1983) (clear and convincing evidence); cf. Hollinger v. Hollinger, 416 Pa. 473,

tional objections by appearance or consent, presence was once required for judicial jurisdiction.[553] In the words of Mr. Justice Holmes, "[t]he foundation of jurisdiction is physical power...."[554]

The view, entertained under the regime of *Pennoyer v. Neff,*[555] that physical presence is necessary for judicial jurisdiction, is now outmoded. The correlate of the necessity of physical presence, that it is a sufficient generally-affiliating basis for jurisdiction,[556] is still with us. Physical presence in the jurisdiction is often linked with other contacts between the defendant and the forum that make it reasonable to exercise jurisdiction[557] either generally, or with regard to the particular cause of action being litigated. Domicile is a generally-affiliating nexus commonly linked with physical presence. Acts done in the forum or consequences caused there are common specifically-affiliating contacts likely to co-exist with physical presence. But physical presence alone, no matter how casual or how transient, is employed in this country as a proper basis for judicial jurisdiction.[558] This view of presence as a generally-affiliating jurisdictional nexus received its *reductio ad absurdum* in *Grace v. MacArthur*[559] when a federal district court denied a motion to quash service that had been made on the defendant while he was a passenger on an airplane in flight above the state in which the court sat. Courts do decline to utilize the defendant's presence as a basis for in personam jurisdiction when that presence is brought about by the plaintiff's force or fraud[560] and many states, in the interest of efficient judicial administration, exempt out-of-state parties and witnesses from service of process while present in the forum in attendance at cases unconnected with the matter in which service is attempted.[561] Generally, however, transient physical presence without more is sufficient for judicial jurisdiction.

---

206 A.2d 1 (1965) (sheriff's return of service is not conclusive as to facts of which the sheriff could not have personal knowledge).

553. Knowles v. Logansport Gaslight & Coke Co., 86 U.S. (19 Wall.) 58, 22 L.Ed. 70 (1874).

554. McDonald v. Mabee, 243 U.S. 90, 91, 37 S.Ct. 343, 61 L.Ed. 608, 609 (1917).

555. 95 U.S. 714, 24 L.Ed. 565 (1878).

556. Currie, 1963 U.Ill.L.Forum 533, 583 (1963).

557. See von Mehren & Trautman, 79 Harv. L. Rev. at 1137–38.

558. See Donald Manter Co., Inc. v. Davis, 543 F.2d 419 (1st Cir.1976); Fisher v. Fielding, 67 Conn. 91, 34 A. 714 (1895) (enforcement of English judgment); Darrah v. Watson, 36 Iowa 116 (1873); Peabody v. Hamilton, 106 Mass. 217 (1870).

559. 170 F.Supp. 442 (E.D.Ark.1959). This assumes that the sole basis for jurisdiction is personal service within the state and that service is not simply a method of giving notice and opportunity to be heard. That the transaction in *Grace* had a "strong connection" to the state over which service was made, see Hazard, *Revisiting the Second Restatement of Judgments: Issue Preclusion and Related Problems,* 66 Cornell L. Rev. 564, 570 n.28 (1981). Moreover, the only issue decided in *Grace* was whether defendant was within the "territorial limits" of Arkansas as required by Federal Rule of Civil Procedure 4(f). The defendant's other objections to personal jurisdiction were reserved for later determination.

560. See Klaiber v. Frank, 9 N.J. 1, 86 A.2d 679 (1952) (abuse of extradition); Restatement, Second, § 82.

561. See § 4.34.

Shaffer v. Heitner,[562] limiting the use of quasi in rem jurisdiction, gave as one of its reasons "that all assertions of state court jurisdiction must be evaluated according to the standards set forth in *International Shoe* and its progeny"[563]—the standards of "fair play and substantial justice."[564] Many commentators thought that transient presence in the forum as a basis for jurisdiction could not withstand scrutiny under this test.[565] *Burnham v. Superior Court*[566] has ended speculation that this basis for jurisdiction violates due process. As indicated in the discussion of *Burnham* in § 4.8, that was a domestic U.S. interstate case. Perhaps in accord with widely held views of exorbitant jurisdiction the Supreme Court of the United States may yet hold that exercising jurisdiction over a citizen of a foreign country on the basis of transient presence in the U.S. is, despite *Burnham,* beyond the pale.

§ 4.11 Domicile, Residence, and Nationality or Citizenship

Domicile is a well-established generally-affiliating basis for in personam judicial jurisdiction.[567] Domicile as a constitutional basis for judicial jurisdiction is discussed in sections 2.15 through 2.15B. The point is there made that, although usually it is fair and reasonable to require absent domiciliaries to appear and defend or have their interests adjudicated in their absence, there may be times when bare technical domicile is not a reasonable basis for personal jurisdiction. This would be true if the defendant has been absent from the forum for a long period of time without any intention of returning, but still retains a technical domicile there because not yet having acquired a new domicile of choice. *Shaffer v. Heitner's* insistence "that all assertions of state court jurisdiction" be evaluated under a "fair play and substantial justice" standard,[568] may, in such circumstances, bar the use of technical domicile alone as a basis for jurisdiction.[569]

---

562. 433 U.S. 186, 97 S.Ct. 2569, 53 L.Ed.2d 683 (1977).

563. Id. at 212, 97 S.Ct. at 2584–85, 53 L.Ed.2d at 703.

564. Id.

565. Sedler, *Judicial Jurisdiction and Choice of Law: The Consequences of Shaffer v. Heitner,* 63 Iowa L. Rev. 1031, 1035 (1978); Vernon, *Single–Factor Bases of In Personam Jurisdiction—A Speculation on the Impact of Shaffer v. Heitner,* 1978 Wash.U.L.Q. 273, 303 (1978); cf. Uniform Foreign Money–Judgments Recognition Act § 4(b)(6) ("A foreign judgment need not be recognized if . . . in the case of jurisdiction based only on personal service, the foreign court was a seriously inconvenient forum for the trial of the action"), 13 U.L.A. 417, 422. But see Brilmayer, *How Contacts Count: Due Process Limitations on State Court Jurisdiction,* 1980 S.Ct.Rev. 77, 82.

566. 495 U.S. 604, 110 S.Ct. 2105, 109 L.Ed.2d 631 (1990) [Discussed supra text accompanying notes 393–438.]

567. Milliken v. Meyer, 311 U.S. 457, 61 S.Ct. 339, 85 L.Ed. 278 (1940). See also McDonald v. Mabee, 243 U.S. 90, 92, 37 S.Ct. 343, 344, 61 L.Ed. 608, 610 (1917) (dictum); Knowles v. Logansport Gaslight & Coke Co., 86 U.S. (19 Wall.) 58, 61, 22 L.Ed. 70, 72 (1874) (dictum). But see Raher v. Raher, 150 Iowa 511, 129 N.W. 494 (1911), overruled in part, Edwards v. Smith, 238 Iowa 1080, 29 N.W.2d 404 (1947).

568. 433 U.S. 186, 212, 97 S.Ct. 2569, 2584–85, 53 L.Ed.2d 683, 703 (1977).

569. See Restatement, Second, § 29 (1988 Revisions) (stating that domicile is not a basis for jurisdiction if "the individual's relationship to the state is so attenuated as to make the exercise of such jurisdiction unreasonable"). But see Developments, 73 Harv. L.

Care must be taken to distinguish cases in which domicile is utilized as a generally-affiliating jurisdictional basis from cases in which, although the court purports to use domicile as a basis for jurisdiction, there is a specifically-affiliating nexus with the forum that makes it reasonable for the court to adjudicate the matter before it. In *Mounts v. Mounts,*[570] for example, in a support action against an absconded divorced husband, the court assumed that the husband had remained domiciled at the marital domicile for fourteen years after he had disappeared. This presumed domicile would be a very questionable basis for general in personam jurisdiction over the missing husband. But the fact that the husband had abandoned his family at the marital domicile should be a sufficient specifically-affiliating circumstance to give a court at the marital domicile jurisdiction over the husband in matters relating to the support of those he has abandoned.[571] In the same manner, cases that appear to rely, at least in part, on former domicile in the forum, when the defendant changed domicile to another state before plaintiff commenced suit, may be explained in terms of a specifically-affiliating nexus that makes it reasonable to adjudicate the matter in issue.[572] For example, a state in which the defendant has caused personal injury to the plaintiff has a constitutional basis for exercising personal jurisdiction over the defendant for causes of action arising out of that injury[573] whether the defendant is domiciled there at the time of suit, was domiciled there at the time of injury but has acquired a new domicile before suit is brought, or was never domiciled at the forum.[574]

Although the United States Supreme Court has not yet had occasion to pass on the question, it is likely that the courts of a state have judicial jurisdiction in personam over individuals resident in the state, but domiciled elsewhere, if the residence is substantial enough to make the exercise of jurisdiction reasonable.[575] The Wisconsin long-arm statute, for example, confers general jurisdiction over a person "engaged in substantial and not isolated activities within this state."[576]

Rev. at 942: "When there is reason to believe that no other state would assume jurisdiction, the plaintiff's overriding interest in having one certain forum makes it reasonable to allow suit in the defendant's domicile."

570. 181 Neb. 542, 149 N.W.2d 435 (1967).

571. Mizner v. Mizner, 84 Nev. 268, 439 P.2d 679 (1968), cert. denied 393 U.S. 847, 89 S.Ct. 130, 21 L.Ed.2d 117 (1968). Cf. Schreiber v. Schreiber, 27 Conn.Sup. 121, 231 A.2d 658 (Fairfield Cty.1967) (service in divorce action made after husband had left home); Venizelos v. Venizelos, 30 A.D.2d 856, 293 N.Y.S.2d 20 (2d Dept.1968) (separation action after husband had returned to Greece).

572. See DeFazio v. Wright, 229 F.Supp. 111 (D.N.J.1964) (boat collision); Owens v. Superior Court, 52 Cal.2d 822, 345 P.2d 921 (1959) (dog bite).

573. See § 4.16.

574. Cf. Schneider v. Linkfield, 389 Mich. 608, 209 N.W.2d 225 (1973) (jurisdiction upheld in suit between former residents based on automobile accident in another state under statute covering actions arising out of "ownership ... of ... personal property situated within the [forum]").

575. See Restatement, Second, § 30.

576. Wisc.Stat.Ann. § 801.05(1)(d).

A person "born or naturalized in the United States"[577] is a citizen of a state only if he is domiciled there. He may be a citizen of the United States, however, while domiciled abroad. Under some circumstances, it may be reasonable for the United States to exercise judicial jurisdiction over an American citizen who is domiciled abroad. Congress has authorized a federal court to issue a subpoena "requiring the appearance as a witness before it, or before a person or body designated by it, of a national or resident of the United States who is in a foreign country, or requiring the production of a specified document or other thing by him"[578] and to punish by contempt proceedings disobedience of such a subpoena.[579] *Blackmer v. United States*[580] affirmed an adjudication of contempt against a United States citizen who had established his residence in France and had disobeyed a subpoena to testify at a criminal trial in the District of Columbia.

§ 4.12   Consent

Consent is a well-established basis for judicial jurisdiction.[581] As used here, "consent" means actual consent. There are some long-arm statutes that unwisely characterize the existence of some specifically-affiliating nexus between forum and defendant, such as a tort committed by the defendant in the forum, as constituting the defendant's "consent" to be subject to the jurisdiction of forum courts in actions arising out of that nexus.[582] Such a specifically-affiliating contact is not consent at all, but an independent basis for judicial jurisdiction.[583]

True consent to jurisdiction may be given either before or after suit is brought.[584] A common form of consent is as part of a contract that later forms the basis for the claim upon which suit is brought. The cognovit clause, discussed above in connection with waiver of notice and

---

577.   U.S.Const. 14th Amend., § 1.

578.   28 U.S.C.A. § 1783(a).

579.   28 U.S.C.A. § 1784.

580.   284 U.S. 421, 52 S.Ct. 252, 76 L.Ed. 375 (1932).

581.   See National Equipment Rental, Ltd. v. Szukhent, 375 U.S. 311, 316, 84 S.Ct. 411, 414, 11 L.Ed.2d 354, 358 (1964) (dictum); New York Fire & Marine Underwriters, Inc. v. Colvin, 241 Ark. 1019, 411 S.W.2d 657 (1967); Walsh v. Walsh, 388 So.2d 240 (Fla.App.2d Dist.1980) (separation agreement); Pacolet Mfg. Co. v. Crescent Textiles, Inc., 219 Ga. 268, 133 S.E.2d 96 (1963); Maxwell Shapiro Woolen Co. v. Amerotron Corp., 339 Mass. 252, 158 N.E.2d 875 (1959); Gilbert v. Burnstine, 255 N.Y. 348, 174 N.E. 706 (1931); Elkin v. Austral American Trading Corp., 10 Misc.2d 879, 170 N.Y.S.2d 131 (Spec.Term 1957); Copin v. Adamson, L.R. 9 Exch. 345 (1874). Cf. In re Sweetapple Plastics, Inc., 77 B.R. 304, 309 (Bankr. M.D. Ga. 1987) (a clause consenting to jurisdiction is an additional term that "materially" alters the agreement within the meaning of U.C.C. § 2–207(2)(b), collecting authority in accord). But see McRae v. J.D./M.D., Inc., 511 So.2d 540 (Fla.1987) (a plaintiff cannot base jurisdiction on consent in the form of a forum-selection clause).

582.   See Chrischilles v. Griswold, 260 Iowa 453, 150 N.W.2d 94 (1967) (refuses to apply tort long-arm statute retroactively because it bases jurisdiction on consent inferred from commission of tort).

583.   See Olberding v. Illinois Cent. R.R., 346 U.S. 338, 341, 74 S.Ct. 83, 85, 98 L.Ed. 39, 43 (1953) (jurisdiction under non-resident motorist statute "does not rest on consent at all").

584.   See cases cited note 581, supra.

opportunity to be heard,[585] is one form of consent to judicial jurisdiction.[586] Other contractual forms of consent to jurisdiction, less oppressive than cognovit clauses, are very common.

In *National Equipment Rental, Ltd. v. Szukhent*[587] a lessor brought suit in New York against a Michigan lessee of farm equipment for an alleged default under the lease. The plaintiff based jurisdiction on a clause in the lease in which the lessee appointed, as his agent for the service of process in New York, the wife of one of the plaintiff's officers. This agent was unknown to the defendant. The clause did not require the agent to notify the defendant of service. In fact, however, both the agent and the plaintiff transmitted such notice to the defendant by certified mail. In a five-to-four opinion, the Supreme Court held that the New York federal court had jurisdiction over the defendant because of service in New York on defendant's "agent authorized by appointment ... to receive service of process" within the meaning of Federal Rule of Civil Procedure 4(d)(1).

Many states have statutes requiring that, as a condition of obtaining a certificate to do business in the state, a corporation appoint a resident agent for service of process. Some courts have construed the resulting appointment as a "consent" to jurisdiction in the courts of the state, even with regard to causes of action not arising out of the business within the state.[588] A number of courts and commentators have questioned the constitutionality of compelling a foreign corporation to consent to general jurisdiction as a condition to doing business in the state.[589] *Bendix Autolite Corp. v. Midwesco Enterprises*[590] invalidated as

---

585. See § 4.5.

586. See, e.g., Egley v. T.B. Bennett & Co., 196 Ind. 50, 145 N.E. 830 (1924); McDade v. Moynihan, 330 Mass. 437, 115 N.E.2d 372 (1953); Hazel v. Jacobs, 78 N.J.L. 459, 75 A. 903 (Errors & App.1910); Gavenda Bros. v. Elkins Limestone Co., 145 W.Va. 732, 116 S.E.2d 910 (1960) (dictum).

It is, however, a defense to a judgment based on a cognovit note that the note is a forgery. Anderson v. Reconstruction Fin. Corp., 281 Ky. 531, 136 S.W.2d 741 (1940).

587. 375 U.S. 311, 84 S.Ct. 411, 11 L.Ed.2d 354 (1964).

588. See, e.g., Pennsylvania Fire Ins. Co. v. Gold Issue Mining & Milling Co., 243 U.S. 93, 37 S.Ct. 344, 61 L.Ed. 610 (1917) (discussed infra this section text accompanying notes 593–594); Bagdon v. Philadelphia & Reading Coal & Iron Co., 217 N.Y. 432, 111 N.E. 1075 (1916) (Cardozo, J.); cf. Mittelstadt v. Rouzer, 213 Neb. 178, 328 N.W.2d 467 (1982) (same with regard to designated agent required by the Motor Carrier Act).

589. See Wenche Siemer v. Learjet Acquisition Corp., 966 F.2d 179, 180–81 (5th Cir. 1992), cert. denied, 506 U.S. 1080, 113 S.Ct. 1047, 122 L.Ed.2d 356 (1993) (obtaining general jurisdiction by service on agent appointed for service of process by a foreign corporation holding a certificate to do business in the state violated due process); Armstrong v. Aramco Services Co., 155 Ariz. 345, 746 P.2d 917 (App.1987); Wallenta v. Avis Rent A Car System, Inc., 10 Conn.App. 201, 522 A.2d 820 (1987) (remand to determine whether exercise of general jurisdiction violates due process); Brilmayer, *Consent, Contract, and Territory*, 74 Minn. L. Rev. 1, 29 (1989) (basing general jurisdiction on a corporation's obtaining a certificate to do business "may be unconstitutional"); Brilmayer, Haverkamp, Logan, Lynch, Neuwirth, & O'Brien, *A General Look at General Jurisdiction*, 66 Texas L. Rev. 723, 758 (1988) (*Pennsylvania Fire Ins.*, discussed in text accompanying notes 593–594, does not seem "viable under today's due process standards"); Hill, *Choice of Law and Jurisdiction in the Supreme Court,* 81 Colum. L. Rev. 960, 981–82 (1981); Shreve, *Interest Analysis as Constitutional Law*, 48 Ohio St.L. J. 51, 60 n.54 (1987) (requiring consent to general jurisdiction as a condition for doing business in the state "seems unreasonable");

an unreasonable burden on interstate commerce the Ohio rule tolling the statute of limitations against a foreign corporation, even though the corporation was subject to long-arm jurisdiction, unless the corporation registered to do business in Ohio. One reason stated for the result was that the Ohio practice "forces a foreign corporation to choose between exposure to the general jurisdiction of Ohio courts or forfeiture of the limitations defense...."[591]

If jurisdiction is based on consent, a court must not exceed the scope of the consent. For example, in *Grover & Baker Sewing–Machine Co. v. Radcliffe*,[592] the Court held that consent that any attorney of a court of record might confess judgment, could not validate, against a nonresident, a confession of judgment done by a court prothonotary who was not an attorney, even though state law permitted this form of confessing judgment. A court's reasonable construction of the consent is likely to be upheld. In *Pennsylvania Fire Insurance Co. v. Gold Issue Mining & Milling Co.*,[593] an insurance company, in order to obtain a license to do business in Missouri, filed with the Missouri Superintendent of Insurance a power of attorney stating that service of process on the Superintendent would be deemed personal service on the company so long as it had any liabilities outstanding in Missouri. The Missouri Supreme Court, construing the statute under which the consent was filed, held that the consent covered service in an action in Missouri on a policy issued in Colorado covering buildings in Colorado. Justice Holmes remarked that "when a power actually is conferred by a document, the party executing it takes the risk of the interpretation that may be put upon it by the courts."[594]

---

cf. Sternberg v. O'Neil, 550 A.2d 1105 (Del.1988) (while court does not believe a minimum contacts analysis is necessary when corporation has qualified to do business in Delaware, it notes that the defendant does have minimum contacts and that Delaware does not penalize a corporation for not qualifying to do business); Anderson Trucking Service, Inc. v. Ryan, 746 S.W.2d 647 (Mo.App. 1988) (obtaining certificate of public convenience and necessity permitting defendant to perform transportation services in the state does not subject defendant to general jurisdiction).

That registering to do business does confer general jurisdiction, see Ranger Nationwide, Inc. v. Cook, 519 So.2d 1087 (Fla.App. 3d Dist.1988), review denied, 531 So.2d 167 (1988); Read v. Sonat Offshore Drilling, Inc., 515 So.2d 1229 (Miss.1987).

590. 486 U.S. 888, 108 S.Ct. 2218, 100 L.Ed.2d 896 (1988).

591. Id. at 893, 108 S.Ct. at 2221, 100 L.Ed.2d at 903.

592. 137 U.S. 287, 11 S.Ct. 92, 34 L.Ed. 670 (1890).

593. 243 U.S. 93, 37 S.Ct. 344, 61 L.Ed. 610 (1917).

594. *Pennsylvania Fire Insurance Co. v. Gold Issue Mining & Milling Co.*. But cf. Frances Hosiery Mills, Inc. v. Burlington Indust., Inc., 285 N.C. 344, 204 S.E.2d 834 (1974) (deny full faith and credit to New York judgment on ground that under § 2–207 of the Uniform Commercial Code, a clause consenting to arbitration in New York was not part of the parties' agreement).

For cases deciding whether the actions of the defendant amount to a consent to jurisdiction, see Schultz v. Schultz, 436 F.2d 635 (7th Cir.1971) (power of attorney given to lawyer does not empower him to accept service of process in a separate action); Johnson v. Superior Court, 14 Ariz.App. 329, 483 P.2d 561 (1971) (accepting service of summons and complaint is not a consent to jurisdiction); Clinic Masters, Inc. v. District Court, 192 Colo. 120, 556 P.2d 473 (1976) (statement that exclusive jurisdiction shall be in a court is a consent to the jurisdiction of that court); Bania v. Royal Lahaina Hotel, 37 Ill.App.3d 661,

Courts have construed an agreement that disputes that may arise under a contract shall be settled by arbitration in F, as an agreement to submit to the jurisdiction of an arbitration board in F[595] and to the jurisdiction of F courts for enforcement of the award.[596] United States courts have not construed an agreement that the law of F shall apply to questions arising under a contract as a submission to the jurisdiction of F courts.[597]

A number of states have by statute limited the use of consent-to-jurisdiction clauses.[598] This raises the question of whether jurisdiction based on "consent" contained in an adhesion contract drafted by the party in the vastly superior bargaining position and permitting litigation in a forum in which it is not convenient for the defendant to defend, should be a violation of due process.[599] Some cases have held it a

---

347 N.E.2d 106 (1975) (telling plaintiff to sue defendant's insurance company is consent to jurisdiction where insurer can be served).

For cases construing the scope of the consent, see Republic Int'l Corp. v. Amco Engineers, Inc., 516 F.2d 161 (9th Cir.1975) (consent to jurisdiction construed as agreement not to bring suit elsewhere); Keaty v. Freeport Indonesia, Inc., 503 F.2d 955 (5th Cir.1974) (ambiguity as to whether consent to jurisdiction is an agreement not to sue elsewhere is construed against party who drafted the agreement); The Plum Tree, Inc. v. Stockment, 488 F.2d 754 (3d Cir.1973) (forum-selection clause does not prevent transfer under 28 U.S.C.A. § 1404(a)); Public Water Supply Dist. v. American Ins. Co., 471 F.Supp. 1071 (W.D.Mo.1979) (selection of county forum prevents removal to federal court); Perini Corp. v. Orion Ins. Co., 331 F.Supp. 453 (E.D.Cal.1971) (consent to jurisdiction of any court of competent jurisdiction waives right to remove to a federal court); Pasquale v. Genovese, 139 Vt. 346, 428 A.2d 1126 (1981) (appointment of agent for service under Motor Vehicle Safety Act is only for service in actions arising under the Act).

595. Gilbert v. Burnstine, 255 N.Y. 348, 174 N.E. 706 (1931); cf. Joseph L. Wilmotte & Co. v. Rosenman Bros., 258 N.W.2d 317 (Iowa 1977) (consent to arbitration "in accordance with the rules of the American Arbitration Association" is consent to jurisdiction in the forum selected by the Association).

596. International Alltex Corp. v. Lawler Creations, Ltd., [1965] Irish R. 264 (H.Ct.).

That a non-resident trustee of a testamentary trust consents to the jurisdiction of the court that appoints him when he accepts the appointment, see Ohlheiser v. Shepherd, 84 Ill.App.2d 83, 228 N.E.2d 210 (1967).

597. See Misco Leasing, Inc. v. Vaughn, 450 F.2d 257 (10th Cir.1971); Agrashell, Inc. v. Bernard Sirotta Co., 344 F.2d 583 (2d Cir.1965); Franklin Nat'l Bank v. Krakow, 295 F.Supp. 910 (D.D.C.1969); Pryles, *Comparative Aspects of Prorogation and Arbitration Agreements,* 25 Int'l & Comp.L.Q. 543, 550 (1976); cf. Burger King Corp. v. Rudzewicz, 471 U.S. 462, 481–82, 105 S.Ct. 2174, 2187, 85 L.Ed.2d 528, 547 (1985) (but choice of a state's law is a factor indicating that the defendant has " 'purposefully invoked the benefits and protections of a State's law' for jurisdictional purposes").

But that a consent to jurisdiction should be construed also as choosing the law of that jurisdiction, see Cowen & Da Costa, *The Contractual Forum: Situation in England and the British Commonwealth,* 13 Am.J.Comp.L. 179, 181 (1964).

598. See B. Curran, *Trends in Consumer Credit Legislation* 41 (1965); Uniform Commercial Code § 2A–106(2) (in lease to consumer, choice of a forum that would not otherwise have jurisdiction over the lessee is not enforceable); Uniform Consumer Credit Code § 1.201(8)(e) (1974 Act) (invalidate consumer consent to jurisdiction of court that does not otherwise have jurisdiction).

599. See May v. Figgins, 186 Mont. 383, 607 P.2d 1132 (1980) (deny full faith and credit to judgment based on unreasonable consent to jurisdiction); *Developments,* 73 Harv. L. Rev. at 944; Schlesinger, *Jurisdictional Clauses in Consumer Transactions: A Multifaceted Problem of Jurisdiction and Full Faith and Credit,* 29 Hastings L. J. 967, 982 (1978) (distinction between jurisdiction and competence based on defendant's consent). Cf. Uniform Model Choice of Forum Act § 2(a)(2), (3), 1968 Handbook of the National Conference

violation of due process for a seller to obtain jurisdiction over an out-of-state buyer at the seller's place of business if the basis for jurisdiction is a long-arm statute conferring jurisdiction over nonresidents who make "a contract to be performed in whole or in part"[600] or who transact business[601] in the forum. It would be strange if these decisions could be avoided by the simple device of inserting into mail-order contracts a boiler-plate clause in which the buyer "consents" to the jurisdiction of courts in the seller's state. The Brussels Regulation denies jurisdiction based solely on a consumer's consent unless the consumer consents after the dispute has arisen.[602]

§ 4.13 Appearance

The defendant's appearance in an action, either in person or by an attorney authorized[603] to appear, is a constitutional basis for exercising judicial jurisdiction.[604] One exception to this statement is that, if the defendant appears in a state court for the sole purpose of removal to a federal court, the appearance does not subject the defendant to the jurisdiction of the state court.[605] Moreover, a defendant does not, by appearing and moving to quash, waive a contention that compelling

---

of Commissioners on Uniform State Laws [Act withdrawn in 1975 by National Conference of Commissioners on Uniform State Laws] (court will accept jurisdiction based on agreement if "this state is a reasonably convenient place for the trial" and "the agreement . . . was not obtained by misrepresentation, duress, the abuse of economic power, or other unconscionable means"); cf. Colonial Leasing Co. v. Pugh Bros. Garage, 735 F.2d 380 (9th Cir.1984) (refuse to enforce consent to jurisdiction in contract between merchants); Spiegel, Inc. v. Federal Trade Comm'n, 540 F.2d 287 (7th Cir.1976) (although whether mail-order seller's exercising long-arm jurisdiction over nonresident consumers violates due process depends on the facts of each case, the Commission may forbid the practice in all cases as "unfair"); Paragon Homes, Inc. v. Carter, 56 Misc.2d 463, 288 N.Y.S.2d 817 (Spec.Term.1968), aff'd mem., 30 A.D.2d 1052, 295 N.Y.S.2d 606 (2d Dep't) (refuses to accept jurisdiction under "unconscionable" agreement). But see AAACon Auto Transport, Inc. v. Teafatiller, 334 F.Supp. 1042 (S.D.N.Y.1971) (upholding consent to arbitration).

600. Fourth Northwestern Nat'l Bank v. Hilson Ind., Inc., 264 Minn. 110, 117 N.W.2d 732 (1962). But cf. Electric Regulator Corp. v. Sterling Extruder Corp., 280 F.Supp. 550 (D.Conn.1968) (jurisdiction over buyer upheld when risk of loss of goods passed to buyer at shipping point in forum).

601. Oswalt Ind., Inc. v. Gilmore, 297 F.Supp. 307 (D.Kan.1969).

602. Brussels Regulation, supra § 4.1 note 6, art. 17(1).

603. Vilas v. Plattsburgh & M.R.R., 123 N.Y. 440, 25 N.E. 941 (1890). But see Brown v. Nichols, 42 N.Y. 26 (1870) (attorney employed by ill defendant's family without defendant's knowledge).

604. See Sugg v. Thorton, 132 U.S. 524, 10 S.Ct. 163, 33 L.Ed. 447 (1889); Knowles v. Logansport Gaslight & Coke Co., 86 U.S. (19 Wall.) 58, 62, 22 L.Ed. 70 (1874) (dictum); In re Morgan Guaranty Trust Co., 28 N.Y.2d 155, 320 N.Y.S.2d 905, 269 N.E.2d 571 (1971), cert. denied, 404 U.S. 826, 92 S.Ct. 58, 30 L.Ed.2d 55 (1971); Myers v. Mooney Aircraft, Inc., 429 Pa. 177, 240 A.2d 505 (1967); cf. Konigsberg v. Shute, 435 F.2d 551 (3d Cir.1970) (lack of jurisdiction cannot be asserted for first time in amended answer); City of New Haven v. Indiana Suburban Sewers, Inc., 257 Ind. 609, 277 N.E.2d 361 (1972) (objection to lack of notice is waived by appearance).

605. Michigan Cent. R.R. v. Mix, 278 U.S. 492, 49 S.Ct. 207, 73 L.Ed. 470 (1929); Cain v. Commercial Publishing Co., 232 U.S. 124, 34 S.Ct. 284, 58 L.Ed. 534 (1914); Goldey v. Morning News, 156 U.S. 518, 15 S.Ct. 559, 39 L.Ed. 517 (1895).

defense in the forum would place an unreasonable burden on interstate commerce.[606]

York v. Texas[607] held that a state may, consistently with due process, refuse to permit a defendant to make a special appearance. In a special appearance, the defendant appears solely to contest the court's jurisdiction and does not thereby waive jurisdictional objections. Today, however, all states[608] permit some form of appearance in which the defendant can contest jurisdiction. Special appearance as a self-imposed limitation on a state's judicial jurisdiction is discussed in section 4.37.

The defendant, by appearing, submits to the jurisdiction of the forum court as to all causes of action pleaded in the complaint at the time of his appearance. The defendant does not submit to jurisdiction with regard to new causes of action that the plaintiff subsequently adds by amending the complaint.[609]

The plaintiff, by bringing the action, submits to the court's jurisdiction not only as to matters that the plaintiff has pleaded in his complaint, but also as to any causes of action that, "may in fairness be determined concurrently with that action."[610]

§ 4.14   Doing Business

Although "doing business" has long been articulated as a basis for judicial jurisdiction over out-of-state corporations,[611] at least as to causes of action arising from transactions in the forum, at one time, doing business was not recognized as a distinct specifically-affiliating[612] nexus sufficient to confer judicial jurisdiction. It was assumed that jurisdiction over foreign corporations was based on the forum's power to exclude them from acting within the forum except upon terms reasonably imposed by the forum. One such reasonable term was the foreign

---

606.   Michigan Cent. R.R. v. Mix, 278 U.S. 492, 49 S.Ct. 207, 73 L.Ed. 470 (1929).

607.   137 U.S. 15, 11 S.Ct. 9, 34 L.Ed. 604 (1890).

608.   The last states to permit special appearances were Mississippi (Mladinich v. Kohn, 250 Miss. 138, 164 So.2d 785 (1964)) and Texas (Tex.R.Civ.Proc. 120a (1962)).

609.   See Vickery v. Garretson, 527 A.2d 293 (D.C.App.1987) (refuse full faith and credit to judgment based on theory that was changed after party signed waiver of appearance, when no notice of change given to the party); Chapman v. Chapman, 284 A.D. 504, 132 N.Y.S.2d 707 (1954) (dictum) (amend separation suit to one for divorce); Restatement, Second, § 34, comment *c*; cf. In re Einstoss, 26 N.Y.2d 181, 309 N.Y.S.2d 184, 257 N.E.2d 637 (1970) (appearance in action to foreclose mortgage does not subject defendant to unrelated cross claim for taxes). But see Everitt v. Everitt, 4 N.Y.2d 13, 171 N.Y.S.2d 836, 148 N.E.2d 891 (1958) (defendant who appeared after summons and notice served but before complaint served was subject to jurisdiction with regard to causes of action stated in the complaint that were not stated in the notice).

610.   Restatement (Second) Judgments § 9 (1982). See Glen, *An Analysis of "Mere Presence" and Other Traditional Bases of Jurisdiction,* 45 Bklyn. L. Rev. 607, 615 (1979); Adam v. Saenger, 303 U.S. 59, 58 S.Ct. 454, 82 L.Ed. 649 (1938) (cross-action); Van Miller v. Hutchins, 118 N.H. 204, 384 A.2d 791 (1978) (resident defendant may file unrelated counterclaim against nonresident plaintiff); Restatement, Second, § 34, comment *c*.

611.   Lafayette Ins. Co. v. French, 59 U.S. (18 How.) 404, 15 L.Ed. 451 (1856); Mutual Reserve Fund Life Ass'n v. Phelps, 190 U.S. 147, 23 S.Ct. 707, 47 L.Ed. 987 (1903).

612.   Doing business as a generally-affiliating basis for jurisdiction is discussed infra this section in text accompanying notes 638–653.

corporation's "consent" to the jurisdiction of local courts.[613] For this reason, it was thought that doing business was not a basis for jurisdiction over individuals as distinguished from corporations, unless the business was of a kind subject to special licensing and regulation. Otherwise there would be no right to exclude individuals from doing business in the forum and thus no basis for extracting "consent" to jurisdiction.[614]

International Shoe Co. v. Washington[615] did much to end the use of a fictitious[616] "consent" as a basis for judicial jurisdiction. A corporation or person may actually consent to the jurisdiction of local courts in return for being permitted to perform activities in the forum that might otherwise be forbidden. If so, this actual consent is a basis for jurisdiction the extent of which depends upon the terms of the consent and often upon construction of a statute imposing those terms.[617] But without any such power of the state to forbid the local business activity and completely aside from actual consent, doing business is now recognized as a distinct basis for judicial jurisdiction grounded upon activities in the forum that are sufficiently substantial to make it reasonable to require a person to appear and defend causes of action arising from those local activities or have those causes adjudicated in the defendant's absence.[618]

The traditional jurisdictional definition of "doing business" "is doing a series of acts for the purpose of thereby realizing pecuniary benefit, or otherwise accomplishing an object, or doing a single act for such purpose with the intention of thereby initiating a series of such acts."[619] In the words of the Utah Supreme Court, this standard requires "a continuity of dealing and activity not too dissimilar from that indulged by local business people attending to their own business pursuits."[620] A view stated by the Second Circuit Court of Appeals is that:

> A foreign corporation is doing business in New York "in the traditional sense" when its New York representative provides services beyond "mere solicitation" and these services are sufficiently important to the foreign corporation that if it did not have a representative to perform them, the corporation's own officials would undertake to perform substantially similar services.[621]

---

613.   Lafayette Ins. Co. v. French, 59 U.S. (18 How.) 404, 15 L.Ed. 451 (1856).

614.   See Henry L. Doherty & Co. v. Goodman, 294 U.S. 623, 55 S.Ct. 553, 79 L.Ed. 1097 (1935); Flexner v. Farson, 248 U.S. 289, 39 S.Ct. 97, 63 L.Ed. 250 (1919).

615.   326 U.S. 310, 66 S.Ct. 154, 90 L.Ed. 95 (1945).

616.   Id. at 318, 66 S.Ct. at 159, 90 L.Ed. at 103.

617.   See Pennsylvania Fire Ins. Co. v. Gold Issue Mining & Milling Co., 243 U.S. 93, 37 S.Ct. 344, 61 L.Ed. 610 (1917) (construing Missouri statute under which consent to jurisdiction filed).

618.   See International Shoe Co. v. Washington, 326 U.S. 310, 66 S.Ct. 154, 90 L.Ed. 95 (1945).

619.   Restatement, Second, § 35, comment *a*.

620.   Dykes v. Reliable Furniture & Carpet, 3 Utah 2d 34, 37, 277 P.2d 969, 972 (1954). See also State Tax Comm'n v. Cord, 81 Nev. 403, 404 P.2d 422 (1965).

621.   Gelfand v. Tanner Motor Tours, Ltd., 385 F.2d 116 (2d Cir.1967), cert. denied, 390 U.S. 996, 88 S.Ct. 1198, 20 L.Ed.2d 95 (1968). See also Bryant v. Finnish Nat'l Airline, 15

Although a few courts have construed their "doing business" statutes very broadly to reach to the limits that due process will allow,[622] the traditional definition of "doing business" noted above, requiring a course of substantial commercial activity in the forum, is far more restrictive. The "doing business" statutes contrast with newer legislation referring to a person who "transacts any business within the state." These "transact" business statutes are generally construed more broadly than the older "doing" business acts,[623] sometimes reaching non-commercial activities in the forum,[624] and are more frequently,[625] though not always,[626] held to reach as far as the Constitution will permit.

Once "doing business" is recognized as a basis for judicial jurisdiction distinct from "consent" to jurisdiction based on the power to exclude a business from the forum, it is apparent that "doing business" for jurisdictional purposes should reach activities that would not be sufficient for the forum to require an out-of-state corporation to obtain a certificate entitling it to conduct its activities in the forum.[627]

The fact that an officer or director of a foreign corporation is served while present in the forum is not sufficient to confer jurisdiction over the corporation if the officer or director was not in the forum on corporate business and the action does not arise out of that business.[628] It is often stated that "mere solicitation" of orders in the forum without other activities conducted there by a foreign corporation is not sufficient to

---

N.Y.2d 426, 432, 260 N.Y.S.2d 625, 628–29, 208 N.E.2d 439, 441 (1965) ("The test for 'doing business' is and should be a simple pragmatic one. . . .").

622. See Henry R. Jahn & Son, Inc. v. Superior Court, 49 Cal.2d 855, 323 P.2d 437 (1958); cf. B.K. Sweeney Co. v. Colorado Interstate Gas Co., 429 P.2d 759 (Okl.1967).

623. See Liquid Carriers Corp. v. American Marine Corp., 375 F.2d 951 (2d Cir.1967); Nix v. Dunavant, 249 Ark. 641, 460 S.W.2d 762 (1970); Griffiths & Sprague Stevedoring Co. v. Bayly, Martin & Fay, Inc., 71 Wn.2d 679, 430 P.2d 600 (1967).

624. See Warren v. Warren, 249 Ga. 130, 287 S.E.2d 524 (1982) (to determine validity of separation agreement); Van Wagenberg v. Van Wagenberg, 241 Md. 154, 215 A.2d 812, cert. denied, 385 U.S. 833, 87 S.Ct. 73, 17 L.Ed.2d 68 (1966) (child support).

625. See Southern Mach. Co. v. Mohasco Indus. Inc., 401 F.2d 374 (6th Cir.1968) (Tenn.Act); Woodring v. Hall, 200 Kan. 597, 438 P.2d 135 (1968); State ex rel. White Lumber Sales, Inc. v. Sulmonetti, 252 Or. 121, 448 P.2d 571 (1968).

626. See Kramer v. Vogl, 17 N.Y.2d 27, 267 N.Y.S.2d 900, 215 N.E.2d 159 (1966). See also Fontanetta v. American Board of Internal Medicine, 303 F.Supp. 427 (E.D.N.Y.1969), aff'd, 421 F.2d 355 (2d Cir.1970); Union Ski Co. v. Union Plastics Corp., 548 P.2d 1257 (Utah 1976).

627. See Mid–Continent Telephone Corp. v. Home Telephone Co., 307 F.Supp. 1014 (N.D.Miss.1969); U.S. Cap & Closure, Inc. v. Superior Court, 265 Cal.App.2d 408, 71 Cal.Rptr. 184 (1968); Librairie Hachette, S.A. v. Paris Book Center, Inc., 62 Misc.2d 873, 309 N.Y.S.2d 701 (S.Ct., N.Y.Co., 1970). But see Hill v. Electronics Corp. of America, 253 Iowa 581, 113 N.W.2d 313 (1962) (statute drafted so as to equate the two); Scranton Grain Co. v. Lubbock Mach. & Supply Co., 167 N.W.2d 748 (N.D.1969) (in determining jurisdiction, court utilizes statutory definition relating to when certificate to do business required).

628. Riverside & Dan River Cotton Mills, Inc. v. Menefee, 237 U.S. 189, 35 S.Ct. 579, 59 L.Ed. 910 (1915); Goldey v. Morning News, 156 U.S. 518, 15 S.Ct. 559, 39 L.Ed. 517 (1895); Hermetic Seal Corp. v. Savoy Electronics, Inc., 290 F.Supp. 240 (S.D.Fla.1967), aff'd mem., 401 F.2d 775 (5th Cir.1968); O'Brien v. Eubanks, 701 P.2d 614 (Colo.App.1984), cert. denied, 474 U.S. 904, 106 S.Ct. 272, 88 L.Ed.2d 233 (1985); cf. Nehemiah v. Athletics Congress of U.S.A., 765 F.2d 42 (3d Cir.1985) (same rule with regard to service on agent of unincorporated association).

constitute "doing business".[629] A number of courts, on this ground of requiring "solicitation plus," have refused to utilize a doing business statute to acquire jurisdiction over a manufacturer that has shipped a defective product into the forum even though the action arises from injury that the product has caused in the forum.[630] Courts have also refused to take jurisdiction in causes of action arising out of defective products if the only basis for applying a "doing business" statute is the defendant's sales of the product to independent dealers in the forum.[631]

Activities that courts have held do not meet the requirements of "doing business" jurisdictional statutes include breach of an agreement settling litigation in the forum, when the breach of the settlement agreement relates to a payment to be made outside the forum;[632] the conduct of inter-corporate affairs between parent and subsidiary corporations when the action for which jurisdiction was sought did not relate to these inter-corporate dealings;[633] sending letters into the forum demanding payment from debtors resident there;[634] and executing contracts outside the forum reinsuring risks in the forum.[635] On the other hand, decisions have held a franchiser subject to suit by the franchisee at the franchisee's place of business for breach of the franchise agreement[636] and have held that painting contractors "transacted" business in a state

629. See, e.g., Green v. Chicago, B. & Q. Ry., 205 U.S. 530, 27 S.Ct. 595, 51 L.Ed. 916 (1907); Lizotte v. Canadian Johns–Manville Co., 387 F.2d 607 (1st Cir.1967); Gelfand v. Tanner Motor Tours, Ltd., 385 F.2d 116 (2d Cir.1967), cert. denied, 390 U.S. 996, 88 S.Ct. 1198, 20 L.Ed.2d 95 (1968) (dictum); Metropolitan Staple Corp. v. Samuel Moore & Co., 278 F.Supp. 85 (S.D.N.Y.1967); cf. Congoleum Corp. v. DLW Aktiengesellschaft, 729 F.2d 1240 (9th Cir.1984) (no general jurisdiction based on sales solicitation); Hughes v. A.H. Robins Co., 490 A.2d 1140 (D.C.App.1985) (same when solicitation not continuous and substantial). But cf. Hutter Northern Trust v. Door County Chamber of Commerce, 403 F.2d 481 (7th Cir.1968) (solicitation sufficient under "transaction of any business" statute when defendant is chamber of commerce having as chief activity the soliciting of trade for its home-town businesses); Oliff v. Kiamesha Concord, Inc., 106 N.J.Super. 121, 254 A.2d 330 (Law Div.1969) (solicitation sufficient under New Jersey long-arm rule designed to stretch to constitutional limits); Laufer v. Ostrow, 55 N.Y.2d 305, 449 N.Y.S.2d 456, 434 N.E.2d 692 (1982) (general jurisdiction over corporation upheld when soliciting and servicing orders constitute its main business).

630. See, e.g., Dykes v. Reliable Furniture & Carpet, 3 Utah 2d 34, 277 P.2d 969 (1954).

631. See Dale Electronics, Inc. v. Copymation, Inc., 178 Neb. 239, 132 N.W.2d 788 (1965) (commercial loss).

632. Dragor Shipping Corp. v. Union Tank Car Co., 361 F.2d 43 (9th Cir.), cert. denied, 385 U.S. 831, 87 S.Ct. 68, 17 L.Ed.2d 66 (1966).

633. Blount v. Peerless Chemicals (P.R.) Inc., 316 F.2d 695 (2d Cir.), cert. denied, 375 U.S. 831, 84 S.Ct. 76, 11 L.Ed.2d 62 (1963).

634. Bowlero, Inc. v. Allen, 205 So.2d 196 (La.App.1967).

635. Perlman v. Great States Life Ins. Co., 164 Colo. 493, 436 P.2d 124 (1968).

636. Hawaii Credit Card Corp. v. Continental Credit Card Corp., 290 F.Supp. 848 (D.Hawaii 1968); cf. Burger King Corp. v. Rudzewicz, 471 U.S. 462, 105 S.Ct. 2174, 85 L.Ed.2d 528 (1985) (franchiser has jurisdiction over franchisee in franchiser's state); Doyn Aircraft, Inc. v. Wylie, 443 F.2d 579 (10th Cir.1971) (manufacturer can obtain jurisdiction over distributor when distributor visited manufacturer to negotiate agreement); Pizza Inn, Inc. v. Lumar, 513 S.W.2d 251 (Tex.Civ.App.1974) N.R.E. (franchiser has jurisdiction over franchisee in franchiser's state). But cf. Hydraulics Unlimited Mfg. Co. v. B/J Mfg. Co., 449 F.2d 775 (10th Cir.1971) (licensee cannot obtain jurisdiction over licensor to rescind agreement and recover damages).

even though the painting was performed on a federal enclave within the state.[637]

Doing business as a specifically-affiliating basis for jurisdiction and the attendant problems of determining just what activities in the forum meet its requirements of substantiality and continuity have lost much of their importance with the advent of "single act" statutes focusing on isolated transactions in the forum or consequences caused in the forum. These new statutes, discussed in section 4.15, are designed to reach or come very close to the due process limits of judicial jurisdiction and render moot many of the questions raised by construction of the more restrictive "doing business" statutes.

Of much more current interest is the utilization of "doing business" as a generally-affiliating basis for jurisdiction. In the words of the Restatement:

> A state has power to exercise judicial jurisdiction over a foreign corporation which does business in the state with respect to causes of action that do not arise from the business done in the state if this business is so continuous and substantial as to make it reasonable for the state to exercise such jurisdiction.[638]

In order for business activities to constitute a generally-affiliating basis for jurisdiction, they must be more continuous and substantial than activities that would justify jurisdiction as to causes of action directly related to activities in the forum.[639] In this regard, doing business may be compared with domicile as a generally-affiliating nexus. The question is whether the defendant is so extensively engaged in business activities within the forum that it is fair to require it to defend there an action not related to forum activities. This is especially likely to be so if the defendant's main office is in the forum,[640] but may occur in other circumstances.

The difficulties of obtaining witnesses and other evidence to defend an action not related to forum activities may, in a particular case, raise valid forum non conveniens objections to permitting suit in the forum.

---

637. Swanson Painting Co. v. Painters Local Union No. 260, 391 F.2d 523 (9th Cir.1968).

638. Restatement, Second, § 47(2). See also International Shoe Co. v. Washington, 326 U.S. 310, 318, 66 S.Ct. 154, 159, 90 L.Ed. 95, 103 (1945) (dictum).

It is not always easy to distinguish between actions that arise out of business within the state and those that do not. See, e.g., Cornelison v. Chaney, 16 Cal.3d 143, 127 Cal.Rptr. 352, 545 P.2d 264 (1976) (jurisdiction over interstate trucker who injured forum resident out of state while trucker was en route to the forum).

639. See Ratliff v. Cooper Labs, Inc., 444 F.2d 745 (4th Cir.), cert. denied, 404 U.S. 948, 92 S.Ct. 271, 30 L.Ed.2d 265 (1971); W.H. Elliott & Sons Co. v. Nuodex Products Co., 243 F.2d 116, 122 (1st Cir.), cert. denied, 355 U.S. 823, 78 S.Ct. 30, 2 L.Ed.2d 38 (1957); Delagi v. Volkswagenwerk AG of Wolfsburg, 29 N.Y.2d 426, 328 N.Y.S.2d 653, 278 N.E.2d 895 (1972); Wainscott v. St. Louis–San Francisco Ry., 47 Ohio St.2d 133, 351 N.E.2d 466, 1 O.O.3d 78 (1976) (solicitation of business in forum not sufficient to subject defendant to suit for personal injuries occurring outside state); Bork v. Mills, 458 Pa. 228, 329 A.2d 247 (1974).

640. Restatement, Second, § 47, comment e.

Sometimes inconvenience to a defendant, despite very extensive business activities in the forum, may be so extreme as to create a due process bar to utilizing doing business as a generally-affiliating basis for jurisdiction.[641] *Asahi Metal Industry Co. v. Superior Court*[642] held that the "burden on the defendant"[643] of defending in the forum may preclude jurisdiction even when the action arises out of or is related to the defendant's forum activities. Nevertheless, doing business, depending upon the facts of a particular case, upon the extent of the defendant's business activities in the forum, upon the inconvenience to the defendant in requiring it to defend there, and upon the forum's legitimate interest in permitting the plaintiff to proceed, may be a valid basis for jurisdiction as to causes of action not related to forum activities.

Perkins v. Benguet Consolidated Mining Company[644] is the case most often cited for the proposition that doing business may be a generally-affiliating basis for jurisdiction. The defendant company was incorporated in the Philippine Islands where it had conducted mining operations. During the Japanese occupation of the islands, the company's operations there were halted. The president of the company returned to his home in Ohio and there supervised the company's limited wartime activities. The plaintiff, who was not an Ohio resident, brought suit against the company in Ohio. She sought unpaid dividends that she claimed were due her as a stockholder and damages for failure to issue share certificates to her. Service was made on the defendant's president while he was in Ohio supervising the defendant's business. The United States Supreme Court answered in the affirmative the question "whether, as a matter of federal due process, the business done in Ohio by the respondent mining company was sufficiently substantial and of such a nature as to *permit* Ohio to entertain a cause of action against a foreign corporation, where the cause of action arose from activities entirely distinct from its activities in Ohio."[645]

The facts in *Perkins* were highly unusual. When sued, the defendant had its main office in the forum. Furthermore, if not amenable to suit in Ohio, it is unlikely that the defendant would be subject to suit anyplace while the occupation of the Philippines continued. Thus *Perkins* is not strong support for the proposition that doing business may be a generally-affiliating basis for judicial jurisdiction.[646] *Helicopteros Nacionales de Colombia v. Hall*,[647] throws further doubt upon the likelihood that the

---

641. See Lau v. Chicago & N.W. Ry., 14 Wis.2d 329, 111 N.W.2d 158 (1961) (discusses and rejects due process argument based on inconvenience to defendant).

642. 480 U.S. 102, 107 S.Ct. 1026, 94 L.Ed.2d 92 (1987).

643. Id. at 114, 107 S.Ct. at 1033.

644. 342 U.S. 437, 72 S.Ct. 413, 96 L.Ed. 485 (1952).

645. Id. at 447, 72 S.Ct. at 416, 96 L.Ed. at 493 (emphasis in original). On remand, the Ohio Supreme Court reversed the quashing of service. 158 Ohio St. 145, 107 N.E.2d 203 (1952).

646. See von Mehren & Trautman, 79 Harv. L. Rev. at 1144; Developments, 73 Harv. L. Rev. at 932.

647. 466 U.S. 408, 104 S.Ct. 1868, 80 L.Ed.2d 404 (1984).

defendant's business contacts with the forum will be sufficiently continuous and substantial to support general jurisdiction.[648]

Before reaching the question of whether the forum may, consistently with due process in a particular case, utilize doing business as a generally-affiliating nexus, it is necessary to focus on the forum's jurisdictional statute. Some doing business long-arm statutes are so drafted that doing business may be used as a basis for jurisdiction only as to causes of action arising out of forum business.[649] If the forum has such a limited statute, that is likely to be the end of any attempt to use the defendant's forum business activities as a basis for jurisdiction in actions unrelated to forum business.[650] Many long-arm statutes, however, do permit the use of doing business as a generally-affiliating basis for jurisdiction[651] and a number of decisions have permitted suits utilizing doing business as a basis for jurisdiction in actions unrelated to the defendant's business activities in the forum.[652] On the other hand, courts have generally refused to exercise jurisdiction over defendants who are not conducting a major portion of their business activities in the forum when the cause of action arises from personal injuries received outside the forum.[653]

---

648. See § 4.8, text accompanying notes 256–268. See also Congoleum Corp. v. DLW Aktiengesellschaft, 729 F.2d 1240 (9th Cir.1984) (no general jurisdiction based on sales solicitation); Land–O–Nod Co. v. Bassett Furniture Ind., Inc., 708 F.2d 1338, 1342–43 (8th Cir.1983) (recent Supreme Court cases "make clear that some nexus between the forum and the subject matter of the litigation is required"). But see Behagen v. Amateur Basketball Assoc. of the U.S.A., 744 F.2d 731 (10th Cir.1984), cert. denied, 471 U.S. 1010, 105 S.Ct. 1879, 85 L.Ed.2d 171 (1985) (whether there is general jurisdiction over amateur athletic association depends on the facts).

649. See Unif. Int. & Int'l P. Act § 1.03(a)(1) and (b); cf. Unif. Int. & Int'l P. Act § 1.02 (providing general jurisdiction if the defendant is incorporated in or has its principal place of business in the state); Precision Polymers, Inc. v. Nelson, 512 P.2d 811 (Okl.1973).

650. See Etheridge v. Grove Mfg. Co., 415 F.2d 1338 (6th Cir.1969) (applying a now superseded Kentucky statute). But see Lindley v. St. Louis–San Francisco Ry., 276 F.Supp. 83 (N.D.Ill.1967), rev'd on other grounds, 407 F.2d 639 (7th Cir.1968) (exercising general jurisdiction over company doing business in Illinois despite limitation of Illinois statute).

651. See, e.g., N.Y.—McKinney's Civil Practice Law & Rules § 301 ("A court may exercise such jurisdiction over persons, property, or status as might have been exercised heretofore"), which has been so construed. Frummer v. Hilton Hotels International, Inc., 19 N.Y.2d 533, 281 N.Y.S.2d 41, 227 N.E.2d 851, cert. denied, 389 U.S. 923, 88 S.Ct. 241, 19 L.Ed.2d 266 (1967).

652. See Hoffman v. Air India, 393 F.2d 507 (5th Cir.1968), cert. denied, 393 U.S. 924, 89 S.Ct. 255, 21 L.Ed.2d 260 (1968); Dunn v. Beech Aircraft Corp., 276 F.Supp. 91 (E.D.Pa.1967) (defendant exercised control over local distributor-dealer); Owen v. Illinois Baking Corp., 235 F.Supp. 257 (W.D.Mich.1964); Bryant v. Finnish National Airline, 15 N.Y.2d 426, 260 N.Y.S.2d 625, 208 N.E.2d 439 (1965) (defendant maintained office in forum to receive reservations for European travel and to advertise; plaintiff, a forum resident, permitted to sue for injuries received in France).

653. See Glater v. Eli Lilly & Co., 744 F.2d 213 (1st Cir.1984); Ratliff v. Cooper Labs, Inc., 444 F.2d 745 (4th Cir.), cert. denied, 404 U.S. 948, 92 S.Ct. 271, 30 L.Ed.2d 265 (1971); Fandel v. Arabian American Oil Co., 345 F.2d 87 (D.C.Cir.1965) (plaintiffs not forum residents, business in forum limited to lobbying activities); Seymour v. Parke, Davis & Co., 423 F.2d 584 (1st Cir.1970) (decedent not forum resident, forum business consisted of marketing products); Richter v. Impulsora De Revolcadero, S.A., 278 F.Supp. 169 (S.D.N.Y.1967) (defendant's forum activities limited to advertising); Fisher Governor Co. v. Superior Court, 53 Cal.2d 222, 1 Cal.Rptr. 1, 347 P.2d 1 (1959) (defendant's products sold in forum through independent manufacturers' agents, persons injured not forum resi-

The insistence of the representatives of the United States in retaining doing business as a generally-affiliating basis for jurisdiction was one a reasons that aborted an attempt by the Hague Conference on Private International Law to draft a multinational judgment-recognition treaty.[654] The only basis for general jurisdiction in the European Union is domicile,[655] which in for a "company or other legal person or association" means the place of its "statutory seat, or central administration, or principal place of business."[656]

§ 4.15   Causing Consequences in the Forum

A frequently used specifically-affiliating basis for judicial jurisdiction is an act done in or outside the forum that causes consequences in the forum. The forum has a constitutional basis for jurisdiction over persons who perform acts causing consequences in the forum as to causes of action arising out of those consequences when jurisdiction is reasonable in the light of the act and its consequences, the forum's interest in providing a remedy to the plaintiff, the interest of plaintiff in seeking a remedy there, and the inconvenience to the defendant if required to defend locally.[657] To give content to this vague standard, this section and sections 4.16 through 4.18 examine various circumstances in which a court has upheld or rejected jurisdiction under this "single act" basis.

As the term "single act" implies, this basis for jurisdiction differs from "doing business" in that it is not necessary that the defendant's contacts with the forum be continuous or last for any substantial period of time. A single consequence in the forum giving rise to a cause of action and resulting from an act of the defendant may be sufficient to confer jurisdiction. If an isolated act of the defendant in the forum is used as the basis for jurisdiction, it is necessary that the act be directly related to the cause of action on which suit is brought. *Peters v. Robin*

---

dents.) But see Lee v. Walworth Valve Co., 482 F.2d 297 (4th Cir.1973) (death of forum resident on high seas); Labbe v. Nissen Corp., 404 A.2d 564 (Me.1979) (trampoline accident in England).

654. See Baumgartner, *Book Review*, 55 Am J. Comp. L. 793, 801 n. 41 (2007).

655. Brussels Regulation, supra § 4.1 note 6, art. 2(1).

656. Id. art. 60(1).

657. See, Asahi Metal Industry Co. v. Superior Court, 480 U.S. 102, 107 S.Ct. 1026, 94 L.Ed.2d 92 (1987); Restatement, Second, §§ 36, 37; Reese & Galston, *Doing an Act or Causing Consequences as Bases of Judicial Jurisdiction*, 44 Iowa L. Rev. 249, 260 (1959).

Some courts have made up a similar check list of factors to use in long-arm cases. A typical three-item list includes (1) the defendant purposefully exercised the privilege of acting in the forum or causing consequences there, (2) the cause of action arises from the consequences in the forum of the defendant's activities, and (3) the activities or consequences are sufficiently related to the forum to make exercise of jurisdiction reasonable. See, e.g., Wilkerson v. Fortuna Corp., 554 F.2d 745 (5th Cir.1977), cert. denied, 434 U.S. 939, 98 S.Ct. 430, 54 L.Ed.2d 299 (1977); State ex rel. Academy Press, Ltd. v. Beckett, 282 Or. 701, 581 P.2d 496 (1978). A typical five-item list includes (1) the quantity of the contacts in the forum, (2) the nature and quality of the contacts, (3) the source and connection of the cause of action with those contacts, (4) the forum's interest in providing a forum, and (5) the convenience of the parties. See, e.g., American Hoechst Corp. v. Bandy Labs, Inc., 332 F.Supp. 241 (W.D.Mo.1970); Ellwein v. Sun–Rise, Inc., 295 Minn. 109, 203 N.W.2d 403 (1972).

Airlines,[658] for example, held it unconstitutional for New York to take jurisdiction of a wrongful death action resulting from an airplane crash in California when the sole basis for that jurisdiction was the fact that the defendant's airplane had departed from a New York airport.

States have enacted a variety of long-arm statutes to permit use of this "single-act" basis for jurisdiction. Tort and contract single-act bases are analyzed in sections 4.16 through 4.18.

§ 4.16 Causing Consequences in the Forum by Tortious Conduct

All of the detailed single-act statutes select the commission of a tort in the forum as a basis for jurisdiction over the tortfeasor. These statutes are more general applications of the older nonresident motorist statutes that focused on one kind of tortious injury in the forum—that caused by a motor vehicle. The nonresident motorist statutes, with their long history[659] in the courts, provided many lessons for the statutory draftsman, not all of which were learned. For example, the motorist cases revealed the undesirability of failing to provide jurisdiction over the resident who becomes a nonresident before suit is brought. This failure usually had to be corrected by redrafting the statute.[660] Yet some states have made this error in their general tort long-arm statutes.[661] Litigation under the motorist statutes also revealed the desirability of clearly providing that a tortfeasor could use the tort long-arm statute to get indemnity or contribution from another tortfeasor,[662] as was the need

---

658.   281 A.D. 903, 120 N.Y.S.2d 1 (1953). See also, Seymour v. Parke, Davis & Co., 423 F.2d 584 (1st Cir.1970) (defendant's sale of defective drug in the forum is not a basis for jurisdiction in wrongful death action when the decedent had purchased and ingested the drug in another state where the decedent resided); Ohio Cas. Ins. Co. v. First Nat'l Bank, 425 P.2d 934 (Okl.1967) (recovery of wrongful death judgment by nonresident widow of airplane owner from those who negligently caused the airplane to crash is not a sufficient basis on which airplane insurer can implead her in suit against insurer by airplane mortgagee).

659.   Nonresident motorist statutes were held consistent with due process in Hess v. Pawloski, 274 U.S. 352, 47 S.Ct. 632, 71 L.Ed. 1091 (1927).

660.   See, e.g., Solis v. Bailey, 139 F.Supp. 842 (S.D.Tex.1956) holding that the Texas statute referring to "a non-resident" motorist could not be used to acquire jurisdiction over a driver who was a resident of Texas at the time of the accident and who subsequently moved to another state, citing numerous cases in other states reaching the same result under similar nonresident motorist statutes. The Texas statute was amended in 1959 to include reference to "a person who was a resident of this State at the time of the accrual of a cause of action but who subsequently removes therefrom." Vernon's Ann.Tex.Civ.Stat., art. 2039a, § 1, now, in slightly modified form, Tex. Civ. Prac. & Rem. C. § 17.062(b).

661.   See Fagan v. Fletcher, 257 Iowa 449, 133 N.W.2d 116 (1965) (construing the Iowa statute before an amendment corrected the problem).

662.   That a suit for indemnity or contribution is permissible under a nonresident motorist statute, see, e.g., Iowa Hardware Mut. Ins. Co. v. Hoepner, 252 Iowa 660, 108 N.W.2d 55 (1961); cf. Marion County Hospital Dist. v. Namer, 225 So.2d 442 (Fla.Dist.Ct. App.1969) (statute includes action by hospital for services to nonresident motorist). For cases permitting actions for indemnity under "tort" long-arm statutes see, e.g., Kroger Co. v. Dornbos, 408 F.2d 813 (6th Cir.1969); Beetler v. Zotos, 388 F.2d 243 (7th Cir.1967); Ehlers v. U.S. Heating & Cooling Mfg. Corp., 267 Minn. 56, 124 N.W.2d 824 (1963); Deutsch v. West Coast Mach. Co., 80 Wn.2d 707, 497 P.2d 1311, cert. denied, 409 U.S. 1009, 93 S.Ct. 443, 34 L.Ed.2d 302 (1972). But cf. the following cases denying defendant

to cover by statute, and thus prevent litigation of, various other subsidiary questions, such as whether the forum's statute that tolled the local statute of limitations when the defendant was "absent" from the state operated when the "absent" defendant was nevertheless subject to in personam jurisdiction in the forum under a long-arm statute.[663]

jurisdiction over third party: Independent Sch. Dist. v. Marshall & Stevens Co., 337 F.Supp. 1278 (D.Minn.1971) (erroneous data supplied to defendant outside forum and defendant made negligent appraisal in forum); Mid–Continent Freight Lines v. Highway Trailer Indus., Inc., 291 Minn. 251, 190 N.W.2d 670 (1971) (third party supplied component part, but defendant is nonresident and injury occurred outside the forum); Hasley v. Black, Sivalls & Bryson, Inc., 70 Wis.2d 562, 235 N.W.2d 446 (1975) (third party supplied component part).

For a related problem, see Comment, *Constitutional Limitations on Vouching,* 118 U.Pa. L. Rev. 237, 268 (1969) discussing "vouching in" of third-party defendants under U.C.C. § 2–607(5)(a) and concluding that this procedure is "subject to the same jurisdictional due process restraints" as impleader. But see Travelers Indem. Co. v. Evans Pipe Co., 432 F.2d 211 (6th Cir.1970) (vouched-in seller bound by prior litigation in court that did not have jurisdiction over seller).

663. For cases adopting the majority view that the nonresident motorist or aircraft operator statute prevented tolling the applicable statute of limitations see, e.g., Rivera v. Taylor, 61 Ill.2d 406, 336 N.E.2d 481 (1975); Kokenge v. Holthaus, 243 Iowa 571, 52 N.W.2d 711 (1952); Hammel v. Bettison, 362 Mich. 396, 107 N.W.2d 887 (1961); Broadfoot v. Everett, 270 N.C. 429, 154 S.E.2d 522 (1967) (nonresident aircraft operator); Ashley v. Hawkins, 293 S.W.3d 175 (Tex. 2009); Tarter v. Insco, 550 P.2d 905 (Wyo.1976) (collecting authority). For a codification of this view, see N.Y.—McKinney's Civ.Prac.L. & Rules § 207(3). Cf. Gray v. Johnson, 165 W.Va. 156, 267 S.E.2d 615 (1980) (limitations tolled during time plaintiff does not have defendant's address for non-resident service). For the opposing view see, e.g., Dew v. Appleberry, 23 Cal.3d 630, 153 Cal.Rptr. 219, 591 P.2d 509 (1979); Walsik v. Brandel, 298 N.W.2d 375 (N.D.1980); Cutino v. Ramsey, 285 S.C. 74, 328 S.E.2d 72 (1985). See also Partis v. Miller Equipment Co., 439 F.2d 262 (6th Cir.1971) (under Ohio law statute is tolled against individuals but not against corporations).

For a danger of treating the nonresident as present when theoretically subject to long-arm service, see Yarusso v. Arbotowicz, 41 N.Y.2d 516, 393 N.Y.S.2d 968, 362 N.E.2d 600 (1977) (statute runs although service by mail not effective because sent to former address). Methods of avoiding this difficulty include making a diligent but unsuccessful attempt to notify defendant sufficient to confer jurisdiction, or, as in Marterie v. Dorado Beach Hotel, 330 F.Supp. 860 (D.P.R.1971), have limitations run only if long-arm service would have been effective. See also Russell v. Balcom Chemicals, Inc., 328 N.W.2d 476, 479 (S.D.1983) (whether limitations tolled depends on whether defendant "could have been located for service of process by reasonably diligent efforts").

Bendix Autolite Corp. v. Midwesco Enterprises, 486 U.S. 888, 108 S.Ct. 2218, 100 L.Ed.2d 896 (1988), invalidated as an unreasonable burden on interstate commerce the Ohio rule tolling the statute of limitations against a foreign corporation, even though the corporation was subject to long-arm jurisdiction. Under the Ohio law, the only way the foreign corporation could escape tolling was to register to do business in Ohio although the corporation was not doing sufficient intrastate business in Ohio to permit Ohio constitutionally to compel the corporation to so register. Cf. Cutler v. Raymark Industries, Inc., 707 F.Supp. 168 (D.N.J.1989) (can toll limitations against nonresident who does not appoint resident agent for service of process when forum permits nonresident to limit designation to cases in which forum would otherwise have jurisdiction). Contra, Juzwin v. Asbestos Corp., Ltd., 900 F.2d 686 (3d Cir.), cert. denied, 498 U.S. 896, 111 S.Ct. 246, 112 L.Ed.2d 204 (1990) (New Jersey statute nevertheless violates the commerce clause because not as narrowly drawn as it might be—for example, tolling limitations only after a diligent effort to effect long-arm service was unsuccessful).

For other issues arising under long-arm legislation that should be, but often are not, covered in the statute, see, e.g., Siemens & Halske v. Gres, 37 A.D.2d 768, 324 N.Y.S.2d 639 (1971) (no provision for subpoena duces tecum); LesCarbeau v. Rodrigues, 109 R.I. 407, 286 A.2d 246 (1972) (no provision for appointing administrator locally if defendant dies and no foreign administrator is appointed). But see Eubank Heights Apts., Ltd. v. Lebow, 615 F.2d 571 (1st Cir.1980) (whether can obtain jurisdiction over deceased debtor's executor

Before legislatures could use the nonresident motorist statutes as a base upon which to erect more general single-act statutes covering all torts, it was necessary to reject the idea, articulated in such landmark nonresident motorist cases as *Hess v. Pawloski*,[664] that the motorist statutes were valid because the activity giving rise to the injury was inherently dangerous or that the activity was of a kind subject to exclusion or regulation under the forum's police power. This rejection is now complete. As stated by Judge Traynor in *Owens v. Superior Court*, "[a]ssumption of jurisdiction is constitutionally justified, however, not because the problem [nonresident motorists causing injury in the forum] is acute and arises often, but because it is reasonable and fair to require a defendant whose voluntary acts have given rise to a cause of action in a state to litigate his responsibility for that conduct at the place where it occurred."[665]

Suppose that the plaintiff asserts jurisdiction over a nonresident defendant under a long-arm statute that includes "the commission of a tortious act" within the forum. The plaintiff alleges that the defendant negligently caused injury in the forum. At trial, the defendant prevails on the ground that the acts in the forum were not negligent. If this is so, then the defendant never committed "a tortious act" in the forum. Is the judgment for the defendant, then, on the merits barring any future suit by the plaintiff on the same cause of action, or is the finding merely jurisdictional, the forum court in effect finding that it did not have judicial jurisdiction?[666] There would seem to be only one sensible answer to this conundrum. The basis for the forum's jurisdiction is, despite the unfortunate wording of the long-arm statute, not the defendant's commission of a tort in the forum, but the defendant's acts in the forum, or, in the product liability cases, for example, the presence in the forum of a product that the defendant has dealt with in the stream of distribution. The forum can then proceed to determine whether the defendant's acts or omissions have caused harmful consequences in the forum and, if so, whether those acts or omissions were tortious. These latter determinations are not jurisdictional but decide the merits of the controversy over which the court has jurisdiction. This is the result reached by the Illinois court and by other courts and commentators that have confronted this

depends on whether under law of domicile at death an executor can represent the estate outside of the domicile).

664. 274 U.S. 352, 355, 47 S.Ct. 632, 633, 71 L.Ed. 1091, 1094 (1927). See also Mueller v. Steelcase, Inc., 172 F.Supp. 416, 418 (D.Minn.1959) holding that it would be unconstitutional to utilize Minnesota's tort long-arm statute to obtain jurisdiction over an out-of-state manufacturer of a defective chair that caused injury to the plaintiff, stating: "It is not suggested that the sale of an ordinary swivel chair to a merchant in this State creates some extraordinary hazard so as to demand the exercise of the State's police power in order to protect its citizens from negligence in their manufacture."

665. 52 Cal.2d 822, 831, 345 P.2d 921, 925 (1959). See also World–Wide Volkswagen Corp. v. Woodson, 444 U.S. 286, 296–97 n.11, 100 S.Ct. 559, 567 n.11, 62 L.Ed.2d 490, 501 n.11 (1980) (jurisdiction over nonresident motorists not based on fact that automobile is a "dangerous instrumentality"); Elkhart Engineering Corp. v. Dornier Werke, 343 F.2d 861, 868 (5th Cir.1965); Nelson v. Miller, 11 Ill.2d 378, 143 N.E.2d 673 (1957).

666. See Leflar, *Conflict of Laws*, 35 N.Y.U. L. Rev. 62, 68 (1960).

problem.[667] The difficulty could be alleviated by wording the long-arm statute to speak not of a "tort" committed in the forum or a "contract" made there or to be performed there, but to speak, instead, of whether the defendant has done an act that is alleged to give rise to the cause of action sued on.[668]

Not every effect manifested in the forum is a "consequence caused" there sufficient to subject the defendant to jurisdiction in suits arising out of the defendant's acts. Under traditional "minimum contacts" analysis, if the defendant acts outside the forum and causes physical

---

667. Nelson v. Miller, 11 Ill.2d 378, 393–94, 143 N.E.2d 673, 679 (1957) ("An act or omission within the State, in person or by an agent, is a sufficient basis for the exercise of jurisdiction to determine whether or not the act or omission gives rise to liability in tort"). See also Restatement, Second, § 36, comment *d* (in an action based on the operation of an automobile in the forum, the operation of the automobile in the forum is jurisdictional, but whether the operation was negligent or was the cause of the plaintiff's injury is not). Cf. Midwest Packaging Corp. v. Oerlikon Plastics, Ltd., 279 F.Supp. 816 (S.D.Iowa 1968) (whether a contract was valid is not a jurisdictional fact under a statute exercising jurisdiction over a defendant who "makes a contract" to be performed in the forum). But cf. Wyatt v. Kaplan, 686 F.2d 276 (5th Cir.1982) (plaintiff must establish a prima facie cause of action before meeting jurisdictional burden). But see Tappen v. Ager, 599 F.2d 376 (10th Cir.1979) (motion to dismiss, based on the theory that no "tort" was committed within the meaning of the long-arm statute, tests the legal sufficiency of each count of the complaint); Schwilling v. Horne, 105 Idaho 294, 669 P.2d 183 (1983) (jurisdiction over seller in Alaska depends on whether repossession was wrongful); Kibby v. Anthony Ind., Inc., 123 N.H. 272, 459 A.2d 292 (1983) (no jurisdiction over manufacturer when plaintiff alleges only that equipment was defectively installed, not that the equipment itself was defective).

An analogous problem arises if the long-arm statute provides jurisdiction over a nonresident who acts in the state through an "agent." Is it a jurisdictional issue whether the person who acted for the defendant is technically an "agent"? See ALP Federal Credit Union v. Ashborn, 477 P.2d 348 (Alaska 1970), denying full faith and credit to a Washington judgment if the repossessor who acted for the defendant in Washington was not an "agent", the term used in the Washington long-arm statute. But the issue in *Ashborn* should have been, not what Alaska would do if it had the Washington statute, but whether Washington would take the same view of the meaning of "agent" as the Alaska Supreme Court and, if so, whether a collateral attack would be permitted in Washington on this basis after a default judgment. There was sufficient nexus with Washington to entitle the Washington judgment to full faith and credit if Washington viewed its default judgment as binding. See also Marsh v. Kitchen, 480 F.2d 1270 (2d Cir.1973) (officers who arrested plaintiff on defendant's complaint were not "agents" and therefore no jurisdiction); Hinson v. Culberson–Stowers Chevrolet, Inc., 244 Ark. 853, 427 S.W.2d 539 (1968) (sheriff not "agent"). "Agent" is a bad word to use in a long-arm statute because of its restricted technical meaning. See Restatement (Second) of Agency § 1 (1958). The defendant should be subject to jurisdiction for the acts of any person in the forum if the defendant can be liable for those acts, whether or not the person who acts is technically an "agent." See Boit v. Emmco Ins. Co., 271 F.Supp. 366 (D.Mont.1967) (repossession).

668. See former Ariz.Rule of Civ.Proc. 4(e)(2) ("When the defendant ... has caused an event to occur in this state out of which the claim which is the subject of the complaint arose...."). This rule, however, appears to have made causation of the plaintiff's injury a jurisdictional fact. Whether it is necessary or desirable to declare causation jurisdictional is more debatable than whether the negligence of the defendant's act should be jurisdictional; negligence should not be jurisdictional. The Arizona Rule now expressly goes to the limits of due process. Id. 4.2(a).

On the question of whether plaintiff's allegations should be sufficient to support jurisdiction, see Continental Nut Co. v. Robert L. Berner Co., 345 F.2d 395 (7th Cir.1965) (plaintiff's unsupported allegation that defendant conspired to publish libel in the forum is, when denied by uncontroverted affidavits, insufficient to establish the jurisdictional requirement); Roskelley & Co. v. Lerco, Inc., 610 P.2d 1307 (Utah 1980) (general allegation of jurisdiction cannot withstand sworn denial).

injury to the plaintiff outside the forum, the forum does not have
jurisdiction over the defendant if the only nexus with the forum is that
the plaintiff is domiciled there and, therefore, the economic and social
effects of the injury are manifested in the forum.[669] In similar fashion, if
the defendant, acting outside the forum, tortiously injures the plaintiff's
business causing the plaintiff economic loss outside the forum, the forum
does not have jurisdiction just because the plaintiff is incorporated in or
has its main place of business in the forum.[670] When the defendant acts
tortiously outside the forum causing, not physical injury, but economic
harm to the plaintiff in the forum, the forum should have jurisdiction
when the defendant intended or should have foreseen that the primary
impact of those acts would be in the forum, or where there is some other
nexus between forum and defendant that makes the exercise of jurisdiction reasonable.[671] Courts have reached mixed results in cases seeking

669.   See Crimi v. Elliot Bros. Trucking Co., 279 F.Supp. 555 (S.D.N.Y.1968) (New York
does not have jurisdiction over defendant in action for wrongful death of New Yorker
whom defendant fatally injured in Connecticut). But cf. Blessing v. Prosser, 141 N.J.Super.
548, 359 A.2d 493 (App.Div.1976) (New York motel at which plaintiff injured listed in tour
book published in forum and this sufficient to confer jurisdiction); Sedler, *The Truly
Disinterested Forum in the Conflict of Laws: Ratliff v. Cooper Laboratories,* 25 S.C. L. Rev.
185, 190 (1973) (proper to provide resident with forum even though not sufficient contacts
to apply own law).

670.   Friedr. Zoellner (New York) Corp. v. Tex Metals Co., 396 F.2d 300 (2d Cir.1968)
(defendant converted property in Louisiana belonging to New York corporation); Spectacu-
lar Promotions, Inc. v. Radio Station WING, 272 F.Supp. 734 (E.D.N.Y.1967) (defendant's
unfair competition in Ohio caused New York corporation to lose revenue in Ohio).

671.   For cases upholding jurisdiction, see, e.g., Waffenschmidt v. MacKay, 763 F.2d 711
(5th Cir.1985), cert. denied 474 U.S. 1056, 106 S.Ct. 794, 88 L.Ed.2d 771 (1986); (non-
parties knowingly aided and abetted party to violate injunction); Vishay Intertechnology,
Inc. v. Delta Int'l Corp., 696 F.2d 1062 (4th Cir.1982) (defendant sued plaintiff outside the
forum but served plaintiff in the forum); Thill Securities Corp. v. New York Stock
Exchange, 283 F.Supp. 239 (E.D.Wis.1968) (antitrust law violations outside the forum by
defendant having slight business contacts with the forum cause economic injury in the
forum); Hull v. Gamblin, 241 A.2d 739 (D.C.App.1968) (defendant conducted improper
patent search in the District of Columbia causing harm in Texas forum where defendant
had advertised her services); Jack O'Donnell Chevrolet, Inc. v. Shankles, 276 F.Supp. 998
(N.D.Ill.1967) (out-of-state bank conspired in check-kiting scheme with person who gave
check to plaintiff in the forum); Shrout v. Thorsen, 470 So.2d 1222 (Ala.1985) (defrauder
made telephone calls and sent letter to forum); Cagle v. Lawson, 445 So.2d 564 (Ala.1984)
(lawyer represented forum client after entering into contract in forum); Meyers v. Hamilton Corp., 143 Ariz. 249, 693 P.2d 904 (1984) (cruise ship advertised in forum and sold
tickets there); Waterval v. District Court, 620 P.2d 5 (Colo.1980), cert. denied, 452 U.S.
960, 101 S.Ct. 3108, 69 L.Ed.2d 971 (1981) (investment adviser who had mail and
telephone contacts with plaintiff in the forum); Cowan v. First. Ins. Co. of Hawaii, Ltd., 61
Hawaii 644, 608 P.2d 394 (1980) (solicited plaintiff to send ship out of state where it
damaged by defendant); Great Atlantic & Pac. Tea Co. v. Hill–Dodge Banking Co., 255
Iowa 272, 122 N.W.2d 337 (1963) (out-of-state bank conspired in check-kiting scheme with
person who gave check to plaintiff in the forum); Mohler v. Dorado Wings, Inc., 675 S.W.2d
404 (Ky.App.1984) (airline sold tickets in forum); Marullo v. Zuppardo, 454 So.2d 268
(La.App. 4th Cir.), writ denied, 458 So.2d 477 (La. 1984) (hotel solicited plaintiffs in the
forum through an independent contractor and flew them in its airplane); Hunt v. Nevada
State Bank, 285 Minn. 77, 172 N.W.2d 292 (1969), cert. denied, 397 U.S. 1010, 90 S.Ct.
1239, 25 L.Ed.2d 423 (1970) (forum has jurisdiction over nonresident participants in
tortious conspiracy that produced harm in the forum); Slivka v. Hackley, 418 S.W.2d 89
(Mo.1967) (defendant bred stallion in Missouri contrary to agreement that he made when
purchasing the horse from the plaintiff in Illinois, causing economic harm in the Illinois
forum); Sybron Corp. v. Wetzel, 46 N.Y.2d 197, 413 N.Y.S.2d 127, 385 N.E.2d 1055 (1978)
(anticipatory injunctive relief against use of trade secrets after hiring plaintiff's former

jurisdiction over nonresident physicians and hospitals[672] and over attor-

employee); Riggs v. Coplon, 636 S.W.2d 750 (Tex.App.—El Paso, 1982, writ ref'd n.r.e.) (telephone plaintiff in forum); Werner v. Werner, 84 Wash.2d 360, 526 P.2d 370 (1974) (negligent notarization of deed to forum land).

But see, the following cases denying jurisdiction: Fielding v. Hubert Burda Media, Inc., 415 F.3d 419, 428 (5th Cir. 2005) (no jurisdiction in Texas over German publishers because "[t]he brunt of the harm of the alleged libel was not suffered in Texas and the publishers did not meaningfully direct their activities toward Texas"); Promotions, Ltd. v. Brooklyn Bridge Centennial Commission, 763 F.2d 173 (4th Cir.1985) (alleged taking of idea set out in letter that plaintiff mailed to defendant from the forum); Paccar International, Inc. v. Commercial Bank of Kuwait, 757 F.2d 1058 (9th Cir.1985) (defendant allegedly making fraudulent claim against forum bank under letter of credit issued to cover obligations of forum seller); Taylor v. Portland Paramount Corp., 383 F.2d 634 (9th Cir.1967) (defendant is actress whose alleged misbehavior outside the forum caused economic harm to film exhibitor in the forum); Green v. Advance Ross Electronics Corp., 86 Ill.2d 431, 56 Ill.Dec. 657, 427 N.E.2d 1203 (1981) (money misappropriated outside the forum had economic effect in the forum on forum corporation); Khalaf v. Bankers & Shippers Ins. Co., 404 Mich. 134, 273 N.W.2d 811 (1978) (defendant is agent who procured wrong insurance for company that committed tort in forum); Fantis Foods, Inc. v. Standard Importing Co., Inc., 49 N.Y.2d 317, 425 N.Y.S.2d 783, 402 N.E.2d 122 (1980) (conversion of goods outside the forum causes economic harm to forum corporation); Roger Williams General Hosp. v. Fall River Trust Co., 423 A.2d 1384 (R.I. 1981) (checks payable to forum corporation converted outside the forum).

As to the degree of foreseeability required, see Leasco Data Processing Equip. Corp. v. Maxwell, 468 F.2d 1326 (2d Cir.1972) (in finding no jurisdiction over English accounting firm whose allegedly inaccurate reports misled plaintiff into buying stock in English firm, Judge Friendly states that "attaining the rather low floor of foreseeability necessary to support a finding of tort liability is not enough ... [defendant] must ... have good reason to know that his conduct will have effects in the [forum]").

Where the defendant's conduct is not tortious, even more nexus with the forum is required. See the following cases denying jurisdiction: Leney v. Plum Grove Bank, 670 F.2d 878 (10th Cir.1982) (over bank that issued letter of credit covering payment for property transferred in the forum); Panos Investment Co. v. District Court, 662 P.2d 180 (Colo. 1983) (over nonresident guarantor of note signed and to be repaid in forum—split of authority discussed); Jahner v. Jacob, 252 N.W.2d 1 (N.D.1977) (over nonresident recipient of transfer in fraud of creditors when recipient not part of scheme to defraud). But cf. Sanditen v. Sanditen, 496 P.2d 365 (Okl.1972) (jurisdiction over recipient of fraudulent transfers of community property when recipient was forum resident at the time of receipt).

672. For cases refusing to exercise jurisdiction see, e.g., Bovino v. Brumbaugh, 221 N.J.Super. 432, 534 A.2d 1032 (App.1987) (to avoid "chilling effect on the availability of professional services to nonresidents"); Valley Wide Health Services, Inc. v. Graham, 106 N.M. 71, 738 P.2d 1316 (1987) (treated outside forum and one telephone call by patient from forum for subsequent treatment advice); Bachman v. Medial Engineering Corp., 81 Or.App. 85, 724 P.2d 858 (1986) (no jurisdiction over hospital or doctors, but jurisdiction over medical supply company that supplied implant); Almeida v. Radovsky, 506 A.2d 1373 (R.I.1986) (patient commutes from forum); Wolf v. Richmond County Hosp. Auth., 745 F.2d 904 (4th Cir.1984) (none over hospital); Wright v. Yackley, 459 F.2d 287 (9th Cir.1972) (physician who had treated plaintiff when plaintiff resident elsewhere mails copies of old prescription to plaintiff without charge); Kilcrease v. Butler, 293 Ark. 454, 739 S.W.2d 139 (1987) (nonresident pathologist negligently analyzed forum patient's tissue sent by forum doctor); Cote v. Gordon, 40 Conn.Supp. 15, 478 A.2d 631 (1984) (none over hospital near border despite yellow page ads and forum patients); Veeninga v. Alt, 111 Ill.App.3d 775, 67 Ill.Dec. 544, 444 N.E.2d 780 (1st Dist.1982) (none by commuting patient over doctor); Muffo v. Forsyth, 37 Ill.App.3d 6, 345 N.E.2d 149 (1976) (prescription given to plaintiff in Missouri filled in Illinois); Woodward v. Keenan, 88 Mich.App. 791, 279 N.W.2d 317 (1979) (examined plaintiff in Indiana and sent report to forum doctor who relied on it); State ex rel. Sperandio v. Clymer, 581 S.W.2d 377 (Mo.1979) (nonresident doctor consulted by mail with forum physician) (changing previous result after United States Supreme Court remanded for further consideration in the light of Kulko v. Superior Court); State ex rel. Wichita Falls General Hospital v. Adolf, 728 S.W.2d 604 (Mo. App.), cert. denied, 484 U.S. 927, 108 S.Ct. 292, 98 L.Ed.2d 252 (1987) (hospital misclassified heart used in transplant operation in forum); Petrik v. Colby, 224 Mont. 531, 730 P.2d 1167 (1986)

neys.[673] In *Touchcom, Inc. v. Bereskin & Parr*,[674] a Canadian company brought a malpractice suit in Virginia against a Canadian law firm and a Canadian lawyer for malpractice in the filing of a patent application with the United States Patent Office in Virginia. The Federal Circuit held that although there were not sufficient minimum contacts with Virginia to permit jurisdiction in Virginia courts, because the claim arose under federal law, Federal Rule of Civil Procedure 4(k)(2) permitted jurisdiction when defendant did not name a state in which the defendant is subject to personal jurisdiction and the contacts with the U.S. are sufficient to satisfy due process. Thus by a wind about route the court reaches the result it should have reached by holding that the negligent filing of a patent application in Virginia permits specific jurisdiction in Virginia courts.

(patient experienced symptoms of malpractice injury after moving to the forum); Etra v. Matta, 61 N.Y.2d 455, 474 N.Y.S.2d 687, 463 N.E.2d 3 (1984) (none over nonresident doctor who prescribed drug and consulted with forum doctor in its administration); Hume v. Durwood Medical Clinic, Inc., 282 S.C. 236, 318 S.E.2d 119 (App.1984), cert. dism'd, 285 S.C. 377, 329 S.E.2d 443, cert. denied, 474 U.S. 848, 106 S.Ct. 141, 88 L.Ed.2d 117 (1985) (none over clinic or doctors who consulted with forum doctor); cf. Hogan v. Johnson, 39 Wn.App. 96, 692 P.2d 198 (1984) (only basis for jurisdiction would be patient's move to the forum).

But see the following cases upholding jurisdiction over nonresident doctors and hospitals: Kennedy v. Freeman, 919 F.2d 126 (10th Cir. 1990) (nonresident doctor analyzed tissue sample and mailed report to forum doctor); Cubbage v. Merchent, 744 F.2d 665 (9th Cir. 1984), cert. denied, 470 U.S. 1005, 105 S.Ct. 1359, 84 L.Ed.2d 380 (1985) (doctor and hospital solicited and served nearby forum patients); Frazer v. McGowan, 198 Conn. 243, 502 A.2d 905 (1986) (hospital has forum doctors with admitting privileges, is close to the forum, and advertises in yellow pages for forum communities); Rossa v. Sills, 493 So.2d 1137 (Fla. App. 4 Dist.1986) (cruise ship doctor for line that regularly operates out of forum ports); Administrators of Tulane Educational Fund v. Cooley, 462 So.2d 696 (Miss.1984) (hospital that treated forum resident part of university that recruits students, solicits alumni contributions, and plays intercollegiate athletics in the forum); Phelps v. Kingston, 130 N.H. 166, 536 A.2d 740 (1987) (nonresident dentist who holds a license in the forum, treats forum residents, and advertises in forum telephone directories); Kathrein v. Parkview Meadows, Inc., 102 N.M. 75, 691 P.2d 462 (1984) (treatment center that advertised in yellow pages and invited the plaintiff to visit her husband there); cf. Parker by and through Parker v. Gulf City Fisheries, Inc., 803 F.2d 828 (5th Cir.1986) (there is admiralty jurisdiction when a land-based doctor gives advice that causes injury at sea); S.R. v. Fairmont, 167 W.Va. 880, 280 S.E.2d 712 (1981) (discovery ordered on issue of whether jurisdiction over doctor).

See also Trail & Maney, *Jurisdiction, Venue, and Choice of Law in Medical Malpractice Litigation*, 7 J.Legal Medicine 403 (1986).

673. For cases upholding jurisdiction, see Lake v. Lake, 817 F.2d 1416 (9th Cir.1987) (attorney who secured modification of a custody decree originally issued in the forum); Alonso v. Line, 846 So.2d 745 (La. 2003) (nonresident attorney accepted representation of plaintiff to recover for injuries in forum and then failed to file complaint before prescriptive period had run); Masada Investment Corp. v. Allen, 697 S.W.2d 332 (Tenn.1985) (alleged mistake affecting forum real estate transaction). For cases denying jurisdiction, see Austad Co. v. Pennie & Edmonds, 823 F.2d 223 (8th Cir.1987) (represented forum client in another state); Wallace v. Herron, 778 F.2d 391 (7th Cir.1985), cert. denied, 475 U.S. 1122, 106 S.Ct. 1642, 90 L.Ed.2d 187 (1986) (no jurisdiction in suit for abuse of process although attorney took discovery and served the plaintiff in the forum); Union Nat'l Bank of Little Rock v. Thornton, 293 Ark. 385, 738 S.W.2d 103 (1987) (same although took deposition in the forum); Rosenblit v. Danaher, 206 Conn. 125, 537 A.2d 145 (1988) (based on construction of forum's long-arm statute); Washington v. Magazzu, 216 N.J.Super. 23, 522 A.2d 1013 (App. Div.1987).

674. 574 F.3d 1403 (Fed. Cir. 2009).

Courts have generally upheld jurisdiction over educational institutions in actions arising out of the institution's acts in the forum or the consequences it caused there.[675] On the other hand, courts have generally declined jurisdiction over nonresident officials whose alleged wrongful acts elsewhere have caused harm in the forum.[676]

The easiest case for jurisdiction under the theory that the defendant has committed a tort in the forum is when the defendant has acted tortiously in the forum and caused harm to the plaintiff in the forum.[677]

The next circumstance in which jurisdiction should be available on a single-act tort theory is that in which a manufacturer produces a defective product outside the forum, sends this product directly into the forum, either to the plaintiff or to a dealer, and the defective product then causes harm to the plaintiff.[678] There has been some difference of

---

675. For cases upholding jurisdiction over out-of-state educational institutions in suits for breach of the educational contract, see Gehling v. St. George's School of Medicine Ltd., 773 F.2d 539 (3d Cir.1985) (delivered student's body to the forum and misrepresented cause of his death—jurisdiction for infliction of mental suffering, but not wrongful death); Hahn v. Vermont Law School, 698 F.2d 48 (1st Cir.1983) (jurisdiction over school that recruited in the forum but not over a professor); Barile v. University of Virginia, 2 Ohio App.3d 233, 441 N.E.2d 608 (1981) (jurisdiction over college that recruited forum athlete in suit arising from medical treatment college provided); Siskind v. Villa Foundation for Education, Inc., 642 S.W.2d 434 (Tex.1982) (school advertised in the forum and plaintiff's son enrolled, but no jurisdiction over employees).

676. See Draper v. Coombs, 792 F.2d 915 (9th Cir.1986) (extradition from the forum); McLeod v. Harmon, 149 Ill.App.3d 378, 102 Ill.Dec. 831, 500 N.E.2d 724 (3d Dist.1986), appeal denied, 113 Ill.2d 576, 106 Ill.Dec. 49, 505 N.E.2d 355 (1987) (convicts escaped from defendants' custody); Drake v. Hammond Square, 525 So.2d 261 (La.App. 1st Cir.1988) (supervision of insurer issuing policy covering forum property); Grange Ins. Ass'n v. State, 110 Wn.2d 752, 757 P.2d 933 (1988), cert. denied, 490 U.S. 1004, 109 S.Ct. 1638, 104 L.Ed.2d 154 (1989) (certified infected cattle).

677. See, e.g., Elkhart Engineering Corp. v. Dornier Werke, 343 F.2d 861 (5th Cir. 1965); Godfrey v. Neumann, 373 So.2d 920 (Fla.1979) (negligent injury in swimming pool); Knight v. San Jacinto Club, Inc., 96 N.J.Super. 81, 232 A.2d 462 (1967); Smyth v. Twin State Improvement Corp., 116 Vt. 569, 80 A.2d 664 (1951); cf. Rosenblatt v. American Cyanamid Co., 86 S.Ct. 1, 15 L.Ed.2d 39 (Goldberg, J., in chambers), appeal dism'd, 382 U.S. 110, 86 S.Ct. 256, 15 L.Ed.2d 192 (1965) (defendant participated in the forum in a conspiracy to steal antibiotic material there from the plaintiff); Brown v. Flowers Ind., Inc., 688 F.2d 328 (5th Cir.1982), cert. denied, 460 U.S. 1023, 103 S.Ct. 1275, 75 L.Ed.2d 496 (1983) (defamatory telephone call to forum where plaintiff resides); Carida v. Holy Cross Hosp., Inc., 424 So.2d 849 (Fla.App. 4th Dist.1982) (series of defamatory calls to the forum where plaintiff resides). But see Mladinich v. Kohn, 250 Miss. 138, 164 So.2d 785 (1964) (forum did not have jurisdiction over a nonresident who made a single speech in the forum slandering forum residents). The New York long-arm provision for tortious acts in the state excludes defamation. N.Y. Civil Practice Law & Rules § 302(a)(2).

678. See, e.g., DeMelo v. Toche Marine, Inc., 711 F.2d 1260 (5th Cir.1983); Beetler v. Zotos, 388 F.2d 243 (7th Cir.1967); Deveny v. Rheem Mfg. Co., 319 F.2d 124 (2d Cir.1963); Vandermee v. District Court, 164 Colo. 117, 433 P.2d 335 (1967); Foye v. Consolidated Baling Mach. Co., 229 A.2d 196 (Me.1967); Atkins v. Jones & Laughlin Steel Corp., 258 Minn. 571, 104 N.W.2d 888 (1960); Farmer v. Ferris, 260 N.C. 619, 133 S.E.2d 492 (1963). But see Bisbee v. Safeway Stores, Inc., 290 F.Supp. 337 (D.Or.1966) (third-party complaint against manufacturer quashed, but harm was remote from product defect, product being waste-disposer that allegedly caused water to back up and wet floor on which customer slipped); cf. Lincoln v. Seawright, 104 Wis.2d 4, 310 N.W.2d 596 (1981) (no jurisdiction over person who sent dog into forum as a gift). For some of the older cases denying jurisdiction, see Trippe Mfg. Co. v. Spencer Gifts, Inc., 270 F.2d 821, 822 (7th Cir.1959) (unfair competition alleged from catalogues that defendant mailed into the forum—the court is much influenced by Hanson v. Denckla, which the court says "demonstrates the McGee

opinion whether, as a matter of statutory construction, this case of the defective product manufactured elsewhere and then sent into the forum is covered by a statute that refers to "the commission of a tortious act within this state" and does not, as does the Uniform Interstate and International Procedure Act, refer specifically to "causing tortious injury in this state by an act or omission outside the state."[679] Because the constitutionality and desirability of the forum's asserting jurisdiction under these circumstances is manifest, it is unfortunate that the New York Court of Appeals, for example, read its long-arm statute restrictively[680] and thus forced the legislature to amend the act to include specifically harm caused in New York by tortious conduct outside New York.[681]

Moreover, a manufacturer who sends a defective product directly into the forum knows that harm resulting from any defect in that product will, in all likelihood, be suffered in the forum. It is therefore desirable and proper for the forum to assert jurisdiction over a manufacturer who sends a defective product directly into the forum even though the manufacturer has little or no other contact with the forum[682] and does little or no other interstate or international business. What is here said of the manufacturer applies also to any entity that is connected with the product in the stream of distribution that sends the product into the forum. It is unfortunate that a number of states provide long-arm jurisdiction over the manufacturer who sends a defective product directly into the forum only if it "regularly does or solicits business, or engages in any other persistent course of conduct, or derives substantial revenue from goods used or consumed or services rendered, in this state." This is the provision in the now withdrawn Uniform Interstate and Internation-

---

case has been limited by the Court to the insurance field"); Mueller v. Steelcase, Inc., 172 F.Supp. 416 (D.Minn.1959); Johns v. Bay State Abrasive Prod. Co., 89 F.Supp. 654 (D.Md.1950).

679. Unif. Int. & Int'l P. Act § 1.03(a)(4).

For cases construing the forum's tort long-arm statute to include a negligent act outside the forum resulting in harm within the forum, see, e.g., Duple Motor Bodies, Ltd. v. Hollingsworth, 417 F.2d 231 (9th Cir.1969) (citing conflicting authorities construing the language "the commission of a tortious act within this state" and finding the majority view in favor of jurisdiction); Czarnick v. District Court, 175 Colo. 482, 488 P.2d 562 (1971) (negligent design and instructions for assembling product); Andersen v. National Presto Indus., Inc., 257 Iowa 911, 135 N.W.2d 639 (1965) (statutory language is "commits a tort in whole or in part in Iowa"); Atkins v. Jones & Laughlin Steel Corp., 258 Minn. 571, 104 N.W.2d 888 (1960) (statutory language is "commits a tort in whole or in part" and court distinguishes this from the "commission of a tortious act within this state"); cf. Gray v. American Radiator & Standard Sanitary Corp., 22 Ill.2d 432, 176 N.E.2d 761 (1961) (defective component part shipped indirectly into the forum; this is the landmark case in which "commission of a tortious act within this State" was held to include negligence outside of the state causing harm in the state).

For cases construing the forum's tort long-arm statute not to include negligence outside the forum causing harm in the forum, see O'Neal Steel, Inc. v. Smith, 120 Ga.App. 106, 169 S.E.2d 827, remanded as moot 225 Ga. 778, 171 S.E.2d 519 (1969); Feathers v. McLucas, 15 N.Y.2d 443, 261 N.Y.S.2d 8, 209 N.E.2d 68 (1965); Hodge v. Sands Mfg. Co., 151 W.Va. 133, 150 S.E.2d 793 (1966) ("commits a tort in whole or in part in this state"); Abbott–Smith v. Governors of Univ. of Toronto, 45 D.L.R.2d 672 (Nova Scotia S.Ct., 1964).

680. Feathers v. McLucas, 15 N.Y.2d 443, 261 N.Y.S.2d 8, 209 N.E.2d 68 (1965).

681. N.Y.—McKinney's Civ.Practice Law & Rules § 302(a)(3).

682. See Foye v. Consolidated Baling Mach. Co., 229 A.2d 196 (Me.1967).

al Procedure Act that describes when there is jurisdiction over a person causing tortious injury in the forum "by an act or omission outside this state"[683] rather than by "an act or omission in this state."[684]

Jurisdiction over the manufacturer who sends the defective product into the forum remains proper and desirable even though the transaction between manufacturer and forum buyer is arranged so that the manufacturer is technically divested of title to the goods before they enter the forum.[685] Moreover, once the defendant sends the defective product directly into the forum and the defective product has been distributed in the forum to a person who is subsequently injured by that product, the forum should have jurisdiction over the foreign manufacturer even though the user carries the product outside the forum and the injury thus fortuitously occurs outside the forum.[686]

A more difficult problem is presented if, instead of sending the defective product directly into the forum, the manufacturer has released a defective product, or the defective component part of a product, into the stream of national distribution and the defective item is then sent into the forum by an agency independent of the manufacturer. In general, if the defendant should have foreseen that the defective product is likely to cause harm in the forum and it does cause such harm, the forum should have jurisdiction over the defendant if the defendant is connected with the product in its stream of distribution in such a way as

---

683.　Unif. Interstate & Int'l Procedure Act § 1.03(a)(4). For a holding that the "substantial revenue" referred to in the section need not include revenue from the product causing the injury, see Liberty Mutual Ins. Co. v. American Pecco Corp., 334 F.Supp. 522 (D.D.C.1971).

684.　Unif. Int. & Int'l P. Act § 1.03(a)(3) (1986).

685.　See, e.g., Vandermee v. District Court, 164 Colo. 117, 433 P.2d 335 (1967); Shepard v. Rheem Mfg. Co., 249 N.C. 454, 106 S.E.2d 704 (1959). For cases denying jurisdiction influenced, in part, by the fact that the F.O.B. point was outside the forum, see, e.g., Agrashell, Inc. v. Bernard Sirotta Co., 344 F.2d 583 (2d Cir.1965); Washington Scientific Indus., Inc. v. Polan Indus., Inc., 302 F.Supp. 1354 (D.Minn.1969); Marvel Products Inc. v. Fantastics, Inc., 296 F.Supp. 783 (D.Conn.1968) (unfair competition by passing off defendant's product as plaintiff's).

686.　See State ex rel. Hydraulic Servocontrols Corp. v. Dale, 294 Or. 381, 657 P.2d 211 (1982) (airplane purchased in forum crashed in California); Callahan v. Keystone Fireworks Mfg. Co., 72 Wn.2d 823, 435 P.2d 626 (1967) (plaintiff was not a forum resident); cf. Burton Shipyard, Inc. v. Williams, 448 F.2d 640 (9th Cir.1971) (ship built by defendant sinks off forum's coast); Williams v. Brasea, Inc., 320 F.Supp. 658 (S.D.Tex.1970) (same and delivery made outside forum); Connelly v. Uniroyal, Inc., 75 Ill.2d 393, 27 Ill.Dec. 343, 389 N.E.2d 155 (1979), appeal dism'd for want of jurisdiction & cert. denied, 444 U.S. 1060, 100 S.Ct. 992, 62 L.Ed.2d 738 (1980) (defendant manufactured tire installed on car shipped into forum, substantial number of defendant's tires sold in forum); Roland v. Modell's Shoppers World of Bergen County, Inc., 92 N.J.Super. 1, 222 A.2d 110 (App.Div.1966) (purchase in the forum was made by a forum resident who was a member of plaintiff's family, but plaintiff was not a forum resident); Singer v. Walker, 15 N.Y.2d 443, 261 N.Y.S.2d 8, 209 N.E.2d 68, cert. denied, 382 U.S. 905, 86 S.Ct. 241, 15 L.Ed.2d 158 (1965) (forum resident injured using product in another state, court utilizes "transaction of any business" provision in forum's statute after construing "commits a tortious act" section as not applicable when negligence did not occur in the forum). But see the following cases denying jurisdiction as a matter of statutory construction: Shon v. District Court, 199 Colo. 90, 605 P.2d 472 (1980); McGowan v. Smith, 52 N.Y.2d 268, 437 N.Y.S.2d 643, 419 N.E.2d 321 (1981).

to make the defendant liable for the harm that the product caused.[687] The limit on the stream-of-commerce basis for jurisdiction, advocated by four justices in *Asahi Metal Industry v. Superior Court*[688] has, however, caused several courts to permit a defendant to insulate itself from jurisdiction by using independent companies to distribute the product in the forum.[689]

---

687. See, e.g., International Paper Co. v. Ouellette, 479 U.S. 481, 107 S.Ct. 805, 93 L.Ed.2d 883 (1987) (Vermont landowners may sue New York polluter in Vermont but Clean Water Act preempted application of Vermont nuisance law although permitting a nuisance claim under New York law); City of Milwaukee v. Illinois and Michigan, 451 U.S. 304, 101 S.Ct. 1784, 68 L.Ed.2d 114 (1981) (jurisdiction over continuous polluter discharging into water flowing into forum); World–Wide Volkswagen Corp. v. Woodson, 444 U.S. 286, 297–98, 100 S.Ct. 559, 567, 62 L.Ed.2d 490, 501–02 (1980) (dictum, "stream of commerce"); Oswalt v. Scripto, Inc., 616 F.2d 191 (5th Cir.1980); Kroger Co. v. Dornbos, 408 F.2d 813 (6th Cir.1969) (action for indemnity against fish processor and trucking companies that transported the fish); Mann v. Frank Hrubetz & Co., Inc., 361 So.2d 1021 (Ala.1978) (carnival ride); International Harvester Co. v. Hendrickson Mfg. Co., 249 Ark. 298, 459 S.W.2d 62 (1970) (component part); Ford Motor Co. v. Atwood Vacuum Mach. Co., 392 So.2d 1305 (Fla.), appeal dism'd for want of jurisdiction & cert. denied, 452 U.S. 901, 101 S.Ct. 3024, 69 L.Ed.2d 401 (1981) (manufacturer impleads maker of component part); Gray v. American Radiator & Standard Sanitary Corp., 22 Ill.2d 432, 176 N.E.2d 761 (1961) (component part); Woods v. Edgewater Amusement Park, 381 Mich. 559, 165 N.W.2d 12 (1969); Ehlers v. U.S. Heating & Cooling Mfg. Corp., 267 Minn. 56, 124 N.W.2d 824 (1963); Smith v. Temco, Inc., 252 So.2d 212 (Miss.1971); Metal–Matic, Inc. v. Eighth Judicial Dist. Ct., 82 Nev. 263, 415 P.2d 617 (1966); State ex rel. Western Seed Production Corp. v. Campbell, 250 Or. 262, 442 P.2d 215 (1968), cert. denied, 393 U.S. 1093, 89 S.Ct. 862, 21 L.Ed.2d 784 (1969) (economic loss); Mallory Engineering, Inc. v. Ted R. Brown & Assoc., 618 P.2d 1004 (Utah), appeal dism'd for want of jurisdiction & cert. denied, 449 U.S. 1029, 101 S.Ct. 602, 66 L.Ed.2d 492 (1980); cf. Honeywell, Inc. v. Metz Apparatewerke, 509 F.2d 1137 (7th Cir.1975) (induce patent infringement); Pegler v. Sullivan, 6 Ariz.App. 338, 432 P.2d 593 (1967) (invasion of privacy by television broadcast).

But cf. Foye v. Consolidated Baling Mach. Co., 229 A.2d 196 (Me.1967) (jurisdiction upheld over manufacturer who shipped product directly into the forum, but court indicates it would be more difficult to obtain jurisdiction over a manufacturer whose product was shipped indirectly into the state). But see Hutson v. Fehr Bros., Inc., 584 F.2d 833 (8th Cir.), cert. denied, 439 U.S. 983, 99 S.Ct. 573, 58 L.Ed.2d 654 (1978) (in a 4–3 en banc decision, the majority holds that due process does not permit reaching an Italian distributor insulated by several layers in the distribution process) (Justice O'Connor's opinion in *Asahi Metal Industry v. Superior Court*, joined by three other justices, cites *Hutson* with approval, 480 U.S. 102, 111–12, 107 S.Ct. 1026, 1032, 94 L.Ed.2d 92 (1987)); Fisher v. Albany Mach. & Supply Co., 261 La. 747, 260 So.2d 691 (1972) (component part); Moss v. Winston–Salem, 254 N.C. 480, 119 S.E.2d 445 (1961) (deny jurisdiction over manufacturer of defective product that was shipped indirectly into the forum and caused harm there); Maschinenfabrik Seydelmann v. Altman, 468 So.2d 286 (Fla.App.2d Dist.1985) (meat grinder); cf. Fidelity & Cas. Co. of N.Y. v. Philadelphia Resins Corp., 766 F.2d 440 (10th Cir.1985) (no jurisdiction over manufacturer when user brings to forum though manufacturer informed of region where use intended); Davis v. C & NW Transp. Co., 266 Pa.Super. 558, 405 A.2d 959 (1979) (plaintiff injured unloading railroad car loaded by defendant).

Courts have denied jurisdiction over the previous owner of a durable machine who sold the machine before it caused harm in the forum. See Schneider v. Sverdsten Logging Co., Inc., 104 Idaho 210, 657 P.2d 1078 (1983); Keech v. Lapointe Machine Tool Co., 200 N.J.Super. 177, 491 A.2d 10 (App.Div.1985); Nissley v. JLG Ind., Inc., 306 Pa.Super. 557, 452 A.2d 865 (1982); cf. Kenny v. Alexson Equip. Co., 495 Pa. 107, 432 A.2d 974 (1981) (defendant sold equipment outside the forum to a firm that leases the equipment in several states including the forum).

688.   480 U.S. 102, 108–13, 107 S.Ct. 1026, 1030–32, 94 L.Ed.2d 92 (1987).

689.   See, e.g. Boit v. Gar–Tec Products, Inc., 967 F.2d 671 (1st Cir. 1992), which denies jurisdiction over the American importer of a paint stripper that caused property damage, when the importer distributed the product thorough a mail order catalogue company. Vargas v. Hong Jin Crown Corp., 247 Mich.App. 278, 636 N.W.2d 291 (2001), denies jurisdiction over South Korean helmet manufacturer that sold helmets to U.S. distributor in Wisconsin. The distributor then sold a helmet to a Michigan retailer from which plaintiff purchased it.

Foreseeability of harm in the forum is the key to satisfaction of the requirements of due process when the defendant has not sent the defective product directly into the forum.[690] It is the same foreseeability of consequences in the forum that has made it proper to extend nonresident motorist statutes to include jurisdiction over the nonresident motorist's liability insurer[691] or over the owner of an automobile[692] who has entrusted the vehicle to a bailee who, in turn, has driven the automobile into the forum. When the bailee has driven into the forum without the owner's permission, jurisdiction over the owner should turn on whether the owner could have foreseen that the automobile might be driven into the forum.[693]

There is at least one circumstance in which a defendant who has sold or serviced a product in the stream of distribution and can foresee that the product or service, if defective, will cause harm in the forum, should not be subject to the jurisdiction of forum courts in actions

---

690. See, e.g., Keckler v. Brookwood Country Club, 248 F.Supp. 645 (N.D.Ill.1965); Buckeye Boiler Co. v. Superior Ct., 71 Cal.2d 893, 80 Cal.Rptr. 113, 458 P.2d 57 (1969); Dornbos v. Kroger Co., 9 Mich.App. 515, 157 N.W.2d 498 (1968) (defendants are trucking companies that mishandled fish); Tavoularis v. Womer, 123 N.H. 423, 462 A.2d 110 (1983) (negligent entrustment of automobile); Roche v. Floral Rental Corp., 95 N.J.Super. 555, 232 A.2d 162 (App.Div.1967), aff'd, 51 N.J. 26, 237 A.2d 265 (1968); Johnson v. Equitable Life Assurance Soc'y, 22 A.D.2d 138, 254 N.Y.S.2d 258 (1st Dept.1964), aff'd, 18 N.Y.2d 933, 277 N.Y.S.2d 136, 223 N.E.2d 562 (1966) (component part); O'Brien v. Comstock Foods, Inc., 123 Vt. 461, 194 A.2d 568 (1963); Restatement, Second, § 37, comment *a*; cf. Deveny v. Rheem Mfg. Co., 319 F.2d 124 (2d Cir.1963) (foreseeability stressed in case where manufacturer sent product directly into the forum); Jack O'Donnell Chevrolet, Inc. v. Shankles, 276 F.Supp. 998 (N.D.Ill.1967) (defendant is co-conspirator in check kiting scheme). But see World–Wide Volkswagen Corp. v. Woodson, 444 U.S. 286, 297, 100 S.Ct. 559, 567, 62 L.Ed.2d 490, 498 (1980): "[T]he foreseeability that is critical to due process analysis is not the mere likelihood that a product will find its way into the forum State. Rather, it is that the defendant's conduct and connection with the forum State are such that he should reasonably anticipate being haled into court there."

691. See Pugh v. Oklahoma Farm Bureau Mut. Ins. Co., 159 F.Supp. 155 (E.D.La. 1958); cf. Commonwealth of Puerto Rico v. SS Zoe Colocotroni, 628 F.2d 652 (1st Cir.1980), cert. denied, 450 U.S. 912, 101 S.Ct. 1350, 67 L.Ed.2d 336 (1981) (jurisdiction to recover clean-up costs from polluter's insurer); Ferrell v. West Bend Mut. Ins. Co., 393 F.3d 786 (8th Cir. 2005) (fact that policy's territory-of-coverage clause expressly included the forum made it reasonable for injured parties to assert jurisdiction over insurer). But cf. Hunt v. Erie Ins. Group, 728 F.2d 1244 (9th Cir.1984) (passenger cannot obtain jurisdiction in state to which she moved to receive medical treatment); United Farm Bureau Mut. Ins. v. United States Fidelity & Guaranty Co., 501 Pa. 646, 462 A.2d 1300 (1983) (no jurisdiction over liability insurer to collect no-fault benefits). But see Torres v. American Serv. Mut. Ins. Co., 294 F.Supp. 635 (D.Puerto Rico 1969) (no jurisdiction in absence of special statutory provision).

692. See Davis v. St. Paul–Mercury Indem. Co., 294 F.2d 641 (4th Cir.1961). But see Clemens v. District Ct., 154 Colo. 176, 390 P.2d 83 (1964) (no jurisdiction over absent owner).

693. See Currie, 1963 U.Ill.L.Forum at 550–51; cf. Scheer v. Rockne Motors Corp., 68 F.2d 942 (2d Cir.1934) (may not apply owner's liability statute of jurisdiction to which bailee drove without owner's authority), disapproved of in § 9.2A.

There have been mixed results in other cases of vicarious liability. See Snyder v. Beam, 380 A.2d 1374 (Del.Super.1977) (jurisdiction over employer when employee acting in course of employment). But see Haker v. Southwestern Ry., 176 Mont. 364, 578 P.2d 724 (1978) (no jurisdiction over employer when employee not acting in scope of employment); Memorial Lawn Cemeteries Assoc. v. Carr, 540 P.2d 1156 (Okl.1975) (no jurisdiction over nonresident parent vicariously liable for tort of child).

arising from that defect. This is when the defendant has sold or serviced the product outside the forum, has then transferred or returned the product outside the forum to a person whom the defendant reasonably regards as a user and not distributor of the product, and the defendant's business is local, rather than interstate, in nature. For example, suppose in California a gasoline station owner installs a new tire on an automobile with New York license plates. The automobile owner, a New York resident, then drives the vehicle back to New York where the tire separates from the rim causing a collision that injures the automobile owner.[694] It would come close to, if not cross, the due process line,[695] for New York to assert jurisdiction over the California gasoline station owner, and New York ought not to assert such jurisdiction.[696] It is in this kind of situation, then, delivery of a defective product out of the state to a user rather than to a distributor, that a long-arm statute should use language, similar to that of the Uniform Interstate and International Procedure Act, that speaks of a defendant who "derives substantial

---

694. A similar hypothetical case involving a California tire dealer and a Pennsylvania tourist was put by Judge Sobeloff in Erlanger Mills, Inc. v. Cohoes Fibre Mills, Inc., 239 F.2d 502, 507 (4th Cir.1956).

695. See World–Wide Volkswagen Corp. v. Woodson, 444 U.S. 286, 296, 100 S.Ct. 559, 566, 62 L.Ed.2d 490, 500 (1980).

696. See Growden v. Ed Bowlin and Associates, Inc., 733 F.2d 1149 (5th Cir.1984) (no jurisdiction over seller of used aircraft when sale outside forum); Insurance Co. of North Amer. v. Marina Salina Cruz, 649 F.2d 1266 (9th Cir.1981) (no jurisdiction over defendant who repaired ship outside forum); Uppgren v. Executive Aviation Services, Inc., 304 F.Supp. 165 (D.Minn.1969) (no jurisdiction over Maryland helicopter distributor); Yules v. General Motors Corp., 297 F.Supp. 674 (D.Mont.1969) (no jurisdiction over Connecticut automobile dealer); Fleet Leasing, Inc. v. District Court, 649 P.2d 1074 (Colo.1982) (no jurisdiction over defendant who repaired truck outside of forum); Tilley v. Keller Truck & Implement Corp., 200 Kan. 641, 438 P.2d 128 (1968) (no jurisdiction over Colorado truck dealer); Sohn v. Bernstein, 279 A.2d 529 (Me.1971) (gift sent into forum); Hapner v. Rolf Brauchli, Inc., 404 Mich. 160, 273 N.W.2d 822 (1978) (no jurisdiction over manufacturer when product purchased outside forum unless manufacturer's products are distributed in the forum); Marion v. Long, 72 N.C.App. 585, 325 S.E.2d 300, review denied, 313 N.C. 604, 330 S.E.2d 612 (1985) (no jurisdiction over defendant who repaired car outside forum even though car picked up in forum); Bev–Mark, Inc. v. Summerfield GMC Truck Co., Inc., 268 Pa.Super. 74, 407 A.2d 443 (1979) (no jurisdiction over defendant who repaired truck outside forum); Pellegrini v. Sachs & Sons, 522 P.2d 704 (Utah 1974) (no jurisdiction over California dealer from whom plaintiff purchased car when plaintiff a California resident); Oliver v. American Motors Corp., 70 Wn.2d 875, 425 P.2d 647 (1967) (no jurisdiction over Oregon automobile dealer—the court draws a distinction between a retailer doing a local business and a manufacturer doing an interstate business); Developments, 73 Harv. L. Rev. at 929. But cf. Garrett v. Key Ford, Inc., 403 So.2d 923 (Ala.Civ.App.1981) (uphold jurisdiction over nearby Florida car dealer who solicited forum customers); Secrest Mach. Corp. v. Superior Court, 33 Cal.3d 664, 190 Cal.Rptr. 175, 660 P.2d 399 (1983) (jurisdiction over seller of machine although plaintiff's employer took possession of it outside of the forum); Duignan v. A.H. Robins Co., 98 Idaho 134, 559 P.2d 750 (1977) (jurisdiction over manufacturer of IUD purchased by plaintiff in California when a resident of that state); Edmundson v. Miley Trailer Co., 211 N.W.2d 269 (Iowa 1973) (jurisdiction over gas station owner who serviced trailer outside forum and over dealer from whom it purchased in another state). Currie, 1963 U.Ill.L.Forum at 559, distinguishes between the buyer who is injured by a product that the buyer purchased elsewhere from a local dealer and a third person whom the product injures, permitting the latter but not the former to sue the dealer in a distant forum. The court in the *Tilley* case, supra, however, did not draw this distinction. Some of the plaintiffs in *Tilley* were forum residents who were in an automobile that collided with the truck that had a defective wheel. Letter to the author from attorneys for the truck dealer, dated November 15, 1968.

revenue from goods used or consumed or services rendered, in this state."[697] The statute would then properly protect the nonresident seller in this type of foreign-localized transaction from forum suits unless the seller's business is interstate rather than essentially local in nature.[698]

A case that arises with some frequency concerns an attempt to obtain jurisdiction over a retail liquor seller, located just across the state line. The seller's customer was a driver who became intoxicated, drove into the forum, and there harmed the plaintiff. Most decisions have denied jurisdiction under these circumstances,[699] but there is some diversity in result depending on the extent to which the defendant has solicited forum customers.[700] *Williams v. Lakeview Co.*[701] went so far as to hold that the border bar's advertising in the forum did not confer jurisdiction because the driver's visit to the bar was not a result of the advertising. Cases denying jurisdiction over border bars seem wrong even by standard "minimum contacts" analysis. The likelihood that the defendant's activities will cause harm in the forum and the defendant's profit from sales to forum residents make jurisdiction reasonable.

Attempts to assert jurisdiction over out-of-state banks have had mixed success.[702] Courts have denied jurisdiction over banks in other states that have cashed checks with forged endorsements even though the forger drew the checks on forum banks.[703] This holding requires the payee to pursue the depository and drawee banks in separate suits and

---

697. Section 1.03(a)(4).

698. See Jonz v. Garrett/Airesearch Corp., 490 P.2d 1197 (Alaska 1971) (jurisdiction over manufacturer whose products used in forum); Fields v. Volkswagen of America, Inc., 555 P.2d 48 (Okl.1976) (jurisdiction over distributors who advertise in forum although car purchased elsewhere); von Mehren & Trautman, 70 Harv. L. Rev. at 1171–72 (stressing importance of whether the defendant engages in multistate activities).

699. See West American Ins. Co. v. Westin, Inc., 337 N.W.2d 676 (Minn.1983), overruling Blamey v. Brown, 270 N.W.2d 884 (Minn.1978), cert. denied, 444 U.S. 1070, 100 S.Ct. 1013, 62 L.Ed.2d 751 (1980); Hennes v. Loch Ness Bar, 117 Wis.2d 397, 344 N.W.2d 205 (App.1983); cf. Perry v. Hamilton, 51 Wn.App. 936, 756 P.2d 150 (1988), rev. denied (no jurisdiction over nonresident social host).

700. See BLC Insurance Company v. Westin, Inc., 359 N.W.2d 752 (Minn.App.1985), cert. denied, 474 U.S. 844, 106 S.Ct. 132, 88 L.Ed.2d 109 (1985) (same bar as in West Amer. Ins. Co. v. Westin, previous note, but different result in the light of advertising in forum since prior decision); cf. Ling v. Jan's Liquors, 237 Kan. 629, 703 P.2d 731 (1985) (uphold jurisdiction over Missouri retail liquor seller as matter of statutory construction).

701. 199 Ariz. 1, 13 P.3d 280 (2000).

702. For cases upholding jurisdiction over banks that conspired in a check-kiting scheme with a person who gave the check to the plaintiff in the forum, see Jack O'Donnell Chevrolet, Inc. v. Shankles, 276 F.Supp. 998 (N.D.Ill.1967); Great Atlantic & Pac. Tea Co. v. Hill–Dodge Banking Co., 255 Iowa 272, 122 N.W.2d 337 (1963). For cases denying jurisdiction over depository banks that paid over forged endorsements, see next note.

This discussion of jurisdiction over banks assumes that there is no bar to jurisdiction other than the usual due process considerations. Federal legislation restricts the venue of actions against national banks. See 12 U.S.C. § 94.

703. See Froning & Deppe, Inc. v. Continental Ill. Nat'l Bk. & Trust Co., 695 F.2d 289 (7th Cir.1982); Roger Williams Gen'l Hosp. v. Fall River Trust Co., 423 A.2d 1384 (R.I. 1981); cf. First National Bank of Lewisville v. First National Bank of Clinton, 258 F.3d 727 (8th Cir. 2001) (issuance of a cashier's check payable to an out-of-state payee does not subject the issuing bank to personal jurisdiction in the payee's state for a claim of wrongful dishonor).

prevents the drawee bank from impleading the depository bank. It seems reasonable to avoid placing these burdens on the legal system by holding that depository banks that cash checks over forged endorsements are subject to jurisdiction in the state where the drawee bank is located.

§ 4.17 Jurisdiction Based on Internet Activities

When does use of the World Wide Web produce sufficient forum contacts to permit the exercise of personal jurisdiction?[704] *Weber v. Jolly Hotels*[705] held that an Italian hotel's establishment of an advertising Web site available in the plaintiff's home state did not render the hotel subject to jurisdiction there in a suit to recover for damages incurred when plaintiff fell at the hotel. The court divided cases dealing with jurisdiction based on Internet contacts into three categories. First, "cases where defendants actively do business on the Internet."[706] Courts have upheld jurisdiction in cases arising out of that business. Second, cases in which "a user can exchange information with the host computer" and jurisdiction depends on "the level of interactivity and commercial nature of the exchange of information that occurs on the Web site."[707] Third, cases involving "passive Web sites; i.e., sites that merely provide information or advertisements to users."[708] The court found this case fell into the third category and that jurisdiction was not available.

In putting internet activities into three categories the *Weber* court followed *Zippo Mfg. Co. v. Zippo Dot Com, Inc.*,[709] which is often cited for this analysis. Whether the *Zippo* analysis is useful is open to question. It seems misplaced as many businesses make sophisticated use of the internet with their Web sites.[710]

---

704. For discussion of jurisdiction based on internet activities see Gilman, *Personal Jurisdiction and the Internet: Traditional Jurisprudence for a New Medium*, 56 Bus. Law. 395 (2000); Rice & Gladstone, *An Assessment of the Effects Test in Determining Personal Jurisdiction in Cyberspace*, 58 Bus. Law. 601 (2003); Stein, *The Unexceptional Problem of Jurisdiction in Cyberspace*, 32 Int'l Law. 167 (1998).

705. 977 F.Supp. 327 (D.N.J.1997).

706. Id. at 333. See Snowney v. Harrah's Entertainment, Inc., 35 Cal.4th 1054, 112 P.3d 28, 29 Cal.Rptr.3d 33 (2005), cert. denied, 546 U.S. 1015, 126 S.Ct. 659, 163 L.Ed.2d 526 (2005) (in an action for damages resulting from failure to provide notice of an energy surcharge imposed on hotel guests, uphold jurisdiction over Nevada hotels some of whose California patrons made reservations using hotels' Web sites).

707. *Weber*, 977 F.Supp. at 333.

708. Id. For examples of such cases see GTE New Media Services Inc. v. BellSouth Corp., 199 F.3d 1343 (D.C. Cir. 2000); Soma Medical Int'l v. Standard Chartered Bank, 196 F.3d 1292 (10th Cir. 1999); Mink v. AAAA Development LLC, 190 F.3d 333 (5th Cir. 1999) (although website provides users with mail-in order form, telephone number, mailing address, and e-mail address, orders were not take through the website); cf. Norris v. Six Flags Theme Parks, Inc., 102 Haw. 203, 74 P.3d 26 (2003) (no jurisdiction when plaintiff did not purchase tickets through defendant's web site although she could have).

709. 952 F.Supp. 1119 (W.D. Pa. 1997).

710. For adverse criticisms of *Zippo* see Borchers, *Internet Libel: The Consequences of a Non–Rule Approach to Personal Jurisdiction*, 98 Nw. U. L. Rev. 473, 489 (2004) ("*Zippo* should be ignored, at least in libel cases"); Stein, *Personal Jurisdiction and the Internet: Seeing Due Process through the Lens of Regulatory Precision*, 98 Nw. U. L. Rev. 411, 431 (2004) ("While courts are paying lip service to *Zippo*, they are increasingly recognizing its conceptual shortcomings").

Gorman v. Ameritrade Holding Corp.[711] upheld general jurisdiction over a defendant who did "continuous and systematic" business in the forum through its Web site even though the suit did not arise from a forum transaction stating: " 'Cyberspace,' however, is not some mystical incantation capable of warding off the jurisdiction of courts built from bricks and mortar. Just as our traditional notions of personal jurisdiction have proven adaptable to other changes in the national economy, so too are they adaptable to the transformations wrought by the Internet."[712] The court applies the *Zippo* sliding scale analysis to determine whether internet contacts are sufficient for general jurisdiction.[713] The circuits are split, however, on whether the *Zippo* test, although perhaps useful for analysis of specific jurisdiction, is appropriate for determining general jurisdiction.[714]

Inset Systems, Inc. v. Instruction Set, Inc.[715] upheld jurisdiction over a defendant whose Internet domain name allegedly infringed the plaintiff's federally registered trademark. A similar case but with more substantial forum contacts, *CompuServe, Inc. v. Patterson,*[716] permitted a plaintiff headquartered in Ohio to sue a Texas defendant in an Ohio federal district court for a declaration that the plaintiff did not violate defendant's trademarks or engage in unfair competition. Defendant had installed his software on plaintiff's system, had signed an agreement

---

711. 293 F.3d 506 (D.C. Cir. 2002).

712. Id. at 510–11. See Graduate Management Admission Council v. Raju, 241 F.Supp.2d 589 (E.D. Va. 2003) (asserting jurisdiction over citizen of India under FRCP 4(k)(2), which considers contacts with entire U.S.). A global survey on Internet jurisdiction revealed that businesses, especially in North America, are avoiding online transactions with some jurisdictions that they regard as presenting high litigation risks. See 72 Law Week 2614 (No. 38 4/13/04).

713. *Gorman*, 293 F.3d at 513.

714. See Lakin v. Prudential Securities, Inc., 348 F.3d 704, 711–12 (8th Cir. 2003) (noting circuit split and rejecting *Zippo* test for general jurisdiction because under that test an interactive Web site might produce contacts that are "continuous, but not *substantial*"). (Emphasis in original).

715. 937 F.Supp. 161 (D.Conn.1996). See also Rio Properties, Inc. v. Rio Int'l Interlink, 284 F.3d 1007 (9th Cir. 2002) (holding that Nevada casino operator can obtain jurisdiction in Nevada federal court to enjoin Costa Rican company that targeted Nevada customers from using the name "RIO" on its gambling Web site); Intercon, Inc. v. Bell Atlantic Internet Solutions, Inc., 205 F.3d 1244 (10th Cir. 2000) (upholding jurisdiction over nonresident provider of Internet service for unauthorized use of plaintiff's e-mail server). But see Carefirst of Maryland, Inc. v. Carefirst Pregnancy Centers, Inc., 334 F.3d 390 (4th Cir. 2003) (defendant's establishment of Web site did not warrant exercise of jurisdiction in suit for infringement of trademark); Quick Technologies, Inc. v. Sage Group PLC, 313 F.3d 338 (5th Cir. 2002) (Texas trademark holder cannot obtain jurisdiction in infringement suit against English company operating Web site providing information about defendant); Pavlovich v. Superior Court, 29 Cal.4th 262, 58 P.3d 2, 127 Cal.Rptr.2d 329 (2002), stay denied, 2003 WL 46660 (U.S. Jan. 3, 2003) (holding 4–3 that California company having sole licensing rights to technology that prevents copying of motion pictures from DVD disks cannot obtain jurisdiction over Texas defendant who posted on Web site a program circumventing plaintiff's technology). Cf. Toys "R" Us, Inc. v. Step Two, S.A., 318 F.3d 446 (3d Cir. 2003) (Spanish defendant's interactive Web site did not establish contacts sufficient for personal jurisdiction in trademark infringement suit, but plaintiff entitled to jurisdictional discovery concerning defendant's business activities in the U.S. including its plans and marketing strategies).

716. 89 F.3d 1257 (6th Cir.1996).

permitting the defendant to do so, and had sent an electronic mail message to plaintiff claiming infringement.

In *Dow Jones & Co. v. Gutnick*,[717] a case that attracted international attention, the High Court of Australia held that a plaintiff could sue Dow Jones in Victoria for defamation. Dow Jones maintained a subscription news site on the World Wide Web. Dow Jones uploaded the allegedly defamatory material on its servers in New Jersey. The plaintiff resided in Victoria, which was the center of his business and social activities. The court also held that the law of Victoria applied. The defamation law of Victoria is more favorable to the plaintiff than the law of any U.S. jurisdiction. Dow Jones has no office or assets in Australia. The plaintiff sued only for harm that he suffered in Victoria and undertook not to sue defendant anyplace else.

Most United States courts have far more difficulty than the High Court of Australia in finding personal jurisdiction over Internet defamers. In *Griffis v. Luban*,[718] plaintiff and defendant were members of an Internet newsgroup on archeology. Members post messages on the group's Web site. Plaintiff lives in Alabama and teaches non-credit courses at the University of Alabama. Defendant resides in Minnesota. Defendant posted comments on the group's Web site disparaging plaintiff's professional qualifications. Plaintiff sued defendant in Alabama and obtained a default judgment. The Minnesota Supreme Court held that it would not enforce the Alabama judgment because the Alabama court did not have jurisdiction over the defendant. The court distinguished *Calder v. Jones*[719] stating that in *Calder*, unlike *Griffis*, there was a "close relationship between the plaintiff's profession and the forum state"[720] and that in *Calder* defendant had "expressly aimed the allegedly tortious conduct at the forum such that the forum was the focal point of the tortious activity."[721] The court also noted that courts have differed on how broadly or narrowly they should apply *Calder*.[722]

---

717. [2002] HCA 56 (Austl. 2002). Dow Jones settled the case before trial by printing a clarification and paying some of the plaintiff's legal fees.

718. 646 N.W.2d 527 (Minn. 2002), cert. denied, 538 U.S. 906, 123 S.Ct. 1483, 155 L.Ed.2d 225 (2003).

719. 465 U.S. 783, 104 S.Ct. 1482, 79 L.Ed.2d 804 (1984), discussed supra § 4.8 text accompanying notes 250–255. See Wagner v. Miskin, 660 N.W.2d 593, 598 (N.D. 2003) (stating that some internet jurisdiction cases apply *Zippo's* "sliding scale" while others apply an "effects test" derived from *Calder*).

720. *Griffis*, 646 N.W.2d at 536.

721. Id. at 535.

722. Id. at 533. See also Revell v. Lidov, 317 F.3d 467 (5th Cir. 2002) (denying Texas resident jurisdiction in Texas over Massachusetts resident who posted defamatory material on Columbia University Web site and also denying jurisdiction over University); Young v. New Haven Advocate, 315 F.3d 256 (4th Cir. 2002) (warden of Virginia prison cannot obtain jurisdiction in Virginia over two Connecticut newspapers that allegedly defamed him in articles posted on their Web sites); Braintech, Inc. v. Kostiuk, 171 D.L.R.4th 46 (B.C. Ct. App. 1999), leave to appeal dism'd (will recognize judgments of foreign countries on the basis of comity but refuse recognition of Texas default judgment on ground Texas court did not have personal jurisdiction over defendant when sole basis for jurisdiction was availability in Texas of Web site on which defendant had posted allegedly defamatory material).

The approach of the High Court of Australia in *Gutnick* is preferable to the approach of the Minnesota Supreme Court in *Griffis*. For personal jurisdiction over Internet defamers it should be sufficient that the defendant can foresee that the forum is the center of plaintiff's activities and that the defendant's communication is available and will cause harm there.[723]

§ 4.18   Contractual Transactions in the Forum

A variety of long-arm statutes permit use of an isolated contractual transaction as a basis for judicial jurisdiction. Some statutes focus on contracts made with forum residents to be performed in whole or in part by either party in the forum.[724] Connecticut permits suit by forum residents against foreign corporations on actions arising "[o]ut of any contract made in this state or to be performed in this state".[725] The Uniform Interstate and International Procedure Act refers to "contracting to supply services or things in this state"[726] and also has a special provision covering a contract "to insure any person, property, or risk located within this state at the time of contracting."[727]

The easiest case in which to uphold an isolated contractual transaction as a basis for *in personam* jurisdiction is that in which the defendant was physically in the forum while defectively performing contractual duties, causing harmful consequences in the forum to the plaintiff who is the obligee under the contract. The plaintiff should be able to sue the defendant in the forum for damages resulting there from the defendant's breach of contract.[728]

By analogy to the tort cases in which the defendant has shipped a defective product into the forum,[729] the plaintiff should be able to obtain jurisdiction over a defendant whose defective performance in the forum consists of shipping into the forum for use there goods that do not conform with a contract between defendant and plaintiff.[730] Some courts,

---

723. See Spencer, *Jurisdiction and the Internet: Returning to Traditional Principles to Analyze Network–Mediated Contacts*, 2006 U. Ill. L. Rev. 71, 100.

724. See, e.g., Tex.Civ.Prac. & Rem.C. § 17.042(1).

725. Conn.Gen.Stat.Ann. § 33–929(f)(1).

726. Unif. Interstate & Int'l P. Act § 1.03(a)(2).

727. Id. § 1.03(a)(6).

728. But see Hartsog v. Robinson, 115 Ga.App. 824, 156 S.E.2d 141 (1967) (California court did not have jurisdiction over Georgia residents in suit by California resident to recover for breach of a contract to repair and improve the plaintiff's dwelling house).

729. See § 4.16, note 677 and accompanying text.

730. See, e.g., Vencedor Mfg. Co., Inc. v. Gougler Industries, Inc., 557 F.2d 886 (1st Cir.1977) (rejecting distinction between tort and contract theories); Jones Enterprises, Inc. v. Atlas Service Corp., 442 F.2d 1136 (9th Cir.1971) (defective materials and designs); Shepler v. Korkut, 33 Mich.App. 411, 190 N.W.2d 281 (1971) (defective design); Murray v. Huggers Mfg., Inc., 398 So.2d 1323 (Miss.1981); cf. A.F. Briggs Co. v. Starrett Corp., 329 A.2d 177 (Me.1974) (plus sale of six other items in five years to other forum customers); John G. Kolbe, Inc. v. Chromodern Chair Co., 211 Va. 736, 180 S.E.2d 664 (1971) (forum dealer can get jurisdiction over manufacturer although goods shipped directly to buyer in another state).

The argument for jurisdiction on a contract theory is especially strong if the same suit involves a claim on a tort theory. See Casad, *Long Arm and Convenient Forum*, 20 Kan. L.

however, have been reluctant to assume jurisdiction over the out-of-state supplier in this kind of case if the supplier's sole nexus with the forum consists of the defective product that the supplier sent there.[731]

Another situation in which the contractual nexus with the forum is sufficient to sustain *in personam* jurisdiction is that in which the plaintiff has, in accordance with a contract with the defendant, performed services in the forum over a substantial period of time, the defendant has promised to compensate the plaintiff in the forum for the plaintiff's services there, and the defendant breaks this promise.[732]

Rev. 1, 17 (1971) ("If defendant will be required to defend one claim in a particular state court, and if substantially similar issues are presented in another claim, it seems fair to adjudicate both claims in that court").

731. See Hall's Specialties, Inc. v. Schupbach, 758 F.2d 214 (7th Cir.1985); Loumar, Inc. v. Smith, 698 F.2d 759 (5th Cir.1983); Iowa Elec. Light & Power Co. v. Atlas Corp., 603 F.2d 1301 (8th Cir.1979), cert. denied, 445 U.S. 911, 100 S.Ct. 1090, 63 L.Ed.2d 327 (1980) (clause choosing forum law not sufficient to confer jurisdiction); Erlanger Mills, Inc. v. Cohoes Fibre Mills, Inc., 239 F.2d 502 (4th Cir.1956); Washington Scientific Indus., Inc. v. Polan, 302 F.Supp. 1354 (D.C.Minn.1969) (no jurisdiction to make supplier third-party defendant); Unarco Ind. v. Frederick Mfg. Co., 109 Ill.App.3d 189, 64 Ill.Dec. 808, 440 N.E.2d 360 (1982); Splaine v. Modern Electroplating, Inc., 17 Mass.App.Ct. 612, 460 N.E.2d 1306 (1984), review denied, 391 Mass. 1106, 464 N.E.2d 74 (1984); Weld Power Ind., Inc. v. C.S.I. Technologies, Inc., 124 N.H. 121, 467 A.2d 568 (1983); Green Thumb Ind. v. Warren County Nursery, Inc., 46 N.C.App. 235, 264 S.E.2d 753 (1980); C.W. Brown Mach. Shop, Inc. v. Stanley Mach. Corp., 670 S.W.2d 791 (Tex.App.—Fort Worth 1984); Hust v. Northern Log, Inc., 297 N.W.2d 429 (N.D.1980); Robinson v. International Ind. Ltd., 139 Vt. 444, 430 A.2d 457 (1981) (drawing distinction between prepaid shipment, as here, and C.O.D.)

732. See, e.g., Madison Consulting Group v. South Carolina, 752 F.2d 1193 (7th Cir.1985) (distinguishing *Lakeside Bridge,* infra this note, on ground defendant solicited the contract); Mississippi Interstate Express, Inc. v. Transpo, Inc., 681 F.2d 1003 (5th Cir.1982) (using plaintiff's shipping service); Nicholstone Book Bindery, Inc. v. Chelsea House Publishers, 621 S.W.2d 560 (Tenn.1981), cert. denied, 455 U.S. 994, 102 S.Ct. 1623, 71 L.Ed.2d 856 (1982) (custom printing); Mouzavires v. Baxter, 434 A.2d 988 (D.C.App. 1981) (en banc), cert. denied, 455 U.S. 1006, 102 S.Ct. 1643, 71 L.Ed.2d 875 (1982) (attorney's work); Bowsher v. Digby, 243 Ark. 799, 422 S.W.2d 671 (1968) (forum real estate broker sues nonresident owner of forum land for commission due when plaintiff, pursuant to his contract with the owner, obtained an offer for the purchase of the land); Danov v. ABC Freight Forwarding Corp., 266 Minn. 115, 122 N.W.2d 776 (1963) (forum employee sues profit-sharing trust and trustees); State ex rel. Metal Service Center of Georgia, Inc. v. Gaertner, 677 S.W.2d 325 (Mo.1984) (finishing metal work); Computac, Inc. v. Dixie News Co., 124 N.H. 350, 469 A.2d 1345 (1983) (processing data); Avdel Corp. v. Mecure, 58 N.J. 264, 277 A.2d 207 (1971) (custom manufacturer); Hi Fashion Wigs, Inc. v. Peter Hammond Adv., Inc., 32 N.Y.2d 583, 347 N.Y.S.2d 47, 300 N.E.2d 421 (1973) (guarantee payment for advertising services); Yankee Metal Prod. Co. v. District Court, 528 P.2d 311 (Okl.1974) (custom manufacture); State ex rel. White Lumber Sales, Inc. v. Sulmonetti, 252 Or. 121, 448 P.2d 571 (1968) (same); Zerbel v. H.L. Federman & Co., 48 Wis.2d 54, 179 N.W.2d 872 (1970), appeal dism'd for want of substantial fed. question, 402 U.S. 902, 91 S.Ct. 1379, 28 L.Ed.2d 643 (1971) (preparation of financial report). But see Mountaire Feeds, Inc. v. Agro Impex, S.A., 677 F.2d 651 (8th Cir.1982) (no jurisdiction over buyer of feed manufactured to specifications in forum); Premier Corp. v. Newsom, 620 F.2d 219 (10th Cir.1980) (tax services, but contract did not require performance in the forum); Barnstone v. Congregation Am Echad, 574 F.2d 286 (5th Cir.1978) (no jurisdiction for payment for plans drafted in forum); Grobark v. Addo Mach. Co., 16 Ill.2d 426, 158 N.E.2d 73 (1959) (distributor denied jurisdiction over manufacturer in suit for manufacturer's breach of exclusive distributorship agreement); Adcock v. Surety Research & Inv. Corp., 344 So.2d 969 (La.1977) (legal drafting); Lakeside Bridge & Steel Co. v. Mountain State Constr. Co., Inc., 597 F.2d 596 (7th Cir.1979), cert. denied, 445 U.S. 907, 100 S.Ct. 1087, 63 L.Ed.2d 325 (1980) (with dissent by White, J. that cites sharp split of authority in federal circuit and state courts) (violation of due process to exercise jurisdiction over buyer of

It is more difficult to justify jurisdiction over the defendant based upon refusal to perform a contract in the forum if the defendant's performance was not the quid pro quo for the plaintiff's performance in the forum over a substantial period of time.[733] One circumstance in which courts have upheld jurisdiction over the nonperforming defendant is that in which the defendant is an out-of-state insurance company insuring persons or risks in the forum and the nonperformance consists of the failure to pay a claim made by an insured who lives in the forum.[734] It may also be reasonable to assert jurisdiction over a defendant who refuses to perform in the forum if the performance that the defendant has promised would require the physical presence of the defendant in the forum over a substantial period of time.[735] Even if the defendant then breaks the contract and does not come to the forum, the defendant was contemplating contacts there that are so substantial that it may be reasonable to require defense there of a suit flowing from the failure to perform.

If, however, the performance that the defendant has refused to make in the forum is a single act, quickly accomplished, such as payment to the plaintiff, and the payment is not for services that the plaintiff has performed in the forum over a substantial period of time, courts are

custom goods if contract did not require plaintiff to perform in the forum); Branstrom & Associates, Inc. v. Community Memorial Hospital, 296 Minn. 366, 209 N.W.2d 389 (1973) (architectural services); Glassman v. Hyder, 23 N.Y.2d 354, 296 N.Y.S.2d 783, 244 N.E.2d 259 (1968) (forum resident denied jurisdiction over nonresident owners of real estate situated outside the forum in suit for services the plaintiff performed in the forum in obtaining an offer to purchase the property); Pecot, Inc. v. Sirianni, 295 Pa.Super. 462, 441 A.2d 1324 (1982) (even though skylight custom made); U–Anchor Advertising, Inc. v. Burt, 553 S.W.2d 760 (Tex.1977), cert. denied, 434 U.S. 1063, 98 S.Ct. 1235, 55 L.Ed.2d 763 (1978) (advertising signs constructed in forum for placement elsewhere); cf. Blanckaert & Willems PVBA v. Trost, [1982] 2 C.M.L.R. 1 (Ct. of Just. of European Communities, 3d Chamber, 1981) (under Brussels Convention, an agent cannot sue for commissions where the agent acts but must sue where the principal is in business).

733. See Patterson v. Dietze, Inc., 764 F.2d 1145 (5th Cir.1985) (finder cannot recover in Texas for services performed in Mexico); Union Ski Co. v. Union Plastics Corp., 548 P.2d 1257 (Utah 1976) (failure to deliver goods). But see Runnels v. TMSI Contractors, Inc., 764 F.2d 417 (5th Cir.1985) (employee solicited in forum has jurisdiction over Saudi Arabian employer for breach of employment contract); N.K. Parrish, Inc. v. Schrimscher, 516 S.W.2d 956 (Tex.Civ.App.1974) (failure to deliver crop to plaintiff in New Mexico).

734. See McGee v. International Life Ins. Co., 355 U.S. 220, 78 S.Ct. 199, 2 L.Ed.2d 223 (1957); Wolfman v. Modern Life Ins. Co., 352 Mass. 356, 225 N.E.2d 598, appeal dism'd, want of substantial federal question, 389 U.S. 153, 88 S.Ct. 689, 19 L.Ed.2d 354 (1967) (*McGee* extended to assignee of policy to whom the defendant insurer delivered a copy of the policy and with whom the insurer corresponded); cf. Travelers Health Ass'n v. Virginia, 339 U.S. 643, 70 S.Ct. 927, 94 L.Ed. 1154 (1950) (forum state has jurisdiction to issue cease and desist order against out-of-state insurer doing a mail-order business in the forum); Zacharakis v. Bunker Hill Mut. Ins. Co., 281 App.Div. 487, 120 N.Y.S.2d 418 (1st Dept.1953) (jurisdiction upheld although property insured was not in the forum, but insurer had delivered the insurance policy to a broker in the forum and the insured was a forum resident). On the other hand, Transwestern Gen'l Agency v. Morgan, 526 P.2d 1186 (Utah 1974) held that in a suit for recovery of a premium, the insurer may not, without other contacts, obtain jurisdiction over a policyholder in the state where the insurer is incorporated.

735. See Mid–America, Inc. v. Shamaiengar, 714 F.2d 61 (8th Cir.1983); *Developments*, 73 Harv. L. Rev. at 927. That the actions of an agent may confer jurisdiction over an undisclosed principal, see Stripling v. Jordan Prod. Co., 234 F.3d 863 (5th Cir. 2000).

divided as to whether this failure to perform is a basis for in personam jurisdiction over the defendant,[736] unless the defendant has some other nexus with the forum[737] that would make the exercise of jurisdiction reasonable. If the defendant is a buyer to whom the plaintiff-seller has

736. See, e.g., Bond Leather Co., Inc. v. Q.T. Shoe Mfg. Co., Inc., 764 F.2d 928 (1st Cir.1985) (over guarantor of payments from forum seller); Misco Leasing, Inc. v. Vaughn, 450 F.2d 257 (10th Cir.1971) (guarantee of rental for machines used outside forum); Sibley v. Superior Court, 16 Cal.3d 442, 128 Cal.Rptr. 34, 546 P.2d 322, cert. denied, 429 U.S. 826, 97 S.Ct. 82, 50 L.Ed.2d 89 (1976) (guarantee of payments from business in Georgia); Moore v. Evans, 196 So.2d 839 (La.App.3d Cir.), writ refused, 250 La. 895, 199 So.2d 914 (1967) (refuse to recognize Texas judgment rendered against Louisiana citizen who had signed a promissory note payable in Texas); Basic Food Indus., Inc. v. Eighth Jud. Dist. Ct., 94 Nev. 111, 575 P.2d 934 (1978) (guarantee payment of debt); Barnes v. Wilson, 580 P.2d 991 (Okl.1978) (accommodation parties); State ex rel. Sweere v. Crookham, 289 Or. 3, 609 P.2d 361 (1980) (contract guarantor); cf. DeLear v. Rozel Packing Corp., 95 N.J.Super. 344, 231 A.2d 232 (1967) (no jurisdiction over lender in borrower's state in suit by trustee in bankruptcy of borrower to undo preferential transfers from borrower to lender). But see National Can Corp. v. K Beverage Co., 674 F.2d 1134 (6th Cir.1982) (guarantors of debtors of forum business); Lewis & Eugenia Van Wezel Foundation, Inc. v. Guerdon Indus., Inc., 450 F.2d 1264 (2d Cir.1971) (replacement notes); Alabama Waterproofing Co. v. Hanby, 431 So.2d 141 (Ala.1983); Tucker v. Vista Fin. Corp., 192 Colo. 440, 560 P.2d 453 (1977) (co-maker); Kagin's Numismatic Auctions, Inc. v. Criswell, 284 N.W.2d 224 (Iowa 1979) (payment for services largely performed outside the forum); Unicon Investments v. Fisco, Inc., 137 N.J.Super. 395, 349 A.2d 117 (1975) (guarantee payments for lease of forum property, collecting authority); Gubitosi v. Buddy Schoellkopf Prod., Inc., 545 S.W.2d 528 (Tex.Civ.App.1976) (guarantee payment of notes).

737. For cases upholding jurisdiction over a defendant who has refused to perform a contract in the forum when the defendant has some other nexus with the forum rendering the exercise of jurisdiction reasonable, see, e.g., Hirschkop & Grad, P.C. v. Robinson, 757 F.2d 1499 (4th Cir.1985) (over client who went to forum to hire plaintiff attorney); August v. HBA Life Ins. Co., 734 F.2d 168 (4th Cir.1984) (defendant insurer mailed new rider to plaintiff who had moved to forum); Southwest Offset, Inc. v. Hudco Publishing Co., Inc., 622 F.2d 149 (5th Cir.1980) (defendant sent copy and returned proofs to forum printer); Elefteriou v. Tanker Archontissa, 443 F.2d 185 (4th Cir.1971) (wages of injured seaman whose ship delivered him to the forum for medical treatment); Gladbach v. Sparks, 468 So.2d 143 (Ala.1985) (over maker of note executed in forum); Giger v. District Ct., 189 Colo. 305, 540 P.2d 329 (1975) (guarantee induces lease of forum realty); Compania de Astral, S.A. v. Boston Metals Co., 205 Md. 237, 107 A.2d 357 (1954), cert. denied, 348 U.S. 943, 75 S.Ct. 365, 99 L.Ed. 738 (1955) (some of contract negotiations were in the forum and the defendant's representative came to the forum with an escrow deposit to deliver the contract to the plaintiff for the plaintiff's signature and to inspect the ships being sold); Carlson Corp. v. University of Vermont, 380 Mass. 102, 402 N.E.2d 483 (1980) (defendant came to forum to sign construction contract); Dahlberg Co. v. Western Hearing Aid Center, 259 Minn. 330, 107 N.W.2d 381, cert. denied 366 U.S. 961, 81 S.Ct. 1921, 6 L.Ed.2d 1253 (1961) (the defendant had been in the forum to negotiate and sign the contract for the goods sold to defendant and to execute the notes on which suit is brought); Town of Haverhill v. City Bank & Trust Co., 119 N.H. 409, 402 A.2d 185 (1979) (over escrow agent for payments to improve forum realty); Parke–Bernet Galleries, Inc. v. Franklyn, 26 N.Y.2d 13, 308 N.Y.S.2d 337, 256 N.E.2d 506 (1970) (bidding over telephone during auction in forum with assistance of plaintiff's employee); State ex rel. Ware v. Hieber, 267 Or. 124, 515 P.2d 721 (1973) (guarantee is part of business transaction with substantial forum contacts); In Matter of All–Star Ins. Corp., 110 Wis.2d 72, 327 N.W.2d 648, appeal dism'd for want of substantial federal question, 461 U.S. 951, 103 S.Ct. 2419, 77 L.Ed.2d 1309 (1983) (receiver over insurer's agents). But see Dollar Savings Bank v. First Security Bank of Utah, N.A., 746 F.2d 208 (3d Cir.1984) (no jurisdiction over commercial borrower where funds originated and were payable); Gordon v. Granstedt, 54 Hawaii 597, 513 P.2d 165 (1973) (refuse to give full faith and credit to California judgment for share of estate erroneously distributed in California to Hawaiian defendant); Dent–Air, Inc. v. Beech Mountain Air Service, 332 N.W.2d 904 (Minn.1983) (no jurisdiction over lessor despite series of leases of plaintiff's airplanes); Dahnken, Inc. v. Marshinsky, 580 P.2d 596 (Utah 1978) (no jurisdiction over person who purchased ring in forum store but was mistakenly charged less than correct price).

shipped goods from the forum, most courts have refused to compel the buyer to defend there a suit for the price, if the buyer has no other contacts with the forum and if the goods were not custom-made to the buyer's specifications.[738] One reason given is that it would be inconvenient for the buyer to defend in the forum on the basis of a breach of warranty that was evidenced in the state where the buyer used the goods.[739] The unreasonableness of jurisdiction over the nonresident buyer who refuses to pay is increased if the buyer is not a merchant, but a consumer, for whom the sale is not part of an interstate commercial transaction for pecuniary gain.[740] It is more reasonable to subject those who profit from interstate commercial transactions to the expense of defending suits against them based on those transactions and brought in distant forums than it is to impose this expense on those who do not earn their income by engaging in interstate transactions. Moreover, the claim against the consumer is unlikely to be sufficiently large to make it practical for the consumer to defend it away from home.[741]

---

738. For cases rejecting jurisdiction over merchant buyers and lessees, see, e.g., Colonial Leasing Co. v. Pugh Bros. Garage, 735 F.2d 380 (9th Cir.1984) (lessee, and consent to jurisdiction invalid in contact of adhesion); Hydrokinetics, Inc. v. Alaska Mechanical, Inc., 700 F.2d 1026 (5th Cir.1983), cert. denied, 466 U.S. 962, 104 S.Ct. 2180, 80 L.Ed.2d 561 (1984) (even though goods custom made); Mountaire Feeds, Inc. v. Agro Impex, S.A., 677 F.2d 651 (8th Cir.1982) (even though custom made); Al–Jon, Inc. v. Garden Street Iron & Metal, Inc., 301 N.W.2d 709 (Iowa 1981) (even though machine returned to forum for repair and forum law chosen); Architectural Woodcraft Co. v. Read, 464 A.2d 210 (Me.1983) (even though custom made, not clear whether merchant buyer); Kreisler Mfg. Corp. v. Homstad Goldsmith, Inc., 322 N.W.2d 567 (Minn.1982) (distinguishing between commercial buyers and sellers); Riverland Hardwood Co. v. Craftsman Hardwood Lumber Co., 259 La. 635, 251 So.2d 45 (1971) (merchant buyer); Neptune Microfloc, Inc. v. First Flo. Util., Inc., 261 Or. 494, 495 P.2d 263 (1972) (merchant buyer, specifically mentions goods not custom-made); NRM Corp. v. Pacific Plastic Pipe Co., 36 Ohio App.2d 179, 304 N.E.2d 248, 64 O.O.2d 114 (1973) (same); Architectural Building Components Corp. v. Comfort, 528 P.2d 307 (Okl.1974) (merchant buyer); State ex rel. Jones v. Crookham, 296 Or. 735, 681 P.2d 103 (1984) (buyer, small sum involved); Pecot, Inc. v. Sirianni, 295 Pa.Super. 462, 441 A.2d 1324 (1982) (even though custom made); Hydroswift Corp. v. Louie's Boats & Motors, Inc., 27 Utah 2d 233, 494 P.2d 532 (1972) (merchant buyer); cf. Sola Basic Industries, Inc. v. Parke County Rural Electric Membership Corporation, 70 N.C.App. 737, 321 S.E.2d 28 (1984) (for repairs of machine purchased from plaintiff). But see the following cases upholding jurisdiction: Mississippi Interstate Express, Inc. v. Transpo, Inc., 681 F.2d 1003 (5th Cir.1982) (trucking services); Empress Int'l, Ltd. v. Riverside Seafoods, Inc., 112 Ill.App.3d 149, 67 Ill.Dec. 891, 445 N.E.2d 371 (1st Dist.1983) (even though seller solicited buyer); Crane v. Rothring, 27 Mich.App. 189, 183 N.W.2d 434 (1970) (defendant purchased machinery and an automobile); Prentice Lumber Co. v. Spahn, 156 Mont. 68, 474 P.2d 141 (1970) (merchant buyer of lumber); Proctor & Schwartz, Inc. v. Cleveland Lumber Co., 228 Pa.Super. 12, 323 A.2d 11 (1974) (merchant buyer of machinery, court notes that risk of loss passed on shipment and contract selected forum law); Nicholstone Book Bindery, Inc. v. Chelsea House Publishers, 621 S.W.2d 560 (Tenn.1981), cert. denied, 455 U.S. 994, 102 S.Ct. 1623, 71 L.Ed.2d 856 (1982) (distinguishing case where buyer consumer and goods not custom made); Sorb Oil Corp. v. Batalla Corp., 32 Wn.App. 296, 647 P.2d 514 (1982) (distinguishing from consumer).

739. See Rath Packing Co. v. Intercontinental Meat Traders, Inc., 181 N.W.2d 184 (Iowa 1970) (merchant buyer); Fourth Northwestern Nat'l Bank v. Hilson Indus., Inc., 264 Minn. 110, 120, 117 N.W.2d 732, 737 (1962).

740. See Developments, 73 Harv. L. Rev. at 937.

741. See Currie, 1963 U.Ill.L.Forum at 577.

If the only contact that the defendant has with the forum is that the contract with the plaintiff was technically "made" in the forum because, for example, that is where the plaintiff has dispatched the acceptance, this contact is not a reasonable basis for in personam jurisdiction over the defendant in actions arising under the contract.[742]

§ 4.19 Ownership and Use of Property

A number of states have special long-arm sections conferring on their courts jurisdiction over a person as to causes of action arising from the person's "having an interest in, using, or possessing"[743] property in the state. Most of these statutes are limited to real property in the state, but some are not so limited.[744]

There are substantial problems of construction in determining what nexus between the defendant, the property, and the cause of action is needed to satisfy the language of the particular "property" statute involved. For example, courts have held that one who guarantees a lease does not "own, use, or possess" the real estate so as to subject the guarantor to jurisdiction in a suit to recover damages for the tenant's default,[745] but that a vendee who enters into a contract to buy realty

---

742. See the following cases denying jurisdiction: Rocke v. Canadian Auto. Sport Club, 660 F.2d 395 (9th Cir.1981) (over association that recruited plaintiff racing driver by advertising in the forum); Frank E. Basil, Inc. v. Guardino, 424 A.2d 70 (D.C.App.1980) (over employer who recruited in forum for breach of employment contract); Keats v. Cates, 100 Ill.App.2d 177, 241 N.E.2d 645 (1968) (no jurisdiction over foreign executor of decedent who had executed in the forum a contract to make a will); Compania de Astral, S.A. v. Boston Metals Co., 205 Md. 237, 255, 107 A.2d 357, 364 (1954), cert. denied, 348 U.S. 943, 75 S.Ct. 365, 99 L.Ed. 738 (1955) (dictum); Perkins v. Bartlett Constr. Co., Inc., 57 Or.App. 817, 646 P.2d 672 (1982) (suit for wages against employer who solicited employee by telephone); Sun–X Int'l Co. v. Witt, 413 S.W.2d 761 (Tex.Civ.App.1967, writ ref'd n.r.e.); cf. Mackender v. Feldia A.G., [1967] 2 Q.B. 590, 599 (Ct. of App.1966) (reliance on a rule of court conferring jurisdiction in an action affecting a contract "made within the jurisdiction" is "a claim which conflicts with the general principles of comity between civilized nations"). But cf. Frank E. Basil, Inc. v. Industrial Comm'n of Ariz., 130 Ariz. 172, 634 P.2d 984 (App.1981) (jurisdiction to enforce workers' compensation on behalf of employee hired in forum); Davis Metals, Inc. v. Allen, 230 Ga. 623, 198 S.E.2d 285 (1973) (jurisdiction over former employee for breach of no competition agreement when employee resided in forum at time of making and worked for employer in forum); Sifers v. Horen, 385 Mich. 195, 188 N.W.2d 623 (1971) (jurisdiction over attorney hired in forum to work in another state, some legal services performed in forum); Pierce v. Foley Bros., Inc., 283 Minn. 360, 168 N.W.2d 346 (1969) (state in which employee was resident and present when he accepted over the telephone a contract of employment, has personal jurisdiction over the employer in a workers' compensation proceeding to compensate the employee for injuries suffered on the job in another state); George Reiner & Co. v. Schwartz, 41 N.Y.2d 648, 394 N.Y.S.2d 844, 363 N.E.2d 551 (1977) (Massachusetts salesman signed employment contract in New York, coming to New York at request and expense of plaintiff).

743. See, e.g., Unif. Interstate & Int'l P. Act § 1.03(a)(5); Pa.C.S.A. tit. 42 § 5322(a)(5); Va.Code § 8.01–328.1(A)(6). Some states substitute "owns" or "ownership" for "having an interest in." See, e.g., N.Y.—McKinney's C.P.L.R. § 302(a)(4) ("owns").

744. See, e.g., Tenn.Code Ann. § 20–2–214(a)(3) ("ownership or possession of any interest in property"). The Wisconsin long-arm statute, in the detail that typifies it, refers with regard to different actions, to "real property," "tangible property" and "any asset or thing of value." Wis.Stat.Ann. § 801.05(6).

745. Weinstein v. Talevi, 4 Conn.Cir. 330, 231 A.2d 660 (1966).

thereby acquires "an interest in" the property so as to be subject to jurisdiction in a suit to recover damages for breach of the contract.[746]

Special long-arm statutes relating to actions arising from interests in or the use of property and the construction problems that they cause seem unnecessary. So far as these statutes provide a specifically-affiliating basis for jurisdiction in actions related to the interest in or use of the property specified in the statute, it would seem that jurisdiction could usually be based on properly drafted "tort"[747] or "contract"[748] long-arm provisions without need for an additional special "property" provision. If the defendant's dealings with property in the forum are so extensive and continuous that it is reasonable for these dealings to provide a generally-affiliating basis for jurisdiction over the defendant as to causes of action unrelated to the property or to dealings with it, a "doing business"[749] or "transaction of business"[750] provision would authorize jurisdiction, again without need for a special "property" provision.

§ 4.20   Long–Arm Jurisdiction in Matters of Alimony, Support, and Custody

Suppose a case in which a husband and wife have lived for a substantial time in state F, their marital domicile. There are minor children of the marriage also living with their parents in state F. Then the father leaves F and does not return. The mother, who has remained in F with the children, sues for divorce in F and also seeks alimony, support, and custody of the children.

F, as the wife's domicile,[751] has jurisdiction to grant her a divorce.[752] In order to make a decree for alimony or support that is personally

---

746.   See Manley v. Fong, 734 F.2d 1415 (10th Cir.1984) (suit for purchase price); Quasha v. Shale Development Corp., 667 F.2d 483 (5th Cir.1982) (damages for breach); Dwyer v. District Court, 188 Colo. 41, 532 P.2d 725 (1975); Carmichael v. Snyder, 209 Va. 451, 164 S.E.2d 703 (1968); cf. Shellcast, Inc. v. Mechanical Equip. Co., 38 Mich.App. 182, 195 N.W.2d 913 (1972) (jurisdiction over buyer of equipment manufactured in forum with tools supplied by buyer); First Nat'l Bk. v. Collins, 372 So.2d 111 (Fla.App. 2d Dist.1979) (deficiency judgment after mortgage foreclosure); Associates Fin. Serv. v. Kregel, 550 P.2d 992 (Okl.App.1976) (jurisdiction for deficiency judgment after foreclosure of mortgage on forum land).

747.   See, e.g., Betcher v. Hay–Roe, 429 Pa. 371, 240 A.2d 501 (1968); Dubin v. Philadelphia, 34 D. & C. 61 (Phil. County 1938). But cf. Schneider v. Linkfield, 389 Mich. 608, 209 N.W.2d 225 (1973) (jurisdiction for action arising out of car accident in another state because defendant's car titled in forum and, at that time, defendant a forum resident).

748.   See, e.g., deLeo v. Childs, 304 F.Supp. 593 (D.Mass.1969) (architect sues for fee for designing and supervising construction of forum building); Hamilton Nat'l Bank v. Russell, 261 F.Supp. 145 (E.D.Tenn.1966) (jurisdiction upheld over those who made and promised to repay notes within the state, but not over those who pledged stock certificates as collateral for the loan); Bowsher v. Digby, 243 Ark. 799, 422 S.W.2d 671 (1968) (suit by real estate broker to recover commission for efforts to sell forum land); Carmichael v. Snyder, 209 Va. 451, 164 S.E.2d 703 (1968).

749.   Cf. Dubin v. Philadelphia, 34 Pa.D. & C. 61, 65 (1938) (jurisdiction over mortgagee under "property" statute explained in terms of "doing business").

750.   See Tandy & Wood, Inc. v. Munnell, 97 Idaho 142, 540 P.2d 804 (1975) (alternate ground in suit to recover commission for sale of forum land).

751.   That, in the United States, a wife may have a domicile separate from that of her husband for divorce and other purposes, see § 2.6.

binding on the husband, however, F must have in personam jurisdiction over the husband.[753] In the circumstances described, F as the last[754] marital domicile, at least for a reasonable time after the husband has left the state,[755] has jurisdiction over the husband to make a decree of alimony and support if it has a statute utilizing this basis for jurisdiction and containing reasonable provisions for giving the husband notice and opportunity to be heard.[756]

---

752. See § 5.2A.

753. See § 5.2E1. Personal jurisdiction over the absent spouse is also desirable to cut off collateral attacks on the finding of domicile as jurisdiction for the divorce itself. See § 5.2D. In the absence of jurisdiction over the absent spouse, relief may be available under the Uniform Interstate Family Support Act. See § 5.2E4. Section 701 of the Act authorizes a determination of paternity. 9 pt. IB U.L.A. 458 (2005).

754. Whether the forum has jurisdiction only if it is the last marital domicile is a question on which courts have divided. For cases rejecting jurisdiction when the last marital domicile was elsewhere, see Nickerson v. Nickerson, 25 Ariz.App. 251, 542 P.2d 1131 (1975), review denied, 113 Ariz. 326, 553 P.2d 1200 (1976) (seven-month residence in New York after leaving forum prevents jurisdiction, but spouses had resided in forum for only seven months while husband in service); Hoerler v. Superior Court, 85 Cal.App.3d 533, 149 Cal.Rptr. 569 (1978) (fact that marital domicile in forum for 14 years not sufficient when last residence was "briefly" in Washington where divorce obtained); Lieb v. Lieb, 53 A.D.2d 67, 385 N.Y.S.2d 569 (1976) (last marital domicile had been established for 12 years in another state, reviewing authorities). The fact that the forum was not the last marital domicile should not prevent jurisdiction if the forum was so firmly established as the former domicile that it was likely that the wife would return there, she has again made it her settled residence, and the last marital domicile was of relatively short duration. See Lontos v. Lontos, 89 Cal.App.3d 61, 152 Cal.Rptr. 271 (1979) (temporary residence in New Mexico while husband in service does not prevent jurisdiction in California which had been marital domicile and domicile of both spouses for many years, doubtful that technical domicile established in New Mexico); Haymond v. Haymond, 60 Ill.App.3d 969, 18 Ill.Dec. 274, 377 N.E.2d 563 (1978), cert. denied (alimony jurisdiction when wife returns after absence of two years); Dillon v. Dillon, 46 Wis.2d 659, 176 N.W.2d 362 (1970) (find wife never intended to make last place of cohabitation her home and therefore she continued to "reside" in the forum within the meaning of its long-arm statute).

755. See Vernon's Tex.C.A., Fam.Code Ann. § 6.305(a)(1) (2 years); Walters v. Walters, 277 Ga. 221, 586 S.E.2d 663 (2003) (jurisdiction after 3½ years); Popple v. Popple, 257 Ga. 98, 355 S.E.2d 657 (1987) (no jurisdiction 20 years after husband has left the forum); cf. Corcoran v. Corcoran, 353 So.2d 805 (Ala.Civ.App.1978) (no jurisdiction after four years, but spouses had resided in forum for only 90 days while husband in service); Stucky v. Stucky, 186 Neb. 636, 185 N.W.2d 656 (1971) (jurisdiction after 4 years, but husband had maintained contacts with the forum, he continued to support his family and make mortgage payments). But see Crowe v. Crowe, 289 S.C. 330, 345 S.E.2d 498 (1986) (jurisdiction after 20 years); cf. Jones v. Jones, 199 Conn. 287, 507 A.2d 88 (1986) (when husband's location in interim unknown, jurisdiction after 15 years to open divorce judgment rendered 5 years after husband left state and enter support order).

756. See Ex parte Brislawn, 443 So.2d 32 (Ala.1983), cert. denied, 464 U.S. 1040, 104 S.Ct. 704, 79 L.Ed.2d 168 (1984) (even though resided there for only 10 days); Whitaker v. Whitaker, 237 Ga. 895, 230 S.E.2d 486 (1976) (give full faith and credit to Florida decree divorcing husband and awarding him family residence); York v. York, 219 Neb. 883, 367 N.W.2d 133 (1985); Mizner v. Mizner, 84 Nev. 268, 439 P.2d 679, cert. denied, 393 U.S. 847, 89 S.Ct. 130, 21 L.Ed.2d 117 (1968) (give full faith and credit to alimony decree rendered by matrimonial domicile against husband who had established a new domicile); Sherwood v. Sherwood, 29 N.C.App. 112, 223 S.E.2d 509 (1976) (alimony); Rogers v. Rogers, 295 Pa.Super. 160, 441 A.2d 398 (1982); Mitchim v. Mitchim, 518 S.W.2d 362 (Tex.1975) (give full faith and credit to alimony decree); cf. Mounts v. Mounts, 181 Neb. 542, 149 N.W.2d 435 (1967) (presumes that missing husband remained domiciled in matrimonial domicile for 14 years until support decree made and gives full faith and credit to that decree).

Section 201 of the Interstate Family Support Act, enacted in all states, the District of Columbia, Guam, Puerto Rico, and the U.S. Virgin Islands provides:

(a) In a proceeding to establish, enforce, or modify a support order or to determine parentage, a tribunal of this State may exercise personal jurisdiction over a nonresident individual [or the individual's guardian or conservator] if:

(1) the individual is personally served with [citation, summons, notice] within this State;

(2) the individual submits to the jurisdiction of this State by consent, by entering a general appearance, or by filing a responsive document having the effect of waiving any contest to personal jurisdiction;

(3) the individual resided with the child in this State;

(4) the individual resided in this State and provided prenatal expenses or support for the child;

(5) the child resides in this State as a result of the acts or directives of the individual;

(6) the individual engaged in sexual intercourse in this State and the child may have been conceived by that act of intercourse;

(7) the individual asserted parentage of a child in the [putative father registry] maintained in this State by the [appropriate agency]; or

(8) there is any other basis consistent with the constitutions of this State and the United States for the exercise of personal jurisdiction.

(b) [Jurisdiction to modify a support order of an other state or a foreign country].[757]

Material in brackets permits local variation. Nineteen states and the District of Columbia omit subsection 7. The comment to the section cautions that "each subsection does contain a possibility that an overly literal construction of the statute will overreach due process." For example, the facts of *Kulko v. Superior Court*[758] literally fit subsection 5, at least with regard to the child to whom the father provided a one-way ticket to California. Nevertheless, the case held that a California court violated due process when it exercised personal jurisdiction over the father to increase his child support obligation.

With regard to the custody decree, matters are more complicated. The need for personal jurisdiction over custody contestants is discussed in section 5.3A.

---

757.   Unif. Int. Support Act (as amended). The Act was revised in 2001. As of January 1, 2008, 21 states and the District of Columbia had enacted the revised Act. The Act was further amended in 2008 to comply with the 2007 Hague Convention on the International Recovery of Child Support and Other Forms of Family Maintenance.

758.   436 U.S. 84, 98 S.Ct. 1690, 56 L.Ed.2d 132 (1978).

In the light of the uncertain state of the law, it is desirable in custody proceedings that a state that has a reasonable basis for *in personam* jurisdiction over an absent spouse also have a statute that utilizes this jurisdiction. The last marital domicile has such a reasonable basis for personal jurisdiction.[759] In *May v. Anderson*,[760] the case at the heart of the present confusion concerning the need for personal jurisdiction over custody contestants, the marital domicile had no long-arm statute that purported to exercise jurisdiction over the absent parent.[761]

§ 4.21 In Personam Jurisdiction Over Corporations

The following bases for jurisdiction over persons are also bases for jurisdiction over corporations: consent, appearance, doing business, an act done or consequences caused in the forum,[1] and ownership of property in the forum. Incorporation in the forum is an additional basis for jurisdiction over corporations that courts have recognized at common law without the need for a statute.[2] Incorporation is a generally-affiliating basis for jurisdiction that provides jurisdiction even as to causes of action unrelated to the corporation's activities in the forum.

It may be questioned whether mere incorporation in the forum should be a generally-affiliating basis for jurisdiction over a corporation if the corporation maintains no business office in the forum and conducts little or no business activities there except those required by the state of incorporation for incorporation there. It would seem, however, that voluntary incorporation in the forum would be sufficient to blunt any constitutional attack on incorporation as a generally-affiliating basis for jurisdiction.[3]

The state of incorporation should also have jurisdiction over officers or directors of a corporation in actions arising out of their conduct as officers or directors, such as actions by the corporation or by stockholders against the officers or directors for improperly conducting corporate affairs.[4] Some long-arm statutes provide for such jurisdiction.[5] The state where the corporation has its main office and where the bulk of its

---

759. See People ex rel. Loeser v. Loeser, 51 Ill.2d 567, 283 N.E.2d 884, cert. denied, 409 U.S. 1007, 93 S.Ct. 436, 34 L.Ed.2d 299 (1972); see cases cited supra notes 753–754.

760. 345 U.S. 528, 73 S.Ct. 840, 97 L.Ed. 1221 (1953). See § 5.3A.

761. See Mitchim v. Mitchim, 518 S.W.2d 362, 365 (Tex.1975) ("The lack of personal jurisdiction over the mother [in *May*] was due, however, to the absence of statutory authority"). But see Pickler v. Pickler, 5 Wn.App. 627, 489 P.2d 932 (1971) (in custody dispute, interprets *May* as indicating that last marital domicile does not have jurisdiction over the absent spouse).

1. Cf. Rees v. Mosaic Technologies, Inc., 742 F.2d 765 (3d Cir.1984) (jurisdiction based on ratified pre-incorporation activity of promoter).

2. See Restatement, Second, ch. 3, Introductory Note at 102.

3. See Developments, 73 Harv. L. Rev. at 933–34.

4. See Ellwein v. Sun–Rise, Inc., 295 Minn. 109, 203 N.W.2d 403 (1972); Folk & Moyer, *Sequestration in Delaware: A Constitutional Analysis*, 73 Colum. L. Rev. 749, 798 (1973).

5. See, e.g., Del.Code Ann. tit. 10 § 3114(a); Wis.Stat.Ann. § 801.05(8) (Wisconsin courts have jurisdiction "[i]n any action against a defendant who is or was an officer, director or manager of a domestic corporation or domestic limited liability company where the action arises out of the defendant's conduct as such officer, director or manager").

managerial functions, such as director meetings, are performed, should also have jurisdiction over officers and directors in actions related to their handling of corporate affairs. *Platt Corporation v. Platt,*[6] however, held that New York had no jurisdiction over a nonresident director of a Delaware corporation with its main office in New York. The suit against the director was to recover damages alleged to have resulted from the defendant's negligent failure to attend directors' meetings in New York and to perform other duties in New York. The *Platt* opinion seems wrong, except, perhaps, as a construction of a narrowly-drawn New York statute.

If the law of the state of incorporation provides that stockholders of a company are liable for the debts of the company to the par value of their stock, and if statutory insolvency proceedings result in an assessment against shareholders, the statutory proceedings are conclusive as to the amount of and the propriety of the assessment against all shareholders.[7] These cases are not based on the notion that the place of incorporation, without more, has *in personam* jurisdiction over stockholders. It does not have such jurisdiction.[8] Even in the assessment cases, a nonresident shareholder who was not a party to the assessment proceedings may assert a personal defense.[9] The state of incorporation may have some other basis for personal jurisdiction over shareholders such as actual, not fictitious, consent.[10]

In applying to corporations those bases for jurisdiction that are also applicable to persons, the statements made above[11] concerning those bases as applied to individuals continue to be pertinent. The landmark United States Supreme Court opinions, from and after *International Shoe,* construing due process limitations on jurisdiction, have drawn no basic distinctions between jurisdiction over individuals and over corporations.[12] Moreover, as indicated above,[13] courts have abandoned the no-

6. 17 N.Y.2d 234, 270 N.Y.S.2d 408, 217 N.E.2d 134 (1966).

7. Chandler v. Peketz, 297 U.S. 609, 56 S.Ct. 602, 80 L.Ed. 881 (1936); Broderick v. Rosner, 294 U.S. 629, 55 S.Ct. 589, 79 L.Ed. 1100 (1935); Marin v. Augedahl, 247 U.S. 142, 38 S.Ct. 452, 62 L.Ed. 1038 (1918); Converse v. Hamilton, 224 U.S. 243, 32 S.Ct. 415, 56 L.Ed. 749 (1912). But cf. Benham v. Woltermann, 201 Mont. 149, 653 P.2d 135 (1982) (no jurisdiction in liquidation proceedings over subscribers in reciprocal insurance exchange when they did not know the name of the company that issued the policy).

8. See Arden–Mayfair, Inc. v. Louart Corp., 385 A.2d 3 (Del.Ch.1978) (no jurisdiction over nonresident stockholders to determine their voting rights); Pope v. Heckscher, 266 N.Y. 114, 194 N.E. 53 (1934); Copin v. Adamson, L.R. 9 Exch. 345 (1874).

9. See Converse v. Hamilton, 224 U.S. 243, 256, 32 S.Ct. 415, 418, 56 L.Ed. 749, 754 (1912) (dictum) ("one against whom it [the assessment] is sought to be enforced is not precluded from showing that he is not a stockholder, or is not the holder of as many shares as is alleged, or has a claim against the corporation which in law or equity he is entitled to set off against the assessment, or has any other defense personal to himself").

10. See Pope v. Heckscher, 266 N.Y. 114, 194 N.E. 53 (1934).

11. See §§ 4.10, 4.12 through 4.19.

12. See McGee v. International Life Ins. Co., 355 U.S. 220, 222, 78 S.Ct. 199, 201, 2 L.Ed.2d 223, 226 (1957) ("a trend is clearly discernible toward expanding the permissible scope of state jurisdiction over foreign corporations and other nonresidents"); Owens v. Superior Ct., 52 Cal.2d 822, 831, 345 P.2d 921, 925 (1959); Thode, *In Personam Jurisdiction,* 42 Texas L. Rev. 279, 300 (1964).

tion that "doing business", as a basis for jurisdiction, rests on the power to exclude a foreign corporation from the forum and thus to require "consent" to the forum's jurisdiction in exchange for the privilege of conducting business activities there. It is more reasonable to exercise personal jurisdiction over a corporation that is widely engaged in interstate business activities and frequently is involved in litigation resulting from those activities, than it is to exercise jurisdiction over an individual who is not engaged in interstate activities. The ability of a large corporation to bear the cost of litigation in a forum distant from the center of its activities may be greater than that of an individual. But the opposite may be true; a wealthy individual engaged in multistate business ventures may be better able to defend an action in a distant forum than a small localized corporation. Perhaps in cases that lie near the due process limits on jurisdiction, subtle differences in the application of what appear to be the same bases for jurisdiction over individuals and over corporations may surface and become decisive.[14]

Cases dating from before *International Shoe Company v. Washington*[15] have held that jurisdiction over a subsidiary corporation does not provide jurisdiction over the parent corporation,[16] nor does jurisdiction over the parent provide jurisdiction over the subsidiary,[17] providing that the separation between subsidiary and parent is real and not a sham.[18]

---

13. See section 4.14, text accompanying notes 615–618; Dykes v. Reliable Furniture & Carpet Co., 3 Utah 2d 34, 36, 277 P.2d 969, 971 (1954) ("same reasoning" in applying "doing business" basis for jurisdiction to individuals and to corporations).

14. See Davis v. St. Paul–Mercury Indem. Co., 294 F.2d 641, 647 (4th Cir.1961); Moreland, *Conflict of Laws—A Rationale of Jurisdiction*, 55 Ky.L. J. 11, 22 (1966); Developments, 73 Harv. L. Rev. at 936.

15. 326 U.S. 310, 66 S.Ct. 154, 90 L.Ed. 95 (1945) (the landmark case ushering in the modern jurisdictional era, discussed in § 4.8).

16. See Cannon Mfg. Co. v. Cudahy Packing Co., 267 U.S. 333, 45 S.Ct. 250, 69 L.Ed. 634 (1925); Kramer Motors, Inc. v. British Leyland, Ltd., 628 F.2d 1175 (9th Cir.), cert. denied, 449 U.S. 1062, 101 S.Ct. 785, 66 L.Ed.2d 604 (1980); Velandra v. Regie Nationale des Usines Renault, 336 F.2d 292 (6th Cir.1964); Miller v. Trans World Airlines, Inc., 302 F.Supp. 174 (E.D.Ky.1969); Hermetic Seal Corp. v. Savoy Electronics, Inc., 290 F.Supp. 240 (S.D.Fla.1967), aff'd mem., 401 F.2d 775 (5th Cir.1968); Dolce v. Atchison, T. & S.F. Ry., 23 F.R.D. 240 (E.D.Mich.1959); Perlman v. Great States Life Ins. Co., 164 Colo. 493, 436 P.2d 124 (1968); Lit v. Storer Broadcasting Co., 217 Pa.Super. 186, 269 A.2d 393 (1970); Conn v. ITT Aetna Fin. Co., 105 R.I. 397, 252 A.2d 184 (1969).

17. See Henry v. Offshore Drilling (W.A.) Pty, Ltd., 331 F.Supp. 340 (E.D.La.1971); Blount v. Peerless Chemicals (P.R.), Inc., 316 F.2d 695 (2d Cir.), cert. denied, 375 U.S. 831, 84 S.Ct. 76, 11 L.Ed.2d 62 (1963); Associated Metals & Minerals Corp. v. S.S. Rialto, 280 F.Supp. 207 (S.D.N.Y.1967); Pauley Petroleum, Inc. v. Continental Oil Co., 43 Del.Ch. 516, 239 A.2d 629 (1968).

18. For cases in which jurisdiction over the subsidiary was held to confer jurisdiction over the parent because proper corporate separation had not been maintained see, Mas v. Orange–Crush Co., 99 F.2d 675 (4th Cir.1938); State ex rel. Grinnell Co. v. MacPherson, 62 N.M. 308, 309 P.2d 981, cert. denied 355 U.S. 825, 78 S.Ct. 32, 2 L.Ed.2d 39 (1957); Mazzoleni v. Transamerica Corp., 313 Pa. 317, 169 A. 127 (1933); Thys Co. v. Harvard Indus., 205 Pa.Super. 472, 210 A.2d 913 (1965); cf. Lakota Girl Scout Council, Inc. v. Havey Fund–Raising Management, Inc., 519 F.2d 634 (8th Cir.1975) (jurisdiction over corporation also provides jurisdiction over sole stockholder whose ego the corporation was); Reul v. Sahara Hotel, 372 F.Supp. 995 (S.D.Tex.1974) (without proper corporate separation, jurisdiction over parent provides jurisdiction over subsidiary). But see Henry v. Offshore Drilling (W.A.) Pty, Ltd., 331 F.Supp. 340 (E.D.La.1971) (jurisdiction over parent does not

Even though the subsidiary corporation maintains its identity separate from that of the parent, the subsidiary may act as an agent for the parent in conducting the parent's business. If this is so, the parent will be "doing business" in the forum through an agent and be subject to jurisdiction on that basis.[19] As stated previously, jurisdiction over a subsidiary should usually confer jurisdiction over the parent when the action is for the wrong of the parent.[20]

Closely related to the agency theory of personal jurisdiction is the conspiracy theory, which attributes the acts of a conspirator to co-conspirators "on the premise that one co-conspirator is acting as the agent of the others."[21]

§ 4.22 Partnerships and Other Unincorporated Associations

If a statute in the forum permits suit against a partnership or other unincorporated association in its firm name,[22] as distinguished from suit against the members of the association as individuals, the following bases for jurisdiction over persons are also bases for jurisdiction over partnerships and other unincorporated associations: consent, appearance, doing business, an act done or consequences caused in the forum, and ownership of property in the forum.

---

provide jurisdiction over subsidiary even without proper corporate separation unless it is shown that the subsidiary directed the local activities of the parent).

19. See Luce & Co., S. En C. v. Alimentos Borinquenos, S.A., 283 F.Supp. 81 (D. Puerto Rico 1968); Maunder v. DeHavilland Aircraft of Canada, Ltd., 102 Ill.2d 342, 80 Ill.Dec. 765, 466 N.E.2d 217, cert. denied, 469 U.S. 1036, 105 S.Ct. 511, 83 L.Ed.2d 401 (1984) (disapproving of *Cannon Mfg. Co.*, supra note 16 and accompanying text); cf. Energy Reserves Group, Inc. v. Superior Oil Co., 460 F.Supp. 483 (D.Kan.1978) (parent acting as agent for subsidiary, disapproves of *Cannon Mfg. Co.*, supra note 16 and accompanying text); Frummer v. Hilton Hotels Int'l, Inc., 19 N.Y.2d 533, 281 N.Y.S.2d 41, 227 N.E.2d 851, cert. denied, 389 U.S. 923, 88 S.Ct. 241, 19 L.Ed.2d 266 (1967) (one subsidiary held to be "doing business" for another); Brilmayer & Paisley, *Personal Jurisdiction and Substantive Legal Relations: Corporations, Conspiracies, and Agency*, 74 Cal. L. Rev. 1, 2–4 (1986) (discussing current viability of *Cannon*).

20. See § 4.8A(1)(E) text accompanying notes 524–528.

21. Mackey v. Compass Marketing, Inc., 391 Md. 117, 129, 892 A.2d 479, 486 (2006) (collecting authority of states that accept and reject the conspiracy theory of personal jurisdiction).

22. See United Mine Workers of America v. Coronado Coal Co., 259 U.S. 344, 385, 42 S.Ct. 570, 574, 66 L.Ed. 975, 984 (1922), which held that plaintiff could sue labor union as unincorporated associations for treble damages for violation of anti-trust laws because provision for such suits was contained in federal anti-trust legislation: "Undoubtedly at common law an unincorporated association of persons was not recognized as having any other character than a partnership in whatever was done, and it could only sue or be sued in the names of its members, and their liability had to be enforced against each member."

The Court indicated that a properly drafted statute could permit suit against an unincorporated association. Id. at 390–92, 42 S.Ct. at 576, 66 L.Ed. at 986–87.

That a statute may permit service on a partnership to be made on an agent of the partnership who is not a partner, see Esteve Bros. & Co. v. Harrell, 272 F. 382 (5th Cir.1921). See also Summa Corp. v. Lancer Indus., Inc., 577 P.2d 136 (Utah 1978) (service on general partner is service on limited partnership); Nutri–West v. Gibson, 764 P.2d 693 (Wyo.1988) (acquire jurisdiction over partnership by serving partner in forum, but not over other partners in their individual capacity). But cf. Lurie v. 8182 Maryland Associates, 282 Mont. 455, 938 P.2d 676 (1997) (do not have jurisdiction over limited partnership simply because a limited partner resides in forum).

§ 4.23 The Time at Which a Basis for Jurisdiction Must Exist

Must the defendant's nexus with the forum, which is used as the basis for jurisdiction, continue to exist at the time process is served on the defendant? The answer depends on the basis for jurisdiction that is utilized.

If the defendant's personal presence within the forum is used as a generally-affiliating basis for jurisdiction, the defendant must be served while still in the forum.[23] If actual consent is used as the basis for jurisdiction (as compared with "consent" as an inaccurate circumlocution to describe some other distinct basis for jurisdiction) jurisdiction must be exercised within the terms of the consent and before it is withdrawn.[24] If the defendant's domicile in the forum is used as a generally-affiliating basis for jurisdiction, this jurisdiction must be exercised while the defendant is still domiciled in the forum.[25] Former Section 417 of the California Code of Civil Procedure, now repealed, did provide for jurisdiction over a person who "was a resident of this State (a) at the time of the commencement of the action, or (b) at the time that the cause of action arose, or (c) at the time of service."[26] Cases involving this statute, in which courts have upheld actions commenced after the defendant was no longer domiciled in California, however, are cases in which there existed a constitutional basis for jurisdiction quite apart from the defendant's domicile.[27] In *Owens v. Superior Court*,[28] for example, the plaintiff sued the defendant in California for injuries that the plaintiff had sustained in California as a result of a bite by the defendant's dog. Before the action was commenced, the defendant had moved from California to Arizona. In approving of service under section 417 on a defendant "resident" in California "at the time that the cause of action arose," Judge Traynor said: "In the present case the cause of action arose out of defendant's activities in this state, namely, his ownership and possession of the offending dog. This alone is sufficient under the Due Process Clause to permit the courts of this state to assert personal jurisdiction over him."[29]

---

23. See Restatement, Second, § 28, comment *a*.

24. See Restatement, Second, § 32, comment *h*.

25. See Lucini v. Mayhew, 113 R.I. 641, 647, 324 A.2d 663 (1974) (both parties forum residents when car accident occurred outside the state, but defendant moved before action brought). But cf. Schneider v. Linkfield, 389 Mich. 608, 209 N.W.2d 225 (1973) (jurisdiction in similar case based on fact defendant's car was titled in forum at the time of the accident).

26. West's Ann.Cal.Code Civ.Proc. § 417 (1967), repealed Cal.Stat.1969, c. 1610, § 21.

27. For cases from other jurisdictions finding bases other than residence for exercising jurisdiction over persons who have moved from the forum since the cause of action arose, see Geelhoed v. Jensen, 277 Md. 220, 352 A.2d 818 (1976) (acts of criminal conversation committed outside the state but with a forum wife); Schneider v. Linkfield, 389 Mich. 608, 209 N.W.2d 225 (1973); Cooke v. Yarrington, 62 N.J. 123, 299 A.2d 400 (1973) (defendant is former resident who collided with another resident in Pennsylvania, jurisdiction based on facts of New Jersey car registry, driver's license, and continued visits to the forum).

28. 52 Cal.2d 822, 345 P.2d 921 (1959).

29. Id. at 830, 345 P.2d at 924. See also Crocker v. Crocker, 103 Ariz. 497, 446 P.2d 226 (1968) (California had jurisdiction, in conjunction with divorce decree, to render money

Doing business in the forum, an act done or consequences caused there, or the ownership or use of property in the forum, when used as specifically-affiliating bases for jurisdiction (in actions that arose out of the business, the act or consequences, or the ownership or use of property) may be utilized as bases for jurisdiction after the business has ceased, the act is completed, and the property is no longer owned or used. Moreover, when these specifically-affiliating bases for jurisdiction confer jurisdiction over a person, they also may be utilized to obtain jurisdiction over that person's executor or administrator, if that person dies before suit is brought or pendente lite.[30] This is so despite the "general rule ... that jurisdiction does not exist to sue a foreign administrator, and that he must be sued in the jurisdiction issuing his letters."[31] Many of the modern long-arm statutes wisely provide for jurisdiction over the personal representative of a deceased defendant.[32]

When "doing business" is used as a generally-affiliating basis for jurisdiction (in a cause of action not arising from the business activities in the forum) jurisdiction must be exercised while the defendant is still doing business in the forum and doing it in a manner that makes it reasonable to use the continued activity there as a generally-affiliating basis for jurisdiction.[33]

---

judgment binding on husband who had left California before being served); Allen v. Superior Court, 41 Cal.2d 306, 259 P.2d 905 (1953) (action arising from automobile accident in California, defendant served after he had moved to Oregon); Mizner v. Mizner, 84 Nev. 268, 439 P.2d 679, cert. denied, 393 U.S. 847, 89 S.Ct. 130, 21 L.Ed.2d 117 (1968) (alimony awarded in California, which was marital domicile, in action commenced after husband had moved to Nevada); cf. DeFazio v. Wright, 229 F.Supp. 111 (D.N.J.1964) (combination of injury from boat collision in the forum and defendant's residence there at the time of injury makes it clear that there is a constitutional basis for jurisdiction over the defendants in an action arising from the collision, even though the defendants moved to another state before they were served).

30. See Crosson v. Conlee, 745 F.2d 896 (4th Cir.1984), cert. denied, 470 U.S. 1054, 105 S.Ct. 1759, 84 L.Ed.2d 822 (1985); Brooks v. National Bank of Topeka, 251 F.2d 37 (8th Cir.1958) (collecting authority under non-resident motorist statutes); Hayden v. Wheeler, 33 Ill.2d 110, 210 N.E.2d 495 (1965) (automobile accident); Williams v. Carter Bros. Co., 390 S.W.2d 873 (Ky.1965) (automobile accident); Rosenfeld v. Hotel Corporation of America, 20 N.Y.2d 25, 281 N.Y.S.2d 308, 228 N.E.2d 374 (1967) (executor substituted for non-resident who died pendente lite in action arising from his transaction of business in the forum).

31. Day v. Wiswall, 11 Ariz.App. 306, 464 P.2d 626, 633 (1970). See also Restatement, Second, § 358: "An action may be maintained against a foreign executor or administrator upon a claim against the decedent when the local law of the forum authorizes suit in the state against the executor or administrator and (a) suit could have been maintained within the state against the decedent during his lifetime because of the existence of a basis of jurisdiction, other than mere physical presence ..., or (b) the executor or administrator has done an act in the state in his official capacity."

32. See, e.g., Smith–Hurd Ill.Ann.Stat., ch. 735, § 5/2–209(a); Wis.Stat.Ann. § 801.05(12).

33. See Klinghoffer v. S.N.C. Achille Lauro, 937 F.2d 44, 52 (2d Cir. 1991) (general "personal jurisdiction depends on the defendant's contacts with the forum state at the time the lawsuit was filed"); Sevits v. McKiernan–Terry Corp., 270 F.Supp. 887 (S.D.N.Y.1967); Keech v. Lapointe Machine Tool Co., 200 N.J.Super. 177, 491 A.2d 10 (App.Div.1985); cf. Radigan v. Innisbrook Resort & Golf Club, 142 N.J.Super. 419, 361 A.2d 610 (Law Div.1976), modified on other grounds, 150 N.J.Super. 427, 375 A.2d 1229 (1977) (solicitation of business in forum after forum resident injured at defendant's resort is sufficient to provide jurisdiction); PHC–Minden, L.P. v. Kimberly–Clark Corp., 235 S.W.3d 163, 169

§ 4.24 In Rem and Quasi In Rem Jurisdiction Defined

A court may have judicial jurisdiction to affect the interest of a person in tangible or intangible property even though the court does not have *in personam* jurisdiction over the person whose interest is being affected. This exercise of judicial jurisdiction to affect a person's interest in property is often spoken of as "judicial jurisdiction over things"[34]—a loose and perhaps misleading method of labeling the relevant concepts. All exercises of judicial jurisdiction affect the interests of persons.[35] A court, however, may have a nexus with property that makes it reasonable to affect the interest of a person in that property although the court does not have a nexus with the person that would make it reasonable to render a judgment *in personam* binding that person beyond an interest in the property involved.[36] For example, the situs has judicial jurisdiction to discharge a mortgage lien on land even though that state's long-arm statute does not provide *in personam* jurisdiction over the mortgagee so as to be able to discharge or otherwise affect the underlying indebtedness that the mortgage secures.[37]

The central question as to the exercise of in rem and quasi in rem jurisdiction is: when does a court have a nexus with property that is sufficient to make it reasonable to affect the interest of a person in the property even though the court does not have *in personam* jurisdiction over the person whose interest the court affects? If the court purports to affect the interests in property of only a specific named person or of specific named persons it is said to be exercising jurisdiction "quasi in rem." If the court purports to affect the interest in property of all persons in the world, whether or not named in the proceedings, as for example, in an action under a land title registration act,[38] the court is said to be exercising jurisdiction "in rem."[39] The same nexus with

---

(Tex. 2007) (for determining whether plaintiff is doing sufficient business in the forum to be subject to general jurisdiction, "the relevant period ends at the time suit is filed").

34. See, e.g., Restatement, Second, ch. 3, topic 2, caption.

35. See Tyler v. Judges of the Ct. of Registration, 175 Mass. 71, 76, 55 N.E. 812, 814 (Holmes, C.J.), writ dism'd, 179 U.S. 405, 21 S.Ct. 206, 45 L.Ed. 252 (1900); von Mehren & Trautman, 79 Harv. L. Rev. at 1135; Restatement, Second, ch. 3, topic 2, Introductory Note at 190.

36. See Freeman v. Alderson, 119 U.S. 185, 7 S.Ct. 165, 30 L.Ed. 372 (1886); In re Estate of Reed, 233 Kan. 531, 664 P.2d 824, cert. denied, 464 U.S. 978, 104 S.Ct. 417, 78 L.Ed.2d 354 (1983).

37. See Combs v. Combs, 249 Ky. 155, 60 S.W.2d 368 (1933); Fitch v. Huntington, 125 Wis. 204, 102 N.W. 1066 (1905); cf. Riley v. New York Trust Co., 315 U.S. 343, 62 S.Ct. 608, 86 L.Ed. 885 (1942) (although Georgia probate court could affect assets in Georgia in rem, assets outside the state are affected only in personam as to parties to the Georgia proceeding or their privies, New York administrator of the state not bound by Georgia finding of domicile at death); Freeman v. Alderson, 119 U.S. 185, 7 S.Ct. 165, 30 L.Ed. 372 (1886); Prudential Ins. Co. v. Berry, 153 S.C. 496, 151 S.E. 63 (1930) (land situs can foreclose equity of buyer but not grant specific performance or damages against the buyer). But see Associates Fin. Serv. v. Kregel, 550 P.2d 992 (Okl.App.1976) (interest in land in forum permits personal jurisdiction for deficiency judgment after foreclosure of mortgage).

38. See Tyler v. Judges of the Ct. of Registration, 175 Mass. 71, 55 N.E. 812, writ of error dism'd, 179 U.S. 405, 21 S.Ct. 206, 45 L.Ed. 252 (1900).

39. See Shaffer v. Heitner, 433 U.S. 186, 194 n.17, 97 S.Ct. 2569, 2577 n.17, 53 L.Ed.2d 683, 694 n.17 (1977): "A judgment *in rem* affects the interest of all persons in designated

property that would make it reasonable to exercise quasi in rem jurisdiction will make it reasonable to exercise in rem jurisdiction. The difference is in the number of persons whose interests are affected and in the kind of notice and opportunity to be heard that is reasonable.

§ 4.25 The Nexus That Makes the Exercise of In Rem or Quasi In Rem Jurisdiction Reasonable

A state that is the situs of land has jurisdiction to affect interests in the land.[40] A state that is the situs of a chattel has jurisdiction to affect interests in the chattel,[41] except, perhaps, when the fact that the goods are in the course of transit through the state in interstate commerce would make the exercise of jurisdiction unreasonable.[42] A state probably has judicial jurisdiction to affect interests in a chattel situated there, even though the title to the chattel is embodied in a document, such as a negotiable warehouse receipt or other document of title, and even though the document of title is not in the state.[43] But a state will elect not to attempt to affect interests in a chattel if the title is embodied in a document and the document is outside the state.[44] The state where a document of title to a chattel,[45] or a document embodying intangible rights,[46] such as a negotiable bond or note, is situated, has jurisdiction to affect interests in that chattel or those intangible rights. A state will rarely attempt to affect intangible rights that are not embodied in a document,[47] with the important exception of garnishment of debts.

---

property. A judgment *quasi in rem* affects the interests of particular persons in designated property." See also State ex rel. Hill v. District Ct., 79 N.M. 33, 34, 439 P.2d 551, 552 (1968): "The cause is plainly *quasi in rem,* the generally-accepted definition being: That which affects only the interests of particular persons in specific property as distinguished from proceedings in rem which determine interests in specific property as against the whole world." See also, Freeman v. Alderson, 119 U.S. 185, 187, 7 S.Ct. 165, 166, 30 L.Ed. 372, 373 (1886) ("quasi in rem"). But see A. Ehrenzweig and D. Louisell, Jurisdiction in a Nutshell 47 (2d Ed.1968) (would use "quasi in rem" only for attachment actions and "in rem" for actions to determine disputes over interests in property whether these latter actions affected the interests of particular persons or of all persons).

40. See Arndt v. Griggs, 134 U.S. 316, 10 S.Ct. 557, 33 L.Ed. 918 (1890); State ex rel. Hill v. District Ct., 79 N.M. 33, 34, 439 P.2d 551, 552 (1968).

41. See Restatement, Second, § 60.

42. Id.; cf. Wilcox v. Richmond, F. & P. R.R., 270 F.Supp. 454 (S.D.N.Y.1967) (finds that attachment of railroad's property did not create an undue interference with the conduct of the railroad's interstate business).

43. See Restatement, Second, § 62, comment *c*.

44. See Uniform Commercial Code § 7–602.

45. See Restatement, Second, § 62.

46. See Hanson v. Denckla, 357 U.S. 235, 78 S.Ct. 1228, 2 L.Ed.2d 1283 (1958) (Florida did not have in rem jurisdiction over a trust consisting of stock, bonds, and notes because it was not the situs of these documents).

47. See Glassman v. Hyder, 23 N.Y.2d 354, 296 N.Y.S.2d 783, 244 N.E.2d 259 (1968) (cannot attach an obligation to pay rent not yet due). But see Atkinson v. Superior Ct., 49 Cal.2d 338, 316 P.2d 960 (1957), cert. denied & appeal dism'd sub nom. Columbia Broadcasting System v. Atkinson, 357 U.S. 569, 78 S.Ct. 1381, 2 L.Ed.2d 1546 (1958) (quasi in rem jurisdiction exercised over trust being administered in another state); Blount v. Metropolitan Life Ins. Co., 190 Ga. 301, 9 S.E.2d 65 (1940) (state where insured resides has jurisdiction to change beneficiary).

Shaffer v. Heitner[48] sharply limits the use of garnishment as a basis for litigating the merits of a claim if there are no specifically or generally affiliating contacts with the forum that make it reasonable to litigate the claim there. The great case of *Harris v. Balk*[49] would be decided differently after *Shaffer* if Balk did not have sufficient business dealings in Maryland to make it reasonable for Balk's Maryland creditor, Epstein, to have personal jurisdiction over Balk in Maryland to collect the debt.[50] But there is still room left for garnishment of debts when this procedure is not used to litigate the merits of the underlying claim. One common use will be in supplementary proceedings to collect an unpaid judgment.[51] It is not clear what bases for garnishment jurisdiction over the garnishee exist beyond the traditional generally-affiliating bases of domicile, presence, doing business, and incorporation. The Court in *Harris v. Balk* indicated that a garnishment proceeding could be brought in a state if "the garnishee could himself be sued by his creditor in that state."[52] Wages may be garnished in a state where the employer is subject to general jurisdiction even though the employee is working elsewhere.[53]

---

48.   433 U.S. 186, 97 S.Ct. 2569, 53 L.Ed.2d 683 (1977) (discussed in § 4.28).

49.   198 U.S. 215, 25 S.Ct. 625, 49 L.Ed. 1023 (1905). This case held that the state in which debtor (Harris) and creditor (Balk) are located must give full faith and credit to a sister state decree garnisheeing the debt. The garnishment was based on personal service on the debtor while he was visiting the other state. The garnishment proceedings were instituted by a resident of the other state (Epstein) to whom the creditor allegedly owed money. Harris' payment to Epstein pursuant to the sister state decree was held a defense to Balk's attempt to collect from Harris.

50.   See §§ 4.14 (doing business) and 4.18 (contractual transactions); Lowenfeld, *In Search of the Intangible: A Comment on Shaffer v. Heitner,* 53 N.Y.U. L. Rev. 102, 104 (1978) (Balk's debt to Epstein was for the purchase price of goods sold by Epstein to Balk). That *Shaffer* does not limit quasi in rem jurisdiction in admiralty, see Trans–Asiatic Oil Ltd. S.A. v. Apex Oil Company, 743 F.2d 956 (1st Cir.1984).

51.   See, e.g., Tumulty v. Tumulty, 516 S.W.2d 530 (Mo.App.1974) (garnishee wages to enforce previously rendered alimony and support decree).

52.   198 U.S. at 222, 25 S.Ct. at 626, 49 L.Ed. at 1026. See, e.g., Huron Holding Corp. v. Lincoln Mine Operating Co., 312 U.S. 183, 61 S.Ct. 513, 85 L.Ed. 725 (1941) (garnishee is domestic corporation); Pierce v. Pierce, 153 Or. 248, 56 P.2d 336 (1936) (garnishee is foreign corporation authorized to do business in the forum); Lang v. Lang, 17 Utah 2d 10, 403 P.2d 655 (1965) (garnishee is foreign executor personally present in the forum); A. von Mehren & D. Trautman, The Law of Multistate Problems 694 (1965) ("The question remains whether all relationships that would ground jurisdiction in an action brought by the true defendant against his debtor are acceptable in a garnishment proceeding.... But the point has received little discussion and apparently arises only rarely in litigation"); Restatement, Second, § 68, comment c ("uncertain").

Jurisdiction to escheat intangibles is discussed in § 9.3B.

When the issue involves jurisdiction to compel the obligor to pay one claimant and not another, personal jurisdiction over the obligor is necessary. See Waite v. Waite, 6 Cal.3d 461, 99 Cal.Rptr. 325, 492 P.2d 13 (1972), overruled on another point, In re Marriage of Brown, 15 Cal.3d 838, 126 Cal.Rptr. 633, 544 P.2d 561 (1976).

53.   See, e.g., Levi Strauss Co. v. Crockett Motor Sales, Inc., 293 Ark. 502, 739 S.W.2d 157 (1987); Garrett v. Garrett, 30 Colo.App. 167, 490 P.2d 313 (1971); United Merchants & Manufacturers, Inc. v. Citizens & Southern Nat'l Bk., 166 Ga.App. 468, 304 S.E.2d 552 (1983); Williams v. Williams, 371 So.2d 297 (La.App.2d Cir.), writ denied, 373 So.2d 526 (1979); Lowenfeld, supra note 49 at 115–16. But cf. Bennett v. Arkansas, 485 U.S. 395, 108 S.Ct. 1204, 99 L.Ed.2d 455 (1988) (Social Security Act prevents Arkansas from attaching social security benefits paid to state prisoners). Contra, Williamson v. Williamson, 247 Ga. 260, 275 S.E.2d 42, cert. denied, 454 U.S. 1097, 102 S.Ct. 669, 70 L.Ed.2d 638 (1981).

The state of incorporation has jurisdiction to affect interests in the shares of the corporation,[54] but most states elect not to do so if the share certificate is in another state.[55]

Some uses of in rem and quasi in rem jurisdiction survive *Shaffer v. Heitner*.[56] For these purposes intangible property is deemed "located" at the owner's domicile.[57] Because intangible property has no physical location, this is a fictional way of stating that the courts at the domicile have jurisdiction to affect interests in the intangible property.

The Anticybersquatting Consumer Protection Act permits use of in rem jurisdiction to protect trademarks on the Internet. 15 U.S.C. § 1125(d)(2) provides:

"(2)(A) The owner of a mark may file an in rem civil action against a domain name in the judicial district in which the domain name registrar, domain name registry, or other domain name authority that registered or assigned the domain name is located if

(i) the domain name violates any right of the owner of a mark registered in the Patent and Trademark Office, or protected under subsection (a) or (c) of this section; and

(ii) the court finds that the owner—

(I) is not able to obtain in personam jurisdiction over a person who would have been a defendant in a civil action under paragraph (1); or

(II) through due diligence was not able to find a person who would have been a defendant in a civil action under paragraph (1) by—

(aa) sending a notice of the alleged violation and intent to proceed under this paragraph to the registrant of the domain name at the postal and e-mail address provided by the registrant to the registrar; and

(bb) publishing notice of the action as the court may direct promptly after filing the action.

(B) The actions under subparagraph (A)(ii) shall constitute service of process.

(C) In an in rem action under this paragraph, a domain name shall be deemed to have its situs in the judicial district in which

(i) the domain name registrar, registry, or other domain name authority that registered or assigned the domain name is located; or

(ii) documents sufficient to establish control and authority regarding the disposition of the registration and use of the domain name are deposited with the court.

---

54. See Restatement, Second, § 64(1).

55. See Uniform Commercial Code § 8–112(a) (1994 rev.). But see tit. 6 Del.Code § 8–112(a); tit. 8 Del.Code §§ 169, 324; tit. 10 Del.Code §§ 365, 366, ch. 35 (can attach certificated shares of Delaware corporations in Delaware even though certificate not in Delaware).

56. See § 4.27.

57. See GP Credit Co. v. Orlando Residence, Ltd., 349 F.3d 976 (7th Cir. 2003) (holding that the location of a legal claim is the domicile of the claim's owner).

(D)(i) The remedies in an in rem action under this paragraph shall be limited to a court order for the forfeiture or cancellation of the domain name or the transfer of the domain name to the owner of the mark.... * * * "

Harrods Ltd. v. Sixty Internet Domain Names[58] held that an English company could bring an in rem action under the statute in the U.S. jurisdiction where an Argentinean company had registered domain names that infringed Harrods' U.S.-registered trademark. The court ruled that the statute's in rem provision authorizes an action not only for claims of bad faith registration of domain names, but also for federal infringement and dilution claims.

§ 4.26   When Property Must Be Attached or Otherwise Brought Under the Court's Control

Pennoyer v. Neff[59] held that a judgment purporting to apply the defendant's interest in land to a debt was void as a quasi in rem adjudication because the plaintiff had not attached the land until after the court rendered the judgment. The opinion stated that "the jurisdiction of the court to inquire into and determine his [the defendant's] obligations at all is only incidental to its jurisdiction over the property [when there is no *in personam* jurisdiction over the defendant]. Its jurisdiction in that respect cannot be made to depend upon facts to be ascertained after it has tried the cause and rendered the judgment."[60] The Court has also held, however, that "[i]n suits for the foreclosure of a mortgage or other lien upon such property, no preliminary seizure is necessary to give the court jurisdiction. The cases in which it has been held that a seizure or its equivalent, an attachment or execution upon the property, is necessary to give jurisdiction are those where a general creditor seeks to establish and foreclose a lien thereby acquired."[61] But *Shaffer v. Heitner*[62] limits the circumstances in which a "general creditor" can seize property to litigate a claim unrelated to the property. Moreover, an injunction issued against a bank ordering it not to make payment from an account is a sufficient seizure of the account to confer in rem jurisdiction.[63]

---

58. 302 F.3d 214 (4th Cir. 2002). See also Porsche Cars North America, Inc. v. Porsche.net, 302 F.3d 248 (4th Cir. 2002) (upholding in rem proceeding by car companies against 128 registered Internet domain names to obtain relief from dilution of trademarks); Allen, *In Rem Jurisdiction from Pennoyer to Shaffer to the Anticybersquatting Consumer Protection Act*, 11 Geo. Mason L. Rev, 243, 287 (2002) ("Congress did not need to enact the ACPA's *in rem* provisions because the *International Shoe* standard, correctly applied, would have allowed United States courts to constitutionally assert jurisdiction over most alleged cybersquatters").

59. 95 U.S. 714, 24 L.Ed. 565 (1878).

60. Id. at 727–28, 24 L.Ed. at 570.

61. Roller v. Holly, 176 U.S. 398, 405, 20 S.Ct. 410, 412, 44 L.Ed. 520, 523 (1900). See also Husband R v. Wife R, 366 A.2d 1193 (Del.1976) (pre-judgment seizure not necessary in suit to divide marital property); Note, 70 Colum. L. Rev. 942, 952 (1970) (collecting authority on when pre-judgment seizure not necessary).

62. 433 U.S. 186, 97 S.Ct. 2569, 53 L.Ed.2d 683 (1977) (discussed in § 4.28).

63. Pennington v. Fourth Nat'l Bank, 243 U.S. 269, 37 S.Ct. 282, 61 L.Ed. 713 (1917). See also Union Shoe Agency, Inc. v. Beacon Shoe Mfg. Corp., 441 S.W.2d 321 (Mo.1969)

The *Pennoyer* doctrine, that quasi in rem jurisdiction to apply the defendant's interest in property to a claim against the defendant turns upon attachment of the property prior to judgment, seems debatable,[64] and in the light of *Shaffer*, may have no further application.[65] If, however, the plaintiff relies upon an attachment of property as the method of giving the defendant notice and opportunity to be heard,[66] then the plaintiff should effect the attachment at the commencement of the proceedings.

§ 4.27 Uses of In Rem Jurisdiction That Survive Shaffer v. Heitner

There are at least four uses of in rem jurisdiction that survive *Shaffer v. Heitner*.[67] First are cases in which "claims to the property itself are the source of the underlying controversy."[68] There are two slightly different circumstances in which this will occur. In one, the plaintiff is attempting to secure a pre-existing claim in the property and to establish the nonexistence of similar interests of all persons (in rem) or of particular persons (quasi in rem).[69] In the other, the plaintiff is seeking to establish his or her rights in the property. An example is the adjudication of marital property rights on divorce.[70] *Dawson–Austin v. Austin*[71] held, however, that a court does not have jurisdiction to

---

(service of process on bank named as co-defendant was sufficient to confer quasi in rem jurisdiction over funds deposited in the bank).

64. See Cooper v. Reynolds, 77 U.S. (10 Wall.) 308, 320, 19 L.Ed. 931, 933 (1870) ("Whether the writ [of attachment] should have been issued simultaneously with the institution of the suit, or at some other stage of its progress, cannot be a question of jurisdiction"); Gruwell v. Hinds, 81 S.D. 6, 130 N.W.2d 92 (1964); Hazard, *A General Theory of State–Court Jurisdiction,* 1965 Sup. Ct. Rev. 241, 260.

65. See Hodge v. Hodge, 178 Conn. 308, 422 A.2d 280 (1979) (*Pennoyer's* requirement of prior attachment is anachronistic in the light of *Shaffer*, discussed in § 4.28).

66. See Pennoyer v. Neff, 95 U.S. 714, 727, 24 L.Ed. 565, 570 (1878) ("The law assumes that property is always in the possession of its owner, in person or by agent; and it proceeds upon the theory that its seizure will inform him, not only that it is taken into the custody of the court, but that he must look to any proceedings authorized by law upon such seizure for its condemnation and sale"). But cf. Schroeder v. New York, 371 U.S. 208, 83 S.Ct. 279, 9 L.Ed.2d 255 (1962) (posting in the vicinity of an unoccupied summer home is not sufficient notice).

67. 433 U.S. 186, 97 S.Ct. 2569, 53 L.Ed.2d 683 (1977) (discussed in § 4.28).

68. Id. at 208, 97 S.Ct. at 2582, 53 L.Ed. at 700.

69. For examples see Arndt v. Griggs, 134 U.S. 316, 10 S.Ct. 557, 33 L.Ed. 918 (1890) (suit to quiet title); Vanstone v. Whitelaw, 196 So.2d 425 (Fla.1967) (action to abate nuisance on realty); State ex rel. Hill v. District Ct., 79 N.M. 33, 439 P.2d 551 (1968) (suit to set aside fraudulent conveyance); Prudential Ins. Co. v. Berry, 153 S.C. 496, 151 S.E. 63 (1930) (suit by vendor to foreclose equity of defaulting buyer). But see Bearden v. Byerly, 494 So.2d 59 (Ala. 1986) (no jurisdiction to adjudicate claim of resident that automobile she drove to the forum was a gift from decedent whose estate is being probated elsewhere).

70. For marital property cases, see, e.g., Husband R v. Wife R, 366 A.2d 1193 (Del.1976); Williams v. Williams, 121 N.H. 728, 433 A.2d 1316 (1981), appeal dism'd, 455 U.S. 930, 102 S.Ct. 1415, 71 L.Ed.2d 639 (1982); Holt v. Holt, 41 N.C.App. 344, 255 S.E.2d 407 (1979). For a different example, see Garfein v. McInnis, 248 N.Y. 261, 162 N.E. 73 (1928) (vendee's action for specific performance).

71. 968 S.W.2d 319 (Tex. 1998), cert. denied, 525 U.S. 1067, 119 S.Ct. 795, 142 L.Ed.2d 657 (1999). But cf. Abernathy v. Abernathy, 267 Ga. 815, 482 S.E.2d 265 (1997) (have

determine marital rights in property than one spouse unilaterally brought into the forum from the marital domicile.

The second surviving use of in rem jurisdiction is the adjudication of claims arising out of ownership of the property "such as suits for injury suffered on the land of an absentee owner."[72] This second use is unlikely to be important because, under these circumstances, a properly drafted long-arm statute will confer personal jurisdiction over the nonresident owner of the property.[73]

The third use will occur when the plaintiff attaches property as security for a judgment the plaintiff is seeking in another forum where there is personal jurisdiction over the defendant.[74] It may be, however, that local procedure will not permit seizing property while a suit is pending in another state.[75]

The fourth situation is that in which the plaintiff seeks enforcement of a judgment rendered by a court that had personal jurisdiction over the defendant. With regard to this fourth surviving use of quasi in rem jurisdiction, footnote 36 in *Shaffer* reads:

> Once it has been determined by a court of competent jurisdiction that the defendant is a debtor of the plaintiff, there would seem to be no unfairness in allowing an action to realize on that debt in a State where the defendant has property, whether or not that State

---

jurisdiction to determine rights of nonresident wife in Georgia property that husband purchased in Georgia after moving there from marital domicile); Restatement, Second, § 60 cmt. *d* (stating that a state will "not usually" exercise jurisdiction to affect interests in a chattel brought there without the consent of the owner).

72. *Shaffer,* 433 U.S. at 208, 97 S.Ct. at 2582, 53 L.Ed.2d at 700. At times it may be difficult to determine whether the ownership of property is sufficiently related to the cause of action. See Travelers Indem. Co. v. Abreem Corp., 122 N.H. 583, 449 A.2d 1200 (1982) (guarantor cannot attach property listed as asset by debtor to induce guarantor to issue performance bond).

73. See, e.g., Betcher v. Hay–Roe, 429 Pa. 371, 240 A.2d 501 (1968).

74. See *Shaffer,* 433 U.S. at 210, 97 S.Ct. at 2583, 53 L.Ed.2d at 701; Carolina Power & Light Co. v. Uranex, 451 F.Supp. 1044 (N.D.Cal.1977); Barclays Bank v. Tsakos, 543 A.2d 802 (D.C.App.1988); cf. ITC Entertainment, Ltd. v. Nelson Film Partners, 714 F.2d 217 (2d Cir.1983) (it is permissible to permit prejudgment attachment against nonresidents when it would not be available against residents); Note, *Attachment Jurisdiction after Shaffer v. Heitner,* 32 Stan. L. Rev. 167, 178 (1979) (if the property is to be seized pending litigation elsewhere, it should be required that "the defendant have directed the property to its location").

Any prejudgment use of quasi in rem jurisdiction must comply with the notice and opportunity to be heard requirements of the *Sniadach–Fuentes–Mitchell–North Georgia Finishing–Doehr* line of cases. See § 4.4, text accompanying notes 58–66; *Shaffer,* 433 U.S. at 210 n.34, 97 L.Ed.2d at 2583 n.34, 53 L.Ed.2d at 701 n.34; Jonnet v. Dollar Savings Bk. of City of New York, 530 F.2d 1123 (3d Cir.1976).

75. See Brittingham v. Ayala, 995 S.W.2d 199 (Tex. App.—San Antonio, 1999, rev. denied) (a Texas court has no power to enjoin defendant from transferring assets in Texas pending the outcome of a suit against defendant in Mexico). Although Grupo Mexicano de Desarrollo, S.A. v. Alliance Bond Fund, Inc., 527 U.S. 308, 119 S.Ct. 1961, 144 L.Ed.2d 319 (1999), held that federal courts have no independent power to grant pre-judgment relief to protect assets in which the plaintiff does not claim a lien or equitable interest, Federal Rule of Civil Procedure 64(a) provides that "every remedy is available that, under the law of the state where the court is located, provides for seizing a person or property to secure satisfaction of the potential judgment."

would have jurisdiction to determine the existence of the debt as an original matter.[76]

Does this statement apply to foreign arbitral awards? The federal circuits do not agree on the answer. *Glencore Grain Rotterdam B.V. v. Shivnath Rai Harnarain Co.*[77] invoked footnote 36 and stated that it would have enforced a United Kingdom arbitration award without jurisdiction over the award debtor, but affirmed dismissal because plaintiff had not identified any assets of the debtor in the jurisdiction.[78] Contrary to *Glencore Grain, Base Metal Trading, Ltd. v. OJSC "Novokuznetsky Aluminum Factory"*[79] affirmed district court rulings that dismissed a suit to enforce a Russian arbitral award and vacated an attachment of aluminum alleged to belong to the award debtor. The Fourth Circuit held that the plaintiff must have personal jurisdiction over the award debtor in order to enforce the award.[80] The plaintiff did not cite *Shaffer*'s footnote 36 to the court.[81]

When the arbitral tribunal has exercised personal jurisdiction over the award debtor in a manner that satisfies due process, U.S. courts should enforce the award against the debtor's assets without requiring a basis for personal jurisdiction over the debtor in the U.S. forum. There is no due process objection to doing so and the U.S., as a signatory of the New York Convention, has a treaty obligation to "recognize arbitral awards as binding and enforce them in accordance with [U.S.] rules of procedure."[82] A major advantage of arbitration to resolve international commercial disputes is that the award is enforceable in any of the 144 countries that, as of 21 July 2009, have ratified the New York Convention. *Base Metal* diminishes that advantage.

Even further dimming the luster of arbitration is *In the Matter of the Arbitration between Monegasque De Reassurances S.A.M. v. Nak Naftogaz of Ukraine,*[83] which affirmed a forum non conveniens dismissal

---

76. *Shaffer,* 433 U.S. at 210 n.36, 97 S.Ct. at 2583 n.36, 53 L.Ed.2d at 702 n.36; Huggins v. Deinhard, 134 Ariz. 98, 654 P.2d 32 (App.1982); Bank of Babylon v. Quirk, 192 Conn. 447, 472 A.2d 21 (1984) (no need for personal jurisdiction over the judgment debtor); Brown v. Rock, 184 Ga.App. 699, 362 S.E.2d 480 (1987). See also United States v. Morton, 467 U.S. 822, 104 S.Ct. 2769, 81 L.Ed.2d 680 (1984) (when debt is garnisheed to enforce judgment, notice to obligor relieves garnishee of the debt if garnishee pays the creditor).

77. 284 F.3d 1114 (9th Cir. 2002).

78. Id. at 1127.

79. 283 F.3d 208 (4th Cir. 2002), cert. denied, 537 U.S. 822, 123 S.Ct. 101, 154 L.Ed.2d 30 (2002).

80. Id. at 212–13. And see Dardana Ltd. v. Yugaskneftegaz, 317 F.3d 202, 206–07 (2d Cir. 2003), remanding suit to enforce Swedish arbitral award for determination of whether there is personal jurisdiction over the arbitral debtor hoping to avoid the "difficult issue" of whether jurisdiction is necessary.

81. See Base Metal Trading Ltd. v. OJSC "Novokuznetsky Aluminum Factory", 47 Fed. Appx. 73, 77 (3d Cir. 2002) (noting failure to cite footnote 36 to the 4th Circuit and rejecting arbitral creditor's attempt to advance an argument based on the footnote when the creditor had failed to make the argument in the District Court).

82. Convention on the Recognition and Enforcement of Foreign Arbitral Awards, art. III, opened for signature June 19, 1958, 21 UST 2517, 330 UNTS 3.

83. 311 F.3d 488 (2d Cir. 2002).

of an action under the New York Convention to confirm an arbitration award rendered by the International Commercial Court of Arbitration in Moscow. The original contract was between two Ukrainian companies. Plaintiff alleged personal jurisdiction over the defendants. The court held that the words of the New York Convention, "enforce them in accordance with the rules of procedure of the territory where the award is relied upon," permit a dismissal. The court might more properly have emphasized the words "enforce them," rather than the Convention's reference to the forum's "rules of procedure."[84]

It is more debatable whether *Glencore Grain* properly dismissed the suit to enforce the foreign arbitral award because the award creditor could not find assets of the debtor in the district. *Lenchyshyn v. Pelko Electric, Inc.*[85] recognized a Canadian judgment under the New York version of the Uniform Foreign Money–Judgments Recognition Act[86] and held that there is no need for personal jurisdiction over defendants in New York. The defendants contended that they had no assets in New York. The court rejected this objection: "Moreover, even if defendants do not presently have assets in New York, plaintiffs nevertheless should be granted recognition of the foreign country money judgment pursuant to [the Uniform Act], and thereby should have the opportunity to pursue all such enforcement steps *in futuro*, whenever it might appear that defendants are maintaining assets in New York, including at any time during the initial life of the domesticated Ontario money judgment or any subsequent renewal period."[87] In similar fashion a court could recognize but not enforce a foreign arbitral award.

An objection to recognition is that if the award debtor has no assets in the forum, recognition is an unfair burden on the debtor and a waste of the court's time. This objection can be eliminated by summary recognition and affording the debtor an opportunity to object to enforcement[88] when the creditor attaches the debtor's assets in the forum. Under most foreign legal systems a court may issue an order recognizing an award under the New York Convention even though the obligor does

---

84. But see Alan Scott Rau, *Provisional Relief in Arbitration: How Things Stand in the United States*, 22 J. Int'l Arb. 1, 22–23 (2005) (stating that the attempt to enforce the award against the government of Ukraine on the ground that the award debtor was Ukraine's agent or alter ego would require extensive discovery). When a country ratifies a convention, it gives a hostage to fortune and is no longer free to do some of things it could do before ratification. See Ulrich Haas, Convention on the Recognition and Enforcement of Foreign Arbitral Awards, New York, June 10, 1958, in Practitioner's Handbook on International Arbitration 473 (2002 Frank–Bernd Weigand ed.) ("the notion 'rules of procedure' is to be construed in a narrow sense").

85. 281 A.D.2d 42, 723 N.Y.S.2d 285 (2001).

86. See § 11.6.

87. *Lenchyshyn*, 281 A.D.2d at 50, 723 N.Y.S.2d at 291. Accord, Haaksman v. Diamond Offshore (Bermuda), Ltd., 260 S.W.3d 476 (Tex. App. [14th Dist.] 2008), pet. rev. denied (to recognize a Dutch judgment under the Texas Uniform Foreign Country Money–Judgment Recognition Act, it is not necessary to have personal jurisdiction over the defendant or for the defendant's property to be present in the forum).

88. Article V of the New York Convention provides bases on which signatory countries can refuse to recognize and enforce the award.

not have assets in the country subject to execution.[89] In the U.S. it is important that the award creditor be able to get a judgment recognizing the arbitral award before locating assets of the award debtor in the forum because 9 U.S.C. § 207 establishes a three-year limit for a federal court to confirm the award.[90] Moreover if the asset is an account receivable, that asset may be whisked away with the stroke a computer key.

§ 4.28   Use of Quasi In Rem Jurisdiction to Apply the Defendant's Interest in Property to a Claim Unrelated to the Property: Shaffer v. Heitner

Although, as indicated in section 4.27, four uses of quasi in rem jurisdiction remain permissible, *Shaffer v. Heitner*[91] sharply limits one classic use. Before *Shaffer,* when the plaintiff could not obtain personal jurisdiction over a defendant, common practice was to search for property of the defendant in the forum. If the plaintiff found property in the state, the plaintiff could seize the property, prove out the claim, and then apply the proceeds of the judicial sale of the property to the claim, even though this claim against the defendant was unrelated to the property.[92] This quasi in rem judgment was not binding personally on the defendant. If, for example, the amount realized from the attached property was not sufficient to satisfy the plaintiff's claim, the plaintiff might proceed again against the defendant, either in a jurisdiction where there was *in personam* jurisdiction over the defendant or in a jurisdiction in which a court had quasi in rem jurisdiction to affect the defendant's interest in other property. In this second action, the defendant, not being personally bound by the first judgment, was free to defend on any basis available and was not bound by any finding of fact on which the prior quasi in rem judgment was based. The first quasi in rem judgment was binding on a non-appearing defendant only to the extent of the defendant's interest in the property attached.[93]

In some jurisdictions, the defendant is privileged to appear specially in the quasi in rem proceeding.[94] A defendant who appears specially is

---

89. Ulrich Haas, Convention on the Recognition and Enforcement of Foreign Arbitral Awards, in Practitioner's Handbook on International Arbitration (Frank–Bernd Weigand ed. 2002) 472–73.

90. Cf. Seetransport Wiking Trader Schiffahrtsgesellschaft MBH & Co. v. Navimpex Centrala Navala, 29 F.3d 79 (2d Cir. 1994) (although too late to enforce the French arbitral award, the court may enforce the French judgment conferring exequatur on the award).

91. 433 U.S. 186, 97 S.Ct. 2569, 53 L.Ed.2d 683 (1977).

92. See Cooper v. Reynolds, 77 U.S. (10 Wall.) 308, 318, 19 L.Ed. 931, 932 (1870).

93. Id., 19 L.Ed. at 933; Restatement (Second) of Judgments § 32(1) (1982) (in an action begun by attachment, the judgment "[i]s conclusive between the parties as to the right to apply the thing to the claim"); cf. Carrington, *The Modern Utility of Quasi In Rem Jurisdiction,* 76 Harv. L. Rev. 303, 316–17 (1962) (suggesting that the defendant in a quasi in rem proceeding should be able to recover against the plaintiff for unjust enrichment if the defendant can show that the plaintiff deliberately brought a groundless claim in a forum in which it was inconvenient for the defendant to defend).

94. See Cheshire Nat'l Bank v. Jaynes, 224 Mass. 14, 112 N.E. 500 (1916); Carrington, supra note 93 at 314; Developments, 73 Harv. L. Rev. at 953.

not subject to the *in personam* jurisdiction of the forum but, neverthe-less, may defend on the merits to the extent of an interest in the property attached. If the defendant does appear specially in a quasi in rem proceeding and loses, the judgment will not, as would a personal judgment, be enforceable against the defendant in other states by simply suing on or registering[95] the first judgment and then collecting any amount of that judgment not already satisfied. The plaintiff will have to bring a new action *in personam* or quasi in rem. The defendant who appeared specially may be bound by any finding of fact necessary for the quasi in rem judgment.[96]

The major objection to this classic use of quasi in rem jurisdiction was that the presence of the defendant's property in a forum is not a reasonable basis for permitting that forum to adjudicate the merits of a claim against the defendant if the claim is so totally unrelated to the property or to anything present, done, or caused in the forum that the forum has no constitutional basis for *in personam* jurisdiction over the defendant.[97] This objection is particularly strong in the light of modern long-arm statutes that have greatly increased the plaintiff's ability to obtain *in personam* jurisdiction over the defendant in an appropriate forum.[98] *Shaffer* is the Supreme Court's response to this objection.

Shaffer was a derivative stockholder suit against the directors of a Delaware corporation.[99] The corporation was headquartered in Arizona and engaged in activities in Oregon that subjected it to criminal and civil antitrust penalties. The suit was to recover the damages to the corpora-tion resulting from the illegal activities. All of the directors were nonresi-dents of Delaware. In order to bring suit in Delaware, the plaintiff stockholder seized the directors' stock, stock options, warrants, and various other rights. The defendants made a special appearance urging that the sequestration of their property violated due process. When the defendants lost in the Delaware state courts, they sought review in the United States Supreme Court.

---

95. See Unif. Enforcement of Foreign Judgments Act (1948 Act) § 2, 13 Pt. I U.L.A. 251 (2002); cf. Revised 1964 Act § 2 ("filing"), 13 U.L.A. Pt. I 163 (2002).

96. See Restatement (Second) of Judgments § 32(3) (1982) (the judgment is "conclu-sive between the parties, in accordance with the rules of issue preclusion, as to any issues actually litigated by them and determined in the action"); cf. Developments, 73 Harv. L. Rev. at 954–55 (plaintiff who loses on the merits after defendant appears specially in quasi in rem proceeding should be barred from relitigating the same claim). But see Cheshire Nat'l Bank v. Jaynes, 224 Mass. 14, 19, 112 N.E. 500, 502 (1916) (dictum): "The plaintiff, by instituting his action and making the effectual attachment of property, offers to the defendant the alternative, first, of coming into court generally and settling all issues by submitting to the jurisdiction of the court with the attendant advantage of ending that cause of action by a final judgment, or second, of appearing specially and protecting only the property attached and settling only that question and nothing else."

97. See Currie, 1963 U.Ill.L.Forum at 583–84; von Mehren & Trautman, 70 Harv. L. Rev. at 1141; cf. Universal Adjustment Corp. v. Midland Bk., Ltd., 281 Mass. 303, 184 N.E. 152 (1933) (forum non conveniens dismissal of attachment).

98. See Carrington, supra note 93, at 306.

99. Some of the defendants were directors of a California subsidiary of the Delaware corporation. Justice Marshall disclaimed basing his opinion on this. 433 U.S. at 214 n.41, 97 S.Ct. at 2585 n.41, 53 L.Ed.2d at 704 n.41.

One might have expected the Supreme Court to have taken either of two polar approaches. The Court might have rendered judgment for the defendants on the ground that the unique Delaware rule that made Delaware the situs for sequestration purposes of stock in a Delaware corporation, even though negotiable stock certificates were located outside the state,[100] was too bizarre and unfair to withstand due process scrutiny.[101] Alternatively, the plaintiff might have prevailed on the ground that, since the state of incorporation should be able to obtain personal jurisdiction over corporate directors in suits alleging breach of their fiduciary obligations to the corporation,[102] it should not matter that Delaware chose to permit assertion of this claim by quasi in rem jurisdiction over the directors' corporate holdings rather than by personal jurisdiction over the directors.[103] The Court, however, declared the Delaware sequestration procedure a violation of due process and limited quasi in rem jurisdiction generally by declaring that "all assertions of state-court jurisdiction must be evaluated according to the standards set forth in *International Shoe* and its progeny"[104]—standards "of fair play and substantial justice."[105]

Section 4.27 discusses uses of quasi in rem jurisdiction that survive *Shaffer*. In other respects the effect of *Shaffer* is not clear. Justice Marshall's majority opinion itself notes that "[t]his case does not raise, and we therefore do not consider, the question whether the presence of a defendant's property in a State is a sufficient basis for jurisdiction when no other forum is available to the plaintiff."[106] But what is the meaning of "no other forum is available"—no forum in the U.S.,[107] no forum here

---

100. Del.Code Ann. tit. 8, § 324; id. tit. 6, § 8–317(1), now tit. 6 Del.Code § 8–112(a); tit. 8 Del.Code §§ 169, 324; tit. 10 Del.Code §§ 365, 366, ch. 35 (can attach certificated shares of Delaware corporations in Delaware even though certificate not in Delaware).

101. Justice Stevens concurred on this ground. 433 U.S. at 217–19, 97 S.Ct. at 2587–88, 53 L.Ed.2d at 706–07.

102. Justice Marshall's majority opinion casts doubt upon this assertion. Id. at 215–16, 97 S.Ct. at 2586–87, 53 L.Ed.2d at 704–05. Justice Brennan dissented from this portion of the opinion. Id. at 219–28, 97 S.Ct. at 2588–2593, 53 L.Ed.2d at 707–13. For the view that jurisdiction can be based on this ground, see § 4.21, note 4 and accompanying text.

103. See Banco Ambrosiano, S.P.A. v. Artoc Bank & Trust Ltd., 62 N.Y.2d 65, 476 N.Y.S.2d 64, 464 N.E.2d 432 (1984) (may use quasi in rem jurisdiction when, because of limited long-arm statute, personal jurisdiction is not available).

104. 433 U.S. at 212, 97 S.Ct. at 2584–85, 53 L.Ed.2d at 703.

105. Id., 97 S.Ct. at 2584, 53 L.Ed.2d at 703.

Use of a constitutionally defective statute for pre-judgment remedy may create a right to recovery under 42 U.S.C.A. § 1983 for deprivation of constitutional rights under color of state law. See Lugar v. Edmondson Oil Co., 457 U.S. 922, 102 S.Ct. 2744, 73 L.Ed.2d 482 (1982); Buller v. Buechler, 706 F.2d 844 (8th Cir. 1983) (private individuals may have good faith immunity from such a 1983 violation, but not an attorney).

106. Id. at 211 n.37, 97 S.Ct. at 2584 n.37, 53 L.Ed.2d at 702 n.37.

107. See Louring v. Kuwait Boulder Shipping Co., 455 F.Supp. 630 (D.Conn.1977) (other forum must be in the United States); Papendick v. Bosch, 389 A.2d 1315 (Del.Super.1978) (under the circumstances, a West German forum is sufficiently available); Leathers, *The First Two Years after Shaffer v. Heitner,* 40 La. L. Rev. 907, 917 (1980) (a foreign forum is sufficient); Silberman, *Shaffer v. Heitner: The End of an Era,* 53 N.Y.U. L. Rev. 33, 77 (1978) (forum abroad "might not offer sufficient protection and might thus justify an assertion of quasi in rem jurisdiction").

or abroad in which it would be reasonably convenient for the plaintiff to sue, no forum in which the plaintiff will receive a just and fair adjudication of the claim?[108] It is unlikely that the *Shaffer* reference to no other "available" forum meant "no forum in the U.S." In *Helicopteros Nacionales de Colombia v. Hall*, the court rejected an argument of "jurisdiction by necessity" by noting that it was not clear "whether suit could have been brought against all three defendants in either Colombia or Peru."[109]

Nor is *Shaffer's* application to tangible property clear. Justice Powell, in his concurring opinion, reserves judgment on applying the case to "forms of property whose situs is indisputably and permanently located within a State ... real property, in particular".[110] Justice Stevens agrees that the opinion "should not be read to invalidate *in rem* jurisdiction where real estate is involved."[111]

Moreover, suppose that a defendant has sufficient contacts with a state so that in personam jurisdiction could be asserted over him for actions arising out of those contacts, if the state had and used a proper long-arm statute. It is difficult to see the objection if the state elects instead the more restrained route of subjecting the defendant to liability for those actions only to the extent of his property found within the state.[112] *Shaffer* is not squarely opposed to this possibility because Justice Marshall suggests that Delaware did not have a basis for personal jurisdiction over the directors.[113] He also says, however, that "Dela-

---

108. See Vernon, *State–Court Jurisdiction: A Preliminary Inquiry into the Impact of Shaffer v. Heitner*, 63 Iowa L. Rev. 997, 1009 n.71 (1978) ("At a minimum, it would seem that the forum that is available must be one that is likely to administer justice evenhandedly").

109. 466 U.S. 408, 419 n.13, 104 S.Ct. 1868, 1874 n.13, 80 L.Ed.2d 404, 414 n.13 (1984).

110. *Shaffer*, 433 U.S. at 217, 97 S.Ct. at 2587, 53 L.Ed.2d at 706 (Powell, J., concurring).

111. Id. at 219, 97 S.Ct. at 2588, 53 L.Ed.2d at 707 (Stevens, J., concurring). See also Rhoades v. Wright, 622 P.2d 343 (Utah 1980), cert. denied, 454 U.S. 897, 102 S.Ct. 397, 70 L.Ed.2d 212 (1981) (*Shaffer* not applicable to attachment of land). For the view that admiralty in rem actions survive *Shaffer*, see Grand Bahama Petro. Co. v. Canadian Transp. Agencies, Ltd., 450 F.Supp. 447 (W.D.Wash.1978) (maritime attachment of defendants' bank account); Bohmann, *Applicability of Shaffer to Admiralty In Rem Jurisdiction*, 53 Tulane L. Rev. 135, 162 (1978) ("Only where a defendant does not have 'minimum contacts' with the United States as a whole will jurisdiction be defeated"); cf. Gulf & Southern Terminal Corp. v. S.S. President Roxas, 701 F.2d 1110 (4th Cir.), cert. denied, 462 U.S. 1133, 103 S.Ct. 3115, 77 L.Ed.2d 1369 (1983) (arrest of vessel by Mexican court permits extinguishing maritime liens without personal jurisdiction over lienholder); Amstar Corp. v. S/S Alexandros T., 664 F.2d 904 (4th Cir.1981) (*Sniadach* not applicable to admiralty); Merchants Nat'l Bank v. Dredge General G.L. Gillespie, 663 F.2d 1338 (5th Cir.1981), cert. dism'd, 456 U.S. 966, 102 S.Ct. 2263, 72 L.Ed.2d 865 (1982) (in rem seizure of vessel without prior hearing constitutional).

Effective August 1, 1985, Admiralty Rules of Civil Procedure B, C, and E were amended to lessen the possibility of objection to seizure of a vessel under the *Sniadach–Fuentes–Mitchell–North Georgia Finishing–Doehr* line of cases. Judicial scrutiny before issuance of an attachment is required except in exigent circumstances and in all cases a prompt post-attachment hearing is provided.

112. See Bank of America Nat. Trust & Sav. Assoc. v. GAC Properties Credit, Inc., 389 A.2d 1304 (Del.Ch.1978); Vernon, supra note 108.

113. See supra note 102 and accompanying text.

ware law bases jurisdiction, not on appellants' status as corporate fiduciaries, but rather on the presence of their property in the State."[114]

Finally, saying that "all assertions of state-court jurisdiction must be evaluated according to the standards set forth in *International Shoe* and its progeny,"[115] is not the same as saying that those standards must provide the same answer no matter what the form of jurisdiction asserted. In cases that would fall close to the due process line if full personal jurisdiction were asserted, the less drastic remedy of allowing the plaintiff to reach the defendant's assets in the state may be reasonable. There is no reason to assume that what is a reasonable nexus between the defendant and the state for one remedy is the same for another remedy.[116]

See the discussion in § 4.8, text accompanying notes 437–438, suggesting that *Shaffer* is ripe for overruling or being limited to its facts, but that an attorney may be reluctant to attempt this because of possible monetary sanctions under 43 U.S.C. § 1983 if the attempt fails.

§ 4.29   Rush v. Savchuk

Rush v. Savchuk[117] extended *Shaffer's*[118] limitation on quasi in rem jurisdiction. Savchuk, then a resident of Indiana, was injured in Indiana while a passenger in an automobile operated by Rush. State Farm insured Rush, also an Indiana resident, under a policy issued in Indiana. A year and a half later, Savchuk moved with his parents to Minnesota where he commenced an action against Rush in a Minnesota state court. Because Savchuk could not obtain personal jurisdiction over Rush, Savchuk garnisheed State Farm's obligation to defend and indemnify Rush. State Farm was doing business in Minnesota and it was as-

---

114. 433 U.S. at 214, 97 S.Ct. at 2585, 53 L.Ed.2d at 704. Delaware has since enacted a long-arm statute exercising jurisdiction over directors of Delaware corporations. Del.Code Ann. tit. 10 § 3114(a).

115. *Shaffer,* 433 U.S. at 212, 97 S.Ct. at 2584–85, 53 L.Ed.2d at 703.

116. See Intermeat, Inc. v. American Poultry Inc., 575 F.2d 1017 (2d Cir.1978) (unnecessary to decide whether the substantial connection of defendant's contract with the forum is sufficient for personal jurisdiction, it is sufficient to permit garnishment of a debt owed the defendant); Hall, Morse, Gallagher & Anderson v. Koch & Koch, 119 N.H. 639, 406 A.2d 962 (1979) (despite *Shaffer,* sufficient forum nexus to permit exercise of quasi in rem jurisdiction although no personal jurisdiction); Risenfeld, *Shaffer v. Heitner: Holding, Implications, Forebodings,* 30 Hast.L. J. 1183, 1204 (1979); Silberman, supra note 107 at 72; cf. Note, 66 Cornell Rev. 595, 605–06 (1981) ("When a defendant's contacts with the forum state suffice to permit the court to exercise quasi in rem jurisdiction, but not in personam jurisdiction over him, the due process clause will not permit the court's judgment to affect more than the defendant's interest in attached property"). But see Justice Marshall's opinion in *Shaffer,* 433 U.S. at 207 n.23, 97 S.Ct. at 2582 n.23, 53 L.Ed.2d at 700 n.23: "It is true that the potential liability of a defendant in an in rem action is limited by the value of the property, but that limitation does not affect the argument. The fairness of subjecting a defendant to state-court jurisdiction does not depend on the size of the claim being litigated."

117. 444 U.S. 320, 100 S.Ct. 571, 62 L.Ed.2d 516 (1980). That *Rush* operates retroactively, see Gager v. White, 53 N.Y.2d 475, 442 N.Y.S.2d 463, 425 N.E.2d 851, cert. denied, 454 U.S. 1086, 102 S.Ct. 644, 70 L.Ed.2d 621 (1981).

118. Shaffer v. Heitner, 433 U.S. 186, 97 S.Ct. 2569, 53 L.Ed.2d 683 (1977). See § 4.28.

sumed[119] that there was generally affiliating jurisdiction there over the company. The United States Supreme Court held that this use of quasi in rem jurisdiction violated due process because there were insufficient contacts between Rush and Minnesota "to satisfy the fairness standard of *International Shoe*."[120]

In some respects, *Rush* was a more justifiable use of quasi in rem jurisdiction than *Shaffer*. The liability of Rush was closely related to the property garnisheed: State Farm's obligation to defend and indemnify Rush.[121] Furthermore, seizure of the property would not have deprived Rush of its use, as would seizure of shares of stock or a bank account.[122]

Perhaps the least satisfactory aspect of *Rush* is the ipse dixit that actions of this type "are not equivalent to direct actions...."[123] Direct actions against the liability insurer are authorized under the law of some states.[124] Savchuk argued that since direct actions were constitutional, this quasi in rem garnishment of the liability insurer's obligations under the policy was permissible because it was the functional equivalent of a direct action.[125] The Court's rejection of this contention simply states an obvious formal distinction. In a direct action, the insurer is a defendant. In *Rush,* the insurer was the garnisheed creditor of the defendant. But why is that of constitutional consequence if the substantive effect of both actions is the same?

The relationship between jurisdiction and choice of law provides a more cogent basis for the unconstitutionality of the suit in *Rush*. The Court noted Rush's contention that if a Minnesota court were permitted to exercise jurisdiction, it would apply the Minnesota comparative negligence law rather than Indiana's contributory negligence rule, and would refuse to apply the Indiana guest statute.[126] This would produce a result far more favorable to Savchuk than he could obtain under the law of the state that was, at the time of injury, the place of injury and the parties' domicile. The Court stated simply that "[t]he constitutionality of a choice-of-law rule that would apply forum law under these circumstances is not before us."[127] But constitutional limitations on choice of law might have provided an answer to the argument that if a statute permitting a direct action against State Farm would have been constitutional, then so is the Minnesota statute, which has the same effect on the parties. There

---

119. This assumption is made doubtful by the limitations that Helicopteros Nacionales de Colombia, S.A. v. Hall, 466 U.S. 408, 104 S.Ct. 1868, 80 L.Ed.2d 404 (1984), imposed on general jurisdiction. See § 4.8, text accompanying notes 260–261.

120. *Rush,* 444 U.S. at 328, 100 S.Ct. at 577, 62 L.Ed.2d at 525.

121. The Court noted that this was the basis on which the Minnesota Supreme Court distinguished *Shaffer.* Id. at 325, 100 S.Ct. at 575, 62 L.Ed.2d at 523.

122. The Court notes this argument. Id. at 330, 100 S.Ct. at 578, 62 L.Ed.2d at 526.

123. Id.

124. See, La.—LSA–Rev.Stat. § 22.1269; Wis.Stat.Ann. §§ 632.24, 631.01(1). See also L. Puerto Rico Ann. tit 26, §§ 2003, 1119(1)(b).

125. *Rush,* 444 U.S. at 330, 100 S.Ct. at 578, 62 L.Ed.2d at 526.

126. Id. at 325 n.8, 100 S.Ct. at 575 n.8, 62 L.Ed.2d at 523 n.8.

127. Id.

is an unwarranted assumption that a Minnesota court could permit a direct action under Minnesota law if no such action was possible under Indiana law. No direct action statute purports to apply to insurance policies issued to nonresidents if the accident occurred outside of the enacting state.[128] *Watson v. Employers Liability Assurance Corp.,*[129] which permitted Louisiana to invalidate a policy provision prohibiting direct actions, stressed that the plaintiff was hurt in Louisiana by a product purchased there, thus giving Louisiana a "legitimate interest in safeguarding the rights of persons injured there."[130] Application of a direct action statute on the facts of *Rush* would come close to, if not cross, the due process line. If in fact, as Judge Friendly stated in *Minichiello v. Rosenberg,*[131] application of a direct action statute would be permitted, there is no convincing reply to the contention that the Minnesota procedure was the functional equivalent of such a statute.[132]

§ 4.30   The Commerce Clause as a Limit on State–Court Jurisdiction

Courts have construed the Commerce Clause of the United States Constitution to forbid a state's placing an unreasonable burden on interstate commerce.[133] At times, the commerce clause has been used to declare unconstitutional a state's exercise of judicial jurisdiction.

Davis v. Farmers' Co–Operative Equity Company[134] is the classic example of the use of the commerce clause to limit state-court jurisdiction. The defendant railroad, a Kansas corporation, did not operate any trains or own any lines in Minnesota. Its activities in Minnesota were

---

128. See this section note 124.

129. 348 U.S. 66, 75 S.Ct. 166, 99 L.Ed. 74 (1954).

130. Id. at 73, 75 S.Ct. at 170, 99 L.Ed. at 82. But see Minichiello v. Rosenberg, 410 F.2d 106, 109–110 (2d Cir.1968), cert. denied, 396 U.S. 844, 90 S.Ct. 69, 24 L.Ed.2d 94 (1969) (dictum that state's interest in protecting its residents and providing them with a forum would permit application of direct action statute when policy issued to nonresident and accident outside the state). *Minichiello* was one of a series of cases applying Seider v. Roth, 17 N.Y.2d 111, 269 N.Y.S.2d 99, 216 N.E.2d 312 (1966), which permitted quasi in rem jurisdiction over the insurer's obligation to indemnify and defend, but without special legislation of the type Minnesota passed to form the basis for *Rush*.

131. *Minichiello*, 410 F.2d at 109–110.

132. The amount sued for was the face amount of the policy. *Rush*, 444 U.S. at 323 n.5, 100 S.Ct. at 575 n.5, 62 L.Ed.2d at 522 n.5. The "functional equivalent" argument also assumes that the garnishment judgment could have no collateral estoppel effect in a subsequent in personam action against Rush. See id. at 334, 100 S.Ct. at 580, 62 L.Ed.2d at 529 (Stevens, J., dissenting). For support of the "functional equivalent" argument, see Silberman, *Can the State of Minnesota Bind the Nation?: Federal Choice-of-Law Constraints After Allstate Insurance Co. v. Hague,* 10 Hofstra L. Rev. 103, 118–19 (1981); Note, 94 Harv. L. Rev. 77, 113 (1980). See also Brilmayer, *How Contacts Count: Due Process Limitations on State Court Jurisdiction,* 1980 Sup.Ct.Rev. 77, 102, stating that a direct action statute "probably" could not be applied, but see id. at 103 where the garnishment procedure is distinguished from a direct action in that garnishment treats multistate cases differently from domestic cases.

133. See, e.g., Davis v. Farmers' Co–Operative Equity Co., 262 U.S. 312, 43 S.Ct. 556, 67 L.Ed. 996 (1923); cf. Wahl v. Pan American World Airways, 227 F.Supp. 839 (S.D.N.Y. 1964) (commerce clause does not limit federal-court jurisdiction).

134. 262 U.S. 312, 43 S.Ct. 556, 67 L.Ed. 996 (1923).

limited to having an agent there who solicited traffic for the railroad's lines in other states. The plaintiff, also a Kansas corporation, brought suit against the railroad in Minnesota for damage to grain that the defendant had carried between two points in Kansas. Pursuant to a Minnesota statute, the defendant was served in Minnesota by delivering a copy of the summons to the defendant's soliciting agent in Minnesota. The Supreme Court, in an opinion by Justice Brandeis, held that the Minnesota statute, as construed by the Minnesota Supreme Court, compelled every railroad to submit to the general jurisdiction of Minnesota courts as a condition of maintaining a soliciting agent in Minnesota. The Court held that "[t]his condition imposes upon interstate commerce a serious and unreasonable burden which renders the statute obnoxious to the commerce clause."[135] Since the *Davis* decision, the United States Supreme Court[136] and other courts[137] have, in a number of opinions, invoked the commerce clause as a limit on state-court jurisdiction.

The question arises whether the limits imposed by the Commerce Clause on state-court jurisdiction are meaningful additions to the limits imposed by due process. If all the factors that a court would consider in holding an exercise of jurisdiction a violation of the Commerce Clause the court would also consider in determining whether due process was violated and if, therefore, the same result would be reached in applying either constitutional concept, the Commerce Clause would be a useless and confusing addition to due process as a limit on judicial jurisdiction.[138]

Scrutiny of the cases relying on the Commerce Clause as a sole or alternative ground for declaring a state's exercise of judicial jurisdiction unconstitutional does indicate that, in all likelihood, most of them could have reached the same result under the banner of due process.[139] A case

---

135. Id. at 315, 43 S.Ct. at 557, 67 L.Ed. at 998.

136. See, e.g., Denver & Rio Grande Western R.R. v. Terte, 284 U.S. 284, 52 S.Ct. 152, 76 L.Ed. 295 (1932); Michigan Cent. R.R. v. Mix, 278 U.S. 492, 49 S.Ct. 207, 73 L.Ed. 470 (1929). But cf. International Milling Co. v. Columbia Transp. Co., 292 U.S. 511, 54 S.Ct. 797, 78 L.Ed. 1396 (1934) (attachment of ship in suit to recover for damage to cargo that occurred outside the forum is not an unreasonable burden on interstate commerce).

137. See, e.g., Scanapico v. Richmond, F. & P. R.R., 439 F.2d 17, 25 (2d Cir.1970) (commerce clause does place greater limits than due process on jurisdiction, but jurisdiction here proper); Erlanger Mills, Inc. v. Cohoes Fibre Mills, Inc., 239 F.2d 502, 507 (4th Cir.1956); White v. Southern Pac. Co., 386 S.W.2d 6 (Mo.1965); Glaser v. Pennsylvania R.R., 82 N.J.Super. 16, 196 A.2d 539 (Law Div.1963).

138. See Lee v. Walworth Valve Co., 482 F.2d 297 (4th Cir.1973) (commerce clause no longer limits judicial jurisdiction); Deutsch v. West Coast Mach. Co., 80 Wash.2d 707, 497 P.2d 1311, cert. denied, 409 U.S. 1009, 93 S.Ct. 443, 34 L.Ed.2d 302 (1972) (in deciding that taking jurisdiction places no undue burden on foreign commerce, the same factors are considered as for due process); cf. Hamburger & Laufer, *Expanding Jurisdiction over Foreign Torts: The 1966 Amendment of New York's Long–Arm Statute,* 16 Buffalo L. Rev. 67, 79 (1966); Southern Mach. Co. v. Mohasco Indus., Inc., 401 F.2d 374, 378, n.6 (6th Cir.1968) (unlikely that Tennessee long-arm statute will be at odds with Commerce Clause).

139. See Michigan Cent. R.R. v. Mix, 278 U.S. 492, 49 S.Ct. 207, 73 L.Ed. 470 (1929) (attempt to use defendant's soliciting activities as generally-affiliating basis for jurisdiction); Erlanger Mills, Inc. v. Cohoes Fibre Mills, Inc., 239 F.2d 502 (4th Cir.1956) (due

that once may have provided an exception is *Denver & Rio Grande Western Railroad v. Terte*,[140] which held that garnishment of a railroad's receivables, as a basis for quasi in rem jurisdiction, violated the commerce clause. In *Terte*, the defendant railroad conducted only soliciting activities in the forum and the claim arose from injury in another state before the plaintiff became a resident of the forum. After *Shaffer v. Heitner*,[141] the *Terte* result can be reached on due process grounds. In *Davis* itself, moreover, the Court concluded that "[s]ince we hold that the Minnesota statute as construed and applied violates the commerce clause, we have no occasion to consider whether it also violated the Fourteenth Amendment."[142]

A conclusion that a particular exercise of jurisdiction violates the Commerce Clause may rest upon a finding that the action imposes an unreasonable inconvenience on the defendant because of the defendant's slight nexus with the forum; or it may rest upon the danger of discouraging the defendant and others similarly situated from engaging in interstate commerce if slight contacts with a state may be the basis for generally-affiliating judicial jurisdiction there. If these are the bases for decision, these same concepts and same results would be available under due process. Nevertheless, the Commerce Clause may be a useful addition to due process concepts. The Commerce Clause may call attention to the national interest in avoiding unreasonable burdens on interstate commerce as distinguished from the defendant's interest in avoiding litigation in an inconvenient forum.[143] For example, if a railroad is compelled to defend an injury claim far from the scene of the accident, not only is the defendant subjected to expense and inconvenience in bringing its witnesses to the forum, but also shippers and passengers may be inconvenienced if the witnesses are railroad employees whose absence from their jobs causes curtailment of service.[144] If the defendant's rolling stock is attached,[145] or if the defendant is garnisheed by a plaintiff having a claim against a shipper whose property the defendant is carrying,[146] the resulting interruption of service until the train is released or the garnisheed shipment located and set aside, imposes a burden on shippers and passengers and conflicts with a national interest

---

process violation found); Glaser v. Pennsylvania R.R., 82 N.J.Super. 16, 196 A.2d 539 (Law Div.1963) (court relies on both due process and commerce clauses to quash service).

140. 284 U.S. 284, 52 S.Ct. 152, 76 L.Ed. 295 (1932).

141. 433 U.S. 186, 97 S.Ct. 2569, 53 L.Ed.2d 683 (1977) (discussed in § 4.28).

142. 262 U.S. at 317, 43 S.Ct. at 558, 67 L.Ed. at 999.

143. See Developments, 73 Harv. L. Rev. at 985.

144. See Davis v. Farmers' Co–Operative Equity Co., 262 U.S. 312, 315, 43 S.Ct. 556, 557, 67 L.Ed. 996, 998 (1923).

145. See Atchison, T. & S.F. Ry. v. Wells, 265 U.S. 101, 44 S.Ct. 469, 68 L.Ed. 928 (1924). But cf. International Milling Co. v. Columbia Transp. Co., 292 U.S. 511, 54 S.Ct. 797, 78 L.Ed. 1396 (1934) (attachment of defendant's ship is not an unreasonable burden on interstate commerce).

146. Cf. Bates v. Chicago, M. & St. P. Ry., 60 Wis. 296, 19 N.W. 72 (1884) (refuse to hold railroad liable as garnishee because shipment that plaintiff attempted to attach was not in forum at the time garnishee summons was served).

in avoiding unreasonable burdens on interstate commerce. This inconvenience to third persons and this national interest add a dimension to the factors that determine due process limitations on judicial jurisdiction. In cases where "[a]n 'estimate of the inconveniences' "[147] to the defendant brings the exercise of jurisdiction in question close to the due process line, but there is doubt as to whether that line has been crossed, the extra Commerce Clause dimension may be sufficient to tip the scales toward a finding that the exercise of jurisdiction is unconstitutional.

§ 4.31 Other Federally–Imposed Limitations on State–Court Jurisdiction

There are numerous other ways in which the federal executive and legislative branches, with their control over the conduct of foreign affairs and over whether or not and in what manner the United States or a federal agency or instrumentality may be sued, limit the jurisdiction of state courts.

For example, a treaty to which the United States is a party may limit the courts in which particular kinds of suits may be brought. The Montreal Convention, dealing with suits to recover damages for injuries suffered on international airplane flights, provides that:

1. An action for damages must be brought, at the option of the plaintiff, in the territory of one of the States Parties, either before the court of the domicile of the carrier or of its principal place of business, or where it has a place of business through which the contract has been made or before the court at the place of destination.

2. In respect of damage resulting from the death or injury of a passenger, an action may be brought before one of the courts mentioned in paragraph 1 of this Article, or in the territory of a State Party in which at the time of the accident the passenger has his or her principal and permanent residence and to or from which the carrier operates services for the carriage of passengers by air, either on its own aircraft, or on another carrier's aircraft pursuant to a commercial agreement, and in which that carrier conducts its business of carriage of passengers by air from premises leased or owned by the carrier itself or by another carrier with which it has a commercial agreement.[148]

Many federal statutes limit the courts in which suits may be brought against the United States or against federal agencies or instrumentalities. For example, the Federal Tort Claims Act requires that tort suits under the act be brought exclusively in federal courts,[149] and, although suits against National Banks, for which the Federal Deposit Insurance

---

147. International Shoe Co. v. Washington, 326 U.S. 310, 317, 66 S.Ct. 154, 158, 90 L.Ed. 95, 102 (1945).

148. Convention for the Unification of Certain Rules for International Carriage by Air, S Treaty Doc No. 106–45 (2000), art. 33.

149. 28 U.S.C.A. § 1346(b)(1).

Corporation has been appointed as receiver, are permitted in state courts, a federal statute controls the venue of these suits.[150]

§ 4.32 Self–Imposed Limitations on Jurisdiction

Even when a state is free to exercise judicial jurisdiction without violating due process or any other constitutional or federally-imposed limitation on its jurisdiction, the state may decline to exercise this jurisdiction. Sometimes the state makes this election, either deliberately or by oversight, by failing to provide a statutory basis for judicial jurisdiction when a statute is needed. Sometimes even when there are no constitutional or statutory impediments to state-court jurisdiction, a court will decide not to exercise that jurisdiction. Sections 4.33 through 4.39 discuss some of the more common grounds on which courts, sometimes acting under rules that they have evolved for their own guidance and sometimes pursuant to statutory direction or authority, have not exercised judicial jurisdiction for which they had a constitutional basis.

§ 4.33 Forum Non Conveniens

Under the doctrine of forum non conveniens, a court may, in the exercise of "sound discretion,"[151] decline to exercise its jurisdiction if the court finds that it is a "seriously inconvenient"[152] forum and that in the light of private and public factors, the court should remit the plaintiff to another more appropriate and available forum. *Gulf Oil Corp. v. Gilbert*[153] contains the classic list of these private and public factors that both state and federal courts use. The factors relating to the private interests of the litigants center on the ease of access to evidence and witnesses.[154] The public interest factors focus on the expenditure of public resources to try the case in the forum and whether the magnitude of this expenditure is greater and its justification less because of the tenuous ties between the forum and the events in litigation.[155] There is a

---

150. 12 U.S.C.A. § 94. See also Federal Uniform Services Former Spouses Protection Act, 10 U.S.C.A. § 1408(c)(4) (may not adjudicate concerning retirement pay unless the court has jurisdiction over the service member because of residence [other than because of military assignment], domicile, or consent).

151. See Piper Aircraft Co. v. Reyno, 454 U.S. 235, 257, 102 S.Ct. 252, 70 L.Ed.2d 419 (1981): ("The *forum non conveniens* determination is committed to the sound discretion of the trial court. It may be reversed only when there has been a clear abuse of discretion").

152. Restatement, Second, § 84.

153. 330 U.S. 501, 67 S.Ct. 839, 91 L.Ed. 1055 (1947).

154. Id. at 508: "An interest to be considered, and the one likely to be most pressed, is the private interest of the litigant. Important considerations are the relative ease of access to sources of proof; availability of compulsory process for attendance of unwilling, and the cost of obtaining attendance of willing, witnesses; possibility of view of premises, if view would be appropriate to the action; and all other practical problems that make trial of a case easy, expeditious and inexpensive."

155. Id. at 508–09: "Factors of public interest also have place in applying the doctrine. Administrative difficulties follow for courts when litigation is piled up in congested centers instead of being handled at its origin. Jury duty is a burden that ought not to be imposed upon the people of a community which has no relation to the litigation.... There is a local interest in having localized controversies decided at home. There is an appropriateness,

split of authority whether a court should consider the private and public factors together or whether consideration of public factors is appropriate only if the private factors do not mandate dismissal.[156]

In federal courts the trial judge's denial of the motion to dismiss is not immediately appealable as of right, although the judge may certify the issue for discretionary review under 28 U.S.C. § 1292(b).[157] Some state courts have held that review after trial of the denial of a motion for forum non conveniens dismissal is not an adequate remedy and an appellate court may grant a writ of mandamus ordering dismissal.[158]

In *Lubbe v. Cape Plc*,[159] the House of Lords rejected consideration of the public interest factors that United States courts weigh in ruling on forum non conveniens motions. Representatives of almost 4,000 South Africans brought a "group action" against an English company for injuries and death suffered in South Africa because of asbestos fibers released into the air by the defendant's manufacturing and mining subsidiaries. The Lords reversed a forum non conveniens stay that the High Court had granted and the Court of Appeal had affirmed. *Lubbe* found that because of the large number of claimants and the need for medical evidence, the defendant had met its burden to "show that England is not the natural or appropriate forum for the trial [and] establish that there is another available forum which is clearly or distinctly more appropriate than the English forum."[160] Nevertheless, the Lords allowed the appeal (reversed) because plaintiffs had met their burden to "establish that substantial justice will not be done in the appropriate forum."[161] The claimants would not receive substantial justice in a South African court because, unlike England, South Africa did not provide legal aid to finance investigation, hiring of expert witnesses, and other litigation expenses.

It will not be easy for a court to determine when depriving the plaintiff of the tactical advantages that the plaintiff will enjoy in the forum rises to the level of denying substantial justice. As Justice Jackson

---

too, in having the trial of a diversity case in a forum that is at home with the state law that must govern the case rather than having a court in some other forum untangle problems in conflict of laws, and in law foreign to itself."

But see Arthur Taylor von Mehren, Theory and Practice of Adjudicatory Authority in Private International Law, in 295 Recuil des Cours D'Académie de Droit International: Collected Courses of the Hague Academy of International Law 58 (2002) (stating that forum may derive net benefit from litigation if public costs of litigation "are more than offset by the income earned, *inter alia*, from court costs assessed on parties, fees earned by local lawyers, and income to hotels and restaurants").

156. See Kedy v. A.W. Chesterton Co., 946 A.2d 1171, 1185 (R.I. 2008) (collecting authority and electing to consider private and public factors together).

157. See Van Cauwenberghe v. Biard, 486 U.S. 517, 108 S.Ct. 1945, 100 L.Ed.2d 517 (1988).

158. See In re Pirelli Tire, L.L.C., 247 S.W.3d 670 (Tex. 2007).

159. [2000] 1 W.L.R. 1545 (H.L. appeal taken from Eng.).

160. Id. at 1554 (Lord Bingham of Cornhill).

161. Id.

stated in *Miles v. Illinois Central R.R.*,[162] "[a]n advantage which it is hoped will be reflected in a judgment is what makes plaintiffs leave home and incur burdens of expense and inconvenience that would be regarded as oppressive if forced upon them."[163]

The Lords also stated that "the principles on which the doctrine of forum non conveniens rest leave no room for considerations of public interest or public policy which cannot be related to the private interests of any of the parties or the ends of justice in the case which is before the court."[164] In this regard, the court declined to follow the practice in the United States of considering public as well as private interests.

One of the public factors considered by United States courts, difficulties of choice of law and the application of foreign law, does impact the parties' interests and the ends of justice. The need to brief the choice-of-law issue and obtain the evidence of experts on foreign law increases the defendant's costs just as surely as locating witnesses in a foreign land and flying them to the forum. The High Court of Australia has also rejected "the selected forum's administrative problems" as a proper factor in forum non conveniens analysis, but has recognized the issue of whether forum law applies as "a very significant factor in the exercise of the court's discretion."[165]

Moreover it is arguable that it is the public factors that should be the primary basis for forum non conveniens analysis. When the court's docket is crowded, forum citizens are further delayed in obtaining adjudication of their cases if local courts are flooded with thousands of litigants from a distant country. Citizens, with their taxes, pay the judges and build and maintain the courts. Justice Jackson emphasized the importance in forum non conveniens decisions of the public interest in efficient administration of justice:

> But the judges with lawyerly indirection have not avowed the interest of the judiciary in orderly resort to the courts as a basis for their decision, and have cast their protective doctrines in terms of sheltering defendants against vexatious and harassing suits. This judicial treatment of the subject of venue leads Congress and the parties to think of the choice of a forum as a private matter between litigants and in cases like the present obscures the public interest in venue practices behind a rather fantastic fiction that a widow is harassing the Illinois Central Railroad.[166]

In *Lubbe* the Lords removed the stay and therefore did not have to decide whether the Brussels Convention[167] precluded a forum non conve-

---

162. 315 U.S. 698, 62 S.Ct. 827, 86 L.Ed. 1129 (1942).

163. Id. at 706 (Jackson, J. concurring).

164. *Lubbe*, [2000] 1 W.L.R. at 1566 (Lord Hope of Craighead).

165. Voth v. Manildra Flour Mills Pty. Ltd., [1990] 171 CLR 538.

166. Miles v. Illinois Central R.R., 315 U.S. 698, 706, 62 S.Ct. 827, 86 L.Ed. 1129 (1942) (Jackson, J., concurring).

167. Convention on Jurisdiction and Enforcement of Judgments in Civil and Commercial Matters, Sept. 27, 1968, as amended, O.J. C 189 (1990), 72 U.N.T.S.

niens stay when an English court has personal jurisdiction over the defendant[168] but the alternative forum, South Africa, is not a Convention country. Lord Bingham thought that if it were necessary to decide that question the Lords would have to seek a ruling from the European Court of Justice because the answer was not clear.[169] He noted that Italian claimants had filed an action against defendant for injuries incurred in Italy. In that case defendant did not contend that the High Court had the power under Brussels to decline jurisdiction in favor of an Italian court.[170] Perhaps the specter of permitting Europeans but not South Africans to sue defendant in England had some influence on the result.

The Brussels Convention, now the Brussels Regulation, bars a European Union court that is exercising personal jurisdiction over a defendant under the Regulation, from granting a forum non conveniens stay or dismissal, whether the alternative forum is within or outside the Union.[171] The United Kingdom and Ireland, Union countries that have a doctrine of forum non conveniens, may use the doctrine only when exercising jurisdiction not permitted in the Regulation over a defendant not domiciled in the Union.

It is not clear whether a European Union court exercising jurisdiction under the Regulation may stay the action because of an action between the same parties previously commenced in a court outside of the Union. If a Union court is "first seised" of the same cause of action between the same parties, article 27 of the Regulation requires that any other Union court stay its action until the jurisdiction of court first seised is established and dismiss the action after jurisdiction of that court is established. The Irish Supreme Court has referred the question to the European Court of Justice as to whether an Irish court may stay an action because of an action first begun in the United States.[172]

§ 4.33A The United States Is A Magnet Forum

As discussed in sections 4.8 and 4.9, in most states in personam jurisdiction is available over defendants to the full constitutional limits. Without a doctrine of forum non conveniens, jurisdictional doctrine would permit opportunities for interstate and international forum shop-

---

168. Id. art. 2 permits suit at defendant's domicile. Id. art. 53 states that a company is domiciled at its "seat." In all European Union countries except Denmark, on March 1, 2002, a Council Regulation replaced the Convention, EN No. 44/2001. The Regulation amends art. 53 (now art. 60) and provides that a company's domicile is where it has its statutory seat, or place of central administration, or principal place of business.

169. *Lubbe,* [2000] 1 W.L.R. at 1562. On 1 March 2005 the Court of Justice of the European Communities answered the question holding that an English court may not grant a forum non conveniens stay of an action against an English defendant when the alternative forum is Jamaica. Case C–281/02, Owusu v. Jackson, [2005] ECR 1–1383.

A 1971 Protocol to the Brussels Convention gave the Court of Justice of the European Communities jurisdiction to rule on interpretations of the Convention. Protocol on the Interpretation by the Court of Justice of the Convention, June 3, 1971, 1971 O.J. (L 304) 97, reprinted in 29 I.L.M. 1439, 1440 (1990).

170. *Lubbe,* [2000] 1 W.L.R. at 1553.

171. See Case C–281/02, Owusu v. Jackson [2005] ECR 1–1383.

172. Goshawk Dedicated Ltd. v. Life Receivables Irl. Ltd., [2009] IESC 7 (2009).

ping. With rare exceptions, such as defamation actions in which the Supreme Court has imposed constitutional limits on liability and recovery,[173] the United States is a magnet forum for injured foreigners. Plaintiffs flock to United States courts for two reasons—higher recoveries and lower barriers to suit. Higher recoveries are facilitated by four features of administration of justice in the United States: trial by jury, choice-of-law rules that are more likely than foreign choice-of-law rules to choose United States law, plaintiff-favoring rules such as liability without fault, and extensive pretrial discovery.[174] The contingent fee and the "American rule" that a losing plaintiff is not liable for the defendant's attorneys' fees lower barriers to suit.[175] The most important of these reasons is trial by jury. In the words of Lord Denning, United States juries are "prone to award fabulous damages."[176]

After years of "tort reform" and the appointment or election of new judges, the situation in United Courts is less favorable to plaintiffs suing to recover for injury or wrongful death. For example, tort victims, such as retired people, who do not lose income, have found that the law of some foreign countries provides more compensation than U.S. law. In Italy, every relative of a decedent has a claim to compensation determined by a regional table. Some regional tables provide higher compensation than others.[177]

Nevertheless, the fact that damage awards in the United States are typically higher than in the country where the foreign plaintiff was injured, affects more than the number of suits filed and litigated to judgment here. It influences settlements of claims. Under what has become known as "the mid-Atlantic formula," European plaintiffs injured in Europe are settling their claims at figures above the likely recovery in the foreign forum. The amount of the settlement turns on the probability that the plaintiff could have obtained jurisdiction over the defendant in the United States and that a motion for forum non conveniens dismissal would not be successful.[178]

---

173. *See* Gertz v. Robert Welch, Inc., 418 U.S. 323, 348–50, 94 S.Ct. 2997, 41 L.Ed.2d 789 (1974) (holding that when assessing damages for libel of a private individual, legislators and courts may not impose liability without fault and may not permit recovery of presumed or punitive damages unless liability is based on knowledge of falsity or reckless disregard for the truth); New York Times v. Sullivan, 376 U.S. 254, 279–80, 84 S.Ct. 710, 11 L.Ed.2d 686 (1964) (holding that a public official cannot recover damages for a defamatory falsehood relating to the official's duties unless he or she proves that the statement was made with actual malice).

174. *See* Piper Aircraft Co. v. Reyno, 454 U.S. 235, 252 n.18, 102 S.Ct. 252, 70 L.Ed.2d 419 (1981).

175. Id.

176. Smith Kline & French Lab. Ltd. v. Bloch, [1983] 1 W.L.R. 730, 734 (C.A. 1982).

177. See Gina Passarella, Bus Crash in Europe Gives Pa. Attorney a Taste of Italian Law, The Legal Intelligencer, February 15, 2008, (Italian law provided twice the damages for death of retired senior citizens than U.S. law provided).

178. See Silva, *Practical Views on Stemming the Tide of Foreign Plaintiffs and Concluding Mid–Atlantic Settlements*, 28 Tex. Int'l L. J. 479, 495–97 (1993).

Even within the European Union, average awards differ greatly from country to country, and forum shopping for the highest recovery is common. The shopping is within the

Even if an American court decides that foreign law applies, including foreign heads of damages (e.g. pain and suffering, lost income), because of a quirk of choice-of-law doctrine that may be surprising to the uninitiated, the foreign litigant may still benefit from the American jury's tendency to award high damages. Determination of the amount to be awarded under the foreign heads of damages is determined under the procedure and practices of the American forum.[179] Typical foreign levels of recovery are irrelevant to this determination unless the foreign rule amounts to a specific monetary limit, such as a statutory cap on wrongful death recovery. If this choice-of-law aberration were corrected, the other advantages of suit in the United States might still draw the afflicted and grieving from abroad, but litigation here would be less likely.

It is a fair question whether any changes are desirable to make the U.S. a less attractive forum. If the quality of justice administered in United States courts is so high that the afflicted and aggrieved of the world flock here, perhaps that should be a point of pride rather than a reason for re-examining what we are doing. Again in the words of Lord Denning referring to the English courts:

> The right to come here is not confined to Englishmen. It extends to any friendly foreigner. He can seek the aid of our court if he desires to do so. You may call this "forum shopping" if you please, but if the forum is England, it is a good place to shop in, both for the quality of the goods and the speed of service.[180]

Nevertheless examination of the reasons why a forum is attractive to foreigners may reveal some aspects of the administration of justice that do not improve "the quality of the goods" and give an unjustifiable advantage to forum shoppers. The bizarre rule with regard to quantification of damages, discussed just above, is one aspect of American law that provides such an unjustifiable advantage. Moreover, the private and public factors that determine whether the court will grant a forum non conveniens dismissal may justify requiring the aggrieved foreigner to sue at home. Particularly in personal injury cases, courts in the plaintiff's country are likely to have easier access than a United States court to evidence concerning the circumstances of injury and the plaintiff's condition.

---

jurisdictional provisions of the Council Regulation on Jurisdiction and the Recognition and Enforcement of Judgments in Civil and Commercial Matters, EC No. 44/2001 adopted by the Council of the European Union on 22 December 2000, entered into force on 1 March 2002 [Brussels Regulation] (art. 2, general jurisdiction, arts 5–6 long-arm jurisdiction, arts 15–17, consumer contracts). Davies Arnold Cooper, a London firm of solicitors, has constructed a chart showing that for loss of sight in one eye to a medical student who is a single woman, aged 20, average product liability awards range from over $150,000 in Ireland, through $25,000 in France, to less than $10,000 in Greece. See *The Legal Profession*, The Economist, July 18 1992, survey section at 8.

179. See supra § 3.2C4.

180. The Atlantic Star, [1973] 1 Q.B. 364, 381–82 (C.A. 1972), *rev'd*, [1974] A.C. 436 (H.L.).

On January 27, 1998, the Congress of Ecuador enacted Law No. 55, which provides: "[I]n case of international concurrent jurisdiction the plaintiff can freely choose to file a complaint in Ecuador or in another country.... In the case that the demand is filed outside of Ecuador, the national competence and the jurisdiction of the Ecuadorian Judges on the case will be terminated forever." An Ecuadorian appellate court has interpreted Law No. 55 as not applying "to cases that a United States court had dismissed because of forum non conveniens."[181] The Eleventh Circuit nevertheless found "arguable uncertainty concerning the future interpretation" of the Ecuadorian law and modified a forum non conveniens dismissal order "to provide that any case dismissed pursuant to the District Court's order may be reinstated in the event that jurisdiction to entertain such a case is rejected by a final decision of a court in Ecuador."[182]

It is a mistake to permit a foreign country to afford its citizens immunity from forum non conveniens dismissals by enacting laws such as the Ecuadorian statute.[183]. Once it is clear that this ploy will not work, it is likely that the foreign law will be construed or repealed to afford an alternative forum following dismissal in the United States. Likely to more effective in deterring forum non conveniens dismissal of foreigner's suits in United States is a law in the plaintiff's country guaranteeing a U.S. level of damages and imposing onerous requirements on foreign defendants.[184]

---

181.   Leon v. Million Air, Inc., 251 F.3d 1305, 1308 (11th Cir. 2001).

182.   Id. at 1316. See also Canales Martinez v. Dow Chemical Co., 219 F.Supp.2d 719 (E.D. La. 2002) (denies defendant's motion to grant a forum non conveniens dismissal of suit by banana plantation workers from Costa Rica, Honduras, and the Philippines because courts in those countries were not available to plaintiffs once they had sued in the U.S. and the courts in Honduras and the Philippines were not adequate because of corruption); Inter–American Juridical Committee of the Organization of American States Annual Report to O.A.S General Assembly, OEA/Ser.Q/VI.31, CJI/doc.45/00 (Latin American law deprives the courts of a country of jurisdiction if a citizen sues in another country and that suit is dismissed on the ground of forum non conveniens).

183.   See The Scotts Co. v. Hacienda Loma Linda, 2 So.3d 1013, 1018 (Fla. App. 3 Dist. 2008), rehearing and rehearing en bank denied: "If the foreign country chooses to turn away its own citizen's lawsuit for damages suffered in that very country, and if the other *Kinney* [forum non conveniens] factors warrant dismissal here, it is difficult to understand why Florida's courts should devote resources to the matter" (collecting authority for granting and refusing the forum non conveniens motion). But see Abad v. Bayer Corp., 563 F.3d 663, 666 (7th Cir. 2009) (court does not believe an Argentine court would refuse to exercise jurisdiction over a case that had been dismissed in the United States, but if so "the plaintiffs could resume suit in the United States"),

184.   See Nicaragua Ley 364 (2000) (creates retroactive no-fault product liability, waives statute of limitations, eliminates need to prove causality, requires defendant to post non-refundable $100,00 bond, establishes escrow account for payment of award, and provides for minimum liability of $25,000 to $100,000 as liquidated damages); Commonwealth of Dominica Transnational Causes of Action (Product Liability) Act no. 16 of 1997 § 12(1) (when suit against a U.S. defendant is dismissed by a U.S. court, a court in Dominica has jurisdiction and in awarding exemplary damages shall be guided by U.S. standards).

§ 4.33B   Federal Forum Non Conveniens: Piper Aircraft Co. v. Reyno[185]

Piper is the leading federal case on the application of forum non conveniens to suits by foreigners injured abroad. It is not good news for plaintiffs and a prime reason for them to invoke tactics to lock the case into state court in a state whose law is not conducive to dismissal.[186]

The case arose from the crash of a small airplane in "mountainous terrain in southern Scotland."[187] Piper manufactured the aircraft in Pennsylvania and Hartzell Propeller manufactured the propellers in Ohio. The passengers, for whose wrongful deaths the suit was brought, were all Scottish citizens. The pilot and the air-taxi company that owned, operated, and maintained the airplane were also Scottish. The suit against Piper and Hartzell claimed defects in the manufacture of the airplane or propellers. The defendants asserted that the crash was the result of pilot error or faulty maintenance.

The tactics employed by plaintiffs and defendants are typical in such cases. The crash occurred in July 1976. A year later a California probate court appointed Gaynell Reyno administratrix of the passengers' estates. Reyno was legal secretary to the plaintiffs' attorney. She brought suit in a California state court. The defendants removed to federal court and moved for transfer to a federal district court in Pennsylvania.[188] The court transferred the action to Pennsylvania and quashed service on Hartzell. Plaintiff served process on Hartzell in Pennsylvania. Both the defendants then moved the Pennsylvania federal district court to dismiss on the basis of forum non conveniens.

The court granted this motion noting that most of the evidence relating to the cause of the crash was in Scotland and that defendants could not implead in the forum the pilot, the owner, or the operating company for determination of fault, as they could in Scotland.[189] The court also found the public interest factors weighed heavily in favor of dismissal, including the necessity of applying Scottish law to some issues affecting Piper and to all issues affecting Hartzell.[190] The Third Circuit

---

185.   454 U.S. 235, 102 S.Ct. 252, 70 L.Ed.2d 419 (1981).

186.   See § 4.33C. The plaintiff will look for a state with no forum non conveniens doctrine or one less favorable to defendants than *Piper*. Even states with robust doctrines differ in their willingness to follow *Piper* and dismiss suits brought against American defendants by foreigners injured abroad. See Picketts v. International Playtex, Inc., 215 Conn. 490, 576 A.2d 518, 525 (1990) (reversing a forum non conveniens dismissal of an action for wrongful death of a Canadian who used the product in Canada, stating that "[w]hile the weight to be given the choice of a domestic forum by foreign plaintiffs is diminished, their entitlement to a preference does not disappear entirely"); Myers v. The Boeing Co., 115 Wash.2d 123, 794 P.2d 1272, 1280–81 (1990) (affirming dismissal of a suit by Japanese nationals for wrongful deaths resulting from a plane crash in Japan, but expressly declining to adopt *Reyno*'s statement that a foreign plaintiff's choice of forum is entitled to less deference than an American plaintiff's).

187.   Reyno v. Piper, 479 F.Supp. 727, 729 (M.D. Pa. 1979), rev'd and remanded, 630 F.2d 149 (3d Cir. 1980), rev'd, 454 U.S. 235, 102 S.Ct. 252, 70 L.Ed.2d 419 (1981).

188.   *Piper*, 454 U.S. at 239–40.

189.   *Piper*, 479 F.Supp. 727, 732–33 (M.D. Pa. 1979).

190.   Id. at 736–37. The court held that Scottish wrongful death law applied to Piper, but that Pennsylvania tort law determined Piper's liability. Scottish law of both wrongful

reversed, deciding that United States law would apply to all issues,[191] that the trial court had abused its discretion in granting the dismissal, and, most significantly, that dismissal is improper whenever it results in the application of law less favorable to the plaintiff.[192] This last factor was controlling because Scotland did not have strict liability in tort and Scottish choice-of-law rules would select Scottish law.[193]

The Supreme Court granted certiorari limited to this last issue—did the fact that the alternative forum would apply law less favorable to the plaintiff preclude dismissal? The Court was unanimously of the opinion that the answer is "no."[194] A bare majority agreed with Justice Marshall that the decision of the Third Circuit should be reversed and the trial judge's dismissal be allowed to stand without remand. The dissenters would have remanded to the Third Circuit for re-examination of the trial court's dismissal under the "abuse of discretion" standard. The dissenters' position is strengthened by the fact that the Third Circuit reversed the trial judge's determination that Scottish law applied to some of the issues and that the trail judge's decision had been influenced by the

---

death and product liability would apply to Hartzell. The explanation for applying different product liability law to Piper and Hartzell lies in the fact that the court applied California choice-of-law rules to Piper, but Pennsylvania choice-of-law rules to Hartzell. This was because the case against Piper had been transferred from California. Van Dusen v. Barrack, 376 U.S. 612, 84 S.Ct. 805, 11 L.Ed.2d 945 (1964) held that after a transfer under 28 U.S.C. § 1404(a), the law applied is the law that would have been applied in the transferor court. The district court in *Piper* held that *Van Dusen* required the application of California conflicts rules to Piper, but because Hartzell was not subject to the jurisdiction of the California court, the *Van Dusen* rule did not apply to Hartzell. 479 F.Supp. at 734. The court found that California applied "the governmental interest approach in resolving conflict of law issues" (id. at 734–35) but that Pennsylvania used the "most significant relationship" approach of the Restatement (Second) of Conflict of Laws (id. at 736).

The court was probably wrong in finding that these "different" approaches to choice of law produced different results. See Borchers, *The Choice of Law Revolution: An Empirical Study*, 49 WASH. & LEE L. REV. 357, 378 (1992) (finding that the results produced by the two approaches are "statistically indistinguishable"). Professor Borchers' survey result is not surprising because both approaches have at their core a focus on the policies underlying domestic laws and whether these policies are made relevant by contacts with the parties or with the transaction. See Weintraub, *An Approach to Choice of Law that Focuses on Consequences*, 56 ALB. L. REV. 701, 714–15 (1993).

191. *Reyno*, 630 F.2d 149, 166–71 (3d Cir. 1980). Ohio products liability law applied to Hartzell and Pennsylvania law to Piper. Id. at 171 n.95.

192. Id. at 164.

193. Id. at 161–62. Times have changed. The Council of the European Communities issued a directive on July 25, 1985, making "[t]he producer . . . liable for damage caused by a defect in his product." Council Directive of 25 July 1985 (85/374/EEC), art. 1; reprinted in 32 I.L.M. 1352, 1353. "Producer" includes "the manufacturer of a finished product, the producer of any raw material or the manufacturer of a component part and any person who, by putting his name, trade mark or other distinguishing feature on the product presents himself as its producer." Id. art. 3, 32 I.L.M. at 1353. It also includes "any person who imports into the Community a product for . . . any form of distribution in the course of his business" and "each supplier of the product" unless the supplier "informs the injured person, within a reasonable time of the identity of the producer or of the person who supplied him with the product." Art. 3, 32 I.L.M. at 1353–54. The United Kingdom has enacted conforming legislation. Consumer Protection Act 1987, 1987 c. 43, part I; reprinted in 32 I.L.M. 1407–13.

194. Justices Powell and O'Connor took no part in the opinion. *Piper*, 454 U.S. at 260–61.

inconvenience of applying Scottish law. If the case had been remanded, the Third Circuit in turn could have remanded to the trial judge for re-determination of the motion now that the specter of Scottish law had been removed. The trial judge might well have taken the hint and denied the motion to dismiss, and that, as a practical matter, would have ended the forum non conveniens issue.

The passage in the Supreme Court opinion that is of greatest comfort to defendants sued by foreign plaintiffs is the one that discriminates against foreigners:

> In *Koster* [*v. Lumbermen's Mut. Cas. Co.*, 330 U.S. 518, 67 S.Ct. 828, 91 L.Ed. 1067 (1947)], the Court indicated that a plaintiff's choice of forum is entitled to greater deference when the plaintiff has chosen the home forum. 330 U.S. at 524. When the home forum has been chosen, it is reasonable to assume that this choice is convenient. When the plaintiff is foreign, however, this assumption is much less reasonable. Because the central purpose of any forum non conveniens inquiry is to ensure that the trial is convenient, a foreign plaintiff's choice deserves less deference.[195]

Discrimination against foreign citizens, if taken literally, would violate United States bilateral Friendship, Commerce, and Navigation treaties with approximately twenty-five countries. These treaties guarantee citizens of the other treaty partner equal access to courts with local citizens. These treaties do not prevent a court from granting a forum non conveniens dismissal of a suit by a foreign non-resident if the court would, under the same circumstances, dismiss a suit by a non-resident citizen.[196]

---

195. Id. at 255–56. See Gemini Capital Group, Inc. v. Yap Fishing Corp., 150 F.3d 1088 (9th Cir. 1998) (affirming dismissal and holding that California corporation's suit in Hawaii is entitled to less deference than suit by a Hawaiian resident). Contra, Iragorri v. United Technologies Corp., 274 F.3d 65 (2d Cir. 2001): "It is not a correct understanding of the rule to accord deference only when the suit is brought in the plaintiff's home district. Rather, the court must consider a plaintiff's likely motivations in light of all the relevant indications. We thus understand the Supreme Court's teachings on the deference due to plaintiff's forum choice as instructing that we give greater deference to a plaintiff's forum choice to the extent that it was motivated by legitimate reasons, including the plaintiff's convenience and the ability of a U.S. resident plaintiff to obtain jurisdiction over the defendant, and diminishing deference to a plaintiff's forum choice to the extent that it was motivated by tactical advantage."; Id. at 73. cf. Adelson v. Hananel, 510 F.3d 43, 53 (1st Cir. 2007) ("A logical extension of that heightened deference in a favor of a plaintiff's 'home forum' applies in cases such as this which involves a U.S. citizen plaintiff who is seeing to litigate in a United States forum" when the plaintiff is not a resident of the forum district and the alternative forum is in a foreign country).

196. See Pollux Holding Ltd. v. The Chase Manhattan Bank, 329 F.3d 64, 73 (2d Cir. 2003), cert. denied, 540 U.S. 1149, 124 S.Ct. 1145, 157 L.Ed.2d 1041 (2004); Stevenson, *Forum Non Conveniens and Equal Access Under FCN Treaties: A Foreign Plaintiff's Rights*, 13 Hastings Int'l & Comp. L. Rev. 267, 277–78 (1990). But cf. Morris v. Crown Equipment Corp., 219 W.Va. 347, 633 S.E.2d 292 (2006), cert. denied, 549 U.S. 1096 (2006) (W. Va. has statute barring nonresidents from suing unless a substantial part of the acts or omissions giving rise to the claim occurred in W. Va.; to avoid violation of the Privileges and Immunities Clause, Art. IV, Sec. 2, of the U.S. Constitution, construe statute not to apply to civil actions against W. Va. citizens and residents)

The United States has also ratified the International Covenant on Civil and Political Rights.[197] Article 2(1) of the Covenant protects foreigners present in the country from discrimination on numerous grounds, such as race, sex, religion, and ends with the inclusion of "other status." Residence is a "status" so that if read literally the Covenant would bar any discrimination against foreigners, resident or non-resident, in granting a forum non conveniens dismissal. The Covenant has not been read literally. The European Court of Human Rights construing the same language in the European Convention for the Protection of Human Rights and Fundamental Freedoms[198] has held that the Convention bars only unreasonable discrimination on the listed grounds, not discrimination that has a "legitimate aim."[199] In like manner the Human Rights Committee, created by the Covenant to administer it, has held that the Covenant bars only irrational prejudice, not discrimination on a stated ground that has a legitimate purpose.[200] Moreover, when the United States ratified the Covenant the Senate reserved the right to discriminate on the grounds stated in the Covenant when the discrimination is "rationally related to a legitimate governmental objective."[201]

In his opinion for the majority in *Piper*, Justice Marshall holds that dismissal is not precluded by the fact that the alternative forum will apply law less favorable to the plaintiff. All the participating judges, including the three dissenters, agree with this proposition. Justice Marshall, however, goes further declaring that "[t]he possibility of a change in substantive law should ordinarily not be given conclusive or even substantial weight in the forum non conveniens inquiry."[202] The reason that he gives is that:

> If the possibility of a change in law were given substantial weight, deciding motions to dismiss on the ground of forum non conveniens would become quite difficult. Choice-of-law analysis would become extremely important, and the courts would frequently be required to interpret the law of foreign jurisdictions. First, the trial court would have to determine what law would apply if the case were tried in the chosen forum, and what law would apply if the case were tried in the alternative forum. It would then have to compare the rights, remedies, and procedures available under the law that would be applied in each forum. Dismissal would be appropriate only if the court concluded that the law applied by the alternative forum is as favorable to the plaintiff as that of the chosen forum. The doctrine of *forum non conveniens*, however, is

---

197. Dec. 19, 1966, 999 U.N.T.S. 171.

198. 213 U.N.T.S.221, art. 14.

199. Darby v. Sweden, 13 Eur. Ct. H.R. 774, 781 (1990).

200. Alina Simunek v. the Czech Republic, U.N. GAOR, 50th Sess., Supp. 40, vol. II, U.N. Doc. A/50/40 at 96; General Comment No. 23, U.N. GAOR, Hum. Rts. Comm., 50th Sess. at 38 ¶ 5.2 U.N. Doc. HRI/gen/1/Rev.1 (1994).

201. 138 Cong. Rec. 8071 (1992).

202. *Piper*, 454 U.S. at 247.

designed in part to help courts avoid conducting complex exercises in comparative law.[203]

A few pages later, however, Justice Marshall concedes what any litigator knows, that choice-of-law analysis is extremely important to the forum non conveniens determination; that the need to apply foreign law, particularly the law of a foreign country, although not controlling, makes it far more likely that a court will grant the motion to dismiss.[204] Typical tactics for the defense would be to move first for partial summary judgment on choice of law hoping to get the court to rule that foreign law applies. If the defense succeeds on choice of law, granting of the motion for dismissal is not guaranteed, but is made much more likely. Even if the court rules that forum law applies, the defense can cite *Piper* itself as a case in which United States law applied and yet the Supreme Court held as a matter of law that the trial judge did not abuse his discretion in dismissing.[205]

Can these two passages from Justice Marshall's opinion be reconciled? How can choice of law be both irrelevant and a key factor? What Marshall seems to be saying is that although he recognizes that the determination that foreign law applies is a factor favoring dismissal, the trial court should not go beyond applying its own choice-of-law rules. The judge should not inquire into the choice-of-law rules in the alternative forum, or, if those rules would select the law of that forum, the content of foreign law.

The problem with this distinction between application of forum and foreign choice-of-law rules is that under modern conflicts methods, choice of law no longer consists of sticking a pin in the map where some key event, such a physical harm, occurred. Choice of law in most states and a growing number of foreign countries now requires knowledge of the content of the competing rules and their underlying purposes.[206] Information on the policies underlying the foreign law is likely to be afforded by choice-of-law determinations in the foreign jurisdiction, particularly if that jurisdiction has, as have most of our states, stopped sticking pins in maps and chooses law in a manner most likely to accommodate different domestic policies.

In *Gulf Oil Corp. v. Gilbert*,[207] Justice Jackson stated that "the doctrine of *forum non* conveniens can never apply if there is absence of

---

203. Id. at 251.

204. Id. at 260. But see Candlewood Timber Group, LLC v. Pan American Energy, LLC, 859 A.2d 989, 999, 1002 (Del. 2004), cert. denied, 543 U.S. 1177, 125 S.Ct. 1314, 161 L.Ed.2d 162 (2005) (although the applicability of Delaware law is a factor against forum non conveniens dismissal, trial court's dismissal because Argentine law applied "minimized a significant Delaware interest in the law suit, which is to make available to litigants a neutral forum to adjudicate commercial disputes against Delaware entities, even where the dispute involved foreign law and [though one plaintiff and the defendant are incorporated in Delaware] the parties and conduct are centered in a foreign jurisdiction").

205. *Piper*, 454 U.S. at 260. (Marshall, J., stating that "[e]ven if the Court of Appeals' conclusion [that Scottish law does not apply] is correct, however, all other public interest factors favored trial in Scotland").

206. See infra § 6.18.

207. 330 U.S. 501, 67 S.Ct. 839, 91 L.Ed. 1055 (1947).

jurisdiction."[208] The Courts of Appeal were split as to whether a district court can grant a defendant's motion for a forum non conveniens dismissal without first determining that it has personal jurisdiction over the defendant and subject matter jurisdiction.[209] *Sinochem Int'l Co. v. Malaysia Int'l Shipping Corp.*[210] resolved this conflict: "where [as in this case] subject-matter or personal jurisdiction is difficult to determine, and *forum non conveniens* considerations weigh heavily in favor of dismissal, the court properly takes the less burdensome course."[211]

Justification for this holding lies in the fact that dismissal for lack of either subject matter jurisdiction or personal jurisdiction will not preclude the plaintiff from litigating any issue affecting the merits when the plaintiff sues elsewhere. A possible merits issue that a court may decide in granting a forum non conveniens issue is choice of law.[212] If there is doubt about a district court's personal or subject matter jurisdiction, the court should resolve it before granting a forum non conveniens motion if the ruling will prejudice the plaintiff on choice of law or another issue that affects the merits. It is not fair that a court without jurisdiction should be able to foreclose the plaintiff on any merits-related issue.

§ 4.33C   Shopping Between State and Federal Courts

Federal courts exercising diversity or alienage jurisdiction[213] have applied federal rather than state *forum non conveniens* doctrine.[214]

---

208. Id. at 504, 67 S.Ct. at 841.

209. See Malaysia Int'l Shipping Corp. v. Sinochem Int'l Co., 436 F.3d 349 (3d Cir. 2006), reversed, 549 U.S. 422, 127 S.Ct. 1184, 167 L.Ed.2d 15 (2007) (holding that may not dismiss before jurisdictional determination and collecting authority from Fifth, Seventh, and Ninth circuits in accord, and from Second and D.C. circuits contra).

210. 549 U.S. 422, 127 S.Ct. 1184, 167 L.Ed.2d 15 (2007).

211. Id. at 436, 127 S.Ct. at 1194.

212. See Chick Kam Choo v. Exxon Corp., 486 U.S. 140, 108 S.Ct. 1684, 100 L.Ed.2d 127 (1988).

213. 28 U.S.C. § 1332(a) provides federal district courts with jurisdiction over civil actions between citizens of different states, citizens of a state and foreigners, citizens of different states when foreigners are "additional parties," and a foreign state as plaintiff against United States citizens, when the amount in controversy exceeds $75,000.

214. See Ravelo Monegro v. Rosa, 211 F.3d 509 (9th Cir. 2000); Royal Bed & Spring Co. v. Famossul Industria e Comercio de Moveis, Ltda., 906 F.2d 45, 50 (1st Cir. 1990); In re Air Crash Disaster Near New Orleans, La., 821 F.2d 1147, 1153–59 (5th Cir. 1987), judgment vacated for further consideration of another issue, 490 U.S. 1032, 109 S.Ct. 1928, 104 L.Ed.2d 400 (1989), remanded for reconsideration of damages, otherwise reinstated, 883 F.2d 17 (5th Cir. 1989); Sibaja v. Dow Chem. Co., 757 F.2d 1215, 1219 (11th Cir. 1985). *Accord*, 15 Charles Alan Wright et al., Federal Practice & Procedure § 3828, at 293–94 (2d ed. 1986). It is doubtful that Learned Hand's statement in Weiss v. Routh, 149 F.2d 193, 195 (2d Cir. 1945), that "we should follow the New York decisions" extends beyond the special rule denying jurisdiction over the "internal affairs" of a foreign corporation, or whether, if it does, the decision is viable. Gilbert v. Gulf Oil Corp., 153 F.2d 883, 885 (2d Cir. 1946), rev'd on other grounds, 330 U.S. 501, 67 S.Ct. 839, 91 L.Ed. 1055 (1947), explains *Weiss* as dealing with the internal affairs rule and states that "New York law should not control" with regard to the application of *forum non conveniens*.

The Supreme Court has not decided whether federal courts exercising diversity jurisdiction must apply state *forum non conveniens* doctrine. *See* Piper Aircraft Co. v. Reyno, 454 U.S. 235, 248 n.13, 102 S.Ct. 252, 70 L.Ed.2d 419 (1981) (stating that the Court "need not

Plaintiffs attempt to defeat dismissal by suing in a state court in a jurisdiction whose *forum non conveniens* doctrine is less robust than the federal version.[215] These plaintiffs then prevent removal to federal court

resolve the *Erie* question" because the relevant state law "is virtually identical to federal law"). For explanation of the "*Erie* question" see chapter 10.

In the converse situation, when state courts must apply federal law, the Court has held that state courts need not adopt the federal view of *forum non conveniens*. American Dredging Co. v. Miller, 510 U.S. 443, 114 S.Ct. 981, 127 L.Ed.2d 285 (1994), held that a Louisiana statute preventing forum non conveniens dismissals of maritime actions in state courts is not pre-empted by federal admiralty law. The opinion stated that the doctrine of forum non conveniens is not "either a 'characteristic feature' of admiralty or a doctrine whose uniform application is necessary to maintain the 'proper harmony' of maritime law." Id. at 447. The court left open the question of whether it would reach the same result in an international case. Id. at 456. *American Dredging* involved a suit by a U.S. sailor injured on the Delaware river.

215. Va. Code Ann. § 8.01–265 (Michie 1992) does not permit dismissal of actions for asbestos-related injury or disease. Fox v. Board of Supervisors of La. State Univ., 576 So.2d 978, 989–91 (La. 1991), rejected forum non conveniens on the ground that it is a common-law doctrine and Louisiana is a civil-law jurisdiction. The Louisiana legislature then amended the Code to permit forum non conveniens dismissals of cases brought by plaintiffs not domiciled in Louisiana when the "cause of action is predicated upon acts or omissions originating outside of the territorial boundaries of this state." La. Code Civ. Proc. Art. 123(B). Montana refuses to apply forum non conveniens to FELA cases, but has left open the question whether it will be applied in other circumstances. Labella v. Burlington Northern R.R., 182 Mont. 202, 595 P.2d 1184 (1979). State ex rel. Burlington Northern R.R. v. District Court, 270 Mont. 146, 891 P.2d 493 (1995), reaffirms *Labella* and states "Montana has yet to apply the common law doctrine of forum non conveniens in any non-FELA case." Id. at 498

In addition to the above states, other states have indicated that they are likely to be more hospitable to suits by foreign plaintiffs than federal courts would be after Piper Aircraft Co. v. Reyno, discussed in the previous section.

Delaware may become especially attractive as a forum because of the large number of United States companies that are incorporated there and therefore cannot remove to federal court if sued in Delaware. Ison v. E.I. DuPont de Nemours & Co., 729 A.2d 832 (Del. 1999) reversed the trial court's forum non conveniens dismissal of a product liability suit brought by foreign nationals whose children suffered birth defects in New Zealand and Great Britain. The court stated that although the presumption in favor of a plaintiff's choice of forum "is not as strong in the case of a foreign national plaintiff," the defendant did not show the "overwhelming hardship" that would justify dismissal.

In applying the "overwhelming hardship" requirement for a forum non conveniens dismissal, Delaware courts apply a modified version of the private and public factors that federal and most state courts apply (see § 4.33), the "*Cryo–Maid*" factors taken from General Foods Corp. v. Cryo–Maid, Inc., 198 A.2d 681, 684 (Del. 1964): (1) the relative ease of access to proof; (2) the availability of compulsory process for witnesses; (3) the possibility of a view of the premises; (4) whether the controversy is dependent upon the application of Delaware law which the courts of this State more properly should decide than those of another jurisdiction; (5) the pendency or nonpendency of a similar action or actions in another jurisdiction; and (6) all other practical problems that would make trial of the case easy, expeditious, and inexpensive. But see Aveta, Inc. v. Delgado Colón, 942 A.2d 603 (Del. Ch. 2008) (stay action because of "overwhelming hardship" to Puerto Rican defendant even though a forum-selection clause chose Delaware).

Myers v. The Boeing Co., 115 Wash.2d 123, 794 P.2d 1272 (1990), affirmed a forum non conveniens dismissal of a suit by Japanese nationals against a Washington manufacturer for wrongful deaths resulting from a plane crash in Japan. The court approved the trial court's finding "that the balance of private and public interest factors weighs heavily in favor of trial of damages in Japan" but "took this opportunity to expressly decline to adopt Reyno.... because it simply is not necessary. Proper application of the Gulf Oil [private and public interest] factors alone will lead to fair and equitable results." (Id. at 1280–81).

Picketts v. International Playtex, Inc., 215 Conn. 490, 576 A.2d 518 (1990), reversed the forum non conveniens dismissal of an action for wrongful death of a Canadian who used

by joining a defendant domiciled in that state[216] or of the same citizenship as a plaintiff. This latter tactic works because *Strawbridge v. Curtiss*[217] held that for federal diversity jurisdiction to attach, complete diversity is required, each defendant being of diverse citizenship from each plaintiff. There are some circumstances in which *Strawbridge's* "complete diversity" requirement does not apply. For example, under the Class Action Fairness Act of 2005 a multistate class action may be removed to federal court on the basis of "minimal diversity"—if any member of the plaintiff class is a citizen of a state different from any defendant.[218]

Defendants respond to these tactics either by removing to federal court and contending that the defendants whose presence would bar diversity jurisdiction should be dismissed as improperly joined,[219] or by combing Title 28 of the United States Code to find some basis other than diversity for removal to federal court.[220]

---

the defendant's product in Canada. The court stated: "While the weight to be given the choice of a domestic forum by foreign plaintiffs is diminished, their entitlement to a preference does not disappear entirely." Id. at 525.

216. See 28 U.S.C. § 1441(b) (providing that a case cannot be removed if any defendant is a citizen of the state in which suit is brought); *id.* § 1332(c)(1) (providing that for diversity purposes, a corporation is a citizen of a state in which it is either incorporated or has its principal place of business). See also Swiger v. Allegheny Energy, Inc., 540 F.3d 179 (3d Cir. 2008) (partnership with U.S. partners and a partner who is a dual U.S. and U.K. citizen domiciled in the U.K. cannot be sued using diversity jurisdiction; for diversity purposes, the court must consult the citizenship of all members of the partnership; the partner with dual citizenship is "stateless" and there is no alienage jurisdiction because that partner is not a "subject of a foreign state"; for diversity purposes the court considers only his U.S. citizenship).

217. 7 U.S. (3 Cranch) 267, 2 L.Ed. 435 (1806), overruled on another issue, Louisville C. & C. R.R. v. Letson, 43 U.S. (2 How.) 497, 11 L.Ed. 353 (1844). Chick Kam Choo v. Exxon Corp., 764 F.2d 1148 (5th Cir. 1985), held that for purposes of this complete diversity requirement, all aliens are treated as if they have the same citizenship, so that a citizen of Singapore could not sue a citizen of Liberia under diversity jurisdiction. Under 28 U.S.C. § 1332(a), as amended in 1988, for purposes of determining diversity jurisdiction, "an alien admitted to the United States for permanent residence shall be deemed a citizen of the State in which such alien is domiciled." *See* Singh v. Daimler–Benz AG, 9 F.3d 303 (3d Cir. 1993) (holding that 1332(a) permits federal courts to hear suits brought by aliens admitted for permanent residence against non-resident aliens). Contra Saadeh v. Farouki, 107 F.3d 52, 60–61 (D.C. Cir. 1997) (refusing to make a "literal interpretation" of the 1988 amendment to § 1332(a), which the court finds was intended to contract, not expand diversity jurisdiction, and holding that the amendment does not create diversity jurisdiction between aliens admitted for permanent residence and non-resident aliens). 28 U.S.C. § 1332(a)(3) permits diversity jurisdiction between "citizens of different states in which citizens or subjects of a foreign state are additional parties." But see 13B Wright, supra note 199, § 3604 at 389 (stating that "the inclusion of a citizen of a state as a party or of citizens of diverse states as parties cannot save jurisdiction of an action in which aliens are the principal adverse parties").

218. 28 U.S.C. § 1332 (d).

219. *See* Cabalceta v. Standard Fruit Co., 883 F.2d 1553 (11th Cir. 1989) (reversing the district court's forum non conveniens dismissal after the district court determined that joinder of a forum defendant was fraudulent and remanding for determination of the fraudulent joinder claim under Costa Rican law). If the fraudulent joinder contention is successful, federal diversity jurisdiction is established and the case can be dismissed under federal forum non conveniens standards.

220. If the defendant can implead a "foreign sovereign" for contribution and indemnity, the sovereign can remove the entire action, not just the contribution and indemnity

Sometimes a plaintiff resident in a state of the United States other than the forum may be better off in a federal district court than in a state court. *Esfeld v. Costa Crociere, S.P.A.*[221] holds that the federal forum non conveniens standard applies in diversity cases even when the federal standard is more permissive of the plaintiff's choice of forum than the Florida standard. The federal standard was more permissive because a federal court would consider the suit's contacts with the entire U.S. but a Florida court would consider only contacts with Florida.

§ 4.33D   Conditions for Dismissal

If the forum non conveniens motion is successful, the next battle ground is the conditions that the court will impose for dismissal. *In re Union Carbide Corporation Gas Plant Disaster at Bhopal, India*[222] and *Harrison v. Wyeth Laboratories Division of American Home Products Corp.*[223] provide an interesting contrast in the imposing of conditions for dismissal. *Bhopal* arose out of the explosion in India at a chemical plant operated by a subsidiary of Union Carbide. The explosion released gas that allegedly killed over 2,000 persons and injured over 200,000 others. Plaintiffs included the injured, representatives of decedents, and the Indian government to which Indian legislation gave the exclusive right to represent the victims. The trial judge granted Union Carbide's motion to dismiss on the grounds of forum non conveniens one hundred and forty-five actions commenced in federal courts in the United States and consolidated for pretrial proceedings in the Southern District of New York. He imposed the following conditions on Union Carbide:

(1) consent to the jurisdiction of the courts of India and continue to waive defenses based on the statute of limitations,

(2) agree to satisfy any judgment rendered by an Indian court against it and upheld on appeal, provided the judgment and affir-

---

claim, to federal court. *See* 28 U.S.C. § 1441(d) (permitting a foreign state, if sued in a state court, to remove to federal court for trial without a jury); Nolan v. Boeing Co., 919 F.2d 1058, 1064 (5th Cir. 1990) (permitting removal of entire action). Impleading a foreign sovereign is not as far-fetched as it may seem because the Foreign Sovereign Immunities Act defines a "sovereign" as including "a separate legal person, corporate or otherwise . . . a majority of whose shares of other ownership interest is owned by a foreign state or political subdivision thereof." 28 U.S.C. § 1603(b). Even outside of communist or formerly communist countries, this includes many manufacturers, airlines, and other commercial entities. In *Nolan*, supra, Boeing, the aircraft manufacturer, impleaded the engine manufacturer, which was owned by the French government.

The federal Bankruptcy Act is another basis for removal to federal court. *See* 28 U.S.C. § 157(b)(5) (providing that a "district court shall order that personal injury tort and wrongful death claims shall be tried in the district court in which the bankruptcy case is pending, or in the district court in the district in which the claim arose"); *In re* Pan Am Corp., 16 F.3d 513, 514 (2d Cir. 1994) (holding that a federal district court may transfer a case against a bankrupt, involving claims by foreigners for personal injury and death, "from a state court to itself after the bankrupt announces its intention to move for *forum non conveniens* dismissal")

221.   289 F.3d 1300 (11th Cir. 2002).

222.   809 F.2d 195 (2d Cir.), cert. denied, 484 U.S. 871 (1987).

223.   510 F.Supp. 1 (E.D. Pa. 1980), aff'd w.o. opinion, 676 F.2d 685 (3d Cir. 1982).

mance "comport with the minimal requirements of due process," and

(3) be subject to discovery under the Federal Rules of Civil Procedure of the United States.[224]

Union Carbide accepted these conditions "subject to its right to appeal them"[225] and the district court dismissed. Although the list of conditions is numbered three, the first item contained two requirements—consent to jurisdiction and waiver of defenses based on limitations.

Although this waiver of limitations is common and courts do not customarily distinguish between foreign limitations that ran before suit was brought in the forum and limitations that ran after suit, requiring waiver of foreign limitations that ran before suit is far more questionable. It is likely to reward the most egregious form of forum shopping— shopping for a long limitation period that the forum will apply on the ground that it is "procedural."[226] If the foreign limitation has run and the defendant has not waived it, the requirement for forum non conveniens dismissal that there be a more convenient alternative forum, is violated. The defendant can rebut this objection by asserting that the plaintiff should choose between forum non conveniens dismissal not on the merits and dismissal on the merits on the ground that under proper choice-of-law analysis, the foreign shorter period would apply in the forum.[227]

---

224. *Bhopal*, 809 F.2d. at 198.

225. Id.

226. See Ferens v. John Deere Co., 494 U.S. 516, 110 S.Ct. 1274, 108 L.Ed.2d 443 (1990) (allowing a Pennsylvania resident injured in Pennsylvania to prevail under the Mississippi statute of limitations after Pennsylvania limitations had run). But see Gschwind v. Cessna Aircraft Co., 161 F.3d 602 (10th Cir. 1998), cert. denied, 526 U.S. 1112, 119 S.Ct. 1755, 143 L.Ed.2d 787 (1999) (affirm dismissal conditioned only on waiver of French limitations that ran after suit brought); Florida Rules of Civil Procedure, Rule 1.061(c): "Statutes of Limitation. In moving for forum-non-conveniens dismissal, defendants shall be deemed to automatically stipulate that the action will be treated in the new forum as though it had been filed in that forum on the date it was filed in Florida, with service of process accepted as of that date."

227. See § 3.2C2. But cf. Norex Petroleum Ltd. v. Access Industries, 416 F.3d 146 (2d Cir. 2005), cert. denied, 547 U.S. 1175, 126 S.Ct. 2320, 164 L.Ed.2d 860 (2006), which reversed a forum non conveniens dismissal of a Canadian company's suit to recover against defendants who allegedly had impaired plaintiff's interest in a Russian oil company. A decision by a Russian court barred plaintiff from pursuing its claim in Russia. "[I]t appears that the district court did not, in fact, find a presently available Russian forum for Norex to pursue its claims against the defendants; rather it found the lack of such a forum excusable in light of Norex's own conduct. We here clarify that a case cannot be dismissed on grounds of forum non conveniens unless there is presently available to the plaintiff an alternative forum that will permit it to litigate the subject matter of its dispute. It may well be that a plaintiff that is precluded from litigating a matter in a foreign jurisdiction because of an adverse earlier judgment by its courts will not be able to pursue the claim further in the United States, but the reason for dismissal in such circumstances is our recognition of the foreign judgment in the interest of international comity, not forum non conveniens.... *[F]orum non conveniens analysis does not concern itself with the reason why an alternative foreign forum is no longer available; its singular concern is the fact of present availability.*" Id. at 158–159 (emphasis added). The court further held that the district court could not recognize the Russian judgment without affording the plaintiff an opportunity to raise a challenge to the Russian court's personal jurisdiction over the plaintiff.

On appeal in *Bhopal* the individual plaintiffs continued to oppose dismissal but India changed its position and supported the district court's order. As a practical matter, India's support of the order limited review to the conditions for dismissal. The Second Circuit then proceeded to eliminate conditions numbered two and three. The condition that Union Carbide agree to satisfy any judgment was stricken on the ground that it was not necessary and, as written, might permit enforcement of a judgment that otherwise would be rejected on due process grounds. In the court's view, the condition was not necessary because under New York law, which in alienage cases controlled recognition of foreign judgments in federal court, an Indian money judgment that complied with due process standards of fairness would be recognized. The condition's reference to *"minimal* requirements of due process" created "the risk that it [would] be interpreted as providing for a lesser [due process] standard than we would otherwise require."[228]

The Second Circuit relieved Union Carbide of the condition that it "be subject to discovery under the Federal Rules of Civil Procedure" unless "Indian authorities will permit mutual discovery pursuant to the Federal Rules...."[229] The court reasoned that "[b]asic justice dictates that both sides be treated equally, with each having equal access to the evidence in the possession or under the control of the other."[230]

Harrison v. Wyeth Laboratories Division of American Home Products Corp.[231] provides an interesting contrast with *Bophal* in regard to the defendant's success in avoiding conditions on dismissal. The court granted a forum non conveniens dismissal of a suit brought for injuries and death allegedly caused in the United Kingdom by oral contraceptives manufactured there by defendant's wholly owned subsidiary. Defendant unsuccessfully opposed the standard condition that it submit to personal jurisdiction in the United Kingdom, but apparently offered no objection to the two conditions avoided in *Bhopal*, making "available, at its own expense, any documents, witnesses, or other evidence under its control that are needed for fair adjudication of any actions brought in the United Kingdom by plaintiffs" and paying "any judgment"[232] obtained by the plaintiffs in the United Kingdom. On the other hand *Harrison* did not mention waiver of limitations, one of the conditions that *Bhopal* imposed.

§ 4.33E   Transfer Under 1404(a)

Section 1404(a) of the Judiciary Act provides that: "For the convenience of parties and witnesses, in the interest of justice, a district court may transfer any civil action to any other district or division where it

---

228. *Bhopal*, 809 F.2d at 205.

229. Id. at 205–06.

230. Id. at 205.

231. 510 F.Supp. 1 (E.D. Pa. 1980), aff'd w.o. opinion, 676 F.2d 685 (3d Cir. 1982).

232. Id. at 6.

might have been brought."[233] Thus, when the alternative forum is another federal district court, a federal court may not dismiss a case under the common law doctrine of forum non conveniens, but instead must transfer it under section 1404(a).[234] The most frequent dismissal in federal court will occur when the alternative forum is in another country, but federal courts have dismissed cases when enforcing a forum-selection clause conferring exclusive jurisdiction on a state court.[235]

The last phrase in 1404(a), "where it might have been brought," has presented some problems of construction. The Supreme Court has held that the case may not be transferred to a district where venue would have been improper at the time that suit was brought, even though the defendant now agrees to waive objection to venue there;[236] that a wrongful death action may be transferred to a district in a state where the plaintiffs have not qualified as personal representatives for bringing such an action,[237] and that joining an in personam action an admiralty with an in rem action against a ship does not prevent transfer to a district where the plaintiff could have brought the in personam but not the in rem action.[238]

Transfer under section 1404(a) and forum non conveniens dismissal involve "similar, but by no means identical, objective criteria."[239] The Supreme Court has held that the requirements for transfer under 1404(a) are not as strict as for dismissal under the common law doctrine, because the remedy of transfer is less onerous on the plaintiff than

---

233. 28 U.S.C.A. § 1404(a).

234. See American Dredging Co. v. Miller, 510 U.S. 443, 449 n.2, 114 S.Ct. 981, 986 n.2, 127 L.Ed.2d 285 (1994) (dictum).

235. See International Software Systems, Inc. v. Amplicon, Inc., 77 F.3d 112 (5th Cir. 1996) (collecting authority); cf. Stewart Org. Inc. v. Ricoh Corp., 487 U.S. 22, 29, 108 S.Ct. 2239, 2244, 101 L.Ed.2d 22 (1988) (when ruling on a motion to transfer under 1404(a), a federal standard controls and a forum-selection clause is "a significant factor" that the court should consider with other public and private interest factors). But see Kerobo v. Southwestern Clean Fuels, Corp., 285 F.3d 531 (6th Cir. 2002) (noting circuit split on whether a forum-selection clause may be enforced by dismissal under Rule 12(b)(3) for improper venue and concluding that it cannot when the case has been removed from state court to federal court).

236. Hoffman v. Blaski, 363 U.S. 335, 80 S.Ct. 1084, 4 L.Ed.2d 1254 (1960).

237. Van Dusen v. Barrack, 376 U.S. 612, 84 S.Ct. 805, 11 L.Ed.2d 945 (1964). *Van Dusen* also held that in diversity cases, after transfer the transferee court applies the state law that would have been applied by the transferor court. Ferens v. John Deere Co., 494 U.S. 516, 110 S.Ct. 1274, 108 L.Ed.2d 443 (1990), held that the law that the transferee court would apply governs even if the plaintiff makes the motion for transfer. See § 10.5A.

238. Continental Grain Co. v. The FBL–585, 364 U.S. 19, 80 S.Ct. 1470, 4 L.Ed.2d 1540 (1960).

239. Parsons v. Chesapeake & Ohio Ry., 375 U.S. 71, 73, 84 S.Ct. 185, 186, 11 L.Ed.2d 137, 139 (1963). But see the reviser's note to 1404(a): "Subsection (a) was drafted in accordance with the doctrine of forum non conveniens...." H.Rep. No. 308, 80th Cong., 1st Sess., A 132 (1947); In re Volkswagen of America, Inc., 545 F.3d 304, 314 (5th Cir. en bank, 2008), cert. denied, ___ U.S. ___, 129 S.Ct. 1336, 173 L.Ed.2d 587 (2009): "That § 1404(a) venue transfers may be granted 'upon a lesser showing of inconvenience' than *forum non conveniens* dismissals, however, does not imply 'that the relevant factors [from the *forum non conveniens* context] have changed or that the plaintiff's choice of [venue] is not to be considered.' "

dismissal.[240] This seems a dubious distinction, considering the flexible procedure available to a state court in staying dismissal until satisfied that all conditions that it has imposed for the protection of the plaintiff are met. It is true that a federal court, even though applying the same standards under 1404(a) as a state court would under forum non conveniens, may reach a different decision on transfer than a state court would on dismissal.[241] The transferee federal court may not be in the same location as the alternative state forum and the federal court docket may be more or less crowded than that of the state court.[242]

§ 4.33F   Internal Affairs of Corporations

Courts have traditionally been reluctant "to interfere with or control by injunction or otherwise the management of the internal affairs of a corporation organized under the laws of another State but will leave controversies as to such matters to the courts of the State of the domicile."[243] Suits involving the "internal affairs" of a corporation include stockholder suits to contest the validity of stock options,[244] derivative stockholder suits,[245] suits by the corporation against its stockholders to compel them to surrender stock certificates in return for new certificates,[246] and suits involving construction of the corporation's obligations on securities that it has issued.[247]

This "internal affairs" rule is not entitled to separate status and should be treated as one facet of the more general forum non conveniens doctrine.[248] A court in a state other than the state of incorporation should permit an "internal affairs" suit unless the same factors that would lead it to dismiss under forum non conveniens cause it to find that it is an inconvenient forum for litigation and that suit in another forum, probably the state of incorporation, would better accord with the legitimate interests of the parties and the public.

---

240.   Norwood v. Kirkpatrick, 349 U.S. 29, 75 S.Ct. 544, 99 L.Ed. 789 (1955).

241.   See Parsons v. Chesapeake & Ohio Ry., 375 U.S. 71, 84 S.Ct. 185, 11 L.Ed.2d 137 (1963).

242.   Id.

243.   Rogers v. Guaranty Trust Co., 288 U.S. 123, 130, 53 S.Ct. 295, 297, 298, 77 L.Ed. 652, 656 (1933). See also Ski Roundtop, Inc. v. Hall, 265 Pa.Super. 266, 401 A.2d 1203 (1979); cf. Bartlett v. Dumaine, 128 N.H. 497, 523 A.2d 1 (1986) (forum should not supervise fiduciary duties of trustees of sister-state trust).

244.   Id.

245.   Koster v. (American) Lumbermens Mut. Cas. Co., 330 U.S. 518, 67 S.Ct. 828, 91 L.Ed. 1067 (1947).

246.   Royal China, Inc. v. Regal China Corp., 304 N.Y. 309, 107 N.E.2d 461 (1952).

247.   Williams v. Green Bay & W.R. Co., 326 U.S. 549, 66 S.Ct. 284, 90 L.Ed. 311 (1946).

248.   See Koster v. (American) Lumbermens Mut. Cas. Co., 330 U.S. 518, 527, 67 S.Ct. 828, 833, 91 L.Ed. 1067, 1076 (1947); Williams v. Green Bay & W.R. Co., 326 U.S. 549, 66 S.Ct. 284, 90 L.Ed. 311 (1946); Restatement, Second, § 84, comment *d*.

§ 4.33G   Enjoining Suit in another Jurisdiction

At times a court has taken the extreme step of enjoining a party from bringing or continuing a suit in another jurisdiction.[249] The most justifiable example is enjoining prosecution of a suit subsequently filed outside the forum when the injunction is necessary to protect the forum's ability to give appropriate relief in the matter before it.[250] The factors that would lead a court to issue such an injunction are similar to those that would lead a court in the other state to dismiss the suit on forum non conveniens grounds.[251] Because of the unseemly clash between courts that such an injunction may engender,[252] a court should be extremely reluctant to grant the injunction and should do so only when necessary to prevent fraud or harassment or to protect the forum's ability to give appropriate relief.[253] A court will often enjoin litigation in

---

249. See, e.g., Seattle Totems Hockey Club, Inc. v. National Hockey League, 652 F.2d 852 (9th Cir.1981), cert. denied, 457 U.S. 1105, 102 S.Ct. 2902, 73 L.Ed.2d 1313 (1982) (enjoin defendant's suit in Canada); Air Products & Chem., Inc. v. Lummus Co., 252 A.2d 543 (Del.1969) (enjoining suit in Puerto Rico provided that the moving party stipulates to the applicability of the Puerto Rican statute of limitations); Brown v. Brown, 120 R.I. 340, 387 A.2d 1051 (1978) (marital domicile enjoins husband from proceeding with divorce action in another state). That such an injunction does not violate full faith and credit, see Cole v. Cunningham, 133 U.S. 107, 10 S.Ct. 269, 33 L.Ed. 538 (1890).

250. See, e.g., Mutual Service Ins. Co. v. Frit Indus., Inc. 358 F.3d 1312, 1324–25 (11th Cir. 2004) (after judgment on merits can enjoin attempt to obtain conflicting judgment abroad); PPG Ind., Inc. v. Continental Oil Co., 492 S.W.2d 297 (Tex.Civ.App.—Houston [1st Dist.] 1973, writ ref'd n.r.e.).

251. See Restatement, Second, § 84, comment *h*. Cf. Cook v. Soo Line R.R., 347 Mont. 372, 198 P.3d 310 (2008) (refusing to give full faith and credit to an Illinois judgment granting a forum non conveniens dismissal and ordering to plaintiff to file the action in Indiana).

252. See James v. Grand Trunk Western R.R., 14 Ill.2d 356, 152 N.E.2d 858, cert. denied, 358 U.S. 915, 79 S.Ct. 288, 3 L.Ed.2d 239 (1958) (Illinois enjoins enforcement of a Michigan injunction that enjoined suit in Illinois); Abney v. Abney, 176 Ind.App. 22, 374 N.E.2d 264 (1978), cert. denied, 439 U.S. 1069, 99 S.Ct. 836, 59 L.Ed.2d 34 (1979) (refuse to accord comity to sister state injunction ordering plaintiff not to sue for divorce in the forum) (collecting authority). But see Janak v. Allstate Ins. Co., 319 F.Supp. 215 (W.D.Wis. 1970) (give full faith and credit to Illinois order enjoining proceeding against insolvent except in receivership proceedings in Illinois); Sterk, *The Muddy Boundaries Between Res Judicata and Full Faith and Credit*, 58 Wash. & Lee L. Rev. 47, 95 (2001): "State courts typically take one of two approaches: Either they refuse to enforce the antisuit injunction [issued by a court of another state], concluding that full faith and credit imposes no obligation to enforce, or they enforce the antisuit injunction on grounds of comity. Although courts might mention full faith and credit in enforcing the antisuit injunction, they do not enforce them because of any constitutional compulsion."

One way to avoid this clash is to stay an action in the forum when there is pending litigation on the same subject in a sister state. See section 4.38. For discussion of the relationship between forum non conveniens standards and stay for a prior pending action in a sister state see McWane Cast Iron Pipe Corp. v. McDowell–Wellman Engineering Co., 263 A.2d 281 (Del.1970) (forum non conveniens principles are not controlling when there is a motion to stay for prior pending action in another state; should grant stay even when would not dismiss; forum non conveniens standards are applicable when the sister state action is filed after the forum suit).

253. See Advanced Bionics Corp. v. Medtronic, Inc., 29 Cal.4th 697, 59 P.3d 231, 128 Cal.Rptr.2d 172 (2002) (California court improperly enjoined employer from suing employee in Minnesota to enforce non-competition agreement even though Minnesota action filed after employee and California employer sued in California seeking declaratory relief from non-competition agreement); Crawley v. Bauchens, 57 Ill.2d 360, 312 N.E.2d 236 (1974) (should enjoin proceedings in other states only when those proceedings would result in "fraud, gross wrong, or oppression"); Arpels v. Arpels, 8 N.Y.2d 339, 207 N.Y.S.2d 663, 170 N.E.2d 670 (1960) (refuse to enjoin divorce proceedings in France, because a French divorce would not be entitled to full faith and credit); Delaware, L. & W. R.R. v. Ashelman,

another forum if that litigation violates a valid forum-selection agreement between the parties.[254]

As noted in *General Electric Co. v. Deutz AG*,[255] federal circuits disagree on when to enjoin litigation abroad:

> The federal Courts of Appeals have not established a uniform rule for determining when injunctions on foreign litigation are justified. Two standards, it appears, have developed. Courts following the "liberal" or "lax" standard will issue an injunction where policy in the enjoining forum is frustrated, the foreign proceeding would be vexatious or would threaten a domestic court's in rem or quasi in rem jurisdiction or other equitable considerations, and finally, where allowing the foreign proceedings to continue would result in delay. The Courts of Appeals for the Fifth, Seventh, and Ninth Circuits generally apply this standard.

> By contrast, the Second, Sixth and District of Columbia Circuits use a more restrictive approach, rarely permitting injunctions against foreign proceedings. These courts approve enjoining foreign parallel proceedings only to protect jurisdiction or an important public policy. Vexatiousness and inconvenience to the parties carry far less weight.

> Our Court is among those that resort to the more restrictive standard.

Paramedics Electromedicina Comercial, Ltda v. GE Medical Systems Information Technologies, Inc.[256] adds a "threshold" requirement for considering a motion to enjoin suit abroad: "An anti-suit injunction against parallel litigation may be imposed only if: (A) the parties are the same in both matters, and (B) resolution of the case before the enjoining court is dispositive of the action to be enjoined."

One attempt to prevent parallel litigation in different countries is the Conflict of Jurisdictions Model Law, promulgated by a subcommittee of the American Bar Association Section on International Law and Practice and proposed for adoption in any state that will have it.[257] Only Connecticut has enacted it.[258] The Act directs local courts to refuse

---

300 Pa. 291, 150 A. 475 (1930) (refuse to enjoin suit in New Jersey in the absence of a showing of fraud or harassment or that the suit was brought in New Jersey to evade Pennsylvania law); Christensen v. Integrity Ins. Co., 719 S.W.2d 161 (Tex.1986) (refuse to enjoin suit filed in California after suit filed in Texas).

254. Cf. Canon Latin America, Inc. v. Lantech (CR), S.A., 508 F.3d 597 (11th Cir. 2007), cert. denied, ___ U.S. ___, 128 S.Ct. 2975, 171 L.Ed.2d 889 (2008) (holding injunction improper because the action in the enjoining court would not be dispositive of action enjoined).

255. 270 F.3d 144, 160–61 (3d Cir. 2001). Cf. Quaak v. Klynveld Peat Marwick Goerdeler Bedrijfsrevisoren, 361 F.3d 11, 18–19 (1st Cir. 2004) (taking a position between the opposing views noted in *Deutz* and listing the factors that would rebut a presumption against the issuance of an order that has the effect of halting foreign judicial proceedings).

256. 369 F.3d 645, 652 (2d Cir. 2004).

257. See Conflict of Jurisdictions Model Law (A.B.A. Section on Int'l Law & Practice 1989).

258. Conn. G. Stat. Ann. §§ 50a–201—50a–203.

recognition of a foreign judgment rendered in a parallel proceeding unless a local court has declared the foreign court the proper "adjudicating forum."[259] The Act requires courts to make this declaration within six months of the time of notice that duplicate suits have been filed, or, in the absence of such early decision, when recognition is sought.[260] The criteria for determining the proper adjudicating forum focus on the convenience of the parties and the interest of the forum.[261] This refusal to recognize foreign judgments goes far beyond the Uniform Foreign Money–Judgments Recognition Act's discretionary basis for non-recognition: "in the case of jurisdiction based only on personal service, the foreign court was a seriously inconvenient forum for the trial of the action."[262] It will be interesting to see what effect the Conflict of Jurisdictions statute has when a litigant seeks recognition of a Connecticut judgment in a country that requires reciprocity as a condition of that recognition.[263]

Although a state court may, on forum non conveniens grounds, dismiss a suit brought under the Federal Employers' Liability Act,[264] it may not enjoin a suit under the Act in another state where venue under the Act is proper.[265] Nor may a state court enjoin proceedings in a federal court having in personam jurisdiction over the parties.[266]

The Anti–Injunction Act limits the circumstances under which a federal court can enjoin state-court proceedings: "A court of the United States may not grant an injunction to stay proceedings in a State Court except as expressly authorized by Act of Congress, or where necessary in

---

259. Id. § 50a–201(a).

260. Id. § 50a–201(b), (d).

261. Id. § 50a–202 (listing as criteria "interest of the affected courts in having proceedings take place in their respective forums," "law likely to be applicable," "the forum likely to render the most complete relief," location of "witnesses . . . documents and other evidence," "[w]hether designation of an adjudicating forum is a superior method to parallel proceedings in adjudicating the dispute").

262. § 4(b)(6), 13 Pt. II U.L.A. 59 (2002).

263. Brand, *Enforcement of Foreign Money–Judgments in the United States: In Search of Uniformity and International Acceptance*, 67 NOTRE DAME L. REV. 253, 255 (1991) (stating that "enforcement of United States judgments overseas is often possible only if the United States court rendering the judgment would enforce a similar decision of the foreign enforcing court").

264. Missouri ex rel. Southern R.R. v. Mayfield, 340 U.S. 1, 71 S.Ct. 1, 95 L.Ed. 3 (1950); Douglas v. New York, N.H. & H.R.R., 279 U.S. 377, 49 S.Ct. 355, 73 L.Ed. 747 (1929); People ex rel. Chesapeake & O.Ry. v. Donovan, 30 Ill.2d 178, 195 N.E.2d 634 (1964); State ex rel. Chicago, R.I. & P.R.R. v. Riederer, 454 S.W.2d 36 (Mo.1970); cf. Labella v. Burlington Northern, Inc., 182 Mont. 202, 595 P.2d 1184 (1979) (although forum could apply forum non conveniens to FELA suits, it will not do so).

That federal courts may transfer an FELA suit under 28 U.S.C.A. § 1404(a), see Ex parte Collett, 337 U.S. 55, 69 S.Ct. 944, 93 L.Ed. 1207 (1949).

That, however, a state court may not simply decline to entertain any FELA suit, see McKnett v. St. Louis & S.F. Ry., 292 U.S. 230, 54 S.Ct. 690, 78 L.Ed. 1227 (1934); Mondou v. New York, N.H. & H. R.R., 223 U.S. 1, 32 S.Ct. 169, 56 L.Ed. 327 (1912).

265. Miles v. Illinois Cent. R.R., 315 U.S. 698, 62 S.Ct. 827, 86 L.Ed. 1129 (1942) (attempt to enjoin suit in another state court); Baltimore & O. R.R. v. Kepner, 314 U.S. 44, 62 S.Ct. 6, 86 L.Ed. 28 (1941) (attempt to enjoin suit in a federal court in another state).

266. Donovan v. Dallas, 377 U.S. 408, 84 S.Ct. 1579, 12 L.Ed.2d 409 (1964).

aid of its jurisdiction, or to protect or effectuate its judgments."[267] As the word "stay" suggests, the Act only applies if the state proceedings are commenced before the federal injunction.[268] Although the Anti–Injunction Act does not apply to enjoining future state proceedings, the district court's granting of an injunction is subject to review for abuse of discretion. *Newby v. Enron Corp.*[269] affirmed the district court's enjoining of future actions without the court's permission. Plaintiffs' lawyer had previously filed "at least seven lawsuits in state courts throughout Texas":

> Although the Anti–Injunction Act is an absolute bar to any federal court action that has the effect of staying a pending state court proceeding unless the action falls within a designated exception, it does not preclude injunctions against a lawyer's filing of *prospective* state court actions. Even so, we are constrained by the overarching principle that federal courts must be wary of infringing on legitimate exercises of state judicial power. The All Writs Act provides that federal courts may "issue all writs necessary or appropriate in aid of their respective jurisdictions and agreeable to the usages and principles of law." 28 U.S.C. § 1651(a)....

> [P]rinciples of federalism lie behind our reluctance to adopt an expansive reading of "necessary in aid of jurisdiction," which extends to injunctions against prospective state court proceedings, even though they escape the reach of the Anti–Injunction Act.... At the same time, it is widely accepted that federal courts possess power under the All Writs Act to issue narrowly tailored orders enjoining repeatedly vexatious litigants from filing future state court actions without permission from the court.[270]

§ 4.33G(1) United Kingdom, the Court of Justice of the European Communities, and Canadian Decisions on Enjoining Suit Abroad

In *Smith Kline & French Laboratories v. Bloch*,[271] Lord Denning affirmed a decree enjoining an English medical researcher from proceeding with his United States suit against an English subsidiary and its American parent. The dispute concerned a contractual dispute with the English company, and related allegations of fraud and interference with contract. The injunction by the court below had triggered a typical response—a counter-injunction by the United States court to prevent the American parent from continuing with the English injunction proceedings. Lord Denning nevertheless found England the "natural forum"

---

267. 28 U.S.C. § 2283.

268. See Villar v. Crowley Maritime Corp., 990 F.2d 1489 (5th Cir. 1993).

269. 302 F.3d 295 (5th Cir. 2002), cert. denied, 537 U.S. 1191, 123 S.Ct. 1270, 154 L.Ed.2d 1024 (2003).

270. Id. at 300–01.

271. [1983] 2 All E.R. 72 (Eng. C.A. 1982).

and declared the benefits to plaintiff of suing in the United States "an illegitimate advantage."[272]

In *Societe Nationale Industrielle Aérospatiale v. Lee Kui Jak*,[273] the Privy Council granted an injunction restraining claimants for the wrongful death of a resident of Brunei from pursuing their suit in Texas. A helicopter crash in Brunei caused the death. One of the defendants, a French company with a Texas subsidiary, had manufactured the helicopter. The court found that Brunei was "the natural forum for the action"[274] and that suit in Texas was "oppressive"[275] because the defendants could not implead the Malaysian company that had serviced and operated the helicopter.

On the other hand, the House of Lords in *British Airways Board v. Laker Airways Ltd.*[276] recognized significant United States interests in permitting a low-fare airline incorporated on the isle of Jersey to pursue in an American court an antitrust action against British Airways, British Caledonian Airways, and others. The Lords discharged the antisuit injunction that the Court of Appeal had granted.

The Court of Justice of the European Communities has held that the Brussels Convention, now the Brussels Regulation, precludes a European Union court from enjoining "a party to proceedings pending before it from commencing or continuing legal proceedings before a court of another Contracting State, even where that party is acting in bad faith with a view to frustrating the existing proceedings."[277]

The Canadian position on enjoining suits by Canadians in other countries is stated in a 1993 decision by the Supreme Court of Canada, *Amchem Products Inc. v. British Columbia (Workers' Compensation Board).*[278] *Amchem* reversed the granting of an injunction by a British Columbia trial judge who ordered British Columbia claimants to desist from pursuing their claims for asbestosis injuries in a Texas state court. With two exceptions, the defendants in the Texas action were United States companies that manufactured asbestos and asbestos products. *Amchem* stated that a Canadian court should grant an antisuit injunction only to prevent "serious injustice [resulting from] the failure of a foreign court to decline jurisdiction."[279] In providing "more specific

---

272. Id. at 78.

273. [1987] 3 All E.R. 510 (P.C. 1987) (appeal taken from Brunei).

274. Id. at 524.

275. Id. at 526.

276. [1985] 1 A.C. 58 (H.L. 1984). See also Donohue v. Armco Inc., [2002] 1 All E.R. 749 (H.L. 2002) (improper to enforce with antisuit injunction a forum-selection clause when New York suit involved claims other than those covered by the clause and New York was forum that could best determine all matters in issue). But cf. Midland Bank v. Laker Airways, [1986] 1 All E.R. 526 (Ct.App.) (enjoining Laker's English liquidator from filing an antitrust action in the United States against an English bank, which had a United States subsidiary).

277. Turner v. Grovit, Case C–159/02, [2004] ECR 1–3565, "Ruling" following ¶ 32.

278. [1993] 102 D.L.R.4th 96 (Can.).

279. Id. at 106.

criteria"[280] to assist in this determination, the Court set out the following guidelines: (1) a Canadian court "should not entertain an application for an injunction if there is no foreign proceeding";[281] (2) a domestic court should then entertain the application for an injunction "only if [the Canadian court] is alleged to be the most appropriate forum and is potentially an appropriate forum";[282] (3) the Canadian court must conclude "that the foreign court assumed jurisdiction on a basis that is inconsistent with principles relating to *forum non conveniens* and that the foreign court's conclusion could not reasonably have been reached had it applied those principles";[283] (4) the Canadian "court must conclude that it provides the natural forum for the trial of the action";[284] and finally, (5) the domestic court must find that granting the injunction will not "deprive the plaintiff of advantages in the foreign forum of which it would be unjust to deprive him."[285] With regard to this last requirement, *Amchem* stated that "[a] party can have no reasonable expectations of advantages available in a jurisdiction with which the party and the subject-matter of the litigation [have] little or no connection."[286]

Applying these criteria to the Texas litigation, the Court found that the British Columbia judge who granted the injunction "gave undue weight to the absence of a *forum non conveniens* rule in Texas and to the anti-anti-suit injunction granted by the Texas court."[287] Although Texas courts could not dismiss tort suits on the basis of *forum non conveniens*,[288] due process requirements of the United States Constitution gave those courts "a responsible way to ensure that suits brought before them neither encroach on the sovereignty of foreign jurisdictions nor subject out-of-state defendants to a forum which has an insufficient connection to the subject matter of the suit...."[289] Thus after *Amchem* Canadian courts will not enjoin suits in United States courts except in the most unusual and justifiable instances.

---

280. Id.

281. Id. at 118.

282. Id.

283. Id. at 119.

284. Id. (quoting Lord Goff in SNI Aerospatiale v. Lee Kui Jak [1987] 3 All E.R. 510, 522 (P.C. 1987) (appeal taken from Brunei)).

285. *Amchem*, 102 D.L.R.4th at 119.

286. Id.

287. Id. at 121.

288. *See* Dow Chem. Co. v. Castro Alfaro, 786 S.W.2d 674 (Tex. 1990) (holding that a Texas statute dating back to 1913 precluded *forum non conveniens* dismissals in tort cases). A statute enacted in 1993 permits forum non conveniens dismissals. Tex. Civ. Prac. & Rem. Code Ann. § 71.051.

289. *Amchem*, 102 D.L.R.4th at 124.

§ 4.34 Immunity from Personal Service

Nonresident parties,[290] witnesses,[291] and attorneys,[292] while present in the forum to attend civil proceedings, have been granted immunity from service of process in unrelated civil proceedings. The reason for this grant of immunity is that it contributes to efficient judicial administration. Nonresident parties and their witnesses and attorneys will be encouraged to attend civil proceedings in the forum, and thus assist in the administration of justice, if they know that their physical presence in attendance at those proceedings cannot be used as a basis for judicial jurisdiction over them.[293] Because immunity is granted primarily for the convenience of forum courts and not for the convenience of the persons on whom service is made, the immunity is generally not granted if the process is served in connection with a matter so related to the pending proceedings that immunity from this service will frustrate an attempt to do complete justice in the pending proceedings.[294] The immunity from service lasts while the parties, witnesses, or attorneys are in the forum to attend civil proceedings and for a reasonable time after their attendance is no longer necessary, in order to give them a chance to leave the forum.[295]

Some courts have rejected this immunity-from-service doctrine on the ground that the defendant's ability to raise fraud and forum non conveniens objections to forum jurisdiction are sufficient protection without need for a special immunity doctrine.[296]

---

290. See Steelman v. Fowler, 234 Ga. 706, 217 S.E.2d 285 (1975); Chase Nat'l Bank v. Turner, 269 N.Y. 397, 199 N.E. 636 (1936) (party in attendance at appellate hearing); cf. Uniform Reciprocal Enforcement of Support Act § 32 (1968 Act), § 31 (1958 Act) (participation in proceeding under Act does not confer jurisdiction over party in any other proceeding); Thompson v. Kite, 214 Kan. 700, 522 P.2d 327 (1974) (former wife's failure to comply with orders in proceeding under Act was not a "tort" subjecting her to long-arm jurisdiction).

291. See Shapiro & Son Curtain Corp. v. Glass, 348 F.2d 460 (2d Cir.), cert. denied, 382 U.S. 942, 86 S.Ct. 397, 15 L.Ed.2d 351 (1965); Youpe v. Strasser, 113 F.Supp. 289 (D.D.C.1953) (witness before Congressional committee).

292. Cf. Lamb v. Schmitt, 285 U.S. 222, 52 S.Ct. 317, 76 L.Ed. 720 (1932) (traditional immunity of attorney denied because the claim was related to the pending suit). But see Lieberman v. Warner, 66 Misc.2d 731, 322 N.Y.S.2d 393 (N.Y. City Civ.Ct.1971) (refuses to extend immunity to attorney, collecting authority).

293. See Lamb v. Schmitt, 285 U.S. 222, 52 S.Ct. 317, 76 L.Ed. 720 (1932); Wangler v. Harvey, 41 N.J. 277, 196 A.2d 513 (1963) (also mentioning, but rejecting, the reason that service on the nonresident during pending proceedings may offend the dignity of the court and interrupt the pending proceedings); Chase Nat'l Bank v. Turner, 269 N.Y. 397, 199 N.E. 636 (1936).

294. See Lamb v. Schmitt, 285 U.S. 222, 52 S.Ct. 317, 76 L.Ed. 720 (1932); McDonnell v. American Leduc Petro., Ltd., 456 F.2d 1170 (2d Cir.1972); Kirtley v. Chamberlin, 250 Iowa 136, 93 N.W.2d 80 (1958); Rheaume v. Rheaume, 107 R.I. 500, 268 A.2d 437 (1970); Bekham v. Johnson, 220 Tenn. 572, 421 S.W.2d 94 (1967); cf. Shapiro & Son Curtain Corp. v. Glass, 348 F.2d 460 (2d Cir.), cert. denied, 382 U.S. 942, 86 S.Ct. 397, 15 L.Ed.2d 351 (1965) (although second proceeding was related to the first, there was no showing that the grant of immunity would obstruct judicial administration in the first proceeding); Anderson v. Ivarsson, 77 Wn.2d 391, 462 P.2d 914 (1969) (deny immunity to a party and a witness when suit in which process served was to recover loans that the party and witness had made in the forum to cover their expenses in attending proceedings in the forum).

295. See Restatement, Second, § 83, comment *b*.

296. See Wangler v. Harvey, 41 N.J. 277, 196 A.2d 513 (1963) (party served is an executor defending suit against an estate, service was in an action against him arising out of the same occurrence). See also Oates v. Blackburn, 430 S.W.2d 400 (Tex.Civ.App.1968), writ ref'd n.r.e.

Because, in the light of the fact that many foreign legal systems consider as exorbitant the use of personal presence as the basis for generally-affiliating judicial jurisdiction,[297] nonresident parties, witnesses, and attorneys should be immune from service when the sole constitutional basis for jurisdiction over them is their personal presence at the time of service. On the other hand, if a valid basis for jurisdiction over the persons served exists independently of their personal presence, service of process on them while they are in the forum, even as parties, witnesses, or attorneys, should be permitted as an efficient and reasonable method of giving them notice of and opportunity to be heard in the proceedings being instituted against them.[298]

In order to facilitate the administration of justice, some courts grant immunity from civil process to parties and witnesses in voluntary attendance at criminal proceedings.[299] Because the reason for this immunity is to encourage voluntary attendance at criminal proceedings, the immunity has sometimes not been granted when the person served was compelled to attend the criminal proceedings.[300]

This refusal to grant immunity from civil process to a criminal defendant whose presence in the forum has been compelled, is partly abrogated by the now withdrawn Uniform Criminal Extradition Act:

> A person brought into this state by, or after waiver of, extradition based on a criminal charge shall not be subject to service of personal process in civil actions arising out of the same facts as the criminal proceeding to answer which he is being or has been returned, until he has been convicted in the criminal proceeding, or, if acquitted, until he has had reasonable opportunity to return to the state from which he was extradited.[301]

The reason for this provision of the Uniform Act is to protect those innocent of crime[302] from the abuse of extradition to compel their

297. See supra § 4.8 text accompanying notes 399–406.

298. See Severn v. Adidas Sportschuhfabriken, 33 Cal.App.3d 754, 109 Cal.Rptr. 328 (1973); Rudd v. Rudd, 278 A.2d 120 (D.C.App.1971).

299. See, e.g., Dwelle v. Allen, 193 F. 546 (S.D.N.Y.1912) (immunity from process of grand jury witness); White v. Henry, 232 Ga. 64, 205 S.E.2d 206 (1974); Thermoid Co. v. Fabel, 4 N.Y.2d 494, 176 N.Y.S.2d 331, 151 N.E.2d 883 (1958). But see the following cases denying criminal defendants, who appeared voluntarily for arraignment, immunity from service in civil actions stemming from the events that produced the criminal charges: Car Lease Inc. v. Kitzer, 276 Minn. 289, 149 N.W.2d 673 (1967); Santos v. Figueroa, 87 N.J.Super. 227, 208 A.2d 810 (App.Div.1965).

300. See Poss v. District Court, 158 Colo. 474, 408 P.2d 69 (1965); Matter of Majuri, 23 Misc.2d 353, 195 N.Y.S.2d 986 (1960), aff'd mem., 10 A.D.2d 611, 197 N.Y.S.2d 419 (1960); cf. State ex rel. Sivnksty v. Duffield, 137 W.Va. 112, 71 S.E.2d 113 (1952) (defendant not immune from service while incarcerated awaiting trial on criminal charges stemming from same incident). But see Northumberland Ins. Co. v. Wolfson, 251 A.2d 194 (Del.1969) (witness responding to grand jury subpoena is immune from civil process in unrelated action).

301. Uniform Criminal Extradition Act § 25 (in force in 41 states, U.S. Virgin Islands, and Puerto Rico as of August 1, 2009).

302. Therefore the immunity granted by the Act has been held to expire after a plea of guilty and before sentencing. Bubar v. Dizdar, 240 Minn. 26, 60 N.W.2d 77 (1953).

presence so that they may be served with civil process.[303] Moreover, because persons extradited are protected against this abuse, governors will be less reluctant to sign extradition papers.[304]

In *Rosenblatt v. American Cyanamid Co.,*[305] Justice Goldberg, in chambers, rejected the plea of a defendant in a civil suit that he should not be subject to long-arm tort service. The defendant claimed that if he appeared to defend the tort suit, he would be arrested in a related criminal action for which he was under indictment.

Another immunity from service of process is that customarily accorded to foreign diplomats, whether at the place where they perform their diplomatic functions or while in transit to or from their posts.[306] The reason for this immunity is to avoid offense to a foreign sovereign and to prevent interference with diplomatic duties.[307]

§ 4.35　Consent to the Exclusive Jurisdiction of a Foreign Court

Only three states hold unenforceable forum-selection provisions that choose a forum outside the state.[308] This marks a dramatic change in U.S. courts largely due to the influence of *M/S Bremen v. Zapata Off–Shore Co.,*[309] which although technically a holding only with regard to

303. See Thermoid Co. v. Fabel, 4 N.Y.2d 494, 176 N.Y.S.2d 331, 151 N.E.2d 883 (1958). But see Poss v. District Court, 158 Colo. 474, 408 P.2d 69 (1965), which first holds that the Uniform Act does not help a defendant who returned for arraignment after being released on bond and then denies him immunity because his appearance was not "voluntary."

304. See Thermoid Co. v. Fabel, 4 N.Y.2d 494, 176 N.Y.S.2d 331, 151 N.E.2d 883 (1958).

305. 86 S.Ct. 1, 15 L.Ed.2d 39, appeal dism'd, 382 U.S. 110, 86 S.Ct. 256, 15 L.Ed.2d 192 (1965).

306. See Bergman v. De Sieyes, 170 F.2d 360 (2d Cir.1948).

307. Id.

308. In Idaho and Montana, the refusal to enforce forum-selection clauses is based on statutes invalidating restrictions on enforcing contractual rights "by the usual proceedings in the ordinary tribunals." See Cerami–Kote, Inc. v. Energywave Corp., 116 Idaho 56, 773 P.2d 1143 (1989); State ex rel. Polaris Industries, Inc. v. District Court, 215 Mont. 110, 695 P.2d 471 (1985). But see Fisk v. Royal Caribbean Cruises, Ltd., 141 Idaho 290, 108 P.3d 990 (2005), enforcing a forum agreement in a cruise contract and holding that federal maritime law, as set out in *Carnival Cruise* (discussed infra this section text accompanying notes 298–300), preempted Idaho law. In Iowa, although a forum-selection clause in not legally binding, it will be one of the factors considered in ruling on a motion for a forum non conveniens dismissal. See Davenport Machine & Foundry Co. v. Adolph Coors Co., 314 N.W.2d 432 (Iowa 1982).

309. 407 U.S. 1, 92 S.Ct. 1907, 32 L.Ed.2d 513 (1972); cf. Scherk v. Alberto–Culver Co., 417 U.S. 506, 94 S.Ct. 2449, 41 L.Ed.2d 270 (1974) (enforce agreement to submit claims arising out of contract to arbitration before International Chamber of Commerce in Paris and treating arbitration agreement as a form of forum-selection clause to which the *Bremen* standards for enforcement apply); Uniform Foreign Money–Judgments Recognition Act § 4(b)(5), 13 Pt. II U.L.A. 59 (need not recognize foreign country judgment if proceeding contrary to forum-selection agreement).

There is a split of authority as to whether in diversity cases a federal court applies state law on the recognition of forum-selection clauses. See Coastal Steel Corp. v. Tilghman Wheelabrator Ltd., 709 F.2d 190 (3d Cir.), cert. denied, 464 U.S. 938, 104 S.Ct. 349, 78 L.Ed.2d 315 (1983) (collecting district court opinions on both sides); Preferred Capital, Inc. v. Sarasota Kennel Club, Inc., 489 F.3d 303 (6th Cir. 2007) (forum-selection clause necessary for personal jurisdiction invalidated under state law because state law deter-

federal admiralty cases, cogently stated the need for enforcing forum-selection clauses to facilitate transjurisdictional commercial transactions. *Union Discount Co. v. Zoller*[310] permitted recovery of costs incurred in a New York proceeding, which enforced a forum-selection clause that chose England.

Bremen involved an agreement by a German corporation to tow a Delaware corporation's Houston-based drilling rig from Louisiana to Italy. The rig was damaged in the Gulf of Mexico and taken to a Florida port. The agreement contained a clause stating that any dispute must be litigated before the High Court of Justice in London, England. The rig owner nevertheless filed suit in admiralty in the United States District Court in Tampa. Both the district court and the Fifth Circuit Court of Appeals, sitting en banc, refused to give effect to the forum-selection clause. The Supreme Court vacated the Fifth Circuit opinion and remanded for reconsideration and to give the plaintiff an opportunity to show that the exclusive jurisdiction agreement was unreasonable. The *Bremen* standard for enforcing forum-selection clauses can be summarized as follows: a forum selection clause is enforceable unless the party wishing to sue in violation of the clause demonstrates that trial in the agreed forum "will be so manifestly and gravely inconvenient that [the party] will be effectively deprived of a meaningful day in court,"[311] with two exceptions: (1) the clause is affected "by fraud, undue influence, or overweening bargaining power,"[312] or (2) "enforcement would contravene a strong public policy of the forum."[313]

In the context of the *Bremen* standard, "fraud" applies only if the party resisting enforcement of the forum-selection clause alleges that "the *inclusion of that clause in the contract* was the product of fraud or

---

mines questions of personal jurisdiction).cf. Stewart Org. Inc. v. Ricoh Corp., 487 U.S. 22, 29, 108 S.Ct. 2239, 2244 101 L.Ed.2d 22 (1988) (when ruling on a motion to transfer under 28 U.S.C. § 1404(a), a federal standard controls and a forum-selection clause is "a significant factor" that the court should consider with other public and private interest factors). But cf. P & S Business Machines, Inc. v. Canon USA, Inc., 331 F.3d 804, 808 (11th Cir. 2003) (except in an " 'exceptional' situation" a federal court will order a 1404(a) transfer to enforce a forum-selection clause).

310.   [2002] 1 All E.R. 693 (Ct. App. 2001).

311.   *Bremen*, 407 U.S. at 18, 92 S.Ct. at 1917, 1918, 32 L.Ed.2d at 525. For discussion of lower-court opinions elaborating on the *Bremen* standards for enforcement of forum-selection clauses, see Mullenix, *Another Choice of Forum, Another Choice of Law: Consensual Adjudicatory Procedure in Federal Court*, 57 Fordham L. Rev. 291, 356–60 (1988).

312.   *Bremen*, 407 U.S. at 12, 92 S.Ct. at 1914, 32 L.Ed.2d at 522.

313.   Id. at 15, 92 S.Ct. at 1916, 32 L.Ed.2d at 523. See Wilder v. Absorption Corp., 107 S.W.3d 181, 185 (Ky. 2003) (refusing, 4–3, to enforce an agreement to arbitrate in Washington and ordering arbitration in Kentucky between a Washington manufacturer and a Kentucky distributor because the "inconvenience and unreasonableness of the choice of forum clause results in manifest injustice"); Beilfuss v. Huffy Corp., 274 Wis.2d 500, 685 N.W.2d 373 (Wis. Ct. App. 2004) (refuse to enforce forum-selection clause when chosen forum would validate agreement not to compete that is invalid under Wisconsin law). But see Boss v. American Express Financial Advisors, Inc., 6 N.Y.3d 242, 844 N.E.2d 1142, 811 N.Y.S.2d 620 (2006) (although wage deductions of New York employees contravene New York law, enforce clause choosing Minnesota forum even though Minnesota statute of limitations has run when another clause chooses Minnesota law).

coercion."[314] Under the federal doctrine, in the light of *Carnival Cruise Lines v. Shute*,[315] there is not much room for refusing enforcement on the ground of "undue influence or overweening bargaining power." That case enforced a forum-selection clause in a cruise ticket forcing a passenger from Washington state, who was injured off the coast of Mexico, to sue the cruise line in Florida. The Brussels Regulation gives wide scope to forum-selection clauses,[316] but would not have enforced the clause in a case like *Shute* because it was a consumer transaction.[317]

Much litigation has centered on the interpretation of poorly drafted forum-selection clauses. In case of ambiguity, an American court, unlike a court bound by the Brussels Regulation,[318] will not interpret a consent to jurisdiction ("prorogation" clause) as a promise not to sue elsewhere ("derogation" clause).[319] The clause should make it clear whether if the plaintiff sues in a state court in the chosen state the defendant may remove to federal court,[320] or if suit is in a federal court, whether the defendant can have the case transferred under 28 U.S.C. § 1404(a) to a federal court in another state.[321] As is true of most good drafting, drafting forum-selection clauses requires studying the cases that have litigated the meaning of such clauses and avoiding the ambiguities litigated in those cases. This process would produce a clause something like the following:

> Any action arising from or in any way related to this transaction shall be brought only in the state courts in the state of _____ and both parties agree that they shall not seek forum non conveniens dismissal of any action so brought and shall not seek removal to federal court[322] or, if removal is effected despite this agreement, they shall not move for transfer from the federal district to which the

---

314. Scherk v. Alberto–Culver Co., 417 U.S. 506, 519 n.14, 94 S.Ct. 2449, 2457 n.14, 41 L.Ed.2d 270, 281 n.14 (1974) (emphasis in original).

315. 499 U.S. 585, 111 S.Ct. 1522, 113 L.Ed.2d 622 (1991).

316. See Brussels Regulation, supra § 4.33A note 178, art. 23.

317. Id. art. 15(3): "This section [establishing a consumer's right to bring suit at the consumer's domicile] shall not apply to a contract of transport other than a contract which, for an inclusive price, provides for a combination of travel and accommodation."

See also Stobaugh v. Norwegian Cruise Line Ltd., 5 S.W.3d 232 (Tex. App.—Houston [14th Dist.] 1999), rev. denied, cert. denied, 531 U.S. 820, 121 S.Ct. 62, 148 L.Ed.2d 28 (2000) (refusing to enforce a clause requiring suit in Florida when plaintiffs received the contract over a month after making full payment and plaintiffs would incur a $400 cancellation charge).

318. See Brussels Regulation, supra § 4.33A note 178, art. 23(1).

319. See Citro Florida, Inc. v. Citrovale, S.A., 760 F.2d 1231 (11th Cir. 1985); Keaty v. Freeport Indonesia, Inc., 503 F.2d 955 (5th Cir. 1974) (ambiguity construed against drafter).

320. See Yakin v. Tyler Hill Corp., 566 F.3d 72 (2d Cir. 2009) (enforce agreement construed to waive removal), pet. cert. 130 S.Ct. 401; Spatz v. Nascone, 364 F.Supp. 967 (W.D. Pa 1973) (removal not permitted).

321. See Plum Tree, Inc. v. Stockment, 488 F.2d 754 (3d Cir. 1973) (transfer permitted).

322. See Yakin v. Tyler Hill Corp. 566 F.3d 72, 76 (2d Cir. 2009): "Parties are free to bind themselves to forum selection clauses that trump what would otherwise be a right to remove cases to federal courts."

case has been removed. This forum-selection agreement applies no matter what the form of action, whether in rem, in personam, or any other, and no matter what the theory of the action, whether tort, contract, or any other, or whether based on any statute, rule, or regulation, now existing or hereafter enacted. If either party is sued without that party's consent or collusion in another forum, that party may implead the other party to this agreement for contribution or indemnity.

Sometimes a statute conferring rights on injured parties has raised the issue of the statute's effect on forum-selection clauses. *Vimar Seguros y Reaseguros, S.A. v. M/V Sky Reefer*[323] construed the provision in the Carriage of Goods by Sea Act[324], which invalidates a clause in a bill of lading "lessening" liability under the Act,[325] as not precluding a derogation clause. On the other hand, the Federal Employers' Liability Act[326] has been construed to invalidate a promise by an injured railroad employee that purports to reduce the employee's choice of forum further than would be done by the venue provisions of the Act.[327]

§ 4.36 Force and Fraud

A court will usually exercise its discretion[328] to decline to exercise jurisdiction based on the presence in the forum of the defendant[329] or the defendant's property,[330] if that presence was secured by the plaintiff's use of fraud or unlawful force.[331] Courts have refused to determine

---

323. 515 U.S. 528, 115 S.Ct. 2322, 132 L.Ed.2d 462 (1995).

324. 46 U.S.C.A. §§ 1300–1315. The Act covers contracts "for the carriage of goods by sea to or from ports of the United States, in foreign trade...." Id. § 1300.

325. Id. § 1303(8).

326. 45 U.S.C.A. §§ 51–60.

327. Boyd v. Grand Trunk Western R.R., 338 U.S. 263, 70 S.Ct. 26, 94 L.Ed. 55 (1949); cf. Krenger v. Pennsylvania R.R., 174 F.2d 556, 561 (2d Cir.), cert. denied, 338 U.S. 866, 70 S.Ct. 140, 94 L.Ed. 531 (1949), in which Chief Judge L. Hand, in a concurring opinion, would avoid the employee's agreement, not on the basis of the Federal Employers' Liability Act, but on the ground that the employee had not been fully advised of the effect of the agreement. In Boyd v. Grand Trunk Western R.R., supra, Justices Frankfurter and Jackson concurred in the result on the ground stated by Chief Judge Hand, 338 U.S. at 266, 70 S.Ct. at 28, 94 L.Ed. at 58.

328. That the force and fraud defenses are not jurisdictional, see Restatement, Second, § 82, comment *f*. Query, however, whether jurisdiction based on force or fraud is a violation of due process.

329. See, e.g., Blandin v. Ostrander, 239 F. 700 (2d Cir.1917) (personal service through fraud of third person working with the plaintiff); Citrexsa, S.A. v. Landsman, 528 So.2d 517 (Fla. App. 3d Dist. 1988) (service on defendants attending settlement negotiations); Klaiber v. Frank, 9 N.J. 1, 86 A.2d 679 (1952) (deny effect to sister state judgment based on service obtained by abuse of extradition on assumption that sister state would permit collateral attack on this ground).

330. See, e.g., Commercial Air Charters, Inc. v. Sundorph Aeronautical Corp., 57 F.R.D. 84 (D.Conn.1972); Abel v. Smith, 151 Va. 568, 144 S.E. 616 (1928) (attached note brought into forum by fraud). See also Sea–Gate Tire & Rubber Co. v. Moseley, 161 Okl. 256, 18 P.2d 276 (1933) (dictum); cf. In re Estate of De Camillis, 66 Misc.2d 882, 322 N.Y.S.2d 551 (Surr.Ct.N.Y.County), aff'd w.o. opinion, 327 N.Y.S.2d 554 (1971) (will not appoint administrator of assets transferred to forum as a result of administratrix's fraud).

331. For the contrary view in criminal cases, that the use of unlawful force is not a reason for declining jurisdiction over a defendant, see, e.g., Frisbie v. Collins, 342 U.S. 519,

marital property rights in property that one spouse has unilaterally brought into the forum.[332]

§ 4.37 Special Appearance

Although due process does not require it,[333] a state will permit a defendant to appear in court for the special purpose of attacking the court's jurisdiction over the defendant. The court will not treat this special appearance as itself sufficient to subject the defendant to the court's jurisdiction, if jurisdiction did not otherwise exist. Now that Texas[334] and Mississippi[335] have joined the fold, all states provide some procedure by which the defendant can contest jurisdiction without waiving jurisdictional objections. The procedure for making the special appearance differs from state to state. To avoid the danger of waiving the defendant's jurisdictional objections, counsel should study local procedure. If the procedure requires anything more complicated than objecting to jurisdiction in the defendant's first pleading, retain a local lawyer experienced in making special appearances.

In the federal courts and in many states, objections to jurisdiction are effective if raised in the defendant's first pleading.[336] In most states, a court's denial of defendant's jurisdictional objections is an interlocutory order and the defendant cannot appeal it until the conclusion of the trial, but some states permit an interlocutory appeal.[337] In federal court, if the trial judge states in the order denying the motion to dismiss for lack of personal jurisdiction "that such order involves a controlling question of law as to which there is substantial ground for difference of opinion and that an immediate appeal from the order may materially advance the ultimate termination of the litigation.... [t]he Court of Appeals ... may thereupon, in its discretion, permit an appeal to be

---

72 S.Ct. 509, 96 L.Ed. 541 (1952); State v. Waitus, 226 S.C. 44, 83 S.E.2d 629 (1954), cert. denied, 348 U.S. 951, 75 S.Ct. 439, 99 L.Ed. 743 (1955).

332. See Carroll v. Carroll, 88 N.C.App. 453, 363 S.E.2d 872 (1988) (no jurisdiction to divide marital property taken to forum by wife's unilateral act); Dawson–Austin v. Austin, 968 S.W.2d 319 (Tex. 1998), cert. denied, 525 U.S. 1067, 119 S.Ct. 795, 142 L.Ed.2d 657 (1999) (no jurisdiction to determine rights in property husband brought to Texas from marital domicile). But cf. Abernathy v. Abernathy, 267 Ga. 815, 482 S.E.2d 265 (1997) (have jurisdiction to determine rights of nonresident wife in Georgia property that husband purchased in Georgia after moving there from marital domicile); Restatement, Second, § 60 cmt. *d* (stating that a state will "not usually" exercise jurisdiction to affect interests in a chattel brought there without the consent of the owner).

333. York v. Texas, 137 U.S. 15, 11 S.Ct. 9, 34 L.Ed. 604 (1890).

334. Texas R.C.P. 120a (effective September 1, 1962).

335. Mladinich v. Kohn, 250 Miss. 138, 164 So.2d 785 (1964).

336. See Fed. R. Civ. P. 12(b): "Every defense to a claim for relief in any pleading must be asserted in the responsive pleading if one is required. But a party may assert the following defenses by motion: ... **(2)** lack of personal jurisdiction."

337. See, e.g., Tex. Civ. Prac. & Rem. C. § 51.014(7); Rose v. Firstar Bank, 819 A.2d 1247 (R.I. 2003) (after granting certiorari quash order denying special appearance); cf. Ex parte Dill, Dill, Carr, Stonbraker & Hutchings, P.C., 866 So.2d 519 (Ala. 2003), cert. denied, 540 U.S. 949, 124 S.Ct. 416, 157 L.Ed.2d 281 (2003) (grant mandamus ordering trial court to vacate its order denying special appearance).

taken from such order."[338] District courts rarely certify rulings on personal jurisdiction for interlocutory appeal and circuit courts even more rarely accept them.[339]

If a defendant makes a special appearance and the court denies the motion to dismiss, the defendant must attack this finding of jurisdiction directly, by appeal, if at all. If the defendant withdraws and allows the judgment that there is jurisdiction to become final, this judgment will be res judicata and entitled to full faith and credit in other states.[340] Moreover, a defendant that makes a special appearance subjects itself to the court's jurisdiction to order discovery on the jurisdictional issue.[341] When the defendant prevails in a special appearance, the plaintiff is ordinarily foreclosed from suing again under the same statute and facts.[342]

Instead of making a special appearance, the defendant can refuse to appear and allow the court to render a default judgment. Then the defendant can make a collateral attack on this judgment when the plaintiff attempts to enforce it. The collateral attack is limited to the personal jurisdiction issue. If the collateral attack fails, the defendant has forfeited any defense on the merits.

Not all legal systems give a defendant a tactical choice between making a special appearance and making a collateral attack on a default judgment. Under the Brussels Regulation, a defendant timely served with a document instituting legal proceedings must make a special appearance and may not make a collateral attack on a default judgment on the ground of lack of personal jurisdiction.[343] Article 26(1) does

---

338. 28 U.S.C. § 1292(b).

339. For the two years, 1994 and 1995, in the Second Circuit there were only "35 motions for leave to appeal under § 1292(b), of which only eight were granted." Koehler v. Bank of Bermuda Ltd., 101 F.3d 863, 866 (2d Cir. 1996) (refusing to entertain interlocutory appeal of the denial of bank's motion to dismiss for lack of personal jurisdiction).

340. See Purser v. Corpus Christi State Nat'l Bk., 258 Ark. 54, 522 S.W.2d 187 (1975); Connell v. Connell, 119 Ga.App. 485, 167 S.E.2d 686, Ga. cert. denied (1969) (cannot make collateral attack even to contend conversion of special to general appearance violated due process); Paffel v. Paffel, 732 P.2d 96 (Utah 1986) (must give full faith and credit to ruling against party who made special appearance in sister state); Restatement, Second, § 81, comment *e*; Developments, 73 Harv. L. Rev. at 997; cf. Baldwin v. Iowa State Traveling Men's Assoc., 283 U.S. 522, 51 S.Ct. 517, 75 L.Ed. 1244 (1931) (finding of jurisdiction in lost special appearance is res judicata in second forum—res judicata and not full faith and credit because both are federal courts). But see Perry v. Perry, 639 S.W.2d 780 (Ky.1982) (lost special appearance not entitled to full faith and credit, distinguishing *Baldwin*, supra this note, as not involving full faith and credit); Erlich Foods Int'l v. 321 Equip. Co., 80 N.C.App. 71, 341 S.E.2d 69 (1986) (refuse to give full faith and credit to ruling in special appearance in California).

341. See Insurance Corp. of Ireland, Ltd. v. Compagnie des Bauxites de Guinee, 456 U.S. 694, 102 S.Ct. 2099, 72 L.Ed.2d 492 (1982) (after defendant has made a special appearance and refuses to obey a discovery order on the jurisdictional issue, it is a proper sanction to shift the burden of proof on that issue from the plaintiff to the defendant).

342. See Swan v. Sargent Ind., 620 P.2d 473 (Okl.App.), cert. denied (Okl.1980); cf. Universal Cooperatives, Inc. v. Tasco, Inc. 300 N.W.2d 139 (Ia.1981) (does not foreclose service under another long arm provision—in first case the constitutional issue was expressly left open); Galle v. Allstate Ins. Co., 451 So.2d 72 (La.App. 4th Cir.1984) (not res judicata against another party in the same case).

343. Brussels Regulation, supra § 4.33A note 178, art 34(2).

provide that a European Union court "shall declare of its own motion that it has no jurisdiction unless its jurisdiction is derived from the provisions of this Regulation." This reflects the civil law tradition in which the trial judge plays a far more active roll than in common law courts, especially in the United States. One of the important civil maxims is jura novit curia, the court knows the law.

Jurisdictional rulings of the courts of foreign countries are not entitled to full faith and credit and the defendant may collaterally attack these rulings under United States due process standards.[344] This distinction concerning foreign judgments does not improperly discriminate against them because the foreign judgment is measured under the same due process standard as a United States judgment; the defendant could not have raised objections under the United States Constitution in the foreign court. The United Kingdom does discriminate against judgments of countries with which it does not have a judgment-recognition treaty, recognizing far fewer bases for personal jurisdiction in foreign courts than are available in United Kingdom courts.[345]

Although U.S. defendants who make special appearances in foreign courts may make collateral attacks in U.S. courts on the foreign basis for jurisdiction, § 5(a)(2) of the Uniform Foreign Money–Judgments Recognition Act provides: "The foreign judgment shall not be refused recognition for lack of personal jurisdiction if ... the defendant voluntarily appeared in the proceedings, other than for the purpose or protecting property seized or threatened with seizure in the proceedings or of contesting the jurisdiction of the court over him."[346] *Nippon Emo–Trans Co. v. Emo–Trans, Inc.*[347] held that this provision bars a collateral attack on the jurisdiction of a Japanese court when the New York defendant made a special appearance in that court to contest personal jurisdiction and, when the court held that it had personal jurisdiction, presented a defense on the merits.[348]

---

344. See Somportex Ltd. v. Philadelphia Chewing Gum Corp., 453 F.2d 435 (3d Cir.1971), cert. denied, 405 U.S. 1017, 92 S.Ct. 1294, 31 L.Ed.2d 479 (1972) (after finding that English court's exercise of jurisdiction satisfied due process, enforce English default judgment after English court ruled defendant's defaulted special appearance in England became a general appearance); Uniform Foreign Money–Judgments Recognition Act § 5(a)(2), 13 U.L.A. pt. II 73 (2002) (can refuse recognition of judgment of foreign country for lack of personal jurisdiction although defendant "voluntarily appeared ... for the purpose of ... contesting the jurisdiction of the court over him").

345. See 1 Dicey & Morris, Conflict of Laws, 487–88 (13th ed. 2000, Lawrence Collins ed.) (Rule 36, stating that only the following four bases are recognized for personal jurisdiction in foreign courts for recognition of judgments from countries with which the United Kingdom has not joined in a judgment-recognition treaty: the plaintiff instituted the proceedings while the defendant was present in the foreign country, the defendant sued or counterclaimed in the proceedings, or voluntarily appeared, or consented before suit to submit to the court's jurisdiction).

346. 13 U.L.A. pt. II 73 (2002).

347. 744 F.Supp. 1215 (E.D. N.Y. 1990).

348. Id. at 1225. As an alternative ground, the court finds that the Japanese court's assertion of jurisdiction was consistent with New York law. Id. at 1233. See in accord with *Nippon*, CIBC Mellon Trust Co. v. Mora Hotel Corp. N.V., 100 N.Y.2d 215, 792 N.E.2d 155, 762 N.Y.S.2d 5 (2003), cert. denied, 540 U.S. 948, 124 S.Ct. 399, 157 L.Ed.2d 279 (2003)

In Washington, a defendant who prevails in a special appearance may recover attorney fees.[349] This is a salutary rule that other states should adopt.

Now that under the federal rules and the procedure in most states a defendant can object to personal jurisdiction by simply including the objection in defendant's first pleading, some courts have made statements like: "Rule 12 has abolished for the federal courts the age-old distinction between general and special appearances."[350] As Arthur Wellesley, the first Duke of Wellington, replied when a minor government official greeted him with "Mr. Jones, I believe", "if you believe that, you'll believe anything."[351] Rule 12 and similar state rules did not abolish the distinction between general and special appearances; they made a special appearance easier. If under such rules the defendant does not object to personal jurisdiction in the defendant's first pleading, the defendant has made a general appearance and waived any objection to the court's jurisdiction.[352]

§ 4.38   Stay Because of Pending Action

The fact that a suit between the same parties on the same claims is pending in another state will not bar an action in the forum.[353] Only a prior final judgment will have this effect.[354] But the pendency of such a suit in another jurisdiction is a basis on which the forum may exercise its discretion to stay the proceeding in the forum until the outcome of the other suit is known.[355] The stay is likely to be granted if it is apparent that the plaintiff may obtain complete relief in the other suit[356]

(under Uniform Act, if defendant does anything more in foreign court than preserve jurisdictional objection, defendant waives right to raise jurisdictional objection in U.S. court).

349.   See Scott Fetzer Co. v. Weeks, 114 Wn.2d 109, 786 P.2d 265 (1990).

350.   Orange Theatre Corp. v. Rayherstz Amusement Corp., 139 F.2d 871, 874 (3d Cir.), cert. denied, 322 U.S. 740, 64 S.Ct. 1057, 88 L.Ed. 1573 (1944).

351.   Elizabeth Longford, Wellington:—Pillar of State 148 (1972, 1st U.S. edition).

352.   See U.S. v. 51 Pieces of Real Property, 17 F.3d 1306, 1314 (10th Cir. 1994) ("Federal Rule of Civil Procedure 12 provides that objections to personal jurisdiction or service of process must be raised in a party's first responsive pleading or by motion before the responsive pleading").

353.   See Mutual Life Insurance Co. v. Brune's Assignee, 96 U.S. 588, 24 L.Ed. 737 (1878); Kerr v. Willetts, 48 N.J.L. 78, 2 A. 782 (1886); Scott v. Demarest, 75 Misc. 289, 135 N.Y.S. 264 (City Ct. of N.Y., Trial Term, 1912).

354.   See Scott v. Demarest, 75 Misc. 289, 135 N.Y.S. 264 (City Ct. of N.Y., Trial Term, 1912) (dictum).

355.   See Microsoftware Computer Systems, Inc. v. Ontel Corp., 686 F.2d 531 (7th Cir.1982) (federal proceeding should be stayed for pending state proceeding absent peculiarly federal interest); P. Beiersdorf & Co. v. McGohey, 187 F.2d 14 (2d Cir.1951) (stay granted in federal court because of pending state case); Mottolese v. Kaufman, 176 F.2d 301 (2d Cir.1949) (stay granted in federal court because of pending state case); Domingo v. States Marine Lines, 253 A.2d 78 (Del.Super.1969); Dodge v. Superior Court, 139 Cal.App. 178, 33 P.2d 695 (1934); Power Train, Inc. v. Stuver, 550 P.2d 1293 (Utah 1976) (stay, but not dismissal, permitted); De Dampierre v. De Dampierre, [1988] 1 A.C. 92 (H.L.) (stay wife's divorce in England when husband's divorce pending in France; Brussels Regulation, discussed in next paragraph, not applicable to matrimonial actions).

356.   See Restatement, Second, § 86, comment *b*.

in a convenient forum[357] and if the stay will alleviate a needless multiplicity of actions and prevent harassment of the defendant.[358]

Under the Brussels Regulation when "proceedings involving the same cause of action and between the same parties are brought in the courts of different Member States, any court other than the court first seised. . . . shall decline jurisdiction in favour of that court."[359]

The "first seised" rule of article 27 has the cost of inducing a race to the courthouse. This cost is increased by several rulings of the Court of Justice of the European Communities that permit debtors to bring defensive suits in a jurisdiction with notoriously slow procedures—the so-called "Italian Torpedo." *Tatry v. The Owners of the Ship Maciej Rataj*[360] holds that the forum first seized has exclusive jurisdiction even though the action is for a negative declaratory judgment of no liability to the natural plaintiff. *Erich Gasser GmbH v. MISAT Srl*[361] holds that even though the parties had agreed that they would litigate only in the court second seized, that court cannot proceed until the court first seized declares that it has no jurisdiction.[362] Nor it is permissible for the court second seized to proceed on the ground that the proceedings in the first forum are "excessively long."[363]

---

357. See Domingo v. States Marine Lines, 253 A.2d 78 (Del.Super.1969).

See the discussion of the doctrine of forum non conveniens in section 4.33. For a discussion of the relationship between standards for staying an action because of a pending action in another state and for forum non conveniens dismissal, see McWane Cast Iron Pipe Corp. v. McDowell–Wellman Engineering Co., 263 A.2d 281 (Del.1970) (will stay for prior action in another state even when forum would not dismiss, but forum non conveniens standards apply if action in other state was brought after forum action).

358. See Mottolese v. Kaufman, 176 F.2d 301 (2d Cir.1949); First Midwest Corp. v. Corporate Finance Associates, 663 N.W.2d 888, 890 (Iowa 2003) (trial court abused its discretion in not granting a stay pending trial in Nebraska because refusal "permitted unreasonable—in fact blatant—forum shopping by the plaintiff").

359. Brussels Regulation, supra § 4.33A note 178, art. 27.

360. Case C–406/92, [1994] ECR I–5439.

361. Case C–116/02, [2003] ECR I–14693.

362. But cf. Speed Investments Ltd. v. Formula One Holdings Ltd., [2005] 1 W.L.R. 1936 (Ct. App. 2004), (the court second seized need not yield to the court first seized if the second-seized court has exclusive jurisdiction under the Brussels Regulation).

363. *Erich Gasser,* supra note 361. But see European Convention for the Protection of Human Rights and Fundamental Freedoms (European Convention on Human Rights) art. 6(1): "In the determination of his civil rights and obligations . . . everyone is entitled to a fair and public hearing within a reasonable time by an independent and impartial tribunal established by law." The European Court of Human Rights has rendered judgments against Italy compensating applicants for pecuniary and non-pecuniary damages resulting from violations of art. 6(1) by excessively long court proceedings. See Capuano v. Italy, 13 E.H.R.R. 271 (1987) (applicant's suit for increasing the burden on the easement she granted to her vendor pending for over 10 years and the Court of Appeal has not yet rendered a judgment after 4 years; applicant granted pecuniary and non-pecuniary compensation); Santilli v. Italy, 14 E.H.R.R. 421 (1991) (applicant not entitled to pecuniary damages because he lost in the Italian courts, but he is entitled to non-pecuniary compensation for the delay); Massa v. Italy, 18 E.H.R.R. 266 (1993) (applicant not entitled to pecuniary damages because Italian law gives full compensation for delay in payment of government pension, but he is entitled to non-pecuniary damages); cf. Paccione v. Italy, 20 E.H.R.R. 396 (1995) (find violation of art. 6(1) because of excessively long proceedings in the Court of Audit, but dismiss claim because applicant did not timely submit his claims for compensation).

The Uniform Law Conference of Canada has codified the law of forum non conveniens in the Court Jurisdiction and Proceedings Transfer Act (CJPTA) § 11.

11(1) After considering the interests of the parties to a proceeding and the ends of justice, a court may decline to exercise its territorial competence in the proceeding on the ground that a court of another state is a more appropriate forum in which to hear the proceeding.

(2) A court, in deciding the question of whether it or a court outside British Columbia is the more appropriate forum in which to hear a proceeding, must consider the circumstances relevant to the proceeding, including

(a) the comparative convenience and expense for the parties to the proceeding and for their witnesses, in litigating in the court or in any alternative forum,

(b) the law to be applied to issues in the proceeding,

(c) the desirability of avoiding multiplicity of legal proceedings,

(d) the desirability of avoiding conflicting decisions in different courts,

(e) the enforcement of an eventual judgment, and

(f) the fair and efficient working of the Canadian legal system as a whole

British Columbia, Nova Scotia, and Saskatchewan have enacted CJPTA. In Lloyd's Underwriters v. Cominco, Ltd.[364], the Supreme Court of Canada held that § 11 applies to parallel litigation. Private individuals and the State of Washington sued a British Columbia company in Washington for environmental damage. The company sued Lloyd's in Washington for a declaratory judgment that its Lloyd's policy covered the claims. Later the same day Lloyd's sued the company in British Columbia for a declaration of the rights of the parties under the policy. The Supreme Court of Canada affirmed the British Columbia trial judge's denial of the company's motion to stay the proceedings until a judgment in the Washington case. The court found that the judge had not abused his discretion in applying § 11

Unlike the Court of Justice of the European Communities, United Courts have refused to defer to a first-filed action in another jurisdiction when that action is by the natural defendant to preempt an imminent action by the natural plaintiff.[365]

The United States Supreme Court has restricted the circumstances in which federal courts may stay or dismiss an action because of pending proceedings in state court. In *Colorado River Water Conservation District v. United States*[366] the United States sued in federal district court in

---

364. 2009 SCC 11 (2009).

365. See Sensient Colors Inc. v. Allstate Ins. Co., 193 N.J. 373, 387–88, 939 A.2d 767, 775 (2008) (collecting authority).

366. 424 U.S. 800, 96 S.Ct. 1236, 47 L.Ed.2d 483 (1976).

Colorado for a declaration of rights to waters in certain Colorado rivers. Colorado provided a state procedure, utilizing Water Referees and Water Judges, for the adjudication of water claims. A pending state adjudication concerned the same rivers involved in the district court suit. The Supreme Court held that although abstention from the exercise of federal jurisdiction because of pending state proceedings "is the exception, not the rule,"[367] this was a rare case in which the district court was correct in dismissing the suit in deference to the state proceedings. A federal statute consented to jurisdiction over the United States in state water rights proceedings.[368] That statute indicated a federal policy of avoiding "piecemeal adjudication of water rights in a river system."[369] The Colorado comprehensive system for adjudicating water rights best serves this policy. Moreover, the motion for dismissal was made soon after the filing of the complaint, the suit affected extensive state water rights, the district court was 300 miles from the area of Colorado where the water rights were disputed, and the United States was already a party to other Colorado state water rights proceedings.

The court gave some examples of situations in which deference to state-court proceedings might be appropriate:

> It has been held, for example, that the court first assuming jurisdiction over property may exercise that jurisdiction to the exclusion of other courts.... In assessing the appropriateness of dismissal in the event of an exercise of concurrent jurisdiction, a federal court may also consider such factors as the inconvenience of the federal forum, the desirability of avoiding piecemeal litigation, and the order in which jurisdiction was obtained by the concurrent forums. No one factor is necessarily determinative; a carefully considered judgment taking into account both the obligation to exercise jurisdiction and the combination of factors counselling against that exercise is required. Only the clearest of justifications will warrant dismissal.[370]

Moses H. Cone Memorial Hospital v. Mercury Construction Corp.[371] emphasized the duty of a district court to adjudicate the matter before it despite pending state litigation. A construction company filed suit in federal court to compel arbitration of a dispute pursuant to an agreement between the company and a hospital for which it was erecting additions to the hospital's building. Before the federal suit, the hospital had filed a suit in state court to resolve the dispute. The district court stayed the action pending resolution of the state-court suit. The Supreme Court held that the district court had abused its discretion in granting the stay. "Applying the *Colorado River* factors to this case, it is

---

367. Id. at 813, 96 S.Ct. at 1244.

368. 43 U.S.C. § 666.

369. *Colorado River*, 424 U.S. at 819, 96 S.Ct. at 1247.

370. Id. at 818–19, 96 S.Ct. at 1246–47 (citations omitted).

371. 460 U.S. 1, 103 S.Ct. 927, 74 L.Ed.2d 765 (1983).

clear that there was no showing of the requisite exceptional circumstances to justify the District Court's stay."[372]

In *Quackenbush v. Allstate Insurance Co.*,[373] the California Insurance Commissioner sued Allstate in state court to recover reinsurance proceeds that he claimed were due to insolvent insurance companies. Allstate removed to federal court on diversity grounds and moved to compel arbitration. The federal district court remanded the case to state court because resolution of the issue required deciding a disputed question of state law. The Supreme Court held that the remand was improper, although it did not determine whether a stay of the federal action pending resolution of the disputed state-law question would have been proper: "Under our precedents, federal courts have the power to dismiss or remand cases based on abstention principles only where the relief being sought is equitable or otherwise discretionary."[374]

These Supreme Court cases involve federal-court deference to pending state proceedings. Federal courts of appeal differ as to whether the principles of these cases apply when the pending litigation is in a foreign country. In *Posner v. Essex Insurance Co.*,[375] the Eleventh Circuit changed a district court's dismissal to a stay pending the outcome of an action in Bermuda. A year before the suit in a federal district court in Florida, a Bermuda insurance company had filed a suit in Bermuda seeking a declaratory ruling on the validity of policies issued to a Florida company. Then the Florida company sued the insurer in Florida for nonpayment of damage claims. The court held that restraints that the Supreme Court had placed on the power of federal courts to abstain because of parallel state proceedings did not apply to parallel proceedings in foreign countries: "The relationship between the federal courts and the states (grounded in federalism and the Constitution) is different from the relationship between federal courts and foreign nations (grounded in the historical notion of comity)."[376] When parallel proceeding were pending in a foreign court the decision whether to stay the action in the United States turned on the application of three factors: "(1) a proper level of respect for the acts of our fellow sovereign nations—a rather vague concept referred to in American jurisprudence as international comity; (2) fairness to litigants; and (3) efficient use of scarce judicial resources."[377] These factors supported the stay pending completion of the Bermuda litigation.

In *Royal and Sun Alliance Insurance Co. of Canada v. Century Int'l Arms, Inc.*,[378] however, the Second Circuit stated:

---

372. Id. at 19, 103 S.Ct. at 939.

373. 517 U.S. 706, 116 S.Ct. 1712, 135 L.Ed.2d 1 (1996).

374. Id. at 731, 116 S.Ct. at 1728.

375. 178 F.3d 1209 (11th Cir. 1999).

376. Id. at 1223.

377. Id. at 1223–24 (quoting Turner Entertainment Co. v. Degeto Film GmbH, 25 F.3d 1512, 1518 (11th Cir. 1994)).

378. 466 F.3d 88 (2d Cir. 2006).

[I]f the parallel proceeding is in a foreign jurisdiction, the district court need not consider the balance between state and federal power dictated by our Constitution. Conversely, if the parallel proceeding is in a state court, the district court need not concern itself with issues of international relations. However, while the relevant factors to be considered differ depending on the posture of the case, the starting point for the inquiry remains unchanged: a district court's "virtually unflagging obligation" to exercise its jurisdiction.[379]

The court held it error for the district court to dismiss an action because of pending Canadian litigation but stated that on remand the trial judge could consider the advisability of issuing a temporary stay until the court could determine whether the Canadian action "will in fact offer an efficient vehicle for fairly resolving all the rights of the parties."[380]

§ 4.39   Local Action

Most states apparently still follow the rule that a forum will not entertain suit on a cause of action to recover compensation for trespass upon or harm done to land in another state.[381] A few courts have rejected the rule that such actions are "local" and must be tried at the situs of the land.[382] New York has changed the rule by statute.[383]

The local action rule, as a complete bar to suit except at the situs, is senseless and originated for reasons that have long ceased to exist.[384] Jurors in England were supposed to have personal knowledge of the facts in issue and all cases had to be tried in the neighborhood of the occurrence. A contemporary "reason" often advanced to justify the rule is that trying such an action may result in questions of title to foreign land with measurements, testimony of local people, and a view desirable.[385] But the same arguments could be advanced in other cases, such as one for conversion of timber, where the defense is based on alleged ownership of the land from which the timber was severed. The conver-

---

379. Id. at 93 (quoting Colorado River Water Conservation District v. United States, 424 U.S. at 817).

380. Id. at 96.

381. See, e.g., Livingston v. Jefferson, 15 Fed.Cas. 660 (No. 8411) (C.C.D.Va.1811); Ellenwood v. Marietta Chair Co., 158 U.S. 105, 15 S.Ct. 771, 39 L.Ed. 913 (1895); Hesperides Hotels Ltd. v. Muftizade, [1978] 3 W.L.R. 378 (House of Lords, 1978).

382. See Wheatley v. Phillips, 228 F.Supp. 439 (W.D.N.C.1964); Reasor–Hill Corp. v. Harrison, 220 Ark. 521, 249 S.W.2d 994 (1952); Little v. Chicago, St.P., M. & O. Ry., 65 Minn. 48, 67 N.W. 846 (1896). See also Ingram v. Great Lakes Pipe Line Co., 153 S.W.2d 547 (Mo.App.1941) (Missouri venue statute construed as ending local action rule); cf. Silver Surprize, Inc. v. Sunshine Mining Co., 74 Wash.2d 519, 445 P.2d 334 (1968) (suit for damages for removal of ore was one for breach of contract and could not be converted to a local action by defendant's alleging in its answer that defendant had title to the ore removed).

383. N.Y. McKinney's Real Prop.Actions & Proc.Law § 121.

384. See Restatement, Second, § 87, comment *a*.

385. See Looper, *Jurisdiction over Immovables: The Little Case Revisited after Sixty Years,* 40 Minn. L. Rev. 191, 197–98 (1956) (repeating, but not agreeing with, this argument).

sion case, however, would not be subject to the local action rule.[386] If in fact a case can be tried more conveniently at the situs of land, application of the flexible doctrine of forum non conveniens would seem to meet the problem better than the local action rule's blanket prohibition.[387]

---

386. See Ellenwood v. Marietta Chair Co., 158 U.S. 105, 15 S.Ct. 771, 39 L.Ed. 913 (1895) (dictum); Hesperides Hotels Ltd. v. Muftizade, [1978] 3 W.L.R. 378 (House of Lords, 1978) (permitting action for conversion of chattels on the foreign realty but not for trespass to the realty).

387. See Looper, supra note 385, at 199–200.

Chapter 5

MARRIAGE, DIVORCE, CUSTODY, AND SUPPORT

§ 5.1A Marriage

Typical circumstances under which it is necessary to choose the law to govern the validity of a marriage are as follows. A man and woman, domiciled in state F, wish to get married. Their marriage would be "void" under F law, because they are closely related—uncle and niece,[1] or first cousins,[2] or one or both of them is too young,[3] or one or both of them has been divorced in F.[4] In order to escape F's interdiction, the couple travel to state X. The law of X permits marriage between persons in their circumstances. The couple marries in state X and then quickly returns to state F where they establish their marital domicile and cohabit until one of them dies intestate. The surviving partner claims a spouse's share in the decedent's estate. This claim is contested by other relatives of the decedent, who contend that the marriage is "void", that the surviving partner is therefore not a "spouse" within the meaning of F's intestacy law, and that, therefore, the estate should go to those who would take in the absence of a spouse. Assuming that, if the marriage had been celebrated in F, this argument would prevail, does the quick trip to state X, many years ago, change the result?

Most of the time, the answer has been "yes". A state in the position of F, the domicile of at least one of the parties before the marriage and the first marital domicile, will, subject to two exceptions, hold the marriage valid if valid under the law of the state where it was celebrated.[5] The first exception occurs under the statutes of several states

---

1. See, e.g., Catalano v. Catalano, 148 Conn. 288, 170 A.2d 726 (1961); In re May's Estate, 305 N.Y. 486, 114 N.E.2d 4 (1953).

2. See, e.g., In re Mortenson's Estate, 83 Ariz. 87, 316 P.2d 1106 (1957); In re Miller's Estate, 239 Mich. 455, 214 N.W. 428 (1927).

3. See, e.g. State v. Graves, 228 Ark. 378, 307 S.W.2d 545 (1957); Wilkins v. Zelichowski, 26 N.J. 370, 140 A.2d 65 (1958).

4. See, e.g., Bogen v. Bogen, 261 N.W.2d 606 (Minn.1977); Randall v. Randall, 216 Neb. 541, 345 N.W.2d 319 (1984); Farber v. U.S. Trucking Corp., 26 N.Y.2d 44, 308 N.Y.S.2d 358, 256 N.E.2d 521 (1970); Garett v. Chapman, 252 Or. 361, 449 P.2d 856 (1969); In re Estate of Lenherr, 455 Pa. 225, 314 A.2d 255 (1974); Korf v. Korf, 38 Wis.2d 413, 157 N.W.2d 691 (1968). Remarriage after divorce should be distinguished from remarriage before the divorce is final. The latter, absent some saving provision in the law of the divorcing state, would result in a polygamous marriage invalid everywhere. See, Restatement, Second, Conflict of Laws § 283 comment *l* (1971) [hereinafter cited as Restatement, Second].

5. See Renshaw v. Heckler, 787 F.2d 50 (2d Cir.1986) (common law marriage valid under law of state in which vacationing, issue one of entitlement to widow's social security benefits, New York law); Etheridge v. Shaddock, 288 Ark. 481, 706 S.W.2d 395 (1986) (no

declaring that if any person residing and intending to continue to reside in the state contracts a marriage in another state that is prohibited and void under the law of the residence, the marriage is void as though entered into in the residence.[6] The second exception applies when an F

---

moral unfitness for custody of child because second marriage to first cousin was valid in state where performed, although not the marital domicile); In re Miller's Estate, 239 Mich. 455, 214 N.W. 428 (1927) (first cousins); Bogen v. Bogen, 261 N.W.2d 606 (Minn.1977) (Minnesota law prohibits remarriage within 6 months after divorce decree but marriage in Nebraska held valid in subsequent divorce action); Gallegos v. Wilkerson, 79 N.M. 549, 445 P.2d 970 (1968) (common-law marriage); Mott v. Duncan Petroleum Trans., 51 N.Y.2d 289, 434 N.Y.S.2d 155, 414 N.E.2d 657 (1980) (common-law marriage); Farber v. U.S. Trucking Corp., 26 N.Y.2d 44, 308 N.Y.S.2d 358, 256 N.E.2d 521 (1970) (remarriage after divorce); In re May's Estate, 305 N.Y. 486, 114 N.E.2d 4 (1953) (uncle and niece); Garrett v. Chapman, 252 Or. 361, 449 P.2d 856 (1969) (dictum) (violation of six-month waiting period after divorce); In re Estate of Lenherr, 455 Pa. 225, 314 A.2d 255 (1974) (remarriage after divorce for adultery); Korf v. Korf, 38 Wis.2d 413, 157 N.W.2d 691 (1968) (divorced husband, having a duty to support his minor children, remarries without court permission); cf. Cook v. Carolina Freight Carriers Corp., 299 F.Supp. 192 (D.Del.1969) (common-law marriage by establishing marital domicile in state where permitted after first cohabiting in state where ceremonial marriage required; court indicates this typical result); Estate of Smart v. Smart, 676 P.2d 1379 (Okl.App.1983) (common-law marriage of parties domiciled elsewhere valid under law of forum where they made frequent visits). But see Grant v. Superior Court, 27 Ariz.App. 427, 555 P.2d 895 (1976) (short stay not sufficient for common-law marriage); Walker v. Yarbrough, 257 Ark. 300, 516 S.W.2d 390 (1974) (same); In re Stahl's Estate, 13 Ill.App.3d 680, 301 N.E.2d 82 (1973) (same, and state where marriage allegedly took place requires more than short stay for common-law marriage); Goldin v. Goldin, 48 Md.App. 154, 426 A.2d 410 (1981) (refuse to recognize common-law marriage under law of state to which couple made skiing trips); Laikola v. Engineered Concrete, 277 N.W.2d 653 (Minn.1979) (same under law of state where temporarily resided); Matter of Marriage of Wharton, 55 Or.App. 564, 639 P.2d 652 (1982) (same under law of state where frequently visited); R. Leflar et al., American Conflicts Law § 220 (4th ed.1986); Restatement, Second, § 283, comment *j*.

For a bizarre blend of the law of the domicile and the place of celebration to invalidate a marriage and deny the putative wife alimony, see Randall v. Randall, 216 Neb. 541, 345 N.W.2d 319 (1984).

Hudson Trail Outfitters v. District of Columbia Dep't of Employment Services, 801 A.2d 987 (D.C. 2002), deals with the converse problem of a marriage invalid under the law of the place of celebration. A widow was receiving worker's compensation death benefits from D.C. After her husband's death she cohabited with a man in Virginia, which had also been the marital domicile. She and the man traveled to, Nicaragua, where they went through a religious marriage ceremony, but did not record the marriage in the civil register. In Nicaragua a marriage is not civilly valid until registered. If the woman's marriage was valid, her D.C. worker's compensation death benefits would end. Held: the widow is entitled to continue receiving death benefits because under Virginia law, which the court applies, the law of the place of celebration determines validity.

6.   See Ill. Comp. Stat. Ann. ch. 750, act 5 § 216; N.H. Rev. Stat. § 457.3; Wisc. Stat. Ann. § 765.04; cf. Ill. Comp. Stat. Ann. ch. 750, act 5 § 217 (marriage in Illinois invalid if nonresident marries in Illinois when marriage invalid in home state).

For the contrary view, see Uniform Marriage and Divorce Act § 210, 9A pt. 1 U.L.A. 194 (1998): "All marriages contracted ... outside this State, that were valid at the time of the contract or subsequently validated by the laws of the place in which they were contracted or by the domicil of the parties, are valid in this State." (Act adopted in 9 states as of January 1, 2006 but one of these states omits § 210).

For an example of a court displaying heroic feats of construction in order to avoid the apparently extraterritorial marriage-invalidating act in its state, see Korf v. Korf, 38 Wis.2d 413, 157 N.W.2d 691 (1968) (marriage by divorced person having duty to support minor children contracted without court permission; Wisconsin had Uniform Marriage Evasion Act and provision in issue referred to a marriage "whether entered into in this state or elsewhere," but the court held that this statute did not apply to a marriage in Illinois, affirming the denial of the husband's motion for a judgment that his marriage was null and

court regards the marriage as not only contrary to F local law but also so offensive to common decency that the court will refuse to validate the marriage under the law of the place of celebration. In order for the marriage to offend the F court's sensibilities so deeply, the marriage will usually have to be polygamous, or between persons so closely related that the court views their marriage with horror.[7] In the absence of an expressly extraterritorial invalidating statute in F,[8] marriages of first cousins have generally not evoked this degree of disfavor;[9] opinion is divided on uncle-niece unions;[10] marriage between brother and sister or between persons in the direct line of consanguinity, such as parent-child or grandparent-grandchild, would be well beyond the pale.[11]

There are two reasons why it is probably unwise to summarize the discussion thus far in a choice-of-law rule such as: "The validity of a marriage is determined by the whole law, including the conflict of laws rules, of the state that was the domicile of at least one partner before marriage and was the first marital domicile. The conflicts rules of this state will usually validate the marriage if valid where celebrated unless either the state prohibits the marriage by an expressly extraterritorial statute or the marriage is contrary to a strongly-held policy of the state."[12]

The first reason why such a generalization is of doubtful value is that it would be based, for the most part, on what courts at the first marital domicile have done, and therefore is not a reliable guide as to

---

void). But see State v. Mueller, 44 Wis.2d 387, 171 N.W.2d 414 (1969) (contra result after amendment of statute to make its extraterritorial application clearer).

7.   See State v. Graves, 228 Ark. 378, 307 S.W.2d 545 (1957) (holding forum's nonage statute inapplicable); In re Miller's Estate, 239 Mich. 455, 214 N.W. 428 (1927) (forum's statute prohibiting first cousins to marry is inapplicable); In re May's Estate, 305 N.Y. 486, 114 N.E.2d 4 (1953) (forum's prohibition of uncle-niece marriages is inapplicable); cf. Westminster City Council v. C, [2009] 2 W.L.R. 185 (Eng. Ct. App. 2008) (declaring invalid a marriage performed over the telephone between the bride in Bangladesh and the groom in England when the groom did not have the intellectual capacity to marry under English standards but the marriage was valid in Bangladesh).

Restatement, Second, § 283, comment *k*: "[T]he only rules that the forum would be likely to find embody a sufficiently strong policy of that state to warrant invalidation of an out-of-state marriage are rules which prohibit polygamous marriages, certain incestuous marriages, or the marriage of minors below a certain age."

8.   See supra note 6 and accompanying text; In re Mortenson's Estate, 83 Ariz. 87, 316 P.2d 1106 (1957) (applying expressly extraterritorial forum statute prohibiting marriages between first cousins).

9.   In re Estate of Loughmiller, 229 Kan. 584, 629 P.2d 156 (1981); Ghassemi v. Ghassemi, 998 So.2d 731 (La. App. 1st Cir. 2008); In re Miller's Estate, 239 Mich. 455, 214 N.W. 428 (1927); Leflar, supra note 5, § 221; Storke, *The Incestuous Marriage—A Relic of the Past*, 36 U.Colo. L. Rev.473, 499 (1964).

10.   See In re May's Estate, 305 N.Y. 486, 114 N.E.2d 4 (1953) (valid); Catalano v. Catalano, 148 Conn. 288, 170 A.2d 726 (1961) (invalid); Leflar, supra note 5, § 221 (majority view validates).

11.   See In re Miller's Estate, 239 Mich. 455, 214 N.W. 428 (1927) (dictum).

12.   Cf. Schwebel v. Ungar, 42 D.L.R.2d 622 (Ont.Ct.App. 1963) (capacity to marry is determined by the law of the domicile at the time of marriage); Act on the General Rules of Application of Laws, Law No. 10 of 1898 as newly titled and amended 21 June 2006 (Japan), art. 24(1): "For each party, the formation of a marriage shall be governed by his or her national law."

what other courts would do. The second reason is that it may be undesirable for a court in a state that is not the first marital domicile to invalidate the marriage just because a court in the first marital domicile would have done so. For example, suppose that an uncle and niece domiciled in X, marry in F, make X their marital domicile for a year and then move to F where they live as husband and wife for twenty years. One partner dies and the other claims in F the inheritance rights of a spouse. F permits uncle-niece marriages, but X does not and an X court would have declared this marriage invalid if the same issue had arisen while X was the marital domicile. Now, however, F not X, has the predominant interest in whether the marriage should be regarded as "valid" for inheritance purposes. It is F that will have to abide the social consequences of permitting or not permitting the surviving partner to inherit. It is therefore undesirable, and unlikely, that F would look to "the whole law" of X to prevent inheritance,[13] and a choice-of-law rule that indicated the contrary would be inaccurate. Moreover, the marital domicile is likely to validate a marriage that is valid under the domicile's law but invalid where celebrated.[14]

§ 5.1B   Distinction between Validity and Incidents

Even though a marriage is valid under the principles just discussed, whether a specific incident of that marriage may be enjoyed in a particular state depends upon whether enjoyment of the incident would offend a strongly held policy of that state. For example, in the days before it was decided that miscegenation statutes are unconstitutional,[15] cohabitation in Tennessee by a white man and a Negro woman, who were married in Mississippi where such marriages were then valid, resulted in an indictment for miscegenetic cohabitation.[16] On the other hand, Mississippi, when it did have a miscegenation statute in force, held that a white man could inherit his Negro wife's Mississippi property because the couple had been married and domiciled in Illinois.[17] Miscegenetic cohabitation would be deeply offensive to local policy, but inheritance would not.

---

13. Cf. In the Matter of the Estate of Murnion, 212 Mont. 107, 686 P.2d 893 (1984) (marriage valid under law of marital domicile at husband's death although not valid under law of marital domicile at time of agreement to enter into common-law marriage); In re Estate of Shippy, 37 Wn.App. 164, 678 P.2d 848 (1984) (marriage held valid under law of marital domicile at husband's death although invalid where celebrated); Restatement, Second, § 283, illustration 2.

14. See McPeek v. McCardle, 888 N.E.2d 171 (Ind. 2008) (holding a marriage performed in Ohio with an Indiana marriage license is valid on the alternative grounds that the marriage is not void in Ohio, but even if invalid under Ohio law, it would be recognized in Indiana).

15. Loving v. Virginia, 388 U.S. 1, 87 S.Ct. 1817, 18 L.Ed.2d 1010 (1967) (Virginia miscegenation statute violates both the due process and the equal protection clauses of the Fourteenth Amendment).

16. State v. Bell, 66 Tenn. (7 Baxter) 9 (1872).

17. Miller v. Lucks, 203 Miss. 824, 36 So.2d 140 (1948). See also In re Dalip Singh Bir's Estate, 83 Cal.App.2d 256, 188 P.2d 499 (1948) (intestate distribution of California personalty to decedent's two wives in India, neither wife contesting the right of the other).

§ 5.1C Is Validation under the Law of the Place of Celebration Desirable?

Why should a marriage that would have been "void" for a particular purpose, if celebrated in the forum between forum domiciliaries, be declared valid for that same purpose just because the forum citizens celebrated their marriage in another state? As we have seen,[18] American courts typically reach this result.

There are a number of grounds on which such a process of validation might be defended. A marriage should be upheld whenever valid to avoid upsetting the expectations of the parties and to legitimate children.[19] In many of the cases resulting in validation of the marriage, the particular incident of the marriage in issue is little related to the purposes of the forum's invalidating statute. For example, if the issue is whether a surviving partner may inherit as a "spouse" despite a forum statute declaring marriages between first cousins "void," the purposes of the statute, whether eugenic,[20] or to avoid abuse of close family relationships, are more directly served by preventing cohabitation than by denying inheritance rights.[21] Refusing to recognize the surviving "spouse" as heir can serve only to punish the survivor and, perhaps, deter others from similar unions.

These same arguments, however, could be made in a completely local non-conflicts case. The only functional difference between a case in which the partners have paid a brief visit to a sister state to speak their vows and one in which they have remained at home is that the parties may have relied upon the law of the place of celebration to validate their marriage. But in a case in which they have gone to another state with the specific purpose of avoiding the interdiction of their domicile, there is doubt as to whether this reliance is justifiable or should be given much weight. The policies underlying the domicile's invalidating rule are just as applicable as if the ceremony had been performed locally and the state that has no contact except as a place of celebration can have only an officious interest in wishing its validating policy to prevail over the contrary policy of the domiciliary state.[22]

---

18. See § 5.1A.

19. See Restatement, Second, § 283, comment *h*.

20. But see Bucca v. State, 43 N.J.Super. 315, 321, 128 A.2d 506, 510 (Ch. 1957): "Geneticists agree generally that the only effect upon offspring would be an increased chance of transmitting any disease or weakness which already existed in the blood line. Such incestuous relationship [uncle-niece in *Bucca*] may be treated not as biologically harmful but only as sociologically improper."

21. See Storke, supra note 9 at 499.

22. See Wilkins v. Zelichowski, 26 N.J. 370, 140 A.2d 65 (1958) (applying New Jersey law to annul for nonage a marriage celebrated in Indiana between New Jersey domiciliaries); Hussain v. Hussain, [1982] 3 All E.R. 369, [1982] 3 W.L.R. 679 (Ct.App.1982) (marriage is not potentially polygamous because law of husband's English domicile, not law of Pakistan where celebrated, would determine whether husband could validly marry a second wife).

Because of the same absence of interest by the place of celebration in the validity of the marriage, a marriage invalid where celebrated should be upheld if valid under the law of the state that is the domicile of the parties before and after marriage. If the parties have

It can be argued that, although analysis of the choice-of-law problem concerning the validity of a marriage in terms of the respective "interests" of the domicile and of the place of celebration would point to invalidation, validation under the law of the place of celebration is nevertheless desirable. By this device, the court is able to escape a draconian forum law with which it has little sympathy and to articulate a "reason" for that result that seems plausible and does not openly flout the legislative will.[23]

There are some problems with this use of conflicts mumbo jumbo for the selective avoidance of a benighted local statute. The statute is left in force for domestic cases. To the extent that escape from the statute is permitted to a favored few who may have the luck, or the knowledge, or the affluence to take advantage of the validating conflicts rule, there is discrimination against the poor and the uninformed and pressure is lessened for change in the bad law.[24] It might be preferable for the court to display its lack of sympathy with the forum's statute by seeking creative and intelligent ways to mitigate the harsher effects of that statute in all cases, domestic and interstate. The court can construe "void" to mean "voidable"[25]—that is, valid unless attacked during

different domiciles before marriage, validation should be under the law of the state that becomes the marital domicile, particularly if this was the domicile of one of the parties before marriage. See Mpiliris v. Hellenic Lines, Ltd., 323 F.Supp. 865 (S.D.Tex.1969), aff'd mem., 440 F.2d 1163 (5th Cir.1971); Radwan v. Radwan (No. 2) [1972] 3 All E.R. 1026 (Family Div.); cf. Fentiman, *The Validity of Marriage and the Proper Law*, 44 Cambridge L. J. 256 (1985) (English cases apply the "proper law" of status); Maddaugh, *Validity of Marriage and the Conflict of Laws: A Critique of the Present Anglo–American Position*, 23 Toronto L. J. 117, 146 (1973) (law of "intended marital domicil" should control); Reese, *Marriage in American Conflict of Laws*, 26 Int. & Comp. L.Q. 952, 955 (1977) ("no marriages have been held invalid [under a law other than that of the place of celebration] except by application of the law of a State where at least one of the spouses was domiciled at the time of marriage and where both made their home thereafter"). An alternative reference rule that would validate under either the law of the place of celebration or the law of the domicile should govern minor formalities, on which the domicile has no very strong policy. A rule invalidating common-law marriages, may reflect a strong interest of the domicile, and not a minor formality. See Metropolitan Life Ins. Co. v. Chase, 294 F.2d 500 (3d Cir.1961); cf. In re Marriage of Reed, 226 N.W.2d 795 (Iowa 1975) (under "significant contacts" test, common-law marriage that was not valid where parties cohabited during most of the period of alleged marriage, not recognized as valid in forum where man domiciled). But see Restatement, Second, § 283, comment c: "the state where the marriage was celebrated may have a real interest in the application to non-residents of a rule regulating the form that a marriage ceremony should take"; Hartley, *The Policy Basis of the English Conflict of Laws of Marriage*, 35 Modern L. Rev. 571, 574 (1972) (same).

23. See von Mehren & Trautman, The Law of Multistate Problems 219 (1965). Professor Myres S. McDougal referred to this process of obfuscation as the "squid function," comparing the use of cryptic legal reasoning to the practice of a squid, which spews an inky cloud when threatened. See Feliciano, *The Application of the Law: Some Recurring Aspects of the Process of Judicial Review and Decision Making*, 37 Am.J.Juris. 17, 35 n.57 (1992) (referring to Professor McDougal's use of the term "to several generations of his students in the classroom").

24. Cf. Sherrer v. Sherrer, 334 U.S. 343, 370 n.18, 68 S.Ct. 1087, 1104 n.18, 92 L.Ed. 1429, 1446 n.18 (1948) (Frankfurter, J., dissenting, making similar arguments against requiring full faith and credit for the jurisdictional finding in a bilateral divorce).

25. See State v. Graves, 228 Ark. 378, 385, 307 S.W.2d 545, 550 (1957). But see In re Mortenson's Estate, 83 Ariz. 87, 89–90, 316 P.2d 1106, 1107 (1957) (rejecting the argument that "void" means voidable when the same statutory section that covered the first cousins in issue, also included parent-child and brother-sister marriages).

coverture. Even better, when a question concerns the enjoyment of some incident normally flowing from marriage, it is time to stop responding to that question by determining whether the marriage is "valid" in some abstract sense for all purposes.[26] A court should compare the purposes of the invalidating rule with the marital incident in issue and not apply the invalidating rule if enjoyment of the incident would not substantially undermine those purposes.[27] It is passing strange, for example, to deprive a woman, who has lived with a man as his wife for twenty years, of her "widow's" claim to workers' compensation benefits on the ground that she was the decedent's first cousin.

If, despite these arguments, courts continue, as they probably will, to use a pseudo-conflicts analysis in order to avoid draconian forum marriage law, this conduct is understandable. There is great temptation to elude the local rule.[28] We should recognize, however, that this sort of adjudication bears about as much resemblance to a consequences-based approach to conflicts problems as reading tea leaves.

§ 5.1D Same–Sex Marriage and Civil Union

Courts will frequently have to face the problem of how to deal with same-sex unions legal in other jurisdictions but not in the forum. The Supreme Judicial Court of Massachusetts has declared "that barring an individual from the protections, benefits, and obligations of civil marriage solely because that person would marry a person of the same sex

---

26. See Meisenhelder v. Chicago & N.W. Ry. Co., 170 Minn. 317, 213 N.W. 32 (1927) (surviving partner not "widow", entitled to compensation under the Federal Employers' Liability Act because a first cousin of the decedent, but the issue of the marriage were "children," applying Uniform Marriage Evasion Act in force at the marital domicile); Restatement, Second, § 283, comment *a*: "the courts have usually acted on the assumption that a decision of questions involving the incidents of a marriage should be preceded by a determination of the validity of the marriage."

27. See Chlystek v. Califano, 599 F.2d 1270 (3d Cir.1979); Estate of Borax v. Commissioner, 349 F.2d 666 (2d Cir.1965), cert. denied 383 U.S. 935, 86 S.Ct. 1064, 15 L.Ed.2d 852 (1966); In re Estate of Lenherr, 455 Pa. 225, 314 A.2d 255 (1974); D. Currie, *Suitcase Divorce in the Conflict of Laws: Simmons, Rosenstiel, and Borax*, 34 U. Chi. L. Rev. 26, 75 (1966); Engdahl, *Proposal for a Benign Revolution in Marriage Law and Marriage Conflicts Law*, 55 Iowa L. Rev. 56, 109 (1969); Fine, *The Application of Issue–Analysis to Choice of Law Involving Family Law Matters in the United States*, 26 Loyola L. Rev. 295, 319 (1980); Maddaugh, supra note 22, at 144; Reese, supra note 22, at 952 ("the validity of a marriage should be determined in the light of the particular issue involved"); Swan, *A New Approach to Marriage and Divorce in the Conflict of Laws*, 24 Univ. Toronto L. J. 17, 53 (1974) (distinguishes question of status from "narrower" question of incident in issue).

28. A good example is Lieblein v. Charles Chips, Inc., 32 A.D.2d 1016, 301 N.Y.S.2d 743 (1969), aff'd mem., 28 N.Y.2d 869, 322 N.Y.S.2d 258, 271 N.E.2d 234 (1971). A woman claiming workers' compensation benefits due a "widow" had married the decedent in New York in violation of a New York divorce decree prohibiting her remarriage without court permission during the life of her divorced husband. The court found that she had contracted a valid common-law marriage during a one-week visit to Georgia.

If a court at the marital domicile decides, in its wisdom, to elude a forum law that prohibits the marriage, no other state should deign to correct the domicile's conflicts technique. In this regard some states are officious in providing that a marriage contracted in the state by a party residing and intending to continue to reside in another state is void if such marriage would be void if contracted in the other state. See, e.g., Ill. Comp. Stat. Ann. ch. 750, act 5, § 217; Wis. Stat. Ann. § 765.04(3)

violates the Massachusetts Constitution."[29] The Court subsequently ruled that proposed legislation permitting civil unions but not same-sex marriages would violate the equal protection and due process requirements of the state Constitution.[30] On May 17, 2004, same-sex couples began marrying in Massachusetts.

The Supreme Court of Alaska has held that affording benefits to spouses of state and municipal employees but not to same-sex partners of employees violates article 1 § 1 of the Alaska constitution, which guarantees "equal rights, opportunities, and protection under the law."[31]

The Vermont legislature has legalized same-sex marriages overriding the governor's veto.[32] Effective January 1, 2010, a New Hampshire statute permits same-sex marriages.[33] The Supreme Courts of Connecticut[34] and Iowa[35] have held that state laws barring marriage between same-sex couples violate the equal protection clauses of the states' constitutions. The Maine legislature passed a law permitting same-sex marriages, but in November 2009 Maine voters repealed it in a referendum.

A New York appellate court has held 3–2 that the surviving member of a Vermont civil union was not entitled to recognition as a "spouse" for purposes of bringing an action under New York's wrongful death statute.[36] The couple was domiciled in New York before and after the marriage ceremony. In 2008, a New York appellate court held that same-sex marriages performed in jurisdiction where they are valid are entitled to recognition in New York.[37] The Governor of New York then issued a directive that state agencies must recognize same-sex marriages performed in jurisdictions where they are valid. New York trial courts have rejected challenges to the legality of the Governor's directive. The New York Court of Appeals has granted leave to appeal an opinion holding valid the Department of Civil Service announcement that it would recognize same-sex marriages valid in the states where the marriages were performed so that same-sex partners of employees are entitled to spousal benefits provided by state employment.[38]

---

29. Goodridge v. Department of Public Health, 440 Mass. 309, 344, 798 N.E.2d 941, 969 (2003)

30. Opinions of the Justices to the Senate, 440 Mass. 1201, 802 N.E.2d 565 (2004).

31. Alaska Civil Liberties Union v. State of Alaska, 122 P.3d 781 (Alaska 2005).

32. Vt. St. 2009 No. 3 §§ 1,2.

33. N.H. Rev. Stat. § 457–1–a.

34. Kerrigan v. Commissioner of Public Health, 289 Conn. 135, 957 A.2d 407 (2008).

35. Varnum v. Brien, 763 N.W.2d 862 (Iowa 2009).

36. Langan v. St. Vincent's Hospital of N.Y., 25 A.D.3d 90, 802 N.Y.S.2d 476 (2005).

37. Martinez v. County of Monroe, 850 N.Y.S.2d 740, 50 A.D.3d 189 (N.Y. App. 4th Dept. 2008), leave to appeal dism'd, action not finally determined, 10 N.Y.3d 856, 859 N.Y.S.2d 617, 889 N.E.2d 496 (2008).

38. Lewis v. New York State Department of Civil Service, 60 A.D.3d 216, 872 N.Y.S.2d 578 (N.Y. App. Div.), leave to appeal granted, 12 N.Y.3d 705, 879 N.Y.S.2d 52, 906 N.E.2d 1086 (2009).

Courts have ruled on the issue of whether they will dissolve a same-sex civil union or marriage formed in another state where it is valid. The Supreme Court of Rhode Island held 3–2 that the Family Court, which has jurisdiction "to grant divorce from the bond of marriage," does not have jurisdiction to divorce a same-sex couple married in Massachusetts because "marriage" does not include same-sex unions.[39] On the other hand, after the Supreme Judicial Court of Massachusetts declared that same-sex couples are entitled to the marital status, the Superior Court of Massachusetts dissolved a civil union formed in Vermont.[40] A New York trial court held that it has subject matter jurisdiction to divorce a same-sex couple married in Canada, where legal, even though New York does not permit such marriages.[41]

In *Lewis v. Harris*[42] the New Jersey Supreme court held 4–3 that although same-sex marriage is not a right under the New Jersey Constitution, same-sex couples must be afforded the same rights and benefits enjoyed by spouses. The court ordered that the state legislature, within 180 days, pass legislation giving same-sex couples such rights and benefits. The dissenters stated that the state Constitution did afford the right to same-sex marriage. On December 14, 2006, the New Jersey legislature enacted a law extending to same-sex couples all the rights, privileges, and duties of married couples, but did not confer the title of "marriage" on the newly authorized civil unions. The governor signed the bill on December 21, 2006; it took effect February 19, 2007.

In May 2008, the Supreme Court of California held that California Family Code provision barring marriages between same-sex couples violated the equal protection clause of the California Constitution.[43] In November 2008, California voters approved an initiative amending the California Constitution to ban same-sex marriages. In May 2009 the California Supreme Court held that the amendment is valid but that same couples who married between the date of the Court's May 2008 decision and the amendment remain validly married.[44]

The California Family Code provides for registration of domestic partners and states: "Registered domestic partners shall have the same rights ... and shall be subject to the same ... duties under law ... as are granted to and imposed upon spouses."[45]

---

39.   Chambers v. Ormiston, 935 A.2d 956 (R.I. 2007).

40.   Salucco v. Alldredge, 17 Mass. L. Rep. 498 (Mass. Super. 2004).

41.   Beth R. v. Donna M., 19 Misc.3d 724, 853 N.Y.S.2d 501 (N.Y.Sup.2008). See also B.S. v. F.B., 25 Misc.3d 520, 883 N.Y.S.2d 458 (N.Y.Sup.2009) (grant defendant's motion to dismiss an action to divorce parties to a Vermont civil union without prejudice to plaintiff's right to file a complaint for dissolution of the civil union).

42.   188 N.J. 415, 908 A.2d 196 (2006).

43.   In re Marriage Cases, 43 Cal.4th 757, 183 P.3d 384 (2008).

44.   Strauss v. Horton, 46 Cal.4th 364, 207 P.3d 48, 93 Cal.Rptr.3d 591 (2009); cf. National Pride at Work, Inc. v. Governor of Michigan, 481 Mich. 56, 748 N.W.2d 524 (2008) (amendment to Michigan Constitution barring same-sex marriage prohibits public employers from providing health insurance benefits to same-sex partners of their employees).

45.   Cal. Family Code § 297.5.

Canadian courts in Quebec,[46] British Columbia,[47] and Ontario[48] have declared that common law and statutory restrictions of marriage to different-sex couples violate the Canadian Charter of Rights and Freedoms. The Supreme Court of Canada ruled that a legislative proposal to extend capacity to marry to persons of the same sex is consistent with the Charter, but, because of the likelihood that the legislation would be enacted, declined to answer the question whether an opposite-sex requirement for marriage would violate the Charter.[49] On July 20, 2005, legislation took effect in Canada legalizing same-sex marriages.[50]

On December 1, 2005, the Constitutional Court of South Africa ruled that defining marriage to exclude same-sex couples was inconsistent with the constitution and invalid.[51] The court gave Parliament one year to effect the necessary changes in the Marriage Act and stated that if Parliament did not correct the "defects" within that time, the word "spouse" would automatically be read into the section of the Act now limiting marriage to unions of "husband" and "wife." On November 14, 2006, the South African National Assembly passed the Civil Unions Bill authorizing same-sex marriages but allowing religious and civil officers to refuse on moral grounds to marry same-sex couples.[52]

Same-sex marriages are also legal in the Netherlands,[53] Spain,[54] and Belgium.[55] In Western Europe, laws now grant same-sex couples many of the same rights as are enjoyed by married couples.[56] On December 5, 2005, legislation took effect in Britain giving same-sex couples the same social security, tax, pension, and inheritance rights as married couples.

Although same-sex marriages cannot be performed in Israel, on November 21, 2006, in *Yosi Ben Ari v. Ministry of the Interior*,[57] the Israeli High Court of Justice held that Israeli same-sex couples who

---

46. Hendricks c. Quebec (Procureur Generale), [2002] R.D.F. 1022 (Cour Superieure du Quiebec, 2002), appeal dismissed. On April 1, 2004, the persons bringing this suit became the first same-sex couple to be married in Quebec.

47. EGALE Canada Inc. v. Canada (Attorney General), 225 D.L.R.4th 472 (B.C. Ct. App. 2003).

48. Halpern v. Toronto, 65 O.R.3d 161 (Ont. Ct. App. 2003).

49. In re Reference by the Governor in Council Concerning the Proposal for an Act Respecting Certain Aspects of Legal Capacity for Marriage for Civil Purposes, 2004 SCC 79, 246 D.L.R.4th 193 (Can. 2004).

50. Bill C–38, An Act Respecting Certain Aspects of Legal Capacity for Marriage for Civil Purposes (2005).

51. Fourie v. Minister of Home Affairs, Case no. 232/2003 ¶ 49 (S.A. Const. Ct. 2005).

52. B 26B–2006.

53. Wet wan 21 December 2000, Stb. 2001 nr. 9 (Neth.).

54. On June 30, 2005, the Spanish Parliament passed legislation legalizing same-sex marriages.

55. Code Civil (Feb. 13, 2003) (Belg.), Moniteur Belge, Feb. 28, 2001, at 9880–82.

56. Y. Merin, Equality for Same–Sex Couples 2–4 (2002); Boele–Woelki, The Legal Recognition of Same–Sex Relationships Within the European Union, 82 Tulane L. Rev. 1949 (2008).

57. Case 05–3045.

married in Canada, where such marriages are valid, are to be registered as married in Israel's population registry.

The United States response to extension of rights to same-sex couples was the passage of the Defense of Marriage Act (DOMA)[58]:

> No State, territory, or possession of the United States, or Indian tribe, shall be required to give effect to any public act, record, or judicial proceeding of any other State, territory, possession, or tribe respecting a relationship between persons of the same sex that is treated as a marriage under the laws of such other State, territory, possession, or tribe, or a right or claim arising from such relationship.

Congress, under the "effect" provision of the Full Faith and Credit Clause,[59] has three times expanded the requirement of recognition of state judgments beyond what the clause itself would require.[60] The effect provision seems to authorize this expansion of the constitutional mandate.[61] It is unlikely, however, that Congress can restrict, rather than expand, what the Constitution requires.[62] The case that would provide

---

58.   28 U.S.C. § 1738C. The Act also contains definitions of "marriage" and "spouse" for all Acts of Congress and all federal regulations. The definitions require persons of opposite sex. (codified as 1 U.S.C. § 7). See Wilson v. Ake, 354 F.Supp.2d 1298 (M.D. Fla. 2005) (as applied to same-sex couple legally married in Massachusetts, DOMA and a Florida statute withholding recognition of same-sex marriages are constitutional); In re Kandu, 315 B.R. 123 (Bankr. W.D. Wash. 2004) (DOMA is constitutional as applied to same-sex couple married in British Columbia and they cannot make a joint filing in bankruptcy as could a married couple); In re Goodale, 298 B.R. 886, 893 (Bankr. W.D. Wash. 2003) (applying 1 U.S.C. § 7 to permit the bankrupt to avoid his former same-sex partner's judgment lien on the bankrupt's homestead, which could not have been avoided if the judgment creditor were a former spouse).

59.   U.S. Const. Art. IV § 1: "Full Faith and Credit shall be given in each State to the public Acts, Records, and judicial Proceedings of every other State. And the Congress may by general Laws prescribe the Manner in which such Acts, Records and Proceedings shall be proved, and the *Effect* thereof." (emphasis added).

60.   See 28 U.S.C. § 1738 (requiring federal courts to recognize state judgments); 28 U.S.C. § 1738A (forbidding modification of sister-state custody award) (see infra text accompanying notes 343–356); 28 U.S.C. § 1738B (forbidding modification of sister-state child support award) (see infra text accompanying notes 158–163).

61.   See Yarborough v. Yarborough, 290 U.S. 202, 215 n.2, 54 S.Ct. 181, 186 n.2, 78 L.Ed. 269, 277 n.2 (1933) (Stone, J. dissenting). But see Sack, *Domestic Violence Across State Lines: The Full Faith and Credit Clause, Congressional Power, and Interstate Enforcement of Protection Orders*, 98 Nw. U. L. Rev. 827, 832 (2004) (Congress cannot either expand or contract full faith and credit in areas where the Supreme Court has already ruled on the Constitution's mandate).

62.   See Thomas v. Washington Gas Light Co., 448 U.S. 261, 272 n.17, 100 S.Ct. 2647, 2656 n.17, 65 L.Ed.2d 757 (1980) ("Thus, while Congress clearly has the power to increase the measure of faith and credit that a State must accord to the laws or judgments of another State, there is at least some question whether Congress may cut back on the measure of faith and credit required by a decision of this Court"); Freund, *Chief Justice Stone and the Conflict of Laws*, 59 Harv. L. Rev. 1210, 1229–30 (1946) (stating that the effect clause "may well be thought to support legislation enlarging the compulsory area of full faith and credit ... but legislation withdrawing from the compulsory area ... may stand on a different footing"); cf. Finstuen v. Crutcher, 496 F.3d 1139 (10th Cir. 2007) (Oklahoma statute preventing recognition of sister-state adoptions by same-sex couples violates the Full Faith and Credit Clause of the U.S. Constitution). But see Wardle, *Non-Recognition of Same–Sex Marriage Judgments under DOMA and the Constitution*, 38 Creighton L. Rev. 365, 410 (2005): "The history of the enactment of the Effects Clause of

the greatest test for the Defense of Marriage Act would be one in which a same-sex spouse obtains a wrongful death judgment against a nonresident who has killed the plaintiff's partner at the couple's domicile. The marriage was performed at the marital domicile, which permits same-sex marriages. Then the plaintiff sues in the nonresident's state demanding full faith and credit for the wrongful death judgment. The wisest course for a court to take under these circumstances is to construe the Act's reference to "a judicial proceeding ... respecting a relationship between persons of the same sex" as not including the wrongful death judgment. This avoidance of the constitutional question may be more difficult under some state homespun versions of the federal Act.[63]

In *Citizens for Equal Protection v. Bruning*[64] the Eighth Circuit rejected the contention that a state constitutional amendment barring same-sex marriage violates the Equal Protection Clause of the Fourteenth Amendment. In *Romer v. Evans*[65] the Supreme Court struck down on equal protection grounds an amendment to the Colorado constitution that prohibited the legislature or any political subdivision from enacting legislation that gave to homosexuals "any minority status, quota preferences, protected status or claim of discrimination." *Romer* stated: "A law declaring that in general it shall be more difficult for one group of citizens than for all others to seek aid from the government is itself a denial of equal protection of the laws in the most literal sense."[66] The Eighth Circuit distinguished *Romer* on the ground that the state constitutional amendment challenged in that case served no legitimate state interest but the Nebraska amendment barring same-sex unions served the purpose of encouraging "heterosexual couples to bear and raise children in committed marriage relationships."[67] This was sufficient to uphold the Nebraska amendment under the proper equal protection standard, which in this instance, the court held, is rational-basis review, rather than a heightened level of judicial scrutiny.

Until the Supreme Court deals with a state constitutional amendment barring same-sex marriage, no one can be certain if that amendment violates the equal protection clause of the Fourteenth Amendment. To conserve ink and paper, please insert "I believe" before every statement concerning that issue in the next paragraph.

Bruning does not discuss the sentence from *Romer* quoted above: "A law declaring that in general it shall be more difficult for one group of

---

the Constitution clearly refutes the [theory that Congress can expand but not contract full faith and credit.]"

63. See, e.g. Tex. Family Code § 6.204(c): "The state or an agency or political subdivision of the state may not give effect to a ... (2) right or claim to any legal protection, benefit, or responsibility asserted as a result of a marriage between persons of the same sex or a civil union in this state or in any other jurisdiction." For the text of laws in 43 states barring same-sex marriages see Koppelman, *Recognition and Enforcement of Same–Sex Marriage,* 153 U. Pa. L. Rev. 2143, 2165–94 (2005).

64.   455 F.3d 859 (8th Cir. 2006).

65.   517 U.S. 620, 116 S.Ct. 1620, 134 L.Ed.2d 855 (1996).

66.   Id. at 633, 116 S.Ct. at 1628.

67.   *Citizens for Equal Protection,* 455 F.3d at 868.

citizens than for all others to seek aid from the government is itself a denial of equal protection of the laws in the most literal sense."[68] In the context of a state constitution this is the essence of the Fourteen Amendment's guaranty of equal protection. As a result of the amendment approved in *Bruning*, Nebraska same-sex couples who wish to marry not only must gain the concurrence of a legislative majority, as is true of other interest groups, but also, unlike others, must undertake the far more arduous task of amending the state constitution. The only state constitutional amendment addressed to same-sex marriage that passes equal protection muster is one that leaves the state constitution neutral on that issue. This would provide a level playing field in the state legislature for proponents and opponents of same-sex marriage. This is why *Bruning* was wrong. It is also the reason that the California Supreme Court in *Strauss v. Horton*[69] should have held that the initiative-induced amendment was unconstitutional. The majority opinion in that case gives only a "cf." citation to *Romer* in the context of addressing the argument that the initiative constituted an invalid revision rather an amendment of the California constitution.[70]

§ 5.2   Divorce

"In other words, settled family relationships may be destroyed by a procedure that we would not recognize if the suit were one to collect a grocery bill."[71]

§ 5.2A   Jurisdiction Based on Domicile

Williams v. North Carolina[72] (referred to as *Williams I* to distinguish it from another decision involving the same parties decided three years later)[73] held that a court in a state in which the petitioner is domiciled at the time that the action for divorce is brought,[74] has

---

68. *Romer,* 517 U.S at 633, 116 S.Ct. at 1628.

69. 46 Cal.4th 364, 207 P.3d 48, 93 Cal.Rptr.3d 591 (2009).

70. Id. at 446, 207 P.3d at 102, 93 Cal. Reptr.3d at 656. The dissent does draw on *Romer* in stating that the "the federal Constitution would likely bar these initiatives." Moreno, J., concurring and dissenting, id. at 497 n.9, 207 P.3d at 139 n.9, 93 Cal.Rptr.3d at 700.

71. Williams v. North Carolina, 317 U.S. 287, 316, 63 S.Ct. 207, 221, 87 L.Ed. 279, 295 (1942) (Jackson, J., dissenting).

72. 317 U.S. 287, 63 S.Ct. 207, 87 L.Ed. 279 (1942).

73. Williams v. North Carolina, 325 U.S. 226, 65 S.Ct. 1092, 89 L.Ed. 1577 (1945).

74. See Slessinger v. Secretary of Health & Human Services, 835 F.2d 937 (1st Cir.1987) (absent estoppel, Rhode Island will not recognize a Dominican divorce not based on domicile); Spalding v. Spalding, 171 Conn. 220, 368 A.2d 14 (1976) (California divorce jurisdiction exists if petitioner had the requisite domicile at the time his petition was filed although he changed his domicile before the decree was granted).

Cf. European Union Council Regulation No. 2116/2004 of 2 December 2004 concerning jurisdiction and the recognition and enforcement of judgments in matrimonial matters and the matters of parental responsibility, art. 3(1)(a): "In matters relating to divorce . . . jurisdiction shall lie in the courts of the member state in whose territory . . . the applicant is habitually resident if he or she resided there for at least a year immediately before the application was made."

jurisdiction to grant a divorce terminating the marital status. The petitioner's domicile alone is a sufficient constitutional basis for divorce jurisdiction even though the spouses did not celebrate the marriage in the forum, never lived there as husband and wife, none of the facts on which the divorce is based occurred in the forum,[75] and even though the other spouse does not appear in the action and there is no other basis for in personam jurisdiction over the absent spouse. In order for the exercise of this domiciliary basis for divorce jurisdiction to accord with due process, the petitioner must give the absent spouse reasonable notice of the divorce proceedings and an opportunity to be heard.[76]

A United States forum that has divorce jurisdiction based solely on the petitioner's domicile will apply its own divorce law in determining whether there are adequate grounds for divorce.[77] This is so even though the events relied on for divorce occurred in other jurisdictions, and although these events are not recognized as grounds for divorce either where they occurred or at the marital domicile.[78]

With the spread of no-fault divorce, it became less likely that grounds for divorce in one state would not also be grounds for divorce in another state.[79] Now, however, the enactment of "covenant marriage"

But cf. Alley v. Parker, 707 A.2d 77 (Me. 1998) (dismissing wife's divorce complaint on the basis of forum non conveniens); Brown v. Brown, 120 R.I. 340, 387 A.2d 1051 (1978) (restrain husband from proceeding with divorce at new domicile when wife had filed first in forum and forum has personal jurisdiction over both spouses); In re Marriage of Ways, 85 Wn.2d 693, 538 P.2d 1225 (1975) (90–day durational residence requirement for members of the armed forces applies to period after the petition is filed); Nicholas v. Nicholas, 94 O.A.C. 21, 139 D.L.R.4th 652 (Ont. Ct. App. 1996) (stay wife's divorce suit because Trinidad was the more appropriate jurisdiction).

75. New Hampshire provides an exception. N.H.Rev.Stat.Ann. § 458:6 requires that the grounds for divorce have occurred while the plaintiff was domiciled in New Hampshire. But id. § 458:7—a permits divorce on the ground of "irreconcilable differences." Woodruff v. Woodruff, 114 N.H. 365, 320 A.2d 661 (1974), held that the "irreconcilable differences" that are a ground for divorce are a "continuing condition" that may persist after one of the spouses becomes domiciled in New Hampshire and as such are proper grounds for divorce. Thus one spouse may move to New Hampshire, become domiciled there, and obtain a divorce under New Hampshire law.

76. See Aleem v. Aleem, 404 Md. 404, 947 A.2d 489 (2008) (refuse to recognize husband's talaq divorce at the Pakistan Embassy in Washington D.C. without notice to the wife); Sanders v. Sanders, 12 Md.App. 441, 278 A.2d 615 (1971) (will not give full faith and credit to Kansas divorce if husband failed to send notice to wife's Maryland address when he knew that address); Restatement, Second, Conflict of Laws § 69 (1971); cf. In re Roedell's Estate, 253 Iowa 438, 112 N.W.2d 842 (1962) (permits collateral attack on sister state divorce decree when petitioner deliberately gave wrong address for mailing notice to absent spouse, but divorcing state would also have permitted a collateral attack on this basis).

77. See Torlonia v. Torlonia, 108 Conn. 292, 142 A. 843 (1928); Restatement, Second, § 285; cf. Shikoh v. Murff, 257 F.2d 306 (2d Cir.1958) (refuse to recognize divorce granted according to the law of the marital domicile, but not of the place where granted). But cf. Whealton v. Whealton, 67 Cal.2d 656, 63 Cal.Rptr. 291, 432 P.2d 979 (1967) (although the law applicable to a divorce is that of the forum, the law applicable to annulment is that of the state in which the marriage was contracted); Goodwine v. Superior Court, 63 Cal.2d 481, 47 Cal.Rptr. 201, 407 P.2d 1 (1965) (in separate maintenance proceeding, the applicable law is not necessarily the forum's).

78. For an exception in New Hampshire, see supra note 75.

79. See Kathleen A. Portuan Miller, *Who Says Muslim Women Don't Have the Right to Divorce?—A Comparison Between Anglo–American Law and Islamic Law*, 22 N.Y. Int'l L.

laws in a few states renews the possibility of significant differences among states in the grounds for divorce.[80]

In other countries, the forum's choice-of-law rules select the law applicable to divorce. The law selected is not invariably forum law. In the European Union, a Council Regulation allows the spouses to agree which of the laws listed in the regulation applies to their divorce or legal separation and indicates the law that applies in the absence of choice by the parties.[81] In Japan divorce is "governed by the spouses' national law, if the national law of each of the spouses is the same. If that is not the case but where the law of the spouses' place of habitual residence is the same, the effect shall be governed by the law of that place. If none of these cases apply, the effect shall be governed by the law of the place with which the spouses are most closely connected. However, a divorce shall be governed by Japanese law if one of the spouses is a Japanese national and has his or her habitual residence in Japan."[82]

Under Japanese law a court in the defendant's domicile has jurisdiction over international divorce cases. The plaintiff may sue for divorce at plaintiff's domicile if the plaintiff is abandoned, the defendant is missing, or in other circumstances when limiting divorce jurisdiction to defendant's domicile would be unjust.[83]

In the European Union, except for Denmark which has opted out, a Council Regulation provides jurisdiction for "divorce, legal separation and marriage annulment" in the following member states: the habitual residence of the spouses; the last habitual residence of the spouses if one spouse retains that residence; the habitual residence of the respondent; if both spouses request relief, where either of them is habitually resi-

---

Rev. 201, 207 (Winter, 2009): "Nowadays, even though divorce laws are based on statutes and vary from state-to-state, most states have adopted some variation of the 'no-fault' divorce. No-fault divorce allows the sole ground for issuing a divorce to be the 'irretrievable breakdown' of a marriage or 'irreconcilable differences' between spouses." (footnotes omitted).

80. Arizona, Arkansas, and Louisiana have enacted laws permitting couples to elect to enter into a covenant marriage or to convert an existing marriage to a covenant marriage. If couples make this election, the laws provide grounds for dissolution of the marriage or granting of separation decrees that are more restrictive than the grounds that apply for other marriages. Az. Stat. Ann. §§ 25–901—25–906; Ark. C. Ann. §§ 9–11–801—9–11–811; La. R. Stat. Ann. §§ 9:272–9:275.1, 9:307–9:309. See Spaht, *Louisiana's Covenant Marriage: Social Analysis and Legal Implications*, 59 La. L. Rev. 63, 105–06 (1998) (stating that although the covenant marriage state must give full faith and credit to a divorce rendered in another state, the divorcing spouse may be liable to the other spouse for breach of contract); cf. Hay, *The American "Covenant Marriage" in the Conflict of Laws*, 64 La. L. Rev. 43, 68 (2003) (raising question of how to quantify damages in such an action).

81. Regulation (EC) No. 2201/2003 as regards jurisdiction and introducing rules concerning applicable law in matrimonial matters ch. IIa, amended by SEC (2006) 949–50 art. 3a(1), further amended by European Parliament P6 TA PROV (2008) 0502.

82. Act on the General Rules of Application of Laws, Law No. 10 of 1898 as newly titled and amended 21 June 2006, arts. 25, 27. For a decision of the Supreme Court of Japan applying Korean law to the divorce of Korean nationals, see Husband v. Wife, 49 Kasai Geppo (7) 56 (1997) (translation in 41 Japanese Ann. Int'l L. 111 (1998)).

83. See Husband v. Wife, H.J. (1696) 120 [2002] (Yokohama Distr. Ct. 1999), English translation in 44 Japanese Ann. Int'l L. 196 (2001) (recognizing validity of Korean divorce when Korean wife of Japanese husband fled to Korea because of spousal abuse and there obtained a divorce).

dent; where the applicant has been habitually resident for a least a year; where the applicant has been habitually resident for at least six months if the applicant is a national of that state or, in the case of the United Kingdom and Ireland, is domiciled there; where both spouses are nationals or, in the case of the United Kingdom and Ireland, are domiciled.[84] In 2006 the Council of the European Union proposed amending the Regulation to permit the spouses to agree that a court of a member state with which spouses have a substantial connection shall have jurisdiction for divorce or legal separation.[85] The amendment lists the contacts that count as a "substantial connection."[86]

In the United States the domicile of the divorce petitioner has the power to grant the petitioner a divorce under its own law and *ex parte*. The rationale for giving this power to the divorce petitioner's domicile is that the forum's nexus as domicile of one of the spouses is sufficient to give the forum a reasonable interest in regulating the marital status of its domiciliary. As will appear in the following sections, the Supreme Court made many adjustments in the constitutional law of divorce before it had, to its satisfaction, reconciled the power to grant an *ex parte* divorce based on petitioner's domicile with the interests of the marital domicile and with fairness to the absent spouse.[87]

---

84. Council Regulation (EC) 2201/2003 of 27 November 2003 concerning jurisdiction and the recognition and enforcement of judgments in matrimonial matters and the matters of parental responsibility, OJ L 338 23/12/2003 p.1, art. 3.

The European Parliament adopted a legislative resolution approving, subject to amendments, the proposal for a Council regulation amending Regulation (EC) No 2201/2003 (Rome III). The report has been tabled for consideration in plenary by Evelyne Gebhardt on behalf of the Committee on Civil Liberties, Justice and Home Affairs.

The amendments would (1) change the title to refer to jurisdiction and the recognition and enforcement of judgments in matrimonial matters and the matters of parental responsibility, as well as the law applicable to divorce and legal separation; (2) define "habitual residence" to mean a person's place of ordinary abode; (3) provide that when the law the parties choose or is otherwise applicable is situated in a Member State whose law makes no provision for divorce or does not recognize the existence or validity of the marriage in question, jurisdiction shall be allocated to the Member State of the nationality of one of the spouses or to the Member State in which the marriage was celebrated; (4) allow the parties to choose the law of the State in which the spouses have their habitual residence at the time when the agreement is concluded, or the law of the State in which the marriage took place, or the law of the State in which the spouses have had their habitual residence for a minimum period of three years—provided that such law is in conformity with the fundamental rights defined in the Treaties and in the Charter of Fundamental Rights of the European Union and the principle of public policy; (5) provide that should the law indicated pursuant to the Regulation not recognize separation or divorce or do so in a form that is discriminatory as regards one of the spouses, the lex fori shall apply.

There a consensus of the members of the European Parliament that judges in the Member States, before enforcing a choice of law by the parties should be aware of the importance of an informed choice on the part of the two spouses concerning the legal implications of the agreement.

85. SEC (2006) 949–50 art. 3a(1), further amended by European Parliament P6 TA PROV (2008) 0502.

86. Id. art 3a(2–4).

87. For an expression of doubt as to the success of these efforts, see Developments in the Law, *State–Court Jurisdiction*, 73 Harv. L. Rev. 909, 971–73 (1960).

Shaffer v. Heitner,[88] raises the question of whether courts must make further adjustments and declare ex parte divorce unconstitutional. *Shaffer* restricted the use of in rem jurisdiction. In the course of enumerating four uses of in rem jurisdiction that survive,[89] the Court leaves open the question of whether *Williams I* remains intact, stating: "We do not suggest that jurisdictional doctrines other than those discussed in text, such as the particularized rules governing adjudications of status, are inconsistent with the standard of fairness. See, e.g. Traynor, supra, at 660–661 [stating that ex parte divorce is justified aside from the in rem characterization]."[90]

The two "adjudications of status" that *Shaffer* is most likely to affect are the ex parte divorce and a determination of child custody without personal jurisdiction over one of the persons whose rights are affected.[91] *Williams I* is likely to emerge unscathed from its encounter with *Shaffer*. The same political and social compromises that resulted in *Williams I* and divisible divorce would be cogent today as an accommodation of different states' interests.[92] The citation to "Traynor" in *Shaffer*'s note 30, quoted just above, is to the pages of an article in which Roger Traynor states that a state should be free to terminate the marital relationship ex parte without the need to "discourse in the jargon of in rem jurisdiction."[93] He reasons that "when a plaintiff asked no more than freedom to remarry", the interests of plaintiff and plaintiff's new domicile outweigh both the other spouse's "purposeless interest in barricading the plaintiff's avenue to freedom" and "the dubious interest of defendant's state in perpetuating a broken marriage."[94]

§ 5.2B   Ex Parte Divorces: Full Faith and Credit and Collateral Attack

If one spouse obtains an ex parte divorce based on that spouse's purported domicile in the divorcing forum, the spouse who did not participate in the divorce proceedings is not bound by the jurisdictional finding of "domicile" and may collaterally attack the validity of the divorce by demonstrating that the purported domicile did not exist.

88.   433 U.S. 186, 97 S.Ct. 2569, 53 L.Ed.2d 683 (1977) (barring the use of in rem jurisdiction to adjudicate the merits of a controversy having no relationship to the forum or to the property seized). *Shaffer* is discussed in § 4.28.

89.   The four uses of in rem jurisdiction that survive *Shaffer* are: (1) the claims being adjudicated are to the property itself; (2) the cause of action, such as injury suffered on the property, is related to rights and duties growing out of property ownership; (3) attachment of property as security for a judgment being sought in another forum in which there is in personam jurisdiction over the defendant; (4) the enforcement of an in personam judgment obtained in another forum. *Shaffer*, 433 U.S. at 208–10, 97 S.Ct. at 2582–83, 53 L.Ed.2d at 700–02.

90.   Id. at 208 n.30, 97 S.Ct. at 2582 n.30, 53 L.Ed.2d at 700 n.30.

91.   The effect of *Shaffer* on custody is discussed in section 5.3A.

92.   See Von Schack v. Von Schack, 893 A.2d 1004 (Me. 2006) (*Shaffer* does not require divorcing forum to have personal jurisdiction over defendant spouse; this is not because judgment is in rem but because of forum's interest in freeing its citizens from marriage) Chamberlin v. Chamberlin, 70 N.C.App. 474, 319 S.E.2d 670 (1984) (*Shaffer* does not prevent ex parte divorce); Smith v. Smith, 459 N.W.2d 785, 788 n.3 (N.D. 1990) (*Williams I* survives *Shaffer*). Contra, Note, *The Divisible Divorce Doctrine Reexamined in Light of Shaffer v. Heitner*, 51 Miss. L. J. 801, 816–17 (1981). Section 5.2E2 discusses "divisible divorce."

93.   Traynor, *Is This Conflict Really Necessary?*, 37 Texas L. Rev. 657, 661 (1959).

94.   Id. at 660–61.

Williams II[95] (the second *Williams v. North Carolina* decision, decided three years after *Williams I*), permitted North Carolina to convict a man and woman of bigamous cohabitation. The defendants journeyed from their North Carolina homes to Nevada, obtained Nevada divorces from their spouses, then married one another in Nevada, and returned to North Carolina, where they cohabited. The Supreme Court held that North Carolina could properly base the bigamous cohabitation conviction on a finding that the defendants in fact were not domiciled in Nevada when they had obtained their divorces and that their divorces, therefore, need not be recognized in North Carolina as freeing them to marry again. The Court explained that "the [ex parte] decree of divorce is a conclusive adjudication of everything except the jurisdictional facts upon which it is founded, and domicile is a jurisdictional fact."[96]

The same day that it decided *Williams II*, the Court made it clear that what the marital domicile could do in collaterally attacking the jurisdictional finding of domicile in an ex parte divorce, the absent spouse could also do. *Esenwein v. Commonwealth*[97] permitted a Pennsylvania wife to show that her husband had not in fact been domiciled in Nevada when he had obtained his ex parte divorce.[98] Because the divorce was invalid, it did not terminate her right to support under an order that had been issued in Pennsylvania before the Nevada proceeding. Under Pennsylvania law, a valid ex parte divorce would have terminated the wife's right to support.

When a collateral attack is made upon the divorcing court's jurisdictional finding of domicile, full faith and credit requires that a court in another state treat the jurisdictional finding with respect. In the words of the court in *Williams II*, the judgment invalidating the divorce must "satisfy our scrutiny that the reciprocal duty of respect owed by the States to one another's adjudications has been fairly discharged, and has not been evaded under the guise of finding an absence of domicile and therefore a want of power in the court rendering the [divorce] judgment."[99] The opinion goes on to state that "[t]he burden of undermining

---

95.   325 U.S. 226, 65 S.Ct. 1092, 89 L.Ed. 1577 (1945).

96.   Id. at 232, 65 S.Ct. at 1096, 89 L.Ed. at 1583.

97.   325 U.S. 279, 65 S.Ct. 1118, 89 L.Ed. 1608 (1945).

98.   See also Colarusso v. Teachers' Retirement Board, 378 Mass. 470, 392 N.E.2d 844 (1979); Meeker v. Meeker, 52 N.J. 59, 243 A.2d 801 (1968) (collateral attack on ex parte divorce permitted in a state that was not the marital domicile); cf. In re Gibson's Estate, 7 Wis.2d 506, 96 N.W.2d 859 (1959) (collateral attack on ex parte Mexican divorce permitted in state that was not the marital domicile). But cf. State v. Drury, 110 Ariz. 447, 520 P.2d 495 (1974) (for purpose of husband-wife testimonial privilege, refuse to permit collateral attack on wife's Texas divorce when husband was in mental hospital and "represented" in divorce proceedings by amicus counsel).

Sometimes the other spouse will be estopped to make a collateral attack on an ex parte divorce. See § 5.2F.

99.   325 U.S. at 233, 65 S.Ct. at 1097, 89 L.Ed. at 1583. See also In re Estate of March, 426 Pa. 364, 231 A.2d 168 (1967) (presumption of validity of Nevada divorce not rebutted).

But cf. Unif. Divorce Recognition Act § 2, (withdrawn in 1978 by the National Conference of Commissioners on Uniform State Laws): "Proof that a person obtaining a divorce from the bonds of matrimony in another jurisdiction was (a) domiciled in this state within

the verity which the Nevada decrees import rests heavily upon the assailant.''[100]

It is unclear how strong this rebuttable presumption of validity is. In *Williams II* itself, the jury had been instructed that the burden was not on the state, but on the criminal bigamy defendants, '' 'to satisfy the trial jury, not beyond a reasonable doubt nor by the greater weight of evidence, but simply to satisfy' the jury from all the evidence, that petitioners [defendants] were domiciled in Nevada at the time they obtained their divorces.'' The court further charged that '' 'the recitation' of *bona fide* domicile in the Nevada decree was 'prima facie evidence' sufficient to warrant a finding of domicile in Nevada but not compelling 'such an inference.' ''[101] Under these circumstances, *Williams II* held that ''[a]ppropriate weight was given to the finding of domicile in the Nevada decrees. . . .''[102]

§ 5.2C   Ex Parte Divorces: Full Faith and Credit to a Successful Collateral Attack

Suppose that a husband comes to Nevada from his marital domicile and obtains an ex parte divorce in Nevada. He then returns to his marital domicile where, in a proceeding in which there is in personam jurisdiction over him,[103] the wife makes a successful collateral attack on the Nevada decree. The marital domicile finds the Nevada decree invalid and declares that the supposedly divorced spouses are still married. Must Nevada now give full faith and credit to this finding that its own decree was invalid? From Supreme Court precedents in other areas, one might expect the answer to be ''yes''.[104] Moreover, this expectation would exist

---

twelve months prior to the commencement of the proceeding therefor, and resumed residence in this state within eighteen months after the date of his departure therefrom, or (b) at all times after his departure from this state, and until his return maintained a place of residence within this state, shall be prima facie evidence that the person was domiciled in this state when the divorce proceeding was commenced.''

It is not clear to what extent this Uniform Act reverses the presumption of validity required by *Williams II*. See Comment, *Statutory Presumptions of Domicile in Divorce: Full Faith and Credit and Due Process*, 67 Colum. L. Rev. 1320, 1325, 1328 (1967). On August 1, 2009 the Uniform Act was in force in Nebraska, New Hampshire, Rhode Island, South Carolina, and Wisconsin.

100. *Williams II*, 325 U.S. at 233–234, 65 S.Ct. at 1096–1097, 89 L.Ed. at 1584. See also Taylor v. Taylor, 168 Conn. 619, 362 A.2d 795 (1975) (there was a denial of full faith and credit to the husband's ex parte divorce when trial court placed on him the burden of proving his domicile in the divorce forum).

101. *Williams II*, 325 U.S. at 235–236, 65 S.Ct. at 1097–1098, 89 L.Ed. at 1585.

102. Id. at 236, 65 S.Ct. at 1098, 89 L.Ed. at 1585.

103. As to the necessity for in personam jurisdiction over the husband in order for him to be bound by the collateral attack, see Rymanowski v. Rymanowski, 105 R.I. 89, 249 A.2d 407 (1969).

104. See Parsons Steel, Inc. v. First Alabama Bank, 474 U.S. 518, 106 S.Ct. 768, 88 L.Ed.2d 877 (1986) (when a state court rules on the preclusive effect of a prior federal judgment, federal courts must give the state judgment the same preclusive effect that it has in courts of that state); Treinies v. Sunshine Mining Co., 308 U.S. 66, 60 S.Ct. 44, 84 L.Ed. 85 (1939) (when there are conflicting state judgments, the last in time is entitled to full faith and credit); Ginsburg, *Judgments in Search of Full Faith and Credit: The Last-in-Time Rule for Conflicting Judgments*, 82 Harv. L. Rev. 798, 803 (1969).

even though the marital domicile, in adjudicating the collateral attack, had itself denied full faith and credit to the Nevada decree by not giving "appropriate weight" to the Nevada finding of domicile. Particularly with regard to full faith and credit to judgments, two wrongs should not make a right. If the husband had his constitutional rights violated by the marital domicile because that forum did not accord full faith and credit to his ex parte divorce decree, his remedy was a direct attack on the marital domicile's judgment.[105] He was subject to the in personam jurisdiction of the court in the marital domicile. Therefore, if he allowed its judgment to become final,[106] he was bound by that judgment, erroneous though it might be. The judgment of the marital domicile, being the last rendered, is entitled to full faith and credit in sister states, including Nevada.

Nevada, however, has rejected this "last-in-time rule" when a spouse makes a successful collateral attack on a Nevada divorce decree. In *Colby v. Colby*,[107] a wife had obtained an ex parte Nevada divorce. Subsequently, her husband obtained a decree of separation in Maryland. The wife appeared in this Maryland proceeding and raised the Nevada divorce as a defense to the Maryland separation action. The Maryland court declared that the Nevada decree was null and void. The husband then brought an action in Nevada to vacate and set aside his wife's Nevada divorce decree, urging that the Nevada court give full faith and credit to the Maryland declaration that the Nevada decree was void. The

---

That the last conflicting judgment is entitled to full faith and credit even though the issue is the validity of a divorce, see Southard v. Southard, 305 F.2d 730 (2d Cir.1962) (federal court sitting in New York must give full faith and credit to Connecticut bilateral divorce even if the Connecticut judgment denied full faith and credit to an earlier ex parte Nevada divorce); DiRusso v. DiRusso, 55 Misc.2d 839, 287 N.Y.S.2d 171 (1968) (gives full faith and credit to Alabama decree vacating an Alabama divorce and rendered after New York had held the Alabama divorce valid); cf. Sutton v. Leib, 342 U.S. 402, 72 S.Ct. 398, 96 L.Ed. 448 (1952) (Illinois must give full faith and credit to a New York annulment decree that declared a Nevada divorce invalid); Sullivan v. Sullivan, 98 Ill.App.3d 928, 54 Ill.Dec. 207, 424 N.E.2d 957 (1981) (give full faith and credit to judgment that modified forum custody and support decree for circumstances predating the decree, which would not be permitted under forum law); Wright Mach. Corp. v. Seaman–Andwall Corp., 364 Mass. 683, 307 N.E.2d 826 (1974) (in contract action, F–3 is bound by F–2's decision that F–1 judgment precludes the claim); Layton v. Layton, 538 S.W.2d 642 (Tex.Civ.App.1976) (must give full faith and credit to Maryland alimony decree that denied full faith and credit to a Texas divorce decree rendered with personal jurisdiction over the wife); Brownlee v. Brownlee, 456 S.W.2d 782 (Tex.Civ.App.1970) (Mississippi habeas corpus proceeding at which wife failed to question validity of prior Texas divorce is res judicata in wife's current attempt to set aside the divorce).

105. Southard v. Southard, 305 F.2d 730 (2d Cir.1962).

106. A possible exception to binding the husband by the judgment of a court at the marital domicile might be made if he had sought review of that judgment by the United States Supreme Court, but certiorari was denied. Because, in this situation, "no impartial arbiter is available to supervise the fair discharge of F–2's obligation to F–1 ... it would seem arbitrary to designate F–2's unchecked rejection of the F–1 judgment as the final, national answer to the matter in controversy." Ginsburg, supra note 103 at 805. But see Porter v. Wilson, 419 F.2d 254 (9th Cir.1969), cert. denied, 397 U.S. 1020, 90 S.Ct. 1260, 25 L.Ed.2d 531 (1970) (applies last-in-time rule to Porter v. Porter, 101 Ariz. 131, 416 P.2d 564 (1966), cert. denied, 386 U.S. 957, 87 S.Ct. 1028, 18 L.Ed.2d 107 (1967), even though in that case certiorari was denied and jurisdiction was quasi in rem).

107. 78 Nev. 150, 369 P.2d 1019, cert. denied, 371 U.S. 888, 83 S.Ct. 186, 9 L.Ed.2d 122 (1962).

Nevada Supreme Court rejected this request remarking that the husband "does not here ask us to merely accord full faith and credit to the Maryland decree. Instead, we are asked to give it a greater credit and respect than the prior decree of our own State lawfully entered. Full faith and credit does not require, nor does it contemplate, such action from us."[108]

Is it clear that *Colby v. Colby* unconstitutionally denied full faith and credit to the Maryland judgment? There are two complicating factors that prevent responding with an unequivocal "yes."

First of all, one might expect that the following would be true: If "domicile" is to be a crucial jurisdictional fact upon which the duty to give full faith and credit to an ex parte divorce decree depends, "domicile," in this context, must have a constitutional definition. If the nexus between petitioner and the divorcing state satisfies this constitutional definition of domicile, the divorce is valid and must be given full faith and credit when collaterally attacked in a sister state. This is so even though the state in which collateral attack is made might impose a stricter test for domicile with regard to its own divorce jurisdiction or for some other purpose under its own law. If, on the other hand, the petitioner's contacts with the divorcing state do not meet the constitutional requirements for "domicile," then the ex parte divorce is invalid because rendered by a court without jurisdiction and the decree need not, perhaps must not, be given full faith and credit in other states. Therefore, because a single constitutional meaning of domicile is involved, if the divorcing court and a court in a sister state arrive at conflicting findings as to the requisite domicile for divorce, one of the findings must be wrong. This would not, for example, be like the finding of domicile as a basis for levying an estate tax on intangible property in

---

108. Id. at 157, 369 P.2d at 1023. See also Tinsley v. Tinsley, 431 So.2d 1304 (Ala.Civ.App.1983) (refuses to enforce Texas judgment dividing defendant's military retirement benefits, which court says conflicts with prior Alabama judgment); Porter v. Porter, 101 Ariz. 131, 416 P.2d 564 (1966), cert. denied, 386 U.S. 957, 87 S.Ct. 1028, 18 L.Ed.2d 107 (1967) (refuses full faith and credit to Idaho divorce decree distributing property in Arizona, in part on the ground that the Idaho judgment did not give full faith and credit to an Arizona separate maintenance decree); Jensen v. Barnes, 33 Colo.App. 333, 519 P.2d 1223 (1974) (deny full faith and credit to Illinois judgment adjudicating rights in marital property that had previously been adjudicated in Colorado divorce); Hayes v. Hayes, 248 Ga. 526, 283 S.E.2d 875 (1981) (South Carolina divorce decree did not terminate prior Georgia separate maintenance decree even if the South Carolina court had personal jurisdiction over both spouses); Clark v. Clark, 80 Nev. 52, 389 P.2d 69 (1964) (wife's Florida separate maintenance decree did not bar husband's subsequent Nevada divorce despite Florida's compulsory counterclaim rule); Meeks v. Meeks, 384 P.2d 902 (Okl.1963) (because the wife's Oklahoma divorce action was filed before the husband's Texas divorce action, the Oklahoma court is not ousted of jurisdiction to grant the wife a divorce even though the Texas divorce is granted first); Pace v. Pace, 222 Va. 524, 281 S.E.2d 891 (1981) (refuse to enforce Missouri judgment for past due child support when contrary to prior Virginia decree terminating support obligations); Kessler v. Fauquier Nat'l Bank, 195 Va. 1095, 81 S.E.2d 440, cert. denied, 348 U.S. 834, 75 S.Ct. 57, 99 L.Ed. 658 (1954) (refuse full faith and credit to Florida decree declaring a Florida divorce invalid after Virginia had declared the Florida divorce valid); cf. Tarnoff v. Jones, 17 Ariz.App. 240, 497 P.2d 60 (1972) (in breach of contract action, deny full faith and credit to Illinois decision that in prior Arizona proceeding the Arizona court had jurisdiction over the defendant).

an estate.[109] In the estate tax situation, more than one state might have a nexus with the intangible property or with the decedent that would make it reasonable for the state to levy a tax on the property.[110] In the tax case, each state could, if it wished, call its own different reasonable nexus "domicile" or, for that matter "red suspenders." But one would not think that this freedom to attach different meanings to domicile exists when the issue is whether the divorcing state had the nexus with the petitioner necessary to render a valid decree entitled to full faith and credit.

With reference to these a priori assumptions as to what one might "expect" concerning a single constitutional meaning of domicile for divorce jurisdiction, Justice Frankfurter's majority opinion in *Williams II* does state that "the proper criteria for ascertaining domicile, should these be in dispute, become matters for federal determination."[111] But he then goes on to say that if the court in which a spouse made the collateral attack on the ex parte divorce accorded proper weight to the finding of domicile in the divorce decree so that the domicile issue "was left for fair determination by appropriate procedure, and that a finding adverse to the necessary foundation for any valid sister-state judgment

---

109. Compare In re Dorrance's Estate, 309 Pa. 151, 163 A. 303, cert. denied, 288 U.S. 617, 53 S.Ct. 507, 77 L.Ed. 990 (1932) (decedent died domiciled in Pennsylvania for purposes of estate tax on intangibles) with In re Estate of Dorrance, 115 N.J.Eq. 268, 170 A. 601 (Prerogative Ct.1934), aff'd, 13 N.J.Misc. 168, 176 A. 902 (1935), aff'd, 116 N.J.Law 362, 184 A. 743, cert. denied sub nom. Dorrance v. Martin, 298 U.S. 678, 56 S.Ct. 949, 80 L.Ed. 1399 (1936) (same decedent died domiciled in New Jersey for same purpose).

110. State Tax Comm'n v. Aldrich, 316 U.S. 174, 62 S.Ct. 1008, 86 L.Ed. 1358 (1942), held that Utah may impose a tax upon the transfer at death of shares of stock in a Utah corporation although the decedent was domiciled at death in New York where he held the share certificates. In rejecting domicile at death as the sole constitutional nexus for taxing the intangible property in the estate, the Court said: "Another State which has extended benefits or protection, or which can demonstrate 'the practical fact of its power' or sovereignty as respects the shares ... may likewise constitutionally make its exaction." Id. at 181–182, 62 S.Ct. at 1012, 86 L.Ed. at 1371. See also Curry v. McCanless, 307 U.S. 357, 59 S.Ct. 900, 83 L.Ed. 1339 (1939) (both domicile of settlor and situs of trust of intangibles may impose death taxes on transfer of an interest in the intangibles). But cf. California v. Texas, 437 U.S. 601, 602–03 n.1, 98 S.Ct. 3107, 3108 n.1, 57 L.Ed.2d 464, 465 n.1 (1978) (Mr. Justice Stewart, concurring in the denial of a complaint under the Court's original jurisdiction in a dispute over the right to tax intangible personalty in the estate of Howard Hughes, suggests that the estate could bring an interpleader action in a federal district court for relief against the tax officials of each state and premises this position in part on the rule that "intangible personal property may, at least theoretically, be taxed only at the place of the owner's domicile. First National Bank v. Maine, 284 U.S. 312, 52 S.Ct. 174, 76 L.Ed. 313 (1932)"). *First National Bank v. Maine* was expressly overruled on this point by State Tax Comm'n v. Aldrich, supra this note, which Justice Stewart did not cite. The administrator of the Hughes estate did file an interpleader, but it was held that the 11th Amendment barred the action. Cory v. White, 457 U.S. 85, 102 S.Ct. 2325, 72 L.Ed.2d 694 (1982). Then the Court reversed its previous denial and granted California leave to file a complaint against Texas under the Court's original jurisdiction. California v. Texas, 457 U.S. 164, 102 S.Ct. 2335, 72 L.Ed.2d 755 (1982). The case was settled when the estate agreed to pay California and Texas about half the tax that would have been due if either state had prevailed in its contentions. [The author was counsel for claimants to the Hughes estate but did not participate in seeking original jurisdiction in the Supreme Court.] But cf. also Tilt v. Kelsey, 207 U.S. 43, 28 S.Ct. 1, 52 L.Ed. 95 (1907) (New York must give full faith and credit to N.J. probate proceedings although New York not a party to the proceedings).

111. *Williams II*, 325 U.S. at 231 n.7, 65 S.Ct. at 1095–96 n.7, 89 L.Ed. at 1587 n.7.

was amply supported in evidence, we cannot upset the judgment before us. And we cannot do so even if we also found in the record of the court of original judgment warrant for its finding that it had jurisdiction."[112] In other words, if the court that hears a collateral attack on the ex parte divorce gives the divorce court's finding of domicile a fair hearing under the proper standard, the Supreme Court will not second guess a determination that the divorce is invalid.

The second reason why the question of whether or not *Colby v. Colby* violated accepted full faith and credit precedents has no definite answer is the possibility that the divorce decree may be valid in Nevada although not entitled to full faith and credit. The concurring and dissenting opinions in *Williams II* contain suggestions that this is so.[113] The same notion of valid at home although not entitled to respect elsewhere appears in other decisions dating back at least to *Haddock v. Haddock*,[114] which Mr. Justice Douglas somewhat prematurely[115] pronounced "overruled"[116] in *Williams I*.

But, should not due process validity at home and full faith and credit abroad be inseparable when the reason for permitting denial of credit is a finding that the divorcing state did not have a constitutional basis for divorce jurisdiction? This is the larger question into which the first question, whether domicile has a single constitutional meaning for the purpose of divorce jurisdiction, merges. This larger question is one upon which scholars have taken different positions.[117]

Can a Nevada divorce meet due process requirements for validity in Nevada and, at the same time, not be entitled to full faith and credit in sister states? The question is much too broad. An intelligent answer cannot be given until it is known for exactly what purpose Nevada

---

112. Id. at 234, 65 S.Ct. at 1097, 89 L.Ed. at 1584.

113. Id. at 242, 65 S.Ct. at 1101, 89 L.Ed. at 1588: "Nevada has a recognizable interest in granting only two types of ex parte divorces: (a) those effective solely within the borders of Nevada, and (b) those effective everywhere on the ground that at least one of the parties had a bona fide domicil in the state at the time the decree was granted." (Murphy, J., concurring); Id. at 244, 65 S.Ct. at 1102, 89 L.Ed. at 1589: "For all that has been determined . . . petitioners are lawful husband and wife in Nevada. . . . They may be such everywhere outside North Carolina." (Rutledge, J., dissenting).

114. 201 U.S. 562, 605, 26 S.Ct. 525, 542, 50 L.Ed. 867, 884 (1906) ("Without questioning the power of the State of Connecticut to enforce within its own borders the decree of divorce which is here in issue. . . ."). See also Sherrer v. Sherrer, 334 U.S. 343, 368 n.16, 68 S.Ct. 1087, 1102–1103 n.16, 92 L.Ed. 1429, 1445 n.16 (1948) (Frankfurter, J., dissenting); Wheat v. Wheat, 229 Ark. 842, 846, 318 S.W.2d 793, 796 (1958).

115. "Premature" in the light of the "divisible divorce" decisions to follow *Williams I* (see infra § 5.2E2) and of the fact that the issue in *Haddock* was whether New York need give full faith and credit to the Connecticut ex parte divorce by refusing to grant alimony to the New York wife. Justice Douglas did note that his disagreement with *Haddock* was "so far as the marital status of the parties is concerned." 317 U.S. at 293, 63 S.Ct. at 210, 87 L.Ed. at 283.

116. *Williams I*, 317 U.S. at 304, 63 S.Ct. at 216, 87 L.Ed. at 289.

117. See R. Leflar et al., American Conflicts Law § 225 (4th ed. 1986) (yes); D. Currie, *Suitcase Divorce in the Conflict of Laws: Simmons, Rosenstiel, and Borax*, 34 U. Chi. L. Rev. 26, 48 (1966) (yes); Foster, *Recognition of Migratory Divorces: Rosenstiel v. Section 250*, 43 N.Y.U. L. Rev. 429, 433 (1968) (no); Powell, *And Repent at Leisure*, 58 Harv. L. Rev. 930, 936 (1945) (no).

wishes to continue to regard its ex parte divorce as "valid" after a bilateral sister-state decision that the divorce is "void."

For example, suppose that the husband, who obtained the ex parte Nevada divorce, owned real estate in Nevada. Another state, with jurisdiction over both the wife and the husband, declares the Nevada divorce void. Then the husband dies and the wife claims a widow's rights in the Nevada property. Nevada decides that she is not a "widow" but a divorcee. There is no constitutional objection to this.[118] Nevada could, if it wished, permit a husband to terminate his wife's inheritance rights in the husband's Nevada realty by running a chartreuse flag up the courthouse flagpole while a judge played "Land of Hope and Glory" on a flute.

Suppose, instead, that the wife serves her husband at their marital domicile and sues him for support. Under the law of the marital domicile, a court cannot award support to a woman already divorced. Under the law of the marital domicile, a valid ex parte divorce would have ended the wife's right to support. The marital domicile finds that the Nevada divorce is void and orders the husband to make monthly support payments to the wife. The husband defaults in his support payments and flees to Nevada. The wife sues him there demanding that Nevada give full faith and credit to the marital domicile's judgment to the extent of accrued and non-modifiable support payments.[119] Nevada refuses on the ground that the divorce is valid in Nevada and that the marital domicile, in rendering the support decree, did not give proper respect to the Nevada judgment. Constitutional? No. Now Nevada has reached beyond its solely domestic concerns and has trespassed upon the strongly held interests of a sister state as articulated in a judgment of that state. This is what the full faith and credit clause is designed to prevent. Moreover, there is no reason to believe that Nevada's interest in keeping its divorce decree inviolable or in protecting the husband from payment of accrued support outweighs the great national interest in full faith and credit to judgments.[120]

§ 5.2D Bilateral Divorces

If both spouses appear in the divorce proceedings, neither spouse can thereafter, in another state, make a collateral attack on the divorce court's jurisdictional finding of domicile,[121] unless the state that granted

---

118. See Williams I, 317 U.S. at 319, 63 S.Ct. at 223, 87 L.Ed. at 297 (Jackson, J., dissenting); cf. Simons v. Miami Beach First Nat'l Bank, 381 U.S. 81, 85 S.Ct. 1315, 14 L.Ed.2d 232 (1965) (ex parte Florida divorce terminates wife's dower rights in Florida estate).

This discussion assumes that the Nevada law has not been changed after the marriage in issue.

119. See Sistare v. Sistare, 218 U.S. 1, 30 S.Ct. 682, 54 L.Ed. 905 (1910) (accrued and non-modifiable installments under support decree entitled to full faith and credit).

120. See § 9.3A.

121. Sherrer v. Sherrer, 334 U.S. 343, 68 S.Ct. 1087, 92 L.Ed. 1429 (1948); Coe v. Coe, 334 U.S. 378, 68 S.Ct. 1094, 92 L.Ed. 1451 (1948); Holm v. Shilensky, 388 F.2d 54 (2d Cir.1968); Cummiskey v. Cummiskey, 259 Minn. 427, 107 N.W.2d 864 (1961).

the divorce would itself permit this kind of collateral attack.[122] Full faith and credit requires that sister states give a divorce decree, rendered by a court having in personam jurisdiction over both parties, the same effect as it has in the state that rendered the judgment.

Not only the participating spouses are barred from collaterally attacking a bilateral divorce. A child of the divorced parents,[123] and a second spouse of one of the divorced parties[124] are also unable to attack the divorce. It would seem that, after a bilateral divorce, anyone whom the divorce forum would bar from collaterally attacking there the jurisdictional finding of fact, is barred by full faith and credit from collateral attack in a sister state.[125] This assumes that the divorce forum's bar is not so extreme as to violate due process.[126]

Full faith and credit does not protect divorces rendered in another country. See U.S. Const. Art. IV § 1. For materials on the recognition of divorces obtained in foreign countries, see Convention of 1 June 1970 on the Recognition of Divorces and Legal Separations, available on the Web Site of the Hague Conference on Private International: Law. On August 1, 2009, in force in 18 countries, but not in the United States; English Domicile and Matrimonial Proceedings Act 1973 § 6 (will recognize divorce obtained in country where neither spouse domiciled if it would be recognized as valid under the law of the domicile of each spouse).

122.   Sherrer v. Sherrer, 334 U.S. 343, 351–352, 68 S.Ct. 1087, 1091, 92 L.Ed. 1429, 1436 (1948) (dictum); Gay v. Gay, 203 So.2d 379 (La.App.1967); Guerieri v. Guerieri, 75 N.J.Super. 541, 183 A.2d 499 (Ch.Div.1962); McLean v. Grabowski, 99 N.J.Super. 209, 239 A.2d 35 (Ch.Div.1968); Donnell v. Howell, 257 N.C. 175, 125 S.E.2d 448 (1962). But cf. Vandervoort, Sams, Anderson, Alper & Post, P.A. v. Vandervoort, 529 F.2d 424 (5th Cir.1976) (although Florida would permit divorce to be attacked for fraud after time for appeal had expired, this attack cannot be made in a federal district court in Texas because under Florida law the attack must be made by filing a motion in the same proceeding in which the questioned judgment was entered).

123.   Johnson v. Muelberger, 340 U.S. 581, 71 S.Ct. 474, 95 L.Ed. 552 (1951) (contest over whether second "wife" of divorced father may take against his will, which left everything to his daughter); Kingdon v. Foster, 238 Ga. 37, 230 S.E.2d 855 (1976), cert. denied, 431 U.S. 916, 97 S.Ct. 2179, 53 L.Ed.2d 226 (1977) (stepchild cannot attack stepmother's Alabama divorce to prevent father's will from being revoked by marriage to stepmother); Goldsmith v. Goldsmith, 19 N.Y.2d 939, 281 N.Y.S.2d 344, 228 N.E.2d 400, cert. denied 389 U.S. 831, 88 S.Ct. 99, 19 L.Ed.2d 90 (1967) (child born after alleged divorce sues for declaration that he is the lawful child of the former husband); von Mehren & Trautman, *Recognition of Foreign Adjudications: A Survey and a Suggested Approach*, 81 Harv. L. Rev. 1601, 1630 (1968) (approving of result in *Johnson v. Muelberger*); cf. Yarborough v. Yarborough, 290 U.S. 202, 54 S.Ct. 181, 78 L.Ed. 269 (1933) (after bilateral divorce at marital domicile, child cannot obtain support decree in child's new residence when the decree would extend father's duty of support beyond lump sum amount awarded in the divorce proceeding; the father still resided at the former marital domicile).

124.   Cook v. Cook, 342 U.S. 126, 72 S.Ct. 157, 96 L.Ed. 146 (1951) (second husband barred from attempt to have his marriage declared void; he wished to show that his wife was not validly divorced from her first husband); Leatherbury v. Leatherbury, 233 Md. 344, 196 A.2d 883 (1964); Virgil v. Virgil, 55 Misc.2d 64, 284 N.Y.S.2d 568 (Trial Term, N.Y.Cty., 1967).

125.   See Cook v. Cook, 342 U.S. 126, 127–28, 72 S.Ct. 157, 159, 96 L.Ed. 146, 149 (1951): "If the defendant spouse appeared in the Florida proceedings and contested the issue of the wife's domicile ... or appeared and admitted her Florida domicile ... or was personally served in the divorce state ... he would be barred from attacking the decree collaterally, and so would a stranger to the Florida proceedings, such as respondent, unless Florida applies a less strict rule of *res judicata* to the second husband than it does to the first."

126.   See Aldrich v. Aldrich, 378 U.S. 540, 543, 84 S.Ct. 1687, 1689, 12 L.Ed.2d 1020, 1023 (1964) (dictum) (a Florida alimony decree "is also binding on those whom Florida

There are various ways in which the defendant spouse can "appear" in a divorce proceeding. The defendant might appear, deny the petitioner's domicile, and vigorously contest this issue. At the other extreme, the defendant might instruct a local attorney to enter a pro forma appearance and to make no attempt to contest the court's jurisdiction. In order to be bound by the divorcing court's jurisdictional finding, it is not necessary that the defendant actually litigate that issue. Language in *Cook v. Cook*[127] indicates that it is sufficient if the divorce court has in personam jurisdiction over the defendant and the defendant has an opportunity to contest the jurisdictional issue. In *Cook*, the Supreme Court went so far as to presume, in the absence of evidence in the record either way, that the divorce was bilateral and not ex parte, thus barring the second husband of the divorced woman from questioning her domicile in the divorcing state. The Court's statement that "[a] judgment presumes jurisdiction over the subject matter and over the persons"[128] seems out of place when, as in divorce, jurisdiction over the defendant is not necessary for a valid decree.

Despite the broad language in *Cook* as to what constitutes an appearance by the defendant spouse sufficient to cut off the possibility of collateral attack, several state courts have refused to regard an unauthorized or involuntary appearance by a spouse in an out-of-state divorce action as sufficient to bar the spouse's collateral attack on the divorce court's jurisdiction. In *Staedler v. Staedler*,[129] the husband selected and paid the Florida attorney who appeared for the wife. The New Jersey Supreme Court subsequently permitted the wife to sue for divorce in New Jersey. The court said that the Florida attorney's appearance "ostensibly on behalf of the wife was an appearance by him as agent for the husband...."[130] *Day v. Day*[131] affirmed a Maryland court's declaratory judgment for the wife that an Alabama divorce was invalid. The wife, at her husband's request, had signed a form in which she consented to the jurisdiction of the Alabama court and waived notice of the proceedings. The wife stated that she had signed because she was emotionally upset and because her husband had represented that he wanted the form only to show to the woman he was seeing and that he would not use it to get a divorce.

Even if a collusive bilateral divorce bars the spouses, children, and subsequent spouses of the divorced couple from collateral attack on the divorce, several scholars have suggested that the marital domicile itself

---

considers to be in privity with [the divorced husband], so long as Florida does not seek to bind those who cannot be bound consistent with due process").

127. 342 U.S. 126, 127–28, 72 S.Ct. 157, 159, 96 L.Ed. 146, 149 (1951) (quoted supra note 124).

128. Id. at 128, 72 S.Ct. at 159, 96 L.Ed. at 150.

129. 6 N.J. 380, 78 A.2d 896 (1951).

130. Id. at 391, 78 A.2d at 902. See also Gherardi De Parata v. Gherardi De Parata, 179 A.2d 723 (D.C.Mun.App.1962) (wife had signed Alabama acceptance of service and waiver of notice form); Pelle v. Pelle, 229 Md. 160, 182 A.2d 37 (1962). But see Restatement, Second, § 73, Reporter's Note (doubting constitutionality of *Staedler* and *Pelle*).

131. 237 Md. 229, 205 A.2d 798 (1965).

would not be barred from attacking the divorce in order to assert some compelling interest of the marital domicile,[132] perhaps in a bigamy prosecution.

§ 5.2E   Alimony and Support

§ 5.2E1   The Need for In Personam Jurisdiction Over the Other Spouse

If one spouse wishes the divorce decree[133] to contain provisions for alimony and support that will be enforceable against the other spouse as a personal obligation, the divorce court must have in personam jurisdiction over that other spouse.[134]

If a spouse is suing for divorce at the marital domicile, even if the other spouse has left the state and established a domicile elsewhere, the absent spouse has a nexus with the marital domicile that makes it reasonable for a court there to exercise jurisdiction over the nonresident spouse for the purpose of making an alimony and support decree for the benefit of the spouse and children left behind.[135] It is necessary that the forum have a long-arm statute that authorizes this exercise of jurisdiction and makes provision for giving the absent spouse reasonable notice and opportunity to be heard.[136]

§ 5.2E2   The Need for In Personam Jurisdiction Over the Other Spouse: "Divisible Divorce"

Just as the divorce court must have jurisdiction over a spouse to impose a personal obligation for alimony and support, it must have in personam jurisdiction over a spouse if it is to make a decree that will

---

132. See Powell, *And Repent at Leisure*, 58 Harv. L. Rev. 930, 1003–04 (1945); W. Rodgers & L. Rodgers, *The Disparity Between Due Process and Full Faith and Credit: The Problem of the Somewhere Wife*, 67 Colum. L. Rev. 1363, 1394 (1967); von Mehren & Trautman, supra note 123 at 1632.

133. Although the focus here is on alimony and support decrees incident to a divorce, the principles discussed here are applicable to such decrees whether or not incident to a divorce.

134. See Armstrong v. Armstrong, 350 U.S. 568, 579, 76 S.Ct. 629, 635–36, 100 L.Ed. 705, 714–15 (1956) (Black, J., concurring) (dictum); Brondum v. Cox, 292 N.C. 192, 232 S.E.2d 687 (1977) (father not bound by paternity and child support portions of Hawaii divorce decree because that court did not have personal jurisdiction over him); Restatement, Second, § 77(1).

Shaffer v. Heitner, 433 U.S. 186, 97 S.Ct. 2569, 53 L.Ed.2d 683 (1977) makes it doubtful that a court without jurisdiction over a spouse can make support and alimony orders and then enforce them against the spouse's property in the forum. For discussion of *Shaffer*, see § 4.28. Vanderbilt v. Vanderbilt, 354 U.S. 416, 77 S.Ct. 1360, 1 L.Ed.2d 1456 (1957) is a pre-*Shaffer* example of alimony awarded by sequestering the husband's property. Cf. Hodge v. Hodge, 178 Conn. 308, 422 A.2d 280 (1979) (alimony awarded to wife in ex parte divorce by assigning to her the husband's real estate in the forum, but the court points out that the husband's only objection was to the lack of pre-judgment attachment of the property).

As a matter of equal protection, alimony and support awards are available against either spouse under comparable circumstances. Orr v. Orr, 440 U.S. 268, 99 S.Ct. 1102, 59 L.Ed.2d 306 (1979).

135. See § 4.20.

136. Id.

preclude the spouse's domicile from awarding that spouse alimony.[137] In *Estin v. Estin*,[138] a New York court, as part of a separation decree, had ordered a husband to make monthly support payments to his wife. Then the husband obtained a valid Nevada ex parte divorce. The Supreme Court held it consistent with full faith and credit to the Nevada decree for New York, the marital domicile, to continue to enforce the support order. The opinion explained that:

> The result in this situation is to make the divorce divisible—to give effect to the Nevada decree insofar as it affects marital status and to make it ineffective on the issue of alimony. It accommodates the interests of both Nevada and New York in the broken marriage by restricting each state to the matters of her dominant concern.[139]

Vanderbilt v. Vanderbilt[140] extended this divisible divorce doctrine in two respects. First, the New York alimony decree, which *Vanderbilt* held consistent with full faith and credit to a valid Nevada ex parte divorce, was issued after the divorce. Second, New York was not the marital domicile. The Vanderbilts had lived in California. When they separated, the husband departed for Nevada and the wife for New York. The wife had acquired her New York residence before her husband had filed for divorce in Nevada.

To go a step beyond *Vanderbilt*, suppose that the wife acquired her domicile in New York after her husband's ex parte Nevada divorce. Could New York, under its law, constitutionally make an alimony award to the wife? No, this should be unconstitutional.[141] The wife's new residence has no interest that, at the time of the divorce, was precluded from protection because the divorce was ex parte and extra-state. Only a state "interest" meeting this test should be of sufficient strength to warrant refusal to give the valid Nevada divorce the same effect in sister states as it has in Nevada.[142] Moreover, a contrary rule would induce divorcees to seek new homes in states that would award them alimony.

---

137. See Nowell v. Nowell, 157 Conn. 470, 254 A.2d 889, cert. denied, 396 U.S. 844, 90 S.Ct. 68, 24 L.Ed.2d 94 (1969) (sister-state divorce decree by court with jurisdiction over wife terminates her entitlement to support under prior forum decree); Welsch v. Gerhardt, 583 S.W.2d 615 (Tex.1979) (Washington bilateral divorce terminated wife's rights to husband's military retirement benefits). But see Seidelson, *Interest Analysis and Divorce Actions*, 21 Buffalo L. Rev. 315, 325 (1972) (domicile of one spouse should be able to bind other spouse with regard to "economic incidents" of divorce).

138. 334 U.S. 541, 68 S.Ct. 1213, 92 L.Ed. 1561 (1948).

139. Id. at 549, 68 S.Ct. at 1218, 92 L.Ed. at 1569.

140. 354 U.S. 416, 77 S.Ct. 1360, 1 L.Ed.2d 1456 (1957).

141. Id. at 434, 77 S.Ct. at 1370, 1 L.Ed.2d at 1468 (Harlan, J., dissenting); See also Loeb v. Loeb, 4 N.Y.2d 542, 176 N.Y.S.2d 590, 152 N.E.2d 36 (1958), cert. denied, 359 U.S. 913, 79 S.Ct. 590, 3 L.Ed.2d 575 (1959) (refuses to extend *Vanderbilt* to case in which wife moved to New York after the divorce); Stumberg, *Foreign Ex Parte Divorces and Local Claims to Alimony*, 34 Wash. L. Rev. 15, 18–19 (1959).

142. It was clear in *Vanderbilt* that the Nevada decree purported to terminate the husband's duty to support his wife.

Suppose that, at the time of the husband's[143] ex parte divorce, the wife is living in a state that would award her alimony after the divorce. Without seeking an alimony award in that state, the wife moves to another state that also grants alimony after extra-state ex parte divorces. It would seem unwise to cut the wife off from the alimony that she would have been entitled to under the law of her domicile at the time of the divorce. Her new home should be able to make an alimony award, applying the law of her domicile at the time of the divorce insofar as this differed from the law of the forum.[144]

Although the wife's domicile at the time of the divorce may assert its interest in her welfare by awarding her alimony after the valid extra-state ex parte divorce, it is within her domicile's discretion whether it will do so. Some states have followed New York in making such alimony awards,[145] but others have not.[146] Some courts have even permitted the

---

143. For convenience the discussion of divisible divorce assumes that it is the husband who has obtained the ex parte decree. As a matter of equal protection, the same protection against ex parte awards is available to either spouse under comparable circumstances. Cf. Orr v. Orr, 440 U.S. 268, 99 S.Ct. 1102, 59 L.Ed.2d 306 (1979) (statutory scheme providing that husbands, but not wives, may be required to pay alimony, violates Equal Protection clause of Fourteenth Amendment).

144. See Vanderbilt v. Vanderbilt, 354 U.S. 416, 434, 77 S.Ct. 1360, 1370, 1 L.Ed.2d 1456, 1468 (1957) (Harlan, J., dissenting).

145. See, e.g., Waite v. Waite, 6 Cal.3d 461, 99 Cal.Rptr. 325, 492 P.2d 13 (1972) (overruled on another point, In re Marriage of Brown, 15 Cal.3d 838, 126 Cal.Rptr. 633, 544 P.2d 561 (1976)); Storer v. Storer, 305 So.2d 212 (Fla.App.1974), cert. discharged, 346 So.2d 994, cert. denied, 434 U.S. 955, 98 S.Ct. 482, 54 L.Ed.2d 314 (1977) (perhaps goes too far because divorce granted at last marital domicile which found that it had personal jurisdiction over the wife); Spadea v. Spadea, 225 Ga. 80, 165 S.E.2d 836 (1969); Schwarz v. Schwarz, 27 Ill.2d 140, 188 N.E.2d 673 (1963); Pope v. Pope, 2 Ill.2d 152, 117 N.E.2d 65 (1954) (leaving open question whether a contrary decision would deprive the wife of due process); Kendall v. Kendall, 224 Kan. 624, 585 P.2d 978 (1978); Lewis v. Lewis, 404 So.2d 1230 (La.1981); Altman v. Altman, 282 Md. 483, 386 A.2d 766 (1978); Owen v. Owen, 389 Mich. 117, 205 N.W.2d 181, cert. denied, 414 U.S. 830, 94 S.Ct. 60, 38 L.Ed.2d 64 (1973); Summers v. Summers, 69 Nev. 83, 241 P.2d 1097 (1952); Linck v. Linck, 31 Ohio Misc. 224, 288 N.E.2d 347, 60 O.O.2d 388 (1972); Matter of Marriage of Anderson & Anderson, 102 Or.App. 169, 793 P.2d 1378, review denied, 310 Or. 422, 799 P.2d 151 (1990) (wife's suit in forum had been filed before California ex parte divorce); Sohmer v. Sohmer, 318 Pa.Super. 500, 465 A.2d 665 (1983) (dictum); Rheaume v. Rheaume, 107 R.I. 500, 268 A.2d 437 (1970) (but see Castellucci v. Castellucci, 116 R.I. 101, 918, 352 A.2d 640 (1976) holding that Nevada ex parte divorce divests Family Court of jurisdiction to enforce property settlement agreement); Nienow v. Nienow, 268 S.C. 161, 232 S.E.2d 504 (1977); Newport v. Newport, 219 Va. 48, 245 S.E.2d 134 (1978); cf. Billingsley v. Billingsley, 285 Ala. 239, 231 So.2d 111 (1970) (title to Alabama land decreed to wife in suit pending at the time of husband's divorce); In re Marriage of Rinderknecht, 174 Ind.App. 382, 367 N.E.2d 1128 (1977) (because forum court does not have jurisdiction over wife, portion of decree adjudicating rights in property in which wife has an interest is vacated); Healey v. Healey, 152 N.J.Super. 44, 377 A.2d 762 (1977) (even though Pennsylvania divorce court had jurisdiction over wife, its decree did not deprive New Jersey courts of power to award wife support, because a Pennsylvania court cannot award support).

Some statutes authorize spousal and child support after an ex parte divorce. See, e.g., Ga. Stat. Ann. § 19–6–27; N.C. Stat. Ann. § 50–11(f); S.C. Code Ann. § 20–3–620.

146. See Gosselin v. Gosselin, 1 Mass.App. 146, 294 N.E.2d 555 (1973); Grant v. Grant, 136 Vt. 9, 383 A.2d 627 (1978) (Virgin Islands proceeding at which both spouses appeared); Brady v. Brady, 151 W.Va. 900, 158 S.E.2d 359 (1967) (existing support order terminated by valid extra-state ex parte divorce); cf. Burton v. Burton, 52 Tenn.App. 484, 376 S.W.2d 504 (1963), cert. denied (1964) (wife's right to support cut off by ex parte divorce at the marital domicile).

spouse who obtained an ex parte divorce to later obtain an alimony award.[147]

Is it permissible for the wife's domicile to refuse to adopt a divisible divorce doctrine?[148] If the state where the husband obtains an ex parte divorce cannot, without violating due process, cut off the wife's right to alimony, does the marital domicile, where the wife has remained, also violate due process if it refuses to recognize the wife's remaining right to alimony? Perhaps a full faith and credit rather than a due process focus provides the answer. Although it is common to speak of the state in which the husband has obtained an ex parte divorce as lacking power to cut off the wife's right to alimony, it might be more accurate to say that the marital domicile's interest in the welfare of the stay-at-home wife outweighs[149] the usual full faith and credit command that the divorce decree be everywhere given the same effect that it has in the forum where rendered. This is why only the wife's domicile at the time of the divorce decree should be able to award her alimony.[150] The wife's domicile need not assert its interest to the constitutional limits and need not adopt a divisible divorce concept.

Can the wife's domicile at the time of a valid ex parte extra-state divorce award her alimony if it would not make such an award after an ex parte divorce that had been granted in that domicile? It could be argued that this would be blatant discrimination against divorces in other states—a refusal to recognize the dissolution of the marriage status, which the valid ex parte divorce effected, and, therefore, a denial of full faith and credit to the divorce.[151] There is, however, a rational basis on which the wife's domicile might discriminate between local and extra-state ex parte divorces that make no alimony award. If the husband gets an ex parte divorce outside the marital domicile, the forum is unlikely to have any interest in providing for the wife, because she is not domiciled at the forum. If she were a forum citizen, she would be subject to the in personam jurisdiction of the forum court[152] and there would be ample opportunity to adjudicate her right to alimony. In the case of an extra-state proceeding in which a local wife is divorced without provision for her support, the wife's domicile has a very real interest in assuring that she is provided for by making an order for her support or by continuing a prior order.

---

147. Blech v. Blech, 6 Ariz.App. 131, 430 P.2d 710 (1967); Woods v. Woods, 285 Ark. 175, 686 S.W.2d 387 (1985). Anglon v. Griffin, 241 Ga. 546, 246 S.E.2d 666 (1978) (child support); Brown v. Brown, 269 N.W.2d 819 (Iowa 1978); Mandelberg v. Mandelberg, 187 Neb. 844, 195 N.W.2d 148 (1972); Portnoy v. Portnoy, 81 Nev. 235, 401 P.2d 249 (1965) (wife's ex parte California divorce does not bar her suit against husband in Nevada for alimony).

148. For cases refusing to adopt divisible divorce, see note 146 supra.

149. See § 9.3A.

150. For the possibility that the award might be made by a subsequent domicile applying the law of the domicile at the time of divorce, see text accompanying note 144 supra.

151. This question is left open by the majority opinion in *Estin.* 334 U.S. at 549, 68 S.Ct. at 1219, 92 L.Ed. at 1569. In his dissent, Mr. Justice Frankfurter declares that this would be a violation of full faith and credit. Id. at 550, 68 S.Ct. at 1219, 92 L.Ed. at 1569.

152. She would also be subject to the jurisdiction of the forum if it were the marital domicile. See § 4.20.

Simons v. Miami Beach First National Bank[153] added new complexity to the divisible divorce doctrine articulated in *Estin* and *Vanderbilt*. *Simons* held that the husband's ex parte Florida divorce could, consistently with due process, terminate his wife's dower rights in his Florida estate. It could be argued that this decision is inconsistent with *Estin* and *Vanderbilt* in that it permits a court, without in personam jurisdiction over the wife, to make a judgment that is res judicata as to the wife's interests in the husband's property.[154] *Estin* and *Vanderbilt*, however, should be read as based, not on Nevada's lack of power to terminate the wife's alimony rights, but on New York's interest in her welfare, which made it desirable to permit New York to give the Nevada decree a different effect in New York than it had in Nevada. *Simons*, then could be explained by Florida's power to adjudicate claims to Florida real estate. Furthermore, if the wife's domicile had jurisdiction over the husband, that state could award the wife alimony and this award would be entitled to full faith and credit in Florida.[155]

If the divorce court does have in personam jurisdiction over the wife, it can terminate her right to alimony, either by decreeing that no alimony be paid or by making provision for a non-modifiable lump-sum payment. This decree is entitled to full faith and credit.[156] If the husband sues the wife for divorce in the marital domicile, after the wife has established a new domicile elsewhere, the marital domicile has a nexus with the wife that makes it reasonable for the marital domicile to exercise jurisdiction over her for the purpose of terminating her alimony rights. This appears, at first, a less compelling case for long-arm jurisdiction in the marital domicile than when the wife is seeking alimony against an absent husband. The marital domicile, nevertheless, has a significant interest in assisting the husband in determining his alimony obligation. The husband should be able to know the extent of his responsibility to his former wife so that he may plan accordingly and decide, for example, whether to marry again.

§ 5.2E3   Full Faith and Credit to Alimony and Support Decrees

Suppose that a court with in personam jurisdiction over the husband orders him to make monthly support and alimony payments. This decree

---

153.   381 U.S. 81, 85 S.Ct. 1315, 14 L.Ed.2d 232 (1965).

154.   See Restatement, Second, § 77. For disapproval of *Simons*, see Currie supra note 117, at 29, 43; Comment, *Divorce Ex Parte Style*, 33 U. Chi. L. Rev. 837, 851 (1966).

155.   See § 5.2E3. In *Simons*, there was a New York maintenance decree that the husband obeyed until his death. 381 U.S. at 84, 85 S.Ct. at 1318, 14 L.Ed.2d at 235.

156.   See Restatement, Second, § 77(2); cf. Yarborough v. Yarborough, 290 U.S. 202, 54 S.Ct. 181, 78 L.Ed. 269 (1933) (child may not have father's duty of support increased over lump sum payment ordered in bilateral divorce at marital domicile; child sued in South Carolina while father still resided in Georgia, the marital domicile). But cf., Elkind v. Byck, 68 Cal.2d 453, 67 Cal.Rptr. 404, 439 P.2d 316 (1968) (*Yarborough* is not applicable when the father has acquired a home and place of business outside the divorcing state); Krueger v. Krueger, 179 Conn. 488, 427 A.2d 400 (1980) (another court with jurisdiction over the wife did not effectively terminate her right to alimony previously awarded by the forum); Thompson v. Thompson, 645 S.W.2d 79 (Mo.App.1982) (after all parties have moved to a new state, that state can extend child support to age 21 although it was only payable to age 18 in the state where originally granted).

is modifiable at the petition of either husband or wife on a showing of changed circumstances. Does this decree possess the necessary finality to be entitled to full faith and credit in sister states? The answer is "yes" as to past due installments that, under the law of the decreeing state, are no longer modifiable. These accrued payments may be enforced against the husband in another state just as any money judgment would be enforceable.[157]

The Full Faith and Credit for Child Support Orders Act[158] directs the "appropriate authorities of each State" to enforce according to its terms and not modify, except as otherwise permitted by the Act, a sister-state child support order[159] if the sister-state court had subject matter jurisdiction to enter the order and personal jurisdiction over the contestants.[160] A state with personal jurisdiction over the party who has not made the modification motion can modify a sister-state decree[161] only if the state of the original decree is no longer the residence of the child or of any individual contestant, or each individual contestant has consented to the court's exercising jurisdiction to modify.[162] This statute gives more full faith and credit to support decrees than the Constitution alone would require because before the Act installments of child support modifiable in the original forum were not entitled in sister states to mandatory enforcement or to protection from modification.[163]

Other federal legislation directs the Secretary of Health, Education and Welfare to certify to the Secretary of the Treasury delinquent child

---

157. Aldrich v. Aldrich, 378 U.S. 540, 84 S.Ct. 1687, 12 L.Ed.2d 1020 (1964); Barber v. Barber, 323 U.S. 77, 65 S.Ct. 137, 89 L.Ed. 82 (1944); Sistare v. Sistare, 218 U.S. 1, 30 S.Ct. 682, 54 L.Ed. 905 (1910); Heron v. Heron, 428 Mass. 537, 703 N.E.2d 712 (1998) (Massachusetts may not modify accrued alimony payments that are modifiable under Massachusetts law but not under the law of Nevada, which awarded the alimony judgment); Mitchim v. Mitchim, 518 S.W.2d 362 (Tex.1975) (will enforce Arizona final alimony installments even though permanent alimony could not be awarded in a Texas divorce); Scott v. Scott, 19 Utah 2d 267, 430 P.2d 580 (1967); cf. Parker v. Parker, 233 Ga. 434, 211 S.E.2d 729 (1975) (final Texas support payments may be enforced by contempt in Georgia once the installments are reduced to judgment in Georgia). But see Nickas v. Nickas, 116 N.H. 498, 363 A.2d 421 (1976) (husband has action against wife for fraud in obtaining Illinois alimony decree); Perry v. Perry, 51 Wash.2d 358, 318 P.2d 968 (1958) (state where husband obtained ex parte divorce refuses to enforce judgment rendered at marital domicile for alimony that accrued after the divorce).

158.   28 U.S.C. § 1738B.

159.   Id. § 1738B(a)(1), (2).

160.   Id. § 1738B(c)(1).

161.   Id. § 1738B(i).

162.   Id. § 1738B(e). See Cavallari v. Martin, 169 Vt. 210, 732 A.2d 739 (1999) (may modify New York child support decree after both parents move to Vermont).

163.   See Sistare v. Sistare, 218 U.S. 1, 30 S.Ct. 682, 54 L.Ed. 905 (1910) (dictum); Dorey v. Dorey, 609 F.2d 1128 (5th Cir.1980) (follows rule of forum state); Worthley v. Worthley, 44 Cal.2d 465, 283 P.2d 19 (1955) (dictum); Gamble v. Gamble, 258 A.2d 261 (D.C.App.1969); Berger v. Hollander 391 So.2d 716, 718–19 (Fla. Ct. App. 1980); Hicks v. Hefner, 210 Kan. 79, 499 P.2d 1147 (1972); Robertson v. Cason, 203 So.2d 743 (La.App. 1967); Windham v. Blakeney, 354 So.2d 786 (Miss.1978); Fox v. Fox, 526 S.W.2d 180 (Tex.Civ.App.1975) (retroactively modifiable alimony); Brazeal v. Renner, 493 S.W.2d 541 (Tex.Civ.App.1973) (retroactively modifiable child support); cf. Cole v. Earon, 26 N.C.App. 502, 216 S.E.2d 422 (1975) (under law of place of making of separation agreement, wife's refusal to allow the exercise of visitation rights is a defense to enforcement of accrued support payments). Contra, Light v. Light, 12 Ill.2d 502, 147 N.E.2d 34 (1958).

support payments that a state has not been able to collect through its own procedures[164] and directs the Secretary of the Treasury to use federal tax collection machinery to recover the amount thus certified.[165] Another federal statute establishes a "Federal Parent Locator Service" in the Department of Health and Human Services to assist in enforcing child support obligations.[166] One reason that all states have so quickly adopted the Uniform Interstate Family Support Act, discussed in the next section, which supersedes the Reciprocal Enforcement of Support Act, is that a federal act mandated such adoption by January 1, 1998 if a state is to remain eligible for its full share of federal funds for support of dependent children.[167] The "Deadbeat Parents Punishment Act" provides fines and imprisonment for willful failure to pay child support.[168] One factor that increases the maximum punishment is that the obligor "travels in interstate or foreign commerce with the intent to evade a support obligation. . . ."[169]

§ 5.2E4   Uniform Interstate Family Support Act

The Uniform Interstate Family Support Act (UIFSA)[170] facilitates the establishment and enforcement of child and spousal support obligations[171] and the modification of child support obligations across state lines. Filing a petition for support establishment or enforcement in an "initiating tribunal sets in motion the Act's procedures."[172] The initiating tribunal forwards the petition to a "responding tribunal" in a state where the obligor is present.[173] The responding tribunal has numerous powers to enforce the support obligation including ordering the obligor to comply,[174] ordering income withholding,[175] employing civil or criminal

---

164.   42 U.S.C. § 652(b).

165.   42 U.S.C. § 6305.

166.   42 U.S.C. § 653.

167.   42 U.S.C. § 666(f).

168.   Pub. L. No. 105–187, 112 Stat. 618 (amending 18 U.S.C. § 228). For a conviction under the statute before this amendment, *see* United States v. Mathes, 151 F.3d 251(5th Cir. 1998) (affirming sentence of fine and imprisonment imposed on Texas resident for willful failure to pay Louisiana child support judgment). Cf. Salahuddin v. Alaji, 232 F.3d 305 (2d Cir. 2000) (the statute does not create a private right of action).

169.   Id. § 2(a)(2).

170.   9 pt. IB.U.L.A. 159 (2001 Act), 281 (1996 Act) (2005). Every state, the District of Columbia, Puerto Rico, and the U.S. Virgin Islands has adopted the Act. On August 1, 2009, 19 states and the District of Columbia had adopted the 2001 Act and it was introduced in New Jersey. In 2008, the Act was amended to conform with obligations under the November 23, 2007 Hague Convention on International Recovery of Child Support and Other Forms of Family Maintenance. On August 1, 2009, 3 states had adopted the 2008 amendments and no country had ratified the Convention.

171.   Id. § 101(3) (1996 Act) (defining "duty of support" as "an obligation imposed or imposable by law to provide support for a child, spouse, or former spouse"); § 102(3) (2001 Act). §§ 401 (petition to establish support order), 611 (modification of child-support order of another state).

172.   Id. § 304.

173.   Id. §§ 304(a)(1), 305.

174.   Id. § 305(b)(2).

175.   Id. § 305(b)(3).

contempt sanctions,[176] issuing a warrant for an obligor who has disobeyed an order to appear,[177] ordering the obligor to seek appropriate employment,[178] and determining parentage.[179] If all else fails, the Act provides for interstate rendition of obligors charged with criminal failure to provide support.[180]

The petitioner need not appear in the responding state but may testify by affidavit.[181] The obligor must contest the validity of a registered support order "in a timely manner"[182] or the order will be confirmed and enforced. A court may send an income-withholding order to the obligor's employer in another state without first filing a petition or registering the order in that state.[183] Courts in different states are encouraged to communicate with one another by telephone and other means.[184] Congruently with the federal Full Faith and Credit for Child Support Orders Act,[185] a court may modify a child support order issued by another state only if that other state is no longer the residence of the child, the obligor, or an individual obligee other than the child, or if all individual parties have consented to have the court make the modification.[186] Unlike the Full Faith and Credit for Child Support Orders Act, UIFSA provides that a court may modify a sister state child-support order only on the petition of a nonresident of the modifying state.[187]

In order "[t]o insure the efficient processing of the huge number of interstate support cases,"[188] a responding tribunal determines "the duty of support and the amount payable in accordance with the law and support guidelines of [its own] State."[189] If this choice-of-law rule seems too favorable to an obligor who resides in a state with lower support guidelines than the obligee's state, it is important to note that the responding state cannot modify the order if that order is not fully enforced.[190] Until a child support decree is validly modified by another

---

176. Id. § 305(b)(5).

177. Id. § 305(b)(9).

178. Id. § 305(b)(10).

179. Id. § 701.

180. Id. § 801.

181. Id. § 316(a), (b).

182. Id. § 605(b)(3).

183. Id. § 501.

184. Id. § 317.

185. See supra note 162 and accompanying text.

186. See UIFSA, supra note 170, § 205. Under § 211(a) of the 2001 Act and § 205(f) of the 1996 Act the tribunal issuing a spousal-support order "has continuing, exclusive jurisdiction to modify the spousal-support order throughout the existence of the support obligation."

187. UIFSA § 611(a)(1)(ii) (1996 Act); § 611(a)(1)(B) (2001 Act); 28 U.S.C.A. § 1738B(e). See LeTellier v. LeTellier, 40 S.W.3d 490 (Tenn. 2001) (28 U.S.C.A. § 1738B(e) does not preempt the nonresidence requirement of UIFSA).

188. Id. § 303 cmt.

189. Id. § 303(2).

190. Id. § 303 cmt.

state,[191] the law of the issuing state determines the nature, extent, amount, and duration of support obligations.[192] Moreover, if the obligee's state does not have a sufficient contact with the obligor to exercise personal jurisdiction over the obligor and make a support order entitled to full faith and credit, it probably does not have sufficient contact to impose its own support obligations on the obligor.[193] UIFSA does have its own long-arm statute facilitating personal jurisdiction over nonresidents.[194]

§ 5.2E5   Enforcement of Support Obligations Incurred in Foreign Countries

Although support orders issued by a court of a foreign country are not entitled to full faith and credit,[195] both federal and state laws assist in enforcing support decrees of foreign countries. A federal statute authorizes the Secretary of State, with the concurrence of the Secretary of Health and Human Services, "to declare any foreign country to be a foreign reciprocating country if the foreign country has established, or undertakes to establish, procedures for the establishment and enforcement of duties of support owed to obligees who are residents of the United States...."[196] The same statute authorizes states to enter into reciprocal support enforcement arrangements with additional foreign countries.[197] Another federal enactment requires that states receiving federal aid to needy families enforce support obligations established in foreign countries that have either been declared "reciprocating countries" by the Secretary of State or with whom the state has its own reciprocal arrangements.[198] The Uniform Interstate Family Support Act extends its enforcement mechanisms to "a foreign jurisdiction that has enacted a law or established procedures for issuance and enforcement of support orders which are substantially similar to the procedures under" the Uniform Act.[199]

---

191.   See supra notes 185–186 and accompanying text.

192.   UIFSA, supra note 170, § 604.

193.   See Yarborough v. Yarborough, 290 U.S. 202, 54 S.Ct. 181, 78 L.Ed. 269 (1933) (holding that South Carolina, where the child was living, could not impose a support obligation greater than that imposed by a court in Georgia, the former marital domicile where the obligor still resided, which had awarded a lump sum as total support).

194.   UIFSA, supra note 170, § 201.

195.   See Nicol v. Tanner, 310 Minn. 68, 256 N.W.2d 796 (1976) (ordering enforcement of accrued installments under a German default decree if the trial court finds that the defendant "could and should have appeared and litigated in the foreign court"). See also Cavers, *International Enforcement of Family Support*, 81 Colum. L. Rev. 994 (1981); Hague Convention of 2 October 1973 on the Recognition and Enforcement of Decisions Relating to Maintenance Obligations (on August 1, 2009 in force in 22 countries, but not in the U.S.). Article 11 of the Convention reads: "If a decision provides for the periodical payment of maintenance, enforcement shall be granted in respect of payments already due and in respect of future payments."

196.   42 U.S.C. § 659a(a)(1).

197.   42 U.S.C. § 659a(d).

198.   Id. § 654(32).

199.   UIFSA, supra note 170, § 101(19)(ii) (1996 Act); § 102(21)(B)(iii) (2001 Act).

On 23 November 2007 the Hague Conference on Private International Law adopted a Convention on the International Recovery of Child Support and other Forms of Family Maintenance.[200] The Convention covers "maintenance obligations arising from a parent-child relationship towards a person under the age of 21"[201] and "with the exception of Chapters II and III, to spousal support."[202] Chapter II requires contracting states to designate a Central Authority to discharge Convention duties. Chapter III routes applications for enforcement and establishment of child maintenance obligations through the Central Authority. Chapter V provides that decisions made in one contracting state regarding child and spousal support shall be recognized and enforced in other contracting states. As of August 1, 2009, only the U.S. has signed the Convention and no country has ratified it. The Convention will enter into force after the second ratification.[203] In 2008 the Uniform Interstate Family Support Act was amended to comply with the Convention. As of October 1, 2009, 3 states had adopted the 2008 amendments contingent on the Convention coming to force in the United States.

§ 5.2F   Estoppel to Make a Collateral Attack on Divorce

As noted above,[204] if the divorce is granted without personal jurisdiction over both spouses, the absent spouse, and others, are not barred by the full faith and credit clause from collaterally attacking the divorce court's jurisdictional finding of domicile. Nevertheless, at times a person attacking the validity of an ex parte divorce has been held estopped to make the attack.[205] Some of the most common situations in which courts have imposed this estoppel include an attempt by the spouse who procured the ex parte divorce to demonstrate that the divorce, and therefore that spouse's subsequent marriage to another, is invalid;[206] an attempt by the non-appearing spouse to invalidate the ex parte divorce after that spouse has taken advantage of the divorce by marrying another;[207] an attack on the divorce by a subsequent spouse who married

---

200. http://www.hcch.net/index_en.php?act=conventions.text&cid=131.

201. Id. art. 2(1)(a).

202. Id. art. 2(1)(c).

203. Id. art. 60(1).

204. See §§ 5.2B and 5.2D.

205. That this form of estoppel is constitutional, see Cook v. Cook, 342 U.S. 126, 131, 72 S.Ct. 157, 161, 96 L.Ed. 146, 151 (1951) (Frankfurter, J., dissenting).

206. See, e.g., Oakley v. Oakley, 30 Colo.App. 292, 493 P.2d 381 (1971), cert. dism'd, 179 Colo. 450, 514 P.2d 633 (1973) (Mexican divorce); Clagett v. King, 308 A.2d 245 (D.C.App.1973) (Mexican divorce); Keller v. Keller, 521 So.2d 273 (Fla.App. 5 Dist.1988) (Mexican divorce); Krause v. Krause, 282 N.Y. 355, 26 N.E.2d 290 (1940) (Nevada divorce); Leflar et al., American Conflicts Law § 226 (4th ed. 1986) ("most states" use this form of estoppel).

207. Carbulon v. Carbulon, 293 N.Y. 375, 57 N.E.2d 59 (1944); cf. Bruneau v. Bruneau, 3 Conn.App. 453, 489 A.2d 1049 (1985) (wife estopped because of her appearance by counsel and acceptance of child support and alimony payments under Mexican decree); In re Estate of Joseph, 27 N.Y.2d 299, 317 N.Y.S.2d 338, 265 N.E.2d 756 (1970) (even if Alabama divorce was not entitled to full faith and credit, wife's delay of nine years in attacking it works an estoppel).

with knowledge of the circumstances that cast doubt upon the validity of the divorce.[208]

In *Rosenstiel v. Rosenstiel*,[209] the New York Court of Appeals took a significant step beyond these estoppel cases. A bilateral Mexican divorce,

---

208. Leatherbury v. Leatherbury, 233 Md. 344, 196 A.2d 883 (1964) (dictum); Newberry v. Newberry, 257 S.C. 202, 184 S.E.2d 704 (1971); cf. Dietrich v. Dietrich, 41 Cal.2d 497, 261 P.2d 269 (1953), cert. denied, 346 U.S. 938, 74 S.Ct. 378, 98 L.Ed. 426 (1954) (decision rests on estoppel although divorce was bilateral). Contra Kazin v. Kazin, 161 N.J.Super. 174, 391 A.2d 536 (App.Div.1978) (deny "wife" divorce or separate maintenance even though "husband" accompanied her on trip during which she obtained Mexican divorce from previous husband).

209. 16 N.Y.2d 64, 262 N.Y.S.2d 86, 209 N.E.2d 709 (1965), cert. denied, 384 U.S. 971, 86 S.Ct. 1861, 16 L.Ed.2d 682 (1966).

See also Perrin v. Perrin, 408 F.2d 107 (3d Cir.1969) (bilateral Mexican divorce upheld against attack of wife who obtained it); Baker v. Baker, 39 Conn.Super. 66, 468 A.2d 944 (1983) (wife who obtained Mexican divorce estopped to attack its validity); Scherer v. Scherer, 405 N.E.2d 40 (Ind.App.1980) (husband estopped to attack Dominican divorce to which he consented); Kazin v. Kazin, 81 N.J. 85, 405 A.2d 360 (1979) (husband who participated in wife's Mexican divorce from former spouse is estopped to attack its validity); Mayer v. Mayer, 66 N.C.App. 522, 311 S.E.2d 659, review denied, 311 N.C. 760, 321 S.E.2d 140 (1984) (same re Dominican divorce); Rosen v. Sitner, 274 Pa.Super. 445, 418 A.2d 490 (1980) (husband estopped to attack wife's Mexican divorce from former spouse); Terrell v. Terrell, 578 S.W.2d 637 (Tenn.1979) (bilateral Haitian divorce prevents wife from obtaining alimony); Dunn v. Tiernan, 284 S.W.2d 754 (Tex.Civ.App.1955, ref. n.r.e.) (spouse who obtained Mexican divorce estopped to challenge its validity in custody action). For comments on *Rosenstiel*, see von Mehren & Trautman, The Law of Multistate Problems 919 (1965); D. Currie, *Suitcase Divorce in the Conflict of Laws: Simmons, Rosenstiel, and Borax*, 34 U. Chi. L. Rev. 26, 60–62 (1966); Leach, *Divorce by Plane–Ticket in the Affluent Society—With a Side-Order of Jurisprudence*, 14 U.Kan. L. Rev. 549 (1966); Comment, *New York–Approved Mexican Divorces: Are They Valid in Other States?* 114 U.Pa. L. Rev. 771 (1966) (concluding that such divorces should be recognized in other states if New York, as marital domicile, had, at the time of the divorce, the sole interest in the validity of the Mexican proceedings).

Cf. Scott v. Scott, 51 Cal.2d 249, 331 P.2d 641 (1958) (recognizes Mexican divorce when petitioner had a bona fide residence in Mexico); McCarthy v. McCarthy, 361 Mass. 359, 280 N.E.2d 151 (1972) (wife who cooperated in husband's Mexican divorce and in exchange received a deed, is barred from petitioning for separate support); Ramm v. Ramm, 28 N.Y.2d 892, 322 N.Y.S.2d 726, 271 N.E.2d 558 (1971) (wife's appearance in Mexico after husband had obtained ex parte divorce renders res judicata the Mexican court's declaration that the divorce was invulnerable to attack); Zwerling v. Zwerling, 270 S.C. 685, 244 S.E.2d 311 (1978) (because the Mexican divorce and subsequent marriage were valid under New York Law, the New York marriage will be recognized in South Carolina).

But cf. Kugler v. Haitian Tours, Inc., 120 N.J.Super. 260, 293 A.2d 706 (Ch.Div.1972) (enjoin sale of Haitian divorce packages in New Jersey, even to New York domiciliaries); Feinberg v. Feinberg, 40 N.Y.2d 124, 386 N.Y.S.2d 77, 351 N.E.2d 725 (1976) (Dominican divorce may be collaterally attacked in New York for fraud if such attack would be permitted in the Dominican Republic, and even if attack there is foreclosed; New York court should decide whether under principles of comity there are sufficient circumstances to justify collateral attack in New York); Aleem v. Aleem, 404 Md. 404, 947 A.2d 489 (2008) (refuse to recognize husband's talaq divorce at the Pakistan Embassy in Washington D.C. without notice to the wife); Schoenbrod v. Siegler, 20 N.Y.2d 403, 283 N.Y.S.2d 881, 230 N.E.2d 638 (1967) (party to bilateral Mexican divorce can collaterally attack it to the extent that collateral attack would be permitted under Mexican law); Tsirlin v. Tsirlin, 19 Misc.3d 1132(A), 866 N.Y.S.2d 96, not published, disposition noted in table at 19 Misc.3d 1132(A), 866 N.Y.S.2d 96 (N.Y., Kings County, 2008) (refuse to recognize divorce by Israeli court without appearance by the parties based upon a "get" obtained from a religious tribunal in Brooklyn); In re Estate of Steffke, 65 Wis.2d 199, 222 N.W.2d 628 (1974) (refuse to recognize Mexican divorce so that subsequent "marriage" is not valid for purpose of qualifying for matrimonial estate tax rate). But see Prudential Ins. Co. v. Lewis, 306 F.Supp. 1177 (N.D.Ala.1969) (refuse to recognize validity of bilateral Mexican divorce so

in which one spouse had appeared in person and the other had appeared by attorney, was recognized for the purpose of precluding an attack on the validity of the Mexican divorce by a subsequent spouse of one of the divorced parties. This was done even though the Mexican decree was not based on a finding of a jurisdictional basis for divorce, such as domicile, that would be recognized in the United States as a constitutional nexus for divorce jurisdiction. Nor did *Rosenstiel* rely on any inequitable conduct of the second spouse to estop him from attacking the validity of the divorce. Although *Rosenstiel* did not rest on this estoppel ground, the second husband in *Rosenstiel*, before his marriage, did know of the circumstances surrounding his wife's Mexican divorce[210] and, in the companion case, *Wood v. Wood*,[211] the second husband did know of the Mexican divorce and had an opportunity to learn of the circumstances that cast doubt on its validity.[212]

§ 5.2G   Divorce Jurisdiction not Based on Domicile

Mr. Justice Frankfurter stated a famous dictum in *Williams II*: "Under our system of law, judicial power to grant a divorce—jurisdiction, strictly speaking—is founded on domicile."[213] This statement reflects what was a widely held belief that domicile of at least one of the parties is the sole constitutional basis for divorce jurisdiction in United States courts.[214]

This notion is fast disappearing. Domicile of one of the parties is a basis for divorce jurisdiction because a forum having this nexus with the marital status has a reasonable interest in affecting that status. Other contacts with one or more of the spouses are also likely to give the forum

---

that "wife" not beneficiary of life insurance policy); Super v. Burke, 374 So.2d 1250 (La.1979) (husband is not estopped to attack his Dominican divorce from prior wife).

Mexican law has been changed so that aliens cannot establish divorce jurisdiction by consent, but Haiti and the Dominican Republic have filled the gap. See Juenger, *Recognition of Foreign Divorces—British and American Perspectives*, 20 Amer.J.Comp.L. 1, 22–23 (1972); Baade, *Marriage and Divorce in American Conflicts Law: Governmental-Interests Analysis and the Restatement (Second)*, 72 Colum. L. Rev. 329, 352 (1972).

210. See the opinion below in *Rosenstiel*, 21 A.D.2d 635, 639, 253 N.Y.S.2d 206, 210 (1964) (Valente, J., concurring).

For subsequent developments in *Rosenstiel*, see Matter of Javits, 35 A.D.2d 442, 316 N.Y.S.2d 943, appeal dism'd, 28 N.Y.2d 923, 323 N.Y.S.2d 172, 271 N.E.2d 701 (1971), cert. denied, 409 U.S. 980, 93 S.Ct. 311, 34 L.Ed.2d 243 (1972) (Mr. Rosenstiel's attorney disciplined for obtaining nullification of Mrs. Rosenstiel's Mexican divorce without notice to Mrs. Rosenstiel); Rosenstiel v. Rosenstiel, 368 F.Supp. 51 (S.D.N.Y.1973), aff'd mem., 503 F.2d 1397 (2d Cir.1974) (Mr. Rosenstiel's ex parte Florida divorce is valid as is an antenuptial agreement ending Mrs. Rosenstiel's interest in Mr. Rosenstiel's estate on termination of the marriage by divorce).

211. 16 N.Y.2d 64, 262 N.Y.S.2d 86, 209 N.E.2d 709 (1965), cert. denied 383 U.S. 943, 86 S.Ct. 1197, 16 L.Ed.2d 206 (1966).

212. See the opinion below in *Wood*, 22 A.D.2d 660, 661, 253 N.Y.S.2d 204, 205 (1964) (Valente, J., concurring).

213. Williams v. North Carolina, 325 U.S. 226, 229, 65 S.Ct. 1092, 1095, 89 L.Ed. 1577, 1581 (1945).

214. See, e.g., Restatement, Conflict of Laws § 111 (1934).

sufficient interest in controlling the marital status to make it reasonable for courts there to exercise divorce jurisdiction.[215]

One basis for divorce jurisdiction that is coming into common use is actual residence of at least one of the spouses in the forum for a substantial period of time.[216] The armed forces divorce statutes are one illustration of this phenomenon.[217] These statutes provide that the time that a person is living in the state while stationed there on military duty shall count as residence in the state for the purpose of fulfilling the state's period of residence, typically one year, required for divorce jurisdiction. The armed forces divorce statutes are not the only examples of actual residence for a substantial period, as distinguished from residence coupled with domiciliary intention, being accepted as a proper basis for divorce jurisdiction.[218]

Alton v. Alton[219] raises the question of whether personal jurisdiction over both spouses is a constitutional basis for divorce jurisdiction. Mrs. Alton sued for divorce in the Virgin Islands. Mr. Alton appeared and did not contest the action. Mrs. Alton had filed for divorce after she had been in the Virgin Islands for six weeks, having come there from her Connecticut domicile. The Virgin Islands divorce statute provided that, if the defendant in a divorce action was personally served or appeared, the court had divorce jurisdiction "without reference to domicile." The trial judge, nevertheless, refused to grant the divorce when the wife did not offer proof of domicile. The trial court's action was affirmed by a four-to-three decision of the Third Circuit Court of Appeals. The majority opinion, by Judge Goodrich, held that the Virgin Islands statute, permit-

---

215. See Scott v. Scott, 51 Cal.2d 249, 254–55, 331 P.2d 641, 644 (1958) (Traynor, J., concurring); R. Leflar et al., American Conflicts Law § 224 (4th ed. 1986); Restatement, Second, § 72.

216. See Restatement, Second, § 72, comment *b*.

217. For cases upholding armed forces divorce statutes, see Lauterbach v. Lauterbach, 392 P.2d 24 (Alaska 1964); Wallace v. Wallace, 63 N.M. 414, 320 P.2d 1020 (1958) (the serviceman's wife is the petitioner); Wood v. Wood, 159 Tex. 350, 320 S.W.2d 807 (1959).

218. See Wheat v. Wheat, 229 Ark. 842, 318 S.W.2d 793 (1958) (upholds divorce statute defining residence to mean actual presence, although the court does consider it possible that divorces so granted may not be entitled to full faith and credit in other states); Scott v. Scott, 51 Cal.2d 249, 331 P.2d 641 (1958) (declares valid a Mexican divorce obtained by a person having a bona fide Mexican residence; Judge Traynor, concurring, states that "although there was a finding of domicile in this case there should be no implication from the court's opinion herein that would preclude contacts with the foreign country other than domicile as a basis of jurisdiction." 51 Cal.2d at 255, 331 P.2d at 644–45); Matrimonial Proceedings Act of 1973 § 5 (U.K.) (either domicile or one year's habitual residence in England or Wales sufficient for divorce jurisdiction).

219. 207 F.2d 667 (3d Cir.1953), appeal dism'd as moot, 347 U.S. 610, 74 S.Ct. 736, 98 L.Ed. 987 (1954) (pending the hearing by the Supreme Court, the husband obtained a bilateral divorce in Connecticut).

Granville–Smith v. Granville–Smith, 349 U.S. 1, 75 S.Ct. 553, 99 L.Ed. 773 (1955), declared invalid the Virgin Islands statute in issue in *Alton* on the ground that the statute exceeded the powers of the Virgin Islands Legislative Assembly under the Virgin Islands Organic Act.

ting divorce based on personal jurisdiction over the defendant, violated due process.[220]

If, as in *Alton*, the defendant does not contest jurisdiction, there are two obstacles to raising a due process barrier to a divorce that is based simply on personal jurisdiction. First, if the defendant does not object to the court's jurisdiction, who is deprived of due process?[221] Surely not the petitioner who has invoked the court's action; and if the defendant has a due process complaint, he or she is not making it. Second, if a United States court grants a bilateral divorce based solely on in personam jurisdiction over the defendant, the defendant may urge a due process objection at trial and on appeal. If the defendant does not, the usual principles of res judicata bar the defendant from making a collateral attack on the court's jurisdiction.[222] In order for the divorcing state to lift this bar, it would have to decide that the policies against a court's granting a divorce in this manner outweigh the policies underlying res judicata.[223] If the divorcing state did not permit collateral attack, a sister state that allowed a collateral attack would have to decide that the interests of the state permitting the collateral attack outweigh the need for full faith and credit to judgments.[224] These are formidable obstacles to collateral attack on the divorce if the defendant is subject to the in personam jurisdiction of the court and does not make timely objection to the court's divorce jurisdiction.

If the defendant does object to divorce jurisdiction based solely on personal jurisdiction over the parties, this objection should prevail at least when the marital domicile does not permit "no fault" divorce. A court with no other nexus with the marital status than personal jurisdiction over the spouses should not undertake to end that status under its own divorce laws. As noted above, unlike courts in some other countries,

---

220. The court also held that a statutory presumption of domicile based on six-weeks residence was invalid because the fact was not reasonably related to the presumption.

221. This same question was raised in *Alton*. The court's only response was: "Nevertheless, if the jurisdiction for divorce continues to be based on domicile, as we think it does, we believe it to be lack of due process for one state to take to itself the readjustment of domestic relations between those domiciled elsewhere." *Alton*, 207 F.2d at 677.

222. See, Restatement, Second, Judgments § 12 (1982) ("Contesting Subject Matter Jurisdiction"):

"When a court has rendered a judgment in a contested action, the judgment precludes the parties from litigating the question of the court's subject matter jurisdiction in subsequent litigation except if:

(1) The subject matter of the action was so plainly beyond the court's jurisdiction that its entertaining the action was a manifest abuse of authority; or

(2) Allowing the judgment to stand would substantially infringe the authority of another tribunal or agency of government; or

(3) The judgment was rendered by a court lacking capability to make an adequately informed determination of a question concerning its own jurisdiction and as a matter of procedural fairness the party seeking to avoid the judgment should have opportunity belatedly to attack the court's subject matter jurisdiction."

See also id., comment *d*: "Even if the issue of subject matter jurisdiction has not been raised and determined, the judgment after becoming final should ordinarily be treated as wholly valid if the controversy has been litigated in any other respect." Cf. Davis v. Davis, 305 U.S. 32, 59 S.Ct. 3, 83 L.Ed. 26 (1938) (wife who appeared is barred from collateral attack on divorce court's jurisdiction).

223. See Restatement, Second, Judgments § 12 (1982).

224. See § 9.3A.

United States courts invariably apply the forum's divorce law.[225] If the marital domicile and the forum both permit "no fault" divorces based on a finding that the marriage is "irretrievably broken",[226] it would be difficult for the forum to misapply the law of the marital domicile,[227] although differences in the application of "no fault" divorce statutes have appeared.[228] If both the forum and the marital domicile grant divorce on mutual consent or unilateral demand, objection would center on a state that is not the domicile of either party passing on questions of support and custody when another state will bear the social consequences of the forum's actions.

David–Zieseniss v. Zieseniss,[229] upheld a former New York statute that based divorce jurisdiction on the fact that the parties were married in New York. Celebration of the marriage, without more is not a nexus with the marital status that gives a state having this contact a reasonable interest in affecting the status.[230]

§ 5.3   Custody

§ 5.3A   Is Personal Jurisdiction Over Custody Contestants Necessary for a Valid Custody Determination?

There are three major related questions concerning interstate treatment of child custody adjudications: the extent to which personal jurisdiction is necessary over all custody contestants; the bases for subject matter jurisdiction; the extent to which custody decrees must or should be enforced and not modified in sister states. The focus in this section is on the need for personal jurisdiction. Section 5.3B discusses subject matter jurisdiction and 5.3C interstate enforcement.

Although there are many contexts for making a custody decision, typically the contestants are spouses or former spouses, the father and mother. The adjudication may be either the initial custody determination, at the marital domicile or elsewhere, or a decision as to whether a prior decree of the forum or of another state should be modified with regard to physical custody, or visiting rights, or both. Should any forum that has a sufficient nexus with the parent-child relationship have the power to make a custody determination that will be enforced against a contestant over whom the court does not have personal jurisdiction? I believe that the answer is "yes" if the need for adjudication in a forum that is the most convenient for determining the best interests of the

---

225. See supra § 5.2A notes 77–78 and accompanying text.

226. See Uniform Marriage & Divorce Act § 302(a)(2), 9A pt.I U.L.A. 200 (1998).

227. See Baade, § 5.2F, note 209, at 340; Garfield, *The Transitory Divorce Action: Jurisdiction in the No–Fault Era*, 58 Texas L. Rev. 501, 524 (1980).

228. See Frank, Berman, & Mazur–Hart, *No Fault Divorce and the Divorce Rate: the Nebraska Experience—An Interrupted Time Series Analysis and Commentary*, 58 Nebr. L. Rev. 1, 63–69 (1979).

229. 205 Misc. 836, 129 N.Y.S.2d 649 (Spec.Term, N.Y.Cty., 1954), constitutionality questioned, Wiener v. Wiener, 19 Misc.2d 470, 472, 191 N.Y.S.2d 280, 282 (Spec.Term, N.Y.Cty., 1959).

230. See Restatement, Second § 72, comment *b*. But cf. Whealton v. Whealton, 67 Cal.2d 656, 63 Cal.Rptr. 291, 432 P.2d 979 (1967) (in annulment actions, the applicable law is that of the state in which the marriage was celebrated).

child outweighs any possible unfairness to an absent contestant. Even if the answer were "no," that would not mean that a forum with a sufficient nexus with the parent-child relationship would not have subject matter jurisdiction to make a valid custody adjudication. It would simply mean that a contestant over whom the forum did not have in personam jurisdiction would have a due process right to a de novo custody determination when that contestant brought the prior adjudication into question either in another state or in the forum.[231] The court conducting the de novo determination of the child's best interests would take account of the child's need for stability and the actual physical custody of the child since the prior decree. Rarely should a long-term custody arrangement be upset because of a theoretical right to de novo review. The threat of such a review would create substantial uncertainty and threaten the primary need of the child—a stable relationship.[232]

There are two United States Supreme Court cases that might be read as giving a due process right of de novo review to a contestant over whom a court adjudicating custody does not have in personam jurisdiction—*May v. Anderson*[233] and *Shaffer v. Heitner*.[234] In *May*, Wisconsin was the marital domicile. The wife left Wisconsin with the children and went to Ohio. The husband then brought suit in Wisconsin for divorce and petitioned for custody of the children. Wisconsin granted the husband a divorce and also gave him custody of the children. At that time, Wisconsin did not have a long-arm statute that would give it personal jurisdiction over the recently departed wife.[235] The Wisconsin court therefore rendered the custody decree without personal jurisdiction over the wife. Nevertheless, armed with this decree and accompanied by an Ohio police officer, the husband obtained the children from their mother. Four years later the wife retained the children in Ohio after their visitation time had expired. The husband filed a petition for habeas corpus in Ohio to regain possession of the children. Under Ohio law, this procedure tested only the husband's immediate right to possession of the children and did not permit a determination of whether, in the light of changed circumstances or otherwise, the father's custody was in the best interest of the children. The Ohio courts ordered the return of the children. The United States Supreme Court reversed.

The Court in *May v. Anderson* split 4–1–2–1 and its members wrote four opinions.[236] The case would, therefore, raise substantial questions as

231. See Garfield, *Due Process Rights of Absent Parents in Interstate Custody Conflicts: A Commentary on In re Marriage of Hudson*, 16 Ind. L. Rev. 445, 480–82 (1983); cf. Goldfarb v. Goldfarb, 246 Ga. 24, 268 S.E.2d 648 (1980) (can adjudicate custody without jurisdiction over the father even though the forum's decree may not be enforceable where the father resides).

232. See Wexler, *Rethinking the Modification of Child Custody Decrees*, 94 Yale L. J. 757, 760 (1985).

233. 345 U.S. 528, 73 S.Ct. 840, 97 L.Ed. 1221 (1953).

234. 433 U.S. 186, 97 S.Ct. 2569, 53 L.Ed.2d 683 (1977).

235. Wisconsin now has such a statute. Wis.Stat.Ann. § 801.05(11).

236. Justice Burton wrote for the plurality of four. *May*, 345 U.S. at 528–35, 73 S.Ct. at 841–44, 97 L.Ed. at 1224–28. Justice Frankfurter concurred. Id. at 535–36, 73 S.Ct. at 844–

to where the court stood even if each opinion were a model of clarity. The plurality opinion by Justice Burton, however, is ambiguous on the crucial issue of whether or not Ohio can defer to the Wisconsin decree if it so desires, or whether the mother, as a matter of due process, is entitled to a de novo determination of custody because the court rendering the original decree did not have personal jurisdiction over her. The opinion begins by focusing on whether the Ohio must enforce the Wisconsin decree:

> The question presented is whether in a habeas corpus proceeding attacking the right of a mother to retain possession of her minor children, an Ohio court must give full faith and credit to a Wisconsin decree awarding custody of the children to their father when that decree is obtained by the father in an *ex parte* divorce in a Wisconsin court which had no personal jurisdiction over the mother.[237]

But Justice Burton's opinion ends by emphasizing the rights of the mother:

> We find it unnecessary to determine the children's legal domicile because, even if it be with their father, that does not give Wisconsin, certainly as against Ohio, the personal jurisdiction that it must have in order to deprive their mother of her personal right to their immediate possession.[238]

To add to the confusion, Justice Frankfurter, in his concurring opinion, assumes that the plurality opinion is simply deciding that full faith and credit does not require Ohio to enforce the Wisconsin decree, but that Ohio may defer to Wisconsin if it so wishes.[239] Justice Jackson, in a dissent in which Justice Reed joins him, assumes that the plurality holds that Ohio could not constitutionally defer to the Wisconsin decree.[240]

45, 97 L.Ed. at 1228. Justice Jackson dissented in an opinion joined by Justice Reed. Id. at 536–42. 73 S.Ct. at 845–47, 97 L.Ed. at 1228–31. Justice Minton dissented separately. Id. at 542–43, 73 S.Ct. at 848, 97 L.Ed. at 1231–32. Justice Clark took no part. Id. at 535, 73 S.Ct. at 844, 97 L.Ed. at 1228.

237. Id. at 528–29, 73 S.Ct. at 841, 97 L.Ed. at 1224.

238. Id. at 534, 73 S.Ct. at 843–44, 97 L.Ed. at 1227.

239. Id. at 535–36, 73 S.Ct. at 844–45, 97 L.Ed. at 1228.

240. Id. at 536–37, 73 S.Ct. at 845, 97 L.Ed. at 1228.

If Justice Jackson's interpretation of *May* is correct, the question arises of whether *May* was overruled sub silentio by Stanley v. Illinois, 405 U.S. 645, 92 S.Ct. 1208, 31 L.Ed.2d 551 (1972). *Stanley* held that an unwed father was deprived of due process when not granted a hearing on his fitness as a parent before his children were taken from him and that denial of such a hearing to an unwed father when granted to all other parents was a denial of equal protection of the laws. The opinion focused on the need for notice and opportunity to be heard and did not mention any requirement of in personam jurisdiction over the father. "Unwed fathers who do not promptly respond [to notice by personal service, certified mail, or by publication when other notice is unavailable] cannot complain if their children are declared wards of the State." Id. at 657 n.9, 92 S.Ct. 1216 n.9, 31 L.Ed.2d 551 n.9. But the contention that *Stanley* supersedes *May* reads *Stanley* out of context. In *Stanley*, there was no question that the father was subject to the in personam jurisdiction of Illinois courts and the only issue was notice and opportunity to be heard. See Sherman, *Child Custody Jurisdiction and the Parental Kidnapping Prevention Act—A Due Process Dilemma?*, 17 Tulsa L. J. 713, 720 (1982). But cf. Wenz v. Schwartze, 183 Mont.

Shaffer v. Heitner[241] restricted the use of in rem jurisdiction. In the course of enumerating four uses of in rem jurisdiction that are still permissible,[242] the Court makes this Delphic utterance: "We do not suggest that jurisdictional doctrines other than those discussed in text, such as the particularized rules governing adjudications of status, are inconsistent with the standard of fairness. See e.g., Traynor, supra, at 660–661."[243]

Is a custody decree one of the "adjudications of status" to which the Court is referring and is one of the "particularized rules" the one subsequently embodied in the Uniform Child Custody Jurisdiction and Enforcement Act (UCCJEA)[244] and 28 U.S.C. § 1738A[245] that an adjudication of status rendered by a court having an appropriate nexus with the parent-child relationship, although without jurisdiction over an absent parent, must be enforced in other states?

The citation to "Traynor" in the quote is to an article by Roger Traynor in which the great judge discusses among many conflict-of-laws issues, ex parte divorces and custody decrees.[246] On the page following those cited by *Shaffer*, Traynor says that despite the importance of the determination to the contestants, "the state where a child is present must be competent to regulate his custody whether his parent is present or not. . . ."[247]

Some courts[248] and commentators[249] have interpreted *Shaffer*'s "status exception" dictum as permitting binding ex parte custody determina-

---

166, 598 P.2d 1086 (1979), cert. denied, 444 U.S. 1071, 100 S.Ct. 1015, 62 L.Ed.2d 753 (1980) (can terminate parental rights without in personam jurisdiction over the parent) (dictum).

241. 433 U.S. 186, 97 S.Ct. 2569, 53 L.Ed.2d 683 (1977) (barring the use of in rem jurisdiction to adjudicate the merits of a controversy having no relationship to the forum or to the property seized). Section 4.28 discusses *Shaffer*.

242. See supra § 5.2A, note 89.

243. *Shaffer*, 433 U.S. at 208 n.30, 97 S.Ct. at 2582 n.30, 53 L.Ed.2d at 700 n.30.

244. Unif. Child Custody Jurisdiction & Enforcement Act, §§ 106, 201, 202, 9 pt. IA U.L.A. 663, 671, 673 (1999). See Sampson & Kurtz, *UIFSA: An Interstate Support Act for the 21st Century and Uniform Interstate Family Support Act (with Unofficial Annotations by John Sampson)*, 27 Fam. L.Q. 85 (Spring 1993).

245. 28 U.S.C. § 1738A(a), (c)(2). Section 1738A is often referred to as the "Parental Kidnapping Prevention Act [of 1980]," but that section is only part of that Act. PL 96–611, 94 Stat. 3568 et seq.

Section 1738A uses the power of Congress under Art. IV, § 1 of the U.S. Const. to "prescribe" "the effect" of state "public acts, records, and judicial proceedings." Under this provision, Congress can extend the scope of full faith and credit beyond what would be required by the Constitution, but it cannot do so in a way that would violate due process. See Yarborough v. Yarborough, 290 U.S. 202, 215 n.2, 54 S.Ct. 181, 186 n.2, 78 L.Ed. 269, 277 n.2 (1933).

246. Traynor, *Is This Conflict Really Necessary?*, 37 Texas L. Rev. 657, 660–62 (1959).

247. Id. at 662.

248. See In re Marriage of Hudson, 434 N.E.2d 107 (Ind.App. 4th Dist.1982), cert. denied, 459 U.S. 1202, 103 S.Ct. 1187, 75 L.Ed.2d 433 (1983); Hudson v. Hudson, 35 Wn.App. 822, 670 P.2d 287 (1983); cf. Wenz v. Schwartze, 183 Mont. 166, 598 P.2d 1086 (1979), cert. denied, 444 U.S. 1071, 100 S.Ct. 1015, 62 L.Ed.2d 753 (1980) (can terminate parental rights without personal jurisdiction over the parent) (dictum); In the Matter of Adoption of J.L.H., Jr., and J.P.H., 737 P.2d 915 (Okla.1987) (adoption permitted without

tions, but others have disagreed.[250] If there is one clear lesson from *Shaffer*, it is that difficult questions are not answered by labels such as "in personam," or "in rem," or "status adjudication" and that "all assertions of state-court jurisdiction must be evaluated according to the standards [of fair play and substantial justice] set forth in *International Shoe* and its progeny."[251]

Shaffer does leave open the question of whether the exercise of jurisdiction struck down in that case would be permissible "when no other forum is available to the plaintiff."[252] It is tempting to make this "jurisdiction by necessity" argument for custody determinations. The state with the most information about the child and the petitioning parent may not have jurisdiction over the other parent. The petitioner can take the other parent's testimony and the other parent can participate without going to the forum determining custody.[253] True jurisdiction by necessity in custody cases would exist only where there were more than two claimants who could not be brought together in the same court.

The idea of adjudicating custody in a court that will have to import its data from afar is closer to nonsense than we should venture. The court with the best access to the facts needed for a sensible decision should adjudicate custody. Moreover, the importance of stability in the child's environment means that other states should enforce this determination and remand claims for modification to the original court, if this court retains the nexus with child and environment necessary for an

---

jurisdiction over mother); Perry v. Ponder, 604 S.W.2d 306 (Tex.Civ.App.—Dallas 1980, no writ) (may, but need not, enforce ex parte custody decree); In re Interest of M.S.B., 611 S.W.2d 704 (Tex.Civ.App.—San Antonio 1980, no writ) (approve ex parte termination of parental rights).

249. See Coombs, *Interstate Child Custody: Jurisdiction, Recognition, and Enforcement*, 66 Minn. L. Rev. 711, 836 (1982) ("the Court will probably hold that even in custody proceedings due process requires either some defendant-forum contacts or, in exceptional cases, other circumstances that make litigation in a forum lacking such contacts fair"); cf. Atwood, *Child Custody Jurisdiction and Territoriality*, 52 Ohio St. L. J. 369, 402 (1991) ("although judicial power over the absent parent is a constitutional necessity, such power, more aptly termed 'territorial jurisdiction,' can arise from child-centered contacts with the forum").

250. See Ex parte Dean, 447 So.2d 733 (Ala.1984) (ex parte custody decree is not entitled to extraterritorial effect); Pasqualone v. Pasqualone, 63 Ohio St.2d 96, 406 N.E.2d 1121, 17 O.O.3d 58 (1980) (refuse recognition of ex parte decree of state to which wife had gone with child when that state did not have jurisdiction over the husband); Garfield, supra note 231 at 446–48; Wasserman, *Parents, Partners, and Personal Jurisdiction*, 1995 U. Ill. L. Rev. 813, 818 ("the status exception should not be used to sanction divorce *or* child custody proceedings in states that lack *in personam* jurisdiction over all interested parties") (emphasis in original).

251. Shaffer v. Heitner, 433 U.S. 186, 212, 97 S.Ct. 2569, 2584–85, 53 L.Ed.2d 683, 703 (1977).

252. Id. at 211 n.37, 97 S.Ct. at 2584 n.37, 53 L.Ed.2d at 702 n.37.

253. See UCCJEA §§ 110 (communication between courts with party participation); 111 (taking testimony in another state); 112 (cooperation between courts in obtaining evidence outside the state).

The provisions of UCCJEA facilitating interstate cooperation also cut in favor of binding ex parte custody decrees because they make it more convenient for the absent parent to be heard.

informed decision. These needs for adjudication and enforcement will usually outweigh due process concerns for possible unfairness to an absent parent. *Shaffer*, however, should increase our sensitivity to is the fact that this is not always so. The balance may tip in favor of the due process rights of the person over whom the petitioned court does not have personal jurisdiction. This is not likely to occur because all U.S. jurisdictions have enacted the UCCJEA, except for Massachusetts and Vermont where it is pending. That Act provides that the home state of the child is the exclusive basis for custody jurisdiction unless no state qualifies as the home or the home state has deferred to the state deciding custody.[254].

An example of ex parte custody adjudication that should violate due process is when one of the parents leaves the marital domicile with the children and within two or three months sues for custody at the new residence.[255] The children have lived at the marital domicile for several years and that is where information concerning their best interests is more readily available. The parent who has remained at the marital domicile should be able to bring a custody suit there within a reasonably short time of the children's departure without the distraction of the other parent's action at the new residence. This could not occur under the UCCJEA because the marital domicile retains exclusive custody jurisdiction until six months after it ceases to be the children's home state.[256]

In most cases the state that is the children's home state should be able to bind an absent contestant with its custody decree. This state typically will be the marital domicile when one parent has remained with the children and the other parent has left. If this is so, a properly drafted long-arm statute and prompt action by the stay-at-home parent will make it unnecessary to decide whether without personal jurisdiction over the absent parent, that parent would be entitled to a de novo determination of custody.[257]

A few courts have interpreted the "status exception" in footnote 30 of *Shaffer v. Heitner*[258] as permitting not only subject matter jurisdiction in child custody matters when there is a nonresident parent, but also as permitting exercise of in personam jurisdiction over the absent parent.[259]

---

254. UCCJEA § 201.

255. But see Farrell v. Farrell, 133 Mich.App. 502, 351 N.W.2d 219 (1984) (approve custody jurisdiction one month after mother arrives in forum from Ireland).

256. UCCJEA § 201(a)(1). See also id. § 102(7), which defines "home state" as a state in which the child has resided for at least six consecutive months or since birth.

257. See Ex parte Dean, 447 So.2d 733 (Ala.1984) (refusing to enforce ex parte custody decree rendered at marital domicile and emphasizing fact that the marital domicile did not have an appropriate long-arm statute).

258. 433 U.S. 186, 208 n.30, 97 S.Ct. 2569, 2582 n.30, 53 L.Ed.2d 683, 700 n.30 (1977) (barring the use of in rem jurisdiction to adjudicate the merits of a controversy having no relationship to the forum or to the property seized but suggesting an exception for "rules governing adjudications of status").

259. See State of Utah in the interest of W.A. v. State of Utah, 63 P.3d 607, 611, 613 (Utah 2002), cert. denied, 538 U.S. 1035, 123 S.Ct. 2092, 155 L.Ed.2d 1065 (2003)

Shaffer's status exception should be limited to subject matter jurisdiction to affect the absent parent's custody rights without personal jurisdiction over that parent.

§ 5.3B   Bases for Custody Jurisdiction

A. OVERVIEW

There is an analytical distinction between the problem discussed in section 5.3A (whether in personam jurisdiction over a custody contestant is necessary to deprive that contestant of a right to a de novo custody determination) and the issues that are the focus of this section.[260] Here the emphasis is on what nexus between a forum and the parent-child relationship is necessary before the forum has subject matter jurisdiction to affect that relationship. The forum might have such subject matter jurisdiction whether or not an absent contestant would be bound by it. The more suitable the forum for custody determination, the less likely it is that a binding determination will violate an absent contestant's due process rights.

There is an important distinction between jurisdiction to render the original custody decree and jurisdiction to amend that decree. The original decree should be made by a forum that has a close connection with the parent-child relationship and easy access to information concerning the best interests of the child. Although several states might have such a nexus, ideally it is the court with the closest connection and best information that should act. After the initial custody determination, a tension arises between the child's need for continuity and stability and the desirability of having custody determinations made by the court in the best position to make informed decisions. The need to have stability and to discourage snatch-and-run relitigation by disappointed contestants, points to keeping custody jurisdiction in the original court as long as possible. On the other hand, keeping jurisdiction there once the child's life is centered elsewhere will interfere with informed modification decisions and may subvert the very stability that motivated jurisdiction retention by producing punitive "home town" decisions against a parent originally awarded custody who has left the state with the child.[261] Obtaining the correct balance between stability and informed modification requires perspicacity and common sense.

(termination of parental rights); In re Termination of Parental Rights to Thomas J.R., 262 Wis.2d 217, 240, 246, 663 N.W.2d 734, 745, 749 (2003) (termination of parental rights).

260.   But see Eicke v. Eicke, 399 So.2d 1231 (La.App.), writ denied, 406 So.2d 607 (1981), cert. dism'd as improvidently granted, 459 U.S. 1139, 103 S.Ct. 776, 74 L.Ed.2d 987 (1983) (refusing to recognize Texas custody decree and confusing Texas bases for in personam and subject matter jurisdiction).

261.   See, e.g., Baird v. Baird, 374 So.2d 60 (Fla.App.3d Dist.1979) (refuse to enforce change of custody decreed by former home state after departed custodial parent found in contempt); Borys v. Borys, 76 N.J. 103, 386 A.2d 366 (1978) (refuse to recognize another state's punitive decree entered 3 years after custodial parent had moved to forum with children).

B. ORIGINAL JURISDICTION

1. HISTORICAL BASES

It was once generally accepted that only the courts of the state in which a child was domiciled had jurisdiction to determine who should have custody of the child.[262] Although the child's domicile remained a widely recognized basis for custody determination,[263] other bases for jurisdiction came to be accepted. These nondomiciliary grounds for custody jurisdiction included in personam jurisdiction over the contestants for custody[264] and the presence of the child in the forum.[265] None of these historical bases for custody jurisdiction were satisfactory because they did not focus sufficiently on the kind of contacts that would both give the forum a reasonable interest in determining a child's custody and facilitate an intelligent judgment as to what would be in the child's best interests.

2. THE UNIFORM CHILD CUSTODY JURISDICTION ACT (UCCJA)

The Conference of Commissioners on Uniform State Laws approved the UCCJA in 1968. Every state, the District of Columbia, and the U.S. Virgin Islands adopted the Act. In 1997 the Conference approved the Uniform Child Custody Jurisdiction and Enforcement Act (UCCJEA) to replace the UCCJA, reconcile the Act with the Parental Kidnapping Prevention Act of 1980, and provide for interstate civil enforcement of custody orders. On January 1, 2009 only Massachusetts, Missouri, New Hampshire, and Vermont had not replaced the UCCJA with the UC-CJEA. The UCCJEA was introduced in the legislatures of these four states in 2009. Missouri and New Hampshire have already enacted it.[266] It has been referred to the Judiciary Committees in the Massachusetts and Vermont legislatures.[267] This edition eliminates the discussions of the UCCJA that appeared in previous editions.

3. THE UNIFORM CHILD CUSTODY JURISDICTION AND ENFORCEMENT ACT (UCCJEA)

UCCJEA § 201 covers "initial child-custody jurisdiction." The major change from UCCJA is that the "home state" of the child is the exclusive basis for jurisdiction unless no state qualifies as the home state

---

262. See, e.g., Brown v. Brown, 105 Ariz. 273, 463 P.2d 71 (1969); Restatement, Conflict of Laws § 117 (1934).

263. See, e.g., Sampsell v. Superior Court, 32 Cal.2d 763, 197 P.2d 739 (1948); Restatement, Second, § 79.

264. See Sampsell v. Superior Court, 32 Cal.2d 763, 197 P.2d 739 (1948).

265. See, e.g., Helton v. Crawley, 241 Iowa 296, 41 N.W.2d 60 (1950); Restatement, Second § 79(b).

266. Mo. HB 481; N.H. HB 695.

267. Mass HB 1578, referred to Joint Committee on the Judiciary; Vt. HB 50, referred to Committee on Judiciary.

or that state has deferred to the jurisdiction of the state exercising jurisdiction.[268] Section 102(7) defines "home state" as "the State in which a child lived with a parent or a person acting as a parent for at least six consecutive months immediately before the commencement of a child-custody proceeding." There is a split of authority as to whether a court should determine "home state" by focusing solely on the child's physical presence or whether the court should consider the parents' intent or "the totality of circumstances."[269]

If no state qualifies as a home state, then exclusive jurisdiction vests in the state with a "significant connection" with "the child and at least one parent or person acting as a parent"[270] unless the state with the significant connection defers to the state exercising jurisdiction.[271] There is a default provision conferring jurisdiction when no other court has jurisdiction.[272] The UCCJEA places the emergency basis for jurisdiction in a separate section that makes it clear that this jurisdiction is for the temporary purpose of protecting the child and not for the purpose of making a custody determination.[273]

C. MODIFICATION JURISDICTION

1. HISTORICAL BASIS

Because a custody decree is subject to modification in the light of changed circumstances, the court that rendered the original decree has been held to retain continuing jurisdiction to modify.[274] Even if there is such continuing jurisdiction, it is unwise for a court to invoke it if the child and one or more parents resides in another state and the court is no longer a convenient forum for the informed determination of what is in the child's best interests.[275] A number of cases have quite sensibly held that continuing custody jurisdiction ends when the parent to whom a court has awarded custody moves with the child to another state.[276]

---

268. UCCJEA § 201(a). See In re D.S., A Minor, 217 Ill.2d 306, 298 Ill.Dec. 781, 840 N.E.2d 1216 (2005) (finding that child has no "home state" and that Illinois has jurisdiction under UCCJEA when mother, a long time resident of Illinois, fearful of losing custody of the child about to be born, left Illinois for Tennessee, but gave birth en route in Indiana).

269. See Powell v. Stover, 165 S.W.3d 322 (Tex. 2005) (focusing solely on child's residence but collecting contrary authority).

270. UCCJEA § 201(a)(2).

271. Id. § 201(a)(3).

272. Id. § 201(a)(4).

273. Id. § 204.

274. See, e.g., Corkill v. Cloninger, 153 Mont. 142, 454 P.2d 911 (1969).

275. See Ratner, *Child Custody in a Federal System*, 62 Mich. L. Rev. 795, 797 (1964).

276. See, e.g., Johnson v. Johnson, 105 Ariz. 233, 462 P.2d 782 (1969).

2. CHILD CUSTODY JURISDICTION AND ENFORCEMENT ACT (UCCJEA)

(a) Modification in the Original Forum

Under UCCJEA a court that makes an original custody determination under § 201 "has exclusive continuing jurisdiction over the determination" so long as (1) "the child, the child's parents, [or] any person acting as a parent" resides in the state or; (2) until a court in that state "determines that neither the child, the child's parents, and any person acting as a parent do not have a significant connection with this State and that substantial evidence is no longer available in this State concerning the child's care, protection training, and personal relationships."[277] A court may decline to exercise its exclusive continuing jurisdiction "if it determines that it is an inconvenient forum under the circumstances and that a court of another State is a more appropriate forum."[278]

(b) Modification in Another Forum

A court of a state that has not made the initial custody determination may not modify the custody decree unless (1) it "determines that the child, the child's parents, and any person acting as a parent do not presently reside in the other State,"[279] or; (2) "the court of the other State determines it no longer has exclusive, continuing jurisdiction";[280] and (3) the state in which the modifying court sits is the child's home state, or the home state has deferred to the modifying state as a more appropriate forum, or there is no home state and the modifying state has a "significant connection" with the child and at least one parent, or a person acting as parent, that enables the court to make an informed decision concerning the child's best interests.[281]

3. THE PARENTAL KIDNAPPING PREVENTION ACT (PKPA)

The PKPA does not purport to supersede state law. It provides, however, that if the state's exercise of custody jurisdiction does not conform to 28 U.S.C. § 1738A, the state custody decree is not entitled to the additional protection resulting from the federal mandate that "every State shall enforce according to its terms, and shall not modify"[282] the decree.

---

277. UCCJEA § 202. But cf. Stewart v. Evans, 332 Mont. 148, 136 P.3d 524 (2006) (the UCCJEA does not govern issue of whether trial court had continuing jurisdiction to rule on grandmother's petition for contact with grandchild; court had jurisdiction after father moved to Kentucky with grandchild).

278. Id. § 207.

279. Id. § 203(a)(2).

280. Id. § 203(a)(1). In re Forlenza, 140 S.W.3d 373 (Tex. 2004) (Texas retains exclusive continuing jurisdiction over custody proceedings when children, who have lived outside of the state for five years, visited their mother in Texas on six occasions, on four of which they lived with their mother for a month, and the mother had visited the children out of state fifteen times).

281. UCCJEA § 203(a).

282. 28 U.S.C. § 1738A(a). But see In Matter of Sayeh R., 91 N.Y.2d 306, 693 N.E.2d 724, 670 N.Y.S.2d 377 (1997) (PKPA does not apply to child protective proceeding and N.Y.

In the subsection that specifies when a custody determination is consistent with the Act and therefore entitled to the protection of the Act's mandate that the decree be enforced and not modified,[283] the PKPA wisely prefers "home State" jurisdiction over that based on "significant connection."[284] Then, however, the Act forbids a state that has become the new home from modifying a prior decree so long as another state, which has rendered a decree within the Act's jurisdictional requirements, purports to retain modification jurisdiction under its law and any contestant continues to live there.[285]

4. INTERNATIONAL CONVENTIONS

Another significant tool for combating child abduction is the 1980 Convention on the Civil Aspects of International Child Abduction[286] promulgated under the auspices of the Hague Conference on Private International Law. Signatory countries promise to summarily return children wrongfully removed from another country in which the child was habitually resident immediately before the removal.[287] "Wrongful removal" includes depriving a person of custody even though no custody decree exists.[288] If a year has elapsed after the wrongful removal, return is not ordered if "the child is now settled in its new environment."[289] Current information on signatory countries is available on the web page that the Hague Conference devotes to the Convention.[290]

The United States has ratified the Convention and has enacted, as implementing legislation, the International Child Abduction Remedies Act (ICARA).[291] ICARA declares that "[t]he provisions of this chapter are in addition to and not in lieu of the provisions of the Convention"[292] and provides concurrent jurisdiction under the Convention to state and federal courts.[293] ICARA covers "burdens of proof."[294] The petitioner has

---

court has jurisdiction despite Florida decree awarding custody to mother who resides in Florida).

283. 28 U.S.C. § 1738A(c)(2)(A), (B).

284. See Foster, *Child Custody Jurisdiction: UCCJA and PKPA*, 27 N.Y.L.Sch. L. Rev. 297, 303–04 (1981) (tracing this home state emphasis to the influence of Professor Brigette Bodenheimer, whose views on this issue did not prevail in the drafting of the UCCJA).

285. 28 U.S.C. § 1738A(c)(1), (d), (f). See Murphy v. Woerner, 748 P.2d 749 (Alaska 1988) (PKPA prevents new home state from modifying custody decree). For cases misapplying these provisions and assuming that the PKPA favors home state jurisdiction for modification as well as for an original decree see Mebert v. Mebert, 111 Misc.2d 500, 444 N.Y.S.2d 834 (Fam.Ct., Onondaga County 1981); Quenzer v. Quenzer, 653 P.2d 295 (Wyo.1982).

286. 19 I.L.M. 1501. See McDonald, *More Than Mere Child's Play: International Parental Abduction of Children*, 6 Dick. J.Int'l.L. 283, 306–311 (1988).

287. Convention arts. 3, 12.

288. Id. art. 3(a).

289. Id. art. 12.

290. <<http://www.hcch.net/e/status/abdshte.html>>.

291. 42 U.S.C. §§ 11601–11611

292. Id. § 11601(b)(2).

293. Id. § 11603(a).

the burden of proving by a preponderance of the evidence that the child has been wrongfully removed or retained and, in the case of rights of access, that the petitioner has such rights. The party opposing return of the child has the burden of establishing by clear and convincing evidence two exceptions to the duty to return the child: (1) return would expose the child to harm,[295] or (2) return "would not be permitted by the fundamental principles of the requested State relating to the protection of human rights and fundamental freedoms."[296] The party opposing return of the child also has the burden of establishing by a preponderance of the evidence various other exceptions to the duty to return the child.[297] ICARA also provides that "[t]he remedies established by the Convention and this chapter shall be in addition to remedies available under other laws or international agreements."[298]

By Executive Order[299] President Reagan designated the Department of State as the Central Authority to discharge the United States' Convention duties. A regulation[300] designates The Office of Citizens Consular Services in the Bureau of Consular Affairs as the Central Authority within the State Department. This office will, in addition to its other functions, assist persons using the Convention to recover children removed from the United States.

The Federal Register contains a Legal Analysis of the Convention including a model form.[301] The Legal Analysis contains frequent references to the report of the official Hague Conference reporter for the Convention, Elisa Perez–Vera,[302] which is available from the Netherlands Government Printing and Publishing Office.[303] Also obtainable

---

294. Id. § 11603(e)

295. See Convention art. 13(b): "there is a grave risk that his or her return would expose the child to physical or psychological harm or otherwise place the child in an intolerable situation" Cf. European Union Council Regulation No. 2116/2004 of 2 December 2004 concerning jurisdiction and the recognition and enforcement of judgments in matrimonial matters and the matters of parental responsibility, art. 11(4): "A court cannot refuse to return a child on the basis of Art. 13b of the 1980 Hague Convention if it is established that adequate arrangements have been made to secure the protection of the child after his or her return."

296. Id. art. 20.

297. These exceptions are (1) one year has elapsed since the date of wrongful removal and "the child is now settled in its new environment" (art. 12); (2) the party petitioning for return of the child "was not actually exercising the custody rights at the time of removal or retention, or had consented to or subsequently acquiesced in the removal or retention" (art. 13(a)); and (3) "the child objects to being returned and has attained an age and degree of maturity at which it is appropriate to take account of its views" (art. 13).

298. 42 U.S.C. § 11603(h).

299. No. 12648, Aug. 11, 1988, 53 F.R. 30637. For discussion of use of the Central Authority see Bruch, *The Central Authority's Role Under the Hague Child Abduction Convention*, 28 Family L.Q. 35, 41–42 (1994) (urging use of the local Central Authority before abduction for help with preventive measures and after abduction for assistance in reaching a foreign Central Authority).

300. 22 CFR § 94.2. See 22 CFR Part 94 for other regulations governing the Convention.

301. 51 Fed. Reg. 10503 (1986).

302. Actes et documents de la Quatorziem Session (1980) Vol. III, Child Abduction.

303. 1 Christoffel Plantijnstraat, P. O. Box 20014, 2500 EA The Hague, Netherlands.

from this source is the report of the Special Commission that met in The Hague on January 18–21, 1993 to study the operation of the Convention. The Report states that at the January 18 session "[a] number of speakers remarked that, despite a few speedy return cases, the excessive time periods for return proceedings remains a major problem to be resolved."[304]

The Report of the Special Commission also discusses another problem with the operation of the Convention—protecting non-custodial parents' rights to access to the children. At the January 19, 1993 session, the First Secretary of the Permanent Bureau of the Hague Conference on Private International Law accepted the criticism that the Convention "does not offer sufficient protection to rights of access." Most U.S. courts have held that rights of access are not enforceable by the Convention's return remedy even though a court in the child's habitual residence has ordered the abducting parent not to remove the child from the country,[305] but courts in other countries have ordered return of children removed in violation of a *ne exeat* order.[306] The Supreme Court of the United States has granted review of a case that raises this issue.[307]

Convention Article 29 and 42 U.S.C. § 11603(h) permit an action for return of the child under law other than the Convention. The primary United States legislation under which such an action would be brought is UCCJEA. Section 105 of the UCCJEA mandates enforcement of foreign custody awards made in substantial conformity with the Act's jurisdictional standards:

> (a) A court of this state shall treat a foreign country as if it were a State of the United States for the purpose of applying Articles 1 and 2.

---

304. A summary of the Report is at 33 I.L.M. 225 (1994). For discussion of experience with the Convention see Silberman, *Hague International Child Abduction Convention: A Progress Report*, 57 Law & Contemp. Probs. 209 (Summer 1994); Silberman, *Hague Convention on International Child Abduction: A Brief Overview and Case Law Analysis*, 28 Family L.Q. 9 (1994).

305. Croll v. Croll, 229 F.3d 133 (2d Cir. 2000), cert. denied, 534 U.S. 949, 122 S.Ct. 342, 151 L.Ed.2d 258 (2001); Gonzalez v. Gutierrez, 311 F.3d 942 (9th Cir. 2002). But see Furnes v. Reeves, 362 F.3d 702 (11th Cir. 2004), cert. denied, 543 U.S. 978, 125 S.Ct. 478, 160 L.Ed.2d 355 (2004). Under Norwegian law the parent with whom the child does not reside retains some decision-making authority over aspects of the child's care. Norwegian law also provides that both parents must consent to the child moving abroad. The court stated: "We conclude that this *ne exeat* right . . . especially in the context of [the] retained rights [of the parent with whom the child is not residing] constitutes a 'right of custody' as defined in the Convention."

306. See Linda Silberman, *The Hague Child Abduction Convention Turns Twenty: Gender Politics and Other Issues*, 33 N.Y.U. J. Int'l L. & Pol. 221, 230 (2000) (stating that "leading decisions in Australia, the United Kingdom, Israel, and France had all interpreted *ne exeat* clauses as conferring 'custody rights' within the meaning of the Child Abduction Convention").

307. Abbott v. Abbott, 542 F.3d 1081 (5th Cir. 2008) (holding that a Chilean Court order requiring that the father authorize the child's leaving the country did not gives "rights of custody" to the father within the meaning of the Convention), cert. granted,___ U.S. ___, 129 S.Ct. 2859, 174 L.Ed.2d 575 (2009).

(b) Except as otherwise provided in subsection (c), a child-custody determination made in a foreign country under factual circumstances in substantial conformity with the jurisdictional standards of this Act must be recognized and enforced under Article 3.

(c) A court of this state need not apply this Act if the child custody law of a foreign country violates fundamental principles of human rights.

The fact that another country has not ratified the Convention may affect a court's determination of custody and visitation. *Al–Zouhayli v. Al–Zouhayli*[308] affirmed the trial judge's order permitting unsupervised visitation by the father with the child. The father was a naturalized United States citizen but retained his Syrian citizenship. A majority thought that the trial judge's discounting the risk of abduction to Syria was not an abuse of discretion, but one of the three judges dissented on this issue. Both majority and dissent noted that Syria is not a party to the Convention, that its courts would not honor a United States custody decree, and that a Syrian court would "be compelled by local law and custom to award custody of the child to" the father.[309] That the child has been taken from a non-Convention country may also affect the standard applied to the decision to order return.[310]

On July 15, 1989, the Fourth Inter–American Specialized Conference on Private International Law Conference approved for submission to the member countries of the Organization of American States the Inter–American (I–A) Convention on International Repatriation of Children. The I–A Convention is similar to the Hague Convention. Nevertheless, some states opposed Article 33 of the I–A Convention, which permits signatories to agree bilaterally among themselves to give priority to the Hague Convention.

The European Convention on Recognition and Enforcement of Decisions Concerning Custody of Children and on Restoration of Custody of Children,[311] unlike the Hague Convention, is premised on the existence of a prior custody determination and is designed to facilitate reciprocal recognition and enforcement of custody decisions, rather than provide for immediate return of an abducted child. Article 1(d) defines "improper removal" as "the removal of a child across an international frontier in breach of a decision relating to his custody which has been given in a Contracting State" and also includes failure to return the child after a visit. The European Convention is open to ratification only by member states of the Council of Europe. If a state has ratified both the Hague and European Conventions, a court in the Netherlands has held "that

---

308. 486 N.W.2d 10 (Minn. App. 1992).

309. Id. at 13.

310. See In re P, [1997] 2 W.L.R. 223, 233 (C.A.) (stating that "one does not proceed upon a basis that it is necessary that the child would be in some obvious moral or physical danger if returned.... [W]elfare [of the child], wide ranging a concept as it is, is the only criterion").

311. Opened for signature May 20, 1980, 19 I.L.M. 273.

the application of the Convention which is most likely to bring about the return of the child should take precedence."[312]

On 1 January 2002 the Hague Convention on Jurisdiction, Applicable Law, Recognition, Enforcement and Co–Operation in Respect of Parental Responsibility and Measures for the Protection of Children entered into force. The Convention includes "rights of custody, including rights relating to the care of the person of the child and, in particular, the right to determine the child's place of residence, as well as rights of access including the right to take a child for a limited period of time to a place other than the child's habitual residence."[313] "The judicial or administrative authorities of the Contracting State of the habitual residence of the child have jurisdiction to take measures directed to the protection of the child's person or property."[314] If, however, the parents agree, "the authorities of a Contracting State exercising jurisdiction to decide upon an application for divorce or legal separation of the parents of a child habitually resident in another Contracting State, or for annulment of their marriage, may ... take measures directed to the protection of the person or property of such child."[315] In taking such measures "the authorities of the Contracting States shall apply their own law" but "may exceptionally apply or take into consideration the law of another State with which the situation has a substantial connection."[316] With listed exceptions including public policy and not giving a parent an opportunity to be heard, "the measures taken by the authorities of a Contracting State shall be recognized by operation of law in all other Contracting States."[317] Although the United States has not ratified the Convention, on August 1, 2009 it was in force in sixteen countries.

In 2007 the United States ratified the Hague Convention on Protection of Children and Co-operation in Respect of Intercountry Adoption.[318] The purpose of the Convention is "to ensure that intercountry adoptions are made in the best interests of the child and with respect for his or her fundamental rights, and to prevent the abduction, the sale of, or traffic in children."[319] Each signatory appoints a Central Authority. The Central Authority of the state of origin determines that the child is adoptable, the custodians of the child have given informed consent to the adoption, intercountry adoption is in the child's best interest, and, if the

---

312. Judgment given by R.H.M. Hooymans-van Oerle, Vice–President and Children's Judge, at the public sitting of 's-Hertogenbosch District Court, 13 February 1991 (applying the Hague Convention to order return of a child removed from England to the Netherlands; the Netherlands and the United Kingdom had ratified both the Hague and European Conventions).

313. Art. 3(b).

314. Art. 5(1).

315. Art. 10.

316. Art. 15

317. Art. 23.

318. Hague Conference on Private Int'l Law, 29 May 1993; on 1 August 2009 in force in 78 countries.

319. Id. Preamble.

child is of a suitable age, that the child has given informed consent.[320] The Central Authority in the receiving state determines that the adoptive parents are suitable.[321]

On November 23, 2007 the Hague Conference concluded the Convention on International Recovery of Child Support and Other Forms of Family Maintenance, but as of August 1, 2009 no country has ratified it.

In the European Union, Council Regulation on Jurisdiction, Applicable Law, Recognition and Enforcement of Decisions and Cooperation in Matters Relating to Maintenance Obligations[322] gives jurisdiction to the country in which either the defendant or the maintenance creditor is habitually resident to make a maintenance order[323] that is enforceable in another European Union without further formalities.[324]

§ 5.3C   Enforcement of Custody Decrees

A.   HISTORY

Until the passage of 28 U.S.C. § 1738A as part of the Parental Kidnapping Prevention Act of 1980 (PKPA),[325] it was an open question whether custody decrees were entitled to full faith and credit.[326] Parties opposing enforcement argued that if ever a state's interest in refusing obedience to a sister-state judgment could outweigh the very strong national interest in full faith and credit to judgments, it would be a state's interest in the welfare of a child when the state has substantial contacts with the child and finds that giving effect to the sister-state decree would not be in the child's best interest.[327] The rebuttal to this argument is that the child's need for stability and certainty makes it especially desirable that a custody decree, even more than other adjudications, be enforced and not modified.[328]

This debate over whether full faith and credit was owed to custody awards was largely academic. Even if full faith and credit were due, the custody award could be modified in another state in the same manner

---

320. Id. art. 4.

321. Id. art. 5.

322. Council Regulation (EC) No. 4/2009 of 18 December 2008, OJ 2009 L7/1 (10/01/2009 p.1).

323. Id. art. 3.

324. Id. art. 17.

325. P.L. 96–611, 94 Stat. 3568 et seq.

326. There were conflicting judicial statements on the issue. For cases giving full faith and credit to custody decrees, see, e.g., Hajovsky v. Hajovsky, 276 Ala. 77, 159 So.2d 194 (1963); Brocker v. Brocker, 429 Pa. 513, 241 A.2d 336 (1968), cert. denied, 393 U.S. 1081, 89 S.Ct. 857, 21 L.Ed.2d 773 (1969). For statements rejecting full faith and credit to custody decrees, see, e.g., Kovacs v. Brewer, 356 U.S. 604, 613, 78 S.Ct. 963, 968, 2 L.Ed.2d 1008, 1015 (1958) (Frankfurter, J., dissenting); Bachman v. Mejias, 1 N.Y.2d 575, 154 N.Y.S.2d 903, 136 N.E.2d 866 (1956).

327. See § 9.3A.

328. See Wexler supra § 5.3A note 232.

that it could be modified in the original forum.[329] In all states, custody judgments can be modified in the light of changes in circumstances after the decree, and, in some states in the light of circumstances existing at the time of the original award but not considered by the court.[330] Thus, any court that wished to modify a sister-state custody decree could do so without raising grave constitutional issues. The new forum could, in good faith, make a finding that a substantial alteration in the situation of the parties required an amendment to the sister-state decree. Or the second state could accomplish this result by making a perfunctory finding of changed circumstances. Even in this latter case, it would be difficult, if not impossible, for the losing party to demonstrate that full faith and credit, even if owed, was denied.

The ease with which courts could modify sister-state custody decrees resulted in the sad spectacle of child snatching, forum shopping, and repeated litigation of custody awards.[331] A parent dissatisfied with the first custody award, or perhaps simply wishing to use the child as a weapon to inflict punishment on the other parent, removed the child to another state or refused to return the child from an authorized visit outside the custody forum. The dissatisfied parent then relitigated the custody issue in the second state. A change in custody invited another round of grabbing, running, and litigating. Whatever chance the child had for stability and happiness was lost amidst the din of the warring parents.

An early effort to mitigate the evils of recurrent interstate custody disputes was the adoption of a "clean hands" doctrine. A number of courts refused to consider a petition for modification of a sister-state custody decree if the petitioner violated that decree.[332] But in some states, the fact that one of the parties had disobeyed the order of a sister state was not accorded much significance in deciding whether to modify an existing decree.[333]

---

329. See Kovacs v. Brewer, 356 U.S. 604, 78 S.Ct. 963, 2 L.Ed.2d 1008 (1958) (state decision remanded to give state court an opportunity to find changed circumstances and obviate the constitutional issue); New York ex rel. Halvey v. Halvey, 330 U.S. 610, 67 S.Ct. 903, 91 L.Ed. 1133 (1947); Note, 73 Yale L. J. 134 (1963).

330. For modification on the basis of circumstances existing at the time of the prior decree but not considered, see New York ex rel. Halvey v. Halvey, 330 U.S. 610, 67 S.Ct. 903, 91 L.Ed. 1133 (1947); Hill v. Hill, 228 Kan. 680, 620 P.2d 1114 (1980) (though court limits holding to a situation in which the prior decree was entered in a default proceeding without full presentation of the facts); Miller v. Miller, 15 Wis.2d 583, 113 N.W.2d 403 (1962); Restatement, Second, § 79, comment *b*.

331. See, e.g., Kern v. Kern, 96 Nev. 20, 604 P.2d 354 (1980); Bodenheimer, *The Uniform Child Custody Jurisdiction Act: A Legislative Remedy for Children Caught in the Conflict of Laws*, 22 Vand. L. Rev. 1207 (1969).

332. See, e.g., Application of Reed, 447 F.2d 814 (3d Cir.1971) (Virgin Islands); Hood v. Hood, 263 Ark. 662, 566 S.W.2d 743 (1978); Strobel v. Thurman, 565 S.W.2d 238 (Tex.1978); State ex rel. Kern v. Kern, 17 Wis.2d 268, 116 N.W.2d 337 (1962).

Some courts read an emergency exception into their clean hands doctrine. See, e.g., Wilson v. Wilson, 172 Colo. 566, 474 P.2d 789 (1970).

333. See, e.g., Scarpetta v. DeMartino, 254 So.2d 813 (Fla.App.1971), cert. denied, 262 So.2d 442 (Fla.), cert. denied, 409 U.S. 1011, 93 S.Ct. 437, 34 L.Ed.2d 305 (1972); People ex rel. Bukovich v. Bukovich, 39 Ill.2d 76, 233 N.E.2d 382 (1968).

There was general agreement that it was imperative to end the interstate custody battles.[334] The rule had to be established that a court would desist from modifying a sister-state custody decree when that decree was rendered by a court that had sufficient contacts with the parties to reach an intelligent decision,[335] when that other court still had these contacts so that it could make an informed determination of the request for modification,[336] and when there was no compelling reason, such as imminent threat of irreparable harm to the child, why the parties should not simply be remitted to that other state for decision on the petition to amend.[337] Even in an emergency, a forum petitioned to amend another jurisdiction's custody decree should make only such orders as are necessary for the protection of the child until a plenary hearing can be held in the other state, if that state is an appropriate forum for modification.[338] These standards were largely met by passage in all states of the Uniform Child Custody Jurisdiction and Enforcement Act[339] and girded with the armor of full faith and credit by the PKPA.[340]

B. THE UCCJEA MODIFICATION PROVISIONS

Modification under UCCJEA is discussed supra in text accompanying notes 274–278. The court making the initial custody determination retains exclusive continuing jurisdiction until the child and all contestants have left the state or the original court has deferred to the jurisdiction of another court.[341] Another court exercising emergency jurisdiction to protect the child may do so only on a temporary basis until a court having jurisdiction to make a custody determination can act.[342]

C. THE PKPA

The PKPA utilizes the power of Congress, under the "effect" clause of the Full Faith and Credit provision of the Constitution,[343] to increase

---

334. See, e.g., Bodenheimer, supra note 331. For an indication of the scope of the problem, see Hearings before the Subcommittee on Juvenile Justice of the Committee on the Judiciary, U.S. Senate, S. Hrg. 98–472 at p. 1 (1983) (opening statement of Senator Specter) (approximately 100,000 children victims of "parental kidnapping" each year).

335. See Turner v. Saka, 90 Nev. 54, 518 P.2d 608 (1974) (decline to enforce ex parte New Jersey decree).

336. See Nesler v. Nesler, 185 N.W.2d 799 (Iowa 1971) (refuse to enforce California decree awarding custody to mother after child had resided with father in Iowa for three years with mother's permission).

337. See State ex rel. Muirhead v. District Court, 169 Mont. 535, 550 P.2d 1304 (1976) (quoting this text).

338. See Ferreira v. Ferreira, 9 Cal.3d 824, 109 Cal.Rptr. 80, 512 P.2d 304 (1973) (dictum); State ex rel. Department of Human Services v. Avinger, 104 N.M. 255, 720 P.2d 290 (1986); Garza v. Harney, 726 S.W.2d 198 (Tex.App—Amarillo, 1987, no writ) (cannot modify Mexican original decree, but can enter temporary order to protect child until steps taken in Mexican forum for protection).

339. See infra § 5.3C(B).

340. See infra § 5.3C(C).

341. UCCJEA § 203.

342. Id. § 204.

343. U.S. Const. Art. IV, § 1: "And the Congress may by general laws prescribe the manner in which such acts, records and proceedings shall be proved, and the effect thereof."

the requirement to recognize sister state custody decrees beyond what the Constitution alone would require.[344] As previously indicated,[345] simply requiring full faith and credit to sister state decrees would not prevent modification on any basis that would permit modification in the original forum. What the relevant provision of the PKPA, 28 U.S.C. § 1738A, does is to forbid modification if the prior decree was rendered in accordance with the Act's standards for custody jurisdiction,[346] unless one of three conditions exist: (1) the state rendering the prior decree, under its law, no longer has jurisdiction to modify; (2) neither the child nor any contestant resides there; (3) the prior state has declined to exercise its power to modify.[347]

The modification provisions of the PKPA differ from those of the UCCJEA. The PKPA accords the state exercising custody jurisdiction consistently with the PKPA exclusive continuing jurisdiction so long as that state "remains the residence of the child or of any contestant."[348] The Act defines "contestant" as "a person, including a parent or grandparent, who claims a right to custody or visitation of a child."[349] Under the UCCJEA the exclusive jurisdiction continues only so long as "the child, the child's parents, [or] any person acting as a parent ... [has] a significant connection" with the state rendering the initial custody decree.[350] Thus if a grandparent remains in the initial state after the child and all parents have moved to another state, under PKPA but not under UCCJEA the first state retains exclusive jurisdiction to determine the grandparent's right to visitation. It may be that this clash between PKPA and UCCJEA will not pose a practical problem. *Troxel v.*

---

344. That Congress has such power, see, e.g., Yarborough v. Yarborough, 290 U.S. 202, 215 n.2, 54 S.Ct. 181, 186 n.2, 78 L.Ed. 269, 277 n.2 (1933); Cook, *The Powers of Congress under the Full Faith and Credit Clause*, 28 Yale L. J. 421 (1919); Freund, *Chief Justice Stone and the Conflict of Laws*, 59 Harv. L. Rev. 1210, 1225 (1946).

345. See supra notes 329–331 and accompanying text.

346. 28 U.S.C. § 1738A(a). See State ex rel. Valles v. Brown, 97 N.M. 327, 639 P.2d 1181 (1981).

A state is also forbidden to exercise custody jurisdiction if a proceeding is pending in the court of another state that is exercising jurisdiction consistently with the Act's provisions. 28 U.S.C. § 1738A(g).

347. Id. § 1738A(d), (f). See Ex parte Blanton, 463 So.2d 162 (Ala.1985) (can exercise jurisdiction when neither child nor any contestant resides in other state in which action is pending); Pierce v. Pierce, 197 Mt. 16, 640 P.2d 899 (1982) (to determine whether Montana may modify Kentucky decree, remand for hearing on whether Kentucky court, under Kentucky law, has jurisdiction to modify); McGee v. McGee, 651 S.W.2d 891 (Tex.App.—El Paso 1983, no writ) (because Mississippi no longer the residence of the child or of any contestant, can modify its decree). But cf. E.E.B. v. D.A., 89 N.J. 595, 446 A.2d 871 (1982), cert. denied, 459 U.S. 110, 103 S.Ct. 1203, 75 L.Ed.2d 445 (1983) (construe Ohio failure to hold hearing on best interest of child as declining to exercise jurisdiction).

348. 28 U.S.C.A. § 1738A(d).

349. Id. (b)(2).

350. UCCJEA § 202(a)(1).

Granville[351] reduced the likelihood that a grandparent may get a court to override a parent's wishes with regard to grandparent-child visits. *Troxel* held that a state statute giving a court the power to order grandparent visits as in the best interest of the child without according deference to the parent's wishes violated a fit parent's due process rights.

Thompson v. Thompson[352] held that there is no federal question jurisdiction under the PKPA to determine which of two conflicting state custody decisions is valid. The remedy for violation of the federal act is by appeal of the offending state decision.

It is probable that *Thompson* reached the right result given the statute's legislative history and absence of any specific creation of a federal cause of action. Part of the Court's reasoning, however, is not cogent. Justice Marshall states that requiring federal courts to enforce 1738A would involve them "in substantive domestic-relations determinations. Under the Act, jurisdiction can turn on the child's 'best interest' or on proof that the child has been abandoned or abused."[353] It is very unlikely that such issues will arise. "Best interest" jurisdiction is available under the PKPA only if the child has no "home state."[354] If the basis for jurisdiction is the presence of an "abandoned or abused" child, the decree is likely to be a temporary order for the protection of the child until a court that has a greater nexus with the parent-child relationship can act.[355]

Thompson, for example, involved a clash of Louisiana and California custody orders. California had made the initial custody order in the context of a divorce proceeding and awarded joint custody. When the mother decided to move to Louisiana, the California court granted her sole custody pending further investigation and the making of another custody determination. The mother took the child to Louisiana and after she was there for only three months, obtained an order from a Louisiana court granting her sole custody and modifying the father's visitation privileges. Five months after mother and child had moved to Louisiana, the California court awarded the father sole custody.

It was clear that when the California court entered the original decree California was the child's "home state," that this decree was entitled to protection under 1738A's mandate that it be enforced and not modified, and that California retained sole jurisdiction to modify its decree because the father continued to reside there.[356] The federal

---

351.   530 U.S. 57, 120 S.Ct. 2054, 147 L.Ed.2d 49 (2000).

352.   484 U.S. 174, 108 S.Ct. 513, 98 L.Ed.2d 512 (1988).

353.   Id. at 186 n.4, 108 S.Ct. at 520 n.4, 98 L.Ed.2d at 524 n.4.

354.   28 U.S.C. § 1738A(c)(2)(B). "Home state" is defined in 1738A(b)(4) as "the State in which, immediately preceding the time involved, the child lived with his parents, a parent, or a person acting as parent for at least six consecutive months, and in the case of a child less than six months old, the State in which the child lived from birth with any of such persons."

355.   See supra note 342 and accompanying text.

356.   28 U.S.C. § 1738A(d), (f)(2). Although irrelevant under the PKPA for modification jurisdiction, California, in the best of custody-jurisdiction worlds, would have had exclusive

district court in which the father sued to enforce the California decree could have made these determinations in summary fashion without any inquiry into the facts of the underlying domestic drama.

Moreover, the remedy of direct attack by appeal up through the Louisiana court system is time-consuming and therefore unsatisfactory when wrongful taking of custody is the issue. A system is on its ear that squanders the time and energies of federal courts to sit as supernumerary state judges in diversity cases, but cannot spare the federal resources for summary correction of state decisions that flout sister-state custody decrees.

---

jurisdiction to modify its own temporary decree because it was the child's "home state" within 6 months before commencement of the Louisiana proceeding. UCCJEA § 201(a)(1).

Chapter 6

TORTS

§ 6.1 Scope of Chapter: A Study of the Place-of-Wrong Rule and its Displacement

It is in the area of choice of law for torts that changes in judicial approaches to conflicts problems have come most swiftly and been most dramatic. Until these sweeping changes were initiated during the mid 1960's, the choice-of-law rule that United States courts most widely accepted and applied was the rule governing liability for tort by the "law of the place of wrong"[1] or, more precisely, the place of injury.[2] It is inconceivable that a single, rigid, territorially-oriented choice-of-law rule could serve adequately over the vast range of tort problems—intentional

---

1. Restatement, Conflict of Laws § 378 (1934).

2. When the defendant acts in one jurisdiction and the harm to the plaintiff occurs in another jurisdiction, courts have applied the law of the place of harm. Rhode Island Hospital Trust Nat'l Bk. v. Swartz, Bresenoff, Yavner & Jacobs, 455 F.2d 847 (4th Cir.1972) (accounting statements negligently prepared in one state but relied on in another); Patch v. Stanley Works, 448 F.2d 483 (2d Cir.1971) (product liability); Doody v. John Sexton & Co., 411 F.2d 1119 (1st Cir.1969) (fraudulent statements made in one state and relied on in another); Hunter v. Derby Foods, Inc., 110 F.2d 970 (2d Cir.1940) (unwholesome canned food); Maryland ex rel. Thompson v. Eis Automotive Corp., 145 F.Supp. 444 (D.Conn.1956) (negligently manufactured brake); Western Newspaper Union v. Woodward, 133 F.Supp. 17 (W.D.Mo.1955) (fraudulent misrepresentation); Jeffrey v. Whitworth College, 128 F.Supp. 219 (E.D.Wash.1955) (negligent failure to warn of danger); Electric Theater Co. v. Twentieth Century–Fox Film Corp., 113 F.Supp. 937 (W.D.Mo.1953) (conspiracy in restraint of trade); Alabama Great So. R.R. v. Carroll, 97 Ala. 126, 11 So. 803 (1892)—followed in Norris v. Taylor, 460 So.2d 151 (Ala.1984); Mann v. Policyholders' Nat'l Life Ins. Co., 78 N.D. 724, 51 N.W.2d 853 (1952) (negligent failure to act on policy application); El Paso & Northwestern Ry. v. McComas, 36 Tex.Civ.App. 170, 81 S.W. 760 (1904) (improperly loaded lumber); Dallas v. Whitney, 118 W.Va. 106, 188 S.E. 766 (1936) (blasting). See also Connecticut Valley Lumber Co. v. Maine Cent. R.R., 78 N.H. 553, 103 A. 263 (1918) (defendant damages bridge in two jurisdictions, damage within each jurisdiction governed by that jurisdiction's law). Cf. Sacra v. Sacra, 48 Md.App. 163, 426 A.2d 7 (1981) (when automobile was hit in Delaware and the impact caused it to strike a telephone pole in Maryland and explode, Delaware is the place of wrong); Cohen v. McDonnell Douglas Corp., 389 Mass. 327, 450 N.E.2d 581 (1983) (when plane crashed in Illinois and mother received news in Massachusetts, Massachusetts is the place of injury for determining whether the mother may recover for emotional distress); Kansas City Star Co. v. Gunn, 627 S.W.2d 332 (Mo.App.1982) (when newspaper with executive offices in Missouri cancelled its independent carrier system causing harm to plaintiff, whose route was in Kansas, the cause of action "arose" in Kansas for purposes of the limitations borrowing statute).

An apparent exception developed in cases involving harm to the incidents of marriage. Courts have applied the law of the place where the defendant acted, rather than the law of the marital domicile. Albert v. McGrath, 278 F.2d 16 (D.C.Cir.1960) (alienation of affections); Orr v. Sasseman, 239 F.2d 182 (5th Cir.1956) (alienation of affections); Gordon v. Parker, 83 F.Supp. 40 (D.Mass.), aff'd 178 F.2d 888 (1st Cir.1949) (alienation of affections). Cf. Darnell v. Rupplin, 91 N.C.App. 349, 371 S.E.2d 743 (1988) (in applying the place-of-injury rule to the tort of alienation of affections when liaisons took place in four states, it is a jury question in which state the alienation occurred); Peru Civil Code of 1984, Book X, Art. 2097 (if the actor is liable under the law of the place of injury but not under the law of the place where the act or omission occurred, apply the law of the place of injury if it was

torts, negligence, liability without fault, capacity to sue, measure of damages, distribution of damages, survival of actions, and more. The result of applying the place-of-wrong rule in so many different contexts has been irrational and worse, unjust, decisions. This chapter will focus on the operation of this place-of-wrong rule, on the changes in conflicts analysis that the inadequacy of that rule has engendered, and on the problems and difficulties that have arisen in attempts to displace the former rule.

First, as a background for what follows, sections 6.2 through 6.9 discuss choice-of-law theory. Sections 6.3 through 6.9 discuss what I refer to as a consequences-based approach to choice of law. This approach chooses law with knowledge of the content of the laws in each of the states that have contacts with the parties and the transaction. The choice seeks to minimize the consequences that any such state is likely to experience if its law is not applied. An approach to choice of law that focuses on consequences is consistent with the positions of almost all major American conflict-of-laws scholars, who differ primarily on whether or not it is feasible to attempt forum-neutral solutions when there is a true clash of state policies, and, if so, what form that forum-neutral solution should take. More important than what the commentators are up to as they deforest the land with their mountains of conflicts articles, is the results that the courts are reaching.

Periodically we are treated to a scholarly analysis of what the courts are doing, typically assigning decisions state-by-state to a conflicts pigeon hole—First Restatement, Second Restatement, interest analysis, or Leflar.[3] Not surprisingly, one survey finds that these seemingly disparate

---

foreseeable that the act or omission would cause injury there). For such holdings on the issue of loss of consortium, see cases cited § 6.11 note 67.

Occasionally, other courts departed from the standard rule, applying the law of the place where the defendant acted. Best Canvas Products & Supplies, Inc. v. Ploof Truck Lines, Inc., 713 F.2d 618 (11th Cir.1983) (Georgia law—when cannot tell where damage occurred, whether privity is necessary for product liability is determined by law of place of manufacture); Telecommunications, Engineering Sales & Service Co. v. Southern Telephone Supply Co., Inc., 518 F.2d 392 (6th Cir.1975) (interference with contract, law of place where employee contacted, not where employer doing business); Bender v. Hearst Corp., 263 F.2d 360 (2d Cir.1959) (wrongful interference with contract); Vrooman v. Beech Aircraft Corp., 183 F.2d 479 (10th Cir.1950) (court follows parties in regarding recovery as controlled by law of place where airplane negligently repaired); Data General Corp. v. Digital Computer Controls, Inc. 357 A.2d 105 (Del.Ch.1975) (where trade secret improperly used); Moore v. Pywell, 29 App.D.C. 312 (D.C.Cir.1907) (negligent filling of prescription); Kelley v. Kokua Sales & Supply, Ltd., 56 Hawaii 204, 532 P.2d 673 (1975) (law of place where relatives killed determines whether cause of action for injuries caused by shock when death reported in another state); Caldwell v. Gore, 175 La. 501, 143 So. 387 (1932) (erection of dam flooding plaintiff's land).

The Federal Tort Claims Act waives the sovereign immunity of the United States to tort claims "under circumstances where the United States, if a private person, would be liable to the claimant in accordance with the law of the place where the act or omission occurred." 28 U.S.C. § 1346(b). Richards v. United States, 369 U.S. 1, 12–13, 82 S.Ct. 585, 592–93, 7 L.Ed.2d 492, 500 (1962), interpreted this language to mean the whole law of that place, including its conflict-of-laws rules.

3. See, e.g., Borchers, *The Choice-of-Law Revolution: An Empirical Study*, 49 Wash. & Lee L. Rev. 357, 367 (1992) (comparing the "apparent preferences" of the conflicts

approaches produce results that are "statistically indistinguishable."[4] This is not surprising because the new approaches have a common consequences-based core—a fact recognized by courts in three states that abandoned the place-of-wrong rule in the 1990's.[5] Without this core, all the modern approaches would be mindless check lists of "things to consider" or banal recitations of territorial contacts.[6]

§ 6.2 The Choice between Territorial and Consequences–Based Rules

Reasonable persons disagree on whether courts should use territorial or consequences-based choice-of-law rules. A territorial rule is one that selects a state's law without regard to the law's content but based on some contact that state has with the parties or the transaction. An example is the rule of the first Restatement of Conflicts that selected the law of the place of injury for torts.[7] A consequences-based rule is one that chooses the law of a state with knowledge of the content of that law and to advance the policies underlying that law. An example is the rule of the Second Restatement of Conflicts choosing the law that validates when a borrower raises the usury defense.[8]

---

approaches of the first Restatement, Second Restatement, interest analysis, and Leflar); Gregory E. Smith, Choice of Law in the United States, 38 HASTINGS L. J. 1041, 1043–49 (1987) (describing the major choice-of-law systems in the United States, which he labels "First Restatement," "Second Restatement," "Center of Gravity Test," "Interest Analysis," and "Leflar"). The reference to "Leflar" is to Professor Robert Leflar, who analyzed the writing of other conflicts scholars and distilled a list of five "choice-influencing considerations." Robert A. Leflar et al., American Conflicts Law 277 (4th ed. 1986), discussed supra § 1.5, notes 62–65 and accompanying text.

4. Borchers, supra note 3, at 378. But see George, *False Conflicts and Faulty Analyses: Judicial Misuse of Governmental Interest in the Second Restatement of Conflict of Laws*, 23 Rev. Litig. 489, 585 (2004) (the Second Restatement and interest analysis will sometimes produce different results); But see Thiel, *Choice of Law and the Home–Court Advantage: Evidence*, 2 Am. L. & Econ. Rev. 291 (2000) (after correcting Borcher's data "to account for the volume of cases and the natural differences of legal culture" (id. 314), finds "Leflar [better law] is relatively strongest in its generosity to plaintiffs and its preference for forum law, and interest analysis is relatively stronger in favoring local parties").

5. See Travelers Indem. Co. v. Lake, 594 A.2d 38, 47 (Del. 1991) (stating that the Second Restatement approach, which it adopts, includes the substance of the other approaches, including interest analysis); Chambers v. Dakotah Charter, Inc., 488 N.W.2d 63, 66 (S.D. 1992) (stating that "all but one of the modern considerations used in government interest and choice-influencing approaches are explicitly recognized in the Restatement (Second), and the omitted consideration, (the better law factor), can be considered under § 6 of the Restatement (Second)"); Hataway v. McKinley, 830 S.W.2d 53, 58 (Tenn. 1992) (stating that the Second Restatement "approach primarily advocates a governmental interest analysis"). But see Glowski v. Allstate Ins. Co., 134 N.H. 196, 589 A.2d 593, 595 (1991) (stating that Leflar's choice-influencing considerations are fine for torts, but adopting the Second Restatement for contract choice-of-law analysis because more certainty is needed).

6. See Hataway, supra note 5, 830 S.W.2d at 58 (stating that "many courts have merely counted contacts rather than engaging in an analysis of the interests and policies listed in the Restatement").

7. RESTATEMENT OF CONFLICT OF LAWS §§ 377, 378 (1934).

8. Restatement (Second) of Conflict of Laws § 203 (1971) [hereinafter Restatement, Second].

My preference is for a consequences-based rule because I do not want a court deciding any issue, even a choice-of-law issue, without regard to the social consequences that are likely to follow from that decision. Some courts and commentators prefer a territorial rule for its certainty and ease of application. The worst choice is for a court to adopt a territorial rule, depart from it in random and unpredictable ways in order to avoid the consequences of applying the law that the rule selects, and not explain the departure in the light of those consequences. A court that does this forfeits the certainty of the territorial rule for "reasons" that defy understanding.

An example is *Grant v. McAuliffe*,[9] which applied forum law to the issue of whether a tort action survived the death of the tortfeasor. Unfortunately the reason stated for applying the law of the forum was not that the forum, as the common domicile of victim and tortfeasor, would alone experience the social consequences of permitting the action to survive. The court said that forum law applied because the issue is procedural.[10]

It may be possible to state territorial rules that minimize the risk of producing results that a consequences-based analysis would reject. If for example, Professor Beale, the Reporter for the first Restatement of Conflicts, had stated his tort rule as "apply the law of the place of injury unless tortfeasor and victim have the same domicile, in which case apply the law of their domicile," there probably would not have been a conflicts revolution. The results produced by this rule would occasionally offend interest-analysis purists, but the rule would eliminate the wrongly-decided "false conflict"[11] cases that sparked the revolt.

§ 6.3   Know the Content of Law before Choosing It

No matter what approach to choice of law a court chooses, the following is sound advice. Do not engage in a choice-of-law analysis until you know the content of the law that one of the parties contends should displace forum law. Do not engage in a choice-of-law analysis if all putatively applicable laws produce the same result.[12] There are two ways

---

9. 41 Cal.2d 859, 264 P.2d 944 (1953).

10. Id. at 946–49.

11. In a "false conflict" case, only one state's policies are affected by the choice of law. An example is Grant v. McAuliffe, discussed supra notes 9–10 and accompanying text, in which the choice only affected California survival policies.

For classic discussions of the concept of the "false" conflict, see B. Currie, *Notes on Methods and Objectives in the Conflict of Laws*, 1959 Duke L. J. 171, 174; Traynor, *Is This Conflict Really Necessary?*, 37 Texas L. Rev. 657, 667–74 (1959). The concept of determining the territorial scope of a rule by reference to its purposes traces back at least to Guy de Coquille, a sixteenth century scholar. See Juenger, *A Page of History*, 35 Mercer L. Rev. 419, 432–33 (1984).

12. See, e.g., Wall v. CSX Transportation, Inc., 471 F.3d 410, 422 (2d Cir. 2006) ("As there is no conflict [between New York and Pennsylvania law], New York, as the forum state, would apply its law"); Interstate Cleaning Corp. v. Commercial Underwriters Ins. Co., 325 F.3d 1024, 1028 (8th Cir. 2003) (because forum and other contact state apply the same legal standards "we need not engage in a conflict of laws analysis" and apply forum law). But cf. Dugan v. Mobile Medical Testing Services, Inc., 265 Conn. 791, 830 A.2d 752

to state the result in such cases. I prefer a statement that you will apply forum law because there is no reason to displace it. An alternative is to say, for example, "it does not make any difference whose law applies, defendant is not liable to plaintiff" or "is not liable unless . . . and I shall instruct the jury accordingly."

These rules are essential if a court is purporting to follow a consequences-based approach. They also are labor-saving suggestions for a court applying territorial rules. There is nothing sillier than a court applying territorial rules to choose between the laws of two states and reaching a result those accords with the law of neither state. An example is *Nelson v. Eckert*[13] in which, by a blend of territorial choice of law and procedural characterization, the court managed to avoid the statutes of limitations for wrongful death of both the forum and of the place where the fatal injuries occurred.

§ 6.4   Requirements for a Consequences–Based Approach

There are four main requirements for a consequences-based approach. First, the court must determine whether one or more states that have a contact with the parties or with the transaction have conflicting laws. Second, if there are conflicting laws, the court must determine the policies underlying those laws. Third, the court must decide whether if a state's law is not applied, that state is likely to experience a consequence that it is its policy to avoid. Fourth, application of the law of a state that will experience consequences must be fair to the parties in the light of their contacts with that state. Now to explain these points.

§ 6.5   Determine Policies Underlying Conflicting Laws

The court should determine the policies underlying the conflicting laws of the states that have contacts with the parties and the transaction. The process of identifying these policies may not be easy, but it is the same process that is undertaken for sensible answers to legal questions outside the conflicts arena. In purely domestic applications there is frequently doubt as to whether a rule applies. For example, should we enforce a contractual promise on the ground that there is sufficient consideration for the promise, or should we deny enforcement on the ground that there is no consideration? The requirement of consideration is an example of a "rule" that is incapable of rational application unless we first answer the questions, "why do we enforce promises with the power of the state and will any of those purposes be served if we enforce this promise?"[14] The major step in a consequences-

---

(2003) (instead of deciding for first time at appellate level whether Connecticut law is the same as New York law, engages in Restatement Second analysis to choose New York law). Contra, Minnesota Mining and Manufacturing Co. v. Nishika Ltd., 953 S.W.2d 733 (Tex. 1997) (after certifying question to Minnesota Supreme Court and receiving response that there is no difference in law, engages in Restatement Second analysis to explain why Minnesota law applies).

13.   231 Ark. 348, 329 S.W.2d 426 (1959), discussed in § 3.2C2.

14.   See Patrick S. Atiyah, Consideration in Contracts: A Fundamental Restatement 7, 48 (1971) (stating that contracts are enforced only for sufficient reasons and "consider-

based conflicts analysis is, therefore, the same process that is the heart of first-year instruction in law school and in which lawyers and judges are continually engaged when applying the laws of their own state.[15] Sources of information on the policies underlying a tort rule include legislative history, if a statute is involved; cases articulating those policies in order to decide whether a particular application of a rule, even in a wholly domestic case, is consistent with the rule's purposes and therefore proper; and the writings of authorities discussing the rule.

§ 6.6 Minimize Consequences that Violate a State's Policies

Ideally, the court should choose the law that will advance the policies of the chosen state and not cause consequences in any other state that that state's laws are intended to avoid. If this is not possible, the court should explain the result in terms of consequences. Why has the court decided to avoid consequences in the chosen state and impose consequences on other states? Reasonable persons may disagree with the court, but at least the opinion will deal directly with the issues that are at the core of sensible choice of law.

Focusing on consequences is necessary if interest analysis is to have any cogent territorial implications. Without these territorial implications, there are no "false conflicts"[16] and we are left with two choices. We can go back to sticking a pin in the map without regard to whether the chosen state will experience the consequences, but this time no cheating.[17] Or we can resolve all conflicts in terms of the effect on the policies of the states that have contacts with the parties and the transaction.

Moreover, it is only in terms of consequences that one can rebut Professor Beal's argument for selecting the law of the place where a cause of action arose, rather than the law of the parties' domicile:

> [E]very law has both a territorial and a personal application: and where a conflict arises, it is because one sovereign wishes to apply his own law to a juridical relation on his territory, while another seeks to throw around his own subject, who is one of the parties to the relation, the protection of his personal law. Which of the two

---

ation" is a "set of guides" to those reasons); Weintraub, *A Survey of Contract Practice and Policy*, 1992 Wɪs. L. Rᴇᴠ. 1, 10 (1992) (stating that "we cannot know what promises to enforce or how to enforce them until we know why we enforce them").

15. See Kramer, *More Notes on Methods and Objectives in the Conflict of Laws*, 24 Cornell Int'l L. J. 245, 277 (1991) (stating that "[t]o decide whether forum law may apply, the court should determine what policy or policies led to its adoption in wholly domestic cases").

16. See Singer, *Real Conflicts*, 69 B.U. L. Rᴇᴠ. 1, 91 (1989) (stating that "[f]alse conflicts analysis rests, to a large extent, on an impoverished conception of state interests [that] wrongly excludes policies based on such fundamental norms as morality, liberty, and nondiscrimination").

17. Courts have evaded the apparently clear mandate of the place-of-wrong rule for torts conflicts by recharacterizing the substantive nature of the problem (e.g. "contract" or "family law"), treating the issue as "procedural" to be resolved by the law of the forum, or rejecting the law of the place of wrong on "public policy" grounds. See infra §§ 6.16–6.17.

independent sovereigns should yield is a question not susceptible of a solution upon which all parties would agree.[18]

The rebuttal is that the sovereign where the "juridical relation" arose is behaving officiously if it wishes to apply its law when only some other state will have to live with the result.

Whether focusing on the policies underlying the conflicting laws is a useful approach to conflicts cases depends on the answers to the following questions. How many typical conflicts cases fall clearly within the "false conflict" end of the spectrum so that this method of analysis quickly and easily disposes of them? For the cases in the rest of the spectrum, cases that present either true or arguably true conflicts, does focusing on the underlying domestic policies at stake assist materially in the rational resolution of those conflicts? Can not only conflicts professors but also courts and lawyers utilize "state interest" analysis? Are the results that this method produces rational, just, and sufficiently predictable to avoid the specter of *ad hoc* adjudications?

Inquirers will have to decide the answers for themselves. Because most states of the United States and a growing list of foreign countries have already adopted this method of analysis,[19] even the most stalwart proponent of territorial choice-of-law rules will wish to understand "interest analysis" and the opinions that have sought to apply it. This chapter seeks to serve that need.

§ 6.7 Avoid Unfair Surprise

One of the strongest factors weighing against resolution of a conflict in favor of liability would be unfair surprise to the defendant. There are two levels of argument available here. On one level, surprise to the defendant should be an element to be considered and perhaps, if sufficiently strong, be controlling in the resolution of a conflict between a rule that would confer liability and one that would deny liability.[20] On the second level, there would be surprise to the defendant so extreme and so outrageous, if liability were found, that there would be a violation of the due process clause of the Fourteenth Amendment of the United States Constitution.[21]

On the first level, surprise as an element to be weighed in resolving a true conflict, there are several points that should be kept in mind. If as in most tort conflicts cases, recovery is sought for negligence, it is very unlikely that a surprise argument will be cogent.[22] Defendants are

---

18. Joseph H. Beale, A Treatise on the Conflict of Laws 1929 (1935).

19. See § 6.18.

20. See Standal v. Armstrong Cork Co., 356 N.W.2d 380 (Minn.App.1984) (to further predictability, product liability of successor corporation is determined by the law of the place where the acquired company was operating); Levin v. Desert Palace Inc., 318 Pa.Super. 606, 465 A.2d 1019 (1983) (to protect defendant's reliance, innkeeper liability for stolen property is determined by law of state where hotel is operating).

21. For discussion of outrageous surprise as a violation of due process when choosing law, see § 9.2A.

22. See J.H.C. Morris, *The Proper Law of a Tort*, 64 Harv. L. Rev. 881, 895 (1951); cf. Fussner v. Andert, 261 Minn. 347, 113 N.W.2d 355 (1961) (refusal to make decision

unlikely to shape their conduct to take account of rules of liability for negligence or of measure of damages.[23] Any realistic discussion of surprise must take account of liability insurance. Insurance may either increase or decrease the element of unfair surprise. Although a negligent defendant cannot reasonably argue that they would have been more careful if they had known of the eventual resolution of a conflict in favor of liability, they may argue that they failed to insure,[24] or failed to take insurance in a greater amount.[25] If so, then the court should certainly consider this. It is more likely that insurance will weaken any argument based on surprise to the nominal defendant. If the defendant is insured, the one who will pay is the liability insurer. It would be more in accord with the facts to speak in terms of surprise to the insurance company.[26] If this is done, then the surprise argument may all but disappear. Insurance actuaries do not base rates upon individual cases, but upon great numbers of cases.[27] That a bizarre event will occur in a given case is unlikely, but that it will not occur in a hundred thousand cases is equally unlikely. Moreover, in setting insurance rates, the "incurred losses" that are used in the computation include not only paid losses but also "loss reserves". The amount of the loss reserve for a particular accident is the amount of probable eventual payment as estimated by the insurer's claim department during the "accident year" in which injury occurs and before payment. This loss reserve is then reviewed and adjusted from time to time in the light of subsequent events until final payment of the claim.[28] The premium set plus investment income is

changing rule of damages for wrongful death of child prospective, defendant's conduct not having been controlled by existing law).

23. Cf. Little, *A Theory and Empirical Study of What Deters Drinking Drivers, If, When and Why*, 23 Admin. L. Rev. 23, 50 (1970) (stating that arrest and loss of license is rated by drivers as far more undesirable than "[a]n accident with minor personal injury").

24. This is the basis upon which courts have made prospective instead of traditional retroactive decisions ending long-standing immunity from liability of charities and governments. See Molitor v. Kaneland Community Unit Dist. No. 302, 18 Ill.2d 11, 163 N.E.2d 89 (1959), cert. denied 362 U.S. 968, 80 S.Ct. 955, 4 L.Ed.2d 900 (1960) (immunity of school district); Williams v. Detroit, 364 Mich. 231, 111 N.W.2d 1 (1961) (immunity of municipal corporation); Parker v. Port Huron Hosp., 361 Mich. 1, 105 N.W.2d 1 (1960); Kojis v. Doctors Hosp., 12 Wis.2d 367, 107 N.W.2d 292 (1961).

25. See the discussion of Victor v. Sperry, 163 Cal.App.2d 518, 329 P.2d 728 (1958), § 6.11, text accompanying notes 77–78. See also Wendelken v. Superior Court, 137 Ariz. 455, 671 P.2d 896 (En banc 1983) (duty to a guest owed by person with possessory interest in realty is measured by standard of common domicile, not situs, defendant being fully insured under domiciliary standards).

26. For conflicts cases in which courts talk of surprise to the insurance company, see, e.g., DeFoor v. Lematta, 249 Or. 116, 121, 437 P.2d 107, 109 (1968); Miller v. Miller, 22 N.Y.2d 12, 21, 290 N.Y.S.2d 734, 741, 237 N.E.2d 877, 882 (1968); Babcock v. Jackson, 12 N.Y.2d 473, 484, 240 N.Y.S.2d 743, 751, 191 N.E.2d 279, 285 (1963).

27. See C.R. Morris, *Enterprise Liability and the Actuarial Process—The Insignificance of Foresight*, 70 Yale L. J. 554, 560–76 (1961). But see Ehrenzweig, *Parental Immunity in the Conflict of Laws: Law and Reason Versus the Restatement*, 23 U. Chi. L. Rev. 474, 477–78 (1956).

28. See McNamara, *Automobile Liability Insurance Rates*, 35 Ins.Counsel J. 398, 401 (1968); Stern, *Ratemaking Procedures for Automobile Liability Insurance*, 52 Proceedings Casualty Actuarial Soc'y 139, 144–45 (1965).

designed to produce an underwriting profit[29] after taking into account all costs, including loss reserves and a "trend factor"[30] that anticipates continuing inflation in settlement costs. In short, to talk of "surprising" the insurer is very likely to be talking nonsense.

§ 6.8   The Foreign Choice-of-Law Rule

At times reference to a choice-of-law rule of one of the contact states may resolve an apparent conflict.[31] Suppose, for example, that a husband and wife, domiciled in X, are present in Y when the husband negligently injures the wife. Under X domestic law, a wife may sue her husband for negligence. Y, a community property state, does not permit such a suit. Is there a real conflict? Does it make any difference where the action is brought? Without more, it is difficult to answer these questions. Y certainly has no interest in preserving the marital harmony of X spouses, if this is the reason for its rule. But if Y's purpose is to prevent collusive suits, Y might legitimately apply its own rule to a suit brought in Y, at least for the purpose of closing the Y forum. The conflict dissolves, however, once we know that the reason for Y's domestic interdicting of wife-husband suits is that the action belongs to the community, and Y will not permit the husband to profit from his own wrong; that Y courts do not consider a wife's cause of action to be community property if it arises in Y between spouses domiciled in noncommunity property states;[32] that Y, rather than fearing collusion, permits such spouses to sue one another in Y courts.

Using another state's choice-of-law rule as a guide to whether that state is "interested" in applying its domestic law to an interstate

---

29. See McNamara, supra note 28 at 401; Stern, supra note 28 at 165.

30. See McNamara, supra note 28 at 403; Stern, supra note 28 at 172–73.

31. See Miller v. White, 167 Vt. 45, 51, 702 A.2d 392, 396 (1997) (applying Vermont law to suit between Vermont residents arising from accident in Quebec and stating that Quebec's common-domicile choice-of-law rules "suggest its weak interest in this type of action"); Hancock, Torts in the Conflict of Laws 179–81 (1942); Hancock, *Three approaches to the Choice-of-Law Problem: The Classificatory, the Functional and the Result–Selective,* in XXth Century Comparative and Conflicts Law 365, 372 n.1 (1961); Katzenbach, *Conflicts on an Unruly Horse: Reciprocal Claims and Tolerances in Interstate and International Law,* 65 Yale L. J. 1087, 1118 (1956). But see the following cases rejecting a reference to another state's choice-of-law rule: Haumschild v. Continental Cas. Co., 7 Wis.2d 130, 95 N.W.2d 814 (1959); Folk v. York–Shipley, Inc., 239 A.2d 236 (Del.1968).

32. Bruton v. Villoria, 138 Cal.App.2d 642, 292 P.2d 638 (1956); cf. Reeves v. Schulmeier, 303 F.2d 802 (5th Cir.1962) (law of marital domicile determines whether husband must be joined in wife's suit); Choate v. Ransom, 74 Nev. 100, 323 P.2d 700 (1958) (law of marital domicile bars wife's action by imputing her husband's negligence to her). But cf. Texas & Pac. Ry. v. Humble, 181 U.S. 57, 21 S.Ct. 526, 45 L.Ed. 747 (1901) (law of place of impact and former marital domicile applied to determine whether wife, injured while leaving to join husband at new marital domicile, must join husband in her suit); Roberson v. U–Bar Ranch, Inc., 303 F.Supp. 730 (D.N.M.1968) (law of place of wrong applied to determine whether husband must join with wife as plaintiff); Redfern v. Collins, 113 F.Supp. 892 (E.D.Tex.1953) (same); Traglio v. Harris, 104 F.2d 439 (9th Cir.1939), petition for cert. dism'd, 308 U.S. 629, 60 S.Ct. 125, 84 L.Ed. 524 (1939) (law of place of impact rather than marital domicile determines whether husband has community interest in wife's cause); Astor Elect. Serv., Inc. v. Cabrera, 62 So.2d 759 (Fla.1952) (same); Maag v. Voykovich, 46 Wn.2d 302, 280 P.2d 680 (1955) (law of place of commission determines whether husband's wrong is a community obligation).

problem may be misleading if that choice-of-law rule is a rigid, territorial rule, such as place of wrong, and is not keyed to the policies underlying that state's tort rules.[33]

§ 6.9   Choice-of-Law Rules

What is said in §§ 6.2 through 6.8 does not mean that every choice-of-law decision must follow anew all the steps necessary for a consequences-based analysis. After a series of decisions dealing with similar conflicts issues, courts and commentators can summarize the results as a rule. A court can then apply that rule to future cases. A statute can enact the rule. The Louisiana Conflict of Laws Code,[34] which took effect on January 1, 1992, is an attempt to codify a consequences-based approach to choice of law. A common-law or statutory choice-of-law rule will work satisfactorily if it is based upon cases that have properly conducted a consequences-based approach and if the rule leaves some flexibility to deal with unforeseen circumstances.

A consequences-based approach will not provide an answer to the choice-of-law problem for cases in which more than one state's policies are affected. The approach may not provide an answer in the so-called "no-interest" case. The classic example of the no-interest case in torts occurs when the law of defendant's state favors the plaintiff the law of plaintiff's state favors the defendant. Section 6.25 discusses no-interest cases.

In true conflict and no-interest cases courts need default rules. These default rules might take many forms: a territorial rule, such as place of injury, that is not consequences-based;[35] a substantive preference, such as the law that favors the plaintiff,[36] or the law that favors the defendant; a "better law" approach rejecting an anachronistic or aberrational rule in favor of a rule that is more in the mainstream of state law;[37] a rule of comparative impairment;[38] a territorial rule that is

---

33. See Pfau v. Trent Aluminum Co., 55 N.J. 511, 526, 263 A.2d 129, 137 (1970); § 3.3.

34. La. Civ. Code Ann. arts. 14, 3515–3549.

35. See Reavley & Wesevich, *An Old Rule for New Reasons: Place of Injury as a Federal Solution to Choice of Law in Single–Accident Mass–Tort Cases*, 71 Tex. L. Rev. 1, 43 (1992) (advocating "a strict place-of-injury rule for single-accident mass-tort cases because it fosters uniformity, neutrality, determinacy, and efficiency in the resolution of these disputes").

36. See Bird, *Mass Tort Litigation: A Statutory Solution to the Choice of Law Impasse*, 96 Yale L. J. 1077, 1079 (1987) (stating that "within certain limits, the proposed statute [for resolving mass tort conflicts problems] requires that a court select the most favorable substantive law available to plaintiffs"); Reese, *Substantive Policies and Choice of Law*, 2 Touro L. Rev. 1, 8, 11–12 (1986) (proposing application of the law that provides a larger recovery).

37. See Cheatham & Reese, *Choice of the Applicable Law*, 52 Colum. L. Rev. 959, 980 (1952); Kramer, *Rethinking Choice of Law*, 90 Colum. L. Rev. 277, 334 (1990) (preferring the law that is not "obsolete"); Singer, *Real Conflicts*, 69 B.U. L. Rev. 1, 6 (1989) (stating "that multistate cases should ordinarily be resolved by application of what the forum considers to be the better law"). But see Laycock, *Equal Citizens of Equal and Territorial States: The Constitutional Foundations of Choice of Law*, 92 Colum. L. Rev. 249, 312 (1992) (stating that a court cannot constitutionally choose law on such better-law grounds); Sedler, *Moffatt Hancock and the Conflict of Laws: An American–Canadian Perspective*, 37

consequences-based because the rule selects a state that is likely to experience the results if its law is not applied, such as an interested forum,[39] or the plaintiff's residence, or the defendant's residence.

At one time I advocated a substantive preference for tort conflicts— the law favorable to the plaintiff.[40] This was really an attempt at "better law" analysis. I still favor a better law approach to default rules, but only when clearly discernible developments in the relevant substantive area permit objective identification of the "better" law. I do not think that the conflicts specialist has any business second guessing changes in other areas of the law of which she or he might disapprove. At the beginning of the "conflicts revolution," the most common conflicts in interstate cases occurred because the law of one state permitted recovery and the law of the other was a rule that was fast disappearing from the American scene, such as a guest statute,[41] or marital immunity,[42] or a statutory limit on wrongful death recovery.[43] Times have changed. Those

U. Toronto L. J. 62, 84 (1987) (stating that "in practice the 'better law' analysis has invariably meant preference for the forum's 'better law' "). For an example that would support critics of better-law analysis, see Wille v. Farm Bureau Mut. Ins. Co., 432 N.W.2d 784 (Minn. Ct. App. 1988) (preferring forum law on the stacking of uninsured motorist coverage even though forum law has been changed after the accident to accord with the law of the other state).

An argument for "better law" resolution of true conflicts is that this is the approach that states might agree upon if they had the opportunity to do so before a specific true conflict arose. Cf. J. Rawls, A theory of Justice 251–57 (1971) (discussing the concept of the "original position" under which principles of justice are selected without knowledge as to how they would affect the selector). Cf. also L. Brilmayer, Conflict of Laws: Foundations and Future Directions 171–72 (1991) (applying game theory to resolution of conflicts problems); Kramer, supra this note, at 280 (suggesting the use of "game theory" for choice of law).

For further discussion of the better law concept, see §§ 6.9, note 37 and accompanying text, 6.29.

38. Under a comparative impairment approach, if both state's policies will be impaired to some degree if their law is not applied, but one state's law will be more impaired, apply the law of that state. Sections 6.26–6.27 discuss comparative impairment.

39. See Lilienthal v. Kaufman, 239 Or. 1, 395 P.2d 543, 549 (1964) (stating that when both the forum and another state have "a substantial interest, which will be served or thwarted, depending upon which law is applied [the] public policy of [the forum] should prevail"); Hay et al., Cases and Materials on Conflict of Laws 507 (12th ed. 2004) (statement prepared by Professor Brainerd Currie to summarize his approach to choice of law); Sedler, *Interest Analysis and Forum Preference in the Conflict of Laws: A Response to the "New Critics"*, 34 Mercer L. Rev. 593, 637–38 (1983) (stating that the law of the forum should be applied to resolve true conflicts); Weinberg, *Against Comity*, 80 Geo. L. J. 53, 71 (1991) (advocating applying forum law as likely to favor the plaintiff and discourage "predatory or injurious conduct"). But see Laycock, supra note 37, at 310 (stating that "any preference for forum law violated the Full Faith and Credit Clause").

40. See Weintraub, *The Future of Choice of Law for Torts: What Principles Should be Preferred?*, 41 Law & Contemp. Probs. 146 (1977). For a sample of the "law and economics" approach to choice of law that cites much of the other literature in the area, see Guzman, *Choice of Law: New Foundations*, 90 Georgetown L. J. 883 (2002), which, at 905, rejects a rule selecting law favorable to the plaintiff because "such an approach would systematically favor liability-producing laws, leading to overregulation."

41. See Beaulieu v. Beaulieu, 265 A.2d 610 (Me.1970).

42. See Schneider v. Schneider, 110 N.H. 70, 260 A.2d 97 (1969).

43. See Griffith v. United Air Lines, Inc., 416 Pa. 1, 203 A.2d 796 (1964).

holdovers from the nineteenth century have all but disappeared[44] and now, certainly for matters of enterprise liability, the pendulum has swung in the opposite direction. Many states have enacted "tort reform" legislation[45] to rein in what has been perceived as doctrines that unduly favor plaintiffs. Nevertheless, in the area of products liability, when the manufacturer's law favors the injured user, courts are likely to apply that law.[46]

§ 6.10 The Second Restatement's Rule

The Second Restatement of Conflict of Laws both reflects and has helped to shape the revolution in choice-of-law analysis. The Restatement rule for torts is:

§ 145. The General Principle.

(1) The rights and liabilities of the parties with respect to an issue in tort are determined by the local law of the state which, with respect to that issue, has the most significant relationship to the occurrence and the parties under the principles stated in § 6.[47]

(2) Contacts to be taken into account in applying the principles of § 6 to determine the law applicable to an issue include:

(a) the place where the injury occurred,

(b) the place where the conduct causing the injury occurred,

(c) the domicil, residence, nationality, place of incorporation and place of business of the parties, and

(d) the place where the relationship, if any, between the parties is centered.

---

44. See infra § 6.11, note 60 and accompanying text.

45. See Kozyris, *Values and Methods in Choice of Law for Products Liability: A Comparative Comment on Statutory Solutions*, 38 Am. J. Comp. L. 475, 476 (1991) (stating that as of February, 1990, at least twenty-one states had enacted special products liability statutes); cf. Gottesman, *Draining the Dismal Swamp: The Case for Federal Choice of Law Statutes*, 80 Geo. L. J. 1, 15 (1991) (stating that today "it is as likely that it is the pro-victim rule that is out of step").

46. See infra § 6.31.

47. Restatement, Second § 6:

"Choice of Law Principles

"(1) A court, subject to constitutional restrictions, will follow a statutory directive of its own state on choice of law.

"(2) When there is no such directive, the factors relevant to the choice of the applicable law include

"(a) the needs of the interstate and international systems,

"(b) the relevant policies of the forum,

"(c) the relevant policies of other interested states and the relative interests of those states in the determination of the particular issue,

"(d) the protection of justified expectations,

"(e) the basic policies underlying the particular field of law,

"(f) certainty, predictability and uniformity of result, and

"(g) ease in the determination and application of the law to be applied."

These contacts are to be evaluated according to their relative importance with respect to the particular issue.[48]

This rule, particularly its last sentence, appears to envision a method of conflicts analysis that focuses on the policies underlying putatively conflicting tort rules. But the list of "contacts to be taken into account" is antithetical to such an analysis. Whether or not a particular contact with a state is significant for conflicts purposes cannot be known until one first knows exactly what domestic tort rules are in conflict and what the policies underlying those rules are. Only then can one intelligently "evaluate" rather than mechanically count the contacts. A dozen contacts with an occurrence may fail to give a state any interest in having its rule applied to determine the consequences of that occurrence. One contact may make the policies underlying a state's rule directly and rationally applicable to the case being decided. Once two or more states have contacts that give those states interests in having different rules applied to determine controversies flowing from an occurrence, there is a real conflict that should be resolved rationally and not by counting contacts.[49] The Restatement formulation, although probably consistent with a consequences-based analysis, has misled courts and lawyers on this most basic element of that analysis. Moreover, to say, as does the Restatement in the very next section, that, when the actor's conduct and the injury occur in the same state "the local law of this state will usually be applied to determine most issues involving the tort"[50] is contrary to a consequences-based analysis.[51] A court should invariably apply the law of

---

48. Restatement, Second § 145.

49. See Katzenbach, supra note 31, at 1127. Cf. Offshore Rental Co. v. Continental Oil Co., 22 Cal.3d 157, 148 Cal.Rptr. 867, 583 P.2d 721 (1978) (California uses "governmental interest analysis" rather than "most significant contact theory"). But cf. Allen v. Gannaway, 294 Minn. 1, 199 N.W.2d 424 (1972) (describing its approach as "center of gravity of the contacts" and resolving the problem without adverting to the policies underlying the conflicting laws); Southwell v. Widing Transp., Inc., 101 Wn.2d 200, 676 P.2d 477 (1984) (remanded for further development of facts without indicating how those facts could affect policies of putatively applicable laws).

50. Restatement, Second § 146, comment *d*. That the law of the place of injury is presumptively applicable under a "most significant relationship" approach, see, e.g., Mason v. Southern New Eng. Conference Assoc. of Seventh–Day Adventists, 696 F.2d 135 (1st Cir.1982) (Maine rule); State Farm Mutual Auto. Ins. Co. v. Olsen, 406 So.2d 1109 (Fla.1981); Cohen v. McDonnell Douglas Corp., 389 Mass. 327, 450 N.E.2d 581 (1983) (even though defendant acted in state other than where plaintiff injured); Morgan v. Biro Mfg. Co., 15 Ohio St.3d 339, 474 N.E.2d 286 (1984); Finch and Smeltzly, *The Restatement Second and Conflict of Laws: Extending the Bishop Approach to Problems in Contract*, 16 Stetson L. Rev. 261, 268–69 (1987) (Florida courts have interpreted the Second Restatement tort rules to apply "the law of the state of injury unless that state has no interest whatsoever in the issue" but this is not consistent with Restatement methodology). For an indication from the Reporter for the Second Restatement of Conflict of Laws that territorial contacts should not be relied upon "without having made any effort to ascertain the policy underlying the" laws of the respective states, See Reese, *Conflict of Laws*, 38 Syracuse L. Rev. 195, 223 (1987).

51. See Proprietors Ins. Co. v. Valsecchi, 435 So.2d 290, 294 (Fla.App.3d Dist.1983), review denied, 449 So.2d 265 (Fla.1984) ("[c]ases applying a Restatement (Second) approach generally do not employ an 'interest analysis' "); Shapira, The Interest Approach to Choice of Law with Special Reference to Tort Problems 214 (1970) (the Second Restatement tort rules "attest to a schizophrenic attitude, that is, an endeavor to erect an essentially jurisdiction-selective structure while, at the same time, to pay lip service to the

the place where the defendant acts to determine whether the defendant's conduct is proper only when that "law" is intended to control conduct in the most direct manner, such as a speed limit or a rule determining the right of way.[52] The landmark cases departing from the place-of-wrong rule, disc are all cases in which the tortfeasor's conduct and the injury occurred in the same state,[53] but nevertheless the court discerned that it made no sense to apply the tort law of that state.

§ 6.11 The Place-of-Wrong Rule in Operation

The classic example of a false conflict is the one involving capacity of the wife to sue the husband in tort. The husband and wife are domiciled in State F, a state that permits the wife to sue the husband when his negligence causes her personal injuries. While a passenger in an automobile driven by the husband in State X, the husband's negligence causes the wife's injuries. Under X law, a wife may not sue her husband in tort. The wife brings suit against the husband in State F. There is no true conflict. F, as the wife's domicile, will advance at least some of the purposes underlying its rule permitting suit—compensation to the wife to prevent her from becoming a public charge and to ease her and the family's financial burden.[54] In the event that the wife has received medical treatment in F, recovery will also provide a pool for the compensation of medical creditors in F. What policies might underlie State X's incapacity rule? On the surface, X might be seeking to preserve marital harmony by preventing husband and wife from becoming adversaries in a public trial. This is a naive appraisal. Almost invariably the real defendant is the husband's liability insurer. Both husband and wife desire recovery in order to help meet the medical and other costs of the wife's injury.[55] But even assuming a marital harmony policy, X is not the forum and has no interest in providing protection for F marriages when F itself does not think protection necessary.[56] Paradoxically, a more

relevance of interests based on rule-supporting purposes"); Leflar, *The Torts Provisions of the Restatement (Second)*, 72 Colum. L. Rev. 267, 269 (1972) ("the *Second Restatement* is misleading to the extent that it may be read to imply that the locus of the wrong is where [the most significant relationship] will ordinarily be found"); cf. Hightower v. Kansas City Southern R.R., 70 P.3d 835 (Okla. 2003) (apply Restatement analysis but reject contention that place of injury and negligence are of overriding importance and apply instead law of forum, where all parties reside and where defendant's train is stationed).

52. See infra § 6.34. But cf. La. Civ. Code Ann. art. 3543 (dealing with issues of "conduct and safety"); Padula v. Lilarn Properties Corp., 84 N.Y.2d 519, 620 N.Y.S.2d 310, 644 N.E.2d 1001 (1994) (refusing to apply New York regulations for constructing a scaffold to an injury in Massachusetts because the New York rule is "conduct regulating" rather than "loss allocating").

53. See § 6.18. Cf. Reese, *American Trends in Private International Law: Academic and Judicial Manipulation of Choice of Law Rules in Tort Cases*, 33 Vand. L. Rev. 717, 763 (1980) (Reporter for Restatement, Second distinguishes between rules determining whether the conduct is tortious and rules providing a defense).

54. The burden is shifted from the family because the husband is only the nominal defendant. It is his liability insurer who will pay. This is discussed just below.

55. See Hancock, *The Rise and Fall of Buckeye v. Buckeye, 1931–1959; Marital Immunity for Tort in Conflict of Laws*, 29 U. Chi. L. Rev. 237, 244 n.36 (1962); Comment, 44 Yale L. J. 1233, 1239 (1935).

56. Hancock, supra note 55 at 244.

realistic policy supporting the X rule might be the prevention of a collusive suit, husband and wife combining to get as much from the insurer as possible. X may desire, in this manner, to keep down the premiums on liability insurance issued to X residents. But in this case the liability insurance covers an automobile principally garaged in F and, therefore, recovery will affect primarily the insurance rates of F residents.[57] Nor does X have even a forum's interest in controlling collusive litigation—something that F may prefer to do by rules concerning presumptions, burden of proof, and quantum of evidence required,[58] rather than by a complete interdicting of suit. Despite all this, the place-of-wrong rule repeatedly resulted in F's denying recovery to the wife.[59]

Guest statutes have all but disappeared from the American scene. As of September 1, 2009, only Alabama retained the statute in its traditional form.[60] Nevertheless, because so much conflicts writing and so many

---

57. The premiums for liability insurance in an amount that complies with each state's financial responsibility law reflect the number and cost of accidents involving cars principally garaged in that state and within a particular rating territory in the state. Loss data in excess of these basic rates is excluded in calculating rates for basic limits coverage. Rates for higher limits of coverage are generally the same in every state since they are determined from nationwide data. See McNamara, *Automobile Liability Insurance Rates*, 35 Insurance Counsel J. 398, 401, 403–06 (1968); Stern, *Ratemaking Procedures for Automobile Liability Insurance*, 52 Proceedings Casualty Actuarial Soc'y 139, 155, 176–77, 183 (1965).

58. See Ford, *Interspousal Liability for Automobile Accidents in the Conflict of Laws: Law and Reason Versus the Restatement*, 15 U.Pitt. L. Rev. 397, 400 (1954).

59. E.g., Dawson v. Dawson, 224 Ala. 13, 138 So. 414 (1931); Landers v. Landers, 153 Conn. 303, 216 A.2d 183 (1966), overruled by statute, Conn.Gen.Stat.Ann § 52–572d; Robinson v. Gaines, 331 S.W.2d 653 (Mo.1960) (but see Kennedy v. Dixon, 439 S.W.2d 173 (Mo.1969) (abandoning place-of-wrong rule in guest statute case)); Gray v. Gray, 87 N.H. 82, 174 A. 508 (1934), overruled, Thompson v. Thompson, 105 N.H. 86, 193 A.2d 439 (1963); Shaw v. Lee, 258 N.C. 609, 129 S.E.2d 288 (1963), overruled by statute, N.C.Gen. Stat. § 52–5.1; Oshiek v. Oshiek, 244 S.C. 249, 136 S.E.2d 303 (1964), overruled, Boone v. Boone, 345 S.C. 8, 546 S.E.2d 191 (2001) (refusing on the ground of public policy to apply the interspousal immunity rule of the place of wrong).

The marital domicile has more readily given effect to its own policies when the situation is reversed, the marital domicile forbidding suit, the place of accident permitting it. When refusing to apply the law of the place of impact, the marital domicile typically avoided a decision on the merits, simply refusing a forum. See Flogel v. Flogel, 257 Iowa 547, 133 N.W.2d 907 (1965); Kircher v. Kircher, 288 Mich. 669, 286 N.W. 120 (1939); Koplik v. C.P. Trucking Corp., 27 N.J. 1, 141 A.2d 34 (1958); Mertz v. Mertz, 271 N.Y. 466, 3 N.E.2d 597 (1936).

60. Ala.Code § 32–1–2. Moreover, the Alabama guest statute is narrowly construed. See Klaber v. Elliott, 533 So.2d 576, 579 (Ala. 1988) (the issue of whether the host's conduct was "willful or wanton" is for the jury if there is "a scintilla of evidence" of such conduct).

There are four states with statutes applying only to certain categories of guests or vehicles. Ill.—S.H.A. ch. 625 act 5 § 10–201 (hitchhikers); Ind. Code Ann. § 34–30–11–1 (West) (family members or hitchhikers); Neb. Stat. Ann. Laws § 3–129.01 (aircraft owners or operators not liable to spouses or relatives within second degree of consanguinity or affinity); § 25–21,237 (same for automobile owners or operators); Or.Rev.Stat. 30.115 (guests in aircraft and watercraft).

All Canadian provinces and territories, including the one figuring most prominently in American cases, Ontario, had repealed their statutes. Nova Scotia shifts the burden of proof concerning negligence from the owner or driver to the guest. N.S. Stat. ch. 293 § 248.

In 1970, 27 states by guest statutes and two additional states by common-law rule, prevented recovery for ordinary host negligence. Since then, 13 statutes have been declared unconstitutional under state constitutional provisions. In addition to the cases from

of the early cases departing from the place-of-injury rule[61] have focused on guest cases, it is worthwhile to illustrate this classic "false conflict." Host and guest are domiciled in State F and host's automobile is principally garaged there. State F permits a guest to recover from a host by showing that the host's ordinary negligence caused the guest's

---

California, Idaho, Kansas, Michigan, Nevada, New Mexico, North Dakota, and Ohio cited in Sidle v. Majors, 429 U.S. 945, 946 n.2, 97 S.Ct. 366, 367 n.2, 50 L.Ed.2d 316 n.2 (1976) (Brennan J. dissenting from denial of cert.), see Bierkamp v. Rogers, 293 N.W.2d 577 (Iowa 1980); Ramey v. Ramey, 273 S.C. 680, 258 S.E.2d 883 (1979); Whitworth v. Bynum, 699 S.W.2d 194 (Tex.1985); Malan v. Lewis, 693 P.2d 661 (Utah 1984); Nehring v. Russell, 582 P.2d 67 (Wyo.1978). Eleven statutes were repealed, two (Iowa and Kansas) after being declared unconstitutional. Ark.Acts 1983, No. 13 §§ 1, 2; 1975 Colo.Sess.Laws p. 1568, § 1; 64 Del.L. c. 59, § 1; 1972 Fla.L. ch. 72–1, § 1; 1984 Ia. (70 G.A.) ch. 1219, § 41; 1974 Kan.Sess.L. c. 32, § 1; 1975 Mont.L. c. 236, § 1; 1978 So.Dak.L. c. 240, § 1; 1970 Vt. Acts No. 194, § 1; Va.Code 1950, § 8.01–63 (changes "gross negligence" to "negligent"); 1974 Wash.L. 1st Ex.Sess. ch. 3 § 1. Georgia and Massachusetts were the two states that restricted recovery by common-law rule. See Bickford v. Nolen, 240 Ga. 255, 240 S.E.2d 24 (1977); Massaletti v. Fitzroy, 228 Mass. 487, 118 N.E. 168 (1917). Legislation in both states now allows the guest to recover for ordinary negligence. Ga. Code Ann. § 51–1–36; Mass.Gen.L.A. ch. 231, § 85L.

This dramatic change from 29 American states that barred guest passengers from recovery for ordinary negligence to 1 (and 4 more with specialized limitations) occurred during the growth of functional conflicts analysis. In at least one instance conflicts methodology that requires scrutiny of policies underlying putatively applicable law was probably the reason for repeal of a guest statute. Clark v. Clark, 107 N.H. 351, 222 A.2d 205 (1966), refused to apply the guest statute of the Vermont place of injury to bar suit between New Hampshire host and guest. In the course of his opinion, Chief Justice Kenison noted that such guest statutes "contradict the spirit of the times." Id. at 357, 222 A.2d at 210. These words "helped induce the legislature of the Green Mountain State to repeal the statute." Juenger, *Leflar's Contributions to American Law*, 34 Ark. L. Rev. 205 (1980). Perhaps the functional resolution of policy differences, which will include disfavoring anachronistic and aberrational rules (see § 6.29) will have the paradoxical effect of eliminating the very conflicts being resolved.

Other rules popular in choice-of-law discussions that are fast disappearing are marital immunity and monetary limits on wrongful death recovery. Only 2 states remain in which there is marital immunity for negligent injury. See Heino v. Harper, 306 Or. 347, 759 P.2d 253, 255 n.1 (1988) citing cases from three states and two state statutes. Since that decision, the Supreme Court of Delaware has overruled the Delaware case cited (Beattie v. Beattie, 630 A.2d 1096 (Del. 1993), overruling Alfree v. Alfree, 410 A.2d 161 (Del 1979)) and the Illinois statute cited has been repealed and replaced by Ill. Stat. Ann. ch. 750 § 65/1, which abolishes marital immunity. Raisen v. Raisen, 379 So.2d 352 (Fla. 1979), upheld marital immunity, but Waite v. Waite, 618 So.2d 1360 (Fla. 1993), abolished it. The two states in which there is marital immunity for negligence suits are Hawaii (Peters v. Peters, 63 Haw. 653, 634 P.2d 586 (1981)), and Louisiana (La. Rev. Stat. Ann. § 9:291).

In 1935 there were seventeen states with monetary limits on wrongful death recovery. See S. Speiser et al., Recovery for Wrongful Death and Injury § 7:2 (1992). As of January 1, 2006, there are no states with a general monetary limit on wrongful death damages. New Hampshire limits recovery if there are no close survivors. New Hampshire and two other states place a monetary limit on some aspects of recovery. See Kan.Gen.Stat. § 60–1903 (except for pecuniary losses sustained by an heir at law, damages may not exceed $250,000 and costs); Me.Rev.Stat.Ann.Tit. 18A § 2–804(b) (damages for loss of comfort, society, and companionship may not exceed $400,000); N.H.Rev.Stat.Ann. § 556:12 ($150,000 limit for loss of comfort, society, and companionship), § 556:13 ($50,000 limit on recovery if no surviving spouse, child, parent, or other dependent relative).

Another disappearing rule that triggered many choice-of-law opinions is the tort of alienation of affection. See Helsel v. Noellsch, 107 S.W.3d 231, 233 n.3 (Mo. 2003) (abolishing the tort and noting that although 48 states once recognized it, only seven still do).

61. See, e.g., Clark v. Clark, 107 N.H. 351, 222 A.2d 205 (1966); Babcock v. Jackson, 12 N.Y.2d 473, 240 N.Y.S.2d 743, 191 N.E.2d 279 (1963).

injuries. Host and guest depart together for a short trip into State X. While in State X, the host's negligent driving causes injury to his guest. State X has a guest statute preventing recovery unless the guest can show "gross" or "wanton" negligence on the part of the host. The guest brings suit against the host in State F. It would make no sense to apply X's guest statute. Two possible policies might underlie the X statute. One is the policy of preventing the guest from manifesting ingratitude toward the host.[62] Two, paradoxically and more realistically, is the prevention of a collusive suit, host aiding guest against the host's liability insurer.[63] Neither of these policies is rationally applicable to a suit in F between an F host and an F guest with the host's liability insurance covering an automobile principally garaged in F. Yet the place-of-wrong rule resulted in the application of the foreign guest statute in just such a situation.[64]

Sestito v. Knop[65] is another typical example of a false conflict resolved incorrectly by application of the place-of-wrong rule In *Sestito*, a husband whose marital domicile was in Michigan, was injured in an automobile collision in Wisconsin and rendered impotent. His wife brought an action in a federal court sitting in Wisconsin for loss of consortium. Defendants were the driver of the other automobile and his liability insurer. The other driver was domiciled in Illinois.[66] Wisconsin did not recognize such an action, but Michigan did. Applying Wisconsin law, as that of the place of wrong, the trial court dismissed the complaint and the dismissal was affirmed on appeal. The wife ingeniously argued that the wrong was an injury to the marital relation and that this occurred in Michigan, the marital domicile. The court rejected this argument, ruling that the place of the wrong was where the defendant injured the husband, this being the last event necessary to create liability.[67] The plaintiff did not urge, nor did the court note, that not only plaintiff's domicile, but also Illinois, the domicile of the other driver, permitted wives actions for loss of consortium.[68] If the defendant driver's

---

62. See 2 Harper & James § 16.15 (1956); Prosser, Torts 191 (3d ed. 1964).

63. Id.

64. E.g., Sharp v. Johnson, 248 Minn. 518, 80 N.W.2d 650 (1957), overruled, Kopp v. Rechtzigel, 273 Minn. 441, 141 N.W.2d 526 (1966); Blount v. Blount, 125 So.2d 66 (La.App.1960); Naphtali v. Lafazan, 8 A.D.2d 22, 186 N.Y.S.2d 1010 (1959), overruled, Babcock v. Jackson, 12 N.Y.2d 473, 240 N.Y.S.2d 743, 191 N.E.2d 279 (1963); cf., Brown v. Seltzer, 424 S.W.2d 671 (Tex.Civ.App.1968), writ ref'd n.r.e. (apply Texas guest statute in suit against New York host on behalf of deceased California guest).

65. 297 F.2d 33 (7th Cir.1961).

66. *Sestito*, Brief for Plaintiff–Appellant, appendix, p. 2.

67. Accord, Jordan v. States Marine Corp., 257 F.2d 232 (9th Cir.1958); McVickers v. Chesapeake & O. Ry., 194 F.Supp. 848 (E.D.Mich.1961); Folk v. York–Shipley, Inc., 239 A.2d 236 (Del.1968); cf., Casey v. Manson Constr. & Eng'r Co., 247 Or. 274, 428 P.2d 898 (1967) (applying law of place where husband injured, but after an interest analysis). See also cases reaching this result when the husband sues for loss of consortium: Harford Mut. Ins. Co. v. Bruchey, 248 Md. 669, 238 A.2d 115 (1968); Conway v. Ogier, 115 Ohio App. 251, 184 N.E.2d 681 (1961). But cf., Lister v. McAnulty, [1944] S.C.R. 317, [1944] 3 D.L.R. 673 (Can.S.Ct.) (law of marital domicile applied to prevent husband's recovery for loss of consortium, though law of place of accident would permit recovery).

68. Dini v. Naiditch, 20 Ill.2d 406, 170 N.E.2d 881 (1960).

home state would not have shielded him from liability, Wisconsin, as place of impact, had no interest in so doing. It is true that the defendant insurer was incorporated in Pennsylvania and licensed to do business in Wisconsin,[69] and that neither of these states permitted a wife to recover for loss of consortium.[70] But neither of these states could have a legitimate interest in insulating the insurer from liability on a policy covering an automobile principally garaged in Illinois with recovery affecting, primarily, Illinois insurance rates.

In *Alabama Great Southern Railroad v. Carroll*,[71] the employees of an Alabama corporation negligently inspected in Alabama a train owned by the corporation. As a result, a coupling parted after the train had crossed the state line into Mississippi injuring a railroad employee who was an Alabama citizen. Alabama had an employer's liability statute making the railroad liable for injuries caused to its employees, but Mississippi retained the common law, "fellow servant" rule that insulated the railroad from such liability. Instead of interpreting the Alabama statute in the light of its purposes[72] of providing compensation for injured employees and encouraging safe practices by employers, both of which were applicable here, the court applied the place-of-injury ruled and held that the statute did not provide compensation.[73] Significantly, the Alabama legislature subsequently amended the statute to cover out-of-state injury in just this situation,[74] but too late to help Mr. Carroll.

Victor v. Sperry[75] provides a fascinating example of the operation of the place-of-wrong rule. Two automobiles driven by California residents collided twenty-seven miles south of the California border in Mexico. The plaintiff, also a California resident, was a passenger in one of the automobiles. The other automobile was owned by and driven with the consent of still another California resident. The severely injured plaintiff brought suit in California against his host and against both the driver and the owner of the other automobile. The accident was the result of the negligence of the drivers of both vehicles.

---

69. *Sestito*, Brief for Plaintiff–Appellant, appendix, p. 2.

70. As to Pennsylvania law, see Neuberg v. Bobowicz, 401 Pa. 146, 162 A.2d 662 (1960).

71. 97 Ala. 126, 11 So. 803 (1892).

72. See Morris, § 6.7 note 22, at 888.

73. The ghost of *Alabama Great Southern R.R.* continues to haunt construction of statutory provisions for compensation of on-the-job injuries. See Boak v. Consolidated Rail Corp., 850 F.2d 110 (2d Cir.1988) (the Federal Employers Liability Act is not applicable unless the railway worker is injured in the United States even though the injury occurred in Canada on a train running between points in Canada and the United States); Powell v. Sappington, 495 So.2d 569 (Ala. 1986) (Alabama employee injured in Georgia is not permitted to sue fellow employees for negligence in inspecting and maintaining truck in Alabama, applying Georgia law rather than Alabama law—Alabama law permits such suits); cf. Union Underwear Co. v. Barnhart, 50 S.W.3d 188 (Ky. 2001) (refusing to apply Kentucky Civil Rights Act to claim by nonresident employed outside of Kentucky though employer headquartered in Kentucky; court notes the employee has claim under Federal Age Discrimination in Employment Act).

74. Ala.Code § 7540 (1928) (when contract of employment made in Alabama).

75. 163 Cal.App.2d 518, 329 P.2d 728 (1958).

Under California law, the plaintiff would have been awarded over $40,000 in damages. Under Mexican law his compensation was only slightly more than $6,000. One reason for this difference in damages was that, under Mexican law, in computing compensation for plaintiff's lost wages and the permanent impairment of his earning capacity, no more than two dollars of wages per day could be taken into account. The court awarded the plaintiff a judgment against both drivers, but not against the owner of the other automobile, in the much lower amount computed under Mexican law, remarking that "[t]he limitation upon the amount of damages imposed by the law of Mexico is not contrary to the public policy of the State of California or injurious to the welfare of the people thereof."[76] This was stated despite the fact that the plaintiff, a laborer, was very likely to become a public charge in California at the expense of California taxpayers and that the Mexican measure of damages was keyed to an entirely different standard of living than that enjoyed in California.

An argument for application of the Mexican measure of damages could be based on a factor not mentioned by the court. Assuming that the defendants had taken out liability insurance in California, it is likely that this insurance did not cover them twenty-seven miles south of the border,[77] and that, if they were insured at the time of the collision, it was by Mexican insurance. The defendants could argue that their Mexican insurance was keyed to the lower compensation available to plaintiffs under Mexican law and that the defendants would be unfairly surprised by the imposition of liability under California standards. This argument would not be very cogent today after the California Supreme Court has abandoned the place-of-wrong rule in favor of interest analysis.[78] A California tourist would be well advised today to key his or her Mexican insurance to California compensation rules.[79]

The Court in *Victor* denied recovery against the California owner of the other automobile on the ground that the Mexican rule, imposing liability without regard to fault on the owner of a "dangerous mechanism" such as an automobile, was contrary to California public policy. The court did not mention the fact that under the California Vehicle Code, in force at the time of the accident, an owner of a motor vehicle was liable for injury resulting from the negligence of "any person using or operating the same with the permission, express or implied, of the

---

76. Id. at 522, 329 P.2d at 732.

77. A standard automobile liability insurance clause read: "This policy applies only to accidents ... while the automobile is within the United States ... or Canada.... It is agreed that the coverage provided by this policy is extended to apply while the automobile insured is being used for occasional trips into that part of the Republic of Mexico lying not more than 25 miles from the boundary line of the United States of America for a period not exceeding 10 days at any one time."

78. See Reich v. Purcell, 67 Cal.2d 551, 63 Cal.Rptr. 31, 432 P.2d 727 (1967).

79. Cf. Contreras v. America, Compania General De Seguros, S.A., 48 Cal.App.3d 270, 121 Cal.Rptr. 694 (1975) (liability policy issued by Mexican company in California and covering liability only while driving in Mexico, must have limits and coverage required under California law).

owner."[80] Thus, since the driver of the other vehicle had been found to be negligent, the court reached a result, non-liability of the owner of that vehicle, which was opposite the result that would have been reached under either Mexican or California law. This despite the fact that the compensation policy underlying California's owner's liability statute was fully applicable and that Mexico would also hold the owner liable. The conflict here was false because the two contact jurisdictions would have reached the same result in an intra-jurisdictional transaction, and, although they would reach this result for different reasons, at least one of these reasons was applicable to the transaction in issue.

One further difficulty was caused by the place-of-wrong rule in *Victor v. Sperry*. The court permitted judgment against the host driver under Mexican law while making only one oblique allusion to the California guest statute, since repealed, which required a showing of "intoxication or willful misconduct" of the driver in order for a guest passenger to recover against the driver or "any other person legally liable for the conduct of the driver."[81] If a purpose of the California guest statute was to protect the host from the guest's ingratitude, this policy was applicable even though the crash occurred in Mexico. If the California act sought to prevent collusive suits, California, as forum, would have an interest in deterring collusive conduct by California residents in California courts. California's anti-collusion policy would be somewhat less relevant if the host was covered by Mexican insurance at the time of the accident so that a collusive recovery would not affect California insurance rates. Thus, at least some of the purposes supporting the California guest statute were applicable, while it was doubtful whether any Mexican policy of compensation or of deterring negligent conduct on Mexican roads would be significantly advanced by permitting recovery by a California plaintiff against a California defendant in California for conduct unlikely to be affected by civil liability.

The failure of the court in *Victor v. Sperry* to hold the owner of the second vehicle liable, even though both Mexico and California would do this in purely domestic cases, presents an interesting by-product of the place-of-wrong rule. The most clearly false conflict occurs when, if the occurrence had been intrastate, all contact states would reach the same result for identical reasons. There is then no rational basis upon which a court can reach a different result because a state line has been crossed.[82]

---

80. Code of 1935, § 402(a), now, in amended form, West's Ann.Cal.Vehicle Code § 17150.

81. Code of 1935, § 403, amended in 1973 to bar only recovery by owner-passenger, except for intoxication or willful misconduct, but declared in violation of state and federal equal protection guarantees even in this amended form. Cooper v. Bray, 21 Cal.3d 841, 148 Cal.Rptr. 148, 582 P.2d 604 (1978).

82. See Harper, *Torts, Contracts, Property, Status, Characterization, and the Conflict of Laws*, 59 Colum. L. Rev. 440, 444 n.14 (1959); M. Traynor, *Conflict of Laws: Professor Currie's Restrained and Enlightened Forum*, 40 Calif. L. Rev. 845, 856 (1961). But see L. McDougal III, *Comprehensive Interest Analysis Versus Reformulated Governmental Interest Analysis: An Appraisal in the Context of Choice-of-Law Problems Concerning Contributory and Comparative Negligence*, 26 UCLA L. Rev. 439, 473, 481 (1979) (would apply pure

Despite the axiomatic quality of such a statement, the traditional, territorially-oriented place-of-wrong rule has, at times, under such circumstances, trapped courts into reaching a result that accords with the law of neither state.

In *Liff v. Hazebroeck*,[83] for example, an Illinois tavern served liquor to a patron, rendering him intoxicated. His intoxication resulted in harm to the plaintiff in Iowa. Both states had dram shop acts imposing civil liability under these circumstances on the seller of the liquor. The court held, nevertheless, that the Iowa statute did not apply because the liquor was not served in Iowa and that the Illinois statute did not apply because the injury was not caused in Illinois. The same thing nearly happened in *Waynick v. Chicago's Last Department Store*.[84] The court held that neither the Illinois nor the Michigan dram shop acts applied to injury caused in Michigan by a drunk who had been served liquor in Illinois, but saved the situation by the heroic device of finding liability under Michigan common law based on a violation of an Illinois criminal statute. In a similar situation, another federal court avoided the need for accomplishing, by such an indirect method, the only rational result. It recognized that there was a "false conflict of laws issue"[85] because both the state where the liquor was served and the state where the harm was caused had statutes that would provide liability in domestic cases.

Maryland Casualty Co. v. Jacek[86] presents a slight variation on this theme. A New Jersey wife was injured in New York while a passenger in an automobile driven by her husband. The wife sued her husband in a federal court sitting in New Jersey. There would have been no liability under New Jersey law because under that law a wife may not sue her husband in tort. Under New York law there was no such disability, but the husband's insurance policy would not insure against liability to a spouse unless the policy expressly so provided. The husband's policy contained no such provision. Nevertheless, there was a summary judgment against the insurer when it sought a declaratory judgment determining its rights and duties under the policy. The court held the New York insurance statute inapplicable to a policy issued in New Jersey.[87] This is a strange result because both the New Jersey marital immunity rule and the New York insurance rule were probably designed to protect the insurer from a collusive husband-wife suit and thus prevent improper recoveries from inflating liability insurance rates. It is true that the two states pursued this policy by different routes and that, once the

comparative negligence rule to all "trans-state" transactions even though this was not the law of any state involved).

83. 51 Ill.App.2d 70, 200 N.E.2d 525 (1964), overruled on another issue, Nelson v. Araiza, 69 Ill.2d 534, 14 Ill.Dec. 441, 372 N.E.2d 637 (1978).

84. 269 F.2d 322 (7th Cir.1959), cert. denied, 362 U.S. 903, 80 S.Ct. 611, 4 L.Ed.2d 554 (1960).

85. Zucker v. Vogt, 329 F.2d 426, 428 (2d Cir.1964).

86. 156 F.Supp. 43 (D.N.J.1957).

87. That a New Jersey court would have applied the New Jersey incapacity rule to a New Jersey wife injured in New York, see Koplik v. C.P. Trucking Corp., 27 N.J. 1, 141 A.2d 34 (1958).

husband's liability to his wife was established, his New Jersey insurer was bound by its contract to defend and indemnify the husband. Perhaps a better result in *Jacek* would have been to decide that, because of the policy that New York shared with New Jersey, New York had no significant reason for imposing its liability rule on a New Jersey husband.[88]

The *Jacek* case reveals another pitfall in conflicts cases that even interest analysis, unless pursued with intelligence and circumspection, will not necessarily avoid. Interest analysis of conflicts problems is an issue-by-issue process. The issues in the case are isolated, the conflicting domestic rules on each issue are identified, and then the policies underlying the domestic laws on each issue are scrutinized for their effect on territorial application of the laws. There is danger that in this process the problem-solver will overlook interrelationships between different rules in the same state, or shared purposes of what appear to be different rules in the same state, or shared purposes of what appear to be different rules in the two states, and thus distort domestic policies while purporting to be guided by them.[89] Such a result would be an abuse of, not a proper application of, interest analysis.

It is possible for an intrastate result to be changed rationally by the crossing of a state line. This occurs when the two contact states would reach the same result, but for different reasons, neither of which is applicable to the interstate transaction. For example, suppose a husband's negligent driving in State X injures his wife, whose marital domicile is in State F. The wife brings suit against her husband in F. X has a rule preventing wives from suing their husbands in tort, but this rule is not rationally applicable when X is neither marital domicile nor forum and the insured automobile is principally garaged in F. The cause of the collision was the husband's violation of an X rule of the road, although he would have been driving properly by F rules. The F rules of the road, however, are not applicable in X. Though there would have been no liability if the occurrence had been an intrastate one within either F or X, there should now be liability.[90]

Reflecting back upon the problems discussed in this section, interspousal tort immunity, guest statute cases, and such cases as *Sestito v. Knop, Alabama Great Southern Railroad v. Carroll*, and *Victor v. Sperry*, an insight emerges that is fundamental to a consequences-based analysis of tort conflicts cases. The place of impact, qua place of impact, has no interest in insulating the defendant from liability, unless it can rationally be argued that the defendant has acted in reliance on that place's insulating rule. Such a reliance argument will almost invariably be

---

88. See Manning v. Hyland, 42 Misc.2d 915, 249 N.Y.S.2d 381 (Spec. Term, Queens City 1964); cf. Urhammer v. Olson, 39 Wis.2d 447, 159 N.W.2d 688 (1968) (family exclusion clause, valid in Minnesota where policy issued, enforced to prevent impleading of insurer by Wisconsin defendant).

89. See section 3.4.

90. See Harper, *Policy Bases of the Conflict of Laws: Reflections on Rereading Professor Lorenzen's Essays*, 56 Yale L. J. 1155, 1162–63 (1947) (suggesting another situation in which there might be an "interstate tort" although no "intrastate tort").

untenable when directed at rules governing liability for unintentional torts, excluding, of course, such purely directory local rules as speed limits, rules of right of way, and the like. In all of the foregoing situations, and in many more,[91] recognizing the place of impact's lack of interest in preventing or in limiting recovery can identify and eliminate false conflicts.

§ 6.12 Interests of the Place of Wrong

Having seen what interests the place of wrong does not have, it might be well to indicate briefly what interests it does have and also to indicate the probable interests of other states having a contact with the parties or with the occurrence in a tort case.[92]

The place of impact may have an interest in compensating the injured party.[93] Compensation will prevent the victim from becoming a public charge within the state and will provide a pool to compensate local medical and other creditors, who have furnished services to the victim.[94]

---

91. See, e.g., Dunn v. Beech Aircraft Corp., 271 F.Supp. 662 (D.Del.1967) (interspousal immunity, contribution sought from husband); Crowder v. Gordons Transports, Inc., 264 F.Supp. 137 (W.D.Ark.1967) rev'd on other grounds, 387 F.2d 413 (8th Cir.1967) (proper party to bring wrongful death suit); Messinger v. Tom, 203 So.2d 357 (Fla.Dist.Ct.App. 1967), cert. denied 210 So.2d 869 (1968) (proper party to bring wrongful death action); De Bono v. Bittner, 13 Misc.2d 333, 178 N.Y.S.2d 419 (N.Y.Cty.1958), aff'd mem., 10 A.D.2d 556, 196 N.Y.S.2d 595 (1st Dept.1960) (whether release of joint tortfeasor validly reserved rights against defendant—law of place of impact shields defendant from the liability that would result under the law of the domicile of all parties) (But see Root v. Kaufman, 48 Misc.2d 468, 265 N.Y.S.2d 201 (N.Y.C.Civ.Ct.1965), suggesting that *De Bono* is no longer applicable in the light of Babcock v. Jackson, 12 N.Y.2d 473, 240 N.Y.S.2d 743, 191 N.E.2d 279 (1963)); Builders Supply Co. v. McCabe, 366 Pa. 322, 77 A.2d 368 (1951) (law of place of wrong determines whether there is contribution between joint tortfeasors), questioned in Elston v. Industrial Lift Truck Co., 420 Pa. 97, 216 A.2d 318 (1966); Goldstein v. Gilbert, 125 W.Va. 250, 23 S.E.2d 606 (1942) (whether covenant not to sue executed for one tortfeasor bars action against joint tortfeasor).

Examples of other issues held governed by the law of the place of the wrong: O'Keeffe v. Atlantic Stevedoring Co., 354 F.2d 48 (5th Cir.1965) (whether Longshoremen's and Harbor Workers' Compensation Act applicable—injury must occur on navigable waters); Southwestern Greyhound Lines, Inc. v. Crown Coach Co., 178 F.2d 628 (8th Cir.1949) (contribution between tortfeasors); Venuto v. Robinson, 118 F.2d 679 (3d Cir.), cert. denied sub nom. Ross, Agent, Inc. v. Venuto, 314 U.S. 627, 62 S.Ct. 58, 86 L.Ed. 504 (1941) (whether master-servant relationship exists for purpose of respondeat superior); Jones v. McKesson & Robbins, Inc., 237 F.Supp. 454 (D.N.D.1965) (whether "probable cause" defense to action for malicious prosecution) (but cf. Weiss v. Hunna, 312 F.2d 711 (2d Cir.1963), cert. denied 374 U.S. 853, 83 S.Ct. 1920, 10 L.Ed.2d 1073 (1963) (distinguishes tort of abuse of process from malicious prosecution)); Zirkelbach v. Decatur Cartage Co., 119 F.Supp. 753 (N.D.Ind.1954) (whether statutory limit on liability for wrongful death); Lumb v. Cooper, 266 A.2d 196 (Del.Super.1970) (proper person to bring wrongful death action); Knight v. Handley Motor Co., 198 A.2d 747 (D.C.App.1964) (whether respondeat superior relationship, but same result under either law); Millsap v. Central Wis. Motor Transp. Co., 41 Ill.App.2d 1, 189 N.E.2d 793 (1963) (contribution between tortfeasors); Ex parte First Pennsylvania Banking & Trust Co., 247 S.C. 506, 148 S.E.2d 373 (1966) (whether injured party has lien on defendant's automobile).

92. See sections 6.13–6.15.

93. See Hutzell v. Boyer, 252 Md. 227, 249 A.2d 449 (1969); Hime v. State Farm Fire & Cas. Co., 284 N.W.2d 829 (Minn.1979), cert. denied, 444 U.S. 1032, 100 S.Ct. 703, 62 L.Ed.2d 668 (1980).

94. See Currie, *The Silver Oar and All That: A Study of the Romero Case*, 27 U. Chi. L. Rev. 1, 71 (1959); Hancock, *Three Approaches to the Choice-of-Law Problem; The Classifica-*

It may be that in an individual case the facts are such that these interests of the place of impact are reduced to the vanishing point. For example, the victim may leave the state of impact immediately, go to another state where he or she is domiciled,[95] and receive medical treatment there. Although, even under such circumstances, the state of impact may retain sufficient interest in providing compensation to prevent our saying that it has no interest and that the application of its law will be unreasonable,[96] the fact that its interest in compensation is thus reduced should certainly be considered in reconciling any true conflict that might exist.[97] The interest of the place of impact in providing compensation is similarly reduced if the victim is killed and recovery is for wrongful death. The proceeds of such recovery, at least when there are close relatives surviving,[98] are typically not subject to the claims of creditors.[99] One matter over which it is clear that the place of impact as such has no interest is in the manner of distributing the

---

tory, The Functional and the Result–Selective, in XXth Century Comparative and Conflicts Law 365, 371 (1961).

95. Commentators have charged that a consequences-based analysis is a complex way of saying that each jurisdiction is interested in making the benefits of its law available to its own citizens but not to others. See Ely, *Choice of Law and the State's Interest in Protecting its Own*, 23 Wm. & Mary L. Rev. 173 (1982). This not only raises grave questions of unfair discrimination, but also focuses on domicile at a time of unprecedented population mobility. See Corr, *Interest Analysis and Choice of Law: The Dubious Dominance of Domicile*, 1982 Utah L. Rev. 651 (1983). But cf. Lopez, *The Law of the Domicile with Greater Compensation Rule: Toward Policy–Oriented Rules for Choice of Law*, 17 Cal.W. L. Rev. 26 (1980) (advocating domicile-based rules without interest analysis).

It is true that in so far as social consequences of applying law are likely to be experienced where the parties reside, consequences-based analysis does focus on residence. But there are other contacts that are relevant to policies underlying local law. See this section and § 6.14. Problems of mobility are discussed § 6.30.

96. Cf. Carroll v. Lanza, 349 U.S. 408, 413, 75 S.Ct. 804, 807, 99 L.Ed. 1183, 1189 (1955) (Missouri employee of sub-contractor, injured in Arkansas, permitted to bring tort suit in Arkansas against general contractor contrary to provisions of Missouri workmen's compensation act): "Arkansas therefore has a legitimate interest in opening her courts to suits of this nature, even though in this case Carroll's injury may have cast no burden on her or on her institutions."

97. See Posnak, *Choice of Law: A Very Well–Curried Leflar Approach*, 34 Mercer L. Rev. 731, 772–73 (1983).

98. See, e.g., Iowa Code § 633.336:

"When a wrongful act produces death, damages recovered therefor shall be disposed of as personal property belonging to the estate of the deceased, however, if the damages include damages for loss of services and support of a deceased spouse and parent, such damages shall be apportioned by the court among the surviving spouse and children of the decedent in such manner as the court may deem equitable consistent with the loss of services and support sustained by the surviving spouse and children respectively. If the decedent leaves a spouse, child or parent, damages for wrongful death shall not be subject to debts and charges of the decedent's estate, except for amounts to be paid to the department of human services for payments made for medical assistance pursuant to chapter 249A, paid on behalf of the decedent from the time of the injury which gives rise to the decedent's death up until the date of the decedent's death."

99. See Currie, *The Constitution and the Choice of Law*, 26 U. Chi. L. Rev. 9, 15 (1958). The fact that it is unnecessary to protect local creditors has made it possible for foreign administrators to sue locally on the wrongful death claim without obtaining local appointment. Gross v. Hocker, 243 Iowa 291, 51 N.W.2d 466 (1952); Howard v. Pulver, 329 Mich. 415, 45 N.W.2d 530 (1951); Ghilain v. Couture, 84 N.H. 48, 146 A. 395 (1929). But see Merchants Distributors, Inc. v. Hutchinson, 16 N.C.App. 655, 193 S.E.2d 436 (1972) (local ancillary administrator necessary to bring wrongful death action).

proceeds of a wrongful death recovery.[100] Any conflict with regard to such distribution between the law of the place of impact and the law of the domicile of the decedent and his next of kin is false. The law of the domicile should control. The rigid standard rule has, however, under such circumstances, resulted in the application of the law of the place of impact.[101]

In addition to its interest in compensating the victim, the place of impact has an interest in shaping its tort rules so as to discourage conduct that will result in harmful impacts within its borders.[102] Such an interest in controlling the tortfeasor's conduct is strongest when dealing with intentional torts[103] and diminishes to the vanishing point when

---

100. See Satchwill v. Vollrath Co., 293 F.Supp. 533 (E.D.Wis.1968); In re Estate of Blanton, 824 So.2d 558, 563 (Miss. 2002) (although Mississippi resident killed in Arkansas "the most substantial relationships of the parties and the dominant interest of the forum require application of Mississippi law" to distribution of settlement proceeds as between the decedent's siblings and children); In re Estate of Wood, 122 N.H. 956, 453 A.2d 1251 (1982); In re Estate of Caccamo, 71 Misc.2d 391, 336 N.Y.S.2d 77 (Surr.Ct.1972). But see Estate of Barnes, 133 Ill.App.3d 361, 88 Ill.Dec. 438, 478 N.E.2d 1046 (Dist. 1 1985) (despite fact that all distributees live in Illinois, wrongful death proceeds are distributed under Michigan law when the suit settled was brought under the Michigan wrongful death statute).

101. See Workman v. Hargadon, 345 S.W.2d 644 (Ky.1961); Matter of Winikoff's Estate, 116 N.Y.S.2d 262 (Surr.Ct.Kings Cty.1952); Breitwieser v. State, 62 N.W.2d 900 (N.D.1954); Restatement, Conflict of Laws § 393, comment c (1934).

102. See Jaffe v. Pallotta TeamWorks, 374 F.3d 1223 (D.C. Cir. 2004) (Virginia has interest in protecting non-resident against negligence in Virginia of out-of-state charities); Vicon, Inc. v. CMI Corp., 657 F.2d 768 (5th Cir.1981) (Mississippi law, misrepresentation); Broome v. Antlers' Hunting Club, 595 F.2d 921 (3d Cir.1979) (Pennsylvania law, injury on property); Kaiser–Georgetown Community Health Plan, Inc. v. Stutsman, 491 A.2d 502 (D.C.1985) (malpractice); Rosett v. Schatzman, 157 Ill.App.3d 939, 109 Ill.Dec. 900, 510 N.E.2d 968 (1st Dist.1987) (situs of realty with regard to liability for negligent maintenance); Barr v. Interbay Citizens Bank of Tampa, 96 Wn.2d 692, 635 P.2d 441 (En banc 1981) (punitive damages for conversion); Baade, *Counter–Revolution or Alliance for Progress? Reflections on Reading Cavers, The Choice-of-Law Process*, 46 Texas L. Rev. 141, 171 (1967); Weinberg, *The Place of Trial and the Law Applied: Overhauling Constitutional Theory*, 59 U.Colo. L. Rev. 67, 79 (1988) ("the place of injury has [an] interest in applying its compensatory laws to those injured while temporarily within its territory"); cf. Barnes Group, Inc. v. C & C Products, Inc., 716 F.2d 1023 (4th Cir.1983) (Ohio law, apply law of place where employee works to determine liability for tort of interference with contract); Estrada v. Potomac Electric Power Co., 488 A.2d 1359 (D.C.App.1985) (apply law of situs to avoid doctrine of attractive nuisance and to encourage use of land).

103. See Acme Circus Operating Co., Inc. v. Kuperstock, 711 F.2d 1538 (11th Cir.1983) (California law, infringement of right to publicity); Houston North Hospital Properties v. Telco Leasing Inc., 688 F.2d 408 (5th Cir.1982) (Texas law, economic duress); Kunstsammlungen Zu Weimar v. Elicofon, 678 F.2d 1150 (2d Cir.1982) (New York law, transfer of stolen property); Brookley v. Ranson, 376 F.Supp. 195 (N.D.Iowa 1974) (alienation of affections); Heaney v. Purdy, 29 N.Y.2d 157, 324 N.Y.S.2d 47, 272 N.E.2d 550 (1971) (malicious prosecution); Kammerer v. Western Gear Corp., 96 Wn.2d 416, 635 P.2d 708 (En banc 1981) (fraud). See also Marra v. Bushee, 317 F.Supp. 972 (D.Vt.1970), rev'd, 447 F.2d 1282 (2d Cir.1971). The reversal was to permit a jury trial of the issue of where the defendant's alleged acts of criminal conversation principally occurred. On whether the jury should decide this choice-of-law fact issue, cf. Chance v. E.I. Du Pont De Nemours & Co., 57 F.R.D. 165 (E.D.N.Y.1972) (court decides choice-of-law fact issues); Amiot v. Ames, 166 Vt. 288, 693 A.2d 675, 679 (1997) (stating that "the facts underlying a choice-of-law decision are generally better left to the judge rather than the jury"); W. Reese, Smit, G. Reese, *The Role of the Jury in Choice of Law*, 25 Case W.Res. L. Rev. 82, 106 (1974) (issue of fact as to location of a contact should be decided by the judge if it arises before jury impaneled or during taking of evidence; after close of evidence "usually" by judge except

dealing with the ordinary automobile negligence case, if one excludes such purely directory rules as speed limits. This is because rules governing civil liability are not likely to shape the conduct of the negligent tortfeasor, particularly the "accident prone" highway menace.[104] The place where the defendant acts, if this is different from the place of impact, has a similar interest in controlling the conduct.[105] The place where the defendant acts will sometimes have a policy of shielding the defendant from liability to encourage economic activity.[106]

Some courts and commentators applying modern choice-of-law approaches distinguish between compensatory and punitive damages.[107] The distinction is based on the argument that the place of wrong's interest in punishing the defendant and deterring similar conduct is strongest when the conduct is sufficiently outrageous to justify punitive damages. On the other hand, higher compensatory damages will also punish and deter.[108] The plaintiff should be able to choose either the law of the place of injury, if foreseeable, or the law of the place where defendant acted to cause the injury. Both jurisdictions have an interest in punishment and deterrence and it is fair to apply their law to the defendant.

§ 6.13 Interests of the Defendant's Domicile

The defendant's domicile, or in the case of a corporation, its place of incorporation, or place of doing business, has an interest in controlling

---

"in those rare situations where the issue could be dealt with simply in the charge and where, in the trial judge's opinion, the jury is better qualified than he to decide the issue"). Cf. Karavokiros v. Indiana Motor Bus Co., 524 F.Supp. 385 (E.D.La.1981) (deny punitive damages under forum law though permitted where defendant negligently entrusted the vehicle that injured plaintiff in the forum); Greco v. Anderson, 615 S.W.2d 429 (Mo.App. 1980) (apply law of state where plaintiff seduced to deny recovery); Myers v. Brickwedel, 259 Or. 457, 486 P.2d 1286 (1971) (when acts occurred in Oregon, Oregon has sufficient interest in applying its law to exercise long-arm jurisdiction in suit between Californians for alienation of affections and criminal conversation, but leave open question whether Oregon law will be applied).

104. See § 6.7, notes 22–23 and accompanying text.

105. See Gaither v. Myers, 404 F.2d 216 (D.C.Cir.1968); Ehrenzweig, *The Place of Acting in Intentional Multistate Torts: Laws and Reason Versus the Restatement*, 36 Minn. L. Rev. 1, 5–6 (1951).

106. See Schumacher v. Schumacher, 676 N.W.2d 685 (Minn. App. 2004) (apply Iowa law to shield Minnesota participant in Iowa horse show from liability to another Minnesota resident).

107. See In re Aircrash Disaster Near Roselawn, Ind. on Oct. 31, 1994, 1997 WL 572897 (N.D. Ill. 1997) (apply punitive damages law to two defendants where they have their principal place of business and most of their misconduct occurred; to two other defendants where most of their misconduct occurred outside of their principal place of business); Dobelle v. National R.R. Passenger Corp., 628 F.Supp. 1518 (S.D. N.Y. 1986) (apply Pennsylvania law to punitive damages, not because it is plaintiff's domicile, which "has little relevance since punitive damages are designed to punish a defendant, not to compensate a plaintiff", but because Pennsylvania was where most of the defendant's actions that caused the accident occurred); Restatement (Second) of Conflict of Laws § 145, cmt. *c* (place of conduct may have "dominant interest" in punitive damages).

108. See In re Air Crash at Belle Harbor, N.Y. on Nov. 12, 2001, 2006 WL 1288298 (S.D.N.Y. 2006) (refusing to apply French law to the issue of punitive damages to victims on ground of air crash in New York; New York has "the paramount governmental interest in having its law applied").

the defendant's conduct. It also has an interest in insulating the defendant from liability.[109] Cases involving charitable immunity illustrate this latter interest. The place of impact has no interest in insulating a charity incorporated elsewhere from tort liability, if the place of impact has no substantial contacts with the charity. This is true, for example, if the charity is merely conducting an outing or tour in a state that has a rule of charitable immunity and the state in which it is incorporated or generally conducts its activities has no immunity rule. The charity should not receive the benefit of the immunity rule for injuries suffered in the state where the short tour or outing is being held.[110] On the other hand, if the charity is generally engaged in beneficial activities within a state, that state has an interest in applying its immunity rule to the charity, even though the charity is incorporated elsewhere.[111]

§ 6.14   Forum Interests

The forum, qua forum, has an interest in preserving the integrity and economy of its judicial process.[112] It may protect this interest by

---

109.   See Gilbert v. Seton Hall Univ., 332 F.3d 105 (2d Cir. 2003) (apply New Jersey charitable immunity rule although student injured in New York was domiciled in Connecticut); Karavokiros v. Indiana Motor Bus Co., 524 F.Supp. 385, 387 n.1 (E.D.La.1981) ("interest in protecting those defendants who do business in Louisiana"); Najarian v. National Amusements, Inc., 768 A.2d 1253 (R.I. 2001) (applying Massachusetts law to negligence suit by Rhode Island resident injured in Massachusetts theater; Massachusetts comparative negligence law denied liability that Rhode Island would confer). But cf. Szalatnay–Stacho v. Fink [1947] K.B. 1 (absolute privilege provided by law of domicile not applicable to official act in England of one official of Czech government-in-exile affecting another such official, but English qualified privilege prevents liability).

110.   See Blum v. American Youth Hostels, Inc., 40 Misc.2d 1056, 244 N.Y.S.2d 351 (Spec.Term, 1963), aff'd on other grounds 21 A.D.2d 683, 250 N.Y.S.2d 522 (1964); Brown v. Church of the Holy Name of Jesus, 105 R.I. 322, 252 A.2d 176 (1969); cf. Prince v. Trustees of University of Pennsylvania, 282 F.Supp. 832, 837 (E.D.Pa.1968). But see Jeffrey v. Whitworth College, 128 F.Supp. 219 (E.D.Wash.1955); Kaufman v. American Youth Hostels, 6 A.D.2d 223, 177 N.Y.S.2d 587 (2d Dept.1958), modified in other respects 5 N.Y.2d 1016, 185 N.Y.S.2d 268, 158 N.E.2d 128 (1959) (same accident as *Blum*, supra this note).

111.   See Menardi v. Thea. Jones Evangelistic Ass'n, 154 F.Supp. 622 (E.D.Pa.1957) (dismiss suit brought where charity transacting business, although no immunity rule at place of impact); Allison v. Mennonite Publications Bd., 123 F.Supp. 23 (W.D.Pa.1954) (dictum); Schultz v. Boy Scouts of America, Inc., 65 N.Y.2d 189, 491 N.Y.S.2d 90, 480 N.E.2d 679 (1985) (applying charitable immunity rule of New Jersey to advance New Jersey's interest in encouraging charitable activity there; where *Schultz* erred is in not recognizing that the place where a charity employee sexually abused children attending camp there had an interest in deterring such conduct). But cf. Heinemann v. Jewish Agricultural Soc'y, 178 Misc. 897, 37 N.Y.S.2d 354 (Chautauqua Cty.1942), aff'd mem., 266 App.Div. 907, 43 N.Y.S.2d 746 (4th Dep't 1943), motion for leave to appeal denied, 266 App.Div. 941, 46 N.Y.S.2d 219 (4th Dep't 1943), motion for leave to appeal granted, 291 N.Y. 828 (1943) (in suit at place of incorporation decline to apply immunity rule of State in which charity running training farm). But see P.V. v. Camp Jaycee, 197 N.J. 132, 962 A.2d 453 (2008) (apply law of Pennsylvania where New Jersey camper was abused rather than law of New Jersey where charity incorporated and has an administrative office; Pennsylvania law does not provide immunity but New Jersey law does); Doctor v. Pardue, 186 S.W.3d 4 (Tex. App.—Houston [1st Dist.] 2006) (Texas rule of immunity not applicable to charity that performs services in Texas when charity is incorporated in another state and conduct in issue occurred outside of Texas and was not directed at Texas residents).

112.   See Karavokiros v. Indiana Motor Bus Co., 524 F.Supp. 385 (E.D.La.1981) (discourage speculative awards of punitive damages); Shapira, supra note 51, at 172.

closing its forum and refusing to render a judgment on the merits if, because of the absence of forum contacts and the presence of foreign contacts, the forum is a seriously inconvenient site for litigation and an appropriate site is available to the plaintiff.[113] Similar forum-closing action may be taken if adjudication at the forum will amount to prosecuting the defendant for a crime committed in another jurisdiction,[114] or if application of relevant foreign law will "violate some fundamental principle of justice, some prevalent conception of good morals, some deep-rooted tradition of the common weal."[115] Rarely, if ever, should this last reason be applicable to the law of a sister state.[116] The forum, qua forum, however, has no interest in affecting the result on the merits by displacing logically applicable foreign law, and it should exert every effort to avoid doing so.[117] The so-called "procedural" category, now including many rules that have high potential for determining the outcome, should be reserved for situations in which the difficulty of ascertaining and applying the foreign rule outweighs the likelihood that the rule will affect the result in such a manner as to trigger forum shopping.[118]

An example of a forum's protection of the integrity of its procedures may be the many refusals by courts in one state to permit suits against insurance companies under the "direct action" statute of a sister state.[119] The reason typically given for this refusal is that the direct

---

113. See § 4.33 (discussing forum non conveniens).

114. See Loucks v. Standard Oil Co., 224 N.Y. 99, 103, 120 N.E. 198 (1918): "The purpose must be, not reparation to one aggrieved, but vindication of the public justice."

115. Id. at 111, 120 N.E. at 202. See § 3.6 discussing public policy.

116. See Gordon v. Parker, 83 F.Supp. 40, 43 (D.Mass.1949), aff'd on other grounds, 178 F.2d 888 (1st Cir.1949) (permitting action for alienation of affections though abolished by Pennsylvania, the marital domicile): "Pennsylvania, was concerned with not having Pennsylvania courts hear this sordid type of controversy.... That is, Pennsylvania has spoken qua possible forum ... but not qua state of matrimonial domicile." Williams v. Jeffs, 57 P.3d 232 (Utah. App. 2002), is a mirror image of *Gordon* but reaches the opposite result. Husband and wife were domiciled in Arizona. The wife divorced her husband after church authorities counseled the wife in Utah. Utah recognizes actions for alienation of affections, but Arizona does not. The husband sued a church trust and church authorities in Utah for alienation of affections. The court affirms a summary judgment for the defendants, applying Arizona law under Restatement Second "most significant relationship" analysis. "Utah's interests are non existent in the personal relationship between two Arizona residents who are husband and wife.... [T]he injury occurred in Arizona because Arizona was the situs of the marriage and where [the husband] would have experienced the alienation of his wife's affections." Id. at 236.

117. But see Comment, 61 Colum. L. Rev. 1497, 1503 (1961) (interest of forum in integrity of its system of administering justice permits use of its outcome-determinative rules of evidence).

118. See § 3.2C(1).

119. Pearson v. Globe Indem. Co., 311 F.2d 517 (5th Cir.1962); Marchlik v. Coronet Ins. Co., 40 Ill.2d 327, 239 N.E.2d 799 (1968); Lieberthal v. Glenn Falls Indem. Co., 316 Mich. 37, 24 N.W.2d 547 (1946); Mech v. General Cas. Co. of Wisconsin, 410 N.W.2d 317 (Minn. 1987) (cannot sue under Wisconsin direct action statute, distinguishing *Myers*, infra this note, as dealing with substantive rights created by Louisiana statute); McNeal v. Administrator of Estate of McNeal, 254 So.2d 521 (Miss.1971); Noe v. United States Fidelity & Guar. Co., 406 S.W.2d 666 (Mo.1966); Morton v. Maryland Cas. Co., 4 N.Y.2d 488, 176 N.Y.S.2d 329, 151 N.E.2d 881 (1958) (Louisiana statute); Penny v. Powell, 162 Tex. 497, 347 S.W.2d 601 (1961). Contra, Collins v. American Auto Ins. Co., 230 F.2d 416

action statute is "procedural" and therefore can be utilized only if the forum has such a statute. A "procedural" label may be an indication that the forum believes that permitting the plaintiff to join the liability insurer as a defendant under a direct action statute is too likely to result in a perversion of justice.[120] This may be naive in view of the known ubiquity of liability insurance. The question of whether permitting suit under another state's direct action statute would too deeply offend the forum's interest in protecting the integrity of its procedures should be faced squarely by the forum, rather than masked under a "procedural" label. New York and Illinois have taken this approach to the direct action problem and have reached different conclusions on the public policy issue, New York permitting suit[121] and Illinois rejecting the direct action.[122] Another factor that the forum should consider in deciding

---

(2d Cir.1956), cert. dism'd, 352 U.S. 802, 77 S.Ct. 20, 1 L.Ed.2d 37 (1956) (permitted a direct action in New York under the Louisiana statute, purporting to apply New York law, which was established to the contrary in *Morton*, supra); Hertz Corp. v. Piccolo, 453 So.2d 12 (Fla.1984) (Louisiana statute); Myers v. Government Employees Ins. Co., 302 Minn. 359, 225 N.W.2d 238 (1974) (La. statute); Oltarsh v. Aetna Ins. Co., 15 N.Y.2d 111, 256 N.Y.S.2d 577, 204 N.E.2d 622 (1965) (Puerto Rican Statute, distinguishing *Morton*, supra this note, on the ground that the Puerto Rican statute, unlike the Louisiana statute, has no venue limitations); cf. Willard v. Aetna Cas. & Sur. Co., 213 Va. 481, 193 S.E.2d 776 (1973) (not against forum policy to permit insured to bring direct action against insurer under uninsured motorist clause, applying North Carolina rather than Virginia law).

Two states and Puerto Rico have generally applicable direct action statutes. La.Rev.Stat. § 22:1269; Wis.Stat.Ann. § 632.24; P.R. Laws Ann. tit. 26, § 2003. The Puerto Rican statute contains the proviso that the direct action "may only be exercised in Puerto Rico". That this kind of limit need not be given full faith and credit in other states, see § 9.3B. See also Ark.Stat.Ann. § 23–89–101(b) (direct action permitted if judgment against insured remains unsatisfied for 30 days); R.I.Gen.Laws § 27–7–2 (permitted if process against insured returned "non est inventus" or insured dead).

For a history of the Louisiana statute, see Johnson, *The Louisiana Direct Action Statute*, 43 La. L. Rev. 1455 (1983).

120.　Cf. Castonzo v. General Cas. Co., 251 F.Supp. 948 (W.D.Wis.1966) (application of guest statute to protect against collusive suits is primarily a forum concern).

121.　Oltarsh v. Aetna Ins. Co., 15 N.Y.2d 111, 256 N.Y.S.2d 577, 204 N.E.2d 622 (1965).

One of the grounds on which the New York court distinguished *Morton*, supra note 117, was that the Puerto Rican direct action statute, unlike the Louisiana statute in *Morton*, contained no provision purporting to limit suit under it to the courts of the enacting state. After *Oltarsh*, the Puerto Rican statute was amended to provide that "[t]he direct action against the insurer may only be exercised in Puerto Rico." Laws P.R.Ann. § 2003(1). That full faith and credit need not be given to statutory provisions purporting to limit suit to the enacting state, see § 9.3B.

122.　Marchlik v. Coronet Ins. Co., 40 Ill.2d 327, 239 N.E.2d 799 (1968).

That a direct action statute may sometimes be applied in the enacting state to an action arising from an injury outside that state, see Scribbins v. State Farm Mut. Auto. Ins. Co., 304 F.Supp. 1268 (E.D.Wis.1969) (Wisconsin statute applicable if policy issued in Wisconsin); Taylor v. Fishing Tools, Inc., 274 F.Supp. 666 (E.D.La.1967) (injury on high seas); Webb v. Zurich Ins. Co., 251 La. 558, 205 So.2d 398 (1967) (when policy issued or delivered in Louisiana even though injury outside Louisiana); Barter v. General Motors Corp., 70 Wis.2d 796, 235 N.W.2d 523 (1975) (product sold in Wisconsin injures plaintiff in Iowa). The Louisiana direct action statute is limited to policies "issued or delivered" in Louisiana and to actions in which "the accident or injury occurred within ... Louisiana." La.Rev.Stat. § 22.1269(B)(2). The Wisconsin act (Wis.Stat.Ann. § 632.24) is limited, by the general territorial scope provision (Id. § 631.01(1)) to insurance policies "delivered or issued for delivery in this state, on property ordinarily located in this state, on persons residing in this state when the policy is issued, or on business operations in this state". Puerto Rico has the only other generally applicable direct action statute (P.R.L.Ann. title

whether to permit a direct action under another state's statute is whether the inconvenience to the insured, who has promised in the insurance policy to cooperate with the insurer in defending the action, outweighs the desirability of providing a local forum for its own citizen.

Article 18 of the European Community Regulation on the Law Applicable to Non–Contractual Obligations[123] provides:

Direct action against the insurer of the person liable

The person having suffered damage may bring his or her claim directly against the insurer of the person liable to provide compensation if the law applicable to the non-contractual obligation or the law applicable to the insurance contract so provides.

If the forum has an interest other than as forum, if it has a rationally applicable rule of its own that conflicts with the rationally applicable rule of another jurisdiction, the forum should face up to the conflict, resolve it one way or another, and render a result on the merits. It should not elect the ostrich-like solution of closing its doors to the problem.[124]

§ 6.15 Interests of Plaintiff's Domicile

The domicile of the plaintiff has an interest in providing compensation.[125] This will prevent the plaintiff from becoming a public charge, or more commonly and less dramatically, assure compensation that the home state regards as appropriate. Compensating the plaintiff will also help guarantee payment for medical creditors who are likely to attend the injured plaintiff at the domicile. The plaintiff's domicile has no interest in applying its law to insulate the defendant from liability unless

---

26 § 2003). P.R.L.Ann. title 26 § 1119(1) forbids a clause precluding a direct action in a "policy delivered or issued for delivery in Puerto Rico and covering a subject of insurance resident, located, or to be performed in Puerto Rico". Hernandez v. Steamship Mut. Underwriting Assoc., Ltd., 388 F.Supp. 312 (D.Puerto Rico 1974) interpreted this provision as indicating the general territorial scope of the direct action statute and did not permit a direct action by a worker injured on a ship docked in Puerto Rico because the ship was owned by an Italian corporation and the insurance had been issued in London.

123. Regulation (EC) No. 864/2007 of the European Parliament and of the Council of 11 July 2007 on the law applicable to non contractual obligations OJ 2007 L 199/46.

124. But see the following examples of refusing a forum for suit against a local citizen: Gaines v. Poindexter, 155 F.Supp. 638 (W.D.La.1957) (alienation of affections); Kircher v. Kircher, 288 Mich. 669, 286 N.W. 120 (1939) (wife suing husband); Koplik v. C.P. Trucking Corp., 27 N.J. 1, 141 A.2d 34 (1958) (wife suing husband); Mertz v. Mertz, 271 N.Y. 466, 3 N.E.2d 597 (1936) (wife suing husband); Herzog v. Stern, 264 N.Y. 379, 191 N.E. 23, cert. denied, 293 U.S. 597, 55 S.Ct. 112, 79 L.Ed. 690 (1934) (survival).

125. See Guillory v. United States, 699 F.2d 781 (5th Cir.1983); Hall v. University of Nevada, 8 Cal.3d 522, 105 Cal.Rptr. 355, 503 P.2d 1363, cert. denied, 414 U.S. 820, 94 S.Ct. 114, 38 L.Ed.2d 52 (1973) (interest in providing a forum where resident may seek redress results in rejection of Nevada claim of sovereign immunity when vehicle operated by Nevada state agency injures Californian in California); (for subsequent history of case see § 6.26 note 283); Struebin v. State, 322 N.W.2d 84 (Iowa 1982), cert. denied, 459 U.S. 1087, 103 S.Ct. 570, 74 L.Ed.2d 933 (1982); Litarowich v. Wiederkehr, 170 N.J.Super. 144, 405 A.2d 874 (Law Div.1979); cf. Sibley v. KLM–Royal Dutch Airlines, 454 F.Supp. 425 (S.D.N.Y.1978) (when Massachusetts residents killed in Canary Islands crash, Massachusetts has a significant interest in insuring adequate compensation, but no interest in recovery of punitive damages).

the defendant relied on the domicile's law. Failure to recognize this resulted in a California court's denying a forum to a California citizen suing a Hawaiian defendant for damage caused in Hawaii by the defendant's child. Refusal was on the ground of substantial conflict between Hawaiian law holding a parent liable for torts of the child and California law denying such liability.[126]

The list of probable or usual interests in sections 6.12 through 6.15 is not a suitable substitute for focusing on the specific rules in supposed conflict and analyzing these rules in terms of their underlying policies.

§ 6.16 Avoidance of the Place-of-Wrong Rule by Recharacterization: "Tort" to "Contract"

One of the commonest methods by which courts have avoided application of the law of the place of wrong to determine the issues presented in a personal injury case, is to switch the label of the problem from "tort" to "contract." *Levy v. Daniels' U–Drive Auto Renting Company*[127] is a classic example. A Connecticut statute made lessors of motor vehicles liable for harm done by the vehicle while leased. An automobile that defendant-lessor had rented to the driver in Connecticut caused harm in Massachusetts. Massachusetts had no lessor-liability statute. The court held the Connecticut statute applicable.[128] The result

---

126. Hudson v. Von Hamm, 85 Cal.App. 323, 259 P. 374 (1927); cf. Le Forest v. Tolman, 117 Mass. 109 (1875) (defendant's domicile applies law of plaintiff's domicile to absolve defendant from liability for dog bite at plaintiff's domicile).

Both of these cases involved questions of vicarious liability. When the defendant was not present at the place of the wrong, a number of cases have refused to subject defendant to various forms of vicarious liability under the law of the place of the wrong. See Siegmann v. Meyer, 100 F.2d 367 (2d Cir.1938) (husband's liability for wife's tort); Lies v. Tuttle, 19 Wis.2d 571, 120 N.W.2d 719 (1963) (negligence of driver under 18 imputed to person who signed driver's license application); cf. Scheer v. Rockne Motors Corp., 68 F.2d 942 (2d Cir.1934) (automobile owner's liability statute not applicable to nonresident owner unless he consented to car being driven into place of wrong). For cases imposing liability on an absent defendant under the vicarious liability rule of the place of wrong, see Watkins v. Cupit, 130 So.2d 720 (La.App.1961) (Mississippi father held liable for his son's tort under Louisiana law); Fischl v. Chubb, 30 Pa. D. & C. 40 (1937) (dog owner liable under statute of state where dog bit victim); cf. Hobbs v. Fireman's Fund Am. Ins. Co., 339 So.2d 28 (La.App.1976) (husband liable for wife's tort while wife on "community mission"). But see Arado v. Central Nat'l Ins. Co., 337 So.2d 253 (La.App.1976) (Florida father not vicariously liable for tort of emancipated daughter in Louisiana); Corley v. Lewless, 227 Ga. 745, 182 S.E.2d 766 (1971) (violation of due process to make even resident parent liable for child's willful and wanton acts).

127. 108 Conn. 333, 143 A. 163 (1928).

128. Cf. Cates v. Creamer, 431 F.3d 456 (5th Cir. 2005) (applies Florida vicarious liability doctrine to permit Texan injured in Texas to recover against Florida lessor); Motor Club of Am. Ins. Co. v. Hanifi, 145 F.3d 170 (4th Cir.1998), cert. denied, 525 U.S. 1001, 119 S.Ct. 509, 142 L.Ed.2d 423 (1998) (predicts Maryland would apply New York owner's liability statute to crash in Maryland despite Maryland's adherence to lex loci delicti); Graham v. Wilkins, 145 Conn. 34, 138 A.2d 705 (1958) (Connecticut statute applicable to injury in Massachusetts even though the contract of bailment was not made in Connecticut, but vehicle was garaged and extensively operated in Connecticut); Stallworth v. Hospitality Rentals, Inc., 515 So.2d 413 (Fla. App. 1st Dist.1987) (under "most significant relationship" test, apply law of state where car rented to permit vicarious liability); Veasley v. CRST Int'l., Inc., 553 N.W.2d 896 (Iowa 1996) (applying Iowa owner's liability statute to Arizona accident); Fu v. Fu, 160 N.J. 108, 733 A.2d 1133 (1999) (applying New York owner's liability statute to crash in New York although car rented in New Jersey);

was commendable. Connecticut's policy was to control the conduct of Connecticut lessors, or perhaps more realistically, to impose the risks created by automobile renting on the lessors as a cost of doing business. Unless Connecticut took an extremely narrow and callous view, its policy was applicable even though the risks created by Connecticut lessors were not realized in Connecticut.[129] Massachusetts had no interest in insulating the Connecticut lessor from liability.[130] The holding in *Daniels' U-Drive*, however, was on the ground that the problem was one of contract, not tort, liability and that the plaintiff was the third party beneficiary of a contract of bailment made in Connecticut, impliedly incorporating the Connecticut statute. It is small wonder that the *Daniels'* rationale has proven unacceptable in another court.[131] What is unfortunate is that the result should fall with the reasoning.

Maffatone v. Woodson, 99 N.J.Super. 559, 240 A.2d 693 (App. Div.), cert. denied, 51 N.J. 577, 242 A.2d 381 (1968) (New York owner's liability statute applicable to crash in New Jersey involving car owned by New York owner and injuring New York residents in another car); Farber v. Smolack, 20 N.Y.2d 198, 282 N.Y.S.2d 248, 229 N.E.2d 36 (1967) (New York owner's liability statute applicable to out-of-state accident injuring passengers in a car belonging to a New York owner); Victoria v. Smythe, 703 A.2d 619 (R.I. 1997) (apply owner's liability doctrine of Florida, where rental company has headquarters, to crash in Rhode Island of car rented in New Jersey). But see Heilmann v. Hertz Corp., 306 F.2d 100 (5th Cir.1962) (disagree with *Levy*; under Florida dangerous instrumentality doctrine claim must be in tort, not contract, and tort statute of limitations has run); Hanseman v. Hamilton, 176 F.Supp. 371 (D.Colo.1959) (lessor's liability under Colorado statute inapplicable to injury in Ohio); Boatwright v. Budak, 625 N.W.2d 483 (Minn. App. 2001) (Minnesota owner-liability statute not applicable to crash in Iowa of car rented in Minnesota, but recovery under Iowa law, which, unlike Minnesota law, does not have statutory limit on liability); Bannister v. Hertz Corp., 316 S.C. 513, 450 S.E.2d 629 (App. 1994), cert. dism'd (New York owner's liability statute not applicable to crash in North Carolina of car rented in New York); Perkins v. Dynasty Group Auto, 2003 WL 22810452 (Tex. App.—El Paso, 2003) (Florida "dangerous instrumentality" doctrine not applicable against Florida defendant when accident in Texas); Jack v. Enterprise Rent–A–Car Co. of Los Angeles, 899 P.2d 891 (Wyo. 1995) (California owner's liability statute not applicable to crash in Wyoming of car rented in California).

129. Cf. J.H.C. Morris, *The Proper Law of a Tort*, 64 Harv. L. Rev. 881, 890 (1951). But see Cheatham & Reese, *Choice of the Applicable Law*, 52 Colum. L. Rev. 959, 967 (1952): "[T]his purpose [incentive to lessor to choose customers with care] would have been substantially achieved even if the scope of the statute's application had been confined to Connecticut accidents."

130. See Garcia v. Plaza Oldsmobile Ltd., 421 F.3d 216 (2005) (Pennsylvania driver injured in Pennsylvania in collision with truck rented from New York company may recover under New York statute imposing vicarious liability on owner; there is a "false conflict" between New York and Pennsylvania law because applying New York law to permit Pennsylvania citizen's recovery does not undermine any Pennsylvania interest); cf. Budget Rent–A–Car System, Inc. v. Chappell, 407 F.3d 166 (3d Cir. 2005), cert. denied, 546 U.S. 978, 126 S.Ct. 567, 163 L.Ed.2d 463 (2005) (when driver rented automobile in Michigan, drove it to New York, and injured passenger in accident in Pennsylvania, New York vicarious liability law applies rather than Michigan law, which places $20,000 limit on lessor's liability; Pennsylvania, which does not impose vicarious liability on lessor, "does not have an interest in applying its law to this dispute" [Id. 177 n.9] and Michigan's interest in the extent of lessor's liability is doubtfully "implicated at all in this case" [id. 177]).

131. Hanseman v. Hamilton, 176 F.Supp. 371, 374 (D.Colo.1959) ("The characterization in the *Levy* case does not accord with the better view."); cf. Kline v. Wheels by Kinney, Inc., 464 F.2d 184 (4th Cir.1972) (New York vicarious liability statute cannot be construed as creating contractual liability, apply law of place of wrong under which renter not vicariously liable); Rogers v. U–Haul Co., 41 A.D.2d 834, 342 N.Y.S.2d 158 (1973) (New York vicarious liability rule not applicable to company that rented car in New York to New

There will be much less occasion to determine the extraterritorial application of a statute making an owner of a motor vehicle vicariously liable for the negligence of the driver. As part of its continuing program of "tort reform", Congress has enacted legislation nullifying any state law that imposes vicarious liability on motor vehicle rental companies.[132]

A group of Texas cases illustrates how, by shifting the problem's label from tort to contract, a court can avoid the undesirable effects of rigid application of the place-of-wrong rule. In *Carter v. Tillery*,[133] a private airplane, owned and operated by a Texas resident and carrying other Texas residents as passengers, crashed in Mexico as a result of losing course while returning to Texas from New Mexico. The injured passengers brought suit in Texas to recover for their injuries, but their action was dismissed for lack of jurisdiction. The court had to apply the Mexican method of computing damages, as the law of the place of wrong, but this was not possible in a Texas court. The Mexican method of computing damages was to provide periodic payments that could be modified from time to time as conditions affecting the plaintiffs' needs changed—somewhat analogous to a common-law alimony or support decree. The court, following a line of cases that included Mr. Justice Holmes' opinion in *Slater v. Mexican National Railroad*,[134] held that the law of the place of wrong was too dissimilar from Texas law to be transplanted to a Texas court. The action was dismissed even though Texas had a compelling interest in measuring the recovery of Texas plaintiffs against Texas defendants by Texas standards and there was no assurance that the airplane owner would be subject to the jurisdiction of a Mexican court.

In *Hudson v. Continental Bus System*,[135] the defendant invoked *Slater* and its ilk in an attempt to avoid a suit brought against a bus company by a passenger who had purchased a Mexican-tour ticket from the bus company in Texas. The plaintiff was injured in Mexico while using transportation arranged for by the defendant. The Texas court reversed a summary judgment for the defendant and refused to follow

---

York resident when accident in Pennsylvania, applying *Neumeier* rule 3—see §§ 6.22–6.23). Contra, Dreher v. Budget Rent–A–Car System, Inc., 272 Va. 390, 634 S.E.2d 324 (2006) (New York vicarious liability statute applies to permit Virginia residents injured in Virginia in collision with car rented in New York to recover against rental companies; the N.Y. statute "resembles a contractual provision" and therefore the Virginia choice-of-law rule, lex loci delicti, does not apply).

132. 49 U.S.C. § 30106(a): "An owner of a motor vehicle that rents or leases the vehicle to a person (or an affiliate of the owner) shall not be liable under the law of any State or political subdivision thereof, by reason of being the owner of the vehicle (or an affiliate of the owner), for harm to persons or property that results or arises out of the use, operation, or possession of the vehicle during the period of the rental or lease, if—(1) the owner (or an affiliate of the owner) is engaged in the trade or business of renting or leasing motor vehicles; and (2) there is no negligence or criminal wrongdoing on the part of the owner (or an affiliate of the owner)."

133. 257 S.W.2d 465 (Tex.Civ.App.1953), writ ref'd n.r.e., overruled, Gutierrez v. Collins, 583 S.W.2d 312 (Tex.1979).

134. 194 U.S. 120, 24 S.Ct. 581, 48 L.Ed. 900 (1904). See also El Paso & Juarez Traction Co. v. Carruth, 255 S.W. 159 (Tex.Com.App.1923), holding approved.

135. 317 S.W.2d 584 (Tex.Civ.App., 1958), writ ref'd n.r.e.

Carter and *Slater*. The court based its refusal to dismiss on the fact that the plaintiff had pleaded a cause of action in contract, not tort, alleging breach of an implied contract to carry her safely. Therefore the law of the place of contracting, Texas, rather than the law of the place of the wrong, Mexico, was applicable to determine whether and, if so, how defendant should compensate plaintiff for her injuries.[136]

In *Daniels' U–Drive* and in *Hudson*, the courts reached good results by switching the characterization of the action from tort to contract. There was a passing reference in *Daniels' U–Drive* to the purpose of the Connecticut bailor's liability statute as "providing an incentive to him who rented motor vehicles to rent them to competent and careful operators...."[137] Aside from this remark, there is little or no indication in *U–Drive* or in *Hudson* that the switch in labels was keyed to underlying domestic purposes or was other than an arbitrary occurrence.

Two Texas cases reveal the effect of switching to a consequences-based approach to choice of law. *Gutierrez v. Collins*[138] abandoned both the dissimilarity doctrine, which *Hudson* circumvented, and the place-of-wrong choice-of-law rule. Then *Trailways, Inc. v. Clark*,[139] which was a twin of *Hudson*, applied Texas law to a Mexican bus company without resorting to recharacterization, but on the grounds that Texas had the "most significant contacts" with the parties and the occurrence; it was fair to apply Texas law to the Mexican bus company in the light of the company's Texas contacts.[140]

§ 6.17 More Recharacterization: The Harbingers of Interest Analysis—Grant, Haumschild, and Kilberg

In the dozen years before the revolution in choice-of-law for torts became dramatically visible, courts decided three cases that, although reminiscent of old label-switchers like *Daniels' U–Drive*, partially articulated the premises for the sweeping changes that were to come. The

---

136. Accord, Garza v. Greyhound Lines, Inc., 418 S.W.2d 595 (Tex.Civ.App.1967).

Whether the liability of a successor corporation should be treated as a "tort" or "contract" issue has arisen in cases applying territorial choice-of-law rules. See In re Asbestos Litigation (Bell), 517 A.2d 697 (Del.Super. 1986) (contract); Brown v. Kleen Kut Mfg. Co., 238 Kan. 642, 714 P.2d 942 (1986) (contract). For cases in jurisdictions taking a functional approach, see Webb v. Rodgers Machinery Manufacturing Co., 750 F.2d 368 (5th Cir.1985) (place of incorporation has more significant relationship than place of injury); but cf. Young v. Fulton Iron Works Co., 709 S.W.2d 927 (Mo.App.1986) (apply tort rules of Second Restatement).

137. 108 Conn. at 336, 143 A. at 164.

138. 583 S.W.2d 312 (Tex. 1979).

139. 794 S.W.2d 479, 486–487 (Tex. App.—Corpus Christi, 1990, writ denied).

140. The Mexican company picked up the Texas passengers in Texas. The court reversed a judgment against a Texas bus company that had transported the passengers to the pick-up point and that had an interlining agreement with the Mexican company. The reason for the reversal was that the plaintiffs had sued the parent corporation instead of its Texas subsidiary and the parent was not liable.

cases are *Grant v. McAuliffe*,[141] *Haumschild v. Continental Casualty Company*,[142] and *Kilberg v. Northeast Airlines*.[143]

Grant concerned a collision in Arizona of two automobiles driven by California citizens. One driver died and, subsequently, plaintiffs, occupants of the other automobile, brought an action in California against his estate. Under California law, but not Arizona law, such an action survived the death of the tortfeasor. The California court, departing from the traditional path, permitted recovery. This result was highly desirable. California, as common domicile of all parties, had the sole interest in determining what balance should be struck between compensation of the injured and protection of the estate. On cursory examination the opinion appears to achieve this rational and just result by the arbitrary switching of the characterization label for the survival problem from "tort", first to "procedure" and then to "administration of estates." Judge Traynor's reference, in the last sentence of his opinion, to the fact that "all of the parties were residents of this state"[144] gave a glimpse of the more cogent reasons for the opinion.[145]

Haumschild v. Continental Casualty Company is a landmark case departing from the place-of-wrong rule on the issue of interspousal tort immunity. While a husband and wife domiciled in Wisconsin were driving in California, the husband's negligence injured the wife. Overruling a long line of Wisconsin cases, the best known of which is *Buckeye v. Buckeye*,[146] the court permitted the wife to sue her husband[147] and his liability insurer under Wisconsin law, although under California law, California being a community property state, a California wife could not then[148] maintain such a suit. The court did advert to the "family

---

141. 41 Cal.2d 859, 264 P.2d 944 (1953).

142. 7 Wis.2d 130, 95 N.W.2d 814 (1959).

143. 9 N.Y.2d 34, 211 N.Y.S.2d 133, 172 N.E.2d 526 (1961).

144. 41 Cal.2d at 867, 264 P.2d at 949.

145. See Traynor, *Is This Conflict Really Necessary?*, 37 Texas L. Rev. 657, 670 n.35 (1959):

"It may not be amiss to add that although the opinion in the case is my own, I do not regard it as ideally articulated, developed as it had to be against the brooding background of a petrified forest. Yet I would make no more apology for it than that in reaching a rational result it was less deft than it might have been to quit itself of the familiar speech of choice of law."

See also Traynor, Book Review, 1965 Duke L. J. 426, 431 (*Grant* was a "false conflicts" case). But see Kahn–Freund, *Delictual Liability and the Conflict of Laws*, II Recueil des Cours, Academy of Int'l Law 111 (1968) (would have solved *Grant* by classifying problem "as one of the law of succession or of administration of estates").

146. 203 Wis. 248, 234 N.W. 342 (1931).

147. The marriage had been annulled after the accident, but the decision does not rest on this ground.

148. The reason why a California wife could not sue her husband for negligence was that her recovery would be community property and the husband would profit from his own wrong. In California, the wife's recovery is no longer community property and a wife may sue her husband for negligence. Cal. Family Code § 781(c); Klein v. Klein, 58 Cal.2d 692, 26 Cal.Rptr. 102, 376 P.2d 70 (1962).

Emery v. Emery, 45 Cal.2d 421, 289 P.2d 218 (1955), held that the capacity of a minor child to sue a parent and whether or not a parent's action is community property, thus causing a husband's negligence to be imputed to the wife, are governed by the law of the

discord" policy for interspousal immunity, but the result seemed to rest upon reclassifying the immunity problem from one of "tort" to one of "family law, where domicile usually controls the law to be applied."[149]

Was there any objection to *Haumschild's* reaching a desirable result by simply changing the characterization label from "tort" to "family law"? After all, a good many commentators had urged achieving such a result by a change in characterization.[150] The answer is that *Haumschild's* articulating a choice-of-law rule in lieu of, instead of as a result of, a policy-centered analysis, created the danger, for a time realized in Wisconsin, that the new "domicile" rule would be applied in a deceptively analogous situation in which it would produce results as unjust and irrational as those it displaced. Three variations of the *Haumschild* problem of interspousal immunity illustrate the need for adjustments in choice-of-law analysis with changes in the law-fact pattern.

Case One. This is *Haumschild* itself and provides the simplest case for consequences-based analysis. The marital domicile permits husband-wife suits for negligence; the place of accident does not; the wife sues her husband at their domicile for negligence. This is a false conflict. The policy of the marital domicile favoring compensation is highly relevant in view of the settled residence of the parties in that place. The possible policies underlying the immunity rule of the state of the crash, preservation of domestic harmony and prevention of collusive suits against liability insurers,[151] are, at best, tangentially and officiously relevant to suits brought, husbands and wives resident, and cars principally garaged in a state that permits husband-wife suits.[152]

Case Two. This time it is the place of the accident that permits husband-wife suits. The marital domicile does not. The place of injury may have more significant interests in permitting recovery than it had in case one in denying it. The wife may have been treated in the state of injury at public expense or there may be local unpaid medical creditors.

---

domicile. The majority of *Haumschild* did not rest on this development in California law, although the concurring opinion stressed it.

Prior to the decision in *Haumschild*, California cases held that a wife's recovery against her husband was not community property if it resulted from a California accident but involved spouses domiciled in non-community-property states. See Bruton v. Villoria, 138 Cal.App.2d 642, 292 P.2d 638 (1956).

149. *Haumschild*, 7 Wis.2d at 137, 95 N.W.2d at 818.

150. See Cook, Logical and Legal Bases of the Conflict of Laws 346 (1942) ("capacity to sue"); Stumberg, Principles of Conflict of Laws 205 (3d ed. 1963) ("domestic relations"); Ford, *Interspousal Liability for Automobile Accidents in the Conflict of Laws: Law and Reason Versus the Restatement*, 15 U.Pitt. L. Rev. 397, 424 (1954) ("status"); Kelso, *Automobile Accidents and Indiana Conflict of Laws: Current Dilemmas*, 33 Ind.L. J. 297, 308 (1958) ("family relations").

151. If the state having a rule forbidding interspousal suits is a community property state, an additional policy underlying the rule may be to prevent the husband from sharing in the wife's recovery if, under that state's law, her recovery is community property. See supra note 148.

152. See, e.g., Potter v. St. Louis–San Francisco Ry., 622 F.2d 979 (8th Cir.1980) (applying Missouri law and stating that the immunity rule of forum, which was place of injury, not applicable to nonresident spouses); Robertson v. Estate of McKnight, 609 S.W.2d 534 (Tex.1980) (same).

The husband's liability policy may be the only available source from which to pay these bills. On the other hand, the marital domicile will have highly relevant policies of preserving marital harmony and preventing collusion. This is, then, a "real" conflict. Both states have, or potentially have, significant relevant and conflicting policies. It may be that the wise resolution of this true conflict will be in favor of application of the law of the marital domicile and the denial of capacity to sue. This will be a particularly appropriate result if, in fact, there are no unpaid medical creditors at the scene of the accident, thereby rendering that state's interest in recovery by the wife more hypothetical than real. In *Johnson v. Johnson*,[153] the Supreme Court of New Hampshire, although recognizing the difference between cases one[154] and two, decided that applying the interspousal immunity rule of Massachusetts, the marital domicile, would not seriously impair the policies of New Hampshire, as the place of the accident.

Case Three. Again the place of accident permits husband-wife suits. The marital domicile does not. This time the wife sues, not her husband, but the driver of the other automobile, who is domiciled in the state where the accident occurred. The issue is whether the defendant can implead the husband to obtain contribution toward payment of the judgment. Such an impleader would not be permitted in a purely domestic case at the marital domicile because the husband lacks the liability to his wife essential to contribution. But in the interstate situation, there is a real conflict that should probably be resolved in favor of the law of the place of the accident. The state where the accident occurred has a very real "interest" in permitting its citizen and his or her insurer, who issued the policy in that state, to obtain contribution in accordance with that state's notions of fairness.[155] The policies of the spouses' domicile in favor of marital harmony and against collusion may still be applicable in the light of the anti-impleader rule in a domestic case at the domicile. At the very least, the dangers of ill feeling between husband and wife or that the wife and husband will invent a story to milk the husband's liability insurer, are greatly attenuated when the wife sues, not her husband, but a third party. The danger of collusion

---

153.   107 N.H. 30, 216 A.2d 781 (1966).

154.   New Hampshire had decided case one in favor of the law of the marital domicile. Thompson v. Thompson, 105 N.H. 86, 193 A.2d 439 (1963); cf. Gordon v. Gordon, 118 N.H. 356, 387 A.2d 339 (1978) (do not apply marital immunity rule in suit between spouses who lived in Massachusetts at the time of the accident in New Hampshire but who have since moved to Maine—Massachusetts has retroactively abolished its marital immunity rule, and Maine has no interest in applying its immunity rule because the risk insured against was not influenced by Maine law); Taylor v. Bullock, 111 N.H. 214, 279 A.2d 585 (1971) (do not apply marital immunity rule of marital domicile at time of accident when spouses have since divorced and when co-defendant is New Hampshire resident).

155.   Cf. Sutton v. Langley, 330 So.2d 321 (La.App.1976), writ denied, no error, 333 So.2d 242 (La.1976) (do not apply Texas host liability standard when Louisiana co-defendants); Griggs v. Riley, 489 S.W.2d 469 (Mo.App.1972), application to transfer to Mo.S.Ct. denied (1973) (do not apply host-guest immunity of domicile when co-defendant is forum resident); Cirelli v. Ohio Cas. Ins. Co., 72 N.J. 380, 371 A.2d 17 (1977) (permit subrogation when this will shift costs to out-of-state insurer); Pierce v. Helz, 64 Misc.2d 131, 314 N.Y.S.2d 453 (1970) (do not apply parental immunity rule of domicile when co-defendants are New York residents).

can be eliminated by allowing the other driver to get contribution from the husband only after that driver has paid more than his or her share of the judgment.

Wisconsin, at first heedless of these distinctions, applied *Haumschild's* "domicile" rule to case three.[156] Later Wisconsin overruled this mistake, having seen that "domicile" as a territorial choice-of-law rule for problems of interspousal immunity is capable of producing results as "mechanical"[157] and unsatisfactory as had been produced by the place-of-wrong rule.

The last of this trio of transitional cases is *Kilberg v. Northeast Airlines.* A New York domiciliary boarded the defendant's airplane in New York, bound for Massachusetts. Defendant airline was incorporated in Massachusetts and transacted much business in both Massachusetts and New York. The airplane crashed in Massachusetts killing the New York passenger. His administrator brought suit in New York. The Massachusetts wrongful death act had a $15,000 limit on recovery and measured this recovery by the culpability of the defendant, rather than by the pecuniary loss to dependents. The administrator sought to avoid the Massachusetts death act's $15,000 limit on recovery by couching his action in contract terms, the theory being that the defendant had broken its implied promise to carry the decedent safely.[158] The Court of Appeals held that the contract count should be dismissed for insufficiency. The court reasoned that a contract action for wrongful death is unknown at common law and that therefore the suit must be brought under the wrongful death statute of the place of the wrong.[159] Then, however, in a considered dictum, the majority declared that the $15,000 limit in the Massachusetts statute was inapplicable. The court noted that in cases involving interstate airplane flights, "[t]he place of injury becomes entirely fortuitous. Our courts should if possible provide protection for our own State's people against unfair and anachronistic treatment of the

---

156. Haynie v. Hanson, 16 Wis.2d 299, 114 N.W.2d 443 (1962). Accord, Pirc v. Kortebein, 186 F.Supp. 621 (D.Wis.1960); cf., Dunn v. Beech Aircraft Corp., 271 F.Supp. 662 (D.Del.1967) (applies law of place of wrong to determine whether defendant can implead husband).

157. Zelinger v. State Sand & Gravel Co., 38 Wis.2d 98, 104, 156 N.W.2d 466, 468 (1968). See also LaChance v. Service Trucking Co., 215 F.Supp. 162 (D.C.Md.1963) (purposes of interspousal immunity are not relevant to a third party complaint against the husband); Restatement, Second § 169, comment *c*; cf. Pennington v. Dye, 456 So.2d 507 (Fla.App. 2d Dist.1984) (immunity rule of domicile applied to prevent contribution, but other driver also resides at spouses' domicile); B. Currie, *Justice Traynor and the Conflict of Laws,* 13 Stan. L. Rev. 719, 732 (1961); Hancock, *The Rise and Fall of Buckeye v. Buckeye,* 29 U. Chi. L. Rev. 237, 253–54 (1962). For a case rejecting the guest statute of the common domicile of host and guest when the issue is whether the host may be impleaded, see Castonzo v. General Cas. Co., 251 F.Supp. 948 (W.D.Wis.1966); cf. Heath v. Zellmer, 35 Wis.2d 578, 151 N.W.2d 664 (1967) (host and guests had different domiciles at time of accident, but both domiciliary states had guest statutes).

158. See Dyke v. Erie Ry., 45 N.Y. 113 (1871) (in recovery for injuries to New York citizen, damages limit of place of impact does not apply when contract of carriage made and completed in New York).

159. But see Griffith v. United Air Lines, Inc., 416 Pa. 1, 203 A.2d 796 (1964) (plaintiff may sue in assumpsit for negligent breach of contract of carriage that caused the death of plaintiff's decedent).

lawsuits which result from these disasters."[160] Instead of further developing these concepts, the court said that imposition of the Massachusetts limit on recovery was contrary to New York public policy and that, moreover, the question of whether or not there should be a limit on damages was "procedural" to be controlled by the law of the forum. Thus a wise and desirable resolution of the true conflict between New York's desire to provide adequate compensation for the death of the New York decedent and the interest of Massachusetts in shielding the defendant from what Massachusetts considered excessive liability[161] was made to appear an unfortunate step backward to the narrowly provincial thinking that relied upon the labels "procedural" and "public policy" to avoid applying a rule different from that of the forum.

Although *Grant, Haumschild*, and *Kilberg* reached desirable results and provided an important bridge between the rigid territorialism of place-of-wrong and the new policy-oriented analysis, their imperfect articulation of their premises created an appearance of arbitrary change from traditional ways. It is not surprising that other courts rejected their reasoning.[162] It is unfortunate that their results were rejected with their reasons.

§ 6.18 Rapid Acceptance of Policy and Interest Analysis

Schmidt v. Driscoll Hotel[163] might be identified as the case that opened the door to the modern replacement of the place-of-wrong rule with a method of analysis that focuses on the policies underlying putatively conflicting domestic tort rules. The defendant operated a bar in Minnesota. Defendant's bar served Mr. Sorrenson liquor until, allegedly, he became intoxicated and, as a result of this intoxication, overturned his automobile while driving in Wisconsin. Sorrenson's passenger, a Minnesota citizen, was injured and brought suit against the bar owners under the Minnesota dram shop act, which imposed civil liability upon liquor sellers under such circumstances. Wisconsin, the place of impact, would not have imposed civil liability.[164] The defendant, citing

---

160. *Kilberg*, 9 N.Y.2d at 39, 211 N.Y.S.2d at 135, 172 N.E.2d at 527–28.

161. For discussions of the desirability of establishing federal substantive law to provide compensation for injuries caused in interstate air flights, see Haller, *Death in the Air: Federal Regulation of Tort Liability a Must*, 54 Am.Bar.Assoc.J. 382 (1968); Tydings, *Air Crash Litigation: A Judicial Problem and a Congressional Solution*, 18 Am.U. L. Rev. 299 (1969). See also Kohr v. Allegheny Airlines, Inc., 504 F.2d 400 (7th Cir.1974), cert. denied, 421 U.S. 978, 95 S.Ct. 1980, 44 L.Ed.2d 470 (1975) (federal common law controls issues of contribution and indemnity in mid-air collision); Smith v. Cessna Aircraft Corp., 428 F.Supp. 1285 (N.D.Ill.1977) (*Kohr* not applicable to intrastate flight of single noncommercial airplane).

162. For rejection of *Grant*, see Allen v. Nessler, 247 Minn. 230, 76 N.W.2d 793 (1956). For rejection of *Kilberg*, see Cherokee Laboratories, Inc. v. Rogers, 398 P.2d 520 (Okl. 1965), overruled, Brickner v. Gooden, 525 P.2d 632 (Okl.1974). For rejection of *Haumschild*, see Shaw v. Lee, 258 N.C. 609, 129 S.E.2d 288 (1963), overruled by statute, N.C.Gen.Stat. § 52–5.1; Oshiek v. Oshiek, 244 S.C. 249, 136 S.E.2d 303 (1964), overruled, Boone v. Boone, 345 S.C. 8, 546 S.E.2d 191 (2001).

163. 249 Minn. 376, 82 N.W.2d 365 (1957).

164. Wis.Stat.Ann. § 176.35 (1955) (applicable only if sale to minor or, after notice to desist, to a habitual drunkard). Section 176.26 did make it a crime to sell to "any person intoxicated or bordering on intoxication."

the place-of-wrong rule, argued that the Minnesota dram shop act did not apply. The court rejected this argument and held that plaintiff could utilize the Minnesota statute. The holding was based on the court's perception that the policies underlying the Minnesota act, control of the activities of Minnesota bartenders and compensation to those injured, were fully applicable even though the plaintiff had been injured out of state.[165]

That the *Schmidt* decision was a landmark case is itself worthy of note. One situation in which it might be expected that a policy-centered analysis of choice of law would be commonplace is in the interpretation of statutes creating civil liability, when the plaintiff seeks to apply such a statute to harm suffered outside the enacting state. If the statute, as is typical, does not expressly cover the choice-of-law problem, the standard process of statutory construction would seem to demand an inquiry into the policies underlying the statute. Although, before the modern revolution in conflicts analysis, the United States Supreme Court had taken such an approach in determining the territorial application of various federal statutes,[166] the record elsewhere was very disappointing.

165. See in accord, Rong Yao Zhou v. Jennifer Mall Restaurant, Inc., 534 A.2d 1268 (D.C.App.1987); Green v. Wilson, 455 Mich. 342, 565 N.W.2d 813 (1997); Pardey v. Boulevard Billiard Club, 518 A.2d 1349 (R.I.1986); cf. Zucker v. Vogt, 329 F.2d 426 (2d Cir.1964) (Connecticut dram shop act permits recovery against owner of Connecticut bar illegally serving liquor causing fatal injuries to a New York resident in New York, New York having a similar dram shop act); Hoeller v. Riverside Resort Hotel, 169 Ariz. 452, 820 P.2d 316 (App. 1991), rev. denied (applying Arizona dram shop act to Nevada casino); Carver v. Schafer, 647 S.W.2d 570 (Mo.App.1983) (Missouri common law rule of unlimited liability rather than Illinois dram shop statutory limit of $20,000 applicable to Illinois bar 10 miles from border when intoxicated Missouri driver hit Missouri resident in Missouri) (Mo. Stat. Ann. § 537.053 modified the common law liability created by *Carver*); Thoring v. LaCounte, 225 Mont. 77, 733 P.2d 340 (1987) (common law liability, deciding that the North Dakota decision in Thoring v. Bottonsek, cited infra in this note, does not prevent suit in Montana).

Illinois has refused to apply its dram shop act to compensate an Illinois resident injured in Wisconsin by an Illinois drunk sold liquor by an Illinois defendant, reasoning that the Illinois act is presumed to have no extraterritorial effect; that Illinois courts have in the past refused to apply the act to out-of-state injuries and the legislature has not amended the statute; that the act "is particularly severe" not requiring any illegal sale of the intoxicating liquor and including among those made liable the owner or lessor of the building in which a bar is located. Graham v. General U.S. Grant Post No. 2665, 43 Ill.2d 1, 248 N.E.2d 657 (1969). See also Waynick v. Chicago's Last Dep't Store, 269 F.2d 322 (7th Cir.1959) cert. denied, 362 U.S. 903, 80 S.Ct. 611, 4 L.Ed.2d 554 (1960) (Illinois statute does not apply when collision in Michigan, nor Michigan statute when liquor served in Illinois, although court bases civil liability on violation of Illinois criminal statute); Estates of Braun v. Cactus Pete's, Inc., 108 Idaho 798, 702 P.2d 836 (1985) (Idaho dram shop statute not applicable to saloon just across border in Nevada although intoxicated driver and victims were Idaho residents and Nevada has no civil liability); Liff v. Haezbroeck, 51 Ill.App.2d 70, 200 N.E.2d 525 (1964) (liquor served in Illinois, drunk caused damage in Iowa, recovery denied under either Illinois or Iowa dram shop acts); Ling v. Jan's Liquors, 237 Kan. 629, 703 P.2d 731 (1985) (apply forum's law as law of place of injury to excuse a Missouri bar for injury to a Kansas citizen even though Missouri has dram shop liability, rejecting the "analytical approach"); Manfredonia v. American Airlines, Inc., 68 A.D.2d 131, 416 N.Y.S.2d 286 (2d Dept. 1979) (New York dram shop statute not applicable when sale occurred outside New York on airplane that had departed from New York); Goodwin v. Young, 34 Hun. 252 (N.Y.S.Ct.1884) (New York statute not applicable when damage in Vermont); Thoring v. Bottonsek, 350 N.W.2d 586 (N.D.1984) (North Dakota dram shop act not applicable although injury in North Dakota to North Dakota resident when drinks served at bar in Montana 8 miles from border).

166. See Romero v. International Terminal Operating Co., 358 U.S. 354, 384, 79 S.Ct. 468, 486, 3 L.Ed.2d 368, 389 (1959) ("The amount and type of recovery which a foreign

It was *Babcock v. Jackson*,[167] decided six years after *Schmidt*, that set the pattern of consequences-based analysis that other courts swiftly followed. A New York host drove his New York guest into Ontario on a weekend trip. In Ontario, the host lost control of the automobile and it went off the highway into a stone wall. The guest sued her host in New York to recover for the harm caused to her by his negligence. Ontario had an extreme form of guest statute, completely barring any action by the guest against the host.[168] New York had no guest statute and permitted the guest to recover for the host's ordinary negligence.

The Court of Appeals held that New York, not Ontario, law governed the right of the guest to recover against the host. The court found that the policy underlying the Ontario guest statute was to prevent collusion between host and guest against the host's liability insurer and noted that "[w]hether New York defendants are imposed upon or their insurers defrauded by a New York plaintiff is scarcely a valid legislative concern of Ontario...."[169] New York's policy of requiring the host to compensate the guest was, moreover, fully applicable to this out-of-state accident involving New York residents. Furthermore, the court announced that thereafter, instead of invariably applying the law of the place of the wrong to torts conflicts cases, it would give "controlling effect to the law of the jurisdiction which, because of its relationship or

seaman may receive from his foreign employer while sailing on a foreign ship should not depend on the wholly fortuitous circumstance of the place of injury."—affirming dismissal of seaman's Jones Act and general maritime claims against his employer); Lauritzen v. Larsen, 345 U.S. 571, 578, 73 S.Ct. 921, 926, 97 L.Ed. 1254, 1265 (1953) (Jones Act) ("We are simply dealing with a problem of statutory construction...."); McCulloch v. Sociedad Nacional de Marineros de Honduras, 372 U.S. 10, 17, 83 S.Ct. 671, 675, 9 L.Ed.2d 547, 553 (1963) ("Since the parties all agree that the Congress has constitutional power to apply the National Labor Relations Act to the crews working foreign-flag ships, at least while they are in American waters ... we go directly to the question whether Congress exercised that power."—held not applicable, possibility of international discord); Steele v. Bulova Watch Co., 344 U.S. 280, 282–83, 73 S.Ct. 252, 254, 97 L.Ed. 319, 323 (1952) (Lanham Act) ("Resolution of the jurisdictional issue in this case therefore depends on construction of exercised congressional power, not the limitations upon that power itself."). But cf., American Banana Co. v. United Fruit Co., 213 U.S. 347, 357, 29 S.Ct. 511, 513, 53 L.Ed. 826, 832 (1909) (Sherman Act) ("The foregoing considerations would lead in case of doubt to a construction of any statute as intended to be confined in its operation and effect to the territorial limits over which the lawmaker has general and legitimate power.") W.S Kirkpatrick & Co. v. Environmental Tectonics Corp., Int'l, 493 U.S. 400, 407, 110 S.Ct. 701, 107 L.Ed.2d 816 (1990) noted that *American Banana*'s holding that the Sherman Act had no extraterritorial application has been "substantially overruled."

167. 12 N.Y.2d 473, 240 N.Y.S.2d 743, 191 N.E.2d 279 (1963). See Comments on *Babcock*, 63 Colum. L. Rev. 1212 (1963) (Professors Cavers, Cheatham, Currie, Ehrenzweig, Leflar, and Reese).

168. The Ontario statute has since been amended to permit recovery for gross negligence or willful misconduct. (Stat.Ont., 1966 c. 64 § 20) and then repealed (Stat.Ont., 1977 c. 54 § 16(1)).

169. *Babcock*, 12 N.Y.2d at 483, 240 N.Y.S.2d at 750, 191 N.E.2d at 284. See also Gordon v. Kramer, 124 Ariz. 442, 604 P.2d 1153 (App.1979) (refuse to apply Utah guest statute to Arizona host and guest when accident in Utah).

contact with the occurrence or the parties has the greatest concern with the specific issue raised in the litigation."[170]

In *Griffith v. United Air Lines*,[171] the Pennsylvania Supreme Court quickly followed the path that New York had marked in *Babcock* and abandoned the place-of-wrong rule for torts "in favor of a more flexible rule which permits analysis of the policies and interests underlying the particular issue before the court."[172] A Pennsylvania domiciliary purchased a round-trip ticket from the airline in Pennsylvania for a flight between Pennsylvania and Arizona. On the trip to Arizona, in the course of landing at Denver, an intermediate scheduled stop, the airplane crashed, causing the immediate death of the Pennsylvania domiciliary. The decedent's executor sued the airline in Pennsylvania.

The issue was whether the Colorado or the Pennsylvania survival act applied. The Colorado survival act would permit no recovery in this case of instantaneous death because that act limited survival recovery to earnings lost and expenses sustained by the decedent between the time of injury and death. The Pennsylvania survival act permitted recovery of the present value of the decedent's probable future earnings for the period of life expectancy, less the cost of decedent's own maintenance during the period that he or she would have lived, and less the amount that decedent would have spent to support a spouse and children. The portion of future earnings that would have been spent to support the wife and children, could then be recovered for them under the Pennsylvania wrongful death act, while the Colorado wrongful death act would limit this item of recovery to $25,000.

In order to avoid Colorado law and the place-of-wrong rule, the executor commenced an action "in assumpsit." In another landmark aspect of this case, the court held "that plaintiff may bring a valid action in assumpsit for the alleged negligent breach of contract of carriage which caused the death of plaintiff's decedent."[173] The plaintiff's hopes may have been temporarily dashed when the court added that "since the action is for negligent breach, not simple breach, of contract . . . the choice of law will be the same whether the action is labeled trespass or assumpsit."[174] But going on to focus on the purposes underlying the Colorado and Pennsylvania wrongful-death laws, the court applied Pennsylvania law, not because of any characterization legerdemain, but because it found that Pennsylvania's policies were highly pertinent while Colorado's had very slight relevance, if any. The court reasoned as follows. Pennsylvania was as interested in applying its more liberal form of recovery for the benefit of the Pennsylvania surviving dependents as if the crash had been in Pennsylvania. Application of Pennsylvania law would not unfairly surprise the defendant, which did not shape its

---

170. *Babcock*, 12 N.Y.2d at 481, 240 N.Y.S.2d at 749, 191 N.E.2d at 283.

171. 416 Pa. 1, 203 A.2d 796 (1964).

172. Id. at 21, 203 A.2d at 805.

173. Id. at 10, 203 A.2d at 800.

174. Id. at 11, 203 A.2d at 800.

conduct in reliance on Colorado law. If the purpose underlying the Colorado restricted recovery for wrongful death was to relieve Colorado courts of the speculative computation of future earnings reduced to present value, this policy was inapplicable in a Pennsylvania forum. If Colorado's purpose was to shield Colorado defendants from large verdicts, Colorado had some interest in protecting United Air Lines and encouraging its activities in Colorado, but this interest seemed slight when placed against the fact that United was not incorporated in Colorado and did business in many other states, including Pennsylvania.

It should be noted that this last link in the Pennsylvania court's chain of reasoning involved weighing Pennsylvania interests against those of Colorado. This is a difficult task for any court to undertake and in any but the clearest case, as perhaps *Griffith* was, the court's announcement that its own interests are found to be weightier is not likely to be particularly cogent. For example, the Pennsylvania court could not have disposed of the problem by dismissing the protective policies of the other state as insignificant if the plane had belonged to Northeast Airlines and the other state had been Massachusetts, the place of incorporation and main office of Northeast. In terms of setting a pattern for future decisions, it might have been preferable for the Pennsylvania court to recognize that both Colorado and Pennsylvania had interests in having their different laws applied. Then the court should have resolved this conflict of interests in favor of Pennsylvania law under a "better law" criterion.[175]

As of September 1, 2009, the courts of forty states plus the District of Columbia and Puerto Rico have followed the way lighted by *Babcock* and *Griffith* and have displaced the place-of-wrong rule as the sole choice-of-law rule for torts.[176] In addition, in North Carolina, when the

---

175. For discussion of the better law concept see §§ 6.9, note 37 and accompanying text, 6.29.

176. Alaska: Ehredt v. DeHavilland Aircraft Co., 705 P.2d 446 (Alaska 1985) (apply Alaska law as that of state with most significant relationship to determine recovery for wrongful death of Alaska resident in Alaska); Armstrong v. Armstrong, 441 P.2d 699 (Alaska, 1968) (interspousal immunity, law of Alaskan domicile applied to permit recovery, but court reserves the question of whether it will apply state-interest analysis in other situations).

Arizona: Bryant v. Silverman, 146 Ariz. 41, 703 P.2d 1190 (1985) (applying Arizona law to increase compensation in suit against Arizona airline to recover for injury and death resulting to Arizona residents in Colorado crash); Wendelken v. Superior Court, 137 Ariz. 455, 671 P.2d 896 (En banc 1983) (liability of person with possessory interest in realty); Schwartz v. Schwartz, 103 Ariz. 562, 447 P.2d 254 (1968) (interspousal immunity, law of Arizona domicile applied to permit recovery, court adopting "contacts" approach of Second Restatement).

Arkansas: Wallis v. Mrs. Smith's Pie Co., 261 Ark. 622, 550 S.W.2d 453 (1977) (apply Arkansas comparative negligence rule rather than Missouri contributory negligence rule to collision in Missouri between Arkansas plaintiff and truck owned by company authorized to do business in Arkansas).

California: Reich v. Purcell, 67 Cal.2d 551, 63 Cal.Rptr. 31, 432 P.2d 727 (1967) (statutory limit on wrongful death recovery) (see comments on *Reich* in 15 U.C.L.A. L. Rev. 552 (1968) by twelve professors); Fuller v. Greenup, 267 Cal.App.2d 10, 72 Cal.Rptr. 531 (1968) (guest statute).

Colorado: First Nat'l Bk. v. Rostek, 182 Colo. 437, 514 P.2d 314 (1973) (refuse to apply guest statute of place of crash when host and guest Colorado spouses and declare that in the future will apply to tort conflicts the most significant relationship test of the Restatement, Second).

Connecticut: O'Connor v. O'Connor, 201 Conn. 632, 519 A.2d 13 (1986) (permitting recovery by Connecticut passenger against Connecticut driver under Connecticut law although barred under the government-funded compensation scheme of Quebec, the place of the accident).

Delaware: Travelers Indem. Co. v. Lake, 594 A.2d 38 (Del. 1991) (applying "most significant relationship" analysis to hold that Delaware law determines amount Delaware insured entitled to recover against unidentified uninsured motorist and not law of Quebec where injury occurred, which would limit recovery to $29,400).

District of Columbia: Gaither v. Myers, 404 F.2d 216 (D.C.Cir.1968) (D.C. statute creating civil liability for harm caused by owner's leaving keys in car applied to harm in Maryland); Williams v. Rawlings Truck Line, Inc., 357 F.2d 581 (D.C.Cir.1965) (whether former owner of automobile estopped to deny ownership for purposes of owner's liability statute). But see Kay, *Theory into Practice: Choice of Law in the Courts*, 34 Mercer L. Rev. 521, 544–45 (1983) (doubt about District of Columbia's continued commitment to interest analysis).

Florida: Bishop v. Florida Specialty Paint Co., 389 So.2d 999 (Fla.1980) (refuse to apply South Carolina airplane guest statute to Florida host and guest, adopting approach of Restatement Second).

Hawaii: Peters v. Peters, 63 Hawaii 653, 634 P.2d 586 (1981) (adopt interest analysis and apply forum spousal immunity rule to New York spouses who rented car in Hawaii).

Idaho: Johnson v. Pischke, 108 Idaho 397, 700 P.2d 19 (1985) (adopts interest analysis to apply forum's longer statute of limitations to wrongful death recovery, quoting from section 6.8 in prior edition, now section 6.10).

Illinois: Esser v. McIntyre, 169 Ill.2d 292, 214 Ill.Dec. 693, 661 N.E.2d 1138 (1996) (applying Illinois law to suit between Illinois residents arising from slip and fall accident in Mexico); Ingersoll v. Klein, 46 Ill.2d 42, 262 N.E.2d 593 (1970) (measure of wrongful death recovery, car owner's liability—adopts "most significant contacts" rule for tort cases); Wartell v. Formusa, 34 Ill.2d 57, 213 N.E.2d 544 (1966) (immunity rule of forum-domicile rather than immunity rule of place of accident precludes wife's action against her husband's estate).

Indiana: Hubbard Mfg. Co., Inc. v. Greeson, 515 N.E.2d 1071 (Ind. 1987) (apply Indiana assumption of risk rule to bar recovery by Indiana citizen injured in Illinois while using product of Indiana manufacturer). Simon v. United States, 805 N.E.2d 798 (Ind. 2004), however, declares that "Indiana is still primarily a *lex loci* state" (id. at 802). The court will displace the law of the place of injury if it finds that another state "has the most significant relationship with the action." In making that determination the court will "simply look at the contacts that exist between the action and the relevant states" and will not "undertake the difficult and ultimately speculative task of identifying the policies underlying the laws of multiple states and weighing the potential advancement of each in the context of the case" (id. at 803).

Iowa: Fuerste v. Bemis, 156 N.W.2d 831 (Iowa 1968) (apply Iowa guest statute to suit between Iowa host and guest when crash in Wisconsin); Fabricius v. Horgen, 257 Iowa 268, 132 N.W.2d 410 (1965) (measure of damages for wrongful death).

Kentucky: Wessling v. Paris, 417 S.W.2d 259 (Ky.1967) (guest statute). And see Arnett v. Thompson, 433 S.W.2d 109, 113 (Ky.1968) (will apply Kentucky law whenever "Kentucky has enough contacts to justify applying Kentucky law"). But cf. Bonnlander v. Leader Nat'l Ins. Co., 949 S.W.2d 618 (Ky. App. 1996), rev. denied (holding that the preference for Kentucky law stated in *Arnett* applies to tort actions but "in contract actions . . . the law of the state with the greatest interest in the outcome of the litigation should be applied").

Louisiana: Jagers v. Royal Indem. Co., 276 So.2d 309 (La.1973) (intrafamily immunity). Choice of law in Louisiana is now codified in a manner that takes a consequences-based approach. La. Civ. Code Ann. arts. 14, 3515–3549.

Maine: Beaulieu v. Beaulieu, 265 A.2d 610 (Me.1970) (guest's recovery against host driver).

Massachusetts: Pevoski v. Pevoski, 371 Mass. 358, 358 N.E.2d 416 (1976) (interspousal immunity).

Michigan: Sutherland v. Kennington Truck Serv., Ltd., 454 Mich. 274, 275, 286, 562 N.W.2d 466, 467, 471 (1997) (applying Michigan's longer statute of limitations to a suit arising from a collision in Michigan of cars driven by residents of Ontario and Ohio, declaring that "because neither Ohio nor Ontario have an interest in having its law applied, Michigan law will apply" and that "we will apply Michigan law unless a 'rational reason' to do otherwise exists"); Olmstead v. Anderson, 428 Mich. 1, 400 N.W.2d 292 (1987) (do not apply limit on wrongful death liability of the state where the crash occurred to a suit involving Michigan and Minnesota parties when neither of these states places a limit on recovery); Sexton v. Ryder Truck Rental, Inc., 413 Mich. 406, 320 N.W.2d 843 (1982) (Michigan owner's liability laws apply when parties are Michigan residents, although automobile or plane crash occurred in state where no liability).

Minnesota: Schneider v. Nichols, 280 Minn. 139, 158 N.W.2d 254 (1968) (guest statute); Balts v. Balts, 273 Minn. 419, 142 N.W.2d 66 (1966) (law of forum-domicile rather than that of place of accident applied to permit mother to sue son); Kopp v. Rechtzigel, 273 Minn. 441, 141 N.W.2d 526 (1966) (guest statute).

Mississippi: Turner v. Pickens, 235 So.2d 272 (Miss.1970) (guest statute); Mitchell v. Craft, 211 So.2d 509 (Miss.1968) (comparative negligence rule of mutual domicile applied rather than contributory negligence rule of place of wrong).

Missouri: Kennedy v. Dixon, 439 S.W.2d 173 (Mo.1969) (guest statute).

Montana: Phillips v. General Motors Corp., 298 Mont. 438, 995 P.2d 1002 (2000) (adopt Restatement Second most significant relationship test; refuse to apply Kansas statute of repose to claim of Montana residents when vehicle purchased in North Carolina crashed in Kansas).

Nebraska: Heinze v. Heinze, 274 Neb. 595, 742 N.W.2d 465 (2007) (apply Nebraska guest statute, which bars actions against a spouse or a person within the second degree of consanguinity except for injuries caused by intoxication or gross negligence; statute barred action between Nebraska spouses for injuries in Colorado because, applying § 146 of the Restatement (Second) of Conflict of Laws, Nebraska has a more significant relationship to the occurrence and the parties); Harper v. Silva, 224 Neb. 645, 399 N.W.2d 826 (1987) (apply Nebraska law to limit liability of Nebraska doctor).

Nevada: General Motors Corp. v. Eighth Judicial District Court, 122 Nev. 466, 134 P.3d 111 (2006), overruled Motenko v. MGM Dist. Inc., 112 Nev. 1038, 921 P.2d 933 (1996) and adopted the Restatement (Second) "most significant relationship test." *Motenko* stated that forum law applies unless another state has an "overwhelming interest" indicated by being the place of at least two of the following contacts: place of conduct, place of injury, domicile or places of incorporation or business of parties, where parties' relationship centered. The court rejected the *Motenko* approach because it "reduces the conflict-of-laws analysis in tort actions to a quantitative comparison of contacts, without any regard to a qualitative comparison of true conflicts-of-law between states." 134 P.3d at 115.

New Hampshire: Schneider v. Schneider, 110 N.H. 70, 260 A.2d 97 (1969) (interspousal immunity); Clark v. Clark, 107 N.H. 351, 222 A.2d 205 (1966) (guest statute); Johnson v. Johnson, 107 N.H. 30, 216 A.2d 781 (1966) (interspousal immunity, apply Massachusetts immunity rule to Massachusetts wife injured in New Hampshire); Thompson v. Thompson, 105 N.H. 86, 193 A.2d 439 (1963) (interspousal immunity).

New Jersey: Pfau v. Trent Aluminum Co., 55 N.J. 511, 263 A.2d 129 (1970) (guest statute, host and guest from different states, neither of which has a guest statute, crash in state with guest statute, hold statute not applicable despite place-of-wrong rule followed in guest's state); Mellk v. Sarahson, 49 N.J. 226, 229 A.2d 625 (1967) (guest statute); Dolan v. Sea Transfer Corp., 398 N.J.Super. 313, 942 A.2d 29 (2008), cert. denied, 195 N.J. 520, 950 A.2d 907 (2008) (New York owner's liability statute applicable to injury in New Jersey to New Jersey resident driving back home from work in New York; N.Y. driver negligently attached cargo in N.Y. to truck based in N.Y.); Van Dyke v. Bolves, 107 N.J.Super. 338, 258 A.2d 372 (App.Div.1969) (motor vehicle owner's liability); Maffatone v. Woodson, 99 N.J.Super. 559, 240 A.2d 693 (App.Div.1968), cert. denied, 51 N.J. 577, 242 A.2d 381 (1968) (owner's liability statute).

New York: Schultz v. Boy Scouts of America, Inc., 65 N.Y.2d 189, 491 N.Y.S.2d 90, 480 N.E.2d 679 (1985) (charitable immunity); Tooker v. Lopez, 24 N.Y.2d 569, 301 N.Y.S.2d 519, 249 N.E.2d 394 (1969) (guest statute); Miller v. Miller, 22 N.Y.2d 12, 290 N.Y.S.2d 734, 237 N.E.2d 877 (1968) (limit on wrongful death recovery); Farber v. Smolack, 20 N.Y.2d 198, 282 N.Y.S.2d 248, 229 N.E.2d 36 (1967) (extraterritorial application of owner's liability statute); James v. Powell, 19 N.Y.2d 249, 279 N.Y.S.2d 10, 225 N.E.2d 741 (1967) (fraudulent conveyance) (for criticism, see Ehrenzweig & Westen, *Fraudulent Conveyances in the Conflict of Laws: Easy Cases May Make Bad Law*, 66 Mich. L. Rev. 1679 (1968)); Long v. Pan American World Airways, Inc., 16 N.Y.2d 337, 266 N.Y.S.2d 513, 213 N.E.2d

796 (1965) (wrongful death); Babcock v. Jackson, 12 N.Y.2d 473, 240 N.Y.S.2d 743, 191 N.E.2d 279 (1963) (guest statute). For a discussion of choice of law in New York under the "*Numeier* rules" see §§ 6.22, 6.23.

North Dakota: Issendorf v. Olson, 194 N.W.2d 750 (N.D.1972) (apply North Dakota contributory negligence rule to suit between North Dakota residents rather than comparative negligence rule of place of wrong).

Ohio: Morgan v. Biro Mfg. Co., 15 Ohio St.3d 339, 474 N.E.2d 286 (1984) (products liability, adopting approach of Restatement Second); Fox v. Morrison Motor Freight, Inc., 25 Ohio St.2d 193, 267 N.E.2d 405, 54 O.O.2d 301 (1971), cert. denied, 403 U.S. 931, 91 S.Ct. 2254, 29 L.Ed.2d 710 (1971) (limit on wrongful death recovery).

Oklahoma: White v. White, 618 P.2d 921 (Okl.1980) (spousal immunity); Brickner v. Gooden, 525 P.2d 632 (Okl.1974) (personal injury suit between Oklahoma residents, "most significant relationship" rule adopted in torts).

Oregon: Oregon has enacted a choice-of-law code for "noncontractual claims." Senate Bill 561, 75th Oregon Legislative Assembly, 2009 Regular Session. The code is generally consistent with applying the law of a jurisdiction if the failure to apply its laws would impair its policies. Earlier case law abandoning the law of the place of wrong: DeFoor v. Lematta, 249 Or. 116, 437 P.2d 107 (1968) (limit on wrongful death recovery); Casey v. Manson Constr. & Eng'r Co., 247 Or. 274, 428 P.2d 898 (1967) (loss of consortium); Nafzinger & Dixon, *Oregon's Choice-of-Law Process*, 60 Ore. L. Rev. 219 (1981).

Pennsylvania: Prince v. Trustees of Univ. of Pennsylvania, 282 F.Supp. 832 (E.D.Pa. 1968) (charitable immunity); Spector v. West Elizabeth Lumber Co., 37 F.R.D. 539 (W.D.Pa.1965) (contribution among joint tortfeasors); Kuchinic v. McCrory, 422 Pa. 620, 222 A.2d 897 (1966) (guest statute); Elston v. Industrial Lift Truck Co., 420 Pa. 97, 216 A.2d 318 (1966) (whether workmen's compensation law precludes third party sued by injured employee from impleading the employer); McSwain v. McSwain, 420 Pa. 86, 215 A.2d 677 (1966) (immunity rule of the forum-domicile rather than the law of the place of accident applied to preclude wife from suing her husband for the wrongful death of their child); Griffith v. United Air Lines, Inc., 416 Pa. 1, 203 A.2d 796 (1964) (wrongful death).

Puerto Rico: Widow of Fornaris v. American Surety Co., 93 P.R.R. 28 (1966) (limit on wrongful death recovery).

Rhode Island: Tiernan v. Westext Transport, Inc., 295 F.Supp. 1256 (D.R.I.1969) (wrongful death); Brown v. Church of the Holy Name of Jesus, 105 R.I. 322, 252 A.2d 176 (1969) (charitable immunity and wrongful death); Woodward v. Stewart, 104 R.I. 290, 243 A.2d 917 (1968), cert. dism'd, 393 U.S. 957, 89 S.Ct. 387, 21 L.Ed.2d 371 (1968) (host's liability).

South Dakota: Chambers v. Dakotah Charter, Inc., 488 N.W.2d 63 (S.D. 1992) (adopting most significant relationship approach and applying stricter South Dakota comparative negligence rule rather than Missouri comparative negligence to deny recovery to South Dakota passenger injured by South Dakota bus company's negligence in Missouri).

Tennessee: Hataway v. McKinley, 830 S.W.2d 53 (Tenn. 1992) (adopting "most significant relationship" approach of Restatement, Second and applying Tennessee law of contributory negligence between Tennessee residents rather than comparative negligence rule of Arkansas where death occurred during scuba dive).

Texas: Gutierrez v. Collins, 583 S.W.2d 312 (Tex.1979) (personal injury suit, "most significant relationship" rule adopted in torts).

Utah: Forsman v. Forsman, 779 P.2d 218 (Utah 1989) (apply law of marital domicile to permit suit between California spouses arising from Utah automobile accident even though the Utah rule is marital immunity).

Vermont: Miller v. White, 167 Vt. 45, 702 A.2d 392 (1997) (in suit between Vermont residents arising out of single-vehicle crash in Quebec, Vermont law determines liability of driver to passenger); Amiot v. Ames, 166 Vt. 288, 693 A.2d 675 (1997) (adopting most significant relationship approach to determine whether Vermont or Quebec law applies to claim of Canadian motorist injured by Vermont motorist just across border in Quebec and remand for determination under that approach).

Washington: Johnson v. Spider Staging Corp., 87 Wn.2d 577, 555 P.2d 997 (1976) (limit on wrongful death recovery); Werner v. Werner, 84 Wn.2d 360, 526 P.2d 370 (1974) (negligence in notarizing deeds).

Wisconsin: Conklin v. Horner, 38 Wis.2d 468, 157 N.W.2d 579 (1968) (guest statute, apply Wisconsin law to permit Illinois guest to sue Illinois host contrary to Illinois law); Zelinger v. State Sand & Gravel Co., 38 Wis.2d 98, 156 N.W.2d 466 (1968) (interspousal immunity); Heath v. Zellmer, 35 Wis.2d 578, 151 N.W.2d 664 (1967) (guest statute, impleader); Wilcox v. Wilcox, 26 Wis.2d 617, 133 N.W.2d 408 (1965) (guest statute); Satchwill v. Vollrath Co., 293 F.Supp. 533 (E.D.Wis.1968) (wrongful death); Angel v. Ray, 285 F.Supp. 64 (E.D.Wis.1968) (comparative negligence); Castonzo v. General Cas. Co., 251 F.Supp. 948 (W.D.Wis.1966) (guest statute); Geehan v. Monahan, 257 F.Supp. 278 (E.D.Wis.1966) (guest statute, host and guest have different residences, but neither residence has a guest statute).

In addition to the clear holdings above, see:

Kansas: In re K.M.H., 285 Kan. 53, 169 P.3d 1025 1032 (2007) ("Kansas courts have often leaned toward a *lex fori*, or law of the forum, approach, opting to apply Kansas law absent a clear showing that another state's law should apply"; applying Kansas law to artificial insemination in Missouri to hold that donor had no parental rights); St. Paul Surplus Lines Ins. Co. v. International Playtex, Inc., 245 Kan. 258, 269, 777 P.2d 1259, 1267 (1989), cert. denied, 493 U.S. 1036, 110 S.Ct. 758, 107 L.Ed.2d 774 (1990) (noting that "[c]ertain states have now abandoned the lex loci rule in favor of the 'most significant relationship' test" and reserving "consideration" of that test "for a later day"; applies Kansas law holding Illinois insurer need not pay punitive damages award assessed against Delaware insured in Kansas suit for death of Kansas citizen on ground that payment would violate Kansas public policy).

Maryland: Wells v. Liddy, 186 F.3d 505, 528 (4th Cir. 1999), cert. denied, 528 U.S. 1118, 120 S.Ct. 939, 145 L.Ed.2d 817 (2000) (noting that "[I]n recent years, the Court of Appeals of Maryland has indicated its willingness to apply more flexible choice-of-law rules from the Second Restatement in situations when the First Restatement rules have become unworkable" and predicting that Maryland would use the rule of the Second Restatement to choose law for multistate defamation); Hauch v. Connor, 295 Md. 120, 453 A.2d 1207 (1983) (although would apply lex loci to torts, apply interest analysis to whether one Maryland employee can sue another for an injury arising in Delaware in the course of employment). But see Erie Ins. Exchange v. Heffernan, 399 Md. 598, 625, 925 A.2d 636, 651 (2007) ("We see no reason to discontinue our adherence to the principles of lex loci delicti").

New Mexico: Ferrell v. Allstate Ins. Co., 144 N.M. 405, 188 P.3d 1156, 1173 (2008) ("the Restatement (Second) is a more appropriate approach for multi-state contract class actions"); Torres v. State, 119 N.M. 609, 613 894 P.2d 386, 390 (1995) (stating that N.M. "generally follows the doctrine of lex loci delicti" but not "if such application would violate New Mexico public policy"; public policy requires that N.M. law apply to determine liability of N.M. officials for death in California); In re Estate of Gilmore, 124 N.M. 119, 125, 946 P.2d 1130, 1136 (App. 1997) (stating that the "approach, if not the result, in *Torres* is consistent with the Restatement Second" and that "we begin with a strong presumption in favor of application of the place-of-wrong rule, but we will not close our eyes to compelling arguments for departure from the general rule in specific circumstances").

North Carolina: Boudreau v. Baughman, 322 N.C. 331, 368 S.E.2d 849 (1988) (the "appropriate relation" under § 1–105 of the Uniform Commercial Code should be determined by the "most significant relationship" test).

South Carolina: Boone v. Boone, 345 S.C. 8, 546 S.E.2d 191 (2001) (refuse on public policy grounds to apply interspousal immunity rule of place of injury to South Carolina spouses).

West Virginia: West Virginia continues to edge toward a Second Restatement approach. See McKinney v. Fairchild Int'l, Inc., 199 W.Va. 718, 728, 487 S.E.2d 913, 923 (1997) (holding that West Virginia rules tolling time limitations apply to action arising when West Virginia resident injured in Kentucky while using machine manufactured by West Virginia company and stating that "where a choice of law question arises about whether the tolling provisions of West Virginia ... or of the place where the claim accrued should be applied, the circuit court should ordinarily apply West Virginia law, unless the place where the claim accrued has a more significant relationship to the transaction and the parties"); Lee v. Saliga, 179 W.Va. 762, 373 S.E.2d 345, 351 (1988) (law of state where insurance policy issued, not place of collision, determines right to uninsured motorist recovery, characterizing problem as one in contract, rather than tort, and stating, "despite some criticism of the Restatement (Second) rules in the tort area, we have utilized Restatement conflict of laws principles in our cases. It cannot be doubted that the Restatement principles do embody what may be termed the modern trend of the law." The court cites *Paul*, discussed below, for "criticism" of the Restatement, but notes that "the author of *Paul* has more recently tempered his view," citing *Oaks*, also discussed below); Oakes v. Oxygen Therapy Services,

courts refused to depart from the old rule in determining marital tort immunity, the legislature directed application of North Carolina law to permit recovery by North Carolina spouses.[177] The Supreme of New Mexico has stated "the Restatement (Second) is a more appropriate approach for multi-state contract class actions."[178]

The Supreme Court of the United States anticipated the cases abandoning the place-of-injury rule by interpreting the language of the Federal Tort Claims Act, "under circumstances where the United States, if a private person, would be liable to the claimant in accordance with the law of the place where the act or omission occurred,"[179] to mean the whole law of that place, including its conflict of laws rules. The main reason given by the Court for this interpretation was to permit the federal courts to utilize the flexibility and rationality that state courts were more and more introducing into a system formerly rigid and irrational.[180]

178 W.Va. 543, 363 S.E.2d 130 (W.Va. 1987) (use "most significant relationship" test to deprive West Virginia employee of a cause of action in tort for retaliatory discharge when employee filed a Maryland workers' compensation claim, but indicate will continue to use place of injury rule for "clear-cut cases of physical injury"); cf. Paul v. National Life, 177 W.Va. 427, 352 S.E.2d 550 (1986) (refuse to apply Indiana guest statute to a suit between West Virginia residents on public policy grounds, but dictum that would apply guest statute of another state if suit between residents of that state).

Caveat: Florida: Although Florida has adopted the Second Restatement approach for torts, see supra this note, Sturiano v. Brooks, 523 So.2d 1126 (Fla. 1988), answered in the affirmative the 11th Circuit's certified question whether the lex loci contractus would apply to insurance coverage, "limiting this answer to contracts for automobile insurance." Two concurring judges noted that on the facts of the case, the same result would be reached under the Second Restatement.

177. N.C.Gen.Stat. § 52–5.1 (spouses domiciled in North Carolina have cause of action against each other for injury or death arising out of acts occurring outside the state). For refusal to apply the immunity rule of the marital domicile to Pennsylvania spouses when the injury occurred in North Carolina and declaring that the statute does not otherwise affect the place-of-wrong rule, see Henry v. Henry, 291 N.C. 156, 229 S.E.2d 158 (1976); cf. Schmidt v. Government Ins. Office of New South Wales, [1973] 1 N.S.W.L.R. 59 (Ct.App. 1973) (New South Wales statute abolishing marital immunity for actions "arising out of the use of a registered motor vehicle" applies whenever vehicle is registered in New South Wales no matter where the accident, but does not apply if the vehicle is not so registered).

178. Ferrell v. Allstate Ins. Co., 144 N.M. 405, 188 P.3d 1156, 1173 (2008).

179. 28 U.S.C.A. § 1346(b).

180. Richards v. United States, 369 U.S. 1, 12–13, 82 S.Ct. 585, 592–93, 7 L.Ed.2d 492, 500 (1962). For cases applying the conflicts rule of the place of act or omission, which selects the law of another state, see, e.g., Guillory v. United States, 699 F.2d 781 (5th Cir.1983) (whole law of Texas points to Louisiana); Loge v. United States, 662 F.2d 1268 (8th Cir.1981), cert. denied, 456 U.S. 944, 102 S.Ct. 2009, 72 L.Ed.2d 466 (1982) (whole law of D.C. points to Arkansas); cf. Beattie v. United States, 756 F.2d 91 (D.C.Cir.1984) (when place of act is Antarctica, which has no law, apply interest analysis to choose law). But cf. Barkanic v. General Administration of Civil Aviation of the People's Republic of China, 923 F.2d 957 (2d Cir.l991) (language in Foreign Sovereign Immunities Act, similar to that in Federal Tort Claims Act, held to refer only to issue of punitive damages and not to general questions of choice of law); Wooton v. Pumpkin Air, Inc., 869 F.2d 848 (5th Cir. 1989) (holding that reference in Outer Continental Shelf Lands Act, 43 U.S.C. § 1333(a)(2)(A), to the laws of the "adjacent" state does not include a reference to that state's choice-of-law rules); In re Hanford Nuclear Reservation Litigation, 780 F.Supp. 1551, 1571 n.36 (E.D. Wash. 1991) (holding that reference in Price–Anderson Act, 42 U.S.C. § 2014 (hh), to "the law of the state in which the nuclear incident involved occurs" does not include a reference to the choice-of-law rules of that state).

Allstate Insurance Company v. Hague,[181] restated constitutional limitations on choice of law. In the course of the opinion, both the four-justice plurality[182] and the three-justice dissent[183] indicated displeasure with the place-of-injury rule. The plurality opinion speaks disparagingly of "the wooden *lex loci delicti* doctrine"[184] and cites with approval cases in the vanguard of modern interest analysis.[185] The three dissenters would go so far as to raise interest analysis to a constitutional requirement.[186]

Article 4 of the Convention on the Law Applicable to Traffic Accidents[187] applies the law of the state where the accident occurred except when only one vehicle is involved or two or more vehicles are involved that are registered in the same State. Under the exceptions, the law of the State of registration applies to determine liability to the driver, owner, a passenger whose habitual residence is in a State other than where the accident occurred, and a victim outside the vehicle whose habitual residence is in the State of registration.

The Convention on the Law Applicable to Traffic Accidents, with its focus on the State of registration of the automobile, will avoid some undesirable effects of a rigid place-of-injury rule. It may produce results contrary to a consequences-based analysis when the single automobile is rented at the place of injury or the two or more vehicles are registered in different states but with laws that produce the same result, which is different from the result reached under the law of the place of injury.

A Regulation of the European Parliament and of the Council of 11 July 2007 on the Law Applicable To Non–Contractual Obligations (Rome II), creates a presumption in favor of "the law of the country in which the damage occurs irrespective of the country in which the event giving rise to the damage occurred and irrespective of the country or countries

---

Gould Elec. Inc. v. United States, 220 F.3d 169 (3d Cir. 2000), discusses five approaches taken by courts choosing law under the Federal Tort Claims Act when the acts or omissions occur in more than one state. Simon v. United States, 341 F.3d 193, 196 (3d Cir. 2003): ("We synthesize the *Gould* approaches into a single inquiry that chooses the rules of the jurisdiction containing the last significant negligent act or omission relevant to the FTCA"). See Patton, *Sisyphus: The Boulder, and the Choice-of-Law Hill*, 71 J. Air L. & Com. 471, 499–509 (2006) (discussing seven different approaches that courts have used to select law under the FTCA when the government's negligence occurred in more than one jurisdiction).

181. 449 U.S. 302, 101 S.Ct. 633, 66 L.Ed.2d 521 (1981).

182. Justice Brennan wrote the plurality opinion joined by Justices White, Marshall, and Blackmun. Justice Stevens concurred in the judgment. Justice Stewart took no part.

183. Justice Powell wrote a dissent joined by Chief Justice Burger and Justice Rehnquist.

184. 449 U.S. at 316 n.22, 101 S.Ct. at 642 n.22, 66 L.Ed.2d at 533 n.22.

185. Id. at 314 n.19, 101 S.Ct. at 641 n.19, 66 L.Ed.2d at 532 n.19.

186. Id. at 334–35, 101 S.Ct. at 651–52, 66 L.Ed.2d at 544.

187. Convention of 4 May 1971 on the Law Applicable to Traffic Accidents. As of September 1, 2009, in force in Austria, Belarus, Belgium, Bosnia and Herzegovina, Croatia, Czech Republic, France, Latvia, Lithuania, Luxembourg, Montenegro, Netherlands, Poland, Serbia, Slovakia, Slovenia, Spain, and Switzerland. Portugal has signed but not ratified the Convention. To update the status of the Convention consult the Web site: <http://www.hcch.net/e/status/stat19e.html>.

in which the indirect consequences of that event occur."[188] Section 6.23 infra discusses this presumption and the circumstances that rebut it. This regulation will replace the choice-of-law rules for non-contractual obligations that previously existed in European Union countries and discussed in previous editions. Article 28 of the regulation states that it does not supersede multilateral conventions, such as the Convention on the Law Applicable to Traffic Accidents. Member states, such as Austria, that are parties to such conventions will continue to be bound by them unless they denounce those conventions.

The codification of Japanese conflict-of-law rules that took effect on 1 January 2007 creates a double actionability requirement similar to the former United Kingdom rule, now displaced by Rome II.[189] Article 17 states the general rule for torts:

> The formation and effect of claims arising from a tort shall be governed by the law of the place where the results of the infringing act are produced. However, if it was not foreseeable under normal circumstances that the results would be produced at that place, the law of the place where the infringing act occurred shall apply.

The next two articles provide special rules for product liability and defamation. Article 20 provides an exception to the place-of-injury rule of article 17:

> Exception for Cases Where a Manifestly More Closely Connected Place Exists
>
> Notwithstanding the provisions of the preceding three articles, the formation and effect of claims arising from a tort shall be governed by the law of the place which is manifestly more closely connected with the tort than the place determined pursuant to the preceding three articles, considering that the parties had their habitual residence in the same jurisdiction at the time when the tort occurs, the tort constitutes a breach of obligations under a contract between the parties, or other circumstances of the case.

The same-habitual-residence provision will produce some decisions that avoid applying the law of a jurisdiction whose policies will not be affected, but as discussed in section 6.17, not enough. There is no magic ruler to measure when a "place ... is manifestly more closely connected with the tort." Unless this term is given an interpretation that focuses on what jurisdictions will have their policies impaired if the court does not apply their law, "more closely connected" will not provide the needed exception to the place-of-injury rule of article 17.

---

188. (EC) No. 864/2007, OJ 2007 L 199/44, art. 4(1).

189. Japanese conflict-of-laws rules: Act on the General Rules of Application of Laws, Law No. 10 of 1898 as newly titled and amended 21 June 2006, art. 22(1): "Where events that should otherwise be governed by the foreign law applicable in tort do not constitute a tort under Japanese law, recovery of damages or any other remedy under the foreign law may not be demanded."

§ 6.19 Retention of the Place-of-Wrong Rule in Some States

Although the great majority of courts that have been asked to reconsider the place-of-wrong rule in the light of an interest-analysis argument have elected to displace the old rule,[190] as of September 1, 2009, five states have decided to retain that rule.[191] Six other states, although formally retaining a place-of-wrong rule, seem to be edging towards its displacement.[192] Courts have retained the place-of-wrong rule for a variety of reasons. Our neighbor to the north, Canada, has reaffirmed the rule of lex loci delicti on the ground that of the two "underlying principles of private international law ... order and fairness, order comes first."[193] Nevertheless, in its opinion, the Supreme Court of Canada provided a possible exception in international cases rather than the interprovincial case with which it was dealing: "However, because a rigid rule on the international level could give rise to injustice, in certain circumstances, I am not averse to retaining a discretion in the court to apply our own law to deal with such circumstances. I can, however, imagine few cases where this would be necessary."[194] The Ontario courts have taken advantage of this exception.[195]

---

190. See supra, § 6.18 note 176.

191. Alabama: Norris v. Taylor, 460 So.2d 151 (Ala.1984) (concurring opinion characterizes "significant interests' rule" as "minority view"—Id. at 152).

Georgia: Dowis v. Mud Slingers, Inc., 279 Ga. 808, 816, 621 S.E.2d 413, 419 (2005) (expressly rejecting "governmental interest" analysis, Leflar, and Second Restatement: "The relative certainty, predictability, and ease of the application of lex loci delicti, even though sometimes leading to results which may appear harsh, are preferable to the inconsistency and capriciousness that the replacement choice-of-law approaches have wrought"); cf. General Telephone Co. of the Southeast v. Trimm, 252 Ga. 95, 311 S.E.2d 460 (1984) (will adhere to place of making in contract conflicts cases "[u]ntil it becomes clear that a better rule exists"—Id. at 462). But cf. Alexander v. General Motors Corp., 267 Ga. 339, 478 S.E.2d 123 (1996) (applying Georgia law of strict liability rather than Virginia law requiring proof of negligence to product liability action by Georgia resident who purchased car in Georgia and was injured by crash in Virginia, declaring Virginia law to be against Georgia's public policy).

South Carolina: Dawkins v. State, 306 S.C. 391, 412 S.E.2d 407 (1991); Lister v. NationsBank, N.A., 329 S.C. 133, 494 S.E.2d 449 (App. 1997).

Virginia: Buchanan v. Doe, 246 Va. 67, 431 S.E.2d 289 (1993); McMillan v. McMillan, 219 Va. 1127, 253 S.E.2d 662 (1979).

Wyoming: Jack v. Enterprise Rent–A–Car Co. of Los Angeles, 899 P.2d 891 (Wyo. 1995).

Counting noses in this manner is necessarily inexact in states without recent opinions, such as the 2005 opinion of the Supreme Court of Georgia, in which the court expressly addresses a request that it abandon the place-of-wrong rule.

192. See cases from Kansas, Maryland, New Mexico, North Carolina, and West Virginia, supra note 176. Note 176 also cites a South Carolina case avoiding the place-or-wrong rule and applying South Carolina law to South Carolina residents on public policy grounds.

193. Tolofson v. Jensen, [1994] 3 S.C.R. 1022, 1058 (Can.). But see Quebec Civil Code art. 3126: "In any case where the person who committed the injurious act and the victim have their domiciles or residences in the same country, the law of that country applies."

194. Id. at 1062–63 (La Forest, J.).

195. Hanlan v. Sernesky, 35 O.R.3d 603 (Ont. Ct. Justice 1997) (permits parents and siblings of an injured Ontario resident to recover damages against an Ontario driver although the law of Minnesota, where the accident occurred, did not permit such recovery), aff'd, 38 O.R.3d 479 (Ont. Ct. App. 1998); Gracey v. Skinner Estate, 53 O.R.3d 559 (Ont. Sup. Ct. J. 2001) (apply Ontario no-fault compensation law to limit recovery for accident in Utah); cf. Lau v. Li, 53 O.R.3d 727 (Ont. Sup. Ct. J. 2001) (invoking the exception in an

So too, the High Court of Australia has declared that "the lex loci delicti is the governing law with respect to torts committed in Australia but which have an interstate element"[196] and has extended this rule to cover international cases.[197]

§ 6.20 Place-of-Wrong Rule through Statutory Construction

One reason for rejection of interest analysis is based on statutory construction. *Marmon v. Mustang Aviation, Inc.*[198] illustrates this reasoning. A private airplane, owned by a Texas corporation and piloted by an employee of the corporation, who was a Texas citizen, departed from Texas with a group of three Texas residents and one Illinois resident as passengers. The group was on a business trip. On the return trip to Texas, because of the pilot's negligence, the airplane crashed in Colorado approximately sixty miles before crossing back into Texas. An action was brought in Texas for the wrongful deaths of the passengers. Colorado had a $25,000 limit on wrongful death recovery, whereas Texas had no statutory limit. The majority of the court seemed sympathetic to an argument that the Colorado limit on recovery should not apply because this would advance no policy underlying the Colorado limitation and would substantially interfere with the interest of Texas in securing adequate compensation for the wrongful death of the Texas passengers.[199] Nevertheless, the majority held that the Colorado wrongful death act, including its limit on recovery, applied. The reason was that for over eighty years Texas court had construed the Texas wrongful death act as inapplicable unless the fatal injury was inflicted in Texas. In the face of this judicial gloss, the legislature had repeatedly re-enacted the Texas death act without any significant change in its wording. Therefore, although the Texas statute contained no express territorial language, the legislature in re-enacting it without change must be presumed to have intended the act to have the meaning given to it by the courts. The majority concluded that:

> The circumstance that we may believe that a case such as this should be controlled by Texas law or that the Legislature, after the

---

interprovincial case and refusing to apply Quebec law, which would prevent recovery by family members, when Quebec's only contact was place of the accident). But see Wong v. Lee, 58 O.R.3d 398 (Ont. Ct. App. 2002) (disagreeing (2–1) with "trend of the case law . . . to broaden what was intended to be a very narrow exception" and applying New York law, the site of the accident, to permit recovery that would be barred under Ontario law)

196. John Pfeiffer Pty Ltd. v. Rogerson, 172 A.L.R. 625, 648 (Austl. 2000).

197. Regie National des Unsines Renault SA v. Zhang [2002] HCA 10.

198. 430 S.W.2d 182 (Tex.1968).

199. As for the Illinois passenger, Illinois had a $30,000 limit on recovery. Nevertheless, if it had been decided that the Colorado limitation was inapplicable, the Illinois decedent should have been entitled to the same unlimited recovery as the Texas passengers. It would be inappropriate for Texas to distinguish between the Texas and the Illinois passengers in the amount of compensation to which they were entitled from a Texas tortfeasor. Moreover, Texas might be regarded as having a policy of placing upon the Texas airplane company the primary responsibility for arranging to have the costs of accidents that result from its operations distributed through insurance, and this purpose would be advanced no matter where or to whom these costs were realized. See § 6.25.

development of the "significant contacts rule," should have amended the statute so as to give it an extra-territorial effect, does not authorize us to enter the legislative field.[200]

On what rational basis could the Texas legislature want the Texas wrongful death act to apply only to deaths caused in Texas, when applying the act to a death caused in another state would advance important Texas policies and not interfere with the policies of any other state? The canon of statutory construction, that a statute is presumed to have no extraterritorial application unless it contains an express provision to that effect,[201] dates from the time when it was thought that only the state where the injury occurred had the power to provide a remedy for the injury. Now this canon is likely to defeat rather than advance the policies underlying a statute. Perhaps in the light of *Marmon*, and similar judicial reactions to arguments that statutes should receive territorial applications in accordance with a consequences-based analysis,[202] the following statute would have a salutary effect:

In appropriate circumstances, a constitutional provision, statute, or non-statutory rule of this state may be applied to persons or events outside this state.

After *Marmon*, the Texas death act was amended to apply to fatal injuries "occurring either within or without this state."[203] The Texas Supreme Court has suggested[204] that this amendment should be construed in conformity with the "most significant relationship" rule of the Second Restatement,[205] and has adopted that rule to govern conflicts concerning common-law tort rules.[206]

In the rare event that a wrongful death or other statute does contain language that limits the remedies provided by the statute to injuries inflicted in the state,[207] a court, if the limitation, though unwise, is

200. *Marmon*, 430 S.W.2d at 187 (Tex.1968).

201. See American Banana Co. v. United Fruit Co., 213 U.S. 347, 357, 29 S.Ct. 511, 513, 53 L.Ed. 826, 832 (1909).

202. See Graham v. General U.S. Grant Post No. 2665, 43 Ill.2d 1, 248 N.E.2d 657 (1969) (one of the reasons given for refusing to apply the Illinois dram shop act to an injury in Wisconsin); State Surety Co. v. Lensing, 249 N.W.2d 608 (Iowa 1977) (rule that statute is presumed not to have extraterritorial effect applied to statute requiring automobile dealers to furnish surety bonds); cf. Shapira, *Rules of Law Delineating Their Own Sphere of Applicability*, § IIB(1) of Israeli Reports to the XI International Congress of Comparative Law 41 (1982) (the Israeli Supreme Court has held "that the 'territorial sovereignty' principle does give rise to a presumption of statutory construction which, however, should give way in the face of a legislative measure with an unequivocal extraterritorial sweep").

203. Tex.Sess.L., 64th Legislature, c. 530, § 1 (1975) (amending Tex.Civ.Stat.Ann. art. 4671). At the same time the statute providing that a cause of action for wrongful death given by the law of the place of injury may be enforced in Texas, was amended to read "the court shall apply such rules of substantive law as are appropriate under the facts of the case." Id. § 2 (amending art. 4678). That these amendments are not retroactive, see Cass v. McFarland, 564 S.W.2d 107 (Tex.Civ.App.1978).

204. Gutierrez v. Collins, 583 S.W.2d 312, 318 n.3 (Tex.1979) (dictum).

205. Restatement, Second § 145.

206. *Gutierrez*, 583 S.W.2d at 318.

207. See Md.Code Ann., Courts & Judicial Proceedings § 3–903(a) ("wrongful death"; "If the wrongful act occurred in another state ... a Maryland court shall apply the

constitutional, must obey the statutory command.[208] It may be that language that appears on its face to have such an effect is not to be taken literally. For example, *Farber v. Smolack*,[209] applied the New York owner's liability statute to an automobile accident in North Carolina despite the reference in the statute to "a vehicle used or operated in this state." The court pointed out that the words "in this state" replaced the former language, "upon a public highway" and that the amendment was intended to include accidents on private roads, not to limit the operation of the statute to accidents in New York.[210]

§ 6.21 Retention of Place-of-Wrong Rule for Certainty

Another reason that courts have given for adhering to the place-of-wrong rule is that the territorial rule is simple and certain in application while an approach to choice of law based on analysis of the policies underlying putatively conflicting domestic rules is likely to produce uncertainty, make the results of litigation unpredictable, and substantially increase the work of an already overburdened judicial system.[211] A

substantive law of that jurisdiction"); Wis.Stat.Ann. § 895.03 ("provided, that such [wrongful death] action shall be brought for a death caused in this state."); cf. Hughes v. Fetter, 341 U.S. 609, 71 S.Ct. 980, 95 L.Ed. 1212 (1951) (Wisconsin proviso may not be used to deny full faith and credit to a sister state death act); Tillett v. J.I. Case Co., 756 F.2d 591 (7th Cir.1985) (inability to apply Wisconsin wrongful death act results in dismissal because action time barred in only other state with both sufficient contacts to apply its law and jurisdiction over defendant); Schnabl v. Ford Motor Co., 54 Wis.2d 345, 195 N.W.2d 602 (1972) (Wisconsin statute applicable when negligence occurred in Wisconsin although fatal injury occurred elsewhere).

208. See Restatement, Second § 6(1); cf. Ellis v. Royal Ins. Co., 129 N.H. 326, 530 A.2d 303 (1987) (cannot apply New Hampshire law to uninsured motorist coverage because statute is unambiguously limited to policies "issued or delivered" in New Hampshire).

209. 20 N.Y.2d 198, 282 N.Y.S.2d 248, 229 N.E.2d 36 (1967).

210. See also Klippel v. U–Haul Co. of Northeastern Michigan, 759 F.2d 1176 (4th Cir.1985) (mere fact that plaintiff resides in New York does not make New York owner's liability statute applicable when the rented vehicle is registered in Michigan and rented in Florida for move to South Carolina where accident occurred); Sexton v. Ryder Truck Rental, Inc., 413 Mich. 406, 320 N.W.2d 843 (1982) (Michigan owner's liability laws apply when parties are Michigan residents, although automobile or plane crash occurred in state where no liability); Ewers v. Thunderbird Aviation, Inc., 289 N.W.2d 94 (Minn.1979) (aircraft owner's liability act language "within the airspace of this state" means at any time during the flight so that statute applies although crash is outside the state); Van Dyke v. Bolves, 107 N.J.Super. 338, 258 A.2d 372 (App.1969) (New York owner's liability act applied to accident in New Jersey when New York owner and New Jersey claimant); Croft v. National Car Rental, 56 N.Y.2d 989, 453 N.Y.S.2d 631, 439 N.E.2d 346 (1982) (New York owner's liability statute is not applicable when the only New York contacts are that the rental company is doing business there and the plaintiff was heading there); cf. Cairns v. Franklin Mint Co., 292 F.3d 1139 (9th Cir. 2002) (in California legislation conferring a post-mortem right of publicity, language that the legislation applies when claims "arise from acts occurring directly in this state" is not a choice-of-law provision and does not confer the right when the decedent resided in England); Reese, *Statutes in Choice of Law*, 35 Amer.J.Comp.L. 395, 399 (1987) ("[b]y and large, detail with respect to a statute's extraterritorial application is better left to the courts").

211. See Kaczmarek v. Allied Chemical Corp., 836 F.2d 1055, 1057 (7th Cir.1987) ("The opponents of mechanical rules of conflict of laws may have given too little weight to the virtues of simplicity") (Posner, J.); Friday v. Smoot, 211 A.2d 594 (Del.1965); White v. King, 244 Md. 348, 223 A.2d 763 (1966); cf. M. de Boer, Beyond Lex Loci Delicti 192, 196 (1987) (displacement of lex loci delicti has resulted in "chaos and crisis", but favors "a much more rational and subtle approach which might eventually yield a number of

court taking this view might, as has the Michigan Supreme Court,[212] point to the chaos resulting in New York after the adoption of interest analysis in *Babcock v. Jackson*.[213]

It is true that choosing law to govern torts by automatic application of the law of the place where the plaintiff was injured is a simple, certain way to dispose of conflicts cases. But there are two difficulties with retaining the place-of-wrong rule for its supposed certainty of application.

First of all, as indicated in section 6.17, although the old rule seemed clear and certain, a number of excellent judges, sensing on the basis of largely unarticulated premises, that the result produced by the settled rule was outrageous, used their ingenuity and the play in the joints of the old system to avoid the law of the place of the wrong. Although such displacements of the place-of-wrong rule were rare, there is every reason to believe that these aberrations would have multiplied if functional, state-interest analysis had not arrived to articulate the unarticulated and to light the path for accomplishing by a predictable reasoning process results that, when accomplished by label-switching, seemed arbitrary and unpredictable.

Second, in response to the simplicity argument for retaining the place-of-wrong rule, there is no doubt that ease of application is a point in favor of any legal rule. Given two rules that respond as well to the underlying social problems to which they are addressed, one rule simple to apply and one very difficult, only an insane person would choose the rule that is difficult to apply. But in shaping legal rules to apply to the complexities of the human condition, a quest for absolute certainty and complete simplicity is a child's dream. Rigid, simple rules produce irrational and dysfunctional solutions to variable, complex problems. Legal rules should be, perhaps inevitably must be, rules that produce socially desirable solutions to the problems to which those rules are addressed and that also are feasible for the members of a learned profession to administer. The place-of-wrong rule focuses on the one contact, injury, that, in unintentional tort cases, is most likely to be unrelated to the policy of any tort rule. The price paid for the simplicity of that rule is, therefore, too high.

Moreover, the pattern of rational and just decisions that will emerge from application of a consequences-based analysis, will provide reason-

---

manageable rules"); Brilmayer, *Governmental Interest Analysis: A House Without Foundations*, 46 Ohio St.L. J. 459 (1985); Hill, *The Judicial Function in Choice of Law*, 85 Colum. L. Rev. 1585, 1647 (1985) (wholesale replacement of traditional rules has resulted in chaos and place-of-wrong rule is too broad, but it should be retained as presumptively applicable "leaving room for the emergence of modifications and particularizations more suited to perceived patterns of controversy"); Symeonides, *Revolution and Counter–Revolution in American Conflicts Laws: Is There a Middle Ground?*, 46 Ohio St.L. J. 549 (1985).

212. Abendschein v. Farrell, 382 Mich. 510, 170 N.W.2d 137 (1969), but see Sexton v. Ryder Truck Rental, Inc., 413 Mich. 406, 320 N.W.2d 843 (1982) (not applying lex loci when both parties reside in forum). See also McMillan v. McMillan, 219 Va. 1127, 253 S.E.2d 662 (1979).

213. Section 6.22 discusses the New York experience.

able certainty and predictability. Much of the alleged uncertainty of interest analysis has resulted from a misunderstanding and misapplication of this analysis.[214]

§ 6.22 Neumeier v. Kuehner: New York's Return to a "Rules" Approach

Between 1963 and 1976, the New York Court of Appeals decided six cases[215] centering on the question of whether a guest's right to recover against a New York host driver is determined by the ordinary negligence standard of New York or by a "guest statute" of another jurisdiction, which bars recovery or requires a heightened degree of wrongdoing, such as "gross negligence." The struggle of the Court with these cases has been awesome to behold—dissents, shifting doctrine, results not easily reconcilable. In short, a law professor's delight but a practitioner's and judge's nightmare. It is quite understandable, then, that weary from this struggle, a majority of the Court felt that the time had come to inject a measure of predictability into New York conflicts doctrine that had been absent since New York discarded the place-of-wrong rule.

Neumeier v. Kuehner[216] provided the setting for the announcement of the new rules for guest-statute cases. In *Neumeier*, a New Yorker was driving his automobile, registered and insured in New York, between two points in Ontario with an Ontario friend as his guest passenger. On this trip a train collided with the car killing both the New York host and his Ontario guest. The personal representative of the deceased Canadian brought a wrongful death action in New York against the estate of the New York host and against the railroad.

An Ontario statute made a driver, other than one in the business of carrying passengers for compensation, liable for injuries to his passengers only if these injuries resulted from the driver's gross negligence. The defendants[217] pleaded this Ontario statute as a defense and the New York Court of Appeals held that the Ontario statute was applicable. Chief Judge Fuld, in his majority opinion, set forth three rules[218] that he

---

214. For example Dym v. Gordon, 16 N.Y.2d 120, 209 N.E.2d 792, 262 N.Y.S.2d 463 (1965), which was overruled by Tooker v. Lopez, 24 N.Y.2d 569, 249 N.E.2d 394, 301 N.Y.S.2d 519 (1969), applied the Colorado guest statute to bar recovery between New Yorkers. The court reasoned that this advanced the Colorado policy of preserving the host's assets for recovery by occupants of the other automobile involved in the accident. No Colorado case and no discussion of guest statutes ever mentioned such a policy.

215. Babcock v. Jackson, 12 N.Y.2d 473, 191 N.E.2d 279, 240 N.Y.S.2d 743 (1963); Dym v. Gordon, 16 N.Y.2d 120, 209 N.E.2d 792, 262 N.Y.S.2d 463 (1965); Macey v. Rozbicki, 18 N.Y.2d 289, 221 N.E.2d 380, 274 N.Y.S.2d 591 (1966); Tooker v. Lopez, 24 N.Y.2d 569, 249 N.E.2d 394, 301 N.Y.S.2d 519 (1969); Neumeier v. Kuehner, 31 N.Y.2d 121, 335 N.Y.S.2d 64, 286 N.E.2d 454 (1972); Towley v. King Arthur Rings, Inc., 40 N.Y.2d 129, 386 N.Y.S.2d 80, 351 N.E.2d 728 (1976).

216. 31 N.Y.2d 121, 335 N.Y.S.2d 64, 286 N.E.2d 454 (1972).

217. The railroad urged application of the Ontario "gross negligence" standard to determine the New York driver's liability because if the statute shielded the driver from liability, the railroad would be insulated from that portion of the damages attributable to the fault of the New York driver. Ont.Rev.Stat. ch. 296, § 2(2) (1970).

218. 31 N.Y.2d at 128, 335 N.Y.S.2d at 70, 286 N.E.2d at 457–58:

indicated would henceforth apply in conflicts cases involving the liability of a host driver to a guest. He quoted these rules from his concurring opinion in a prior case.[219] The rules merit careful examination because although they arose in the context of a choice-of-law problem that has all but disappeared, the guest statute, New York cases have applied the rules by analogy to other tort issues.[220] Colorado has applied the *Neumier* rules in a guest-statute case.[221]

Rule 1 states that if the host and guest are domiciled in the same state and the car is also registered there, the law of that state determines the standard of care that the host owes the guest.

Rule 2 focuses on the situation in which the host resides in a state that has a guest statute and the guest resides in a state that does not have a guest statute. Under these circumstances, if the host's conduct occurs in the host's state then the host should not be liable under the law of the guest's state, but if the host injures the guest in the guest's state, the driver is not entitled "in the absence of special circumstances" to the protection of the guest statute of his own state.[222]

Rule 3 is addressed to other situations when the host and the guest are domiciled in different states. In these circumstances the Court will "normally" apply the law of the state where the accident occurred unless applying a different rule "will advance the relevant substantive law purposes without impairing the smooth working of the multi-state system or producing great uncertainty for litigants."[223]

The Court held that *Neumeier* fell under Rule 3, that the exception to use of the law of the place of accident was not applicable, and that therefore the Canadian statute controlled.[224] A number of courts in

---

"1. When the guest-passenger and the host-driver are domiciled in the same state, and the car is there registered, the law of that state should control and determine the standard of care which the host owes to his guest.

"2. When the driver's conduct occurred in the state of his domicile and that state does not cast him in liability for that conduct, he should not be held liable by reason of the fact that liability would be imposed upon him under the tort law of the state of the victim's domicile. Conversely, when the guest was injured in the state of his own domicile and its law permits recovery, the driver who has come into that state should not—in the absence of special circumstances—be permitted to interpose the law of his state as a defense.

"3. In other situations, when the passenger and the driver are domiciled in different states, the rule is necessarily less categorical. Normally, the applicable rule of decision will be that of the state where the accident occurred but not if it can be shown that displacing that normally applicable rule will advance the relevant substantive law purposes without impairing the smooth working of the multi-state system or producing great uncertainty for litigants."

219. Tooker v. Lopez, 24 N.Y.2d 569, 585, 301 N.Y.S.2d 519, 532–33, 249 N.E.2d 394, 404 (1969).

220. See, e.g., Schultz v. Boy Scouts of America, Inc., 65 N.Y.2d 189, 491 N.Y.S.2d 90, 480 N.E.2d 679 (1985) (charitable immunity).

221. First National Bank in Fort Collins v. Rostek, 182 Colo. 437, 514 P.2d 314 (1973).

222. *Neumeier*, 31 N.Y.2d at 128, 335 N.Y.S.2d at 70, 286 N.E.2d at 458.

223. Id.

224. On remand, plaintiff was granted leave to amend the complaint to allege gross negligence and defendant Kuehner's motion to dismiss on forum non conveniens grounds

states other than New York that have abandoned the lex loci delicti rule have used the place of injury as a tie-breaker when interest or most-significant-relationship analysis does not produce a clear answer.[225]

§ 6.23   Examination of the Neumeier Rules

Rule 1: Host, guest, and car from same state

The most obvious question concerning this rule is why, as between host and guest,[226] it makes any difference where the car is registered. Suppose two New York friends fly on vacation to a state with a guest statute. There one of them rents a car and the other is injured while a passenger. What possible reason could there be for applying that state's guest statute when guest sues host back in New York? Perhaps insurance rates in the vacation state might be affected if the only liability insurance in force is that provided by the rental company.[227] But is this "interest" of the place of accident in protecting insurance rates from the pressures of recoveries under suspiciously collusive circumstances sufficient to make New York abandon its quest for adequate compensation to a New York guest injured by a negligent New York host? Even this reason for applying the law of the place of accident fades if, as is likely, the host elects not to pay the rental company for liability insurance and is covered instead by the host's New York policy.[228] If registry of the car is in fact a major requirement of Rule 1 and not just an unfortunate and

---

was denied. Neumeier v. Kuehner, 43 A.D.2d 109, 349 N.Y.S.2d 866 (1973). See also Miller v. Gay, 323 Pa.Super. 466, 470 A.2d 1353 (1983) (law of guest's residence where crash occurred applied to bar recovery against host). But cf. Danner v. Staggs, 680 F.2d 427 (5th Cir.1982) (apply law of host's state to permit recovery although crash occurred on interstate trip just across line in guest's state).

225.   See, e.g., Nodak Mutual Ins. Co. v. American Family Mutual Ins. Co., 604 N.W.2d 91, 96 (Minn. 2000) ("when all other relevant choice-of-law factors favor neither state's law, the state where the accident occurred has the strongest governmental interest"); Martineau v. Guertin, 170 Vt. 415, 751 A.2d 776, 781 (2000) (because it is a "close and difficult call as to whether Quebec or Vermont law should govern" use the default rule of Restatement (Second) § 145–the place of injury).

226.   For a holding that a company renting an automobile to the host may not, when charged with negligence and breach of warranty, invoke the guest statute of the place of accident and registry, see Pahmer v. Hertz Corp., 36 A.D.2d 252, 319 N.Y.S.2d 949 (1971), aff'd on other grounds, 32 N.Y.2d 119, 296 N.E.2d 243, 343 N.Y.S.2d 341 (1973).

227.   See Peters v. Peters, 63 Hawaii 653, 634 P.2d 586 (1981) (apply Hawaiian law of interspousal immunity to prevent suit between New York spouses who rented car in Hawaii covered by Hawaiian insurance).

228.   The customer's own liability insurance will provide coverage throughout the United States and Canada. See G. Couch, 12 Cyclopedia of Insurance Law (2d Ed. R. Anderson, rev. M. Rhodes 1981) § 45:1, p. 225 (territorial coverage of standard policy is "the United States of America, its territories or possessions, or Canada, or is being transported between ports thereof").

The premiums for liability insurance in an amount that complies with each state's financial responsibility law reflect the number and cost of accidents chargeable to policies covering drivers whose cars are principally garaged in that state and within a particular rating territory in the state. See McNamara, *Automobile Liability Insurance Rates*, 35 Ins. Counsel J. 398, 401, 403–06 (1968); Stern, *Ratemaking Procedures for Automobile Liability Insurance*, 52 Proc.Cas. Actuarial Soc'y 139, 155, 176–77, 183 (1965).

unnecessary afterthought,[229] none of the Court's rules covers the hypothetical of the New Yorkers on vacation.

Rule 1 will work best when a New York guest is injured in a guest-statute state. But if parties from a guest-statute state crash in New York, should New York invariably protect the host under the statute of the home state?[230] Suppose the host collides with a car driven by a New Yorker. The guest sues the New Yorker and the New Yorker impleads the host for contribution. If, as is widely supposed,[231] the New Yorker cannot obtain contribution unless the host is liable to the guest, should New York abandon its contribution policy[232] in favor of the paradoxical purposes of preventing ingratitude and collusion underlying a statute that is fast becoming extinct?[233] Recovery is also desirable if a seriously injured guest is cared for in New York and there are huge medical bills that will remain unpaid unless the host's liability insurance is available.[234]

Four years before *Neumeier*, Wisconsin had abandoned the domicile rule as too "mechanical" for conflicts cases involving marital immunity.[235] There is nothing wrong with choice-of-law rules that are sensitive both to the consequences of choice and to the need for reasonable certainty. The problem with the *Neumeier* rules is that they ignore the lessons of the past and are clumsily drafted.

A regulation of the European Parliament and the Council on the Law Applicable to Non–Contractual Obligations (Rome II)[236] contains the following provision:

---

229. For a holding that despite its mention in *Neumeier*, the place of registry lacks significance, see Gyory v. Radgowski, 82 Misc.2d 553, 369 N.Y.S.2d 583 (1974).

230. The New York intermediate appellate courts are split on this question. See, e.g., Rye v. Kolter, 39 A.D.2d 821, 333 N.Y.S.2d 96 (1972) (apply New York law); Arbuthnot v. Allbright, 35 A.D.2d 315, 316 N.Y.S.2d 391 (1970) (apply Ontario law).

231. See, e.g., Shonka v. Campbell, 260 Iowa 1178, 152 N.W.2d 242 (1967) (citing many cases in accord); Unif. Contribution Among Tortfeasors Act § 1, 12 U.L.A. 194 (1996). In Pennsylvania a defendant may obtain contribution even though the other tortfeasor is insulated from liability. Restifo v. McDonald, 426 Pa. 5, 7 n.1, 230 A.2d 199, 200 n.1 (1967) (intrafamily immunity) (dictum).

For a suggestion that a court resolve this conflict by applying the guest statute to bar any claim by the guest against the host, but permitting the driver of the other car to obtain indemnity from the host to the extent that the other driver pays more than half the verdict, see section 3.5.

232. Holding that New York would apply New York law to all defendants in this situation, see Saleem v. Tamm, 67 Misc.2d 335, 323 N.Y.S.2d 764 (1971). See also Sutton v. Langley, 330 So.2d 321 (La.App.1976), writ denied, no error. 333 So.2d 242 (1976) (when Texas host and guest and Louisiana defendants, do not apply Texas guest statute); Griggs v. Riley, 489 S.W.2d 469 (Mo.App.1972), transfer to Mo.S.Ct. denied (1973) (permit action between Illinois host and guest to protect Missouri defendant).

233. See § 6.11 note 60 and accompanying text.

234. See Bray v. Cox, 39 A.D.2d 299, 333 N.Y.S.2d 783 (1972), appeal dism'd, 33 N.Y.2d 789, 350 N.Y.S.2d 653, 305 N.E.2d 775 (1973) (New York's interests in protecting medical creditors and in assuring that injured nonresidents do not become public charges justifies application of New York law rather than Ontario guest statute to Ontario host and guest); cf. Milkovich v. Saari, 295 Minn. 155, 203 N.W.2d 408 (1973) (likelihood of medical costs justifies application of law of place of crash even though in case at bar the bills have been paid).

235. Zelinger v. State Sand & Gravel Co., 38 Wis.2d 98, 104, 156 N.W.2d 466, 468 (1968). See supra § 6.17, notes 150–157 and accompanying text. But see Quebec Civil Code Book 10 § 3126: "In any case where the person who committed the injurious act and the victim have their domiciles or residences in the same country, the law of that country applies."

Article 4: General Rule

1. Unless otherwise provided for in this Regulation, the law applicable to a non-contractual obligation arising out of a tort/delict shall be the law of the country in which the damage occurs irrespective of the country in which the event giving rise to the damage occurred and irrespective of the country or countries in which the indirect consequences of that event occur.

2. However, where the person claimed to be liable and the person sustaining damage both have their habitual residence in the same country at the time when the damage occurs, the law of that country shall apply.

3. Where it is clear from all the circumstances of the case that the tort/delict is manifestly more closely connected with a country other than that indicated in paragraphs 1 or 2, the law of that other country shall apply. A manifestly closer connection with another country might be based in particular on a pre-existing relationship between the parties, such as a contract, that is closely connected the tort/delict in question.

Article 4(2) is likely to produce the same results that induced the Wisconsin Supreme Court to abandon a domicile-based rule as too "mechanical"[237] when rights of third parties were affected. Nor should the law of the common habitual residence apply if that law denies punitive damages but the jurisdiction where the defendant caused harm has an interest in punishing and deterring the defendant's conduct.

The exception in article 4(3) is difficult to apply. There is no magic ruler to determine when a tort is "manifestly more closely connected with a country other than that indicated in paragraphs 1 or 2." The regulation should make its exception turn on whether a jurisdiction other than that designated by 4(1) or 4(2) would suffer consequences if its law were not applied. That is a matter subject to empirical testing.

The Japanese Code, which took effect on January 1, 1007,[238] has a similar exception to the place of injury rule of article 17 raising the same objection:

Article 20

Exception for Cases Where a Manifestly More Closely Connected Place Exists

Notwithstanding the provisions of the preceding three articles, the formation and effect of claims arising from a tort shall be governed by the law of the place which is manifestly more closely connected

---

236. Regulation (EC) No. 864/2007 of the European Parliament and of the Council of 11 July 2007 on the law applicable to non contractual obligations. OJ 2007 L 199/40.

237. Zelinger v. State Sand & Gravel Co., 38 Wis.2d 98, 104, 156 N.W.2d 466, 468 (1968).

238. Act No. 78 of 2006.

with the tort than the place determined pursuant to the preceding three articles, considering that the parties had their habitual residence in the same jurisdiction at the time when the tort occurs, the tort constitutes a breach of obligations under a contract between the parties, or other circumstances of the case.

The Oregon choice-of-law Code for noncontractual claims[239] avoids this objection by having a consequences-based exception to same domicile rule and including persons domiciled in different states if the laws of the domiciles produce the same result.[240]

Rule 2: Host's state has statute, guest's state does not, and crash is in one of these states

Applying the law of the place of accident[241] produces a result that at least is defensible in most circumstances; but suppose that the trip during which the accident occurs is one that has touched or is intended to touch on both states. Do we really want the result to depend on which side of the state line the car happened to be on when the guest was injured?[242] Would this case fall under the cryptic "special circumstances" exception in the rule?

Alas, that exception is addressed only to injury in the guest's state and means that under those circumstances the host driver will not always be subjected to the ordinary negligence rule of the guest's state. Perhaps in our hypothetical involving driving in both states we could interpret the first words of the rule—"when the driver's conduct occurred in the state of his domicile"—to mean "all of his conduct, actual and intended, during the events preceding the injury." Rule 2 again ignores the lessons of decided cases and reflects clumsy drafting in referring the "special circumstances" to the situation when the injury is in the guest's state. It should refer to a case when the injury is in the host's state. Drafting of exceptions in choice-of-law rules is a fine art[243] that the *Neumeier* rules do not exhibit.

---

239. Senate bill 561, 75th Oregon Legislative Assembly, 2009 Regular Session.

240. Id. §§ 8(2)(a) (same domicile), 8(2)(b) (different domiciles but their laws produce the same outcome), 8(4) and 9 (determine whether another state's law is substantially more appropriate by the effect on the policies of the contact states).

241. See Bader v. Purdom, 841 F.2d 38 (2d Cir.1988) (construe *Neumeier* rule 2 as creating a strong presumption in favor of the law of the place of wrong and apply it to issue of parental immunity); Byrn v. American Universal Ins. Co., 548 S.W.2d 186 (Mo.App.1977) (apply Iowa guest statute when Missouri guest injured on intrastate Iowa trip with Iowa host).

242. But see Cipolla v. Shaposka, 439 Pa. 563, 267 A.2d 854 (1970) (apply Delaware guest statute when Delaware host, Pennsylvania guest, Pennsylvania destination, crash in Delaware; court disclaims considering the place of the accident as a "relevant contact"). But cf. Bennett v. Macy, 324 F.Supp. 409 (W.D.Ky.1971) (apply law of guest's domicile where trip began and was to end rather than guest statute of host's domicile where injury occurred); Foster v. Leggett, 484 S.W.2d 827 (Ky. 1972) (apply law of guest's domicile to permit recovery rather than law of place of accident where host domiciled when trip began at guest's domicile and was planned to end there); Felix, *Symposium on Cipolla*, 9 Duq. L. Rev. 413, 421 (1971) (*Cipolla* arguably a sufficiently multi-state case to justify application of Pennsylvania law).

243. See Symeonides, *Exception Clauses in American Conflicts Law*, 42 Am. J. Comp. L. 813 (1994).

Rule 3: Apply the law of the place of accident in other situations in which host and guest are domiciled in different states

The Court holds that *Neumeier* does not fall within the vague exception articulated at the end of the rule. This result raises the question when the exception will apply and, despite Chief Judge Fuld's disclaimer, invites the accusation of invidious discrimination against guests who are unlucky enough not to live in New York.[244]

If ever the exception of Rule 3 is to apply, it should be in the case in which host and guest come from different states, neither state has a guest statute, but the crash is in a guest-statute state.[245] In the first major guest statute case decided by the Court after *Neumeier*, however, Iowa guest met New York host while both were vacationing in Colorado.[246] The Court applied the Colorado guest statute to a one-car crash[247] in Colorado without even pausing to inquire whether Iowa had a guest statute[248] or had one different in terms[249] or application[250] from the Colorado statute. Nor did the Court note that the Colorado guest statute had been repealed after the accident but more than a year before its opinion.[251]

§ 6.24   The Rhode Island "Rules" Approach

The New York Court of Appeals' quest for conflicts rules is understandable. Given the complexity that is possible in a consequences-based conflicts analysis, a court may well wish to avoid treating every conflicts case as a new problem to be analyzed from scratch.[252] The safest way to implement a rules approach is to wait until the court has decided a

---

244. See Leflar, *Choice of Law: A Well–Watered Plateau*, 41 L. & Contemp.Prob. 10, 21 (1977); Trautman, *Rule or Reason in Choice of Law: A Comment on Neumeier*, 1 Vt. L. Rev. 1, 18 (1976).

245. See, e.g., Chila v. Owens, 348 F.Supp. 1207 (S.D.N.Y.1972).

246. Towley v. King Arthur Rings, Inc., 40 N.Y.2d 129, 386 N.Y.S.2d 80, 351 N.E.2d 728 (1976).

247. This made the case more like Tooker v. Lopez, 24 N.Y.2d 569, 301 N.Y.S.2d 519, 249 N.E.2d 394 (1969) (New York host and guest, crash in Michigan, New York law applied) than Dym v. Gordon, 16 N.Y.2d 120, 262 N.Y.S.2d 463, 209 N.E.2d 792 (1965) (New York host and guest, crash in Colorado, Colorado law applied). I disapprove of the distinction between one-car and two-car crashes suggested by the reasoning of *Dym* and so does *Tooker*.

248. It did. Iowa Code Ann. § 321.494, which was subsequently declared unconstitutional (Bierkamp v. Rogers, 293 N.W.2d 577 (Iowa 1980)) and then repealed (1984 Ia. (70 G.A.) ch. 1219, § 41).

249. Colo.Rev.Stat. § 42–9–101 (1963) (formerly § 13–9–1; now repealed, see infra note 267): "willful and wanton disregard of the rights of others". Iowa Code § 321.494: "reckless operation", now repealed, see supra note 248.

250. The Court did decide that, in the light of Colorado opinions applying the Colorado statute, it could not be said as a matter of law that the trial court erred in leaving the question of whether the host's conduct was "willful and wanton" to the jury. The Court remitted the case to the Appellate Division for a review of the facts. The Appellate Division had reversed the judgment against the driver and dismissed the complaint.

251. 1975 Colo.Sess.Laws, p. 1568, § 1.

252. See Reese, *Choice of Law: Rules or Approach*, 57 Cornell L. Rev. 315, 322–23 (1972).

variety of cases focusing on the same choice-of-law problem. If the results of these cases can be succinctly and clearly summarized,[253] this summary of the pattern of decided cases can provide "rules" to guide the court, lower courts, and attorneys. When a rule articulated by a court purports to be broader than the pattern of already decided cases, this is a more hazardous undertaking. At the very least, the court should think through the fact patterns that are likely to occur in future cases and see whether in those situations it would desire the result dictated by the new rules.

This process of stating a rule to cover yet undecided fact situations and doing so in a manner that the court is reasonably certain will not prove embarrassing in the future is very difficult, but as *Labree v. Major*,[254] decided by the Rhode Island Supreme Court, indicates, is not impossible for an able and imaginative court. *Labree* presented a fact pattern similar to that in *Neumeier*, was decided by a court embarking on a rules approach, but reached the opposite result.

In *Labree*, a Rhode Island driver was taking some Massachusetts friends between two points in Massachusetts. There was a collision with another car in Massachusetts and the guests were injured. At the time, under a Massachusetts judicially-created rule,[255] a guest passenger could recover against a host driver only for gross negligence. Under Rhode Island law, there could be recovery for ordinary negligence. The Rhode Island Supreme Court held that the Rhode Island rule, favoring recovery, applied. The Court noted that this case would fall under the third rule in *Neumeier*, but rejected that rule. The Rhode Island judges viewed the third rule as a thinly-disguised place-of-wrong standard containing an exception so vague that it destroyed the certainty of application that a rules approach seeks. The Court created its own rule for guest-statute cases in lieu of Judge Fuld's third rule: "where a driver is from a state which allows a passenger to recover for ordinary negligence, the plaintiff should recover, no matter what the law of his residence or the place of accident."[256] The Court suggested that no other state could have a reasonable objection to the defendant's home state holding the defendant to a stricter standard of conduct even when the defendant ventured abroad. This seems a defensible proposition and makes it unlikely that the Rhode Island Court will find its narrowly-drawn rule unworkable in unforeseen circumstances.

§ 6.25 "No Interest" Cases

One of the difficulties with *Neumeier* and *Labree* is that they are

---

253. This is not true of the New York cases cited in § 6.22 note 215.

254. 111 R.I. 657, 306 A.2d 808 (1973).

255. Massaletti v. Fitzroy, 228 Mass. 487, 118 N.E. 168 (1917). Doctrine abolished by Mass.Gen.Laws c. 231, § 85L.

256. *Labree*, 111 R.I. at 673, 306 A.2d at 818. See also Danner v. Staggs, 680 F.2d 427 (5th Cir.1982) (Arkansas guest recovers against Texas host for injuries in Arkansas applying Texas law and not Arkansas guest statute).

"unprovided"-for[257] or "no interest" cases. The classic "no interest" case is one in which the plaintiff's state has a law favorable to the defendant and the defendant's state has a law favorable to the plaintiff. The term "no interest" comes from the argument that neither state is interested in having its own law apply. The plaintiff's state has no interest in protecting the defendant who comes from another state and the defendant's state has no reason to give the plaintiff more compensation than the law of the plaintiff's state would provide. As the discussion in the preceding section indicates, this is an unduly parochial reading of state interests that has led some commentators to decry the "no interest" label.[258]

Perhaps the best known of the no-interest cases is *Hurtado v. Superior Court.*[259] In *Hurtado*, a Mexican resident, while visiting California, died when the car in which he was a passenger collided with a parked car. A wrongful death action was brought against the driver of the car in which the decedent was a passenger and against the owner of the parked automobile. Both defendants were California residents. Under the law of the Mexican state in which the decedent was domiciled at the time of his death, the maximum recovery was just under $2,000. California placed no monetary limit on recovery. The California Supreme Court held that the California measure of recovery for wrongful death should apply.

Hurtado contains a factual distinction from both *Neumeier* and *Labree*—a distinction on which the California Supreme Court focused. In *Hurtado*, the California defendants performed their allegedly negligent acts in California. The court saw deterrence of negligent conduct as one of the reasons for California's rule of full compensation for wrongful death. This deterrence policy applied when a California resident acted tortiously in California.[260]

Is *Hurtado's* deterrence argument cogent? If a California driver does not drive carefully because of fear for his or her own safety, or for fear of the safety of loved ones and friends who are passengers, or for fear of the sanctions of criminal law, is the driver likely to be more careful because of the specter of California's unlimited recovery?[261] Perhaps the effect of an accident on the cost and availability of liability insurance is some

---

257. See B. Currie, Selected Essays on the Conflict of Laws 152 (1963).

258. See Kramer, *The Myth of the Unprovided–For Case*, 75 Va. L. Rev. 1045 (1989) (contending, contrary to the discussion in the preceding section, that the plaintiff should lose unless some state has an interest in providing relief); Symeonides, *The American Choice-of-Law Revolution in the Courts: Today and Tomorrow*, in Hague Academy of Int'l L. Collected Courses 340 (2002) (most U.S. courts apply the law of a state that has plaintiff-affiliating contacts whether or not that law favors the plaintiff).

259. 11 Cal.3d 574, 114 Cal.Rptr. 106, 522 P.2d 666 (1974).

260. Id. at 583, 114 Cal.Rptr. at 112, 522 P.2d at 672; cf. Hernandez v. Burger, 102 Cal.App.3d 795, 162 Cal.Rptr. 564 (1980), (applying lower Mexican measure of damages when Mexican plaintiff injured in Mexico by California defendant).

261. See Veazey v. Doremus, 103 N.J. 244, 510 A.2d 1187, 1190 (1986) ("'[a] motor vehicle operator's concern for his or her own safety and that of others on the highway is sufficiently strong, so that judicial recognition of interspousal immunity as declared in another state will not endanger highway safety in New Jersey"). But see Ledesma v. Jack

incentive for more prudent driving.[262] There is very little empirical data that throws light upon the question of whether a combination of civil liability and insurance practices deters careless driving.[263] I find such a proposition counterintuitive.[264] In the meantime, I would prefer a more compelling argument to support the *Hurtado* result.

One tempting basis for resolving the "unprovided-for" case is to fall back upon the core legal concepts that are common to both jurisdictions. Both states have a general background of liability for wrongful conduct. The rule of the plaintiff's state limiting that liability is an exception to the general rule of liability—an exception that is not applicable if its sole purpose is to protect defendants resident in that state or in states with similar rules. If the exception is not applicable, the rule, liability, is and this is then the common result under the law of both states.[265]

The difficulty with this "common core" basis for resolving no-interest cases is that there is danger of begging the question by attach-

---

Stewart Produce, Inc., 816 F.2d 482, 486 (9th Cir.1987) ("drivers tend to be more careful when their chances of incurring liability are more substantial").

262. See Cramton, *Driver Behavior and Legal Sanctions: A Study of Deterrence*, 67 Mich. L. Rev. 421, 445, 453 (1969); McKean, *Products Liability: Trends and Implications*, 38 U. Chi. L. Rev. 3, 41 (1970); Trautman, supra note 260, at 5.

263. See Little, *A Theory and Empirical Study of What Deters Drinking Drivers, If, When and Why*, 23 Ad. L. Rev. 23, 50 (1970):

When asked to select which alternative they would mind less in a series of all possible pairings of four undesirable consequences, the drivers showed their preferences from least undesirable to most undesirable to be:

(1) A $250 accident with no injuries (selected on 70% of 606 binary choices).

(2) An accident with minor personal injury (selected 56%).

(3) A drunk driving arrest (selected 34%).

(4) Loss of driving privileges for one year (selected 33%).

264. I am admittedly on very shaky ground here. A distinguished court has referred to my doubts about the efficacy of deterrence in this context as the "naive product of wishful thinking." Hunker v. Royal Indem. Co., 57 Wis.2d 588, 604 n.2, 204 N.W.2d 897, 905–06 n.2 (1973).

For cases permitting the plaintiff to recover under the law of the place of the crash, partly because of an interest in deterring negligent driving, see Gagne v. Berry, 112 N.H. 125, 290 A.2d 624 (1972) (New Hampshire law applied to permit Massachusetts guest to recover against Massachusetts host); Bray v. Cox, 39 A.D.2d 299, 333 N.Y.S.2d 783 (1972), appeal dism'd, 33 N.Y.2d 789, 350 N.Y.S.2d 653, 305 N.E.2d 775 (1973) (New York law applied to permit Ontario guest to sue Ontario host). But see Gordon v. Eastern Air Lines, Inc., 391 F.Supp. 31 (S.D.N.Y.1975) (place of crash has no interest in measure of recovery when defendant's standard of conduct is not in issue); Tower v. Schwabe, 284 Or. 105, 585 P.2d 662 (1978) (place of injury interest in safety "abstract" and adequately protected by its criminal law). See also supra note 254 and accompanying text.

For commentators approving of a deterrence interest, see D. Cavers, The Choice-of-Law Process 144 (1965); Horowitz, *The Law of Choice of Law in California—A Restatement*, 21 U.C.L.A. L. Rev. 719, 757 (1974). But see Ratner, *Choice of Law: Interest Analysis and Cost–Contribution*, 47 S.Cal. L. Rev. 817, 840 (1974) ("If automobile accident recovery policies did deter careless driving, narrower recovery by a small number of nonresidents from restrictive-recovery states would not significantly diminish the local deterrent effect.")

265. See Sedler, *Interstate Accidents and the Unprovided for Case: Reflections on Neumeier v. Kuehner*, 1 Hofstra L. Rev. 125, 138 (1973); cf. Baade, *The Case of the Disinterested Two States: Neumeier v. Kuehner*, 1 Hofstra L. Rev. 150, 167 (1973) (not a proper basis for decision in *Neumeier* so long as Ontario applies its guest statute to uninsured Ontario motorists).

ing one label rather than another. Why is it not just as accurate to say that the background rule is no liability for conduct unless there is a rule specifically imposing liability?[266] This objection seems especially appropriate when addressed to liability for wrongful death in the light of the great differences in compensable losses and methods of computing damages that exist even between states of the United States.[267] There are times when the "common core" concept may be especially attractive. For example, one could argue with some force that all states have a policy of validating wills and that if a state has a particular invalidating rule, which in the light of its underlying policies does not apply to the law-fact pattern in litigation, the common policy of validation should prevail. But this kind of argument should be used with great caution to avoid illogical leaps to results that are desired for unarticulated reasons.

Another way of deciding the unprovided-for case is to re-examine the tentative conclusion that neither state has a policy that applying its law will advance. By finding a deterrence policy, the court in *Hurtado* converted a "no interest" case into a "false conflict" in which California had an interest in imposing liability but the Mexican state had no interest whatever in preventing full liability. In the same manner, it would be possible to reanalyze both *Neumeier* and *Labree* and defend the result in each as the only sensible resolution of a false conflict. In *Neumeier*, the New York Court of Appeals suggested that although New York has no interest in giving an Ontario citizen recovery not available under Ontario law, Ontario certainly has an interest in seeing to it that its citizens behave graciously in Ontario and do not manifest their ingratitude by extracting compensation from hosts who are only ordinarily negligent.[268] On the other hand, the *Labree* result could be defended on the basis of the "altruism" policy articulated in that opinion: a state has an interest in having its drivers bear the primary responsibility for distributing the cost of their injurious conduct no matter where this conduct occurs or who is injured by that conduct.

---

266. See Milhollin, *The Forum Preference in Choice of Law; Some Notes on Hurtado v. Superior Court*, 10 U.S.F. L. Rev. 625, 646–47 (1976).

267. See S. Speiser et al., Recovery for Wrongful Death and Injury § 1:9 (1992).

268. *Neumeier*, 31 N.Y.2d 121, 125–26, 335 N.Y.S.2d 64, 68, 286 N.E.2d 454, 456. But see Baade, supra note 265, at 156 ("the sole apparent legislative purpose of the Ontario guest statute . . . is to protect insurance companies against claims which would necessitate an increase of motor vehicle insurance rates in Ontario").

For a case attributing a more altruistic policy to New York, see Erny v. Estate of Merola, 171 N.J. 86, 792 A.2d 1208 (2002). The negligence of two New York drivers caused a multi-car crash in New Jersey that injured a New Jersey resident. A jury determined that one New York driver's negligence was 60% responsible for the injuries and that the other driver's negligence was 40% responsible. The 60% responsible driver had only $100 thousand in liability insurance; the 40% responsible driver had $1.5 million insurance coverage. Under New Jersey law, plaintiff could only recover 40% of his non-economic damages from the driver 40% responsible. Under New York law, that driver would be jointly and severally liable for 100% of all damages. The court held that New York law applied. New York has a "policy of providing for recovery to plaintiffs injured in accidents caused by its residents driving automobiles registered and insured in New York." Id. at 1218.

The question then becomes which of the policies articulated to resolve the unprovided-for cases, *Neumeier* (deter ingratitude by denying recovery), *Labree* (extend benefits of recovery rule to nonresidents), or *Hurtado* (deter negligent driving by imposing civil liability), is the most credible. I vote for *Labree*.[269]

§ 6.26 Comparative Impairment in California: Bernhard v. Harrah's Club

The opposite of the "no interest" case is the "true conflict" in which each of two or more states would advance its policies by applying its own

---

269. For holdings that defendant's state should make the benefits of its law available to nonresidents, see Broome v. Antlers' Hunting Club, 595 F.2d 921 (3d Cir.1979) (Pennsylvania law—deterrence, retribution, equal protection); Gravina v. Brunswick Corp., 338 F.Supp. 1 (D.R.I.1972) (invasion of privacy, "better rule"); Decker v. Fox River Tractor Co., 324 F.Supp. 1089 (E.D.Wis.1971) (products liability, "better rule"); Dworak v. Olson Constr. Co., 191 Colo. 161, 551 P.2d 198 (1976) (effect on other defendant of covenant not to sue, forum preference in the absence of more contacts elsewhere); McCrossin v. Hicks Chevrolet, Inc., 248 A.2d 917 (D.C.App.1969) (D.C. rule dispensing with privity requirement is for benefit of all who buy in the District, not just for residents); Bolgrean v. Stich, 293 Minn. 8, 196 N.W.2d 442 (1972) (guest statute; center of gravity, better law; plaintiff has since resumed former residence in defendant's state); Gantes v. Kason Corp., 145 N.J. 478, 679 A.2d 106 (1996) (applying New Jersey time limitations rather than Georgia statute of repose because of "substantial interest in deterrence"); Frummer v. Hilton Hotels Int'l, Inc., 60 Misc.2d 840, 304 N.Y.S.2d 335 (1969) (England would not be so "parochial" as to claim it has no interest in compensating a New York plaintiff at the expense of an English defendant); Hepp v. Ireland, 66 Civ. 2128 (S.D.N.Y.1970) (unreported, discussed in D. Cavers, *Contemporary Conflicts Law in American Perspective*, in 131 Collected Courses of the Hague Academy of Int'l L. 179 n. 24 (1970 III), and excerpt from opinion quoted in Ausubel, *Conflict of Laws Trends—Torts*, 19 DePaul L. Rev. 684, 692 (1970)) (the New York policy of financial responsibility for motorists extends to all people injured by the negligence of motorists reachable by the New York policy); Brown v. Market Development, Inc., 41 Ohio Misc. 57, 322 N.E.2d 367 (1974) (action by Ohio Attorney General, Ohio statute applies to deceptive and unconscionable practices directed at nonresidents); Erwin v. Thomas, 264 Or. 454, 506 P.2d 494 (1973) (automobile accident, loss of consortium, forum preference); Johnson v. Spider Staging Corp., 87 Wn.2d 577, 555 P.2d 997 (1976) (products liability, deterrence); Lichter v. Fritsch, 77 Wis.2d 178, 252 N.W.2d 360 (1977) (liability of owner for leaving keys in car); cf. In re Paris Air Crash, 399 F.Supp. 732 (C.D.Cal.1975) (products liability, California law applied to California defendants both increase and limit liability). See also Shapira, *"Manna for the Entire World" or "Thou Shalt Love Thy Neighbor as Thyself"—Comment on Neumeier v. Kuehner*, 1 Hofstra L. Rev. 168, 172 (1973); Note, *Choice of Law in Tort Cases: Neumeier v. Kuehner*, 37 Alb. L. Rev. 173, 187 (1972); cf. von Mehren, *Special Substantive Rules for Multistate Problems: Their Role and Significance in Contemporary Choice of Law Methodology*, 88 Harv. L. Rev. 347, 369 (1974) (*Neumeier* could be solved by giving plaintiff recovery for one-half of the damage).

But see Vaz Borralho v. Keydril Co., 696 F.2d 379 (5th Cir.1983) (recovery under United States law not available for death of Brazilian killed while working on fixed drilling rig off coast of Brazil); Gordon v. Eastern Air Lines, 391 F.Supp. 31 (S.D.N.Y.1975) (New York dependents of New Yorker killed in Florida crash limited to items compensable under New York wrongful death law); Stutsman v. Kaiser Foundation Health Plan, 546 A.2d 367 (D.C.1988) (apply law of marital domicile to deny claim for loss of consortium rather than recovery rule of the forum where the defendant is incorporated); Goetz v. Wells Ford Mercury, Inc., 405 N.W.2d 842 (Iowa 1987) (apply Iowa law to a claim by an Iowa plaintiff to deny vicarious liability of Minnesota car dealer); Cavers, *Cipolla and Conflicts Justice*, 9 Duquesne L. Rev. 360, 370 (1971) ("quixotic" to give guest benefit of law of host's state when relationship created and ended in guest's state); Ratner, supra note 264 at 836 (nonresidents who do not contribute to local taxes, prices, and insurance premiums should not benefit from local law more favorable than that in their home states); cf. Baade, supra note 265 at 162 (although in *Neumeier* New York might apply New York law in a spirit of altruism, Ontario should not apply New York law if New York would not).

law rather than the different rule of the other state. The California Supreme Court and the Louisiana Conflict of Laws Code[270] have adopted a "comparative impairment" approach to the true conflict.

In *Bernhard v. Harrah's Club*,[271] a California plaintiff was injured when his motorcycle collided in California with an automobile driven by another California resident. The automobile driver had allegedly become intoxicated at a Nevada gambling establishment from which she was driving home. The Nevada club advertised in California and solicited the business of California residents. Under Nevada law, service of liquor to a drunken person did not render the server civilly liable for harm caused by the drunk. Under California law, service of intoxicating beverages to a person obviously intoxicated was regarded as a proximate cause of injury resulting from the drunk's conduct and the server was liable.

The California Supreme Court recognized that both Nevada and California were interested in having their own rules applied. Nevada wished to protect the bar owner from civil liability because that was Nevada's policy and the defendant was a Nevada corporation that served the beverages in Nevada. California wished to "prevent tavern keepers from selling alcoholic beverages to obviously intoxicated persons who are likely to act in California in the intoxicated state."[272] The Court resolved this dilemma in favor of application of the California rule making the bar owner civilly liable.[273] The method adopted by the Court to do this is to

---

270. See La. Civ. Code Ann. art. 3515 (stating that an issue in a transjurisdictional occurrence is "governed by the law of the state whose policies would be most seriously impaired if its law were not applied to that issue").

271. 16 Cal.3d 313, 128 Cal.Rptr. 215, 546 P.2d 719, cert. denied, 429 U.S. 859, 97 S.Ct. 159, 50 L.Ed.2d 136 (1976).

272. 16 Cal.3d at 322, 128 Cal.Rptr. at 221, 546 P.2d at 725. See Sloan et al., *Liability, Risk Perceptions, and Precautions at Bars*, 43 J. L. & Econ. 473, 484, 495–97 (2000) (strict dramshop laws increase bar owners' and managers' perceptions of the probability of being sued and this in turn increases the level of precaution to avoid serving obviously intoxicated adults); cf. Nelson & Roethe, *Driving under the Influence of Alcohol: A Wisconsin Study*, 1970 Wis. L. Rev. 495, 510 (if the California policy were simply to provide an additional and probably solvent defendant for the victim to sue, comparative impairment analysis should require the Court to determine whether the driver's assets, including insurance coverage, were sufficient to compensate plaintiff without looking to the Nevada club).

273. See also Carver v. Schafer, 647 S.W.2d 570 (Mo.App.1983) (Missouri rule of unlimited liability rather than Illinois rule of limited liability applicable to Illinois bar 10 miles from border when intoxicated Missouri driver hit Missouri resident in Missouri). But see Estates of Braun v. Cactus Pete's, Inc., 108 Idaho 798, 702 P.2d 836 (1985) (Idaho dram shop statute not applicable to bar just across border in Nevada although intoxicated driver and victims were Idaho residents and Nevada has no civil liability); Manfredonia v. American Airlines, Inc., 68 A.D.2d 131, 416 N.Y.S.2d 286 (2d Dep't 1979) (New York dram shop statute not applicable when sale occurred outside New York on airplane that had departed from New York); Thoring v. Bottonsek, 350 N.W.2d 586 (N.D.1984) (North Dakota dram shop act not applicable although injury in North Dakota to North Dakota resident when drinks served at bar in Montana 8 miles from border); cf. Interprovincial Co–Operatives, Ltd. v. The Queen, 53 D.L.R.3d 321 (Can.S.Ct.1975) (only the Canadian Parliament has power to deal with pollution that affects province other than one in which pollution originated).

For other cases involving liability of bar owners for injuries caused in another state by drunks, see § 6.18 n.162.

measure the "comparative impairment"[274] of the policies of the two states if the law of the other state were applied. The Court found that California's interest in protecting its residents would be very seriously impaired if California law did not reach out-of-state tavern keepers who, like defendant, regularly and purposefully sell intoxicating beverages to California residents when it is reasonably certain that these residents will return to California and act in California while still intoxicated. The Court found, on the other hand, that Nevada's interest in protecting its tavern keepers would not be significantly impaired when, as in the instant case, liability is imposed only on tavern keepers who actively solicit California business. Moreover, the Court reasoned, since the act of selling alcoholic beverages to obviously intoxicated persons is already a crime in Nevada, the application of California's rule of civil liability will not impose an entirely new duty on Nevada bar owners requiring the ability to distinguish between California residents and other patrons.

I do not find this reasoning cogent. The most obvious difficulty is that the Court failed to note that the Nevada statute imposing criminal sanctions for serving liquor to inebriated persons had been repealed after the accident but almost three years before the opinion.[275] Unless the Court is issuing a one-trip ticket, it is imposing on Nevada bartenders a new duty.

The Court suggests that its decision will affect few Nevada tavern keepers. In the absence of empirical data, is there any reason not to believe that relatively few Californians injured in California would be affected if the decision had gone the other way?[276] One can certainly imagine a Nevada court applying what purports to be exactly the same method of analysis and coming to the opposite conclusion.[277] Unless

---

274. See Baxter, *Choice of Law and the Federal System*, 16 Stan. L. Rev. 1, 18 (1963); Horowitz, § 6.25 note 264, at 752–53; cf. Kearney v. Salomon Smith Barney, Inc., 39 Cal.4th 95, 137 P.3d 914, 45 Cal.Rptr.3d 730 (2006) (apply California law to Georgia defendant to enjoin conduct but not to allow damages or restitution); Hall v. University of Nevada, 74 Cal.App.3d 280, 141 Cal.Rptr. 439 (1977), hearing denied, Cal. (1977), aff'd, 440 U.S. 410, 99 S.Ct. 1182, 59 L.Ed.2d 416 (1979) (apply California law denying sovereign immunity and eliminating limit on liability to Nevada state agency operating vehicle that caused injuries in California—court declares this an even stronger case than *Bernhard* for applying California law because the defendant's conduct occurred in California). See also Biscoe v. Arlington County, 738 F.2d 1352 (D.C.Cir.1984), cert. denied, 469 U.S. 1159, 105 S.Ct. 909, 83 L.Ed.2d 923 (1985) (using comparative impairment analysis to apply forum law to permit recovery against county in adjoining state); Liew v. Official Receiver and Liquidator, 685 F.2d 1192 (9th Cir.1982) (California comparative impairment analysis is applicable only after a true conflict is found); Barringer v. State, 111 Idaho 794, 727 P.2d 1222 (1986) (using comparative impairment); Hicks v. Graves Truck Lines, Inc., 707 S.W.2d 439 (Mo.App.1986) (using comparative impairment analysis); cf. Lee v. Miller County, Ark., 800 F.2d 1372 (5th Cir.1986) (give comity to sister state immunity rule when a Texas county would have been completely or partially immune from liability—Texas law). But see Kay, *The Use of Comparative Impairment to Resolve True Conflicts: An Evaluation of the California Experience*, 68 Cal. L. Rev. 577, 578 (1980) ("if the California Supreme Court wishes to use Currie's methodology to resolve choice of law cases, it should reject comparative impairment analysis as inconsistent with that approach").

275. 1973 Nev.Stats. 1062, c. 604, § 8, S.B. 359. Effective July 1, 1973. Nev.Rev.Stat. § 218.530 (1975).

276. See Note, *After Hurtado and Bernhard: Interest Analysis and the Search for a Consistent Theory for Choice-of-Law Cases*, 29 Stan. L. Rev. 127, 146 (1976).

277. Id.; Note, *Choice of Law for True Conflicts*, 65 Cal. L. Rev. 290, 303 (1977); cf. Kramer, *Rethinking Choice of Law*, 90 Colum. L. Rev. 277, 318 (1990) (stating that "we cannot rely on comparative impairment to resolve all or even most true conflicts").

supplemented by specific objective criteria, "comparative impairment" is unlikely to be a method that is cogent, feasible to administer, and predictable. It is noteworthy that *Bernhard* has been repudiated in one of the rare United States statutes to state by name the cases that it abrogates.[278]

§ 6.27   Objective Bases for a "Comparative Impairment" Method

What are specific objective criteria that can guide comparative impairment analysis? The failure to apply a state's law does not impair its policies if the law in issue does not in fact advance the policies on which it purports to be based.[279] For example, it can be contended that a guest statute does not prevent collusive suits or shield hosts from ungrateful guests. In the absence of clear empirical verification, such a route is very hazardous. It should be traveled, if at all with great caution.[280]

Another objective basis for comparing policy impairment is to determine whether the policies advanced by the laws of one state are eliminated or greatly attenuated by the facts of the case at bar.[281] For example, even if one concedes that guest statutes prevent collusion, if the guest is killed in the crash, the guest cannot be a party to collusion.[282] Or if the place of injury has a hypothetical interest in providing recovery in order to insure the payment of local medical creditors, this interest disappears if the medical creditors are paid or if there are sufficient funds to pay them without resort to the tortfeasor or the liability insurer.[283]

---

278.   West's Ann.Cal.Bus. & Prof.C. § 25602:

"... (b) No person who sells, furnishes, gives, ... any alcoholic beverage pursuant to subdivision (a) [misdemeanor if to habitual drunkard or obviously intoxicated person] shall be civilly liable to any injured person or the estate of such person for injuries inflicted ... as a result of intoxication by the consumer of such alcoholic beverage.

"(c) The Legislature hereby declares that this section shall be interpreted so that the holdings in cases such as Vesely v. Sager (5 Cal.3d 153) [95 Cal.Rptr. 623, 486 P.2d 151 (1971) imposing civil liability for committing the misdemeanor], Bernhard v. Harrah's Club ... and Coulter v. Superior Court (21 Cal.3d 144) [145 Cal.Rptr. 534, 577 P.2d 669 (1978) (social host held liable for serving liquor to intoxicated guest who causes harm to others)] be abrogated in favor of prior judicial interpretations finding the consumption of alcoholic beverages rather than the serving of alcoholic beverages as the proximate cause of injuries inflicted upon another by an intoxicated person." (Amendment enacted by Stats. 1978 ch. 929 p. 2903 § 1).

See also Cable v. Sahara Tahoe Corp., 93 Cal.App.3d 384, 155 Cal.Rptr. 770 (2d Dist. Div. 3 1979) (Nevada hotel not civilly liable for injury in Nevada to California passenger by intoxicated Nevada driver—although amendments to California alcoholic beverage act are not retroactively applicable to this case, "the impairment of such a repudiated policy has a minimal effect upon California's governmental interest").

279.   See Horowitz, section 6.25 note 264 at 756–58; L. McDougal, *Choice of Law: Prologue to a Viable Interest–Analysis Theory*, 51 Tul. L. Rev. 207, 213 (1977).

280.   See Trautman, § 6.23 note 244 at 15.

281.   See Horowitz, § 6.25 note 264 at 753–54.

282.   See Trautman, § 6.23 note 244 at 11.

283.   But see Milkovich v. Saari, 295 Minn. 155, 203 N.W.2d 408 (1973) (place of injury gets interest from likelihood of medical bills whether or not they have been paid in case at bar).

Another cogent basis for comparative impairment analysis is present if the state with the opposing rule has, since the occurrence in issue, changed its rule for future cases to accord with the rule of the other state.[284] This is most likely to occur if the changed rule was objectively anachronistic or aberrational because most states that had the rule have abandoned it or no other state had the rule. The fact that the other state has joined the clearly discernible movement simply adds cogency to the "anachronism" or "aberrational" argument.

There is at least one circumstance in which it is plausible to argue that applying Y's law will less impair the purposes of state X's law than the application of X law will impair the policies underlying state Y's law. This is when both states share a common policy but differ in its detailed application. If a transaction would be valid under Y law but invalid under X law, validation under Y law will protect X's basic policy, because that policy is shared by Y, but invalidation under X law will completely undermine Y's policy of validation.

For example, suppose X's rule against perpetuities is "lives of persons in being or twenty-five years." Y's rule is the more typical "lives in being plus twenty years."[285] A testamentary trust that suspends the vesting of title to property free of the trust for a period of named lives plus twenty years will be valid under Y's rule, but invalid under X's rule. If a testator dies domiciled in Y and the trust res is land in X, both states

---

284. For cases in which the court notes a change in the law of one state and applies the law of the other state, see, e.g., Rosenthal v. Warren, 374 F.Supp. 522 (S.D.N.Y.1974) (charitable immunity); Wallis v. Mrs. Smith's Pie Co., 261 Ark. 622, 550 S.W.2d 453 (1977) (contributory negligence); Cable v. Sahara Tahoe Corp., 155 Cal.Rptr. 770, 93 Cal.App.3d 384 (2d Dist.1979) (removal of civil liability under forum law); DeMeyer v. Maxwell, 103 Idaho 327, 647 P.2d 783 (App.1982) (guest statute of place of accident subsequently amended); State ex rel. Broglin v. Nangle, 510 S.W.2d 699 (Mo.1974) (limit on wrongful death damages) (change in forum law); LaBounty v. American Ins. Co., 122 N.H. 738, 451 A.2d 161 (1982) (suit against co-employee barred by workers' compensation); Gagne v. Berry, 112 N.H. 125, 290 A.2d 624 (1972) (gross negligence for guest's recovery); Fisher v. Huck, 50 Or.App. 635, 624 P.2d 177 (1981), appeal dism'd by stipulation, 291 Or. 566, 632 P.2d 1260 (1981) (repeal of forum's guest statute); Labree v. Major, 111 R.I. 657, 306 A.2d 808 (1973) (gross negligence for guest's recovery); Central Mut. Ins. Co. v. H.O., Inc., 63 Wis.2d 54, 216 N.W.2d 239 (1974) (statute of limitations). But see Hanley v. Tribune Pub. Co., 527 F.2d 68 (9th Cir.1975). In *Hanley*, the choice was between the libel rules of California (newspaper incorporated and published) and Nevada (plaintiff's domicile where some papers circulated). California law required the plaintiff to allege special damages unless retraction of the libel was demanded and not forthcoming. At the time of publication, Nevada law did not require that special damages be pleaded. The court applied Nevada law as of the time of publication even though the Nevada rule had since been changed to conform to the California law. But see also Dalton v. McLean, 137 Me. 4, 14 A.2d 13 (1940) (refuses to apply expressly retroactive survival statute of place of impact); Allen v. Nessler, 247 Minn. 230, 76 N.W.2d 793 (1956) (refuses to apply survival statute of place of impact passed since the occurrence); cf. Zurzola v. General Motors Corp., 503 F.2d 403 (3d Cir.1974) (apply marital immunity rule of marital domicile even though that state has since abolished that rule prospectively); Berghammer v. Smith, 185 N.W.2d 226 (Iowa 1971) (apply law of marital domicile but not that aspect of it that makes overruling of marital immunity prospective only); Mager v. Mager, 197 N.W.2d 626 (N.D.1972) (applying Minnesota law of interspousal immunity to Minnesota spouses although law abrogated five days after accident in Minnesota).

285. See In re Chappell's Estate, 124 Wash. 128, 213 P. 684 (1923). A rule against perpetuities invalidates a will or trust that suspends the power to transfer title to property if the suspension is for a period longer than that permitted by the rule.

will have an interest in having their perpetuities rules applied. Y will wish to uphold a will of a Y testator when that will is valid under Y law. X will want to prevent the vesting of title to the land from being delayed past the time that X deems proper. Validating the will under Y's rule against perpetuities will uphold Y's validation policy and, because of Y's perpetuities rule, it is unlikely that social consequences will occur in X that the X rule seeks to avoid. On the other hand, invalidating the will under X law will completely frustrate Y's policy of freedom of testation.[286]

§ 6.28　The Nexus Problem

One of the difficulties with *Bernhard*[287] is that it raises a tough question for which the new method of conflicts analysis has no ready answer: what contact, if any, other than residence of the plaintiff, should the forum have before applying its own law in favor of the plaintiff? In *Bernhard*, should a Nevada tavern keeper be held civilly liable under California law for conduct in Nevada that under Nevada law would have been immune from civil liability?

There are several other well known cases that raise the question of whether the plaintiff's state has sufficient nexus with the defendant or with the defendant's course of conduct to make it fair and reasonable to hold the defendant liable under the plaintiff-favoring rule of the plaintiff's state. In *Rosenthal v. Warren*,[288] a world-renowned Boston surgeon operated on a New York resident in a Boston hospital. The plaintiff died after the surgery and a wrongful death action was brought in New York against the doctor and the hospital. At the time of the death, Massachusetts limited recovery to $50,000, but New York had no limit. A majority of the court held that the Massachusetts limit was not applicable[289] and justified the result in part on the ground that the Massachusetts hospital and the famous surgeon treated patients from all over the world.

Schwartz v. Consolidated Freightways Corporation[290] raises the nex-

---

286. Cf. Barringer v. State, 111 Idaho 794, 727 P.2d 1222 (1986). Idaho law was applied to permit reduction of the verdict against an Idaho tortfeasor. The reduction was in the amount represented by the percent of contribution to the injury by the deceased worker's Washington employer. This did not increase the amount the employer had to pay, did not change the amount recovered by the dependents, and only slightly reduced the amount of reimbursement to Washington for its workers' compensation benefits.

287. See § 6.26.

288. 475 F.2d 438 (2d Cir.1973), cert. denied, 414 U.S. 856, 94 S.Ct. 159, 38 L.Ed.2d 106 (1973), on remand, 374 F.Supp. 522 (S.D.N.Y.1974) (defense based on Massachusetts charitable immunity rule stricken). See Reese, *Legislative Jurisdiction*, 78 Colum. L. Rev. 1587, 1605 (1978) (*Rosenthal* wrongly decided and may violate due process).

289. See also Tyminski v. United States, 481 F.2d 257 (3d Cir.1973) (apply New Jersey law to measure recovery for New Jersey resident treated at Veterans Administration hospital in New York); cf. Wall v. Noble, 705 S.W.2d 727 (Tex.App—Texarkana, 1986, writ refd. n.r.e.) (Texas has most significant relationship when Louisiana doctor, who operated in Louisiana, examined Texas patient in doctor's branch office in Texas). Contra, Blakesley v. Wolford, 789 F.2d 236 (3d Cir.1986) (apply law of state where doctor operated although he examined the patient in the forum on a visit there—Pennsylvania conflicts law); Bannowsky v. Krauser, 294 F.Supp. 1204 (D.Colo.1969).

290. 300 Minn. 487, 221 N.W.2d 665 (1974), cert. denied sub nom. Spector Freight System, Inc. v. Schwartz, 425 U.S. 959, 96 S.Ct. 1740, 48 L.Ed.2d 204 (1976).

us problem in an extreme form. The plaintiff, a Minnesota resident, was driving a truck in Indiana when he was involved in a three-truck collision. Both of the other trucks were garaged and maintained in Ohio. The plaintiff went back to Minnesota and there sued the two corporations that owned the two trucks with which he had collided in Indiana. The only connection between the defendants and Minnesota that the court mentions is stated as follows: "[B]oth defendant corporations, although foreign to Minnesota, are licensed to do business in this state, and presumably exercise this privilege."[291] The court nevertheless held that the Minnesota comparative negligence rule was applicable rather than the Indiana contributory negligence rule, which completely barred recovery by the Minnesota plaintiff.

It is interesting to compare the plaintiff-favoring results of cases like *Bernhard, Rosenthal,* and *Schwartz*[292] with *Maguire v. Exeter & Hampton Electric Company*[293]—a case in which the defendant's state got to appraise the nexus problem. In *Maguire,* a Maine resident who was an employee of a New Hampshire firm, was killed in the course of his employment in New Hampshire. Under New Hampshire law at the time, the limit on recovery was $20,000, but under the law of Maine there was no limit on recovery. The New Hampshire court found that the New Hampshire limit on recovery was applicable despite the fact that the New Hampshire court had abandoned the place-of-wrong rule; that to resolve a real conflict it would apply the law that it deemed the "better" rule; and that in this case it found that the New Hampshire rule was not the "better" law, but, on the contrary, that its "limitation death statute lies in the backwater of the modern stream."[294] What was the reason for

---

291. 300 Minn. at 492, 221 N.W.2d at 668.

292. See also Foster v. Maldonado, 315 F.Supp. 1179 (D.N.J.1970), leave to appeal denied, 433 F.2d 348 (3d Cir.1970) (Pennsylvania resident killed in New Jersey in collision with New Jersey resident—more generous Pennsylvania measure of recovery applied); Wallis v. Mrs. Smith's Pie Co., 261 Ark. 622, 550 S.W.2d 453 (1977) (Arkansas plaintiff collides in Missouri with truck owned by Pennsylvania defendant—Arkansas comparative negligence rule applied); Kasel v. Remington Arms Co., 24 Cal.App.3d 711, 101 Cal.Rptr. 314 (1972) (California products liability law applied in favor of California resident injured in Mexico by product manufactured and sold in Mexico by defendant's affiliate); DeRemer v. Pacific Intermountain Express Co., 353 N.W.2d 694 (Minn.App.1984) (apply forum law to favor forum plaintiff injured in neighboring state in collision with truck of company licensed to do business in the forum and in fact doing business there); Tjepkema v. Kenney, 31 A.D.2d 908, 298 N.Y.S.2d 175, motion to appeal dism'd, 24 N.Y.2d 942, 302 N.Y.S.2d 580, 250 N.E.2d 68 (1969) (New Yorker killed in Missouri by Missouri driver—Missouri statutory limit on damages not applied); MacKendrick v. Newport News Shipbuilding & Dry Dock Co., 59 Misc.2d 994, 302 N.Y.S.2d 124 (1969) (New Yorker sent by New York employer to work on equipment of Virginia defendant in Virginia killed on job by defendant's alleged negligence—Virginia limit on recovery not applied) (subsequently judgment was rendered for the defendant on a finding of no negligence, 40 A.D.2d 798, 338 N.Y.S.2d 41 (1972), aff'd mem., 35 N.Y.2d 681, 361 N.Y.S.2d 158, 319 N.E.2d 421 (1974)); Cunningham v. McNair, 48 A.D.2d 546, 370 N.Y.S.2d 577 (1975) (New York owner's liability law applies although automobile rented in Maryland, registered in Virginia, and accident in Maryland); Slawek v. Stroh, 62 Wis.2d 295, 215 N.W.2d 9 (1974) (cause of action for seduction under Wisconsin law for Wisconsin woman although all acts took place elsewhere).

293. 114 N.H. 589, 325 A.2d 778 (1974).

294. 114 N.H. at 592, 325 A.2d at 780.

this result? The court stated: "What this case comes down to is that the only relationship or contact with Maine is the fact that the decedent was a resident of Maine. Surely this is not enough, standing alone, to warrant the application of Maine law to the issue of damages."[295]

Is there any reason why, as a limit on consequences-based analysis, the plaintiff's state should have some reasonable nexus with the defendant or the defendant's course of conduct before its law is applied to the defendant, or is this requirement just an atavistic retreat to territorial dogma?[296] In extreme cases the defendant may be able to make a realistic unfair surprise argument; that he or she would have acted differently or obtained different insurance if there was any reason to take plaintiff's law into account. This surprise argument is not likely to be cogent when addressed to unintentional torts with all contacts in the United States. The unintentional nature of the tort makes it unlikely that the defendant shaped his or her conduct to conform with a tort rule, and standards of recovery between states are sufficiently similar, so that it is unlikely that the defendant has procured $5,000 worth of liability insurance rather than $500,000 in reliance on the defendant-favoring rule of defendant's home state. Nor is it realistic to speak of the insurer as being surprised. The loss is just grist for its actuarial mill.[297]

Even in cases in which a nexus requirement cannot be tied to a realistic unfair surprise argument, it is likely that the defendant will perceive the result as unfair if the plaintiff's state applies its law for no other reason than that the victim is a resident of that state.[298] It is not

---

295. Id. See also Klippel v. U–Haul Co. of Northeastern Michigan, 759 F.2d 1176 (4th Cir.1985) (mere fact that plaintiff resides in New York does not make New York owner's liability statute applicable when the rented vehicle is registered in Michigan and rented in Florida for move to South Carolina where accident occurred); Rice v. Dow Chem. Co., 124 Wash.2d 205, 216, 875 P.2d 1213, 1219 (1994) (refusing to apply Washington law to action by Washington resident who moved to forum after most of his exposure to defendant's chemical occurred in Oregon and stating "[a]lthough [an interest in compensating residents] is a real interest, recognizing this as an overriding concern, despite the lack of contacts, would mean that Washington law would be applied in all tort cases involving any Washington resident, regardless of where all the activity relating to the tort occurred").

296. See Sedler, *Weintraub's Commentary on the Conflict of Laws: The Chapter on Torts*, 57 Iowa L. Rev. 1229, 1236 (1972) ("territorial hang-up"); Sedler, *The Truly Disinterested Forum in the Conflict of Laws: Ratliff v. Cooper Laboratories*, 25 S.C. L. Rev. 185, 188 n.19 (1973) (application of forum law justified whenever nominal defendant's insurer does business in the forum).

297. See § 6.7, text accompanying notes 26–30.

298. See Tramontana v. S.A. Empresa De Viacao Aerea Rio Grandense, 350 F.2d 468 (D.C.Cir.1965), cert. denied, 383 U.S. 943, 86 S.Ct. 1195, 16 L.Ed.2d 206 (1966) (Brazilian recovery limits applicable to collision over Brazil between United States Navy plane and Brazilian airliner); Bannowsky v. Krauser, 294 F.Supp. 1204 (D.Colo.1969) (recovery limit of place where operation performed); Satchwill v. Vollrath Co., 293 F.Supp. 533 (E.D.Wis. 1968) (apply Wisconsin limit to Ohio resident killed in Wisconsin while installing equipment for Wisconsin company); Ciprari v. Servicos Aereos Cruzeiro, 245 F.Supp. 819 (S.D.N.Y.1965), aff'd, 359 F.2d 855 (2d Cir.1966) (Brazilian limit on recovery applied to New Yorker injured in crash of Brazilian airliner flying between two Brazilian points); Byrn v. American Universal Ins. Co., 548 S.W.2d 186 (Mo.App.1977) (fact of guest's Missouri residence not sufficient to avoid Iowa guest statute when Iowa host and injury during intrastate Iowa trip); Casey v. Manson Constr. & Eng'r Co., 247 Or. 274, 428 P.2d 898 (1967) (law of place where husband injured applied to deprive forum wife of action for loss of consortium); Restatement, Third, Foreign Relations Law of the United States § 402,

likely that the defendant's state would resolve the choice-of-law problem in that manner. Before the defendant will perceive this treatment under plaintiff's law as fair, it is necessary that there exist reasonable contacts between the plaintiff's state and the defendant,[299] or at least that the defendant be able to foresee that in many, not just extraordinary, cases his or her conduct will have an effect in the plaintiff's state.[300] This perception of fairness is important to any choice-of-law methodology.

§ 6.29 The "Better Law"

A number of courts that have abandoned the place-of-wrong rule and have adopted a functional or interest analysis approach to choice of law have adopted as one criterion for choice of law, "application of the better rule of law"[301] often citing Professor Leflar's clear articulation of

cmt. *g* (1987) ("The principal [that a state may apply its law to events in other states whenever the victim is its national] has not been generally accepted for ordinary torts or crimes"); D. Cavers, The Choice-of-Law Process 146 (1965); Reese, supra note 268 at 330; Trautman, *Concluding Remarks*, 32 Hast.L. J. 1678, 1680 (1981); von Mehren, *Recent Trends in Choice-of-Law Methodology*, 60 Cornell L. Rev. 927, 961 (1975); Comment, 40 U.Colo. L. Rev. 577, 597 (1968).

299. See Malena v. Marriott Int'l, Inc., 264 Neb. 759, 651 N.W.2d 850 (2002). A hypodermic needle that had been left under a nightstand in defendant's hotel in California stuck plaintiff, a Nebraska citizen. Plaintiff was repeatedly tested for AIDS for eighteen months after the incident, finally testing negative. She sued defendant for damages attributable to her fear of contracting AIDS. Under California law she could not recover unless it was more likely than not that she would contract AIDS from the needle stick. Under Nebraska law she could recover if the fear of AIDS was reasonable. The court applied California law under the "most significant relationship" test of the Restatement. "[A] foreign state has the dominant interest in having its tort rules applied when the forum state's only interest in the litigation is compensating its residents." Id. at 858. Cf. Carris v. Marriott Int'l, Inc., 466 F.3d 558 (7th Cir. 2006) (that defendant's web site is accessible in forum is not sufficient to justify applying forum law).

Brilmayer, *Rights, Fairness, and Choice of Law*, 98 Yale L. J. 1277, 1308 (1989) (stating that "[t]he territorial factor that is chosen must reflect the aggrieved party's voluntary submission to the law that is chosen"). In extreme cases, application of the forum's law without contacts with the defendant or the defendant's course of conduct may violate due process. See §§ 9.2 and 9.2A.

300. See Schneider v. Nichols, 280 Minn. 139, 158 N.W.2d 254 (1968) (North Dakota guest statute is not applicable to injury suffered in North Dakota by Minnesota guest of North Dakota host when ride began and was intended to end in Minnesota). But see Cipolla v. Shaposka, 439 Pa. 563, 267 A.2d 854 (1970) (Delaware host, Pennsylvania guest, crash in Delaware on way to Pennsylvania, Delaware guest statute applied); cf. Pryor v. Swarner, 445 F.2d 1272 (2d Cir.1971) (apply guest statute of place of injury when host's state also has such a statute, although guest's state does not and trip did touch there).

301. Tiernan v. Westext Transport, Inc., 295 F.Supp. 1256 (D.R.I.1969) (limit on wrongful death recovery and measure of damages); Schneider v. Nichols, 280 Minn. 139, 158 N.W.2d 254 (1968) (guest statute); McDaniel v. Ritter, 556 So.2d 303 (Miss.1989) (comparative negligence); Clark v. Clark, 107 N.H. 351, 222 A.2d 205 (1966) (guest statute); American Standard Ins. Co. of Wisconsin v. Cleveland, 124 Wis.2d 258, 369 N.W.2d 168 (1985) (Wisconsin law, which does not deduct insurance payments from the recovery, is better than Minnesota's law, which does); Conklin v. Horner, 38 Wis.2d 468, 157 N.W.2d 579 (1968) (guest statute); Zelinger v. State Sand & Gravel Co., 38 Wis.2d 98, 156 N.W.2d 466 (interspousal immunity, contribution) (1968); Heath v. Zellmer, 35 Wis.2d 578, 151 N.W.2d 664 (1967) (guest statute, contribution). For approval of the "better law" approach, see Juenger, *Choice of Law in Interstate Torts*, 118 U.Pa. L. Rev. 202, 235 (1969); Kramer, *Rethinking Choice of Law*, 90 Colum. L. Rev. 277, 336 (1990).

In Minnesota there is some confusion over the viability of the "better law" criterion. See Nodak Mutual Ins. Co. v. American Family Mutual Ins. Co., 604 N.W.2d 91, 96 (Minn.

that concept.[302] The use of a "better law" criterion is commendable and is to be encouraged provided that two conditions on its use are met. First, it is necessary that the conflict in state laws, which the court is attempting to resolve, not be a false conflict; the two states between whose law the forum is attempting to choose by the "better law" criterion should each have a policy underlying its different domestic law that would be significantly and legitimately, not hypothetically and officiously, advanced by application of its domestic law.[303] Second, the better law should be selected by an objective determination that the disfavored law is anachronistic or aberrational. A law is objectively anachronistic if many states that formerly had the rule have abandoned it. The classic example is the guest statute.[304] A law is aberrational if no other jurisdiction has the same rule and sufficient time has passed so that it is unlikely that other states will adopt the rule. Failure to observe these two limitations on the "better law" approach has generated new conflicts between states that have adopted a state-interest analysis of conflicts problems and has deterred other courts from abandoning the place-of-wrong rule.[305]

Conklin v. Horner[306] is an example misapplying the better law concept. An Illinois guest passenger sued an Illinois host driver for injuries sustained in Wisconsin on an automobile trip that began and was to end in Illinois. Illinois had a guest statute requiring "willful and wanton misconduct" by the host in order for the guest to recover, while Wisconsin would permit recovery for the host's ordinary negligence. It was clear that the possible policies underlying the Illinois guest statute, to protect the Illinois host from the ingratitude of the Illinois guest and to prevent a collusive suit in order to keep down Illinois insurance rates, were, whether one regards them as silly and benighted or wise and enlightened, fully applicable to the crash in Wisconsin. The *Conklin* court then proceeded to convince itself that Wisconsin had policies that would be significantly advanced in this case if the guest recovered under

---

2000) ("this court has not placed any emphasis on [the better law] factor in nearly 20 years"); cf. Boatwright v. Budak, 625 N.W.2d 483, 490 (Minn. App. 2001) (noting that the better law factor "has not been given any emphasis for many years" but then using it to choose law).

302. See R. Leflar et al., American Conflicts Law 95 (4th ed. 1986).

303. For examples of needless use of the "better law" criterion to resolve false conflicts as they should have been resolved without that criterion, see Mitchell v. Craft, 211 So.2d 509 (Miss.1968); Clark v. Clark, 107 N.H. 351, 222 A.2d 205 (1966). But cf. L. McDougal, *Toward Application of the Best Rule of Law in Choice of Law Cases*, 35 Mercer L. Rev. 483, 484 (1984) (courts should be free to construct and apply a rule that accommodates competing interests and promotes common interests better than the law of any of the states involved).

304. See supra § 6.11 note 60 and accompanying text.

305. See Abendschein v. Farrell, 382 Mich. 510, 521, 170 N.W.2d 137, 141 (1969) (rejecting interest analysis because it would "authorize the trial judge to make discretionary choices from one or indeed more of several conflicting jurisdictions, of laws he as a matter of discretion deems more equitable"). But see Sexton v. Ryder Truck Rental, Inc., 413 Mich. 406, 320 N.W.2d 843 (1982) (Michigan owner's liability laws apply when parties are Michigan residents, although automobile or plane crash occurred in state where no liability).

306. 38 Wis.2d 468, 157 N.W.2d 579 (1968).

Wisconsin's ordinary negligence rule. Wisconsin's policy was that the wrongdoer should bear the cost of the injury, not the injured party, and not the taxpayers or medical creditors, if the victim receives care for which he or she cannot pay. Furthermore, "[t]he deterrent effect that it is hoped our negligence laws exercise upon driver misconduct will be defeated by allowing negligent misconduct to go unpunished."[307] Then, having decided that there was "a serious conflict"[308] between the Illinois and Wisconsin policies, the court went on to resolve this conflict in favor of Wisconsin's "better law"[309] remarking that "guest statutes are anachronistic."[310]

It is not surprising that in *Fuerste v. Bemis*, when the domicile of host and guest was the forum, it reached a result opposite that in *Conklin*, applying its own guest statute rather than the ordinary negligence rule of Wisconsin, the place of injury, declaring that "Wisconsin has no significant relationship with the parties nor any interest in any issue herein presented."[311]

Perhaps the most questionable view is that stated in *Arnett v. Thompson*[312] when, in permitting recovery under its own law as place of injury, contrary to both the interspousal immunity rule and the guest statute of the marital domicile, the court declared that the law of the forum would be applied whenever an accident occurs in the forum, and that forum law would also be applied whenever the forum has an interest in applying its law to an accident in another state:

> The fact that we will apply Kentucky law where Kentucky people have an accident in Ohio or Indiana does not require that we apply Ohio or Indiana law where people of one of those states have an accident here, because the basis of the application is not a weighing of contacts but simply the existence of enough contacts with Kentucky to warrant applying our law.[313]

---

307. Id. at 477, 157 N.W.2d at 583. For disagreement with this deterrence theory, see § 6.25, note 264 and accompanying text. See also Johnson v. Johnson, 107 N.H. 30, 32, 216 A.2d 781, 783 (1966) (application of immunity rule of Massachusetts marital domicile will not make drivers "less careful on our highways since their own and their wives' safety will still be jeopardized by carelessness").

308. *Conklin*, 38 Wis.2d at 477, 157 N.W.2d at 583.

309. Id. at 483, 157 N.W.2d at 586.

310. Id. See also Arnett v. Thompson, 433 S.W.2d 109 (Ky.1968); Kell v. Henderson, 26 A.D.2d 595, 270 N.Y.S.2d 552 (1966) (holding the Ontario guest statute inapplicable to a suit based on a New York accident involving an Ontario host and guest). For comments on *Kell*, see 67 Colum. L. Rev. 459, 465 (1967) (Professors Rosenberg and Trautman); Ehrenzweig, *Foreign Guest Statutes and Forum Accidents: Against the Desperanto of State "Interests"*, 68 Colum. L. Rev. 49 (1968).

311. 156 N.W.2d 831, 833 (Iowa, 1968). Accord, Witherspoon v. Salm, 142 Ind.App. 655, 237 N.E.2d 116 (1968), rev'd on other grounds, 251 Ind. 575, 243 N.E.2d 876 (1969); Vick v. Cochran, 316 So.2d 242 (Miss.1975) (apply guest statute of domicile, not ordinary negligence rule of Mississippi where injury occurred). See also Cardin v. Cardin, 14 Ill.App.3d 82, 302 N.E.2d 238 (1973) (would apply Illinois guest statute to Illinois residents when accident out of state) (dictum).

312. 433 S.W.2d 109 (Ky.1968).

313. Id. at 113. Despite this language, the result in *Arnett* may be sound. The Arnetts were native Kentuckians who were residing in Ohio for the time being because Mr. Arnett

In short, consequences-based analysis should not be a subterfuge for "the plaintiff wins" or "apply the law of the forum."[314] Such a misuse of

could find suitable employment there but not in Kentucky. They thought of themselves as Kentuckians, hoped to return to live in Kentucky as soon as employment conditions permitted, and returned "home" frequently to see relatives and friends. They remained in Kentucky after the litigation and were still living there five years later. (Information supplied to Professor Robert Sedler by attorney for Edna Arnett.) The Kentucky compensation policy had a legitimate, not officious, claim to recognition because denial of compensation was extremely likely to have a significant impact in Kentucky. For further statements giving effect to forum law when there are competing state interests, see Satchwill v. Vollrath Co., 293 F.Supp. 533, 537 (E.D.Wis.1968); Castonzo v. General Cas. Co., 251 F.Supp. 948, 954 (W.D.Wis.1966). For a defense of this practice, see Sedler, *On Choice of Law and the Great Quest: A Critique of Special Multistate Solutions to Choice-of-Law Problems*, 7 Hofstra L. Rev. 807 (1979). That litigants choosing a forum with the hope of having forum law applied will "rarely [be] disappointed by courts favoring interest analysis", see Juenger, *Conflict of Laws: A Critique of Interest Analysis*, 32 Am. J. comp. L. 1, 13 (1984); Weinberg, *On Departing from Forum Law*, 35 Mercer L. Rev. 595, 599 (1984) (applying forum law will promote multistate policies of compensation, deterrence of wrongdoing, and enforcement of agreements, because the plaintiff has the power to select a forum with favorable law).

314. For examples of courts finding the law of another state better than the forum law, see Schlemmer v. Fireman's Fund Ins. Co., 292 Ark. 344, 730 S.W.2d 217 (1987) (Tennessee law permitting recovery by guest, but this is after repeal of the Arkansas guest statute); Offshore Rental Co. v. Continental Oil Co., 22 Cal.3d 157, 148 Cal.Rptr. 867, 583 P.2d 721 (1978) (Louisiana law applied to deny recovery to California employer for injury to employee in Louisiana); Gate City Fed. Sav. & Loan Ass'n v. O'Connor, 410 N.W.2d 448 (Minn.App.1987) (North Dakota law, which does not permit recovery of a deficiency judgment until the fair market value of the collateral is deducted, is better than Minnesota law, which simply deducts the resale price, but court notes that although the realty is in Minnesota, both debtor and creditor reside in North Dakota and all choice factors point to North Dakota law); Bigelow v. Halloran, 313 N.W.2d 10 (Minn.1981) (applies Iowa survival statute as "better" than Minnesota's when Minnesota statute does not permit an action for intentional tort to survive the death of the tortfeasor); Victoria v. Smythe, 703 A.2d 619 (R.I. 1997) (Florida law, which holds car rental company vicariously liable for negligence of lessee is better than Rhode Island which does not); cf. Zelinger v. State Sand & Gravel Co., 38 Wis.2d 98, 113, 156 N.W.2d 466, 473 (1968) (forum law is applied because it is better, not because it is the forum's law).

For cases utilizing interest analysis and not applying forum law when forum policies are impinged, see Casey v. Manson Constr. & Eng'r Co., 247 Or. 274, 428 P.2d 898 (1967) (applying law of place of injury to deny forum wife a cause of action for loss of consortium); Cipolla v. Shaposka, 439 Pa. 563, 267 A.2d 854 (1970) (Delaware guest statute applied to deny recovery to Pennsylvania guest injured by Delaware host in Delaware although trip was intended to reach Pennsylvania).

Offshore Rental Co. v. Continental Oil Co., cited above, is less impressive in the light of I.J. Weinrot & Son, Inc. v. Jackson, 40 Cal.3d 327, 220 Cal.Rptr. 103, 708 P.2d 682 (1985). *Weinrot* decided that the California statute involved in *Offshore* did not afford a cause of action to the employer, a question left open in *Offshore*.

With regard to Bigelow v. Halloran, cited above, Thompson v. Estate of Petroff, 319 N.W.2d 400 (Minn.1982), held that the Minnesota survival statute's discrimination against intentional torts violated the equal protection provision of the Minnesota constitution. That this weakens *Bigelow* as an indication that Minnesota will sometimes find another state's law "better" as a basis for resolving true conflicts, see Morrison, *Death of Conflicts*, 29 Villanova L. Rev. 313, 328 (1984).

There may be a justifiable presumption in favor of forum law. This presumption can be rebutted by showing either that the interests of the forum will not be advanced by application of forum law and the interests of another state will be advanced if the law of that state is applied, or that both states' interests are implicated and that, under all the circumstances, forum interests should yield. See Allstate Ins. Co. v. Hague, 449 U.S. 302, 326, 101 S.Ct. 633, 647, 66 L.Ed.2d 521, 539 (1981) (Stevens, J., concurring): "I question whether a judge's decision to apply the law of his own State could ever be described as wholly irrational. For judges are presumably familiar with their own state law and may

interest analysis will, as it already has, generate new disparities in the treatment of conflicts problems and will, as it already has, discourage needed reform in the conflict of laws.

§ 6.30   A Post–Accident Change in Residence

Suppose that a party changes his or her state of residence after the injury for which compensation is sought. Should this change of residence be taken into account in assessing the interest of the prior or of the subsequent residence in assuring the plaintiff adequate compensation or in protecting the defendant from liability? Several cases have asserted that state interests should be judged as of the time of injury without taking into account post-accident changes in residence[315] and the Second Restatement tentatively takes this position.[316]

This is painting with too broad a brush. We would not want to take such post-accident residence changes into account in such a manner as to create unfair surprise by subjecting defendant's conduct to standards that were not foreseeable when defendant acted; nor would we wish to encourage forum-shopping, or, perhaps more accurately in this circumstance, house-shopping; nor do we desire to discourage a change in residence that is otherwise in the best interests of one of the parties. But if these objections can be put to rest, there is no reason why post-accident changes in residence should not be considered insofar as they affect state-interest analysis.[317] To make this abstract proposition more concrete, it will be useful to review some of the contexts in which, after

---

find it difficult and time consuming to discover and apply correctly the law of another State. The forum State's interest in the fair and efficient administration of justice is therefore sufficient, in my judgment, to attach a presumption of validity to a forum State's decision to apply its own law to a dispute over which it has jurisdiction." See also Piamba Cortes v. American Airlines, Inc., 177 F.3d 1272, 1303 (11th Cir.), rehearing en banc denied, 193 F.3d 525 (11th Cir. 1999), cert. denied, 528 U.S. 1136, 120 S.Ct. 980, 145 L.Ed.2d 930 (2000) (stating that the ease of determining and applying Florida law compared with the disagreement between experts over Colombian law "weighs heavily in favor of applying Florida law"); Smith v. Pierpont, 123 Mich.App. 33, 38, 333 N.W.2d 165, 167–68 (1983): "[I]n a tort action commenced in this state, the law of this state is to be applied unless the court determines that a superior foreign state interest exists which calls for the application of the foreign law in order to reach a just resolution of the controversy."

315.   See Gore v. Northeast Airlines, Inc., 373 F.2d 717, 723 (2d Cir.1967); Tiernan v. Westext Transport, Inc., 295 F.Supp. 1256, 1264 n.6 (D.R.I.1969); Reich v. Purcell, 67 Cal.2d 551, 555, 63 Cal.Rptr. 31, 34, 432 P.2d 727, 730 (1967); Doiron v. Doiron, 109 N.H. 1, 4–5, 241 A.2d 372, 374–75 (1968); cf. Raskulinecz v. Raskulinecz, 357 A.2d 330, 141 N.J.Super. 148 (Law Div.1976) (although New Jersey may no longer have interest in parties who have moved from the state, it did have an interest when action filed and Ontario, where accident occurred, had no interest).

316.   Restatement, Second, ch. 7, topic 1, Introductory Note at 414.

317.   See Allstate Ins. Co. v. Hague, 449 U.S. 302, 101 S.Ct. 633, 66 L.Ed.2d 521 (1981); Huff v. Lasieur, 571 S.W.2d 654 (Mo.App.1978); Corr, *The Frailty of Interest Analysis*, 11 Geo. Mason. L. Rev. 299, 308–09 (2002) (businesses relocate frequently); Sedler, *The Governmental Interest Approach to Choice of Law: An Analysis and a Reformulation*, 25 UCLA L. Rev. 181, 241–242 (1977); Note, *Post Transaction or Occurrence Events in Conflicts of Laws*, 69 Colum. L. Rev. 843, 865 (1969) ("Considerations of fairness, predictability, and the existence of forum shopping should all be considered. Consequently, it is as wrong categorically to give effect to post occurrence events as it is categorically to deny their relevance").

the event in issue, courts that have adopted state-interest analysis have considered the effect of a change in residence.

The first situation is that in which a plaintiff moves out of a state that has a sufficient nexus with the parties or with the occurrence to assert an interest in securing more adequate compensation for the plaintiff than plaintiff would receive under the law of the place of wrong.[318] The plaintiff moves to a state that either has no such nexus or, if it has, would nevertheless apply the law of the place of wrong. *Gore v. Northeast Airlines*[319] is an example. A New Yorker was killed on a flight that left New York for Massachusetts and that crashed in Massachusetts. The surviving dependents of the deceased New Yorker moved from New York to Maryland a month after the crash. Maryland would apply the law of the place of wrong, Massachusetts, limiting recovery to $15,000. New York, following *Kilberg v. Northeast Airlines*,[320] a case involving the same crash, would reject the Massachusetts ceiling on damages. In *Gore*, the court applied New York law despite the move from New York to Maryland. The *Gore* court's argument, that application of the law of the plaintiffs' domicile at the time of the crash would avoid "forum-shopping by changing domicile after the decedent's death prior to commencing a wrongful death action,"[321] was inapplicable because the new domicile provided a lesser recovery. The court's suggestion that the *Gore* result would protect New York citizens by inducing common carriers to exercise more care than they might if recovery were limited seems unrealistic. The result in *Gore*, nevertheless, was correct. We would not want the widow's move to more congenial surroundings at a time of bereavement to have the draconian effect of reducing compensation for the dependents by many hundreds of thousands of dollars.[322] If unforeseen, this reduction in recovery would be especially cruel. If the possible impact of change of residence on choice of law is adverted to, we would not want this possibility to deter the widow from a move otherwise in the best interests of herself and the children.[323]

---

318. See § 6.28.

319. 373 F.2d 717 (2d Cir.1967).

320. 9 N.Y.2d 34, 211 N.Y.S.2d 133, 172 N.E.2d 526 (1961).

321. *Gore*, 373 F.2d at 723.

322. In *Gore*, after the Second Circuit decided that the $15,000 Massachusetts limitation was not applicable, the case was settled for $760,000. N.Y. Times, May 2, 1967, p. 41, col. 1 (city ed.). See also Huddy v. Fruehauf Corp., 953 F.2d 955, 957 (5th Cir.), cert. denied, 506 U.S. 828, 113 S.Ct. 89, 121 L.Ed.2d 52 (1992) (applying Texas law to facilitate recovery in product liability action and stating that "[t]o hold that Texas loses its interest in this case because [plaintiff] chose to move to another state during the litigation process would chain litigants to the state of residence at the time of the accident lest they lose the protection of its laws").

323. See also Foster v. United States, 768 F.2d 1278 (11th Cir.1985) (Illinois retains an interest in compensating a resident who moves away—Illinois law); Comment, 81 Harv. L. Rev. 1342, 1345–46 (1968) (arguing that New York had an interest in securing adequate compensation for the decedent's dependents after they moved to Maryland because New York's standards for wrongful death compensation were "analogous . . . to a life insurance policy—a form of security which the state gives its citizens against wrongful death, insuring them that their survivors may be provided for through institution of suit against the tortfeasor"). But see Dent v. Cunningham, 786 F.2d 173 (3d Cir.1986) (remand to

For somewhat the same reason, avoiding penalizing a change of residence otherwise in the best interest of the plaintiff, *Doiron v. Doiron*[324] was probably correct in permitting a wife to sue her husband for negligence. After the accident in New Hampshire, the Doirons shifted their marital domicile from New Hampshire, which permitted such suits, to Massachusetts, which had a rule of interspousal immunity.[325] Moreover, insofar as the Massachusetts immunity rule was designed to prevent collusive interspousal suits and thus keep down Massachusetts insurance rates, the change of residence to Massachusetts would not give Massachusetts a reason for asserting this interest, because the insurance would have been issued to a New Hampshire driver and payment would be chargeable to New Hampshire loss experience. Massachusetts would acquire an interest in preventing marital discord between its new residents, if this were one of the policies underlying the Massachusetts rule, but because of the inadvisability of discouraging a change of residence, this Massachusetts interest should not be asserted.

The opposite situation involving a move by the plaintiff is a move to a state that has a sufficient nexus with the defendant or with the defendant's conduct to assert an interest in giving the plaintiff a larger recovery than the plaintiff would have been awarded by either the former domicile or by the place of injury.[326] To take a hypothetical situation suggested by *Reich v. Purcell*,[327] suppose that the plaintiff lives in X and is injured in Y by a defendant who resides in Z; X would place a $10,000 limit on the plaintiff's recovery, as would Y, but under Z law, there would be no limit on recovery and the plaintiff would recover $50,000. After the accident, the plaintiff moves to Z. If the plaintiff had been a Z resident at the time of injury, he or she should recover under Z law, except in the unlikely situation in which the Z defendant's conduct

---

determine if plaintiffs move from the forum deprived the forum of interest in the action— New Jersey law); Seidelson, *Interest Analysis and an Enhanced Degree of Specificity: The Wrongful Death Action*, 10 Duq. L. Rev. 525, 530–31 (1972).

324.   109 N.H. 1, 241 A.2d 372 (1968).

325.   But see Kjeldsen v. Ballard, 52 Misc.2d 952, 277 N.Y.S.2d 324 (Spec.Term, Suffolk Cty. 1967) (woman domiciled in New York at the time that she was injured by defendant in New Jersey and who then married the defendant in Virginia and lived with him in Virginia may not sue the defendant because of Virginia's rule of interspousal immunity); Manning v. Hyland, 42 Misc.2d 915, 249 N.Y.S.2d 381 (S.Ct., Spec.Term, Queens Cty. 1964) (woman domiciled in New York at the time that she was injured by the defendant in New Jersey and who then married the defendant in New Jersey and lived with him in New Jersey may not sue the defendant because of New Jersey's rule of interspousal immunity).

326.   See Mills v. State Farm Mut. Auto. Ins. Co., 827 F.2d 1418 (10th Cir.1987) (apply law of new marital domicile to permit interspousal suit—Oklahoma law); Bates v. Superior Court of Maricopa County, 156 Ariz. 46, 749 P.2d 1367 (1988) (apply law of insured's new domicile to permit recovery for bad faith refusal to continue insurance benefits paid at former domicile where insurance was issued and injury occurred); Pine v. Eli Lilly & Co., 201 N.J.Super. 186, 492 A.2d 1079 (App.Div.1985) (plaintiff, who was born in New York where his mother ingested defendant's drug that allegedly harmed plaintiff, is entitled to New Jersey's discovery rule to extend the period of limitations if he has acquired a domicile in New Jersey); cf. Brown v. Cities Service Oil Co., 733 F.2d 1156 (5th Cir.1984) (move to Texas after injury on job in Louisiana does not remove Louisiana workers' compensation statute bar to tort suit).

327.   67 Cal.2d 551, 63 Cal.Rptr. 31, 432 P.2d 727 (1967).

was shaped in reliance on Y law.[328] But should the plaintiff receive the larger recovery permitted by Z law if plaintiff moves to Z after the accident? Would this not be likely to induce house-hunting in Z by the plaintiff? Perhaps, but if domicile-shopping is our major concern, it should not deter us from applying Z law if, on the facts of the case before us, it is unlikely that the move to Z was made in order to influence the choice of applicable law.[329] For example, there might be a case, perhaps *Reich* was such a case, in which the plaintiff was in the process of moving from X to Z when he or she collided with the defendant in Y. Moreover, perhaps Z should give the X plaintiff the benefit of the larger recovery available under Z law, even if the plaintiff does not move to Z. Z's liberal compensation standards may reflect a Z policy that Z drivers should bear the primary responsibility of assuring full compensation for injuries caused by the Z drivers, no matter where those injuries are caused or to whom.[330] Furthermore, a case like *Reich*, in which a plaintiff is injured en route to the defendant's residence, warns that if Z does not make its higher compensation standards available to a person who is not a Z resident and who is not injured in Z, when applying Z's law would not interfere with another state's interests, Z could be creating undesirable social consequences that may some day be Z's problem if the injured person moves to Z.

---

328. See section 6.28.

329. See Allstate Ins. Co. v. Hague, 449 U.S. 302, 319 n.28, 101 S.Ct. 633, 643 n.28, 66 L.Ed.2d 521, 534 n.28 (1981): "The dissent suggests that considering respondent's post-occurrence change of residence as one of the Minnesota contacts will encourage forum shopping. . . . This overlooks the fact that her change of residence was bona fide and not motivated by litigation considerations." See also Goede v. Aerojet General Corp., 143 S.W.3d 14 (Mo. App. 2004) (under "most significant relationship" test, when decedent was exposed to asbestos in California but diagnosed and treated for cancer after her move to Missouri, apply Missouri law, which unlike California law, permits recovery for pain and suffering in wrongful death action); Haines v. Mid–Century Ins. Co., 47 Wis.2d 442, 177 N.W.2d 328, 332 (1970) (rejecting house-hunting argument after the plaintiff moved to a forum with more favorable law).

In Nesladek v. Ford Motor Co., 46 F.3d 734 (8th Cir.), cert. denied 516 U.S. 814, 116 S.Ct. 67, 133 L.Ed.2d 28 (1995), a products liability action, the majority refused to take into account the plaintiffs' move to Minnesota because plaintiffs "admitted that they moved to Minnesota in part because they consulted an attorney and were aware that their case was a non-starter [under the law of Nebraska, where they then lived, because of a ten-year statute of repose], whereas Minnesota's law [a 'useful life' statute of repose] was more favorable." Id. at 738.

To avoid "forum shopping," HM Holdings, Inc. v. Aetna Casualty & Surety Co., 154 N.J. 208, 712 A.2d 645 (1998), refused to take account of the insured's move to New Jersey in determining which state's law applied to determine the extent of pollution coverage. The court did, however, consider the move to New Jersey in deciding to apply the New Jersey rule that late notice to the insurance company does not eliminate coverage unless the late notice has prejudiced the insurer. The court noted that the late notice occurred after the insured had moved to New Jersey. See also Hall v. General Motors Corp., 229 Mich.App. 580, 588, 582 N.W.2d 866, 869 (1998), appeal denied, 459 Mich. 986, 593 N.W.2d 556 (1999) (as a matter of first impression, to avoid encouraging "forum shopping," do not use plaintiff's post-accident move to forum as factor in interest analysis).

See Brilmayer, *Rights, Fairness, and Choice of Law*, 98 Yale L. J. 1277, 1291 (1989) (stating that "[t]he defendant, who is required to pay simply because the plaintiff moved to another state, is in a situation similar to that of the innocent defendant sent to jail for deterrent purposes").

330. See § 6.24.

A change of domicile problem that is the converse of those discussed above is one in which it is the defendant who moves from a state that has a sufficient nexus with the parties and with the occurrence to assert its interest in shielding the defendant from liability. Assuming that a court would apply the law of the defendant's former domicile if the defendant had not moved, will the post-accident change in his or her residence change the result? *Miller v. Miller*[331] gives an affirmative answer to this question. In *Miller*, the decedent, a New Yorker, was fatally injured in Maine while a passenger in an automobile driven by his brother and owned by his sister-in-law, both Maine residents. At the time of the accident,[332] Maine placed a $20,000 limit on wrongful death recovery. The brother and sister-in-law then moved to New York where a wrongful death action was brought against them. In a four-to-three opinion, the New York Court of Appeals held that the change in the defendant's residence would be taken into account, that it removed any Maine interest in shielding the defendants from liability,[333] and that therefore the court would not apply the Maine limit on wrongful death recovery. As for arguments that this result would discourage tortfeasors from moving to New York and would encourage collusive changes in residence, the majority dismissed these objections on the ground that they "contradict each other, are speculative and are insufficient to move us to disregard the change in domicile."[334]

§ 6.31　Products Liability

I have proposed the following choice-of-law rule for international product liability disputes and would apply the same rule to interstate cases:

331.　22 N.Y.2d 12, 290 N.Y.S.2d 734, 237 N.E.2d 877 (1968). See also Purcell v. Kapelski, 444 F.2d 380 (3d Cir.1971), cert. denied, 404 U.S. 940, 92 S.Ct. 283, 30 L.Ed.2d 254 (1971) (law of marital domicile at time of accident not applicable to provide immunity when, before suit brought, spouses have divorced and husband has left the state). But cf. Tiernan v. Westext Transport, Inc., 295 F.Supp. 1256, 1265 n.6 (D.R.I.1969) (Massachusetts has no interest in limiting recovery against the estate of a defendant whose wife moved to Massachusetts after the accident); Schultz v. Boy Scouts of America, Inc., 65 N.Y.2d 189, 491 N.Y.S.2d 90, 480 N.E.2d 679 (1985) (apply charitable immunity rule of state from which defendant has since moved, distinguishing *Miller* on ground that change was not to New York nor was New York the plaintiff's domicile).

332.　After the accident the Maine limit on recovery was first raised to $30,000 (Me.Law 1961, c. 315) and then removed completely (18 Me.Rev.Stat.Ann. § 2552, Me.Law 1965, c. 255). It is not clear how large a part this change in Maine law played in the result. The majority assumed that Maine would not apply the repeal of the liability limitation retroactively (22 N.Y.2d at 15 n.1, 290 N.Y.S.2d at 736 n.1, 237 N.E.2d at 878 n.1), but then remarked that "[a]ny claim that Maine has a paternalistic interest in protecting its residents against liability for acts committed while they were in Maine, should they move to another jurisdiction, is highly speculative and ignores the fact that for the very same acts committed today Maine would now impose the same liability as New York." 22 N.Y.2d at 21–22, 290 N.Y.S.2d at 742, 237 N.E.2d at 882.

333.　The majority also decided that there was no other reason to apply the Maine law because there had been no reliance on that law by either the tortfeasors or their liability insurer and recovery in excess of the Maine limit would have "an infinitesimal effect, if that, on insurance rates in Maine". 22 N.Y.2d at 21, 290 N.Y.S.2d at 741, 237 N.E.2d at 882.

334.　22 N.Y.2d at 22, 290 N.Y.S.2d at 742, 237 N.E.2d at 883.

To determine liability and the measure of compensatory and punitive damages for injuries caused by a product, apply the law of the injured person's habitual residence, whether this law is more or less favorable to the injured person than the law of other countries that have contacts with the defendant and the product, except:

1. The injured person is not entitled to the favorable law of his or her habitual residence if the defendant could not reasonably have foreseen that the product or the defendant's products of the same type would be available there through commercial channels.

2. Law of a country that is not the injured person's habitual residence, but is where the defendant has acted and is favorable to the injured person, should be applied when this is desirable to punish and deter the defendant's outrageous conduct.[335]

The reasons for this rule are: (1) it is fair to both the victim and the manufacturer to apply the law of the victim's habitual residence under the circumstances provided in the rule; (2) the countries where the manufacturer designs and produces the product should not discourage those activities if the basis for recovery is "liability without fault"[336] or negligence; (3) a court should apply law more favorable to the victim than the victim's home law when the activities of the manufacturer are so blameworthy that the locus of those activities wishes to deter and punish them.

The Hague Convention on the Law Applicable to Products Liability[337] also applies the law of the victim's habitual residence, whether favorable or unfavorable to recovery, when that residence has an additional contact as the location of the place of injury, the defendant's principal place of business, or the place where the victim acquired the product.[338]

---

335. Weintraub, *A Proposed Choice-of-Law Standard for International Products Liability Disputes*, 16 Brook. J. Int'l L. 225, 238 (1990).

336. *See* Restatement (Third) of Torts: Products Liability § 1 cmt. *a* (1998) (stating that "[c]ourts early began imposing liability without fault on product sellers for harm caused by [manufacturing] defects"); id. § 1 (stating that "[o]ne engaged in the business of selling or otherwise distributing products who sells or distributes a defective product is subject to liability for harm to person or property caused by the defect"); id. § 2 (stating that "[a] product is defective when, at the time of sale or distribution, it contains a manufacturing defect" and that a product "contains a manufacturing defect when the product departs from its intended design even though all possible care was exercised in the preparation and marketing of the product").

337. Opened for signature Oct. 2, 1973, 11 I.L.M. 1283. [hereinafter Hague Convention]. As of September 1, 2009, the Convention is in force in Finland, France, Luxembourg, Montenegro, Netherlands, Norway, Serbia, Spain, and three successor states to the former Yugoslavia—Croatia, Macedonia, Slovenia. It has been signed but not ratified by Belgium, Italy, and Portugal. <http://www.hcch.net/e/status/stat22e.html>.

338. Hague Convention, supra note 337, arts. 4–5. There is an exception under which the law of the victim's habitual residence does not apply even if it is the place of injury if the defendant "could not reasonably have foreseen that the product or his own products of the same type would be made available in that State through commercial channels." Id. art. 7. See Kozyris, *Conflicts Theory for Dummies: Après le Deluge, Where Are We on*

The European Union Regulation on the Law Applicable to Non–Contractual Obligations (Rome II)[339] applies the law of the victim's habitual residence if the product was marketed in that country.[340] Article 28 provides that it does not "prejudice the application of international conventions to which one or more Member States are parties at the time when this Regulation is adopted and which lay down conflict-of-laws rules relating to non-contractual obligations." Thus a member state that is a party to the Hague Convention on the Law Applicable to Products Liability will continue to be bound by that convention unless the state denounces the Hague convention.

In products liability cases the codification of Japanese conflict-of-law rules that took effect on 1 January 2007 applies "the law of the place where the injured person has been delivered the product."[341] There is an exception in favor of the "law of the place with which they are clearly more closely connected in light of the circumstances such as where at the time of the tort both of the parties had their habitual residence in a place under the same law, or where the tort occurred by breaching obligations in a contract between the parties."[342]

The Oregon Code for choice of law in noncontractual liability provides:

Product liability civil actions.

(1) Notwithstanding sections 8 and 9 of this 2009 Act, Oregon law applies to product liability civil actions, as defined in ORS 30.900, if:

(a) The injured person was domiciled in Oregon and the injury occurred in Oregon; or

(b) The injured person was domiciled in Oregon or the injury occurred in Oregon, and the product:

(A) Was manufactured or produced in Oregon; or

(B) Was delivered when new for use or consumption in Oregon.

(2) Subsection (1) of this section does not apply to a product liability civil action if a defendant demonstrates that the use in Oregon of the product that caused the injury could not have been foreseen and that none of the defendant's products of the same type were avail-

---

Producers Liability?, 60 La. L. Rev. 1161, 1176 (2000) (apply law of victim's home state if product acquired or available there); cf. Symeonides, *Party Choice of Law in Product–Liability Conflicts*, 12 Willamette J. Int'l L. & Disp. Resol. 263, 268 (2004) (permit injured party to choose law where product made only if that also either place of injury, place of residence of injury party, or place in which first delivered to user).

339. Regulation (EC) No. 864/2007 of the European Parliament and of the Council of 11 July 2007 on the law applicable to non-contractual obligations (Rome II), OJ 2007 L 199/40.

340. Id. art. 5(1)(a).

341. Japanese conflict-of-laws rules: Act on the General Rules of Application of Laws, Law No. 10 of 1898 as newly titled and amended 21 June 2006, art. 18. If that place of delivery "could not usually be foreseen, the law of the principal place of business of the producer" applies. Id.

342. Id. art. 20.

able in Oregon in the ordinary course of trade at the time of the injury.

(3) If a party demonstrates that the application of the law of a state other than Oregon to a disputed issue is substantially more appropriate under the principles of section 9 [focuses on the pertinence of the policies of contact states] of this 2009 Act, that issue shall be governed by the law of the other state.

(4) All noncontractual claims or issues in product liability civil actions not provided for or not disposed of under this section are governed by the law of the state determined under section 9 of this 2009 Act.[343]

The Oregon code provision for the law applicable to products liability is likely to produce the same results as the rule recommended in the first paragraph of this section.

Some product liability conflicts cases are contrary to both my proposal and the Hague Convention. Courts have applied the law of manufacturer's state that is favorable to foreign plaintiffs even when the manufacturer's liability is based on liability without fault or simple negligence. Although in these circumstances an interest in deterring the manufacturer's improper conduct is slight, courts have found that interest sufficient to apply law favorable to a nonresident victim.[344]

Gantes v. Kason Corp.[345] is typical. A worker "in a chicken processing plant in Georgia, was killed when struck in the head by a moving part of a machine."[346] The machine "was manufactured in and then shipped from [New Jersey] by the defendant-manufacturer."[347] "Representatives of the decedent, asserting that the machine was defective, brought [a] personal-injury action based on claims of survivorship and wrongful death against the New Jersey manufacturer...."[348] The action was timely under New Jersey's two-year statute of limitations but was

---

343. Senate Bill 561, 75th Oregon Legislative Assembly, 2009 Regular Session.

344. See Reyno v. Piper Aircraft Co., 630 F.2d 149, 168 (3d Cir. 1980), rev'd on another issue, 454 U.S. 235, 102 S.Ct. 252, 70 L.Ed.2d 419 (1981) (applying Pennsylvania and California choice-of-law rules and basing the result on an "interest in the regulation of manufacturing [and] in deterring defects in products"); cf. Quebec Civil Code Book 10 § 3128: "The liability of the manufacturer of a movable, whatever the source thereof, is governed, at the choice of the victim, (1) by the law of the country where the manufacturer has his establishment or, failing that, his residence, or (2) by the law of the country where the movable was acquired." Id. § 3129: "The application of the rules of this Code is imperative in matters of civil liability for damage suffered in or outside Quebec as a result of exposure to or the use of raw materials, whether processed or not, originating in Quebec." But see Symeonides, *Choice of Law for Products Liability*: The 1990s and Beyond, 78 Tulane L. Rev. 1247, 1348 (2004) (in cases decided from 1990 to 2003, "[m]ost cases (76%) applied the law of a state with plaintiff-affiliating contacts, but in most of those cases (58%) that state had a pro-defendant law").

345. 145 N.J. 478, 679 A.2d 106 (1996).

346. Id. at 107.

347. Id. at 113. There was some evidence that the manufacturer had produced the machine in New York but for the ruling on a motion for summary judgment, which was before the court, the court assumed manufacture in New Jersey. Id. at 118 (Garibaldi, J., dissenting).

348. Id. at 107.

barred if the court applied Georgia's ten-year statute of repose.[349] The court applied New Jersey law favorable to the Georgia claimants reasoning that "New Jersey ... has a cognizable and substantial interest in deterrence that would be furthered by the application of its statute of limitations, and that interest is not outweighed by countervailing concerns over creating unnecessary discriminatory burdens on domestic manufacturers or by fears of forum shopping and increased litigation in the courts of this State."[350] Other courts have used this "deterrence" rationale to apply the law of the manufacturer's state that is favorable to a foreign plaintiff.[351]

Twenty-three years before deciding *Gantes* the Supreme Court of New Jersey, in *Heavner v. Uniroyal, Inc.*,[352] had applied the North Carolina statute of limitations to bar a product liability suit against a manufacturer incorporated in New Jersey.[353] *Gantes* distinguished *Heavner* on the ground that in *Heavner* the manufacturer's "only contact with New Jersey was that it was incorporated in this State."[354]

Harrison v. Wyeth Laboratories[355] held that United Kingdom law, not the law of Pennsylvania, where the defendant had its principal place

---

349. Id. The Georgia statute barred a product liability action "ten years from the date of the first sale for use or consumption" of the product, even though the product had not yet caused the injury on which the plaintiff based the action. GA. CODE ANN. § 51-1-11(b)(2).

350. *Gantes*, 679 A.2d at 113.

351. *See* Baird v. Bell Helicopter Textron, 491 F.Supp. 1129, 1141 (N.D. Tex. 1980) (applying Texas law in favor of a Canadian injured in Surinam by the crash of a helicopter manufactured in Texas and stating that "Texas is certainly interested in seeing that Bell markets the safest product possible"); Johnson v. Spider Staging Corp., 87 Wash.2d 577, 555 P.2d 997, 1002 (1976) (applying Washington law, which permitted unlimited wrongful death recovery, rather than Kansas law, which had a $50,000 limit on recover, in suit for wrongful death of Kansan killed in Kansas when using scaffold manufactured in Washington by Washington company and stating "[u]nlimited recovery will deter tortious conduct and will encourage [the defendant manufacturer] to make safe products for its customers"). Contra, Vasquez v. Bridgestone/Firestone, Inc., 325 F.3d 665 (5th Cir. 2003) (applying Texas "most significant relationship" test, holds Mexican law applies to action against U.S. manufacturers of products that allegedly caused death in Mexico); Townsend v. Sears, Roebuck and Co., 227 Ill.2d 147, 316 Ill.Dec. 505, 879 N.E.2d 893 (2007) (applying law of Michigan where injury occurred to Michigan resident rather than law of Illinois where defendant headquartered resulting in application of negligence rather than strict liability standard, statutory caps on noneconomic damages, and barring of punitive damages).

352. 63 N.J. 130, 305 A.2d 412 (1973).

353. *Heavner* was one of the first cases to reject the Restatement (Second) of Conflict of Laws position that statutes of limitations are procedural so that the limitations of the forum always applied. Id. at 415 (noting rules of both original and Second Conflicts Restatements), 418 (applying interest analysis and selecting North Carolina limitations because "New Jersey has no substantial interest in the matter"). The court also held, alternatively, that the action was barred even under New Jersey time limitations. Id. at 418–27. In 1988, the Restatement abandoned the procedural characterization of time limitations. Restatement, Second, § 142 (Rev. 1989) (publishing revisions adopted and promulgated in 1988).

354. *Gantes*, 679 A.2d at 111. See also Hughes v. Wal–Mart Stores, Inc., 250 F.3d 618, 621 (8th Cir. 2001) (fact that defendant's principal place of business is in Arkansas is not sufficient to choose Arkansas law to determine liability for injury from product sold in Louisiana).

355. 510 F.Supp. 1 (E.D. Pa. 1980), aff'd w.o. opinion, 676 F.2d 685 (3d Cir. 1982).

of business, applied to a suit brought on behalf of women injured in the United Kingdom by oral contraceptives manufactured there under defendant's license. The plaintiffs contended that the warnings accompanying the pills were not adequate under Pennsylvania law. The court reasoned that "the United Kingdom, and not Pennsylvania, has the greater interest in the control of drugs distributed and consumed in the United Kingdom."[356]

Thus applying Pennsylvania law in *Harrison* would interfere with the United Kingdom's interest in having the drug distributed there. This is one of the grounds on which *Rowe v. Hoffman–La Roche, Inc.*[357] distinguished *Gantes*. In *Rowe* a Michigan resident sued New Jersey drug manufacturers claiming inadequate warnings of the drug's risks. The drug had been approved by the federal Food and Drug Administration. Under Michigan law, FDA approval barred the suit. Under New Jersey law, the approval created a rebuttable presumption that the warnings were adequate. *Rowe* also stated that the New Jersey deterrence policy was not as strong in that case as in *Gantes* because New Jersey created a presumption that the warnings were adequate.[358]

Rowe's distinction of *Gantes* on the ground of Michigan's interest in facilitating the availability of affordable prescription drugs is subject to the objection that the same could be said of any product or service. Perhaps in the case of prescription drugs this consideration is especially compelling.

It is difficult to reconcile *Harrison* with *Reyno v. Piper Aircraft Co.*,[359] which was decided later the same month by the circuit court in the same circuit and which used deterrence rationale to apply United States law favorable to foreign plaintiffs. The Third Circuit nevertheless affirmed *Harrison* without opinion two years after that circuit decided *Reyno*. Therefore *Harrison* is some support for the proposition that a court should apply the law of the victim's country even though this is less favorable to recovery than the law of the manufacturer's country. It should be noted, however, that in *Harrison* the holding that the Third Circuit affirmed was the granting of a motion for forum non conveniens dismissal and choice-of-law was only one factor, though an important one, leading to the dismissal.

It would greatly diminish the attractiveness of a United States forum in product liability cases if all United States courts applied the law of the victim's home country when that law is less favorable to recovery than American law. In the light of current decisions it is an

356. Id. at 5. See Hall v. General Motors Corp., 229 Mich.App. 580, 588, 582 N.W.2d 866, 869 (1998), appeal denied, 459 Mich. 986, 593 N.W.2d 556 (1999) (state where manufacturer headquartered has no interest in affording North Carolina resident greater rights than North Carolina).

357. 189 N.J. 615, 917 A.2d 767 (2007).

358. Id. at 625–26, 917 A.2d at 773–74.

359. 630 F.2d 149, 168 (3d Cir. 1980), rev'd on another issue, 454 U.S. 235, 102 S.Ct. 252, 70 L.Ed.2d 419 (1981).

uphill battle in some states to convince a court to adopt this choice-of-law position.

Another possibility is to argue that although United States law determines liability, damages should be quantified under the standards of the victim's home country. It is the injured person's habitual residence, its standard of living, its social services, that should determine whether, for example, one thousand dollars or one million dollars is appropriate compensation for pain and suffering.[360] Thus United States law determines liability but foreign law determines the proper level of damages. Accomplishing this dépeçage[361] will be especially difficult in view of the fact that courts have traditionally considered quantification of damages "procedural" so that the forum's standards apply even though another state's law governs liability.[362] Thus the accepted rule is exactly the reverse of the approach suggested here. Perhaps *Gasperini v. Center for Humanities, Inc.*,[363] which requires federal courts exercising diversity jurisdiction to refer to state judgments when quantifying damages, will help end characterizing quantification of damages as procedural and will assist distinguishing the liability and quantification issues.

Characterizing the quantification of damages as substantive is important whether or not the change reduces recoveries against United States manufacturers sued by foreigners injured abroad. Even when a foreign defendant injures a foreigner abroad, the victim has an incentive to sue in the United States. Though foreign law applies to all substantive issues, if American standards determine the proper level of compensation, recovery is likely to exceed that in a court abroad.[364] All over the world the settlement value of lawsuits is determined by the likelihood that the plaintiff will obtain personal jurisdiction over the defendant in a United States court and will defeat defendant's attempt to obtain a forum non conveniens dismissal.[365] The most effective way to stop making every law suit's value turn on the availability of a United States forum is to treat the level of compensation as a substantive issue for choice-of-law purposes.

---

360. See Markesinis, *Litigation–Mania in England, Germany and the U.S.A.: Are We So Very Different?*, 49 Cambridge L. J. 233, 243 (1990) (stating that one reason for large jury verdicts in the U.S. may be that the jury is aware that American does not have "a strong welfare state system" and that injured plaintiffs are likely to have to rely on tort recovery for compensation, support, and medical treatment).

361. Dépeçage refers to applying the law of different states to different issues in the same case. See § 3.4.

362. See § 3.2C4.

363. 518 U.S. 415, 116 S.Ct. 2211, 135 L.Ed.2d 659 (1996), discussed in § 3.2C4, text accompanying notes 146–150.

364. See Silva, *Practical Views on Stemming the Tide of Foreign Plaintiffs and Concluding Mid–Atlantic Settlements*, 28 Tex. Int'l L. J. 479, 497 (1993) (stating that "[a] conservative estimate of the relationship between United States and Scottish awards typically is seven to one").

365. See Baade, *Foreign Oil Disaster Litigation Prospects in the United States and the "Mid–Atlantic Settlement Formula,"* 7 J. Energy & Nat. Resources L. 125, 135 (1989) (discussing whether foreign plaintiff can obtain jurisdiction over foreign defendant in U.S. court), 140 (discussing forum non conveniens).

§ 6.32 The Multiple–State Torts of Invasion of Privacy, Libel, and Infringement of the Right of Publicity

The policy-centered analysis for resolving conflicts problems, which is described in this chapter, is concerned mainly with giving maximum effect to the policies underlying each state's domestic laws. There may be other goals for a court to achieve in a given case that are even more important than this main concern of state-interest analysis. This is true, for example, when dealing with the multiple-state torts of invasion of privacy,[366] libel,[367] and infringement of the right of publicity.[368] If the defendant has published the same damaging material in many jurisdictions, there is no reason, in order to give effect to each state's policies concerning privacy and libel, why every jurisdiction should not be free to determine for itself the consequences of the harm caused within it, some granting recovery, some denying it, some applying liberal damages rules, some restricting damages. But to permit these diverse results when the publication has caused harm in many jurisdictions[369] would produce an unintelligible babble of rules if an attempt were made to try all of the resulting transitory causes of action in one suit, or cause multiple litigation at much cost to the parties and harassment of the defendant. For these reasons, it may be desirable to select one jurisdiction,[370] such

---

366. See Motschenbacher v. R.J. Reynolds Tobacco Co., 498 F.2d 821 (9th Cir. 1974); Ettore v. Philco Television Broadcasting Corp., 229 F.2d 481 (3d Cir.1956), cert. denied, 351 U.S. 926, 76 S.Ct. 783, 100 L.Ed. 1456 (1956); Gravina v. Brunswick Corp., 338 F.Supp. 1 (D.R.I.1972); Negri v. Schering Corp., 333 F.Supp. 101 (S.D.N.Y.1971); Strickler v. National Broadcasting Co., 167 F.Supp. 68 (S.D.Cal.1958); Bernstein v. National Broadcasting Co., 129 F.Supp. 817 (D.D.C.1955), aff'd, 232 F.2d 369 (D.C.Cir.1956), cert. denied, 352 U.S. 945, 77 S.Ct. 267, 1 L.Ed.2d 239 (1956); Schumann v. Loew's Inc., 135 N.Y.S.2d 361 (Supp.Ct.N.Y.Cty.1954) (also libel).

367. See Moore v. Greene, 431 F.2d 584 (9th Cir.1970); Association for Preservation of Freedom of Choice v. Simon, 299 F.2d 212 (2d Cir.1962); Hartmann v. Time, Inc., 166 F.2d 127 (3d Cir.1947), cert. denied 334 U.S. 838, 68 S.Ct. 1495, 92 L.Ed. 1763 (1948); Willenbucher v. McCormick, 229 F.Supp. 659 (D.Colo.1964); Tocco v. Time, Inc., 195 F.Supp. 410 (E.D.Mich.1961); Brewster v. Boston Herald–Traveler Corp., 188 F.Supp. 565 (D.Mass.1960); Palmisano v. News Syndicate Co., 130 F.Supp. 17 (S.D.N.Y.1955); Dale Sys., Inc. v. Time, Inc., 116 F.Supp. 527 (D.Conn.1953); Dale Sys., Inc. v. General Teleradio, Inc., 105 F.Supp. 745 (S.D.N.Y.1952); O'Reilly v. Curtis Publishing Co., 31 F.Supp. 364 (D.Mass.1940); Velle Transcendental Research Assoc., Inc. v. Esquire, Inc., 41 Ill.App.3d 799, 354 N.E.2d 622 (1976); Lewis v. Reader's Digest Assoc., Inc., 162 Mont. 401, 512 P.2d 702 (1973).

368. See Bi–Rite Enterprises v. Bruce Miner Co., Inc., 757 F.2d 440 (1st Cir.1985); Acme Circus Operating Co., Inc. v. Kuperstock, 711 F.2d 1538 (11th Cir.1983); Groucho Marx Productions v. Day and Night Co., 689 F.2d 317 (2d Cir.1982); Factors Etc., Inc. v. Pro Arts, Inc., 652 F.2d 278 (2d Cir.1981), cert. denied, 456 U.S. 927, 102 S.Ct. 1973, 72 L.Ed.2d 442 (1982).

369. See Schumann v. Loew's Inc., 135 N.Y.S.2d 361 (Supp.Ct.N.Y.Cty.1954) (61 jurisdictions); Bernstein v. National Broadcasting Co., 129 F.Supp. 817 (D.D.C.1955), aff'd, 232 F.2d 369 (D.C.Cir.1956), cert. denied, 352 U.S. 945, 77 S.Ct. 267, 1 L.Ed.2d 239 (1956) (28 jurisdictions); O'Reilly v. Curtis Publishing Co., 31 F.Supp. 364 (D.Mass.1940) (38 jurisdictions).

370. See Uniform Single Publication Act, 14 U.L.A. 469 (2005) (as of September 1, 2009, adopted in Arizona, California, Idaho, Illinois, New Mexico, North Dakota, and Pennsylvania). This Act gives the plaintiff "one cause of action" for a tort "founded upon any single publication" (§ 1), and provides that the judgment in this action "shall bar any other action for damages by the same plaintiff against the same defendant founded upon the same publication" (§ 2), but the Act contains no indication of what law applies to the

as the plaintiff's domicile, or, if the plaintiff has suffered most harm in some other jurisdiction, that jurisdiction,[371] to provide rules to govern

plaintiff's "one cause of action". See Dominiak v. National Enquirer, 439 Pa. 222, 266 A.2d 626 (1970) (under Uniform Act plaintiff is permitted to select the publication that starts the statute of limitations running); cf. Keeton v. Hustler Magazine, Inc., 131 N.H. 6, 549 A.2d 1187 (1988) (adopting a single publication rule under which any one edition of a book, magazine, or newspaper constitutes a single publication and there is only one action for damages suffered in all jurisdictions); Rinaldi v. Viking Penguin, Inc., 52 N.Y.2d 422, 438 N.Y.S.2d 496, 420 N.E.2d 377 (1981) (under New York's common law single publication rule, paperback edition of earlier hardcover book is a separate publication for limitations purposes). But cf. Brinkley & West, Inc. v. Foremost Ins. Co., 499 F.2d 928 (5th Cir.1974) (when suit is for tort of interference with contracts in several states, the law of each state is applied to the tort within it).

Firth v. State, 98 N.Y.2d 365, 775 N.E.2d 463, 747 N.Y.S.2d 69 (2002), interpreted the "separate publication" exception to the single publication rule in the context of Internet publication. The court held that the statute of limitations began to run on the defamation action when defendant first posted the material on the Internet. The addition of unrelated information to a Web site is not a separate publication that restarts limitations. See also Nationwide Bi–Weekly Administration, Inc. v. Belo Corp., 512 F.3d 137 (5th Cir. 2007) (limitations period for libel action began when article posted on web site); Traditional Cat Assoc. v. Gilbreath, 118 Cal.App.4th 392, 13 Cal.Rptr.3d 353 (2004) (because statements giving rise to cause of action were posted on Web site for more than period of limitations action is barred). But see Loutchansky v. Times Newspapers Ltd., [2002] Q.B. 783, [2002] 1 All E.R. 652 (Ct. App. 2001), which holds that limitations begin anew each time a user accesses the site.

A series of United States Supreme Court decisions place constitutional limitations on recovery for defamation. These cases will reduce the number of actionable multiple-state torts. See Harte–Hanks Communications, Inc. v. Connaughton, 491 U.S. 657, 109 S.Ct. 2678, 105 L.Ed.2d 562 (1989) (a public figure plaintiff in a libel action must prove by clear and convincing evidence that the defendant published the false and defamatory material with knowledge of falsity or with a reckless disregard for the truth, and a reviewing court must exercise independent judgment in determining whether the record establishes this knowledge or disregard with convincing clarity); Philadelphia Newspapers, Inc. v. Hepps, 475 U.S. 767, 106 S.Ct. 1558, 89 L.Ed.2d 783 (1986) (when a newspaper publishes statements of public concern about a private figure, due process requires that the plaintiff has the burden of proving that the statements are false); Gertz v. Robert Welch, Inc., 418 U.S. 323, 94 S.Ct. 2997, 41 L.Ed.2d 789 (1974) (when imposing damages for libel of private individual in discussion of matter of public concern, states may not impose liability without fault and may not permit recovery of presumed or punitive damages unless liability is based on knowledge of falsity or reckless disregard for the truth); New York Times Co. v. Sullivan, 376 U.S. 254, 84 S.Ct. 710, 11 L.Ed.2d 686 (1964) (a public official cannot recover damages for a defamatory falsehood relating to official conduct unless the official proves that the statement was made with actual malice). Cf. Dunn & Bradstreet, Inc. v. Greenmoss Builders, Inc., 472 U.S. 749, 105 S.Ct. 2939, 86 L.Ed.2d 593 (1985) (false statements in credit report did not involve matters of public concern and did not require a showing of actual malice for recovery of presumed and punitive damages).

That diversity still exists within the constitutional limits imposed by the Supreme Court see Anderson, *An American Perspective*, in Tort Law 721, 730 (Deakin, Johnston, & Markesinis eds., 5th ed. 2003) ("It is probably safe to say that, despite the imposition of a complex set of federal constitutional limits, there is less uniformity [in U.S. defamation law] today than ever before"); Rose, *Interstate Libel and Choice of Law: Proposals for the Future*, 30 Hastings L. J. 1515, 1525–27 (1979) (variations in meaning of "fault").

For a discussion of due process limitations on the forums in which the plaintiff may bring actions based on multiple-state publication, see § 4.8 text accompanying notes 237–255.

371. See, e.g., Fuqua Homes, Inc. v. Beattie, 388 F.3d 618 (8th Cir. 2004) (under Missouri most significant relationship approach apply law of manufacturer's principal place of business to deny cause of action for alleged libel published on internet); Wood v. Hustler Magazine, Inc., 736 F.2d 1084 (5th Cir.1984), cert. denied, 469 U.S. 1107, 105 S.Ct. 783, 83 L.Ed.2d 777 (1985) (defamation and privacy, Texas law, plaintiff's domicile); Reeves v. American Broadcasting Co., Inc., 719 F.2d 602 (2d Cir.1983) (defamation, New York

liability for the damage done everywhere. This may be desirable for reasons of economy of judicial administration when, otherwise, the result might be justly criticized for incorrectly resolving a false conflict. For instance, if the law of the plaintiff's domicile is selected, it may insulate the defendant from liability under the law of other states where the defendant has published and caused consequences that those other states seek to compensate and deter by their law. Applying the law of the plaintiff's domicile to protect the defendant from liability is not likely to advance significantly any domestic policy of the domicile. By its rule insulating the defendant from liability, the plaintiff's domicile may wish to encourage free discussion and dissemination of information, but this policy will not be advanced significantly in the case of a statement that is published in many states, some of which would hold the statement actionable. The defendant is deterred by the law of libel from nationwide publication if any substantial number of states would hold the publication actionable. If the law of the plaintiff's domicile is applied to shield the defendant from liability, without significantly advancing any substantive policy of the domicile, it may conflict with the interests of other

conflicts law, apply privilege rule of California where plaintiff domiciled); Groucho Marx Productions v. Day and Night Co., 689 F.2d 317 (2d Cir.1982) (right of publicity, New York law, where deceased performers domiciled and plaintiffs reside and incorporated); Fleury v. Harper & Row, Publishers, Inc., 698 F.2d 1022 (9th Cir.1983), cert. denied, 464 U.S. 846, 104 S.Ct. 149, 78 L.Ed.2d 139 (1983) (libel, privacy, California law, plaintiffs' domicile); Hanley v. Tribune Pub. Co., 527 F.2d 68 (9th Cir.1975) (libel, law of plaintiff's domicile); Strickler v. National Broadcasting Co., 167 F.Supp. 68 (S.D. Cal. 1958) (privacy—law of domicile); Bernstein v. National Broadcasting Co., 129 F.Supp. 817 (D.D.C 1955), aff'd, 232 F.2d 369 (D.C. Cir. 1956), cert. denied, 352 U.S. 945, 77 S.Ct. 267, 1 L.Ed.2d 239 (1956) (privacy—law of domicile or where plaintiff has most of his contacts); Palmisano v. News Syndicate Co., 130 F.Supp. 17 (S.D. N.Y. 1955) (libel—place of plaintiff's principal reputation); Dale Sys., Inc. v. Time, Inc., 116 F.Supp. 527 (D. Conn. 1953) (libel—law of domicile); Restatement, Second § 150 (domicile or principal place of business); Stumberg, *"The Place of Wrong" and the Conflict of Laws*, 34 Wash. L. Rev. 388, 393 (1959) ("place where the plaintiff is likely to incur the most harm"); cf. Bi–Rite Enterprises v. Bruce Miner Co., Inc., 757 F.2d 440 (1st Cir.1985) (right of publicity, Massachusetts law, place where musicians' exclusive licensee incorporated rather than domicile of musicians); Acme Circus Operating Co., Inc. v. Kuperstock, 711 F.2d 1538 (11th Cir.1983) (right of publicity, California law, plaintiff's domicile determines whether right exists, but more liberal recovery rule of place where defendant acted would apply if right did exist); System Operations, Inc. v. Scientific Games Development Corp., 555 F.2d 1131 (3d Cir.1977) (product disparagement, plaintiff's principal place of business when that is also one of the places of publication and the forum); Nader v. General Motors Corp., 25 N.Y.2d 560, 307 N.Y.S.2d 647, 255 N.E.2d 765 (1970) (privacy and intentional infliction of emotional distress, but not based on a multiple-state publication—place where plaintiff domiciled and where most of defendant's acts were performed is "the place which has the most significant relationship with the subject matter of the tort charged"). But cf. Association for the Preservation of Freedom of Choice v. Simon, 299 F.2d 212 (2d Cir. 1962) (libel—law of place of first publication); Gravina v. Brunswick Corp., 338 F.Supp. 1 (D.R.I.1972) (privacy, law of defendant's headquarters, which recognized right of recovery contra law of plaintiff's domicile); Negri v. Schering Corp., 333 F.Supp. 101 (S.D.N.Y.1971) (privacy, law of forum where published and which recognized action); Brewster v. Boston Herald–Traveler Corp., 188 F.Supp. 565 (D. Mass. 1960) (libel—law of each state where newspaper distributed); Dale Sys., Inc. v. General Teleradio, Inc., 105 F.Supp. 745 (S.D. N.Y. 1952) (libel—law of place where there is a grouping of dominant contacts).

That under United States Supreme Court libel decisions choice of law should focus on the place where defendant acted rather than on plaintiff's domicile, see Rose, *Interstate Libel and Choice of Law: Proposals for the Future*, 30 Hastings L. J. 1515, 1532, 1537–38 (1979).

states that would hold the defendant liable. Nevertheless, as indicated above, policies of judicial economy may sometimes justify applying the law of the plaintiff's domicile to insulate the defendant from liability for a multiple-state tort.

Granting all this one should not lose sight of the fact that such policies of judicial economy do not exist in every case of interstate publication. The defendant may have published in only two or three states, or the facts may be such that it is clear that a cause of action exists under the law of only one or a very few states.[372] If so, there is no reason to apply a rule of the plaintiff's domicile that would relieve the defendant from liability existing under the laws of other states having an interest in compensating the plaintiff and in discouraging such publications within their borders.

When the defamation is published on the Internet, many U.S. courts have denied jurisdiction at the plaintiff's domicile unless the publication is expressly aimed at the domicile. Foreseeability that the defamatory material is accessible at the domicile and will cause harm there is not sufficient for judicial jurisdiction over the tortfeasor.[373] If defendant's contacts with the domicile are not sufficient to confer judicial jurisdiction on the domiciliary courts, then a fortiori it should be unconstitutional to apply the law of the domicile.

It is true that the Supreme Court of the United States has repeatedly insisted that contacts with a jurisdiction may be sufficient for application of its law but not for jurisdiction of its courts.[374] Such statements are nonsense. The relationship between constitutional limits on choice of law and judicial jurisdiction is just the opposite. It may be that a forum, because of the defendant's close ties with the forum, may have general jurisdiction over the defendant in a cause of action unrelated to the forum, but that the forum does not have a sufficient nexus to apply its law to the unrelated activity.[375] It is inconceivable, however, that a court can have specific jurisdiction over a defendant for a cause of action arising out or related to forum events and not have sufficient contacts to make application of its law constitutional. The converse should also be true—sufficient contacts to apply forum law to defendant equals sufficient contacts for personal jurisdiction over defendant. To state otherwise, as the Supreme Court has done, is, as Professor Silberman has written, "to believe that an accused is more concerned with where he will be hanged than whether."[376]

---

372. See Donahue v. Warner Bros. Pictures, 194 F.2d 6 (10th Cir.1952) (heirs' action for invasion of the right of privacy existed, if at all, only under Utah law); Gorton v. Australian Broadcasting Commission, 22 F.L.R. 181 (Australian S.Ct., Capital Territory, 1973) (broadcast in three jurisdictions, separate tort in each).

373. See § 4.17.

374. See § 4.8 text accompanying notes 175–176, 182.

375. See § 4.2.

376. Silberman, *Shaffer v. Heitner: The End of an Era*, 53 N.Y.U. L. Rev. 33, 88 (1978).

Far more sensible with regard to both jurisdiction and choice of law is the opinion of the High Court of Australia in *Dow Jones & Co. v. Gutnick*.[377] *Gutnick* found that a Victoria resident had personal jurisdiction in the courts of Victoria over a U.S. company that had uploaded the allegedly defamatory material on its servers in New Jersey. The court also held that the law of Victoria applied. The defamation law of Victoria is more favorable to the plaintiff than the law of any U.S. jurisdiction. The plaintiff eliminated the multi-state choice-of-law problem by suing only for harm that he suffered in Victoria and undertaking not to sue defendant anyplace else.

The "single publication rule," now widely adopted in the U.S., provides that a plaintiff has only one cause of action for a tort founded on a single publication, although the defendant may have distributed the publication to many persons.[378] When the publication is over the internet, the New York Court of Appeals has held that the statute of limitations begins to run on the day of first publication and that modification of the site to add unrelated material does not constitute a republication.[379] In England, however, each individual publication of a libel gives rise to a new cause of action and the same is true of internet publication—limitations begin anew each time a user accesses the site.[380]

In defamation cases the codification of Japanese conflict-of-law rules that took effect on 1 January 2007 applies "the law of the injured person's habitual residence (i.e., the law of its principal place of business where the injured person is a juridical person or other corporate association.)"[381] There is an exception in favor of the "law of the place with which [the tort] is clearly more closely connected in light of the circumstances such as where at the time of the tort both of the parties had their habitual residence in a place under the same law, or where the tort occurred by breaching obligations in a contract between the parties."[382]

The European Union Regulation on the Law Applicable to Non–Contractual Obligations excludes defamation, leaving it for further study.[383]

§ 6.33 Mass Torts and Class Actions

A "mass tort" is one in which the same wrongful conduct injures many victims—dozens, hundreds, or, with increasing frequency, thou-

---

377. [2002] HCA 56 (Austl. 2002).

378. See supra note 370.

379. Firth v. State of New York, 98 N.Y.2d 365, 775 N.E.2d 463, 747 N.Y.S.2d 69 (2002).

380. See Loutchansky v. Times Newspapers Ltd., [2002] Q.B. 783, [2002] 1 All E.R. 652 (Ct. App. 2001).

381. Act on the General Rules of Application of Laws, Law No. 10 of 1898 as newly titled and amended 21 June 2006, art. 19.

382. Id. art. 20.

383. European Parliament and of the Council of 11 July 2007 on the law applicable to non-contractual obligations (Rome II) arts. 1(2)(g) (exclusion), 30(2) (further study), OJ 2007 L 199.

sands. Plaintiffs "come not single spies, but in battalions"[384] that threaten to overwhelm our systems for administering justice. The explosion of the Union Carbide Gas Plant at Bhopal, India, allegedly killed over 2,000 people and injured more than 200,000.[385] Claims against asbestos manufacturers have resulted in the filing of tens of thousands of suits, peaking at a rate of 500 a month.[386]

As the Bhopal and asbestos examples indicate, there are two forms of mass tort. In one, the same event killed or injured the victims. In the other, injuries occur over a period to time at different locations but have the same cause, typically a defective product.

The most common example of the single-event mass tort is the airplane crash.[387] Although the number of claims resulting from an airplane accident may be insignificant compared with the Bhopal thousands, the Bhopal victims shared a common domicile. In the typical United States air crash litigation, passengers are likely to come from a dozen or more states and from several foreign countries.[388] Single cause but geographically and temporally dispersed mass torts also present the problem of many plaintiffs with diverse domiciles.

In the United States, one common method for litigating mass torts is the class action. Federal Rule of Civil Procedure 23 provides:

Class Actions

(a) Prerequisites to a Class Action. One or more members of a class may sue or be sued as representative parties on behalf of all only if (1) the class is so numerous that joinder of all members is impracticable, (2) there are questions of law or fact common to the class, (3) the claims or defenses of the representative parties are typical of the claims or defenses of the class, and (4) the representative parties will fairly and adequately protect the interests of the class.

(b) Class Actions Maintainable. An action may be maintained as a class action if Rule 23(a) is satisfied, and in addition: .... (3) the court finds that the questions of law or fact common to class members predominate over any questions affecting only individual members, and that a class action is superior to other available methods for fairly and efficiently adjudicating the controversy. The matters pertinent to these findings include: (A) the class members' interests in individually controlling the prosecution or defense of separate actions; (B) the extent and nature of any litigation concerning the controversy already begun by or against class members; (C) the desirability or undesirability of concentrating the litigation of

---

384. W. Shakespeare, Hamlet Prince of Denmark, act IV, scene V, l. 78: "When sorrows come, they come not single spies, but in battalions...."

385. See In re Union Carbide Corp. Gas Plant Disaster at Bhopal, India, 809 F.2d 195, 197 (2d Cir.), cert. denied, 484 U.S. 871, 108 S.Ct. 199, 98 L.Ed.2d 150 (1987).

386. See Rubin, *Mass Torts and Litigation Disasters*, 20 Ga. L. Rev. 429, 430 (1986).

387. See, e.g. In re Air Crash Disaster Near Chicago, 644 F.2d 594 (7th Cir.) cert. denied, 454 U.S. 878, 102 S.Ct. 358, 70 L.Ed.2d 187 (1981).

388. Id.

the claims in the particular forum; and (D) the likely difficulties in managing a class action.

Many state rules are modeled on the federal rule.

Choice of law is a potential roadblock to a class action. *Castano v. American Tobacco Co.*[389] reversed the trial court's certification of a class action filed on behalf of all United States cigarette smokers and their survivors against seven tobacco companies. The court ordered the district court to dismiss the class complaint stating that "[i]n a multi-state class action, variations in state law may swamp any common issues and defeat predominance [of questions of law or fact common to the members of the class]."[390]

Even in a national class action, choice of law may not create an insurmountable barrier. Plaintiffs may be able to demonstrate that there are no or few relevant variations in state law. The court may be able to divide plaintiffs and defendants into a manageable number of subclasses.[391] On the other hand, state-by-state tort reform produces many disparities on such key issues as elements of proof, affirmative defenses, joint and several liability, comparative fault, and punitive damages. The American Law Institute has recommended the following choice-of-law rule for actions that "involve one or more common questions of fact"[392] and are consolidated from cases filed in two or more United States district courts[393] or in more than one state court and removed to federal court:[394]

§ 6.01. Mass Torts

. . . .

(c) In determining the governing law ... the court shall consider the following factors for purposes of identifying each state having a policy that would be furthered by the application of its laws:

(1) the place or places of injury;

(2) the place or places of the conduct causing the injury; and

(3) the primary places of business or habitual residences of the plaintiffs and defendants.

(d) If, in analyzing the factors set forth in subsection (c), the court finds that only one state has a policy that would be furthered by the application of its law, that state's law shall govern. If more

---

389. 84 F.3d 734 (5th Cir. 1996).

390. Id. at 741.

391. See, e.g., Miner v. Gillette Co., 87 Ill.2d 7, 56 Ill.Dec. 886, 428 N.E.2d 478 (1981), cert. dismissed, 459 U.S. 86, 103 S.Ct. 484, 74 L.Ed.2d 249 (1982); Kramer, *Choice of Law in Complex Litigation*, 71 N.Y.U. L. Rev. 547, 549 (1996) (stating that "whatever choice-of-law rules we use to define substantive rights should be the same for ordinary and complex cases").

392. Complex Litigation: Statutory Recommendations and Analysis § 3.01(a)(1) (1994).

393. Id. § 3.01(a).

394. Id. § 5.01(a).

than one state has a policy that would be furthered by the application of its law, the court shall choose the applicable law from among the laws of the interested states under the following rules:

(1) If the place of injury and the place of the conduct causing the injury are in the same state, that state's law governs.

(2) If subsection (d)(1) does not apply, but all of the plaintiffs habitually reside or have their primary places of business in the same state, and a defendant has its primary place of business or habitually resides in that state, that state's law governs the claims with respect to that defendant. Plaintiffs shall be considered as sharing a common habitual residence or primary place of business if they are located in states whose laws are not in material conflict.

(3) If neither subsection (d)(1) nor (d)(2) applies, but all of the plaintiffs habitually reside or have their primary places of business in the same state, and that state also is the place of injury, then that state's law governs. Plaintiffs shall be considered as sharing a common habitual residence or primary place of business if they are located in states whose laws are not in material conflict.

(4) In all other cases, the law of the state where the conduct causing the injury occurred governs. When conduct occurred in more than one state, the court shall choose the law of the conduct state that has the most significant relationship to the occurrence.

(e) To avoid unfair surprise or arbitrary results, the transferee court may choose the applicable law on the basis of other factors that reflect the regulatory policies and legitimate interests of a particular state not otherwise identified under subsection (c), or it may depart from the order of preferences for selecting the governing law prescribed by subsection (d).

In a national class action sections (d)(1) through (d)(3) will not apply. Conduct and injury are not in the same state and plaintiffs "habitually reside" in different states. Therefore (d)(4) governs and if a court uses a choice-of-law rule modeled on § 6.01 it will apply "the law of the state where the conduct causing the injury occurred." In a product liability case this will be the state where the manufacturer designed and made the product.

An obvious objection is that this is unfair to those plaintiffs who would fare better under the law of the state where they purchased, used, and were injured by the product. In addition, rule (d)(4), if widely adopted, may trigger a race to the bottom with states vying to adopt defendant-friendly liability law in order to attract manufacturers. 6.01(e) does provide the court some wiggle room in this regard, but applying the law of fifty states will produce the very barriers to a class action that 6.01 attempts to avoid. Nevertheless, a plaintiff who is prejudiced by 6.01(d)(4) can opt out of the class action.[395] Moreover, (d)(4), by making

---

395. Fed. R. Civ. P. 23(c)(2). See Issacharoff, *Settled Expectations in a World of Unsettled Law: Choice of Law after the Class Action Fairness Act*, 106 Colum. L. Rev. 1839,

a national class action feasible, may provide plaintiffs with a remedy when otherwise there would be none because each claim is too small for prosecution of individual actions or even state-wide class actions.

Ignoring the fact that small claims may produce "negative value" cases if plaintiffs have to litigate them individually, *In re Bridgestone/Firestone*[396] provides the occasion for Judge Frank Easterbrook to reject the ALI choice-of-law rules and class actions in general:

> Plaintiffs share the premise of the ALI's Complex Litigation Project (1993), which devotes more than 700 pages to an analysis of means to consolidate litigation as quickly as possible, by which the authors mean, before multiple trials break out. The authors take as given the benefits of that step. Yet the benefits are elusive. The central planning model—one case, one court, one set of rules, one settlement price for all involved—suppresses information that is vital to accurate resolution. What *is* the law of Michigan, or Arkansas, or Guam, as applied to this problem? * * * And if the law were clear, how would the facts (and thus the damages per plaintiff) be ascertained? One suit is an all-or-none affair, with high risk even if the parties supply all the information at their disposal. Getting things right the first time would be an accident. Similarly Gosplan[397] or another central planner may hit on the price of wheat, but that would be serendipity. Markets instead use diversified decision making to supply and evaluate information. Thousands of traders affect prices by their purchases and sales over the course of a crop year. This method looks "inefficient" from the planner's perspective, but it produces more information, more accurate prices, and a vibrant, growing economy.[398]

The court reversed the trial judge's certification of a national class action for the risk of failure of one defendant's allegedly defective tires on the other defendant's allegedly defective Sport Utility Vehicles. The trial judge committed error in ruling that the laws of the two states in which defendants were headquartered applied to all claims. The Seventh Circuit held that the class action was not manageable because the trial court would have to apply the laws of each jurisdiction in which injuries occurred. The court also cautioned plaintiffs not to refile a class action involving claimants resident in the same state because there were too many factual variations to make the class manageable.

Then, the following year, the court ordered the trial judge to enjoin all members of the class and their lawyers "from again attempting [in any court, state or federal] to have nationwide classes certified over

---

1869 (2006) ("any plaintiff could choose to sue under more suitable home state law by excluding herself from the class action").

396. 288 F.3d 1012 (7th Cir. 2002), cert. denied, 537 U.S. 1105, 123 S.Ct. 870, 154 L.Ed.2d 774 (2003).

397. Gosplan was the committee for economic planning in the Soviet Union. "Gosplan" is an acronym formed from Russian words meaning "state committee for planning." Ed.

398. Id. at 1020.

defendants' opposition with respect to the same claims."[399] The court did, however, hold that its warning not to file a statewide class action was not binding on plaintiffs in other jurisdictions because that issue was not before the court at the time of the previous opinion.[400]

Contrary to *Bridgestone/Firestone*, courts utilizing interest and most-significant-relationship analysis have sometimes facilitated certification of a national class action by applying to all claims the law of the state that was the center of defendant's wrongful conduct.[401] It is easiest to justify this result when the law of the state where defendant's conduct is centered is so favorable to plaintiffs that no member of the class would recover more under the law of the member's home state.[402]

Reasonable persons might differ as to whether it is desirable to facilitate certification of a multi-state class action by applying to all claims the law of a single state where defendant's acts originated. Defendants often contend that it is not only unwise to do so but also unconstitutional, citing *Phillips Petroleum Co. v. Shutts*.[403] *Shutts* does not support such a claim. Phillips produced natural gas from land in eleven states. The royalty recipients brought a class action against Phillips in a Kansas state court for interest on royalty payments that Phillips had withheld pending Federal Power Commission approval of new rates. The Kansas courts held that Kansas law determined the amount of interest payable on proceeds from wells in all eleven states to

---

399. In re Bridgestone/Firestone, Inc., 333 F.3d 763, 769 (7th Cir. 2003).

400. Id. at 766.

401. See Hall v. Sprint Spectrum L.P., 376 Ill.App.3d 822, 315 Ill.Dec. 446, 876 N.E.2d 1036 (2007), app. denied, 226 Ill.2d 614, 317 Ill.Dec. 503, 882 N.E.2d 77 (2008), cert. denied, ___ U.S. ___, 129 S.Ct. 50, 172 L.Ed.2d 23 (2008) (apply Kansas law selected in choice-of-law clause in contract drafted by defendant); Ysbrand v. DaimlerChrysler Corp., 81 P.3d 618 (Okla. 2003), cert. denied, 542 U.S. 937, 124 S.Ct. 2907, 159 L.Ed.2d 812 (2004) (permitting certification as to warranty claims but not for the claim for fraud and deceit), but see Cuesta v. Ford Motor Co., 209 P.3d 278, 284 (Okla. 2009), cert. denied, 130 S.Ct. 258 (apply Michigan law to national class action and state "Plaintiffs' request for only economic damages makes it unnecessary to consider Plaintiffs' tort theories of recovery in our choice of law analysis"); Grider v. Compaq Computer Corp., Case No. 102,693 (Okla. App. 2006) (not for official publication, but summarized in petition for certiorari, 2007 WL 2220382 at 4), cert. denied, 552 U.S. 949, 128 S.Ct. 378, 169 L.Ed.2d 261 (2007); cf. In re Warfarin Sodium Antitrust Litigation, 391 F.3d 516, 529 (3d Cir. 2004) (distinguish *Bridgestone/Firestone* on ground this "a class solely for purposes of settlement"); Liggett Group Inc. v. Affiliated FM Ins. Co., 788 A.2d 134, 144 (Del. Super. 2001) (in determining liability insurers' obligation to defend and indemnify tobacco manufacturer in suits throughout the United States "[t]he interests of economy, ease of application, and uniformity of result favor a global choice of law"—the manufacturer's principal place of business); Citizens Ins. Co. of America v. Daccach, 217 S.W.3d 430 (Tex. 2007) (although Texas Securities Act by it terms applied to sales from Texas to nonresidents in violation of the Act, class decertified and remanded to trial court to determine issues other than choice of law that might preclude class action). But see, Goshen v. Mutual Life Ins. Co. of New York, 98 N.Y.2d 314, 774 N.E.2d 1190, 746 N.Y.S.2d 858 (2002) (nonresidents defrauded by New York insurance company do not have claims under New York's Consumer Protection Act although the deceptive scheme originated in New York). Contra Barbara's Sales, Inc. v. Intel Corp., 227 Ill.2d 45, 316 Ill.Dec. 522, 879 N.E.2d 910 (2007) (applying Restatement (Second), Illinois law, which is less favorable to recovery than law of California, the center of defendant's activities, governs actions of Illinois consumers).

402. See In re St. Jude Medical, Inc., 2006 WL 2943154 (D. Minn. 2006).

403. 472 U.S. 797, 105 S.Ct. 2965, 86 L.Ed.2d 628 (1985).

recipients in fifty states, the District of Columbia, and several foreign countries. Phillips contested this ruling on due process and full faith and credit grounds. The court reversed holding that it was a violation of due process to apply Kansas law if Kansas law was more favorable to the class members than the laws of the states where the wells were located.

In *Shutts* less than 1,000 of the over 28,000 class members resided in Kansas and only one quarter of one per cent of the gas leases were on Kansas land. Under *Shutts* it is unconstitutional to select the law of a state where some class members live and apply that law to a national class action when that law is more favorable to class members than the laws of other states having more significant relationships with the other class members and with the defendant. It is not unconstitutional in a national class action to apply the law of a single state if that is the state where the defendant's wrongful acts were centered. Whose constitutional rights are violated? The state where the defendant misbehaved has an interest in punishing and deterring such conduct and it is not unfair to the defendant to apply the law of that state even in favor of nonresident plaintiffs. How about those members of the class that would recover more under the law of their home state? Those members of the class can opt out. Moreover, in the typical national class action the claims of any individual class member or even of a state-wide class are so small as to make a national class action the only feasible route to recovery.

In *Ysbrand v. DaimlerChrysler Corp.* the Supreme Court of Oklahoma correctly rejected the constitutional *Shutts* argument and on the warranty issue applied to the national class action the laws of the states where defendants were headquartered.[404] Unfortunately in *In re St. Jude Medical, Inc.* the Eight Circuit gave *Shutts* as the reason why it would be unconstitutional to apply the law of Minnesota, where defendant was headquartered, to the claims of class members whose home state laws differed from those of Minnesota.[405]

Equally unfortunate is that a passing remark in *State Farm Mutual Automobile Ins. Co. v. Campbell*[406] could be cited (it was not cited) in support of the Eight Circuit's opinion in *St. Jude Medical*. *Campbell* continued the elaboration of constitutional limits on punitive damages begun in *BMW of North America, Inc. v. Gore*.[407] In *Campbell* the court the court barred the trier of fact, when considering the quantification of punitive damages, from including a sanction for defendant's unlawful acts in another state:

> Nor, as a general rule, does a State have a legitimate concern in imposing punitive damages to punish a defendant for unlawful acts committed outside of the State's jurisdiction. Any proper adjudication of conduct that occurred outside Utah to other persons would

---

404. 81 P.3d 618, 626 (Okla. 2003), cert. denied, 542 U.S. 937, 124 S.Ct. 2907, 159 L.Ed.2d 812 (2004).

405. 425 F.3d 1116, 1120 (8th Cir. 2005).

406. 538 U.S. 408, 123 S.Ct. 1513, 155 L.Ed.2d 585 (2003).

407. 517 U.S. 559, 116 S.Ct. 1589, 134 L.Ed.2d 809 (1996).

require their inclusion, and, to those parties, the Utah courts, in the usual case, *would need to apply the laws of their relevant jurisdiction.*[408]

Another important factor in nationwide class actions is which party has the burden of proving that the laws of states in which class members reside differ from the law of the forum. In this regard *Washington Mutual Bank v. Superior Court*[409] is favorable to certification of a national class action. The court held that if class members sue under California law, California law applies until the defendant both demonstrates that other states have different laws and that the court should apply those laws instead of California law:

> Amici curiae in support of [the defendant] argue that the [usual] burdens [of displacing California law, which fall on the party seeking displacement,] should not apply when a nationwide class action is at issue. In their view, the law of the other states in which class members reside should presumably govern their claims unless the proponent of class certification affirmatively demonstrates that California law is more properly applied. To support this position, amici curiae point out that nationwide class actions may be, and often are, used to resolve the claims of nonresidents who lack the minimum contacts in the forum state normally needed to support personal jurisdiction. In such cases, they argue, California may not constitutionally weigh the scales in favor of applying its own law. We disagree.
>
> As amici curiae acknowledge ... a forum state may constitutionally apply its own law to the claims of nonresident class members if the state has a " 'significant contact or significant aggregation of contacts' to the claims asserted by each member of the plaintiff class, contacts 'creating state interests,' in order to ensure that the choice of [the forum's] law is not arbitrary or unfair." (*Phillips Petroleum Co. v. Shutts*, 472 U.S. [797] at pp. 821–822 [1985]) Accordingly, so long as the requisite significant contacts to California exist, a showing that is properly borne by the class action proponent, California may constitutionally require the other side to shoulder the burden of demonstrating that foreign law, rather than California law, should apply to class claims.[410]

One objection to this statement is the threshold requirement that the party suing under California law bears the burden of demonstrating that California has sufficient contacts with the parties and the transaction to make it constitutional to apply California law. It is constitutional to apply California law until a party wishing to displace that law shows

---

408. *Campbell*, 538 U.S. at 421–22, 123 S.Ct. at 1522 (emphasis added).

409. 24 Cal.4th 906, 15 P.3d 1071, 103 Cal.Rptr.2d 320 (2001).

410. Id. at 920–21, 15 P.3d at 1081, 103 Cal.Rptr.2d at 331. Cf. Ferrell v. Allstate Ins. Co., 144 N.M. 405, 418, 188 P.3d 1156, 1169 (2008) (if the plaintiff proves there are no significant variations among the laws of the states connected to the class action, if there is any ambiguity, the defendant must "show that the laws of relevant states actually conflict through clearly established, plainly contradictory law").

that the law of another state would produce a different result from that reached under California law. Then the court must find that in the light of the difference in law, it would be unconstitutional to apply California law rather than the law of another state. *Phillips Petroleum Co. v. Shutts*[411] blundered in reversing a Kansas court's application of Kansas law to a multi-state class action when there was no showing that the laws of the other states differed from Kansas law. In dissenting from this portion of the opinion Justice Stevens futilely attempted to derail this silliness:

> Again, however, a constitutional claim of "unfair surprise" cannot be based merely upon an unexpected choice of a particular State's law—it must rest on a persuasive showing of an unexpected result arrived at by application of that law. Thus, absent any conflict of laws, in terms of the results they produce, the Due Process Clause simply has not been violated. . . .

> In this case it is perfectly clear that there has been no due process violation because this is a classic "false conflicts" case. Phillips has not demonstrated that any significant conflicts exist merely because Oklahoma and Texas state case law is silent concerning the equitable theories developed by the Kansas courts in this litigation, or even because the language of some Oklahoma and Texas statutes suggests that those States would "most likely" reach different results.[412]

Predictably, on remand the Kansas Supreme Court decided that, in the absence of any evidence to the contrary, Texas and Oklahoma courts were sufficiently fair and wise to reach the same result that Kansas courts had reached and reaffirmed its former opinion.[413] This time the Supreme Court of the United States did what it should have done in the first place. It denied certiorari.[414]

Thus *Washington Mutual Bank* is wrong in stating that a California court cannot apply California law unless California has constitutionally sufficient contacts with the parties and the transaction. This omits the necessity of showing that the laws of other states would produce different results.

There is another false note in the opinion. The court held that because the action was based on contracts containing enforceable choice-of-law agreements that selected the law of each state where a class member resides, "the burden rests upon the party seeking nationwide class certification to identify any variations of applicable state law and to meaningfully demonstrate how a trial on the class causes of action can

---

411. 472 U.S. 797, 105 S.Ct. 2965, 86 L.Ed.2d 628 (1985).

412. Id. at 837–38, 105 S.Ct. at 2987–88 (Stevens, J., concurring and dissenting).

413. Shutts v. Phillips Petroleum Co., 240 Kan. 764, 732 P.2d 1286 (1987) (except for post-judgment interest, which was awarded under the laws of the states where the leases were situated).

414. Phillips Petroleum Co v. Shutts, 487 U.S. 1223, 108 S.Ct. 2883, 101 L.Ed.2d 918 (1988).

be conducted fairly and efficiently in light of those variations."[415] This is a non sequitur. If in the absence of a choice-of-law clause the party seeking to displace California law has the burden of showing that applying the law of another state will change the result, that party should retain the burden even though the laws of other states are selected by the parties' agreement.

The lex loci delicti rule will not ease certification of a class action, even if all members of the class reside in the same state, if the class members have been injured in different states.[416]

On February 18, 2005, President George W. Bush signed into law the Class Action Fairness Act of 2005.[417] The Act applies to "any civil action commenced on or after the date of enactment."[418] It permits removal from state court and gives federal district courts original jurisdiction on the basis of minimal diversity[419] of any class action in which the amount in controversy exceeds $5,000,000. Thus the plaintiffs' attorney can no longer prevent removal from state to federal court by joining a defendant of the same citizenship as any plaintiff[420] or by suing in a state court in a state where any defendant is a citizen.[421] The only exception to federal jurisdiction is if "greater than two-thirds of the members of all proposed plaintiff classes in the aggregate are citizens of the State in which the action was originally filed."[422]

Although state courts will no longer be viable forums for national class actions, the Act does not contain a choice-of-law provision. Therefore federal district courts in which plaintiffs file national class actions or to which defendants remove such actions from state court will have to apply the choice-of-law rules of the state in which the court is sitting.[423] This means that where the action is filed still matters and may be the difference between certification and dismissal. States where courts apply

---

415. *Washington Mut. Bank*, 24 Cal.4th at 928, 15 P.3d at 1086, 103 Cal.Rptr.2d at 337.

416. See Philip Morris Inc. v. Angeletti, 358 Md. 689, 752 A.2d 200 (2000) (decertifying a class action by Maryland residents because Maryland law not applicable to class members who suffered manifestations of disease before moving to Maryland or who became addicted elsewhere).

417. Pub. L. No. 109–002, 119 Stat.4 (2005).

418. Id. § 9.

419. 28 U.S.C. 1332(d)(2)(A).

420. Strawbridge v. Curtiss, 7 U.S. (3 Cranch) 267, 2 L.Ed. 435 (1806), overruled on other grounds, Louisville R.R. v. Letson, 43 U.S. 497, 11 L.Ed. 353 (1844) (holding that for federal diversity jurisdiction to attach, complete diversity is required, each defendant being of diverse citizenship from each plaintiff).

421. See 28 U.S.C. § 1441(b), which provides that a case cannot be removed from state court under federal diversity jurisdiction if any defendant is a citizen of the state in which suit is brought.

422. 28 U.S.C. 1332(d)(4)(A). Class Action Fairness Act § 4. A district court is also given discretion to decline to exercise jurisdiction "over a class action in which greater than one-third but less than two-thirds of the members of all proposed plaintiff classes in the aggregate and the primary defendants are citizens of the State in which the action was originally filed." Id. d(3).

423. *See* Klaxon Co. v. Stentor Elec. Mfg. Co., 313 U.S. 487, 61 S.Ct. 1020, 85 L.Ed. 1477 (1941).

to all class members the law of the state where defendant's conduct was centered will be attractive forums under the Act.[424]

There are commentators who disagree that under the Act federal courts must apply the choice-of-law rules of the state in which they sit. Professor Samuel Issacharoff urges federal courts to adopt a federal choice-of-law rule that applies the law of defendant's home state.[425] Professor Linda Silberman, although stating that "it may be that the federal courts will continue to apply *Klaxon* to CAFA cases as the decisions under the Act indicate,"[426] advocates the adoption of federal rule like "the Restatement (Second) of Conflict of Laws with an emphasis on 'contacts' and 'interests' ".[427] Such a rule, in typical class actions presenting many differences in state laws that cannot be accommodated by a manageable number of subclasses, would result in a refusal to certify.[428] The Report of the Senate Judiciary Committee on the Class Action Fairness Act also assumed that a federal court having jurisdiction under the Act was free to adopt its own choice-of-law rule.[429]

The Report's assumption is unfounded. The issue arose when CAFA's predecessor, the Multiparty, Multi-forum Trial Jurisdiction Act, provided that "district courts shall have original jurisdiction of any civil action involving minimal diversity between adverse parties that arises from a single accident, where at least 75 natural persons have died in the accident at a discrete location."[430] There were many attempts to put in the Act a provision freeing federal courts to adopt their own choice-of-law rules,[431] all of which failed. An attempt to address choice of law in

424. See supra notes 401–402 and accompanying text.

425. Issacharoff, *Settled Expectations in a World of Unsettled Law: Choice of Law After the Class Action Fairness Act*, 106 Colum. L. Rev. 1839, 1869 (2006).

426. Silberman, *Choice of Law in National Class Actions: Should CAFA Make a Difference?*, 14 Roger Williams U. L. Rev. 54, 71 (2009).

427. Id. at 70.

428. Id at 71.

429. Cong. Record Vol. 151, S. Rep. No. 109–14, Feb. 28, 2005, §§ IV (discussing state decisions applying the law of a single state to multi-state class actions), VII (Response to Critics' Contention No. 9) (federal courts will not "botch these critical choice-of-law issues" as some state courts have done).

430. 28 U.S.C. § 1369.

431. See, e.g., See H.R. Rep. 100–889 at 42–3, 1988 U.S.C.C.A.N 5982 at 6002–003 (emphasis added):

Section 305 of the bill adds a new § 1658 to address the problems of choice of law determinations in actions within the proposed jurisdiction. Because the jurisdiction is for multiparty, multiforum actions, the substantive law of several states and even foreign nations will often be potentially applicable to different aspects of the litigation before the Federal court. In general, Federal courts in state law cases are bound by the choice of law rules of the state in which they sit. That rule, however, is extremely hard to defend for actions like those within the proposed jurisdiction, in which a Federal court would not be largely acting as a surrogate state court but rather serving a nationwide function that often could not have been served by any state court. When the purpose of the jurisdiction is to use the Federal courts to do what no state court may be able to do, it makes no sense to have a Federal court bound by the conflicts laws of a single state. (The Federal court may, of course, end up following the same conflicts rules or substantive law that would have governed in the courts of the forum state; but it should not invariably be required to do so.)

CAFA also failed.[432]

Section 10.8, infra, states that federal courts, when applying state law, should be free to apply a federal choice-of-law rule when, as in federal interpleader, the federal court has personal jurisdiction over a party that is not subject to jurisdiction in the forum's state courts.[433] The Supreme Court has nevertheless held that *Klaxon* applies in federal interpleader.[434] Moreover, state courts have personal jurisdiction over nonresident members of a national class.[435] It would be political rather judicial for a court to rule that federal choice-of-law rules apply under CAFA when repeated legislative attempts to achieve that result have failed and federal courts have not utilized far more cogent circumstances in which to fashion a *Klaxon* exception.

Contrary to the statements of many commentators,[436] choice of law should favor aggregation. If a national company defrauded each of its million customers in the amount of $100, the company would have a substantial ill-gotten gain, but the only way for the customers to get redress and deter future frauds is in a national class action. Even in one of the many states that would permit a customer to recover multiple damages and attorneys' fees,[437] the only practical course is a class action. If a single customer sues under the consumer fraud statute, the company's lawyers will mount a vigorous defense including requiring plaintiff's attorney to respond to numerous pre-trial motions—all within the bounds of ethical practice, of course.

Under the Class Action Fairness Act, will an attorney representing a national class improve the chances of certification by suing in a state like California that even in such actions presumes that the law of other states is the same as that of California unless the defendant shows

Section 1658, accordingly, specifically provides that the district court in which the § 1367 action is pending is not bound by the choice of law rules of any state. The section does not dictate any particular rule for choosing the jurisdiction or jurisdictions whose substantive law will be applied in a § 1367 action. It does, however, effectively create a presumption in favor of uniformity by requiring in subsection (b) that the responsible district court enter an order designating a single jurisdiction whose law would be applied in all § 1367 actions before the court arising from the same incident, except where federal law governed a matter or the order specifically authorized a departure from uniformity with respect to particular cases or matters. This section identifies various factors that may be relevant for such choice of law determinations but does not attempt to legislate a single governing law or methodology, preferring to leave this complex matter to judicial development. The Federal courts' discretion on this point is limited to choosing the jurisdiction whose substantive law will apply; the section does not authorize the creation of federal substantive common law for mass torts.

432. 151 Cong. Rec. S1166 (daily ed. Feb. 9, 2005).

433. 28 U.S.C. § 2361.

434. Griffin v. McCoach, 313 U.S. 498, 61 S.Ct. 1023, 85 L.Ed. 1481 (1941). See also Bank of New York v. Janowick, 470 F.3d 264, 270 n.3 (6th Cir. 2006), cert. denied, 552 U.S. 825, 128 S.Ct. 195, 169 L.Ed.2d 36 (2007) ("under the federal interpleader statute's minimal diversity requirement ... we apply the choice-of-law provisions of the forum state").

435. Phillips Petroleum Co. v. Shutts, 472 U.S. 797, 808–814, 105 S.Ct. 2965, 2972–2976, 86 L.Ed.2d 628 (1985).

436. See, e.g., Silberman, supra note 426, at 61–62.

437. See, e.g., N.J.S.A. § 56:8–19 (triple damages and reasonable attorneys' fees).

otherwise? On this issue must the judge must follow California law or is the court free to apply federal procedural law, which places on the plaintiff the burden of demonstrating that in the light of variations in state law and choice-of-law analysis, "any problems with predominance or superiority can be overcome."[438]

The answer is likely to be in favor of following the federal placement of burden on the plaintiff to explore variations in state laws. There is a somewhat analogous problem under Federal Rule of Civil Procedure 44.1, which states that when determining the law of a foreign country, the court "may consider any relevant material or source ... whether or not submitted by a party...." The Advisory Committee Notes on 44.1 state: "There is no requirement that the court give formal notice of its intention to engage in its own research on an issue of foreign law which has been raised by them, or of its intention to raise and determine independently an issue not raised by them."[439]

Moreover, under Federal Rule of Civil Procedure 23, which requires that a class action be efficient, that common questions of law or fact predominate, and that the class action will present no great difficulties of management,[440] there are, pursuant to *Byrd v. Blue Ridge Rural Electric Cooperative, Inc.,*[441] "affirmative countervailing considerations"[442] militating against the use of state presumptions. Concerns with the quality of justice administered in a federal court justify putting the burden on the plaintiff to deal with choice of law before certification. Further, under *Hanna v. Plumer,*[443] Congress in enacting FRCP 23 and federal courts in interpreting the rule have the "power to regulate matters which, though falling within the uncertain area between substance and procedure, are rationally capable of classification as either."[444]

In rebuttal it might be argued that the state-law presumption that other laws are the same as the forum's eliminates choice-of-law problems and assures that the requirements of Rule 23 are met insofar as they are affected by variations in state law. Nevertheless, a federal court might wish to preclude such problems from arising when addressed by the defendant and to accomplish this by placing the burden on the plaintiff at the outset.

---

438.   Castano v. American Tobacco Co., 84 F.3d 734, 741 (5th Cir. 1996).

439.   See also Keller, *Interpreting Foreign Law Through an Erie Lens: A Critical Look at United States v. McNab,* 40 Tex. Int'l L. J. 157, 172 (2004) ("In order to avoid the parochial view that foreign law is similar to our law ... federal courts must determine foreign law when it is feasible to do so").

440.   FRCP 23(b)(3).

441.   356 U.S. 525, 78 S.Ct. 893, 2 L.Ed.2d 953 (1958), discussed in § 10.3.

442.   Id. at 537, 78 S.Ct. at 900, 2 L.Ed.2d at 962.

443.   380 U.S. 460, 85 S.Ct. 1136, 14 L.Ed.2d 8 (1965), discussed in § 10.3.

444.   Id. at 472, 85 S.Ct. at 1144. But see Principles of the Law of Aggregate Litigation, Discussion Draft 81–86 (Amer. L. Inst. April 21, 2006) (a court should be free to ignore the choice-of-law issue until a party demonstrates the need to decide it); Woolley, *Erie and Choice of Law After the Class Action Fairness Act,* 80 Tul. L. Rev. 1723, 1724 (2006) ("the claim that Rule 23 permits federal courts to ignore state law presumptions in favor of forum law is paper-thin and may not survive review by the United States Supreme Court").

Ironically, while in the United States, because of judicial hostility, it is becoming difficult to certify a class action and almost impossible to certify a nation-wide class action, European countries are using similar devices to dispose of mass litigation.[445] Britain has permitted "group actions" since 2000.[446] The Netherlands allows court-approved settlements for classes of plaintiffs, using as a basis the award to one or two class members who have litigated their claims.[447] Germany permits court-ordered settlements based on test cases in securities actions.[448]

§ 6.34 "Conduct Regulating" Rules Versus "Loss Allocating Rules"

Babcock v. Jackson,[449] the case that sparked the revolution in choice of law, compares rules regulating conduct with rules affecting compensation for improper conduct.[450] In subsequent New York cases, this concept developed into a distinction between "conduct regulating" rules and "loss allocating" rules. If a rule is conduct regulating, the law of the place where the defendant acted is applicable. If a rule is loss allocating, choice of law follows an approach modeled on *Neumeier v. Kuehner*.[451]

A case that epitomizes this distinction is *Padula v. Lilarn Properties Corp.*[452] A worker, domiciled in New York, was injured by a fall from a scaffold at a construction site in Massachusetts. A New York corporation owned the site. The scaffold did not conform to specifications promulgated under New York law for worker safety. The New York Labor Law provided "strict and vicarious liability of the owner of the property"[453] if a worker was injured because of a non-conforming scaffold. The court affirmed a summary judgment for the property owner, holding that because the scaffold requirements were "conduct regulating" rather than "loss allocating," Massachusetts law applied.[454]

---

445. See C. Hodges, The Reform of Class and Representative Actions in European Legal Systems (2008).

446. See Lubbe v. Cape PLC, [2000] 1 W.L.R. 1545 (H.L.); R. Mulheron, The Class Action in Common Law Legal Systems: A Comparative Perspective (2004).

447. See The Economist, *Class Actions*, Bälz & Felix Blobel, Coll: *If You Can't Beat Them, Join Them*, 56–57 (Feb. 17, 2007).

448. Gesetz über Musterverfahren in kapitalmarktrechtlichen Stretgkeiten [Act on Model Proceedings in Capital Market Disputes], Aug. 16, 2005, Bundesgesetzblatt I [Federal Gazette, Part I] at 2437; Moritz Bälz & Felix Blobel, *Collective Litigation German Style*, in Conflict of Laws in a Globalized World, 126 (Eckart Gottschalk et al., eds., 2007).

449. 12 N.Y.2d 473, 240 N.Y.S.2d 743, 191 N.E.2d 279 (1963).

450. See id. at 483, 240 N.Y.S.2d at 750–51, 191 N.E.2d at 284 (stating that if the issue had "related to the manner in which the defendant had been driving his car at the time of the accident.... it is appropriate to look to the law of the place of the tort so as to give effect to that jurisdiction's interest in regulating conduct within its borders, and it would be almost unthinkable to seek the applicable rule in the law of some other place").

451. 31 N.Y.2d 121, 335 N.Y.S.2d 64, 286 N.E.2d 454 (1972), discussed in § 6.22.

452. 84 N.Y.2d 519, 620 N.Y.S.2d 310, 644 N.E.2d 1001 (1994).

453. Id. at 522, 620 N.Y.S.2d at 312, 644 N.E.2d at 1003.

454. Id. at 522–23, 620 N.Y.S.2d at 312, 644 N.E.2d at 1003. See also Collins v. Trius, Inc., 663 A.2d 570, 573 (Me. 1995) (Canadian law limiting recovery for pain and suffering

The Louisiana Conflict of Laws Code distinguishes "issues of conduct and safety"[455] from "issues of loss distribution and financial protection."[456] If conduct and injury occur in the same state, the law of that state governs issues of conduct and safety. Issues of loss distribution and financial protection are governed by the law of the domicile of the injured person and the person who caused the injury if both are domiciled in the same state or in different states that have "substantially identical" laws on the relevant issue. Whether violation of a rule of conduct constitutes negligence per se is also treated as a rule of conduct.[457]

The categories of "conduct regulating" rules under New York law and "issues of conduct and safety" under the Louisiana Code should be limited to directory rules intended to regulate conduct in the most immediate manner. Examples are speed limits and rules determining right of way.[458] Once a court finds that the defendant has violated a directory rule, the court should not necessarily determine the consequences of that violation by the law of the place of conduct and injury. A per se negligence rule is not likely to affect a motorist's conduct. If the New York caselaw and Louisiana Code provisions that require application of the law where defendant acted are not limited to directory rules, those provisions will flout the most important insight that emerges from interest analysis of thousands of torts conflicts cases. A state whose sole contact is as place of conduct and injury never has an interest in applying its law to insulate the defendant from liability, unless the defendant has acted in reliance on that law. Except for purely directory rules, a reliance argument is likely to be untenable when directed at liability for unintentional torts.

---

applies to suit between Canadian parties arising out of Maine bus accident because "[a]lthough Maine has a significant interest in regulating conduct on its highways, the rule at issue is primarily 'loss allocating' rather than 'conduct regulating' "); Allen & O'Hara, *Second Generation Law and Economics of Conflict of Laws: Baxter's Comparative Impairment and Beyond*, 51 Stanford L. Rev. 1011, 1044 (1999) ("the First Restatement could be modified to include a common domicile rule for 'loss distribution' rules while retaining a 'place of injury' rule for those laws directed toward conduct"); Borchers, *The Return of Territorialism to New York's Conflict Law: Padula v. Lilarn Properties Corp.*, 58 Albany L. Rev. 775 (1995).

455. La.Civ.C. art. 3543.

456. Id. art. 3544.

457. Id. art. 3543, Revision Comment *e*. For comments on these and other aspects of the Louisiana conflicts code, see Symeonides, *Louisiana's New Law of Choice of Law for Tort Conflicts: An Exegesis*, 66 Tul. L. Rev. 677 (1992).

458. See K.T. v. Dash, 37 A.D.3d 107, 827 N.Y.S.2d 112 (2006) (apply N.Y. law to suit by N.Y. plaintiff against N.Y. defendant to recover damages for rape in Brazil) (in situations other than rules of the road "the analysis is less one-sided, and the competing concerns of the two jurisdictions must be considered"); cf. Currie, Selected Essays on the Conflict of Laws 69 (1963) (distinguishing between a "rule of conduct" and a "rule of decision" and treating a rule of conduct as a factual datum on which the rule of decision will operate).

A regulation of the European Parliament and the Council on the Law Applicable to Non–Contractual Obligations (Rome II),[459] contains the following provision:

Article 17: Rules of Safety and Conduct

In assessing the conduct of the person claimed to be liable, account shall be taken, as a matter of fact and in so far as is appropriate, of the rules of safety and conduct which were in force at the place and time of the event giving rise to the liability.

Paragraph 34 of the recitals preceding the text of the Regulation states:

The term "rules of safety and conduct" should be interpreted as referring to all regulations having any relation to safety and conduct, including, for example, road safety rules in the case of an accident.

These provisions seem flexible enough so that only purely directory rules of the place where the defendant acts will be applied without considering the policies of other jurisdictions that have contacts with the parties and the occurrence.

§ 6.35 Workers' Compensation

A "multilateral" approach to choice of law attempts to prevent forum shopping and choose the single most appropriate law, whether that of the forum or of some foreign state. A "unilateral" approach to choice of law focuses solely on forum law and policies to determine whether the forum has sufficient contacts with the parties and the transaction so that application of forum law will advance forum policies and be fair to the parties. The approach for workers' compensation is unilateral. In dispensing compensation, every state having sufficient contact with the employer-employee relationship to make it desirable that the employee be protected under its law and reasonable to require the employer to insure in the state should feel free to provide protection under its workers' compensation law.[460] The local administrative ma-

---

459. Regulation (EC) No. 864/2007 of the European Parliament and of the Council of 11 July 2007 on the law applicable to non-contractual obligations (Rome II) art. 17, OJ 2007 L 199/46.

460. See Gustafson v. International Progress Enterprises, 832 F.2d 637 (D.C.Cir.1987) (the D.C. workers' compensation act was intended to have the widest possible application); Williams v. Johnson Custom Homes, 374 Ark. 457, 288 S.W.3d 607 (2008) (an agreement signed by employee selecting Ohio workers' compensation law as exclusive remedy is void); Harlow v. Emery Waterhouse Co., 484 A.2d 1002 (Me.1984); cf. Iowa Beef Processors, Inc. v. Miller, 312 N.W.2d 530 (Iowa 1981) (cannot recover under compensation law of domicile if no meaningful connection there with employment relationship).

Courts apply the workers' compensation law of a jurisdiction with which the employment relationship is substantially connected to preclude common law recovery under the law of another state. See Paulo v. Bepex Corp., 792 F.2d 894 (9th Cir.1986) (Ontario law applied to prevent Ontario employee from bringing product liability action against manufacturer of machine—California law); Brown v. Cities Service Oil Co., 733 F.2d 1156 (5th Cir.1984) (Texas law); Jaiguay v. Vasquez, 287 Conn. 323, 948 A.2d 955 (2008) (New York law bars wrongful death action against fellow employee and employer although death occurred in Connecticut and Connecticut law would allow action based on negligence of fellow employee); Vickrey v. Caterpillar Tractor Co., 146 Ill.App.3d 1023, 100 Ill.Dec. 636, 497 N.E.2d 814 (4th Dist.1986) (machine manufacturer cannot implead employer, applying law of Missouri where employee killed on the job, rather than Illinois law); Saharceski v. Marcure, 373 Mass. 304, 366 N.E.2d 1245 (1977) (law of place of common domicile and location of

chinery for enforcement of a state's compensation statute will usually preclude the confusion of litigating in the same proceeding claims under different laws.[461] Any subsequent award under the statute of another state will take account of the first award. The conflicts problem in the workers' compensation area is the articulating of the circumstances under which a forum does have sufficient connection with the employer-employee relationship to make it reasonable and desirable to apply its workers' compensation statute to claims arising from that relationship.[462] These factors make workers' compensation cases dangerously misleading bases upon which to build general conclusions about choice-of-law problems.[463]

---

employer applied to give fellow servant immunity from suit contrary to law of place of injury); LaBounty v. American Ins. Co., 122 N.H. 738, 451 A.2d 161 (1982); Eger v. E.I. Du Pont DeNemours Co., 110 N.J. 133, 539 A.2d 1213 (1988) (apply law of employee's place of employment to prevent suit against general contractor by employee of subcontractor); Busby v. Perini Corp., 110 R.I. 49, 290 A.2d 210 (1972) (law of plaintiff's domicile and place of incorporation of general contractor and subcontractor applied to shield general contractor from common law recovery contrary to law of place of injury); cf. American Interstate Ins. Co. v. G & H Service Center, Inc., 112 Ohio St.3d 521, 861 N.E.2d 524 (2007) (the law of the state under which compensation is granted governs subrogation claims arising from workers' compensation payments. But cf. Spearing v. National Iron Co., 770 F.2d 87 (7th Cir.1985)) (permit Ontario employee to bring tort action against United States affiliate of the company that manufactured the vehicle that caused injury—Wisconsin law); Simaitis v. Flood, 182 Conn. 24, 437 A.2d 828 (1980) (law of state of employees' domicile, where they work in the home office about half the time, applied to permit tort action between them rather than law of place where they were on field assignment when injury occurred).

For exceptions from a unilateral approach to choosing workers' compensation law see Janet's Cleaning Service v. Roynon, 311 Md. 686, 537 A.2d 256 (1988) (the Maryland act exempts employees injured in Maryland if the employer and employee reside in another state where the employment contract was entered into, if that state exempts Maryland employees under similar circumstances); Neumer v. Yellow Freight System, Inc., 220 Kan. 607, 556 P.2d 202 (1976) (employee hired over telephone not covered by forum statute because contract was "made" in state where employer spoke rather than in forum where employee spoke); cf. LaBombard v. Peck Lumber Co., 141 Vt. 619, 451 A.2d 1093 (1982) (law of state under which compensation benefits were recovered determines whether the cost of recovery by the employee against a third person is to be borne by the employee or apportioned between employee and insurer).

461. For exceptions see Crider v. Zurich Ins. Co., 380 U.S. 39, 85 S.Ct. 769, 13 L.Ed.2d 641 (1965) (an Alabama court has jurisdiction to award damages under the Georgia Workers' Compensation Act to an Alabama resident who was injured while working in Alabama for a Georgia corporation, even though the remedy provided by the Georgia act is an exclusive one that can be afforded only by the Georgia compensation board); Overstreet v. Liberty Mutual Ins. Co., 263 So.2d 528 (Miss.1972) (worker's claim under Alabama court-administered act may be heard by Mississippi court).

462. See Cleveland v. U.S. Printing Ink, Inc., 218 Conn. 181, 192, 588 A.2d 194, 200 (1991) (quoting report by National Commission on State Workmen's Compensation Laws that "in the majority of states, the local statute will be applied if the place of injury, the place of hiring, or the place of employment relation is within the state").

463. But see B. Currie, *The Verdict of Quiescent Years; Mr. Hill and the Conflict of Laws*, 29 U. Chi. L. Rev. 258, 274 (1961).

Chapter 7

CONTRACTS

§ 7.1 Introduction

It was common for American Conflicts scholars to refer to contracts as the most complex and confused area of choice-of-law problems.[1] In part, this complexity was caused, as stated by the Second Restatement of Conflict of Laws, "by the many different kinds of contracts and of issues involving contracts and by the many relationships a single contract may have to two or more states."[2] A more significant reason for the scholars' sighs of despair was the confusing diversity of choice-of-law rules applied by United States courts in resolving contracts-conflicts problems.

This chapter examines choice-of-law rules in the contracts area. Most attention will be given to the two rules that have emerged from the welter of contending rules as kings of the hill. These two rules are, first, that the parties may, in the contract, choose the governing law, and second, that in the absence of such a choice by the parties, the applicable law is that of the state that has the most significant relationship to the transaction and the parties. This scrutiny of contracts choice-of-law rules will include an inquiry into which rules are capable of responding to conflicts problems with solutions that are socially desirable and responsive to the needs of a global commercial community.

§ 7.2 The Distinctions between "Validity", "Construction", and "Interpretation"

The distinction between the validity of a contract and the construction of a contract is important for useful discussion of contracts-conflicts problems. A choice-of-law problem involving the validity of a contract arises when, under the domestic law of one state having some contact with the problem, a provision in a contract is invalid, but under the law of another contact state, the same provision is enforceable. The actual intention of the parties on the issue is known or can realistically be ascertained, but one state refuses to give effect to that intention. Whether the provision in issue is enforced or not depends upon which law is "chosen" to govern its validity.

If the choice-of-law problem concerns construction rather than validity, the difficulty arises because the intention of the parties on some

---

1. See G. Stumberg, Conflict of Laws 225 (3d ed. 1963); cf. A. Ehrenzweig, Conflict of Laws 453 (1962) ("this confusion . . . is one of language rather than substance").

2. Restatement (Second), Conflict of Laws, Ch. 8, Introductory Note (1971) [hereinafter cited as Restatement (Second)].

important aspect of their agreement is unknown and unknowable.[3] For example, after a manufacturer has agreed to sell air conditioners to a wholesaler, the manufacturer's factory burns down and the manufacturer is not able to deliver as promised. Is the manufacturer excused from performance or must it pay damages to the wholesaler because the wholesaler's expectation of profit has been disappointed by the missed shipment? The parties could have settled this issue either way in their contract. If they have not manifested their intention on this issue, the court must fill in the blank that the parties have left. If the transaction has contacts with both states X and Y, a choice-of-law problem arises if state X would excuse the manufacturer, but state Y would not. Either X or Y would give effect to the parties' intention on this issue if that intention were known, but in the absence of knowledge concerning the parties' actual intention, the two states would construe the contract differently.

As contrasted with "construction," "interpretation" is the process of finding and giving effect to the actual intention of the parties. For this reason, interpretation, as such, presents no choice-of-law problem,[4] although, of course, conflicts problems can arise concerning the admissibility of evidence bearing upon the intention of the parties and concerning other rules governing the determination of their intention. This chapter first focuses on choice of law to determine questions of contract validity and then turns to construction problems. This chapter does not give further attention to interpretation because interpretation presents no discrete "contract" conflict problem.

Choice of law is sometimes necessary to determine the appropriate remedy for breach of contract.[5] This topic is treated as part of the other topics in the chapter.

§ 7.3A The Confusing Diversity of Rules for Determining Validity

One once widely adopted rule to determine the law governing the validity of a contract is the rule pointing to the law of the place where the contract was made. The place of making is the geographical location where, according to the law of contracts, the acceptance of the offer to contract became effective, or, more accurately in this context, would be effective if the choice-of-law problem were resolved in favor of the

---

3. Id. § 204, comment *a*. Courts do not always recognize these distinctions. See, e.g., American Inst. of Marketing Systems, Inc. v. Brooks, 469 S.W.2d 932 (Mo.App.1971) (treating clause selecting law to govern construction as also covering matters of validity). It is sometimes difficult to distinguish between validity and construction. See, e.g., Duncan v. Cessna Aircraft Co., 665 S.W.2d 414 (Tex. 1984) (whether reference in release to "any other corporations or persons" included aircraft manufacturer not specifically named); McGill v. Hill, 31 Wn.App. 542, 644 P.2d 680 (1982) (whether settlement agreement pursuant to divorce includes husband's retirement benefits in the absence of specific mention of them).

4. Restatement (Second) § 204, comment *a*.

5. See Reicher v. Berkshire Life Ins. Co. of America, 360 F.3d 1 (1st Cir.2004) (applying eclectic Massachusetts "functional approach" to choice law, choose law of policy holder's residence, Maryland, rather than law of Massachusetts, where insurer headquartered, to deny recovery for unfair settlement practices).

validity of the contract. This place of contracting rule is the rule of the first Restatement of Conflict of Laws[6] and of such classic cases as *Milliken v. Pratt.*[7]

Daniel Pratt and his wife were life-long residents of Massachusetts. Daniel, who was in business in Massachusetts, applied to a Maine partnership for credit to facilitate Daniel's purchase of goods from the partnership. The partners would not grant Daniel's request until his wife guaranteed payment. Daniel procured this guarantee in writing from his wife and mailed it from Massachusetts to the partners in Maine. The partners then sold goods to Daniel, shipping them by express from Maine to Massachusetts, the buyer paying the shipping charges. Daniel failed to pay for the goods and the Maine partners brought suit in Massachusetts to enforce the wife's guaranty.

At the time of the sale, the wife did not have capacity under Massachusetts law to contract as a surety, although Maine law permitted

---

6. Restatement, Conflict of Laws § 332 (1934).

7. 125 Mass. 374 (1878). For other cases applying the place of making choice-of-law rule see, e.g., Modern Farm Serv., Inc. v. Ben Pearson, Inc., 308 F.2d 18 (5th Cir.1962) (apply law of place where title to goods passed to invalidate oral warranty); Sturiano v. Brooks, 523 So.2d 1126, 1129 (Fla. 1988) (on certified question from 11th Circuit, "limiting this answer to contracts for automobile insurance"); Goodman v. Olsen, 305 So.2d 753 (Fla. 1974), cert. denied, 423 U.S. 839, 96 S.Ct. 68, 46 L.Ed.2d 58 (1975) (apply law of New York where contract to purchase shares made to validate transaction against a charge of usury); Menendez v. Perishable Distributors, Inc., 254 Ga. 300, 329 S.E.2d 149 (1985), overruled on another issue, Posey v. Medical Center–West, Inc., 257 Ga. 55, 354 S.E.2d 417 (1987) (parol evidence rule); General Telephone Co. of the Southeast v. Trimm, 252 Ga. 95, 311 S.E.2d 460 (1984) (the law of the place of contracting applies unless it appears from the contract itself that it is to be performed elsewhere, rejecting a change from this "traditional approach" to a "center of gravity" system); Stark v. Marsh, 314 So.2d 465 (La.App.1975) (under law of Texas where agreement made, it is not effective as a novation), superseded by La Civ. Code tit. VI arts. 3537–3541 dealing with conflict of laws concerning "conventional obligations"; Bethlehem Steel Corp. v. G.C. Zarnas & Co., Inc., 304 Md. 183, 498 A.2d 605 (1985) (but refuse to apply that law because contract to indemnify the promisee against the promisee's own negligence is against Maryland public policy); Goulet v. Goulet, 105 N.H. 51, 192 A.2d 626 (1963) (apply law of place where wife signed covenant not to sue husband, which was also the marital domicile, to determine whether seal sufficient to make covenant enforceable); Suitt Constr. Co., Inc. v. Seaman's Bk. for Savings, 30 N.C.App. 155, 226 S.E.2d 408 (1976) (apply law of New York where "last act . . . essential to a meeting of the minds" occurred to validate agreement against charge it provided for a penalty); Briggs v. United Serv. Life Ins. Co., 80 S.D. 26, 117 N.W.2d 804 (1962) (law of place where insurer's main office located and where application approved applied to invalidate provision making good health in fact a condition precedent to policy's taking effect); cf. Okla.Stat. Ann. tit. 15, § 162 ("[a] contract is to be interpreted according to the law and usage of the place where it is to be performed or, if it does not indicate a place of performance, according to the law and usage of the place where it is made"); Great Amer. Ins. Co. v. Hartford Accident & Idem. Co., 519 S.W.2d 579 (Tenn.1975) (law of New York where policy issued determines whether it will be treated as affording primary coverage).

When the contract is made over the telephone, it is usually deemed "made" where the acceptor spoke. See, e.g., Neumer v. Yellow Freight System, Inc., 220 Kan. 607, 556 P.2d 202 (1976) (forum's workers' compensation statute not applicable because contract of employment not made there); Linn v. Employers Reinsurance Corp., 397 Pa. 153, 153 A.2d 483 (1959) (validate against statute of frauds defense); Tolley v. General Accident, Fire & Life Ins. Corp. Ltd., 584 S.W.2d 647 (Tenn.1979) (forum workers' compensation statute applies because contract made there); Restatement, Conflict of Laws § 326 comment c (1934); cf. Brinkibon, Ltd. v. Stahag Stahl und Stahlwarenhadels GmbH, [1982] 1 All E.R. 293, [1982] 2 W.L.R. 264 (H.L.) (a contract made by telex is made where the acceptance is

married women to so contract. Whether the plaintiffs won or lost turned on whether the court chose the Maine or the Massachusetts rule. The court applied the law of Maine because that was the place where the contract was "made"[8] and judgment was for the plaintiffs.

Why was the contract "made" in Maine? The court states that the contract "was complete when the guaranty had been received and acted on by them [plaintiffs] at Portland, and not before."[9] In traditional contract terms, the wife's guaranty was an offer for a unilateral contract, the acceptance of which would be the extension of credit to the husband by a sale of goods. Because the husband was to pay the express charges, title to the goods passed to the husband in Maine when the seller delivered them to the express carrier.

The Court rejected a proposal to adopt a choice-of-law rule selecting the law of the domicile to determine contractual capacity, remarking that:

> It is more just, as well as more convenient, to have regard to the law of the place of the contract, as a uniform rule operating on all contracts of the same kind, and which the contracting parties may be presumed to have in contemplation when making their contracts, than to require them at their peril to know the domicile of those with whom they deal, and to ascertain the law of that domicile, however remote....[10]

This justification of the place-of-making rule in terms of commercial convenience is open to question if the court in fact meant to define place of making for choice-of-law purposes in the same technical manner in which contract and sales law would determine the time of effective acceptance or passage of title. If the goods had been delivered to Daniel's store on the plaintiff's own wagon, title would have passed in Massachusetts and the contract would have been "made" there. If the wife's guaranty were not an offer for a unilateral contract, but rather her promise constituted the acceptance of the sellers' offer for a bilateral contract, the contract would have been "made" in Massachusetts. This might have occurred, for example, if the sellers had promised to sell the husband a specific amount of goods if his wife would guaranty payment. These circumstances, resulting in changing the technical place of making of the guaranty contract to Massachusetts, could have no bearing on the reasonable expectations of the parties as to the applicable law or the validity of their agreement. Yet, in the hypothetical cases just put, application of the place-of-making rule would have reversed the result reached in *Milliken v. Pratt.*

It is probably an injustice to a wise and perceptive court to suppose for a moment that the Supreme Judicial Court of Massachusetts would

---

received, for the purpose of determining whether the contract was "made within the jurisdiction" within the meaning of the English long-arm statute).

8. *Milliken*, 125 Mass. at 375.

9. Id. at 376.

10. Id. at 382.

have followed such a mechanical and simplistic path to invalidate the contract. In the first place, the court wisely left open the question of what it would do in a case that was the converse of *Pratt*. This converse case is one in which the wife's domicile grants her capacity to contract, but the law of the creditor's domicile and place of business, where the contract is "made", denies contractual capacity to wives. The court remarked that applying the incapacity rule of the creditor's domicile would be carrying the place of making rule "far,"[11] thus revealing half-articulated insights into the choice-of-law process that are the corner-stone of modern "state-interest" or "consequences-based" analysis. This converse of *Pratt* would be, in current parlance, a "false" conflict, because the state of the creditor's domicile and place of business would have no "interest" in applying its incapacity rule. The contract, there-fore, in the absence of any applicable invalidating rule, should be enforced.

It seems odd to speak of a state's "interest" when referring to private law rules such as those involved in contract cases.[12] "Interest" in this context is a term of art intended to encapsulate a method of choice-of-law analysis that has won wide acceptance by American scholars and courts and has influenced developments abroad. If the domestic laws of two states having contacts with the parties or the transaction differ on an issue affecting the validity of the contract, resolving the conflict begins with determining the purposes or policies underlying those do-mestic laws. Then, the next step in analysis is to determine whether these domestic policies would be meaningfully advanced by application to the conflicts case in issue. For example, the converse of *Pratt* (wife's domicile granting capacity, creditor's state denying capacity) is labeled as a "false"[13] conflict on the assumption that the purpose of the rule depriving wives of contractual capacity is to protect wives against their own inexperience and, in the guaranty case, their husbands' importuni-ties. If so, the argument goes, this policy of protection is inapplicable, or at best, officiously and offensively applicable, to wives whose home states do not think such protection necessary. Moreover, the creditor's state, having no interest in protecting the nonresident wife, has a residuary interest in enforcing a commercial transaction deliberately entered into and in protecting the expectations of its creditor.

This analysis is open to debate. It may be that there are policies underlying a state's incapacity rule other than the protection of its own wives.[14] The state may wish to deter creditors from conduct that it

---

11. Id. at 381.

12. See A. Ehrenzweig, Conflict of Laws 350 (1962); cf. D. Cavers, The Choice-of-Law Process 99–102 (1965).

13. See Currie, *Notes on Methods and Objectives in the Conflict of Laws*, 1959 Duke L. J. 171, 174; Traynor, *Is This Conflict Really Necessary?*, 37 Texas L. Rev. 657, 667–74 (1959).

14. See Kramer, *Interests and Policy Clashes in Conflict of Laws*, 13 Rutgers L. Rev. 523, 540–41 (1959). For discussions of the problems of choosing law to determine contrac-tual capacity of married women, see Currie, *Married Women's Contracts: A Study in*

considers unconscionable.[15] If so, this deterrence policy would be fully applicable to the converse of *Pratt*. Perhaps a policy of controlling creditors might underlie a rule incapacitating idiots or infants, but seems farfetched when applied to married women, even in 1878.

Debatable or not, the above analysis of the wife's guaranty contract illustrates three premises that form the basis for "state interest" or "consequences-based" choice-of-law analysis. First, we can usually determine, realistically and sensibly, the policies that underlie domestic rules including, in the context of this chapter, rules validating or invalidating contracts. Second, we will be able to appraise the relevance of these policies to specific physical contacts that the parties or the transaction have with the state whose policies are in issue. Third, frequently this analysis will provide a simple and direct answer to the choice-of-law problem, because the putative conflict between domestic laws will be exposed as a "false" one. The policies underlying the domestic laws of all but one state will be irrelevant. A court should apply the relevant law, whether it validates or invalidates, and should reject the irrelevant law.[16]

This kind of analysis, even assuming only a wife-protecting policy underlying the Massachusetts incapacity rule, would not provide an answer to *Milliken v. Pratt* itself. In *Pratt* the wife's domicile denied her capacity; the creditor's state granted capacity. This was, then, a "true" conflict. One of the difficult problems facing proponents of interest analysis property is whether such "true" conflicts, when one contact state would significantly advance its invalidating policies and another would significantly advance its validating policies, are susceptible to rational and practical solution and, if so, how.

In deciding that applying the Maine validating rule did not violate Massachusetts public policy the *Pratt* opinion stated:

> But it is not true at the present day that all civilized states recognize the absolute incapacity of married women to make contracts. The tendency of modern legislation is to enlarge their capacity in this respect, and in many states they have nearly or quite the same powers as if unmarried. In Massachusetts, even at the time of the making of the contract in question, a married woman was vested by statute with a very extensive power to carry on business by herself, and to bind herself by contracts with regard to her own, business and earnings; and, before the bringing of the present action, the power had been extended so as to include the making of

---

Conflict-of-Laws Method, 25 U. Chi. L. Rev. 227 (1958); Ehrenzweig, *Contractual Capacity of Married Women and Infants in the Conflict of Laws*, 43 Minn. L. Rev. 899 (1959).

15. See A. Jaffey, *Essential Validity of Contracts in the English Conflict of Laws*, 23 Int'l & Comp.L.Q. 1, 10 (1974) (distinguishing between invalidating rules aimed at "preventing some act or activity" and those intended "to protect the interests of a party"); cf. Reding v. Texaco, Inc., 598 F.2d 513 (9th Cir.1979) (state where drilling occurred has an interest in invalidating an indemnity agreement for the purpose of deterring negligence).

16. See Cirelli v. Ohio Cas. Ins. Co., 72 N.J. 380, 371 A.2d 17 (1977) (New Jersey statute invalidating subrogation clause in insurance policy does not apply when a New Jersey insurer seeks subrogation against a nonresident tortfeasor because the purpose of the statute is no longer served).

all kinds of contracts, with any person but her husband, as if she were unmarried. There is therefore no reason of public policy which should prevent the maintenance of this action.[17]

It would be well to keep these words in mind. We shall return to them after reviewing and evaluating rules that have been suggested from time to time for resolving choice-of-law problems affecting the validity of contracts.[18] It will then be time to articulate several factors that are useful in the rational resolution of true conflicts.

§ 7.3B The Law Intended by the Parties

Pritchard v. Norton[19] is another classic case. It appears to stand for the rule that if two states having contacts with the parties or the contract differ on the enforceability of the contract, a court should apply the law that the parties intended. The case involved a promise by a New York resident to indemnify a Louisiana resident from loss on an appeal bond that the Louisiana resident had executed in connection with litigation in a Louisiana court. The indemnity contract was executed and delivered in New York. The New York resident received no consideration for his promise, the appeal bond having been executed before the promise of indemnity. Under New York common law the indemnity promise was unenforceable, but under Louisiana civil law it was valid. The Supreme Court held that Louisiana law applied. The Court cited "[t]he principle that in every forum a contract is governed by the law with a view to which it was made,"[20] and then quoted the common-sense observation that "[t]he parties cannot be presumed to have contemplated a law which would defeat their engagements."[21] Therefore the Court presumed that the parties must have intended the validating Louisiana law to apply, a presumption reinforced by the circumstance that the indemnity contract was to be performed in Louisiana.[22]

----

17. *Milliken*, 125 Mass. at 383.

18. See § 7.4B.

19. 106 U.S. 124, 1 S.Ct. 102, 27 L.Ed. 104 (1882).

20. Id. at 136, 1 S.Ct. at 112, 27 L.Ed. at 108. See also Ark–La–Tex Timber Co. v. Georgia Gas. & Sur. Co., 516 So.2d 1217 (La.App. 2d Cir. 1987) (insurance policy to be interpreted by the law intended by the parties and this is an issue of fact); Austin Building Co. v. National Union Fire Ins. Co., 432 S.W.2d 697 (Tex.1968) (effect of contract determined by law intended by the parties and presumption is that they contracted with regard to the law of the place where the contract was made), superseded by Duncan v. Cessna Aircraft Co., 665 S.W.2d 414 (Tex. 1984) (apply law of state with most significant relationship to the particular substantive issue unless a valid choice-of-law clause selects the law of another state); cf. Hill, *The Judicial Function in Choice of Law*, 85 Colum. L. Rev. 1585, 1635 (1985) ("it may sometimes be fairly inferable that the parties did in fact have an actual intent [with regard to the applicable law]").

21. *Pritchard*, 106 U.S. at 137, 1 S.Ct. at 112, 27 L.Ed. at 108.

22. **The law of the place of performance has sometimes emerged as a distinct choice-of-law rule.** See Dr. Franklin Perkins School v. Freeman, 741 F.2d 1503 (7th Cir.1984) (if performance is in one state and place of making in another, apply the law of place of performance, but if performance is in more than one state, apply the law of the state with the most significant relationship—Illinois conflicts rule); General Telephone Co. of Southeast v. Trimm, 252 Ga. 95, 311 S.E.2d 460 (1984) (if performance is not where contract made, apply law of place of performance); First Nat'l Bk. v. Dreher, 202 N.W.2d

The Court's combination of the statements that "a contract is governed by the law with a view to which it was made" and "the parties cannot be presumed to have contemplated a law which would defeat their engagements" is simply a circumlocution for "apply the law that will validate the contract." At least in the absence of a choice-of-law clause in the contract, a problem we will turn to next, the parties' primary intention is not in terms of choice of law. Unless they are engaged in some ridiculous charade, their intention is the enforcement of every promise they have made in the contract. The choice-of-law "presumption" that would best accord with reality is a rebuttable presumption in favor of the law that will validate the contract. In interest terms, this presumption is most clearly rebutted when there is a "false" conflict and the only state whose contacts with the parties or with the transaction make the policies underlying its domestic law relevant is the state with the invalidating rule. In true conflict cases, when one state would significantly advance its invalidating policies and the other its validating policies, the question is exactly what factors should strengthen or rebut this presumption in favor of validation.

§ 7.3C The Law Chosen by the Parties

Of the many choice-of-law rules for determining contract validity that have vied for favor in conflicts jurisprudence, one has sprinted ahead of the field both in the United States and abroad. This is the rule giving the parties to the contract the power, either by a choice-of-law clause in the contract or by some other clear manifestation of their intention,[23] to choose the law to govern the validity of the contract.

---

670 (N.D.1972) (validate against claim of usury, purporting to apply statute, since repealed, that chose law for interpretation); Matarese v. Calise, 111 R.I. 551, 305 A.2d 112 (1973); Jones v. Tri–County Growers, Inc., 179 W.Va. 218, 366 S.E.2d 726 (1988) (validity of provision relating to performance is determined by law of place of performance); cf. Okla.Stat.Ann. tit. 15, § 162 (1971), supra note 7; Cf. Mont. Code Ann. § 28–3–102, which is same as Okla. Stat. Ann. Tit. 15, § 162, supra note 7. Mitchell v. State Farm Ins. Co., 315 Mont. 281, 68 P.3d 703 (2003), applied the statute to determine that Montana law governed a Montana resident's rights under uninsured motorist coverage for injuries suffered in Montana, although the policy covered cars garaged in California and was issued to the plaintiff's parents, who are California residents. The court concluded that "Montana is the place of performance." Id. at 289, 68 P.3d at 709. Peru Civil Code of 1984 Book X Art. 2095 (contracts are governed by the law expressly chosen by the parties, and, if no express choice, by law of the place of performance, or, if the place of performance is not clear from the nature of the obligation, by the law of the place of execution).

The original Conflicts Restatement referred to the law of the place of performance to determine the manner and methods of performance and excuse for nonperformance. Restatement, Conflict of Laws § 358 (1934). The Restatement noted that "the point at which initiation ceases and performance begins is not a point which can be fixed by any rule of law of universal application to all cases." Id. at § 332 Comment c. For criticism of the place of performance rule, see Morris, *The Eclipse of the Lex Loci Solutionis—A Fallacy Exploded*, 6 Vand. L. Rev. 505 (1953); Nussbaum, *Conflict Theories of Contracts: Cases Versus Restatement*, 51 Yale L. J. 893, 916 (1942).

23. A court has sometimes interpreted a **clause submitting to jurisdiction** as indicating an intention that the law of that place should apply. See Scherk v. Alberto–Culver Co., 417 U.S. 506, 519 n.13, 94 S.Ct. 2449, 2457 n.13, 41 L.Ed.2d 270, 280 n.13 (1974) ("under some circumstances, the designation of arbitration in a certain place might also be viewed as implicitly selecting the law of that place to apply to that transaction", but here a choice-of-law clause selected a different law); Lummus Co. v. Commonwealth Oil

In formulating rules governing the ability of the parties to choose law for validity, three issues emerge. First, are the parties limited to choosing the law of a jurisdiction that has some significant relationship to the parties or the transaction, or may they shop the world for applicable law? Second, when should a court refuse to apply the law that the parties have chosen because the rule of validity involved is too important to be pushed aside by the parties? Third, should parties in an inferior bargaining position, such as consumers, be protected from a choice that would deprive them of the protective laws of their home state or country?

Refining Co., 280 F.2d 915 (1st Cir.1960), cert. denied, 364 U.S. 911, 81 S.Ct. 274, 5 L.Ed.2d 225 (1960) (provision for arbitration in New York "indicates a choice of law"); Compagnie Tunisienne de Navigation SA v. Compagnie d'Armement Maritime SA, [1970] 3 All E.R. 71, [1970] 3 W.L.R. 389 (House of Lords) (rebuttable presumption that forum-choosing clause is intended also to choose forum law).

For discussion of the converse question of whether a choice-of-law clause should be considered a consent to the jurisdiction of that legal system, see Pryles, *Comparative Aspects of Prorogation and Arbitration Agreements*, 25 Int'l & Comp.L.Q. 543, 550–51 (1976).

For cases dealing with other clauses that are claimed to be choice-of-law provisions see Burchett v. MasTec North America, Inc., 322 Mont. 93, 98, 93 P.3d 1247, 1250 (2004) (employer by agreeing to pay income taxes, unemployment insurance premiums, and wages to Montana "manifested its intent to be governed by Montana law"); DeCesare v. Lincoln Benefit Life Co., 852 A.2d 474 (R.I. 2004) (provision in annuity contract that it was subject to the laws of the state in which the application was signed and would be treated as complying with the laws of that state was not a choice-of-law clause; therefore a national class action could be certified applying on behalf of all class members the law of the state where the annuity company accepted the applications); cf. Shamil Bank of Bahrain EC v. Beximco Pharmaceuticals Ltd., [2004] 4 All E.R. 1073 (Ct. App. 2004) (choice-of-law clause stating that "subject to the principles of" Islamic law the financing agreement was governed by English law chose English law and not Islamic law, which would invalidate a promise to pay interest).

For other issues concerning construction of choice-of-law clauses see Peugeot Motors of America, Inc. v. Eastern Auto Distributors, Inc., 892 F.2d 355 (4th Cir.1989), cert. denied, 497 U.S. 1005, 110 S.Ct. 3242, 111 L.Ed.2d 752 (1990) (clause choosing New York law to govern validity of dealership agreement does not include New York Dealer Act, which would invalidate provision giving franchisor right to terminate, because the Act limits its territorial effect to dealers doing business in New York); Scientific Holding Co., Ltd. v. Plessey Inc., 510 F.2d 15 (2d Cir.1974) (choice-of-law clause applied to an amendment of the contract); McCabe v. Great Pacific Century Corp., 222 N.J.Super. 397, 537 A.2d 303 (App.Div. 1988) ("made under Indiana law" is not a choice-of-law clause); cf. Whitworth Street Estates v. James Miller & Partners Ltd. (Manchester) Ltd., [1970] 1 All E.R. 796 [1970] 2 W.L.R. 728 (House of Lords) (use of English rather than Scottish contract form indicated parties intended English law to apply); Twohy v. First National Bank Of Chicago, 758 F.2d 1185 (7th Cir.1985) (at trial, the parties are free to stipulate the applicable law—Illinois).

For an alternative designation of law, see Musgrave v. HCA Mideast, Ltd., 856 F.2d 690 (4th Cir.1988) (employee may recover under the law of either Saudi Arabia or of the country of which he is a citizen, but if suit is brought under one law, the other is waived).

When the choice-of-law clause is in an order or acceptance form, whether the clause becomes part of an agreement for the sale of goods may depend on **Uniform Commercial Code § 2–207**. See Coastal Ind. v. Automatic Steam Prod. Corp., 654 F.2d 375 (5th Cir.1981) (holding that a choice-of-law clause is not a "material" alteration within the meaning of § 2–207(2)(b), but the clause produced consequences adverse to the party that inserted it); Glyptal Inc. v. Engelhard Corp., 801 F.Supp. 887 (D. Mass. 1992) (refuse to apply choice-of-law clause in seller's acknowledgement form to determine whether other terms in the forum are part of the contract); cf. Avedon Eng'g, Inc. v. Seatex, 126 F.3d 1279 (10th Cir. 1997) (choice-of-law analysis necessary because relevant states differ on whether an arbitration term is "material" under 2–207).

Can the Parties Choose the Law of an Unconnected Jurisdiction?

For the first issue, whether the parties must choose the validating law from a jurisdiction connected to them or the transaction, the emerging answer is "no". An example is the general choice-of-law section for the Uniform Commercial Code formerly promulgated by the American Law Institute and the National Council of Commissioners on Uniform State Laws to replace section 1–105:

SECTION 1–301. TERRITORIAL APPLICABILITY; PARTIES' POWER TO CHOOSE APPLICABLE LAW

(a) In this section:

(1) "Domestic transaction" means a transaction other than an international transaction; and

(2) "International transaction" means a transaction that bears a reasonable relation to a country other than the United States.

(b) This section applies to a transaction to the extent that it is governed by another article of the [Uniform Commercial Code]. Except as otherwise provided in this section:

(1) an agreement by parties to a domestic transaction that any or all of their rights and obligations are to be determined by the law of this State or of another State is effective, whether or not the transaction bears a relation to the State designated; and

(2) an agreement by parties to an international transaction that any or all of their rights and obligations are to be determined by the law of this State or of another State or country is effective, whether or not the transaction bears a relation to the State or country designated.

The section exhibits a degree of chauvinism in limiting parties to a U.S. transaction to choice of U.S. law. This limitation is inappropriate at least with regard to choice of law for construction. Section 1–301, however, does not distinguish between validity and construction. A New York seller and a Massachusetts buyer should be able to choose English law to construe a contract for the sale of goods. English law is likely to give clearer answers to issues such as excuse for impossibility or frustration of purpose.

The freedom given by the section to choose any U.S. law for validity is too broad in one respect. Parties to a purely local transaction can bargain out of the validity rules of their home state.

Perhaps these problems and others are why in 2007 the National Conference of Commissioners on Uniform State Laws approved of withdrawing the text of § 1–301 and reverting to the wording of former section 1–105. At its annual meeting in May 2008, the American Law Institute (ALI) concurred in the amendment of the wording completing the formal reversion to the wording of section 1–105. At the time of the ALI action, 29 states and the Virgin Islands had adopted the revised article I of the Uniform Commercial Code. Only the Virgin Islands adopted the wording of 1–103. The 29 states retained the wording of 1–105.

It was unwise to revert to the wording of 1–105, which was drafted in the 1950s. Sections 187 and 188 of the Restatement and the European Union Regulation on the Law Applicable to Contractual Obligations afford models that could have been used to improve the terms of 1–105.

Because the language of former 1–105 has been retained by states otherwise enacting a revised article 1, and 1–301 has been withdrawn, it is desirable to analyze 1–105:

Territorial Application of the Act Parties'
Power to Choose Applicable Law

(1) Except as provided hereafter in this section, when a transaction bears a reasonable relation to this state and also to another state or nation the parties may agree that the law either of this state or of such other state or nation shall govern their rights and duties.[24]

Although 1–105 does not clearly refer to matters of validity, as distinguished from construction, it is reasonably certain that the party autonomy provided by the Code is intended to embrace issues ordinarily beyond the contractual capacity of the parties. The title to section 1–105 refers to the "Territorial Application of the Act,"[25] which would include Code provisions that the parties are not free to change by a contrary manifestation of intention. Moreover, Comment 1 in the official text states that the "reasonable relation" limitation on choice of law is not applicable to matters that the parties can control by a manifestation of intention. This comment would be meaningless unless the first sentence of section 1–105 is intended to include issues of validity. The answer to the question of whether 1–105 permits the parties to choose a law not connected to them or the transaction is that it does not.

The Second Restatement of Conflict of Laws deals with party autonomy in section 187:

Law of the State Chosen by the Parties.

---

24. Uniform Commercial Code § 1–105(1). See Calloway v. Manion, 572 F.2d 1033 (5th Cir.1978) ("agree" in 1–105(1) includes trial stipulation that forum law applies); County Asphalt, Inc. v. Lewis Welding & Engineering Corp., 323 F.Supp. 1300 (S.D.N.Y.1970), aff'd, 444 F.2d 372 (2d Cir.), cert. denied, 404 U.S. 939, 92 S.Ct. 272, 30 L.Ed.2d 252 (1971) (although construction was to take place in New York, contract has "reasonable relation" with Ohio where builder had its headquarters and choice of Ohio law governs right to prejudgment interest).

Note that literally under 1–105(1) the parties may agree on the application of non-forum law only if the transaction also bears a reasonable relation to the forum. This makes no sense. See Prebble, *Choice of Law to Determine the Validity and Effect of Contracts: A Comparison of English and American Approaches to the Conflict of Laws*, 58 Cornell L. Rev. 433, 533 (1973).

25. See Uniform Commercial Code § 1–109: "Section captions are parts of this Act" (omitted from revised article 1).

(1) The law of the state chosen by the parties to govern their contractual rights and duties will be applied if the particular issue is one which the parties could have resolved by an explicit provision in their agreement directed to that issue.

(2) The law of the state chosen by the parties to govern their contractual rights and duties will be applied, even if the particular issue is one which the parties could not have resolved by an explicit provision in their agreement directed to that issue, unless ...

> (a) the chosen state has no substantial relationship to the parties or the transaction and there is no other reasonable basis for the parties' choice.

Section 187 wisely distinguishes between validity and construction and allows the parties to choose any law for construction. For validity, however, the chosen law must have a "substantial relation to the parties or the transaction" unless there is another "reasonable basis for the parties' choice." The example that is provided for an exception to the "substantial relationship" requirement is that "when contracting in countries whose legal systems are strange to them as well as relatively immature, the parties should be able to choose a law on the ground that they know it well and that it is sufficiently developed."[26] The implication is that for validity, with rare exceptions, the parties are limited in the law that they can choose.

The Regulation on the Law Applicable to Contractual Obligations (Rome I), in force between members of the European Union,[27] allows the parties to shop the world for law to govern validity. Unlike withdrawn UCC 1–301, however, the Regulation does not accord this freedom to parties to a purely domestic transaction:

Article 3

Freedom of choice

1. A contract shall be governed by the law chosen by the parties. The choice shall be made expressly or clearly demonstrated by the terms of the contract or the circumstances of the case. By their choice the parties can select the law applicable to the whole or to part only of the contract.

* * *

3. Where all other elements relevant to the situation at the time of the choice are located in a country other than the country whose law has been chosen, the choice of the parties shall not prejudice the

---

26. Restatement (Second) § 187(2)(a) cmt. *f.* This comment finds support in a dictum in Vita Food Prods., Inc. v. Unus Shipping Co., [1939] A.C. 277, 291 (P.C.).

27. Regulation (EC) No. 593/2008 Of the European Parliament and of the Council of 17 June 2008 on The Law Applicable To Contractual Obligations (Rome I) [hereinafter cited as Rome I].

application of provisions of the law of that other country which cannot be derogated from by agreement.

The Inter–American Convention on the Law Applicable to International Contracts,[28] six UCC choice-of-law provisions,[29] the Uniform Computer Information and Transactions Act,[30] and the Louisiana Conflict of Laws Code[31] also permit the parties to choose any law to govern validity. The New York General Obligations Law,[32] permits the parties to choose New York law although that state has no contacts with the parties or the transaction.

The Contract Law of the People's Republic of China provides similar freedom for choice of law, with stated exceptions:

> The parties to a contract involving foreign interests may choose the law applicable to the settlement of their contract disputes, except as otherwise stipulated by law. If the parties to a contract involving foreign interests have not made a choice, the law of the country to which the contract is most closely connected shall be applied.

> The contracts for Chinese-foreign equity joint ventures, for Chinese-foreign contractual joint ventures and for Chinese-foreign cooperative exploration and development of natural resources to be performed within the territory of the People's Republic of China shall apply the laws of the People's Republic of China.[33]

Section 81.120 of Oregon's Code for Choice of Laws for Contracts also gives the parties freedom to choose any law.

---

28.   OEA/Ser. K/XXI.5, CIDIP–V/doc.34/94 rev. 3 corr.2, 17 March 1994, reprinted in 33 I.L.M. 732, 734, art. 7: "The contract shall be governed by the law chosen by the parties" [hereinafter cited as Inter–American Convention].

29.   See §§ 4A–507(b) (rights and obligations of parties to funds transfers), 5–116(a) (liability under letter of credit), 8–110(d) (rights and duties of issuer of investment security), 8–110(e)(1), (2) (rights and duties of securities intermediary), 9–304(b)(1) (perfection of security interest in a deposit account), 9–305(b)(1), (2), (perfection of security interest in investment property).

30.   UCITA, 7 U.L.A. Pt. II, pocket part, § 109(a) (with exception for consumer contract).

31.   La. Civ. C. ch. 3, Book IV art. 3540: "All other issues of conventional obligations [other than form and capacity] are governed by the law expressly chosen or clearly relied upon by the parties, except to the extent that law contravenes the public policy of the state whose law would otherwise be applicable under Article 3537 ['the state whose policies would be most seriously impaired if its law were not applied']."

32.   N.Y. Gen. Oblig. Law § 5–1401 (permitting choice of New York law for transactions of $250,000 or more with exceptions for agreements concerning labor or personal services, consumer transactions, and to the extent that UCC 1–105(2) limits party autonomy in choice of law). But see Lehman Brothers Commercial Corp. v. Minmetals Int'l Non–Ferrous Metals Trading Co., 179 F.Supp.2d 118, 134 (S.D.N.Y. 2000) (applying 5–1401 but noting that "[t]he power of courts to enforce that choice ... remains restricted within constitutional bounds").

33.   Contract Law art. 126 (adopted at the Second Session of the Ninth People's Congress on March 15, 1999). See also Trans–Tec Asia v. M/V Harmony Container, 518 F.3d 1120 (9th Cir. 2008), cert. denied, 129 S.Ct. 628, 172 L.Ed.2d 639 (2008) (an agreement choosing U.S. law enables a foreign supplier who supplied fuel to a foreign-flagged ship in a foreign port to obtain a maritime lien under the U.S. Federal Maritime Lien Act on the vessel docked in a U.S. port).

When Should A Court Refuse To Apply The Law That The Parties Have Chosen?

UCC section 1–105(2) subordinates the parties' power to choose law to the choice-of-law rules in other sections of the Code:

> Where one of the following provisions of this Act specifies the applicable law, that provision governs and a contrary agreement is effective only to the extent permitted by the law (including the conflict of laws rules) so specified: [sections 2–402, 2A–105, 2A–106, 4–102, 4A–507, 5–116, 6–103, 8–110, 9–103, and 9–301 through 9–307].

Otherwise 1–105 places no limits on the applicability of the law chosen by the parties other than the "reasonable relation" requirement of 1–105(1).

Second Restatement section 187(2)(b) provides that a court should override the parties' choice of law when:

> application of the law of the chosen state would be contrary to a fundamental policy of a state which has a materially greater interest than the chosen state in the determination of the particular issue and which, under the rule of § 188 [the state that "has the most significant relationship to the transaction and the parties"], would be the state of the applicable law in the absence of an effective choice of law by the parties.

Comment *g* provides the following guidance in determining when a policy is sufficiently strongly held to override the parties' choice:

> To be "fundamental," a policy must in any event be a substantial one. Except perhaps in the case of contracts relating to wills, a policy of this sort will rarely be found in a requirement, such as the statute of frauds, that relates to formalities. Nor is such policy likely to be represented by a rule tending to become obsolete, such as a rule concerned with the capacity of married women, or by general rules of contract law, such as those concerned with the need for consideration. On the other hand, a fundamental policy may be embodied in a statute which makes one or more kinds of contracts illegal or which is designed to protect a person against the oppressive use of superior bargaining power. Statutes involving the rights of an individual insured as against an insurance company are an example of this sort. To be "fundamental" within the meaning of the present rule, a policy need not be as strong as would be required to justify the forum in refusing to entertain suit upon a foreign cause of action under the rule of § 90 [public policy].

Under this and similar concepts courts have refused to apply the law chosen by the parties in wide variety of circumstances.[34]

---

34. Haisten v. Grass Valley Medical Reimbursement Fund, Ltd., 784 F.2d 1392 (9th Cir.1986) (contract chose Cayman Island law, which would excuse insurer of California doctors if doctor's malpractice liability is discharged in bankruptcy—California law); Matte v. Zapata Offshore Co., 784 F.2d 628 (5th Cir.), cert. denied, 479 U.S. 872, 107 S.Ct. 247, 93

L.Ed.2d 171 (1986) (choice of general maritime law contrary to Louisiana and federal statutes seeking to protect oilfield safety); Industrial Indem. Ins. Co. v. United States, 757 F.2d 982 (9th Cir.1985) (chose law under which a clause reducing the period of limitations would be valid, contrary to forum law—Idaho law); Barnes Group, Inc. v. C & C Prod., Inc., 716 F.2d 1023 (4th Cir.1983) (refuse to apply chosen law to validate covenant not to compete); Federal Deposit Ins. Corp. v. Bank of America Nat'l Trust & Savings Ass'n, 701 F.2d 831 (9th Cir.1983), cert. denied, 464 U.S. 935, 104 S.Ct. 343, 78 L.Ed.2d 310 (1983) (clause subordinating bank capital notes to claims of bank's creditors); Dothan Aviation Corp. v. Miller, 620 F.2d 504 (5th Cir.1980) (covenant not to compete); Oceanic Steam Nav. Co. v. Corcoran, 9 F.2d 724 (2d Cir.1925) (violation of forum's public policy); Ex parte Alabama Oxygen Co., Inc., 433 So.2d 1158 (Ala.1983), vac'd and remanded on another point, 465 U.S. 1016, 104 S.Ct. 1260, 79 L.Ed.2d 668 (1984) (arbitration clause); Long v. Holland America Line Westours, Inc., 26 P.3d 430 (Alaska 2001) (refuse to enforce choice in tour contract); Hall v. Superior Ct., 150 Cal.App.3d 411, 197 Cal.Rptr. 757 (4th Dist.1983) (cannot avoid forum's Securities Law); Ashland Chem. Co. v. Provence, 129 Cal.App.3d 790, 181 Cal.Rptr. 340 (4th Dist.1982) (chosen law of Kentucky does not apply to statute of limitations when Kentucky has no interest in that issue); Frame v. Merrill Lynch, Pierce, Fenner & Smith, Inc., 20 Cal.App.3d 668, 97 Cal.Rptr. 811 (1971) (refuse to apply chosen law to validate covenant not to compete); J.S. Alberici Constr. Co. v. Mid-West Conveyor Co., 750 A.2d 518 (Del. 2000) (refuse to enforce clause choosing law that would permit indemnity for own negligence); Convergys Corp. v. Keener, 276 Ga. 808, 582 S.E.2d 84 (2003) (refusing to enforce clause choosing law of place of employment to govern non-competition clause and invalidating clause under Georgia law even though employee moved to Georgia after employment terminated); Nasco, Inc. v. Gimbert, 239 Ga. 675, 238 S.E.2d 368 (1977) (law that would validate covenant not to compete); Donaldson v. Fluor Eng'rs, Inc., 169 Ill.App.3d 759, 120 Ill.Dec. 202, 523 N.E.2d 1113 (1st Dist.1988) (indemnity against own negligence); Robinson v. Robinson, 778 So.2d 1105 (La. 2001) (refuse to apply chosen law affecting spouse's pension benefits); Turner v. Aldens, Inc., 179 N.J.Super. 596, 433 A.2d 439 (App.Div.1981) (time-price differential ceiling of forum's Retail Installment Sales Act cannot be avoided by choice-of-law clause); Fiser v. Dell Computer Corp., 144 N.M. 464, 188 P.3d 1215 (2008) (refusing to apply Texas law, which would validate the agreement of consumer buyer not to bring any claim against the phone company as a class action); Giltner v. Commodore Contract Carriers, 14 Or.App. 340, 513 P.2d 541 (1973) (choice-of-law clause cannot remove applicability of forum's workers' compensation act); Johnston v. Commercial Travelers Mut. Acc. Ass'n, 242 S.C. 387, 131 S.E.2d 91 (1963) (stipulation contra forum's insurance statute); Schick v. Rodenburg, 397 N.W.2d 464 (S.D.1986) (release agreement that settling defendant will loan plaintiff money to be repaid out of recovery from other party); McKee v. AT & T Corp., 164 Wash.2d 372, 191 P.3d 845 (2008) (refusing to apply New York law, which would validate the agreement of telephone customers not to bring any claims against the phone company as a class action).

DeSantis v. Wackenhut Corp., 793 S.W.2d 670 (Tex.1990), cert. denied, 498 U.S. 1048, 111 S.Ct. 755, 112 L.Ed.2d 775 (1991) refused to apply Florida law to validate a Texas employee's covenant not to compete. For an example of drafting the employment contract to avoid the result in *DeSantis*, see In re AutoNation, Inc., 228 S.W.3d 663 (Tex. 2007). The Supreme Court of Texas enforced a clause choosing Florida as the exclusive forum and issued a writ of mandamus directing "the trial court to dismiss this suit in favor of the first-filed Florida action in the parties' contracted-for forum" (Id. at 667). The court stated: "Even if *DeSantis* requires Texas courts to apply Texas law to certain employment disputes, it does not require suit to be brought in Texas when a forum-selection clause mandates venue elsewhere. No Texas precedent compels us to enjoin a party from asking a Florida court to honor the parties' express agreement to litigate a non-compete agreement in Florida, the employer's headquarters and principal place of business." (Id. at 669).

Opposed to *AutoNation* is Beilfuss v. Huffy Corp., 274 Wis.2d 500, 685 N.W.2d 373 (App. 2004). A former employee, residing in Wisconsin, sued his former employer, an Ohio corporation, in a Wisconsin state court seeking a declaration that provisions in the employment contract were unenforceable. The provisions limited the employee's ability to work for a competitor of the employer. The employer moved to dismiss based on provisions in the contract limiting litigation of disputes concerning the employment contract to Ohio courts and selecting Ohio law as governing the contract. The trial judge granted the motion to dismiss. Held: reversed. "[T]he choice of law provision is unenforceable because it violates Wisconsin's long-standing public policy controlling covenants not to compete, in that [the noncompetition agreements are invalid under Wisconsin and valid under Ohio law]. Moreover, we hold that because important public policy considerations are involved, it is unreasonable to enforce the forum selection provision." Id. at 379.

Article 9 of the Rome Regulation provides for overriding the parties' choice:

Article 9 Overriding mandatory provisions

1. Overriding mandatory provisions are provisions the respect for which is regarded as crucial by a country for safeguarding its public interests, such as its political, social or economic organisation, to such an extent that they are applicable to any situation falling within their scope, irrespective of the law otherwise applicable to the contract under this Regulation.

2. Nothing in this Regulation shall restrict the application of the overriding mandatory provisions of the law of the forum.

3. Effect may be given to the overriding mandatory provisions of the law of the country where the obligations arising out of the contract have to be or have been performed, in so far as those overriding mandatory provisions render the performance of the contract unlawful. In considering whether to give effect to those provisions, regard shall be had to their nature and purpose and to the consequences of their application or non-application.

Article 9 covers rules that are internationally mandatory—rules of validity that a member state would insist on applying to an international transaction although the parties had chosen the law of another country that would validate the agreement. Some rules of validity a forum might not insist on applying internationally. For example, suppose that a forum business borrows funds from a lender in another country. The interest is usurious under forum law, which would prevent the lender from recovering principal or interest. The interest is legal under the law of the lender's home country. A forum court is unlikely to insist on applying its own law because this would deprive local businesses of the ability to borrow funds abroad that they could not borrow at home.[35] On the other hand, the forum is likely to insist on protecting a local franchisee under domestic law even though the franchisee has signed a

---

Most courts have refused to enforce choice-of-law clauses in franchise or dealership agreements that deprive the franchisee or dealer of the protection of its own state's law. See Ticknor v. Choice Hotels Int'l, Inc., 265 F.3d 931 (9th Cir. 2001) (applying Montana conflicts law refuses to enforce choice-of-law clause in franchise agreement); Wright–Moore Corp. v. Ricoh Corp., 908 F.2d 128 (7th Cir. 1990); Solman Distributors, Inc. v. Brown–Forman Corp., 888 F.2d 170 (1st Cir. 1989); Instructional Sys., Inc. v. Computer Curriculum Corp., 130 N.J. 324, 614 A.2d 124 (1992); Bush v. National School Studios, Inc., 139 Wis.2d 635, 407 N.W.2d 883 (1987). Contra, United Wholesale Liquor Co. v. Brown–Forman Distillers Corp., 108 N.M. 467, 775 P.2d 233 (1989).

See Ribstein, *From Efficiency to Politics in Contractual Choice of Law*, 37 Ga. L. Rev. 363 (2003) (summarizing the results in 697 cases that decided whether to enforce choice-of-law clause).

35. Cf. Restatement (Second) § 203:

The validity of a contract will be sustained against the charge of usury if it provides for a rate of interest that is permissible in a state to which the contract has a substantial relationship and is not greatly in excess of the rate permitted by the general usury law of the state of the otherwise applicable law under the rule of § 188 ["most significant relationship to the transaction and the parties"].

franchise agreement selecting law that would that would negate those protections.[36]

Should Parties In An Inferior Bargaining Position, Such As Consumers, Be Protected From A Choice That Would Deprive Them Of The Protective Laws Of Their Home State Or Country?

Section 1–105 of the Uniform Commercial Code contains no exception for adhesion contracts. One would hope, though, that this omission can be remedied, at least in contracts for the sale of goods, by applying to choice-of-law clauses the provisions of section 2–302 giving a court power to deny effect to an "unconscionable" clause.

A question similar to that of whether a court may invalidate a choice-of-law clause as unconscionable is whether the court may do so on the ground of fraudulent inducement. Restatement (Second) § 201 comment *c* states that to invalidate the choice-of-law clause, the fraud must have induced agreement to that clause. Thus fraudulent inducement of the contract does not necessarily invalidate a choice-of-law provision in the contract.[37] This is also the rule for arbitration and forum-selection clauses.[38]

In the comments on section 187, the Second Restatement states that in deciding whether to give effect to the choice of law clause "[a] factor which the forum may consider is whether the choice of law provision is contained in an 'adhesion' contract, namely one that is drafted unilaterally by the dominant party and then presented on a 'take-it-or-leave-it' basis to the weaker party who has no real opportunity to bargain about its terms."[39]

The Rome Regulation protects consumers,[40] holders of insurance contracts,[41] and employees[42] from choice-of-law provisions. The consumer provision, article 6, states:

---

36. See franchise cases cited supra note 34. Cf. Ingmar GB Ltd. v. Eaton Leonard Technologies, Inc. [2000] ECR I–9305 (Case C–381/98) (European Community Directive guaranteeing certain rights to commercial agents after termination of agency contracts is mandatory and must be applied when a United Kingdom company is a commercial agent for a California company even though the contract between the parties stipulated that it was governed by California law).

37. See Mazzoni Farms, Inc. v. E.I. DuPont De Nemours & Co., 761 So.2d 306 (Fla. 2000) (applying § 201 cmt. *c*).

38. See Scherk v. Alberto–Culver Co., 417 U.S. 506, 519 n.41, 94 S.Ct. 2449, 2457 n.14, 41 L.Ed.2d 270 (1974): "This qualification [that a forum-selection clause affected by fraud is unenforceable] does not mean that any time a dispute arising out of a transaction is based upon an allegation of fraud ... the clause is unenforceable. Rather, it means that an arbitration or forum-selection clause in a contract is not enforceable if the inclusion of that clause in the contract was the product of fraud or coercion."

39. Restatement (Second) § 187, comment *b*. Cf. Uniform Commercial Code § 2A–106(1) (in a lease to a consumer, will not enforce choice of law other than that of a jurisdiction in which the goods are to be used, the lessee resides at the time the lease agreement becomes enforceable, or resides within 30 days thereafter). But see Sekeres v. Arbaugh, 31 Ohio St.3d 24, 508 N.E.2d 941 (1987) (enforce choice of New York law in brokerage contract with Ohio customer).

40. Rome I, supra note 27, art. 6.

41. Id. art. 7.

Article 6 Consumer contracts

1. Without prejudice to Articles 5 [contracts of carriage] and 7 [insurance contracts], a contract concluded by a natural person for a purpose which can be regarded as being outside his trade or profession (the consumer) with another person acting in the exercise of his trade or profession (the professional) shall be governed by the law of the country where the consumer has his habitual residence, provided that the professional:

(a) pursues his commercial or professional activities in the country where the consumer has his habitual residence, or

(b) by any means, directs such activities to that country or to several countries including that country, and the contract falls within the scope of such activities.

2. Notwithstanding paragraph 1, the parties may choose the law applicable to a contract which fulfils the requirements of paragraph 1, in accordance with Article 3 [freedom of choice]. Such a choice may not, however, have the result of depriving the consumer of the protection afforded to him by provisions that cannot be derogated from by agreement by virtue of the law which, in the absence of choice, would have been applicable on the basis of paragraph 1.

3. If the requirements in points (a) or (b) of paragraph 1 are not fulfilled, the law applicable to a contract between a consumer and a professional shall be determined pursuant to Articles 3 and 4 [applicable law in the absence of choice].

4. Paragraphs 1 and 2 shall not apply to:

(a) a contract for the supply of services where the services are to be supplied to the consumer exclusively in a country other than that in which he has his habitual residence;

(b) a contract of carriage other than a contract relating to package travel within the meaning of Council Directive 90/314/EEC of 13 June 1990 on package travel, package holidays and package tours (1);[43]

(c) a contract relating to a right *in rem* in immovable property or a tenancy of immovable property other than a contract relating to the right to use immovable properties on a timeshare basis within the meaning of Directive 94/47/EC;

(d) rights and obligations which constitute a financial instrument and rights and obligations constituting the terms and conditions governing the issuance or offer to the public and public take-over bids of transferable securities, and the subscription and redemption of units in collective investment un-

---

42. Id. art. 8.

43. The Council Directive referred to in art. 6(4)(b) defines "package" as including in the price transportation and accommodation when trip covers a period of more than twenty-four hours or includes overnight accommodation.

dertakings in so far as these activities do not constitute provision of a financial service;

(e) a contract concluded within the type of system falling within
the scope of Article 4(1)(h)[interests in financial instruments].

The Oregon code for choice of law for contracts gives Oregon
consumers even wider protection. Section 81.105(4) provides that Oregon
law applies to:

(a) A consumer contract, if:

(A) The consumer is a resident of Oregon at the time of
contracting; and

(B) The consumer's assent to the contract is obtained in Oregon, or the consumer is induced to enter into the contract in
substantial measure by an invitation or advertisement in Oregon.

(b) For the purposes of this subsection, a consumer contract is a
contract for the supply of goods or services that are designed
primarily for personal, familial or household use.

In addition section 81.150 allows Oregon residents to revoke a forum
selection clause or an arbitration clause in a consumer contract that
requires the Oregon resident to consent to a forum not in Oregon.

Drafting the choice-of-law clause.

Giving the parties freedom to choose law for validity tests their
drafting skills. One problem is that the parties may inadvertently choose
a jurisdiction whose laws will invalidate the contract in whole or in part.
This phenomenon of mistaken choice is already observable in many
reported cases.[44] Now that choice-of-law clauses are becoming ubiquitous
boilerplate in commercial contracts, the number of cases in which the

---

44. See, e.g., Milanovich v. Costa Crociere, S.p.A, 954 F.2d 763 (D.C. Cir. 1992) (apply
law chosen on cruise ticket to invalidate time limit on bringing suit); Moyer v. Citicorp
Homeowners, Inc., 799 F.2d 1445 (11th Cir.1986) (apply chosen law to invalidate for
usury—Georgia law); Boatland, Inc. v. Brunswick Corp., 558 F.2d 818 (6th Cir.1977)
(Tennessee forum) (construe choice-of-law clause as including substantive law although it
refers only to interpretation and construction, and then apply chosen law to invalidate
provision governing termination of dealership—contract drafted by party disfavored by
chosen law); Foreman v. George Foreman Associates, Ltd., 517 F.2d 354 (9th Cir.1975)
(California forum) (invalidate boxing contract under chosen law); Meltzer v. Crescent
Leaseholds, Ltd., 315 F.Supp. 142 (S.D.N.Y.1970), aff'd, 442 F.2d 293 (2d Cir.1971) (under
forum law chosen in contract, unlicensed plaintiff could not recover finder's fee provided in
the contract) (perhaps no conflict of laws); Pisacane v. Italia Societa Per Azioni Di
Navigazione, 219 F.Supp. 424 (S.D.N.Y.1963) (passenger ticket's provision of one-year limit
on suit for injury invalid under Italian law also designated in ticket); Jones v. Tindall, 216
Ark. 431, 226 S.W.2d 44 (1950) (lender forfeits principal and interest under usury law of
chosen state); Fairfield Lease Corp. v. Pratt, 6 Conn.Cir. 537, 278 A.2d 154 (1971) (lease
unenforceable under chosen law) (perhaps no conflict of laws); Department of Motor
Vehicles For Use of Fifth Ave. Motors, Ltd. v. Mercedes–Benz of North America, Inc., 408
So.2d 627 (Fla.App.2d Dist.1981) (apply chosen New Jersey law to invalidate clause in
franchise agreement restricting changes in ownership or management of franchise); Punzi
v. Shaker Advertising Agency, Inc. 601 So.2d 599 (Fla. App. 1992) (employment contract
chooses law that invalidates employee's promise not to compete); Atlas Subsidiaries, Inc. v.
O. & O., Inc., 166 So.2d 458 (Fla. App. 1964) (promissory note chooses law under which it
is usurious); Hardy v. Monsanto Enviro–Chem Systems, 414 Mich. 29, 323 N.W.2d 270

law-choosing clause stipulates the invalidating law may be expected to increase.

This problem of the inadvertent stipulation of invalidating law is easily resolved. A court should disregard a stipulation of invalidating law as an obvious mistake and choose the proper law by some other means. The Second Restatement makes this sensible exception to section 187.[45] When fully translated, section 187 means that the parties' choice of law will be given effect if it selects the validating law, but not if it selects the invalidating law. This is a partial rule of validation. If it is desirable to apply the validating law when chosen by the parties, it is just as desirable to choose that law whether or not it is referred to in a choice-of-law clause. Commercial convenience and upholding of expectations are served whenever the validating rule is applied and disserved whenever invalidating law is invoked.

(1982) (apply chosen Illinois law to invalidate indemnity clause); Robertson v. Burnett, 172 Neb. 385, 109 N.W.2d 716 (1961), vacated on other grounds and remanded sub nom. Michigan Nat'l Bank v. Robertson, 372 U.S. 591, 83 S.Ct. 914, 9 L.Ed.2d 961 (1963) (conditional sales contract designates law under which interest is usurious and principal and interest are forfeited); cf. Peugeot Motors of America, Inc. v. Eastern Auto Distributors, Inc., 892 F.2d 355 (4th Cir.1989), cert. denied, 497 U.S. 1005, 110 S.Ct. 3242, 111 L.Ed.2d 752 (1990) (clause choosing New York law to govern validity of dealership agreement does not include New York Dealer Act, which would invalidate provision giving franchisor right to terminate, because the Act limits its territorial scope to dealers doing business in New York); Coastal Ind. v. Automatic Steam Prod. Corp., 654 F.2d 375 (5th Cir.1981) (under chosen New York law, arbitration clause in seller's form did not become part of the agreement); Ocean S.S. Co. v. Queensland State Wheat Bd., [1941] 1 All Eng.R. 158 (C.A.1940) (choice-of-law clause designating English law invalidated by Australian Carriage of Goods by Sea Act which bill of lading also incorporated by reference).

See also infra notes 60–70 and accompanying text for discussion of the unintended consequences of choice-of-law clauses in arbitration agreements.

For interesting attempts to avoid the embarrassment of selecting invalidating law, see Tex. Bus. & Commerce C. § 35.51(e) (in transactions with an aggregate value of at least $1,000,000, if the parties select a law that would invalidate a provision of the contract, the law of the jurisdiction with the most significant relationship to the transaction applies if that law would validate the provision); Leasing Service Corp. v. River City Constr., Inc., 743 F.2d 871, 874 (11th Cir.1984) ("enforceability and effectiveness of each provision shall be determined by the law of the state of residence or principal place of business of Lessee [Alabama] or Lessor [New York] or the original lessor [Georgia], whichever may render each such provisions effective").

45. Restatement (Second) § 187, Comment *e.* See also Tex. Bus. & Commerce C. § 35.51(e); Kipin Indus. v. Van Deilen Int'l, Inc., 182 F.3d 490 (6th Cir. 1999) (applying Michigan choice-of-law rules, disregards parties' choice of Michigan law as mistake because it would invalidate waiver of right to file mechanics' liens, which is valid under otherwise applicable Kentucky law) (quoting this text); cf. Bense v. Interstate Battery System of America, Inc., 683 F.2d 718 (2d Cir.1982) (choice-of-law clause construed as not applying when Texas law chosen would invalidate a clause choosing Texas as exclusive forum); Temporarily Yours–Temporary Help Services, Inc. v. Manpower, Inc., 377 So.2d 825 (Fla.App.1979) (clause choosing Wisconsin law for "interpretation and construction" held not applicable to validity when Wisconsin law would invalidate); Kronovet v. Lipchin, 288 Md. 30, 415 A.2d 1096 (1980) (between conflicting choice-of-law clauses, apply the one that selects validating law). But see General Elec. Credit Corp. v. Beyerlein, 55 Misc.2d 724, 286 N.Y.S.2d 351 (Monroe Cty.1967) (applying law chosen to invalidate clause that cut off defenses against assignee); Ehrenzweig, *Contracts in the Conflict of Laws*, 59 Colum. L. Rev. 973, 991–92 (1959) (suggests applying the law designated by the parties even though it invalidates part of the agreement); Sedler, *The Contracts Provisions of the Restatement (Second): An Analysis and a Critique*, 72 Colum. L. Rev. 279, 294 (1972) ("fair" to apply invalidating law chosen by dominant party).

Some courts distinguish cases in which the law that the parties choose invalidates part of the contract from cases in which the chosen law invalidates the whole contract. These courts apply the law chosen to invalidate part, but not the whole, contract.[46] This distinction is without merit. The parties could avoid having the chosen applied to invalidate any part of the contract by a properly drafted choice-of-law agreement, such as that infra accompanying note 54.

There are other problems in the drafting of choice-of-law clauses that arise repeatedly. Courts have differed as to whether a choice-of-law clause includes tort claims related to the contract and, if so, whether the stipulation is effective. The consensus seems to be that a court will enforce a clause that includes tort claims.[47] In *Kuehn v. Children's Hospital, Los Angeles*,[48] Chief Judge Posner finds that the choice-of-law clause did not cover torts and states: "One can, it is true, find cases that say that contractual choice of law provisions govern only contractual disputes and not torts. E.g. Lazard Freres & Co. v. Protective Life Ins. Co., 108 F.3d 1531, 1540 (2d Cir. 1997). But what the cases actually hold is that such a provision will not be construed to govern tort as well as contract disputes unless it is clear that this is what the parties intended." He then indicates that he would have enforced the choice of law if it had clearly included torts.[49]

A regulation of the European Parliament and the Council on the Law Applicable to Non–Contractual Obligations (Rome II)[50] permits parties to a contract to choose law governing tort claims arising from their commercial activity. Even parties not pursuing a commercial activity can agree on choice of law for torts after the damage has occurred. If the parties and the transaction are within the European Union, the choice may not avoid mandatory Community law.

Most courts have held that a choice-of-law clause does not cover issues that U.S. courts have traditionally characterized as "procedural"

---

46. CS–Lakeview at Gwinnett, Inc. v. Simon Property Group, Inc., 283 Ga. 426, 659 S.E.2d 359 (2008), reconsideration denied (2008) (applying chosen law to invalidate part of contract; dissent cites and quotes the passage on p. 495 of the main volume).

47. See Cooper v. Meridian Yachts, Ltd., 575 F.3d 1151, 1162 (11th Cir. 2009) ("disputes arising out of or in connection with" shipbuilding contract includes a claim for negligent construction); Watkins & Son Pet Supplies v. Iams Co., 254 F.3d 607 (6th Cir. 2001) (choice-of-law clause that does not mention torts does include "promissory fraud"— making promises with no intention to keep them); Rayle Tech, Inc. v. Dekalb Swine Breeders, Inc., 133 F.3d 1405, 1409 (11th Cir. 1998) (clause did not cover torts, but if it did, Georgia conflicts rules would not enforce it); Northwest Airlines, Inc. v. Astraea Aviation Servs., Inc., 111 F.3d 1386 (8th Cir. 1997) (construe clause to cover torts arising from failure to perform contract and enforce it); Krock v. Lipsay, 97 F.3d 640 (2d Cir. 1996) (construe clause as not covering fraud claim); Nedlloyd Lines B.V. v. Superior Court, 3 Cal.4th 459, 834 P.2d 1148, 11 Cal.Rptr.2d 330 (1992) (construe clause to cover tort claim and enforce it; two dissenters differed on construction but indicated they would enforce the clause if it covered torts); Barrow v. ATCO Mfg. Co., 524 N.E.2d 1313 (Ind.App. 1st Dist.1988) (the law chosen applies although plaintiff sues in "tort" for misrepresentation).

48. 119 F.3d 1296 (7th Cir. 1997).

49. Id. at 1302.

50. Regulation (EC) No. 864/2007 of 11 July 2007, OJ 2007 L199/46, art. 14.

for conflict-of-laws purposes, such as statutes of limitations and burden of proof.[51]

Yavuz v. 61 MM, Ltd.[52] held that when a contract contains both choice-of-law and choice-of-forum clauses, the forum clause is construed under the chosen law. *Finance One Public Co. Ltd. v. Lehman Brothers Special Financing, Inc.*,[53] however, held that the scope of a choice-of-law agreement is determined by forum law, not the law designated in the agreement.

The following choice-of-law agreement avoids these ambiguities:

> The parties select the law of X, excluding the conflict-of-laws rules of X, to govern: (1) the construction and validity of this contract; (2) any action arising from or in any way related to this contract no matter what the theory of the action, whether tort, contract, or any other; (3) any issue that will affect the result in a manner that would influence choice of the forum if the law of X will not be unusually difficult for a court in another jurisdiction to apply, such as statutes of limitations, burden of proof, attorneys' fees, prejudgment interest, and other similar issues; (4) the scope of this choice-of-law agreement; (5) the construction of the choice-of-forum agreement in [designate paragraph number in the contract].

> If the law of X invalidates any term of the contract, the parties stipulate that the choice of X law is a mistake as to that term and should be disregarded. Instead the law applicable to that term is the local law of the state that, with respect to that term, has the most

---

51. See Schwan's Sales Enterprises, Inc. v. SIG Pack, Inc., 476 F.3d 594 (8th Cir. 2007) (under Minnesota law, prejudgment interest is procedural to be governed by the law of the Minnesota forum despite a choice-of-law provision designating Wisconsin law); Woodling v. Garrett Corp., 813 F.2d 543 (2d Cir.1987) (the law designated applies to the "substantive" issues of rescission and parol evidence rule, but not to the "procedural" issue of burden of proof—New York); Federal Deposit Insurance Corp. v. Petersen, 770 F.2d 141 (10th Cir.1985) (absent an express statement of contrary intention, a choice-of-law clause does not apply to statutes of limitation); Juran v. Bron, 2000 WL 1521478 (Del Ch. 2000) (choice-of-law clause does not, without express reference, include statutes of limitations); Nez v. Forney, 109 N.M. 161, 783 P.2d 471 (1989) (choice-of-law clause does not, without express reference, include statutes of limitations). Contra, Cooper v. Meridian Yachts, Inc., 575 F.3d 1151, 1162 (11th Cir. 2009) ("disputes arising out of or in connection with" shipbuilding contract includes the statute of limitations for negligence—federal choice of law in admiralty); Hughes Electronics Corp. v. Citibank Delaware, 120 Cal.App.4th 251, 15 Cal.Rptr.3d 244 (2004), rev. denied (Cal. 2004) (choice-of-law clause reference to "laws" of New York includes both the New York statute of limitations and borrowing statute, which would borrow the California limitations and bar the action); Hambrecht & Quist Venture Partners v. American Medical Int'l, Inc., 38 Cal.App.4th 1532, 46 Cal.Rptr.2d 33 (1995) (because California no longer adheres to the traditional characterization of statutes of limitations as procedural, a choice-of-law clause referring to "laws" includes statutes of limitations); Intellectual Property: Principles Governing Jurisdiction, Choice of Law, and Judgments in Transnational Disputes § 326 cmt. *a* (American L. Inst. Discussion Draft April 10, 2006): "Where the parties have designated the law applicable to their contract, that law will also govern the statute of limitations."

52. 465 F.3d 418 (10th Cir. 2006).

53. 414 F.3d 325 (2d Cir. 2005), cert. denied, 548 U.S. 904, 126 S.Ct. 2968, 165 L.Ed.2d 951 (2006) (applying forum law to hold that the choice-of-law provision in a master derivatives contract is not broad enough to cover setoff rights).

significant relationship to the transaction and the parties. As to all other matters stated above, the law of X shall apply.[54]

This choice-of-law agreement will not be effective in Oregon. The code covering choice of law for tort and other noncontractual claims permits the parties to choose law only "after the parties had knowledge of the events giving rise to the dispute."[55] Moreover, section 81.120 of the Oregon code covering choice of law for contracts permits the parties to choose law that governs only their "contractual rights and duties." Dean and Professor of Law Symeon Symeonides of the Willamette University College of Law, which participated in the code project, has stated:

> The use of ["contractual"] was deliberate: it is intended to exclude from the scope of party autonomy non-contractual issues, such as tort claims, unfair trade practices, statutes of limitation, attorney fees, and prejudgment interest. It is one thing to allow parties to jointly pre-select the law that will govern their contractual dispute and another thing to allow them to do so with regard to a future tort between them. The latter is a much more serious matter, especially in contracts in which one party is likely to be in a weak bargaining position, such as employment contracts, consumer contracts, or insurance contracts. The protection traditionally afforded to these parties should not be evaded through the ostensible "choice" of another law.[56]

I believe this limitation on the parties' choice is unfortunate. Especially puzzling is exclusion of choice for statutes of limitations when more U.S. courts are re-characterizing the statutes as substantive and within the scope of a choice-of-law clause.[57] Certainly the law should protect parties in an inferior bargaining position from having their

---

54. See Restatement (Second) § 187, cmt. *e*: ". If the parties have chosen a law that would invalidate the contract, it can be assumed that they did so by mistake. If, however, the chosen law is that of the state of the otherwise applicable law under the rule of § 188 [most significant relationship], this law will be applied even when it invalidates the contract. Such application will be by reason of the rule of § 188, and not by reason of the fact that this was the law chosen by the parties."

55. Senate Bill 561, 75th Oregon Legislative Assembly, 2009 Regular Session, § 11. See also id. § 6(1) (parties can agree to application of Oregon law "after the events giving rise to the dispute").

56. Symeonides, *Oregon's Choice-of-Law Codification for Contract Conflicts: An Exegesis*, 44 Willamette L. Rev. 205, 223 (2007).

57. See, e.g., Hambrecht & Quist Venture Partners v. American Medical Int'l, Inc., 38 Cal.App.4th 1532, 46 Cal.Rptr.2d 33 (1995).

At the time Symeonides, supra note 56 was published, the Uniform Conflict of Laws—Limitations Act had been in force in Oregon for 20 years. ORS §§ 12.410–12.480. Section 12:430 provides:

(1) Except as provided by ORS 12.450 [limitation chosen by Act is substantially different from Oregon's and is unfair to the plaintiff or the defendant], if a claim is substantively based:

(a) Upon the law of one other state, the limitation period of that state applies; or

(b) Upon the law of more than one state, the limitation period of one of those states, chosen by the law of conflict of laws of this state, applies.

(2) The limitation period of this state applies to all other claims.

rights undermined by a choice-of-law agreement. The way to do that is provide in the code that a choice-law-agreement cannot deprive such parties of the law of their home state if there are designated contacts with that state. As noted above, article 14 of Rome II permits the parties to choose law for future torts, but only in commercial transactions.

Article 21 of the Japanese Act on the General Rules of Application of Laws,[58] like the Oregon code, permits the parties to choose the law that applies to tort only "[a]fter a tort occurs."

"Floating" forum-selection clauses give one or both parties a choice of fora in which to sue and frequently provide that the applicable law is that of the chosen forum. Art. 3(2) of the Rome Regulation permits the parties to make a choice of law after initially contracting, including changing an earlier choice.

A company rented telecommunications equipment to businesses in different states. The rental agreement provided that it was governed by the law of the state where the rental company's principal offices are located and that any suit relating to the rental contract would be brought in that state. The rental company reserved the rights to assign the right to receive rental payments, in which event the rental contract would be governed by the law of the state in which the assignee's principal offices are located and any suit relating to the rental contract would be brought in that state. Actions in different states litigated the right of various assignees to enforce the combined choice-of-law and choice-of-forum agreement. The results varied.[59]

Choice-of-Law Clauses in Arbitration Agreements

Choice-of-law clauses in arbitration agreements require particularly careful drafting. If the law of the chosen state limits the powers of arbitrators or the scope of arbitration, dispute settlement is likely to take a prolonged detour to litigate the interaction of the parties' agreement to arbitrate, their choice-of-law clause, and the arbitration law of the chosen state.

In *Mastrobuono v. Shearson Lehman Hutton, Inc.*,[60] clients of a securities dealer had signed an agreement proffered by the dealer that submitted all disputes to arbitration "in accordance with the rules of the National Association of Securities Dealers (NASD)" and chose New York law to govern. NASD rules permitted arbitrators to assess punitive damages, but under New York law only courts could do so. It took a trip up to the Supreme Court of the United States to decide whether the arbitrators' award of punitive damages was foreclosed by the agreement. The Court upheld the award on the ground that the choice-of-law clause "might include only New York's substantive rights and obligations, and

---

58. Law No. 10 of 1898 as newly titled and amended 21 June 2006.

59. See IFC Credit Corp. v. Rieker Shoe Corp., 378 Ill.App.3d 77, 317 Ill.Dec. 214, 881 N.E.2d 382 (2007), which enforced the agreement but collects contra authority.

60. 514 U.S. 52, 115 S.Ct. 1212, 131 L.Ed.2d 76 (1995).

not the State's allocation of power between alternative tribunals."[61] The Court also invoked "the common-law rule ... that a court should construe ambiguous language against the interest of the party that drafted it."[62]

Six years to the day before *Mastrobuono*, the Supreme Court had decided *Volt Information Sciences v. Board of Trustees of Stanford University*.[63] In *Volt*, Stanford University had entered into a construction contract with Volt. The contract contained a provision agreeing to arbitrate all disputes and a clause choosing "the law of the place where the Project is located," which was California. Volt demanded arbitration of a dispute and Stanford responded by suing Volt for fraud and breach of contract. The University also sought indemnity from two other companies with whom it did not have arbitration agreements. California law permits a court to stay arbitration in a case of this kind involving parties to an arbitration agreement and other litigants who have not agreed to arbitrate. The California courts interpreted the arbitration agreement to include the California rule on staying arbitration and denied Volt's motion to compel arbitration. The Supreme Court affirmed.

In *Mastrobuono*, the Court distinguished *Volt* on the basis of a different interpretation of the interaction between the arbitration and choice-of-law clauses. The *Mastrobuono* opinion pointed out that in *Volt* the Supreme Court of the United States deferred to an interpretation of the agreement by a California state court, while in *Mastrobuono* it was reviewing a federal court's interpretation "and our interpretation accords with that of the only decision-maker arguably entitled to deference—the arbitrator."[64] Justice Thomas dissented in *Mastrobuono* on the ground that "the choice-of-law provision here cannot reasonably be distinguished from the one in *Volt*."[65]

To add to the confusion, under New York law, whether a claim is barred by passage of time is an issue for the courts, not arbitrators. *PaineWebber Inc. v. Bybyk*[66] held that if an agreement contains both an arbitration clause and a clause choosing New York law, the issue of timeliness is for the arbitrators. The court also held that a recent contrary opinion from the New York Court of Appeals was not persuasive because it relied on the Seventh Circuit decision in *Mastrobuono*, which was reversed by the United States Supreme Court. This despite *Mastrobuono*'s distinction of *Volt* on the ground that in *Volt* the Supreme Court had deferred to a state court's interpretation of the agreement.

---

61.   Id. at 59, 115 S.Ct. at 1217.

62.   Id. at 62, 115 S.Ct. at 1219.

63.   489 U.S. 468, 109 S.Ct. 1248, 103 L.Ed.2d 488 (1989).

64.   *Mastrobuono*, 514 U.S. at 59 n.4, 115 S.Ct. at 1217 n.4.

65.   Id. at 64, 115 S.Ct. at 1219 (Thomas, J., dissenting).

66.   81 F.3d 1193 (2d Cir. 1996).

These cases suggest that a choice-of-law clause in an arbitration agreement should exclude the law of the chosen state that governs the powers of arbitrators and the scope of arbitration.[67]

Preston v. Ferrer[68] will lessen the clash between arbitration agreements and state law that limits the powers of arbitrators or the scope of arbitration. Ferrer, an entertainer, and Preston, who renders services to entertainers, agreed to arbitrate any dispute in accordance with American Arbitration Association rules and California law. California law vests exclusive original jurisdiction over the dispute in the California Labor Commissioner. The Supreme Court reversed California state court opinions enjoining arbitration and held that "when parties agree to arbitrate all questions arising under a contract, state laws lodging primary jurisdiction in another forum, whether judicial or administrative, are superseded by the F[ederal] A[rbitration] A[ct]."[69] With regard to *Volt*, the court stated:

> [W]e are guided by our more recent decision in *Mastrobuono*. Although the contract in *Volt* provided for "arbitration in accordance with the Construction Industry Arbitration Rules of the American Arbitration Association," Volt never argued that incorporation of those rules trumped the choice-of-law clause contained in the contract. Therefore, neither our decision in *Volt* nor the decision of the California appeals court in that case addressed the import of the contract's incorporation by reference of privately promulgated arbitration rules.[70]

Nevertheless, a choice-of-law clause in an arbitration agreement should exclude law of the chosen state that governs the powers of arbitrators or the scope of arbitration.

§ 7.3D The Law of the State With the Most Significant Relationship

In the absence of a choice-of-law clause in the contract in issue, the emerging consensus in the United States and abroad appears to be that questions of validity should be controlled by the law of the state having the most significant or closest relationship with the parties and with the transaction.[71] Section 188 of the Second Restatement reflects this con-

---

67. See Roadway Package System, Inc. v. Kayser, 257 F.3d 287 (3d Cir. 2001) (clause choosing Pennsylvania law does not choose Pennsylvania Uniform Arbitration Act rather than Federal Arbitration Act standards for vacating arbitration award; award vacated because arbitrator exceeded scope of his authority—a ground available under FAA but not under PUAA); Portland General Electric Co. v. U.S. Bank Trust Nat'l Assoc., 218 F.3d 1085 (9th Cir. 2000) (when clause chooses Oregon law, that law determines whether appraisal is an "arbitration" subject to the Federal Arbitration Act); Diamond Waterproofing Systems, Inc. v. 55 Liberty Owners Corp., 4 N.Y.3d 247, 826 N.E.2d 802, 793 N.Y.S.2d 831 (2005) (when arbitration agreement stated that the contract was governed by New York law and did not state that New York law governed the agreement's "enforcement", the question of whether the demand for arbitration was timely was for the arbitrator and not for the courts).

68. 552 U.S. 346, 128 S.Ct. 978, 169 L.Ed.2d 917 (2008).

69. Id. at 981.

70. Id. at 988.

71. For U.S. cases see, e.g., Palmer v. Beverly Enterprises, 823 F.2d 1105 (7th Cir.1987) (predicting that an Illinois court would so hold); Williams v. State Farm Mut. Auto. Ins.

sensus that the section itself, in prior tentative drafts, had helped to shape:

Law Governing in Absence of Effective Choice by the Parties.

(1) The rights and duties of the parties with respect to an issue in contract are determined by the local law of the state which, with respect to that issue, has the most significant relationship to the transaction and the parties under the principles stated in § 6.[72]

Co., 737 F.2d 741 (8th Cir.1984) (Arkansas rule); Aries v. Palmer Johnson, Inc., 153 Ariz. 250, 735 P.2d 1373 (App. 1987); Wood Bros. Homes, Inc. v. Walker Adjustments Bureau, 198 Col. 444, 601 P.2d 1369 (1979); In re Asbestos Litigation (Bell), 517 A.2d 697 (Del.Super. 1986) (determined with aid of choice-of-law clause); Baybutt Constr. Corp. v. Commercial Union Ins. Co., 455 A.2d 914 (Me.1983); Protective Cas. Ins. Co. v. Cook, 734 S.W.2d 898 (Mo.App.1987); Boardman v. United Services Automobile Association, 470 So.2d 1024 (Miss.1985); Consolidated Mut. Ins. Co. v. Radio Foods Corp., 108 N.H. 494, 240 A.2d 47 (1968); Bernick v. Frost, 210 N.J.Super. 397, 510 A.2d 56 (App.Div.1986); Sotirakis v. United Service Automobile Ass'n, 106 Nev. 123, 787 P.2d 788 (1990) (validity of family-exclusion clause); Terry v. Pullman Trailmobile, 92 N.C.App. 687, 376 S.E.2d 47 (1989) (breach of warranty); Gries Sports Enterprises, Inc. v. Modell, 15 Ohio St.3d 284, 473 N.E.2d 807 (1984), cert. denied, 473 U.S. 906, 105 S.Ct. 3530, 87 L.Ed.2d 654 (1985) (expiration of agreement between majority and minority stockholders—not state of incorporation); Knauer v. Knauer, 323 Pa.Super. 206, 470 A.2d 553 (1983); Duncan v. Cessna Aircraft Co., 665 S.W.2d 414 (Tex.1984); New v. Tac & C Energy, Inc., 177 W.Va. 648, 355 S.E.2d 629 (1987) (when contract not both made and to be performed in same state); Peterson v. Warren, 31 Wis.2d 547, 143 N.W.2d 560 (1966), overruled on another point, Allen v. Ross, 38 Wis.2d 209, 156 N.W.2d 434 (1968); cf. Casanova Club v. Bisharat, 189 Conn. 591, 458 A.2d 1 (1983) (defer deciding whether to abandon traditional rule and adopt most significant relationship test because record lacks factual basis for application of Restatement (Second) § 188).

For cases applying the law of the "center of gravity" of the transaction, see, e.g., Fleet Messenger Service, Inc. v. Life Ins. Co. of No. Am., 315 F.2d 593 (2d Cir.1963) (N.Y. rule); W.H. Barber Co. v. Hughes, 223 Ind. 570, 63 N.E.2d 417 (1945).

But see Sturiano v. Brooks, 523 So.2d 1126 (Fla. 1988), answering in the affirmative the 11th Circuit's certified question whether the lex loci contractus would apply to insurance coverage, "limiting this answer to contracts for automobile insurance." Two concurring judges noted that on the facts of the case, the same result would be reached under the Second Restatement. Florida has adopted the Second Restatement approach for torts. But see also St. Paul Surplus Lines Ins. Co. v. International Playtex, Inc., 245 Kan. 258, 777 P.2d 1259, 1267 (1989), cert. denied, 493 U.S. 1036, 110 S.Ct. 758, 107 L.Ed.2d 774 (1990) (whether policy may validly cover punitive damages—"reserve consideration of the Restatement's 'most significant relationship' test for a later day", resting choice of forum law, precluding coverage, on public policy and on conclusion that forum, where fatally injured consumer resided, has greater interest than Delaware, where manufacturer has its principal place of business and which would permit coverage); Ellis v. Royal Ins. Co., 129 N.H. 326, 530 A.2d 303 (1987) (cannot apply most significant relationship test because of "issued or delivered" territorial limit in insurance statute) (apparently inconsistent with Mathena v. Granite State Ins. Co., 129 N.H. 249, 525 A.2d 284 (1987)—although both opinions are by Chief Justice Brock, *Mathena is* not cited in *Ellis*).

72. Restatement (Second), Conflict of Laws § 6 provides:

"Choice of Law Principles

"(1) A court, subject to constitutional restrictions, will follow a statutory directive of its own state on choice of law.

"(2) When there is no such directive, the factors relevant to the choice of the applicable rule of law include

"(a) the needs of the interstate and international systems,

"(b) the relevant policies of the forum,

"(c) the relevant policies of other interested states and the relative interests of those states in the determination of the particular issue,

(2) In the absence of an effective choice of law by the parties (see § 187), the contacts to be taken into account in applying the principles of § 6 to determine the law applicable to an issue include:

(a) the place of contracting,

(b) the place of negotiation of the contract,

(c) the place of performance,

(d) the location of the subject matter of the contract, and

(e) the domicil, residence, nationality, place of incorporation and place of business of the parties.

These contacts are to be evaluated according to their relative importance with respect to the particular issue.

(3) If the place of negotiating the contract and the place of performance are in the same state, the local law of this state will usually be applied, except as otherwise provided in §§ 189–199 and 203.[73]

The great merit of section 188 is that it is consistent with the a consequences-based conflicts analysis that begins by focusing on the particular domestic rules of contract law in putative conflict and on their underlying purposes. Section 188 invites this process of inquiry into substantive contract policies. The section states that the enumerated "contacts are to be evaluated according to their relative importance with respect to the particular issue."

Despite this wise injunction, there is grave danger that section 188 will be interpreted to direct the counting of physical contacts with the parties and with the transaction and the awarding of the palm to the state with the "most" contacts. To the judge or lawyer, not expert in conflicts theory and working under time pressures that prevent scrutiny of the Second Restatement in all its detailed commentary on the black letter, this counting seems invited by section 188's listing of contacts "to be taken into account." It is inconsistent with functional analysis to list any contact as "significant" a priori, without first knowing the domestic law of the state having that contact and the policies underlying that domestic law. Even more antithetical to proper analysis is subsection three's announcement that if the place of negotiation and place of performance coincide, "the local law of this state will usually be applied."[74]

"(d) the protection of justified expectations,

"(e) the basic policies underlying the particular field of law,

"(f) certainty, predictability and uniformity of result, and

"(g) ease in the determination and application of the law to be applied."

73. Restatement (Second) § 188.

74. Other statements in the comments to section 188, which appear to be inconsistent with a functional analysis, include the following:

Comment c:

"Frequently, it will be possible to decide a question of choice of law in contract without paying deliberate attention to the purpose sought to be achieved by the relevant contract

It may well be that subsection three is a correct statistical description of the results of the proper functional analysis of, let us say, a thousand contracts-conflicts cases picked at random from the reports. But this form of statement invites confusion between the end product of proper analysis and its beginning; confusion that, in view of the ordinary court's or lawyer's lack of experience with modern choice-of-law analysis, is likely to be fatal to the chances for intelligent decisions.

Two cases cited in the Reporter's Note to section 188 illustrate this confusion, with its hallmark of Ouija Board manipulation of physical contacts without advertence to the domestic laws in putative conflict or to their underlying purposes. The first case, *Auten v. Auten*,[75] was one of the principal sources from which the section drew its "significant relationship" concept. The second case, *Baffin Land Corporation v. Monticello Motor Inn, Incorporated*,[76] falls at the other end of the historical thread connecting the Second Restatement with the emerging consensus of decided cases. The Reporter characterizes Baffin as "citing and applying the rule of this Section."

Auten involved a suit by a former wife of the defendant to collect unpaid installments allegedly due under a separation agreement that the parties had signed in New York. The defendant had deserted his wife and children in England, the marital domicile. The wife came to New York to bargain with her former spouse concerning support. In the resulting agreement, the husband promised to pay a certain sum per month to a New York trustee for forwarding to the wife who was to return to England and not "cause any complaint to be lodged against [the husband] in any jurisdiction by reason of the said alleged divorce or remarriage."[77] After the wife had returned to England, the promised support payments quickly stopped. The wife was advised to sue the husband in an English court for separation. She did so, but the case was never tried and she realized not one cent in support money for her efforts.

The *Auten* decision results from the wife's attempt to enforce the support agreement in New York. The issue to which the court addresses itself is whether the wife had repudiated the agreement by bringing the support suit in England. The lower courts, finding that under New York

---

rules of the interested states. This will be so whenever by reason of the particular circumstances one state is obviously that of the applicable law."

Comment *e*:

"*Domicil, residence, nationality, place of incorporation, and place of business of the parties.* These are all places of enduring relationship to the parties. Their significance depends largely upon the issue involved and upon the extent to which they are grouped with other contacts."

See Del Monte Fresh Produce (Hawaii), Inc. v. Fireman's Fund Ins. Co., 117 Hawai'i 357, 183 P.3d 734, 741 (2007) (rejecting § 188 in favor of a "flexible approach [that] places primary emphasis on deciding which state would have the strongest interest in seeing its laws applied to the particular case").

75. 308 N.Y. 155, 161–63, 124 N.E.2d 99, 102–03 (1954).

76. 70 Wn.2d 893, 425 P.2d 623 (1967).

77. *Auten*, 308 N.Y. at 158, 124 N.E.2d at 100.

law the wife had repudiated the agreement, limited her recovery to any cause of action accruing prior to the English suit. The Court of Appeals reversed and remanded declaring that "it is English law which must be applied" because England "has all the truly significant contacts."[78] The court thus fixed on English law as the law that "must" be applied without any finding as to what that English law was,[79] or, for that matter, whether the lower courts were correct in their statement of New York law. Moreover, the opinion leaves in doubt whether the court viewed the problem as one of construction of the separation agreement or one of invalidation of an unconscionable promise in that agreement. If both New York and England would have given effect to a promise by the wife clearly interdicting her English separation suit, the court's explanation of its "grouping of contacts" theory as giving "the place 'having the most interest in the problem' paramount control over the legal issues,"[80] rings somewhat false.

In *Baffin*, a motel had been community property of husband and wife. The spouses divorced and the wife received as a property settlement some of the property previously held as community property. The case concerns the question whether a judgment creditor of the motel can satisfy the judgment out of the former community property taken by the wife in the divorce settlement. The contract had been "made" in New York where the creditor had its main office.

Using the place of making choice-of-law rule, the trial court applied New York law, which recognized no obligation on the contract by either the former marital community or the wife. The trial court therefore held that the creditor could not reach any of the wife's property, either her separate property or her former community property. The Supreme Court of Washington reversed, abandoning the place of making rule and adopting the rule of the Second Restatement. Under this new approach the Court found that "Washington is the state of the applicable law because it is the state with the most significant relationship to the contract."[81]

It is significant that only after making this pronouncement that Washington law is applicable does the court "come now to the question of what the applicable Washington law is"[82] and find that under Washington law the creditor can reach the property that the wife received in the divorce settlement. This order of decision is inconsistent with a functional analysis. The court does state that "the approach is *not* to count contacts, but rather to consider which contacts are most signifi-

---

78. Id. at 161, 124 N.E.2d at 102.

79. Because the decision arose on dismissal of the wife's complaint, the wife had gone no further in her proof of English law than the submission of affidavits by English lawyers stating that, under English law, the separation suit in England did not constitute a repudiation of the separation agreement. Id. at 164 n.2, 124 N.E.2d at 103 n.2.

80. Id. at 161, 124 N.E.2d at 102.

81. *Baffin*, 425 P.2d at 629.

82. Id.

cant and to determine where those contacts are found."[83] The court fails to realize that a contact is "significant" only in terms of its relevance to a specific domestic law and the policies underlying that law. Despite its good intentions, the court does "count" contacts when it proceeds to list them without relating each contact to a specific domestic policy.

If the court had applied a proper functional analysis of the problem, it would have found the decision far easier to write and Washington lawyers would have found the decision far easier to understand and apply to future contracts-conflicts cases. The problem before the court was functionally a "false" one.[84] The defendant might contend that under New York law the creditor cannot recover against the wife's former community property because the concept of "community property" is alien to New York jurisprudence. But an intelligent appraisal of New York views on the issue would require a complete, not misleadingly partial, translation of the problem into New York common-law terms. If the motel had been a New York partnership, the creditor could have reached the wife's assets and would not even have been limited to those assets of the wife that were formerly partnership assets. Under Washington law, as found by the court, the creditor of the community can reach former community assets in the divorced wife's hands and no settlement agreement between husband and wife can affect this right. Therefore, both Washington and New York would reach the same results on the issue before the court and for essentially the same reasons. Only a magician could manufacture a conflict and resolve it against the creditor. Under its former "place of making" rule, the Washington Court had performed just such magic[85] until it recognized the folly of its past practices in another case decided the same day as *Baffin*.[86]

Once the significant relationship concept degenerates into contact counting, other evils follow in addition to the aberration illustrated in *Auten* and *Baffin* of selecting the controlling law without knowledge of its content. If it is the gross number of contacts that matter, then contact building is encouraged. One of the most dramatic examples of this piling up of contacts with an eye to possible litigation is *Haag v. Barnes*.[87] The defendant, an Illinois resident, while on a business trip to

---

83. Id. at 628.

84. See P. Trautman, *Evolution in* Washington *Choice of Law—A Beginning*, 43 Wash. L. Rev. 309, 314 (1967).

85. See Escrow Service Co. v. Cressler, 59 Wn.2d 38, 365 P.2d 760 (1961).

86. Pacific States Cut Stone Co. v. Goble, 70 Wn.2d 907, 425 P.2d 631 (1967). See Bainum v. Roundy, 21 Ariz.App. 534, 521 P.2d 633 (1974) (following *Goble*); cf. Pacific Gamble Robinson Co. v. Lapp, 95 Wn.2d 341, 622 P.2d 850 (1980) (when spouses move from non-community state to Washington, the law of their prior domicile determines what property is subject to claims for husband's separate debt incurred before the move, citing this text); Potlatch No. 1 Federal Credit Union v. Kennedy, 76 Wn.2d 806, 459 P.2d 32 (1969) (apply Washington rather than Idaho community property rule to protect Washington wife's share of community property from debt incurred by husband, court states this not a "false conflict" like *Goble*); Colorado Nat'l Bank v. Merlino, 35 Wn.App. 610, 668 P.2d 1304 (1983) (when Washington spouse signs contract in Washington to buy land in Colorado, Washington law applies to protect community property from execution to satisfy default judgment obtained in Colorado).

87. 9 N.Y.2d 554, 216 N.Y.S.2d 65, 175 N.E.2d 441 (1961).

New York, had sexual intercourse in New York with a secretary, a New York resident. The secretary became pregnant. Following the orders of the defendant's attorney, she had her baby in Chicago and there signed an agreement releasing all claims against the defendant for child support in exchange for the defendant's promise to pay her $275 per month until the child was sixteen. The agreement recited that it "shall in all respects be interpreted, construed and governed by the laws of the State of Illinois." The mother then went to California where she stayed for two years before resuming her New York residence. The defendant supported the mother and child in compliance with the agreement and made large additional payments.

The mother commenced support proceedings against the defendant in New York. Under Illinois law, the support agreement was binding. Under New York law, the agreement was subject to judicial review for fairness. The Court of Appeals affirmed dismissal of the proceedings. Illinois law governed because, in the light of the large number of contacts with Illinois, Illinois was "the 'center of gravity' of this agreement."[88] It may well be that the support agreement in issue, especially in view of the father's substantial additional payments, would have passed muster under New York's rule providing for judicial scrutiny of support agreements and that there was thus no conflict for the New York court to resolve. But if there were a conflict, to suggest that the lawyer-manufactured contacts, including particularly the choice-of-law clause, would control, is to exalt a rigid formalism above New York's interest in the welfare of the child and the mother.

Article 4 of the Rome Regulation[89] chooses law when the parties have not exercised their power under article 3 to select the law:

Applicable law in the absence of choice

1. To the extent that the law applicable to the contract has not been chosen in accordance with Article 3 and without prejudice to Articles 5 to 8, the law governing the contract shall be determined as follows:

(a) a contract for the sale of goods shall be governed by the law of the country where the seller has his habitual residence;

(b) a contract for the provision of services shall be governed by the law of the country where the service provider has his habitual residence;

(c) a contract relating to a right *in rem* in immovable property or to a tenancy of immovable property shall be governed by the law of the country where the property is situated;

---

88. Id. at 560, 216 N.Y.S.2d at 69, 175 N.E.2d at 444; cf. In re Adoption of MM, 652 P.2d 974 (Wyo.1982) (under most significant relationship test, court applies law of forum where adoptive parents reside, not law of New York where natural mother resides and child born, and adoption agreement cannot be rescinded).

89. See supra note 27.

(d) notwithstanding point (c) a tenancy of immovable property concluded for temporary private use for a period of no more than six consecutive months shall be governed by the law of the country where the landlord has his habitual residence, provided that the tenant is a natural person and has his habitual residence in the same country;

(e) a franchise contract shall be governed by the law of the country where the franchisee has his habitual residence;

(f) a distribution contract shall be governed by the law of the country where the distributor has his habitual residence; goods by auction shall be governed by the law of the country where the auction takes place, if such a place can be determined;

(g) a contract for the sale of goods by auction shall be governed by the law of the country where the auction takes place, if such a place can be determined;

(h) a contract concluded within a multilateral system which brings together or facilitates the bringing together of multiple third-party buying and selling interests in financial instruments, as defined by Article 4(1), point (17) of Directive 2004/39/EC, in accordance with non-discretionary rules and governed by a single law, shall be governed by that law.

2.   Where the contract is not covered by paragraph 1 or where the elements of the contract would be covered by more than one of points (a) to (h) of paragraph 1, the contract shall be governed by the law of the country where the party required to effect the characteristic performance of the contract has his habitual residence.

3.   Where it is clear from all the circumstances of the case that the contract is manifestly more closely connected with a country other than that indicated in paragraphs 1 or 2, the law of that other country shall apply.

4.   Where the law applicable cannot be determined pursuant to paragraphs 1 or 2, the contract shall be governed by the law of the country with which it is most closely connected.

In the absence of choice of law by the parties, article 4 chooses "the law of the country with which it is most closely connected." Subsections 1 and 2 create presumptions as to the identity of that country. These presumptions are subject to rebuttal under subsection 3 "[w]here it is clear from all the circumstances of the case that the contract is manifestly more closely connected with a country other than that indicated in paragraphs 1 or 2." "Most closely connected" is a vague metaphor that cannot be empirically tested. Article 4 would do better to take a consequences-based approach keyed to impairment or non-impairment of the policies underlying the different law of the countries having contacts with the parties and the transaction. Ironically this is the focus of the language in article 9(3) dealing with when internationally mandatory rules of countries other than the forum trump the law otherwise chosen by articles 3 and 4: "regard shall be had to their nature and purpose and to the consequences of their application or non-application."

Subsection 1(c), creating that a presumption in favor of the situs in a contract dealing with immovable property, is especially undesirable. The situs qua situs is unlikely to have a policy that would be impaired if its law is not applied to the various issues which article 12 lists as within the scope of the law selected by the regulation including interpretation, time limitations on suit for breach, and remedies for breach.[90] Subsection 1(c) is surprising because civil countries are free of the situs myth that has infected common law countries and do not apply the law of the situs to issues such as testate and intestate succession to realty.[91]

Article 8(3) of the Japanese Act on the General Rules of Application of Laws[92] also creates a presumption that the law of the situs applies to "the formation and effect of a juristic act" concerning immovables.

§ 7.3E Apply the Law of the Forum

As indicated above,[93] the basic choice-of-law rule of the Uniform Commercial Code is one permitting the parties to choose a law having a "reasonable relation" to the transaction. The Code then provides that "[f]ailing such agreement this Act applies to transactions bearing an appropriate relation" to the forum to justify such insistence on forum law "is left to judicial decision."[94] The forum is invited to be freer in applying its own Code than it would ordinarily be in applying other forum law not as distinguished as is the Code "by its comprehensiveness . . . and by the fact that it is in large part a reformulation and restatement of the law merchant and of the understanding of a business community which transcends state and even national boundaries."[95]

There may have been some basis for such preference for the forum's Uniform Commercial Code when conflicts were likely between a state that had adopted the Code and one that had not yet adopted it. Today, however, all states have adopted a version of the Uniform Commercial Code.[96] There are, in the various state versions, numerous variations from the official text.[97] Moreover, even if two states have what appears to be an identical Code section, variations in construction and applica-

---

90. See § 8.22.

91. See Droz, *Commentary on the Questionnaire on Succession in Private International Law*, in II Proceedings of the 16th Session, Hague Conference on Private International Law 19–29; van Loon, *Update of the Commentary with Special Reference to Recent Laws and Drafts Concerning Private International Law*, id. at 107–111 (1990).

92. Law No. 10 of 1898 as newly titled and amended 21 June 2006.

93. See text accompanying note 24.

94. Uniform Commercial Code § 1–105, Official Comment 3.

95. Id. For an example of a strong preference for forum law under the "appropriate relation" standard, see Cherry Creek Dodge, Inc. v. Carter, 733 P.2d 1024 (Wyo. 1987).

96. Louisiana has not adopted Articles 2 (Sales) or 2A (Leases).

97. See Permanent Editorial Board (PEB) for the Uniform Commercial Code, Report No. 2, at 11 (1965) ("far too many unofficial amendments were enacted"): Minutes of PEB meeting of April 8, 2004, agenda item 2 re enactment of Revised Article 1: "typically

tion of the section are likely to occur despite the presence of a Permanent Editorial Board and the Code's injunction (Section 1–102(1), (2)(c)) to construe with uniformity as a goal.[98] Therefore the forum-favoring rule of the second sentence of 1–105 will have its greatest operation between two states of the United States that have, through differences in enactment or construction, disparate versions of the Code provision in issue.

Under such circumstances it is not tenable to defend, as does the official Code comment, the widest possible application of the forum's rule on the ground that it is better attuned to the needs of a modern commercial community than the competing foreign rule. The other application of the second sentence of section 1–105 will be in international conflicts cases. Blanket insistence on application of the law of the American forum is likely to impress our foreign trading partners as parochial. It is desirable, therefore, that the words "appropriate relation" be construed, despite the official comment, so as to reach functional rather than parochial results.[99]

Closely related to the forum-centered rule of the Uniform Commercial Code is the suggestion advanced by the late Brainerd Currie that, if functional analysis of a conflict problem reveals it to be a "true" conflict, the forum should apply its own rule.[100] This is because, if the forum and

[enactments] have not followed the official text with respect to conflict of laws issues ... and ... in some states, the former definition of 'good faith' has been retained."

98. See Slavenburg Corp. v. Kenli Corp., 36 U.C.C.R.Serv. 8 (E.D.Pa.1983) (choice of law necessary under 1–105 because New York and Pennsylvania interpret 1–207 differently).

99. See General Electric Credit Corp. v. R.A. Heintz Constr. Co., 302 F.Supp. 958, 962 (D.Or.1969) ("appropriate relation" has the same meaning as "significant contacts"); Travenol Laboratories, Inc. v. Zotal, Ltd., 394 Mass. 95, 474 N.E.2d 1070 (1985) ("appropriate relation" means "most significant relationship"); Boudreau v. Baughman, 322 N.C. 331, 368 S.E.2d 849 (1988) (same); Collins Radio Co. of Dallas v. Bell, 623 P.2d 1039 (Okl.App.1980), cert. denied (Okl.1981) ("appropriate relation" is the same as the most significant relationship test of Restatement Second); Nordstrom & Ramerman, *The Uniform Commercial Code and the Choice of Law*, 1969 Duke L. J. 623, 641; Siegel, *The U.C.C. and Choice of Law: Forum Choice or Forum Law?*, 21 Amer.U. L. Rev. 494, 496, 506–07 (1972); Note, *Conflict of Laws and the "Appropriate Relation" Test of Section 1–105 of the Uniform Commercial Code*, 40 Geo.Wash. L. Rev. 797, 799, 802–03 (collecting state comments to 1–105 some of which refer to 1–105(1) as strongly forum oriented and some of which indicate no change in prior conflicts approaches).

But see the following cases finding an "appropriate relation" with the forum based on physical contacts there without policy analysis: Barclays Discount Bank Ltd. v. Levy, 743 F.2d 722 (9th Cir.1984) (whether holder to whom note negotiated in Israel held in due course); Mann v. Weyerhaeuser Co., 703 F.2d 272 (8th Cir.1983) (privity requirement of Nebraska forum applied to prevent action by Iowa commercial buyer); Whitaker v. Harvell-Kilgore Corp., 418 F.2d 1010 (5th Cir.1969) (apply Georgia privity requirement to prevent recovery by soldier injured there by grenade manufactured and sold elsewhere); Bernick v. Jurden, 306 N.C. 435, 293 S.E.2d 405 (1982) (1–105 changes North Carolina conflicts rules and forum law applies to hockey player injured there to determine whether privity necessary to recover for breach of warranty although product purchased elsewhere); cf. Madaus v. November Hill Farm, Inc., 630 F.Supp. 1246 (W.D.Va. 1986) (no indication that "appropriate relation" supersedes Virginia's established rule that the law of the place of performance governs issues of performance).

100. Currie, *Survival of Actions: Adjudication versus Automation in the Conflict of Laws*, 10 Stan. L. Rev. 205, 245 (1958); cf. Frank Briscoe Co., Inc. v. Georgia Sprinkler Co.,

a foreign state each have a domestic rule, the underlying policies of which are applicable to the interstate case in issue, it is improper for a court to give effect to the policies of another state in preference to those of its own state. Professor Currie did urge that the forum should, whenever possible, avoid the decision that there was a true conflict. This avoidance is achieved by a "moderate and restrained interpretation"[101] of the forum's own law and policies so that a court would not extend them to cover all hypothetically possible forum interests, but only those policies actually represented by the forum's laws. If, however, in light of this "moderate and restrained interpretation" of forum law, a real conflict remained, the only proper solution for a court was to apply the forum's law.

Lilienthal v. Kaufman[102] illustrates this forum-preference reasoning. After a court at his Oregon residence had declared the defendant a spendthrift, he journeyed to California. There he borrowed money from the plaintiff, a California resident, to finance a business venture. The California creditor was unaware that the defendant had been declared a spendthrift and placed under guardianship. Under Oregon but not California law, the guardian could avoid the obligation of the spendthrift. When the California creditor brought suit against the spendthrift in Oregon, the guardian declared void the promissory note executed and payable in California. The Supreme Court of Oregon affirmed a judgment for the defendant under Oregon's spendthrift law reasoning that:

> We have, then, two jurisdictions, each with several close connections with the transaction, and each with a substantial interest, which will be served or thwarted, depending upon which law is applied. The interests of neither jurisdiction are clearly more important than those of the other. We are of the opinion that in such a case the public policy of Oregon should prevail and the law of Oregon should be applied; we should apply that choice-of-rule which will 'advance the policies or interests of' Oregon.[103]

By the same reasoning, of course, if the case were litigated in a California court, that court would have reached an opposite result.

The *Lilienthal* decision may be explained in part by the fact that the previous year an Oregon creditor suing the same spendthrift under circumstances that, except for the extra-state contacts, were the same, had been unable to recover the money loaned.[104] The court may have felt reluctant to treat a California creditor better than an Oregon creditor. Nevertheless, the main purpose of conflicts analysis is to determine

---

Inc., 713 F.2d 1500 (11th Cir.1983) (although under Georgia conflicts rules an insurance contract is construed under the law of the place of delivery and that was New Jersey, Georgia common law applies rather than the common law of another state) [compare the discussion of Swift v. Tyson, 41 U.S. (16 Pet.) 1, 10 L.Ed. 865 (1842) § 10.2].

101. Currie, *The Disinterested* Third State, 28 Law & Contemp.Prob. 754, 757 (1963).

102. 239 Or. 1, 395 P.2d 543 (1964).

103. Id. at 16, 395 P.2d at 549.

104. Olshen v. Kaufman, 235 Or. 423, 385 P.2d 161 (1963).

when an interstate case should be decided differently than a completely domestic case. In the prior case involving the Oregon creditor, there was no way for the court to avoid application of the Oregon spendthrift law short of holding the Oregon statute unconstitutional. In *Lilienthal*, faced, as the court noted, with a true clash of policies underlying different domestic laws, the court was free to seek a way of resolving this conflict that was in keeping with the proper behavior of states in a federal nation when dealing with interstate commercial transactions. Was the Oregon spendthrift law unusual? Was the California creditor unfairly surprised? What is the preferred national solution that should be acceptable to any forum trying this case? These were questions that were appropriate in the interstate case although foreclosed by the legislature in the wholly Oregon case. Proper responses would have prevented the *Lilienthal* result.[105] The Oregon legislature has enacted a comprehensive choice-of-law code for contracts that would have prevented the result in *Lilienthal* because of unfair surprise to the California creditor.[106]

There is some indication that the Oregon court has repented of its decision in *Lilienthal*. *Casey v. Manson Construction and Engineering Company*[107] was an action by Mrs. Casey to recover for the loss of consortium sustained as a result of an injury suffered by her husband in the State of Washington. The Caseys were domiciled in Oregon. Manson and Osberg, two Washington companies that also did business in Oregon, formed a joint venture to construct a dam in Washington about 60 miles from the Oregon border. Plaintiff's husband, a business invitee,

---

105. See D. Cavers, The Choice-of-Law Process 192 (1965) (disapproving of result in *Lilienthal*); cf. Baade, *Counter–Revolution or* Alliance *for Progress? Reflections on Reading Cavers, the Choice-of-law Process*, 46 Texas L. Rev. 141, 160 (1967): "If California had a modern long-arm statute covering contracts to be performed by natural persons, Mr. Lilienthal could have sued at home. He would undoubtedly have recovered; and the judgment—whatever the law applied to the claim underlying it—would have been entitled to full faith and credit in Oregon."

Cf. R. Cramton, D. Currie, H. Kay, Conflict of Laws 253 (4th ed. 1987) (two Portland banks that had investigated Kaufman's credit for Lilienthal reported it good and did not mention that Kaufman had been declared a spendthrift). But see Kramer, *Rethinking Choice of Law*, 90 Colum. L. Rev. 277, 323 (1990) ("*Lilienthal* was correctly decided, but for the wrong reasons"); Weinberg, *On Departing From Forum Law*, 35 Mercer L. Rev. 595, 605 (1984) (the *Lilienthal* decision "is not an unreasonable result, as long as little could be done to eliminate the defense for domestic as well as interstate cases").

For other cases insisting on applying forum law, see Davis v. Ebsco Indus., Inc., 150 So.2d 460, 463–64 (Fla.Dist.Ct.App.1963) (refuse to enforce in the forum a contract not to compete because it is "contrary to public policy of the forum"); Lowe v. Jones, 414 Pa. 466, 469–670, 200 A.2d 880, 882 (1964) (refuse to permit garnishment of payments from pension fund administered at the forum, upholding the fund's spendthrift clause in favor of a nonresident beneficiary).

106. O.R.S. § 81.112(2): "A party that lacks capacity to enter into a contract under the law of the state in which the party resides may assert that incapacity against a party that knew or should have known of the incapacity at the time the parties entered into the contract." Cf. art. 4(2) of the Japanese Act on the General Rules of Application of Laws, Law No. 10 of 1898 as newly titled and amended 21 June 2006, applies the law of the place where a juristic act is performed to determine a person's legal capacity if all the parties are situated there.

107. 247 Or. 274, 428 P.2d 898 (1967).

was injured while driving a tractor loaded with pipe on an access road to the construction site. The access road gave way causing the tractor to tip over into a deep ravine. Washington adhered to the common law rule that denied to a wife a right of action for the loss of her husband's consortium. Oregon conferred such a right by statute. The court recognized that Washington's policies were applicable to protect the Washington defendants from liability and that Oregon's policies were relevant to compensate the Oregon wife for the consequences of her husband's injuries. Nevertheless, the court applied Washington law as that of the state having "the most significant relationship with the occurrence and with the parties"[108] and affirmed a judgment for the defendant declaring that:

> The view has been expressed, though not, so far as we are aware, by any court,[109] that if both the forum state and the foreign state have legitimate interests in the application of their laws the court should apply the law of the forum: Currie, Selected Essays on the Conflict of Laws, 189. That, it would seem, is the policy expressed in the Uniform Commercial Code with respect to transactions controlled by that enactment.... Nevertheless, we are warned by highly regarded authority that "[s]tate chauvinism and interstate retaliation are dangers to be avoided": Clark v. Clark [222 A.2d 205, 208 (N.H.1966)]....[110]

Perhaps the court could have reached the same result by deciding that in the light of the fact that the husband was not an employee of the defendants, there were not sufficient contacts with Oregon to make it reasonable to apply Oregon law to Manson or to Osberg.

Moreover if, as the court states, "state chauvinism and interstate retaliation" are not to prevail in conflicts analysis, there will have to be rational bases for the resolution of true conflicts concerning the validity of interstate contracts. These bases for conflict resolution must also be so objective and fair that they can be expected to be applied by any forum, even one whose local law would be compelled to yield under their application. Sections 7.4A through 7.4F attempt to articulate such standards.

§ 7.4   Rational Bases for Resolving True Conflicts Concerning the Validity of Contracts

As the title to this section indicates, we are here concerned only with validity problems that create "true" conflicts. That is, one state, because of some contact with the parties or with the transaction, would advance the policies underlying its rule invalidating the contract and

---

108.   428 P.2d at 907.

109.   But see the quotation from the *Lilienthal* case in the text accompanying note 103 supra.

110.   *Casey*, 428 P.2d at 907. But see Straight Grain Builders v. Track N' Trail, 93 Or.App. 86, 760 P.2d 1350 (1988), rev. den. 307 Or. 246, 767 P.2d 76 (1988) (method of resolving real conflict is in favor of Oregon law, quoting *Lilienthal*).

another contact state has a legitimate interest in upholding this particular interstate transaction. The following bases, drawn largely from some of the classic conflicts decisions, are suggested for the resolution of true conflicts-contracts-validity problems.

§ 7.4A   A Rebuttable Presumption of Validity

The party autonomy rule that has emerged in choice-of-law rules and codes both in the U.S. and abroad reflects a legitimate concern for facilitating the planning of interstate and international commercial transactions. This purpose is also served by a rebuttable presumption that the contract will be valid under the local law of any contact state provided that the validating policies underlying that law will be advanced by application to the transaction in issue.[111] This presumption gives the parties the benefits that they would receive under a party autonomy rule except a rule, such as that of the Rome Regulation, which permits a choice of the law of an unconnected jurisdiction to validate. The presumption of validity does not limit the search for validating law to a single state named in a choice-of-law clause and focuses on a policy that all states share—making commercial transactions convenient and reliable by enforcing commercial contracts in the absence of compelling countervailing considerations articulated in a particular invalidating rule.[112]

---

111. For discussion of a choice-of-law rule that would select law with the purpose of validating a contract whenever reasonable to do so, see Kossick v. United Fruit Co., 365 U.S. 731, 741, 81 S.Ct. 886, 893, 6 L.Ed.2d 56, 64 (1961); Dailey v. Transitron Electronic Corp., 475 F.2d 12 (5th Cir.1973); Credit Bur. Management Co. v. Huie, 254 F.Supp. 547, 553–56 (E.D.Ark.1966); Cook Associates, Inc. v. Colonial Broach & Mach. Co., 14 Ill.App.3d 965, 304 N.E.2d 27 (1973); G. Stumberg, Conflict of Laws, 239 (3d Ed.1963); Ehrenzweig, *The Statute of Frauds in the Conflict of Laws: The Basic Rule of Validation*, 59 Colum. L. Rev. 874, 875–80 (1959); Reese, *Some Thoughts on the Drafting of Choice-of-Law Rules*, in International Law at the Time of Its Codification—Essays in Honour of Roberto Ago, 249, 253 (1987) ("absent strong countervailing considerations, the court will seek to apply a law that would uphold the contract"); cf. Briggs, *An Institutional Approach to Conflict of Laws: "Law and Reason" versus Professor Ehrenzweig*, 12 U.C.L.A. L. Rev. 29, 48–67 (1964); Currie, *Ehrenzweig and the Statute of Frauds: An Inquiry into the "Rule of Validation"*, 18 Okl. L. Rev. 243, 339 (1965); Leflar, *Conflict of Laws Contracts, and the New Restatement*, 15 Ark. L. Rev. 163, 172 (1961).

For an example of application of the validating law, see Northrop Corp. v. Triad Int'l Marketing S.A., 811 F.2d 1265 (9th Cir.1987), cert. denied, 484 U.S. 914, 108 S.Ct. 261, 98 L.Ed.2d 219 (1987), order amended, 842 F.2d 1154 (9th Cir.1988) (contract to pay commission on sales to Saudi airforce enforced although commission illegal under Saudi law). But see Wong v. Tenneco, Inc., 39 Cal.3d 126, 216 Cal.Rptr. 412, 702 P.2d 570 (1985) (refuse to enforce produce-marketing contact illegal under Mexican law where California grower's farm was located); Miller v. Fallon County, 222 Mont. 214, 721 P.2d 342 (1986) (invalidate a waiver of liability agreement between nonresidents when accident occurred while driving through Montana).

112. See Woods–Tucker Leasing Corp. v. Hutcheson–Ingram Dev. Co., 626 F.2d 401 (5th Cir.1980), vac'd, 642 F.2d 744 (5th Cir.1981). In *Woods–Tucker*, which concerned choice of law for usury, the court refused to give effect to a clause selecting the law of the lender's state. Some of the largest commercial law firms in Texas, the borrower's state, filed amicus briefs with the court urging a rehearing and a different result on the ground that the opinion would have a disastrous impact on Texas commercial borrowers. On rehearing, the court vacated the previous opinion and gave effect to the choice-of-law clause. The loan may have been usurious under the law of either state, but if this were so, the penalties under the law of the lender's state were less. But see Sedler, *Interest Analysis*

§ 7.4B Anachronism

Some rules invalidating contracts, such as, formerly in the U.S., a rule depriving a married woman of the capacity to contract, are anachronistic lags in the development of a state's law. They run counter to objectively determinable trends in the development of contract law, trends that are very likely to be generally shared by the two states whose domestic rules on a particular issue are in conflict. Resolution of the conflict in favor of the validating rule and away from the anachronistic invalidating rule is the solution that any forum should prefer, even the forum with the invalidating rule.[113] A similar result should be reached if, as in *Lilienthal v. Kaufman*, the invalidating rule is aberrational.[114] The anachronism standard is not dependent on subjective judgments as to which law is "better."[115] One need not agree that a particular general trend in the law of contracts is socially desirable in order to be able to determine whether or not the trend exists.

This suggestion that courts resolve conflicts in accordance with widely shared substantive developments is not a new concept. The Massachusetts Supreme Judicial Court, in *Milliken v. Pratt*, when holding that the Maine validating rule did not violate Massachusetts public policy, noted the trend in the law regarding the contractual capacity of married women.[116]

Not all invalidating rules are anachronistic. Sometimes an invalidating rule represents a viable trend in the law of contracts. Contract doctrine has shown increasing concern for protecting the party in a markedly inferior bargaining position.[117] The Uniform Commercial Code provision giving a court authority to refuse to enforce an "unconscionable" contract or clause also seems to mirror this concern.[118] If the

---

and Forum Preference in the Conflict of Laws: A Response to the "New Critics", 34 Mercer L. Rev. 593, 602 (1983): "The decision of a court in a particular conflicts case, or for that matter, all the decisions of all the courts in all the conflicts cases that arise, will have no effect at all on the 'harmonious relations between states' or on 'commercial intercourse between them.' The cases are simply too few in number to make any difference."

113. See Cheatham & Reese, *Choice of the Applicable Law*, 52 Colum. L. Rev. 959, 980 (1952).

114. See supra notes 102–106 and accompanying text.

115. Cf. Haines v. Mid–Century Ins. Co., 47 Wis.2d 442, 177 N.W.2d 328 (1970) (invalidate clause excluding liability to member of same household when wife injured in Wisconsin has since moved to Wisconsin and Wisconsin invalidating rule is "better rule of law" than that of Minnesota where policy issued). But see Urhammer v. Olson, 39 Wis.2d 447, 159 N.W.2d 688 (1968) (enforce such a clause in case where wife had not become Wisconsin resident).

116. See supra text § 7.3A accompanying note 17.

117. See Henningsen v. Bloomfield Motors, Inc., 32 N.J. 358, 404, 161 A.2d 69, 95 (1960), where the court articulated such a concern: "The lawmakers did not authorize the automobile manufacturer to use its grossly disproportionate bargaining power to relieve itself from liability and to impose on the ordinary buyer, who in effect has no real freedom of choice, the grave danger of injury to himself and others that attends the sale of such a dangerous s instrumentality as a defectively made automobile."

118. Uniform Commercial Code § 2–302. But cf. id. at Comment 1, which states: "The principle is one of the prevention of oppression and unfair surprise ... and not of disturbance of allocation of risks because of superior bargaining power."

invalidating rule is of a kind designed to protect against the harsher consequences of adhesion contracts, it will serve to rebut the presumption of validity.

The importance of the adhesion factor[119] in resolving interstate conflicts concerning the validity of contracts is well illustrated in the usury cases. The Second Restatement, reflecting a long line of judicial

---

119. For cases in which the adhesion factor has influenced choice of law, see, e.g., Boat Town U.S.A., Inc. v. Mercury Marine Div. of Brunswick Corp., 364 So.2d 15, 18 (Fla.App. 1978) (Wisconsin fair dealership law applicable to protect a Florida dealer because Wisconsin has an interest in controlling the Wisconsin supplier "to prevent overreaching"); Lewkowicz v. El Paso Apparel Corp., 625 S.W.2d 301 (Tex.1981) (an agreement and judgment by consent obtained while defendant was imprisoned in Mexico and in exchange for dropping charges is not enforceable in Texas because against public policy as constituting compounding a felony if done in Texas).

For influence of the adhesion factor in **life insurance** cases, see Zogg v. Penn Mut. Life Ins. Co., 276 F.2d 861, 864 (2d Cir.1960) ("If any trend is discernible in these cases, it is that of a forum to apply its own law to adhesion contracts of insurance entered into by its residents."); Daniels v. National Home Life Assur. Co., 103 Nev. 674, 747 P.2d 897 (1987) (distinguishing this "franchise insurance" from group insurance, because there was no employer here to negotiate on behalf of the insured).

Litigation concerning **group insurance** policies, bargained for by an employer on behalf of many employees, has typically resulted in applying the law of the state where the policy was issued or the law stipulated in the policy. Perhaps this is in part due to the greater bargaining power of the employer. See Assicurazioni Generali, S.P.A. v. Clover, 195 F.3d 161, 165 (3d Cir. 1999) (giving effect to choice-of-law provision in policy and stating that "a choice of law made by the insurer is less suspect in the group insurance context as the greater bargaining leverage possessed by the group agent should protect the insureds from unfavorable law"); Pound v. Insurance Co. of North Amer., 439 F.2d 1059 (10th Cir.1971) (policy construed under law of place where master policy issued to employer, not where employee resided); Hofeld v. Nationwide Life Ins. Co., 59 Ill.2d 522, 322 N.E.2d 454 (1975) (give effect to choice-of-law clause in policy); Simms v. Metropolitan Life Ins. Co., 9 Kan.App.2d 640, 685 P.2d 321 (1984) (group health policy construed by law of place where it was made and this is where the master policy was delivered); Miller v. Home Ins. Co., 605 S.W.2d 778 (Mo.1980) (law of place where employer has principal place of business, not law of employee's domicile, governs validity of group accident policy, but recovery not available under either law); Woelfling v. Great–West Life Assur. Co., 30 Ohio App.2d 211, 285 N.E.2d 61 (1972) (give effect to choice-of-law clause); cf. H.S. Equities, Inc. v. Hartford Accident & Idem. Co., 334 So.2d 573 (Fla.1976) (policy covering liability of insured to its clients—apply law of state where policy issued to determine effect of late notice of loss, not state where loss occurred). But see Krauss v. Manhattan Life Ins. Co. of New York, 643 F.2d 98 (2d Cir.1981) (law of New York where master life policy delivered does not apply to permit recovery by an Illinois domiciliary because New York has no interest in recovery); Harrison v. Insurance Co. of N. Amer., 294 Ala. 387, 318 So.2d 253 (1975) (apply law of employee's residence under which he did not receive sufficient notice of a change in policy terms); Breeding v. Massachusetts Indem. & Life Ins. Co., 633 S.W.2d 717 (Ky.1982) (apply law of place where car rented to invalidate exclusion rather than law of renter's headquarters, applying most significant relationship test); Guardian Life Ins. Co. of America v. Insurance Comm'r of Md., 293 Md. 629, 446 A.2d 1140 (1982) (cannot avoid mandatory coverage by setting up an out-of-state insurance trust that does not qualify as a multiple-employer trust permitted under Maryland law); The Travelers Ins. Co. v. Fields, 451 F.2d 1292 (6th Cir.1971), cert. denied, 406 U.S. 919, 92 S.Ct. 1772, 32 L.Ed.2d 118 (1972) (law of state where divorce obtained, not law of state where group policy issued, determines whether divorce decree abrogated divorced wife's interest as named beneficiary).

For an apparent failure to advert to the adhesion aspects of the contract, see Sayers v. International Drilling Co., [1971] 3 All E.R. 163, [1971] 1 W.L.R. 1176 (Ct. of Appeal) (enforce English employee's agreement to accept compensation payments in lieu of cause of action for injury applying Dutch law applicable to "international" contracts, although such a promise would be unenforceable under the domestic law of both England and Holland— employer is a Dutch company drilling off the coast of Nigeria).

decisions,[120] applies the validating law of any state with which "the contract has a substantial relationship."[121] The Restatement's usury

120. The classic case is Seeman v. Philadelphia Warehouse Co., 274 U.S. 403, 47 S.Ct. 626, 71 L.Ed. 1123 (1927). For other cases choosing law so as to uphold a loan agreement against a charge of usury, see Woods–Tucker Leasing Corp. of Ga. v. Hutcheson–Ingram Devel. Co., 642 F.2d 744 (5th Cir.1981) (Texas, give effect to choice-of-law clause); Moody v. Bass, 357 F.2d 730, 732 (6th Cir.1966) (place of making); Consolidated Jewelers, Inc. v. Standard Fin. Corp., 325 F.2d 31, 34–35 (6th Cir.1963) (law stipulated by parties, transaction having substantial connection with state indicated); Fahs v. Martin, 224 F.2d 387, 397–399 (5th Cir.1955) (income tax refund granted, interest being valid under applicable state law chosen by alternative-reference validating rule); Arkansas Appliance Distributing Co. v. Tandy Electronics, Inc., 292 Ark. 482, 730 S.W.2d 899 (1987) (apply choice-of-law clause to validate against charge or usury); Stacy v. St. Charles Custom Kitchens, 284 Ark. 441, 683 S.W.2d 225 (1985) (alternative reference to validate against charge of usury); Ury v. Jewelers Acceptance Corp., 227 Cal.App.2d 11, 17–18, 38 Cal.Rptr. 376, 380–81 (Dist.Ct.App.1964) (law stipulated by parties, transaction having substantial connection with state indicated); Peragallo v. Sklat, 39 Conn.Supp. 510, 466 A.2d 1200 (App.1983); Continental Mortgage Investors v. Sailboat Key, Inc., 395 So.2d 507 (Fla.1981); Dairy Equipment Co. v. Boehme, 92 Idaho 301, 442 P.2d 437 (1968) (in absence of attempt to evade forum law); West Side Motor Express, Inc. v. Finance Discount Corp., 340 Mass. 669, 671, 165 N.E.2d 903, 904 (1960) (follow reference of whole law of place of making to law of state where mortgage security located); Green v. Northwestern Trust Co., 128 Minn. 30, 37–39, 150 N.W. 229, 232 (1914) (law of state where transaction has substantial connection, location of land securing debt); Ferdie Sievers & Lake Tahoe Land Co., Inc. v. Diversified Mortgage Investors, 95 Nev. 811, 603 P.2d 270 (1979) (validate under chosen law with which substantial relationship); Anderson v. Taurus Financial Corp., 268 N.W.2d 486 (S.D.1978); Goodwin Bros. Leasing, Inc. v. H & B Inc., 597 S.W.2d 303 (Tenn.1980) (validate under law chosen); High Fashion Wigs Profit Sharing Trust v. Hamilton Investment Trust, 579 S.W.2d 300 (Tex.Civ.App.—Eastland 1979) (validate under law chosen with which there is a reasonable relationship); Pioneer Credit Corp. v. Carden, 127 Vt. 229, 245 A.2d 891 (1968) (forum usury law not applicable in absence of attempt to evade forum law unless contract both made and to be performed in forum, but in absence of proof to the contrary, presume that foreign law is the same as forum law). But see Equilease Corp. v. Belk Hotel Corp., 42 N.C.App. 436, 256 S.E.2d 836 (1979), review denied, 298 N.C. 568, 261 S.E.2d 121 (1979) (apply forum law to invalidate when loan secured by forum realty); Commercial Credit Equipment Corp. v. West, 677 S.W.2d 669 (Tex.App—Amarillo, 1984, writ ref'd n.r.e.), disagreed with on another issue, Coppedge v. Colonial Sav. & L. Ass'n, 721 S.W.2d 933 (Tex.App.—Dallas, 1986, writ ref'd n.r.e.) (apply "most significant relationship" test to declare loan to purchase an airplane was usurious under Texas law and assess triple damages and attorney's fees); General Electric Co. v. Keyser, 166 W.Va. 456, 275 S.E.2d 289 (1981) (refuse to validate under law chosen when no contact with that state except lender's incorporation).

There is authority that if the interest is usurious under the laws of all contact states, the law should be applied that provides the lightest penalty. See Woods–Tucker Leasing Corp. of Ga. v. Hutcheson–Ingram Devel. Co., 642 F.2d 744 (5th Cir.1981) (Texas rule); Speare v. Consolidated Assets Corp., 367 F.2d 208 (2d Cir.1966) (New York conflicts rule); Wiltsek v. Anglo–American Properties, Inc., 277 F.Supp. 78 (S.D.N.Y.1967); Continental Mortgage Investors v. Sailboat Key, Inc., 395 So.2d 507, 513 n.9 (Fla.1981); Wood v. Sadler, 93 Idaho 552, 468 P.2d 42 (1970); Restatement (Second) § 203, comment d.

A number of cases concern the special problem of interest on the margin accounts of customers of brokerage houses. Most cases have validated under the law chosen in the brokerage contract. Zerman v. Ball, 735 F.2d 15 (2d Cir.1984) (New York rule); U.S. Manganese Corp. v. Merrill Lynch, Pierce, Fenner & Smith, Inc., 576 F.2d 153 (8th Cir.1978) (Arkansas rule); Gamer v. DuPont Glore Forgan, Inc., 65 Cal.App.3d 280, 135 Cal.Rptr. 230 (1976); Mell v. Goodbody & Co., 10 Ill.App.3d 809, 295 N.E.2d 97 (1973); Black v. Kidder Peabody & Co., Inc., 559 S.W.2d 669 (Tex.Civ.App.1977). See also Shull v. Dain, Kalman & Quail Inc., 201 Neb. 260, 267 N.W.2d 517 (1978) (validated under law of broker's home office). To the contrary is O'Brien v. Shearson Hayden Stone, Inc., 93 Wn.2d 51, 605 P.2d 779 (1980) (refuse to validate under chosen New York law when no interest stipulated in contract and under New York law interest might be greatly in excess of that permitted in Washington).

121. Restatement (Second) § 203.

section, however, is "uncertain"[122] whether the same support should be accorded loans interdicted by small loan statutes as distinguished from general usury statutes. This uncertainty is warranted in view of the distinction between small loan and general usury statutes drawn in some cases,[123] and by many of the special statutory choice-of-law provisions governing small loans.[124] One difference between general commercial loans and small loans is that the former may, or may not, be contracts of adhesion, depending on the circumstances of the parties, but the latter, the small loan to the necessitous consumer-borrower, is almost surely one whose terms are dictated by the lender to one who has not the social or economic power to demur.

§ 7.4C   Is the Difference between the Validating and Invalidating Rule One of Detail or Basic Policy?

The justifiable difference in treatment between commercial loan and small loan cases also illustrates another important factor that will rebut or strengthen the presumption of validity. If the difference between the conflicting rules can fairly be described as one of detailed application of the same general policy, the presumption of validity is strengthened. The contrary is true if the difference between the two laws is one of basic policy rather than detail. The general usury statutes are likely to vary little in permissible interest rates, differences of one or two percent in interest being the norm in a conflicts case.[125]

Of course, even a few percentage points can amount to a great deal of money, especially if the loan is large and repayable over a long term. Moreover, a rise or fall of a few points in the prevailing rate of interest is likely to cause substantial economic consequences.[126] But the fact that the difference in interest is slight does give a court sitting in the borrower's state some assurance that enforcement of the loan will not cause grave social consequences that the forum's law is designed to prevent and that the lender is not acting unconscionably and greedily far beyond the bounds permitted by local law.[127]

---

122.   Id. cmt. *f.*

123.   See, Kinney Loan & Fin. Co. v. Sumner, 159 Neb. 57, 66–68, 65 N.W.2d 240, 247–49 (1954); Turner v. Aldens, Inc., 179 N.J.Super. 596, 433 A.2d 439 (App.Div.1981); Whitaker v. Spiegel, Inc., 95 Wn.2d 661, 637 P.2d 235 (1981), appeal dism'd for want of substantial federal question, 454 U.S. 958, 102 S.Ct. 496, 70 L.Ed.2d 374 (1981); cf. Anderson v. Taurus Financial Corp., 268 N.W.2d 486, 489 (S.D.1978) (financing of doctor's equipment—validating rule "particularly appropriate" when borrower "not making these arrangements because he was lacking any of the necessities of life, but simply because he was seeking some savings on his federal income taxes"). But see Walker v. Associates Financial Serv. Corp., 588 S.W.2d 416 (Tex.Civ.App.—Eastland, 1979, writ ref'd n.r.e.) (apply law chosen in mail order loan contract).

For further discussion of small loan cases see §§ 7.6 and 7.7.

124.   See § 7.7.

125.   See B. Curran, Trends in Consumer Credit Legislation 15 (1965) "majority of states . . . have maximum rates between 6% and 12%".

126.   See Sedler, supra note 45 at 320.

127.   See, e.g., Ury v. Jewelers Acceptance Corp., 227 Cal.App.2d 11, 21, 38 Cal.Rptr. 376, 383 (1964) (interest charged not "unconscionable" in the light of California rates);

Small loans, on the other hand, with their higher interest, leave much more room for variations in permissible rates from state to state.[128] Moreover, because one of the purposes of small loan legislation is to prevent extortion and oppression, the states are likely to differ greatly, aside from interest rates, on just what practices the lender may employ when dealing with a necessitous borrower.[129]

Another example of a difference in laws that may represent basic policy is whether it is permissible to insure against punitive damages. The cases deciding whether to apply the law of the forum where punitive damages were awarded or the law of the state having the most significant relationship to the issuance of the insurance policy have reached inconsistent conclusions. Courts in states where the punitive damages were awarded have applied their law both to deny[130] and to permit coverage.[131] In *Fluke Corp. v. Hartford Accident & Indemnity Co.*,[132] on the other hand, when the insured sued at its principal place of business where the policy was negotiated and issued, the court permitted coverage of punitive damages awarded in California, where a statute barred coverage.

This disagreement is predictable. Both states have interests in applying their own law. The state where the insured inflicted injury and where punitive damages were awarded has an interest in precluding insurance coverage in order to deter wrongful conduct. It has an interest in permitting coverage in order to facilitate compensation awarded in its courts to its citizens. The insured's home state has an interest in applying its law. If it permits coverage, this accords with the expectation of the parties. If it denies coverage as a matter of public policy, this policy applies to corporations headquartered there and acquiring coverage there.

§ 7.4D Unfair Surprise

Any time that a provision in a contract, valid under the law of some contact state, is invalidated, the expectations of the party who would benefit from that provision are to some extent disappointed. That party is surprised. But the degree of surprise and its unfairness may differ

---

Green v. Northwestern Trust Co., 128 Minn. 30, 38, 150 N.W. 229, 232 (1914) ("no greed for interest" in the light of Minnesota rates).

128. See B. Curran, supra note 125 at 20–35.

129. Id. at 37–42.

130. See St. Paul Surplus Lines Ins. Co. v. International Playtex, Inc., 245 Kan. 258, 777 P.2d 1259, 1267 (1989), cert. denied, 493 U.S. 1036, 110 S.Ct. 758, 107 L.Ed.2d 774 (1990) ("reserve consideration of the Restatement's 'most significant relationship' test for a later day," resting choice of forum law, which precludes coverage, on public policy and on conclusion that forum, where fatally injured consumer resided, has greater interest than Delaware, where manufacturer has its principal place of business and which would permit coverage).

131. See American Home Assur. v. Safway Steel Prod., 743 S.W.2d 693 (Tex.App— Austin 1987, error denied) (applying Tex. Ins. Code Ann. art. 21.42 requiring application of Texas law to any policy of insurer doing business in Texas that is payable to Texas resident).

132. 145 Wash.2d 137, 34 P.3d 809 (2001).

markedly from one situation to another. The more unfair it is to one of the parties to invalidate some provision of the contract, the stronger the presumption of validity becomes.

At one extreme, for example, we might have a lender with an office in state X who makes a small loan to an X resident. The loan agreement provides for interest rate twenty per cent higher than that permitted under X law and requires the borrower to give the lender a power of attorney to confess judgment. X law forbids these terms. The lender also has an office in state Y under whose law the transaction would be valid. The lender arranges the transactions so that the loan is "made" and payable at the Y office.[133] The "surprise" of the lender when either an X or a Y court applies X law to invalidate the loan contract is not of an order sufficient to strengthen a presumption of validity. At the other extreme would be a transaction such as that in *Lilienthal v. Kaufman*[134] in which the Oregon borrower journeyed to California to solicit advances for a joint business venture from a California lender. The surprise of the lender in being told that the promissory notes were uncollectable because the debtor was an adjudicated Oregon spendthrift should have made the presumption of validity compelling.[135] The Oregon legislature

---

133. See § 7.6 suggesting different treatment of the lender in small loan cases depending on the lender's nexus with the borrower's home state.

134. 239 Or. 1, 395 P.2d 543 (1964) (discussed supra notes 102–106 and accompanying text).

135. See von Mehren, *Recent Trends in Choice-of-Law Methodology*, 60 Cornell L. Rev. 927, 938 (1975) (calling attention to the policies "of protecting legitimate expectations" and "the facilitation of multistate activity"); Reese, *Legislative Jurisdiction*, 78 Colum. L. Rev. 1587, 1597 (1978) (*Lilienthal* violates due process); cf. Roesgen v. American Home Prod. Corp., 719 F.2d 319 (9th Cir.1983) (refuse to apply forum law to invalidate clause valid where employee worked when employee moved to the forum after terminating employment).

The **construction and validity of automobile insurance policies** raise problems of unfairness to the insurer if the law applied is that of the place of accident rather than the place where the car is principally garaged and the insured resident. For cases applying the law of the place where the car is principally garaged, see, e.g., Moore v. United Services Auto. Assoc., 808 F.2d 1147 (5th Cir.1987) (Mississippi law); Williams v. State Farm Mut. Auto. Ins. Co., 737 F.2d 741 (8th Cir.1984) (Arkansas rule); Aetna Cas. and Sur. Co. v. Diamond, 472 So.2d 1312 (Fla.App. 3d Dist.1985); Champagne v. Ward, 893 So.2d 773 (La. 2005) (law of Mississippi, where plaintiff resided and policy issued, determines plaintiff's right to recover underinsured insurance coverage for damages resulting in collision in Louisiana with Louisiana resident); Zurich Amer. Ins. Co. v. Goodwin, 920 So.2d 427 (Miss. 2006) (apply law of Iowa where motor carrier had principal place of business to reduce recovery for Mississippi accident); State Farm Auto. Ins. Co. v. MFA Mut. Ins. Co., 671 S.W.2d 276, 277 (Mo.1984) ("[i]t would be strange indeed if contract obligations imposed by law would change whenever a state line is crossed"); State Farm Mut. Auto. Ins. Co. v. Simmons' Estate, 84 N.J. 28, 417 A.2d 488 (1980) (apply law of state where serviceman was domiciled and obtained the insurance rather than law of state where he was stationed and car crashed—dissent on ground that heavily regulated nature of business makes it unlikely that the insurer relied on law of place where policy issued); Nationwide Mut. Ins. Co. v. Ferrin, 21 Ohio St.3d 43, 487 N.E.2d 568 (1986); Caputo v. Allstate Ins. Co., 344 Pa.Super. 1, 495 A.2d 959 (1985), appeal denied (1986); cf. Diamond Int'l Corp. v. Allstate Ins. Co., 712 F.2d 1498 (1st Cir.1983) (industrial accident, New Hampshire rule); Atlanta Casualty Co. v. Gagnon, 174 Ga.App. 452, 330 S.E.2d 390 (1985) (insured not entitled to full forum no-fault benefits although he was a forum resident because policy was issued in Tennessee). But cf. Bates v. Superior Court of Maricopa County, 156 Ariz. 46, 749 P.2d 1367 (1988) (apply law of forum to which insured moved after the accident but before insurance benefits were allegedly terminated in bad faith); USAA Life Ins. Co. v. Boyce, 294 Ark. 575,

has enacted a comprehensive choice-of-law code for contracts that would have prevented the result in *Lilienthal* on precisely those grounds.[136]

It is difficult to speak of unfairly surprising a party to a contract by validating the contract, but sometimes the party wishing to enforce knows that the other party did not advert to the provision, the validity of which is in dispute.[137] This is especially likely to be true with a contract of adhesion. Such factors as adhesion and non-advertence may make it proper to resolve a conflict in favor of invalidity.

§ 7.4E How "Commercial" is the Contract?

The more commercial the context of the transaction, for example a contract between manufacturer and wholesaler, the greater the need for validation and the stronger the presumption of validity. But some "contracts" are of a distinctly noncommercial character, such as promises by uncles to pay nephews for refraining from drinking and gambling until twenty-one[138] or take-care-of-me-for-the-rest-of-my-life-and-you-can-have-the-farm-when-I-am-gone contracts. A perceptive court will draw distinctions between these kinds of arrangements in purely domestic cases in assessing proper sanctions for promise breaking and should surely do so in evaluating the rebuttable presumption of validity in conflict cases. Obviously there is no sharp line that can be drawn between a "commercial" and a "noncommercial" contract, any more than, with regard to another conflict-resolution factor suggested above, a clear distinction can be drawn between differences in laws that represent a matter of detail and differences that are matters of basic policy.[139]

---

745 S.W.2d 136 (1988) (apply forum's law to permit award of prejudgment interest and attorneys fees when insured and beneficiary were forum residents, although life insurance policy issued in Texas and insured killed while stationed in Georgia).

But for cases applying the law of the place of the crash, see, e.g., Abramson v. Aetna Cas. & Sur. Co., 76 F.3d 304 (9th Cir. 1996) (to invalidate anti-stacking provision); Wilson v. State Farm Ins. Co., 448 So.2d 1379 (La.App. 2d Cir.1984); Kemp v. Allstate Ins. Co., 183 Mont. 526, 601 P.2d 20 (1979); Hime v. State Farm Fire & Cas. Co., 284 N.W.2d 829 (Minn.1979), cert. denied, 444 U.S. 1032, 100 S.Ct. 703, 62 L.Ed.2d 668 (1980); Pate v. MFA Mut. Ins. Co., 649 P.2d 809 (Okl.App.1982); cf. Allstate Ins. Co. v. Hague, 449 U.S. 302, 101 S.Ct. 633, 66 L.Ed.2d 521 (1981) (holding constitutional applying law of state where insured worked) (discussed infra § 9.2A).

136. O.R.S. § 81.112(2): "A party that lacks capacity to enter into a contract under the law of the state in which the party resides may assert that incapacity against a party that knew or should have known of the incapacity at the time the parties entered into the contract."

137. See Oceanic Steam Nav. Co. v. Corcoran, 9 F.2d 724, 727 (2d Cir.1925). In affirming judgment for an injured passenger despite an exception clause on the ticket, the court stated: "The passengers named in the ticket did not see this ticket until the trial." But the court added: "We do not attach importance to the fact that this plaintiff never saw the ticket. . . . They are bound to know what is printed as part of the ticket."

138. Hamer v. Sidway, 124 N.Y. 538, 27 N.E. 256 (1891).

Premarital agreements are a common kind of non-commercial contract. See Lewis v. Lewis, 69 Hawaii 497, 748 P.2d 1362 (1988) (invalidate under law of new marital domicile, using "most significant relationship" analysis); cf. Uniform Premarital Agreement Act § 3(a)(7) 9C ULA 35, 43 ("[p]arties to a premarital agreement may contract with respect to . . . the choice of law governing the construction of the agreement").

139. See § 7.4C.

Whether these factors are useful in conflict resolution depends not on their litmus paper certainty, but on whether they are sufficiently objective and relevant to underlying social policies to make practicable their reasonable and sensible use by courts and lawyers.

A trio of famous statutes of frauds cases illustrates the interplay of the "commercial" and other factors in conflict resolution. Moreover, the factors enumerated above facilitate the reconciliation of the results in these three cases. The cases are *Lams v. F.H. Smith Company*,[140] *Emery v. Burbank*,[141] *and Bernkrant v. Fowler*.[142]

In *Lams*, a Delaware corporation sold securities to the plaintiffs. The contract of sale and sale were made in New York. An agent of the seller had written a letter giving the buyers a three-year resale option. The buyers sought to exercise their resale option and, upon the Delaware corporation's refusal to buy, brought suit in a Delaware court. The defendant pleaded the Delaware Statute of Frauds provision that "no action shall be brought" on any agreement not to be performed within one year from the making thereof unless there is a written memorandum of the agreement signed by the party to be charged "or some other person thereunto by him lawfully authorized in writing." New York also required that agreements running longer than one year be evidenced by a written memorandum signed by the party to be charged or the party's authorized agent, but did not require, as did Delaware, that the agent's authority be in writing. The written memorandum in this case satisfied the New York, but not the Delaware Statute of Frauds. Sustaining the plaintiff's demurrer to the plea of the Delaware statute, the court stated that although the wording of the Delaware statute, "no action shall be brought," sounded procedural and therefore applicable to any suit in Delaware, maximum protection of Delaware residents over the long run would result from construing the statute as substantive and therefore applicable only to contracts made in Delaware. This contract was not made in Delaware and hence the Delaware Statute of Frauds did not apply.

In *Emery*, the plaintiff alleged that the testatrix had made an oral agreement in Maine. The agreement provided that if the plaintiff would care for the testatrix in Massachusetts, the testatrix would bequeath property to the plaintiff. The testatrix did not keep her promise and the plaintiff brought suit in Massachusetts, the testatrix's domicile, to enforce the alleged agreement. Massachusetts, but not Maine, required a contract to make a will to be in writing. Judge Holmes affirmed a judgment for the defendant, stating that, despite the apparently "substantive" wording of the Massachusetts Statute of Frauds ("no agreement ... shall be binding, unless ... in writing"), in view of the strong interest of Massachusetts as the domicile of the testatrix in protecting

140. 36 Del. 477, 178 A. 651 (1935).

141. 163 Mass. 326, 39 N.E. 1026 (1895).

142. 55 Cal.2d 588, 12 Cal.Rptr. 266, 360 P.2d 906 (1961).

her estate against fraud and mistake, the Massachusetts statute "implies a rule of procedure broad enough to cover this case."[143]

Bernkrant also involved a contract to make a will. The testator had met with the plaintiffs in Nevada and orally promised them that, if they would refinance loans secured by the plaintiffs' Nevada realty and prepay a substantial part of their indebtedness to the testator, he would provide in his will that any indebtedness remaining at the time of his death would be canceled. The decedent's will contained no such provision and the plaintiffs brought suit against his estate to enforce the oral promise. California, but not Nevada, required contracts to make a will to be in writing.[144] Judge Traynor held the California Statute of Frauds inapplicable. There was no finding as to where the decedent was domiciled at the time the contract was made, although he died domiciled in California. If he was not domiciled in California at the time the contract was made, Judge Traynor thought it would be unfair to the plaintiffs to impose on them the requirements of the California statute. Even if the decedent was a resident of California at the time the promise was made, the California Statute of Frauds still should not apply for "[s]ince California ... would have no interest in applying its own statute of frauds unless Granrud [the decedent] remained here until his death, plaintiffs were not bound to know that California's statute might ultimately be invoked against them."[145]

Thus we have three statute of frauds cases in which the forums reach varying results as to the application of the forums' statutes of frauds to contracts "made" elsewhere. In *Lams*, the contract for the sale and option to resell securities was highly commercial. Both New York and Delaware had statutes of frauds requiring signed memoranda of contracts not to be performed within a year. The difference between the New York and Delaware statutes, in terms of whether the signing agent had to have written authority, was one of detail rather than basic policy. Both states shared a policy of enforcing contracts to make commercial dealings predictable and reliable.

In *Emery*, the contract to make a will in exchange for personal care was decidedly less commercial. The absence of a commercial element in

---

143. *Emery*, 163 Mass. at 329, 39 N.E. at 1027. But see Bushkin Associates, Inc. v. Raytheon Co., 393 Mass. 622, 635, 473 N.E.2d 662, 671 (1985) ("the Statute of Frauds involves a question of substantive law and is not a procedural rule governed by the law of the forum (but see Emery v. Burbank)").

144. For a suggestion that, although Nevada did not have a special Statute of Frauds for promises to make a will, the Nevada Dead Man's Statute may have excluded testimony concerning decedent's promise, see Cavers, *Oral Contracts to Provide by Will and the Choice-of-Law Process: Some Notes on Bernkrant, in Perspectives of Law—Essays for Austin Wakeman Scott* 38, 67–68 (R. Pound, E. Griswold & A. Sutherland ed. 1964); cf. Alexander, *The Concept of Function and the Basis of Regulatory Interests under Functional Choice-of-Law Theory: The Significance of Benefit and the Insignificance of Intention*, 65 Va. L. Rev. 1063, 1085 (1979) (both Nevada and California required "that agreements to make wills satisfy the clear and convincing evidence requirement").

145. *Bernkrant*, 55 Cal.2d at 596, 12 Cal.Rptr. at 270, 360 P.2d at 910.

the typical contract to make a will was pointed out in *Rubin v. Irving Trust Company*,[146] which applied the New York wills statute of frauds provision to an oral contract made by a New York testator in Florida: "It is clear, also, that in reaching our decision here we are not to be guided by the same considerations as we would in determining the applicability of our statute of frauds to the ordinary or commercial contract."[147]

In *Bernkrant*, although again we are dealing with a contract to make a will, the context is decidedly more commercial than in *Emery*. The agreement involves the refinancing of a loan secured by realty. The use of the creditor's will to perform the promise to release the remaining indebtedness was an unnecessary and unwise feature of the arrangement. Rather than apply the California Statute of Frauds, Judge Traynor preferred to "give effect to the common policy of both states to enforce lawful contracts...."[148] To be sure, there are distinctions between *Emery* and *Bernkrant* other than the difference in commercialism. In *Emery* the plaintiff performed at the forum; in *Bernkrant*, the plaintiff did his refinancing in Nevada. This difference in place of performance may have affected the courts' judgments as to whether the plaintiffs would be unfairly surprised by application of the forum statute. In *Bernkrant*, Judge Traynor stressed the importance of preventing surprise.

---

146.   305 N.Y. 288, 113 N.E.2d 424 (1953).

147.   Id. at 300, 113 N.E.2d at 428. But cf. Talmudical Academy v. Harris, 238 So.2d 161 (Fla.App.1970) (refuse to enforce promise to make a bequest on the ground that the Florida statute of frauds is "procedural" and applicable to all actions brought in Florida although the promise was made in another state).

148.   *Bernkrant*, 55 Cal.2d at 596, 12 Cal.Rptr. at 270, 360 P.2d at 910.

But cf. Rosenthal v. Fonda, 862 F.2d 1398 (9th Cir.1988) (apply New York statute of frauds to protect a California defendant against a New York agent—California law); Intercontinental Planning, Ltd. v. Daystrom, Inc., 24 N.Y.2d 372, 300 N.Y.S.2d 817, 248 N.E.2d 576 (1969) (using state-interest analysis to apply the New York statute of frauds and deny a New York broker a finder's fee sought from out-of-state clients); Andover Realty, Inc. v. Western Electric Co., Inc., 64 N.Y.2d 1006, 489 N.Y.S.2d 52, 478 N.E.2d 193 (1985) (apply New Jersey statute of frauds to protect New Jersey resident against New York broker).

In connection with *Daystrom*, supra, see Cavers, *Symposium: the Value of Principled Preferences*, 49 Texas L. Rev. 211, 222 (1971) (the court "rightly regarded the transaction as centered in" New York); cf. Hutner v. Greene, 734 F.2d 896 (2d Cir.1984) (New York would apply California law to determine whether California resident must obtain a broker's license to be compensated for services—exempt from New York finder's statute of frauds because licensed to practice law in New York); Denny v. American Tobacco Co., 308 F.Supp. 219 (N.D.Cal.1970) (apply New York statute to protect New York-based defendants against claim by California finder); J. Zeevi & Sons, Ltd. v. Grindlays Bank (Uganda), Ltd., 37 N.Y.2d 220, 371 N.Y.S.2d 892, 333 N.E.2d 168 (1975), cert. denied, 423 U.S. 866, 96 S.Ct. 126, 46 L.Ed.2d 95 (1975) (on reasoning similar to *Daystrom*, apply New York law to enforce letter of credit issued against funds deposited in Uganda to protect New York's position as "the financial capital of the world"). But cf. Havenfield Corp. v. H & R Block, Inc., 509 F.2d 1263 (8th Cir.1975), cert. denied, 421 U.S. 999, 95 S.Ct. 2395, 44 L.Ed.2d 665 (1975) (applying Missouri "most significant contacts" rule, enforce contract in favor of New York finder against Missouri defendant—apply Missouri or Ohio law under which contract enforceable, not New York law which required a writing); Bushkin Associates, Inc. v. Raytheon Co., 393 Mass. 622, 630, 473 N.E.2d 662, 667; (1985) (New York finder permitted to recover against a Massachusetts client under Massachusetts law, the court rejecting "the Empire State's imperial reach" manifested in *Daystrom*).

In short, the factors here suggested for strengthening or rebutting the presumption of validity are not only useful tools for the solution of future conflicts problems, but also make the results of many decided cases easier to understand.

§ 7.4F   What Functional Information Does the Other State's Choice–Of–Law Rule Provide?

Sometimes the choice-of-law rule of the other state can assist the forum in determining that a real conflict can be resolved in favor of the forum's law without seriously impairing the policies of the other state. For example, suppose a case involving usury in the making of a commercial loan. The borrower's state permits interest less than that charged, but the agreement is valid under the law of the lender's state, which is the forum. This problem is resolved by a decision of the highest court in the borrower's state refusing to apply its usury law in just such an interstate case. Another example is *Bernkrant v. Fowler.*[149] In the light of Judge Traynor's decision, a Nevada court should have no hesitancy in applying the Nevada validating law to a case that, except for the Nevada forum, is the twin of *Bernkrant.*[150]

It is unwise, however, to conclude that every time the other state's choice-of-law rule points to the forum this is a declaration by the other state that it has no domestic policy that application of the forum's rule would substantially impair. It is necessary to appraise the extent to which the other state's choice-of-law rule reflects functional considerations rather than rigid territorial dogma. If the wife's domicile has an incapacitating rule, but would apply the law of the place of making to determine her capacity, this may either, as in *Milliken v. Pratt,*[151] be a half-articulated expression of a functional preference for the resolution of interstate conflicts or be a parroting of territorial notions that were once thought to be implicit in the nature of things.

§ 7.5   A Suggested Choice–Of–Law Rule for Validity of Contracts

A choice-of-law rule intended to encapsulate the foregoing discussion of the proper resolution of conflicts-contracts-validity problems in the absence of choice of law by the parties is the following:

> A CONTRACT IS VALID IF VALID UNDER THE DOMESTIC LAW OF ANY STATE HAVING A CONTACT WITH THE PARTIES OR WITH THE TRANSACTION SUFFICIENT TO MAKE THAT STATE'S VALIDATING POLICIES RELEVANT, UNLESS SOME OTHER STATE WOULD ADVANCE ITS OWN POLICIES BY INVALIDATING THE CONTRACT AND ONE OR MORE OF

---

149. 55 Cal.2d 588, 12 Cal.Rptr. 266, 360 P.2d 906 (1961) (discussed supra § 7.4E).

150. See Freund, *Characterization with Respect to Contracts in the Conflict of Laws, in The Conflict of Laws and International Contracts* 158, 162–63 (1951) (discussing University of Chicago v. Dater, 277 Mich. 658, 270 N.W. 175 (1936)).

151. 125 Mass. 374 (1878) (discussed supra notes 7–17 and accompanying text).

THE FOLLOWING FACTORS SUGGEST THAT THE CONFLICT BETWEEN THE DOMESTIC LAWS OF THE TWO STATES SHOULD BE RESOLVED IN FAVOR OF INVALIDITY:

1) THE INVALIDATING RULE REFLECTS A VIABLE, CURRENT TREND IN THE LAW OF CONTRACTS SUCH AS PROTECTION OF THE PARTY IN THE INFERIOR BARGAINING POSITION;

2) THE INVALIDATING RULE DIFFERS IN BASIC POLICY, RATHER THAN MINOR DETAIL, FROM THE VALIDATING RULE;

3) THE PARTIES SHOULD HAVE FORESEEN THE SUBSTANTIAL INTEREST THAT THE STATE WITH THE INVALIDATING RULE WOULD HAVE IN CONTROLLING THE OUTCOME;

4) THE CONTEXT OF THE CONTRACT IS NONCOMMERCIAL;

5) THE COURTS OF THE STATE WITH THE VALIDATING RULE HAVE, IN SIMILAR INTERSTATE CASES, DEFERRED TO THE POLICIES UNDERLYING THE FOREIGN INVALIDATING RULE.

Here is a simpler form of the rule:

A CONTRACT IS VALID IF VALID UNDER THE LAW OF THE PRINCIPAL PLACE OF BUSINESS OR HABITUAL RESIDENCE OF THE PARTY WISHING TO ENFORCE THE CONTRACT UNLESS THE PRINCIPAL PLACE OF BUSINESS OR HABITUAL RESIDENCE OF THE OTHER PARTY HAS A RELEVANT INVALIDATING RULE DESIGNED TO PROTECT AGAINST CONTRACTS OF ADHESION.

The other factors stated in the longer version are unlikely to be present except in a small number of cases when they can be trotted out as exceptions to the rule.

§ 7.6 The New Rule Approach[152] Applied to Interstate Small Loan Transactions

As indicated in sections 7.4B and 7.4C, the problem of when to invalidate in whole or in part an interstate contract for the repayment of money falls into two subclasses: the large business loan and the small consumer loan. For the reasons discussed in those sections, the arguments for applying the validating law to the large business loan are more compelling than for upholding the consumer loan. As the next section (7.7) indicates, in many states special statutory provisions control choice of law for small loans. This section will examine the problem of the interstate consumer loan as background for judging the desirability of the statutory choice-of-law rules covered in the next section. This discus-

---

152. See § 3.5.

sion may also assist in shaping desirable constructions of the statutory rules and in making choice-of-law decisions in the minority of states without statutory conflicts provisions.

Although there are cogent arguments for giving the small borrower the full protection of his or her home-state law, there are two situations in which it is most arguable that a court should not subject the lender to the full rigor of the law of the consumer borrower's home state: when the borrower's residence changes and when the loan transaction occurs exclusively in the lender's state.

The less debatable of these propositions is when the borrower was either a resident of the lender's state at the time that the loan was made or has misrepresented to the lender that he or she is resident there. Under these circumstances, the law of the lender's state should ordinarily apply to validate a loan legally made there, although the borrower subsequently moves to or is discovered to live in a state with a more restrictive small loan law.[153]

The more difficult problem occurs when the borrower travels to the lender's state and there negotiates, receives, and promises to repay the loan, and the lender has not solicited the loan in the borrower's state either directly,[154] through intermediaries, or through advertising intended to reach residents of the borrower's state. If the loan agreement would be completely valid under the law of the lender's state but would be invalid as to both principal and interest under the law of the borrower's state, the choice of borrower's or lender's law is especially difficult.

In favor of invalidation under the law of the borrower's state are the following arguments: This is a contract of adhesion with a consumer, and the invalidating rule represents a recognition of the need for protecting the necessitous individual in these circumstances. The lender knows or can easily determine the law of the borrower's state. To permit the lender to recover would subject similar lenders in the borrower's state to competition that they are powerless to meet.[155] Moreover, if the borrower does go to even a nearby city across the state line to make the

---

153. See Uniform Consumer Credit Code § 1.201(6) & (7) (1968 Act), § 1.201(4), (5) & (6) (1974 Act) [hereinafter cited as UCCC]; Comment, *Usury in the Conflict of Laws: The Doctrine of the Lex Debitoris*, 55 Calif. L. Rev. 123, 246–47 (1967). But see Lyles v. Union Planters Nat'l Bank, 239 Ark. 738, 393 S.W.2d 867 (1965); N.Y.—McKinney's Banking Law § 356 (if borrower moves into New York after transaction, cannot collect charges in excess of those permitted in local transactions).

154. For an example of a lender sending an agent into the borrower's state to engage in door-to-door solicitation, see Jones v. Tindall, 216 Ark. 431, 226 S.W.2d 44 (1950) (Arkansas law applied to invalidate—choice-of-law clause selected Arkansas law).

155. See Comment, supra note 153, at 175–76; cf. Robertson v. California, 328 U.S. 440, 457, 66 S.Ct. 1160, 1169, 90 L.Ed. 1366, 1378–79 (1946) (permitting defendant to act as an agent for a non-admitted insurer "could only result in placing domestic and complying foreign insurers at great disadvantage and eventually in nullifying all controls unless or until Congress should take over the regulation"); Washington Nat'l Bldg., Loan & Inv. Ass'n v. Stanley, 38 Or. 319, 63 P. 489 (1901) (apply forum law to small loan when all contacts in forum except incorporation of lender and place of payment, noting that otherwise lender would have advantage over local lenders).

loan, this indicates that borrower is even more necessitous, desperate, and in need of protection than if he or she had stayed home.[156]

There are also arguments for validation under the lender's law: the law of the borrower's state may set interest rates and other terms that are unrealistic in the light of the risk of making the kind of loan in issue.[157] The borrower's state does not have a sufficient nexus with the lender to make it fair and reasonable to subject the lender to its law.[158] It is unlikely, however, that this unfairness is of constitutional dignity, that the Commerce Clause,[159] the Due Process clause,[160] or the Full Faith and Credit clause[161] would prohibit the borrower's state from applying its own law to the stay-at-home lender.

Under the commerce clause, it is questionable whether the borrower's state could impose penalties on the lender for failing to obtain a certificate to do business there or for otherwise not complying with registration, filing, and other regulations applicable to lenders doing business there. There is probably not sufficient contact with the borrower's state for the lender to be held to be "localized" there for any of these purposes.[162] It is another large step to contend that the borrower's state cannot apply its small loan law to invalidate nonconforming loans made to resident borrowers. The lender can continue to do its interstate business, but when it deals with borrowers from another state, it must shape its agreements to their laws. That the lender cannot do this in some cases, because it is subject to conflicting requirements of its own

---

156. See Comment, supra note 153, at 244–45.

157. See UCCC, Prefatory Note at xii–xiv (Working Redraft No. 5, 1973), reprinted in 28 Personal Finance L.Q.Rep. 2, 3, 30 (1973).

158. See supra § 6.28.

159. U.S. Const. Art. I, § 8, cl. 3.

160. U.S. Const. Amend. 14, § 1.

161. U.S. Const. Art. IV, § 1.

162. See Allenberg Cotton Co. v. Pittman, 419 U.S. 20, 95 S.Ct. 260, 42 L.Ed.2d 195 (1974) (cannot condition use of courts on authorization to do business when company's cotton was in local warehouse only temporarily for sorting and classification for out-of-state shipment); International Text–Book Co. v. Pigg, 217 U.S. 91, 30 S.Ct. 481, 54 L.Ed. 678 (1910) (correspondence school doing interstate business, but with local agents, cannot be made to file statement of condition in order to use forum courts to collect debt from local student); cf. Eli Lilly & Co. v. Sav–On–Drugs, Inc., 366 U.S. 276, 81 S.Ct. 1316, 6 L.Ed.2d 288 (1961) (can deny use of courts as sanction for failing to obtain certificate to do intrastate as distinguished from interstate business); Robertson v. California, 328 U.S. 440, 66 S.Ct. 1160, 90 L.Ed. 1366 (1946) (upheld prosecution of defendant acting as unlicensed local agent for nonadmitted foreign insurer); Union Brokerage v. Jensen, 322 U.S. 202, 210, 64 S.Ct. 967, 972, 88 L.Ed. 1227, 1233 (1944) (permitted exclusion of custom-house broker from state courts until authorized to do business: "It has localized its business, and to function effectively it must have a wide variety of dealings with people in the community"); People v. Fairfax Family Fund, Inc., 235 Cal.App.2d 881, 47 Cal.Rptr. 812 (1964), appeal dism'd, 382 U.S. 1, 86 S.Ct. 34, 15 L.Ed.2d 6 (1965) (enjoined unlicensed lender from soliciting small loans by mail from forum residents, local credit investigation conducted by independent contractor); cf. Horowitz, *The Commerce Clause as a Limitation on State Choice-of-Law Doctrine*, 84 Harv. L. Rev. 806, 814 (1971) (commerce clause may control choice of law when "the principle of facilitating multistate transactions would require that a single state's law or a group of compatible state laws, should govern"—e.g. rights of shareholders of an interstate enterprise—or when application of one state's law rather than that of another "would tend to facilitate interstate commercial activity").

law and the law of the borrower's state, does not necessarily mean that the borrower's state is imposing an unreasonable burden on commerce. The fault may be in the statute of the lender's state if it does not make an exception when a local lender is dealing with a foreign borrower and conforming to the law of the borrower's state.[163]

The constitutional unfairness argument seems best made in due process terms. The borrower's state, to use the language of *Home Insurance Co. v. Dick*,[164] "may not abrogate the rights of parties beyond its borders having no relation to anything done or to be done within them."[165] But *Dick* can be distinguished. Texas, the forum, wished to apply its own law to invalidate a stipulation in the policy that suit must be brought within one year of a loss. Mr. Dick, at all relevant times, resided in Mexico. The only nexus with Texas was that it was Dick's domicile while he was actually residing in Mexico. Moreover, the boat insured was covered by the policy only in Mexican waters. In the stay-at-home lender case, the borrower's state has more nexus with the transaction. It is, after all, the borrower's residence, the place where social and economic effects sought to be avoided by its small loan law are most likely to manifest themselves if that law is not applied.

Moreover, *Dick* may have given too much emphasis to the place of making and performance of the contract and too little to the foreseeable[166] interest of Texas in protecting its citizen, Mr. Dick. A later case, *Hoopeston Canning Co. v. Cullen*,[167] held that New York could require out-of-state reciprocal insurers that insured New York risks to adopt prescribed forms of accounting and provide for the election of a management committee at an annual subscriber's meeting. Although the holding in *Hoopeston* can be explained in terms of the very broad powers that a state has for imposing conditions on foreign corporations that wish to do business within the state,[168] the following language in the opinion reflects a sensible view of the role of constitutional limitations on choice of law:

> In determining the power of a state to apply its own regulatory laws to insurance business activities, the question in earlier cases became involved by conceptualistic discussion of theories of the place

---

163. See UCCC § 1.201(8)(a) (1968 Act), § 1.201(7)(a) (1974 Act) (creditor not subject to Code if consumer is nonresident and law of consumer's residence is stipulated).

164. 281 U.S. 397, 50 S.Ct. 338, 74 L.Ed. 926 (1930).

165. Id. at 410, 50 S.Ct. at 342, 74 L.Ed. at 935.

166. Although the policy was issued to one Bonner, of Tampico, Mexico, the loss was made "payable to the Texas Gulf Steamship Company of Galveston, Texas, and C.J. Dick, as their respective interests may appear." Record at 38–39, Home Ins. Co. v. Dick. See also *Dick*, 281 U.S. at 403 n.2, 50 S.Ct. at 340 n.2, 74 L.Ed. at 931 n.2. Moreover, not only was Dick named along with a Texas company in the original policy, but also, before the policy could be assigned to Dick, the insurer had to give its written consent. Record at 38.

167. 318 U.S. 313, 63 S.Ct. 602, 87 L.Ed. 777 (1943).

168. Cf. Watson v. Employers Liab. Assurance Corp., 348 U.S. 66, 74, 75 S.Ct. 166, 171, 99 L.Ed. 74, 83 (1954) (Frankfurter, J., concurring in application of forum's direct action statute to foreign insurer on ground insurer had consented to direct suit in order to get a certificate to do business in the forum).

of contracting or of performance. More recently it has been recognized that a state may have substantial interests in the business of insurance of its people or property regardless of these isolated factors. This interest may be measured by highly realistic considerations such as the protection of the citizen insured or the protection of the state from the incidents of loss.[169]

Absent a cogent argument by lender that at the time of the loan it could not have foreseen that borrower's state would have an interest in applying its law to invalidate the repayment obligation, there is no viable due process argument. Such an "outrageous surprise" argument is not likely to be available. It might be raised if, for example, the borrower moved after the making of the loan and borrower's new domicile applied its law to invalidate principal and interest of a loan perfectly valid by the law of both borrower's and lender's residence at the time of making.[170]

If there is no tenable due process argument on behalf of the stay-at-home lender, it is not likely that invoking full faith and credit to a "public act" (the small loan statute)[171] of the lender's state will advance the lender's cause. There is not a sufficient need for a nationally uniform result under the small loan statute of the lender's state to outweigh the interest of the borrower's state in protecting the borrower under its own law.[172]

There does not seem to be, then, any constitutional barrier to the borrower's state applying the full force of its law even to the stay-at-home lender.[173] This is just as well. Once before, then current notions of

169. *Hoopeston*, 318 U.S. at 316, 63 S.Ct. at 604, 87 L.Ed. at 781 (footnote omitted). See also Allstate Ins. Co. v. Hague, 449 U.S. 302, 312–13, 101 S.Ct. 633, 640, 66 L.Ed.2d 521, 531 (1981) ("for a State's substantive law to be selected in a constitutionally permissible manner, that State must have a significant aggregation of contacts, creating state interests, such that choice of its law is neither arbitrary nor fundamentally unfair"); Clay v. Sun Ins. Office, Ltd., 377 U.S. 179, 84 S.Ct. 1197, 12 L.Ed.2d 229 (1964); Richards v. United States, 369 U.S. 1, 15, 82 S.Ct. 585, 594, 7 L.Ed.2d 492, 501 (1962) (dictum): "Where more than one State has sufficiently substantial contact with the activity in question, the forum State, by analysis of the interests possessed by the States involved, could constitutionally apply to the decision of the case the law of one or another state having such an interest in the multistate activity."

But see Apodaca v. Banco Longoria, S.A., 451 S.W.2d 945 (Tex.Civ.App.1970, writ refused n.r.e.) (permitting recovery against forum resident under higher Mexican interest rates).

170. Cf. John Hancock Mut. Life Ins. Co. v. Yates, 299 U.S. 178, 57 S.Ct. 129, 81 L.Ed. 106 (1936). But cf. Allstate Ins. Co. v. Hague, 449 U.S. 302, 101 S.Ct. 633, 66 L.Ed.2d 521 (1981) (listing widow's move to forum after husband's death as one factor upholding application of forum law to determine recovery for death) (discussed infra § 9.2A).

171. For authority that a statute is a "public act" within the meaning of the Full Faith and Credit clause, see Bradford Elec. Light Co. v. Clapper, 286 U.S. 145, 154–55, 52 S.Ct. 571, 573, 76 L.Ed. 1026, 1032 (1932).

172. This is the standard for applying full faith and credit to statutes articulated in Order of United Commercial Travelers of America v. Wolfe, 331 U.S. 586, 624, 67 S.Ct. 1355, 1373, 91 L.Ed. 1687, 1708 (1947). For dictum that outside of the area of enforcement of interstate judgments, full faith and credit and due process limitations on choice of law are the same, see Allstate Ins. Co. v. Hague, 449 U.S. 302, 308 n.10, 101 S.Ct. 633, 637–38 n.10, 66 L.Ed.2d 521, 527–28 n.10 (1981). See also section 9.3A.

173. Cf. Aldens, Inc. v. Miller, 610 F.2d 538 (8th Cir.1979), cert. denied, 446 U.S. 919, 100 S.Ct. 1853, 64 L.Ed.2d 273 (1980) (no violation of commerce clause to apply interest

proper choice-of-law rules were frozen into constitutional imperatives.[174] We should not rush to repeat that error of the early decades of the twentieth century. Nevertheless, everything that is constitutional is not wise. Applying the full force of the borrower's law to the stay-at-home lender can be unfair without being sufficiently outrageous to call down a constitutional thunderbolt.

Because of the seeming unfairness of subjecting the stay-at-home lender to the borrower's law,[175] it is unlikely that a court in the lender's state would apply the invalidating law of the borrower's home. The very factors that support this unfairness argument also make it likely that, under modern long-arm statutes, the lender will be able to obtain in personam jurisdiction over the borrower in the lender's state[176] without resorting to the constitutionally questionable[177] device of an adhesion "consent" to jurisdiction in the loan agreement. Borrowers, however, also can and do sue lenders[178] to have the loan transaction declared

---

limits of buyer's home state to mail-order seller); Aldens, Inc. v. LaFollette, 552 F.2d 745 (7th Cir.), cert. denied, 434 U.S. 880, 98 S.Ct. 236, 54 L.Ed.2d 161 (1977) (no violation of Commerce Clause or Due Process in applying interest limit of buyer's home state to transactions with mail-order seller).

174. See, e.g., New York Life Ins. Co. v. Dodge, 246 U.S. 357, 38 S.Ct. 337, 62 L.Ed. 772 (1918). See also section 9.2A.

175. See Commercial Credit Plan, Inc. v. Parker, 152 Ga.App. 409, 263 S.E.2d 220 (1979) (validate under law of neighboring state to which borrower went after mail solicitation); Sedler, *The Contracts Provisions of the Restatement (Second): An Analysis and a Critique*, 72 Colum. L. Rev. 279, 324–25 (1972).

176. See Hamilton Nat'l Bank v. Russell, 261 F.Supp. 145 (E.D.Tenn.1966) (defendants executed note in forum and the proceeds were received by the defendants in the forum); Oxford Consumer Discount Co. v. Stefanelli, 55 N.J. 489, 500, 262 A.2d 874, 880 (dissent, Weintraub, C.J.: "If a Pennsylvania lender obtains judgment against a New Jersey borrower by service under a Pennsylvania long-arm statute, what then? We need not invite this discord to vindicate our State policy"), appeal dism'd for want of final judgment, 400 U.S. 923, 91 S.Ct. 183, 27 L.Ed.2d 182 (1970); cf. Banco Espanol de Credito v. DuPont, 24 A.D.2d 445, 261 N.Y.S.2d 233 (1965) (the defendant was an accommodation endorser of notes to make available his credit in the production of motion pictures by forum partnerships of which the defendant was a special partner). But see Hubbard, Westervelt & Mottelay, Inc. v. Harsh Bldg. Co., 28 A.D.2d 295, 284 N.Y.S.2d 879 (1967) (no jurisdiction over maker of note payable to the plaintiff in the forum even though part of the service for which the note was given was rendered in the forum).

177. Cf. Swarb v. Lennox, 405 U.S. 191, 92 S.Ct. 767, 31 L.Ed.2d 138 (1972) (affirming invalidation on due process grounds of cognovit clauses in agreements with low-income consumers, but the creditors had not appealed); Trauger v. A.J. Spagnol Lumber Co., Inc., 442 So.2d 182 (Fla.1983) (must give full faith and credit to Pennsylvania cognovit judgment for commercial debt although judgment would be void under Florida law). But cf. National Equip. Rental, Ltd. v. Szukhent, 375 U.S. 311, 84 S.Ct. 411, 11 L.Ed.2d 354 (1964) (uphold service by agent appointed by defendant although agent not known by defendant).

178. For interstate commercial loan cases in which the borrower has sued for relief on the ground of usury, see Consolidated Jewelers, Inc. v. Standard Financial Corp., 325 F.2d 31 (6th Cir.1963); Yarbrough v. Prentice Lee Tractor Co., 252 Ark. 349, 479 S.W.2d 549 (1972); Cooper v. Cherokee Village Dev. Co., 236 Ark. 37, 364 S.W.2d 158 (1963) (suit by borrower's stockholder against borrower and lender); Ury v. Jewelers Acceptance Corp., 227 Cal.App.2d 11, 38 Cal.Rptr. 376 (1964); Crisafulli v. Childs, 33 A.D.2d 293, 307 N.Y.S.2d 701 (1970); Securities Inv. Co. v. Finance Acceptance Corp., 474 S.W.2d 261 (Tex.Civ.App.1971, writ refused n.r.e.). For similar suits in small loan cases, see Mell v. Goodbody & Co., 10 Ill.App.3d 809, 295 N.E.2d 97 (1973) (class action on behalf of margin account customers); Oxford Consumer Discount Co. v. Stefanelli, 55 N.J. 489, 262 A.2d

invalid and for recovery of already paid installments of principal and interest. It is likely that, because of the following factors, the borrower will be able to get jurisdiction over the lender in the borrower's state: the nearness of the lender's place of business, the large volume of similar loans by lender to residents of borrower's state, the fact that enforcement of the loan will have consequences in the borrower's state that were foreseeable when the loan was made,[179] and the probability that the lender, at least to sue on and execute the judgments that it recovers at home, employs lawyers in and litigates in the borrower's state.

We have the stage set then for a particularly grating and unseemly clash of conflicting state policies. There is likely to be a rush to judgment by borrower and lender, each in their own courts, so that the swifter may carry the judgment into the other state with the Full Faith and Credit clause as their protector and champion. To remove the inducement for this race to judgment, it is desirable that there be some accommodation of the policies of the two states that the courts of either state might find acceptable. Such an accommodation lies in shaping a new rule for the stay-at-home lender case that is the law of neither the borrower's nor the lender's state. Whichever state is the forum should enforce the repayment agreement but in an amount and manner that accords with the limits and requirements of the borrower's state.[180] There is authority for this kind of judicial reformation of the loan agreement, even in intrastate cases, when either the borrower's misconduct or other circumstances make the penalties for violation of the loan law appear to the court as inappropriate.[181]

Against this New Rule approach in the difficult small loan conflicts case it can be argued that partial validation will encourage the lender to continue to write loans under its own law and collect as much as it can. In the few cases in which it meets a litigious borrower, it will still be able to salvage the lion's share of the loan. In short, there is not sufficient deterrence to out-of-state lenders that violate the laws of the borrower's

---

874, appeal dism'd for want of final judgment, 400 U.S. 923, 91 S.Ct. 183, 27 L.Ed.2d 182 (1970) (intervenors in action against Stefanelli).

179. See Restatement (Second) § 37; People v. Fairfax Family Fund, Inc., 235 Cal. App.2d 881, 885, 47 Cal.Rptr. 812, 814 (1964), appeal dism'd, 382 U.S. 1, 86 S.Ct. 34, 15 L.Ed.2d 6 (1965) (dictum); Stubbs v. Security Consumer Discount Co., 146 N.J.Super. 160, 369 A.2d 44 (Law Div.1976) (jurisdiction over Pennsylvania assignee of New Jersey second mortgages).

180. See Oxford Consumer Discount Co. v. Stefanelli, 55 N.J. 489, 499–500, 262 A.2d 874, 880 (dissent, Weintraub, C.J.), appeal dism'd for want of final judgment, 400 U.S. 923, 91 S.Ct. 183, 27 L.Ed.2d 182 (1970); cf. Comment, supra note 153, at 238.

181. See Turney v. Roberts, 255 Ark. 503, 501 S.W.2d 601 (1973) (reforms loan agreement drafted by borrower, no reference by court to law of Florida where loan made); Davidson v. Commercial Credit Equip. Corp., 255 Ark. 127, 499 S.W.2d 68 (1973) (small error in calculating interest); cf. HIMC Inv. Co. v. Siciliano, 103 N.J.Super. 27, 246 A.2d 502 (Law Div.1968) (interstate case, apply New Jersey law to invalidate, but will not cancel mortgage unless borrower returns $500 received on understanding rest of principal would be paid); Washington Nat'l Bldg., Loan & Inv. Ass'n v. Stanley, 38 Or. 319, 63 P. 489 (1901) (interstate case, permit equitable reformation of agreement in the light of prior uncertainty whether a court would apply forum law). But see First Nat'l Bank v. Thompson, 249 Ark. 972, 463 S.W.2d 87 (1971) (no relief to lender who computed interest from wrong date).

state.[182] This is a cogent point. Nevertheless, the New Rule approach is suggested only for the most difficult small loan conflicts case in which there are reasonable arguments for both borrower's law and lender's law and in which the alternative is a race to don the armor of full faith and credit to judgments.

§ 7.7   Statutory Choice–Of–Law Rules Concerning Small Loans

Assuming that the New Rule approach (see § 7.6) to otherwise intractable small loan conflicts problems is desirable, to what extent is it possible? In most states statutes control choice of law in small loan cases. A symbol of this phenomenon is the subsequent history of the controversy that split the New Jersey Supreme Court four to three in *Oxford Consumer Discount Co. v. Stefanelli.*[183] In an action brought in the borrower's state, the court decided a stay-at-home lender problem, with the additional forum nexus of a second mortgage on the Stefanelli home. A bare majority of the court held that the New Jersey Secondary Mortgage Loan Act applied to invalidate the obligation to repay, both principal and interest.[184] Today the result reached by the majority would be compelled by a subsequent amendment to the New Jersey Act defining its territorial scope.[185]

Most states have either the Uniform Consumer Credit Code or other special small loan legislation that includes a provision controlling territorial application. These provisions span a broad spectrum that at one end affords little assurance that local residents will receive the protection of their home state's laws and at the other end gives the full protection of forum law even to persons who were nonresidents when the transaction in issue occurred.

Points in this spectrum, from little to much protection of residents, may be traced as follows:

Oregon, except for payday loans, exempts from its law "loans made or payable in other jurisdictions and lawful where made or payable."[186]

Five states permit enforcement of loans lawful where "made".[187]

---

182. See Comment, supra note 153, at 238.

183. 55 N.J. 489, 262 A.2d 874, appeal dism'd for want of final judgment, 400 U.S. 923, 91 S.Ct. 183, 27 L.Ed.2d 182 (1970).

184. The impact of this ruling on the Philadelphia small loan industry was somewhat softened by the court's ruling on the retroactivity of the decision. If the foreign lender made the loan to the New Jersey resident exclusively at the lender's out-of-state office with "no intermediation of any kind by others" (55 N.J. at 492, 262 A.2d at 876) in New Jersey, the decision was not retroactive to affect loans made prior to the first decision in the case on September 11, 1968; except that borrowers who were on that date in litigation contesting the validity of the loans, would repay principal without interest (id. at 493, 262 A.2d at 877).

185. N.J.Stat.Ann. 17:11C–45.

186. Or.Rev.Stat. § 725.370.

187. Ala.Code § 5–18–19; Ky.Rev.Stat. § 286.4–620; Minn.Stat.Ann. § 56.18; Nev.Rev. Stat.Ann. § 675.310; N.H.Rev.Stat.Ann. § 399–A:11.

North Carolina exempts small loans made elsewhere only if "all contractual activities, including solicitation ... occur entirely outside" the state.[188]

Several states enforce loans lawfully made in another state under a small loan law "similar in principle" to the forum's act.[189] This, incidentally, is the language of a "Uniform" Small Loan Law[190] drafted by the Department of Remedial Loans of the Russell Sage Foundation and for a time, during the 1920's and 1930's, sponsored by the American Association of Personal Finance Companies.[191]

Two states enforce a loan legal where "made" but only up to the amount of interest and other charges permitted by forum law.[192]

Maryland enforces loans legal where made if made under a law similar in principle to theirs, but only up to their own limits on interest and charges, and only if the loan transaction itself did not have a significant nexus with the forum.[193] This is essentially the New Rule approach.

New Jersey will enforce a loan legally made under another act similar in principle to its own, but only up to the New Jersey limits on interest and charges if the borrower was a New Jersey resident at the time the loan was made.[194]

New Mexico will enforce a loan violating domestic law only if legal where made and if the borrower was a nonresident of the forum when the loan was made.[195]

Ohio will enforce a loan violating its act only if legal where made under a law similar in principle to its own and with a borrower not resident in Ohio at the time of the loan.[196]

Eleven states and Guam have some version of the Uniform Consumer Credit Code.[197] This Code, in section 1.201, has a comprehensive

---

188. N.C.Gen.Stat. § 53–190(a).

189. Alaska Stat. § 06.20.310; R.I.Gen.Laws Ann. § 19–14.2–1.

Michigan adds to its act a provision subjecting to Michigan law all loans made by mail to Michigan residents. Mich.Comp.Laws Ann. § 493.18(3).

The most famous case applying this type of statute is Kinney Loan & Finance Co. v. Sumner, 159 Neb. 57, 65 N.W.2d 240 (1954). See also Grady v. Denbeck, 198 Neb. 31, 251 N.W.2d 864 (1977).

190. Uniform Small Loan Law § 18 (6th draft 1935), reprinted in F. Hubachek, Annotations on Small Loan Laws 111 (1938).

191. Id. at 192–93.

192. La.—LSA—Rev.Stat.Ann. § 9:3511(B); W.Va.Code, 46A–1–104(2) (but West Virginia law applies if a "resident is ... induced to enter into a consumer [credit transaction] by personal or mail solicitation and the goods, services or proceeds are delivered to the consumer in this State and payment ... is to be made from this State"—id. (1)).

193. Md.Ann.Code, Commercial Law § 12–314(c) (applies if borrower "is a Maryland resident and the application for the loan originated in Maryland").

194. N.J.Stat.Ann. title 17, § 17:11C–41(f).

195. N.Mex.Stat.Ann. § 58–15–24.

196. Ohio Rev.Code Ann. § 1321.17.

197. As of January 1, 2009, Indiana, Oklahoma, South Carolina, Utah, Wisconsin, Wyoming, and Guam had adopted the 1968 version of the UCCC. In 1975 the Colorado Act

territorial application provision that warrants further discussion.

One subsection of 1.201 is close to the New Rule approach. It provides that if a covered transaction is made in another state with a person resident in the enacting state at the time of the transaction, the creditor may not collect charges in excess of those permitted by the Code.[198]

Resident creditors are subject to the Code, but escape is sensibly permitted if the consumer is a nonresident at the time of the transaction, and if the creditor is sufficiently well counseled to insert a choice-of-law clause in the agreement stipulating the law of the consumer's residence.[199]

The territorial provision that merits closest scrutiny is the subsection that applies certain Code provisions to any action brought in the enacting state although that state has no contact except as forum with the consumer, the creditor, or the transaction.[200] The least objectionable application of this qua forum concept is in the prohibition against prejudgment garnishment (section 5.104)[201] and limitation on wages subject to garnishment (section 5.105). The subsection's incorporation by reference of section 5.103,[202] however, seems to insulate from a deficiency judgment a consumer who has moved into the enacting state after the goods have been repossessed in a state where both creditor and consumer then resided and where the creditor did not have to choose between repossession and judgment.

Also incorporated is section 5.107, which makes "unenforceable" repayment obligations if there are, at the time credit is extended, threats of criminal harm as a sanction for nonpayment. The word "unenforceable" should be interpreted as simply closing the forum to suit, not as entitling the consumer to a judgment canceling principal and interest, if the enacting state's only nexus is as forum and there is no similar sanction for extortion in the states otherwise connected with the parties and with the transaction. Incorporation of section 5.106 subjects any employer who can be sued in the enacting state to that state's absolute bar on discharging an employee because the employee's wages have been

---

was amended to include many of the provisions of the 1974 Act. Idaho, Iowa, Kansas, and Maine had adopted the 1974 version of the UCCC.

198. UCCC § 1.201(5)(a) (1968 Act), § 1.201(4)(a) (1974 Act).

199. UCCC § 1.201(8)(a) (1968 Act), § 1.201(7)(a) (1974 Act).

200. UCCC § 1.201(4) (1968 Act); § 1.201(3) (1974 Act). In both versions these subsections make applicable to all suits in the state "[t]he Part on Limitations on Creditors' Remedies (Part 1) of the Article on Remedies and Penalties (Article 5)".

201. See Sniadach v. Family Fin. Corp., 395 U.S. 337, 89 S.Ct. 1820, 23 L.Ed.2d 349 (1969) (prejudgment garnishment violates due process if no hearing). See also North Ga. Finishing, Inc. v. Di–Chem, Inc., 419 U.S. 601, 95 S.Ct. 719, 42 L.Ed.2d 751 (1975); Mitchell v. W.T. Grant Co., 416 U.S. 600, 94 S.Ct. 1895, 40 L.Ed.2d 406 (1974); Fuentes v. Shevin, 407 U.S. 67, 92 S.Ct. 1983, 32 L.Ed.2d 556 (1972).

202. UCCC § 5.103(2) (both versions) provides that if the seller repossesses goods that were sold for less than the designated cash price and in which the seller had a security interest, the buyer is not subject to a deficiency judgment.

garnished, a bar much stricter than the garnishment discharge provision of the Federal Consumer Protection Act.[203]

Finally, the provision that the enacting state would be least justified in applying simply qua forum is section 5.108, which empowers the court to "limit the application of any unconscionable" clause "as to avoid any unconscionable result." The exercise of this power will almost certainly affect the result on the merits. Thus, when section 5.108 is applied qua forum, the sanctions should be limited to closing the forum to enforcement of all or part of an agreement that the court finds "unconscionable." This would leave the creditor free to enforce those parts of the agreement in other states that have the appropriate contacts with the parties and the transaction and where the provision in issue is not deemed "unconscionable." This is not impossible under section 5.108, for it does provide that as alternatives to modifying the agreement "to avoid any unconscionable result," the court "may refuse to enforce the agreement," or it may "enforce the remainder of the agreement without the unconscionable" clause.

In general, sections 1.201(4) of the 1968 Act and 1.201(3) of the 1974 Act should be redrafted to make it clear that the only rules of the enacting state that apply when that state is acting solely qua forum are rules that concern procedure and remedy and are unlikely to alter the creditor's rights under the agreement. The application of forum law beyond this should be limited to closing the forum's courts to enforcement of agreements that offend the forum's notions of basic morality and justice, but without deciding the merits of the controversy.

Section 1.201(6) of the 1968 Act,[204] with the exceptions just discussed,[205] permits enforcement in the enacting state of an agreement made elsewhere with consumers who were nonresidents at the time of the transaction, if the agreement "is valid and enforceable under the laws of the state applicable to the transaction." This last clause frees the court to articulate and apply its own choice-of-law concepts. The comparable provision in the 1974 version, section 1.201(5), enforces a transaction entered into in another state "to the extent that it is valid and enforceable under the laws of the other jurisdiction." This limits the forum to a rigid territorial choice-of-law rule unless "laws" refers to the conflicts rules of the other state.[206] If "laws" includes choice-of-law rules, the forum must defer to the other state's conflicts analysis. The 1968 version is preferable.

---

203. 15 U.S.C. § 1674(a): "No employer may discharge any employee by reason of the fact that his earnings have been subjected to garnishment for any one indebtedness."

204. UCCC § 1.201(6) (1968 Act): "Except as provided in subsection (4), a sale, lease, loan, or modification thereof, made in another state to a person who was not a resident of this State when the sale, lease, loan, or modification was made is valid and enforceable in this State according to its terms to the extent that it is valid and enforceable under the laws of the state applicable to the transaction."

205. See text accompanying notes 201–204, supra.

206. Cf. Richards v. United States, 369 U.S. 1, 82 S.Ct. 585, 7 L.Ed.2d 492 (1962), which gave this interpretation to "law" in the choice-of-law clause of the Federal Tort Claims Act, 28 U.S.C.A. § 1346(b).

§ 7.8 Choice of Law to Determine the Construction of a Contract

When the conflicts problem concerns the construction of a contract,[207] there is no reason why the parties should not be able to use the choice-of-law clause as a shorthand expression of their intention on all matters they have not otherwise covered in the contract. Because the choice-of-law clause serves only to incorporate by reference into the contract matters that the parties were free to spell out at length, the parties should be able to refer to the law of any jurisdiction for this purpose, even one having no contacts with the parties or with the transaction.[208] Moreover, if the choice-of-law clause must be utilized to determine the meaning of the contract, there is no way that the "actual" intention of the parties on the issue can realistically be ascertained.[209] Therefore, there is no danger that giving effect to the choice-of-law clause will disappoint the discoverable expectations of the parties. In addition, any contact state would allow the parties to settle the issue one way or another by a full manifestation of their intention in the contract. Therefore, a state's rule of construction that fills a gap the parties have left in their arrangement, if it reflects any policy of that state, represents a policy that the state would immediately subordinate to the parties' manifestation of a contrary intention.

Under such circumstances, when neither the intentions of the parties nor the policies of contact states are of major importance, the primary goal for adjudication is to reach a uniform and predictable result no matter where the forum. The choice-of-law clause provides a method of accomplishing this.

The parties to an international agreement should be able be able to divorce themselves from national laws and choose instead rules that are generally accepted by those engaged in international transactions, such as the UNIDROIT Principles of International Commercial Contracts.[210]

207. For cases involving choice of law for construction see Atlantic Mut. Ins. Co. v. Truck Ins. Exch., 797 F.2d 1288 (5th Cir.1986) ("most significant relationship" analysis to construe insurance policy—Texas law); Pound v. Insurance Co. of N.Amer., 439 F.2d 1059 (10th Cir. 1971) (N.Mex. law, "accidental bodily injury", where master policy issued); Raymond v. Monsanto Co., 329 F.Supp. 247 (D.N.H.1971) (insurer's duty to defend under product liability policy, where injury occurred, not where policy issued, most significant relationship); Becker Pretzel Bakeries, Inc. v. Universal Oven Co., 279 F.Supp. 893 (D.Md.1968) (whether clause exempting manufacturer from liability includes liability for negligence, place of making); Menendez v. Perishable Distributors, Inc., 254 Ga. 300, 329 S.E.2d 149 (1985) (law of place of contracting to determine effect of release), overruled on another issue, Posey v. Medical Center–West, Inc., 257 Ga. 55, 354 S.E.2d 417 (1987); Crown Center Redevelopment Corp. v. Occidental Fire & Cas. Co. of N.C., 716 S.W.2d 348 (Mo.App.1986) (place where insured risk is located); Bjerken v. Ames Sand & Gravel Co., 189 N.W.2d 366 (N.D.1971) (applying statutory rule since repealed); American Home Assur. v. Safway Steel Prod., 743 S.W.2d 693 (Tex.App—Austin 1987, error denied) (whether punitive damages covered—law of Texas where torts occurred and claimants reside).

208. See Uniform Commercial Code § 1–105(1), Comment 1; Restatement (Second) § 187(1).

209. Restatement (Second) § 204, comment *a.*

210. The International Institute for the Unification of Private Law (UNIDROIT), with headquarters in Rome, published the amended Principles in 2004. The Principles are set

The Rome Regulation on the Law Applicable to Contractual Obligations, which is in force in the European Community, gives contracting parties substantial freedom to choose the national law to govern their rights and duties,[211] but not the freedom to choose anational rules such as the Principles.[212] There is no reason for this limitation. By adopting the Principles the parties are simply incorporating by reference details of their agreement. If instead of this shorthand the parties had spelled out these provisions at length, any state that has a contact with the parties or the transaction would enforce that portion of the contract. Article 1.4 states: "Nothing in these Principles shall restrict the application of mandatory rules, whether of national, international or supranational origin, which are applicable in accordance with the relevant rules of private international law."[213]

The Second Restatement of Conflict of Laws gives contracting parties the power to choose the law of any "state" to govern an issue that "the parties could have resolved by an explicit provision in their agreement"[214] and notes that this Restatement provision "is a rule providing for incorporation by reference and is not a rule of choice of law."[215] Therefore there is no reason to read this Restatement provision literally as restricting the parties to the law of a "state."

If there is no choice-of-law clause in the contract, the problem of resolving a conflict problem concerning the construction of a contract becomes more difficult. It may be that there is a "false" conflict in

---

out in 37 UCC L. J. 91 (2004). See also The Principals of European Contract Law (1999), prepared by the Commission on European Contract Law, http://www.cbs.dk/departments/law/staff/ol/commission_on_ecl.

211. Regulation on the Law Applicable to Contractual Obligations art. 3, EC No. 593/2008 O.J. (L 177).

212. Cf. these comments on the Convention that preceded the Regulation: M. Giuliano & P. Lagarde, Report on the Convention on the Law Applicable to Contractual Obligations, 1980 O.J. (C 282) at 15 (referring to the parties' freedom for "localization of the contract in a specific legal system") (comment by Mario Giuliano); Lagarde, *The European Convention on the Law Applicable to Contractual Obligations*, 22 Va. J. Int'l L. 91, 93 (1981) (stating that "[t]he negotiators have adopted the method of bilateral choice-of-law rules, resorting neither to the method of substantive rules of private international law (lex mercatoria) nor to governmental interests analysis") (citations omitted); cf. Juenger, *The UNIDROIT Principles of Commercial Contracts and Inter–American Contract Choice of Law*, in Contratación International: Commentarios a los Principios Sobre Los Contratos Comerciales Internacionales del UNIDROIT 229, 234 (1998) (stating that "[w]hile the Rome Convention does not *prohibit* the parties from designating the *lex mercatoria* or the UNIDROIT Principles, such choice-of-law clauses are treated as if the parties had failed to make a selection, so that their validity depends on the otherwise applicable law") (emphasis in original).

Professor Juenger also points out that art. 7 of the Mexico City Treaty on the Law Applicable to Contracts "grants the parties to a contract full autonomy to select any law they wish, be it the law of some state or nation or a non-positive law such as the Principles." Id. at 235. For the text of art. 7 *see* Organization of American States Fifth Inter–American Specialized Conference on Private International Law: Inter–American Convention on the Law Applicable to International Contracts, OAS Doc.–OEA/Ser. K/XXI.5 (Mar. 17, 1994), 33 I.L.M. 732, 734.

213. UNIDROIT Principles supra note 210 art. 1.4.

214. Restatement (Second) § 187(1).

215. Id. § 187 cmt. *c*.

somewhat the same sense as that term is used in connection with validity problems.[216] Domestic rules of construction, though they represent policies less strongly held than policies underlying invalidating rules, may nevertheless seek to advance specific social purposes. For example, assume a rule that, in the absence of a contrary manifestation of intention in the contract, a manufacturer is excused from its promise to sell its product if its factory is destroyed before manufacture is completed. This rule of construction probably represents a policy that risks of the type covered by the rule should not be borne by the seller unless it has specifically agreed to bear them. If both buyer and seller have their home offices in the state having the rule described and the contacts with a state having a contrary rule of construction would give that state no interest in distributing the risk of impossibility of performance between buyer and seller, the policy of the home state is exclusively relevant.

If two or more states have different rules of construction the underlying purposes of which would be advanced by application to the interstate contract in issue, there is a "true" conflict concerning construction. Of the factors indicated above for resolving true validity problems,[217] only "anachronism" seems relevant. If one of the rules of construction, when compared with the other rule, seems clearly out of step with modern trends in such matters and unresponsive to the practical needs of the commercial community, the conflict should be resolved in favor of the rule that does not have these defects.

If there is a true conflict between two rules of construction and one does not seem clearly anachronistic or aberrant in comparison with the other, the sole remaining goal of conflicts analysis is to insulate the result from the selection of the forum. If any choice-of-law rule is to be applied at this point, it should be one that is simple and gives substantial assurance that it will be uniformly interpreted and applied. These are not characteristics one would associate with the rule that the Second Restatement supplies for construction problems in the absence of a choice-of-law clause—the law of the state that "has the most significant relationship to the transaction and the parties."[218] If the forum wishes above all else to reach the same result as would be reached if the case were litigated in the other contact state, it should inquire directly into how the other state would in fact decide the interstate case in issue and copy this result.[219] There are two situations in which the forum will not be able to achieve uniformity of result by thus placing itself in the place of the foreign court. One situation is that in which the foreign court would insist on making the same reference to the forum's result as the forum is attempting to make to the foreign result. The two mirrors that

---

216. See text accompanying notes 11–16, supra.

217. See §§ 7.4A–7.4F.

218. Restatement (Second) §§ 204(b), 188(1).

219. See In re Schneider, 198 Misc. 1017, 1021, 96 N.Y.S.2d 652, 657, adhered to 198 Misc. 1017, 100 N.Y.S.2d 371 (Surr.Ct.1950); In re Annesley, [1926] Ch. 692, 708; Griswold, *Renvoi Revisited*, 51 Harv. L. Rev. 1165 (1938).

the courts are holding up to one another give a glimpse of infinity, but no answer. The other situation in which the forum cannot achieve uniformity of result by sitting and judging as would the foreign court is when there is more than one foreign contact state and the foreign courts differ from one another on the result to be reached.

If the forum is unable to resolve a conflicts-contracts-construction problem by reference to policies underlying the domestic rules of construction and is also unable to insulate the result from the selection of the forum, there is no conflicts policy that can be attained. The time has come to apply the law of the forum, thus providing a rule of decision most convenient for local judges and lawyers. This assumes that the forum is not neutral—that its contacts with the transaction are such as to make its law rationally applicable.

§ 7.9   Elimination of Conflicts by Unification: The U.N. Convention

There are three methods for dealing with the problems posed by differences in domestic rules when contracts have contacts with more than one jurisdiction. First and most common is the method discussed in this chapter. Develop choice-of-law rules to determine which jurisdiction's law applies to a particular issue.[220] Second, eliminate the conflict by unifying the domestic laws of different jurisdictions. This is the goal, only partially attained,[221] of the Uniform Commercial Code. A third method is to leave the diverse domestic rules as they are but develop a special set of substantive rules for transjurisdictional contracts. An important example of this third method has now come on the scene with the United States' ratification in 1986 of the United Nations Convention for the International Sale of Goods.[222]

The Convention was adopted at a 62–nation United Nations (U.N.) conference in 1980 after twelve years of preparatory work by the U.N. Commission on International Trade Law. The Convention was ratified by more than the necessary ten countries[223] and entered into force on

220. It is also possible to formulate a "new rule" that better accommodates the policies of the contact states than would the domestic laws of any of the states. See §§ 3.5, 7.6.

221. Louisiana has not adopted Uniform Commercial Code Articles 2 and 2A, and there are many variations from state to state both in the adoption of Code language and in the interpretation of identical language.

222. See 98th Congress, 1st Session, Senate Treaty Doc. No. 98–9; April 11, 1980, 1489 U.N.T.S. 3, 19 I.L.M. 671 [hereinafter cited as U.N. Convention].

The Convention is intended to supersede the Hague Convention on a Uniform Law on the Formation of Contracts for the International Sale of Goods and the Hague Convention on a Uniform Law on the International Sale of Goods. See U.N. Convention Art. 99(3). [Unless otherwise indicated, all references are to the U.N. Convention.]; J. Honnold, Uniform Law for International Sales Under the 1980 United Nations Convention (1982).

See also UN Convention on the Use of Electronic Communications in International Contracts, General Assembly Resolution A/Res/60/21; U.N. Doc. A/CN.9/577 (2005). As of September 1, 2009, 18 countries had signed the Convention, none had ratified it, and it was not in force

223. Art. 99(2).

January 1, 1988. Discussion here will be limited to the Convention's scope, when it applies, and some of its more interesting sales law rules.

The Convention does not apply to consumer sales or to the sales of certain items such as securities.[224] It covers formation of the contract, but not the validity of its provisions[225] and it does not apply to the liability of the seller for death or personal injury.[226]

The parties to the contract may exclude the operation of the Convention or "derogate from or vary the effect of any of its provisions."[227] In order to do so the parties must either choose the law of a non-signatory country or express their intention that the Convention does not apply. If their contract has a choice-of-law clause choosing the law of a signatory country or a political subdivision of a signatory country, the Convention applies because it is part of the law chosen.[228]

In the absence of effective exclusion by the contracting parties, the "Convention applies to contracts of sales of goods between parties whose places of business are in different States" if those states have ratified the Convention.[229] The Convention also applies if the forum's conflicts rules lead to the application of the law of a ratifying country.[230] The United States, as permitted by Article 95 of the Convention, has declared that it will not be bound by this latter provision. The reasons given are the uncertainty that would be introduced by reference to conflicts rules and the one-sided operation of the provision.[231] If the United States had not rejected the Convention's conflicts-rules provision and a United States business dealt with a business located in a country that had not ratified the Convention, United States domestic law would be replaced by the Convention if the conflicts rules of the United States forum pointed to the United States. If suit had been in the non-ratifying country, the Convention would not apply.

---

224. Art. 2. Also excluded are auction and execution sales and sales of ships, vessels, hovercraft, aircraft, and electricity. Id.

225. Art. 4.

226. Art. 5.

227. Art. 6. The parties may not, however, depart from the Article 12 provision permitting a Contracting State to insist that the making and modification of contracts be in writing.

See BP Oil Int'l, Ltd. v. Empresa Estatal Petroleos de Ecuador, 332 F.3d 333, 337 (5th Cir. 2003) (stating that the parties "must affirmatively opt-out of the" Convention and holding that they do not do so by choosing the law of a country that has ratified the Convention).

228. See Ajax Tool Works, Inc. v. Can–Eng Manufacturing Ltd., 2003 WL 223187 (N.D. Ill. 2003) (choice of Ontario law does not exclude the Convention because the Convention is part of Ontario law).

229. Art. 1. See also Art. 10 (if more than one place of business, the place referred to is "that which has the closest relationship to the contract and its performance"; if a party has no place of business, the reference is to his or her habitual residence).

A Contracting State may exclude operation of the Convention between it and other States that "have the same or closely related legal rules on matters governed by" the Convention. Art. 94.

230. Art. 1(1)(b).

231. See 98th Congress, 1st Session, Senate Treaty Doc. No. 98–9, Appendix B.

The sales rules of the Convention resemble those of Article 2 of the Uniform Commercial Code (UCC). When there is a deviation from a Code provision, the change is usually for the better. Following are comments on some of the Convention rules.

There is no statute of frauds. On the contrary, the Convention disclaims a writing requirement.[232] Although the Convention permits a ratifying country to disclaim this provision,[233] the United States has wisely accepted it.

There is a firm-offer provision, similar to that of section 2–205 of the Code, but without the Code's three-month limit on the effectiveness of the promise not to revoke an offer to buy or sell.[234] The Convention makes clear that a rejection terminates the power of accepting a firm offer,[235] a question not addressed in the Code.

Modification of a sales agreement is permitted without additional consideration, similar to UCC section 2–209, but, consistent with the Convention's avoidance of writing requirements, there is missing section 2–209's requirement that modification satisfy the statute of frauds.[236]

The Convention's counterpart to UCC section 2–207, the "battle of the forms" provision, limits itself to acceptance by a communication that does not contain a material addition.[237] Thus the Convention, unlike § 2–207, limits itself to keeping a party in who is attempting to take advantage of a minor variation between exchanged forms to repudiate what in commercial understanding is a completed agreement. Other problems with which section 2–207 attempts to deal,[238] at the cost of much complexity and confusion, are wisely left to the courts to sort out by basic principles concerning the making of express and implied-in-fact agreements.

In some respects the Convention's treatment of the battle of the forms is less desirable than the UCC's section 2–207. Article 19(3) sets out "[a]dditional or different terms [that] are considered to alter the terms of the offer materially." There is no provision for possible exceptions. The language "unless the offeree by virtue of the offer or the particular circumstances of the case has reason to believe they are acceptable to the offeror," which appeared in an earlier version of the

---

232. Art. 11 (formation); Art. 29 (modification or termination). A written contract may provide that it must be modified or terminated in writing. Art. 29(2).

233. Art. 96.

234. Art. 16(2)(a).

235. Art. 17.

236. Art. 29(1).

237. Art. 19(2).

238. Two other purposes ascribed to UCC § 2–207 are to end the "last shot advantage" of the sender of the second form and to prevent implied-in-fact contract arguments unrealistically based on fine-print forms not read by anyone with actual or apparent authority to contract for the recipient. See Weintraub, *Disclaimer of Warranties and Limitation of Damages for Breach of Warranty Under the UCC*, 53 Texas L. Rev. 60, 70–72 (1974).

Convention,[239] has been deleted. It is unwise to attempt to set in concrete, incapable of being modified by trade usage, course of dealing, or course of performance, what is "material." For example, one of the terms labeled "material" in 19(3) is any term relating to "payment." This contrasts unfavorable with UCC section 2–207, comment 5, which gives as an example of a clause that does not materially alter the agreement, "a clause providing for interest on overdue invoices or fixing the seller's standard credit terms where they are within the range of trade practice and do not limit any credit bargained for...." Comment 4 to 2–207, which gives examples of clauses that constitute material alteration, modifies its list with words such as "standard," "normally," "usage of trade," "customary or reasonable."

Article 19(2) provides that if "a reply to an offer ... contains additional or different terms which do not materially alter the terms of the offer," the new terms become part of the contract "unless the offeror, without undue delay, objects orally to the discrepancy or dispatches a notice to that effect." These words seem to require a notice after the reply has been received. This assumes that someone reads the fine print on the seller's[240] form. Under 2–207, the buyer can prevent the seller's non-material additions from automatically becoming part of the contract by including in the buyer's order form the statement "this offer expressly limits acceptance to the terms of the offer and you are hereby given notification of the offeror's objection to any additional or different terms."[241]

Both Article 19 and 2–207 are probably tilting against windmills. There is no problem with the battle of the forms that common-sense application of reasonable standards of interpretation cannot resolve. It is not possible to legislate common sense. It is possible to legislate lunacy and some excellent courts, in struggling with the 2–207 monster, have said some strange things.[242] The best way to improve both 2–207 and Article 19 is to repeal them and trust to the good sense of courts to keep the repudiator in and to avoid unwarranted findings of implied-in-fact acceptances of fine-print terms.

The normal Convention remedy if either buyer or seller breaks the contract is specific performance.[243] The forum need not, however, order

---

239. See United Nations Commission on International Trade Draft Convention on Contracts for the International Sale of Goods (1978), reprinted in 27 Am.J. Comp.L. 325, 328–29 (1979), Art. 17(3).

240. Although the offer may come from the seller, typically it is the seller who is responding to the buyer's offer.

241. UCC § 2–207(2)(a), (c).

242. See, e.g., C. Itoh & Co. (America) Inc. v. Jordan Int'l Co., 552 F.2d 1228, 1237 (7th Cir.1977), which states that the 2–207(3) language, "any other provisions of this Act," refers only to "the standardized 'gap filler' provisions of Article Two." The only example given in 2–207 comment 6 of a UCC provision that might supply a term is 2–207(2), which would make the seller's non-material additions part of the contract unless the buyer objected or competently drafted the buyer's form to exclude them—hardly a "standardized 'gap filler.'"

243. Art. 46 (buyer's remedy); Art. 62 (seller's remedy).

specific performance if this is contrary to its normal procedures.[244] The Convention's preference for specific performance is in accord with the arguments of some commentators that this remedy is efficient and less likely to under compensate the aggrieved party.[245]

The "perfect tender" rule of the English law merchant, which was carried forward in the UCC,[246] is happily absent.[247]

Parties engaged in international sales of goods should carefully consider whether they wish the Convention to control their rights and duties. Much thanks is due to the group of experts who drafted the Convention and, in the United States, especially to Professors John Honnold and Allan Farnsworth.[248]

§ 7.10   Conclusion

The Rome Regulation (Rome I) provides a good model for affording freedom to choose law governing the construction or validity of the contract and in setting limits on this freedom. In the absence of a choice by the parties: (1) problems of validity should be approached with a rebuttable presumption that the validating law of a jurisdiction connected to the parties or the transaction applies; (2) courts and lawyers should be directed to specific, objectively determinable factors that will strengthen or rebut this presumption.

---

244.   Art. 28.

245.   See, e.g., Schwartz, *The Case for Specific Performance*, 89 Yale L. J. 271 (1979).

246.   See UCC § 2–601 ("if the goods or the tender of delivery fail in any respect to conform to the contract, the buyer may (a) reject the whole...."). There is a substantial impairment requirement for rejection of an installment delivered under an installment contract (§ 2–612(2)) and the seller has the right, under certain circumstances, to cure a non-conforming tender (§ 2–508).

247.   Art. 46(2).

248.   See S.Hrg. 98–837, p. 20 (1984) outlining Professor Honnold's participation in the drafting of the Convention from the first working session to its completion. Professor Allan Farnsworth represented the United States during much of the work on the Convention. Id.

Chapter 8

PROPERTY

I. REAL PROPERTY ("IMMOVABLES")

§ 8.1 The Situs Rule

It follows that the right to redemption as of course under a foreclosure sale is a rule of property in the State of Iowa. It has no extra-territorial force, but dies at the State boundary, as the trees about Troy, under the mandate of the gods, grew no higher than the walls.[1]

Thus, in his typically colorful fashion, Judge Henry Lamm epitomizes the common law's almost mystical acceptance of the law of the situs as the law that determines all matters concerning real property. In the mid nineteenth century Joseph Story said that "the general principle of the common law is, that the laws of the place, where such [real] property is situate, exclusively govern in respect to the rights of the parties, the modes of transfer, and the solemnities, which should accompany them."[2] Although there are a few earlier examples, it is primarily in the late 1970's and early 1980's that courts began to subject Story's statement to the kind of functional reappraisal[3] that began in the early 1960's for tort choice-of-law problems.[4] The Second Restatement of Conflict of Laws, which made dramatic departures from the rigid rules of the First Restatement in articulating choice-of-law rules for torts[5] and contracts,[6] refers almost[7] every question concerning "immovables,"[8]

---

1. Hughes v. Winkleman, 243 Mo. 81, 91, 147 S.W. 994, 996 (1912).

2. Story, Conflict of Laws § 424, at 708 (3d ed. 1846). For a more recent statement of the same conclusion, with approval, see Goodrich, *Two States and Real Estate*, 89 U.Pa. L. Rev. 417, 418 (1941). Baxter, *Conflicts of Law and Property*, 10 McGill L. J. 1, 34–35 (1964), gives reluctant approval to the situs rule because its wide use leads to uniformity and predictability. Carnahan, *Tangible Property and the Conflict of Laws*, 2 U. Chi. L. Rev. 345, 347 (1935), so favors the situs rule as to urge its extension to questions of succession of personal property. But cf. Note, 38 Colum. L. Rev. 1049, 1050 (1938) (noting "substantial deflections" from the situs rule in cases concerning covenants not running with the land, contracts to convey, and mortgages, but concluding "there is no denying the fact that the situs rule is dominant").

3. See § 8.21A.

4. See, e.g., Babcock v. Jackson, 12 N.Y.2d 473, 240 N.Y.S.2d 743, 191 N.E.2d 279 (1963).

5. Restatement (Second) Conflict of Laws § 145 (1971) [hereinafter cited as Restatement (Second)] ("the state which ... has the most significant relationship to the occurrence and the parties").

6. Restatement (Second) § 188(1) ("the local law of the state which ... has the most significant relationship to the transaction and the parties").

7. Construction of an instrument of conveyance is "in accordance with the rules of construction of the state designated for this purpose in the instrument". Restatement

whether arising from inter vivos transactions or on testate or intestate succession, to the whole law[9] of the situs of the realty, including the conflicts rules of the situs. This reference to the whole law of the situs is not itself a choice-of-law rule, for it provides no guidance to a court at the situs, the most probable forum.[10] Despite this circumlocution, the Second Restatement notes that the domestic law of the situs is usually applied to the full gamut of choice-of-law problems concerning realty.[11]

This most monolithic of all choice-of-law rules is further buttressed by the very conflicts jargon used in the property area. Instead of "realty" and "personalty" we speak of "immovables" and "movables." The term "immovables"[12] is likely to encompass matters such as leaseholds,[13] which would be classified as "personalty" for domestic purposes, and "it is a firmly established principle that questions involving interests in immovables are governed by the law of the situs."[14]

The real property portion of this chapter will review and appraise the cogency of the reasons commonly given for favoring the law of the situs to control interests in realty. Then it will scrutinize the results actually obtained by application of the situs rule to a number of classic choice-of-law problems to determine whether those results are rational and just. Criticism of the results of applying the situs rule is accompanied by suggestions for more functional resolution of conflicts problems involving interests in realty.

Civil law jurisdictions do not share the common law countries' fixation on the situs of realty. A survey of countries that are members of

---

(Second) § 224(1). "A will insofar as it devises an interest in land is construed in accordance with the rules of construction of the state designated for this purpose in the will." Id. § 240(1).

"The local law" of the situs, excluding the conflicts law of the situs, is used to determine acquisition by adverse possession or prescription (Id. § 227), the method for foreclosure of a mortgage (Id. § 229), and whether there is escheat (Id. § 243).

8. Restatement (Second), ch. 9, Topic 2.

9. Id., Introductory Note at 7.

10. See Susi v. Belle Acton Stables, Inc., 360 F.2d 704, 710 (2d Cir.1966). (Friendly, J.) (in case of chattels, referral to whole law of situs "gives us a method of approach but little more"); Cook, The Logical and Legal Bases of the Conflict of Laws 264 (1942).

11. Restatement (Second), ch. 9, Topic 2, Introductory Note at 8.

An occasional functional insight emerges even in the Second Restatement's treatment of choice of law to determine interests in realty. See, e.g., Restatement (Second) § 233, comment *b* (the marital domicile "is the state which has the dominant interest in" the spouses and its local law should determine whether the husband can deprive the wife "of any marital interest she might have in his land").

12. Restatement (Second), ch. 9, Topic 2, Introductory Note at 7: "The term 'immovables,' as used in the Restatement of this Subject, refers to land and to things that are so attached, or otherwise related, to the land as legally to be regarded a part of it."

13. See Duncan v. Lawson, 41 Ch.D. 394 (1889); Restatement (Second) § 278, comment *e* at 218 (indicating some split of authority with regard to conflicts treatment of leaseholds).

Other problems may arise in characterizing property as movable or immovable. See, e.g., Denney v. Teel, 688 P.2d 803 (Okl.1984) (the right to receive a royalty from mineral leases is an interest in unpossessed minerals in the ground and is realty).

14. Restatement (Second), ch. 9, Topic 2, Introductory Note at 7.

the Hague Conference on Private International Law revealed that most civil law jurisdictions applied the same law to both personal and real property (unity principle) for testate and intestate succession. Most applied the law of the decedent's nationality, but some applied the law of the decedent's domicile at death.[15]

§ 8.2 Reasons for the Situs Rule

Courts and commentators most frequently advance two reasons for a choice-of-law rule invariably pointing to the law of the situs to govern all questions that may arise concerning realty. The first of these reasons has to do with modern recording systems and the necessity of keeping title search simple and feasible by allowing the searcher to apply the law of the situs to all legal problems that the search may uncover. The record will not reveal many of the factors that might favor application of law other than that of the situs, such as the fact that the parties to a transaction have a settled residence elsewhere. Even if such matters were revealed, it would substantially complicate the title search and enormously increase its cost to require the searcher to ferret out the foreign law, gain an understanding of its nuances, and apply it to the problem at hand. In short, the recording system would be thrown into chaos and transactions in realty would become impossibly expensive, risky, and impractical if any law but that of the situs were to govern.[16]

This is indeed an imposing reason for adherence to the situs rule when there is a bona fide purchaser who has relied upon record title and situs law. This argument based on the needs of the recording system has no relevance to the original parties to the transaction for which we are seeking the governing law. But it is here, between the original parties, that almost all the conflicts problems in the cases and the literature arise and here that the situs rule has been dominant. The fundamental distinction that would eliminate the cogency of the expediency reason for the situs rule is the distinction between immediate and subsequent parties to the transaction for which a choice-of-law question arises.[17] It is this distinction that this chapter draws.

---

15. Droz, Commentary on the Questionnaire on Succession in Private International Law, and Van Loon, Update of the Commentary, in Proceedings of the Sixteenth Session of the Hague Conference on Private International Law. See also the Japanese Act on the General Rules of Application of Laws, Law No. 10 of 1898 as newly titled and amended 21 June 2006, art. 36 (succession governed by national law of the decedent), art. 37 (formation and effect of a will governed by testator's national law at the time of will's formation, revocation of will governed by testator's national law at the time of revocation).

16. Succession of Simms, 250 La. 177, 218, 195 So.2d 114, 129 (1965), cert. denied sub nom. Kitchen v. Reese, 389 U.S. 850, 88 S.Ct. 47, 19 L.Ed.2d 120 (1967); Sinclair v. Sinclair, 99 N.H. 316, 318, 109 A.2d 851, 852 (1954); Restatement (Second), ch. 9, Topic 2, Introductory Note at 8; Cook, supra note 10, at 262; Goodrich, supra note 2, at 419; Note, 111 U.Pa. L. Rev. 482, 486, 490 (1963).

17. See Matter of Courtney, Mont. & C. 239, 252 (Ch.1840) (law of England, residence of creditor and debtor, not the law of the situs, Scotland, determines whether creditor acquired a lien on Scottish land superior to succession rights of debtor): "The transaction is in no respect impeached, and there is no competition with any person having obtained a title under the law of Scotland."; Hancock, *Conceptual Devices for Avoiding the Land Taboo in Conflict of Laws: The Disadvantages of Disingenuousness*, 20 Stan. L. Rev. 1, 22–

If a court applied some law other than that of the situs to a transaction between the original parties, the victor, in order to preserve the victory against subsequent bona fide purchasers, would have to record the judgment at the situs.[18] Nevertheless, the substantial law-and-economics literature now centered on choice of law, typically selects the law of the situs to preserve certainty of title.[19]

A cogent indication that the law of the situs is not a rule written in heaven is that civil law jurisdictions apply the same law to testate and intestate succession of both realty and personalty. Most apply the law of the decedent's nationality, but some apply the law of the decedent's domicile at death.[20]

The second reason for applying the law of the situs is well stated in an early draft of the Second Restatement:

> [L]and and things attached to the land are within the exclusive control of the state in which they are situated, and the officials of that state are the only ones who can lawfully deal with them

23 (1967); cf. Lorenzen, *Application of Full Faith and Credit Clause to Equitable Decrees for the Conveyance of Foreign Land*, 34 Yale L. J. 591, 611 (1925), (drawing distinction between immediate and remote parties for requirement of full faith and credit to non-situs land decree).

18. See Matson v. Matson, 186 Iowa 607, 622–623, 173 N.W. 127, 132 (1919) (dictum); B. Currie, *Full Faith and Credit to Foreign Land Decrees*, 21 U. Chi. L. Rev. 620, 639 (1954); Hopkins, *The Extraterritorial Effect of Probate Decrees*, 53 Yale L. J. 221, 254 (1944).

In Hughes v. Winkleman, 243 Mo. 81, 147 S.W. 994 (1912), the court refused to enforce an Iowa right of redemption against a Missouri citizen to whom the Iowa creditor had negotiated a note and mortgage on Missouri real estate, the court noting that there was no showing that the Missouri holder knew that the mortgagor was an Iowa citizen or that a right of redemption existed under Iowa law. In Jennings v. Jennings, 21 Ohio St. 56, 62–63 (1871), one R.P. Ranney, attorney for the plaintiff, in arguing brilliantly but unsuccessfully that the law of the domicile of all parties, not the situs, should govern the question whether provisions in the husband's will for the widow are in lieu of dower, contended: "the legislature has intended in this as in many other directions, to allow the citizens of such States to dispose of property held here in accordance with their own laws, simply requiring them to place the evidence of their title upon our public records...." X v. Y, [1994] 48 Minshu (3) 835, [1994] H.J. (1493) 80 (S.Ct. of Japan), translation in 18 Japanese Ann. Int'l L. 144 (1995), held that although the law of China as the nationality of a decedent determines succession to the decedent's land in Japan, the rights of a purchaser of the land are determined by Japanese law.

19. See Allen & O'Hara, *Second Generation Law and Economics of Conflict of Laws: Baxter's Comparative Impairment and Beyond*, 51 Stan. L. Rev. 1011, 1046 (1999) ("without a clear choice-of-law rule regarding these disputes [over personal rights in realty], certainty of title is threatened, and the land becomes less valuable as the cost of title insurance rises"); O'Hara & Ribstein, *From Politics to Efficiency in Choice of Law*, 67 U. Chi. L. Rev. 1151, 1220 (2000) ("situs states also have a comparative regulatory advantage regarding title issues because clarity of title affects the price and availability of title insurance and therefore the transferability of land to its most highly valued uses").

20. See supra § 8.1 note 15. See also Convention on the Law Applicable to Succession to the Estates of Deceased Persons, Aug. 1, 1989, art. 3 (succession to both realty and personalty governed by law of habitual residence or law of nationality). The Convention does not have the three ratifications that art. 28(1) requires for the Convention to enter into force. It has been ratified by the Netherlands and signed by Argentina, Luxembourg, and Switzerland. http://www.hcch.net/e/status/stat32e.html (visited 9/25/09). Cf. Germany, Bundesgesetzblatt 1999, I, 1026, art. 46 (stating that if there is a substantially closer connection to a state other than the situs of property, the law of that state applies to govern rights in the property).

physically. Since interests in immovables cannot be affected without the consent of the state of the situs, it is natural that the latter's law should be applied by the courts of other states.[21]

Even if it were true that only a court at the situs of realty has constitutional jurisdiction over the subject matter when litigation affects interests of persons in that realty, this would not logically compel application of the law of the situs. For example, if the situs courts believed that they would reach a more rational result by applying the law of some other state, they would be free to apply that other law.[22]

Of course, if the situs had exclusive jurisdiction of the subject matter, the Restatement's reference to the whole law of the situs would be a constitutionally-compelled truism. But much more than this, such a jurisdictional requirement would seriously weaken any argument to change the situs rule. If nothing else, the simple convenience and economy in judicial administration flowing from the only competent forum's applying its own law would raise a presumption in favor of situs law that only the most compelling circumstances should rebut.

It is necessary then, before focusing directly on the choice-of-law problem, to scrutinize the alleged constitutional reasons why, as between states of the United States, only situs courts have jurisdiction over the subject matter in adjudications affecting interests in real property and why in personam jurisdiction over all persons whose interests are to be affected is not sufficient. The United States Supreme Court opinions most often cited for such a proposition provide a place to begin.

§ 8.3 Jurisdiction of the Non–Situs Court: Early Supreme Court Decisions

One of the earliest cases discussing the jurisdiction of a non-situs court to issue a decree affecting interests in land, *Massie v. Watts*,[23] supported such jurisdiction, at least under certain circumstances. Watts, a citizen of Virginia, sued Massie, a citizen of Kentucky in a federal court in Kentucky to compel Massie to convey to Watts land in Ohio to which Massie held legal title. Watts claimed that Massie had acquired legal title with notice of Watts' equitable title. In affirming a decree that Watts should recover the land from the defendant, Chief Justice Marshall said:

> Was this cause, therefore, to be considered as involving a naked question of title . . . the jurisdiction of the Circuit Court of Kentucky would not be sustained. But where the question changes its character, where the defendant in the original action is liable to the plaintiff, either in consequence of contract, or as trustee, or as the holder of a legal title acquired by any species of *mala fides* practiced on the plaintiff, the principles of equity give a court jurisdiction wherever the person may be found, and the circumstance, that a

---

21. Restatement (Second) ch. 7, Topic 2, at 12–13 (Tent. Draft No. 5, 1959).

22. See Hancock, *Equitable Conversion and the Land Taboo in Conflict of Laws*, 17 Stan. L. Rev. 1095, 1096 n.4 (1965).

23. 10 U.S. (6 Cranch) 148, 3 L.Ed. 181 (1810).

question of title may be involved in the inquiry, and may even constitute the essential point on which the case depends, does not seem sufficient to arrest that jurisdiction.[24]

In *Watts v. Waddle*,[25] a sequel to *Massie v. Watts*, the Court held that Watts was not entitled to land he had won in *Massie v. Watts*. The refusal was based on clouds on Watts' title unrelated to his decree against Massie. Banks, who claimed an interest in the Ohio land, was suing Watts in Kentucky. Watts tried to dissipate this cloud by arguing that "the court of Kentucky has not jurisdiction of the subject-matter, so as to transfer the title to land in Ohio."[26] The Court replied that: "The general court of Kentucky have [sic] jurisdiction of the controversy; and as process was served on the defendant Watts, their powers are ample to enforce their decree, in personam, or to direct the execution of a deed, should the land be decreed, by a commissioner, as the statute of Kentucky authorizes."[27]

There was dictum to the same effect in *Cheever v. Wilson*,[28] a case involving the impact of an Indiana divorce decree on District of Columbia realty: "The decree rendered in Indiana, so far as it related to the real property in question, could have no extraterritorial effect; but, if valid, it bound personally those who were parties in the case, and could have been enforced in the *situs rei*, by the proper proceedings conducted there for that purpose."[29]

Thus far then, the Supreme Court cases seemed to support the power of a non-situs court to affect interests in realty between parties over whom it has in personam jurisdiction. *Robertson v. Pickrell*,[30] holding that a District of Columbia court at the situs of realty need not give full faith and credit to a Virginia proceeding that validated a will devising the realty, permitted attack on the will by persons who (as the Court was careful to point out)[31] were not parties to the Virginia proceeding.

Carpenter v. Strange[32] began the movement away from this early line of cases. The plaintiff sued her sister, the executrix of her father's estate. She sued in New York, the common domicile of the sisters and of the father at death. The plaintiff sought to recover a sum that the father had held for her benefit as trustee, but for which he had never accounted. The father had made a devise to the plaintiff on condition that she renounce this claim against his estate. He conveyed land in Tennessee to the executrix without consideration.

---

24. Id. at 158, 3 L.Ed. at 185.

25. 31 U.S. (6 Pet.) 389, 8 L.Ed. 437 (1832).

26. Id. at 397, 8 L.Ed. at 441.

27. Id.

28. 76 U.S. (9 Wall.) 108, 19 L.Ed. 604 (1869).

29. Id. at 121, 19 L.Ed. at 607.

30. 109 U.S. 608, 3 S.Ct. 407, 27 L.Ed. 1049 (1883).

31. Id. at 609, 613, 3 S.Ct. at 410, 27 L.Ed. at 1051.

32. 141 U.S. 87, 11 S.Ct. 960, 35 L.Ed. 640 (1891).

The New York court held that the plaintiff had not accepted the provision in her father's will, that she was entitled to recover the full amount she claimed from her father's estate, and that the deed of the Tennessee land to the executrix was null and void insofar as it purported to affect the assets against which the plaintiff might press her claim. Then, in a Tennessee equity proceeding in which the plaintiff and her executrix-sister again were parties, the Supreme Court of Tennessee made just the opposite ruling on every point. It held that the plaintiff had elected to take the devise, that therefore she could no longer press her claim, and that a New York court was without power to declare a deed of Tennessee land null and void. On writ of error, the Supreme Court of the United States held that the Tennessee court had improperly denied full faith and credit to the New York decree insofar as the New York decree determined that plaintiff had not elected to take her father's devise and was not barred from pressing her claim. But then, emphasizing the form of the New York decree, the Court upheld Tennessee's refusal to recognize that portion of the sister-state decree that declared the deed of Tennessee land void:

> By its terms no provision whatever was made for its enforcement against Mrs. Strange [the executrix] in respect of the real estate. No conveyance was directed, nor was there any attempt in any way to exert control over her in view of the conclusion that the court announced. Direct action upon the real estate was certainly not within the power of the court, and as it did not order Mrs. Strange to take any action with reference to it, and she took none, the courts of Tennessee were not obliged to surrender jurisdiction to the courts of New York over real estate in Tennessee, exclusively subject to its laws and the jurisdiction of its courts.[33]

There then followed the two cases upon which the doctrine that the non-situs court lacks jurisdiction over the subject matter is primarily based, *Clarke v. Clarke*[34] and *Fall v. Eastin.*[35]

§ 8.4　Jurisdiction of the Non–Situs Court: The *Clarke* and *Fall* Decisions

In the *Clarke* case, Mrs. Clarke had died domiciled in South Carolina survived by two minor daughters and her husband. Her daughters and husband were also South Carolina citizens. Mrs. Clarke's will left all of her estate, real and personal, wherever situated, in three equal shares to her husband and two daughters. When one of the daughters died shortly after Mrs. Clarke, Mr. Clarke, as executor and testamentary trustee

---

33. Id. at 106, 11 S.Ct. at 966, 35 L.Ed. at 648. For similar emphasis on the failure of the non-situs court to shape its decree in the form of an order to convey see Fire Ass'n v. Patton, 15 N.M. 304, 107 P. 679 (1910); Rozan v. Rozan, 129 N.W.2d 694 (N.D.1964); cf. Whitmer v. Whitmer, 243 Pa.Super. 462, 365 A.2d 1316, allocatur ref'd (1976); cert. denied, 434 U.S. 822, 98 S.Ct. 67, 54 L.Ed.2d 79 (1977) (non-situs court cannot directly affect the title to personal property).

34. 178 U.S. 186, 20 S.Ct. 873, 44 L.Ed. 1028 (1900).

35. 215 U.S. 1, 30 S.Ct. 3, 54 L.Ed. 65 (1909).

under his wife's will, brought an action in South Carolina to construe the will. The surviving daughter was represented by a guardian ad litem. The South Carolina Supreme Court affirmed the finding of the lower court that Mrs. Clarke intended that her realty, including that situated in other states, should be sold and the proceeds distributed as personalty—the will thus working an equitable conversion of the realty everywhere into personalty.[36] In so holding, the court specifically adverted to the choice-of-law issue, concluding that the equitable conversion made South Carolina law applicable to all questions of testate succession of the realty situated in Connecticut, New York, and Kansas, and, more important, made South Carolina law applicable to the intestate succession of the father and surviving daughter to the deceased daughter's share in the mother's estate.[37] Under South Carolina law, the father and surviving daughter divided equally the share that the deceased daughter would have taken in the mother's estate.

Mr. Clarke then brought suit in Connecticut as administrator of his deceased daughter's estate and asked directions for distribution. The Connecticut Probate Court decreed that the surviving daughter should take the entire share that the deceased daughter would have taken in the mother's estate. Mr. Clarke appealed in his own name, claiming that the Connecticut court was bound by the prior South Carolina determination between the same parties. The Connecticut Supreme Court of Errors, however, affirmed the Connecticut probate decree.[38] The Supreme Court of Errors indicated that the South Carolina courts did not have subject-matter jurisdiction to control intestate succession to Connecticut land, citing *Carpenter v. Strange*.[39] It avoided meeting the issue of full faith and credit head-on by reading the South Carolina opinion as purporting to affect only realty in South Carolina,[40] an interpretation that is extremely doubtful in the light of the express reference by the South Carolina court to the Connecticut realty and the choice of law for intestacy. Further, the Connecticut court pointed out that the parties were not the same because the husband had not appeared in his individual capacity in South Carolina and therefore would not have been bound if the South Carolina decision had gone against him, citing no South Carolina decisions to support such a statement. The Connecticut court therefore felt it:

> [U]nnecessary to inquire whether, if he had been a party individually to the South Carolina suit, and the principal administrator of the estate of Julia Clarke [the deceased daughter] had also been brought in, the court would have had jurisdiction to make a final and conclusive determination as to the effect of the will upon lands in

---

36. Clarke v. Clarke, 46 S.C. 230, 24 S.E. 202 (1896).

37. Id. at 233–38, 24 S.E. at 203–05.

38. Clarke's Appeal, 70 Conn. 195, 39 A. 155 (1898).

39. Id. at 210, 39 A. at 159.

40. Id. at 212, 39 A. at 160.

other States and their descent upon the decease of those in whose favor the testatrix disposed of them.[41]

Upon writ of error the United States Supreme Court went directly to the jurisdictional issue in meeting Mr. Clarke's full-faith-and-credit objections to the Connecticut judgment. The doctrine was "firmly established that the law of a State in which land is situated controls and governs its transmission by will or its passage in case of intestacy."[42] Mr. Clarke's argument was "but to contend that what cannot be done directly can be accomplished by indirection."[43] The guardian ad litem appointed for the surviving daughter in South Carolina did not have "authority to act for her *quo ad* her interest in real estate beyond the jurisdiction of the South Carolina court, and which was situated in Connecticut." And finally, "the decree of the South Carolina court, in the particular under consideration, was not entitled to be followed by the courts of Connecticut, by reason of a want of jurisdiction in the court of South Carolina over the particular subject-matter which was sought to be concluded in Connecticut by such decree."[44]

In *Fall v. Eastin*, Mrs. Fall had obtained a divorce from her husband in a contested proceeding in Washington, where both spouses were then domiciled. As part of its decree, the Washington court set apart for Mrs. Fall, as her separate property, land in Nebraska owned jointly by the couple. It ordered the husband to convey his interest in the Nebraska land to his wife and, when he failed to do so, appointed a commissioner who did execute such a deed. Four months before the Washington decree, Mr. Fall mortgaged the Nebraska land to his brother and, after the decree, deeded the land to his sister. Mrs. Fall brought suit in Nebraska to quiet title to the land in herself, contending that the mortgage and deed were attempts to defraud her of the interest in the land that she had acquired under the Washington decree. Although Mr. Fall was served by publication,[45] he was not served personally and did not appear. The Nebraska Supreme Court first affirmed a judgment in favor of Mrs. Fall, quieting her title in the land,[46] but then, after a decisive change in membership of the court, reversed on rehearing.[47] The opinion held that the Washington court was without jurisdiction to affect the title to Nebraska land: "To say that the decree binds the conscience of the party, so that persons to whom he may convey the land thereafter take no title, is the same as saying that the decree affects the title. . . ."[48]

---

41. Id. at 212–13, 39 A. at 160.

42. Clarke v. Clarke, 178 U.S. 186, 190, 20 S.Ct. 873, 874, 44 L.Ed. 1028, 1031 (1900).

43. Id. at 191–92, 20 S.Ct. at 875, 44 L.Ed. at 1031.

44. Id. at 195, 20 S.Ct. at 876, 44 L.Ed. at 1033. See also In re Estate of Roberg, 396 So.2d 235 (Fla.App.1981) (validity of will may be contested at situs of realty although the contestant was a party to a proceeding at the testator's domicile in which the will was held valid).

45. Fall v. Fall, 75 Neb. 104, 123, 113 N.W. 175, 176 (1907).

46. Fall v. Fall, 75 Neb. 104, 106 N.W. 412 (1905).

47. Id. at 120, 113 N.W. at 175.

48. Id. at 132, 113 N.W. at 180.

On writ of error, the United States Supreme Court affirmed. Mr. Justice McKenna sounded somewhat reluctant: "however plausibly the contrary view may be sustained, we think that the doctrine that the court, not having jurisdiction of the *res*, cannot affect it by its decree, nor by a deed made by a master in accordance with the decree, is firmly established."[49]

It is possible to attempt to explain away *Fall v. Eastin* on the ground that the wife mistook her remedy.[50] Instead of suing the husband's grantees directly, she should first have sued upon the Washington decree in Nebraska asking a Nebraska court to establish and enforce it as a decree from a Nebraska court, much as is the practice with sister-state money judgments. Mr. Justice McKenna remarked: "Plaintiff seems to contend for a greater efficacy for a decree in equity affecting real property than is given to a judgment at law for the recovery of money simply."[51] The Nebraska court made a similar point in expressing concern over a hypothetical bona fide purchaser, who might be misled by the record title in Nebraska if a Washington court "can so adjudicate the rights of parties to land in this state that a title apparently clear upon the official records could be made null and void by its action. . . ."[52] If this is all that was bothering the Nebraska court, requiring Mrs. Fall to go through what Nebraska considered the proper procedural steps would seem, within broad reasonable bounds, consistent with the mandate of full faith and credit.

Since *Fall v. Eastin*, the Supreme Court has done little to dispel the notion that only the situs has subject-matter jurisdiction to affect title to land. In a 1963 opinion holding that full faith and credit must be given to the jurisdictional finding that the land is within the adjudicating state, Mr. Justice Stewart stated that the first forum, Nebraska, "had jurisdiction over the subject matter of the controversy only if the land in question was in Nebraska."[53] This same notion is reflected in many decisions of situs courts refusing to recognize sister-state adjudications

---

49. Fall v. Eastin, 215 U.S. 1, 11, 30 S.Ct. 3, 7, 54 L.Ed. 65, 70 (1909).

50. See, e.g., Restatement (Second) § 102, Reporter's Note; Goodrich, supra note 2, at 428 n.50.

51. Fall v. Eastin, 215 U.S. at 12, 30 S.Ct. at 8, 54 L.Ed. at 71.

52. Fall v. Fall, 75 Neb. at 133, 113 N.W. at 180.

53. Durfee v. Duke, 375 U.S. 106, 108, 84 S.Ct. 242, 243, 11 L.Ed.2d 186, 189 (1963). The effect of this statement is mitigated because the action was quasi in rem to quiet title. Personal jurisdiction over the defendant was obtained because he made a general appearance. The Court notes that neither party disputed the proposition that Nebraska had jurisdiction only if the situs of the land. See id. at 108 n.3, 111 n.8, 84 S.Ct. at 243 n.3, 254 n.8, 11 L.Ed.2d at 189 n.3, 191 n.8. But see Baker v. General Motors Corp., 522 U.S. 222, 235, 118 S.Ct. 657, 665, 139 L.Ed.2d 580, 593–94 (1998): "Thus, a sister State's decree concerning land ownership in another State has been held ineffective to transfer title, see Fall v. Eastin, 215 U.S. 1, 30 S.Ct. 3, 54 L.Ed. 65 (1909), although such a decree may indeed preclusively adjudicate the rights and obligations running between the parties to the foreign litigation, see, e.g., Robertson v. Howard, 229 U.S. 254, 261, 33 S.Ct. 854, 856, 57 L.Ed. 1174 (1913) ('[I]t may not be doubted that a court of equity in one State in a proper case could compel a defendant before it to convey property situated in another State.')."

purporting to affect the interests in realty of parties before the non-situs court.[54]

It remains to be seen whether such refusal can withstand analysis under proper constitutional standards. A hint is given in the Supreme Court's more recent statement on the effect of non-situs judgments affecting interests in realty. *Baker v. General Motors Corp.*[55] held that a Missouri court did not have to give full faith and credit to a Michigan judgment enjoining an expert witness from testifying in other states. In the opinion, Justice Ginsburg states:

> Orders commanding action or inaction have been denied enforcement in a sister State when they purported to accomplish an official act within the exclusive province of that other State or interfered with litigation over which the ordering State had no authority. Thus, a sister State's decree concerning land ownership in another State has been held ineffective *to transfer title*, see *Fall v. Eastin*, 215 U.S. 1, 30 S.Ct. 3, 54 L.Ed. 65 (1909), although such a decree may indeed preclusively adjudicate the rights and obligations running between the *parties* to the foreign litigation, see, *e.g., Robertson v. Howard*, 229 U.S. 254, 261, 33 S.Ct. 854, 856, 57 L.Ed. 1174 (1913) ("[I]t may not be doubted that a court of equity in one State in a proper case could compel a defendant before it to convey property situated in another State.").[56]

§ 8.5 Full Faith and Credit for Non–Situs Decrees: Proper Constitutional Standards

One ground upon which it might be contended that the situs state need not give full faith and credit to the judgment of a sister state affecting interests in realty at the situs is that this would deprive the

---

54. Courtney v. Henry, 114 Ill.App. 635 (1904); Fire Ass'n v. Patton, 15 N.M. 304, 107 P. 679 (1910); McRary v. McRary, 228 N.C. 714, 47 S.E.2d 27 (1948); Rozan v. Rozan, 129 N.W.2d 694 (N.D.1964); Sharp v. Sharp, 65 Okl. 76, 166 P. 175 (1916); Williams v. Williams, 83 Or. 59, 162 P. 834 (1917) (but reaching the same conclusion as the non-situs court). See also Bullock v. Bullock, 52 N.J.Eq. 561, 30 A. 676 (Err. & App.1894). (But see refusal to follow *Bullock* in Higginbotham v. Higginbotham, 92 N.J.Super. 18, 222 A.2d 120 (App.Div.1966)); Welch v. Trustees of the Robert A. Welch Foundation, 465 S.W.2d 195 (Tex.Civ.App.—Houston [1st Dist.] 1971, writ ref'd n.r.e.) (Foundation trustees not bound by South Carolina judgment that will creating charitable trust of Texas realty is invalid) (but see *McElreath*, infra this note). Cf. Porter v. Porter, 101 Ariz. 131, 416 P.2d 564 (1966), cert. denied, 386 U.S. 957, 87 S.Ct. 1028, 18 L.Ed.2d 107 (1967) (but non-situs court had also refused to recognize prior situs judgments) [see Porter v. Wilson, 419 F.2d 254 (9th Cir.1969), cert. denied, 397 U.S. 1020, 90 S.Ct. 1260, 25 L.Ed.2d 531 (1970) holding second Arizona decision in *Porter* now entitled to full faith and credit]; In re Goar's Estate, 252 Iowa 108, 106 N.W.2d 93 (1960) (refusal to determine whether Texas land was part of estate of Iowa testator on ground that only Texas courts have such power) (Ironically, the next year the Texas Supreme Court recognized an Oklahoma divorce decree ordering the husband to convey Texas land to the wife, McElreath v. McElreath, 162 Tex. 190, 345 S.W.2d 722 (1961)); Second Nat'l Bk. v. Thomson, 455 S.W.2d 51 (Ky.1970) (local beneficiaries not bound by Texas domiciliary probate decision that a will disposing of Kentucky realty was void, but heirs at law may be bound); French v. Short, 207 Va. 548, 151 S.E.2d 354 (1966) (assumes that non-situs judgment did not purport to extend to situs land).

55. 522 U.S. 222, 118 S.Ct. 657, 139 L.Ed.2d 580 (1998).

56. Id. at 235–236, 118 S.Ct. at 665.

situs of control over its realty and would conflict with the strong and legitimate interests of the situs. The answer to such a contention must begin with recognition that the mandate of full faith and credit, even as to judgments, is not absolute; it requires weighing the interests of the situs in refusing to recognize the decree of a sister state affecting the title to situs land against the very strong national interest in according full faith and credit to judgments.[57] The situs, moreover, does not have the last word as to the balance to be struck. The standard is federal.[58]

We may dismiss at once the argument that by refusing to recognize the sister-state decree as between the original parties and their privies, the situs is simply protecting hypothetical bona fide purchasers who might rely on a record title that does not note the sister-state decree. When bona fide purchasers exist, the situs is free to protect them on the same basis as it would in wholly domestic transactions that are improperly recorded. It may not, however, create imaginary bogies to mask what is simply hostility to a sister-state decree.[59]

The situs may, under a proper full faith and credit standard, refuse to recognize a sister-state judgment affecting the interests of persons in realty (this is the true meaning of an adjudication of title)[60] only when recognizing a particular interest as validly created will conflict with its own interests as situs and when this conflict with its interests is so gross as to outweigh the need for full faith and credit. Although full discussion of this point must await analysis of the choice-of-law issues below, almost never will the situs qua situs have any legitimate interest in having its own law applied to the matter in hand. When the situs qua situs does have such an interest, it will typically be when the foreign decree affecting the interest of persons in the land will also affect the nature of the use of the land in ways not permitted by the law of the situs. Even in such very rare instances, it will be at least debatable whether this conflict with the interest of the situs is sufficient to outweigh the very great national need for full faith and credit to judgments. It is inconsistent with any rational view of full faith and credit to raise an irrefutable presumption that the interest of the situs advanced by refusing recognition will always outweigh the national need for full faith and credit.

It might be argued that non-situs land decrees are not entitled to full faith and credit because of their special nature. Equity decrees act upon the conscience of the defendant, and of old the only enforcement of

---

57. For statements of this full faith and credit standard on matters other than land decrees, see Hughes v. Fetter, 341 U.S. 609, 612, 71 S.Ct. 980, 982, 95 L.Ed. 1212, 1216 (1951); Milwaukee County v. M.E. White Co., 296 U.S. 268, 276–277, 56 S.Ct. 229, 233, 234, 80 L.Ed. 220, 228 (1935); Restatement (Second) § 103; Reese, *Full Faith and Credit to Foreign Equity Decrees*, 42 Iowa L. Rev. 183, 187 (1957); infra section 9.3A.

58. See Currie, supra note 18, at 623.

59. Cf. Hughes v. Fetter, 341 U.S. 609, 71 S.Ct. 980, 95 L.Ed. 1212 (1951) (forum may not be closed to wrongful death action under statute of sister state if only basis for refusal of forum is hostility to the statute).

60. See Restatement (Second), ch. 3, Introductory Note at 102: "Every valid exercise of judicial jurisdiction, as here defined, affects the interests of persons."

such decrees was by coercion upon defendant's person.[61] But to argue today "that a foreign decree ordering the conveyance of land creates no obligation but merely a duty owed by the defendant to the court" is to assume "that equity has made no progress since the time of Coke."[62] Since *Sistare v. Sistare*,[63] moreover, it has been clear that at least equity decrees in the form of past due unmodifiable alimony installments are entitled to full faith and credit.

Indeed, in one respect it is circular to talk in terms of full faith and credit not being owed to non-situs decrees affecting interests in land because the decreeing court lacks subject-matter jurisdiction. If full faith and credit were required, the non-situs court would have subject-matter jurisdiction. This point is well illustrated in one of the fountainheads of the doctrine of lack of jurisdiction, Joseph Story's treatise on Conflict of Laws.[64] In section 543, widely cited by situs courts denying recognition to non-situs decrees,[65] he does state:

> [A]lthough the person may be within the territorial jurisdiction; yet it is by no means true, that, in virtue thereof, every sort of suit may there be maintainable against him. A suit cannot, for instance, be maintainable against him, so as absolutely to bind his property situate elsewhere; and, *a fortiori*, not so as absolutely to bind his rights and titles to immovable property situate elsewhere.

Little noticed, however, is Story's statement in section 551 having important implications for courts bound by the mandate of full faith and credit:

> In respect to immovable property every attempt of any foreign tribunal to found a jurisdiction over it must, from the very nature of the case, be utterly nugatory, and its decree must be forever incapable of execution *in rem*. We have seen, indeed, that by the Roman law a suit might in many cases be brought, either where the property was situate, or where the party had his domicil. This might well be done within any of the vast domains, over which the Roman empire extended; for the judgments of its tribunals would be every where respected and obeyed. But among the independent nations of modern times there would be insuperable difficulties in such a course.

In order to break the circle of reasoning that concludes non-situs courts lack subject matter jurisdiction, it would be necessary to establish that permitting a non-situs court to affect the interests of persons before

---

61. See Penn v. Lord Baltimore, 1 Ves.Sen. 444, 27 Eng.Rep. 1132 (Ch.1750); J.R. v. M.P., Y.B. 37 Hen. VI, f. 13, pl. 3 (Common Pleas, 1459); Cook, *The Powers of Courts of Equity*, 15 Colum. L. Rev. 37, 48 (1915).

62. Barbour, *The Extra–Territorial Effect of the Equitable Decree*, 17 Mich. L. Rev. 527, 528 (1919).

63. 218 U.S. 1, 30 S.Ct. 682, 54 L.Ed. 905 (1910).

64. Story, Conflict of Laws (3d ed.1846).

65. See, e.g., Courtney v. Henry, 114 Ill.App. 635, 639 (1904). Cf. Page v. McKee, 66 Ky. (3 Bush) 135, 138–40 (1867) (but the situs court will enforce equities growing out of invalid decree).

it in realty is so unfair, so inappropriate, so outrageous, as to deprive the party adversely affected of due process of law. One difficulty with such a proposition is that it proves far too much. If this were so, the decree of the non-situs court affecting interests in realty would be void, and recognition of it not only would not be required under the full-faith-and-credit clause, but also would be forbidden as a violation of due process.[66] Yet many courts at the situs of real estate have given effect in various ways to decrees rendered in other jurisdictions by courts exercising in personam jurisdiction to affect the interests in the realty of the parties before the non-situs courts.[67] Some courts have held the losing party estopped to relitigate facts found as the basis for the non-situs decrees;[68] some have, on the basis of comity, recognized the interests declared by

66. But cf. Roller v. Murray, 234 U.S. 738, 34 S.Ct. 902, 58 L.Ed. 1570 (1914) (no substantial federal questions raised if forum erred by giving conclusive effect to sister-state judgment). Professor Currie points out, however, that *Roller v. Murray* was decided before the Supreme Court had jurisdiction to review state decisions that favored rights asserted under the Constitution. Currie, supra note 18, at 648 n.102.

67. For examples of the exercise of in personam jurisdiction to adjudicate interests in realty in another state, see, e.g., State v. Henderson, 149 Ariz. 254, 717 P.2d 933 (App. 1986) (order conveyance of land in Colorado); Goldman v. Bloom, 90 Wis.2d 466, 280 N.W.2d 170 (1979) and cases cited in note 86, infra this section; cf. Kountouris v. Varvaris, 476 So.2d 599 (Miss.1985) (forum court may adjudicate interest of parties in Greek realty, but on remand should decide whether this is feasible); Hamlin v. Hamlin, [1985] 3 W.L.R. 629 (C.A.) (forum divorce court may enjoin husband from disposing of Spanish realty). But cf. Furman v. Mascitti, 714 F.2d 299 (4th Cir.1983) (non-situs decree that wife has one-half interest in realty but not ordering the husband to convey this interest to her, operates neither in rem nor in personam and therefore is not entitled to full faith and credit and does not estop the husband from relitigating the issue at the situs); Miller v. Miller, 715 S.W.2d 786 (Tex.App.—Austin 1986, writ ref'd n.r.e.) (forum court does not have jurisdiction to order conveyance of Oklahoma realty).

European Community Regulation on Jurisdiction and the Enforcement of Judgments in Civil and Commercial Matters, EC No. 44/2001, [2001] OJ art. 22(1) (situs courts have "exclusive jurisdiction ... in proceedings which have as their object rights *in rem* in immovable property or tenancies of immovable property" with exception for tenancies for "private use for a maximum period of six consecutive months" if the tenant is a natural person and the landlord and tenant are domiciled in the same member state). Cases decided under art. 16(1) of the Convention that preceded the Regulation. The original Convention of 1968 did not the exception. It was added after the Court of Justice of the European Communities decided Rösler v. Rottwinkel, infra this note: Case C–343/04, Land Oberösterreich v. CEZ A.S., [2006] ECR 4557 (Brussels Convention article that places exclusive jurisdiction of "proceedings which have as their object rights in rem in immovable property or tenancies of immovable property" in situs courts does not prevent a suit in Austria to enjoin a nuisance resulting from radiation emitted by a nuclear power plant in the Czech Republic); Case C–294/92, Webb v. Webb, [1994] 5 E.C.R. 1717 (nor does the restriction article apply to a suit for a declaration that the defendant holds the property in trust for the plaintiff and for an order directing the defendant to execute documents to vest legal ownership in the plaintiff);. Case 214/83, Rösler v. Rottwinkel, [1985] 1 E.C.R. 99 (Eur.Ct.Justice) (Italy has exclusive jurisdiction of suit on a lease of Italian realty between German landlord and German tenant for landlord's claim for damage, for missing property, and for charges incurred by the tenant, but the landlord's claim for loss of enjoyment of a holiday and traveling expenses, being only incidental to the lease, were not within the Italian courts' exclusive jurisdiction); Hay, *The Situs Rule in European and American Conflicts Law—Comparative Notes*, in Property Law & Legal Education 109, 121 (P. Hay & M. Hoeflich eds.) (1988) (criticizing European Court of Justice for not limiting Art. 16(1) to title-related damage claims).

68. Norton v. House of Mercy, 101 F. 382 (5th Cir.1900); Kline v. Heyman, 309 So.2d 242 (Fla.App.1975), cert. denied, 317 So.2d 767 (1975), cert. denied, 423 U.S. 1034, 96 S.Ct. 567, 46 L.Ed.2d 408 (1975) (res judicata); Arthur v. Arthur, 625 S.W.2d 592 (Ky.App.1981) (enforce the equities growing out of the non-situs decree); Dunlap v. Byers, 110 Mich. 109, 67 N.W. 1067 (1896); Lyle Cashion Co. v. McKendrick, 227 Miss. 894, 87 So.2d 289 (1956);

the non-situs court;[69] and some have even thought the non-situs decree entitled to full faith and credit.[70]

Section 55 of the Restatement provides that a court may exercise its personal jurisdiction to order a person to do or refrain from doing an act "although the carrying out of the decree may affect a thing in another state."[71]. Comment *b* states that a court may issue such a decree "whenever the defendant is under a personal obligation, subject to enforcement by a court of equity, to do the act in question."[72] The two

Small v. Carey, 269 Or. 35, 522 P.2d 1202 (1974) (res judicata); Bailey v. Tully, 242 Wis. 226, 7 N.W.2d 837 (1943). Cf. Redwood Inv. Co. v. Exley, 64 Cal.App. 455, 459, 221 P. 973, 975 (Dist.Ct.App.1923) (decree is "record evidence of the equities therein determined"); Page v. McKee, 66 Ky. (3 Bush) 135, 140 (1867) (decree invalid to affect interest in land, but situs court will "enforce the equities growing out of it").

69. Allis v. Allis, 378 F.2d 721 (5th Cir.1967), cert. denied, 389 U.S. 953, 88 S.Ct. 337, 19 L.Ed.2d 363 (1967); Phelps v. Williams, 192 A.2d 805 (D.C.App.1963); McElreath v. McElreath, 162 Tex. 190, 345 S.W.2d 722 (1961).

70. Barber v. Barber, 51 Cal.2d 244, 247, 331 P.2d 628, 630–31 (1958) (dictum); Andre v. Morrow, 106 Idaho 455, 680 P.2d 1355 (1984); Meents v. Comstock, 230 Iowa 63, 296 N.W. 721 (1941); Fagone v. Fagone, 508 So.2d 644 (La.App. 2d Cir.1987) (full faith and credit to Ohio divorce decree dividing Louisiana realty); DeVlieg v. DeVlieg, 492 A.2d 605 (Me. 1985) (full faith and credit to Ohio divorce decree dividing Maine realty); Weesner v. Weesner, 168 Neb. 346, 95 N.W.2d 682 (1959); Burnley v. Stevenson, 24 Ohio St. 474 (1873); Mallette v. Scheerer, 164 Wis. 415, 160 N.W. 182 (1916). But cf. Estate of Waitzman, 507 So.2d 24 (Miss. 1987) (give Florida judgment declaring a will valid res judicata effect because it affected personalty in Mississippi, but dictum that it would not be conclusive as to Mississippi realty); Matter of Estate of Reed, 768 P.2d 566 (Wyo. 1989) (permit will contest at situs after will declared valid at domicile, though apparently domiciliary probate proceedings did not purport to deal with out-of-state realty).

The problem of full faith and credit to judgments affecting land outside the forum is complicated by uncertainty concerning the extent to which a judgment binds a foreign administrator or executor. See Restatement (Second) § 356(1): "if a person asserting a claim against a decedent recovers a judgment against an executor or administrator of the decedent's estate, such judgment does not usually establish the claim in another state unless a statute of that other state so provides.... (2) When the defendant is an executor of the decedent, a judgment for the claimant can be proved as a claim against the same person as executor in another state in which he is also executor of the decedent...." The Reporter's Note to this section comments: "The rule ... may lead to unjust and inconvenient results and is stated only because of what is thought to be compelling, though comparatively ancient, authority." Riley v. New York Trust Co., 315 U.S. 343, 62 S.Ct. 608, 86 L.Ed. 885 (1942), permitted the New York administrator to relitigate the issue of where the testator had died domiciled even though this had already been decided in a Georgia probate proceeding in which all the real parties in interest appeared, but to which the New York administrator was not a party. Estate of Torian v. Smith, 263 Ark. 304, 564 S.W.2d 521 (1978), cert. denied, 439 U.S. 883, 99 S.Ct. 223, 58 L.Ed.2d 195 (1978) held that the executor of an Arkansas estate was not a party to Mississippi probate proceedings qua Arkansas executor, despite the fact that the executor, a bank, had taken part in the Mississippi litigation. As a result, neither the executor nor the Arkansas estate was held bound by the Mississippi decision concerning apportionment of estate taxes. Uniform Probate Code § 3–408, 8 pt. 2 U.L.A. 91 (1998), makes a ruling in the domiciliary administration binding on all interested parties. Section 4–401, id. at 320, makes adjudications elsewhere in favor of or against a personal representative of the estate binding on the local representative. See also Restatement (Second) § 358 (when an action may be maintained against a foreign executor or administrator); Day v. Wiswall, 11 Ariz.App. 306, 464 P.2d 626 (1970) (although California probate judgment entitled to full faith and credit against individual distributees even as to Arizona land, it does not bind Arizona administrator).

71. Restatement (Second) of Conflict of Laws § 55.

72. Id. cmt. *b*. See also J.G. Castel, Canadian Conflict of Laws 465 (4th ed. 1997): Non-situs court "will grant decrees imposing a personal obligation on a defendant with respect

illustrations that follow deal with specific performance of a contract to convey land in another state and ordering reconveyance of land in another state that the defendant has obtained title to by fraud.

Miller v. Miller[73] interpreted these Restatement provisions literally and held that it did not have subject matter jurisdiction to adjudicate a dispute over title to Oklahoma realty between a Texas widow and a Texas son by a former marriage. The widow claimed the right to elect against her husband's will and take a forced one-half share in the realty under Oklahoma law. The son claimed that Texas law applied and that he was entitled to take all of the property under his father's will. The court stated: "the power of a court of one state to compel a party to convey real property located in another state has always been limited in its application [to situations such as those in the Restatement illustrations], subject to the ultimate restriction that it cannot be applied in cases which involve a direct adjudication as to title to real property."[74]

Although the non-situs court cannot directly affect the title to the realty it can adjudicate the rights in that realty of parties over whom it has personal jurisdiction.[75] Moreover, the many cases in which non-situs courts in divorce cases award one spouse or both interests in realty are cases that adjudicate title to the realty and do not merely enforce a pre-existing equitable claim.[76]

It is indeed ironic that Nebraska, the state whose refusal to recognize a non-situs decree led to the decision in *Fall v. Eastin*, falls into this last category. *Weesner v. Weesner*,[77] like *Fall*, involved a non-situs divorce decree purporting to alter the interests of husband and wife in Nebraska land they had previously owned jointly, transferring the husband's interest to the wife as part of an alimony award. This time, however, the Nebraska Supreme Court said:

> [W]here all necessary parties are before a competent court in the land situs state, such an order will be given force and effect under

---

to a contractual or equitable obligation arising out of a transaction involving a foreign immovable."

73.   715 S.W.2d 786 (Tex. Ct. App.—Austin, 1986), writ ref'd n.r.e. (1987). I was losing counsel in *Miller*.

74.   Id. at 789.

75.   See Baker v. General Motors Corp., 522 U.S. 222, 235, 118 S.Ct. 657, 665, 139 L.Ed.2d 580 (1998) ("a sister State's decree concerning land ownership in another State has been held ineffective to *transfer title*, although such a decree may indeed preclusively adjudicate the rights and obligations running between the *parties* to the foreign litigation") (dictum, emphasis in original, citations omitted).

Cf. Pattni v. Ali, [2007] 2 A.C. 85 (Privy Council, 2006) (Kenyan judgment ordering party over whom the court had jurisdiction to transfer ownership of shares in a Manx company entitled to recognition on the island of Man; also stating (¶ 26) "an English court may, as between the parties before it, give an in personam judgment to enforce contractual or equitable rights in respect of immovable property situate in a foreign country").

76.   See infra note 89. The *Miller* court dismissed these cases as "analogous to the personal obligations—to rectify fraud or to enforce a trust or contract—which have traditionally conferred jurisdiction on courts to compel conveyances of out-of-state property." 715 S.W.2d at 790.

77.   168 Neb. 346, 95 N.W.2d 682 (1959).

the full faith and credit clause ... and [the] same may in a proper case be pleaded as a defense, or as a cause of action to enforce the obligation of the order, if the related public policy of the situs state is in substantial accord with that of the other state.[78]

As this quote indicates, one ground on which the Nebraska court attempted to distinguish its former decision in *Fall v. Eastin* was that at the time of *Fall* a Nebraska court did not have the power to award real estate to the wife as alimony. Because this was no longer so, recognizing the sister-state decree now violated no substantial interest of Nebraska. This distinction is unconvincing. Nebraska's reasons for formerly denying the divorced wife alimony rights in the husband's Nebraska realty are unrelated to spouses domiciled elsewhere.[79] It is difficult to articulate an interest of Nebraska *qua situs* that would be sufficiently undermined to outweigh the federal need for recognition of the sister-state decree. The further distinction by the *Weesner* court, that in *Fall* the husband had not been subject to the in personam jurisdiction of the Nebraska court,[80] is untenable because the situs of real estate as such, upon giving reasonable notice and opportunity to be heard, has judicial jurisdiction to affect the interest of all persons in the world in land at the situs.[81]

Another distinction between *Weesner* and *Fall* is that in *Weesner* the wife's quiet-title action was directly against the husband whereas in *Fall* it was against his grantees. It is difficult to see how this difference could be of constitutional dignity unless one is prepared to argue that the wife's action in *Weesner* was in effect one to reduce the sister-state decree to judgment in Nebraska, as is done with money judgments preparatory to local execution, and that this detail of procedural etiquette had been omitted in *Fall*.

Traditionally, great importance has been attached to the distinction between in personam and in rem decrees by non-situs courts. A non-situs court could act "in personam" to adjudicate the interests of parties before it in foreign realty and make "in personam" orders to effectuate its determination, such as ordering one party to make a conveyance to the other in accordance with the interests adjudicated. It would be "improper," however, for a non-situs court to act "in rem" by, for example, declaring a prior conveyance of foreign realty "void" and relying only on its own decree to effect a change in the title.[82] Although prevailing counsel should mind their "in personam" etiquette and shape the court's decree to declare rights of parties before the court and order

---

78. Weesner v. Weesner, 168 Neb. 346, 357, 95 N.W.2d 682, 689–90 (1959).

79. See B. Currie, *Full Faith and Credit to Foreign Land Decrees*, 21 U. Chi. L. Rev. 620, 637 (1954).

80. *Weesner*, 168 Neb. at 356–57, 95 N.W.2d at 689.

81. See Avery v. Bender, 124 Vt. 309, 204 A.2d 314 (1964); Restatement (Second) § 59.

82. See Sylvester v. Sylvester, 723 P.2d 1253 (Alaska 1986) (trial erred in declaring conveyance of Hawaiian land "null and void"—remanded for entry of order to convey and record).

a conveyance, there is no reason why the wrong form of decree should be fatal.[83]

As a further indication that the non-situs court is not so outrageously inappropriate a forum as to raise due process impediments to the enforcement of its decree, situs states have consistently given effect to a deed actually executed by a party under the compulsion of such a decree.[84] In *Fall* itself the Nebraska court said:

> [I]f Fall had obeyed the order of the Washington court and made a deed of conveyance to his wife of the Nebraska land, even under the threat of contempt proceedings, or after duress by imprisonment, the title thereby conveyed to Mrs. Fall would have been of equal weight and dignity with that which he himself possessed at the time of the execution of the deed.[85]

It is difficult to see how such circumstances could remove legitimate due process objections based on the inappropriateness of the forum.

A similar notion of the inappropriateness of the non-situs forum for adjudication of title is at least partially responsible for the "local action" doctrine—that actions for trespass to land are "local" and triable only at the situs of the land.[86] Several jurisdictions, however, have abandoned the local action rule either by judicial decision[87] or statute[88] and, it is submitted, without running afoul of the due process clause.

---

83. See Allis v. Allis, 378 F.2d 721, 726 (5th Cir.1967), cert. denied, 389 U.S. 953, 88 S.Ct. 337, 19 L.Ed.2d 363 (1967) (power of court to declare personal rights in foreign realty does not depend on "the mere form of a decree"); McKay v. Palmer, 170 Mich.App. 288, 427 N.W.2d 620 (1988) (Massachusetts decision declaring conveyance of Michigan land "void" was binding determination of parties' interest in the land); Willis v. Willis, 104 N.M. 233, 719 P.2d 811 (1986) (Texas court validly determined interest of parties in New Mexico realty although no conveyance was ordered). Cf. Ashurst v. Pollard, [2001] 2 W.L.R. 722 (Ct. App. Eng. 2000) (English court had jurisdiction to order sale of Portuguese realty because this was not a proceeding having as its "object rights in rem in immovable property," for which the European Union Convention on Jurisdiction and Enforcement of Judgments would confer exclusive jurisdiction on Portuguese courts).

84. See Gilliland v. Inabnit, 92 Iowa 46, 60 N.W. 211 (1894); Steele v. Bryant, 132 Ky. 569, 116 S.W. 755 (1909); Bullock v. Bullock, 52 N.J.Eq. 561, 569, 30 A. 676, 677 (App.1894) (dictum); Sharp v. Sharp, 65 Okl. 76, 78, 166 P. 175, 177 (1916) (dictum); Barbour, supra note 59, at 549; Lorenzen, *Application of Full Faith and Credit Clause to Equitable Decrees for the Conveyance of Foreign Land*, 34 Yale L. J. 591, 608–09 (1925); cf. Douglass v. First Nat'l Realty Corp., 351 F.Supp. 1142 (D.D.C.1972), vac'd in part and remanded without opinion, 505 F.2d 475 (D.C.Cir.1974) (order defendant to convey land outside the forum); Matarese v. Calise, 111 R.I. 551, 935, 305 A.2d 112 (1973) (same, land in Italy). Contra, Porter v. Porter, 101 Ariz. 131, 416 P.2d 564 (1966), cert. denied, 386 U.S. 957, 87 S.Ct. 1028, 18 L.Ed.2d 107 (1967). For the proposition that the situs would be free to refuse recognition of such a deed, see Irving Trust Co. v. Maryland Cas. Co., 83 F.2d 168, 172 (2d Cir.1936) (dictum, L. Hand, J.), cert. denied, 299 U.S. 571, 57 S.Ct. 34, 81 L.Ed. 421 (1936); Note, *Validity of Deed Given under Compulsion of "Foreign" Court*, 12 Mont. L. Rev. 59, 71 (1951).

85. Fall v. Fall, 75 Neb. 104, 128, 113 N.W. 175, 178 (1907), aff'd sub nom. Fall v. Eastin, 215 U.S. 1, 30 S.Ct. 3, 54 L.Ed. 65 (1909).

86. Livingston v. Jefferson, 15 Fed.Cas. 660 (No. 8411) (C.C.D.Va.1811); see Ehrenzweig, Conflict of Laws § 39 (1962).

87. Reasor–Hill Corp. v. Harrison, 220 Ark. 521, 249 S.W.2d 994 (1952); Little v. Chicago, St.P., M. & O. Ry., 65 Minn. 48, 67 N.W. 846 (1896). See also Ingram v. Great Lakes Pipe Line Co., 153 S.W.2d 547 (Mo.App.1941) (Missouri venue statute construed as

Moreover, it is simply not true that the non-situs forum is always an extremely inappropriate setting for adjudicating the interests in realty of persons before the court. In cases such as *Fall* and *Weesner*, when the forum is granting a divorce and dividing the property of the warring spouses, it is highly desirable that a court make the division with a view of the full picture and includes property of the couple wherever situated.[89] If a non-situs forum in a particular case proves to be an inconvenient place to litigate interests in land, because a view of the land is desirable or because witnesses available at the situs are necessary, the doctrine of forum non conveniens is available to prevent a miscarriage of justice. In rare cases the inconvenience might be so severe as to violate due process.[90] But none of the cases cited in this chapter presents such a problem.

It is at this point that the interrelationship between the problems of judicial jurisdiction and choice of law for adjudicating interests in realty becomes apparent. If the situs court is the only court competent to hear such matters, this will support the argument that it is most expedient to apply situs law—the law of the forum. Conversely, if the non-situs court must or should apply the law of the situs, then this will buttress a contention that the non-situs court is an incompetent forum. Therefore, this chapter now turns to the choice-of-law problem itself.

Non-situs decrees affecting the interests in land of persons before the court should be entitled to the same recognition at the situs under full faith and credit as other judgments. Rarely, if ever, will the situs have so great an interest in denying full recognition to non-situs decrees

---

ending local action rule); cf. Kane v. Kane, 198 Mont. 335, 646 P.2d 505 (1982) (situs court dismisses suit for damages resulting from refusal to comply with non-situs decree and finds that non-situs court is more appropriate forum).

88. N.Y.—McKinney's Real Prop.Actions & Proc.Law § 121.

89. For divorce courts adjudicating interests in land outside the forum, see, e.g., Ivey v. Ivey, 183 Conn. 490, 439 A.2d 425 (1981) (order conveyance); Dority v. Dority, 645 P.2d 56, 58 (Utah 1982) ("it has been held in the majority of American jurisdictions that the equitable powers of divorce courts extend to the award and disposition of real property in other states insofar as the parties' interests therein are concerned"); Brock v. Brock, 586 S.W.2d 927 (Tex.Civ.App.—El Paso 1979) (order sale); In re Marriage of Kowalewski, 163 Wash.2d 542, 182 P.3d 959 (2008 en banc) (Divorce court with personal jurisdiction over both spouses can adjudicate their interest in land in Poland); cf. In re Marriage of Fink, 25 Cal.3d 877, 160 Cal.Rptr. 516, 603 P.2d 881 (1979) (California statute establishes a preference for division of community property in a manner that avoids changing interests in realty outside the state, but if this cannot be done, the court may order conveyance of the realty and if this order is not obeyed, award the money value of the property to the other party).

See also Vernon's Tex.C.A., Family Code § 7.002 (in divorce or annulment, Texas court's power to divide marital property extends to real property "wherever situated"); Cameron v. Cameron, 641 S.W.2d 210 (Tex.1982) (adopting rule of Family Code as a common law rule for cases arising before the effective date of the statute); McElreath v. McElreath, 162 Tex. 190, 345 S.W.2d 722, 724 (1961) ("[q]uite obviously one authority must settle these [marital property] rights if anything approaching fairness and equity is to be secured"—enforcing an Oklahoma divorce decree ordering husband to convey Texas land to his wife).

90. Cf. Asahi Metal Indus. Co. v. Superior Court, 480 U.S. 102, 113–14, 107 S.Ct. 1026, 1033, 94 L.Ed.2d 92, 105 (1987) (holding exercise of personal jurisdiction violated due process despite defendant's "minimum contacts" with the forum and citing as one reason "the burden on the defendant").

that it should be permitted to disregard them. The following sections will attempt to demonstrate that the reason why it is especially important that this result, long advocated,[91] now be realized, is to permit the functional re-analysis of choice-of-law problems, having such salutary effects in other areas, to enter the mists of the real property realm. Once false dogmas about jurisdiction of the subject matter are consigned to the bonfire, it becomes apparent that proper solution of the choice-of-law problem will rarely, if ever, result in the application of the law of the situs qua situs.[92]

§ 8.6   A Consequences–Based Approach to Choosing Law for Determining Interests In Land

The primary focus of choice-of-law analysis for problems concerning real property should be on the purposes underlying putatively conflicting domestic rules of property law. Although two states have domestic rules pointing to different results if applied to interests in realty, analysis of the purposes underlying those domestic rules may reveal that the conflict is apparent rather than real. Applying one domestic rule to the transaction in issue may not advance the purposes underlying the rule; the policies of the other domestic rule, on the other hand, may be fully applicable. When this occurs, a rational and just result can be achieved only by applying the domestic rule whose purposes are relevant to the transaction in issue and rejecting the domestic rule whose policies would not be meaningfully advanced by application. This is true without regard to which rule is that of the forum or that of the situs of the realty. When, on the other hand, the domestic property rules of two or more states point to different results and each rule has an underlying policy that would be meaningfully advanced by application to the case at bar, there is a real, not apparent, conflict-of-laws problem. A rational solution will turn primarily on interests and policies that the two jurisdictions have in common and on clearly discernible trends and developments in the substantive area involved.

§ 8.7   Intestate Distribution of Realty

The classic choice-of-law problem involving the intestate distribution of realty runs as follows: The real estate is situated in state X. Mr. Smith owns it in fee simple. Mr. Smith has a settled residence in state Y, as do

---

91.   See Barbour, supra note 62, at 532–33; B. Currie, *Full Faith and Credit, Chiefly to Judgments: A Role for Congress*, in 1964 Supreme Court Review 89, 108 (1964); Currie, supra note 79, at 623–66; Hancock, *Full Faith and Credit to Foreign Laws and Judgments in Real Property Litigation: The Supreme Court and the Land Taboo*, 18 Stan. L. Rev. 1299, 1321 (1966); Hancock, *In the Parish of St. Mary le Bow, in the Ward of Cheap*, 16 Stan. L. Rev. 561, 571 n.33 (1964); Lorenzen, supra note 84, at 597, 607; Reese, supra note 57, at 201; B. Schwartz, *Fall v. Eastin Revisited: Extraterritorial Effect of Foreign Land Decrees*, 54 Dick. L. Rev. 293, 299 (1950).

92.   Cf. Janeen M. Carruthers, The Transfer of Property in the Conflict of Laws 281–82 (2005) (presumption in favor of applying law of situs to transfers of immovable property rebutted when "it is more appropriate" to apply non-situs law or when "the transfer or issue is more closely connected with another country"); von Mehren & Trautman, The Law of Multistate Problems 197 (1965).

his wife and three minor children. Mr. Smith dies intestate. Under the intestacy statute of State X, the widow would take a one-third interest in the real estate and the other two-thirds would be divided equally among the children. Under Y intestacy law, however, the widow would take a one-half interest in the realty and the other one-half would go to the children. Should X or Y law be applied to the intestate distribution of the X realty?

Y, the settled residence of all the claimants, has as much interest in determining the proportions in which the claimants shall take as it would if the land in question were in that state. Y has indicated who shall take on intestacy and in what shares in accordance with its own notions of what would be fair in the light of the claimant's needs and legitimate expectations. If a Y resident does not receive a share that Y thinks sufficient and as a consequence becomes a public charge, it is Y and Y's citizens who will pay the bill. If the distribution does not comport with Y's ideas of fairness and the Y claimants quarrel, it is Y's peace that is disturbed.

Does X, the situs, have any interest in controlling the intestate distribution in this case? No. It can be of no legitimate concern to X in what shares the Y widow and children take. The conflict is a false one, only Y law being rationally applicable.[93] Yet the situs dogma has here uniformly resulted in the wrong answer.[94]

If the intestacy laws of X and Y speak of "wife" and "children" but do not specify what wives and children, whether only wives and children with settled residences there or all the wives and children in the world, the above approach might be taken as an exercise in statutory construction.[95] "Wife" and "children" have, in this territorial context, more than one reasonable meaning and that meaning should be adopted that best advances the purposes of the statute. The situs dogma has, however,

---

93. See Baxter, *Choice of Law in the Federal System*, 16 Stan. L. Rev. 1, 16 (1963); Hancock, *Equitable Conversion and the Land Taboo in Conflict of Laws*, 17 Stan. L. Rev. 1095, 1115 (1965); J.H.C. Morris, *Intestate Succession to Land in the Conflict of Laws*, 85 L.Q.Rev. 339, 340 (1969).

94. See, e.g., Sinclair v. Sinclair, 99 N.H. 316, 109 A.2d 851 (1954); Matter of Estate of Sendonas, 62 Wn.2d 129, 381 P.2d 752 (1963). Cf. McCollum v. Smith, 19 Tenn. 342 (1838) (same result classifying slaves as immovables). See also Restatement (Second) § 236.

Once the claimant's status (e.g., "widow", "legitimate child", "illegitimate child") is determined, situs law determines the intestate rights of a person having that status. The status itself is determined by the domicile at the relevant time of the parties whose status is in issue. See Wickware v. Session, 538 S.W.2d 466 (Tex.Civ.App.—Tyler 1976, writ ref'd n.r.e.); In re Estate of Duquesne, 29 Utah 2d 94, 505 P.2d 779 (1973); Restatement (Second) § 287 (law determining legitimacy); discussion of "the incidental question", section 3.4A note 281.

95. Cf. Williamson's Adm'rs v. Smart, 1 N.C. 355, 362 (1801). In applying the law of the state where the master died domiciled to the question of intestate distribution of slaves, the court dismissed the argument that the law of the state where the slaves were located was to be applied, the situs state's rules causing slaves to descend like realty to heirs-at-law: "there can be no reason wherefore that State [situs] should be concerned about the manner in which strangers hold that sort of property, which they may freely carry away with them. All that, as a State, they can be interested in ascertaining is, whether the party asserting a claim has really a right, according to the laws of his own country...."

been frozen into a number of intestacy statutes.[96] Such statutes would have to be amended before a rational result could be reached.

The situs, which has no interest in the fractions in which the interests in realty are divided among non-residents, also has no interest in deciding whether one or another non-resident shall take. In this latter situation, applying the situs law is likely to be even more inimical to the interest of the home state of the claimants in treating them according to its own notions of fairness. But in *In re Berchtold*[97] the situs rule resulted in an English court applying English law to give the Hungarian widow the entire interest in the English realty rather than giving all to the Hungarian sister subject to a usufruct for life in the widow, as would have been the result under Hungarian law.

Can the situs ever have a legitimate interest qua situs in controlling the intestate distribution of interests in realty? Not today as between states of the United States. Their laws on intestacy are too similar in both letter and purpose, differing on details that do not concern a state that has no contact except as situs. It is theoretically possible for the intestacy law of the situs to differ from that of another jurisdiction in a manner that may affect the use of the land as land and, therefore, affect the economy and vital interests of the situs. For example, the situs might have a rule designed to prevent the land from being broken up into parcels too small to be utilized economically. Its intestacy law might, instead of dividing the interests in the land among relatives of the same degree in equal shares, select some one or a few persons to take all—as, for example, the English rule of primogeniture gave all to the oldest son.[98] Such concentration of the interests in realty might also increase the likelihood that the land will eventually escheat to the situs. The situs as such has an interest in intestate distribution only if that distribution will in some way be reasonably likely to affect the use of the land and the economy of the situs, or to increase the likelihood of escheat.

The Connecticut Supreme Court in Errors in *Clarke's Appeal* indicated that it had an interest as situs in controlling the intestate distribution of Connecticut realty between the South Carolina father and daughter:

> Succession to the real estate of a deceased person is regulated at the will of the sovereign within whose territory it is embraced. It has always been regarded as a matter of grave political consequence.... Ownership of land controls its occupancy, and largely influences the character of the population. It determines the source to which governments ordinarily look for their surest, if not their principal, means of financial support. It had, in former times, in England and in all her American colonies, an intimate relation to the right of

---

96. Smith–Hurd Ill.Ann.Stat. ch. 775, § 5/2–1. Cf. N.Y.—McKinney's Estates, Powers & Trusts Law § 3–5.1(b)(1) (whole law of situs).

97. [1923] 1 Ch. 192.

98. See In re Cutcliffe's Will Trusts, [1940] Ch. 565.

suffrage, and in this State is still a qualification for it under at least one of our municipal charters.[99]

None of this justifies the decision in the context of that case. Connecticut's ability to collect land taxes does not turn on which non-resident takes and, even if the "right of suffrage" could constitutionally turn on land ownership,[100] it is irrelevant when apportioning interests in the land among non-residents who do not in any event vote at the situs.

§ 8.8 Apportionment of Estate Taxes

A somewhat analogous problem occurs when an inter vivos trust is treated as part of the gross estate for federal estate tax purposes, and the situs of the trust property and the settled residence of the settlor-decedent differ on whether the beneficiaries of the trust and the distributees of the estate should share the tax burdens. Although it does not deal with a trust corpus consisting of realty, the Seventh Circuit case of *Doetsch v. Doetsch*,[101] chooses the law of the decedent's domicile and articulates a reason for its selection of that law that is relevant to our purposes:

> Finally, referring to the law of decedent's domicile results in observing that state's policy with respect to protecting the widow and family.... Protection of the widow and family is a matter in which the domiciliary state has a dominant interest, and without reference by the situs state to the state of decedent's domicile, this policy can not be fulfilled.[102]

§ 8.9 Equitable Conversion

The equitable conversion fiction has sometimes resulted in choice of domiciliary rather than situs law.[103] This doctrine, which is rooted in the notion that the law will regard as done what ought to have been done, may be applicable to a question of intestate succession if, in an inter

---

99. Clarke's Appeal, 70 Conn. 195, 210–11, 39 A. 155, 159 (1898), aff'd sub nom. Clarke v. Clarke, 178 U.S. 186, 20 S.Ct. 873, 44 L.Ed. 1028 (1900).

100. But see Cipriano v. Houma, 395 U.S. 701, 89 S.Ct. 1897, 23 L.Ed.2d 647 (1969) (Louisiana law giving only "property taxpayers" right to vote in elections called to approve issuance of revenue bonds by city utility is unconstitutional denial of equal protection); Kramer v. Union Free School Dist. No. 15, 395 U.S. 621, 89 S.Ct. 1886, 23 L.Ed.2d 583 (1969) (New York law limiting right to vote in school district elections to owners or lessees of taxable realty and parents of school children is unconstitutional denial of equal protection).

101. 312 F.2d 323 (7th Cir.1963).

102. Id. at 328. Accord, Mazza v. Mazza, 475 F.2d 385 (D.C.Cir.1973); In re Royse's Estate, 118 N.Y.S.2d 421 (Surr.Ct. New York County 1952); First Nat'l Bank v. Wells, 267 N.C. 276, 148 S.E.2d 119 (1966); cf. In re Estate of Torian, 321 So.2d 287 (Miss.1975) (apportionment controlled by law of situs, which decedent regarded as her home although it was not her formal domicile at death) [but see Estate of Torian v. Smith, 263 Ark. 304, 564 S.W.2d 521 (1978), cert. denied, 439 U.S. 883, 99 S.Ct. 223, 58 L.Ed.2d 195 (1978) (domicile at death refuses to follow Mississippi apportionment)]. See also Scoles, *Apportionment of Federal Estate Taxes and Conflict of Laws*, 55 Colum. L. Rev. 261, 295 (1955). Contra, Beatty v. Cake, 236 Or. 498, 387 P.2d 355 (1963) (corpus was realty, but court assumed that most of the beneficiaries were residents of the situs).

103. See Hancock, *In the Parish of St. Mary le Bow, in the Ward of Cheap*, supra note 91, at 574.

vivos or testamentary document, the decedent has directed the sale of the realty and its conversion into personalty. Even though the sale has not yet taken place at the death of the intestate, by "regarding as done what ought to have been done" the court may view the realty as equitably converted into personalty. This, in turn, would invoke another classic but quite different choice-of-law rule: the law of the decedent's domicile at death determines the intestate distribution of personal property.[104] Such an argument was offered but rejected in *In re Berchtold:* "But this equitable doctrine of conversion only arises and comes into play where the question for consideration arises as between real estate and personal estate. It has no relation to the question whether property is movable or immovable."[105]

Acceptance of the doctrine of equitable conversion is not the answer. The equitable conversion argument is an advocate's trick that should be remembered and stored away for possible use in undermining the situs monolith when all else fails. It is true that on the average, over a great number of cases, more just and rational decisions will be reached by accepting this argument of equitable conversion than by rejecting it. This is because the domicile of the decedent at death will usually have the predominant interest, often the sole interest, in regulating the intestate distribution of his or her property. But this would leave untouched the greater number of cases in which, because of the absence of any direction or discretion to sell, the equitable conversion game cannot be played. Moreover, the substitution of one rigid, territorially-oriented choice-of-law rule, "domicile at death," for another, is not desirable. "Domicile" itself is a flawed concept for choice-of-law purposes. Because it is used on so many different occasions—choice of law for intestate distribution of personalty, validity of a will of personalty, judicial jurisdiction, estate tax on intangibles in the estate—the slightest insight into the legal process will reveal that the meaning of "domicile" must shift with these very different contexts.[106] In order to choose rationally among different possible meanings, we must advert to the purposes we seek to serve by our choice. If this is done, "domicile," when determined, is the label for the result, not the reason.[107]

Finally, even if we were so naive as to believe that domicile had a single, unitary meaning that, once determined, could be plugged in as needed to any legal problem requiring it for solution, we would find

---

104. See Restatement (Second) § 260 (whole law of domicile); cf. Moore v. Livingston, 148 Ind.App. 275, 265 N.E.2d 251 (1970) (because of equitable conversion, construe will under law of domicile at death).

105. [1923] 1 Ch. 192, 206. Accord, Re Burke, 22 Sask. 142 [1928] 1 D.L.R. 318 (Sask.K.B.1927); cf. Landmark First Nat'l Bk. v. Commissioner of Corp. & Tax., 6 Mass.App.Ct. 902, 378 N.E.2d 458 (1978) (equitable conversion does not apply to avoid tax on Massachusetts realty in estate of nonresident decedent). But see Re Hole, 56 Man. 295, 312–13 [1948] 4 D.L.R. 419, 433 (Man.K.B.) (disapproving *Re Burke* for its rejection of equitable conversion and holding rights of vendor in contract for sale of Saskatchewan land escheated to vendor's domicile, Manitoba).

106. Restatement (Second) § 11, comment *o*; 3 ALI Proceedings 227 (1925) (Cook's Statement); § 2.16.

107. See § 2.16.

many instances in which the domicile at death did not have the predominant interest in the distribution of the intestate property.[108] *Matter of Wright's Estate*[109] probably reached the correct result by applying the law of the situs of realty to intestate succession, rather than the law of the intestate's domicile at death. The contest was between an illegitimate child of the decedent and an illegitimate child of his sister. The decedent had died domiciled in New York. However, both children had been born in the Virgin Islands, the situs of the brother's realty, and had resided there all their lives.

Although adoption of the fiction of equitable conversion is, therefore, not the answer to our problem,[110] it should be recognized that actual or imminent sale of the realty may terminate whatever interests the situs qua situs does have in intestate distribution. For example, *In re Cutcliffe's Will Trusts*[111] involved the distribution on the intestacy of an Ontario resident of his interests under a trust of property situated in England. The intestate had seven children. Under the then English rule of primogeniture only his oldest son would take, but under Ontario law his seven children would take equal shares. If, as was true at the time the English trust was created by his aunt, the corpus had consisted solely of realty, England as situs might claim some interest in having its rule of primogeniture applied to avoid fractionizing the interests in English realty into uneconomically small units. But, at the time that the case was heard, part of the realty had been sold and the proceeds used to buy stocks. Only the distribution of the stocks was in issue. Even if England had an interest as situs in the application of its rule of primogeniture to land, it had no such interest where only stock was involved. The English statute that the court relied on may have precluded recognition of the functional shift in situs interests caused by the sale of the land. The statute provided that proceeds of the sale of land "shall, for all purposes of disposition, transmission, and devolution, be considered as land, and the same shall be held for and go to the same persons successively, in the same manner and for and on the same estate, interests, and trusts, as the land wherefrom the money arises would, if not disposed of, have been held and have gone."[112]

Although actual sale of the realty may terminate an interest of the situs in affecting its distribution, some care will have to be taken that the discretion to sell or hold is not exercised by parties in interest to affect that very distribution.[113] Such a danger exists only when such

---

108. See § 2.12 (personalty, discussing In re Estate of Jones, 192 Iowa 78, 182 N.W. 227 (1921) and White v. Tennant, 31 W.Va. 790, 8 S.E. 596 (1888)).

109. 207 F.Supp. 912 (D.Virgin Islands 1962).

110. See Hancock, *Conceptual Devices for Avoiding the Land Taboo in Conflict of Laws: The Disadvantages of Disingenuousness*, 20 Stan. L. Rev. 1, 38 (1967) (use of equitable conversion fiction may obscure real ground for decision and mislead judges in subsequent cases).

111. [1940] 1 Ch. 565.

112. Settled Land Act, 1882, 45 & 46 Vict., c. 38, § 22(5).

113. Cf. Matter of Schneider's Estate, 198 Misc. 1017, 1021, 96 N.Y.S.2d 652, 657 (1950), adhered to on reargument, 198 Misc. 1017, 100 N.Y.S.2d 371 (Surr.Ct. New York County 1950) (fortuitous conversion of land should not affect its disposition).

discretion exists. When a decision to sell or hold can be made, *Norris v. Loyd*[114] is the kind of horrible example that should be avoided. That case involved a contest between an illegitimate child of the testator on one side, and the testator's widow and twelve legitimate children on the other. Under the law of California, the domicile at death of the testator, the bastard would take an intestate share in the estate as a pretermitted heir because he was not mentioned in the will. Under the law of Iowa, the situs of the land and domicile of the bastard, he would take nothing. The will directed the executors to sell the Iowa land and divide the proceeds among the legitimate children. In order to avoid the change into personalty and the possible shift from the law of the situs by use of the equitable conversion fiction, the legitimate children and the widow (who had elected to take a share against the will) agreed to take and hold the land as land and so notified the executors who consented. This plan succeeded, the Iowa court stating: "It is well settled by authority that, though a will work an equitable conversion of land, the beneficiaries of the devise may, at any time before actual conversion, work a reconversion into land, by so electing and agreeing among themselves."[115]

Such manipulation of the decision to sell or hold the land will not occur if the choice of law is not affected by the change in ownership of the realty. Sale of the realty should not affect the conflicts analysis if, as is typically the case in intestacy, the situs as such would have no interest in having its law applied even if the interests of the claimants had remained interests in realty.[116] The settled residence of the claimants will in every case have valid interests to promote: concern for the welfare of the claimants and of the society of which they are a part. This concern is a policy underlying the intestacy laws of both situs and claimants' residence, but in this context only the concern of the residence is relevant.

§ 8.10 Validity of a Will Devising Realty

The traditional rule is that the law of the situs of realty determines the validity of a will disposing of interests in realty.[117] Here the situs rule is especially unsatisfactory. There are many domestic rules affecting the validity of wills. The policies underlying these laws are as various as the rules. Solving all problems concerning the validity of a will of land with a single choice-of-law rule is to ignore the underlying diversity of rules and

---

114. 183 Iowa 1056, 168 N.W. 557 (1918).

115. Id. at 1061, 168 N.W. at 558.

116. Cf. von Mehren & Trautman, supra note 92, at 406: "In former days, of course, the concern of the situs was greater. For example, the rule of primogeniture, with its function of precluding the splitting up of land into small estates, represented a significant concern of the situs. However, few rules representing comparable concerns of the situs can be found today."

117. See Guidry v. Hardy, 254 So.2d 675 (La.App.1971), writ ref'd, no error of law, 260 La. 454, 256 So.2d 441 (1972) (will disposing of Louisiana land upheld against charge of undue influence after it has been declared invalid in California domiciliary administration); Mitchell v. Cloyes, 620 P.2d 398 (Okl.1980) (will not offered for probate at the domicile within that state's period of limitations, may be admitted to probate at the situs); Restatement (Second) § 239 (whole law of situs).

policies and to make just and rational results extremely improbable.[118] This is illustrated in the discussion in sections 8.11 through 8.13 of some of the validity rules that most often appear in the wills conflicts cases.

§ 8.11 Applicability of a Mortmain Statute to a Devise of Realty

The bizarre results obtained from applying situs law to determine the applicability of a mortmain statute to a devise of realty are epitomized in *Toledo Society for Crippled Children v. Hickok*.[119] Mr. Hickok died domiciled in Ohio survived by a wife and two children, also Ohio domiciliaries.[120] In a will that he executed within one year of his death he established a trust, the income to be paid to his widow and two adult children for twenty years and then the corpus to be divided among twenty charities. An Ohio statute invalidated any devise to charity by a testator with surviving children if the will was not executed at least one year prior to death. The charities sought to establish their rights under the will to certain Texas land and mineral interests. Mr. Hickok owned some of the land and mineral interests individually at his death, but the most valuable interests were owned by a partnership of which he was a member. Before his death, Mr. Hickok had contracted with his partner to form a corporation and to convey the partnership assets to the corporation in exchange for stock. His will incorporated this contract by reference and directed compliance with it. By the time of trial, his executors had carried out Mr. Hickok's instructions and all of his interest in the partnership had been conveyed to the corporation in exchange for stock.[121] As to the land and mineral interests that Mr. Hickok owned individually at his death, the trustees of the testamentary trust were given the power, but not directed, to sell any assets and reinvest the proceeds.

Under Texas law, the devise to the charities would be valid. In order to avoid the situs rule, Mr. Hickok's widow and two children argued that both the discretion to sell the land owned individually by Hickok and the actual exchange of his partnership interests for corporate stock resulted in an equitable conversion of the interests in Texas realty into interests in personalty, so that the law of the domicile at death would determine the validity of the will. The Texas Supreme Court rejected the equitable conversion argument, applied Texas law as the law of the situs, and, with respect to the Texas land and mineral interests, held valid the testamentary gift over to the charities. It concluded:

> If this view should impress some as legalistic . . . it is hardly more of a "technical" approach than that of regarding "as done" that which

---

118. See Hancock, *In the Parish of St. Mary le Bow, in the Ward of Cheap*, supra note 91, at 566.

119. 152 Tex. 578, 261 S.W.2d 692 (1953), cert. denied 347 U.S. 936, 74 S.Ct. 631, 98 L.Ed. 1086 (1954).

120. Reply Brief for Appellees, pp. 80–81, Toledo Soc'y for Crippled Children v. Hickok, 252 S.W.2d 739 (Tex.Civ.App.1952).

121. Toledo Soc'y for Crippled Children v. Hickok, 252 S.W.2d 739, 740 (Tex.Civ.App.—Eastland 1952), reversed, 152 Tex. 578, 261 S.W.2d 692 (1953).

was *not* done, in order to deprive the [charities] of the last remnant of benefits the testator obviously intended them to have, and, in effect, to enforce here a legislative policy of Ohio, which is contrary to the policy of our own Legislature.[122]

What policy of the Texas legislature? Not one of the twenty charities was a Texas charity. Eighteen of them were Ohio corporations and two had headquarters in Michigan.[123] There was no indication that any of the charities conducted any activities in Texas. Texas did not have any interest in validating the devise for the benefit of the charities when to do so would undermine the highly relevant purposes of Ohio to protect the Ohio wife and children and "to prevent undue influence enhanced by the apprehension of approaching death."[124]

Sometimes the law of the situs will provide the wrong answer to a false conflict in such a manner that charities will be deprived of benefits that they should have received. *Lowe v. Plainfield Trust Co.,*[125] provides an example. At the time of his death, the testator was domiciled in New Jersey and owned realty in New York. His will left the realty to one New Jersey and two New York charities. He was survived by a wife and two children. A New York statute prohibited any person having a spouse or child from devising more than one-half of his estate to a charity. The will gave the executor a power to sell the New York realty and, pursuant to that power, the executor had entered into a written contract providing for the sale of all except one parcel of the realty.

---

122. Toledo Soc'y for Crippled Children v. Hickok, 152 Tex. at 593, 261 S.W.2d at 702.

123. Appendix to Application for Writ of Error, pp. 40–41, Toledo Soc'y for Crippled Children v. Hickok, 152 Tex. 578, 261 S.W.2d 692.

124. Kirkbride v. Hickok, 155 Ohio St. 293, 302, 98 N.E.2d 815, 820 (1951). The Ohio Supreme Court held that the corpus would pass as intestate property at the end of the twenty year period, but left undisturbed the Ohio Court of Appeals reservation that whether this was true as to the Texas realty was up to the Texas courts. See Respondents' Supplemental Argument in Supreme Court of Texas, p. 5, quoting from the opinion of the Court of Appeals of Lucas County, Ohio: "The opinion of this court as to the equitable conversion, however, cannot be a controlling judgment. The courts of Texas will determine the effect of the will as it relates to real estate located in that state."

See Hancock, *In the Parish of St. Mary le Bow, in the Ward of Cheap*, supra note 91, at 573 characterizing the *Hickok* result as "officious intermeddling."

For similar "intermeddling", see N.Y.—McKinney's Estates, Powers & Trusts Law § 3–5.1(h): "Whenever a testator, not domiciled in this state at the time of death, provides in his will that he elects to have the disposition of his property situated in this state governed by the laws of this state, the intrinsic *validity*, including the testator's general capacity, effect, interpretation, revocation or alteration of any such disposition is determined by the local law of this state." [Emphasis added.] In re Estate of Clark, 21 N.Y.2d 478, 288 N.Y.S.2d 993, 236 N.E.2d 152 (1968) construed a predecessor of this statute, which covered "testamentary dispositions" and the "validity and effect of such dispositions." The court held that the prior statute did not apply to the right of a Virginia widow of a Virginia testator to elect against a will disposing of intangible personalty because her election was not a "testamentary disposition." In Matter of Estate of Renard, 56 N.Y.2d 973, 453 N.Y.S.2d 625, 439 N.E.2d 341 (1982), however, the court construed the quoted successor provision as preventing a son's election against his mother's will, approving a Surrogate's opinion that emphasized the change in wording of the statute from "testamentary dispositions" to the broader "disposition of his property."

125. 216 A.D. 72, 215 N.Y.S. 50 (1st Dep't 1926).

Rejecting the contention of the charities that this resulted in the conversion of the realty into personalty, thus avoiding the situs choice-of-law rule, the court held that New York law controlled as to the interests in the New York realty and its proceeds, and that the son and daughter (the wife now also having died) were entitled to one half of the New York realty unless they had waived their rights under an alleged settlement agreement.

The New York statute involved in *Lowe* seems to be directed at protecting the natural objects of the testator's bounty from having the bulk of the estate diverted from them to charities. New York had no interest in providing this protection for citizens of New Jersey if their own state did not think such protection necessary. It might be argued that New York had an interest in controlling the soliciting activities of New York charities and that this statute was designed, in part, to mitigate the harm of overzealous fundraising. This is possible, but it does not seem nearly so likely a purpose of the New York statute in *Lowe* as it might have been of the Ohio statute in *Hickok*, the latter being aimed at deterring deathbed solicitations and at protecting the family from the testator's late-coming religious fervor. Moreover, the *Lowe* decision affected the New Jersey charity as well and New York could have no interest in policing that charity's solicitations of New Jersey citizens in New Jersey.

Mortmain statutes of the type involved in *Hickok* and *Lowe* are primarily designed to protect the family from undue depletions of the estate by devises to charity. It is the settled residence of the testator and his family that is primarily concerned with the application of such a statute.[126] Another state, in which the charity is incorporated or conducts a substantial amount of its activities, may be interested in application of such a statute if, as in *Hickok*, it seems reasonable to view the statute also as controlling the soliciting activities of the charity. The situs does not have a legitimate countervailing interest in validating the will unless the charity conducts a substantial amount of its activities at the situs.

Another type of mortmain statute, representing the original meaning of the term, limits the total value of property that a charity may hold.[127] Both the situs qua situs and a state in which the charity conducts substantial activities are interested in enforcing such a statute.

---

126. See Crum v. Bliss, 47 Conn. 592, 600 (1880) ("the [New York mortmain] statute was intended to protect the interest of parents, wives and children, and inasmuch as it could have no extraterritorial effect, it could have no application to testators domiciled in other states than New York").

If the testator has died domiciled in a state having a mortmain statute, but all claimants (charity and heirs) reside in a state without such a statute and the charity has not solicited the devise, applying the statute will not advance its policies. But see Memphis State Univ. v. Agee, 566 S.W.2d 283 (Tenn.App.1977), cert. denied (Tenn.1978) (applying Mississippi statute prohibiting bequest of more than one-third of estate to charity, although the charity is a Tennessee university and heirs are Tennessee residents—voids bequest of personal property in Tennessee).

127. For an early case pointing out the differences in types and policies of such statutes, see Trustees of Amherst College v. Ritch, 151 N.Y. 282, 45 N.E. 876 (1897).

The situs may wish to keep realty in the stream of commerce. The scene of the charity's activities may wish to protect itself from what it considers excessive economic and political power of charities. The settled residence of the testator and his family has little interest in application of this type of statute. *Norton v. House of Mercy*[128] reached a result similar to that which would have been achieved by analysis of the purposes of this latter type of statute. The permissive law of the situs was avoided by classifying the question as one of the capacity of the charity to take. The issue of capacity to take was resolved by the law under which the charity was organized, New York, rather than that of the situs of the realty, Texas.

§ 8.12 Perpetuities Problems Concerning Realty

The situs qua situs has an interest in having its own rules on perpetuities and accumulations applied. Restrictions on use may adversely affect the economy of the situs by removing land from the stream of commerce.[129]

This legitimate interest of the situs qua situs is terminated if the land, whether because of directions or discretion under the will or otherwise, is sold and thus freed from what the situs considers undesirable provisions as to alienation or accumulation. The effect of sale in eliminating the interest of the situs, basic to any functional analysis of the problems in this area, has been recognized by a number of courts for over a century.[130]

A true conflict occurs when the testator makes provisions in his will concerning land that violate the perpetuities rules of the situs but not of the state where the testator and the beneficiaries under the will have settled residences. The situs is interested in freeing its land from fetters. The state where the claimants reside has an interest in giving effect to

128. 101 F. 382 (5th Cir.1900).

129. See Cook, The Logical and Legal Bases of the Conflict of Laws 290 (1942); Restatement (Second) § 239, comment *f*; Baxter, supra note 90 at 16–17; Re, *The Testamentary Disposition of Land in the Conflict of Laws*, 27 St. John's L. Rev. 36, 54 (1952). *Cf.* Wilson v. Smith, 373 S.W.2d 514 (Tex.Civ.App.—San Antonio 1963, writ refused n.r.e.), cert. denied sub nom. Burrows v. Carr, 379 U.S. 973, 85 S.Ct. 663, 13 L.Ed.2d 564 (1965) (trust of Texas land and personal property invalid in providing proceeds to be used to operate chiropractic hospitals, which are prohibited in Texas, even though the hospitals were to be operated in California where they were legal).

130. See Ford v. Ford, 80 Mich. 42, 55–56, 44 N.W. 1057, 1061 (1890): "The object of our statute was to prevent the lands within this State from being taken out of the channels of trade and the accumulation of large landed estates to be held in perpetuity, or for a long series of years. The only act which the executor is required to perform in Michigan is to make the sale; the proceeds to be taken to Missouri, and there invested. Our statute is in no sense violated by the direction in the will that the estate, after conversion here, is to be invested in Missouri lands, and there held for any number of lives."

Cf. Equitable Trust Co. v. Ward, 29 Del.Ch. 206, 48 A.2d 519 (Ch.1946) (rents from situs land transmitted to another state for accumulation); Hope v. Brewer, 136 N.Y. 126, 32 N.E. 558 (1892) (vagueness rules of situs not violated when situs land to be sold and proceeds administered in Scotland); Despard v. Churchill, 53 N.Y. 192 (1873) (fact that New York leaseholds soon to terminate makes New York perpetuities policy inapplicable). But see Penfield v. Tower, 1 N.D. 216, 46 N.W. 413 (1890) (trustee's discretion to sell does not make situs' perpetuities policy inapplicable).

the desires of the testator and having the claimants conform to his estate plan. This true conflict, at least as between states of the United States, should be resolved in favor of the validity of the will. The differences between the perpetuities rules of the various states are differences in detail rather than of basic policy.[131] The usual variations are the common law rule of lives in being plus twenty-one years,[132] a lives-in-being rule, or a two-lives rule. In view of the shared interest in giving effect to the intention of the testator and the largely-shared policies on perpetuities, the situs may defer to the more permissive perpetuities rule of the testator's residence without vitally affecting its own land policy.[133]

§ 8.13   Formalities of Execution and Revocation of a Will Devising Realty

One of the most objectionable applications of the situs rule is to invalidate, because of lack of requisite formalities, a will that satisfies the formalities indicated by the law of the testator's settled residence where it was executed. In reaching such a result, the situs not only upsets the expectation of the testator and the policy of a sister state in giving effect to those expectations, but also advances no conceivable interest that it, qua situs, can have.[134]

This is clearly true when the situs invalidates the will because of some variance on a matter of detail from the situs' statute of wills. For example, the will may have two witnesses as required at the testator's residence but lack the three witnesses required by the situs.[135] But invalidation under situs law is still undesirable even when the will violates in some very substantial way the formalities requirements of the situs. For example, the will is nuncupative or holographic, valid at the residence of the testator but not permitted by the situs.[136] The situs' rejection of nuncupative and holographic wills, designed to assure appro-

---

131. See von Mehren & Trautman, supra note 92 at 200; cf. Shannon v. Irving Trust Co., 275 N.Y. 95, 103–04, 9 N.E.2d 792, 794 (1937) (accumulations of proceeds from personalty: "Our policy in that connection is substantially the same as that of New Jersey"); Cross v. United States Trust Co. of N.Y., 131 N.Y. 330, 30 N.E. 125 (1892) (personalty).

132. See Atkinson v. Kettler, 372 S.W.2d 704 (Tex.Civ.App.—Dallas 1963), modified, 383 S.W.2d 557 (Tex.1964) (common law rule applicable in Texas described as twenty-one years after some life in being at the time of the creation of the interests, plus a period of gestation).

133. Cf. Matter of Bauer, 14 N.Y.2d 272, 278, 251 N.Y.S.2d 23, 26–27, 200 N.E.2d 207, 210–211 (1964) (dissent, Fuld, J.) (urging more flexible choice-of-law approach to perpetuities problem concerning personalty). But cf. Succession of Simms, 250 La. 177, 195 So.2d 114 (1965), cert. denied sub nom. Kitchen v. Reese, 389 U.S. 850, 88 S.Ct. 47, 19 L.Ed.2d 120 (1967) (invalidate will of Texas testatrix under "substitution" rule of Louisiana situs).

134. See In re Estate of Janney, 498 Pa. 398, 446 A.2d 1265 (1982) (does not apply law of situs, which would invalidate a bequest to an attesting witness).

135. See Melon v. Entidad Provincia Religiosa De Padres Mercedarios De Castilla, 189 F.2d 163 (1st Cir.1951) (nuncupative will denied effect because it had only the four witnesses required by the testatrix's domicile, not the five required by the situs).

136. For cases applying the situs law under such circumstances, see Trotter v. Van Pelt, 144 Fla. 517, 198 So. 215 (1940); Matter of McDougal's Will, 49 N.J.Super. 485, 140 A.2d 249 (Probate Div.1958), aff'd, 55 N.J.Super. 36, 149 A.2d 801 (1959) aff'd, 29 N.J. 586, 151 A.2d 540 (1959).

priate deliberation on the part of the testator and to prevent mistake and fraud, is understandable for the protection of citizens of the situs, but is misplaced paternalism when directed at citizens of other states when those states would strike a balance in such cases in favor of the intention of the decedent, even though that intention is somewhat informally expressed.[137] This is true whether the testamentary act in question is the only will, a will revoking a prior will,[138] or some other act intended to revoke a will.[139]

Suppose the situation is reversed, and the law of the situs would validate the will but the law of the testator's residence would not. Is application of the situs law justified? Perhaps validation under situs law is proper if the situs law differs from that of the settled residence on what might fairly be described as a matter of detail—number of witnesses, necessity for attestation clause, whether witnesses must sign in the presence of one another, and so forth. Here the situs and the residence share the basic policy of giving effect with appropriate safeguards to the intention of the testator or testatrix and are in substantial agreement on what those safeguards should be. This would seem to justify an alternative-reference rule validating the will if valid under either the law of the place of residence or of the situs.[140] If the difference between situs and decedent's residence is more basic, the situs, for

---

137.   See Hancock, supra note 22, at 1099–1100, rejecting the argument that the situs, as forum, has an interest in preventing fraud in its courts; the reliability of such informal wills may turn on whether they are sanctioned and customary in the community with which the testator is most closely related.

138.   See cases cited supra note 136.

139.   See In re Barrie's Estate, 240 Iowa 431, 35 N.W.2d 658 (1949) (revocation by writing "void" invalid under situs law though valid under law of domicile, rejecting equitable conversion argument); Hancock, *Conceptual Devices for Avoiding the Land Taboo in Conflict of Laws: The Disadvantages of Disingenuousness*, 20 Stan. L. Rev. 1, 1–11 (1967) (disapproving of result in *In re Barrie's Estate*); Scoles & Rheinstein, *Conflict Avoidance in Succession Planning*, 21 Law & Contemp.Probs. 499, 501–06 (1956). Cf. Matter of Estate of Wimbush, 41 Colo.App. 289, 587 P.2d 796 (1978) (no claimants resident at situs, but situs law applied so that subsequent marriage does not revoke will—apparently neither testator nor his attorney was aware of contrary rule at testator's domicile); In re Barrie's Estate, 331 Ill.App. 443, 73 N.E.2d 654 (1947) (concerning same will as in first case cited in this note and holding revocation valid under Illinois law, but permitting withdrawal from Illinois probate files so that it may be probated at the Iowa situs); Cox v. Harrison, 535 S.W.2d 78 (Ky.1975) (under situs law, subsequent marriage revokes will insofar as it disposes of realty in Kentucky, but under law of domicile at death, will not revoked as to personalty in Kentucky); Succession of Martin, 147 So.2d 53 (La.App.1962), cert. denied (result correct), 243 La. 1003, 149 So.2d 763 (1963) (renunciation of will by testator's widow, though in proper form under law of domicile of testator and widow, invalid under law of situs).

See also Owen v. Younger, 242 S.W.2d 895 (Tex.Civ.App.—Amarillo 1951) (Texas situs rejects rule of domicile that subsequent marriage revokes the will, but beneficiaries were Texas citizens). But see Gailey v. Brown, 169 Wis. 444, 171 N.W. 945 (1919) (applying law of domicile, contra law of situs, that subsequent marriage revoked the will, but result based on construction of situs statute admitting to probate at the situs wills of situs land probated elsewhere).

140.   Uniform Probate Code § 2–506, 8 pt. 1 U.L.A. 151 (1998) validates with regard to the method of execution if valid under any of the following laws: forum; place of execution at time of execution; place of domicile, abode, or nationality at time of either execution or death. See also Rees, *American Wills Statutes*, 46 Va. L. Rev. 856, 905–06 (1960) (listing thirty-two states with statutes making some alternative references for formal validity).

example, accepting holographic or nuncupative wills and the residence completely rejecting them, then validation under situs law is far more questionable.[141] It would seem to be an unwise interference in matters with which the situs qua situs has no interest.

§ 8.14　Marital Property

The following rules have traditionally determined interests in property acquired during marriage. The law of the marital domicile at the time that the property is acquired determines rights in personalty.[142] The law of the situs determines rights in realty.[143] Once rights in property are determined by these rules, the rights are not affected by moving the property or its proceeds to another state.[144] Because the

---

141. For application of situs law under such circumstances, see McCaughna v. Bilhorn, 10 Cal.App.2d 674, 52 P.2d 1025 (Dist.Ct.App.1935); In re Briggs' Estate, 148 W.Va. 294, 134 S.E.2d 737 (1964) (but holding instrument did not qualify even under more liberal law of situs).

142. See Restatement (Second) § 258; cf. Travelers Ins. Co. v. Fields, 451 F.2d 1292 (6th Cir.1971), cert. denied, 406 U.S. 919, 92 S.Ct. 1772, 32 L.Ed.2d 118 (1972) (under law of marital domicile, divorce terminates wife's interest in group life insurance policy, though this not result under law of state where policy issued). Until 1980, under Louisiana law, the law of the Louisiana situs determined the rights of nonresidents in both movables and immovables. See Dawson v. Capital Bank & Trust Co., 261 So.2d 727 (La.App.1972) (right of surviving nonresident spouse in Louisiana joint bank account); Crichton v. Succession of Crichton, 232 So.2d 109 (La.App.1970), writ ref'd, result correct, 256 La. 274, 236 So.2d 39 (1970), cert. denied, 400 U.S. 919, 91 S.Ct. 172, 27 L.Ed.2d 159 (1970) (New York opinion erroneously failed to apply Louisiana law to determine right of New York widow to take Louisiana personalty against her husband's testament, but the erroneous opinion is entitled to full faith and credit); Comment, *Conflict of Laws: Property Acquired after Marriage*, 35 La. L. Rev. 125, 131 (1974). This rule has now been changed by statute so that "movables, wherever situated, acquired by either spouse during marriage are governed by the law of the domicile of the acquiring spouse at the time of acquisition." La. Civ. C. art. 3523.

Sometimes federal law preempts state marital property rules. See, e.g., McCarty v. McCarty, 453 U.S. 210, 101 S.Ct. 2728, 69 L.Ed.2d 589 (1981) (there are no marital property rights in military retirement payments); Hisquierdo v. Hisquierdo, 439 U.S. 572, 99 S.Ct. 802, 59 L.Ed.2d 1 (1979) (benefits under Railroad Retirement Act may not be divided as community property). Both of these results have been changed by subsequent statutory amendments that, within certain limits imposed by the amendments, permit recognition of marital property rights. See 10 U.S.C.A. § 1408(c)(1) (military retirement); 45 U.S.C.A. § 231m(b)(2) (railroad retirement).

143. See La. Civ. C. art. 3524 (immovables situated in Louisiana); Strang v. Strang, 258 Ark. 139, 523 S.W.2d 887 (1975) (in Arkansas divorce, law of Oklahoma situs determines wife's interest in land); Morton v. Morton, 297 So.2d 79 (Fla.App.), cert. denied, 304 So.2d 131 (Fla.1974) (widow's dower rights whole law of situs); Restatement (Second) § 234. But cf. La Civ. C. art. 3525 (on termination of community while either spouse domiciled in Louisiana, immovable property in another state acquired while spouse domiciled in Louisiana treated as community property if it would be community property under Louisiana law); Williams v. Williams, 390 A.2d 4 (D.C.App.1978) (interest of wife on divorce, applies law of situs not qua situs but qua last marital and husband's domicile pursuant to interest analysis).

144. See Jones v. Jones, 293 Ala. 39, 299 So.2d 729 (1974) (proceeds of sale of realty when marital domicile changed from Florida to Alabama); McDowell v. Harris, 107 S.W.2d 647 (Tex.Civ.App.—Dallas 1937, writ dism'd) (Texas realty acquired with separate funds by husband domiciled in Illinois is husband's separate property); Restatement (Second) §§ 259 (personalty), 234, comment *a* (land). Contra, Savelle v. Savelle, 650 So.2d 476 (Miss. 1995) (when husband granted divorce in Mississippi, wife entitled only to equitable distribution of husband's retirement benefits under Mississippi law and not community property share

rights remain immutable, rights in realty trace to the rights in the proceeds with which the realty was acquired. Thus, if a husband domiciled in a non-community property state buys realty in a community property state with the proceeds of his earnings, the realty takes the same "separate property" status as the assets with which it was purchased.[145] This tracing rule saves the situs rule for marital property rights from creating as many dysfunctional results as it otherwise might. But there is likely to be a presumption at the community property situs that all property acquired in the state during marriage is community property unless the contrary is shown.[146] Moreover, as the following discussion demonstrates, the basic situs rule for determining marital property rights in realty causes many undesirable results that the tracing rule does not avoid.

The situs qua situs has no interest in applying its own rules to determine whether a surviving spouse may elect against the will, the share in realty to which the survivor is entitled upon such election, and whether provisions in the will for the spouse should be construed as in lieu of or in addition to dower. The law of the settled residence of the spouses should control these issues.[147] Yet the situs dogma has tradition-

---

under Louisiana law although Louisiana was marital domicile at time of husband's employment).

145. See McCarver v. Trumble, 660 S.W.2d 595 (Tex.App.—Corpus Christi 1983).

146. See, e.g., Vernon's Tex.C.A. Family Code § 3.003: "(a) Property possessed by either spouse during or on dissolution of marriage is presumed to be community property. (b) The degree of proof necessary to establish that property is separate property is clear and convincing evidence." See also Gilchrist, *Washington Disinherits the Non–Native Wife*, 46 Wash. L. Rev. 283, 287 (1971).

An "inception of title" rule may increase the scope of tracing by characterizing property under the law of the marital domicile when first acquired, even though payments have been continued after the domicile has changed. An example would be an insurance policy acquired by the husband when domiciled in a non-community state with some premiums paid for out of income earned after a move to a community property state. See Baade, *Annual Survey of Texas Law—Conflict of Laws*, 28 Sw.L. J. 166, 241 (1974).

147. See Uniform Probate Code §§ 2–202, 2–203, 8 pt. 1 U.L.A. 102–04 (1998) (the right to elective shares for all property is determined under the law of the decedent's domicile at death); Federal Republic of Germany: Act on the Revision of the Private Int'l Law 27 I.L.M. 1 (1988) Art. 14 (legal effects of marriage determined by law of nationality or residence); In re Estate of Clark, 21 N.Y.2d 478, 288 N.Y.S.2d 993, 236 N.E.2d 152 (1968) (marital domicile has predominant interest in determining whether wife can elect against will disposing of intangible personalty); cf. Vernon's Tex.C.A., Family C. § 7.002 (division of property in a decree of divorce or annulment). But cf. Hague Convention on the Law Applicable to Matrimonial Property Regimes, 14 March 1978 art. 3 (matrimonial property regime is governed by law designated by spouses, which may include law of nationality, habitual residence, and in the case of immovables, the law of the situs); Matter of Estate of Renard, 56 N.Y.2d 973, 453 N.Y.S.2d 625, 439 N.E.2d 341 (1982) (after amendment of statute applied in *Clark*, supra, cannot protect nonresident son from disinheritance under law of the New York situs of the personalty); In re Estate of Erickson, 368 N.W.2d 525 (N.D. 1985) (agreement by Washington spouses that all property would be community is not valid as to North Dakota realty).

Under modern conditions, it is increasingly likely that spouses will be domiciled in different states while married. In this situation, there will not be a single "settled residence of the spouses." The law that should be applied depends on the issue on which the laws of the two jurisdictions differ and the policies underlying the different laws. See, e.g., Lane–Burslem v. Commissioner of Internal Revenue, 659 F.2d 209 (D.C.Cir.1981) (apply law of jurisdiction with the most significant relationship to the spouses and their earnings); Keller

ally resulted in displacing the residence's rules on such matters with the rules of the situs.[148] If objection is made that creditors, in extending credit, may have relied upon the law of the situs and its less liberal provisions for the widow,[149] the answer is to protect them under situs law, but only when they actually exist and when their right to payment in full would be threatened by applying the law of the settled residence.[150] This is consistent with the distinction between original parties and remote parties, which is the basis for all of this chapter's choice-of-law discussion concerning realty.

Applying the law of the situs to determine the rights of the widow as against other claimants to the testator's bounty is bad enough when it provides the wrong answer to a conflict over interests in situs land. It becomes doubly pernicious when the threat of application of situs law hangs as blackmail over the widow's head, preventing her from freely exercising her rights to non-situs property under non-situs law. This is very likely to happen. The widow's election against the will, when made at the settled residence of the testator and the natural objects of his bounty, is binding against the widow at the situs of the land.[151]

Singleton v. St. Louis Union Trust Co.[152] illustrates what the result is when a large portion of the estate consists of interests in land. In *Singleton*, the testator died resident in Missouri owning as his separate property valuable real estate in a community-property state, Texas. Not

---

v. Department of Revenue, 292 Or. 639, 642 P.2d 284 (1982) (wife domiciled in non-community state is taxable on half the earnings of her husband, who lives in a community property state).

148. See Colvin v. Hutchison, 338 Mo. 576, 92 S.W.2d 667 (1936) (whether in absence of express preference wife, on electing against the will, to be given dower or alternative fee interest); Jennings v. Jennings, 21 Ohio St. 56 (1871) (whether to presume provision in will is in lieu of dower, despite argument by widow's counsel, one R.P. Ranney, that the Ohio statutes "have no application to wills made and proved in other States, or to the rights of widows resident there." Id. at 60); Pfau v. Moseley, 9 Ohio St.2d 13, 222 N.E.2d 639 (1966) (following *Jennings*); Ing v. Cannon, 398 S.W.2d 789 (Tex.Civ.App.—Amarillo 1965, writ ref'd n.r.e.) (interest in land acquired during coverture; effect of electing to take under husband's will); Singleton v. St. Louis Union Trust Co., 191 S.W.2d 143 (Tex.Civ.App.—Waco 1945, writ ref'd n.r.e.) (effect of electing against the will); Restatement (Second) §§ 241 (interest of surviving spouse), 242 (forced share and election); cf. Matter of Schneider's Estate, 198 Misc. 1017, 96 N.Y.S.2d 652 (1950), adhered to on reargument, 198 Misc. 1017, 100 N.Y.S.2d 371 (Surr.Ct. New York County 1950) (avoidance of situs law of "legitime" by renvoi device); Matter of Stackman's Estate, 388 P.2d 305 (Okl.1963) (widow's allowance during administration, but court stresses that widow is a resident of the situs); Scoles, *Conflict of Laws and Elections in Administration of Decedents' Estates,* 30 Ind.L. J. 293 (1955); Scoles, *Conflict of Laws and Nonbarrable Interests in Administration of Decedents' Estates,* 8 U.Fla. L. Rev. 151 (1955).

149. See Ester & Scoles, *Estate Planning and Conflict of Laws,* 24 Ohio St.L. J. 270, 280 (1963); Scoles, *Conflict of Laws and Creditors' Rights in Decedents' Estates,* 42 Iowa L. Rev. 341 (1957).

150. But cf. Colorado Nat'l Bank v. Merlino, 35 Wn.App. 610, 668 P.2d 1304 (1983) (default judgment obtained by bank at situs cannot be enforced at marital domicile against community property—bank is assignee of promissory note signed by husband for price of land).

151. Colvin v. Hutchison, 338 Mo. 576, 92 S.W.2d 667 (1936). But cf. In re Estate of Miller, 541 P.2d 28 (Wyo.1975) (election against will at domicile not effective at situs when situs formalities for election not followed).

152. 191 S.W.2d 143 (Tex.Civ.App.—Waco 1945, writ ref'd n.r.e.).

satisfied with the provisions made for her in the will, the widow elected against the will in Missouri and filed this declaration in Texas. The latter was probably a tactical error, but it made no difference as she would have been bound at the situs by her election at home in any event. Under Missouri law, on her rejection of the will, the wife was entitled to a one-third life dower interest in her husband's realty or, in lieu of dower, a fee in a share equal to the share of a child of the deceased husband. In Texas the widow lost all her rights under the will to the Texas realty and, because in Texas a wife has no rights in the separate property of her husband, a gift over after the widow's life to the children was accelerated and she took nothing. It is evident that in such a situation the widow cannot exercise her rights under the law of the home state to property there without weighing against her gains under that law losses that she will suffer under the law of the situs.[153]

Ing v. Cannon[154] demonstrates the appalling mess that results from applying the law of the situs qua situs to the rights of the widow. The husband and wife were domiciled in Oklahoma at all relevant times. Before his marriage, the husband owned Oklahoma land, which he traded after marriage for Texas land, taking title in his own name. The court stated that under Texas law all land acquired in the state during coverture is presumed to be community property unless the conveyance otherwise indicates.[155] At this point, then, the wife owned one-half of the Texas realty. The husband died leaving his wife a life interest in his realty wherever situated, remainder to his son. When the wife died intestate, her mother and then her mother's heirs claimed the wife's one-half interest in Texas realty. The court held that having accepted the benefits of her husband's will, which purported to dispose of the wife's interest in the Texas realty, and having taken other rights under the will that she would not otherwise have, the wife and her successors in interest were estopped to question the husband's disposition of the wife's property. Thus, by giving the wife an interest she probably never knew she had and having her make an election she never knew she made, the court circuitously arrives at the result that could have been reached directly by applying Oklahoma law to determine the wife's interests in the Texas realty.

A far more undesirable example of applying situs law to determine the widow's protection against disinheritance is the following. A husband and wife live all their lives in X, a common-law state. The husband prospers and accumulates considerable wealth in X, including realty in X. Under X law, the husband has sole title to the realty and the wife is protected against disinheritance by her inchoate dower rights in the realty and by a right to take a forced share of her husband's estate if not

---

153. See Banks v. Junk, 264 So.2d 387 (Miss.1972) (husband's statutory share in realty after electing against will governed by law of situs, not domicile).

154. 398 S.W.2d 789 (Tex.Civ.App.—Amarillo 1965, writ ref'd n.r.e.).

155. Id. at 790–91. But see McDowell v. Harris, 107 S.W.2d 647 (Tex.Civ.App.—Dallas 1937, writ dismissed) (realty in Texas acquired with separate funds by husband domiciled in Illinois is separate property of the husband).

satisfied with the provisions of his will. In their later years, husband and wife sell out their interests in X property, the wife releasing her dower rights. Husband and wife then move to the sunnier climate of Y, a community-property state. The husband invests most of the savings of his X income and the proceeds of the sale of X property in reliable income-producing securities and with the remainder buys a modest home in Y. On the husband's death it is discovered that in his will he has left everything to persons other than his wife. The wife takes nothing and has no right to elect against the will. Because the marital domicile is no longer in X and the husband does not own X realty, the wife has lost the protection of X law. Under Y law, all of the husband's property is his "separate" property, because purchased with the proceeds of his X income and the sale of his X property, which was not "community" property. If it were community property, the wife would be entitled to one-half of it.

Thus the wife falls between the protections that both X and Y have provided for their wives.[156] California has now corrected this aberration with regard to personal property wherever situated and with regard to realty in California by a statute treating the wife for purposes of inheritance as if husband and wife were residents of California at all relevant times.[157] Except for the exclusion of out-of-state realty, this

---

156. See Estate of O'Connor, 218 Cal. 518, 23 P.2d 1031 (1933) (personalty). For a similar mixture of common law and community property law burdening the husband's creditor with the worst features of each and reaching a result untenable under either law, see Escrow Service Co. v. Cressler, 59 Wn.2d 38, 365 P.2d 760 (1961), overruled, Pacific States Cut Stone Co. v. Goble, 70 Wn.2d 907, 425 P.2d 631 (1967). See also Bainum v. Roundy, 21 Ariz.App. 534, 521 P.2d 633 (1974) (following *Goble*).

157. West's Ann.Cal.Prob.Code §§ 66, 101. An earlier version reclassifying the property as "community" for all purposes was declared unconstitutional. In re Thornton's Estate, 1 Cal.2d 1, 33 P.2d 1 (1934) (personalty). A similar fate was met by the provision that attempted to give the wife the power to dispose by will of one-half of the property if she pre-deceased her husband. Paley v. Bank of America, 159 Cal.App.2d 500, 324 P.2d 35 (Dist.Ct.App.1958). But see Addison v. Addison, 62 Cal.2d 558, 565–566, 43 Cal.Rptr. 97, 101, 399 P.2d 897, 901 (1965), which held constitutional West's Ann.Cal.Civ.Code § 4803 providing that property acquired by a California spouse while domiciled in a common-law state shall be treated as "quasi-community property" for purposes of distribution in matrimonial actions, (see also Vernon's Tex.C.A., Family C.Ann. § 7.002) and stated, in regard to *Thornton*: "the correctness of the rule of Thornton is open to challenge." But cf. Roesch v. Roesch, 83 Cal.App.3d 96, 147 Cal.Rptr. 586 (1st Dist.1978), cert. denied, 440 U.S. 915, 99 S.Ct. 1232, 59 L.Ed.2d 465 (1979) (it is a violation of due process and the privileges and immunities clause to treat marital property as quasi community when only one spouse, the husband, has moved to California); cf. Martin v. Martin, 156 Ariz. 440, 752 P.2d 1026 (App. 1986), modified on other grounds and aff'd, 156 Ariz. 452, 752 P.2d 1038 (1988) (apply Arizona law to husband's post-separation earnings even though husband retained his California domicile—court erroneously holds that husband's appearance waives his choice-of-law objection—there may have been a sufficient husband-forum nexus to make choice of Arizona law constitutional [husband gave wife money for living expenses and to pay mortgage on Arizona house to which he had planned to retire], but court does not focus on this); Ismail v. Ismail, 702 S.W.2d 216 (Tex.App.—Houston [1st Dist.] 1985, writ ref'd n.r.e.) (only wife is domiciled in Texas at time of divorce proceeding, but before her return to Texas from Egypt, husband and wife had a marital domicile in Texas for six years).

For discussions of the problem, see Abel, Barry, Halsted & Marsh, *Rights of a Surviving Spouse in Property Acquired by a Decedent While Domiciled Outside California*, 47 Calif. L. Rev. 211 (1959); Andrews, *Washington's New Quasi–Community Property Act: Protecting*

seems the sensible way to protect the wife and give effect to the now predominant interest of the new home in her welfare. It is a result that, barring insurmountable local statutory or constitutional obstacles in the form of definitions of "separate" and "community" property, should be reached in Y without need for a statute.[158] If there are such obstacles, they should be removed at once. Here, in the light of Y's interests other than as situs, it is not the application of situs law that is undesirable, but the application of a weird amalgam of situs and non-situs law. If, under state statutory or constitutional provisions, the wife cannot be protected under the law of her new domicile, she should be accorded the same rights in her husband's estate as she had under the law of the former marital domicile. Just as it is alleged to be improper to change the husband's separate property to community property when the property or its proceeds crosses state lines,[159] it is unfair to deprive the wife of the protections against disinheritance that she had under the law of the

---

the Immigrant Spouse, 15(3) Community Prop.J. 50 (1988); De Funiak, *Conflict of Laws in the Community Property Field*, 7 Ariz. L. Rev. 50 (1965); Schreter, *"Quasi–Community Property" in the Conflict of Laws*, 50 Calif. L. Rev. 206 (1962); Comment, *Marital Property and the Conflict of Laws: The Constitutionality of the "Quasi–Community Property" Legislation*, 54 Calif. L. Rev. 252 (1966); Weisberger, *Selected Conflict of Laws Issues in Wisconsin's New Marital (Community) Property Act*, 35 Am.J.Comp.L. 295 (1987); Note, 5 Natural Resources J. 373 (1965).

Legislation treating property acquired before a marital domicile was acquired in the forum as community property for purposes of divorce or inheritance, does not resolve the problem of treating the property as separate property during marriage. For a proposal to treat all property of forum spouses under forum law, no matter when or where the property was acquired, see Bassett, *Repealing Quasi–Community Property: A Proposal to Readopt a Unitary Marital Property Scheme*, 22 U. San Francisco L. Rev. 463 (1988).

For the converse problem of a move by spouses from a community property to a non-community state, see Unif. Disposition of Community Property Rights at Death Act §§ 1, 3, 8A U.L.A. (one half of property that would have been community property under laws of another jurisdiction is the property of the surviving spouse and not subject to testamentary disposition by the decedent) (adopted by 14 states as of January 1, 2006); Pascoe v. Keuhnast, 642 S.W.2d 37 (Tex.App.—Waco 1982, writ ref'd no rev. error), appeal dism'd for want of juris., 463 U.S. 1201, 103 S.Ct. 3528, 77 L.Ed.2d 1381 (1983) (not only does realty acquired at the marital domicile remain community property when the spouses moved to a non-community state, but also the validity of the wife's conveyance of the property is determined by situs law); Juenger, *Marital Property and the Conflict of Laws: A Tale of Two Countries*, 81 Col. L. Rev. 1061, 1075 (1981); Lay, *Migrants from Community Property States—Filling the Legislative Gap*, 53 Cornell L. Rev. 832 (1968). For aberrant treatment of the problem, see Savelle v. Savelle, 650 So.2d 476 (Miss. 1995) (when husband granted divorce in Mississippi, wife entitled only to equitable distribution of husband's retirement benefits under Mississippi law and not community property share under Louisiana law although Louisiana was marital domicile at time of husband's employment).

158. See Cameron v. Cameron, 641 S.W.2d 210 (Tex.1982) (adopting statutory quasi community property rule as common law rule for cases arising before effective date of statute); cf. Dority v. Dority, 645 P.2d 56 (Utah 1982) (apply law of forum, to which husband has moved, to give wife an interest in realty at the former marital domicile that she would not have under situs law). But see Estate of Hanau v. Hanau, 730 S.W.2d 663 (Tex. 1987) (although *Cameron*, supra, applied Texas' quasi-community property statute as a common law rule to cases arising before the effective date of the statute, the statute and *Cameron* deal with divorce, and similar treatment will not be given to a spouse's inheritance rights) For discussion of *Hanau* see Weintraub, *Obstacles to Sensible Choice of Law for Determining Marital Property Rights on Divorce or in Probate: Hanau and the Situs Rule*, 25 Houston L. Rev. 1113 (1988)

159. See cases cited supra note 144.

former domicile if no reasonable substitute for these protections is accorded to her.[160]

The same factors just discussed with regard to inheritance of marital property also apply to division on divorce. Spouses frequently move from non-community state to a community state and then divorce. If the state from which they came permits equitable distribution on divorce, it may make no practical difference whether the court is theoretically applying the law of the former residence to the property acquired there or is treating all the property as quasi-community.[161]

If the property acquired before the spouses moved to the forum is realty, it is doubtful that the typical "quasi-community" property legislation will permit division of that property or its proceeds, even if that would have been the result under forum law for forum realty and forum spouses. For example, the Texas act refers to property "that would have been community property if the spouse who acquired the property had been domiciled in this state at the time of the acquisition."[162] Unless Texas courts follow the courts that have abandoned the situs choice-of-law rule for realty,[163] Texas law would not apply to marital property rights in out-of-state realty even if the acquiring spouse were domiciled in Texas; the law of the situs would apply.[164] One way to correct this,

---

160. See Rau v. Rau, 6 Ariz.App. 362, 432 P.2d 910 (1967) (on divorce, wife's right to share of real property purchased in forum with proceeds of property and earnings acquired in former marital domicile is determined by the rights she would have had under law of former domicile); McHugh v. McHugh, 108 Idaho 347, 699 P.2d 1361 (1985) (apply law of Maryland, the situs of realty and the marital domicile when it was acquired, to determine rights of spouses in the realty for purposes of division on divorce); Hughes v. Hughes, 91 N.M. 339, 573 P.2d 1194 (1978) (same); Marsh, Marital Property in Conflict of Laws 229 (1952) (wife's rights should be determined under law of former domicile); cf. Berle v. Berle, 97 Idaho 452, 546 P.2d 407 (1976) (when husband has moved to community property forum and wife has remained at non-community marital domicile, the law of the marital domicile determines the wife's rights in property acquired there); Hand v. Hand, 834 So.2d 619 (La. App. 1st Cir. 2002) (when only husband moved to Louisiana and there filed for divorce, Louisiana community property regime did not determine spouses' rights in personal property acquired by husband while he resided in Louisiana); Braddock v. Braddock, 91 Nev. 735, 542 P.2d 1060 (1975) (when husband has moved to community property forum and wife has remained at non-community marital domicile, the law of the marital domicile determines the wife's rights in property acquired there and antenuptial agreement invalid under law of marital domicile where it made and to be performed).

161. See Kreimeyer v. Kreimeyer, 125 Ariz. 16, 606 P.2d 834 (App.1980); Cameron v. Cameron, 641 S.W.2d 210, 222–23 (Tex.1982); Oldham, *Property Division in a Texas Divorce of a Migrant Spouse: Head He Wins, Tails She Loses?*, 19 Houston L. Rev. 1, 42–43 (1981) (only four non-community states do not permit equitable distribution of property owned by either spouse).

162. Tex.Fam.Code Ann. § 7002(1) (dissolution or marriage). See also Cal. Fam.Code § 125(a) (definition of "quasi community property") (same as Texas wording). The analogous provision in the California Probate Code refers only to "real property situated in this state." Cal.Prob.Code § 66(a). It is true that in probate, as in divorce, the court will not always have jurisdiction to affect interests in realty outside the forum, but it does have this power when it has personal jurisdiction over the parties whose interest it is affecting. See § 8.5.

163. See § 8.21A.

164. It is not certain that if the situs rule is used, this result can be avoided by a "tracing" argument that realty acquired with earnings is community because the earnings would have been community if the spouse had been domiciled in the forum at the time. Situs law would determine whether interests in situs realty will be traced to proceeds of

other than hoping that forum courts will abandon the situs rule for all purposes, is to add to the current statutory provision, the words "and if the property, real or personal, had been situated in this state at the time of its acquisition."[165]

§ 8.15 Construction of the Will Devising Realty

In administering the estate, issues often arise that the testator or testatrix could have controlled with a proper manifestation of intention but on which intention is either non-existent, or, if there was an intention, it is unknown and unknowable. Such questions have included, whether a bastard of the testator's son qualifies as an "heir of the body" of the son after written recognition,[166] or as "lawful issue" of the son when legitimized by the son's subsequent marriage of the mother;[167] whether a bastard[168] or legitimate child[169] of the testator, not mentioned in the will, should take as a pretermitted heir; whether, if devisees predecease the testator, the heirs of such devisees are to take under an anti-lapse statute;[170] whether a devise of mortgaged realty is intended to pass the property clear of the mortgage.[171]

A glance at the cases cited to illustrate these problems will indicate that this is one area in which a sizeable crack has appeared in the monolith of the situs rule. As an early draft of the second Restatement puts it:

> Authority is nearly equally divided as to whether in situations where there is no satisfactory evidence of the testator's intentions, the meaning of the words in question should be determined according to usage in the state where the testator was domiciled at the time the will was executed, or according to usage prevailing at the situs of the land.[172]

The reasons advanced for the rule pointing to the domicile of the testator or testatrix on questions of construction of the will are that the domicile's rule will be most likely to coincide with the actual intention of

personalty acquired in another state and characterized under the law of the marital domicile. See Restatement (Second) § 234.

165. Cf. Wash Code Ann. § 26.16.220(2)(b) (defines as quasi-community property "[r]eal property situated outside this state if the law of the state where the real property is located provides that the law of the decedent's domicile at death shall govern the rights of the decedent's surviving spouse").

166. Keith v. Eaton, 58 Kan. 732, 51 P. 271 (1897) (law of testator's domicile).

167. Olmsted v. Olmsted, 216 U.S. 386, 30 S.Ct. 292, 54 L.Ed. 530 (1910) (law of testator's domicile and situs but not son's domicile).

168. Norris v. Loyd, 183 Iowa 1056, 168 N.W. 557 (1918) (situs law).

169. Peet v. Peet, 229 Ill. 341, 82 N.E. 376 (1907) (situs law).

170. Duckwall v. Lease, 106 Ind.App. 664, 20 N.E.2d 204 (1939) (law of testatrix's domicile applied after court accepted "equitable conversion" argument); Zombro v. Moffett, 329 Mo. 137, 44 S.W.2d 149 (1931) (law of testator's domicile).

171. Higinbotham v. Manchester, 113 Conn. 62, 154 A. 242 (1931) (law of testator's domicile).

172. Restatement (Second), Conflict of Laws § 251, comment *b* (Tent.Draft No. 5, 1959).

the testator or testatrix.[173] Moreover, in a case in which the testator or testatrix has made the same cryptic provision concerning land situated in several states, with differing domestic rules of construction, applying the law of the domicile will avoid the absurdity of construing the will differently at each situs.[174] An example of the bizarre effects of the situs dogma is *Craig v. Carrigo*,[175] in which the Supreme Court of Arkansas construed the will one way, under Arkansas law, as to interests in realty in Arkansas, and another way, under the law of Alberta, Canada, the testator's domicile at death, as to interests in cash deposits in Arkansas.

Neither of these reasons is a convincing argument for looking to the law of the domicile on such matters. It is highly unrealistic in a genuine construction problem, when intention is either non-existent or unknown and unknowable, to assume that the testator or testatrix formulated any intention in terms of the domicile's rule of construction—a rule of which he or she is probably unaware.[176] If an attorney has drafted the will, the attorney should know the domicile's rule of construction, but should not rely on such a rule to express an intention communicated to the attorney by the testator. It is true that applying the law of the testator's or testatrix's domicile will avoid different constructions of the will when the land is situated in several states. This, however, is only an argument for some non-situs choice-of-law rule, not necessarily a rule pointing to the domicile.

Which choice-of-law rule should be adopted for construction of a will disposing of interests in real property—the law of the situs or the law of the testator's or testatrix's domicile at the time of execution of the will? Neither. The law that should be applied is the law of the state predominantly concerned with the matters with which the issue of construction deals. This may be the testator's or testatrix's domicile at the time he or she executed the will, or at the time of death, even though it is not concerned qua domicile; it may be the situs, though not qua situs; or it may be none of these. If all of the claimants under the will have settled residences in a single state, it will be that state.[177]

---

173. See Higinbotham v. Manchester, 113 Conn. 62, 154 A. 242 (1931); Keith v. Eaton, 58 Kan. 732, 51 P. 271 (1897). Contra, In re Estate of Hannan, 246 Neb. 828, 523 N.W.2d 672 (1994) (applying law of situs to hold, contrary to law of testatrix's domicile, that an adopted daughter is "issue").

174. Restatement (Second) § 240, comment *f*.

175. 340 Ark. 624, 12 S.W.3d 229 (2000).

176. See Matter of Estate of Wimbush, 41 Colo.App. 289, 587 P.2d 796 (1978) (situs law applied when neither decedent nor his attorney were aware of domicile's rule of construction).

177. But see Ford v. Newman, 77 Ill.2d 335, 33 Ill.Dec. 150, 396 N.E.2d 539 (1979) (adopted children held not "lawful issue" under law of trust situs although all claimants reside in California and adopted children would take under California law); Matter of Estate of Allen, 237 Mont. 114, 772 P.2d 297 (1989) (law of situs, not testator's domicile, determines whether residuary clause exercised power of appointment over mineral royalties); Hill, *The Judicial Function in Choice of Law*, 85 Colum. L. Rev. 1585, 1641 (1985) (situs law should apply because of the wishes "real or constructive" of the testator).

In *Keith v. Eaton*,[178] the testator died domiciled in Missouri and owning land in Kansas, Missouri, Illinois, and Colorado. His will left a life estate in all his land to his son Lanson with remainder to the "heirs of his [Lanson's] body." Lanson resided in Kansas from the death of the testator until his own death. He was survived by his wife, a son, two grandchildren, and the plaintiff, his bastard. The bastard sued for partition between himself and the other lineal descendants of Lanson of the land in Kansas devised by the testator to the heirs of Lanson's body. The illegitimate son would have prevailed under Kansas law, but not under Missouri law. The court applied Missouri law, the law of the testator's domicile, and held against the bastard. The court explained its choice on the ground that the testator presumably used the words "heirs of his body" in the sense given to them by the laws of his own domicile, not of the situs; he was presumably more familiar with the law of his own domicile.

One difficulty with this was that the illegitimate son was born four years after execution of the will and months after the death of the testator. The court candidly admitted: "Of the possibility of his [plaintiff's] birth we cannot presume the testator had knowledge, neither can we conceive that the testator understood as a fact that the will made provision for the illegitimate offspring of his son."[179] Under the circumstances, then, it would have made far more sense to apply Kansas law under which the illegitimate son, because recognized in writing by his father, would have participated in the estate. Kansas is where Lanson resided at all relevant times and presumably was where the other claimants had settled residences. As the home of the claimants, not as situs of the land, Kansas had the predominant interest in determining the rights in land, wherever situated, as among Lanson's illegitimate and legitimate lineal descendants.[180]

§ 8.16 Inter Vivos Transactions Concerning Realty: The Contract–Conveyance Distinction

Another major crack in the situs monolith appears when we focus on inter vivos transactions affecting interests in realty. This crack is in the form of the contract-conveyance distinction.[181] Courts have drawn dis-

---

178. 58 Kan. 732, 51 P. 271 (1897).

179. Id. at 740, 51 P. at 274.

180. But see Hancock, *Conceptual Devices for Avoiding the Land Taboo in Conflict of Laws: The Disadvantages of Disingenuousness*, 20 Stan. L. Rev. 1, 23–24 (1967) (although "a gross legal fiction" to talk of domicile's rule as indicating testator's probable intention, Missouri law was properly applied because "the testator was a member of the Missouri political community, whose legislature had attempted to fill this and other potential gaps in his will according to the notions of propriety prevailing in that community").

181. See Note, 38 Colum. L. Rev. 1049, 1050 (1938). Most commentators adverting to the distinction have not had a good word to say for it. See, e.g., Goodrich, *Two States and Real Estate*, 89 U.Pa. L. Rev. 417, 422 (1941) ("civilization would not crumble if the distinction disappeared and both the contractual and the conveyancing sides of the transfer of land were referred to the law of the place where the land is"); Stumberg, Conflict of Laws 344 (3d ed. 1963) ("difficulties encountered in attempting to draw a clear line of demarcation between matters of title and contract"); Note, 111 U.Pa. L. Rev. 482 (1963) ("the fact that many land transactions can fit comfortably into either characterization demonstrates the inadequacy of the contract-conveyance dichotomy as the sole choice-of-law rule").

tinctions between the contract to convey and the conveyance itself,[182] between a promissory note and the mortgage securing the note,[183] and between covenants personal to the parties and those running with the land.[184] The effect of such distinctions has often been to treat the second item in each set as a "land" problem to which the law of the situs is applicable and the first item as a "contract" problem to be resolved by a choice-of-law rule appropriate to contracts—typically, in the old cases, the law of the place of making of the contract.

One result of this contract-conveyance dichotomy is to give added flexibility to choice of law in dealing with inter vivos land transactions, just as flexibility is added to problems of decedents' estates by the equitable conversion fiction. Is this added flexibility sufficient to produce just and rational results in choice of law for inter vivos land transactions? The answer lies in a functional analysis of the usual circumstances in which such choice-of-law problems have arisen. Sections 8.17 through 8.21 examine these circumstances.

§ 8.17   Capacity to Affect Interests in Realty

In the old cases, one of the most frequent problems involving capacity to affect interests in realty concerned the capacity of the wife to contract with her husband or as surety for her husband. If the wife and husband have settled residences in state X under whose law the wife has such capacity, and the land is in state Y where wives may not so contract, the decision should be in favor of the wife's capacity. This is so whether the transaction is classified as a contract or a conveyance. The purpose behind the situs statute—to protect wives from the impositions of impecunious husbands—is not relevant for wives whose home states

---

182. Liljedahl v. Glassgow, 190 Iowa 827, 180 N.W. 870 (1921); Polson v. Stewart, 167 Mass. 211, 45 N.E. 737 (1897) (Holmes, J.); Mallory Associates, Inc. v. Barving Realty Co., 300 N.Y. 297, 90 N.E.2d 468 (1949); cf. Hill v. Hill, 269 A.2d 212 (Del.1970) (validity of antenuptial contract to convey situs realty determined by law of place of making).

The contract-conveyance distinction is constitutionally permissible in that the situs may cancel a deed given elsewhere to a foreign corporation not qualified to own land under situs law, Munday v. Wisconsin Trust Co., 252 U.S. 499, 40 S.Ct. 365, 64 L.Ed. 684 (1920), and the place of contracting may give damages for forfeiture of a contract to convey if forfeiture is improper under its own law but proper under the law of the situs. Selover, Bates & Co. v. Walsh, 226 U.S. 112, 33 S.Ct. 69, 57 L.Ed. 146 (1912). But the distinction is not compelled, for the situs may apply its own law to determine the proper procedure to cancel a contract to convey land made elsewhere, Kryger v. Wilson, 242 U.S. 171, 37 S.Ct. 34, 61 L.Ed. 229 (1916). See also Widmer v. Wood, 243 Ark. 457, 420 S.W.2d 828 (1967) (law of situs determines damages for breach of contract to sell land).

Cf. Irving Trust Co. v. Maryland Cas. Co., 83 F.2d 168 (2d Cir.1936), cert. denied 299 U.S. 571, 57 S.Ct. 34, 81 L.Ed. 421 (1936) (although the validity of a conveyance is determined by the law of the situs, place where conveyance made may declare it tortious and order specific reparation); James v. Powell, 19 N.Y.2d 249, 279 N.Y.S.2d 10, 225 N.E.2d 741 (1967) (situs law determines whether New York judgment creditor can recover compensatory damages from New York judgment debtor who conveyed Puerto Rican realty to defraud the creditor, but New York, not situs law, applies to deny punitive damages).

183. Thomson v. Kyle, 39 Fla. 582, 23 So. 12 (1897); Burr v. Beckler, 264 Ill. 230, 106 N.E. 206 (1914); Union Savings Bk. v. DeMarco, 105 R.I. 592, 254 A.2d 81 (1969).

184. Beauchamp v. Bertig, 90 Ark. 351, 119 S.W. 75 (1909).

do not think such protection necessary.[185]

Sometimes, as in *Polson v. Stewart*,[186] the situs court has reached this rational result by use of the contract-conveyance distinction. *Polson* enforced a contract between husband and wife made in North Carolina, their marital domicile. The contract would have been invalid under the law of Massachusetts, the situs. Thus the contract-conveyance dichotomy may, as was the case with the equitable conversion fiction, be more likely than the situs rule to produce proper results. This is because the place of contracting is likely to coincide with the settled residence of the wife, and the settled residence of the wife is likely to have the predominant interest in the capacity to contract. But because this distinction between contract and conveyance is unrelated to the purposes of the particular domestic rule denying the wife capacity, there is no assurance that it will lead to a correct decision. In *Burr v. Beckler*,[187] for example, application of the law of the place of contracting resulted in invalidating a wife's note and the trust deed securing it, though the instruments were valid at her marital domicile, which was also the situs of the land. The place where she executed the note while sojourning denied wives capacity to so contract. The decision may be explainable in terms of the strong sympathies for the wife created by her husband's fraudulent conduct, but relief, if needed, should have come from the law of the forum-domicile-situs.

On the other hand, if wife, husband, and husband's creditor have settled residences in X, another state cannot have any legitimate interest, as situs of the land on which the wife issues a mortgage to secure her husband's debt, in validating the mortgage in the face of an invalidating rule of the common residence, unless it seems likely that the creditor has relied on situs law in extending credit. In a case in which the husband, wife, and creditor had a common non-situs residence, the Florida court in *Thomson v. Kyle*[188] was misled by the contract-conveyance distinction into validating the wife's mortgage, although stating that her note, made and payable at her domicile, was probably void. The New Hampshire court in *Proctor v. Frost*[189] came much closer to the mark without drawing a contract-conveyance distinction, for it started at the heart of the problem—the purpose of the situs statute denying a wife

---

185. See Restatement (Second) § 223, comment *b*; Note, 111 U.Pa. L. Rev. 482, 486 (1963). But see Swank v. Hufnagle, 111 Ind. 453, 12 N.E. 303 (1887) (situs law invalidates wife's mortgage executed in Ohio where wife apparently domiciled); Story, Conflict of Laws 720 (3d ed. 1846) (situs should invalidate even though wife has capacity at her domicile); cf. Mott v. Eddins, 151 Ariz. 54, 725 P.2d 761 (App.1986) (apply situs law to prevent husband from charging community with debt, but situs is also new marital domicile where spouses had intended to move at time purchase contract signed); Pascoe v. Keuhnast, 642 S.W.2d 37 (Tex.App.—Waco, 1982, writ ref'd n.r.e.), appeal dism'd for want of juris., 463 U.S. 1201, 103 S.Ct. 3528, 77 L.Ed.2d 1381 (1983) (realty acquired in Texas while spouses domiciled there remains community property after they move to Iowa and wife's conveyance of it, executed in Iowa, is invalid under Texas law).

186. 167 Mass. 211, 45 N.E. 737 (1897).

187. 264 Ill. 230, 106 N.E. 206 (1914).

188. 39 Fla. 582, 23 So. 12 (1897).

189. 89 N.H. 304, 197 A. 813 (1938).

capacity to mortgage her land to secure her husband's debt. The court validated the mortgage saying: "The primary purpose of the statute ... was not to regulate the transfer of New Hampshire real estate, but to protect married women in New Hampshire...."[190] If the court had not stressed the fact that the contract was executed in Massachusetts rather than that the wife had a settled residence there, the opinion would have scored a bull's-eye.

A true conflict concerning the capacity of a married woman to affect her interests in realty occurs when her residence has an interest in protecting her under its invalidating rule and the situs has an interest in holding her to her promise in order to protect the expectations of a creditor resident at the situs. Assuming that the creditor's expectations are justifiable, that he has not, for example, jerry-built the situs contact with the wife's transaction in a deliberate attempt to evade the law of the wife's home where the creditor is doing business, this conflict should probably be resolved in favor of validating the wife's contract or conveyance. Both the wife's residence and the situs-creditor's residence share an interest in making commercial transactions convenient and reliable and enforcing agreements deliberately entered into. The unmistakable march of the law in this area is to increase the contractual competence of married women. This trend the two states share, although one has not advanced as far along this road as the other.

Problems sometimes occur concerning the capacity of minors to affect their interests in realty. The false conflicts here are the same as those discussed just above in the context of the wife—the minor's domicile and settled residence grants capacity,[191] or it denies capacity and no other jurisdiction has any legitimate interest in validating what the minor has done. The true conflict between protective minor's residence and enforcing creditor's residence may call for the same response as when dealing with a wife. If the conflict is between a state that has kept the age of capacity at 21 and a state that has lowered it to 18 or 19, the lower age may better reflect current trends.[192]

§ 8.18 Inter Vivos Transactions Concerning Realty: Formal and Substantial Validity

Again, as in the case of wills, rules invalidating inter vivos transactions purporting to affect interests in land come in many different forms, and the policies underlying the rules are quite diverse. In such circumstances, rational results must begin with an inquiry into the purposes of the particular rule that is alleged to invalidate the transaction and into whether these purposes would be advanced in the case at hand in view of

---

190. Id. at 307, 197 A. at 815.

191. Cf. Sun Oil Co. v. Guidry, 99 So.2d 424 (La.App.1957) (for purpose of terminating tolling of situs statute of limitations for minority, situs recognizes domiciliary decree emancipating the minor). But see Beauchamp v. Bertig, 90 Ark. 351, 119 S.W. 75 (1909) (situs invalidates conveyance despite judgment of residence removing disabilities of nonage).

192. Cf. Note, 38 Colum. L. Rev. 1049, 1055 (1938).

contacts between the state having the rule, the parties, and the transaction.[193]

There is no better example of the fruits of blind adherence to a situs formula in determining validity than *Smith v. Ingram.*[194] A wife, whose marital domicile was in South Carolina, joined with her husband in deeding North Carolina land to a purchaser for value. The wife was not given privy examination regarding her willingness to make the conveyance, as was required by the situs, North Carolina, but not by her home, South Carolina. Under North Carolina law, absence of such examination made a wife's deed void. Seventeen years later, after a town had been built on the land conveyed, the wife sued to recover the land. She prevailed under situs law, and the defendants, subsequent bona fide purchasers, did not even receive a refund of their purchase money. One may marvel at the force of the situs rule that could cause Judge Douglas to say: "I concur in the opinion of the Court with reluctance, on account of the great and unmerited hardship it inflicts upon so many individuals; but I am forced to concur because, in my opinion, it is the law."[195] It was the law of the situs, but if its purpose was to protect North Carolina wives from the importunities of their husbands, it had no relevance to South Carolina wives if that state did not deem such protection necessary.[196]

Mallory Associates, Inc. v. Barving Realty Co.[197] reached better results. One New York company leased a hotel in Virginia from another New York company. The lease provided that the landlord could spend the tenant' $65,000 deposit to purchase the premises. A New York statute invalidated any clause purporting to waive the landlord's duty to hold such deposits in trust for the tenant. A majority of the court thought the statute precluded use of the money to purchase the premises. Having so decided, it applied the New York statute even though the realty leased was in Virginia, saying: "The need for protection is obviously no less, but rather more, when the land to which the lease relates is situated outside of this State."[198]

---

193. See Cook, The Logical & Legal Bases of the Conflict of Laws 274 (1942); cf. Warner v. Kressly, 9 Wn.App. 358, 512 P.2d 1116 (1973) (validity of real estate broker's contract determined not by law of situs, but under law of defendant's domicile pursuant to "most significant contacts" test).

194. 130 N.C. 100, 40 S.E. 984 (1902), rehearing denied 132 N.C. 959, 44 S.E. 643 (1903) (leaving open question whether equitable remedy for improvements is available to purchasers).

195. Id. at 108, 40 S.E. at 986. See also Gray v. Gray, 189 So.2d 735 (La.App.1966), writ denied, no error 249 La. 766, 191 So.2d 142 (1966), (situs refuses to enforce property settlement executed before divorce by wife who had left the situs and marital domicile and established a residence in the state where she executed the instrument and where it was valid); Hall v. Tucker, 414 S.W.2d 766 (Tex.Civ.App.—Eastland 1967, writ ref'd n.r.e.) (law of Texas situs invalidates deed of Mississippi wife when deed did not comply with formalities required by Texas law for married women's deeds).

196. See Cook, supra note 193, at 272.

197. 300 N.Y. 297, 90 N.E.2d 468 (1949).

198. Id. at 302, 90 N.E.2d at 471. But cf. Alachua Inn Corp. v. Cooper, 66 Misc.2d 479, 321 N.Y.S.2d 222 (1971), aff'd mem., 38 A.D.2d 796, 327 N.Y.S.2d 1006 (1972) (Florida law

There is a real conflict concerning substantial or formal validity when one state has an interest in protecting some of the parties with its invalidating rule and another state has an interest in validating to protect the expectations of other parties. Again, as in the case of the wife's capacity, resolution should probably be in favor of validity. This probability increases when the difference in domestic laws is one of detail[199] and decreases when there are more fundamental policy differences between the two jurisdictions. Resolution of the conflict in favor of validity is less likely if the invalidating rule is one designed to protect a resident party from contracts of adhesion.[200] Again, the more justifiable are the expectations that the parties have formulated in terms of the validating law, the more justifiable is the validation.[201]

James v. Powell[202] misapplies the kind of choice-of-law analysis suggested in this chapter. The result is a bizarre blend of the law of the situs qua situs and of non-situs law qua "the jurisdiction with the strongest interest in the resolution of the particular issue presented."[203] The plaintiff, a New York resident, had obtained a libel judgment against Powell, also a New York resident. The plaintiff alleged that Powell's wife, acting with Powell's power of attorney, transferred realty, which the wife and Powell owned in Puerto Rico, to the wife's aunt and uncle with the intention of defrauding the plaintiff by preventing collection of the libel judgment. The plaintiff sued Powell and his wife demanding compensatory and punitive damages for this fraudulent conveyance. The Court of Appeals reversed a judgment for compensatory and punitive damages that applied New York law and remanded the case for further proceedings.

The court held New York law properly applicable to the issue of punitive damages, because New York "has the 'strongest interest' in the protection of its judgment creditors."[204] On the facts of this case, the court said that there was not sufficient moral culpability for recovery of punitive damages under New York law. The court further held that Puerto Rican law determined whether the plaintiff could recovery compensatory damages, not, as both parties had assumed, New York law.

The Court was correct when it said that Puerto Rican law, as the law of the situs, determined whether the plaintiff had a right to levy on

---

governs Florida landlord's right to retain security deposit of New York corporate lessee of Florida realty—result based in part on prior judgment in Florida action).

199. See Ideal Structures Corp. v. Levine Huntsville Dev. Corp., 396 F.2d 917 (5th Cir.1968) (situs validates contract meeting statute of frauds requirements of place of making though not of situs); Rees, *American Wills Statutes*, 46 Va. L. Rev. 856, 906 n.829 (1960) (list of statutes providing alternative choice-of-law references for deed formalities).

200. See § 7.4B.

201. See Liljedahl v. Glassgow, 190 Iowa 827, 180 N.W. 870 (1921) (whether deed with grantee's name blank binds grantee to mortgage assumption clause determined not by law of situs but by law of state where two of three grantees and lender resided and where lending contract executed and to be performed).

202. 19 N.Y.2d 249, 279 N.Y.S.2d 10, 225 N.E.2d 741 (1967).

203. Id. at 259, 279 N.Y.S.2d at 18, 225 N.E.2d at 746–47.

204. Id. at 260, 279 N.Y.S.2d at 18, 225 N.E.2d at 747.

the land before the conveyance in issue[205] and, if so, whether the conveyance impaired this right or made it more costly. It was a non sequitur to conclude that therefore, if the plaintiff had been injured under Puerto Rican law, "her remedy, if any, must arise under the law of Puerto Rico."[206] Once it was determined that the conveyance made it impossible or more costly for the plaintiff to levy on the land in Puerto Rico, New York, as the home of both judgment debtor and creditor, had a substantial interest in determining to what extent, if any, the creditor should be compensated for her loss.[207] Puerto Rico, as situs of the land or as the scene of acts constituting an intentional tort, might have a legitimate interest in imposing liability for the fraudulent conveyance. Liability might discourage acts in Puerto Rico that Puerto Rico considered improper and that might cloud Puerto Rican titles and impose a burden on Puerto Rican Courts. Puerto Rico, as situs, however, would have no reason to insulate the New York debtor from liability for the harm he had caused.[208]

§ 8.19 Construction of Inter Vivos Transfers of Interests in Land

As was the case with testamentary dispositions, the situs rule is less than universally established on matters of construction of inter vivos transfers of interests in land.[209] In a way, this is ironic, for it is in

---

205. The situs' choice-of-law rule might refer to the common domicile of debtor and creditor to determine what assets were exempt from execution. See Uniform Exemptions Act § 3(a), 13 pt. I U.L.A.: "Residents of this State are entitled to the exemptions provided by this Act. Nonresidents are entitled to the exemptions provided by the law of the jurisdiction of their residence." (Adopted in Alaska). Cf. Restatement (Second) § 132 (forum law determines exemptions unless another state, such as the common domicile of creditor and debtor, "has the dominant interest in the question of exemption.")

206. James v. Powell, 19 N.Y.2d at 257, 279 N.Y.S.2d at 16, 225 N.E.2d at 745.

207. See Comment, *Choice of Law in Fraudulent Conveyance*, 67 Colum. L. Rev. 1313, 1315 (1967); cf. Irving Trust Co. v. Maryland Cas. Co., 83 F.2d 168 (2d Cir.1936), cert. denied, 299 U.S. 571, 57 S.Ct. 34, 81 L.Ed. 421 (1936); Rudow v. Fogel, 12 Mass.App.Ct. 430, 426 N.E.2d 155 (1981) (law of common domicile, not situs, determines whether there was a constructive trust resulting from conveyance); Werner v. Werner, 84 Wn.2d 360, 526 P.2d 370 (1974) (law of California, where notary performed negligently, determines his liability, rather than law of situs of land which had its title clouded by the negligence); Ehrenzweig & Westen, *Fraudulent Conveyances in the Conflict of Laws: Easy Cases May Make Bad Law*, 66 Mich. L. Rev. 1679, 1688 (1968): "Whatever its possible virtues or shortcomings otherwise, the lex situs has no bearing on the issue of whether a conveyance valid under the law of Puerto Rico (lex situs) is a tort under the law of New York (lex fori). The validity of a conveyance is relevant only as a datum establishing the existence of a tortious injury."

208. This assumes that Puerto Rico would not grant compensation for the harm caused. The court did not make any finding as to the content of Puerto Rican law on this issue before holding that Puerto Rican law was applicable. This is inconsistent with proper functional conflicts analysis. See section 3.7. For cogent criticism of the Court on this ground and an indication that Puerto Rico would provide compensation, see Ehrenzweig & Westen, supra note 207, at 1685.

209. See Restatement (Second) § 224, comment *f*: "When the conveyance is a gift, the transferor's intentions are particularly important. Here authority is divided as to whether the meaning of the words used in the conveyance should, in situations where the actual intentions of the transferror are unascertainable, be determined in accordance with the

relation to questions of the construction of inter vivos transfers that the situs rule has special strengths—and special weaknesses.

The special weakness of the situs rule in this area stems from the fact that it is not supported on matters of construction by considerations of expediency and ease of title search, even as to remote parties, for "although a title searcher can rely on a statute which determines legal effect regardless of the intention of the parties, he cannot so rely on a rule of construction which can be overcome by evidence of a contrary intent."[210]

But the situs rule has special appeal in dealing with the construction of inter vivos transactions affecting the interests of persons in realty. There is less likelihood than there was in the case of testamentary dispositions that some one state will stand out as the state predominantly concerned with the results of the construction. If there is, its law should be applied. If there is no such state, by definition in problems of "construction," no state is sufficiently opposed to the construction that would result under the law of another state to invalidate such a result if it were clearly manifested as the intention of the parties. Again by definition, the intention of the parties is nonexistent or unknown and unknowable. The primary goals of choice-of-law, to advance the legitimate interests of contact states and to give effect to the justifiable expectations of the parties, recede into the background. There remains another purpose of conflicts analysis—uniformity of result. If this is left as the sole consideration, the situs of land emerges as the natural source of the domestic rule to insulate the result from the selection of the forum. The situs is certain, easily identified, and the most probable forum.[211]

§ 8.20 Servitudes on Realty

If the parcels of land are in different states, one state imposing a servitude on one parcel with the other parcel dominant and the other state imposing no such servitude, it is not possible to seek a mechanical solution in terms of the law of the situs. Which situs? Nor will rational solutions likely result from mechanical insistence on always looking to the law of the situs of the servient estate, or to the law of the situs of the dominant estate. Again, focusing on the actual domestic rules in putative conflict and on their underlying policies is the key.

Such analysis may reveal that the conflict is only apparent. For example, A owns land in state X where A is resident and B owns adjoining land in state Y, where B is resident. A dams a stream that runs onto A's land from B's land, causing a flood on B's land. Under X law,

rules of construction of the domicil of the transferor at the time of the conveyance or of the situs."

210. Note, 111 U.Pa. L. Rev. 482, 495 (1963).

211. For discussion of the "more probable forum" concept, see Freund, *Characterization with Respect to Contracts in the Conflict of Laws*, in The Conflict of Laws and International Contracts 158, 161 (1951).

A's land would have a servitude of drainage and A would be liable in damages for harm caused to upper riparian owners by interfering with the natural drainage. Under Y law there is no such servitude and if everything had occurred in Y, A would have no liability. There is no real conflict. X has no interest in imposing a servitude on A's land when the state where the owner of the alleged dominant estate is resident and the injured land is situated has no rule conferring such a benefit on lands there.[212]

If, in the above hypothetical case, the laws of X and Y are reversed, a true conflict appears. X has an interest in permitting A to use land to the limit permitted by X law, and Y wishes to protect B and Y land. If one state's rule is not clearly anachronistic and if the servitude does not stem from any transaction between the parties, there seems to be little opportunity for reaching a rational solution to this true conflict on the basis of shared policies, trends in the substantive area, or the legitimate expectations of the parties. Nor is the situs a natural focus for achieving the one remaining goal of conflicts analysis, insulation of the result from the selection of the forum. Again, which situs? Perhaps then, the sitting-and-judging rule will prove useful in this context.[213] The forum, X or Y, if it decides that achieving uniformity of result is more important to it than insistence on application of its domestic rule, should put itself in the position of the other state's courts and decide the case just as it finds that they would have decided it. This will not work if the other state would be so uncooperative as to use this same sitting-and-judging rule, for then the references back and forth would be circular and infinite. If so, then no goal of the conflict of laws can be achieved and the time has come for the forum to apply the law most convenient for it to apply and most in consonance with its domestic policies—its own.

§ 8.21 Rights of Creditors with Security Interests in Realty

Choice-of-law problems have frequently arisen concerning the rights of creditors who hold obligations secured by mortgages or other liens on land. Such questions have included, for example, whether the creditor may obtain a deficiency judgment after foreclosure,[214] whether the credi-

---

212. But cf. Caldwell v. Gore, 175 La. 501, 143 So. 387 (1932), which reached the opposite result while differing from the hypothetical only in that both owners were residents of the state where the alleged servient estate was located. The court did note that it was likely that there was no practical difference between the laws of the two states, there being liability in each though by different routes.

213. Cf. Matter of Schneider's Estate, 198 Misc. 1017, 1020, 96 N.Y.S.2d 652, 656 (1950), adhered to on reargument, 198 Misc. 1017, 100 N.Y.S.2d 371 (Surr.Ct. New York County 1950); Griswold, *Renvoi Revisited*, 51 Harv. L. Rev. 1165 (1938).

214. Younker v. Manor, 255 Cal.App.2d 431, 63 Cal.Rptr. 197 (1967) (no, applying law of debtor's residence and forum, not situs; but evidence that creditor had assured debtor before transaction that situs law was the same as forum law); Goodman v. Nadler, 113 Ga.App. 493, 148 S.E.2d 480 (1966) (yes, applying situs law); California Fed. Sav. & Loan Assoc. v. Bell, 6 Hawaii App. 597, 735 P.2d 499 (1987) (no, applying situs law for predictability); Gate City Fed. Sav. & Loan Ass'n v. O'Connor, 410 N.W.2d 448 (Minn.App. 1987) (no, applying law of residence of creditor and debtor); Eufaula Bank & Trust Co. v. Wheatley, 663 P.2d 393 (Okl.App.1983) (no, applying forum law to give forum debtor a

tor must first foreclose the lien and not sue directly on the secured obligation,[215] whether the debtor has a right to redeem after foreclosure,[216] and whether the form of the mortgage is sufficient to create a valid security interest.[217]

If the law of the situs gives the creditor greater rights than does the law of some other state having a contact with the parties and with the transaction, such as the debtor's settled residence, there is good reason to apply situs law when the creditor is likely to have relied on it in extending credit.[218] Reliance on the law of the situs is especially likely when the creditor is a remote holder, having taken by mesne assignments from the original creditor.[219]

If the situation is reversed, the situs giving the creditor fewer rights in regard to the security than does a state with which the parties and the transaction have all other contacts, there seems to be no purpose in making available to the debtor a rule that is designed primarily for the protection of situs citizens and that may upset the expectations of the creditor.

§ 8.21A Functional Analysis of Conflicts Problems Concerning Realty

Perhaps because of the situs fixation of the Second Restatement,[220] functional resolutions of conflicts problems concerning realty are not as widespread as in cases involving torts and contracts. A few courts have inquired into the policies underlying apparently conflicting situs and

---

setoff equal to the fair market value of the land); Note, *Application of California's Antideficiency Statutes in Conflict of Laws Contexts*, 73 Cal. L. Rev. 1332 (1985).

215. Maxwell v. Ricks, 294 F. 255 (9th Cir.1923) (yes, applying forum law on theory that action was "transitory"); Provident Savings Bank & Trust Co. v. Steinmetz, 270 N.Y. 129, 200 N.E. 669 (1936) (yes, applying situs law).

216. Hughes v. Winkleman, 243 Mo. 81, 147 S.W. 994 (1912) (no, applying situs law).

217. See Bank of Oak Grove v. Wilmot State Bank, 279 Ark. 107, 648 S.W.2d 802 (1983) (no, applying situs law rather than law of place where loan made and mortgage executed).

218. Cf. Pacific Gamble Robinson Co. v. Lapp, 95 Wn.2d 341, 622 P.2d 850 (1980) (when spouses have moved to the community property forum from a non-community state, the husband's earnings remain subject to the claim of a creditor for the husband's separate debt incurred before the move).

219. Id; cf. Colorado Nat'l Bank v. Merlino, 35 Wn.App. 610, 668 P.2d 1304 (1983) (default judgment for husband's separate debt incurred in purchase of real estate outside the community-property marital domicile cannot be enforced at the domicile except out of the husband's separate property, and he has none).

220. The Second Restatement refers almost every question concerning immovables to the whole law of the situs, with the expectation that the situs would generally apply its own law. Restatement (Second), ch. 9, Topic 2, Introductory Note at 7–8. There are a few shafts of light that penetrate even the Restatement treatment. The Restatement says that situs courts "might" apply the law of the marital domicile in determining marital property rights in realty and explains that they "might do so for the reason that [the marital domicile] is the state which has the dominant interest in the parties and that accordingly its local law should be applied to determine whether by means of such a conveyance [a husband] could deprive [his wife] of any marital interest she might have in his land." Id. § 233, comment *b*.

non-situs law and shaping their opinions to effect a maximum accommodation of those policies.

An early straw in the wind was *McElreath v. McElreath.*[221] Texas enforced an Oklahoma divorce decree ordering an Oklahoma husband to convey his Texas land to his Oklahoma wife. Texas law forbade divesting title to separate realty when dividing property on divorce. Oklahoma permitted awarding the husband's realty as alimony. The Supreme Court of Texas perceived that only Oklahoma policies were affected and ordered the Oklahoma decree enforced with regard to the Texas land:

> We expect other states to recognize our system of marital property ownership, so should we respect their schemes of property ownership and attendant plans for the adjustment of property rights upon the dissolution of a marriage. Texas public policy does not relate to and is not concerned with the settlement by Oklahoma courts of marital property problems which arise between Oklahoma citizens.[222]

After *McElreath*, the Texas legislature recognized the interest of Texas in applying its law to the marital property rights of Texas spouses, even as to realty situated in other states. In actions of divorce and annulment, Texas courts are directed to dispose of "real and personal property, wherever situated" under Texas law if the property would have been community property if it had been acquired while the martial domicile was in Texas even though the spouse acquiring the property was not domiciled in Texas at the time that the property was acquired.[223] *Cameron v. Cameron*[224] adopts this statutory rule of distribution as a common law rule applicable to cases arising before the effective date of the statute.

In re Estate of Janney[225] applied Pennsylvania law to uphold the validity of a will of a Pennsylvania domiciliary as to the disposition of New Jersey land, though under New Jersey law the will would have been invalid because the chief devisee was also an attesting witness. The reasons given were that only Pennsylvania policies were affected, and that New Jersey's interest in regulating the transfer of title to New Jersey land was not affected because the land had been sold and only the proceeds were in issue.[226] The court noted that "[i]n fulfilling the intention of the testatrix we neither offend the principle [of situs interest in the integrity of real property records] nor depart from the

---

221. 162 Tex. 190, 345 S.W.2d 722 (1961).

222. Id. at 193–94, 345 S.W.2d at 724.

223. Tex.Fam.Code Ann. § 7002(1). See supra notes 162–165 and accompanying text indicating why this provision might not produce desirable results with regard to out-of-state realty and recommending that the statute also provide for reaching the same result that would be reached if the land were in Texas.

224. 641 S.W.2d 210, 222 (Tex.1982).

225. 498 Pa. 398, 446 A.2d 1265 (1982).

226. Id. at 402, 446 A.2d at 1266–67.

mainstream of accelerating liberalization of conflict of laws principles."[227]

Dority v. Dority,[228] awarded a divorce to a husband who had moved to Utah from Pennsylvania, the marital domicile. Under Pennsylvania law, only one half of Pennsylvania realty, owned by the spouses as tenants by the entireties, could go to the wife. Under Utah law, the court could make such disposition of the property as was equitable. The court affirmed an award of all the Pennsylvania realty to the wife and rejected the husband's contention that the law of the situs must be applied.

Williams v. Williams[229] did apply the law of the situs in determining marital property rights on divorce, but the court made it clear that it was applying that law, not because it was that of the situs, but because that state had been the martial domicile and was still the domicile of the husband. The court explained that it reached its result under a conflicts analysis that "requires us to evaluate the governmental policies underlying the applicable conflicting laws and to determine which jurisdiction's policy would be most advanced by having its law applied to the facts of the case under review."[230]

Rudow v. Fogel[231] applied the law of the New York common domicile rather than the Massachusetts situs to determine whether there was a constructive trust in realty. The court found that New York had "the dominant contacts and the superior claim for application of its law"[232] because only New York domiciliaries were involved and no innocent third party had relied on Massachusetts record title.

Wendelken v. Superior Court[233] applied interest analysis to choose the law to determine what compensation a person with a possessory interest in realty owed to a guest injured on the land. Both parties were domiciled in Arizona. The guest had been injured at a vacation home the defendant had in Mexico. Under Mexican law, the guest's compensation for lost wages would be limited to 25 pesos per day, about sixteen cents at the time of the decision. Full recovery was available under Arizona law. The court noted that Mexico had an interest in affording protection to someone with a possessory interest in Mexican real estate and therefore this was not a "false" conflict, but resolved the conflict in favor of Arizona law. Mexico's interest was not as strong as it would be if the parties were Mexican citizens and wage earners participating in Mexico's socialized system of health care. Arizona had a strong interest

227. Id., 446 A.2d at 1266.

228. 645 P.2d 56 (Utah 1982).

229. 390 A.2d 4 (D.C.Ct.App.1978). See also Sarbacher v. McNamara, 564 A.2d 701 (D.C.1989) (law of D.C. domicile, not Florida situs, determines whether husband's estate is entitled to contribution from wife's estate toward payment of mortgage).

230. *Williams*, 390 A.2d at 5–6.

231. 12 Mass.App.Ct. 430, 426 N.E.2d 155 (1981).

232. Id. at 437, 426 N.E.2d at 160.

233. 137 Ariz. 455, 671 P.2d 896 (1983). But cf. Rosett v. Schatzman, 157 Ill.App.3d 939, 109 Ill.Dec. 900, 510 N.E.2d 968 (1 Dist.1987) (apply law of situs under most significant relationship analysis to permit social guest to recover).

in assuring adequate compensation to its citizen and making sure that Arizona medical providers would be paid and that Arizona taxpayers would not have to bear the burden of caring for the injuries. The court also noted that defendant carried $300,000 in liability insurance on the Mexican property through an Arizona insurance carrier.

In re French v. Liebmann[234] affirmed a bankruptcy court's setting aside the debtor's transfer of real property in the Bahamas. The debtor had transferred the property to her children without consideration. The debtor and the transferees were at all times resident in the U.S. Under U.S. law the transfer was fraudulent and could be set aside. The transferees contended that Bahamian law permitted avoidance of the transfer only if there is proof of an actual intent to defraud. The court held that U.S. law applied: "The United States has a strong interest in extending these personal protections [of debtors and creditors] to its residents—including the vast majority of the interested parties here. The Bahamas, by contrast, has comparatively little interest in protecting nonresidents."[235]

In re Bankruptcy Estate of Midland Euro Exchange[236] disagrees with In re French on the ground that the section of the Bankruptcy Act under which the trustee in bankruptcy can recover fraudulent transfers of the bankrupt's property cannot be applied extraterritorially. If a court cannot apply the section permitting the avoidance of fraudulent transfers to transfers in other countries, anyone who wishes to shield assets from the trustee in bankruptcy has an easy way to accomplish this.

The Florida Probate Code, § 731.106(2), before its amendment in 2001 provided:

> When a nonresident decedent who is a citizen of the United States or a citizen or subject of a foreign country provides in her or his will that the testamentary disposition of her or his tangible or intangible personal property having a situs within this state, or of her or his real property in this state, shall be construed and regulated by the laws of this state, the validity and effect of the dispositions shall be determined by Florida law.

Saunders v. Saunders,[237] construed this provision to mean that because the testator's will did not choose Florida law, the law of Colorado, the testator's domicile, not the law of Florida, the situs, determined whether the testator's widow had rights as a pretermitted spouse.[238]

---

234.   440 F.3d 145 (4th Cir. 2006).

235.   Id. at 154.

236.   347 B.R. 708 (Bankr.C.D. Cal. 2006).

237.   796 So.2d 1253 (Fla. App., 1st Dist. 2001), rev. denied, 819 So.2d 139 (Fla. 2002).

238.   See Fla. Stat. Ann. § 732.301: "Pretermitted spouse. When a person marries after making a will and the spouse survives the testator, the surviving spouse shall receive a share in the estate of the testator equal in value to that which the surviving spouse would have received if the testator had died intestate, unless: (1) Provision has been made for, or

Willis Reese, the Reporter for the Second Conflicts Restatement,[239] and Robert Leflar[240] have repudiated the situs rule for real property.

Mississippi has declared the "most significant relationship" rule applicable to determine contractual rights in realty in other states, but these opinions departing from the situs rule enumerate physical contacts with the states involved rather than focusing on the differences in domestic law and the policies underlying those differences.[241]

§ 8.22 Conclusion: The Situs Rule is Undesirable

There is no constitutional basis for reserving to the situs of realty exclusive judicial jurisdiction to affect the interests of persons in property. The situs will rarely, if ever, have so substantial an interest qua situs in refusing to recognize a non-situs land decree that the situs' interest should be permitted to override the great national interest in recognition of sister-state judgments. Once false constitutional dogmas concerning jurisdiction of the subject matter are swept aside, a functional analysis reveals that the situs qua situs, with rare exceptions, has an interest in applying its own law to affect the interest of persons in property only when choice of law will affect the use of the land. Even when land use is affected, as between states of the United States, the situs rule should probably yield to the conflicting rule of another state that has a genuine interest in validating a transaction that the situs would invalidate.

II. PERSONAL PROPERTY ("MOVABLES")

§ 8.23 The Situs Rule is Less Dominant

The situs rule has not been as dominant in resolving choice-of-law problems concerning personal property as it has in matters touching real estate. In terms of traditional territorial conflicts rules, both situs and domicile have been looked to for the appropriate law. In recent years, judicial treatment of choice-of-law problems concerning personal property has demonstrated a welcome trend toward functional analysis of the problems based on inquiry into policies underlying putatively conflicting domestic rules. This movement toward more thoughtful solutions to personal property conflicts problems was threatened, at least in commercial cases, by the poorly drafted and regressive choice-of-law provisions of Article 9 of the Uniform Commercial Code. 1972 and 1999 revisions of Article 9 substantially improved these sections. In commenting on these matters, it will be useful to distinguish between donative and commercial transactions.

---

waived by, the spouse by prenuptial or postnuptial agreement; (2) The spouse is provided for in the will; or (3) The will discloses an intention not to make provision for the spouse."

239. Reese, *Review of M. Hancock. Studies in Modern Choice-of-Law*, 9 Dalhousie L. J. 181, 183–84 (1984) (courts "have fared worst when they have disregarded [the purposes underlying conflicting laws] and unthinkingly applied some broad choice-of-law rule, such as one calling for application of the law of the situs").

240. Leflar, *Review*, 34 Amer.J. Comp.L. 387 (1986) ("rigid reliance on situs law . . . is wrong").

241. See Tideway Oil Programs, Inc. v. Serio, 431 So.2d 454 (Miss.1983) (alleged breach of partnership agreement concerning mineral leases in another state); Spragins v. Louise Plantation, Inc., 391 So.2d 97 (Miss.1980) (validity of contracts to exchange realty and broker's contract).

§ 8.24   Intestate Succession to Personalty

In the United States, the almost universally accepted choice-of-law rule for intestate distribution of personalty selects the domicile at death of the decedent.[242] There are, even concerning this well-accepted domiciliary rule, some situs overtones. A Mississippi statute directs that all personal property situated in Mississippi be distributed according to Mississippi law.[243] In the case of chattels and rights embodied in a document, the standard choice-of-law reference to the law of the domicile at death for intestate distribution of personalty is often explained as a tacit preliminary reference to the whole law of the situs and then a referral by the choice-of-law rule of the situs to the law of the domicile at death.[244] The situs does have control over tangible movables,[245] the power to administer such assets in the event of intestacy,[246] and probably

---

242.   Restatement (Second), Conflict of Laws § 260, comment *b*.

Once the claimant's status (e.g. "widow", "legitimate child", "illegitimate child") is determined, the law of the domicile at death of the decedent determines the intestate rights of a person having that status. The status itself is determined by the domicile at the relevant time of the parties whose status is in issue. See discussion of "the incidental question", § 3.4A, note 228. Cf. Wilmington Trust Co. v. Chichester, 369 A.2d 701 (Del.Ch.1976), aff'd, 377 A.2d 11 (Del.1977) (law of place of adoption determines whether claimant was adopted, law of testator's domicile at death determines whether adopted child is "issue" within meaning of will and trust); In re Estate of Stewart, 131 Ill.App.2d 183, 268 N.E.2d 187 (1971) (whether child is legitimate so that natural father can inherit is determined by law of domicile at death of child); § 8.7, note 91 (incidental question with regard to inheritance of realty).

243.   Miss.Code Ann. § 91–1–1.

244.   See Boyd v. Curran, 166 F.Supp. 193, 196–197 (S.D.N.Y.1958) (whole law of situs refers to domicile to determine wife's forced share); Robertson, Characterization in the Conflict of Laws 208 (1940); Stumberg, Conflict of Laws 374 (3d ed. 1963); Briggs, *"Renvoi" in the Succession to Tangibles: A False Issue Based on Faulty Analysis*, 64 Yale L. J. 195, 197 (1954); Griswold, *Renvoi Revisited*, 51 Harv. L. Rev. 1165, 1194 (1938); cf. Stimson, *Conflict of Laws and the Administration of Decedents' Personal Property*, 46 Va. L. Rev. 1345, 3180 (1960) (finding substantial evidence that situs law is being applied).

Some support for explanation of the domicile rule as a transmission from the whole law of the situs stems from the fact that escheat is to the situs. See Matter of Menschefrend's Estate, 283 App.Div. 463, 128 N.Y.S.2d 738 (1954), aff'd mem., 8 N.Y.2d 1093, 208 N.Y.S.2d 453, 170 N.E.2d 902 (1954), remittitur amended, 8 N.Y.2d 1156, 209 N.Y.S.2d 836, 171 N.E.2d 909 (1960), cert. denied sub nom. Brown v. Lefkowitz, 365 U.S. 842, 81 S.Ct. 801, 5 L.Ed.2d 808 (1961); O'Keefe v. State Dept. of Revenue, 79 Wn.2d 633, 488 P.2d 754 (1971) (bank account); In re Barnett's Trusts, [1902] 1 Ch. 847; Restatement (Second) § 266, comment *a* (chattels and rights embodied in a document). There is some authority to the contrary. See Estate of Nolan, 135 Cal.App.2d 16, 286 P.2d 899 (Dist.Ct.App.1955) (bank accounts); California v. Tax Comm'n, 55 Wn.2d 155, 346 P.2d 1006 (1959) (stock in Washington corporation escheats to state of nonresident's domicile). There is even some authority that escheat will not be to the situs if the law of the domicile treats the domiciliary government as an heir for purposes of escheat. See In re Utassi's Will, 15 N.Y.2d 436, 261 N.Y.S.2d 4, 209 N.E.2d 65 (1965) [changed by statute: N.Y.—McKinney's Est.P. & T.L. § 4–1.5 (escheat to New York situs in all cases)]; Re Maldonado, [1953] 2 All E. R. 1579 (Ct.App.). For criticism of this latter trend, see Ehrenzweig, *Characterization in the Conflict of Laws—An Unwelcome Addition to American Doctrine*, in XXth Century Comparative and Conflicts Laws 395, 403 (1961).

245.   Restatement (Second) § 60.

246.   See Iowa v. Slimmer, 248 U.S. 115, 39 S.Ct. 33, 63 L.Ed. 158 (1918); Stimson, supra note 240 at 1380; cf. Matter of Estate of De Lano, 181 Kan. 729, 315 P.2d 611 (1957)

the power to apply its own law on distribution should it wish to do so.[247] These situs overtones notwithstanding, it is to the law of the domicile at death that most American courts, including situs courts, look on matters of intestate distribution of personalty.

Sections 2.12 to 2.12C analyze this domiciliary rule and criticize some of the leading cases applying the rule. This chapter will not repeat that discussion. The domiciliary rule for intestate succession will usually produce functional results. This is because it is the domicile at death of the intestate that will usually have the predominant interest, often the only interest, in the distribution of decedent's personalty. Sometimes, however, the technical domicile at death will have no legitimate concern with intestate distribution. This will be so in cases such as *White v. Tenant*,[248] when the last domicile has been acquired only shortly before death and all the possible distributees have long-settled residences in the state that was also the long-settled residence of the decedent until shortly before death. The domicile at death will not have the predominant interest in intestate distribution, even when it has been the long-settled residence of the decedent, if, as in *In re Estate of Jones*,[249] there is no reason to believe that its intestacy laws better accord with the probable wishes of the decedent than the intestacy laws of another jurisdiction where all the possible distributees have long-settled residences. It is this latter jurisdiction's views on distribution that should prevail. In short, the rule on intestate distribution that would best correspond with functional realities would be "the law of the state with the predominant interest in intestate distribution", or a rule of thumb that would do minimum violence to traditional notions, "the law of the domicile at death unless some other state has the predominant interest in intestate distribution."

§ 8.25 Validity and Effect of a Will Bequeathing Personalty

Section 8.15 discusses construction of a will disposing of real estate. Much of that discussion is applicable to construction of a will disposing of personal property. The domiciliary law that is most likely to be applied to construction of wills of personalty is that of the domicile of the testator or testatrix at the time of the execution of the will if this is different from the domicile at death,[250] on the theory that this rule of

---

(situs court has option to administer personalty under will itself or permit administrators at domicile to take possession); Newcomb v. Newcomb, 108 Ky. 582, 57 S.W. 2 (1900) (power to probate will at situs).

247. Cf. Pullmans Palace Car Co. v. Pennsylvania, 141 U.S. 18, 22, 11 S.Ct. 876, 877–878, 35 L.Ed. 613, 616 (1891) (dictum).

248. 31 W.Va. 790, 8 S.E. 596 (1888).

249. 192 Iowa 78, 182 N.W. 227 (1921).

250. See McKinney's New York Estate, Powers & Trusts Law § 3–5.1(e); Restatement (Second) § 264, comment *f*; cf. In re Nicholas' Will, 50 Misc.2d 76, 269 N.Y.S.2d 623 (Surr.Ct.1966) (construction of will of donee of power of appointment controlled by law of domicile at death of donor, but no showing that this law differed from law of donee's domicile); Toledo Trust Co. v. Santa Barbara Foundation, 32 Ohio St.3d 141, 512 N.E.2d 664 (1987), cert. denied, 485 U.S. 916, 108 S.Ct. 1089, 99 L.Ed.2d 250 (1988) (whether

construction is most likely to accord with the intentions of the decedent. Assuming that the court is dealing with a genuine construction problem in which the actual intention of the decedent is either nonexistent or unknown and unknowable, it is unrealistic to assume that the decedent knew of the rule of construction or that his or her lawyer relied on a rule of construction to express an intention communicated to the lawyer by the decedent.[251] If one state has the predominant interest in the effect on the distributees of the construction of the will, the rule of construction of that state should be applied. Such a state, for example, will be one where all the distributees have settled residences. This state is more likely to be the decedent's domicile at death than the domicile at the time the will was executed, if those domiciles are different.

The law of the domicile at death is also commonly applied to determine the validity of a will disposing of personal property.[252] Sections 2.13 to 2.13B discuss this domiciliary rule, and much of the discussion in section 8.10 concerning the validity of a will of realty is also applicable to wills of personalty. Once again, sensible solutions to choice-of-law problems are obtainable only if attention is paid to the purposes underlying seemingly conflicting domestic rules concerning the validity of wills. If only one state's policies are relevant, its law should be applied. If two or more states have relevant conflicting policies on validity, some rational accommodation of this conflict should be sought. Frequently the difference between validating and invalidating rules will be one of degree, not basic policy, and resolution of the conflict in favor of validity will not seriously conflict with a strongly-held policy of any state and will give effect to the estate plan of the testator.

There is some evidence that courts have acted consistently with this suggested rule of validation. *In re Chappell's Estate*[253] applied the law of the situs of the personalty, which was also the place where the testamentary trust was to be administered, to uphold the trust against the claim that it violated the rules of the testator's alleged domicile at death limiting restraints on alienation. The court regarded the traditional domiciliary rule as designed to apply the law most likely to be in accord with the intentions of the testator—a policy obviously inapplicable when the domiciliary law would invalidate a term of the will. In his thoughtful study of international conflicts cases, Professor Yiannopoulos concludes: *"whenever the will does not violate superior policies of the forum essen-*

---

testamentary power of appointment has been exercised is determined by the law of beneficiary's domicile, not the locus of the trust).

251. Cases should be distinguished in which application of the law of the domicile at the time of the execution of the will serves to give effect to the decedent's manifested intention. See, e.g., Royce v. Estate of Denby, 117 N.H. 893, 379 A.2d 1256 (1977) (do not apply rule of domicile at death that child must be named in will in order to be disinherited); In re Estate of Garver, 135 N.J.Super. 578, 343 A.2d 817 (App.Div.1975) (law of prior domicile applied to revoke will by divorce, this according with advice testator received from counsel and with statement by testator to second wife).

252. See Restatement (Second) § 263.

253. 124 Wash. 128, 213 P. 684 (1923).

tial validity is governed by the law upholding the will...."[254] The Second Restatement suggests an alternative reference to the place of administration in order to validate a testamentary trust of movables[255] and indicates that courts are even more willing to make this alternative reference in the case of charitable trusts.[256] In regard to formal validity, many states have statutes that, in addition to the law of the domicile at death, make alternative references for the purposes of validation to either the law of the place of execution of the will or the law of the place of the testator's domicile at the time of execution.[257]

Matter of Bauer,[258] rather than following this sensible policy of validating the will whenever validation can be accomplished under a relevant law without violating a strongly held policy of the state with the predominant interest in the will's validity, invalidated the will. The court applied the law of New York as the state where the trust donor was domiciled at the time the trust instrument was executed and as the place of execution. The testatrix, while a resident of New York, had there executed a trust indenture in which she gave herself the power to appoint in her will the persons to receive the trust principal. Her will left the trust fund to two nieces for life with the remainder to a United Kingdom charitable corporation. At the time of her death, the testatrix had been domiciled in England for a number of years. The disposition violated the New York rule limiting the suspension of the power of alienation to two lives. The vesting of the trust res had been suspended for three lives, that of the donor-testatrix and her two nieces. Therefore the testamentary disposition was held invalid and, under a residuary clause in the trust, the res was distributed to the settlor's next of kin pursuant to New York statutes. Under both the law of England, the testatrix's domicile at death and for a substantial period before death, and under the revised New York law at the time of the decision in *Bauer*, the will would have been valid. As Judge Fuld said in his dissent: "Since no discernible New York policy or interest dictates the application of its law to invalidate the disposition by the English testatrix valid under her personal law—and, indeed, now valid under present New York law—such intention should be given effect."[259] A New York statute would now

---

254. Yiannopoulos, *Wills of Movables in American International Conflicts Law: A Critique of the Domiciliary "Rule"*, 46 Calif. L. Rev. 185, 206 (1958) (emphasis in original). See also Note, *The Testator's Intention as a Factor in Determining the Place of Probate of His Estate*, 33 Ind.L. J. 591, 599, 608 (1958); cf. Lanius v. Fletcher, 100 Tex. 550, 101 S.W. 1076 (1907) (situs law applied to prevent beneficiary from dissolving trust under law of domicile).

255. Restatement (Second) § 269(b)(ii).

256. Id. comment *h*. See also Farmers & Merchants Bank v. Woolf, 86 N.M. 320, 523 P.2d 1346 (1974), quoting comment *h* with approval and validating a charitable testamentary trust under the law of the place where the trust was to be administered, though the testator died domiciled elsewhere.

257. See § 8.13, note 140. But cf. In re Estate of Reed, 233 Kan. 531, 664 P.2d 824 (1983), appeal dism'd for want of jurisdiction & cert. denied, 464 U.S. 978, 104 S.Ct. 417, 78 L.Ed.2d 354 (1983) (a will that is not subscribed declared invalid although held valid and admitted to probate where executed).

258. 14 N.Y.2d 272, 251 N.Y.S.2d 23, 200 N.E.2d 207 (1964).

259. Id. at 279, 251 N.Y.S.2d at 28, 200 N.E.2d at 211.

require a different result on the facts of *Bauer*. In order to determine the validity of a will exercising a testamentary power of appointment, the statute selects the law of the domicile at death of a person who is both the donor and donee of the power.[260]

It is possible to carry this policy of validation too far. If, for example, the long-settled residence of the testator or testatrix and all the natural objects of his or her bounty would invalidate a provision of the will for reasons the domicile thinks essential to the protection of the decedent's family, no other state should apply its own law to validate the will. A New York statute, however, provides that:

> Whenever a testator, not domiciled in this state at the time of death, provides in his will that he elects to have the disposition of his property situated in this state governed by the laws of this state, the intrinsic *validity*, including the testator's general capacity, effect, interpretation, revocation or alteration of any such disposition is determined by the local law of this state.[261]

Such a provision may attract business to New York, but it is also likely, officiously and selfishly, to override the strongly-held policies of sister states.[262]

In *Clark's Estate*,[263] the New York Court of Appeals was able to construe a predecessor of this statutory provision to avoid this officious effect. The prior language covered "testamentary dispositions" and the "validity and effect of such dispositions." The court held that this language did not apply to the right of a Virginia widow of a Virginia testator to elect against a will disposing of intangible personalty because the availability or nonavailability of her election was not a "testamentary disposition." The court said: "In sum, Virginia's overwhelming interest in the protection of surviving spouses domiciled there demands that we apply its law to give the widow in this case the right of election provided for her under that law."[264]

---

260. N.Y.—McKinney's Estates, Powers & Trusts Law § 3–5.1(g)(2)(C).

For a discussion of what law applies to determine whether the donee has exercised a power of appointment when donor and donee are domiciled in different states, see White v. United States, 680 F.2d 1156 (7th Cir.1982) (reject rule that law of donor's domicile governs and apply law of donee's domicile on ground this likely to reflect donee's intention under the circumstances of this case—held not exercised).

261. Id. § 3–5.1(h) (emphasis added).

262. See also N.Y.—McKinney's General Obligations Law §§ 5–1401 (in transaction involving $250,000 or more, can agree that New York law governs "whether or not such contract ... bears a reasonable relation to" New York), 5–1402 (provides New York forum for 5–1401 agreements if amount covered by transaction is 1 million dollars or more and nonresident agrees to submit to the jurisdiction of New York courts).

For a discussion of the provision quoted in the text accompanying note 257, supra, see Hendrickson, *Choice-of-Law Directions for Disposing of Assets Situated Elsewhere than the Domicile of Their Owner—The Refractions of Renard*, 19 Real Property, Probate & Trust J. 407, 408 (1984) (helps avoid "outdated domiciliary restrictions" on disinheritance of spouses and children).

263. 21 N.Y.2d 478, 288 N.Y.S.2d 993, 236 N.E.2d 152 (1968).

264. Id. at 489, 288 N.Y.S.2d at 1001–02, 236 N.E.2d at 158; cf. In re Crichton, 20 N.Y.2d 124, 133, 281 N.Y.S.2d 811, 819, 228 N.E.2d 799, 805 (1967) (New York law

The amended provision, quoted just above, uses the more general term "disposition of his property." In *Matter of Estate of Renard*,[265] the court approved a Surrogate's opinion that construed the successor provision as choosing New York law and thus preventing a son's election against his mother's will. The opinion emphasized the change in wording of the statute. This reasoning would suggest the opposite result in *Clark's Estate* if litigated under the new statute, although *Renard* was a less outrageous interference with the interests of another jurisdiction. In *Renard*, not only was the claimant a son rather than a spouse, but also the son was not domiciled in France and it was under French law that he claimed a forced share of his mother's estate.

§ 8.26 Inter Vivos Trusts of Personalty

In dealing with inter vivos transactions, the New York Court of Appeals has not always been as careful as it was in *In re Estate of Clark* to avoid undermining the strongly-held policies of other jurisdictions. *Wyatt v. Fulrath*[266] is a classic example. A husband and wife, the Duke and Duchess of Arion, who were life-long nationals and domiciliaries of Spain, had from time to time sent money and securities to be held for safekeeping and investment by New York banks. The spouses themselves never entered the United States. Three of the bank accounts were originally in the names of both husband and wife, although later the contents of two of the accounts were transferred to accounts in the sole name of the wife. The New York bank forms that were signed by husband and wife provided that the assets in the account would go to the survivor on the death of one of the spouses. One of the forms, though not the others, provided that the rights of all parties were governed by New York law.[267] Under New York law, these survivorship agreements were valid. The husband died and then the wife died. Under Spanish law, the property in the accounts was community property, only half of the property would have gone to the wife on her husband's death and at least two thirds of the remaining half would pass to the heirs of the deceased husband. Any agreement to the contrary between husband and wife would be void. The New York ancillary administrator of the hus-

---

determines right of widow of New York testator to take against the will, not the law of Louisiana situs) ("The choice of law problem here should be resolved by an examination of the contacts which Louisiana and New York have with this controversy for the purpose of determining which of those jurisdictions has the paramount interest in the application of its law."). [But see Crichton v. Succession of Crichton, 232 So.2d 109 (La.App.1970), writ ref'd, result correct, 256 La. 274, 236 So.2d 39 (1970), cert. denied, 400 U.S. 919, 91 S.Ct. 172, 27 L.Ed.2d 159 (1970) (New York opinion wrong in concluding that Louisiana law does not apply to determine rights of New York widow, but New York opinion given full faith and credit)]. Cf. also Boyd v. Curran, 166 F.Supp. 193 (S.D.N.Y.1958) (apply whole law of situs of administration of National Maritime Union Pension and Welfare Plan to determine alleged widow's rights to death benefits, situs conflicts rule referring to law of domicile of spouses when property acquired).

265. 56 N.Y.2d 973, 453 N.Y.S.2d 625, 439 N.E.2d 341 (1982).

266. 16 N.Y.2d 169, 264 N.Y.S.2d 233, 211 N.E.2d 637 (1965).

267. Wyatt v. Fulrath, 38 Misc.2d 1012, 239 N.Y.S.2d 486 (Spec.Term. 1963), aff'd mem., 22 A.D.2d 853, 254 N.Y.S.2d 216, modified, 16 N.Y.2d 169, 264 N.Y.S.2d 233, 211 N.E.2d 637 (1965).

band's estate brought suit against the executor of the wife's will to establish a claim to one half of the property held in the New York accounts. The wife's will had disposed of this property.[268] The court held that the law of New York, as the situs selected by the spouses for the safekeeping of their property, applied to validate the survivorship agreements that would be void under Spanish law. As Judge McGivern said in his trial court opinion in *Wyatt*, "[t]he public policy of New York appears to be one of encouragement to non-residents to do business with New York banks, in accordance with New York law."[269] In this case, this "encouragement" permitted about $2,000,000 to be transferred contrary to the mandatory scheme of Spanish family inheritance.[270]

The majority in *Wyatt* was much influenced by the same court's opinion over thirty years earlier in *Hutchison v. Ross*.[271] In *Hutchison*, by an antenuptial agreement, a husband had established a $125,000 trust for his wife and future children. At all relevant times, the settlor and his wife were domiciled in Quebec. Subsequently, the husband established a $1,000,000 trust for the benefit of his wife and children, with a New York bank as trustee. An instrument executed in Quebec by husband and wife recited that the new trust was in lieu of the antenuptial settlement and that the wife renounced her rights under the antenuptial settlement. Later the husband, in financial distress, brought an action to revoke the $1,000,000 trust on the ground that under Quebec law the transfer during coverture from husband to wife was invalid. When a petition in bankruptcy was filed against the husband, the trustee in bankruptcy was substituted for the husband as plaintiff. The court applied New York law as situs law to validate the trust. In his dissent, Judge Kellogg pointed out that since, under Quebec law, the wife's renunciation of the original trust was invalid, she would now have the benefit of both trusts.

In *National Shawmut Bank v. Cumming*,[272] the Massachusetts court applied the law of Massachusetts, as the situs of an inter vivos trust. The court rejected the claim of the Vermont wife of the Vermont settlor that

---

268. See Appellant's Brief, New York Supreme Court, Appellate Division, Wyatt v. Fulrath, p. 17, n.*: "The Duchess's New York will, after a bequest of $5,000 to her grandson, Gonzalo, leaves one-half of her New York assets in equal shares to Campbell [a banker who had assisted the Duke and Duchess in their financial affairs], a Mme. Dastot (Campbell's former secretary who afterwards acted as secretary to the Duchess) and a Mlle. Boisard (the Duchess's personal maid and traveling companion), and the other one-half in equal shares to her children, Hilda and Jaime."

269. *Wyatt*, 38 Misc.2d at 1016, 239 N.Y.S.2d at 491.

270. Under Spanish law, the children and descendents would have taken a two-thirds forced heirship in the husband's estate. Spanish Civil Code, Art. 807(1). The wife's will did leave the children, though not the grandchild, who was the offspring of a deceased oldest son, at least as much of the New York assets as they would have taken under the Spanish forced heirship provision. See note 264 supra. The one-third of the husband's portion of the Spanish community property over which, under Spanish law, he had the power of testamentary disposition, he left to the wife for life. She renounced the life estate to permit the immediate delivery of the corpus to her children and to the grandson. Wyatt v. Fulrath, Appellant's Brief, New York Supreme Court, Appellate Division, p. 16.

271. 262 N.Y. 381, 187 N.E. 65 (1933).

272. 325 Mass. 457, 91 N.E.2d 337 (1950).

the trust, under Vermont law, was an invalid attempt to deprive the estranged wife of her forced share in the husband's estate.[273]

Wyatt and *Cumming* and, perhaps, because creditors, not family were the real losers, to a lesser extent *Hutchison*, are misguided applications of the law of the situs as an alternative reference to validate an inter vivos trust. Validation and alternative references for that purpose are to be applauded when they save the settlor's plan from foundering on the shoals of some minor difference in policy between two jurisdictions, such as a slightly stricter rule against perpetuities.[274] But validation under situs law should not set at naught important policies of the settled residence of the affected parties.[275]

§ 8.27   Commercial Transactions: The Uniform Commercial Code Will Not Eliminate Conflicts Problems

The adoption in all states[276] of Article 9 of the Uniform Commercial Code, which covers Secured Transactions, will reduce the incidence of interstate conflict of laws problems concerning security interests in personal property and fixtures This is because of the uniformity in applicable law that the Code creates, whether we are concerned about rights and duties as between the secured creditor and the debtor[277] or

---

273. But cf. In re Estate of Danz, 444 Pa. 411, 283 A.2d 282 (1971) (deed of gift valid under law of place where executed, though invalid under law of forum where bank account situated); Ossorio v. Leon, 705 S.W.2d 219 (Tex.Civ.App—San Antonio 1985, no writ) (apply law of Mexican marital domicile to determine marital property rights in Texas account); Tirado v. Tirado, 357 S.W.2d 468 (Tex.Civ.App.—Texarkana 1962, writ dism'd for want of juris.) (law of marital domicile applied to determine whether wife's interests in oil and gas leases were separate or community property for purposes of partition of property in divorce proceedings).

274. See Wilmington Trust Co. v. Wilmington Trust Co., 26 Del.Ch. 397, 24 A.2d 309 (1942) (apply law of place to which administration shifted after first being administered at domicile of donor to validate provisions of inter vivos trust that would be invalid under perpetuities rule of domicile of donor and beneficiaries); Shannon v. Irving Trust Co., 275 N.Y. 95, 103–104, 9 N.E.2d 792, 794 (1937) (apply law of state chosen in inter vivos trust instrument, which was also domicile of settlor and beneficiaries, to validate trust invalid under rule on accumulations of situs of trust administration) ("our policy in that connection [accumulations] is substantially the same as that of New Jersey"). In regard to Wilmington Trust Co., supra this note, cf. Application of New York Trust Co., 195 Misc. 598, 87 N.Y.S.2d 787 (Spec. Term, 1949) (situs of trust administration can be shifted from forum as provided in trust instrument, even though after situs shift, trust should continue to be governed by forum law because instrument refers to forum intestacy law to fill in distribution scheme under certain contingencies).

275. Cf. Uniform Trust Code § 107(1), 7C U.L.A. pocket part: "The meaning and effect of the terms of a trust are determined by: (1) the law of the jurisdiction designated in the terms unless the designation of that jurisdiction's law is contrary to a strong public policy of the jurisdiction having the most significant relationship to the matter at issue; or (2) in the absence of a controlling designation in the terms of the trust, the law of the jurisdiction having the most significant relationship to the matter at issue."

276. Article 9 has also been adopted in the District of Columbia, Guam, and the Virgin Islands

277. See, e.g., Uniform Commercial Code §§ 9–503 (1972 Code), 9–609 (2000 Code) (secured party's right to take possession after default); 9–504 (1972 Code), 9–610, 9–611, 9–615, 9–617 (secured party's right to dispose of collateral after default and effect of disposition); 9–505 (1972 Code), 9–620, 9–621, 9–624 (2000 Code) (limitation on creditor's right to retain the collateral without reselling it and accounting for the proceeds).

between the secured creditor and third parties who challenge the secured creditor's right to enforce the security interest.[278]

Although the Uniform Commercial Code, by unifying substantive law, will decrease the frequency of conflicts problems in commercial property transactions, there are several reasons why there remain a substantial number of secured transactions in which the need to choose the governing law arises.

First of all, the various state versions of the Code are not uniform. The state variations from the "official" text are most numerous in Article 9. For example, when California enacted the 1972 version and the 1977 amendments, that state departed from the official text in twenty-six of the fifty-five sections of Article 9[279] in ways that affect the substance of the provisions, going beyond clarification or minor changes in wording.

An additional important reason for lack of uniformity has been the state-by-state enactment of Article 9. The Commissioners on Uniform State Laws first promulgated Article 9 in 1962. In 1972 the Commissioners and the American Law Institute approved a major revision of Article 9. A few additional changes were promulgated in 1977. It took thirty years for all the states that had adopted the 1962 version to enact the 1972 Code. During those three decades, the different versions of Article 9 produced major choice-of-law problems.

In 2000 another major revision was promulgated. In an attempt to avoid the conflicts caused by the lag in state adoptions of the 1962, 1972, and 1977 versions of Article 9, the Commissioners proposed July 1, 2001 as the uniform effective date for the new version.[280] The hope was that by that date all states would have adopted the new Article 9. All states did enact the new Article by that date although it took effect in four states soon thereafter.[281] Therefore there is minimum likelihood of problems caused when, because of time lags in adoption of a new official version, states have different provisions for secured transactions.[282] The problem of non-uniform enactments, however, remains.[283]

---

278. See, e.g., §§ 9–103 (1972 Code), 9–301, 9–303, 9–305, 9–306, 9–307, 9–316, 9–337 (2000 Code) (choice of law to determine validity and perfection of security interests), 9–301–18 (rights of third parties) (1972 Code), 9–317–39 (priority) (2000 Code).

279. There are 55 sections in the 1972 official text of Article 9 and 53 sections in the 1962 official text, which the 1972 text superseded.

280. U.C.C. § 9–701 (2000).

281. Revised Article 9 took effect in Connecticut on October 1, 2001 and in Alabama, Florida, and Mississippi on January 1, 2002.

282. In anticipation of these problems, the Permanent Editorial Board for the Uniform Commercial Code issued a Report: Article 9 Perfection Choice of Law Analysis Where Revised Article 9 Is Not in Effect in All States by July 1, 2001, reprinted in 56 Bus. Law. 1725 (2001).

283. See 3 U.L.A. containing the latest official version of article 9. After most of the sections, under the heading "Action in Adopting Jurisdictions", there is a note detailing non-uniform enactments. Some of the variations from the official text are matters of form, but many create substantive differences.

Moreover, as will become apparent in this discussion, the meanings of Code provisions and an understanding of the manner in which the various Articles relate to one another do not leap from the page. Much construction and interpretation of the Code is needed. There is great likelihood that, despite the salutary injunction of section 1–102 to construe with uniformity as a goal and the existence of a Permanent Editorial Board to oversee the operation of the Code, states will differ in their construction of various Code provisions.

Another factor requiring choice of law is that the Code leaves in force various nonuniform state enactments concerning usury, small loans, and retail installment sales,[284] thus excluding some aspects of vast numbers of commercial property transactions from the Code's unifying influence. Finally, transactions with foreign countries will continue to present conflicts problems.

It is therefore desirable, before discussing the Article 9 choice-of-law provisions, to discuss the pre-Code conflict of laws rules both in terms of the non-Code transactions to which they will continue to apply and as background for understanding the Article 9 conflicts rules. The Code choice-of-law rules in turn will influence the future development of non-Code conflicts rules. A useful division of this discussion is first, choice of law to determine the rights and duties as between a secured creditor and his debtor, and then, what law determines whether the rights of a secured creditor prevail over those of third parties who claim an interest in the collateral.[285]

§ 8.28 The Debtor and the Secured Creditor: Pre–Code Conflicts Rules

It is often said that the standard choice-of-law rule for determining rights and duties as between the secured creditor and the debtor refers to the situs of the chattel at the time that the security interest attached.[286] This situs rule does find some support in a few of the older cases.[287] It is doubtful, however, that the situs rule ever represented the

---

284. See § 9–201(1972 Act); § 9–201(b) (2000 Act).

285. But see In re Howards Appliance Corp., 91 B.R. 208 (E.D.N. Y. 1988) (a debtor-in-possession under chapter 11 of the Bankruptcy Act is deemed a lien creditor without notice, and an unperfected security interest is not enforceable against the debtor).

286. See Restatement, Conflict of Laws § 272 (1934) (conditional sale); cf. Restatement (Second) § 251 ("the state which ... has the most significant relationship"; "[i]n the absence of an effective choice of law by the parties, greater weight will usually be given to the location of the chattel at the time that the security interest attached than to any other contact...."). See also § 8.31, notes 307–309 and accompanying text. Contra, Istim, Inc. v. Chemical Bank, 78 N.Y.2d 342, 581 N.E.2d 1042, 575 N.Y.S.2d 796 (1991) (applying New York law to determine validity of attorney's lien on proceeds of settlement of Illinois litigation when dispute is between New York law firm and New York creditor, expressly rejecting Restatement (Second) § 251).

287. See, e.g., United States v. Rogers & Rogers, 36 F.Supp. 79 (D.Minn.), appeal dism'd 121 F.2d 1019 (8th Cir.1941) (whether mortgagor may sell property; situs also debtor's residence); Youssoupoff v. Widener, 246 N.Y. 174, 190–191, 158 N.E. 64, 69 (1927) (whether contract of sale will be construed as a mortgage) ("the construction and legal effect of a contract for the transfer of, or the creation of a lien upon, property situated in the jurisdiction where the contract is made is governed by the law of that jurisdiction").

position of a majority of United States jurisdictions.[288] The trend of modern choice-of-law analysis has been markedly away from any such rigid situs approach.[289] This can be illustrated by three cases spanning thirty years of developments in choice of law to determine rights as between debtor and secured creditor—*Thomas G. Jewett, Jr. Inc. v. Keystone Driller Co.*,[290] *Shanahan v. George B. Landers Construction Co.*,[291] and *Universal C.I.T. Credit Corp. v. Hulett.*[292]

In *Jewett*, the debtor was incorporated in and had its headquarters in Massachusetts. The creditor was a Pennsylvania corporation with headquarters in Pennsylvania. The debtor and the creditor's local agent executed in Massachusetts a conditional sales contract for a power shovel. As agreed, the shovel was delivered to the debtor in New Hampshire where the debtor was working on a construction project. After the project was finished, the debtor stored the shovel in New Hampshire. Nine months after the shovel had been delivered to the debtor, it was still in New Hampshire where the creditor repossessed it. The creditor then shipped the shovel to Connecticut where it was resold. The debtor sued the creditor for conversion of the shovel, claiming that under New Hampshire law the debtor's right to redeem the collateral after default could not be cut off unless the debtor is given fourteen days notice before resale. No such notice was given. The Massachusetts Supreme Judicial Court affirmed a judgment for the creditor, holding that Massachusetts law, not New Hampshire law, determined the debtor's right to redeem the collateral. Under Massachusetts law, the debtor lost its right to redeem when it failed to tender to the creditor, within fifteen days after repossession, the full amount due. The court characterized the problem as one of "contract" and held that the law of the place of making of the contract applied because it did not appear that the contract was entered into with reference to the law of any other state. Judge Lummus dissented, contending that the law of New Hampshire, the situs of the chattel from delivery until repossession, should have been applied.

In *Shanahan*, a Massachusetts seller made a conditional sale of a power trench hoe to a New Hampshire buyer. The contract was technically "made" in Massachusetts, where the seller signed, and thus accepted, the conditional sales contract that had previously been executed by the buyer in New Hampshire. The hoe was, as agreed between buyer and seller, although not stated in the conditional sales contract, delivered to the buyer in Vermont. The buyer used the hoe in Vermont and then moved it to New Hampshire where the machine was in use when the seller repossessed it because the buyer had defaulted in payment. The seller, within ten days after repossessing the hoe, removed it to Massa-

---

288. See infra note 299.

289. See R. Leflar et al., American Conflicts Law § 177 (4th ed. 1986) (situs dogma "rapidly disappearing").

290. 282 Mass. 469, 185 N.E. 369 (1933).

291. 266 F.2d 400 (1st Cir.1959).

292. 151 So.2d 705 (La.App.1963).

chusetts and resold it. This resale was proper under Massachusetts law, but violated a New Hampshire requirement that, after being repossessed, the collateral remain in New Hampshire for ten days during which the vendee may redeem by tendering to the creditor the amount owed. The buyer brought suit in the United States District Court in Massachusetts against the seller and others[293] for conversion.

The District Court applied New Hampshire law and gave judgment for the plaintiff. On appeal, the First Circuit Court of Appeals approved the application of New Hampshire law, but vacated the judgment and remanded for re-computation of damages under New Hampshire law. Because trial was held in Massachusetts, under *Erie*[294] and *Klaxon*,[295] the court was compelled to apply Massachusetts conflicts law. The court was thus called upon to construe *Jewett* and apply it to these facts. The court first decided that *Jewett* required it to disregard the fortuitous location of the collateral at the time that the conditional sales contract was made. This situs was somewhere in the Midwest where the hoe was manufactured. The *Jewett* majority had made no mention of where the shovel was at the time of contracting. Further, the *Shanahan* court decided that it should disregard the fact that the hoe was delivered to a job site in Vermont, just as the *Jewett* court was not controlled by the delivery of the shovel to a job site in New Hampshire. The difficult problem for the federal court was whether it should read *Jewett* as articulating a place of contracting rule and apply the law of Massachusetts where the conditional sales contract was "made". The court referred to a more recent Massachusetts decision, *Budget Plan, Inc. v. Sterling A. Orr, Inc.*,[296] in which the Massachusetts Supreme Judicial Court had spoken of *Jewett* as being "contrary to the prevailing view."[297] The *Shanahan* opinion stated:

> But it does seem to us that the remarks in the later case [*Budget Plan*] indicate that the Supreme Judicial Court of Massachusetts now would not be disposed to extend the rule of the *Jewett* case to facts like those in the case at bar, where the purchaser of the chattel was not a Massachusetts corporation but a New Hampshire corporation with its headquarters in that state and where in addition the shovel was not only located in New Hampshire when it was repossessed, but also where the shovel would presumably be kept when not in use on out-of-state jobs.[298]

Shanahan then applied New Hampshire law. For reasons indicated at the end of this section, this result is desirable. *Shanahan's* use of the

---

293. The other defendants were the finance company to whom the contract and note had been assigned with recourse and a Mr. Shanahan who repossessed the hoe, bought it from Shanahan, Inc., the secured creditor, and then resold it.

294. Erie R.R. v. Tompkins, 304 U.S. 64, 58 S.Ct. 817, 82 L.Ed. 1188 (1938).

295. Klaxon Co. v. Stentor Elec. Mfg. Co., 313 U.S. 487, 61 S.Ct. 1020, 85 L.Ed. 1477 (1941). See chapter 10.

296. 334 Mass. 599, 137 N.E.2d 918 (1956).

297. Id. at 601, n.1, 137 N.E.2d at 920, n.1.

298. *Shanahan*, 266 F.2d at 405.

intervening *Budget Plan* case to avoid the place of contracting rule of *Jewett* was, however, puzzling. When the Massachusetts court in *Budget Plan* said that *Jewett* seemed "contrary to the prevailing view", the court was referring to the rule choosing the law of the situs of the collateral at the time of delivery to the buyer.[299] In *Shanahan*, this would have meant application of the Vermont law that the federal court had rejected in reliance on *Jewett*. The federal court had thus used *Budget Plan* to avoid the place of contracting rule of *Jewett* and *Jewett* to avoid the situs rule hinted at in *Budget Plan*.

In *Hulett*, the defendants, Louisiana spouses, had purchased an automobile in Indiana from an Indiana firm. The purchase was under a conditional sales contract executed in Indiana and immediately assigned to the Indiana office of the plaintiff finance company. The contract indicated that the buyers were Louisiana residents and that the automobile would be brought to Louisiana and kept there. Five months later the automobile was repossessed in Louisiana with the wife's written consent. The automobile was then returned to Indiana where it was sold at a public sale. The finance company then brought suit against the buyers in Louisiana for a deficiency judgment. Under Indiana law the plaintiff had preserved its right to a deficiency judgment by giving defendants prior written notice of the repossession sale and posting notice of the sale. Under Louisiana law an appraisal of the automobile, fixing the minimum resale price, was necessary before the creditor was entitled to a deficiency judgment. No such appraisal had been made.

The Louisiana court held that Louisiana law was applicable and affirmed the trial court's granting of defendants' motion for summary judgment. The court reviewed various choice-of-law rules that courts had applied in determining rights as between secured creditor and debtor—

---

299. The *Budget Plan* opinion cites the following sources for the "prevailing view", all advocating the situs rule: "See Restatement: Conflict of Laws, § 272 [1934]; Goodrich, Conflict of Laws, § 157 [3d Ed.1949]; and cases cited in the dissenting opinion of Lummus, J., in the *Jewett* case at page 479." *Budget Plan*, 334 Mass. at 601 n.1, 137 N.E.2d at 920 n.1.

The citation to Judge Lummus' dissenting opinion is to the following statement and string citation. It is ironic that not a single case in this string citation supports the situs rule in determining rights as between the secured creditor and the debtor. Every case cited deals with the rights of the secured creditor, not against the debtor, but against various third parties. A description of the third party in each case is inserted in brackets: "Ordinarily the law of the place of delivery, at least where it does not appear that no further presence or use of the chattel there is contemplated, governs the rights of the parties under a conditional sale. Cleveland Machine Works v. Lang, 67 N.H. 348[, 31 A. 20 (1893)] [attaching creditor]. Knowles Loom Works v. Vacher, 28 Vroom 490, 30 Vroom 586, [57 N.J.L. 490, 31 A. 306 (S.Ct.1895), aff'd mem., 59 N.J.L. 586, 39 A. 1114 (1896)] [subsequent mortgagee]. Cooper v. Philadelphia Worsted Co., 2 Robb. (N.J.) 622[, 68 N.J.Eq. 622, 60 A. 352 (1905)] [judgment creditors]. Eli Bridge Co. v. Lachman, 124 Or. 592[, 265 P. 435 (1928)] [bona fide purchaser]. Mergenthaler Linotype Co. v. Hull, 239 F. 26 [(1st Cir.1916)] [trustee in bankruptcy]. Smith's Transfer & Storage Co. v. Reliable Stores Corp., 58 F.2d 511 [(D.C.Ct.App.(1932))] [warehouseman]. United States Fidelity & Guaranty Co. v. Northwest Engineering Co., 146 Miss. 476[, 112 So. 580 (1927)] [execution creditor]. James Beggs & Co. v. Bartels, 73 Conn. 132[, 46 A. 874 (1900)] [buyers at execution sale]. H.G. Craig & Co. v. Uncas Paperboard Co., 104 Conn. 559[, 133 A. 673 (1926)] [receiver for benefit of creditors]...." *Jewett*, 282 Mass. at 479, 185 N.E. at 373 (dissent, Lummus, J.).

the law of the place of contracting, the law of the place where the contract was intended to have effect, the law of the place where the collateral was intended to be kept, the law of the place where the collateral was repossessed—and found all these rules too rigid to be satisfactory. The court noted that Louisiana had a significant interest in protecting the Louisiana residents from a deficiency judgment when an appraisal had not been made prior to resale and that there were sufficient contacts with Louisiana, the residence of the defendants, the place where the automobile was intended to be kept and where it was repossessed, to make it reasonable for Louisiana to give effect to its own policy.[300]

Thus, in each of these three leading cases, despite disparate reasoning, in order to determine the manner in which the secured creditor should repossess and resell the goods to avoid liability to the debtor or to preserve the creditor's right to a deficiency judgment, the court applies the law of the debtor's residence or principal place of business when, as will usually be the case, that is where the creditor had reason to expect that the goods would be kept when not in use elsewhere. This same pattern, applying the law of the debtor's home state if the goods have a nexus with that state that the creditor should have foreseen, emerges from a great many of the modern cases dealing with rights as between secured creditors and their debtors.[301] This choice of law makes eminent functional sense.[302] The debtor's state will have a legitimate concern in extending the protection of its repossession and resale requirements to the debtor when this protection will not unfairly surprise the creditor

---

300. Cf. General Motors Acceptance Corp. v. Robinson, 263 A.2d 302 (Del.Super.1970) (legality of repossession determined by law of state to which buyer moved after default and where repossession took place—no indication of whether the events took place before the 1967 effective date of the Delaware UCC, which is not cited, but the court does cite *Hulett* and a pre-UCC Delaware case); Murdock Acceptance Corp. v. S & H Distributing Co., Inc., 331 So.2d 870 (La.App.1976), writ ref'd, no error in result, 334 So.2d 435 (La. 1976) (deficiency judgment against guarantor denied because of failure to obey Louisiana requirement of appraisal before sale although only Louisiana party is the defendant guarantor; seller, buyer, and assignee all incorporated in states with no appraisal rule).

301. See Susi v. Belle Acton Stables, Inc., 360 F.2d 704 (2d Cir.1966) (method of foreclosure as between Maine creditor and Maine debtor governed by Maine law although the horses mortgaged were not in Maine either at time security interest attached or foreclosure made); United Sec. Corp. v. Tomlin, 198 A.2d 179 (Del.Super.1964) (whether creditor entitled to deficiency judgment after private sale of automobile; law of debtor's residence rather than of seller's place of business); Phillips v. Englehart, 437 S.W.2d 158 (Mo.App.1968) (whether buyer of repair equipment entitled to refund after default; law of buyer's state to which equipment moved with consent of seller); Industrial Credit Co. v. J.A.D. Constr. Corp., 29 A.D.2d 952, 289 N.Y.S.2d 243 (1969) (whether rights of buyer violated by private sale after default; law of buyer's state where goods were to be shipped, although their situs at all relevant times was elsewhere); General Acceptance Corp. v. Lyons, 125 Vt. 332, 215 A.2d 513 (1965) (in absence of choice-of-law clause in conditional sales contract, apply law of "center of gravity" of contract to determine whether vendor entitled to deficiency judgment, this being law of place where both vendor and vendee have business headquarters, not place where boat was repossessed and resold); Pioneer Credit Corp. v. Morency, 122 Vt. 463, 177 A.2d 368 (1962) (method of resale to preserve creditor's right to deficiency judgment determined by law of state to which conditional buyer, with permission of creditor, moved house trailer about a year after sale).

302. See Cavers, *The Conditional Seller's Remedies and the Choice-of-Law Process—Some Notes on Shanahan*, 35 N.Y.U. L. Rev.1126, 1140–42 (1960).

and when the law that the creditor wishes applied provides significantly less protection to the debtor.[303] The debtor is likely to rely on being able to redeem the collateral in the manner provided by the law of his or her home state. If the creditor acts properly under the law of the debtor's state, no other state is likely to have a significant reason for affording the debtor any greater protection, except in the unusual situation in which the creditor acts in another state contrary to the law of that state and in such a manner as to make it likely that a breach of the peace of that state will occur.[304] This may be the case if the debtor's state permits self-help repossession, but the situs of the goods at the time of retaking forbids self help.

§ 8.29　The 1962 Code Conflicts Rules

Under the 1962 Uniform Commercial Code, there were three major problems of interpretation in applying the Code to determine the rights and duties of secured creditor and debtor in the event of default: (1) which choice-of-law provision governed, the general Code conflicts rule of 1–105(1) or the special secured transactions rules of 9–102 and 9–103;[305] (2) if an Article 9 choice-of-law rule selects the law to govern default rights, which Article 9 rule applies, 9–102 or 9–103;[306] (3) if 9–102 governs, the situs of the goods provides the applicable law, but situs when, at the time of adjudication, the time of when the security interest attached, or the time when the conduct in question, repossession, resale,

---

303. For a thoughtful criticism of *Hulett* on the ground that Indiana law, although different from Louisiana law, shared with Louisiana the basic policy of protecting the vendee against inflated deficiency judgments, see Dainow, *Variations on a Theme in Conflict of Laws,* 24 La. L. Rev. 157, 163 (1964).

304. See Associates Discount Corp. v. Cary, 47 Misc.2d 369, 372, 262 N.Y.S.2d 646, 650 (N.Y.Civ.Ct., 1965) (although it was resale without notice that was in issue).

305. Professor Grant Gilmore stated that 1–105 is "irrelevant to any choice of law problem which involves any Article 9 security interest." II Gilmore, Security Interests in Personal Property § 44.11 at 1278 (1965). Atlas Credit Corp. v. Dolbow, 193 Pa.Super. 649, 165 A.2d 704 (1960), allocatur ref'd (1961), held that 1–105(1) selects the law to govern debtor-creditor rights even though the controversy centers on issues covered by Article 9. (Pennsylvania adopted the U.C.C. before the 1962 version, which Pennsylvania later adopted. The pre–1962 version presented the same problems of construction regarding debtor-creditor rights as the 1962 version). Skinner v. Tober Foreign Motors, Inc., 345 Mass. 429, 187 N.E.2d 669 (1963) applied 1–105(1) because the issue was whether consideration was necessary to make a modification binding and this was covered by 2–209. The court stated that if the issue concerned the validity or perfection of the security interest, 9–103 would apply. Id. at 432–33, 187 N.E.2d at 671.

I took the position that under the 1962 Code, 1–105(1) governed if the problem concerned an issue covered by a provision in Article 2; 9–102 and 9–103 applied if the issue was covered by a provision in Article 9. Commentary § 8.29 at 478 (3rd ed. 1986).

306. 9–102(1)(a) provided that the forum's Code applies "so far as concerns any personal property and fixtures within this state." 9–103 chose law to determine the "validity" and "perfection" of the security interest. Professor Gilmore took the position that the word "validity" meant that 9–103 chose the law to govern the debtor's rights after default. II Gilmore, Security Interests § 44.11 at 1276–77. Associates Discount Corp. v. Cary, 47 Misc.2d 369, 262 N.Y.S.2d 646 (N.Y. Civ. Ct. 1965) applied 9–102 to choose the law determining whether resale without notice is proper. I took the position that 9–102 governs default rights as between creditor and debtor. Commentary § 8.30 at 483 (3rd ed. 1986).

or redemption, occurred?[307] The 2000 version, now in force in every state, eliminates these problems of interpretation.[308] Therefore, this edition deletes the detailed discussion of these problems that is contained in sections 8.29 through 8.31 of the third edition.

§ 8.30   Choice of Law Between the Debtor and the Secured Creditor Under the 2000 Code

Under the 2000 Code, choice-of-law issues arising between the debtor and the secured creditor are governed by the general Code conflicts provisions in Article 1.[309] This shift to the more flexible and potentially functional provisions of Article 1 is a salutary change from the 1962 Code.[310]

§ 8.31   The Secured Creditor and Third Parties: Pre–Code Conflicts Rules

The classic triangle, involving secured creditor, debtor, and third party can be sketched as follows. Creditor acquires a security interest in goods situated in state X. Creditor records the interest as required by X law so that, in X, the security interest would be preferred over the claims of third parties who thereafter might deal with the goods in X. Debtor transports the goods to state Y where a third person, perhaps a bona fide purchaser or another creditor of the debtor, enters into a transaction involving the goods. On the basis of this transaction, the third person claims an interest in the goods superior to the security interest of the first creditor. The first creditor has not recorded its security interest in Y or done whatever else might be required by Y law for secured creditors to be protected against having their security interests superseded by the claims of persons dealing with the goods in Y. As between the secured creditor and the third person, who prevails?

The almost universally recognized common law rule was that the interest that a person acquires in personal property is determined by the

---

307. 9–102(1) stated that "this Article applies so far as concerns any personal property and fixtures within the jurisdiction of this state." This cannot refer to situs at the time of adjudication if the forum has no other contacts with the parties or the transaction. Such an application would be arbitrary, unfair, and unconstitutional See infra § 9.2A. For a suggestion that the provision refers to the location of the collateral at the time that the security interest attached, see I Gilmore, Security Interests § 10.8 at 318 n.5. Several decisions took the position that 9–102 referred to the location of the collateral at the time that the conduct in question, repossession, resale, or redemption, occurred. See, e.g., Lewis v. First Nat'l Bank, 134 Ga.App. 798, 216 S.E.2d 347 (1975) (Georgia law applies as site of repossession and resale although debtor purchased the collateral in Florida and then moved to Georgia). I took the position that 9–102 referred to the location of the collateral at the time of repossession, although I found this rule unsatisfactory. Commentary § 8.31 at 485 (3rd ed. 1986).

308. See infra § 8.30.

309. This is § 1–105. The Conference of Commissioners on Uniform State Laws and the American Law Institute withdrew a proposed replacement, § 1–301, when state legislatures refused to enact it. For discussion of the Article 1 choice-of-law provisions see §§ 7.3C and 7.3E.

310. See §§ 9–109 (Scope, replacing 9–102), 9–301 through 9–306 (replacing 9–103 and limited to "law governing perfection and priority of security interests").

law of the situs of the property at the time of the transaction on which that person bases a claim.[311] This did not mean that in our introductory

---

311. See Hervey v. Rhode Island Locomotive Works, 93 U.S. 664, 23 L.Ed. 1003 (1877); Green v. Van Buskirk, 72 U.S. 307, 18 L.Ed. 599 (1866), 74 U.S. 139, 19 L.Ed. 109 (1868) (New York is compelled to give full faith and credit to law of Illinois situs, which prefers New York attaching creditor over secured creditor who was not a party to Illinois attachment suit); In re Herold Radio & Electronics, 327 F.2d 564 (2d Cir.1964); Fred E. Cooper, Inc. v. Farr, 165 So.2d 605 (La.App.), writ ref'd, result correct, 246 La. 838, 167 So.2d 667 (1964); Craig v. Columbus Compress & Warehouse Co., 210 So.2d 645 (Miss. 1968) (whether warehouse receipts are negotiable is determined by the situs of the goods, not place of negotiation; court also notes result consistent with "center of gravity" rule); Marvin Safe Co. v. Norton, 48 N.J.L. 410, 7 A. 418 (1886) (situs rule carried to extreme of giving secured creditor more protection against bona fide purchaser under situs law than under law of creditor's state); Zendman v. Harry Winston, Inc., 305 N.Y. 180, 111 N.E.2d 871 (1953) (situs rule stated for determining whether factor could convey title to bona fide purchaser, but probably no conflict in laws); Torrance v. Third Nat'l Bank, 70 Hun 44, 23 N.Y.S. 1073 (S.Ct., Gen.Term, 1893) (conditional vendor loses to attaching creditor under situs law); W.H. Applewhite Co. v. Etheridge, 210 N.C. 433, 187 S.E. 588 (1936) (situs law applied although it defeats interest of forum creditor recorded at the forum); Cammell v. Sewell, 5 Hurl. & N. 728 (Exch.Ch.1860) (whether bona fide purchaser gets good title through unauthorized sale by ship's master); Restatement (Second), Conflict of Laws § 245; Vernon, *Recorded Chattel Security Interests in the Conflict of Laws*, 47 Iowa L. Rev. 346, 355 (1962); cf. Ford Motor Co. v. National Bond & Inv. Co., 294 Ill.App. 585, 14 N.E.2d 306 (1938) (secured creditor wins under situs law, but he could lose only by combining elements of laws of both situs and place of contracting); Clark Equip. Co. v. Poultry Packers, Inc., 254 Miss. 589, 181 So.2d 908 (1966) (whether conditional sale must be recorded to protect vendor against attaching creditor determined in vendor's favor by law of place of contracting, which was same as law of place where truck trailers were temporarily located when attached, but contrary to law of debtor's principal place of business where trailers based); Hornthall v. Burwell, 109 N.C. 10, 13 S.E. 721 (1891) (permits chattel mortgagee to recover against attaching creditor who had sold the goods, but assumes that situs court would reach same decision); DeLaney Furniture Co. v. Magnavox Co., 222 Tenn. 329, 435 S.W.2d 828 (1968) (whether receiver can recover preferential transfer); Cherry Creek Dodge, Inc. v. Carter, 733 P.2d 1024 (Wyo. 1987) (under 1–105(1), law of state where consumer purchased automobile applied to allow consumer to prevail over dealer who knew that automobile might be taken there for resale). But cf. Charles T. Dougherty Co. v. Krimke, 105 N.J.L. 470, 144 A. 617 (1929) (refuse to give owner more protection under situs law against person to whom factor pledged the goods than owner would receive under law of owner's state); Leflar, American Conflicts Law § 178, n.9 (3d ed. 1977) (result in *Krimke* partially explained by "misinterpretation of the facts of *Marvin Safe*", supra, this note). Contra, Forgan v. Bainbridge, 34 Ariz. 408, 274 P. 155 (1928) (refuses to apply law of situs where bona fide purchaser acquired automobile when that law would prefer purchaser over mortgagee); Edgerly v. Bush, 81 N.Y. 199 (1880) (refuses to apply situs law under which purchaser would prevail over mortgagee, all parties being forum citizens).

There has been resistance to application of situs law when that law has permitted a thief to deprive the owner of title and the owner has done nothing to subject the property to this risk. See Brown & Root, Inc. v. Ring Power Corp., 450 So.2d 1245 (Fla.App. 5th Dist.1984) (refuse to apply law of Louisiana situs that bona fide purchaser from a thief is entitled to reimbursement by the owner); cf. Kunstsammlungen Zu Weimar v. Elicofon, 678 F.2d 1150 (2d Cir.1982) (apply situs statute of limitations more favorable to owner than law of owner's country because the situs has an interest in discouraging transfers of stolen property); Winkworth v. Christie Manson & Woods Ltd., [1980] 1 All E.R. 1121 (Ch. Div. 1979) (apply situs law, but when that law is proved it may be found contrary to forum public policy or situs conflicts rules may refer to forum law); Cammell v. Sewell, supra this note.

As a sign of departure from a rigid situs rule, the issue of whether furnishing goods or services to a ship results in a maritime lien on the ship has been subjected to functional analysis, including appraisal of the reasonable expectations of the parties, rather than being automatically determined by the law of the place where the goods or services were delivered. See Ocean Ship Supply, Ltd. v. MV Leah, 729 F.2d 971 (4th Cir.1984) (under either lex loci or modern multi-factor approach, no lien for supplies after ship sold,

hypothetical case the secured creditor would lose. Almost as universally recognized as the situs rule was the rule that the situs would recognize rights that a secured creditor had perfected in another state where the property was formerly situated[312] if the property had been removed to

applying law of place where supplies delivered and seller incorporated); Gulf Trading & Transportation Co. v. M/V Tento, 694 F.2d 1191 (9th Cir.1982), cert. denied, 461 U.S. 929, 103 S.Ct. 2091, 77 L.Ed.2d 301 (1983) (vessel is subject to liens for expenses incurred by a sub-charterer, choosing United States law under a contacts approach although goods and services delivered in Egypt and Italy); Gulf Trading & Transportation Co. v. Vessel Hoegh Shield, 658 F.2d 363 (5th Cir.1981), cert. denied, 457 U.S. 1119, 102 S.Ct. 2932, 73 L.Ed.2d 1332 (1982) (apply law of United States, where fuel delivered, to impose lien and advance United States interest in protecting the United States supplier). For an example of the most dysfunctional approach possible, see Bankers Trust Int'l Ltd. v. Todd Shipyards Corp., [1980] 3 All E.R. 197, 3 W.L.R. 400 (Privy Council) (right to enforce a maritime lien is determined according to the law of the forum whose court was distributing the proceeds of the sale of the ship).

The law of a person's domicile has traditionally been applied to determine whether that person has rights in intangible property. In selecting the law that determines whether a person has a "right to publicity" that survives his or her death, recent cases have focused on various contacts deemed significant, including the celebrity's domicile at death. See, e.g., Groucho Marx Productions v. Day & Night Co., Inc., 689 F.2d 317 (2d Cir.1982) (law of place where celebrity lived, place of incorporation of the company to which the alleged right was assigned, and where the assignment was made); Factors Etc., Inc. v. Pro Arts, Inc., 652 F.2d 278 (2d Cir.1981), cert. denied, 456 U.S. 927, 102 S.Ct. 1973, 72 L.Ed.2d 442 (1982) (domicile of celebrity and place where alleged right assigned). For application of a governmental interest test to determine rights in intangible property, see Liew v. Official Receiver and Liquidator, 685 F.2d 1192 (9th Cir.1982) (validity of assignment of interest in stock as security for loan is determined by law of Singapore, where assignor and assignee resided, not by the law of the forum in which the companies that issued the stock are incorporated).

312. Forgan v. Bainbridge, 34 Ariz. 408, 274 P. 155 (1928); Merchants & Farmers State Bank v. Rosdail, 257 Iowa 1238, 131 N.W.2d 786 (1964), modified, 257 Iowa 1238, 136 N.W.2d 286 (1965); Scott Truck & Tractor Co., Inc. v. Daniels, 401 So.2d 590 (La.App. 3d Cir.1981), cert. denied, 409 So.2d 617 (1981); Brawner v. Elkhorn Prod. Credit Ass'n, 78 Nev. 483, 376 P.2d 426 (1962); Churchill Motors, Inc. v. A.C. Lohman, Inc., 16 A.D.2d 560, 229 N.Y.S.2d 570 (1962); J.A. Tobin Constr. Co. v. Grandview Bank, 424 P.2d 81 (Okl.1966); Bank of Atlanta v. Fretz, 148 Tex. 551, 226 S.W.2d 843 (1950) (Texas adopts "majority rule"); Re Union Acceptance Corp., 16 West. Weekly R. (N.S.) 283 (Alberta S.Ct.App.Div.1955). See Raphael, *Extra-territoriality of a Chattel Security Interest: A Plea for the Bona Fide Purchaser,* 28 Fordham L. Rev. 419, 420 (1959); Vernon, supra note 311, at 350. Cf. Wells v. City Nat'l Bank, 233 Ark. 868, 349 S.W.2d 668 (1961) (refuse to recognize mortgage recorded in another state when mortgage not refiled in forum within period other state would require for refiling of out-of-state mortgages); Hornthall v. Burwell, 109 N.C. 10, 13 S.E. 721 (1891) (assumes that situs of attachment proceedings would recognize prior mortgage recorded at forum); Hardware Mut. Cas. Co. v. Gall, 15 Ohio St.2d 261, 240 N.E.2d 502 (1968) (bona fide purchaser from thief who obtained a clean title certificate loses to owner from whom car had been stolen in another state); Hannah v. Pearlman & Selchen, [1954] 1 D.L.R. 282 (B.C.S.Ct.1953) (bona fide purchaser at forum prevails over conditional vendor who did not comply with conditional sales statute of jurisdiction where conditional sale made, "Chevrolet" not meeting requirement of that statute that "manufacturer's name" be "plainly attached" to goods). But cf. Fincher Motors, Inc. v. Northwestern Bank & Trust Co., 166 So.2d 717 (Fla.Dist.Ct.App.1964) (although interest of foreign mortgagee protected, forum "procedure" denies him remedy of replevin); Fred E. Cooper, Inc. v. Farr, 165 So.2d 605 (La.App.), writ ref'd, result correct 246 La. 838, 167 So.2d 667 (1964) (conditional seller loses to forum's materialmen) [but see Ford Motor Credit Co. v. Partee, 514 So.2d 640 (La.App.2d Cir.1987) (secured creditor prevails over Louisiana repairer when creditor did not know of or consent to removal of truck from Ohio)]; Universal Credit Co. v. Marks, 164 Md. 130, 163 A. 810 (1933) (garageman's lien prevails over conditional sales contract recorded out of state); Johnson v. Eastern Precision Resistor Corp., 19 Ohio Op.2d 150, 182 N.E.2d 59 (Ct.Common Pleas), aff'd , 182 N.E.2d 59, 19 Ohio Op.2d 150 (1961) (assignee of accounts receivable loses to creditor who garnishees at forum). But see Leary, *Horse and Buggy Lien Law and*

the new situs without the knowledge or consent of the creditor and if the creditor, after learning of the new location of the property, acted with reasonable dispatch to perfect the interest under the law of the new situs, typically by recording it there.[313]

These rules gave the secured creditor a substantial amount of protection. They shifted from the creditor the risk that the debtor would abscond with the goods to another state and there trick someone into parting with value for what that person believed was an interest in unencumbered goods. The argument most frequently advanced in favor of these creditor-protecting rules was that a state that did not recognize rights perfected elsewhere would quickly become a dumping ground for stolen property. Buyers of mobile goods, such as automobiles, would have no incentive to exercise care in determining whether there was an outstanding security interest in the goods.[314]

This argument has a certain amount of surface appeal. It might justify shifting from secured creditor to third person who has dealt with the goods the burden of proof on the issue of the good faith of the third person. It might justify charging a person, particularly a used car dealer, with whatever that person could learn by diligent inquiry to recording officials of a sister state if an automobile is offered for sale bearing the license plate of that sister state.[315] One might also prefer the first secured creditor over subsequent creditors who, like the first creditor, could be expected to make a thorough credit investigation before parting with value for a security interest in the goods.[316] But it was nothing

---

Migratory Automobiles, 96 U.Pa. L. Rev. 455, 457 (1948) (despite lip service to supposed majority rule, courts found ways to protect the bona fide purchaser). Contra, GFC Corp. v. Antrim, 2 Pa.D. & C.2d 377 (C.P.Ct., Luzerne County, 1955).

313. See Uniform Conditional Sales Act § 14, superseded by Uniform Commercial Code (must refile "within ten days after the seller has received notice of the filing district to which the goods have been removed"); In re Hoover, 447 F.2d 195 (5th Cir.1971) (security interest valid under law of place where sale made but not under Louisiana law, is invalid when vendor shipped goods into Louisiana); Brown v. Universal C.I.T. Credit Corp., 331 F.2d 246 (7th Cir.1964) (law of situs to which creditor knew truck to be removed determines whether recording necessary); Davis v. P.R. Sales Co., 304 F.2d 831 (2d Cir.1962) (situs to which equipment moved with consent of conditional vendor applies own law to prefer trustee in bankruptcy over creditor, but no indication that law of vendor's state would produce different result); Enterprise Optical Mfg. Co. v. Timmer, 71 F.2d 295 (6th Cir.1934) (law of situs to which creditor knew chattels to be removed determines whether recording necessary); J.A. Tobin Constr. Co. v. Grandview Bank, 424 P.2d 81 (Okl.1966) (decision in favor of secured creditor who did not record lien at situs based on finding he did not know that machine to be moved there); Restatement (Second), Conflict of Laws § 253, comment *b*; Davis, *Conditional Sales and Chattel Mortgages in the Conflict of Laws*, 13 Int'l & Comp.L.Q. 53 (1964) (reviewing English and United States cases); Raphael, supra note 308, at 420; Vernon, supra note 311, at 353–55; cf. Figuero v. Figuero, 303 So.2d 801 (La.App.1974) (Texas creditor's security interest not recognized when creditor did not use due diligence to determine that automobile was in Louisiana at time interest granted).

314. See Forgan v. Bainbridge, 34 Ariz. 408, 413–14, 274 P. 155, 157 (1928); Merchants & Farmers State Bank v. Rosdail, 257 Iowa 1238, 1245–46, 131 N.W.2d 786, 790 (1964), modified, 257 Iowa 1238, 136 N.W.2d 286 (1965); Commercial Credit Corp. v. Pottmeyer, 176 Ohio St. 1, 13, 197 N.E.2d 343, 351 (1964) (dissent); Bank of Atlanta v. Fretz, 148 Tex. 551, 560, 226 S.W.2d 843, 849 (1950).

315. See Leary, supra note 312, at 472, 483.

316. See Vernon, supra note 311, at 364–65.

short of madness to shift, as was frequently done, the risk of the debtor's misconduct from the secured creditor to a consumer who purchased an automobile in the consumer's home state bearing license plates of that state, when no lien was recorded in that state and there was no way that the consumer could, by reasonable inquiry, learn of the existing lien. Comparison of the opportunity to investigate the debtor's background and to distribute losses caused by fraudulent debtors would indicate that in this latter situation the bona fide consumer purchaser should have prevailed.[317] That the consumer did not prevail was the great weakness of the pre-Code rules. The great strength of those rules was that the creditor had to act with reasonable dispatch to protect third persons in a new state once the creditor knew that the goods had been removed to that state. What changes in this pattern has Article 9 wrought?

§ 8.32 The Secured Creditor and Third Persons under Article 9

The central choice-of-law issue between a secured creditor and a third person making competing claims to the same collateral is what law should be applied to determine whether the creditor's interest is "perfected" so that it "cannot be defeated in insolvency proceedings or in general by creditors"[318] and the effect of perfection or nonperfection. The Code choice-of-law rules on these matters are set forth in sections 9–301 through 9–307 of the 2000 Code. Which of these Code rules applies, depends, in part, upon the type of collateral in which a security interest is claimed.

There are three basic situations that require resort to Article 9 choice-of-law provisions. First, differences in Article 9 provisions from state to state may mean that a security interest is perfected under the law of one state, but not of another. Now that all states have enacted the 2000 Code, these differences result from a state's departing from the official version in its codification.[319]

The second kind of problem requiring resort to Article 9 choice-of-law rules is when steps have been taken in a state that would be sufficient to perfect a security interest, but it is contended that these steps should have been taken in some other state. Finally, the most common secured transaction choice-of-law problem occurs when the security interest is perfected by taking the proper steps in the correct state, but either the debtor or the collateral or both move to another state and the question arises whether the original perfection is lost.

§ 8.33 Uncertificated Securities: The 2000 Code

The practice of issuing shares of stock that are not embodied in a share certificate ("uncertificated") has grown rapidly. Article 8, dealing

---

317. See Leary, supra note 312, at 483; Raphael, supra note 312, at 426–28; Vernon, supra note 311, at 363.

318. U.C.C. § 9–301, official comment 1 (1972 Code).

319. See, e.g., 3 U.L.A. 157–58 (2002) ("variations from official text" of § 9–301 in 8 states).

with "Investment Securities", has been revised to deal with this phenomenon.

The 2000 version of article 9 and the 1994 revisions of article 8 alleviate problems created by the former references in those articles to the "whole law", which included the conflict-of-laws rules, of the state in which the issuer is organized to govern the rights and duties of the issuer (former 8–106) and the effect of perfection or non-perfection of a security interest in uncertificated securities (former 9–103(3)). These references to the "whole law" created the possibility of a "renvoi" problem,[320] the conflicts rules of two states pointing to one another in an endless circle. Section 9–305(a)(2) provides that the "local law," not the "whole law" of the issuer's jurisdiction, as defined in 8–110(d), "governs perfection, the effect of perfection or nonperfection, and the priority of a security interest in an uncertificated security." Section 8–110(a)(2) of the 1994 amendments states that the "local law," not the "whole law," of the issuer's jurisdiction, governs "the rights and duties of the issuer with respect to registration of transfer."

The lesson taught by these problems and their correction is that transition difficulties created by new U.C.C. enactments are aggravated by Code choice-of-law rules that select the whole law, rather than the local law, of the designated jurisdiction.

8.34 Choice of Law for Security Interests Under the 2000 Code

This section summarizes the major provisions of the 2000 Code. Section 9–301 states the general rules for determining what law "governs perfection, the effect of perfection or nonperfection, and the priority of a security interest in collateral."[321] Sections 9–302 through 9–306 provide different rules for specific kinds of collateral.

The general rule is that the local law of the debtor's location governs.[322] Section 9–307 determines where the debtor is located. Location depends on the type of debtor as follows:

Type of Debtor	Location
1. individual	principal residence [323]
2. organization not organized under state or federal law (i.e. NOT a corporation or limited partnership)	at place of business if only one place of business, otherwise at chief executive office [324]
3. registered organization organized under law of a State (e.g. a corporation or limited partnership)	State where organized [325]

---

320. See § 3.3.

321. 9–301(1).

322. Id.

323. 9–307(b)(1).

324. 9–307(b)(2), (3)(e), (3)(f).

325. 9–307(e), Official Comment 4.

Rules 1 and 2 do not apply if the debtor is not located in a jurisdiction "whose law generally requires information concerning the existence of a nonpossessory security interest to be made generally available in a filing, recording or registration system as a condition or result of the security interest's obtaining priority over the rights of a lien creditor with respect to the collateral."[326] If the debtor is not located in such a jurisdiction, it is located in the District of Columbia.[327] The three rules above refer to the most common classes of debtors. Section 9–307 provides special rules for registered organizations organized under federal law,[328] bank branches and agencies not organized under the law of a State or of the United States,[329] foreign bank branches and agencies,[330] and foreign air carriers.[331]

If the debtor moves, the security interest remains perfected for four months during which the secured creditor may perfect by filing at the new location.[332] If the debtor transfers the collateral to another person who is located in a state other than the state in which the debtor is located, the security interest remains perfected for one year during which the secured creditor may perfect by filing at the new location.[333] The difference between the four month and one year periods reflects the common sense notion that it is easier to keep track of the location of debtors than it is of collateral.

The location of the debtor does not govern with regard to a **possessory security interest** in collateral.[334] The local law of the location of the collateral governs.[335] The effect of perfection or nonperfection, but not perfection, is governed by the local law of the location of **negotiable instruments, goods, instruments, money, or tangible chattel paper**.[336] Thus if a security interest in equipment located in Pennsylvania is perfected by filing at the debtor's location in Illinois, the law of Pennsylvania determines the priority between an execution lien and the

---

326. 9–307(c).

327. Id.

328. 9–307(f) (in District of Columbia unless U.S. law designates some other state, or organization designates some other state under authorization of U.S. law).

329. Id. (same).

330. 9–307(i) (in state in which licensed if all branches and agencies of the bank are licensed in only one state).

331. 9–307(j) ("at the designated office of the agent upon which service of process may be made on behalf of the carrier").

332. 9–316(a)(2).

333. 9–316(a)(3); 9–102(a)(28)(A) (defining as "debtor" "a person having an interest, other than a security interest or other lien, in the collateral, whether or not the person is an obligor").

334. 9–313 permits perfection by possession of a security interest in negotiable instruments, documents, goods, instruments, money, tangible chattel paper, and certificated securities.

335. 9–301(2).

336. 9–301(3).

security interest.[337] Because all states have enacted the 2000 version of article 9, this distinction between perfection and the effect of perfection is not likely to harm secured creditors if the collateral is located within the United States. The secured creditor is subject to the risk that the collateral will be moved to a foreign jurisdiction that either does not give effect to security interests or requires filing there.[338]

The local law of the jurisdiction where the collateral is located also governs perfection of a security interest by filing a **fixture filing**[339] or in timber to be cut.[340] The local law of the jurisdiction in which a wellhead or minehead is located "governs perfection, the effect of perfection or nonperfection, and the priority of a security interest in **as-extracted collateral**."[341]

If **goods are covered by** a **certificate of title**, "[t]he local law of the jurisdiction under whose certificate of title the goods are covered governs perfection, the effect of perfection or nonperfection, and the priority of a security interest in goods covered by a certificate of title from the time the goods become covered by the certificate of title until the goods ceased to be covered by the certificate of title."[342] "Goods become covered by a certificate of title when a valid application for the certificate of title and the applicable fee are delivered to the appropriate authority. Goods cease to be covered by a certificate of title at the earlier of the time the certificate of title ceases to be effective under the law of the issuing jurisdiction or the time the goods become covered subsequently by a certificate of title issued by another jurisdiction."[343] The fact that a new title certificate has been issue in another state does not mean, however, that the security interest perfected by the first title certificate is unperfected. Except against a purchaser for value, the security interest remains perfected until the perfection would have lapsed under the law of the first state.[344] Against a purchaser for value, the secured creditor has four months to perfect in the new state, but if the four months lapse the security interest is "deemed never to have been perfected as against" the purchaser.[345] Moreover, under 9–337(1), a "buyer of the goods, other than a person in the business of selling goods of that kind, takes free of the security interest if the buyer gives value and receives delivery of the goods after issuance [of a clean certificate by the new state] and without knowledge of the security interest." Under 9–337(2) the same protection is given to a secured creditor that records

---

337. 9–301, Official Comment 7.

338. See Bull, *Operation of the New Article 9 Choice of Law Regime in an International Context*, 78 Texas. L. Rev. 680, 710–15 (2000).

339. 9–301(3)(A).

340. 9–301(3)(B).

341. 9–301(4).

342. 9–303(c).

343. 9–303(b).

344. 9–316(d).

345. 9–316(e).

its interest on the new certificate without knowledge of the prior security interest.

§ 8.35 The Need for Federalization

It is desirable to stop tying perfection to nineteenth century technology—pieces of paper in filing cabinets—and have national, centralized, computerized records[346] in lieu of, or at least in addition to, individual state records.

The need for centralized national records is, however, only a symptom of a much more serious malady affecting Article 9 and the rest of the "Uniform" Commercial Code. It is easy to sit on the sidelines and take pot shots at the drafting efforts of the hardworking and intelligent experts who have revised Article 9. But it is probably not possible to draft a Code with the specificity and explicitness demanded of Article 9 and have a product with a life expectancy of more than a few years. Commercial transactions are too complex and techniques and technology change at amazing speed. New problems arise faster than we can solve old ones. If we must have a Code that needs redrafting every few years, at least let us have a single national code that will be in effect in all states and the amendments to which will take effect uniformly. In 1986, for example, there were four versions of the conflicts provisions for Article 9 in effect in some states.[347] And these were just conflicts about what to do about conflicts. It is past time to brush off the old idea of a commercial code enacted by federal legislation. Another possibility is to stop chasing the phantom of absolute certainty, codify a few central principles, and trust to the good sense of lawyers and judges to fill in the details.

§ 8.36 International Conventions and Model Laws Affecting Security Interests

There has been much recent activity intended to facilitate security interests in international commercial transactions. On 12 December 2001 a resolution of the United Nations General Assembly adopted the Convention on the Assignment of Receivables in International Trade.[348] The Convention sets out the rights and duties of assignors, assignees and debtors. Article 4 contains "exclusions and other limitations." The Convention does not apply, for example, to assignments made "to an individual for his or her personal, family or household purposes"[349] or to "receivables arising under or from . . . bank deposits, a letter of credit or

---

346. See Coogan, *Article 9–An Agenda for the Next Decade*, 87 Yale L. J. 1012, 1051–52 (1978); Comment, 18 Wayne L. Rev. 737, 769 (1972).

347. Adoptions as of January 1, 1986: 1962 Code, 7 states; 1972 Code without 1977 amendments to Article 8, to section 9–103, and to certain other sections in Articles 9, 1, and 5, 30 states; 1972 Code with 1977 Amendments, 12 states; Uniform Motor Vehicle Certificate of Title and Anti-theft Act § 20, 11 states, but the Connecticut section incorporated 9–103 by reference—Conn. G.S.Ann. §§ 14–185, 42a–9–103a.

348. G.A. Res. 56/81, UN GAOR, 56th Sess., Agenda Item 161.

349. Id. art. 4(1)(a).

independent guarantee."[350] Article 22 provides that the law where the assignor is located governs the priority of the right of an assignee in the assigned receivable over the rights of competing claimants. Under Article 23 a forum may refuse to apply the law of the assignor's State, as provided in Article 22, only if the law is "manifestly contrary to the public policy of the forum State."[351] Article 42 requires signatory countries to declare that they are bound by one of the rules set out in the Convention for determining the priority between assignees of the same receivable from the same assignor and between the assignee and the insolvency administrator or creditors of the assignor. Unfortunately this permits a choice between quite different priority rules. The best choice, and one that ideally should have been required of all signatories, is to base priority on the order of registration in an international register that can be searched by the identity of the assignor.[352] Other priority choices given to signatories include "the order of conclusion of the respective contracts of assignment,"[353] and "the order in which notification of the respective assignments is received by the debtor."[354] The Convention enters into force after ratification by five nations.[355]

The Inter–American Conference on Private International Law, at its meeting in Washington D.C. in February 2002, approved the Model Inter–American Law on Secured Transactions.[356] The Model Law regulates security interests in movable property. The Law requires establishment of a uniform registration system. A creditor can perfect a security interest either by registration or by taking possession or control of the collateral.

The International Institute for the Unification of Private Law (UNIDROIT), with headquarters in Rome, in 2001 promulgated a Convention on International Interests in Mobile Equipment.[357] The Convention sets out rules for creating an interest in mobile equipment and establishes an International Registry for noting interests in the equipment.

The Hague Convention of 5 July 2006 on the Law Applicable to Certain Rights in Respect of Securities Held with an Intermediary[358] is designed to provide legal certainty and predictability to financial mar-

---

350. Id. art. 4(2)(f), (g).

351. Id. Art. 23(1).

352. Id. Art. 42 1(a), Annex Sections I, II.

353. Id. Annex Section III.

354. Id. Annex Section IV.

355. Id. art. 45. On 23 March 2006 only Liberia had ratified the Convention.

356. Available at http://www.oas.org. by choosing in turn Documents, Treaties–Conventions, Sixth Inter–American Specialized Conference on Private International Law, Final Act.

357. http://www.unidroit.org/english/conventions/c-main.htm.

See also id. Protocol to the Convention on Matters Specific to Aircraft Equipment (Cape Town 2001); Luxembourg Protocol to the Convention on International Interests in Mobile Equipment on Matters Specific to Railway Rolling Stock (Luxembourg 2007).

358. http://www.hcch.net/index_en.php?act=conventions.text&cid=72.

kets with respect to the law governing securities held in clearing and settlement systems and other intermediaries, as well as to reduce risk and costs associated with transactions across borders. Under article 19(2), the Convention will go into force after the third ratification. As of October 1, 2009, the Convention has been ratified by Switzerland and signed but not ratified by the United States and Mauritius.

Chapter 9

CONSTITUTIONAL LIMITATIONS ON CHOICE OF LAW

§ 9.1 Introduction

In analyzing conflicts problems, it is important to have in mind the limits that the United States Constitution imposes on choice of law. Which choices are forbidden and which are required by the Constitution?

The materials in this chapter focus, for the most part, on the Due Process Clause of the Fourteenth Amendment[1] and on the Full Faith and Credit Clause of Article IV.[2] The reason for this emphasis is that it mirrors that of the United States Supreme Court opinions dealing with constitutional limitations on choice of law. This historical emphasis on full faith and credit and especially on due process is understandable, given the territorially-oriented choice-of-law rules, which until the 1960's prevailed in every state, and given the "vested rights" theory that formed the philosophical foundation for the territorial rules. Under this theory, rights "vested" at a particular moment under the law of the state in which a key event occurred, such as the place of injury in torts. If this theory is accepted, any tampering with those vested rights by applying the law of some state other than that of the locus of the key event selected by the standard choice-of-law rule would raise serious due process and perhaps full faith and credit problems.

As the discussion that follows will indicate, for a time the Supreme Court did attempt to translate rigid territorial choice-of-law dogmas into equally rigid constitutional dogmas. The Court's retreat from these attempts to impose strict constitutional limitations on choice of law has eased the way for the "functional" and "state-interest," or, as I would prefer to call them, "consequences based," choice-of-law approaches that other chapters examine.

The purpose here is to appraise the current scope of due process and full faith and credit limitations on choice of law and to inquire into the relevance of these and other constitutional provisions, particularly the Equal Protection Clause of the Fourteenth Amendment,[3] to a method of

---

1. U.S. Const. Amend. 14, § 1: "No State shall ... deprive any person of life, liberty, or property, without due process of law...."

2. U.S. Const. Art. IV, § 1: "Full Faith and Credit shall be given in each State to the public Acts, Records and judicial Proceedings of every other State. And the Congress may by general Laws prescribe the Manner in which such Acts, Records and Proceedings shall be proved, and the effect thereof."

3. U.S. Const. Amend. 14, § 1: "No State shall ... deny to any person within its jurisdiction the equal protection of the laws."

654

choice-of-law analysis that focuses on the policies underlying the domestic laws in putative conflict.

§ 9.2   Due Process Limitations on a State's Choice of Law

§ 9.2A   General Considerations

New York Life Insurance Company v. Dodge[4] represents an early attempt by the Supreme Court to control a state's choice of law by means of the Due Process Clause. Mr. Dodge, a resident of Missouri, made application in Missouri to the New York Life Insurance Company for a policy insuring his life. The insurance company was incorporated in New York where its main office was located. The company approved Mr. Dodge's application and delivered to him in Missouri a policy naming his wife as beneficiary. The policy contained the following provisions regarding the ability of the insured to obtain loans from the insurance company:

> Cash loans can be obtained by the insured on the sole security of this policy on demand at any time after this policy has been in force two full years.... Application for any loan must be made ... to the Home Office ... and the loan will be subject to the terms of the company's loan agreement.... Any indebtedness to the company ... will be deducted in any settlement of this policy....[5]

Mr. Dodge took advantage of these provisions and, after the policy had been in force for two years, he borrowed money annually from the insurance company. The procedure for making these loans was as follows. Mr. Dodge filled out an application for a loan and signed a loan agreement in Missouri. The insurance company's Missouri office forwarded the loan application and agreement, together with a pledge of the policy, to the main office in New York. The company then drew a check for the proceeds on a New York bank and mailed the check to Mr. Dodge in Missouri. The loan agreement provided that "principal and interest are payable at said Home Office, and that this contract is made under and pursuant to the laws of the State of New York, the place of said contract being said Home Office of said Company."

After several years of this borrowing, Mr. Dodge missed paying the premium on the insurance policy. The insurance company thereupon, as permitted by New York law, applied the cash surrender value of the policy to payment of Mr. Dodge's indebtedness. This exhausted the cash surrender value of the policy and the insurance was canceled. Following this cancellation, Mr. Dodge died.

Mrs. Dodge sued the insurance company in a Missouri court claiming the full amount of the policy less the unpaid loans and premiums. Her theory was that under Missouri law, as it existed at the time that the policy had been issued, although not when the loan in question was

---

4.   246 U.S. 357, 38 S.Ct. 337, 62 L.Ed. 772 (1918).

5.   Id. at 368–69, 38 S.Ct. at 338–339, 62 L.Ed. at 779–780.

made,[6] the insurance company was not permitted to subtract, as it had, the full amount of Mr. Dodge's indebtedness from the cash surrender value of the policy. A Missouri statute,[7] designed to avoid forfeiture of insurance for nonpayment of premiums, required that after payment of three annual premiums, three quarters of the net value of the policy, minus indebtedness to the company on account only of past premium payments, be used to purchase insurance for the face amount of the policy. If the Missouri statute applied to Mr. Dodge's policy, the insurance would still have been in force at Dodge's death. Only a portion of Mr. Dodge's debt to the company had been applicable to past premiums.

The Missouri courts decided that the Missouri statute did apply and gave judgment for Mrs. Dodge. The Supreme Court of the United States, in a five-to-four decision, reversed the Missouri courts. Justice McReynolds, writing for the majority, reasoned as follows. True, the policy itself was a "Missouri contract" subject to Missouri law. However, the policy provision that "cash loans can be obtained by the insured" imposed no obligation upon the company to make such a loan. Therefore, the loan agreement was a completely separate transaction, and the loan agreement, unlike the policy, was "made" in New York. Missouri could not have prevented Mr. Dodge from entering into the loan contract out of the state of Missouri without violating Mr. Dodge's constitutional freedom of contract. To apply the Missouri statute to the loan agreement "made" in New York,

> transcends the power of the state. To hold otherwise would permit destruction of the right—often of great value—freely to borrow money upon a policy from the issuing company at its home office, and would, moreover, sanction the impairment of that liberty of contract guaranteed to all by the Fourteenth Amendment.[8]

Missouri, then, was forbidden to substitute its own law for that of "the place of making" of the loan agreement. This was so despite the fact that the insured was a Missouri resident would significantly advance

---

6. In 1903, three years after the policy was issued and three years before the loan in question was made, the Missouri law was changed, affecting policies "hereafter issued". This change brought it about that under Missouri law, as under New York law, the insurer could deduct all indebtedness from the cash surrender value of the policy before computing the period of paid-up insurance, not just indebtedness for premiums as under the prior Missouri law. 246 U.S. at 367, n. 1, 38 S.Ct. at 338, n. 1, 62 L.Ed. at 779, n. 1.

This change in Missouri law, making it the same as New York law, might have been utilized by a Missouri court to resolve any conflict between relevant Missouri and New York "interests" in favor of that of New York. Missouri, however, would still retain a reasonable interest in giving Mrs. Dodge the same protection under Missouri law that Missouri residents similarly situated (that is, holding life insurance policies issued before 1903) received under the Missouri insurance law.

7. Laws of Mo.1899, § 11 at 247.

8. *Dodge*, 246 U.S. at 377, 38 S.Ct. at 341, 62 L.Ed. at 783. Cf. Bigelow v. Virginia, 421 U.S. 809, 95 S.Ct. 2222, 44 L.Ed.2d 600 (1975) (violation of First Amendment for Virginia to punish advertisement in Virginia of abortion services available in New York and legal in New York—dictum that Virginia could not punish its own citizens for obtaining the services in New York); § 7.6 for discussion of regulating the interest charged to residents by out-of-state lenders and whether this regulation violates due process or the Commerce Clause (U.S. Const. Art. I, § 8, cl. 3).

the purpose underlying the Missouri cash-surrender-value statute. More-over, Missouri's reasonable interest in applying its own law could come as no surprise to the insurer. Mr. Dodge was a citizen of Missouri during the entire time that he had dealings with the insurance company. In the course of these dealings he never set foot outside of Missouri.

Mutual Life Insurance Company v. Liebing[9] demonstrated the fantastic results that would obtain if due process were made to turn upon the technical place of making of a contract. In the *Liebing* case, the facts paralleled those in *Dodge* with one important difference. In *Liebing* the policy read: "the company will ... loan amounts within the limits of the cash surrender value,"[10] whereas in *Dodge* the provision was that "cash loans can be obtained." The Supreme Court seized upon this difference in wording to make the result in *Liebing* opposite that in *Dodge*. In *Liebing*, Missouri was allowed to apply its own statute to regulate the terms of the loan agreement. Justice Holmes explained:

> The policy now sued upon contained a positive promise to make the loan if asked, whereas, in the one last mentioned [the one in *Dodge*] it might be held that some discretion was reserved to the company.... On this distinction the Missouri court seems to have held that as soon as the application [for the loan] was delivered to a representative of the company in Missouri the offer in the policy was accepted and the new contract complete, and therefore subject to Missouri law.... In whichever way regarded the facts lead to the same conclusion, and although the circumstances may present some temptation to seek a different one by ingenuity, the Constitution and the first principles of legal thinking allow the law of the place where a contract is made to determine the validity and the consequences of the act.[11]

Could it really be then that, in a case like *Dodge*, a state was prevented from applying its own law to protect its own citizens just because the insurance company had so arranged the loan transaction that the last event necessary to complete the loan contract had taken

---

9. 259 U.S. 209, 42 S.Ct. 467, 66 L.Ed. 900 (1922).

10. Id. at 214, 42 S.Ct. at 468, 66 L.Ed. at 907.

11. Id. at 213, 42 S.Ct. at 468, 66 L.Ed. at 907. For the suggestion that Holmes did not intend to endorse the "place of making" as a choice-of-law rule of constitutional dignity, see Freund, *Chief Justice Stone and the Conflict of Laws*, 59 Harv. L. Rev. 1210, 1234–35 (1946): "The climactic statement ... becomes somewhat anticlimactic when stress is put on 'allow' and when it is observed that the action of the state court was sustained." Holmes, however, stood with the majority in *Dodge*.

Alaska Packers Assoc. v. Industrial Accident Comm'n, 294 U.S. 532, 55 S.Ct. 518, 79 L.Ed. 1044 (1935), upheld an award of California workers' compensation to a Mexican alien injured in Alaska in the course of employment. The employment contract provided that the worker elected to be bound by the Alaska workers' compensation act and that act recited that it was the exclusive remedy for covered workers. The Court rejected the employer's contention that application of the California act violated both due process and full faith and credit. In dismissing the due process objection, the Court did not rely solely on the fact that the employment contract was made in California. The contract required the worker to return to California to be paid. California therefore might wish to guard against the possibility that he would become a public charge in California. Id. at 542, 55 S.Ct. at 521, 79 L.Ed. at 1049.

place elsewhere? If a state that had contacts with the parties and with the transaction as relevant to the purposes underlying its own law as Missouri had in *Dodge* could be prevented by the Due Process Clause from applying that law in adjudicating a controversy, perhaps the way was open for a single choice-of-law rule in each substantive area— contracts, torts, property, all—to be raised to constitutional dignity.

Nothing of the sort has come to pass because the Supreme Court has retreated from the position that it took in the *Dodge* case. Although that case has not been expressly overruled, *Dodge* cannot be reconciled with later decisions including *Allstate Insurance Company v. Hague*,[12] the case that set current standards for constitutional limits on choice of law.

Hoopeston Canning Company v. Cullen[13] concerned the power of New York to regulate out-of-state reciprocal insurance companies that wished to issue contracts affecting New York risks. All contracts of insurance were signed in Illinois and losses were paid by checks mailed from that state. Nevertheless, it was decided that New York might, among other forms of regulation, validly require that out-of-state recip- rocals insuring New York risks adopt prescribed forms of accounting and provide for the election of a management committee at an annual subscribers' meeting.

Although the holding in *Hoopeston Canning* can be explained in terms of the very broad powers that a state has for imposing conditions on foreign corporations that wish to do business within the state, the following language in the opinion indicates a view of due process quite different from that in *Dodge*:

> In determining the power of a state to apply its own regulatory laws to insurance business activities, the question in earlier cases became involved by conceptualistic discussion of theories of the place of contracting or of performance. More recently it has been recog- nized that a state may have substantial interests in the business of insurance of its people or property regardless of these isolated factors. This interest may be measured by highly realistic consider- ations such as the protection of the citizen insured or the protection of the state from the incidents of loss.[14]

Watson v. Employers Liability Assurance Corporation[15] also indicates an attitude quite different from that in *Dodge*. A home permanent kit injured the plaintiff, a Louisiana citizen, in Louisiana. An insurance company that was not incorporated or headquartered in Louisiana insured the manufacturer of the home permanent against product liabili- ty. The insurance policy was negotiated and delivered to the manufactur-

---

12.   449 U.S. 302, 101 S.Ct. 633, 66 L.Ed.2d 521 (1981), discussed infra text accompany- ing notes 23–43.

13.   318 U.S. 313, 63 S.Ct. 602, 87 L.Ed. 777 (1943).

14.   Id. at 316, 63 S.Ct. at 604, 87 L.Ed. at 781. Accord, State Farm Mut. Auto. Ins. Co. v. Duel, 324 U.S. 154, 65 S.Ct. 573, 89 L.Ed. 812 (1945) (upholding the Wisconsin's right to deny a license to do business to a foreign insurance company that refused to comply with Wisconsin requirements for the computation of unearned premium reserve and the form of the annual statement).

15.   348 U.S. 66, 75 S.Ct. 166, 99 L.Ed. 74 (1954).

er out of Louisiana. The policy contained a provision that suit could not be brought against the insurance company until the liability of the manufacturer had first been determined. This provision negating direct suit against the insurance company was valid in the jurisdictions where the policy was negotiated and delivered. Nevertheless, the Supreme Court held that Louisiana might permit its injured citizen to sue the insurance company directly.

The result in *Watson* might be reconciled with *Dodge* by pointing out that the insurance company had consented to direct suit in order to get a certificate to do business in Louisiana.[16] Furthermore, here suit in violation of the policy provisions was not being brought by one so closely identified with the insured as was Mrs. Dodge. In meeting the due process objection, the opinion focused on neither of these distinctions but said simply: "What has been said is enough to show Louisiana's legitimate interest in safeguarding the rights of persons injured there. In view of that interest, the direct action provisions here challenged do not violate due process."[17]

Pacific Employers Insurance Company v. Industrial Accident Commission[18] is another case that one would not expect to find in the same legal universe with *Dodge*. The Massachusetts workers' compensation act covered a Massachusetts employee. The Massachusetts act permitted an employee, by giving written notice to his or her employer, to elect to retain common-law tort rights against the employer in case of injury. If this election was not made, the employee lost the common-law rights and received in their stead workers' compensation coverage. Such coverage was the exclusive remedy for all injuries received by the employee in the course of employment whether within or without Massachusetts. The employee did not elect to retain his common-law rights. Subsequently, the employee was injured while on temporary duty for his employer in California. California was permitted to give the employee compensation under the California workers' compensation act in defiance of the exclusive remedy provisions of the Massachusetts statute. Since the Massachusetts act was elective, the analogy to the out-of-state contract in *Dodge* is apparent. True, the constitutional attack in *Pacific Employers* was based on the Full Faith and Credit Clause rather than on the Due Process Clause, but there is no reason to believe that the Due Process Clause would have prevailed where the requirement of full faith and credit did not.[19]

---

16. Justice Frankfurter rested his concurrence on this ground. Id. at 74, 75 S.Ct. at 171, 99 L.Ed. at 83. See also National Mut. Bldg. & Loan Ass'n v. Brahan, 193 U.S. 635, 24 S.Ct. 532, 48 L.Ed. 823 (1904), where the Court permitted a Mississippi court to apply Mississippi usury law to a loan made with a New York loan company, partly on the ground of the company's having qualified to do business in Mississippi.

17. *Watson*, 348 U.S. at 73, 75 S.Ct. at 170, 99 L.Ed. at 82.

For cases applying the forum's direct action statute even though the injury was in another state, see § 6.14, note 122

18. 306 U.S. 493, 59 S.Ct. 629, 83 L.Ed. 940 (1939).

19. See § 9.3A, text accompanying notes 215–218, stating that the Full Faith and Credit Clause sometimes invalidates a choice of law than the Due Process Clause would permit.

Another indication of a departure from the *Dodge* view of due process appears in *Richards v. United States*,[20] holding that the wording of the Federal Tort Claims Act, "under circumstances where the United States, if a private person, would be liable to the claimant in accordance with the law of the place where the act or omission occurred,"[21] refers to the whole law of that place, including its conflict of laws rules. The Court remarked:

> Where more than one State has sufficiently substantial contact with the activity in question, the forum State, by analysis of the interests possessed by the States involved, could constitutionally apply to the decision of the case the law of one or another state having such an interest in the multistate activity.[22]

Allstate Insurance Company v. Hague[23] should dispel any lingering arguments that rigid territorial concepts such as place of contracting determine constitutional limitations on choice of law. Mr. Hague lived in Wisconsin, commuted to work in Minnesota, and was killed in Wisconsin when an uninsured motorist struck the motorcycle on which he was taking a pleasure ride. The operator of the motorcycle also was uninsured. Mr. Hague owned three automobiles and his insurance on each vehicle provided $15,000 compensation for losses caused by uninsured motorists. Mr. Hague paid three premiums for this coverage. Each of his policies had an "other insurance" clause that made the $15,000 uninsured motorist coverage available only to the extent that recovery could not be had under "other similar insurance available" to Mr. Hague.[24]

After the accident, Mr. Hague's widow moved to Minnesota, was appointed personal representative of her husband's estate, and then sued Allstate to recover under the uninsured motorist provisions of the policies. The issue was whether the "other insurance" clause prevented her from recovering more than $15,000 or whether the three coverages could be "stacked" to produce a recovery of $45,000.

The Supreme Court of the United States held that neither the Due Process nor Full Faith and Credit clauses prevented the Minnesota courts from applying Minnesota law to produce the higher recovery. The Court assumed, erroneously, that it made a difference whether it applied Minnesota or Wisconsin law and that under Wisconsin law, plaintiff could recover only $15,000. In fact, it made no difference. Under Minne-

---

20. 369 U.S. 1, 82 S.Ct. 585, 7 L.Ed.2d 492 (1962).

21. 28 U.S.C.A. § 1346(b).

22. *Richards*, 369 U.S. at 15, 82 S.Ct. at 594, 7 L.Ed.2d at 501. See also, e.g., Ingersoll v. Klein, 46 Ill.2d 42, 262 N.E.2d 593 (1970) (no violation of due process or full faith and credit to apply forum law to an out-of-state occurrence when the forum has a substantial relationship to the activity); Fox v. Morrison Motor Freight, Inc., 25 Ohio St.2d 193, 267 N.E.2d 405, cert. denied, 403 U.S. 931, 91 S.Ct. 2254, 29 L.Ed.2d 710 (1971) (constitutional to apply Ohio wrongful death act to fatal injury in Illinois when trip on which trucks collided began and would have ended in Ohio).

23. 449 U.S. 302, 101 S.Ct. 633, 66 L.Ed.2d 521 (1981).

24. I am grateful to Professor Andreas Lowenfeld, New York University School of Law, for providing me with a copy of the policy. Professor Lowenfeld argued for the insured before the United States Supreme Court and was counsel on the brief.

sota law, the "other insurance" clause would not have prevented stacking because it was invalid if so applied.[25] Moreover, the clause was ambiguous concerning whether it applied to "other insurance" issued by the same insurer to the same insured. Under Wisconsin law, this ambiguity would be construed against the insurer.[26]

To discuss *Hague*, however, we must join in the Court's error and assume that whether Minnesota or Wisconsin law is applied makes a difference in the result. The three key assumptions are: (1) under Minnesota law the "other insurance" clause does not prevent stacking because as so applied, it is invalid (correct);[27] (2) under Wisconsin law, on the facts of *Hague*, the clause would be construed to prevent stacking (nonsense),[28] and; (3) if so construed, would be valid (probably correct).[29]

The standard that both the plurality and the three dissenters[30] agreed should determine whether the Due Process Clause or the Full Faith and Credit Clause prevented application of Minnesota law was:

---

25. See Van Tassel v. Horace Mann Ins. Co., 296 Minn. 181, 207 N.W.2d 348 (1973).

26. Cases holding that an "other insurance" clause identical to the one in *Hague* did not refer with sufficient specificity to uninsured motorist coverage issued by the same insurer on the insured's other cars are: Safeco Ins. Co. of Am. v. Robey, 399 F.2d 330 (8th Cir.1968); Woolston v. State Farm Mut. Ins. Co., 306 F.Supp. 738 (W.D.Ark.1969); Glidden v. Farmers Auto Ins. Ass'n, 57 Ill.2d 330, 312 N.E.2d 247 (1974); United Services Auto Ass'n v. Dokter, 86 Nev. 917, 478 P.2d 583 (1970). Contra Sammons v. Nationwide Mut. Ins. Co., 267 A.2d 608 (Del.Super.1970) (trial court).

Wisconsin construes ambiguities in insurance policies against the insurer. Ehlers v. Colonial Penn Ins. Co., 81 Wis.2d 64, 259 N.W.2d 718 (1977). For a strong indication that Wisconsin would follow the cases cited supra, finding the "other insurance" clause ambiguous in the context of *Hague*, see Rosar v. General Ins. Co. of Am., 41 Wis.2d 95, 163 N.W.2d 129 (1968), in which the court refused to allow stacking of liability coverage but distinguished medical payments for which "recovery is completely independent of liability on the part of the insured." Id. at 101–02, 163 N.W.2d at 132.

27. See Van Tassel v. Horace Mann Ins. Co., 296 Minn. 181, 207 N.W.2d 348 (1973).

28. See supra note 26 and cases cited therein.

29. Wisconsin construed an earlier version of its statute requiring minimum uninsured motorist coverage to permit the parties to contract against stacking. Nelson v. Employers Mut. Cas. Co., 63 Wis.2d 558, 217 N.W.2d 670 (1974). This statute had been amended before the accident in *Hague*. Id. at 562 n.1, 217 N.W.2d at 672 n.1. The Minnesota Supreme Court, in deciding *Hague*, refused to find that the Wisconsin Supreme Court would construe the rather inconclusive changes in the wording of the Wisconsin statute as changing Wisconsin law. Hague v. Allstate Ins. Co., 289 N.W.2d 43, 48 (Minn.1978), aff'd, 449 U.S. 302, 101 S.Ct. 633, 66 L.Ed.2d 521 (1981). After the accident, the Wisconsin statute was amended again so that it unambiguously invalidated "other insurance" clauses for uninsured motorist coverage. See Landvatter v. Globe Sec. Ins. Co., 100 Wis.2d 21, 300 N.W.2d 875 (1980).

For a suggestion that this change in Wisconsin law to accord with Minnesota law would have caused even a Wisconsin court to apply Minnesota law in *Hague*, see Weinberg, *Conflicts Cases and the Problem of Relevant Time: A Response to the Hague Symposium*, 10 Hofstra L. Rev. 1023, 1042 (1982).

Ironically, Minnesota now forbids stacking of uninsured motorist coverage. Minn.Stat. Ann. § 65B.49(3a)(6). See Stenzel v. State Farm Mut. Auto. Ins. Co., 379 N.W.2d 674 (Minn.App.1986), rev. denied March 25, 1986 (refuse to apply prior Minnesota stacking requirement to South Dakota employee commuting to work in Minnesota when accident occurred before effective date of statute forbidding stacking).

30. Justice Brennan wrote the plurality opinion joined by Justices White, Marshall, and Blackmun. Justice Stevens concurred in the judgment. Justice Powell wrote a dissent joined by Chief Justice Burger and Justice Rehnquist. Justice Stewart took no part.

application of Minnesota law was constitutional if "Minnesota had a significant aggregation of contacts with the parties and the occurrence, creating state interests, such that application of its law was neither arbitrary nor fundamentally unfair."[31] The plurality found the necessary contacts in Mr. Hague's commuting to work in Minnesota for fifteen years,[32] Allstate's extensive business contacts in Minnesota,[33] and Mrs. Hague's subsequent move to Minnesota.[34]

It is apparent that the plurality was not using the term "state interests" in the sense of a policy or policies underlying a state's law.[35] Mr. Hague's commuting and Allstate's business contacts did not implicate any policy underlying the Minnesota statute. Mrs. Hague's subsequent move gave Minnesota an "interest" in giving her additional compensation because, after she became a Minnesota resident, the amount of her recovery would have social consequences in Minnesota. But if it were not for the prior commuting and business contacts, even the plurality in *Hague* probably would have thought it so outrageous as to be unconstitutional for Minnesota to assert this late—acquired interest in compensation.[36]

---

31. *Hague*, 449 U.S. at 320, 101 S.Ct. at 644, 66 L.Ed.2d at 535 (Brennan, J.); 449 U.S. at 332, 101 S.Ct. at 650, 66 L.Ed.2d at 543 (Powell, J., dissenting) (dissent's disagreement is not over the standard articulated by the plurality, but concerns its application to the facts). Justice Stevens concurred in the judgment, but would apply a different constitutional standard to full faith and credit than he would apply to due process. 449 U.S. at 322–24, 101 S.Ct. at 645–46, 66 L.Ed.2d at 536–38. (Stevens, J., concurring).

32. Id. at 313–17, 101 S.Ct. at 640–42, 66 L.Ed.2d at 531–33.

33. Id. at 317–18, 101 S.Ct. at 642–43, 66 L.Ed.2d at 533–34.

34. Id. at 318–19, 101 S.Ct. at 643–44, 66 L.Ed.2d at 534–35.

35. This is the sense in which "interest" is used in the "interest analysis" approach to choice of law. For a description of this method, see § 6.2. The *Hague* dissenters do give "interest" the same meaning as in "interest analysis." See 449 U.S. at 334–35, 101 S.Ct. at 651, 66 L.Ed.2d at 544 (Powell, J., dissenting).

For analyses demonstrating the absence of relevant Minnesota policies in *Hague*, see Brilmayer, *Legitimate Interests in Multistate Problems: As Between State and Federal Law*, 79 Mich. L. Rev. 1315, 1342–46 (1981); Shreve, *In Search of a Choice-of-Law Reviewing Standard—Reflections on Allstate Insurance Co. v. Hague*, 66 Minn. L. Rev. 327, 352–53 (1982); Note, 81 Cal. L. Rev. 1134, 1142 (1981). But see L. McDougal, *Toward Application of the Best Rule of Law in Choice of Law Cases*, 35 Mercer L. Rev. 483, 501–02 (1984) ("[a] state in which the individual is a regular member of the work force also has a sufficient relationship with the individual to have an interest in protecting or enhancing the individual's or his family's value position").

36. The plurality was very cagey about this. It distinguished John Hancock Mut. Life Ins. Co. v. Yates, 299 U.S. 178, 57 S.Ct. 129, 81 L.Ed. 106 (1936) on the ground that in *Hague*, Mrs. Hague's "bona fide residence in Minnesota was not the sole contact Minnesota had with this litigation," 449 U.S. at 319, 101 S.Ct. at 643, 69 L.Ed.2d at 535, but the plurality also said that "[w]e express no view whether the first two contacts [Mr. Hague's commuting and Allstate's doing business], either together or separately, would have sufficed to sustain the choice of Minnesota law...." 449 U.S. at 320 n.29, 101 S.Ct. at 644 n.29, 69 L.Ed.2d at 535 n.29.

In *Yates*, the Court did not discuss the wife's move to Georgia has having any bearing on the result. In terms of the then prevailing vested rights choice-of-law theory, domicile at any time might be irrelevant, although the Court did refer to the fact that the insured's death occurred in New York, thus indirectly referring to the husband's domicile. The Court indicated as follows what contacts it thought important: "The contract of insurance was made, and the death of the insured occurred in [New York]." *Yates*, 299 U.S. at 182, 57 S.Ct. at 130, 81 L.Ed. at 107. See Hancock, *The Effect of a Post–Occurrence Change of*

The reason Mr. Hague's fifteen years of commuting to work did not give Minnesota an interest in applying its stacking statute is that, if this were the only Minnesota contact, no social consequence would be felt in Minnesota if Mr. Hague's estate recovered only $15,000 instead of $45,000.[37] No Minnesota resident would be undercompensated and thus in danger of becoming a public charge. Higher recovery would not encourage others to commute to work in Minnesota, thus enhancing the Minnesota economy. In considering the fringe benefits of Minnesota employment, no prospective employee would consider Minnesota's stacking and conflicts rules concerning uninsured motorist compensation. More adequate compensation would not speed Mr. Hague's recovery and return to the Minnesota work force because his injuries were fatal.[38]

Minnesota might assert an "interest" in protecting an insured from an insurance contract of adhesion and might regard a member of their work force as sufficiently affiliated with Minnesota to merit this protection. This may be a sufficient interest to prevent application of Minnesota law from being so arbitrary as to violate due process, but it is surely pushing the "interest" envelope. Undercompensated Minnesota residents cause social consequences in Minnesota; undercompensated commuters do not.

Nor could Minnesota base an interest in applying its law on the fact that Allstate did so much business there that the company was subject to generally affiliating personal jurisdiction in Minnesota courts.[39] It might be argued that Minnesota has an interest in regulating the conduct of insurers that do business there so that they do not impose unconscionable adhesion contracts on those they insure, whether or not the customers reside in Minnesota. It is officious, however, for Minnesota to make this choice between greater coverage and higher premiums when both the costs and the benefits will be experienced only in other states. Even the Minnesota legislature recognized this with a choice-of-law clause in the stacking statute, a clause that was ignored by all of the courts in *Hague*. The statute that the Minnesota Supreme Court interpreted as invalidating the "other insurance" clause in Mr. Hague's policies read: "[n]o ... policy ... shall be delivered or issued for delivery in this state with respect to any motor vehicle registered or principally garaged in

---

Domicile upon a Choice of Law Determining the Validity of Other–Insurance Clauses in an Accident Policy, 7 Dalhousie L. J. 653, 683 (1983); Weinberg, supra note 29 at 1029 (suggesting that because of its choice-of-law approach *Yates* is "obsolete"). *Yates* is further discussed infra text accompanying notes 91–95.

37. See von Mehren & Trautman, *Constitutional Control of Choice of Law: Some Reflections on Hague*, 10 Hofstra L. Rev. 35, 43 (1981).

38. Mr. Hague was dead on arrival at the Minnesota hospital to which he was taken after the accident. Transcript of Oral Argument at 21, Allstate Ins. Co. v. Hague, 449 U.S. 302, 101 S.Ct. 633, 66 L.Ed.2d 521 (1981) (statement by Mr. Lowenfeld).

39. A contact is "generally affiliating" if it permits exercise of jurisdiction over the defendant in any action, even one not related to the particular contact. See A. von Mehren & D. Trautman, *The Law of Multistate Problems* 656 (1965); cf. Helicopteros Nacionales de Colombia, S.A. v. Hall, 466 U.S. 408, 104 S.Ct. 1868, 80 L.Ed.2d 404 (1984), limiting generally affiliating jurisdiction. *Helicopteros* is discussed in § 4.8, text accompanying notes 256–283.

this state unless [uninsured motorist coverage of at least $15,000] is provided."[40]

In the hands of the plurality in *Hague*, therefore, "a significant aggregation of contacts with the parties and the occurrence, creating state interests"[41] means simply sufficient contacts so that a reasonable person, unschooled in the niceties of "interest analysis", would not regard the application of the law of that state as arbitrary or as resulting in unfair surprise to one of the parties.[42] "Arbitrary" does not mean that there is also unfair surprise, although any choice of law that works unfair surprise is also arbitrary. Two illustrations help understand how choice of law may be arbitrary without creating unfair surprise.

First an example of arbitrariness without unfair surprise: The defendant negligently injures the plaintiff in state X, where both parties reside. The defendant then moves to Y, where the plaintiff brings suit. Under Y law, plaintiff is entitled to compensation that he would not be entitled to under X law. It would be arbitrary for a Y court to apply Y law, even though the defendant cannot claim unfair surprise in the sense that his conduct was affected by the different legal regime in X. The defendant's injurious conduct was unintentional, and his insurance coverage was the same as he would have obtained if he had lived in Y.

Next an example of unfair surprise: The defendant burns trash in X and the smoke injures the plaintiff's property in X. Under X law, the

---

40. Minn.Stat.Ann. § 65B.22(1) (1968) (repealed by 1974 Minn.Laws 408, § 33 (effective Jan. 1, 1975)).

The Minnesota No–Fault Insurance Law, which displaced, i.a., former § 65B.22(1), provided that "[e]very contract of liability insurance for injury, *wherever issued*, includes [the coverage required by Minnesota's no-fault law] while the vehicle is in this state...." Minn.Stat.Ann. § 65B.50(2) (emphasis added). For a suggested distinction between first-party insurance, such as uninsured motorist coverage or no-fault coverage, and third-party insurance, such as liability insurance, see Kozyris, *Justified Party Expectations In Choice-of-Law and Jurisdiction: Constitutional Significance or Bootstrapping?*, 19 San Diego L. Rev. 313, 335 (1982) (proper to make the law of the place of accident apply to third-party but not to first-party insurance).

41. *Hague*, 449 U.S. at 320, 101 S.Ct. at 644, 69 L.Ed.2d at 535.

42. See Gerling Global Reinsurance Corp. of America v. Gallagher, 267 F.3d 1228 (11th Cir. 2001) (violation of due process to make insurer doing business in Florida liable under Florida Holocaust Victims Insurance Act for non-payment of claim by A German company that Florida company does not control, but with which it is affiliated); Haisten v. Grass Valley Medical Reimbursement Fund, Ltd., 784 F.2d 1392 (9th Cir.1986) (California interest in regulating malpractice insurance of California doctors makes it constitutional to apply California law despite clause in policy choosing Cayman Island law); Bowers v. National Collegiate Athletic Assoc., 151 F.Supp.2d 526 (D. N.J. 2001) (constitutional to apply N.J. Law Against Discrimination to out-of-state organizations and educational institutions that corresponded with plaintiff's high school and that recruit athletes in N.J. when their conduct could be expected to cause harm in N.J.); Kogan, *Toward a Jurisprudence of Choice of Law: The Priority of Fairness over Comity*, 62 N.Y.Univ. L. Rev. 651, 656, 677 (1987) (lack of affiliating contacts may make it unfair to apply a state's law even though there is no unfair surprise); Sedler, *Constitutional Limitations on Choice of Law: The Perspective of Constitutional Generalism*, 10 Hofstra L. Rev. 59, 72 (1981). But cf. Shreve, *Interest Analysis as Constitutional Law*, 48 Ohio St.L. J. 51, 72 (1987) (a disinterested state should be forbidden to apply law conflicting with that of an interested state); Weinberg, *The Place of Trial and the Law Applied: Overhauling Constitutional Theory*, 59 U.Colo. L. Rev. 67, 69 (1988) (application of the law of an uninterested state is "fundamentally unfair").

defendant is not liable for this injury because he has obtained a permit and conformed to all other X rules regulating the burning of trash. The defendant relied on the X law when he decided to burn the trash. It would be arbitrary and would produce unfair surprise to apply Y law to the defendant's conduct.

In *Hague*, a common sense reaction to the facts might be that Mr. Hague's fifteen years of commuting to Minnesota gave Minnesota an interest in protecting Hague from an insurance contract of adhesion. This interest, though minimal, prevented the application of Minnesota law to determine the validity of the "other insurance" clause from being arbitrary. There was no unfair surprise to the insurer for two reasons. First, because the "other insurance" clause was ambiguous, Allstate could not be surprised if it were construed not to cover insurance issued by Allstate—a result several courts had already reached.[43] As Justice Stevens stated in his concurring opinion: "In this case, no express indication of the parties' expectations is available."[44] Second, the $45,000 payment in *Hague* was just grist for the actuarial mill to determine premiums in the Wisconsin rating district where Mr. Hague's cars were principally garaged.[45]

Home Insurance Company v. Dick[46] is another landmark case imposing a due process limitation on a state's choice of law. It is more difficult, however, to appraise the current viability of *Dick* than it is to make that judgment about *Dodge*.

Justice Brandeis, who had dissented in *Dodge*, wrote the *Dick* opinion for a unanimous court. Mr. Dick was a Texan. While in Mexico, Dick acquired an interest in a vessel in Mexican waters and received an assignment of a policy of fire insurance covering the vessel. The policy had originally been issued by a Mexican insurance company to a Mexican resident and covered the vessel only while it was in Mexican waters. Any claim was payable in Mexico. The policy contained a clause stipulating that any suit for the collection of a claim must be filed within one year from the date of loss. This one-year contractual limitation was valid under Mexican law to which the policy was expressly made subject.

---

43. See supra note 26 and accompanying text.

44. *Hague*, 449 U.S. at 329, 101 S.Ct. at 649, 66 L.Ed.2d at 541 (Stevens, J. concurring). Justice Stevens was referring to an indication of the parties' expectations either in the form of a clear statement in the policy that other insurance covered the insurance from Allstate on Mr. Hague's other cars, or in the form of a choice-of-law clause stating that Wisconsin law would apply to construe any ambiguity. Id. at 328, 101 S.Ct. at 648, 66 L.Ed.2d at 540. A clause choosing Wisconsin law would not have helped Allstate because a Wisconsin court would have construed the ambiguity against the insurer. See supra note 26 and accompanying text. Incidentally, the policy did contain a choice-of-law clause: "Such terms of this policy as are in conflict with statutes of the state in which this policy is issued are hereby amended to conform" Policy at 12. This means that Wisconsin law governs validity.

45. Cf. McNamara, *Automobile Liability Insurance Rates*, 35 Ins.Couns.J. 398, 401, 403–06 (1968).

46. 281 U.S. 397, 50 S.Ct. 338, 74 L.Ed. 926 (1930).

Mr. Dick returned to his native Texas. He brought suit on the policy in a Texas court more than one year after the alleged loss had occurred. He obtained jurisdiction by garnisheeing two American insurance companies that had reinsured part of the policy risk. The garnishees pleaded in defense the one-year contractual limitation.

The Texas courts, over the due process objections of the garnishees, refused to recognize the limitations defense. In the view of the Texas courts, a period of limitations was a matter of procedure. Therefore, the law of the forum applied. According to Texas law, no contractual limitation shorter than two years was valid. Judgment was entered for Dick. On appeal, the Supreme Court reversed the Texas courts because Texas did not have any contact with the controversy that was sufficient to make it reasonable to use Texas law in the adjudication:

> All acts relating to the making of the policy were done in Mexico. . . . Neither the Texas laws nor the Texas courts were invoked for any purpose, except by Dick in the bringing of this suit. The fact that Dick's permanent residence was in Texas is without significance. At all times here material, he was physically present and acting in Mexico. Texas was therefore, without power to affect the terms of contracts so made.[47]

On the face of it then, *Home Insurance Company v. Dick* does not seem greatly emancipated from the rigid, territorial conceptualism of Dodge. There is no talk of whether, because the plaintiff is a Texas citizen, Texas has a reasonable interest in applying its rule striking down what it considers an unreasonable limitation on the period in which suit can be brought against the insurer. The focus, instead, is on physical contacts. The insurance contract was not made or to be performed in Texas. The plaintiff, although at all times domiciled in Texas, was actually residing in Mexico from the time that the insurance policy was issued until the loss to the boat.

It is tempting to explain the result in *Dick* in terms of unfair surprise to the insurers. Although Dick was a Texas citizen, the policy had originally been issued in Mexico to a Mexican resident. Therefore, the argument might run, neither the Mexican insurance company nor the American reinsurers had any reason to foresee that Texas would have a reasonable interest in striking down the contractual time limitations. The application of Texas law to invalidate was an outrageous surprise to the insurers.

On closer examination, this "outrageous surprise" explanation of *Dick* seems very doubtful. First of all, although the policy was issued to one Bonner, of Tampico, Mexico, the loss was made "payable to the Texas Gulf Steamship Company of Galveston, Texas, and C.J. Dick, as their respective interests may appear."[48] Moreover, not only was Dick named, along with a Texas company, in the original policy, but also,

---

47. Id. at 408, 50 S.Ct. at 341, 74 L.Ed. at 933.

48. Home Ins. Co. v. Dick, transcript of record, pp. 38–39. See also 281 U.S. at 403 n.2, 50 S.Ct. at 340 n.2, 74 L.Ed. at 931 n.2.

before the policy could be assigned to Dick, the insurer had to give its written consent.[49] This consent was given. An endorsement to the policy, noted on the insurer's register eight years before the insured boat burned and sank, stated, "[i]t is hereby declared and agreed that as from July 12th, 1921, all the interests, rights and obligations of the above mentioned Policy, are transferred to and solely vest in Mr. C.J. Dick as Lessee of the Insured Craft."[50]

Thus, an explanation of *Dick* in terms of unfair surprise to the insurer seems unlikely.[51] *Dick* is cogent only if it was not reasonable for Texas to extend the protection of its own laws to one of its own citizens when those laws invalidated a term of an insurance contract issued elsewhere, and insuring property at all times located in another jurisdiction where the term was valid. In short, the application of Texas law violated due process because the contacts that Texas had with the parties and with the transaction were not sufficient to make it reasonable for Texas to assert the interest that it did have in applying Texas law.[52]

One of the cases relied on by the majority in the *Dodge* case may be explained in terms of this due process standard. The case is *New York Life Insurance Company v. Head*.[53] Mr. Head, a citizen of New Mexico, while temporarily in Missouri, applied for a policy with a New York insurance company. The application stipulated that the policy when issued should be considered as having been issued in New York and should be treated as a New York contract. The policy was delivered in Missouri to a friend of Mr. Head. The friend turned the policy over to Mr. Head when Head next visited Missouri. Mr. Head returned to New Mexico and transferred the policy to his daughter. In New Mexico, the daughter borrowed money from the insurance company against the cash

---

49. Home Ins. Co. v. Dick, transcript of record, p. 38 (quoting from the policy): "It is further understood ... that if the interests of the assured ... are sold or transferred, then, and except the assuring company gives its written consent to such ... transfer, this Policy shall by that act become cancelled as from the date of such ... transfer...."

50. Id. at 39. The ship burned and sank on July 27, 1929. Id. at 9. Moreover, the brief for the appellants (insurers) states, p. 3: "On March 18, 1921, in Mexico, C.J. Dick procured a policy of insurance...."

51. For a suggestion that the insurer could not have foreseen the availability of a Texas forum and that no other forum would have applied Texas law, see Kirgis, *The Roles of Due Process and Full Faith and Credit in Choice of Law*, 62 Cornell L. Rev. 94, 108 n. 53 (1976). See also Redish, *Due Process, Federalism, and Personal Jurisdiction: A Theoretical Evaluation*, 75 Nw. L. Rev. 1112, 1127 (1981) ("the Court's lack of emphasis on the defendant's awareness of Texas contacts may imply that the Court itself was proceeding on the assumption that surprise was a factor in the case").

52. See Kirgis, supra note 51, at 108: "The key is the insurer's attempt to localize the transaction in Mexico, without receiving any actual or potential benefit from Texas; it would be manifestly unfair to apply Texas law to undo a perfectly valid (in Mexico) contractual provision, even if the insurer somehow could have foreseen that Texas law might ultimately be applied to some aspects of the transaction." Cf. Restatement, Second, Conflict of Laws § 9 (1971): "A court may not apply the local law of its own state to determine a particular issue unless such application of this law would be reasonable in the light of the relationship of the state and of other states to the person, thing or occurrence involved."

53. 234 U.S. 149, 34 S.Ct. 879, 58 L.Ed. 1259 (1914).

surrender value of the policy. As in *Dodge*,[54] there was a default in payment of the premium, the entire cash surrender value was applied to the indebtedness, and the policy canceled.

Like Mrs. Dodge, Mr. Head's daughter sued in Missouri in an attempt to take advantage of the Missouri statute that, upon non-payment of a premium, allowed only that portion of indebtedness due for past premiums to be deducted from the cash surrender value before the purchase of paid-up insurance. The Missouri courts did apply the Missouri statute and gave judgment for plaintiff. The Supreme Court reversed. Missouri did not have a contact with the transaction sufficient to make the application of the Missouri statute reasonable. In the words of Brandeis' dissent in *Dodge*,

> if this court had held constitutional the statute of Missouri as construed . . . in that case, it would have sanctioned, not regulation by the State of the insurance of its citizens, but an arbitrary interference by one State with the rights of citizens of other States.[55]

The converse of the rule drawn from the *Dick* case is that if a state has sufficient contact with the parties or with the facts to make it reasonable for that state to enforce its own policies in adjudicating a controversy arising between the parties on those facts, application of the law of that state will not violate the Due Process Clause of the Fourteenth Amendment to the Federal Constitution.

Kryger v. Wilson,[56] another Brandeis opinion, is a good illustration. Plaintiff sued to quiet title to land in North Carolina. The defendant was claiming an interest in the land under a contract for purchase that he had entered into with the plaintiff in Minnesota. After the defendant-buyer had defaulted, the plaintiff had attempted to cancel the contract. The steps that plaintiff had taken were sufficient under North Carolina law to terminate the contract, but those acts were not enough to effect a contract cancellation under Minnesota law. The North Carolina courts applied North Carolina law, held the contract properly canceled, and gave judgment for the plaintiff. The Supreme Court affirmed, stating:

> [There is] no lack of due process. . . . The most that the plaintiff in error can say is that the state court made a mistaken application of the doctrines of the conflict of laws in deciding that the cancellation of a land contract is governed by the law of the *situs* instead of the place of making and performance. But that, being purely a question of local common law, is a matter with which this court is not concerned.[57]

The reason why North Carolina's use of local law to adjudicate the controversy did not violate due process was that the Court believed that

---

54. *Dodge* is discussed supra notes 4–8 and accompanying text.

55. New York Life Ins. Co. v. Dodge, 246 U.S. 357, 384–85, 38 S.Ct. 337, 342, 62 L.Ed. 772, 786 (1918).

56. 242 U.S. 171, 37 S.Ct. 34, 61 L.Ed. 229 (1916).

57. Id. at 176, 37 S.Ct. at 35, 61 L.Ed. at 231.

North Carolina as situs had a sufficient contact with the facts to keep its use of North Carolina law within the bounds of reason.

When, then, is it a denial of due process to apply the law of a state to an interstate transaction? The safest, but not very helpful, answer is when it is not reasonable to apply the law of that state. Reasonableness is the basic, core concept of due process. Any further elaboration of this "reasonableness" standard attempts to give this vague standard more specific content in order to facilitate its application to specific cases. The Supreme Court was applying this reasonableness standard in *Dodge*. The answer that the Court arrived at in *Dodge* was that it is not reasonable to use the law of a state to invalidate a provision in a contract unless that state was the place of making of the contract. Today, the Supreme Court and most scholars would reject this gloss on the basic reasonableness standard. It can be reasonable, in fact may be the wiser and preferable solution to a contracts conflict-of-laws problem, to apply the law of a state to invalidate even though that state is not the technical place of making of the contract. But once this "place-of-making" gloss for contracts, or the "place-of-wrong" gloss for torts is rejected, the question becomes what other elaboration of the basic reasonableness standard is desirable.

Allstate Insurance Company v. Hague[58] indicates that, for now at least, only minimal constitutional scrutiny will be imposed on a state's conflicts decisions.[59] Choice of law is likely to run afoul of due process standards only in the two relatively narrow circumstances discussed above in connection with *Hague*.[60] First, a person who plans his or her conduct in justifiable reliance on the law of one state, should not have that reliance frustrated by the application of the law of another state if, at the time the person acted, that other state did not have a contact with the parties or with the transaction that would make use of its law reasonable. Second, even though conduct has not been shaped by expectations as to governing law, a state may have so little contact with the parties or with the transaction that application of its law will be arbitrary and therefore violate due process. The dissenters in *Hague* would give this arbitrariness standard the specific content of the "false conflict" dear to advocates of interest analysis. Application of the law of a state would violate due process if no social consequences sought to be achieved by that law would be experienced in that state. The *Hague* plurality, however, gives "arbitrary" a less rigorous and more impressionistic content than interest analysis would demand.

It is probably just as well that *Hague* defined "state interests" in these common sense terms.[61] There are a lot of intelligent people who do

---

58. 449 U.S. 302, 101 S.Ct. 633, 66 L.Ed.2d 521 (1981), discussed supra notes 23–45 and accompanying text.

59. See Weinberg, *Choice of Law and Minimal Scrutiny*, 49 U. Chi. L. Rev. 440 (1982).

60. See supra text accompanying notes 41–45.

61. See Sedler, *Constitutional Limitations on Choice of Law: The Perspective of Constitutional Generalism*, 10 Hofstra L. Rev. 59, 61, 78–79 (1981). But see Kirgis, *A Wishful Thinker's Rehearing in the Hague Case*, 10 Hofstra L. Rev. 1059, 1070 (would require a

not regard interest analysis as the greatest thing since sliced bread.[62] Once before, the Supreme Court raised then current notions of choice of law to constitutional status with results that today seem bizarre.[63] Until there is something approaching a consensus in the legal profession concerning the proper approach to choice of law, it is wise to use caution in imposing one view or another by constitutional fiat.

There is, however, a cost in leaving the states free to experiment with choice of law. There are two ways to employ constitutional controls to mitigate the worst aspects of forum shopping in interstate litigation. One is to place restrictions on the judicial jurisdiction of state courts. The other is to focus on one very important factor in forum shopping, choice of law. The convenience of travel and the availability of techniques such as video-taping and remote televised or internet appearances suggest, in the words of Justice Brennan, that due process limits on the jurisdiction of state courts based on "minimum contacts" between defendant and forum "may already be obsolete."[64] There is a strong argument that, at least as far as litigation between citizens of different states is concerned,[65] the plaintiff's choice of a forum that has a contact with a party or the transaction should be upset only in the light of some specific unfairness to the defendant other than having to cross a state line.[66]

This suggests that in interstate litigation, parochialism and unfairness should be combated primarily by federalizing choice of law and removing most restrictions on judicial jurisdiction. Instead, in opinions such as *World–Wide Volkswagen v. Woodson*[67] and *Helicopteros Nacio-*

"contact or affiliation relevant to the particular rules involved"); Kozyris, *Reflections on Allstate—The Lessening of Due Process in Choice of Law*, 14 U.C. Davis L. Rev. 889, 892 (1981); Martin, *Personal Jurisdiction and Choice of Law*, 78 Mich. L. Rev. 872 (1980) ("[t]he time has come for the Supreme Court to declare that a state may not apply its own law to a case unless it has the 'minimum contacts' required by *International Shoe* for the exercise of specific personal jurisdiction over the defendant"); Silberman, *Can the State of Minnesota Bind the Nation?: Federal Choice-of-Law Constraints after Allstate Insurance Co. v. Hague*, 10 Hofstra L. Rev. 103, 130 (1981) (suggests judicial development of "choice-of-law restraints" that "[l]ike the negative commerce clause restraints ... would be subject to revision and displacement at the hands of Congress").

62. See, e.g., Brilmayer, *Methods and Objectives in the Conflict of Laws: A Challenge*, 35 Mercer L. Rev. 555 (1984); Ely, *Choice of Law and the State's Interest in Protecting Its Own*, 23 William & M. L. Rev. 173 (1982); Juenger, *Conflict of Laws: A Critique of Interest Analysis*, 32 Amer.J.Comp.L. 1 (1984); Korn, *The Choice-of-Law Revolution: A Critique*, 83 Colum. L. Rev. 772 (1983); Laycock, *Equal Citizens of Equal and Territorial States: The Constitutional Foundations of Choice of Law*, 92 Colum. L. Rev. 249 (1992).

63. See discussion supra accompanying notes 4–11.

64. World–Wide Volkswagen Corp. v. Woodson, 444 U.S. 286, 299, 100 S.Ct. 559, 581, 62 L.Ed.2d 490, 503 (1980) (Brennan, J., dissenting). See also Carrington, *Virtual Civil Litigation: A Visit to John Bunyan's Celestial City*, 98 Colum. L. Rev. 1516 (1998).

65. With regard to jurisdiction over foreign defendants, some reasonable nexus between the defendant and the United States is important for reasons of international comity.

66. Section 4.8A(1)(D) explores this idea and suggests a new standard for personal jurisdiction in interstate cases.

67. 444 U.S. 286, 100 S.Ct. 559, 62 L.Ed.2d 490 (1980), discussed supra § 4.8 text accompanying notes 208–236.

nales de Colombia v. Hall[68] the Court imposes restrictions on state court jurisdiction that many commentators regard as unduly narrow[69] and in cases such as *Allstate Insurance Company v. Hague*[70] leaves the states free to do what they will with choice of law so long as they do not do it in the street and scare the horses. This bit of the judicial world may be on its ear.[71] The time is ripe for movement on both fronts—greater jurisdictional freedom but more restrictions on choice of law.

Phillips Petroleum Company v. Shutts[72] may indicate the start of greater constitutional control of choice of law, although it may not be an auspicious circumstance in which to embark on this venture. It was the first case in thirty-eight years to declare a forum's application of its own law unconstitutional,[73] but it was far from clear whether or not, and if so, how, the forum's law differed from that of the other states involved. It would have been preferable to reserve this new constitutional activism for a case in which it was clearer that a different result would have been reached under the law of a state other than the forum. A clear difference would make more cogent a finding that applying forum law is unreasonable both because of lack of forum interest in advancing its own policies and also because of unfairness to the party disfavored by forum law.

Phillips produced natural gas from land in eleven states. Shutts and others held rights to leases from which Phillips produced the gas and the lease owners were entitled to royalty payments. The Federal Power Commission (FPC) had to approve any increase by Phillips in the price of the gas Phillips could collect an increased price pending approval by the

---

68. 466 U.S. 408, 104 S.Ct. 1868, 80 L.Ed.2d 404 (1984), discussed supra § 4.8 text accompanying notes 256–283.

69. With regard to *Volkswagen*, see, e.g. Lilly, *Jurisdiction over Domestic and Alien Defendants*, 69 Va. L. Rev. 85, 114–15 (1983); von Mehren, *Adjudicatory Jurisdiction: General Theories Compared and Evaluated*, 63 B.U. L. Rev. 279 (1983).

70. 449 U.S. 302, 101 S.Ct. 633, 66 L.Ed.2d 521 (1981).

71. See Peterson, *Jurisdiction and Choice of Law Revisited*, 59 U.Colo. L. Rev. 37, 64–5 (1988) (should be greater restriction on choice of law than on jurisdiction); Silberman, *Shaffer v. Heitner: The End of an Era*, 53 New York U. L. Rev. 33, 88 (1978) ("To believe that a defendant's contacts with the forum state should be stronger under the due process clause for jurisdictional purposes than for choice of law is to believe that an accused is more concerned with where he will be hanged than whether"). But see Maltz, *Visions of Fairness—The Relationship Between Jurisdiction and Choice-of-Law*, 30 Ariz. L. Rev. 751 (1988) ("fairness is adequately vindicated through restrictions on personal jurisdiction rather than on choice of law").

72. 472 U.S. 797, 105 S.Ct. 2965, 86 L.Ed.2d 628 (1985).

73. Not included in the calculation are summary dispositions without full opinion. See, e.g., McCluney v. Jos. Schlitz Brewing Co., 454 U.S. 1071, 102 S.Ct. 624, 70 L.Ed.2d 607 (1981) affirming without opinion 649 F.2d 578 (8th Cir.1981) (unconstitutional to apply Missouri service letter statute when employment from which employee requesting the letter was discharged was in another state). The last full opinion before *Shutts* that struck down a forum's application of its own law is Order of United Commercial Travelers of America v. Wolfe, 331 U.S. 586, 67 S.Ct. 1355, 91 L.Ed. 1687 (1947), discussed infra text accompanying notes 209–214. Cf. Hughes v. Fetter, 341 U.S. 609, 71 S.Ct. 980, 95 L.Ed. 1212 (1951) and First Nat'l Bank v. United Air Lines, 342 U.S. 396, 72 S.Ct. 421, 96 L.Ed. 441 (1952) (*Hughes* is discussed infra notes 242–249 and accompanying text) in which the forum was held required by full faith and credit not to dismiss but to entertain an action for wrongful death occurring in another state and based on the wrongful death act of that state.

FPC, but if the increase was denied, Phillips would have to refund the increase plus interest. The interest was set by federal regulation. Before FPC approval, royalties on the tentatively increased prices were received only by those owners who provided Phillips with a bond or indemnity for the royalties plus interest at the rate set in the federal regulation for refunds to customers. Three times Phillips raised prices and withheld royalties from the vast majority of lease owners who did not provide the required indemnity. When approval was received, Phillips paid the withheld royalties to the lease owners, but without interest although Phillips had used the money for several years.

The lease owners brought a class action against Phillips in a state court in Kansas to recover interest. Notice of the suit was mailed to all owners. The final class consisted of those owners who received notice and who did not elect to opt out of the class. The members of the class lived in all fifty states, the District of Columbia, and several foreign countries. Less than one thousand of the over twenty-eight thousand class members resided in Kansas and approximately one quarter of one per cent of the gas leases involved were on Kansas land.

The trial court found that under Kansas contract and equity principles, Phillips had to pay the royalty recipients interest at the same rate that, in the event of FPC disapproval, federal regulations required Phillips to pay customers and that Phillips had demanded by way of indemnity from lease owners who elected to receive the royalties pending approval.

Phillips contended that it was denial of due process to include in the class royalty recipients who did not have sufficient contact with Kansas to permit in personam jurisdiction over them. Phillips also contended that it was a violation of due process and full faith and credit to apply Kansas law to determine the applicable interest.

The Kansas courts ruled against Phillips and certiorari was granted. An opinion by Justice Rehnquist held that Phillips had standing to raise the constitutionality of including absent owners in the class action, because Phillips had an interest in having those owners bound by any decision that would bind Phillips. The Court then upheld the constitutionality of including nonresident owners in the class action. Their rights were protected by mailed notice, an opportunity to opt out, adequate representation by the class representatives, and court supervision. The application of Kansas law, however was held unconstitutional. Justice Stevens joined in the ruling on the class action, but dissented with regard to the unconstitutionality of applying Kansas law.

The Court itself noted that "[t]here can be no injury in applying Kansas law if it is not in conflict with that of any other jurisdiction connected to this suit."[74] The majority then found that the conflicts on applicable interest rates between Kansas law and that of Oklahoma and Texas, where most of the leases were situated, could not be "labeled

---

74. *Shutts,* 472 U.S. at 816, 105 S.Ct. at 2976, 86 L.Ed.2d at 645.

'false conflicts' without a more thorough-going treatment than was accorded them by the Supreme Court of Kansas."[75] And if lower interest is payable under the law of those states, Kansas did not have a sufficient reason for applying its law to prevent that application from being unconstitutionally "arbitrary and unfair."[76] It was unfair because "[t]here is no indication that when the leases involving land and royalty owners outside of Kansas were executed, the parties had any idea that Kansas law would control."[77]

The Court thus realizes[78] that on remand the Supreme Court of Kansas may well determine that there is insufficient showing of any difference between Kansas law and that of Texas and Oklahoma. In which case, this landmark opinion on constitutional limitations on choice of law would end with a whimper. In all fairness, the Kansas Supreme Court invited this slap by not stating that it was applying Kansas law in default of any clear showing that a Texas or Oklahoma court would reach a different result on the specific facts of this case.[79] The Kansas Supreme Court noted that "[t]he trial court did not determine whether any difference existed between the laws of Kansas and other states or whether another state's law should be applied."[80] The Kansas court then stated that because of the nature of the case, a nationwide class action, "the law of the forum should be applied unless compelling reasons exist for applying a different law."[81] It found no such compelling reasons, but did not base this on lack of any showing of difference from forum law. Instead the opinion concluded that "[t]he common fund nature of the lawsuit provides an excellent reason to apply a uniform measure of damages to the class as a whole" and "[t]he plaintiff class members have indicated their desire to have this action determined under the laws of Kansas."[82] Just before this passage, however, the Kansas Supreme Court did refer to a similar previous case[83] which had specifically found that the Texas and Oklahoma statutes providing for interest at six per cent did not apply because those "statutes refer to situations where there is no agreement as to the rate of interest. Here that situation does not exist."[84] Moreover, the principal Texas case on which Phillips relied[85]

---

75. Id. at 818, 105 S.Ct. at 2978, 86 L.Ed.2d at 646.

76. Id. at 822, 105 S.Ct. at 2979, 86 L.Ed.2d at 648.

77. Id. at 822, 105 S.Ct. at 2980, 86 L.Ed.2d at 649.

78. See text accompanying note 75 supra.

79. The specific facts would include the undertaking that Phillips had made with the FPC to pay regulatory interest to customers. Justice Stevens dissented on the ground that a difference in law was not apparent. *Shutts*, 472 U.S. at 824, 105 S.Ct. at 2981, 86 L.Ed.2d at 650.

80. Shutts v. Phillips Petroleum Co., 235 Kan. 195, 220, 679 P.2d 1159, 1180 (1984), rev'd, 472 U.S. 797, 105 S.Ct. 2965, 86 L.Ed.2d 628 (1985).

81. Id. at 221, 679 P.2d at 1181.

82. Id. at 221–22, 679 P.2d at 1181.

83. Id. at 221, 679 P.2d at 1181. The previous case is Shutts v. Phillips Petroleum Co., 222 Kan. 527, 567 P.2d 1292 (1977), cert. denied, 434 U.S. 1068, 98 S.Ct. 1246, 55 L.Ed.2d 769 (1978) (*Shutts I*).

84. *Shutts I*, 222 Kan. at 564, 567 P.2d at 1319.

was one in which the royalty owner asked only for the statutory six per cent interest, which the Texas Supreme Court found due.

Shutts did end with a whimper. On remand the Kansas Supreme Court decided that Texas and Oklahoma courts were sufficiently fair and wise to reach the same result that had been reached in Kansas and reaffirmed its former result.[86] In *Sun Oil Company v. Wortman*[87] almost a twin of *Shutts*, Justice O'Connor dissented from allowing Kansas to apply its own law under the subterfuge that there is no discernible difference from the law of the states where the oil leases were situated:

> [A] court that does not like [the law of a sister state that the court is constitutionally obligated to apply] apparently need take only two steps to avoid applying it. First, invent a legal theory so novel or strange that the other State has never had an opportunity to reject it; then, on the basis of nothing but unsupported speculation, "predict" that the other State would adopt that theory if it had the chance.[88]

The question is whether this is a fair criticism of the Kansas court. In the light of the lack of close precedents in Texas or Oklahoma, I do not think so. Thus *Shutts* used the cannon of constitutional limits on choice of law to slay a gnat—to teach the Supreme Court of Kansas conflicts etiquette rather than to prevent an arbitrary and unfair deprivation of rights clearly available under appropriate law.

Defendants in multi-state class actions frequently cite *Shutts* as precluding the application of the law of any single state to the claims of all class members. In *Shutts* less than 1,000 of the over 28,000 class members resided in Kansas and only one quarter of one per cent of the gas leases were on Kansas land. Under *Shutts* it is unconstitutional to select the law of a state where some class members live and apply that law to a national class action when that law is more favorable to class members than the laws of other states having more significant relationships with the other class members and with the defendant. It is not unconstitutional in a national class action to apply the law of a single state if that state is the center of defendant's wrongful acts.[89]

Unfair surprise as a limitation on choice of law has a substantial history in Supreme Court litigation culminating in the "neither arbitrary nor fundamentally unfair" standard stated in *Allstate Insurance v.*

---

85. Phillips Petroleum Co. v. Stahl Petroleum Co., 569 S.W.2d 480 (Tex.1978).

86. Shutts v. Phillips Petroleum Co., 240 Kan. 764, 732 P.2d 1286 (1987), cert. denied, 487 U.S. 1223, 108 S.Ct. 2883, 101 L.Ed.2d 918 (1988) (except for post-judgment interest which is to be awarded under the laws of the states where the leases are situated).

87. 486 U.S. 717, 108 S.Ct. 2117, 100 L.Ed.2d 743 (1988). *Sun Oil is* discussed infra text accompanying notes 157–177.

88. Id. at 749, 108 S.Ct. at 2136, 100 L.Ed.2d at 769–70. Cf. Miller & Crump, *Jurisdiction and Choice of Law in Multistate Class Actions After Phillips Petroleum v. Shutts*, 96 Yale L. J. 1, 61 (1986) ("more pragmatic" to find "conflicts on the basis of law that other states 'most likely' would follow").

89. See section 6.33 text accompanying notes 403–408.

Hague.[90] Perhaps the best known of these prior cases is *John Hancock Mutual Life Insurance Company v. Yates.*[91] John Hancock issued a life insurance policy to Mr. Yates while he was a resident of New York. Under New York's insurance statute,[92] if a false answer was written on the insurance application, there could be no recovery on the policy, even if a true answer had been given to the examiner. The insurance company's agent had no power to waive this requirement. In his application for insurance, Mr. Yates had stated falsely that he had not recently been under medical care, when in fact he was being treated for cancer. Mr. Yates died soon after the policy was issued. Mrs. Yates, the beneficiary, moved to Georgia and brought suit on the policy in a Georgia court.

The Georgia trial judge permitted Mrs. Yates to testify over objection that Mr. Yates had orally given true answers to the insurance agent and the judge submitted to the jury the question of whether, under the circumstances, the false written recital in the application was material, charging that "if a policy is issued with knowledge by the agent of a fact or condition which, by the terms of the contract, would render it void, the insurer will be held to have waived the existence of such fact or condition, and the policy will not be voided thereby."[93] The Georgia Supreme Court affirmed a judgment for Mrs. Yates holding that under Georgia "procedure" materiality of misrepresentation is a question of fact to be decided by the jury in the light of knowledge imputed to the insurer.

If the action of the Georgia courts were allowed to stand, Mrs. Yates, simply by moving to Georgia after the death of her husband, would have been able to pull a statutory defense out from under the insurance company. In a unanimous opinion, the Supreme Court reversed the Georgia courts. "In respect to the accrual of the right asserted under the contract ... there was no occurrence, nothing done, to which the law of Georgia could apply."[94] Although *Yates* is based on denial of full faith

---

90. 449 U.S. 302, 320, 101 S.Ct. 633, 644, 66 L.Ed.2d 521, 535 (1981), discussed supra text accompanying notes 23–45.

91. 299 U.S. 178, 57 S.Ct. 129, 81 L.Ed. 106 (1936).

92. N.Y.—McKinney's Consol.Laws 1909, ch. 28, §§ 58, 59, 107.

93. *Yates*, 299 U.S. at 180, 57 S.Ct. at 130, 81 L.Ed. at 107.

94. Id. at 182, 57 S.Ct. at 131, 81 L.Ed. at 108. The Court did not focus on the timing of the widow's move to Georgia. Under the then prevailing vested rights approach to choice of law, domicile at any time was irrelevant. See supra note 36.

See Sedler, *The Governmental Interest Approach to Choice of Law: An Analysis and a Reformulation*, 25 UCLA L. Rev. 181, 241 (1977): "if a different standard were to be applied, the insurer presumably would have taken steps to cancel the policy at an earlier time when proof of materiality was more likely to have been available." See also McCluney v. Joseph Schlitz Brewing Co., 649 F.2d 578, 582 (8th Cir.1981), aff'd without opinion, 454 U.S. 1071, 102 S.Ct. 624, 70 L.Ed.2d 607 (1981) (cannot apply Missouri service letter statute to create rights in favor of employee who moved to Missouri after he was discharged—"when [the parties'] rational expectations are not based upon the laws of some other state, it violates due process to breach those expectations by applying the unexpected law") (citing this text); Hay, *Reflections on Conflict-of-Laws Methodology*, 32 Hastings L. J. 1644, 1646 (1981) ("there must be a nexus of defendant, litigation, and forum"); Martin, *The Constitution and Legislative Jurisdiction*, 10 Hofstra L. Rev. 133, 139 (1981) ("due process analysis in the choice-of-law area ought to be limited to cases ... containing an

and credit to the New York insurance statute, the language just quoted
is a paraphrase of language in *Home Insurance Company v. Dick*,[95] which
Yates cites. *Dick*, because it involved a refusal to apply Mexican law,
rested solely on due process. It seems, therefore, that *Yates* would have
reached the same result if it had relied on due process rather than on
full faith and credit.

In *Aetna Life Insurance Company v. Dunken*,[96] a Connecticut insurance company issued life insurance to Mr. Dunken. At the time that the
policy was issued, Mr. Dunken was a citizen of Tennessee. Mr. Dunken
then moved to Texas and, after becoming a citizen of Texas, exercised an
option to convert the policy to twenty-payment life. Mr. Dunken died
and suit was brought on the policy in a Texas court. In awarding the
judgment for plaintiff, the Texas court included in the judgment an
additional twelve per cent of the face value of the policy and plaintiff's
attorney's fee. Such additions were permissible under Texas law if an
insurance company failed to pay a proper claim promptly, but were
unknown under the law of Tennessee where the policy had been issued.
The Supreme Court reversed. The Court's language recalled the rigid
"vested rights" theorizing that had resulted in the *Dodge* decision:

> The contract contained in the original policy was a Tennessee
> contract. The law of Tennessee entered into it and became a part of
> it. The Texas statute was incapable of being constitutionally applied
> to it since the effect of such application would be to regulate
> business outside the State of Texas and control contracts made by
> citizens of other States in disregard of their laws under which
> penalties and attorney's fees are not recoverable.[97]

One might attempt to explain *Dunken* in terms of refusing to allow
the defendant's obligation to be substantially affected in a way that the

---

element of genuine unfair surprise. The remaining cases ought to be analyzed under full
faith and credit"); Reese, *Legislative Jurisdiction*, 78 Colum L. Rev. 1587, 1597, 1605–06
(1978). But cf. Manuel v. Convergys Corp., 430 F.3d 1132 (11th Cir. 2005) (not unconstitutional to apply Georgia law to invalidate employee's noncompetition agreement even
though employee moved to Georgia after resigning from employment in Florida and
agreement required application of the law of Ohio, where employer had its principal place
of business); Lettieri v. Equitable Life Assurance Soc'y, 627 F.2d 930 (9th Cir.1980)
(permits application of California rather than New York law to determine effect of false
statements in insurance application by New York insured—beneficiary moved to California
after her husband's death and another beneficiary resided there at the time of the
application).

95. 281 U.S. 397, 408, 50 S.Ct. 338, 341, 74 L.Ed. 926, 933 (1930) ("nothing in any way
relating to the policy sued on, or to the contracts of reinsurance, was ever done or required
to be done in Texas").

96. 266 U.S. 389, 45 S.Ct. 129, 69 L.Ed. 342 (1924).

97. Id. at 399, 45 S.Ct. at 132, 69 L.Ed. at 349. The Court seems to be talking in terms
of due process at this point, citing New York Life Ins. Co. v. Head, 234 U.S. 149, 34 S.Ct.
879, 58 L.Ed. 1259 (1914). See supra text accompanying notes 52–53. Previously, however,
the Court had said: "[T]he contention that the contract is controlled by the law of
Tennessee or Connecticut ... clearly presents a substantial question under the full faith
and credit clause of the Constitution." 266 U.S. at 393, 45 S.Ct. at 130, 69 L.Ed. at 346. See
also Austin Bldg. Co. v. National Union Fire Ins. Co., 432 S.W.2d 697 (Tex.1968) (Texas
law could not constitutionally be applied to determine the efficacy of a defense to coverage
raised by the insurer of Kansas property even though the plaintiff, a Texas corporation,
was named in the policy as one of those insured, citing *Dunken*).

defendant, when issuing the policy, did not foresee or have any reason to foresee. This unfair surprise gloss on *Dunken*, however, seems to ignore the fact that the insurer could have foreseen that Mr. Dunken might change his residence (he had been born in Texas)[98] and that his new domicile would then have a significant interest in protecting the policy beneficiaries against the insurer's unjustified refusal to pay. Moreover, the viability of *Dunken* seems doubtful in the light of *Clay v. Sun Insurance Office, Ltd.*[99]

In *Clay*, the plaintiff, while he was a citizen and resident of Illinois, insured personal property, then in Illinois, against loss by fire. The insured then moved to Florida, taking his property with him. The insured property was destroyed by fire in Florida. When the insurer refused to pay, the insured brought suit in Florida on the policy. The plaintiff brought the suit more than a year after the discovery of the loss. The policy contained a clause barring a suit on the policy more than twelve months after the discovery of a loss. This clause was valid under Illinois law, but Florida law nullified such clauses if they limited the time for suit to less than five years. The insurer defended on the basis of the twelve-month clause.

The Supreme Court held that Florida law could be applied to invalidate this provision. The Court distinguished two other insurance cases, *Hartford Accident & Indemnity Company v. Delta & Pine Land Company*[100] and *Home Insurance Company v. Dick*.[101]

The *Dick* case has been examined above.[102] In the *Delta & Pine Land* case, the defendant insurance company issued a policy to the plaintiff in Tennessee bonding plaintiff's workers, including an employee then working for the plaintiff in Tennessee and twenty-one employees who were then working in Mississippi.[103] After the policy had been issued, the Tennessee employee was transferred to the plaintiff's Mississippi office and there embezzled funds. In a suit on the bonding policy, the Court held that the Mississippi court could not apply local law to invalidate a policy provision that required suit on the policy to be brought within fifteen months after termination of the suretyship. This clause was valid under the law of Tennessee where the policy had been issued. In its *Delta & Pine Land* opinion the Court gave lip service to the significance of the forum's interest in applying its own law, but was apparently controlled by the same notions of "vested rights" that had prevailed in *Dodge*. The *Delta & Pine Land* opinion declared:

---

98. See *Dunken*, supra note 96, Record, p. 47 (in answer to question 4 on the insurance application, Mr. Dunken stated that he had been born in Sherman, Texas).

99. 377 U.S. 179, 84 S.Ct. 1197, 12 L.Ed.2d 229 (1964).

100. 292 U.S. 143, 54 S.Ct. 634, 78 L.Ed. 1178 (1934).

101. 281 U.S. 397, 50 S.Ct. 338, 74 L.Ed. 926 (1930).

102. See text accompanying notes 46–52.

103. The fact that, in *Delta & Pine Land*, twenty-one of the insured's employees were working in Mississippi when the policy was issued is pointed out by Justice Frankfurter in Watson v. Employers Liab. Assur. Corp., 348 U.S. 66, 77, 75 S.Ct. 166, 172, 99 L.Ed. 74, 84 (1954) (concurring opinion).

Conceding that ordinarily a state may prohibit performance within its borders even of a contract validly made elsewhere . . . it may not . . . ignore a right which has lawfully vested elsewhere, if, as here, the interest of the forum has but slight connection with the substance of the contract obligations.[104]

Thus, confronted with the *Dick* and *Delta & Pine Land* opinions, the Court in *Clay* disposed of those former opinions by saying:

Those were cases where the activities in the State of the forum were thought to be too slight and too casual, as in the *Delta & Pine Land Co.* case . . . to make the application of local law consistent with due process, or wholly lacking, as in the *Dick* case. No deficiency of that order is present here.[105]

Significantly, the *Clay* opinion went on to emphasize that the insurer was not unfairly surprised by the application of Florida law:

In this very case the policy was sold to Clay with knowledge that he could take his property anywhere in the world he saw fit without losing the protection of his insurance. In fact, his contract was described on its face as a "Personal Property Floater Policy (World Wide)." The contract did not even attempt to provide that the law of Illinois would govern when suits were filed anywhere else in the country. Shortly after the contract was made, Clay moved to Florida and there he lived for several years. His insured property was there all that time. The company knew this fact. Particularly since the company was licensed to do business in Florida, it must have known it might be sued there. . . .[106]

There is one respect in which the unfair surprise argument might have been slightly more cogent in *Dunken* than in *Clay*. The policy in

---

104. 292 U.S. at 150, 54 S.Ct. at 636, 78 L.Ed. at 1181. See Security Ins. Group v. Emery, 272 A.2d 736 (Me.1971) (Maine law could not be applied to extend notice period stipulated in automobile liability policy issued in Connecticut to Connecticut motorist although collision was in Maine with a Maine motorist and insured subsequently moved to Maine, citing *Delta & Pine Land*).

In *Delta & Pine Land*, the Mississippi statute that was held unconstitutional as applied read: "All contracts of insurance on property, lives or interests in this state shall be deemed to be made therein." Miss. Code § 5131 (1930). In American Fire Ins. Co. v. King Lumber & Mfg. Co., 250 U.S. 2, 39 S.Ct. 431, 63 L.Ed. 810 (1919), the Court upheld application of a Florida statute that provided: "[A]ny person who solicits insurance and procures applications therefor . . . shall be held to be the agent of the party issuing . . . anything in the application or policy to the contrary notwithstanding." Fla.Gen.Stat. § 2777 (1906).

105. 377 U.S. at 181–182, 84 S.Ct. at 1198–1199, 12 L.Ed.2d at 231–32.

106. Id. at 182, 84 S.Ct. at 1198–1199, 12 L.Ed.2d at 232. The Court's opinion, by Justice Douglas, was, at this point, quoting from Justice Black's dissent when the case had previously been before the Court. 363 U.S. 207, 221, 80 S.Ct. 1222, 1230, 1231, 4 L.Ed.2d 1170, 1181 (1960). Cf. Travelers Ins. Co. v. Fields, 451 F.2d 1292 (6th Cir.1971), cert. denied, 406 U.S. 919, 92 S.Ct. 1772, 32 L.Ed.2d 118 (1972) (although accidental death policy was issued in Ohio to Kentucky resident working in Ohio, Kentucky law can constitutionally be applied in holding that Kentucky divorce terminates rights of first wife as beneficiary under the policy); Carver v. Schafer, 647 S.W.2d 570 (Mo.App.1983) (because harm there was foreseeable, can apply law of place of accident to increase liability of bar owner in neighboring state).

Clay could be canceled by the company on five day's notice.[107] When the insurer failed to cancel after being notified that Mr. Clay had moved to Florida and taken the insured property with him, this was the functional equivalent, so far as the constitutional arguments in *Clay* were concerned, of issuing a new policy in Florida. In *Dunken*, the insurer could not cancel the seven-year term insurance except for nonpayment of premium or suicide within one year.[108] The right to convert to another form of insurance, which Dunken exercised in the fifth year of coverage,[109] was granted in the original policy.[110] No court opinion and no brief in *Clay* took note of the fact that the insurer had the power to cancel the policy when notified that Clay had moved to Florida.

As for a due process argument based on surprise, there is much confusion and not a little nonsense stemming largely from Learned Hand's opinion in *Scheer v. Rockne Motors Corporation*.[111] In this case a New York corporation owned an automobile. In New York, it entrusted the possession of the vehicle to one of its employees. The employee drove into Ontario where he crashed injuring the plaintiff, a passenger. The passenger sued the owner. Both New York and Ontario had statutes making the owner responsible for the negligence of someone to whom the owner had entrusted an automobile. In New York the owner was relieved of responsibility if the driver violated geographical restrictions that the owner had imposed on the authority to drive. Under Ontario law, once having entrusted possession of the automobile to the driver, the owner would not be relieved of liability by the driver's violation of restrictions on where the owner permitted the driver to take the automobile.

The trial judge instructed the jury that if the defendant had given possession of the automobile to the driver, it was liable for his negligence. Judge Hand reversed the resulting verdict and judgment for the plaintiff, ruling that the Ontario statute "could not"[112] be applied to the defendant unless the plaintiff proved that the driver was not exceeding his authority in entering Ontario.[113]

Judge Hand relied for his conclusion largely upon *Young v. Masci*.[114] There a New Jersey owner had loaned his automobile in New Jersey,

---

107. See *Clay*, Record p. 3c.

108. See *Dunken*, Record pp. 40–41 (paragraphs 7 and 9 of policy).

109. Id. Record p. 76.

110. Id. Record p. 41 (paragraph 10 of policy).

111. 68 F.2d 942 (2d Cir.1934).

112. Id. at 944.

113. It is not clear from the opinion whether Judge Hand would require express or only implied-in-fact authority. See Cavers, *The Two "Local Law" Theories*, 63 Harv. L. Rev. 822, 827–28 (1950). See also O'Connor v. Wray, [1930] Can.Sup.Ct. 231, [1930] 2 D.L.R. 899 (refuses to apply Ontario statute to Quebec owner who was not himself in Ontario although he gave the driver of his automobile authority to drive there). But cf. Fischl v. Chubb, 30 Pa.D. & C. 40 (Montgomery County Ct. 1937) (applies New Jersey absolute liability statute to Pennsylvania dog owner whose dog bit the plaintiff in New Jersey).

114. 289 U.S. 253, 53 S.Ct. 599, 77 L.Ed. 1158 (1933).

without restriction on its use, to a driver who took it into New York. The plaintiff, injured by the driver's negligence in New York, sued the owner in New Jersey. The New Jersey courts compensated the plaintiff, applying the New York owner's responsibility statute. The Supreme Court affirmed, rejecting due process, equal protection, and freedom of contract arguments.

Judge Hand's opinion in *Scheer* led the Minnesota Supreme Court to suggest in a dictum that, even if Wisconsin and Minnesota had similar dram shop acts, a Minnesota bar that served liquor in Minnesota to a drunk who caused damage in Wisconsin could not be subjected to liability under the Wisconsin statute absent a finding that the bar had "consented to be bound by Wisconsin law."[115]

First of all, *Young v. Masci* did not hold that the owner's authorizing the driver to drive into the state of impact was a constitutional condition precedent to applying to the owner the owner's responsibility statute of the state of impact. The Court very carefully pointed out that all it was deciding was that, at least when authority was given, there was no constitutional problem. It was not drawing a line for future decisions.[116] Secondly, the kind of outrageous surprise that will provide the basis for a tenable due process argument in choice-of-law problems can occur only under the two circumstances previously discussed[117]—upsetting reasonable reliance on the law of a particular jurisdiction and application of the law of a state that has no reasonable nexus with the party affected by that application.[118]

Thus far in this chapter, with the exception of *Scheer v. Rockne Motors Corporation* and *Young v. Masci*,[119] the cases reviewed for having imposed due process limitations on a state's choice of law have involved contracts, most often insurance contracts. Courts have sometimes cited the "telegraph cases," decided by the Supreme Court,[120] as indicating a constitutional requirement that the law of the place where harm occurred governs liability for a tort.

In *Western Union Telegraph Company v. Chiles*,[121] defendant telegraph company received in Virginia a message for transmission to a sailor aboard a ship in Norfolk Navy Yard. The telegram was transmit-

---

115. Schmidt v. Driscoll Hotel, Inc., 249 Minn. 376, 380, 82 N.W.2d 365, 367–68 (1957).

116. *Masci*, 289 U.S. at 260, 53 S.Ct. at 602, 77 L.Ed. at 1162.

117. See supra text accompanying notes 41–45.

118. See Hutchings v. Bourdages, 291 Minn. 211, 189 N.W.2d 706 (1971) (fact that owner forbade driving car into forum does not prevent application of forum's owner's liability statute). But cf. Watkins v. Cupit, 130 So.2d 720 (La.App.1961) (Mississippi father held liable for his son's tort under Louisiana law).

119. See supra text accompanying notes 111–118.

120. See Alaska Packers Ass'n v. Industrial Acc. Comm'n, 294 U.S. 532, 541, 55 S.Ct. 518, 521, 79 L.Ed. 1044, 1049 (1935): "While similar power to control the legal consequences of a tortious act committed elsewhere has been denied, Western Union Telegraph Co. v. Brown, 234 U.S. 542, 547 [1914]; Western Union Telegraph Co. v. Chiles, 214 U.S. 274, 278 [1909]; compare Western Union Telegraph Co. v. Commercial Milling Co., 218 U.S. 406 [1910], the liability under workmen's compensation acts is not for a tort."

121. 214 U.S. 274, 29 S.Ct. 613, 53 L.Ed. 994 (1909).

ted as far as Portsmouth, Virginia, adjoining the navy yard, but was never received by the sailor. The sailor sued the telegraph company in a Virginia court attempting to recover under a Virginia statute imposing a forfeiture of one hundred dollars for failure to deliver a message. The Virginia court allowed recovery, but the Supreme Court reversed. The Court relied, not on the Due Process Clause, but on Article I, section 8 of the Constitution, giving Congress "power . . . to exercise exclusive legislation" over the District of Columbia and military bases.[122]

Western Union Telegraph Company v. Brown,[123] reversing recovery under a South Carolina statute for a telegram mishandled in the District of Columbia, is similarly explained in terms of Congress' exclusive jurisdiction over federal territory.[124] More than this should not be read into *Chiles* and *Brown*. True, Holmes' opinion in *Brown* was pitched in the vested rights key,[125] but this was hardly the basis for decision.

Another case decided during the same period indicates that *Brown* and *Chiles* are not imposing strict constitutional limitations on choice of law in tort cases. In *Western Union Telegraph Company v. Commercial Milling Company*,[126] freed from the mandate of the Exclusive Jurisdiction Clause, the Court permitted recovery under a Michigan statute for negligent handling of telegram in Illinois. The telegram had been delivered to the defendant in Michigan and was mishandled after reaching Chicago.[127]

Moreover, if there ever was a viable notion that the place-of-wrong rule for resolving tort conflicts problems was required by due process, that notion is dead. *Richards v. United States*,[128] in construing the

---

122. U.S.Const.Art. I, § 8: "The Congress shall have Power. . . . To exercise exclusive legislation in all Cases whatsoever, over such District (not exceeding ten Miles square) as may, by Cession of particular States . . . become the Seat of the Government of the United States, and to exercise like Authority over all Places purchased by the Consent of the Legislature of the State in which the Same shall be, for the Erection of Forts, Magazines, Arsenals, Dock–Yards, and other needful Buildings. . . ."

123. 234 U.S. 542, 34 S.Ct. 955, 58 L.Ed. 1457 (1914).

124. Justice Holmes, who wrote the opinion, also indicated a possible improper regulation of interstate commerce. Id. at 547, 34 S.Ct. at 956, 58 L.Ed. at 1459.

125. Id.: "[W]hen a person recovers in one jurisdiction for a tort committed in another he does so on the ground of an obligation incurred at the place of the tort that accompanies the person of the defendant elsewhere, and that is not only the ground but the measure of the maximum recovery. . . . [W]hen a State attempts in this manner to affect conduct outside its jurisdiction or the consequences of such conduct, and to infringe upon the power of the United States, it must fail. . . ."

126. 218 U.S. 406, 31 S.Ct. 59, 54 L.Ed. 1088 (1910).

127. But see Tucker v. Texas Co., 203 F.2d 918 (5th Cir.1953). A laborer, employed by a Texas subcontractor was working in Louisiana pursuant to the subcontractor's contract with a general contractor. The laborer was injured in Louisiana. The Louisiana workers' compensation act barred a common-law remedy against the general contractor, but the Texas act did not. The employee sued the general contractor in Texas in tort. In reviewing summary judgment for the general contractor, the circuit court said: "[I]t is clear that the cause of action for tort can be given only by the law of the place where the tort was committed. . . ." Id. at 921. (The summary judgment was reversed on the ground that there was an issue of fact.)

128. 369 U.S. 1, 82 S.Ct. 585, 7 L.Ed.2d 492 (1962), discussed supra, text accompanying notes 20–22.

choice-of-law provision in the Federal Tort Claims Act,[129] noted the spread of interest analysis in the solution of torts conflicts problems and stated that if a state had a "sufficiently substantial contact with the activity in question" to give that state "an interest" in having its law applied to the tort, application of that state's law would not violate due process whether or not that state was the place of wrong.[130] *Allstate Insurance Company v. Hague*[131] ended whatever doubt might have remained about the constitutional imperative of the place-of-wrong rule by referring to it as "the wooden *lex loci delicti* doctrine."[132]

An issue of constitutional limitations on choice of law concerns the extent to which an award of punitive damages may seek to punish defendant's conduct outside the forum. Does it make any difference whether the conduct is lawful or unlawful in the other state?

BMW of North America v. Gore[133] held that a punitive damages award of two million dollars was so grossly excessive in the light of compensatory damages of four thousand dollars that it violated due process. BMW had not informed Gore that the automobile he purchased as new had been repainted to repair minor damage during delivery. BMW's policy was not to give such notice when, as in *Gore*, the cost of repair did not exceed 3% of the suggested retail price. This policy was in accord with disclosure statutes in 25 states. Alabama, Gore's residence and the state in which he purchased the automobile, did not have such a statute.

The jury apparently based its punitive damages award on the number of refinished automobiles that BMW sold not only in Alabama, but also in all other states. The Supreme Court stated: "While each State has ample power to protect its own consumers, none may use the punitive damages deterrent as a means of imposing its regulatory policies on the entire Nation."[134] *Gore* also stated: "Given that the verdict was based in part on out-of-state conduct that was lawful where it occurred, we need not consider whether one State may properly attempt to change a tortfeasor's *unlawful* conduct in another State."[135]

In *State Farm Mutual Auto. Ins. Co. v. Campbell*[136] the Supreme Court of the United States returned to the issue of whether in deciding whether or not to award punitive damages and if so in what amount a jury may consider the defendant's conduct in other states. The court reversed as a violation of due process an award of $145 million for

---

129.   28 U.S.C.A. § 1346(b).

130.   *Richards*, 369 U.S. at 15, 82 S.Ct. at 585, 7 L.Ed.2d at 501.

131.   449 U.S. 302, 101 S.Ct. 633, 66 L.Ed.2d 521 (1981).

132.   Id. at 316 n.22, 101 S.Ct. at 642 n.22, 66 L.Ed.2d at 533 n.22.

133.   517 U.S. 559, 116 S.Ct. 1589, 134 L.Ed.2d 809 (1996).

134.   Id. at 585, 116 S.Ct. at 1604, 134 L.Ed.2d at 832–33.

135.   Id. at 573 n.20, 116 S.Ct. at 1598 n.20, 134 L.Ed.2d at 825 n.20 (emphasis in original).

136.   538 U.S. 408, 123 S.Ct. 1513, 155 L.Ed.2d 585 (2003).

punitive damages when the award for compensatory damages was $1 million.

Defendant refused to settle a claim against plaintiff within policy limits resulting in a judgment in excess of policy limits. Evidence admitted at trial concerned defendant's conduct nationwide that allegedly attempted to minimize payments without regard to the merits of a claim. The Court stated that "as a general rule" a State does not "have a legitimate concern in imposing punitive damages to punish a defendant for unlawful acts committed outside of the State's jurisdiction."[137] The opinion added, however, that in determining the reprehensibility of defendant's conduct, which is a proper consideration in determining punitive damages, the jury might consider the defendant's conduct in other instances but that "dissimilar acts, independent from the acts upon which liability was premised, may not serve as the basis for punitive damages.... Although evidence of other acts need not be identical to have relevance in the calculation of punitive damages, the Utah court erred here because evidence pertaining to claims that had nothing to do with a third-party lawsuit was introduced at length. Other evidence concerning reprehensibility was even more tangential."[138]

On the consideration of out-of-state conduct that was lawful where it occurred, the Court gave confusing directions:

> A State cannot punish a defendant for conduct that may have been lawful where it occurred....
>
> Lawful out-of-state conduct may be probative when it demonstrates the deliberateness and culpability of the defendant's action in the State where it is tortious, but that conduct must have a nexus to the specific harm suffered by the plaintiff. A jury must be instructed, furthermore, that it may not use evidence of out-of-state conduct to punish a defendant for action that was lawful in the jurisdiction where it occurred.[139]

Boyd v. Goffoli,[140] stated that "this Court does not believe that the *Campbell* Court's broadly worded dictum that a state does not have a legitimate concern imposing punitive damages to punish a defendant's unlawful out-of-state conduct applies to the instant case."[141] In *Boyd* the plaintiffs were West Virginia citizens whom the defendant told to use a fictitious Pennsylvania address and to train in Pennsylvania for Pennsylvania commercial drivers' licenses. The defendant allegedly misinformed the plaintiffs that the Pennsylvania licenses could then be transferred to

---

137. 538 U.S. at 421, 123 S.Ct. at 1522, 155 L.Ed.2d at 603. See also Philip Morris USA v. Williams, 549 U.S. 346, 127 S.Ct. 1057, 1064, 166 L.Ed.2d 940 (2007) (stating that the jury may consider harm to nonparties in determining whether defendant's conduct is reprehensible, but "a jury may not go further than this and use a punitive damages verdict to punish a defendant directly on account of harms it is alleged to have visited on nonparties").

138. 538 U.S. at 422–24, 123 S.Ct. at 1523, 155 L.Ed.2d at 604–05.

139. 538 U.S. at 420–22, 123 S.Ct. at 1521–23, 155 L.Ed.2d at 603–04.

140. 216 W.Va. 552, 608 S.E.2d 169 (2004).

141. Id. at 178.

West Virginia without violating Pennsylvania law. The scheme did violate Pennsylvania law.

The jury awarded each plaintiff $250,000 in punitive damages. The defendant claimed that the jury improperly awarded punitive damages "on the basis of an out-of-state 'scheme' to violate Pennsylvania law."[142] The court rejected this argument:

> Appellees were all West Virginia residents who were initially informed of the Pennsylvania scheme, and wrongly assured that it was legal by Appellant's agent who was a resident of West Virginia. Further, Appellees' economic losses occurred in West Virginia. Therefore, West Virginia has a significant contact with the claims asserted by Appellees. As a result, the fact that a portion of Appellant's misconduct occurred in Pennsylvania is legally insignificant. Certainly, a West Virginia court has an interest in protecting its citizens from tortious conduct and is not precluded from doing so simply because some of the tortious conduct occurred in another state.[143]

§ 9.2B Effect of Procedural Classification on Due Process Limitations

If a state does not have sufficient contact with the parties or with the facts to make it reasonable for its law to be used in adjudicating a controversy arising between the parties on those facts, application of the law of that state will violate the Due Process Clause of the Fourteenth Amendment to the Federal Constitution. But what does "law" mean in this context? Does it include only substantive law and exclude what might normally be regarded as local procedure?

We have already seen two cases in which the forum's procedural classification of the law applied did not prevent the decision from being overturned on constitutional grounds. In *Home Insurance Company v. Dick*,[144] classifying the one-year contractual limitation in the insurance policy as "procedural" did not make it any less unreasonable for Texas to ignore that limitation. In *John Hancock Mutual Life Insurance Company v. Yates*,[145] although the decision formally relied on full faith and credit rather than due process, classifying both the materiality of the misrepresentation and whether the materiality issue should be submitted to the jury as "procedural" did not prevent reversal. From these cases it might be supposed that "law" in our definition of due process limitations on a state's choice of law is to receive the same outcome-determinative interpretation that "law of the state in which it sits" received under the rule of *Erie Railroad v. Tompkins*.[146] Such, however, is not the case.

---

142. Id. at 176.

143. Id. at 179.

144. 281 U.S. 397, 50 S.Ct. 338, 74 L.Ed. 926 (1930), discussed supra, text accompanying notes 46–52.

145. 299 U.S. 178, 57 S.Ct. 129, 81 L.Ed. 106 (1936), discussed supra, text accompanying notes 91–95.

146. 304 U.S. 64, 58 S.Ct. 817, 82 L.Ed. 1188 (1938). But see Hanna v. Plumer, 380 U.S. 460, 85 S.Ct. 1136, 14 L.Ed.2d 8 (1965).

McElmoyle v. Cohen[147] decided that a forum that has no substantial connection with a cause of action might apply its own statute of limitations to bar a cause of action that would not be barred under a statute of limitations of the state with which the cause does have its significant contacts. In that case, suit was brought in Georgia on a judgment obtained in South Carolina. *McElmoyle* held that Georgia could refuse to enforce the judgment on the grounds that the Georgia statute of limitations for suits on judgments had run, despite the fact that South Carolina limitations had not expired. The Court relied for its result on the standard conflicts characterization of a general statute of limitation as procedural: "[W]e think it well settled to be a plea to the remedy; and consequently that the lex fori must prevail."[148]

Wells v. Simonds Abrasive Company[149] confirmed this conclusion. Mr. Wells was killed in Alabama when the grinding wheel with which he was working burst. A Pennsylvania corporation had manufactured the wheel. Unable to serve process on the manufacturer in Alabama, the decedent's administratrix brought suit in a federal court in Pennsylvania under the Alabama death act. The Alabama act contained within it a two-year period of limitation. The comparable Pennsylvania act had a one-year limit. Suit was brought more than one year but less than two years after death. The federal court, following what it decided was the Pennsylvania conflicts rule, applied the Pennsylvania one-year statute and ordered summary judgment for the defendant. The Supreme Court affirmed. Review was limited to the question of whether there had been a denial of full faith and credit to the Alabama death act, but, in this context, if there was no denial of full faith and credit, there would be no violation of due process.[150]

On the surface, it might appear that this application of the forum's shorter statute of limitations unreasonably changed the result when the forum did not have a sufficient contact with the controversy to apply its law. It should be noted, however, that the forum's dismissal based on the forum's shorter statute of limitations need not be on the merits. Furthermore, even if the forum has no contact with the controversy except as forum, simply as forum it has an interest in preventing the prosecution of what its own statute of limitations would label as a stale claim. This interest qua forum may be sufficient to make application of the

---

147.   38 U.S. (13 Pet.) 312, 10 L.Ed. 177 (1839).

148.   Id. at 327, 10 L.Ed. at 184; cf. Watkins v. Conway, 385 U.S. 188, 87 S.Ct. 357, 17 L.Ed.2d 286 (1966) (forum may apply a shorter statute of limitations to sister state judgments than it does to domestic judgments); Newhouse v. Newhouse, 271 Or. 109, 530 P.2d 848 (1975) (forum may apply its own statute of limitations to a sister-state judgment); Potomac Leasing Co. v. Dasco Technology Corp., 10 P.3d 972 (Utah 2000) (noting a split of authority as to whether the forum statute of limitations for enforcing sister-state judgments applies to sister-state judgments registered under the Uniform Enforcement of Foreign Judgments Act and holding that it does); Carter v. Carter, 232 Va. 166, 349 S.E.2d 95 (1986) (the forum may apply a shorter statute of limitations to a sister-state judgment than to a forum judgment and need not permit revival of a sister-state judgment).

149.   345 U.S. 514, 73 S.Ct. 856, 97 L.Ed. 1211 (1953).

150.   Full faith and credit may invalidate a choice of law that due process permits. See § 9.3A.

forum's shorter statute reasonable enough to accord with minimum due process standards.

It may be urged that the fact that the forum's dismissal is theoretically not on the merits is of little consequence if, as a practical matter, the plaintiff cannot find any other jurisdiction where the courts will have a basis for in personam jurisdiction over the defendant.[151] Perhaps the way to meet this objection is not to use the Due Process Clause to prevent a forum from asserting whatever legitimate interests it may have as forum in closing its doors. It would be preferable for the state whose law is functionally relevant to the controversy to enact a long-arm statute that would confer jurisdiction on its courts. It is also desirable that the Due Process Clause be applied to problems of judicial jurisdiction in such a manner as to facilitate the obtaining of jurisdiction over the defendant in the state whose law ought to be applied.[152]

Therefore, the Due Process Clause should not be utilized to prevent a forum from applying its own shorter statute of limitations. Suppose, however, that the forum, having no contact with the controversy except as forum, seeks to apply its own longer statute of limitations to permit an action barred by the statute of limitations of a jurisdiction that has a legitimate interest in protecting the defendant from suit. The application of the forum's longer statute cannot be justified in terms of a forum interest in preventing the litigation of stale claims. Application of a longer period of limitations, unlike a mere denial of a forum, will result in a judgment on the merits. Is, therefore, the application of the forum's longer limitations period to a controversy with which the forum has no significant contact so unreasonable as to constitute a violation of due process of law?

In *Home Insurance Company v. Dick* there is a dictum by Justice Brandeis that it is not unconstitutional for a forum to apply its longer statute of limitations. Although Justice Brandeis finds a violation of due process in the Texas court's ignoring of the one-year contractual limitation, he says: "And, in the absence of a contractual provision, the local statute of limitation may be applied to a right created in another jurisdiction even where the remedy in the latter is barred."[153]

Is this distinction between a limit contracted for by the parties and a limit set by the statute of another jurisdiction valid? It might be argued that realistically the parties are more likely to formulate justifiable

---

151. See Vernon, *Some Constitutional Problems in the Conflict of Laws and Statutes of Limitation*, 7 J.Pub.L. 120, 124 (1958).

152. See Jackson, *Full Faith and Credit—The Lawyer's Clause of the Constitution*, 45 Colum. L. Rev. 1, 30 (1945): "Occasions which require the forum to make a choice between application of its own law and that of some other state would be diminished if courts were free to decline cases that might more appropriately be litigated elsewhere, and also if appropriate courts were enabled better to get jurisdiction of the persons concerned."

153. 281 U.S. 397, 409, 50 S.Ct. 338, 341, 74 L.Ed. 926, 934 (1930) (dictum). Accord, Canadian Pac. Ry. v. Johnston, 61 Fed. 738 (2d Cir.1894) (permitting tort action to proceed although barred by statute of limitations of place of injury). The court's theory was that the plaintiff had moved out of the foreign jurisdiction before the bar of its statute became effective.

expectations in terms of a limitation period that they themselves set than in terms of a statutory period of which they may not even be aware. Furthermore, use of procedural classification to apply the forum's longer limitation period has been a traditional conflicts rule.[154] A court is not likely to be readily convinced that a common-law rule of such long standing is so unreasonable as to constitute a violation of due process of law. Moreover, the common distinction between a general statute of limitations and one specifically related to the right[155] is not of constitutional dignity. "Differences based upon whether the foreign right was known to the common law or upon the arrangement of the code of the foreign state are too unsubstantial to form the basis for constitutional distinctions under the Full Faith and Credit Clause"[156]—or under due process.

Sun Oil Company v. Wortman[157] supports the view that there are no constitutional limitations on a state's freedom to apply its own longer statute of limitations. *Sun Oil* held that a state could apply its own longer statute of limitations even though limitations had expired in the states whose law it was constitutionally compelled to apply to "substantive"[158] issues. The basis for the opinion was so narrow, however, that the case may be of only temporary significance.

The three states whose limitations had run, Louisiana, Oklahoma, and Texas, "view[ed] their own statutes as procedural for choice-of-law purposes."[159] There is a growing realization that statutes of limitations should be treated as "substantive" and subjected to full choice-of-law analysis.[160] Therefore it is less likely that in the future the state whose statute has run will affix the "procedural" label to that statute. If Louisiana, Oklahoma, and Texas had already taken this step, all of the opinions in *Sun Oil*[161] would have to be rewritten, and perhaps the opposite result reached.

---

154. For cases abandoning the procedural classification of statutes of limitations, see § 3.2C2, note 62 and accompanying text.

155. See § 3.2C2, text accompanying notes 51–52.

156. Wells v. Simonds Abrasive Co., 345 U.S. 514, 518, 73 S.Ct. 856, 858, 97 L.Ed. 1211, 1216 (1953).

157. 486 U.S. 717, 108 S.Ct. 2117, 100 L.Ed.2d 743 (1988).

158. Id. at 722, 108 S.Ct. at 2121, 100 L.Ed.2d at 752. Accord, Goad v. Celotex Corp., 831 F.2d 508 (4th Cir.1987), cert. denied, 487 U.S. 1218, 108 S.Ct. 2871, 101 L.Ed.2d 906 (1988); cf. Keeton v. Hustler Magazine, Inc., 131 N.H. 6, 549 A.2d 1187 (1988) (although longer forum statute of limitations is "procedural," would reach same result if "substantive" because libel was published in the forum as well as in the states whose limitations had run); Hay, *Judicial Jurisdiction and Choice of Law: Constitutional Limitations*, 59 U.Colo. L. Rev. 9, 32 (1988) ("assuming 'state interest' in New Hampshire, reinstating liabilities time-barred in the states that created them would appear to violate the defendant's due process rights"); Pielemeier, *Constitutional Limitations on Choice of Law: The Special Case of Multistate Defamation*, 133 Pa. L. Rev. 381, 383 (1985) (application of forum's defamation law in *Keeton* "would substantially jeopardize constitutional values").

159. Id. at 729 n.3, 108 S.Ct. at 2125 n.3, 100 L.Ed.2d at 757 n.3.

160. See supra § 3.2C2.

161. Justice Scalia wrote for the Court. On the limitations issue, Chief Justice Rehnquist, and Justices White, Stevens, and O'Connor joined, although O'Connor wrote a separate opinion in which Rehnquist joined, concurring on limitations and dissenting on

In his opinion on the limitations issue, Justice Scalia noted that "[i]t cannot possibly be a violation of the Full Faith and Credit Clause for a State to decline to apply another State's law where that other State *itself* does not consider it applicable."[162] Therefore Kansas could be constitutionally compelled to apply the shorter statutes of limitations of the other three states only if they themselves were compelled by either due process or full faith and credit to regard their statutes as substantive and the running of those statutes as barring suits not only in their own forum but also in any other state. Quite understandably, Justice Scalia declined to find any such constitutional compulsion that a state insist on the application of its own law in other states. "Moreover, [defendant] could in no way have been unfairly surprised by the application to it of a rule [the forum applies its own period of limitations] as old as the Republic."[163]

On the other hand, suppose, as will more likely be so in the future, the state whose statute has run regards its limitations as "substantive"? Two examples illustrate the full faith and credit and due process issues. First, full faith and credit: The case that will most directly throw the full-faith-and-credit fat in the fire is one in which the same parties have already litigated the same claim in a sister state. The first court expressly declared that its limitation period should apply to bar suit between plaintiff and defendant not only in its own forum but also in any place else.[164] Defendant demands full faith and credit to this decision when sued in the second state.

Second, due process: Four years after the claim accrues, plaintiff sues in F, which has a five-year statute of limitations. F does not have a sufficient nexus with the parties or with the transaction to have any legitimate interest in providing relief barred in X. X, the residence of both parties, has a three-year limitations period. It is clear from X decisions that if X had decided the case pending in F, X would have declared its shorter period controlling everywhere.

Just as Justice Scalia would have to rethink his opinion in these latter circumstances, so would the other justices who concurred in the

---

whether Kansas had constitutionally decided that the other states would reach the same result as Kansas on the amount of interest due on suspended royalties. On the limitations issue, Justice Brennan concurred only in the result, joined by Justices Marshall and Blackmun. Justice Kennedy took no part.

162. *Sun Oil*, 486 U.S. at 729 n.3, 108 S.Ct. at 2125 n.3, 100 L.Ed.2d at 757 n.3 (emphasis in original).

163. Id. at 730, 108 S.Ct. at 2126, 100 L.Ed.2d at 757.

164. If the forum wishes to bar suit in another state, it is important that this intention be clearly expressed. Declaring that the running of the forum's limitations bars suit "on the merits" is ambiguous because it does not make clear whether this bar extends beyond forum courts. See Semtek Int'l Inc. v. Lockheed Martin Corp., 531 U.S. 497, 121 S.Ct. 1021, 149 L.Ed.2d 32 (2001) (Federal Rule of Civil Procedure making a judgment dismissing an action because time limitations have run an "adjudication upon the merits" only bars refiling the same claim in the same United States District Court); Lee v. Swain Bldg. Materials Co., 529 So.2d 188 (Miss. 1988) (deny full faith and credit to Louisiana judgment of dismissal "with prejudice" that was based on running of limitations—dismissal "on the merits" because of limitations applies only to courts in same state).

result on limitations. Justice O'Connor, with whom Chief Justice Rehnquist joined, expressly left open the question of whether she would reach a different result "if Texas, Oklahoma, or Louisiana regarded its own shorter statute of limitations as substantive."[165] Justice Brennan, with whom Justices Marshall and Blackmun joined, concurred in the result with a Zen-like meditation on the complexity and mystery of limitations reality.

Brennan reasoned that if the state whose law would properly apply to the underlying claim ("the claim state") has a shorter statute of limitations than that of the state in which suit is brought, it is not clear that the claim state would wish its limitations applied to bar suit in the sister-state forum because "a claim State may have a substantive interest in vindicating claims that, at a particular period, outweighs its substantive interest in repose standing alone but not the combination of its interest in repose and avoiding the adjudication of stale claims."[166] This Gordian knot of forum-procedural-staleness and substantive-justice issues would be cut if it were clear that, yes indeed; the state with the shorter statute of limitations wishes its concepts of repose to control elsewhere, as well as in its own courts.

Justice Scalia cites three opinions for the proposition that "[t]his Court has long and repeatedly held that the Constitution does not bar application of the forum State's statute of limitations to claims that in their substance are and must be governed by the law of a different State"[167]—*Wells v. Simonds Abrasive Company*,[168] *Townsend v. Jemison*,[169] and *McElmoyle v. Cohen*.[170]

Wells and *McElmoyle* were cases in which, unlike *Sun Oil*, the forum's statute of limitations was shorter than in the other state. *Townsend* did permit suit in Alabama on a contract made in Mississippi when the Mississippi statute of limitations had run. The court in *Townsend* refers to a case also referred to by Justice Scalia[171]—Joseph Story's Circuit Court opinion in *Le Roy v. Crowninshield*.[172] Justice Wayne, the author of the *Townsend* opinion, said: "We will now venture to suggest the causes which misled the learned judge [Story] in Leroy v. Crowninshield.... We do not find him pressing his argument in Leroy v. Crowninshield in the Conflict of Laws [Story's treatise], in which it might have been appropriately done, if his doubts, for so he calls them,

---

165. *Sun Oil*, 486 U.S. at 743, 108 S.Ct. at 2133, 100 L.Ed.2d at 766.

166. Id. at 738, 108 S.Ct. at 2139, 100 L.Ed.2d at 762.

167. Id. at 722, 108 S.Ct. at 2121, 100 L.Ed.2d at 752. Cf. Hall v. Summit Contractors, Inc., 356 Ark. 609, 158 S.W.3d 185 (2004) (legislature may retroactively lengthen time to sue for claims not already barred but may not, by repealing statute that borrowed time limitations of another state, lengthen time for suit on a claim already barred under the borrowed law).

168. 345 U.S. 514, 73 S.Ct. 856, 97 L.Ed. 1211 (1953).

169. 50 U.S. (9 How.) 407, 13 L.Ed. 194 (1850).

170. 38 U.S. (13 Pet.) 312, 10 L.Ed. 177 (1839).

171. *Sun Oil*, 486 U.S. at 723, 108 S.Ct. at 2122, 100 L.Ed.2d at 753.

172. 15 Fed.Cas. 362 (No. 8,269) (D.Mass.1820).

had not been removed.... [W]e find him, in the Conflict of Laws, stating the law upon the point, in opposition to his former doubts, not in deference to authority alone, but from declared conviction."[173]

Le Roy v. Crowninshield, the Story circuit opinion, invoked, at an interval of 138 years, by both Justices Scalia and Wayne, was a suit in Massachusetts on a contract made in New York. Justice Story overruled defendant's plea that the New York statute of limitations had run. Justice Wayne is referring to the fact that despite the holding in *Crowninshield*, Justice Story said in the opinion that he was compelled to do so by precedent and that "if the question were now entirely new [I would hold] [t]hat where all remedies are barred, or discharged by the lex loci contractus, and have operated on the case there, the bar may be pleaded by the debtor in a foreign tribunal, to repel any suit brought to enforce the debt."[174] Justice Wayne then says that Story's famous treatise on Conflict of Laws abandoned this notion that a state with no interest in the merits should not be able to apply its own longer statute of limitations. Justice Wayne was mistaken. Although Wayne does not cite to any portion of the treatise, in section 582, which retained the identical wording through the three editions published during Story's lifetime, Story takes the same position as he did in *Crowninshield*.[175]

It is unreasonable for a forum that has no significant contact with the controversy to employ its own longer statute to extend the limitations period.[176] Such conduct serves no substantial interest of the forum. Application of the foreign statute of limitations is not likely to enmesh the forum in the details of foreign procedure.[177] Application of the forum's longer limitation period results in a judgment on the merits different from the judgment that could have been obtained in the jurisdiction with which the controversy is most closely connected. Due process should preclude a state from applying its own law to a case on the sole ground that the law applied is "procedural" if application of forum law advances no relevant forum policy and if failure to apply the foreign rule will trigger forum shopping to change the result.

---

173.   *Townsend*, 50 U.S. at 415–16, 13 L.Ed. at 198.

174.   *Crowninshield*, 15 Fed.Cas. at 371 (Story, J.)

175.   J. Story, Commentaries on the Conflict of Laws § 582 (1834), (2d ed. 1841), (3d ed. 1846).

176.   See Martin, *Constitutional Limitations on Choice of Law*, 61 Cornell L. Rev. 185, 221 (1976). Cf. Keeton v. Hustler Magazine, Inc., 465 U.S. 770, 104 S.Ct. 1473, 79 L.Ed.2d 790 (1984). *Keeton* upheld jurisdiction in a libel action against a magazine that distributed a small percentage of its copies in the forum. Although the action was by a nonresident, the Court found that New Hampshire had an interest in deterring deception of its citizens. It was argued that it would be unfair to apply New Hampshire's statute of limitations to permit suit when the limitation periods in all other jurisdictions had run. The Court found that this did not affect the jurisdictional issue and said: "There has been considerable academic criticism of the rule that permits a forum State to apply its own statute of limitations regardless of the significance of contacts between the forum State and the litigation. [Citing i.a. this text.] But we find it unnecessary to express an opinion at this time as to whether any arguable unfairness rises to the level of a due process violation," Id. at 778 n.10, 104 S.Ct. at 1480 n.10, 79 L.Ed.2d at 800 n.10.

177.   See Morgan, *Choice of Law Governing Proof*, 58 Harv. L. Rev. 153, 195 (1944).

§ 9.3 Full Faith and Credit Limitations on a State's Choice of Law

§ 9.3A General Considerations

Suppose that a state has sufficient contact with the parties or with the facts so that, within the limits of due process, its law may be used in adjudicating a controversy arising between the parties on those facts. Under what circumstances will the use of that state's law nevertheless violate the requirements of full faith and credit? Perhaps we can formulate a working hypothesis by juxtaposing two groups of cases in which the mandate of full faith and credit has been involved in attempts to limit a state's choice of law. These cases deal with workers' compensation awards and the obligations of fraternal beneficiary societies.

Probably the best known cases discussing the extent to which full faith and credit will prevent the forum from applying its own law are the workers' compensation decisions beginning with *Bradford Electric Light Company v. Clapper*.[178] A Vermont utility company employed a Vermont resident who performed work for the company in both Vermont and New Hampshire. The Vermont workers' compensation act covered the employment. The act provided statutory compensation for workers killed or injured in the course of employment. There was also a provision that the statutory remedy was the sole remedy against the employer for injury anywhere in the course of employment. The employee was killed in the act of restoring fuses at a substation in New Hampshire. The New Hampshire workers' compensation act gave the worker an election, even after injury, of suing his or her employer at common law for negligence.

The employee's executrix elected common law recovery. She brought suit in a New Hampshire state court. Defendant removed the case to federal court, which rendered a judgment for the plaintiff. Defendant objected that the common-law judgment denied full faith and credit to the provision of the Vermont workers' compensation act that declared the act the exclusive remedy in such a situation.[179] In an opinion written by Justice Brandeis, the Supreme Court reversed.

Brandeis reasoned thusly. A statute is a "public act" within the meaning of the Full Faith and Credit Clause. New Hampshire was only the place of injury of a nonresident employee, working in New Hampshire temporarily and leaving no dependents there. Therefore, "[i]t is difficult to see how the state's interest would be subserved, under such

---

178. 286 U.S. 145, 52 S.Ct. 571, 76 L.Ed. 1026 (1932).

179. Ohio v. Chattanooga Boiler & Tank Co., 289 U.S. 439, 53 S.Ct. 663, 77 L.Ed. 1307 (1933), illustrates why a statutory exclusive remedy provision is important to a full faith and credit defense. Decided the year after *Bradford* and also written by Brandeis, *Chattanooga Boiler* held that an Ohio court did not deny full faith and credit to the Tennessee workers' compensation act although the facts were similar to those in *Bradford*. There was no denial of full faith and credit because, as construed by the Tennessee courts, the Tennessee act did not purport to deny a remedy under other workers' compensation acts for injuries suffered out of state. "And the full faith and credit clause does not require that greater effect be given the Tennessee statute elsewhere than is given in the courts of that State." Id. at 443, 53 S.Ct. at 665, 77 L.Ed. at 1310.

circumstances, by burdening its courts with this litigation."[180] Or, one might add, by applying its law permitting recovery in excess of that permitted under the Vermont workers' compensation statute. In addition to New Hampshire's lack of interest, if the plaintiff were permitted to recover under the New Hampshire tort remedy an amount in excess of that permitted under the Vermont workers' compensation statute, "the effectiveness of the Vermont act would be gravely impaired."[181]

This last statement by Brandeis, concerning the grave impairment that would have resulted to Vermont interests if full faith and credit were not required for the exclusive remedy clause in the Vermont workers' compensation statute, is important to an understanding of the full faith and credit standard that Brandeis was using in *Clapper*. The need for full faith and credit is directly proportional to the extent to which the policies of a state, as articulated in its public acts, records, and judicial proceedings, would be impaired if credit is denied to those acts, records, and proceedings. In Brandeis' view, therefore, the interest of New Hampshire in having its law applied to permit a tort recovery was outweighed by the national need for full faith and credit to the Vermont workers' compensation statute, in order to prevent grave impairment to the policies underlying the Vermont statute.

Justice Brandeis states:

> Moreover, there is no adequate basis for the lower court's conclusion that to deny recovery would be obnoxious to the public policy of New Hampshire. No decision of the state court has been cited indicating that recognition of the Vermont statute would be regarded in New Hampshire as prejudicial to the interests of its citizens.[182]

It does not seem that Brandeis intended this reference to what would be "obnoxious" to New Hampshire policy as a test of the requirement of full faith and credit. This remark follows his discussion of the difference between a forum's using its public policy to "decline to enforce a foreign cause of action" and using public policy "to refuse to give effect to a substantive defense under the applicable law of another state, as under the circumstances here presented".[183] Closing the forum to enforcement of a foreign cause of action on public policy grounds leaves the plaintiff "free to enforce it elsewhere", but refusal to recognize a defense "subjects the defendant to irremediable liability." After stating this important difference between two circumstances in which a forum might invoke its public policy to deny effect to foreign law, Brandeis notes that, in any event there is no indication that enforcement of the defense based on the exclusive remedy provision of the Vermont workers' compensation statute "would be obnoxious to the public policy of New Hampshire."

---

180. *Bradford*, 286 U.S. at 162, 52 S.Ct. at 577, 76 L.Ed. at 1037.

181. Id. at 159, 52 S.Ct. at 575, 76 L.Ed. at 1035.

182. Id. at 161, 52 S.Ct. at 576, 76 L.Ed. at 1036.

183. Id. at 160, 52 S.Ct. at 576, 76 L.Ed. at 1036.

The next significant case in the series of workers' compensation opinions is *Alaska Packers Association v. Industrial Accident Commission*.[184] A nonresident alien and a company doing business in California executed a written employment contract in California. The worker agreed to work for the company in Alaska during the salmon-canning season. The company agreed to transport the worker to Alaska and, at the end of the season, to return him to California where he was to be paid. The contract recited that the worker elected to be bound by the Alaska workers' compensation act. The worker, covered by the Alaska act, was injured while working in Alaska. The Alaska act, like the Vermont act in *Bradford*, had a provision making it the exclusive remedy for covered workers against employers. The injured worker waited until he returned to California and there applied for and was awarded compensation under the California workers' compensation act. The award was made over objections that it denied full faith and credit to the exclusive remedy provision of the Alaska act.

The Supreme Court affirmed a refusal of the California high court to set aside the award. The opinion was written by Justice Stone. Stone had concurred in *Bradford* solely on the ground that a New Hampshire state court would have honored voluntarily the defense under the Vermont compensation act and that a federal court sitting in New Hampshire should do the same.[185] He saw no basis for applying the Full Faith and Credit Clause to compel an unwilling New Hampshire court to bow to the Vermont statute. New Hampshire's interest as the place of the injury was sufficient to prevent this.[186]

Now Stone, upholding California's refusal to bow to Alaska law, nodded in passing to the "obnoxiousness" language used by Brandeis in *Bradford*. In *Alaska Packers*, what Justice Stone apparently perceived as an "obnoxiousness" test was held to be satisfied. The highest court of California had specifically "declared it to be contrary to the policy of the State to give effect to the provisions of the Alaska statute and that they conflict with its own statutes."[187] Thus Stone found an "obnoxiousness" test satisfied between two states that would keep the worker's recovery within the framework of workers' compensation legislation, while Brandeis found no obnoxiousness existing between New Hampshire, which would allow escape from the statutory system, and Vermont, which would not.[188]

The explanation for this seeming paradox is that Stone reformulated the "obnoxiousness" test that he thought Brandeis had employed and produced a "weighing" test. Because both the Alaska and the California workers' compensation statutes contained exclusive remedy provisions,

184. 294 U.S. 532, 55 S.Ct. 518, 79 L.Ed. 1044 (1935).

185. *Bradford*, 286 U.S. at 163, 52 S.Ct. at 577, 76 L.Ed. at 1037.

186. Id. at 164, 52 S.Ct. at 577, 76 L.Ed. at 1038.

187. *Alaska Packers*, 294 U.S. at 549, 55 S.Ct. at 524, 79 L.Ed. at 1053.

188. See 4 Larson, The Law of Workmen's Compensation § 86.40: "Oddly enough, the only case in which there was a deep-seated policy difference between the two statutes was the one case in which 'obnoxiousness' was found to be absent—the *Bradford* case."

there was a direct conflict between the California and Alaska statutes. In such a situation:

> [A] rigid and literal enforcement of the full faith and credit clause, without regard to the statute of the forum, would lead to the absurd result that, wherever the conflict arises, the statute of each state must be enforced in the courts of the other, but cannot be in its own. . . .
>
> . . . [T]he conflict is to be resolved . . . by appraising the governmental interests of each jurisdiction, and turning the scale of decision according to their weight.
>
> . . . *Prima facie* every state is entitled to enforce in its own courts its own statutes, lawfully enacted. One who challenges that right, because of the force given to a conflicting statute of another state by the full faith and credit clause, assumes the burden of showing, upon some rational basis, that of the conflicting interests involved those of the foreign state are superior to those of the forum. . . .[189]
>
> . . . [Here California's] interest is sufficient to justify its legislation and is greater than that of Alaska, of which the employee was never a resident and to which he may never return. . . .
>
> The interest of Alaska is not shown to be superior to that of California.[190]

Under this "weighing" standard, when each of two states has sufficient interest in a controversy to apply its own law without violating due process, full faith and credit will impose no additional limitation on choice of law unless the interest of one state, embodied in a "public act" of that state, can be shown to "outweigh" the interest of the other state.

The next step in the rise and fall of full faith and credit in workers' compensation cases was *Pacific Employers Insurance Company v. Industrial Accident Commission.*[191] The facts recall the *Bradford* case. Here a resident of Massachusetts, regularly employed in Massachusetts by a Massachusetts corporation, was injured while on temporary duty in California. The Supreme Court upheld California's award of compensation under the California act in disregard of the exclusive remedy provision of the Massachusetts act. Again, Justice Stone wrote the opinion and nodded to the *Bradford* "obnoxiousness" language by pointing out that here the Supreme Court of California had specifically declared it obnoxious to its policy to remit one in the position of the instant employee to recovery under the compensation act of another state.[192] Far more significant was the decreased emphasis on comparing the interests of California and Massachusetts and the greatly increased

---

189. *Alaska Packers*, 294 U.S. at 547–548, 55 S.Ct. at 523–524, 79 L.Ed. at 1052.

190. Id. at 549–550, 55 S.Ct. at 524–525, 79 L.Ed. at 1053. Cf. Kirgis, *The Roles of Due Process and Full Faith and Credit in Choice of Law*, 62 Cornell L. Rev. 94, 120 (1976) (the forum cannot apply its own law if "another state has an interest in applying its law that is overwhelming by comparison with the interest of the forum").

191. 306 U.S. 493, 59 S.Ct. 629, 83 L.Ed. 940 (1939).

192. Id. at 504, 59 S.Ct. at 633, 83 L.Ed. at 946.

emphasis on the important interests of California viewed separately. The injured employee, after all, was in California, receiving medical treatment and constituting a burden on California institutions—a burden that the California compensation act was designed to lighten.

This change in analysis was highlighted in *Cardillo v. Liberty Mutual Insurance Company*.[193] A District of Columbia firm employed a resident of the District. The employee had previously worked in the District of Columbia and was subject to reassignment there, but for the past three years he had been working only in Virginia, commuting daily between the job in Virginia and his home in the District of Columbia. He was killed in Virginia while driving home from work. The Supreme Court upheld an award to the employee's dependents under the District of Columbia compensation act although that award disregarded the exclusive remedy provision of the Virginia act. The opinion, by Justice Murphy, did not utilize the "obnoxiousness" test, nor was there a weighing of Virginia and District of Columbia interests a la *Alaska Packers*. The District of Columbia, viewed apart from any other jurisdiction, had an important interest in the matter and that was that.

> [T]he District's legitimate interest in providing adequate workmen's compensation measures for its residents does not turn on the fortuitous circumstance of the place of their work or injury.... Rather it depends upon some substantial connection between the District and the particular employee-employer relationship, a connection which is present in this case.... And as so applied the statute fully satisfies any constitutional questions of due process or full faith and credit.[194]

See also Franchise Tax Board of California v. Hyatt, 538 U.S. 488, 123 S.Ct. 1683, 155 L.Ed.2d 702 (2003) (Nevada need not give full faith and credit to California statute immunizing California tax collection agency from suit for intentional torts when the Nevada Supreme Court found that affording immunity would "contravene Nevada's policies and interests"); Nevada v. Hall, 440 U.S. 410, 99 S.Ct. 1182, 59 L.Ed.2d 416 (1979) (in personal injury suit by California residents against instrumentality of State of Nevada, California need not surrender jurisdiction nor give full faith and credit to Nevada $25,000 limit on damages because it would be "obnoxious" to California's policy of full recovery); Biscoe v. Arlington County, 738 F.2d 1352 (D.C.Cir.1984) (a D.C. court has jurisdiction over a Virginia county for harm caused in D.C. by a county police officer and need not give full faith and credit to the Virginia law of sovereign immunity); Mianecki v. Second Judicial Dist. Ct., 99 Nev. 93, 658 P.2d 422 (1983), cert. dism'd for want of final judgment, 464 U.S. 806, 104 S.Ct. 195, 78 L.Ed.2d 171 (1983) (Nevada court has jurisdiction over Wisconsin in suit for harm caused in Nevada by released sex offender and need not give full faith and credit to the Wisconsin law of sovereign immunity); Cf. Sam v. Estate of Sam, 139 N.M. 474, 134 P.3d 761 (2006) (as a matter of comity dismiss suit against Arizona governmental entity as not timely under time limitations in New Mexico Tort Claims Act when time limitations in Arizona Tort Claims Act have also expired); Hansen v. Scott, 687 N.W.2d 247 (N.D. 2004) (applying the same level of immunity as public employees would have under North Dakota law, which is less than the immunity under Texas law, employees of Texas Department of Criminal Justice are immune from suit for deaths caused in North Dakota).

193. 330 U.S. 469, 67 S.Ct. 801, 91 L.Ed. 1028 (1947).

194. Id. at 476, 67 S.Ct. 805, 91 L.Ed. 1035. See also Dissell v. Trans World Airlines, 511 A.2d 441 (Me.1986), cert. denied, 479 U.S. 948, 107 S.Ct. 433, 93 L.Ed.2d 382 (1986)

It was becoming increasingly difficult to distinguish the requirements of full faith and credit from those of due process in the workers' compensation field.

Any remaining distinction was all but obliterated by *Carroll v. Lanza*.[195] The employee here was a resident of Missouri employed by a Missouri contractor. The employment contract had been made in Missouri. The Missouri contractor agreed to subcontract some work in Arkansas and sent the employee to Arkansas to work. While on the job in Arkansas, the employee was injured. The employee was immediately removed to a Missouri hospital. Arkansas had a compensation act that removed the worker's common-law tort remedy against his employer but not against one in the position of the general contractor for whom the employee in this case had been working when injured. The Missouri compensation statute provided the exclusive remedy against both the employer and the general contractor.[196] Contrary to the provisions of the Missouri act, the employee sued the general contractor in tort in Arkansas and recovered a judgment for common-law damages. The Supreme Court permitted this judgment to stand over objections that it denied full faith and credit to the provisions of the Missouri statute making the Missouri act the exclusive remedy against someone in the position of the general contractor. The majority opinion by Justice Douglas did not speak in terms of the "obnoxiousness" of the Missouri act nor did it purport to weigh the interests of Missouri and Arkansas under the actual facts of this case. Arkansas as the place of injury had a significant contact with the controversy and was likely to have an important interest in the resolution of that controversy. "Arkansas therefore has a legitimate interest in opening her courts to suits of this nature, even though in this case Carroll's injury may have cast no burden on her or on her institutions."[197] Douglas went to the extent of declaring: "[W]e write not only for this case and this day alone, but for this type of case."[198] At this point it would seem that, in the workers' compensation area, the full faith and credit clause imposes no further limitation on a

_____

(employee's residence may constitutionally apply its own workers' compensation law); Martin v. Furman Lumber Co., 134 Vt. 1, 346 A.2d 640 (1975) (Vermont compensation benefits may be made available for death of Vermont employee killed in Vermont in the course of his employment for a Massachusetts employer under a contract entered into in Massachusetts).

195. 349 U.S. 408, 75 S.Ct. 804, 99 L.Ed. 1183 (1955).

196. In his dissent, Justice Frankfurter expressed doubt that the Missouri statute would have barred the tort remedy against this particular general contractor because this general contractor was not subject to the Missouri compensation act. If this were so, and Frankfurter would remand for clarification of this point, there would be no conflict between the Missouri and Arkansas statutes and therefore no occasion to invoke the command of full faith and credit. Id. at 422–26, 75 S.Ct. at 812–814, 99 L.Ed. at 1193–1196.

197. Id. at 413, 75 S.Ct. at 807, 99 L.Ed. at 1189.

198. The injured employee, unaware that he had a remedy under Arkansas law, accepted 34 compensation payments made voluntarily by his employer's insurer pursuant to the Missouri statute, without formal proceedings or an award. Both majority and dissent agreed that, under these circumstances, the employee's receipt of payments did not bar any other remedy that he might have.

state's choice of law than is imposed by the basic requirements of due process.[199]

While in the workers' compensation area the Supreme Court was eliminating the Full Faith and Credit Clause as a significant constitutional limitation on a state's choice of law, in a series of cases involving fraternal beneficiary societies, the Court was using that clause to raise to constitutional dignity a single choice-of-law rule.

Supreme Council of the Royal Arcanum v. Green[200] was the first in this series of fraternal beneficiary society cases. The plaintiff had joined a New York lodge of a Massachusetts-incorporated fraternal beneficiary society. After the plaintiff joined, the society twice raised its assessment rates. Sixteen members of the society brought an action against the society in Massachusetts seeking to set aside as ultra vires the bylaws under which assessments had been increased. Judgment in the Massachusetts action was in favor of the society. The plaintiff then sued the society in New York seeking to enjoin it from collecting at the higher rates. The society defended on two grounds. One, the validity of the increase in rates must be determined under Massachusetts law under which it was admittedly valid. Two, the Massachusetts judgment was rendered in a class suit, which foreclosed the plaintiff's interest.

The New York Court of Appeals decided that New York law was applicable to determine the validity of the assessments and that under New York law the plaintiff was entitled to the relief asked. Without finding it necessary to decide the res judicata effect of the Massachusetts judgment, the Supreme Court reversed. The Full Faith and Credit Clause required that the validity of the assessment be determined under Massachusetts law which, as indicated in the Massachusetts judgment, permitted the assessments.

> The contradiction in terms is apparent which would rise from holding on the one hand that there was a collective and unified standard of duty and obligation on the part of the members themselves and the corporation, and saying on the other hand that the duty of members was to be tested isolatedly and individually by

---

199. For a suggestion that there may still be some vitality left in the *Bradford* decision, see note 221 infra and accompanying text.

200. 237 U.S. 531, 35 S.Ct. 724, 59 L.Ed. 1089 (1915). *Green* is the first in the series of cases finding a special need for uniformity of result under the law of the place of incorporation of the society. Supreme Lodge, Knights of Pythias v. Meyer, 198 U.S. 508, 25 S.Ct. 754, 49 L.Ed. 1146 (1905), is an earlier fraternal beneficiary society case that is not completely consistent in result with this later series of cases. In the *Meyer* case, the society was incorporated under an act of Congress and had its main office in Illinois. The society's Illinois office issued the certificate in question to a resident of New York. A death claim by the beneficiary was defended on the ground that death had been due to suicide. The society attempted to introduce the testimony of doctors who had attended the dying member, but the evidence was rejected when the plaintiff invoked the doctor-patient privilege. The membership certificate contained a clause waiving the privilege. This waiver was valid under Illinois law but invalid under a New York statute. The Court held that application of the New York rule of evidence did not result in an unconstitutional impairment of a contract obligation. The Court rejected an argument by the society that use of the New York rule of evidence rather than the Illinois rule would make the rights of society members and the obligations of the society vary from state to state.

resorting not to one source of authority applicable to all but by applying many divergent, variable and conflicting criteria.[201]

Because of this necessity for keeping uniform the duty of members of the society, no matter where resident, full faith and credit must be given "to the Massachusetts charter and to the laws of that State...."[202]

Modern Woodmen of America v. Mixer[203] followed this same pattern. The plaintiff and her husband had been residents of South Dakota when a fraternal beneficiary society incorporated in Illinois issued a membership certificate to the husband. The certificate was issued in South Dakota. After her husband had disappeared and had not been heard from for ten years, the plaintiff brought suit in a Nebraska court to recover the death benefits due under the terms of her husband's membership. The society defended on the basis of a bylaw that it had adopted after the husband had become a member and cited an Illinois decision upholding the retroactive effect of the bylaw. The bylaw declared that no death benefit was due the dependent of a missing member until the full life expectancy of the member had expired. The Nebraska high court affirmed a judgment for the plaintiff, declaring that the bylaw was unreasonable and in any event recovery depended upon a rule of evidence which, like all rules of evidence, must be determined by the law of the forum. The Supreme Court promptly reversed on the ground that the Nebraska court denied full faith and credit to the Illinois charter as construed by the Illinois courts.

> The act of becoming a member is something more than a contract, it is entering into a complex and abiding relation, and as marriage looks to domicil, membership looks to and must be governed by the law of the State granting the incorporation.[204]

This doctrine was reaffirmed in *Sovereign Camp of the Woodmen of the World v. Bolin*.[205] A fraternal beneficiary association organized under the laws of Nebraska had issued a certificate of membership to Mr. Bolin, a resident of Missouri. A bylaw of the association entitled Mr. Bolin to life membership without payment of further assessments after his certificate of membership had been outstanding 20 years. After Bolin's death, his beneficiaries brought an action to recover upon the certificate. The association defended on the ground that Mr. Bolin had defaulted in paying dues after his certificate had been outstanding for 20 years. The bylaw providing for life membership in such a circumstance without payment of dues had been declared ultra vires by the high court

---

201. *Green*, 237 U.S. at 542, 35 S.Ct. at 727, 728, 59 L.Ed. at 1100.

202. Id. at 546, 35 S.Ct. at 729, 59 L.Ed. at 1102. See Kirgis, supra note 190 at 120 (the forum cannot apply its own law if "there is an overwhelming reason to decide all similar claims according to one legal system, and one state other than the forum clearly would be the bellwether"); cf. Horowitz, *The Commerce Clause as a Limitation on State Choice-of-Law Doctrine*, 84 Harv. L. Rev. 806, 814 (1971) (the Commerce Clause may require application of the law of a single state if this would facilitate multistate transactions).

203. 267 U.S. 544, 45 S.Ct. 389, 69 L.Ed. 783 (1925).

204. Id. at 551, 45 S.Ct. at 389, 390, 69 L.Ed. at 785.

205. 305 U.S. 66, 59 S.Ct. 35, 83 L.Ed. 45 (1938).

of Nebraska in a class suit brought by one Trapp. The association declared that the Missouri court must give full faith and credit to the Nebraska decision. The Missouri courts, however, gave a judgment for the beneficiaries. The Missouri decision was based, in part, on treating the association as an old line insurance company rather than as a fraternal beneficiary society because, at the time that the certificate in issue was executed, there was no Missouri statute providing for the licensing of foreign fraternal beneficiary societies. Whether the defendant was a fraternal beneficiary society when sued in Missouri was declared to be a question of local law. This characterization legerdemain did not prevent prompt reversal by the Supreme Court. Though the opinion rested partly on the conclusive effect of the class action that had been litigated in Nebraska,[206] it also declared:

> Another State, wherein the certificate of membership was issued, cannot attach to membership rights against the society which are refused by the law of the domicile [of the society].[207]
>
> ... [T]he court below failed to give full faith and credit to petitioner's charter embodied in the statutes of Nebraska as interpreted by its highest court.[208]

The last decision in this series is *Order of United Commercial Travelers of America v. Wolfe.*[209] The Supreme Court held that South Dakota must honor a six-month period of limitations set forth in the constitution of an Ohio fraternal society. The claim held barred by the short limitation period was one based on a membership certificate that had been issued to a lifelong South Dakota citizen. The short contractual limitation was valid under Ohio law but invalid under South Dakota law. In holding that Ohio law must be applied, Justice Burton, writing for the majority, said: "If full faith and credit are not given to these provisions, the mutual rights and obligations of the members of such societies are left subject to the control of each state. They become unpredictable and almost inevitably unequal."[210]

This time, four members of the court dissented. In an opinion written by Justice Black, the dissenters pointed out that traditionally the forum had been allowed to apply its own statute of limitations[211] and that South Dakota, as the lifelong domicile of the member, had a considerable interest in the controversy.[212] The dissenters further claimed that the limitation appearing in the society's constitution was not a "public act" within the meaning of the Full Faith and Credit Clause[213] and that no reason was apparent why fraternal beneficiary

---

206. Id. at 78–79, 59 S.Ct. at 39–40, 83 L.Ed. at 51–52.

207. Id. at 75, 59 S.Ct. at 37, 83 L.Ed. at 50.

208. Id. at 79, 59 S.Ct. at 39, 83 L.Ed. at 52.

209. 331 U.S. 586, 67 S.Ct. 1355, 91 L.Ed. 1687 (1947).

210. Id. at 592, 67 S.Ct. at 1357, 91 L.Ed. at 1692.

211. Id. at 627, 67 S.Ct. at 1374, 91 L.Ed. at 1710.

212. Id. at 628, 67 S.Ct. at 1375, 91 L.Ed. at 1710.

213. Id. at 629, 637, 67 S.Ct. at 1376, 1380, 91 L.Ed. at 1711, 1715.

societies should receive "unique constitutional protection."[214] Despite these arguments the consistent pattern of the fraternal beneficiary society cases was maintained. The forum was required to yield to the law of the state of the society's incorporation.

We have seen then, that in the workers' compensation cases the Full Faith and Credit Clause appears to impose no constitutional limitation on a state's choice of law beyond that of the reasonable connection with a controversy required by due process. During the same period, in the same Court, the Full Faith and Credit Clause consistently requires the forum state, no matter how relevant its policies to the matter before it, to yield to the law of the state where a fraternal beneficiary society is incorporated. A full faith and credit standard that would explain this phenomenon is stated in a sentence from the opinion of Justice Burton who wrote for the majority in the *Wolfe* case:

> The weight of public policy behind the general statute of South Dakota, which seeks to avoid certain provisions in ordinary contracts, does not equal that which makes necessary the recognition of the same terms of membership for members of fraternal benefit societies wherever their beneficiaries may be.[215]

To determine whether the Full Faith and Credit Clause imposes a further limitation on a state's choice of law than is imposed under due process, a weighing of interests is called for. But it is not the weighing of the interests of one state against another in an attempt to determine whether the law of one state is "obnoxious" to another or whether the interest of one state is "outweighed" by the interest of another. If the problem is to determine what limitation the Full Faith and Credit Clause imposes on a state's choice of law, the answer lies in the policy behind that clause.

The purpose of the Full Faith and Credit Clause was and is to help forge a federal nation out of individual sovereign states. If the United States is to be more than just a loose alliance of independent sovereignties, if it is to be a nation, then the individual states must act as parts of a nation. In many crucial areas there is need for national uniformity of conduct. The Full Faith and Credit Clause articulates one respect in which national uniformity is required: one state is not free to ignore the public acts, records, or judicial proceedings of another, nor to subject them to the gantlet of local "public policy", as it may the acts, records, and judicial proceedings of a sovereign with which it is not combined in a federation.[216] In order to determine whether the Full Faith and Credit

---

214. Id. at 637, 67 S.Ct. at 1380, 91 L.Ed. at 1715.

215. Id. at 624, 67 S.Ct. at 1373, 91 L.Ed. at 1708.

216. But cf. Banco Nacional de Cuba v. Sabbatino, 376 U.S. 398, 84 S.Ct. 923, 11 L.Ed.2d 804 (1964) ("act of state doctrine" precludes United States court from inquiring into the validity of the public acts a recognized foreign sovereign power commits within its own territory); 22 U.S.C.A. § 2370(e)(2) ("Hickenlooper" amendment to Foreign Relations Act proclaims act of state doctrine inapplicable if act of foreign country violates "principles of international law" in confiscating property unless President determines that foreign policy interests of the United States require application of the doctrine).

Clause places a further limitation on a state's choice of law than is imposed by the Due Process Clause, the interest of the state that makes application of its law consistent with due process is to be weighed against the need for national uniformity of result under a public act, record, or judicial proceeding of a sister state.[217] The need for national uniformity may depend on the strength of the sister state's interest in requiring full faith and credit to its statute or judicial proceeding. The less legitimate the sister-state's interest, the less the need for compelled national recognition of that interest.[218]

In this light it is possible to reconcile the apparently conflicting results reached by the Supreme Court in the workers' compensation cases and in the fraternal beneficiary cases. The system and theory of workers' compensation is not seriously threatened if the employee recovers under the compensation act of any state having a significant contact with the employer-employee relationship. So long as the employee remains within the workers' compensation system the employer has, to some extent, the protection of the "limited and determinate"[219] liability that has been substituted for unlimited common-law liability. If the employee is permitted to leave the framework of workers' compensation to bring a common-law suit against a third party, contrary to the provisions of the "home" statute, as was done in *Carroll v. Lanza*, the compensation system is perhaps weakened,[220] but it is not completely

---

217. See Justice Stone's language in Milwaukee County v. M.E. White Co., 296 U.S. 268, 276–277, 56 S.Ct. 229, 233–234, 80 L.Ed. 220, 228 (1935): "The very purpose of the full faith and credit clause was to alter the status of the several states as independent foreign sovereignties, each free to ignore obligations created under the laws or by the judicial proceedings of the others, and to make them integral parts of a single nation throughout which a remedy upon a just obligation might be demanded as of right, irrespective of the state of its origin. That purpose ought not lightly to be set aside out of deference to a local policy which, if it exists, would seem to be too trivial to merit serious consideration when weighed against the policy of the constitutional provisions and interest of the state whose judgment is challenged."

Milwaukee County held that full faith and credit to judgments included judgments for taxes.

Cf. Greenstein, *Is the Proposed U.C.C. Choice of Law Provision Unconstitutional?*, 73 Temple L. Rev. 1159 (2000) (suggesting that § 1–301 of the revised Uniform Commercial Code may violate the Full Faith and Credit Clause by permitting the parties to choose law having no relationship to the transaction contrary to the sovereignty interests of a state having a significant relationship to the transaction) (§ 7.3C contains a detailed criticism of UCC § 1–301); von Mehren & Trautman, *Constitutional Control of Choice of Law: Some Reflections on Hague*, 10 Hofstra L. Rev. 35, 55 (1981) (interest of forum in applying its own law may be required by full faith and credit "to defer to the superior interest of another state").

218. See infra text accompanying notes 231–238 discussing the minor interest of a state where a worker is injured while temporarily working there in precluding a supplementary workers' compensation award under the law of the state that is the worker's home and also the center of the employee-employer relationship.

219. Bradford Elec. Light Co. v. Clapper, 286 U.S. 145, 159, 52 S.Ct. 571, 575, 76 L.Ed. 1026, 1035 (1932).

220. See Stone, *The Forum's Policy and the Defense of Full Faith and Credit to Workmen's Compensation Acts*, 41 Iowa L. Rev. 558, 591 (1956): "Risk shifting so as to place the ultimate burden on the negligent party is costly; and it is reflected in the cost to the consumer to the extent that members of the state's compensation system are made

undermined. On the other hand, the workers' compensation system would be more seriously threatened if some state having only slight contact with the employer-employee relationship permitted the employee to bring a common-law action directly against his or her employer contrary to the exclusive remedy provisions of the compensation act of the state having the most significant contacts with the employer-employee relationship. Perhaps, then, there is some life left in the *Bradford* decision.[221]

In contrast with the workers' compensation area, the Supreme Court has consistently found a special need that the rights of members of the same fraternal beneficiary society be adjudicated in the same manner under the same law—the law of the state of incorporation of the society.

It may be that the fraternal beneficiary society cases were wrongly decided; that there is no reason to treat this form of insurance differently from other insurance[222] or to command respect for the law of the place

---

potential risk bearers, who, in addition to workmen's compensation insurance, must carry reserves or insurance to meet contingent tort liability as well."

Although by the time the *Cardillo* case was decided in 1947, the Supreme Court, in the workers' compensation area, had ceased to measure the requirement of full faith and credit by weighing the interest of one state against the interest of another state, this form of the "weighing" test reappeared in a different context. In Watson v. Employers Liab. Assur. Corp., 348 U.S. 66, 75 S.Ct. 166, 99 L.Ed. 74 (1954), the Court decided that the Louisiana direct action statute could constitutionally be used to permit direct suit against an out-of-state liability insurer even though the policy itself contained a provision against such direct suit. Justice Black wrote for the majority: "The insurance contract was formally executed in [Massachusetts] . . . and Gillette has an office there. But plainly these interests cannot outweigh the interest of Louisiana in taking care of those injured in Louisiana. Since this is true, the Full Faith and Credit Clause does not compel Louisiana to subordinate its direct action provisions to Massachusetts contract rules." Id. at 73, 75 S.Ct. at 170, 99 L.Ed. at 82–83.

221. See Stone, supra note 220 at 592: "No national policies were found to compel subordination of the forum's affirmative interest in granting workmen's compensation benefits to exclusive remedy provisions in foreign states' compensation acts. The wisdom of constitutionally requiring denial of a tort remedy in the state of injury, in recognition of conflicting immunity provisions, may involve vastly different considerations, however. It is believed that as to this question there are stronger national policies, which can be served only through limitation of the forum's autonomy under the governmental interest doctrine."

See also Fleet Transport Co. v. Insurance Co. of N. Amer., 340 F.Supp. 158 (M.D.Ala. 1972) (availability of remedy under Georgia workers' compensation act precludes recovery under Alabama employers' liability act or under common law for fatal injury in Alabama of Georgia resident whose employment contract was made in Georgia); Jaiguay v. Vasquez, 287 Conn. 323, 948 A.2d 955 (2008) (New York law bars wrongful death action against fellow employee and employer although death occurred in Connecticut and Connecticut law would allow action based on negligence of fellow employee); cf. Tucci v. Club Mediterranee, S.A., 89 Cal.App.4th 180, 107 Cal.Rptr.2d 401 (2d Dist. 2001), rev. denied (California resident hired in California to work in Dominican Republic and covered by Dominican Republic workers' compensation insurance may not bring tort action against employer when insurer is not licensed to write insurance in California).

222. See Leflar, *Constitutional Limits on Free Choice of Law*, 28 Law & Contemp. Prob. 706, 716 (1963); cf. Mayo v. Hartford Life Ins. Co., 354 F.3d 400 (5th Cir. 2004) (law of employee's residence applied to invalidate for lack of insurable interest employer's claim to life insurance covering employee); Sedler, *Constitutional Limitations on Choice of Law: The Perspective of Constitutional Generalism*, 10 Hofstra L. Rev. 59, 99–100 (1981) (distinguishing between the rights of the member against the association, when there is no special need

of incorporation of the society. Even if the fraternal beneficiary society cases did misjudge the need for national uniformity of result and even if they are some day overruled, this does not mean that the full faith and credit standard revealed by juxtaposing those cases with the workers' compensation cases is wrong. It would merely mean that the fraternal society cases had misapplied that standard.

In the workers' compensation cases, the full faith and credit standard here suggested is unlikely to limit a state's choice of law beyond the limit already imposed by due process. The same standard creates doubt concerning the continued viability of the fraternal society cases.[223] This does not mean, as was suggested by the plurality opinion in *Allstate Insurance Company v. Hague*,[224] that full faith and credit does not impose a limitation on a state's choice of law distinct from and in addition to the limitation imposed by due process. In the case of judgments, for example, it is clear that full faith and credit interdicts what due process would permit. State X may have a highly relevant policy that it wishes to advance by applying its law to a controversy and application of its law may, in all other respects, be eminently reasonable, so that it is beyond debate, if that state were the first to adjudicate the controversy, due process would not prevent it from applying its own law. If, however, that same controversy is first adjudicated in a sister state, state Y, that has jurisdiction over the subject matter and the parties, and the law of Y, not X, is applied in the Y adjudication, state X must accord that Y judgment full faith and credit.[225] X is no longer free to apply its own law to the controversy. This is because the national need for full faith and credit to sister state judgments is greater than X's interest in advancing its own domestic policies by applying its own law.

The same full faith and credit standard that applies to Y judicial proceedings applies to Y public acts. It may be that the standard,

---

for uniformity of treatment, and the validity of an assessment against a member, when there is such a need).

223.   Cf. Clay v. Sun Ins. Office, Ltd., 377 U.S. 179, 183, 84 S.Ct. 1197, 1199, 12 L.Ed.2d 229, 232 (1964): "We do not extend that rule [referring to Order of United Commercial Travelers v. Wolfe] nor apply it here . . . ."

224.   449 U.S. 302, 308 n.10, 101 S.Ct. 633, 637–38 n.10, 66 L.Ed.2d 521, 527–28 n.10 (1981): "Although at one time the Court required a more exacting standard under the Full Faith and Credit Clause than under the Due Process Clause for evaluating the constitutionality of choice-of-law decisions, . . . the Court has since abandoned the weighing-of-interests requirement. . . . Different considerations are of course at issue when full faith and credit is to be accorded to acts, records, and proceedings outside of the choice-of-law area, such as in the case of sister state-court judgments." For arguments that due process and full faith and credit should have the same effect on choice of law, see B. Currie, *The Constitution and the Choice of Law: Governmental Relations and the Judicial Function*, 26 U. Chi. L. Rev. 9, 15 (1958); Reese, *The Hague Case: An Opportunity Lost*, 10 Hofstra L. Rev. 195, 197 (1981); Walker, *A Criticism of Professor Weintraub's Presentation of Full Faith and Credit to Laws*, 57 Iowa L. Rev. 1248, 1249 (1972).

225.   See Fauntleroy v. Lum, 210 U.S. 230, 28 S.Ct. 641, 52 L.Ed. 1039 (1908); Miller v. Kingsley, 194 Neb. 123, 230 N.W.2d 472 (1975) (full faith and credit must be given to a sister state's judgment for punitive damages even though such damages could not be granted by a forum court); Conquistador Hotel Corp. v. Fortino, 99 Wis.2d 16, 298 N.W.2d 236 (App.1980) (give full faith and credit to Puerto Rico judgment for gambling debt when would not have given a remedy on the underlying claim).

properly applied, would rarely, if ever, require X to yield its own law in favor of a Y statute,[226] just as that standard, properly applied, would rarely, if ever, permit X to apply its own law contrary to a Y judgment, but the full faith and credit *standard* is the same. It simply produces different answers when one or more of the variables that it includes—a state's interest in applying its own law or the national need for deference to the public act, record, or judicial proceeding of a sister state—are different.

There may be rare instances in which the need for a nationally uniform result is so compelling that the Full Faith and Credit Clause should require application of a particular state's law to an issue not yet adjudicated. An example might be the determination of issues concerning the internal affairs of a corporation by the law of the state of incorporation. *VantagePoint Venture Partners v. Examen, Inc.*[227] concerned the imminent merger of two Delaware corporations. A preferred shareholder of one of the corporations claimed that the corporation was a "quasi-California corporation" under the California Corporation Code because more than 50% of its property, payroll payments, sales, and stockholders were in California. As a quasi-California corporation the shareholder claimed that that the corporation was governed by California law under which, unlike Delaware law, preferred shareholders were entitled to vote as a separate class on the merger.

The Delaware Supreme Court held that Delaware law controlled and that the Due Process and Commerce Clauses of the U.S. Constitution mandated this result. The court could have reached the result under the Full Faith Clause; although California had a reasonable and foreseeable interest in applying its law to quasi-California companies, there is a compelling national need for uniform treatment of shareholder rights under the law of the state of incorporation.[228]

---

226. But see in support of a wider role for full faith and credit as a limit on choice of law, Hay, *Full Faith and Credit and Federalism in Choice of Law*, 34 Mercer L. Rev. 709, 718–19 (1983); Simson, *State Autonomy in Choice of Law: A Suggested Approach*, 52 S.Cal. L. Rev. 61, 73 (1978).

227. 871 A.2d 1108 (Del. 2005).

228. See McDermott Inc. v. Lewis, 531 A.2d 206 (Del. 1987) (full faith and credit, due process, and commerce clauses require application of the law of the state of incorporation of the parent corporation to determine whether a parent can vote the shares the subsidiary owns in the parent); cf. Palmer v. Arden–Mayfair, Inc., CCH Corp. Law Guide ¶ 11,047, 47 LW 2055 (Del.Ct.Ch. 7/6/78), in which the court directed a Delaware corporation to elect directors in accordance with Delaware law, which prohibited cumulative voting. The court refused to rule on the applicability or constitutionality of a California statute, which, because of the extent of the company's property, payroll, and sales in California, applied to the corporation, and which required cumulative voting. Cf. Case C–208/00, Uberseering BV v. Nordic Construction Co. Baumanagement GmbH, [2002] ECR 1–9919 (Ct. of Justice of European Communities) (under European Union law Germany may not require a company incorporated in the Netherlands with its actual center of administration in Germany to re-incorporate in Germany in order to be able to sue in German courts). But cf. Jefferson Industrial Bank v. First Golden Bancorp., 762 P.2d 768 (Colo.App. 1988) (stockholder's right to inspect shareholder lists is governed by the law of the forum where corporation has its principal place of business, not by the law of the state of incorporation); Gries Sports Enterprises, Inc. v. Modell, 15 Ohio St.3d 284, 473 N.E.2d 807 (1984), cert. denied, 473 U.S. 906, 105 S.Ct. 3530, 87 L.Ed.2d 654 (1985) (duration of voting agreement between

Thinking of the limitation imposed by full faith and credit on a state's choice of law in terms of weighing the interests of the state, not against the interests of a sister state, but against the need for national uniformity, is more than a slight shift in emphasis. It will prove of practical value generally in dealing with full faith and credit problems. Some examples follow.

Magnolia Petroleum Company v. Hunt[229] decided that Louisiana must give full faith and credit to a final Texas workers' compensation award just as full faith and credit must be given to a sister state judgment. Thus Louisiana could not award compensation in addition to that already granted. In writing for the bare majority of five, Justice Stone said:

---

majority and minority shareholders is determined by law of Ohio, the principal place of business, under a "most significant relationship" analysis, not by the law of the state of incorporation). But see Wilson v. Louisiana–Pacific Resources, Inc., 138 Cal.App.3d 216, 187 Cal.Rptr. 852 (1982) (California statute requiring cumulative voting for directors constitutionally may be applied to a Utah corporation with a majority of payroll, property, sales, and stockholders in California although Utah permits cumulative voting only if a corporation's articles of incorporation so provide and the articles had no such provision); Western Air Lines, Inc. v. Sobieski, 191 Cal.App.2d 399, 12 Cal.Rptr. 719 (1961) (California Commissioner of Corporations has jurisdiction to act on a change in voting rights attempted by a Delaware corporation with its principal place of business in California); State ex rel. Weede v. Iowa S. Utils. Co. of Delaware, 231 Iowa 784, 2 N.W.2d 372 (1942), modified, 4 N.W.2d 869 (1942) (Iowa law forbidding issuance of stock without monetary consideration is applied to a Delaware corporation operating a public utility in Iowa); Beloit Liquidating Trust v. Grade, 270 Wis.2d 356, 677 N.W.2d 298 (2004) (law of Wisconsin, where corporation has its headquarters, rather than law of Delaware, the state of incorporation, determines whether directors have a fiduciary duty to the corporation's creditors). For discussion, see DeMott, *Perspectives on Choice of Law for Corporate Internal Affairs*, 48 Law & Contemp. Problems 161 (1985); Ebke, *The "Real Seat" Doctrine in the Conflict of Corporate Laws*, 36 Int'l Law. 1015, 1016 (2002) (most European Union countries recognize the country where a corporation has its "real seat"—"where the central management decisions are being implemented on a day-to-day basis"—as the only state that has the authority to regulate a corporation's internal affairs).

Perhaps the Commerce Clause, in cases such as the internal affairs of a corporation, can prevent choice of law from imposing an unreasonable burden on interstate commerce. U.S. Const., Art. I, § 8, cl. 3: "Congress shall have Power ... [t]o regulate Commerce ... among the several states." Cf. Edgar v. MITE Corporation, 457 U.S. 624, 102 S.Ct. 2629, 73 L.Ed.2d 269 (1982) (Illinois Business Takeover Act, even though the target company is incorporated in Illinois, not only is preempted by federal legislation, but also violates the commerce clause); Hyde Park Partners v. Connolly, 839 F.2d 837 (1st Cir.1988) (affirm preliminary injunction against enforcement of Massachusetts statute because it was probably preempted by the Williams Act and portions of it probably violated the commerce clause). But cf. CTS Corp. v. Dynamics Corp. of America, 481 U.S. 69, 107 S.Ct. 1637, 95 L.Ed.2d 67 (1987) (Indiana business takeover act covering corporations chartered in Indiana is valid). For discussion, see Kozyris, *Corporate Wars and Choice of Law*, 1985 Duke L. J. 1 (1985); Kozyris, *Some Observations on State Regulation of Multistate Takeovers—Controlling Choice of Law Through the Commerce Clause*, 14 Dela. J. Corp. L. 499 (1989); Kozyris, *Corporate Takeovers at the Jurisdictional Crossroads: Preserving State Authority over Internal Affairs While Protecting the Transferability of Intestate Stock Through Federal Law*, 36 UCLA L. Rev. 1109 (1989).

Cf. International Paper Co. v. Ouellette, 479 U.S. 481, 107 S.Ct. 805, 93 L.Ed.2d 883 (1987) (in order to avoid subjecting alleged water polluters to a variety of rules established by different states along interstate waterways, the Clean Water Act pre-empts application of state law other than the law of the source state).

229. 320 U.S. 430, 64 S.Ct. 208, 88 L.Ed. 149 (1943).

No convincing reason is advanced for saying that Louisiana has a greater interest in awarding compensation for an injury suffered in an industrial accident, than North Carolina had in determining the marital status of its domiciliary against whom a divorce decree had been rendered in another state. Williams v. North Carolina, [317 U.S. 287, 63 S.Ct. 207, 87 L.Ed. 279 (1942)] ... or Mississippi in stamping out gambling within its borders, Fauntleroy v. Lum, [210 U.S. 230 (1908)] ... or South Carolina in requiring a parent to support his child who was domiciled within that state, Yarborough v. Yarborough [290 U.S. 202, 54 S.Ct. 181, 78 L.Ed. 269 (1933)].[230]

Justice Jackson in his concurrence remarked:

Is Louisiana's social interest in seeing that its labor contracts carry adequate workmen's compensation superior constitutionally to North Carolina's interest in seeing that people who contract marriage there are protected in the rights they acquire?[231]

A possible reply to both Justices is that, although Louisiana's interest was perhaps not stronger than the interests of the various states that were compelled, in the cited cases, to give full faith and credit to the judgments of other states, the need for national uniformity in the form of giving conclusive and binding effect to the Texas workers' compensation award is far less than the comparable need when the usual judgment is involved.

Consider a case like *Magnolia Petroleum*, in which the first state to make a workers' compensation award is the site of Worker's injury but Worker usually is on the job in another state where Worker is domiciled and where the employment relationship is centered. The injury state has an interest in permitting recovery under its law to assure medical services and compensation for the injured worker. If, however, Worker's home state provides greater compensation benefits than the injury state, the injury state has only a miniscule interest, at best, in barring the home state from providing that additional compensation. If the injury state claims an "interest in placing a limit on the potential liability of companies that transact business within its borders,"[232] this interest is slight in these circumstances because it is easily defeated if Worker first seeks compensation in Worker's home state.[233] The injury state has an "interest in the welfare of the injured employee,"[234] but "the interest in providing adequate compensation to the injured worker would be fully served by the allowance of successive awards."[235] Finally, the injury state "has an interest in having the integrity of its formal determinations of

---

230. Id. at 440–41, 64 S.Ct. at 214, 215, 88 L.Ed. at 156.

231. Id. at 446, 64 S.Ct. at 217, 88 L.Ed. at 159.

232. Thomas v. Washington Gas Light Co., 448 U.S. 261, 277, 100 S.Ct. 2647, 2659, 65 L.Ed.2d 757, 770 (1980).

233. Id. at 279–80, 100 S.Ct. at 2659–60, 65 L.Ed.2d at 771–72.

234. Id. at 277, 100 S.Ct. at 2659, 65 L.Ed.2d at 770.

235. Id. at 280, 100 S.Ct. at 2660, 65 L.Ed.2d at 772.

contested issues respected by other sovereigns."[236] This interest is not affected because "[a] supplemental award gives full effect to the facts determined by the first award and also allows full credit for payments pursuant to the earlier award."[237] The only viable interest of the injury state in preventing a supplemental award in the home state is to discourage use of its agencies and courts when more adequate recovery is available in Worker's home state. It is doubtful that there is a national interest in compelling all other states to enforce this policy and forego their own policies of providing what they consider adequate compensation to Worker and Worker's family. Moreover, Worker's decision to seek compensation first in the injury state was probably made because Worker was uninformed that Worker's home state would make a more adequate award.[238]

Thus the majority in *Magnolia Petroleum* did not focus adequately on whether the home state's interest in providing supplemental recovery was outweighed by a national interest in compelling full faith and credit to the injury state's award. It is perhaps not surprising then that *Industrial Commission v. McCartin*[239] distinguished *Magnolia Petroleum* in such a manner that the *Magnolia Petroleum* facts would probably produce a different result under the *McCartin* formula.[240] *McCartin*

---

236. Id. at 277, 100 S.Ct. at 2659, 65 L.Ed.2d at 773.

237. Id. at 281, 100 S.Ct. at 2661, 65 L.Ed.2d at 770.

238. Id. at 284–85, 100 S.Ct. at 2662–63, 65 L.Ed.2d at 775.

For a suggested statutory provision that would reduce the likelihood of an uninformed choice, see Cowan, *Extraterritorial Application of Workmen's Compensation Laws—A Suggested Solution*, 33 Texas L. Rev. 917, 923 (1955): "[I]f it appears, from a consideration of the circumstances ... that the employee is also entitled to recover under the laws of another state, the Administrator shall so inform the employee, in writing, and shall notify him that the recovery to which he may be entitled under the laws of another state may be more advantageous."

There are some states that regard receipt of workers' compensation benefits under the law of another state as a binding election of remedies. See, e.g., Cofer v. Industrial Comm'n, 24 Ariz.App. 357, 359, 538 P.2d 1158, 1160 (1975) (citing *Magnolia Petroleum*); United States Fidelity & Guaranty Co. v. North Dakota Workmen's Compensation Bureau, 275 N.W.2d 618 (N.D.1979); True v. Amerail Corp., 584 S.W.2d 794 (Tenn.1979).

239. 330 U.S. 622, 67 S.Ct. 886, 91 L.Ed. 1140 (1947).

240. See Kindle v. Cudd Pressure Control, Inc., 792 F.2d 507 (5th Cir. 1986), cert. denied, 479 U.S. 1030, 107 S.Ct. 873, 93 L.Ed.2d 828 (1987) (neither Texas workers' compensation act nor decisions interpreting it contain unmistakable language that would prevent Louisiana from making an award under its act to deceased worker's parents after Texas had made an award to the worker's spouse); Griffin v. Universal Underwriters Ins. Co., 283 So.2d 748 (La.1973), cert. denied, 416 U.S. 904, 94 S.Ct. 1607, 40 L.Ed.2d 108 (1974) (Texas employee injured in Louisiana may recover benefits under Louisiana compensation act after benefits under Texas act have been terminated); Wood v. Aetna Cas. & Sur. Co., 260 Md. 651, 273 A.2d 125 (1971) (Maryland exclusive remedy provision does not prohibit claimant from pursuing additional compensation benefits in another state under whose statute he qualifies); Cramer v. State Concrete Corp., 39 N.J. 507, 511, 189 A.2d 213, 215 (1963): "We are satisfied we should accept the view, now so widely held, that *McCartin* did in practical effect overrule *Magnolia* and that there is no constitutional barrier to a second proceeding here unless the law of the state of earlier award was unmistakably designed to bar relief under the laws of another jurisdiction." But see Plante v. North Dakota Workers Compensation Bureau, 455 N.W.2d 195 (N.D. 1990) (North Dakota statute forbidding recovery under North Dakota statute if worker has recovered in another state unless that state's benefits are awarded as a "supplement" to the North

decided that a workers' compensation award does not bar a subsequent award in a sister state unless the statute of the first state purports in "unmistakable language" to bar such a subsequent award. A plurality in *Thomas v. Washington Gas Light Company*[241] would go even further and hold that the Full Faith and Credit Clause does not prevent a second state from making a supplementary workers' compensation award no matter how clearly the first state purported to bar such relief.

Hughes v. Fetter[242] demonstrates that articulation of the proper full faith and credit standard does not always produce the correct result. A Wisconsin resident was a passenger in an automobile driven in Illinois by another Wisconsin resident.[243] The administrator of the passenger's estate brought suit in Wisconsin under the Illinois wrongful death statute against the driver and against the driver's liability insurer, a Wisconsin corporation. The Wisconsin courts dismissed the suit on the ground that the Wisconsin wrongful death act requirement "that such action shall be brought for a death caused in this state" barred the action in Wisconsin.[244] The Supreme Court, in a five-to-four opinion, reversed, holding that dismissal of the action denied full faith and credit to the Illinois wrongful death act. Justice Black, writing for the majority, utilized the full faith and credit standard here suggested—a weighing of Wisconsin's legitimate interest in dismissing the suit against the nation-

---

Dakota benefits, prevents the employee from recovering temporary total disability payments for a longer period under the North Dakota statute than he has already received under the Minnesota statute).

241. 448 U.S. 261, 100 S.Ct. 2647, 65 L.Ed.2d 757 (1980). This is the position taken by Justice Stevens, joined by Justices Brennan, Stewart, and Blackmun. Id. at 263–86, 100 S.Ct. at 2652–63, 65 L.Ed.2d at 762–76. Justice White, with whom Chief Justice Burger and Justice Powell joined, concurred in the judgment on the ground that the act under which the first award was made lacked "unmistakable language" precluding a subsequent award and that *McCartin* required such language. Id. at 290–91, 100 S.Ct. at 2665, 65 L.Ed.2d at 778. Justice Rehnquist, joined by Justice Marshall, dissented on the ground that a workers' compensation award should be entitled to the same full faith and credit as "any other judicial award." Id. at 295, 100 S.Ct. at 2668, 65 L.Ed.2d at 782.

There have been conflicting interpretations of the effect of Thomas v. Washington Gas Light. See, e.g., Landry v. Carlson Mooring Service, 643 F.2d 1080 (5th Cir.1981), cert. denied, 454 U.S. 1123, 102 S.Ct. 970, 71 L.Ed.2d 109 (1981) (because only a plurality would displace *McCartin*, *McCartin* remains the rule); Southland Supply Co., Inc. v. Patrick, 397 So.2d 77 (Miss.1981) (no full faith and credit bar to a supplementary award); United Airlines, Inc. v. Kozel, 33 Va.App. 695, 536 S.E.2d 473 (Va. App. 2000) (relies on *Thomas* in awarding employee additional workers' compensation despite Illinois award incorporating settlement that expressly included any claim for Virginia worker's compensation). See also Comment, *Full Faith to Administrative Judgments: Courts Illuminate Thomas v. Washington Gas Light Co.*, 9 George Mason U. L. Rev. 351, 368 (1987) (Supreme Court should abandon full faith and credit requirement for supplemental workers' compensation awards).

242. 341 U.S. 609, 71 S.Ct. 980, 95 L.Ed. 1212 (1951).

243. These facts appear in the Wisconsin Supreme Court opinion, Hughes v. Fetter, 257 Wis. 35, 36, 42 N.W.2d 452, 453 (1950), rev'd, 341 U.S. 609, 71 S.Ct. 980, 95 L.Ed. 1212 (1951).

244. The Wisconsin trial court dismissed the plaintiff's complaint "on the merits". It appears that this was intended only to bar further suit in Wisconsin and not to prevent subsequent suit in Illinois. The Wisconsin Supreme Court framed the issue as follows: "The question is now raised whether for a death in Illinois this action can be maintained in Wisconsin notwithstanding that provision [that death be caused in Wisconsin] in our state." 257 Wis. at 37, 42 N.W.2d at 453.

al need for Wisconsin to give recognition to the Illinois wrongful death act by providing a forum for enforcement of the cause of action created by the Illinois statute.[245]

No matter how light the need for full faith and credit in this form to a sister state statute, this need for full faith and credit would outweigh Wisconsin's legitimate interest in dismissing the suit, if that interest was, as Justice Black thought, zero. Wisconsin, the opinion reasoned, having a death act of its own, had no general policy against wrongful death actions. Moreover, because all the parties were Wisconsin residents or companies, Wisconsin could not have a valid *forum non conveniens* basis for dismissal.[246]

The difficulty with *Fetter* is not with the full faith and credit standard utilized, but with the application of that standard. Wisconsin's *forum non conveniens* interest in dismissal was not eliminated by the fact that all parties were Wisconsin residents. The fatal automobile crash occurred in Illinois. Thus, trial might have required the testimony of witnesses who were Illinois residents. Moreover, given the place-of-wrong conflicts rule then applicable to wrongful death actions and the Wisconsin statutory proviso limiting recovery under the Wisconsin death act to death caused in Wisconsin, the Wisconsin court would have been compelled to apply Illinois wrongful death law if it had provided a forum for the action. This application of the Illinois death act rather than the Wisconsin act to an action between the administrator of a Wisconsin passenger on one side and a Wisconsin driver and his Wisconsin insurer on the other, may, in the focus of modern interest or functional choice-of-law analysis appear unwise, but, for the present at least, not so unwise as to be unconstitutional.[247] It would seem then, to give the Wisconsin court its then understandable choice-of-law assumptions, that

---

245. 341 U.S. at 612, 71 S.Ct. at 982, 95 L.Ed. at 1216: "On the one hand is the strong unifying principle embodied in the Full Faith and Credit Clause looking toward maximum enforcement in each state of the obligations or rights created or recognized by the statutes of sister states; on the other hand is the policy of Wisconsin, as interpreted by its highest court, against permitting Wisconsin courts to entertain this wrongful death action."

246. Justice Black also said: "We think it relevant, although not crucial here, that Wisconsin may well be the only jurisdiction in which service could be had as an original matter on the insurance company defendant. And while in the present case jurisdiction over the individual defendant apparently could be had in Illinois by substituted service, in other cases Wisconsin's exclusionary statute might amount to a deprivation of all opportunity to enforce valid death claims created by another state." Id. at 613, 71 S.Ct. at 983, 95 L.Ed. at 1217.

First Nat'l Bank v. United Air Lines, 342 U.S. 396, 72 S.Ct. 421, 96 L.Ed. 441 (1952), indicated that this possible inability to obtain jurisdiction over the defendant in another jurisdiction was not a necessary basis for the *Fetter* result. In *First Nat'l*, the Court reversed the denial of an Illinois forum for an action based on the wrongful death of an Illinois resident in Utah. The Illinois statute, on which judgment for the defendant had depended, provided that "no action shall be brought ... for a death occurring outside of this State where a right of action ... exists under the laws of the place where ... death occurred and service of process ... may be had upon the defendant in such place."

247. But see B. Currie, *The Constitution and the "Transitory" Cause of Action*, 73 Harv. L. Rev. 36, 60–62 (1959) (Wisconsin was required by the Equal Protection Clause to afford the action for the wrongful death of its resident access to its courts and was then required by due process to apply the Wisconsin wrongful death statute).

the foreign facts, possibly foreign witnesses, and the need to apply foreign law,[248] were valid bases for dismissal on *forum non conveniens* grounds. This Wisconsin interest in dismissal should have been enough to counterbalance the relatively slight national need for according full faith and credit to a sister state statute by providing a forum for suit on a statutory cause of action not yet reduced to judgment.[249]

§ 9.3B Other Uses of a Proper Full Faith and Credit Standard

The importance of weighing the interests of the forum against the need for national uniformity can be discerned in still other areas.

A state may grant a forum to a cause of action in disregard of a provision of the statute of a sister state that purports to limit suit to the courts of the enacting state.[250] This is explained, in part at least, by the fact that there is little national interest in obedience to such a provision.

The Supreme Court has given debtors protection against multiple escheat of intangible property when that property is in the form of obligations that the debtors owe to creditors who have not claimed the amount owed and whose whereabouts are unknown. *Texas v. New*

---

248. See Gulf Oil Co. v. Gilbert, 330 U.S. 501, 509, 67 S.Ct. 839, 91 L.Ed. 1055 (1947): "There is an appropriateness, too, in having the trial of a diversity case in a forum that is at home with the state law that must govern the case rather than having a court in some other forum untangle problems in conflict of laws, and in law foreign to itself." See also In re Kernot, [1964] 3 All Eng.R. 339, 342 (Ch.1964). In rejecting an argument that, because all witnesses were in Italy, the English court was an inconvenient forum in which to determine the custody of a child, the court remarked: "In considering questions of forum conveniens I think that the court has to take into consideration not only such matters as the physical convenience of the parties and the witnesses and matters attendant on the trial and things of that kind, but also the system of law which is to be applied, and must consider what court is really the appropriate tribunal to reach a proper answer in applying that system of law. That seems to me as much relevant for consideration as are considerations of personal convenience and questions of expense."

249. But cf. Kirgis, supra note 190 at 120 (a state may not "refuse to provide a forum for adjudication of a transitory dispute arising out of an occurrence or relationship in another state, solely because it arose in another state or solely as a subterfuge for some disguised policy applicable to the merits of the dispute").

250. Tennessee Coal, Iron & R.R. Co. v. George, 233 U.S. 354, 34 S.Ct. 587, 58 L.Ed. 997 (1914); Atchison, T. & S.F. Ry. v. Sowers, 213 U.S. 55, 29 S.Ct. 397, 53 L.Ed. 695 (1909); cf. Crider v. Zurich Ins. Co., 380 U.S. 39, 85 S.Ct. 769, 13 L.Ed.2d 641 (1965) (an Alabama court has jurisdiction to award damages under the Georgia workers' compensation act to an Alabama resident who was injured while working in Alabama for a Georgia corporation, even though the remedy provided by the Georgia act purported to be an exclusive one that could be afforded only by the Georgia compensation board); Codo, Bonds, Zumstein & Konzelman v. FDIC, 148 Ill.App.3d 698, 102 Ill.Dec. 227, 499 N.E.2d 1007 (3d Dist.1986) (need not recognize purported exclusive jurisdiction of sister-state receivership proceeding); Eastern Indemnity Co. v. Hirschler, Fleischer, Weinberg, Cox & Allen, 235 Va. 9, 366 S.E.2d 53 (1988) (need not give full faith and credit to a sister-state decree that stayed proceedings against insolvent insurer); cf. Baker v. General Motors Corp., 522 U.S. 222, 118 S.Ct. 657, 139 L.Ed.2d 580 (1998) (the Full Faith and Credit Clause does not prevent a U.S. District Court in Missouri from compelling the testimony of a witness that a Michigan state court had enjoined from testifying). But cf. Herstam v. Board of Directors of Silvercreek Water and Sanitation Dist., 895 P.2d 1131 (Colo. App. 1995) (give full faith and credit to decree issued in Arizona receivership proceedings enjoining making claim against insolvent in other proceedings); The Coca–Cola Co. v. Harmar Bottling Co., 218 S.W.3d 671 (Tex. 2006) (cannot sue in Texas under antitrust law of another state).

Jersey[251] utilized the original jurisdiction of the Supreme Court[252] to settle the question of which state could escheat sums that a corporation owed to various creditors who failed to claim or cash checks for payment of various company obligations, such as dividends or wages. The Court held that only the state of the creditor's last known address, as shown on the debtor's books and records, had jurisdiction to escheat the abandoned intangible personal property. If the debtor's records failed to show any such address, or if the state of the creditor's last address had no applicable escheat law, then the "State of corporate domicile"[253] of the debtor could escheat the obligation, subject to later escheat in the state of the creditor's last known address if that state proves that such an address is within its borders and provides for escheat of the property.

It is interesting to compare this protection against double escheat of intangibles with the lack of protection against multiple taxation of intangibles. An estate tax on intangible personalty in an estate may be levied by the state of the owner's domicile at death,[254] by the state of incorporation if the intangible personalty consists of shares of stock in a corporation,[255] and by the state in which an inter vivos trust of the intangibles was being administered at the time of the beneficiary's death.[256]

Why should there be constitutional protection against multiple escheat of an intangible, but no such protection against multiple taxation

---

251. 379 U.S. 674, 85 S.Ct. 626, 13 L.Ed.2d 596 (1965).

252. U.S.Const. Art. III, § 2: "In all Cases ... in which a State shall be Party, the Supreme Court shall have original Jurisdiction." See also 28 U.S.C.A. § 1251(a).

253. Texas v. New Jersey, 379 U.S. at 682, 85 S.Ct. at 631, 13 L.Ed.2d at 602. See also Commonwealth of Pennsylvania v. New York, 407 U.S. 206, 92 S.Ct. 2075, 32 L.Ed.2d 693 (1972) (Western Union's state of incorporation may escheat unclaimed funds for money orders even though, because Western Union does not regularly record the addresses of its money-order creditors, the state of incorporation will receive an unusually large share of the funds). But cf. State v. Liquidating Trustees of Republic Petroleum Co., 510 S.W.2d 311 (Tex.1974) (Texas may escheat funds in Texas bank of dissolved New Mexico corporation although the present addresses of the stockholders entitled to the funds are unknown and although the last known addresses were not in Texas). Cf. cases holding that a state may not constitutionally tax the income that a non-domiciliary parent corporation doing business in the state receives from subsidiaries not doing business in the state unless there is a "unitary business" relationship between the parent and the subsidiaries, e.g., F.W. Woolworth Co. v. Taxation and Revenue Department of the State of New Mexico, 458 U.S. 354, 102 S.Ct. 3128, 73 L.Ed.2d 819 (1982); ASARCO Inc. v. Idaho State Tax Comm'n, 458 U.S. 307, 102 S.Ct. 3103, 73 L.Ed.2d 787 (1982).

254. Curry v. McCanless, 307 U.S. 357, 59 S.Ct. 900, 83 L.Ed. 1339 (1939). As to whether the domicile at death may levy an estate tax on an unexercised special power of appointment, see In re Estate of Ward, 168 Mont. 396, 543 P.2d 382 (1975) (yes, but citing authority on both sides of the question).

255. State Tax Comm'n v. Aldrich, 316 U.S. 174, 62 S.Ct. 1008, 86 L.Ed. 1358 (1942).

256. Curry v. McCanless, 307 U.S. 357, 59 S.Ct. 900, 83 L.Ed. 1339 (1939).

But cf. California v. Texas, 437 U.S. 601, 603–04 n.1, 98 S.Ct. 3107, 3109 n.1, 57 L.Ed.2d 464, 465 n.1 (1978), in which Justice Stewart, concurring in the denial of original jurisdiction in a dispute over the right to tax intangible personalty in the estate of Howard Hughes states: "intangible personal property may, at least theoretically, be taxed only at the place of the owner's domicile." Justice Stewart cites for this proposition City First Nat'l Bank v. Maine, 284 U.S. 312, 52 S.Ct. 174, 76 L.Ed. 313 (1932), which had been overruled 36 years before Justice Stewart's opinion by State Tax Commission of Utah v. Aldrich, 316 U.S. 174, 62 S.Ct. 1008, 86 L.Ed. 1358 (1942). The Court denied original jurisdiction but later granted it in California v. Texas, 457 U.S. 164, 102 S.Ct. 2335, 72 L.Ed.2d 755 (1982).

of the intangible? Because there is far greater need for nationally uniform recognition of the exclusive power of a single state in the case of escheat than in the case of taxation. It may be reasonable for several states, each of which "has extended benefits or protection, or which can demonstrate 'the practical fact of its power' or sovereignty"[257] with respect to intangible property, to tax that property, but once one state has taken all by escheat, there is nothing left to apportion among other states without taking it out of the hide of the stakeholder.

Several cases have established the proposition that if the law of the state of incorporation provides that stockholders of a company are liable for the debts of the company to the par value of their stock, and if statutory insolvency proceedings have been taken against a corporation during which an assessment has been made against shareholders, the statutory proceedings are conclusive as to the amount of and the propriety of the assessment against all shareholders, whether personally parties to the proceedings or not.[258] Another state may not close its courts to a suit against a resident shareholder based on the statutory assessment.[259] This is because of the need for national uniformity in determining whether shareholders in a corporation, no matter where resident, are liable for the debts of the company, and, if liable, in what amount. Still there is some room for recognition of the justifiable interest of the state where the shareholder resides. Georgia was permitted to shield its residents from liability for debts of a New York mutual insurance company when the policies of the company did not on their face carry warning of such liability:[260] "But the full faith and credit clause is not an inexorable and unqualified command. It leaves some

---

257. State Tax Comm'n v. Aldrich, 316 U.S. 174, 181–182, 62 S.Ct. 1008, 1012, 86 L.Ed. 1358, 1371 (1942). See also Worcester County Trust Co. v. Riley, 302 U.S. 292, 299, 58 S.Ct. 185, 188, 82 L.Ed. 268, 275 (1937): "Neither the Fourteenth Amendment nor the full faith and credit clause requires uniformity in the decisions of the courts of different states as to the place of domicil, where the exertion of state power is dependent upon domicil within its boundaries."

But see Texas v. Florida, 306 U.S. 398, 59 S.Ct. 563, 83 L.Ed. 817 (1939). In this case the Court accepted original jurisdiction of a dispute between several states as to where Edward Green, son of the legendary Hetty Green, died domiciled for purposes of estate taxation. The combined state and federal estate taxes would have exceeded the size of the estate. The Court confirmed a master's finding that Green had died domiciled in Massachusetts. See also California v. Texas, 457 U.S. 164, 102 S.Ct. 2335, 72 L.Ed.2d 755 (1982) (approve original jurisdiction to determine where Howard Hughes was domiciled at death—the combined Texas, California, and federal tax rates were 101%) (the matter was settled pending proceedings before a special master appointed by the Court). For a suggestion that the due process clause be used to compel fair apportionment among states of estate taxes on intangibles, see Farage, *Multiple Domiciles and Multiple Inheritance Taxes—A Possible Solution*, 9 Geo.Wash. L. Rev. 375, 383 (1941).

258. Chandler v. Peketz, 297 U.S. 609, 56 S.Ct. 602, 80 L.Ed. 881 (1936); Broderick v. Rosner, 294 U.S. 629, 55 S.Ct. 589, 79 L.Ed. 1100 (1935); Marin v. Augedahl, 247 U.S. 142, 38 S.Ct. 452, 62 L.Ed. 1038 (1918); Converse v. Hamilton, 224 U.S. 243, 32 S.Ct. 415, 56 L.Ed. 749 (1912). See also Hancock Nat'l Bank v. Farnum, 176 U.S. 640, 20 S.Ct. 506, 44 L.Ed. 619 (1900) (suit by creditor of insolvent corporation against nonresident shareholder based on shareholder's statutory liability).

259. Broderick v. Rosner, 294 U.S. 629, 55 S.Ct. 589, 79 L.Ed. 1100 (1935).

260. Pink v. A.A.A. Highway Express, Inc., 314 U.S. 201, 62 S.Ct. 241, 86 L.Ed. 152 (1941).

scope for state control within its borders of affairs which are peculiarly its own."[261]

§ 9.3C Effect of a Procedural Classification on Full Faith and Credit Limitations

A court ought not to be able to escape the mandate of full faith and credit through the device of classifying the rule that it wishes to apply as "procedural." The court's actions should be looked at realistically. Will the procedural classification be outcome-determinative? If so, is the interest of the forum in refusing to apply the sister state rule less than the national need for recognition of a public act, record, or judicial proceeding of a sister state? An affirmative answer to this question should preclude avoidance of the requirement of full faith and credit under the guise of conforming to local "procedure."

Several cases support this suggestion. *Modern Woodmen of America v. Mixer*[262] held that a Nebraska court could not award death benefits to the dependents of a long-missing member of a fraternal beneficiary society, when to allow such benefits would violate a society bylaw. The claim that the court was merely applying a local rule of evidence fell on deaf ears. Another fraternal beneficiary society case prevented a Missouri court from altering the result by reclassifying the society as an old line insurance company.[263] *Broderick v. Rosner*[264] held that New Jersey could not, by insisting upon an impossible joinder of parties, close its courts to stockholder liability claims arising under the statute of a sister state.[265]

Further, a court ought not to be able to escape the mandate of full faith and credit through the device of classifying as "procedural" the rule that it wishes to apply, even though such classification would accord with a standard rule of the conflict of laws. The reasoning in *Order of United Commercial Travelers of America v. Wolfe*,[266] which required South Dakota to obey the short limitations period in the constitution of a fraternal beneficiary society, would have been no less apt, perhaps more apt,[267] if the short limitations period had been embodied in an Ohio statute.

---

261. Id. at 210, 62 S.Ct. at 246–247, 86 L.Ed. at 158. See People v. Laino, 32 Cal.4th 878, 87 P.3d 27, 11 Cal.Rptr.3d 723 (2004) (full faith and credit does not prevent California from considering guilty plea in Arizona as a "strike" for purposes of enhancing criminal sentence even though Arizona court had dismissed the criminal prosecution there after the defendant completed an anger-management program).

262. 267 U.S. 544, 45 S.Ct. 389, 69 L.Ed. 783 (1925).

263. Sovereign Camp of the Woodmen of the World v. Bolin, 305 U.S. 66, 59 S.Ct. 35, 83 L.Ed. 45 (1938).

264. 294 U.S. 629, 55 S.Ct. 589, 79 L.Ed. 1100 (1935).

265. But cf. Klaxon Co. v. Stentor Elec. Mfg. Co., 313 U.S. 487, 498, 61 S.Ct. 1020, 1022, 85 L.Ed. 1477, 1481 (1941), holding that the full faith and credit clause does not require a Delaware court to apply the New York statute on judgment interest "if such application would interfere with its local policy."

266. 331 U.S. 586, 67 S.Ct. 1355, 91 L.Ed. 1687 (1947).

267. See Black's dissent: "[T]he 'state of vassalage' to which the Court's decision here reduces South Dakota is not even in subordination to the laws of another state.... The

The decision in *Wells v. Simonds Abrasive Company*[268] does not necessarily indicate a different result.[269] In *Wells*, the Court held that the Full Faith and Credit Clause did not require Pennsylvania to apply Alabama's longer limitations period. As already indicated in the discussion of *Hughes v. Fetter*,[270] the need for national uniformity in the manner of an available forum in every jurisdiction for every cause of action is relatively weak. This need may be outweighed by a significant interest of the forum. In *Wells*, Pennsylvania was refusing to litigate what in its eyes was a state claim.[271]

§ 9.3D   Historical Problems in the Application of the Full Faith and Credit Clause

The Full Faith and Credit Clause concludes: "And the Congress may by general Laws, prescribe the Manner in which such Acts, Records and Proceedings shall be proved, and the Effect thereof."[272] Congress quickly acted under this constitutional authority and passed a statute[273] that prescribed the method of authenticating legislative acts and of proving records and judicial proceedings. The statute concluded:

> And the said records and judicial proceedings shall have such faith and credit given to them in every court of the United States, as they have by law or usage in the courts of the State from whence the said records are, or shall be taken.

Omitted was any reference to "acts." It was not until the 1948 amendment to the Judicial Code that the word "acts" was added to the "effect" clause of the federal statute.[274]

Bradford Electric Light Company v. Clapper[275] and *John Hancock Mutual Insurance Company v. Yates*[276] declared that a statute is a "public act" within the meaning of the Full Faith and Credit Clause and held the clause self-executing in this context. If these decisions are correct, it is difficult to see how anything important turned upon the

---

nearest that this private association's law comes to being a law of Ohio is that Ohio permits but does not require it." Id. at 629, 67 S.Ct. at 1376, 91 L.Ed. at 1711.

268.   345 U.S. 514, 73 S.Ct. 856, 97 L.Ed. 1211 (1953).

269.   But see Rhoades v. Wright, 622 P.2d 343, 350 (Utah 1980), cert. denied, 454 U.S. 897, 102 S.Ct. 397, 70 L.Ed.2d 212 (1981) (permit action after dismissal in sister state when that state's statute of limitations had run, even if that state characterized the limitations issue as substantive, citing *Wells*).

270.   See supra text accompanying notes 242–249.

271.   But see Vernon, *Some Constitutional Problems in the Conflict of Laws and Statutes of Limitation*, 7 J.Pub.L. 120, 133 (1958). With regard to the fraternal beneficiary society cases, Professor Vernon states: "I suggest the forum's 'state of vassalage' extends to denying to it the right to refrain from hearing a claim on the basis of the running of its local statute of limitations. . . . If barred by the law of the state of incorporation, the claim is barred everywhere. If not so barred, it must be heard everywhere."

272.   U.S. Const. Art. IV, § 1.

273.   Rev.Stat. § 905 (1875); 1 Stat. 122 (1790).

274.   Judicial Code, 28 U.S.C.A. § 1738; 62 Stat. 947 (June 25, 1948, ch. 646).

275.   286 U.S. 145, 154, 52 S.Ct. 571, 573, 76 L.Ed. 1026, 1032 (1932).

276.   299 U.S. 178, 183, 57 S.Ct. 129, 132, 81 L.Ed. 106, 109 (1936).

absence from the statute of the word "acts". Nor, in view of the limited scope of the federal statute's "effect" clause,[277] should very much turn upon the word's subsequent inclusion.[278] Nevertheless, there have been judicial[279] and other scholarly statements[280] indicating that something of moment turns upon the presence or absence of the word "acts" in the federal statute. It is true that the 1948 amendment to the Judicial Code might become crucial if for historical,[281] or other reasons, it is decided that the *Bradford* and *Yates* decisions were wrong, and that the Full Faith and Credit Clause is not self-executing.

Even if the 1948 amendment provided no basis for a change in previously existing law, it may be that the second sentence of the Full Faith and Credit Clause provides Congress with the power to extend the scope of full faith and credit beyond the range of the narrow and

---

277. Judicial Code, 28 U.S.C.A. § 1738: "Such Acts, records and judicial proceedings or copies thereof, so authenticated, shall have the same full faith and credit in every court within the United States and its Territories and Possessions as they have by law or usage in the courts of such State, Territory or Possession from which they are taken."

278. See Schmidt v. Pittsburgh Plate Glass Co., 243 Iowa 1307, 1311, 55 N.W.2d 227, 229 (1952). In rejecting the employer's argument that the Full Faith and Credit Clause prevented the court from applying the Iowa workers' compensation act in disregard of the exclusive remedy provisions of the South Dakota act, the court referred to the 1948 revision to the Judicial Code and remarked: "We do not think the cited revision has met the decision in Pacific Employers Ins. Co. v. Industrial Accident Comm...."

279. Alaska Packers Ass'n v. Industrial Acc. Comm'n, 294 U.S. 532, 547, 55 S.Ct. 518, 523, 79 L.Ed. 1045, 1052 (1935): "In the case of statutes, the extra-state effect of which Congress has not prescribed, where the policy of one state statute comes into conflict with that of another, the necessity of some accommodation of the conflicting interests of the two states is still more apparent."

Pacific Employers Ins. Co. v. Industrial Acc. Comm'n, 306 U.S. 493, 502, 59 S.Ct. 629, 633, 83 L.Ed. 940, 945 (1939): "And in the case of statutes, the extra-state effect of which Congress has not prescribed, as it may under the constitutional provision, we think the conclusion is unavoidable that the full faith and credit clause does not require one state to substitute for its own statute, applicable to persons and events within it, the conflicting statute of another state...."

Hughes v. Fetter, 341 U.S. 609, 613–14 n. 16, 71 S.Ct. 980, 983 n. 16, 95 L.Ed. 1212, 1217 n. 16 (1951): "In certain previous cases [citing the above-quoted portions of *Pacific Employers* and *Alaska Packers*] ... this court suggested that under the Full Faith and Credit Clause a forum state might make a distinction between statutes and judgments of sister states because of Congress' failure to prescribe the extra-state effect to be accorded public acts. Subsequent to these decisions the Judicial Code was revised.... In deciding the present appeal, however, we found it unnecessary to rely on any changes accomplished by the Judicial Code revision."

Carroll v. Lanza, 349 U.S. 408, 422, 75 S.Ct. 804, 812, 99 L.Ed. 1183, 1193 (1955) (Frankfurter, J., dissenting): "Furthermore, the new provision of 28 U.S.C.A. § 1738 cannot be disregarded. In 1948 Congress for the first time dealt with the full faith and credit effect to be given statutes. The absence of such a provision was used by Justice Stone to buttress the Court's opinions both in Alaska Packers ... and Pacific Employers.... Hence, if § 1738 has any effect, it would seem to tend toward respecting Missouri's legislation."

280. Freund, *Chief Justice Stone and the Conflict of Laws*, 59 Harv. L. Rev. 1210, 1225 (1946); Reese, *Full Faith and Credit to Statutes: The Defense of Public Policy*, 19 U. Chi. L. Rev. 339, 342 (1952).

281. For suggestions that historically "acts" was meant to apply only to legislative exercise of judicial power, see McGrath v. Tobin, 81 R.I. 415, 421, 103 A.2d 795, 798 (1954); Note, *Conflict of Laws—Full Faith and Credit to Public Acts*, 30 N.Y.U. L. Rev. 984 (1955). For a suggestion that the clause is not self-executing, see Nadelmann, *Full Faith and Credit to Judgments and Public Acts*, 56 Mich. L. Rev. 33, 75 (1957).

somewhat cryptic provisions of the constitutional clause itself,[282] and, of course, beyond the scope of full faith and credit as sketched in this chapter. An example is that portion of the Parental Kidnapping Prevention Act of 1980 that prohibits modification of sister-state custody decrees.[283]

§ 9.4   Equal Protection Limitations on a State's Choice of Law

Most states have moved from the use of rigid, territorial choice-of-law rules to evolve new rules based on an appraisal of the extent to which states with putatively conflicting domestic laws have some legitimate concern with giving effect to the policies underlying those laws. This conflict-of-laws focus on relevant state "interests" raises the question of the extent to which a state may make choice-of-law decisions that apply its domestic law to extra-state events involving its own residents, but refuse to make similar applications of its law to residents of other states for the reason that it is "interested" in protecting or compensating its own residents but not others. When is this discrimination based on residence reasonable and when, if ever, is the classification so

---

282.   See Yarborough v. Yarborough, 290 U.S. 202, 215 n.2, 54 S.Ct. 181, 186 n.2, 78 L.Ed. 269, 277 n.2 (1933) (Stone, J. dissenting): "The constitutional provision giving Congress power to prescribe the effect to be given to acts, records and proceedings would have been quite unnecessary had it not been intended that Congress should have a latitude broader than that given the courts by the full faith and credit clause alone."

Cook, *The Powers of Congress Under the Full Faith and Credit Clause*, 28 Yale L. J. 421 (1919); Freund, supra note 280 at 1229–30: "The constitutional power to 'prescribe the manner in which such acts, records, and proceedings shall be proved, and the effect thereof' may well be thought to support legislation enlarging the compulsory area of full faith and credit beyond the bounds set by the present statute ... but legislation withdrawing from the compulsory area what the Court has held is encompassed by the constitutional mandate may stand on a different footing."

Nadelmann, supra note 281 at 86: "Currently without practical interest but provoking arguments about its possible effect, the amendment detracts from the real task which confronts us: the study of what if anything can be achieved by *proper* legislation under the clause...."

But see Sack, *Domestic Violence Across State Lines: The Full Faith and Credit Clause, Congressional Power, and Interstate Enforcement of Protection Orders*, 98 Nw. U. L. Rev. 827, 832 (2004) (Congress cannot either expand or contract full faith and credit in areas where the Supreme Court has already ruled on the Constitution's mandate); Wardle, *Non-Recognition of Same-Sex Marriage Judgments under DOMA and the Constitution*, 38 Creighton L. Rev. 365, 410 (2005): "The history of the enactment of the Effects Clause of the Constitution clearly refutes the [theory that Congress can expand but not contract full faith and credit]."

In addition to the "effect clause" in the Full Faith and Credit provision, other possible constitutional bases for federal legislation controlling which state's law shall apply are the Commerce Clause, Art. I, § 8, cl. 3, (see supra note 228), and the Necessary and Proper Clause, Art. I, § 8, cl. 18. See American Law Institute, Complex Litigation: Statutory Recommendations and Analysis with Reporter's Study 310 (1994).

283.   28 U.S.C.A. § 1738A. See §§ 5.3B and 5.3C. For the much more doubtful attempt to restrict the effect of the Full Faith and Credit Clause, see 28 U.S.C.A. § 1738C: "No State, territory, or possession of the United States, or Indian tribe, shall be required to give effect to any public act, record, or judicial proceeding of any other State, territory, possession, or tribe respecting a relationship between persons of the same sex that is treated as a marriage under the laws of such other State, territory, possession, or tribe, or a right or claim arising from such relationship."

unreasonable as to violate the Equal Protection Clause of the Fourteenth Amendment?

One form of this equal protection problem may be put as follows. State F has a dram shop act making an owner of a saloon liable for injury caused by the intoxication of patrons who became inebriated in the owner's bar. State X, bordering state F, has no dram shop act and under X law an owner of a bar is not liable for damages caused by persons who became intoxicated in the owner's tavern. State F has applied its dram shop act to hold F bar owners liable when liquor is sold in F bars to F drunks who injure F residents in state X.[284] The reason stated by F courts for this extraterritorial application of the F statute is that the two policies underlying the statute, deterrence of liquor sales to those who are drunk or almost drunk and assuring an adequate source of compensation to those injured by the conduct sought to be deterred, are fully applicable when the only contact not in state F is the place of injury.

A case subsequently arises in which an X resident is injured in X by an F drunk who became intoxicated in an F bar. Can an F court, without making an unreasonable classification[285] and thus violating the Equal Protection Clause, now refuse to hold the F tavern owner liable under the F statute? The F court might say that its primary purpose in applying the F statute extraterritorially is one of compensation to F residents and that it is not "interested" in compensating an X resident, especially when under X law no compensation is available. But refusal to extend the benefits of F law to a nonresident is likely to be most discriminatory when, as here, it means that the nonresident will have no recovery available anywhere. The problem would be different if the F court were dealing, for example, with workers' compensation, for there then would be a greater likelihood that, if denied compensation under one state's statute because a nonresident, the injured person will have compensation available under the statute of a state with which he or she is more closely identified. Moreover, granting recovery under the F dram shop act will not interfere with any applicable policy of state X.[286] For these reasons, denial of recovery to the X resident under the F dram shop act when an F resident would be given compensation should be held

---

284.   See Schmidt v. Driscoll Hotel, Inc., 249 Minn. 376, 82 N.W.2d 365 (1957).

285.   See Currie & Schreter, *Unconstitutional Discrimination in the Conflict of Laws: Equal Protection*, 28 U. Chi. L. Rev. 1, 11 (1960); Currie & Schreter, *Unconstitutional Discrimination in the Conflict of Laws: Privileges and Immunities*, 69 Yale L. J. 1323, 1348 (1960); Kramer, *Interests and Policy Clashes in Conflict of Laws*, 13 Rutgers L. Rev. 523, 536 (1959). Cf. Canadian No. Ry. v. Eggen, 252 U.S. 553, 559, 40 S.Ct. 402, 403, 64 L.Ed. 713, 715 (1920) (borrowing statute's exclusion of local citizens is not an "arbitrary or vexatious discrimination against non-residents"); supra § 2.10, text accompanying notes 61–69 suggesting that the impact of equal protection varies depending on the right asserted and the extent to which the challenged law impairs that right. But cf. Haughton v. Haughton, 76 Ill.2d 439, 31 Ill.Dec. 183, 394 N.E.2d 385 (1979), cert. denied, 444 U.S. 1102, 100 S.Ct. 1069, 62 L.Ed.2d 789 (1980) (tolling statute, which applies only if one of the parties was a resident of Illinois at the time the action accrued, violates equal protection).

286.   Cf. Currie & Schreter, supra note 285, 69 Yale L. J. at 1366 n.172 (F need not apply its dram shop act if the bar were incorporated in X but did business in F where it sold the liquor).

an unreasonable classification that denies to the X resident the equal protection of the laws.

Sometimes permitting a nonresident to recover under F law may officiously interfere with the policy of the injured person's home state. For example, suppose that the victim, a resident of state X, is employed by an X corporation and performs duties mainly in X, although occasionally working in state F. The employer has qualified as a self-insurer under X's workers' compensation system, but has failed to apply or qualify as required by F's workers' compensation statute. The victim is injured while working in F. F would permit an employee of an uninsured employer to sue the employer at common law, escaping from the limited and definite liability of the workers' compensation system. F should not permit this victim to do so, and perhaps if F did permit recovery under F common law, this action should be held a denial of full faith and credit to the "exclusive remedy" provision in X's workers' compensation statute.[287] There would not be a similar objection to F's making compensation available under its own workers' compensation act.

An equal protection problem would arise if a state applied interest analysis only to favor its own citizens, but applied territorial choice-of-law rules when non-citizens were involved. *Skahill v. Capital Airlines, Inc.*[288] illustrates the problem. A passenger, domiciled in Massachusetts with his wife and children, boarded the defendant's airplane in Virginia for a flight between two points in Virginia. The airplane crashed in Virginia killing the passenger. A wrongful death action was brought against the airline in New York. The Virginia death act had a $30,000 limit on recovery. The defendant moved for summary judgment in favor of the plaintiff in the amount of $30,000. The plaintiff argued that in *Kilberg v. Northeast Airlines, Inc.*,[289] the New York Court of Appeals had rejected, as contrary to New York public policy, the Massachusetts $15,000 limit on wrongful death recovery. In *Kilberg*, the decedent was a New York citizen who had boarded the fatal flight in New York. Therefore, the plaintiff argued, a court in New York should similarly reject the Virginia limit on death recovery and failure to do so just because the decedent was not a New York resident would be unconstitutional, violating *inter alia* the Equal Protection Clause of the Fourteenth Amendment. The court rejected this argument and granted the motion for summary judgment saying:

> The New York Court of Appeals pointed to residents of New York as the natural objects of New York's public policy....
>
> The question for decision here is whether New York's contacts or interests are sufficient to justify the superposition of the New

---

287. See supra § 9.3A, text accompanying note 221.

288. 234 F.Supp. 906 (D.N.Y.1964), aff'd without opinion (2d Cir.), cert. denied, 382 U.S. 878, 86 S.Ct. 161, 15 L.Ed.2d 119 (1965).

289. 9 N.Y.2d 34, 211 N.Y.S.2d 133, 172 N.E.2d 526 (1961). Full faith and credit objections to *Kilberg* were rejected in Pearson v. Northeast Airlines, Inc., 307 F.2d 131, 309 F.2d 553 (2d Cir.1962), cert. denied, 372 U.S. 912, 83 S.Ct. 726, 9 L.Ed.2d 720 (1963).

York damage policy on the Virginia statute. The answer must be in the negative. Neither the decedent nor his dependents were residents of New York at any relevant time. Further, New York's concern for users of its transportation facilities is of no help because the flight did not touch New York. . . .

I conclude that the classification here, based on contacts with or interest in the transaction from which the litigation arose and incidentally resulting in the dissimilar treatment of residents and non-residents of the forum state is reasonable under both the Equal Protection and Privileges and Immunities[290] criteria.[291]

---

290. U.S. Const. Art. IV, § 2: "The Citizens of each State shall be entitled to all Privileges and Immunities of Citizens in the several States." See also U.S.Const. Amend. XIV, § 1: "No State shall make or enforce any law which shall abridge the privileges or immunities of citizens of the United States. . . ." (Footnote added).

291. *Skahill,* 234 F.Supp. at 908–909. Accord, Campbell v. Trans World Airlines, Inc., 9 Av.Cas. 18, 223 (S.D.N.Y.1965), aff'd without opinion (2d Cir.), cert. denied, 385 U.S. 824, 87 S.Ct. 57, 17 L.Ed.2d 61 (1966). Cf. Moan v. Coombs, 47 N.J. 348, 221 A.2d 10 (1966) refusing to extend New Jersey Unsatisfied Claim and Judgment Fund Law benefits to motorists from a state that would not extend reciprocal benefits to New Jersey citizens. An uninsured New Jersey motorist injured Pennsylvania residents in New Jersey. The court held that there was no violation of equal protection in so limiting the benefits under the New Jersey statute; Holly v. Maryland Auto. Ins. Fund, 29 Md.App. 498, 349 A.2d 670 (1975) (same, and no violation of privileges and immunities under Art. IV § 2 or of privileges or immunities under 14th amend.); Law v. Maercklein, 292 N.W.2d 86 (N.D. 1980) (no violation of equal protection or of privileges and immunities to deny recovery from unsatisfied judgment fund to nonresident mother bringing suit to recover for wrongful death of her resident son).

For discussion of whether a "state-interest" approach to choice of law is constitutional, see Brilmayer, *Carolene, Conflicts, and the Fate of the "Inside–Outsider",* 134 U.Pa. L. Rev. 1291, 1303 (1986) ("[s]ooner or later, the Court will have to address the privileges and immunities clause, the commerce clause, and the equal protection issues that lurk within the modern view of choice of law"); Ely, *Choice of Law and the State's Interest in Protecting Its Own,* 23 Wm. & Mary L. Rev. 173, 185–86 (1981) (stating that the requirements of the Privileges and Immunities Clause are not met when a citizen is denied the benefits of local law although getting "what his home state would give him"); Gergen, *Equality and the Conflict of Laws,* 73 Iowa L. Rev. 893, 934 (1988) (with minor exception, interest analysis "passes constitutional muster"); Laycock, *Equal Citizens of Equal and Territorial States: The Constitutional Foundations of Choice of Law,* 92 Colum. L. Rev. 249, 285 (1992) (stating that "the first principle of interest analysis is antithetical to the first principle of the [Privileges and Immunities] Clause, and antithetical to the Union"); Roosevelt, *The Myth of Choice of Law: Rethinking Conflicts,* 97 Mich. L. Rev. 2448 (1999); cf. Neuman, *Territorial Discrimination, Equal Protection, and Self–Determination,* 135 U.Pa. L. Rev. 261, 329 (1987) (the privileges and immunities clause is relevant to "claims of discrimination against citizens of sister states" but "[t]he equal protection clause still has an independent role to play . . . when state residents or corporations or resident aliens are disfavored by residence classifications, because they are *not* protected by the privileges and immunities clause").

Application of a tolling statute to companies subject to long-arm jurisdiction in the state but not required to obtain a license to do business there may impose an unreasonable burden on interstate commerce and violate the Commerce Clause even if there is no equal protection violation. See Bendix Autolite Corp. v. Midwesco Enterprises, Inc., 486 U.S. 888, 108 S.Ct. 2218, 100 L.Ed.2d 896 (1988) (tolling the statute of limitations against a foreign corporation that does not register to do business violates the Commerce Clause if the corporation is subject to long-arm jurisdiction and compelling it to appoint an in-state agent for service of process would subject it to general jurisdiction); Juzwin v. Asbestos Corp., Ltd., 900 F.2d 686 (3d Cir.1990), cert. denied, 498 U.S. 896, 111 S.Ct. 246, 112 L.Ed.2d 204 (1990) (New Jersey statute tolling limitations against nonresident who does not appoint resident agent for service of process and permitting nonresident to limit designation to cases in which forum would otherwise have jurisdiction nevertheless violates

On the facts in *Skahill*, this conclusion seems correct. Because the flight did not originate in New York, it is not even clear that a New York court would have displaced the Virginia damages limitation even if the decedent had been a New York resident. Moreover, when *Skahill* was decided, Massachusetts, the decedent's home state, would have applied Virginia law because it was the law of the place of the wrong.[292] Suppose, however, that the decedent had been resident in state X, where he boarded the airplane, and that state X would mirror the New York result in *Kilberg* and refuse to apply the Virginia recovery limit if suit were brought in X. Under these circumstances, a refusal by a New York court to reach the result that it would reach if the decedent were a New York resident, or that state X, decedent's domicile, would reach, should be held a denial of equal protection.[293] This objection is removed if the decedent's domicile would apply Virginia law.

Another form of equal protection problem arises if the forum would refuse to apply its own law to its own residents because the forum's traditional choice-of-law rule points to some other geographical location as having the decisive "contact." Such a refusal may be based upon an unreasonable classification of forum residents if the policies underlying the forum rule would be advanced by applying it and if such application would not interfere with the legitimate interests of any other state or unfairly surprise any party. For example, suppose that a husband and wife, domiciled in state F, are driving in state X with the husband at the wheel. Because of the husband's negligence, the wife is injured. Under F law, a wife may sue her husband for negligence. In X, such a suit would be barred by a rule of marital immunity. The wife sues her husband in F

---

the Commerce Clause because not as narrowly drawn as it might be—for example, tolling limitations only after a diligent effort to effect long-arm service was unsuccessful); cf. G.D. Searle & Co. v. Cohn, 455 U.S. 404, 102 S.Ct. 1137, 71 L.Ed.2d 250 (1982) (remand for consideration of Commerce Clause argument after deciding tolling statute did not violate equal protection); New Energy Co. of Indiana v. Limbach, 486 U.S. 269, 108 S.Ct. 1803, 100 L.Ed.2d 302 (1988) (Ohio statute violates the Commerce Clause in awarding a tax credit only for fuel produced in the state or in another state that grants similar tax advantages to fuel produced in Ohio); Horowitz, *The Commerce Clause as a Limitation on State Choice-of-Law Doctrine*, 84 Harv. L. Rev. 806, 814 (1971).

292. See In re Air Crash Disaster at Boston, Mass. on July 31, 1973, 399 F.Supp. 1106, 1115 (D. Mass. 1975) ("Massachusetts adheres to the traditional lex loci delicti rule"). Since then Massachusetts has changed its approach to choice of law. See Pevoski v. Pevoski, 371 Mass. 358, 360, 358 N.E.2d 416, 417 (1976) (applying Massachusetts law to determine the issue of interspousal immunity between Massachusetts spouses although the injury was suffered outside the state because Massachusetts "has the strongest interest in the resolution of the particular issue presented").

Although in *Skahill* the decedent had been a resident of Massachusetts, by the time that the action was commenced, his widow and three minor children had moved to Rhode Island. 234 F.Supp. at 907. Rhode Island has, since *Skahill*, applied its own wrongful death act in a suit to recover against a Rhode Island defendant for fatal injury to a Rhode Island resident in Massachusetts. Brown v. Church of Holy Name of Jesus, 105 R.I. 322, 252 A.2d 176 (1969); Woodward v. Stewart, 104 R.I. 290, 243 A.2d 917 (1968), cert. dism'd, 393 U.S. 957, 89 S.Ct. 387, 21 L.Ed.2d 371 (1968).

293. Cf. Note, *Unconstitutional Discrimination in Choice of Law*, 77 Colum. L. Rev. 272, 286 (1977): "A choice-of-law rule that expressly required application of whichever law was most favorable to the party from the forum state would violate the privileges and immunities clause because its discrimination would be based on nothing other than a desire to prefer its own citizens."

and F gives judgment for the husband, applying the law of X as the place of the wrong. This application of X law defeats the F policy of compensation and serves no relevant X policy of preserving marital harmony or protecting the insurer, who issued the policy in F, from a collusive suit. An F wife who had been similarly injured in F would have been permitted to recover. The time may be approaching when discriminating in the treatment of the two F wives because they were injured in different states will be recognized as the kind of irrational classification that runs afoul of the Equal Protection Clause.[294]

---

294. See Currie & Schreter, supra note 285, 28 U. Chi. L. Rev. at 11; cf. Tussman & TenBroek, *The Equal Protection of the Laws*, 37 Calif. L. Rev. 341, 344 (1949). But cf. Szlinis v. Moulded Fiber Glass Companies, Inc., 80 Mich.App. 55, 263 N.W.2d 282 (1977) (Michigan statute borrowing shorter limitations period of place of fatal injury and containing no exception for Michigan residents does not violate equal protection). But see Allstate Insurance Co. v. Hague, 449 U.S. 302, 101 S.Ct. 633, 66 L.Ed.2d 521 (1981) (minimal scrutiny of choice of law under due process and full faith and credit) (discussed in § 9.2A); Greider v. Pennsylvania Assigned Claims Plan, 316 Pa.Super. 146, 462 A.2d 836 (1983) (no due process or equal protection violation in denying no-fault coverage to forum residents injured in another state when they would be covered if injured in the forum).

Chapter 10

CHOICE OF LAW IN THE
FEDERAL COURTS

§ 10.1 The Erie Doctrine and State Conflict-of-Laws Rules

The focus here is upon that aspect of the *Erie*[1] doctrine that compels a federal district court, on issues not governed by federal law, to apply the conflict-of-laws rules of the state in which it sits. The purpose is to appraise some of the desirable and some of the undesirable effects of this rule. First it is necessary to tell enough of the *Erie* story to provide a background for what is to follow.

§ 10.2 Development of the Outcome—Determinative Test

There are three major sources of limitations on federal courts applying a different rule of decision than found in state law when the case is not governed by a federal statute, a treaty, or the U.S. Constitution. Such a case would usually be one in which federal subject matter jurisdiction is based on diversity of citizenship of the parties. These three sources are (1) the U.S. Constitution; (2) the Judiciary Act of 1789; and (3) the Rules Enabling Act.

There are two approaches to constitutional limits on applying a federal rule of decision in such cases. First there is what might be called a "federalism" limit, as stated by Justice Brandeis in *Erie Railroad Co. v. Tompkins*:

> Congress has no power to declare substantive rules of common law applicable in a state whether they be local in their nature or "general," be they commercial law or a part of the law of torts. And no clause in the Constitution purports to confer such a power upon the federal courts.[2]

Another constitutional approach is the due process limitation on choice of law, which precludes selection of a law that, if applied, would be arbitrary or unfair. As stated in *Allstate Insurance Co. v. Hague*:

> In order to ensure that the choice of law is neither arbitrary nor fundamentally unfair, the Court has invalidated the choice of law of a State which has had no significant contact or significant aggregation of contacts, creating state interests, with the parties and the occurrence or transaction.[3]

---

1. Erie R.R. v. Tompkins, 304 U.S. 64, 58 S.Ct. 817, 82 L.Ed. 1188 (1938).
2. Id. at 78, 58 S.Ct. at 822.
3. 449 U.S. 302, 308, 101 S.Ct. 633, 638, 66 L.Ed.2d 521 (1981) (citation omitted).

In the *Erie* context, this second constitutional approach is epitomized by Justice Harlan's concurring opinion in *Hanna v. Plumer*:

> To my mind the proper line of approach in determining whether to apply a state or a federal rule, whether "substantive" or "procedural," is to stay close to basic principles by inquiring if the choice of rule would substantially affect those primary decisions respecting human conduct which our constitutional system leaves to state regulation. If so, *Erie* and the Constitution require that the state rule prevail, even in the face of a conflicting federal rule.[4]

Section 34 of the Judiciary Act of 1789 provided a statutory check on the law applied in federal courts: "The laws of the several states, except where the constitution, treaties or statutes of the United States shall otherwise require or provide, shall be regarded as rules of decision in trials at common law in the courts of the United States in cases where they apply."[5] An amendment in 1948 changed the words "trials at common law" to "civil actions,"[6] thus rendering moot any further debate as to whether the section or the doctrine it embodied applied to equity cases[7] and eliminating one possible basis for distinguishing between the mandate of the statute and the commands of the United States Constitution.[8] In its present form, the section reads: "The laws of the several states, except where the Constitution or treaties of the United States or Acts of Congress otherwise require or provide, shall be regarded as rules of decision in civil actions in the courts of the United States, in cases where they apply."[9]

A second statutory check on the law applied by federal courts is the Rules Enabling Act, which authorized the Federal Rules of Civil Procedure. The Act provided: "Said rules shall neither abridge, enlarge, nor modify the substantive rights of any litigant."[10]

Swift v. Tyson[11] held that "laws," the second word of section 34 of the Judiciary Act of 1789, did not include the decisions of state courts upon matters of general common law, which the federal courts were as

---

4. 380 U.S. 460, 475, 85 S.Ct. 1136, 1146, 14 L.Ed.2d 8 (1965) (footnote omitted) (Harlan, J., concurring).

5. Act of September 24, 1789, ch. 20, § 34, 1 Stat. 92.

6. H.R. 3214, 80th Cong., 2d Sess. (1948).

7. See, e.g., Russell v. Todd, 309 U.S. 280, 287, 60 S.Ct. 527, 531, 84 L.Ed. 754, 759 (1940) ("The Rules of Decision Act does not apply to suits in equity"); Ruhlin v. New York Life Ins. Co., 304 U.S. 202, 205, 58 S.Ct. 860, 861, 82 L.Ed. 1290, 1292 (1938) ("The doctrine [*Erie*] applies though the question of construction arises not in an action at law, but in a suit in equity"); Mason v. United States, 260 U.S. 545, 559, 43 S.Ct. 200, 204, 67 L.Ed. 396, 401 (1923) (statute merely declarative of the rule that would exist in the absence of statute; state laws as rules of decision in equity suits not excluded from the statute by implication).

8. See Kurland, *Justice Frankfurter, The Supreme Court and the Erie Doctrine in Diversity Cases*, 67 Yale L. J. 187, 193 (1957).

9. 28 U.S.C. § 1652.

10. 48 Stat. 1064 (1934), now, slightly reworded, 28 U.S.C. § 2072(b):"Such rules shall not abridge, enlarge or modify any substantive right."

11. 41 U.S. 1, 10 L.Ed. 865 (1842).

competent as the state courts to decide. Justice Story's opinion explained:

> It never has been supposed by us, that the section did apply, or was designed to apply to questions of a more general nature, not at all dependent upon local statutes, or local usages of a fixed and permanent operation, as, for example, to the construction of ordinary contracts or other written instruments, and especially to questions of general commercial law, where the state tribunals are called upon to perform the like functions as ourselves, that is, to ascertain, upon general reasoning and legal analogies, what is the true exposition of the contract or instrument, or what is the just rule furnished by the principles of commercial law to govern the case.[12]

Tyson was a suit on a bill of exchange dated in Maine, taken in payment for Maine land, and drawn on and accepted by the defendant in New York. It held that a federal court sitting in New York need not follow the New York rule concerning the adequacy of a preexisting debt as consideration to make a taker of a note one in due course. The purpose may have been to foster uniformity in an area where uniformity then, as now, was very important to the young nation—interstate commercial transactions. Quite often, following *Swift v. Tyson*, the Court sounded this theme of national uniformity. For example, in *Baltimore & Ohio Railroad v. Baugh*, holding that a federal court sitting in Ohio need not follow the Ohio fellow-servant rule as it applied to an action against a railroad for injuries suffered by an employee in a collision in Ohio, the Court asked: "As it [the railroad] passes from State to State, must the rights, obligations and duties subsisting between it and its employees change at every state line?"[13] Even Justice Holmes, who, in a series of dissents, opposed extensions of *Tyson*, was willing to acquiesce in its application to "those principles which it is desirable to make uniform throughout the United States."[14]

No such uniformity resulted. The Court stopped short of requiring the state courts to follow the "general law" as articulated by the federal courts, and the state courts continued to go their own way. More significantly, the *Tyson* concept of general law was applied to essentially intrastate transactions. Horrible examples began to accumulate in which a litigant could step across the courthouse square into the federal court

---

12.   Id. at 18–19, 10 L.Ed. at 871. See Borchers, *The Origins of Diversity Jurisdiction, the Rise of Legal Positivism, and a Brave New World for Erie and Klaxon,* 72 Tex. L. Rev. 79, 81 (1993) (stating that "the drafting and ratification history supports the conclusion that diversity was intended at least in part as a protection against aberrational state laws, particularly those regarding commercial transactions").

Georgia takes a similar position and will apply its own common law rather than the common law of the state indicated by Georgia's choice-of-law rule. See Frank Briscoe Co., Inc. v. Georgia Sprinkler Co., Inc., 713 F.2d 1500 (11th Cir.1983); Motz v. Alropa Corp., 192 Ga. 176, 15 S.E.2d 237 (1941); Rees, *Choice of Law in Georgia: Time to Consider a Change?,* 34 Mercer L. Rev. 787, 789–90 (1983).

13.   149 U.S. 368, 378, 13 S.Ct. 914, 918, 37 L.Ed. 772, 778 (1893).

14.   Kuhn v. Fairmont Coal Co., 215 U.S. 349, 371, 30 S.Ct. 140, 148, 54 L.Ed. 228, 239 (1910) (Holmes, J., dissenting).

under the aegis of diversity jurisdiction and thus avoid a state rule applicable to an intrastate transaction. *Kuhn v. Fairmont Coal Co.*[15] involved the duty of a coal company to provide support for surface land during mining operations in West Virginia. The Court refused to direct a federal court sitting in West Virginia to follow a decision of West Virginia's highest court, directly in point, which had become final after suit had been filed in the federal court, but before the decision by the Court of Appeals.[16] Probably the best known of the "horrible examples" is Black & White Taxicab & Transfer Co. v. Brown & Yellow Taxicab & Transfer Co.[17] In this case, a Kentucky corporation, by dissolving and reincorporating in Tennessee, manufactured diversity of citizenship jurisdiction and enforced in a federal court, sitting in Kentucky, a contract made and to be performed in Kentucky that no Kentucky state court would have enforced.

Many commentators recognized that the situation was intolerable.[18] The forum shopping involved was bad, but much worse, at the core of the problem was the fact that individuals, in their everyday activities and dealings, were subjected to two inconsistent bodies of law. At the nadir of Black & White Taxicab, Tyson entered its last decade. It was slain by the "sledge-hammer"[19] blows of *Erie Railroad v. Tompkins.*[20]

Mr. Tompkins, a Pennsylvania citizen, was walking alongside the defendant's railroad tracks in Pennsylvania when he was struck by some projection from a passing train. On the jurisdictional basis of diversity of citizenship, Tompkins sued the railroad in a federal court in New York. The defendant urged that under Pennsylvania law the plaintiff, being a trespasser, could not recover. This point of Pennsylvania law was disputed, but in deciding to affirm a verdict for the plaintiff, the Court of Appeals held that it was unnecessary to consider whether the Pennsylvania law was as defendant had contended, because the question was one of general law upon which the federal courts were free to exercise their independent judgment. When certiorari was granted, the parties focused their arguments on the extent of the *Tyson* doctrine. Justice Brandeis, however, seized the opportunity to overrule *Tyson*.

---

15.   215 U.S. 349, 30 S.Ct. 140, 54 L.Ed. 228 (1910).

16.   For a post-*Erie* case to the contrary on the duty of a federal court to conform to state decisions pendente lite, see Vandenbark v. Owens–Illinois Glass Co., 311 U.S. 538, 61 S.Ct. 347, 85 L.Ed. 327 (1941).

See also Pierce v. Cook & Co., 518 F.2d 720 (10th Cir.1975), cert. denied, 423 U.S. 1079, 96 S.Ct. 866, 47 L.Ed.2d 89 (1976) (relief granted under Fed.R.Civ.P. 60(b)(6) from federal judgment rendered 3 years previously when, in case arising from same accident, state court overrules precedent on which federal had relied).

17.   276 U.S. 518, 48 S.Ct. 404, 72 L.Ed. 681 (1928).

18.   See, e.g., Mills, *Should Federal Courts Ignore State Laws?*, 34 Am. L. Rev. 51, 68–69 (1900) (urging amendment of the Judiciary Act to compel federal courts to use as rules of decision both "statutes and decisions of the courts of last resort of such States").

19.   Clark, *State Law in the Federal Courts: The Brooding Omnipresence of Erie v. Tompkins*, 55 Yale L. J. 267, 295 (1946).

20.   304 U.S. 64, 58 S.Ct. 817, 82 L.Ed. 1188 (1938).

Charles Warren had demonstrated that, in the original draft of Section 34 of the Judiciary Act of 1789, the words "statute law" and "unwritten or common law" had been stricken and the single word "laws" inserted in their place.[21] But Justice Brandeis was not content to overturn *Tyson* simply on a matter of statutory construction. He believed that *Tyson* had produced unconstitutional results:

> *Swift v. Tyson* introduced grave discrimination by noncitizens against citizens. It made rights enjoyed under the unwritten "general law" vary according to whether enforcement was sought in the state or in the federal court; and the privilege of selecting the court in which the right could be determined was conferred upon the noncitizen. Thus, the doctrine rendered impossible equal protection of the law. In attempting to promote uniformity of law throughout the United States, the doctrine had prevented uniformity in the administration of the law of the State.
>
> . . .
>
> If only a question of statutory construction were involved, we should not be prepared to abandon a doctrine so widely applied throughout nearly a century. But the unconstitutionality of the course pursued has now been made clear and compels us to do so.... Except in matters governed by the Federal Constitution or by Acts of Congress, the law to be applied in any case is the law of the State. And whether the law of the State shall be declared by its legislature in a statute or by its highest court in a decision is not a matter of federal concern. There is no federal general common law. Congress has no power to declare substantive rules of common law applicable in a State whether they be local in their nature or "general," be they commercial law or part of the law of torts. And no clause in the Constitution purports to confer such a power upon the federal courts.[22]

The case was remanded to the Court of Appeals with directions to determine the issue of state law it had thought irrelevant.[23]

Ironically, less than five months after the *Erie* opinion, the new Federal Rules of Civil Procedure took effect.[24] The stage was thus set for exploring in depth the "substance"-"procedure" dichotomy in the context of *Erie* and the Judiciary Act. To what extent would federal courts now be free to apply the new Federal Rules of Civil Procedure and other

---

21. C. Warren, *New Light on the History of the Federal Judiciary Act of 1789*, 37 Harv. L. Rev. 49, 86 (1923).

22. *Erie*, 304 U.S. at 74–78, 58 S.Ct. at 820–822, 82 L.Ed. at 1192–1194.

23. Id. at 80, 58 S.Ct. at 823, 82 L.Ed. at 1195. On remand, the Second Circuit panel held that Tompkins could not recover under Pennsylvania law and remanded to the trial court with directions to enter a judgment for the defendant. Tompkins v. Erie R.R., 98 F.2d 49 (2d Cir.1938), cert. denied, 305 U.S. 637, 59 S.Ct. 108, 83 L.Ed. 410 (1938).

24. See Kane, *The Golden Wedding Year: Erie Railroad Company v. Tompkins and the Federal Rules*, 63 Notre Dame L. Rev. 671, 673 (1988) ("Justice Brandeis was the sole member of the Court to dissent from the adoption of the Federal Rules in 1938. The reasons [practical or constitutional] are not clear.... ").

rules and procedures formerly common in those courts and to what extent would these rules and procedures have to be displaced by state law? What was to be "procedural" and what "substantive"?

The first battle was a victory for the new rules. *Sibbach v. Wilson & Co.*[25] held that a federal district court could, pursuant to Rule 35,[26] order the plaintiff in a personal injury suit to submit to a physical examination by a court-appointed physician, despite the fact a state court in the state in which the case was tried could not make such an order.[27] The Court found that the rule was within the mandate of the Rules Enabling Act[28] authorizing the Supreme Court to prescribe uniform rules of civil procedure for the federal district courts: "Said rules shall neither abridge, enlarge, nor modify the substantive rights of any litigant."[29] The plaintiff was wrong in translating "substantive" into "important" or "substantial."[30]

It was apparent that deeper analysis would soon be required. "Substance" and "procedure" are chameleon-like words, changing their meaning with changed context. The Court had yet to indicate what meaning they bore in this new context.

Klaxon Co. v. Stentor Electric Manufacturing Co.[31] pointed the direction in which the Court was to move. Pursuant to an agreement executed in New York, a New York corporation transferred its business to a Delaware corporation. The Delaware corporation promised to use its best efforts to further the manufacture and sale of certain patented devices and to pay the New York corporation a share of the profits. The assets were transferred in New York and performance was commenced there. Subsequently, the New York corporation sued the Delaware corporation in a Delaware federal court for violating the agreement. Upon recovering judgment, plaintiff moved for addition of interest under the New York Civil Practice Act. Without inquiry into what a Delaware court would have done, the federal court granted the motion. The Supreme Court reversed. Delaware was not constitutionally compelled to apply the New York rule on interest and therefore, under the *Erie* doctrine, the federal court was bound to determine and to follow the

---

25. 312 U.S. 1, 61 S.Ct. 422, 85 L.Ed. 479 (1941).

26. Fed.R.Civ.P. 35.

27. See Schlagenhauf v. Holder, 379 U.S. 104, 85 S.Ct. 234, 13 L.Ed.2d 152 (1964) (extending *Sibbach v. Wilson* to defendants).

28. See Burbank, *The Rules Enabling Act of 1934*, 130 Pa. L. Rev. 1015 (1982): "The primary limitation imposed by the Act was intended to allocate lawmaking power between the Supreme Court as rule-maker and Congress and did not have any independent federalism purpose" (at page 1187); "if lawmaking in an area necessarily involves the consideration of public policy—policies extrinsic to the process of litigation—the choices in that area are for Congress" (at page 1190); Carrington, *"Substance" and "Procedure" in the Rules Enabling Act*, 1989 Duke L. J. 281.

29. Act of June 19, 1934, ch. 651, § 1, 48 Stat. 1064. Now, as amended, 28 U.S.C. § 2072: "Such rules shall not abridge, enlarge or modify any substantive right...."

30. *Sibbach*, 312 U.S. at 11, 61 S.Ct. at 425, 85 L.Ed. at 483–484.

31. 313 U.S. 487, 61 S.Ct. 1020, 85 L.Ed. 1477 (1941).

Delaware conflicts rule.[32] "Otherwise, the accident of diversity of citizenship would constantly disturb equal administration of justice in coordinate state and federal courts sitting side by side."[33]

In the same vein, stressing the avoidance of state and federal courts in the same state reaching different results, the Court decided a series of cases resulting in what has come to be called the "outcome-determinative" test for application of the *Erie* doctrine. The Court held that in a suit by a stakeholder under the Federal Interpleader Act,[34] despite the nation-wide service of process provided in the Act, the federal district court would have to reach the same result as would be reached in the state courts of the state in which it sat.[35] Similarly, state law governed the burden of proving contributory negligence even though under Rule 8(c) of the Federal Rules of Civil Procedure,[36] contributory negligence had to be pleaded as an affirmative defense.[37] *Guaranty Trust Co. v. York*,[38] holding that in a diversity case a federal court cannot try a case barred by a state statute of limitations, stated the outcome-determinative test in classic fashion. "In essence, the intent of that decision [*Erie*] was to insure that, in all cases where a federal court is exercising jurisdiction solely because of the diversity of citizenship of the parties, the outcome of the litigation in the federal court should be substantially the same, so far as legal rules determine the outcome of a litigation, as it would be if tried in a State court."[39] In further applications of this doctrine, the Court held that in diversity cases a federal court must obey a state forum-closing rule;[40] that although Rule 3 of the Federal Rules of Civil Procedure states that "filing a complaint with the court" commences an action,[41] such filing does not toll the local statute of limitations if the state rule requires service of the summons for tolling;[42] that

---

32. On remand, the court below reached the same result that it had before, finding "from all the available data" that a Delaware court would probably apply the New York rule on interest as "substantive." Stentor Elec. Mfg. Co. v. Klaxon Co., 125 F.2d 820 (3d Cir.), cert. denied 316 U.S. 685, 62 S.Ct. 1284, 86 L.Ed. 1757 (1942). See also Jarvis v. Johnson, 668 F.2d 740 (3d Cir.1982) (although state prejudgment interest rule has been characterized as "procedural" by state courts in construing limitations that state constitution imposes on judicial rule making, the rule is outcome determinative and must be applied in federal diversity cases).

33. *Klaxon*, 313 U.S. at 496, 61 S.Ct. at 1021–1022, 85 L.Ed. at 1480.

34. 28 U.S.C. §§ 1335, 1397, 2361.

35. Griffin v. McCoach, 313 U.S. 498, 61 S.Ct. 1023, 85 L.Ed. 1481 (1941).

36. Fed.R.Civ.P. 8(c).

37. Palmer v. Hoffman, 318 U.S. 109, 63 S.Ct. 477, 87 L.Ed. 645 (1943). See also Dick v. New York Life Ins. Co., 359 U.S. 437, 446, 79 S.Ct. 921, 927, 3 L.Ed.2d 935, 942 (1959) ("presumptions (and their effects) and burden of proof are 'substantive'"); Cities Service Oil Co. v. Dunlap, 308 U.S. 208, 60 S.Ct. 201, 84 L.Ed. 196 (1939) (burden of proof in equity action to remove cloud on title).

38. 326 U.S. 99, 65 S.Ct. 1464, 89 L.Ed. 2079 (1945).

39. Id. at 109, 65 S.Ct. at 1470, 89 L.Ed. at 2086.

40. Angel v. Bullington, 330 U.S. 183, 67 S.Ct. 657, 91 L.Ed. 832 (1947).

41. Fed.R.Civ.P. 3.

42. Ragan v. Merchants Transfer & Warehouse Co., 337 U.S. 530, 69 S.Ct. 1233, 93 L.Ed. 1520 (1949). But cf. Morel v. DaimlerChrysler AG, 565 F.3d 20 (1st Cir. 2009) (relation back of amendment substituting defendants is determined by federal rule, under

if the state court is closed to a plaintiff who has not qualified to do business within the state, the federal court is likewise closed;[43] that a state statute requiring a plaintiff in a derivative stockholder's action to give security for costs at the demand of the corporation must be followed, although no such requirement is contained in rule 23;[44] and, in what may be the high-water mark of the outcome-determinative test in the Supreme Court, that if a contract that contains an arbitration clause is not covered by the Federal Arbitration Act because the agreement does not affect interstate commerce, a federal court should not stay a suit pending arbitration if a state court would not.[45]

There are many questions concerning application of this outcome-determinative test that are still open, causing debate and often disagreement in the lower courts. *Dick v. New York Life Insurance Co.*[46] left open the question of whether, in a diversity case, a state or a federal standard should determine the sufficiency of the evidence to support a jury verdict.[47] Problems that have raised the question of whether a federal or state standard applies include the permissibility of a verdict in excess of the ad damnum clause,[48] indispensability of parties,[49] election of reme-

which it is timely, rather than by Puerto Rican rule, under which time limitations for suit would have expired); S.J. v. Issaquah School Dist. No. 411, 470 F.3d 1288 (9th Cir. 2006) (in an action under federal law when there is no federal statute of limitations and a federal court borrows the state's statute of limitations, the federal rule applies, which, unlike the state rule, tolls the statute when suit is filed rather than when process is served); Atkins v. Schmutz Mfg. Co., 435 F.2d 527 (4th Cir.1970), cert. denied, 402 U.S. 932, 91 S.Ct. 1526, 28 L.Ed.2d 867 (1971) (the tolling effect of a suit in federal court in another district is a matter of federal law).

That *Ragan* is still viable after Hanna v. Plumer, 380 U.S. 460, 85 S.Ct. 1136, 14 L.Ed.2d 8 (1965), see Walker v. Armco Steel Corp., 446 U.S. 740, 100 S.Ct. 1978, 64 L.Ed.2d 659 (1980), discussed in § 10.3.

43. Woods v. Interstate Realty Co., 337 U.S. 535, 69 S.Ct. 1235, 93 L.Ed. 1524 (1949). But cf. Grand Bahama Petroleum Co. v. Asiatic Petroleum Corp., 550 F.2d 1320 (2d Cir.1977) (state forum-closing rule does not bar suit brought pursuant to Federal Arbitration Act).

44. Fed.R.Civ.P. 23; Cohen v. Beneficial Industrial Loan Corp., 337 U.S. 541, 69 S.Ct. 1221, 93 L.Ed. 1528 (1949); cf. Feinstein v. Massachusetts General Hospital, 643 F.2d 880 (1st Cir.1981) (federal court must apply state rule that, as conditions precedent to suit for malpractice, plaintiff must submit the claim to a special tribunal and post a bond for costs).

45. Bernhardt v. Polygraphic Co. of America, 350 U.S. 198, 76 S.Ct. 273, 100 L.Ed. 199 (1956). 9 U.S.C. § 2 provides that arbitration agreements in "a contract evidencing a transaction involving commerce ... shall be valid, irrevocable and enforceable." 9 U.S.C. § 3 provides that United States courts shall stay suits brought in violation of such an arbitration agreement. Cf. Prima Paint Corp. v. Flood & Conklin Mfg. Co., 388 U.S. 395, 87 S.Ct. 1801, 18 L.Ed.2d 1270 (1967) (if contract covered by Federal Arbitration Act because it evidences transactions in interstate commerce, federal court is correct in applying federal standard to stay action pending arbitration).

46. 359 U.S. 437, 444–445, 79 S.Ct. 921, 926, 3 L.Ed.2d 935, 941–942 (1959). See also Mercer v. Theriot, 377 U.S. 152, 156, 84 S.Ct. 1157, 1160, 12 L.Ed.2d 206, 209 (1964).

47. Most cases passing on the issue have favored a federal standard. See, e.g., Fairley v. American Hoist & Derrick Co., 640 F.2d 679 (5th Cir.1981); Safeway Stores v. Fannan, 308 F.2d 94 (9th Cir.1962); 5 Moore, Federal Practice ¶ 38.10 (discussing split of authority in courts of appeal and advocating a federal standard); Annotation, 10 A.L.R.Fed. 451. Contra, Gold v. National Savings Bank of City of Albany, 641 F.2d 430 (6th Cir.1981), cert. denied, 454 U.S. 826, 102 S.Ct. 116, 70 L.Ed.2d 100 (1981) (but same result under federal standard).

48. Riggs, Ferris & Geer v. Lillibridge, 316 F.2d 60 (2d Cir.1963) (dictum) (federal).

dies,[50] and others.[51] The Supreme Court has granted certiorari to determine whether a New York rule prohibiting class actions to recover a statutory penalty is binding on a federal court exercising diversity jurisdiction.[52]

The former uncertainty whether federal or state rules of evidence apply[53] has in part been resolved by enactment of the Federal Rules of Evidence in title 28 of the United States Code. The rules "apply generally to civil actions and Proceedings" in federal courts and before federal magistrates.[54] Presumptions[55] testimonial privileges,[56] and competency of witnesses,[57] however, are determined under state law, if there is in issue an element of a claim or defense to which state law supplies the rule of decision.[58] But problems remain.

49. Kuchenig v. California Co., 350 F.2d 551 (5th Cir.1965), cert. denied, 382 U.S. 985, 86 S.Ct. 561, 15 L.Ed.2d 473 (1966) (state); Resnik v. La Paz Guest Ranch, 289 F.2d 814 (9th Cir.1961) (federal).

50. Berger v. State Farm Mut. Auto. Ins. Co., 291 F.2d 666 (10th Cir.1961) (state).

51. See Maddox v. American Airlines, Inc., 298 F.3d 694 (8th Cir. 2002), cert. denied, 537 U.S. 1192, 123 S.Ct. 1273, 154 L.Ed.2d 1026 (2003) (federal rather than state law determines whether the plaintiff can recover post-judgment interest and the interest rate); Northrop Corp. v. Triad Int'l Marketing, 842 F.2d 1154 (9th Cir.1988) (apply state law on prejudgment interest); Thornhill v. Donnkenny, Inc., 823 F.2d 782 (4th Cir.1987) (same); Vishipco Line v. Chase Manhattan Bank, N.A., 660 F.2d 854 (2d Cir.1981), cert. denied, 459 U.S. 976, 103 S.Ct. 313, 74 L.Ed.2d 291 (1982) (apply state law to determine proper date for conversion of foreign currency to determine amount of judgment); Dorey v. Dorey, 609 F.2d 1128 (5th Cir.1980) (whether will enforce sister-state judgment for future installments of alimony). For cases applying a state rule that before suit is brought, a malpractice claim must be submitted to a special medical panel, see, e.g., Feinstein v. Massachusetts General Hospital, 643 F.2d 880 (1st Cir.1981); DiAntonio v. Northhampton–Accomack Memorial Hospital, 628 F.2d 287 (4th Cir.1980); Edelson v. Soricelli, 610 F.2d 131 (3d Cir.1979) (despite argument that state procedure is so slow as to deprive plaintiff of relief).

Although the Supreme Court has not ruled on whether federal courts must apply state rules on forum non conveniens dismissals, federal courts have thus far ruled that a federal standard controls. For discussion of this issue and the forum shopping between state and federal courts that it has triggered, see supra § 4.33C. For discussion of the split of authority as to whether state or federal standards control enforcement of choice-of-forum clauses, see supra § 4.35 note 309.

52. Shady Grove Orthopedic Associates, P.A. v. Allstate Ins. Co., 549 F.3d 137 (2d Cir. 2008) (state law governs), cert. granted, ___ U.S. ___, 129 S.Ct. 2160, 173 L.Ed.2d 1155 (2009).

53. See, e.g., Dallas County v. Commercial Union Assur. Co., 286 F.2d 388 (5th Cir.1961) (hearsay-federal); Massachusetts Mut. Life Ins. Co. v. Brei, 311 F.2d 463 (2d Cir.1962) (physician-patient privilege-state).

54. Rule 1101(b). But see Equitable Life Assur. Soc'y v. McKay, 306 Or. 493, 760 P.2d 871 (1988) (Oregon court would not bar evidence under Washington's Dead Man's Statute, answering question certified by 9th Circuit).

55. Rule 302. See Travelers Ins. Co. v. Riggs, 671 F.2d 810 (4th Cir.1982) (state law determines applicability of res Pisa).

56. Rule 501.

57. Rule 601.

58. But cf. von Bulow v. von Bulow, 811 F.2d 136 (2d Cir.), cert. denied, 481 U.S. 1015, 107 S.Ct. 1891, 95 L.Ed.2d 498 (1987) (federal privilege rule applies when the same evidence is applicable to federal, diversity, and pendent claims); Wm. T. Thompson Co. v. General Nutrition Corp., Inc., 671 F.2d 100 (3d Cir.1982) (state accountant's privilege does not apply in an action on claims based upon both federal and state law); Memorial Hospital for McHenry County v. Shadur, 664 F.2d 1058 (7th Cir.1981) (state privilege for testimony

It is not always easy to distinguish a state rule of evidence from state substantive law.[59] *Conway v. Chemical Leaman Tank Lines, Inc.,*[60] provides a good example. This case held that in a diversity wrongful death suit, the federal court should apply Texas law under which evidence of the widow's remarriage was relevant. The court found this rule of "evidence" "so bound up with state substantive law that federal courts sitting in Texas should accord it the same treatment as state courts in order to give full effect to Texas' substantive policy."[61]

Moreover, the presumption, privileges, and competency rules do not indicate which state's law controls[62] or whether state or federal choice-of-law rules select that law. This last question should be resolved in accord with *Klaxon*[63] (the conflicts rules of the forum state), if that doctrine is limited as suggested in this chapter.[64] These issues are as likely as any other to engender the kind of intrastate forum shopping between state and federal court that *Erie* and *Klaxon* seek to control.

The question naturally arose whether there was any logical stopping point for the outcome-determinative test. Any difference in method of administering justice might be outcome-determinative. Would there be a halt to extensions of *Erie* or would the doctrine continue to grow until, at least in diversity cases, it strangled the last vestige of independent responsibility of federal courts for the integrity and economy of judicial administration in those courts? Moreover, the implications of the answer to this question extend beyond diversity cases. Although it is largely in diversity cases that the gloss upon *Erie* has been written, the Judiciary Act does not so limit its "rules of decision" section. The *Erie* doctrine or, perhaps more correctly, a close analogue of it, is applicable whenever federal courts turn to state law to supply the rule for decision because "the Constitution or treaties of the United States or Acts of Congress"

given in hospital disciplinary hearings does not apply in federal antitrust action); Lewis v. Capital Mortgage Investments, 78 F.R.D. 295 (D.Md.1977) (state accountant-client privilege is not applicable in suit alleging violation of Securities Exchange Act even though one plaintiff in class action brings a pendent state claim).

59. See Feldman v. Allstate Ins. Co., 322 F.3d 660, 667 (9th Cir. 2003), cert. denied, 540 U.S. 875, 124 S.Ct. 222, 157 L.Ed.2d 137 (2003) (California Penal Code provision limiting the admissibility of illegally intercepted conversations "is an integral component of California's substantive state policy of protecting the privacy of its citizens, and is properly characterized as substantive law within the meaning of *Erie*"); Moe v. Avions Marcel Dassault–Breguet Aviation, 727 F.2d 917 (10th Cir.1984), cert. denied, 469 U.S. 853, 105 S.Ct. 176, 83 L.Ed.2d 110 (1984) (Federal Rule of Evidence 407 barring admission of evidence of subsequent remedial measures is not applicable in a diversity case when state law permits admission); Dixon v. 80 Pine St. Corp., 516 F.2d 1278 (2d Cir.1975) (whether testimony at official inquest is privileged is governed by state law, but federal law rejects state requirement of "special circumstances" for disclosure); Wellborn, *The Federal Rules of Evidence and the Application of State Law in the Federal Courts,* 55 Texas L. Rev. 371, 450 (1977) (substantive law indicates "what propositions are material" and a rule of evidence indicates "whether an offer tends sufficiently to prove a material proposition").

60. 540 F.2d 837 (5th Cir.1976).

61. Id. at 838.

62. See Seidelson, *The Federal Rules of Evidence: Rule 501, Klaxon and the Constitution,* 5 Hofstra L. Rev. 21, 22 (1976).

63. See Samuelson v. Susen, 576 F.2d 546 (3d Cir.1978).

64. See §§ 10.7A–7D, 10.8.

do not "otherwise require or provide,"[65] whatever the basis for federal jurisdiction.[66] Recognizing that the problems discussed in this chapter are not limited to diversity cases will be particularly important if one of the recurring attempts to abolish[67] or diminish[68] diversity jurisdiction is successful.

§ 10.3   Byrd and Hanna: New Light?

Byrd v. Blue Ridge Rural Electric Cooperative, Inc.[69] is the case that seemed to provide the pin to prick the *Erie* bubble. The plaintiff's employer, an electric contractor, had agreed to erect electrical power lines for Blue Ridge. Plaintiff was injured while performing this job. The plaintiff recovered benefits from the electric contractor under the South Carolina workers' compensation act. Then the plaintiff, on the jurisdictional basis of diversity of citizenship, sued Blue Ridge in a federal court in South Carolina for common-law negligence. The defense was that plaintiff's exclusive remedy against Blue Ridge was under the South Carolina workers' compensation act, a remedy that plaintiff had already exhausted. Under the South Carolina statute, the defendant was entitled to the limited and definite liability of an employer if in the past it had performed work for itself similar to the work it had here contracted to the company for which plaintiff worked. The Court of Appeals decided this fact question adversely to the plaintiff and rendered judgment for

---

65.   28 U.S.C. § 1652.

66.   See Commissioner v. Estate of Bosch, 387 U.S. 456, 87 S.Ct. 1776, 18 L.Ed.2d 886 (1967) (28 U.S.C. § 1652 applicable where federal estate tax liability turns on character of a property interest held and transferred by decedent under state law); Meredith v. Winter Haven, 320 U.S. 228, 237, 64 S.Ct. 7, 12, 88 L.Ed. 9, 15 (1943): "*Erie R. Co. v. Tompkins* . . . did not free the federal courts from the duty of deciding questions of state law in diversity cases. Instead it placed on them a greater responsibility for determining and applying state laws in all cases within their jurisdiction in which federal law does not govern"; Watson v. McCabe, 527 F.2d 286 (6th Cir.1975) (applicability of Rules of Decision Act does not depend on the jurisdictional basis of the action, but on the issue under consideration); Austrian v. Williams, 198 F.2d 697, 700 (2d Cir.1952), cert. denied, 344 U.S. 909, 73 S.Ct. 328, 97 L.Ed. 701 (1952); United States v. Neal, 443 F.Supp. 1307 (D.Neb. 1978) (state tort and conflicts law applies in suit under Federal Medical Care Recovery Act); Clark, *State Law in the Federal Courts: The Brooding Omnipresence of Erie v. Tompkins*, 55 Yale L. J. 267, 281 (1946); Hart & Wechsler, The Federal Courts and the Federal System 697 (1953); Vestal, *Erie R.R. v. Tompkins: A Projection*, 48 Iowa L. Rev. 248, 257 (1963); cf. Kelly v. Kosuga, 358 U.S. 516, 79 S.Ct. 429, 3 L.Ed.2d 475 (1959) (effect of illegality under a federal statute a matter of federal law, even in diversity actions); Bank of America Nat'l Trust & Sav. Ass'n v. Parnell, 352 U.S. 29, 77 S.Ct. 119, 1 L.Ed.2d 93 (1956) (in action for alleged conversion of bonds of federal agency, burden of proof and good faith issues governed by state law, but not whether bonds overdue). But see United States v. Williams, 441 F.2d 637 (5th Cir.1971) (*Erie* is not applicable to suit by United States to protect its interest in land, but absent contrary federal statute or policy, state law of the situs governs); Rothenberg v. H. Rothstein & Sons, 183 F.2d 524 (3d Cir.1950) (since not a diversity case, remedy not barred in federal court although barred in state court); Young v. Minton, 344 F.Supp. 423 (W.D.Ky.1972) (jurisdiction in custody case based on fact defendant resident of federal reservation—the court is not sitting as a diversity court and is not bound to follow local state law, but "it would be appropriate to use it as a vehicle in determining this case").

67.   See, e.g., 95th Cong., 1st sess., H.R. 9622 (not passed).

68.   See, e.g., 95th Cong., 1st sess., S. 2094 (would eliminate in-state plaintiff, not voted out of Committee on the Judiciary).

69.   356 U.S. 525, 78 S.Ct. 893, 2 L.Ed.2d 953 (1958).

the defendant. The Supreme Court reversed, holding that in a federal court the fact issue should have been submitted to a jury, even though under South Carolina practice the court decides this issue. In the course of his opinion for the majority, Justice Brennan uttered words that were welcome to those who thought that the outcome-determinative test had been carried to undesirable extremes:

> Therefore, were "outcome" the only consideration, a strong case might appear for saying that the federal court should follow the state practice.
>
> But there are affirmative countervailing considerations at work here. The federal system is an independent system for administering justice to litigants who properly invoke its jurisdiction. An essential characteristic of that system is the manner in which, in civil common-law actions, it distributes trial functions between judge and jury and, under the influence—if not the command—of the Seventh Amendment, assigns the decisions of disputed questions of fact to the jury.[70]

The way seemed open for viewing the outcome-determinative gloss upon *Erie* as a policy against forum shopping between a state court and a federal court in the same state. This policy might, in appropriate circumstances, yield to sufficient "countervailing considerations."

Even in the *Byrd* opinion, however, this hope of mitigating the outcome-determinative test was dimmed by indications that the "countervailing considerations" language was limited in scope and not a broad mandate for change. The result was reached "under the influence—if not the command—of the Seventh Amendment." If there ever was doubt, it now seems clear, in the light of subsequent Supreme Court decisions, that the Seventh Amendment to the United States Constitution[71] required the *Byrd* result.[72] Moreover, *Byrd's* reliance on "countervailing considerations" was hedged by a statement that the South Carolina practice of deciding such fact questions by judge rather than jury "appears to be merely a form and mode of enforcing the immunity ... and not a rule intended to be bound up with the definition of rights

---

70. Id. at 537, 78 S.Ct. at 900, 2 L.Ed.2d at 962.

71. "In Suits at common law, where the value in controversy shall exceed twenty dollars, the right of trial by jury shall be preserved, and no fact tried by a jury, shall be otherwise reexamined in any Court of the United States, than according to the rules of the common law." U.S. Const. Amend. VII.

72. See Simler v. Conner, 372 U.S. 221, 83 S.Ct. 609, 9 L.Ed.2d 691 (1963) (in federal courts, in diversity as well as other actions, right to a jury trial determined as a matter of federal law under the Seventh Amendment); Atlantic & Gulf Stevedores, Inc. v. Ellerman Lines, Ltd., 369 U.S. 355, 82 S.Ct. 780, 7 L.Ed.2d 798 (1962) (suit by longshoreman on law side of federal court by reason of diversity carried with it a right to trial by jury under the Seventh Amendment); A.E. Smith, *Blue Ridge and Beyond: A Byrd's–Eye View of Federalism in Diversity Litigation*, 36 Tul. L. Rev. 443, 451 (1962); Whicher, *The Erie Doctrine and the Seventh Amendment: A Suggested Resolution of Their Conflict*, 37 Texas L. Rev. 549, 560–61 (1959). But cf. Justice v. Pennzoil Co., 598 F.2d 1339 (4th Cir.1979) (in West Virginia, whether the owner of mineral rights has improperly damaged the surface is a question of law, not fact, and should not be submitted to the jury, even in federal court).

and obligations of the parties."[73] Further, in view of the extensive powers of a federal judge to comment on the evidence and witnesses and to grant a new trial if the verdict seemed contrary to the weight of the evidence, Justice Brennan did not think the right to trial by jury rather than judge was very likely to affect the outcome.[74]

Notwithstanding these built-in limitations on *Byrd* as a possible change in the outcome-determinative doctrine, a few circuit court decisions have seized upon the "countervailing considerations" concept as an aid in rejecting arguments made under the *Erie* gloss,[75] and some commentators saw in *Byrd* hope for basic shifts in attitude.[76] Even if the "countervailing considerations" concept of *Byrd* was a viable basis for relief from an over-rigid outcome-determinative rule, it seemed likely to be largely limited to preserving those aspects of federal trial court procedures and practices essential to the integrity and economy of judicial administration in the federal courts as a separate system. Further encroachment of *Erie* on the Federal Rules of Civil Procedure might be prevented, but much beyond this, concerning rules traditionally deemed "substantive," the reform value of *Byrd* seemed, at best, doubtful.[77]

Hanna v. Plumer[78] strengthened the presumption in favor of applying the Federal Rules of Civil Procedure when those rules conflicted with a state rule. The plaintiff, basing jurisdiction upon diversity of citizenship, brought suit in a Federal District Court in Massachusetts against the estate of an alleged tortfeasor. The plaintiff served the executor of the estate by leaving copies of the summons and complaint with the executor's wife at his residence pursuant to Federal Rule of Civil Procedure 4(d) (1) authorizing service on an individual by leaving the papers "at his dwelling house or usual place of abode with some person of suitable age and discretion then residing therein. . . ." The defendant answered alleging that the action could not be maintained because

---

73. *Byrd*, 356 U.S. at 536, 78 S.Ct. at 900, 2 L.Ed.2d at 961–62. See also Magenau v. Aetna Freight Lines, Inc., 360 U.S. 273, 79 S.Ct. 1184, 3 L.Ed.2d 1224 (1959). But cf. Justice v. Pennzoil Co., 598 F.2d 1339 (4th Cir.1979), cert. denied, 444 U.S. 967, 100 S.Ct. 457, 62 L.Ed.2d 380 (1979) (follow state rule that whether the owner of mineral interest in land exceeded his rights is a question of law for the judge).

74. *Byrd*, 365 U.S. at 539–40, 78 S.Ct. at 901–02, 2 L.Ed.2d at 963–64 (1958).

75. See Snead v. Metropolitan Property & Cas. Ins. Co., 237 F.3d 1080, 1092 (9th Cir. 2001), cert. denied, 534 U.S. 888, 122 S.Ct. 201, 151 L.Ed.2d 142 (2001) (in suit under Oregon disability discrimination law, apply federal rather than state standard for summary judgment because applying the state standard requiring only that the plaintiff present prima facie evidence of discrimination would only postpone the inevitable loss for the plaintiff and provide "an increased burden on the district courts' already crowded trial dockets"); Brown v. Pyle, 310 F.2d 95, 97 (5th Cir.1962) (rejecting argument that, despite improper venue, federal court must hear case if state court would); Monarch Ins. Co. of Ohio v. Spach, 281 F.2d 401, 406–407 (5th Cir.1960) (may admit pre-trial deposition in evidence even though state court would not).

76. Meador, *State Law and the Federal Judicial Power*, 49 Va. L. Rev. 1082, 1098–99 (1963); Storke, *Conflicts Erie Cases*, 32 Rocky Mt. L. Rev. 20, 36 (1959); Vestal, supra note 66.

77. But see Vestal, supra note 66, at 269.

78. 380 U.S. 460, 85 S.Ct. 1136, 14 L.Ed.2d 8 (1965).

brought contrary to a Massachusetts statute providing that "an executor . . . shall not be held to answer to an action by a creditor of the deceased which is not commenced within one year from the time of his giving bond for the performance of his trust, or to such an action which is commenced within said year unless before the expiration thereof the writ in such action has been served by delivery in hand upon such executor. . . ."[79] The answer was filed before one year had elapsed from the day the defendant had met the bonding requirement, but the plaintiff took no further action and, after the year had elapsed, the defendant moved for summary judgment.[80] This motion was granted and the Court of Appeals affirmed.

The Supreme Court reversed. Chief Justice Warren's opinion first indicates that, even if the service here had not been authorized by a Federal Rule, it is "doubtful" that *Erie* would require application of the Massachusetts in-hand service rule:

> "Outcome-determination" analysis was never intended to serve as a talisman.
>
> . . .
>
> The "outcome-determination" test therefore cannot be read without reference to the twin aims of the *Erie* rule: discouragement of forum shopping and avoidance of inequitable administration of the laws.[81]

Availability of the federal method of service was not likely to lead to forum shopping between state and federal courts and did not result in unfair treatment of the Massachusetts defendant.

But whether or not *Erie*, in the absence of the specific provisions of Rule 4(d) (1), would have required application of Massachusetts service methods, it was clear that in *Hanna* the Federal Rule controlled. The Rule did not unconstitutionally usurp state substantive authority and did not violate the Enabling Act injunction that Rules "not abridge, enlarge or modify any substantive right". A Rule of Civil Procedure avoids this constitutional and Enabling Act interdiction even if it falls "within the uncertain area between substance and procedure [and is] rationally capable of classification as either."[82]

If, as *Hanna* indicates, a federal court is more likely to apply state law if the issue is not covered by a Federal Rule of Civil Procedure, much

---

79. Mass.Gen.Laws Ann. c. 197, § 9 (emphasis added).

80. Hanna v. Plumer, 331 F.2d 157, 159 (1st Cir.1964), rev'd, 380 U.S. 460, 85 S.Ct. 1136, 14 L.Ed.2d 8 (1965).

81. *Hanna*, 380 U.S. at 466–68, 85 S.Ct. at 1141–42, 14 L.Ed.2d at 14–15.

82. Id. at 472, 85 S.Ct. at 1144, 1145 14 L.Ed.2d at 17. Cf. Ely, *The Irrepressible Myth of Erie*, 87 Harv. L. Rev. 693, 698 (1974) distinguishing between the controls on choice of law in federal courts exerted by the Constitution, the Rules of Decision Act, and the Enabling Act: "The United States Constitution . . . constitutes the relevant text only where Congress has passed a statute creating law for diversity actions and it is in this situation alone that *Hanna's* 'arguably procedural' test controls. . . . [W]here there is no relevant Federal Rule of Civil Procedure . . . the Rules of Decision Act [controls]. Where the matter in issue is covered by a Federal Rule . . . the Enabling Act . . . constitutes the relevant standard."

will turn on the construction of the Federal Rule. *Walker v. Armco Steel Corp.*,[83] is a good example. Federal Rule of Civil Procedure 3 provides that "[a] civil action is commenced by filing a complaint with the court." Under Oklahoma law, an action is not "commenced" for the purposes of tolling the running of the statute of limitations until service of summons on the defendant, but there is a 60–day grace period for service if the action is filed within the limitations period. In *Walker*, the diversity action was filed in an Oklahoma federal court within the Oklahoma period of limitations, but service was not effected until both the limitations and the 60–day grace period had expired. The Supreme Court held that Rule 3 did not conflict with Oklahoma law. Although "in diversity actions Rule 3 governs the date from which various timing requirements of the federal rules begin to run, . . . [it] does not affect state statutes of limitations."[84] Therefore, the state policy governing tolling of limitations applied in order to prevent "inequitable"[85] differences in the administration of the law between state and federal courts.[86]

Semtek International Inc. v. Lockheed Martin Corp.[87] provides another example of the Court construing a Federal Rule of Civil Procedure so as to avoid a clash with state law. A federal district court in California had dismissed plaintiff's action on the ground that the California statute of limitations had run. Federal Rule 41(b) provides that "[u]nless the court in its order for dismissal otherwise specifies, a dismissal . . . operates as an adjudication upon the merits." The California federal court not only did not otherwise specify, but also stated that the dismissal was "on the merits." Plaintiff then sued in a Maryland state court, which held that the California federal dismissal was res judicata and dismissed plaintiff's suit. The Supreme Court reversed, holding that dismissal under 41(b) did not have claim-preclusive effect but simply prevented suit on the same claim in the same federal district court.[88] The Court held that federal common law determined the claim-preclusive effect of the federal dismissal on limitations grounds, but federal law incorporated the law of the state in which the federal court was sitting.[89] The Court remanded to the Maryland state court to apply the California law of claim preclusion following a limitations dismissal.

In *Semtek* Justice Scalia suggested that if Rule 41(b) effected a claim-preclusive dismissal when California law would not, the rule would violate the Rules Enabling Act mandate that the rules "shall not abridge, enlarge, or modify any substantive right" and would unconstitutionally violate federalism principles:

---

83. 446 U.S. 740, 100 S.Ct. 1978, 64 L.Ed.2d 659 (1980).

84. Id. at 751, 100 S.Ct. at 1985, 64 L.Ed.2d at 668.

85. Id. at 753, 100 S.Ct. at 1986, 64 L.Ed.2d at 669, quoting from Hanna v. Plumer, 380 U.S. at 468, 85 S.Ct. at 1142, 14 L.Ed.2d at 15.

86. Thus reaffirming the pre-*Hanna* decision, Ragan v. Merchants Transfer & Warehouse Co., 337 U.S. 530, 69 S.Ct. 1233, 93 L.Ed. 1520 (1949).

87. 531 U.S. 497, 121 S.Ct. 1021, 149 L.Ed.2d 32 (2001).

88. Id. at 505, 121 S.Ct. at 1027.

89. Id. at 507–08, 121 S.Ct. at 1028.

In the present case, for example, if California law left petitioner free to sue on this claim in Maryland even after the California statute of limitations had expired, the federal court's extinguishment of that right (through Rule 41(b)'s mandated claim-preclusive effect of its judgment) would seem to violate this [Enabling Act] limitation.

Moreover, as so interpreted, the Rule would in many cases violate the federalism principle of *Erie R. Co. v. Tompkins*, 304 U.S. 64, 78–80, 58 S.Ct. 817, 82 L.Ed. 1188 (1938), by engendering " 'substantial' variations [in outcomes] between state and federal litigation" which would "[l]ikely . . . influence the choice of a forum," *Hanna v. Plumer*, 380 U.S. 460, 467–468, 85 S.Ct. 1136, 14 L.Ed.2d 8 (1965).[90]

A question that arises in national class actions in federal court is whether the federal court can permit recovery under the Deceptive Trade Practices Act or Consumer Protection Act of a state that permits recovery by non-residents but only in individual suits, not in a class action. *In re Bridgestone/Firestone, Inc. Tires Products Liability Litigation*[91] answered "yes." The court held that Federal Rule of Civil Procedure 23, not the Michigan Consumer Protection Act, determined whether a class action remedy was available to non-residents asserting claims under the Act. "Whether that substantive right [conferred by the Act] can be vindicated through a class action or whether it must be pursued individually, is a procedural question."[92] This result accords with *Byrd* and *Hanna*. Under *Byrd*, Rule 23 reflects "affirmative countervailing considerations" of efficient procedures. Under *Hanna*, Rule 23 both conflicted with the Michigan Act and was "rationally capable of classification" as procedural.

Gasperini v. Center for Humanities, Inc.[93] provides another example of a possible clash between a federal rule of civil procedure and state law. In *Gasperini*, the plaintiff sued in the federal district court for the Southern District of New York to recover damages for the loss of his property. Applying New York law, which required rejecting a verdict that "materially deviates from what is reasonable compensation," the Second Circuit ordered a new trial unless the plaintiff agreed to reduce the judgment entered on the jury's verdict. The United States Supreme Court unanimously agreed that "[t]he Second Circuit correctly recognized that when New York substantive law governs a claim for relief, New York law and decisions guide the allowable damages."[94] The justices disagreed on how federal courts should apply state decisions in reviewing

---

90. Id. at 503–04, 121 S.Ct. at 1026 (brackets after first set in original).

91. 205 F.R.D. 503 (S.D. Ind. 2001), rev'd on another issue, 288 F.3d 1012 (7th Cir. 2002), cert. denied, 537 U.S. 1105, 123 S.Ct. 870, 154 L.Ed.2d 774 (2003). Contra, Shady Grove Orthopedic Associates, P.A. v. Allstate Ins. Co., 549 F.3d 137 (2d Cir. 2008) (state law governs), cert. granted, ___ U.S. ___, 129 S.Ct. 2160, 173 L.Ed.2d 1155 (2009).

92. Id. at 515.

93. 518 U.S. 415, 116 S.Ct. 2211, 135 L.Ed.2d 659 (1996).

94. Id. at 437, 116 S.Ct. at 2224, 135 L.Ed.2d at 680.

jury verdicts. A majority held that the trial judge should apply the state review standard and compare the verdict with awards in comparable cases in state courts. The circuit court should then review the trial judge's decision under an abuse of discretion standard.[95] Justice Stevens stated that the circuit court should review the trial judge's decision de novo applying the state standard.[96] Justice Scalia, joined by Chief Justice Rehnquist and Justice Thomas, would have the district judge apply a federal standard when comparing the verdict with comparable state awards.[97] Justice Scalia found this standard in Federal Rule of Civil Procedure 59, which provides that "[a] new trial may be granted . . . in an action in which there has been a trial by jury for any of the reasons for which new trials have heretofore been granted in actions at law in the courts of the United States. . . ." He noted that district judges in the Second Circuit had interpreted Rule 59 to authorize a new trial when " 'it is quite clear that the jury has reached a seriously erroneous result' and letting the verdict stand would result in a 'miscarriage of justice.' "[98] He stated that he had "no reason to question that this is a correct interpretation of what Rule 59 requires."[99]

Thus, although *Hanna* represented a further setback for the "outcome-determinative" test, it was hardly a mortal blow for that *Erie* gloss. After *Hanna* it is unlikely that any direct clash between a Federal Rule of Civil Procedure and a state rule will be resolved in favor of the state rule, although, as Justice Scalia indicated in *Semtek*, it is possible for a Federal Rule to violate both the Constitution and the Rules Enabling Act.[100]

---

95. Id. at 438–39, 116 S.Ct. at 2225, 135 L.Ed.2d at 680–81.

96. Id. at 439, 116 S.Ct. at 2225, 135 L.Ed.2d at 681 (Stevens, J., dissenting).

97. Id. at 467–68, 116 S.Ct. at 2239, 135 L.Ed.2d at 698–99 (Scalia, J., dissenting).

98. Id. at 468, 116 S.Ct. at 2239, 135 L.E.2d at 699 (Scalia, J., dissenting) (quoting Koerner v. Club Mediterranee, S.A., 833 F.Supp. 327, 331 (S.D.N.Y. 1993), which quoted Bevevino v. Saydjari, 574 F.2d 676, 684 (2d Cir. 1978)).

99. *Gasperini*, 518 U.S. at 468, 116 S.Ct. at 2239, 135 L.E.2d at 699 (Scalia, J., dissenting).

100. See supra note 90 and accompanying text.

For discussion of apparent conflicts between federal and state rules, see Freund v. Nycomed Amersham, 347 F.3d 752 (9th Cir. 2003) (F.R.C.P. 50(b), which prevents a party from making a post-trial motion for judgment as a matter of law on grounds not covered in the party's pre-verdict motion, prevents defendant from making post-trial motion for judgment as a matter of law on issue of punitive damages despite California rule that appealability of punitive damages award is not waivable); Houben v. Telular Corp., 309 F.3d 1028 (7th Cir. 2002) (in suit for violation of Illinois Wage Payment Act, 28 U.S.C. § 1961 rather than Wage Payment Act determines amount of post-judgment interest, and F.R.C.P 62 rather than Act determines date at which post-judgment interest begins); Cohen v. Office Depot, Inc., 204 F.3d 1069 (11th Cir. 2000) (Rule 8(a)(3)'s requirement that "[a] pleading which sets forth a claim for relief . . . shall contain . . . a demand for judgment for the relief the pleader seeks" prevails over the conflicting Florida law that a request for punitive damages requires leave of court); Gil de Rebollo v. Miami Heat Assocs., 137 F.3d 56 (1st Cir. 1998) (Rule 68 rather than contrary Puerto Rican law applies to deny defendants recovery of their attorney's fees when plaintiff did not recover more than amount defendants offered in settlement); Burlington Northern R.R. v. Woods, 480 U.S. 1, 107 S.Ct. 967, 94 L.Ed.2d 1 (1987) (Rule 38's discretionary sanctions for frivolous appeals govern in diversity rather than Alabama's mandatory 10 percent penalty upon affirming a money judgment without substantial modification); Olympic Sports Products, Inc. v.

Hanna distinguishes between cases like it, involving "housekeeping rules",[101] such as those enacted under the authority of the Rules Enabling Act,[102] and other cases. It is in these latter cases that the "outcome-determinative" test has shaped "the typical, relatively unguided *Erie* choice...."[103] The *Hanna* opinion made only brief citation to the "countervailing considerations" language of *Byrd*, without quoting that language.[104] Choice-of-law rules could hardly be called "housekeeping rules" and differences in conflicts rules might very well prompt the intrastate forum shopping that Mr. Chief Justice Warren delineated in *Hanna* as one of "the twin aims of the *Erie* rule."

§ 10.4   "Countervailing Considerations": The Key to Use of State Conflict-of-Laws Rules in Federal Courts

Conceding the weakness of *Byrd* and *Hanna* as reeds upon which to rest an argument for pervasive change of the outcome-determinative rule, *Byrd's* "countervailing considerations" concept is useful, indeed essential, for achieving wise and desirable answers to the question of when, in choosing applicable state law, a federal court should utilize the conflict-of-laws rules of the state in which it sits. The *Byrd* rationale has very special strengths here that it may not have elsewhere.

Neither of the two basic reasons given by Justice Brandeis in *Erie* for overruling *Swift v. Tyson*, the constitutional pronouncement or the

---

Universal Athletic Sales Co., 760 F.2d 910 (9th Cir. 1985), cert. denied, 474 U.S. 1060, 106 S.Ct. 804, 88 L.Ed.2d 780 (1986) (Federal Rule 41(b), not state rule, controls dismissal for lack of prosecution); Travelers Ins. Co. v. Riggs, 671 F.2d 810 (4th Cir.1982) (Rule 17, not state law, determines whether suit can be brought in name of insureds rather than insurer as real party in interest); Platis v. Stockwell, 630 F.2d 1202 (7th Cir.1980) (Rule 51, not state law, determines whether there is reversible error when no objection is made to an instruction before the jury retires); Product Promotions, Inc. v. Cousteau, 495 F.2d 483 (5th Cir.1974) (Rule 12(b)(2), not state law, determines burden of proof when defendant objects to the exercise of personal jurisdiction); Johnson Chem. Co. v. Condado Center, Inc., 453 F.2d 1044 (1st Cir.1972) (Rule 60(b) permits federal court to reconsider amount of bond despite contrary Puerto Rican Rule); Hopkins v. Metcalf, 435 F.2d 123 (10th Cir.1970) (15(b) permits issues tried by consent to be treated as if pleaded); Follenfant v. Rogers, 359 F.2d 30 (5th Cir.1966) (Rule 11, not state law, controls whether pleadings need be verified); Troutman v. Modlin, 353 F.2d 382 (8th Cir.1965) (Rule 54(c) permits recovery in excess of demand notwithstanding contrary state rule); Urbano v. News Syndicate Co., 358 F.2d 145 (2d Cir.1966), cert. denied, 385 U.S. 831, 87 S.Ct. 68, 17 L.Ed.2d 66 (1966) (rule of forum state depriving plaintiff sentenced to life imprisonment of capacity to sue not applicable in view of Rule 17(b)); Note, Choice of Procedure in Diversity Cases, 75 Yale L. J. 477 (1966); but cf. Reibor Int'l Ltd. v. Cargo Carriers Ltd., 759 F.2d 262 (2d Cir.1985) (New York attachment statute governs as to property that garnishee acquired after order was served when Admiralty Rules do not address the issue); Moe v. Avions Marcel Dassault–Breguet Aviation, 727 F.2d 917 (10th Cir.1984), cert. denied, 469 U.S. 853, 105 S.Ct. 176, 83 L.Ed.2d 110 (1984) (refuse to apply Federal Rule of Evidence 407 in diversity when Rule bars evidence of subsequent remedial measures but state law does not).

See, generally, J. McCoid, *Hanna v. Plumer: The Erie Doctrine Changes Shape*, 51 Va. L. Rev. 884 (1965).

101.   *Hanna*, 380 U.S. at 473, 85 S.Ct. at 1145, 14 L.Ed.2d at 17–18.

102.   For an example of a "housekeeping rule" not enacted under the Enabling Act, see Donovan v. Penn Shipping Co., Inc., 429 U.S. 648, 97 S.Ct. 835, 51 L.Ed.2d 112 (1977) ("a plaintiff in federal court, whether prosecuting a state or federal cause of action, may not appeal from a remittitur order he has accepted").

103.   *Hanna*, 380 U.S. at 471, 85 S.Ct. at 1143–44, 14 L.Ed.2d at 16–17.

104.   Id. at 467, 85 S.Ct. at 1141–42, 14 L.Ed.2d at 14–15.

interpretation of "laws" to include decisional law, is applicable to use of state conflicts rules. There has been much debate concerning the soundness of Brandeis' remarks on the "unconstitutionality of the course pursued"[105] under *Tyson*. His reasoning here seems to have been, in part, that Congress, when unauthorized by any provision of the Constitution of the United States, could not make laws applicable to essentially intrastate transactions. If Congress could not do this, neither could the federal courts: "Congress has no power to declare substantive rules of common law applicable in a State whether they be local in their nature, or 'general,' be they commercial law or part of the law of torts. And no clause in the Constitution purports to confer such a power upon the federal courts."[106] This argument, which might conveniently be labeled a "federalism" or "Tenth Amendment"[107] argument,[108] also appeared in several of the pre-*Erie* dissents to applications of *Tyson*.[109] A possible reply to this constitutional argument is that, although Congress cannot legislate except within the bounds of its constitutional authority, the "necessary and proper" clause[110] combined with the judiciary article[111] may in fact be sufficient constitutional authority for Congress to make substantive law for diversity cases.[112]

Even conceding the validity of a "federalism" argument in *Erie*,[113] it is not applicable to conflict-of-laws rules, which involve interstate rather than intrastate transactions and which Congress can enact under the Commerce[114] and Full Faith and Credit[115] clauses. Justice Brandeis was

---

105.   *Erie*, 304 U.S. at 77–78, 58 S.Ct. at 822, 82 L.Ed. at 1193–94.

106.   Id. at 78, 58 S.Ct. at 822, 82 L.Ed. at 1194.

107.   U.S. Const. Amend. 10: "The powers not delegated to the United States by the Constitution, nor prohibited by it to the States, are reserved to the States respectively, or to the people." See Gelfand & Abrams, *Putting Erie on the Right Track*, 49 U.Pitt. L. Rev. 937, 941 (1988) (*Erie* rests on the two "similar but not entirely overlapping" objectives of "promoting federalism and eliminating forum shopping between federal and state courts").

108.   See Iovino v. Waterson, 274 F.2d 41, 48 (2d Cir.1959), cert. denied sub nom. Carlin v. Iovino, 362 U.S. 949, 80 S.Ct. 860, 4 L.Ed.2d 867 (1960); Silving, *Analogies Extending and Restricting Federal Jurisdiction; Erie R. Co. v. Tompkins and the Law of Conflict*, 31 Iowa L. Rev. 330, 345 (1946).

109.   Black & White Taxicab & Transfer Co. v. Brown & Yellow Taxicab & Transfer Co., 276 U.S. 518, 532–33, 48 S.Ct. 404, 408–09, 72 L.Ed. 681, 686–87 (1928) (Holmes, J., dissenting); Baltimore & Ohio R.R. v. Baugh, 149 U.S. 368, 399, 13 S.Ct. 914, 926, 37 L.Ed. 772, 785 (1893) (Field, J., dissenting).

110.   U.S. Const. Art. I, § 8, cl. 18.

111.   U.S. Const. Art. III.

112.   See Erie R. Co. v. Tompkins, 304 U.S. 64, 91, 92, 58 S.Ct. 817, 828, 82 L.Ed. 1188, 1201–02 (1938) (Reed, J., concurring). But see Ely, supra note 82 at 713; Quigley, *Congressional Repair of the Erie Derailment*, 60 Mich. L. Rev. 1031, 1059 (1962); Whicher, § 10.3 note 72, at 553.

113.   See Bernhardt v. Polygraphic Co. of America, 350 U.S. 198, 202, 76 S.Ct. 273, 275–76, 100 L.Ed. 199, 204–05 (1956) (construing United States Arbitration Act as not applicable, to avoid constitutional question presented by *Erie*).

114.   U.S. Const. Art. I, § 8, cl. 3. See Silving, supra note 108, at 351.

115.   U.S. Const. Art. IV, § 1. See Cook, *The Powers of Congress Under the Full Faith and Credit Clause*, 28 Yale L. J. 421 (1919); Freund, *Chief Justice Stone and the Conflict of Laws*, 59 Harv. L. Rev. 1210, 1229–30 (1946).

addressing application of an alien rule to an essentially intrastate transaction which, under the Constitution, was solely of state concern. It was surely only in this limited context that he meant "there is no federal general common law."[116] In a case decided the same day as *Erie*, Justice Brandeis himself applied what he called "federal common law" to apportion an interstate stream.[117] Moreover, *Erie* itself involved a choice-of-law problem. The injury had been in Pennsylvania while the federal forum was in New York. Without paying the New York choice-of-law rule even the respect of mention, the case was remanded to permit the circuit court to determine and apply Pennsylvania tort law.[118] This is especially striking in view of the fact that the question of the applicability of *Erie* to choice-of-law rules was specifically reserved in a case decided less than a month after *Erie* and *sub judice* at the time the Court decided *Erie*.[119]

Justice Brandeis also raised an "equal protection" argument against *Tyson*. A non-resident's power to select a federal forum and thus change the applicable law provided an unfair advantage over a resident and "rendered impossible equal protection of the law."[120] This objection is met by an analysis that focuses on "countervailing considerations". Treating a local citizen differently than he or she would be treated in a state court is not based on an irrational classification if there are cogent "countervailing considerations" that outweigh the possible evil of intrastate forum shopping.

Another argument in support of a constitutional basis for *Erie* is that, although Congress has constitutional power to make substantive law for diversity cases, the federal courts, on their own, do not,[121] save in those few areas where the necessity for a uniform national result achieved by adherence to a federal rule requires the shaping of "federal

116. *Erie*, 304 U.S. at 78, 58 S.Ct. at 822, 82 L.Ed. at 1194.

117. Hinderlider v. La Plata River & Cherry Creek Ditch Co., 304 U.S. 92, 110, 58 S.Ct. 803, 810–11, 82 L.Ed. 1202, 1212–13 (1938). See also, e.g., United States v. Standard Oil Co. of Calif., 332 U.S. 301, 67 S.Ct. 1604, 91 L.Ed. 2067 (1947) (government's right to recover for injury to soldier governed by federal law even though Congress had not acted on the question) (Congress now has—42 U.S.C. § 2651(a)); National Metropolitan Bank v. United States, 323 U.S. 454, 65 S.Ct. 354, 89 L.Ed. 383 (1945) (even in absence of statute, rights and liabilities on commercial paper issued by the federal government determined by federal law); Clearfield Trust Co. v. United States, 318 U.S. 363, 63 S.Ct. 573, 87 L.Ed. 838 (1943) (same); Fulton Nat'l Bank v. United States, 197 F.2d 763 (5th Cir.1952) (same); § 10.9.

118. *Erie*, 304 U.S. at 80, 58 S.Ct. at 823, 82 L.Ed. at 1195. For similar pre-*Klaxon* statements, see Sibbach v. Wilson & Co., 312 U.S. 1, 10–11, 61 S.Ct. 422, 424–25, 85 L.Ed. 479, 483–84 (1941); Hudson v. Moonier, 304 U.S. 397, 58 S.Ct. 954, 82 L.Ed. 1422 (1938). That, because of echoes of *Tyson* in New York opinions, reference to New York law might have produced a different result, see Hill, *The Erie Doctrine and the Constitution*, 53 Nw.U. L. Rev. 427, 541, 598 (1958).

119. Ruhlin v. New York Life Ins. Co., 304 U.S. 202, 208 n.2, 58 S.Ct. 860, 862 n.2, 82 L.Ed. 1290, 1293 n.2 (1938).

120. *Erie*, 304 U.S. at 74, 58 S.Ct. at 820, 82 L.Ed. at 1192. See U.S. Const. Amend. 14, § 1: "No state shall ... deny to any person within its jurisdiction the equal protection of the laws."

121. See Mishkin, *Some Further Last Words on Erie—The Thread*, 87 Harv. L. Rev. 1682, 1685 (1974); Quigley, supra note 112; Whicher, supra note 72, at 551; Note, 52 Harv. L. Rev. 1002, 1003 (1939).

common law."[122] Again, even assuming that conflicts rules do not present such a need for national uniformity, this reason is not cogent when applied to such rules. The contrary attitude, that the federal courts can act to shape conflicts law different from state law until the Congress occupies the field, seems more consistent with the traditional view that the forum applies its own choice-of-law rules, even choice-of-law rules that a federal forum would not impose on the states as constitutionally required.

Finally, and strongest of all, a constitutional argument for *Erie* can be made by analogy to those cases establishing due process limitations on a state's choice of law.[123] A forum may not apply its own law to a case so as to affect the result on the merits, if no policy of the forum would be advanced in so doing and application of forum law would be unfair to one of the parties.[124] Justice Harlan, in his concurring opinion in *Hanna*, seems to have had a similar constitutional test in mind for the *Erie* doctrine when, in disagreeing with the emphasis that the majority opinion gave to forum-shopping, he said:

> To my mind the proper line of approach in determining whether to apply a state or a federal rule, whether "substantive" or "procedural," is to stay close to basic principles by inquiring if the choice of rule would substantially affect those primary decisions respecting human conduct which our constitutional system leaves to state regulation.[125]

Such a constitutional argument is not applicable to choice-of-law rules if those rules select a domestic law, the application of which meets the requirements of due process.

As for *Erie's* interpretation of "laws" to including court-made law—this does not foreclose the argument, especially in view of Justice Brandeis' failure to advert to the conflicts element in *Erie*, that such court-made laws include only the ordinary domestic laws of the appropriate state, not the conflicts rules of the state in which the district court is sitting. This contention is buttressed by the last phrase in the Rules of Decision Act: "in cases where they apply." The federal court, the argument might run, is free to decide for itself to which controversies, having contacts with more than one state, the domestic law of any particular state applies.

Having said all this is still not to say that a federal district court should never apply the conflicts rules of the state in which it is sitting. The outcome-determinative gloss written upon *Erie* in subsequent Supreme Court cases represents a policy that, if unopposed by "counter-

---

122.   See supra note 117 and accompanying text.

123.   See, e.g., Allstate Ins. Co. v. Hague, 449 U.S. 302, 101 S.Ct. 633, 66 L.Ed.2d 521 (1981); Home Ins. Co. v. Dick, 281 U.S. 397, 50 S.Ct. 338, 74 L.Ed. 926 (1930). See also, Leathers, *Erie and its Progeny as Choice of Law Cases*, 11 Houston L. Rev. 791, 803 (1974).

124.   See § 9.2A.

125.   *Hanna*, 380 U.S. at 475, 85 S.Ct. at 1146, 14 L.Ed.2d at 19 (Harlan, J., concurring).

vailing considerations," should prevail—the policy against making the result depend upon the selection of forum.[126] Different conflicts rules are likely to lead to different results in litigation as surely as different substantive domestic laws. The following sections examine various circumstances in which a federal district court, in a diversity case might be asked to apply the conflicts rules of the state in which it is sitting. The purpose will be to determine in what situations the non-constitutional, non-statutory policy against forum-shopping between state and federal court is outweighed by conflicting policies that point to the federal court's applying its own conflicts rules.

§ 10.5 The Argument Against the Application of Erie to any Conflicts Problem

§ 10.5A The Danger of Interstate Forum–Shopping

It might be argued that the policy against intrastate forum shopping is always outweighed by the danger of interstate forum shopping if a federal district court is required to conform to local state conflicts law. Application of the local conflicts rule will reflect the parochial views of the forum state and provide a convenient forum, additional to the state court, where, by application of inappropriate and outcome-determinative forum rules, the result is made dependent upon the selection of the forum. Classic examples of this undesirable practice are *Sampson v. Channell*[127] and the landmark Supreme Court case extending Erie to conflicts rules, *Klaxon Co. v. Stentor Electric Manufacturing Co.*[128] In each of these cases, the federal court was required to apply an outcome-determinative rule of the state in which it was sitting if that state would classify the rule as "procedural." This was true even though the forum state would agree that all "substantive" issues should be decided under the law of another jurisdiction whose contacts with facts and parties made use of the other state's law more appropriate. In *Sampson* this resulted in applying the Massachusetts rule on burden of proof as to contributory negligence when, for resolution of all "substantive" issues, a Massachusetts court would have looked to Maine law. In *Klaxon*, such a view required remand to determine whether a Delaware court would insist on applying the Delaware rule on pre-judgment interest to a contract made and performed in New York, the only contact with Delaware being that Delaware was the place of the defendant's incorporation.[129] A more recent example is *Ferens v. John Deere Co.*,[130] in which

---

126. "If the decree would have been right in a court of the State of Texas it was right in a District Court of the United States sitting in the same State." Union Trust Co. v. Grosman, 245 U.S. 412, 418, 38 S.Ct. 147, 148, 62 L.Ed. 368, 372 (1918) (Homes, J.).

127. 110 F.2d 754 (1st Cir.), cert. denied, 310 U.S. 650, 60 S.Ct. 1099, 84 L.Ed. 1415 (1940).

128. 313 U.S. 487, 61 S.Ct. 1020, 85 L.Ed. 1477 (1941).

129. On remand it was held that Delaware would regard the New York rule as "substantive" and apply it. Stentor Electric Mfg. Co. v. Klaxon Co., 125 F.2d 820 (3d Cir.1942), cert. denied, 316 U.S. 685, 62 S.Ct. 1284, 86 L.Ed. 1757 (1942).

130. 494 U.S. 516, 110 S.Ct. 1274, 108 L.Ed.2d 443 (1990).

a Pennsylvania farmer, injured while using a Deere combine, was able to shop in Mississippi for a tort statute of limitations that had not run. Then the farmer compelled the Pennsylvania federal district court to which the case was transferred under 28 U.S.C.A. § 1401(a) to apply the Mississippi procedural characterization of the limitations issue.[131] The transfer joined the farmer's tort claims with the contract claims already pending in Pennsylvania and avoided the inconvenience to the plaintiff of having to litigate his tort and contract claims in different states.

There are several possible answers to an argument that compelling a federal court to apply the choice-of-law rules of the forum state provides an additional convenient forum for application of parochial state conflicts doctrines. First of all, as Professor Freund has pointed out,[132] the argument may be based on an assumption as to the plaintiff's freedom of choice of forum that is unrealistic in view of the venue limitations on diversity suits.[133] Furthermore, a state's choice-of-law rules are important expressions of its domestic policy.[134] It is as important for the state to decide to what interstate transactions its domestic laws are applicable as it is for it to decide what intrastate transactions invoke those laws.[135] Displacement of a state conflicts rule by the federal court's own view as to appropriate choice of law, although it may be proper under certain circumstances, should not be made cavalierly or as a matter of course. Moreover, although labeling as "procedural" a rule with high potential for affecting the outcome may seem a wild and irrational aberration of the local state's conflicts doctrine, it may mask a poorly articulated but quite reasonable policy decision that the local domestic rule is the one most appropriate for application to the interstate transaction in dispute.

---

131. Van Dusen v. Barrack, 376 U.S. 612, 84 S.Ct. 805, 11 L.Ed.2d 945 (1964), held that when a federal court grants a defendant's motion to transfer a case under 28 U.S.C. 1404(a) to another federal court, the law of the transferor state applies. *Ferens* extended this rule to a case in which the plaintiff moved for the transfer.

132. Freund, *Federal–State Relations in the Opinions of Judge Magruder*, 72 Harv. L. Rev. 1204, 1212 (1959).

133. 28 U.S.C. § 1391(a): "A civil action wherein jurisdiction is founded only on diversity of citizenship may, except as otherwise provided by law, be brought only in (1) a judicial district where any defendant resides, if all defendants reside in the same State, (2) a judicial district in which a substantial part of the events or omissions giving rise to the claim occurred, or a substantial part of property that is the subject of the action is situated, or (3) a judicial district in which any defendant is subject to personal jurisdiction at the time the action is commenced, if there is no district in which the action may otherwise be brought." See also 28 U.S.C. § 1391(c): "For purposes of venue under this chapter, a defendant that is a corporation shall be deemed to reside in any judicial district in which it is subject to personal jurisdiction at the time the action is commenced. In a State which has more than one judicial district and in which a defendant that is a corporation is subject to personal jurisdiction at the time an action is commenced, such corporation shall be deemed to reside in any district in that State within which its contacts would be sufficient to subject it to personal jurisdiction if that district were a separate State, and, if there is no such district, the corporation shall be deemed to reside in the district within which it has the most significant contacts."

134. See Cavers, *Change in Choice-of-Law Thinking and Its Bearing on the Klaxon Problem*, in ALI Study of the Division of Jurisdiction Between State and Federal Courts 154, 166 (Tent.Draft No. 1, 1963); Currie, *Change of Venue and the Conflict of Laws: A Retraction*, 27 U. Chi. L. Rev. 341, 344 (1960).

135. See Freund, supra note 115, at 1217–1219.

A notorious example of this is the statement in *Kilberg v. Northeast Airlines, Inc.*[136] that the $15,000 limit on recovery contained in the Massachusetts wrongful death act was not applicable to a suit in New York by the administrator of a deceased New York domiciliary who had boarded the fatal airplane flight in New York, because the measure of damages was "procedural."

At bottom, the argument that federal courts should always apply their own conflicts rules assumes that federal courts, being by nature less parochial than the courts of the state in which they are sitting, are likely to evolve better choice-of-law rules, selecting domestic rules more appropriate than those that would be selected by a local state court.[137] This assumption may have been weakened by the fact that courts in most states have turned from rigid, territorially oriented choice-of-law rules to choice of law based upon analysis of the policies underlying putatively conflicting domestic rules.[138]

In extreme cases when the state conflicts rule results in an irrational selection of inappropriate law, a remedy may lie in cautious extension of established constitutional limitations on a state's choice of law. One area where such extension might occur is that mentioned above. It should be a violation of due process for a forum, by the device of affixing a "procedural" label, to avoid the application of another state's rule, if the policies underlying the other state's rule would be advanced by applying that rule to the case at bar, the rule is of a kind that has high potential for affecting the outcome on the merits, the foreign rule is not inordinately difficult for the forum to find and apply, and application of the forum's different rule will not advance any rationally applicable policy of the forum.[139] Ironically, one of the first candidates for overruling under such a view of due process would be *Klaxon* itself.[140] A similar due process argument might be made if the forum state would apply its own "substantive" law to a controversy as indicated by a traditional, territorially-oriented choice-of-law rule, such as the place of injury for torts, but analysis reveals that no policy of the forum's rule is applicable to the case at bar and that a different and rationally applicable rule

---

136. 9 N.Y.2d 34, 42, 211 N.Y.S.2d 133, 137, 172 N.E.2d 526, 529 (1961).

137. See Wolkin, *Conflict of Laws in the Federal Courts: The Erie Era*, 94 U.Pa. L. Rev. 293, 295 (1956). But see Cavers, supra note 134, at 182–191 (reasons why unlikely federal courts could develop a unitary system of choice-of-law rules better than states have done); Cavers, The Choice-of-Law Process 216–24 (1965).

138. See § 6.18. Danger of parochialism remains if the forum insists on advancing its own interests without regard either to the impairment of the interests of other states or to some reasonable nexus between the forum and the party disfavored by the forum's rule. See §§ 6.27 and 6.28.

139. Cases that present the greatest danger of such irrational choice of law are those in which the court bases its jurisdiction over the defendant on a generally-affiliating basis, such as doing business, that is unrelated to the transaction in issue. See, e.g., Ferens v. John Deere Co., 494 U.S. 516, 110 S.Ct. 1274, 108 L.Ed.2d 443 (1990) (Mississippi longer limitations period applies to injury in Pennsylvania because Mississippi, where defendant does business, regards its limitations as procedural).

140. See Cavers, supra note 134, at 210.

exists elsewhere.[141]

Again, if the forum would refuse to apply its own rule because the forum's traditional choice-of-law rule points to some other geographical location as having the decisive "contact," such a refusal may be based upon an unreasonable classification if in fact the policies underlying the forum rule would be advanced by applying it and if application would not interfere with the legitimate interests of any other state or unfairly surprise any party. The "equal protection" clause of the Fourteenth Amendment should preclude such unreasonableness.[142]

In the light of *Allstate Insurance Co. v. Hague*,[143] it seems unlikely that this "cautious extension of established constitutional limitations on a state's choice of law" will occur in the near future. Adopting the Court's erroneous[144] assumption in *Hague* that the amount of recovery turned on whether Minnesota or Wisconsin law applied, the Court permitted higher uninsured motorist recovery under Minnesota law even though the policy was issued in Wisconsin to a Wisconsin domiciliary who was killed by an accident in Wisconsin. A majority found that "Minnesota had a significant aggregation of contacts with the parties and the occurrence, creating state interests, such that application of its law was neither arbitrary nor fundamentally unfair."[145] Two of the contacts on which the majority relied were Mr. Hague's commuting to work in Minnesota for fifteen years before his death and Allstate's extensive business contacts there. Neither of these contacts created "state interests" in Minnesota in the proper choice-of-law sense. No policy sought to be advanced by Minnesota's requirement that uninsured motorist coverage be stacked would be affected by these "contacts" with the state. The third contact on which the majority relied was Mrs. Hague's post-accident move to Minnesota. This move did give Minnesota an "interest" in higher compensation to Mrs. Hague. If this were the only contact with Minnesota, however, it was acquired too late to make assertion of Minnesota's interest reasonable.[146] Thus the plurality[147]

---

141. See § 9.2A.

142. See § 9.4.

143. 449 U.S. 302, 101 S.Ct. 633, 66 L.Ed.2d 521 (1981). For a detailed discussion, see § 9.2A.

144. The "other insurance" clause in the policy, which purported to reduce recovery, was invalid under Minnesota law and, even if valid under Wisconsin law, was ambiguous and would have been construed not to apply on the facts of *Hague*. See Safeco Ins. Co. of Am. v. Robey, 399 F.2d 330 (8th Cir.1968) (identical clause held inapplicable); Ehlers v. Colonial Penn Ins. Co., 81 Wis.2d 64, 259 N.W.2d 718 (1977) (ambiguities in insurance policies construed against insurer); Rosar v. General Ins. Co. of Am., 41 Wis.2d 95, 101–02, 163 N.W.2d 129, 132 (1968) (stacking of liability coverage not allowed but court distinguishes medical payments because "recovery is completely independent of liability on the part of the insured").

145. *Hague*, 449 U.S. at 320, 101 S.Ct. at 644, 66 L.Ed.2d at 535. Four justices, Brennan, White, Marshall, and Blackmun, found both due process and full faith and credit requirements satisfied under this standard. Justice Stevens, who concurred in the judgment, applied a different full faith and credit standard.

146. See John Hancock Mutual Life Ins. Co. v. Yates, 299 U.S. 178, 57 S.Ct. 129, 81 L.Ed. 106 (1936).

147. See, supra, note 145.

opinion in *Hague* used "state interests" to mean physical contacts of a kind that would lead a reasonable person, unschooled in the niceties of "interest analysis," to regard the application of the law of the state with those contacts as neither arbitrary nor unfair. Under this view the most maligned of territorial choice-of-law rules, place of wrong, passes constitutional muster.

§ 10.5B   The Danger of Intrastate Forum–Shopping

Paradoxically, requiring the federal district court to apply the conflicts law of the state in which it is sitting may result in the very intrastate forum shopping that such a requirement is designed to prevent. This is because although most states have abandoned territorial choice-of-law rules, the conflicts area is still in a state of flux.[148] In this atmosphere, a party who would benefit from application of a standard, territorially oriented choice-of-law rule reflected in the most recent pronouncement of the highest court of the state would do well to choose the federal district court as forum. Conversely, a party will have greater chance of success in the state supreme court, if he or she wishes to argue that the conflicts rule formerly accepted in the state would produce an irrational and unjust result in the case and should be changed in accord with current trends elsewhere.[149] It is sobering to reflect that only five years before *Kilberg v. Northeast Airlines, Inc.*[150] and seven years before *Babcock v. Jackson*[151] so able a federal judge as Jerome Frank felt compelled, despite his sympathy with arguments that the result was unjust, to sanction the dismissal of a complaint brought by an American plaintiff against an American defendant in an American court if the plaintiff could not prove the tort law of Saudi Arabia, the place of injury. New York had consistently applied the law of the place of wrong to tort conflicts problems and Judge Frank could "see no signs that the New York decisions pertinent here are obsolescent."[152]

---

148.   See, e.g., American Motorists Ins. Co. v. ARTRA Group, Inc., 338 Md. 560, 659 A.2d 1295 (1995) (using renvoi to escape forum's lex loci contractus rule and stating that the court may have to reevaluate that rule in the future).

149.   See Quigley, supra note 112, at 1036. Able litigators are fully aware of the importance of making innovative choice-of-law arguments in state rather than federal court. Two tactics to remain in state court are to destroy diversity by joining defendants who have the same citizenship as the plaintiff and to prevent removal by suing defendants who are citizens of the forum. For example, in Griffith v. United Air Lines, Inc., 416 Pa. 1, 203 A.2d 796 (1964), the landmark Pennsylvania case abandoning the place-of-wrong rule, Lee Kreindler, plaintiff's attorney, joined the airline's mechanics who had serviced the plane, guessing correctly that at least one of them would prove to be a citizen of Pennsylvania. United Air Lines was a Delaware corporation with its principal place of business in Illinois and it could have removed but for the joinder of the mechanics. Kilberg v. Northeast Airlines, Inc., 9 N.Y.2d 34, 211 N.Y.S.2d 133, 172 N.E.2d 526 (1961), which refused to apply the Massachusetts wrongful death act despite the place-of-wrong rule, was not removed to federal court because a settlement had apparently been reached with plaintiff's attorney, who was then replaced by Mr. Kreindler. Kreindler, Luncheon Address, American Association of Law Schools Workshop on Conflict of Laws, Program 8032R Tape 10, July 9, 1988.

150.   9 N.Y.2d 34, 211 N.Y.S.2d 133, 172 N.E.2d 526 (1961).

151.   12 N.Y.2d 473, 240 N.Y.S.2d 743, 191 N.E.2d 279 (1963).

152.   Walton v. Arabian Am. Oil Co., 233 F.2d 541, 543 (2d Cir.1956), cert. denied, 352 U.S. 872, 77 S.Ct. 97, 1 L.Ed.2d 77 (1956). Although Judge Frank wrote the opinion that

The reason for this unhappy state of affairs is that federal courts have been given too little freedom to adapt to current trends in state law. In the words of Justice Black:

> But the Circuit Courts of Appeals do not have the same power to reconsider interpretations of state law by state courts as do the highest courts of the state in which a decision has been rendered. The Mississippi Supreme Court had the power to reconsider and overrule its former interpretation, but the court below did not. And in the absence of a change by the Mississippi legislature, the court below could reconsider and depart from the ruling of the highest court of Mississippi on Mississippi's statute of limitations only to the extent, if any, that examination of the later opinions of the Mississippi Supreme Court showed that it had changed its earlier interpretation of the effect of the Mississippi statute.[153]

Unless "convinced by other persuasive data that the highest court of the state would otherwise decide," the federal court is required to follow the opinions, not only of the state supreme court, but also of the lower state courts of record.[154] To aggravate the situation, in diversity cases the Supreme Court has, except in exceptional circumstances such as avoidance of a constitutional issue, disapproved a federal court's staying proceedings until a question of state law could be determined by the parties in a declaratory proceeding in a state court.[155] It is not surprising, then, to find federal judges saying such things as: "Nor can we apply, in diversity cases, a rule of stare decisis which permits us to weigh the degree of authority belonging to a precedent by its agreement with the spirit of the times. The Georgia courts can overrule their prior decisions. The Federal Courts cannot do so."[156]

---

affirmed the dismissal of the complaint, he voted to remand in order to give the plaintiff another opportunity to prove Saudi–Arabian law.

153.   Moore v. Illinois C.R.R., 312 U.S. 630, 633, 61 S.Ct. 754, 755, 85 L.Ed. 1089, 1091–1092 (1941).

154.   West v. American Tel. & Tel. Co., 311 U.S. 223, 237, 61 S.Ct. 179, 183, 85 L.Ed. 139, 144 (1940). See also Fidelity Union Trust Co. v. Field, 311 U.S. 169, 61 S.Ct. 176, 85 L.Ed. 109 (1940); cf. Commissioner v. Estate of Bosch, 387 U.S. 456, 87 S.Ct. 1776, 18 L.Ed.2d 886 (1967) (even though nature of property interest on which federal estate tax liability turns is determined by state law, the United States is not bound by a determination of that interest by a state trial court in a proceeding to which the United States was not a party) (annotation in 18 L.Ed.2d 1602–30); King v. Order of United Commercial Travelers of America, 333 U.S. 153, 68 S.Ct. 488, 92 L.Ed. 608 (1948) (need not follow decision of court not of record and not constituting precedent in any state court); cf. Factors Etc., Inc. v. Pro Arts, Inc., 652 F.2d 278 (2d Cir.1981), cert. denied, 456 U.S. 927, 102 S.Ct. 1973, 72 L.Ed.2d 442 (1982) (on novel question of state law, federal circuit court defers to view of federal circuit in which state located).

155.   Sutton v. Leib, 342 U.S. 402, 72 S.Ct. 398, 96 L.Ed. 448 (1952); Meredith v. Winter Haven, 320 U.S. 228, 64 S.Ct. 7, 88 L.Ed. 9 (1943); Spector Motor Service, Inc. v. McLaughlin, 323 U.S. 101, 65 S.Ct. 152, 89 L.Ed. 101 (1944) (avoidance of constitutional question—suit to enjoin enforcement of state tax).

156.   Polk County, Ga. v. Lincoln Nat'l Life Ins. Co., 262 F.2d 486, 490 (5th Cir.1959). See also Ideal Structures Corp. v. Levine Huntsville Dev. Corp., 396 F.2d 917 (5th Cir.1968) (refuse to predict adoption by Alabama of "most significant relationship test" for contract choice-of-law problems); Schultz v. Tecumseh Prods., 310 F.2d 426, 432 (6th Cir.1962); Hausman v. Buckley, 299 F.2d 696, 704 (2d Cir.1962), cert. denied, 369 U.S. 885,

If the question is how to avoid this weird form of intrastate forum shopping, the answer does not lie in giving federal courts complete freedom to disregard the law of the state in which they are sitting. The answer does lie in removal of artificial limitations that have impeded their efforts to reflect viable current trends and changes in conflicts law not discernible in state opinions that are ripe for overruling. Professor Moore has put it well: "Although there must be faithful adherence to state substantive law in non-federal matters, it should be a wise and discerning loyalty, something in the nature of a 'prophetic judgment' as to what the highest court would now do."[157] In an area that is changing as rapidly as is the conflict of laws, there should be a reversal of the current attitude that prevents federal courts from obtaining direct information on the state view of the matter in controversy by staying, for declaratory proceedings in a state court. When a state statute permits,[158] certifying the question directly to the state's highest court may work, but only if recent decisions of that court create doubt as to the prevailing choice-of-law rule.[159]

§ 10.5C   The Loss of Federal Judicial Talent in Developing Conflicts Rules

It might be urged that requiring federal courts in diversity cases to follow the law of the state in which they are sitting destroys the creativity of federal courts in a major fraction of their business and squanders the talents of federal judges, whose ranks include many of our most able jurists.[160] This is an especially serious waste of intellectual resources in an area, such as conflicts, where the complexity of the problems and the rapidity of current growth and change require as much talent as can be recruited.

Much of the answer to such an argument lies in what has been said just above concerning the desirability of giving federal judges in diversity cases reasonable freedom to take account of developing trends so that

---

82 S.Ct. 1157, 8 L.Ed.2d 286 (1962); Fry v. Lamb Rental Tools, Inc., 275 F.Supp. 283 (W.D.La.1967) (refuse to anticipate Louisiana's abandonment of the place-of-wrong rule, despite Louisiana appellate dicta indicating a change).

157. Moore, Commentary on the United States Judicial Code 338 (1949). See also Cooke v. E.F. Drew & Co., 319 F.2d 498, 505 (2d Cir.1963) (Friendly, J., dissenting); Cavers, supra note 134, at 211; Quigley, supra note 112, at 1067.

158. As of October 1, 2009, eight states had adopted the 1995 revision and the District of Columbia and nine states had adopted the 1967 version of the Uniform Certification of Questions of Law Act. Other states have non-uniform provisions for certification. See, e.g., Tex. Const. Art. 5 § 3–c(a); implemented by Tex. R. App. Proc. 114. See also Note, *Civil Procedure—Scope of Certification in Diversity Jurisdiction*, 29 Rutgers L. Rev. 1155 (1976); Note, *The Ascertainment of State Law in a Federal Diversity Case*, 40 Ind.L. J. 541 (1965); cf. Kurland, *Justice Frankfurter, The Supreme Court and the Erie Doctrine in Diversity Cases*, 67 Yale L. J. 187, 214 (1957) (federal certification statute would be permissible).

159. See, e.g., American Motorists Ins. Co. v. ARTRA Group, Inc., 338 Md. 560, 659 A.2d 1295 (1995) (using renvoi to escape forum's lex loci contractus rule and stating that court may have to reevaluate that rule in the future).

160. See Hart, *The Relations Between State and Federal Law*, 54 Colum. L. Rev. 489, 510 (1954); Corbin, *The Judicial Process Revisited: Introduction*, 71 Yale L. J. 195, 200 (1961); Note, 71 Yale L. J. 344, 353 (1961).

they do not march several leagues behind the very state courts whose pace they are attempting to match. But there is another vast area where full advantage may be taken of the creative talents of federal judges in solving conflicts problems. This is the area in which, in the interstitial augmenting of federal common or statutory law, the federal court turns to state law as the rule for decision.[161] The federal court should be free here to determine for itself which state will supply the rule most appropriate for the case at bar.[162] In admiralty cases when there is no established admiralty rule and no pressing need for a uniform federal rule, federal courts have used a federal choice-of-law rule to select the governing law.[163] The Supreme Court has left open the question of whether *Klaxon* is applicable to cases in which federal jurisdiction is not based on diversity of citizenship.[164] This doubt should be resolved in favor of freedom for federal judges to lend their talents to the efforts to solve conflicts problems. Intrastate forum-shopping between state and federal court would be minimized if, once the federal choice-of-law rule had been established, the state court, having concurrent jurisdiction of the issue arising under federal law, would be compelled to follow suit.

It may be that there will be fewer occasions for federal courts to fashion federal common law in the light of decisions such as *O'Melveny & Meyers v. Federal Deposit Insurance Corp.*[165] *O'Melveny* held that

---

161.   See, e.g., Commissioner v. Stern, 357 U.S. 39, 78 S.Ct. 1047, 2 L.Ed.2d 1126 (1958) (recovery of estate's tax deficiencies from beneficiary of life insurance policy held by decedent depends upon law of decedent's domicile); Helvering v. Fuller, 310 U.S. 69, 60 S.Ct. 784, 84 L.Ed. 1082 (1940) (whether husband taxable on income from alimony trust depends on whether, under appropriate state law, the husband can be compelled to make additional payments in the future); Huber v. Baltimore & O.R.R., 241 F.Supp. 646 (D.Md.1965) ("children" under FELA—uses conflicts rule of forum state); Tune v. Louisville & N.R.R., 223 F.Supp. 928 (M.D.Tenn.1963) ("children" under FELA—apparent use of federal choice-of-law rule); cf. Bell v. Tug Shrike, 332 F.2d 330 (4th Cir.1964), cert. denied, 379 U.S. 844, 85 S.Ct. 84, 13 L.Ed.2d 49 (1964) ("widow" under Jones Act—law of domicile, which "normally governs", applied). For a split of authority as to whether in choosing law under the Foreign Sovereign Immunities Act a federal court should use a federal choice-of-law rule or the choice-of-law rule of the state in which the federal court is sitting, see Barkanic v. General Administration of Civil Aviation of People's Republic of China, 923 F.2d 957 (2d Cir. 1991) (state rule); Liu v. Republic of China, 892 F.2d 1419 (9th Cir. 1989), cert. dism'd, 497 U.S. 1058, 111 S.Ct. 27, 111 L.Ed.2d 840 (1990) (federal rule). For a similar split of authority under the Edge Act, which authorizes federal chartering of corporations engaged in international financial operations and grants federal courts jurisdiction over suits against such corporations, see A.I. Trade Finance, Inc. v. Petra Int'l Banking Corp., 62 F.3d 1454 (D.C. Cir. 1995) (applying choice-of-law rules of D.C. and noting contrary decisions in First and Second Circuits).

162.   See In re L.M.S. Associates, Inc., 18 B.R. 425, 428 (Bankr. S.D. Fla. 1982) (when a bankruptcy court "is applying federal law which refers to state law ... the court should use federal conflicts rules (its independent judgment) as part of the overall federal law it is applying"). Contra, In re Merritt Dredging Co., 839 F.2d 203 (4th Cir. 1988) (bankruptcy court should apply conflicts rule of state in which it sits). See also Freund, supra note 115, at 1236 n.62; Mishkin, *The Variousness of "Federal Law": Competence and Discretion in the Choice of National and State Rules for Decision*, 105 U.Pa. L. Rev. 797, 807–08 (1957).

163.   See, e.g., Lien Ho Hsing Steel Enterprise Co. v. Weihtag, 738 F.2d 1455 (9th Cir. 1984).

164.   D'Oench, Duhme & Co. v. Federal Deposit Ins. Corp., 315 U.S. 447, 456, 62 S.Ct. 676, 679, 86 L.Ed. 956, 961 (1942).

165.   512 U.S. 79, 114 S.Ct. 2048, 129 L.Ed.2d 67 (1994). See also Atherton v. Federal Deposit Ins. Corp., 519 U.S. 213, 117 S.Ct. 666, 136 L.Ed.2d 656 (1997) (state law standard,

California law, not federal common law, determined whether bank officers' knowledge of fraud can be imputed to the FDIC as the bank's receiver, stating that a federal court should not "adopt a court-made rule to supplement federal statutory regulation that is comprehensive and detailed; matters left unaddressed in such a scheme are presumably left subject to the disposition provided by state law."[166]

The ideal situation in which to develop federal choice-of-law rules is that in which federal law looks to state law for the final rule of decision, but jurisdiction is exclusively in the federal courts. Suits against the federal government under the Federal Tort Claims Act[167] fit this description exactly. Unfortunately, this chance for creative federal contributions to the common law of conflicts has been wasted because the statute contains a choice-of-law reference to "the law of the place where the act or omission occurred."[168] In order to restore at least a chance for flexibility and rationality to the statutory rule, the Supreme Court of the United States has interpreted the statute as referring to the whole law of the state where the "act or omission occurred" including that state's choice-of-law rule.[169] It would be better to amend the statute so as to leave federal courts free to fashion their own conflicts rules in tort claims cases. This might be done, for example, by having the quoted provision read simply "the appropriate law."

There is a possible rebuttal to this position that in choosing state law to augment federal law, the federal courts should be free to apply their own choice-of-law rules. It might be argued that once it is determined that state law should be looked to for the rule of decision, the

---

which is stricter than federal statutory standard, applies to determine whether behavior of bank officers and directors was improper). Neither opinion cited D'Oench Duhme & Co. v. Federal Deposit Ins. Corp., 315 U.S. 447, 62 S.Ct. 676, 86 L.Ed. 956 (1942), which held that federal common law governed the civil liability of an accommodation maker of notes taken by the FDIC as collateral.

There is a split of authority as to whether *D'Oench* survives *O'Melveny* and the enactment of the Federal Institutions Reform, Recovery, and Enforcement Act of 1989 (FIRREA). See F.D.I.C. v. O'Melveny & Myers, 61 F.3d 17, 19 (9th Cir. 1995) (*D'Oench* "overruled"). Contra, Motorcity of Jacksonville, Ltd. v. Southeast Bank N.A., 120 F.3d 1140 (11th Cir. 1997), cert. denied, 523 U.S. 1093, 118 S.Ct. 1559, 140 L.Ed.2d 791 (1998). For the FDIC's view as to when *D'Oench* applies, see 62 FR 5984, 5985, 1997 WL 49242: "the FDIC will assert the D'Oench doctrine for pre-FIRREA claims to the extent section [12 U.S.C.] 1823(e) (as it existed prior to FIRREA) is inapplicable but the claim nevertheless runs afoul of the D'Oench doctrine. For claims that relate to agreements or arrangements entered into after the effective date of FIRREA, the FDIC will apply only [12 U.S.C. §§ 1821(d)(9)(A) and 1823(e) as amended by FIRREA]."

166. *O'Melveny*, 512 U.S. at 85, 114 S.Ct. at 2054, 129 L.Ed.2d at 74.

167. 28 U.S.C. §§ 1346(b), 2671–80.

168. 28 U.S.C. § 1346(b). See also In re Gaston & Snow, 243 F.3d 599, 601–02 (2d Cir. 2001), cert. denied, 534 U.S. 1042, 122 S.Ct. 618, 151 L.Ed.2d 540 (2001): "Because federal choice of law rules are a type of federal common law, which federal courts have only a narrow power to create, we decide that bankruptcy courts confronting state law claims that do not implicate federal policy concerns should apply the choice of law rules of the forum state." But see In re Lindsay, 59 F.3d 942, 948 (9th Cir. 1995), cert. denied, 516 U.S. 1074, 116 S.Ct. 778, 133 L.Ed.2d 730 (1996) ("In federal question cases with exclusive jurisdiction in federal court, such as bankruptcy, the court should apply federal, not forum state, choice of law rules").

169. Richards v. United States, 369 U.S. 1, 82 S.Ct. 585, 7 L.Ed.2d 492 (1962).

whole law of the state should be applied, including its conflicts rules.[170] Conflicts rules express the policies of the state as surely as the purely domestic rules of the state and often provide a vital clue to the policies underlying the domestic rules. Nevertheless, saying that federal courts, in federal question cases where reference to state law is required, should be free to fashion their own conflicts rules is not saying that they should deliberately disregard state conflicts rules. They should examine the state conflicts rules for any clue those state rules afford as to the policies underlying the putatively conflicting state domestic rules. Any rational choice-of-law decision must begin with a consideration of those underlying policies. Also, any proper choice-of-law rule will avoid unfair surprise to the parties. If a federal court decides to fashion a conflicts rule different from that of the state in which it is sitting, it will be because the federal court's rule is thought to be more "appropriate"—more concerned with the policies underlying the conflicting domestic rules of the states having relevant contacts with the controversy and less likely to upset the reasonable expectations of the parties.

A split of authority has occurred as to whether a state or federal choice-of-law rule selects the law applicable under the Foreign Sovereign Immunities Act.[171] *Liu v. Republic of China*[172] applied a federal choice-of-law rule, modeled on the "most significant relationship" rule of the Restatement (Second) of Conflict of laws. *Barkanic v. General Administration of Civil Aviation of People's Republic of China*[173] applied the choice-of-law rule of the state in which the federal court was sitting, finding that this is the meaning of the 28 U.S.C. § 1606 provision that "the foreign state shall be liable in the same manner and to the same extent as a private individual under like circumstances." The court also held that the language in 1606, "the law of the place where the action or omission occurred,"[174] applies only to punitive damages and not to the general issue of choice of law. The court distinguished *Richards v. United States*,[175] in which similar language in the Federal Tort Claims Act[176] was held to refer to the whole law of the place of act or omission,

---

170. See 1A Moore, Federal Practice ¶ 0.325.

171. 28 U.S.C. §§ 1330, 1391(f), 1441(d), 1602–1611.

172. 892 F.2d 1419 (9th Cir. 1989), cert. dism'd, 497 U.S. 1058, 111 S.Ct. 27, 111 L.Ed.2d 840 (1990).

173. 923 F.2d 957 (2d Cir. 1991).

174. 28 U.S.C. § 1606: "As to any claim for relief with respect to which a foreign state is not entitled to immunity under section 1605 or 1607 of this chapter, the foreign state shall be liable in the same manner and to the same extent as a private individual under like circumstances; but a foreign state except for an agency or instrumentality thereof shall not be liable for punitive damages; if, however, in any case wherein death was caused, the law of the place where the action or omission occurred provides, or has been construed to provide, for damages only punitive in nature, the foreign state shall be liable for actual or compensatory damages measured by the pecuniary injuries resulting from such death which were incurred by the persons for whose benefit the action was brought."

175. 369 U.S. 1, 82 S.Ct. 585, 7 L.Ed.2d 492 (1962)

176. 28 U.S.C. § 1346(b)(1): "[T]he district courts ... shall have exclusive jurisdiction of civil actions on claims against the United States, for money damages, accruing on and after January 1, 1945, for injury or loss of property, or personal injury or death caused by

including the choice-of-law rules of that place. The court stated that the provision in the Federal Tort Claims Act was expressly a choice-of-law rule, unlike the passage in § 1606 of the FSIA.

State law applies in admiralty cases if there is no established admiralty rule and there is no need for a uniform federal rule governing the particular issue. An example of the application of state law in admiralty is the construction of a maritime insurance policy.[177]. When federal courts use admiralty choice-of-law rules to select state law, they usually utilize a most significant relationship approach modeled after the Restatement (Second) of Conflict of Laws.[178]

§ 10.5D Across-the-Board Refusal to Apply State Conflicts Rules Unjustified

For the reasons stated above, a blunderbuss attack on federal courts' ever applying state conflicts rules should be repulsed. It cannot be said that there is any one policy or any combination of policies that, in all circumstances, will outweigh the policy against intrastate forum shopping that requires a federal court to use the conflicts rules of the state in which it is sitting. What is necessary is separate scrutiny of various diversity jurisdiction situations to determine in which circumstances the policy against intrastate forum shopping is overcome by countervailing considerations. Now to turn to this task.

§ 10.6   State Forum–Closing Conflicts Rules

§ 10.6A   General Diversity Jurisdiction

Out of the rather complex circumstances in *Angel v. Bullington*[179] arose the rule that, in a diversity case, a federal court must follow the conflicts rule of the state in which it is sitting, even if that state rule

---

the negligent or wrongful act or omission of any employee of the Government while acting within the scope of his office or employment, under circumstances where the United States, if a private person, would be liable to the claimant in accordance with the law of the place where the act or omission occurred."

177. See Wilburn Boat Co. v. Fireman's Fund Ins. Co., 348 U.S. 310, 314, 75 S.Ct. 368, 370, 99 L.Ed. 337 (1955).

178. Albany Ins. Co. v. Anh Thi Kieu, 927 F.2d 882 (5th Cir.), cert. denied, 502 U.S. 901, 112 S.Ct. 279, 116 L.Ed.2d 230 (1991), held that state law on the effect of misrepresentations by the insured is not pre-empted by federal admiralty law and stated: "Modern choice of law analysis, whether maritime or not, generally requires the application of the law of the state with the 'most significant relationship' to the substantive issue in question." Id. at 891. See also Lien Ho Hsing Steel Enterprise Co. v. Weihtag, 738 F.2d 1455, 1458 (9th Cir.1984) (whether a maritime insurance broker is the insurer's agent is determined by "the law of the state with the greatest interest in the issue"); Edinburgh Assur. Co. v. R.L. Burns Corp., 479 F.Supp. 138, 152–53 (C.D.Cal.1979), aff'd in part and rev'd in part on other grounds, 669 F.2d 1259 (9th Cir.1982) (applying "the points of contact analysis of *Lauritzen* [v. Larsen, 345 U.S. 571, 73 S.Ct. 921, 97 L.Ed. 1254 (1953)] and *Romero* [v. Int'l Terminal Operating Co., 358 U.S. 354, 79 S.Ct. 468, 3 L.Ed.2d 368 (1959)]" and holding that English law determines the meaning of "actual total loss" in an insurance policy covering maritime risks because England has "the most significant relationship to the transaction," citing Restatement (Second) of Conflict of Laws §§ 188 and 193). *Lauritzen* and *Romero* determined when injured foreign seamen could recover under the federal Jones Act or U.S. maritime law.

179. 330 U.S. 183, 67 S.Ct. 657, 91 L.Ed. 832 (1947).

merely closes the state forum to suit and does not produce a result on the merits. In *Angel*, the plaintiff, a citizen of Virginia, had sold land in Virginia to the defendant, a North Carolina citizen. The defendant made a down payment and then defaulted on one of a series of notes given for the balance of the purchase price. The land was sold under a power of sale contained in a deed of trust securing the notes. Because the proceeds of sale were less than the amount owed on the notes, the plaintiff brought suit in a state court in North Carolina for the deficiency. The defendant demurred, relying on a North Carolina statute that provided: "In all sales of real property by ... trustees under powers of sale contained in any ... deed of trust ... the ... holder of the notes secured by such ... deed of trust shall not be entitled to a deficiency judgment...."[180] The trial court overruled the demurrer, but on appeal the North Carolina Supreme Court held that the statute denied the state courts jurisdiction to grant the relief sought and dismissed the suit. The North Carolina high court rejected the plaintiff's claim under the United States Constitution that North Carolina was precluded from closing the doors of its courts to him. The court stated that it was merely denying a forum and not passing on any question of substantive law that affected the merits

Without appealing this decision to the Supreme Court of the United States, the plaintiff, utilizing diversity jurisdiction, brought a new suit for the deficiency judgment in a federal district court sitting in North Carolina. The Supreme Court reversed a judgment for the plaintiff. The Court held that the issue of whether North Carolina could constitutionally close its courts to plaintiff was res judicata, having been decided adversely to the plaintiff in the North Carolina high court opinion that plaintiff had allowed to become final. If North Carolina state courts were not open to the plaintiff, then, to avoid a difference in result, a federal district court sitting in North Carolina was similarly closed to him.

A contrary argument that a federal court in a diversity case should not be bound by any forum-closing state rule, might be based upon the current wording of section thirty-four of the Judiciary Act of 1789.[181] State forum-closing rules are not "rules of decision" because they do not produce a judgment on the merits. Moreover, the Judicial Code, in stating that "district courts shall have original jurisdiction"[182] of diversity cases, does "otherwise require or provide."

The real issues run deeper than these surface arguments suggest. Important state policies designed for the protection of citizens of the state may be expressed in terms of forum-closing rules. If a state has an applicable rule insulating its citizen from liability flowing from a transaction having some contacts abroad, it might be more desirable for the state to resolve any conflict between the policies underlying its rule and the policies underlying the applicable liability-producing rule of another

---

180. N.C.Gen.Stat. § 45–21.38.

181. 28 U.S.C. § 1652. (Quoted in § 10.2, text accompanying note 9.)

182. 28 U.S.C. § 1332(a)(1).

state and come to a decision on the merits, applying one rule or the other. By abandoning the ostrich-like solution of simply closing its courts to the problem, the chances are increased that conflicts involving commercial agreements will be resolved in favor of validity, especially if the difference in domestic rules producing the conflict reflects a difference in detail rather than basic policy.[183] The fact remains, however, that states do utilize the forum-closing device to express their strongly held policies. Moreover, although theoretically not a decision on the merits, closing the forum may effectively insulate the local citizen from liability, for the plaintiff may not be able to find a court elsewhere that has jurisdiction to adjudicate the matter in a state whose statute of limitations has not run.

In the typical diversity case, a federal district court should respect the policies underlying the forum-closing rules of the state in which it is sitting unless these policies are those of the state only qua possible forum and do not rationally flow from some contact that the state has with the parties or with the transaction. Typical of rationally applicable rules that should be respected is one protecting a local citizen from contractual liability entered into abroad, when the interest of his or her domicile was at all times apparent.[184] Another such rule is one insulating a citizen of the state from tort liability to another local citizen when, although the injury fortuitously happened abroad, the policies underlying the rule denying liability remain fully applicable.[185] State forum-closing rules that are rationally applicable only when trial is held in the state, should not be followed when the forum is shifted to a federal court sitting in the state. Forum non conveniens is one such solely forum-centered policy.[186] Perhaps another would be a rule designed to keep offensive testimony from being heard in state courts.[187]

An argument that a state forum-closing rule is, in view of the policies it advances, applicable only in the state courts qua possible forums and is inapplicable in another forum, even a federal court sitting in the state, deserves serious consideration. *Angel v. Bullington* rejected the argument that the North Carolina statute, as construed by the North Carolina Supreme Court, was intended only to close the courts of that state and not federal courts sitting there. *Angel* characterized as "obsolete"[188] *David Lupton's Sons Co. v. Automobile Club of America*,[189] which had accepted such an argument and had held that a corporation, which

---

183. See §§ 7.4A and 7.4C.

184. See Union Trust Co. v. Grosman, 245 U.S. 412, 38 S.Ct. 147, 62 L.Ed. 368 (1918).

185. See, e.g., Kircher v. Kircher, 288 Mich. 669, 286 N.W. 120 (1939); Koplik v. C.P. Trucking Corp., 27 N.J. 1, 141 A.2d 34 (1958); Mertz v. Mertz, 271 N.Y. 466, 3 N.E.2d 597 (1936); Herzog v. Stern, 264 N.Y. 379, 191 N.E. 23 (1934), cert. denied, 293 U.S. 597, 55 S.Ct. 112, 79 L.Ed. 690 (1934).

186. See § 4.33C describing how federal courts exercising diversity or alienage jurisdiction have applied federal rather than state forum non conveniens doctrine.

187. Cf. Gordon v. Parker, 83 F.Supp. 40, 43 (D.Mass.1949), aff'd, 178 F.2d 888 (1st Cir.1949) (action for alienation of affections).

188. *Angel*, 330 U.S. at 192, 67 S.Ct. at 662, 91 L.Ed. at 838.

189. 225 U.S. 489, 32 S.Ct. 711, 56 L.Ed. 1177 (1912).

could not sue in New York state courts because it was not authorized to do business in New York, could maintain a suit in a federal court in that state. In view of North Carolina's strong interest in protecting its citizens from a deficiency judgment, this argument may have been properly rejected in Angel. Its rejection is more debatable in *Woods v. Interstate Realty Co.*,[190] which reached a result opposite that of David Lupton's Sons under a similar state statute. It should not be assumed that there is never any merit to the argument that a state's forum-closing rule is rationally applicable only in courts of that state.

The argument based on the Judiciary Act provision, "except where the Constitution, treaties or statutes of the United States shall otherwise require or provide," is weakest when it claims that the general provision for diversity jurisdiction is license to override a strong and rationally applicable state policy when that policy is expressed in a forum-closing conflicts rule, rather than one that points to the law of the state for a judgment on the merits. Such an argument gains strength, in cases like *Allstate Insurance Co. v. Charneski*,[191] which denied relief under the federal Declaratory Judgments Act[192] because a Wisconsin court would not let an insurance company, subject to direct suit in Wisconsin, obtain a preliminary declaration of its policy's coverage.[193] The argument becomes compelling when a state attempts to restrict certain proceedings to the state courts of general jurisdiction, withdrawing jurisdiction from all other courts, including federal courts within the state.[194]

§ 10.6B Constitutional Limitations on Forum Closing

A state's forum-closing rule should withstand constitutional attack under the due process clause if the policy underlying the rule will be advanced by applying it to the case at bar, and if its application will not be fundamentally unfair to the plaintiff.[195] This test is usually satisfied if the state seeks to protect its citizens from liability on agreements made in other states that would be unenforceable if entered into within the

---

190. 337 U.S. 535, 69 S.Ct. 1235, 93 L.Ed. 1524 (1949).

191. 286 F.2d 238 (7th Cir.1960).

192. 28 U.S.C. §§ 2201–2202.

193. But see Horton v. Liberty Mut. Ins. Co., 367 U.S. 348, 360, 81 S.Ct. 1570, 1577, 6 L.Ed.2d 890, 898 (1961) (dictum).

194. See Thompkins v. Stuttgart School District No. 22, 787 F.2d 439 (8th Cir. 1986) (state statute creating a right and vesting exclusive jurisdiction in a specific state court cannot preclude a federal court from exercising pendent jurisdiction over state law claims based on the statute); Markham v. Newport News, 292 F.2d 711 (4th Cir.1961) (refuses to follow state rule limiting suits against municipalities to state courts established under state constitution); Baton Rouge Contracting Co. v. West Hatchie Drainage Dist., 279 F.Supp. 430 (N.D.Miss.1968) (rejects state rule that would limit suit against drainage district to state court); Linn County v. Hiawatha, 311 N.W.2d 95 (Iowa 1981) (state legislature cannot restrict review of zoning decisions to state courts). But cf. Yarber v. Allstate Ins. Co., 674 F.2d 232 (4th Cir.1982) (Virginia statute tolling limitations if a voluntary nonsuit is taken and the action is refiled in the same court within six months, does not apply if the suit is refiled in federal court after a nonsuit has been taken in state court); Zeidner v. Wulforst, 197 F.Supp. 23 (E.D.N.Y.1961) (obeys New York statute limiting suit against New York Throughway Authority to the New York Court of Claims).

195. See § 9.2A.

state. Unless the defendant's domicile has changed since the transaction in issue, a fundamental unfairness argument would be difficult for the plaintiff to maintain.

A state's forum-closing rule should be immune from attack under the Full Faith and Credit Clause unless the state's interest in the application of that rule is outweighed by the national need for a uniform result under the public act, record, or judicial proceeding of another state.[196] In the area of judgments, where the national full faith and credit policy is especially strong, local forum-closing rules will generally have to bow to permit enforcement of the judgment of a sister state.[197] It is only in exceptional circumstances, if any, that a state's rationally applicable forum-closing rule should have to yield to permit suit on a statutory or non-statutory cause of action arising under the law of another state and not reduced to judgment. *Hughes v. Fetter*[198] did hold that Wisconsin could not close its courts to a suit under the Illinois wrongful death act.[199] This holding was based on a finding that Wisconsin had no interest whatever to weigh in the balance against the need to give full faith and credit to the Illinois statute by providing a forum for the action. Wisconsin had no policy against wrongful death actions generally because suit could be brought there for a death caused in Wisconsin. Wisconsin had no valid forum non conveniens policy here applicable because all the parties were Wisconsin residents.

Even in *Hughes v. Fetter*, this conclusion is debatable. A rational forum non conveniens policy may be based not only upon foreign parties, but also upon foreign facts, the need for calling foreign witnesses, and the problems involved in applying foreign law. The rationale of *Hughes v. Fetter* should not be applicable to situations in which a state's forum-closing rule advances a policy of the state, and surely not if a state has such an interest in the matter that a judgment on the merits for the defendant would withstand constitutional attack, but the state elects instead to close its courts to the plaintiff.

§ 10.6C   State Forum–Closing Rules in Federal Interpleader Actions

Griffin v. McCoach[200] discusses the interplay between the Federal Interpleader Act[201] and the outcome-determinative *Erie* gloss. Colonel

---

196. See § 9.3A.

197. See Fauntleroy v. Lum, 210 U.S. 230, 28 S.Ct. 641, 52 L.Ed. 1039 (1908). But see Anglo–American Provision Co. v. Davis Provision Co. No. 1, 191 U.S. 373, 24 S.Ct. 92, 48 L.Ed. 225 (1903) (New York permitted to refuse forum for suit by one Illinois corporation against another Illinois corporation on an Illinois judgment). *Fauntleroy* distinguished *Anglo–American Provision* stating that the New York statute involved in that case denied jurisdiction to N.Y. courts but the Mississippi statute in *Fauntleroy* "seems to us only to lay down a rule of decision." *Fauntleroy*, 210 U.S. at 235, 28 S.Ct. 642.

198. 341 U.S. 609, 71 S.Ct. 980, 95 L.Ed. 1212 (1951).

199. Accord, First Nat'l Bank v. United Air Lines, 342 U.S. 396, 72 S.Ct. 421, 96 L.Ed. 441 (1952).

200. 313 U.S. 498, 61 S.Ct. 1023, 85 L.Ed. 1481 (1941).

201. 28 U.S.C. §§ 1335, 1397, 2361.

Robert D. Gordon, a citizen of Texas, interested several persons in Texas oil development and those persons formed a syndicate for this purpose. The syndicate advanced money to Gordon and paid premiums on an insurance policy on his life. Gordon promised to repay the syndicate, but no repayment was ever made. Because of financial reverses, the syndicate was dissolved and a new association formed for the sole purpose of paying premiums on the life insurance policy and receiving and distributing the proceeds among the members, one-eighth to Gordon's widow and seven-eighths to members of the syndicate or their assignees. The application for the insurance policy had been signed by Gordon in New York and accepted in New Jersey at the home office of the insurer; the policy had been delivered in New York. The final change of beneficiaries incorporating the agreement to divide the proceeds eight ways was effected by forms signed in Texas by Gordon and in New York by syndicate members, the insurer's endorsement on the policy in New Jersey, and return of the policy to the New York beneficiaries. Upon Gordon's death, his personal representatives sued the insurer on the policy in a federal district court in Texas. The insurer, acting under the Federal Interpleader Act, impleaded the other beneficiaries who claimed a seven-eighths share in the proceeds.

The Federal Interpleader Act permits a stakeholder, such as the insurer here, if there are two or more adverse claimants of diverse citizenship, to bring a bill of interpleader in any judicial district in which a claimant resides. Service of process under the act is nation-wide.

The district court distributed the proceeds of the policy, one-eighth to Gordon's widow and the remainder to the other beneficiaries, as indicated in the policy. The estate's representatives appealed, contending that under Texas law the claimants adverse to the widow did not have an insurable interest in Gordon's life. The Court of Appeals affirmed, holding that the policy and subsequent changes were governed by New York law, under which the policy's terms concerning distribution were enforceable. The Supreme Court reversed and remanded to the Court of Appeals for determination of Texas law. The implication was that the federal court should do whatever a Texas court would do under the same circumstances.

A Texas court, however, would probably never have a case under the same circumstances. It is unlikely that the insurer could file an effective bill of interpleader in a Texas state court because a Texas court would probably not have personal jurisdiction over nonresident claimants.[202] The case that might occur in a Texas state court would be a suit by the New York beneficiaries against Gordon's estate to recover seven-eighths of the policy proceeds. Even this is very unlikely, as the wisest course for the New York beneficiaries to follow would be to stay out of Texas and sue the insurer in New York.

Assuming, however, a suit in a Texas court involving the New York beneficiaries against the estate, there are two possible courses of action

---

202.   See New York Life Ins. Co. v. Dunlevy, 241 U.S. 518, 36 S.Ct. 613, 60 L.Ed. 1140 (1916).

for a Texas court to take in enforcing the Texas rule on insurable interest: (1) close the Texas forum to the suit and dismiss but not on the merits; (2) render a judgment on the merits for the estate. The federal court in the interpleader action would have no difficulty mirroring the Texas judgment on the merits for the estate, although such a result would raise grave questions that are discussed in the next section.

What, though, is the federal court to do in its interpleader action if the Texas courts would simply close their doors and not render a decision on the merits? One possibility is to deliver the proceeds to the representative of the estate, leaving the adverse claimants theoretically free to pursue the proceeds in the hands of the representative, but cutting off any claim that the New York beneficiaries might have had against the insurer. Though nominally not a decision on the merits, such a decision would, for all practical purposes, end the New York beneficiaries' chances of obtaining the proceeds, since a Texas state forum would be closed to them and their rights against the insurer would be terminated. This raises questions substantially identical with the propriety of the federal court, in an interpleader action, mirroring a Texas judgment on the merits. This is discussed in the next section. In fact, on remand, the Court of Appeals awarded the proceeds to Gordon's administrator, but it is not clear whether the New York beneficiaries would be free to pursue the proceeds in his hands, if they could find some way to do so.[203]

Another possibility, if the Texas rule is a forum-closing one, is to dismiss the bill of interpleader and return the funds to the stakeholder. This should not be the result. Federal interpleader is one circumstance under which the federal forum should not be closed in deference to a state forum-closing rule. Because of the nation-wide service of process available under the Federal Interpleader Act, upon dismissal, the stakeholder could simply bring suit again in another judicial district where a claimant resided, obtain in personam jurisdiction over all claimants, and enjoin pending[204] or future action against it in a state court. It should not be necessary to act out such a farce. In view of the futility of attempting to follow a state forum-closing rule by dismissing a bill of interpleader, the argument that the Federal Interpleader Act does "otherwise require or provide"[205] is particularly strong.

§ 10.7   Application of State Law on the Merits When the Federal Court Has Wider Jurisdiction Than a State Court

§ 10.7A   Interpleader Actions

Griffin v. McCoach also raises the question of whether a federal court, in an interpleader case, having nation-wide service of process,

---

203. Griffin v. McCoach, 123 F.2d 550 (5th Cir.1941), cert. denied, 316 U.S. 683, 62 S.Ct. 1270, 86 L.Ed. 1755 (1942).

204. See Holcomb v. Aetna Life Ins. Co., 255 F.2d 577 (10th Cir.1958), cert. denied sub nom. Fleming v. Aetna Life Ins. Co., 358 U.S. 879, 79 S.Ct. 118, 3 L.Ed.2d 110 (1958) (prior state court suit enjoinable).

205. 28 U.S.C. § 1652 (section 34 of the Judiciary Act of 1789).

should invariably apply the choice-of-law rules of the state in which it is sitting, if these rules produce a judgment on the merits. Commentators have urged that the federal court should not do so because this would make federal interpleader a device for interstate forum-shopping. The first claimant to sue could fix the forum and pick the law.[206]

This is not quite true. Only the stakeholder may bring a bill in federal interpleader.[207] The bill may be brought in any judicial district where a claimant resides.[208] The federal court within which the bill is brought has jurisdiction to enjoin claimants anywhere in the nation[209] from instituting or continuing[210] actions in state courts against the stakeholder. The stakeholder is required to deposit in the court the funds or property it is holding[211] to be divided among the claimants and will usually have no incentive for interstate forum-shopping, except, perhaps, on matters unrelated to the merits, such as whether the stakeholder may recover its attorneys' fees.[212]

Nevertheless, there remains compelling force to the argument that, in federal interpleader, the federal court should not be required to apply the choice-of-law rules of the state in which it is sitting. Although, theoretically, the stakeholder may sue anywhere a claimant resides, it is likely that the bill of interpleader will be filed as a reflex action in the judicial district in which the first claimant sues the stakeholder.[213] This is what happened in *Griffin v. McCoach*. Moreover, the power of nationwide service of process obligates the federal court to act as a neutral forum, not as the vassal of the state in which it is sitting.[214] Otherwise

---

206. See, e.g., Clark, *State Law in the Federal Courts: The Brooding Omnipresence of Erie v. Tompkins*, 55 Yale L. J. 267, 287 (1946); Harper, *Policy Bases of the Conflict of Laws: Reflections on Rereading Professor Lorenzen's Essays*, 56 Yale L. J. 1155, 1175 n.63 (1947).

207. 28 U.S.C. § 1335(a)(2).

208. 28 U.S.C. § 1397.

209. 28 U.S.C. § 2361.

210. See id.; Holcomb v. Aetna Life Ins. Co., 255 F.2d 577 (10th Cir.1958), cert. denied sub nom., Fleming v. Aetna Life Ins. Co., 358 U.S. 879, 79 S.Ct. 118, 3 L.Ed.2d 110 (1958) (prior state court suit enjoinable).

211. 28 U.S.C. § 1335(a)(2).

212. See Aetna Life Ins. Co. v. Johnson, 206 F.Supp. 63 (N.D.Ill.1962) (whether stakeholder entitled to attorneys' fees out of fund depends on local state law). Contra, Palomas Land & Cattle Co. v. Baldwin, 189 F.2d 936 (9th Cir.1951); Minnesota Mut. Life Ins. Co. v. Gustafson, 415 F.Supp. 615 (N.D.Ill.1976).

213. For an example of a case in which the interpleader action was not filed where the stakeholder was first sued, see Sanders v. Armour Fertilizer Works, 292 U.S. 190, 54 S.Ct. 677, 78 L.Ed. 1206 (1934).

214. See ALI Study of the Division of Jurisdiction Between State and Federal Courts 45–46 (O.D.1965) [hereinafter cited as ALI Study] (recommending that 28 U.S.C. § 2361 be amended so that when state law supplies the rule of decision, the district court may make its own determination as to which state rule is applicable); Study of the Division of Jurisdiction Between State and Federal Courts 211–12, 402–03 (1969) (disapproving of *Griffin*); Freund, supra note 132, at 1211. For the expression of this idea in a pre-*Erie* case, see Sanders v. Armour Fertilizer Works, 292 U.S. 190, 200, 54 S.Ct. 677, 680, 78 L.Ed. 1206, 1210 (1934): "The purpose of the interpleader statute was to give the stakeholder protection, but in no wise to change the rights of the claimants by its operation.... The decision should be the same whether the interpleader is filed in Illinois or in Texas."

the policies of that state might prevail over claimants who, but for the nation-wide service, could never have been subjected to those policies. Moreover, if federal interpleader is available, it is unlikely that the requisite personal jurisdiction exists over conflicting claimants so that an interpleader action could be brought in a state court.[215] Indeed, this is the reason we have federal interpleader. Therefore, it is false and misleading, in this context, to talk of the danger of intrastate forum-shopping if the federal court refuses to apply the conflicts rules of the state in which it is sitting.

It is not suggested that in federal interpleader the federal court ignore the conflicts rules of the state in which it is sitting, but merely that the court be free to depart from those rules. The federal court should act as a responsible neutral forum. A neutral forum should not apply its own choice-of-law rule if that rule differs from the rule in all states that have contacts with the parties and with the event and all contact states would reach an identical result. The federal court should also scrutinize the conflicts rules of the states involved for clues to the policies underlying conflicting domestic laws.

If the federal court decides that it should apply its own conflicts rule, *Griffin v. McCoach* provides a compelling circumstance for resolving any conflict against local law. The Texas insurable interest rule was anachronistic and "unique."[216]

§ 10.7B   Federal Rule 4(k)

If, when the action is brought by a usually neutral stakeholder, a federal court, whose process runs beyond that of local state courts, should not be required to apply the conflicts rules of the state in which it is sitting, this is true a fortiori when extra-state federal process is available to parties contending on the merits and this federal process provides jurisdiction over parties that state process would not reach.[217] Under conditions of such extended federal process, the danger of inter-state forum-shopping is dramatically increased.[218]

This danger of interstate forum-shopping has been created to a limited extent by a change in Rule 4 of the Federal Rules of Civil Procedure that became effective on July 1, 1963. As subsequently amended, it reads, in part, as follows:

4(k) Territorial Limits of Effective Service.

---

215. See New York Life Ins. Co. v. Dunlevy, 241 U.S. 518, 36 S.Ct. 613, 60 L.Ed. 1140 (1916).

216. See Clark, supra note 206, at 287.

217. See Sprow v. Hartford Ins. Co., 594 F.2d 412 (5th Cir.1979) (personal jurisdiction exists under Rule 4(f) if defendant's contacts are with the bulge area outside of the state in which the court sits).

In diversity cases, a federal court's jurisdiction is, absent special federal jurisdictional provisions such as interpleader or Rule 4(f), dependent on long-arm statutes of the state in which it sits. See § 4.7, note 142.

218. See Freund, supra note 132, at 1211–12; Vestal, *Erie R.R. v. Tompkins: A Projection*, 48 Iowa L. Rev. 248, 269 (1963).

(1) *In General.* Serving a summons or filing a waiver of service establishes personal jurisdiction over a defendant:.... (B) who is a party joined under Rule 14 [brought in by defendant as third-party defendants] or Rule 19 [persons who ought to be parties to avoid prejudice to themselves or if complete relief is to be accorded between those already parties] and is served within a judicial district of the United States and not more than 100 miles from the place from where the summons was issued....[219]

Although there is a limit of 100 miles on the out-of-state service under this rule, Professor Vestal has pointed out that in many of our multi-state metropolitan areas "the federal court will be able to reach vast population centers outside the state in which the court is sitting."[220] When 4(k) takes the federal court beyond the reach of state process, the federal court should act as a responsible neutral forum in choosing governing state law.[221]

§ 10.7C   Section 1404(a) Transfers

A somewhat similar danger of subjecting a party to the law of a state the party might not otherwise have been subjected to is presented by section 1404(a) of the Judicial Code: "For the convenience of parties and witnesses, in the interest of justice, a district court may transfer any civil action to any other district or division where it might have been brought."[222] But what conflicts rules apply—those of the state from which the action is transferred, those of the state to which it is transferred, or those fashioned by the federal courts?

Before *Van Dusen v. Barrack,*[223] the few federal cases in point had decided in favor of the law of the state from which transfer is made, at least so far as the applicable statute of limitations was concerned.[224] *H.L. Green Co. v. MacMahon*[225] reached this same result for the law applicable generally to claims that could have been brought by the plaintiff in the transferor state. The ALI study referred to above recommends codifying this result in the Judicial Code on the ground that, "[s]o long as *Klaxon* stands (and the Reporters remain of the opinion that it should stand), an independent federal choice-of-law rule applicable in transfer

---

219. Fed.R.Civ.P. 4(k). See Quinones v. Pennsylvania General Ins. Co., 804 F.2d 1167 (10th Cir.1986) (rule 4(f)'s (now 4k's) extension of personal jurisdiction does not violate due process).

220. Vestal, *Expanding the Jurisdictional Reach of the Federal Courts: The 1963 Changes in Federal Rule 4*, 38 N.Y.U. L. Rev. 1053, 1065 (1963).

221. See supra, text accompanying notes 215–216.

222. 28 U.S.C. § 1404(a). Cf. 28 U.S.C. § 1407(a) (transfer for consolidated pretrial proceedings of multidistrict litigation).

223. 376 U.S. 612, 84 S.Ct. 805, 11 L.Ed.2d 945 (1964).

224. H.L. Green Co. v. MacMahon, 312 F.2d 650 (2d Cir.1962), cert. denied, 372 U.S. 928, 83 S.Ct. 876, 9 L.Ed.2d 736 (1963); Headrick v. Atchison, T. & S.F. Ry., 182 F.2d 305 (10th Cir.1950); Gomez v. The S.S. Dorothy, 183 F.Supp. 499 (D.Puerto Rico 1959); Hargrove v. Louisville & Nashville R.R. Co., 153 F.Supp. 681 (W.D.Ky.1957).

225. 312 F.2d 650 (2d Cir.1962), cert. denied, 372 U.S. 928, 83 S.Ct. 876, 9 L.Ed.2d 736 (1963). But cf. Goranson v. Kloeb, 308 F.2d 655, 656–657 (6th Cir.1962) (dictum) (law of transferee state).

cases only seems logically impossible to justify."[226] Furthermore, "[t]he effect is to give the plaintiff the benefit which traditionally he has had in the selection of a forum with favorable choice-of-law rules."[227]

There are several answers that might be made to this argument. First of all, the plaintiff is not "traditionally" entitled to select an inconvenient forum. But for the flexibility that 1404(a) provides when the plaintiff has selected an inconvenient forum, the remedy would be dismissal of the complaint and with it the plaintiff's advantage in being able to select the law with the forum. Because transfer under section 1404(a) is made for "the convenience of parties and witnesses, in the interest of justice," the state to which transfer is made is likely to have far closer connections with the parties and the transaction in controversy and the probabilities are that its law will be more appropriate for application. From this standpoint, it would seem preferable to apply the law of the state to which transfer is made, including its conflicts rules.[228] Such a result, however, might turn defendant's motion for transfer under 1404(a) into a device for interstate forum-shopping of the kind condemned above. In view of all this, it may be that the best solution in cases transferred on the motion of the defendant, when a court of the state in which the transferor federal court is sitting would have dismissed the action on the ground of *forum non conveniens*, is to permit the federal courts to act as responsible neutral forums[229] in determining which state law is most appropriately applicable to the case at bar.

This suggestion is not necessarily inconsistent with *Van Dusen v. Barrack*.[230] In *Van Dusen*, an airplane, destined for Philadelphia, had crashed into Boston Harbor on takeoff. The plaintiffs, Pennsylvania fiduciaries representing the estates of Pennsylvania decedents, brought suit against the airline and others in the United States District Court for the Eastern District of Pennsylvania. The defendants moved under section 1404(a) to transfer the case to the Massachusetts District Court alleging that most of the witnesses resided in that district and that over one hundred other actions were pending there.[231] The District Court granted this transfer motion, holding it immaterial whether Pennsylvania or Massachusetts conflicts and domestic rules would govern the action after transfer. The Court of Appeals held that the order of

---

226. ALI Study, supra note 214, at 97.

227. Id. at 96.

228. See Braucher, *The Inconvenient Federal Forum*, 60 Harv. L. Rev. 908, 937 (1947); Freund, supra note 132, at 1211; Note, *Choice of Law in Federal Court after Transfer of Venue*, 63 Cornell L. Rev. 149, 163 (1977).

229. See supra text accompanying notes 215–216. Another factor that should limit the transferee federal court's freedom to apply its own conflicts rules is if the state courts in the transferee state are the only courts in which the plaintiff could get jurisdiction over the defendant and which would not have dismissed. Under these circumstances, the law that should be applied is that of the transferee state.

230. 376 U.S. 612, 84 S.Ct. 805, 11 L.Ed.2d 945 (1964).

231. The plaintiffs thought it likely that the defendants' "ultimate reason for seeking transfer is to move to a forum where recoveries for wrongful death are restricted to sharply limited punitive damages rather than compensation for the loss suffered." Id. at 626, 84 S.Ct. at 814, 11 L.Ed.2d at 955.

transfer should be vacated because the plaintiff fiduciaries had not qualified to sue in Massachusetts and therefore Massachusetts was not a district where the suit "might have been brought" within the meaning of 1404(a). The Supreme Court reversed and remanded holding that 1404(a) did permit transfer to the Massachusetts district[232] but that if transfer were granted, the transferee court should look to the law, including the conflicts law, of Pennsylvania as the situs of the transferor court. On remand, the District Court was to decide whether the fact that the law of the transferor state would be applied made the transfer inappropriate.[233] In holding that the law of the transferor state applied, the Court found that, under *Erie*, "the critical identity to be maintained is between the federal district court which decides the case and the courts of the State in which the action was filed."[234] In his majority opinion,[235] however, Justice Goldberg specifically left open the question of whether the same result would follow if a state court in the transferor

---

232. "[T]he words 'where it might have been brought' must be construed with reference to the federal laws delimiting the districts in which such an action 'may be brought' and not with reference to laws of the transferee State concerning the capacity of fiduciaries to bring suit." Id. at 624, 84 S.Ct. at 813, 11 L.Ed.2d at 954.

233. On remand the motion to transfer was denied on the grounds that the plaintiffs were Pennsylvania residents, Pennsylvania compensatory damages witnesses would provide much of the testimony, and the controlling conflicts law would be that of Pennsylvania. Popkin v. Eastern Air Lines, Inc., 253 F.Supp. 244 (E.D.Pa.1966).

That the crash was on navigable waters would not, under an admiralty choice-of-law rule, require application of Massachusetts law. See Scott v. Eastern Air Lines, Inc., 399 F.2d 14 (3d Cir.1967), cert. denied, 393 U.S. 979, 89 S.Ct. 446, 21 L.Ed.2d 439 (1968). For creation of an admiralty action for wrongful death resulting from violation of maritime duties, see Moragne v. States Marine Lines, Inc., 398 U.S. 375, 90 S.Ct. 1772, 26 L.Ed.2d 339 (1970).

See also Calhoun v. Yamaha Motor Corp., 216 F.3d 338 (3d Cir. 2000), cert. denied, 531 U.S. 1037, 121 S.Ct. 627, 148 L.Ed.2d 536 (2000). A jet ski accident killed a Pennsylvania child in Puerto Rican waters. After remand by Yamaha Motor Corp. v. Calhoun, 516 U.S. 199, 116 S.Ct. 619, 133 L.Ed.2d 578 (1996), which held that state remedies remain applicable in wrongful death and survival actions arising from injuries in territorial waters to persons who are not seamen, the Third Circuit held that Pennsylvania law determined compensatory damages, Puerto Rican law punitive damages, and federal maritime law determined liability.

234. *Van Dusen*, 376 U.S. at 639, 84 S.Ct. at 820, 821, 11 L.Ed.2d at 962. Cf. In re Air Crash Disaster Near Hanover, N.H., 314 F.Supp. 62 (Jud.Pan.Mult.Lit.1970) (must also apply law of transferor state in 1407(a) transfer). But cf. In re Methyl Tertiary Butyl Ether Products Liability Litigation, 2005 WL 106936 (S.D. N.Y. 2005), which applies the law of its transferee circuit to determine constitutional limits on personal jurisdiction and holds that application of the law of the transferee circuit to cases transferred under 28 U.S.C. § 1407 for consolidated pre-trial proceedings is not precluded by Lexecon v. Milberg Weiss Bershad Hynes & Lerach, 523 U.S. 26, 118 S.Ct. 956, 140 L.Ed.2d 62 (1998). *Lexecon* held that after conclusion of pre-trial proceedings in cases transferred under 28 U.S.C. § 1407 the transferee court cannot transfer the cases to itself for trial under 28 U.S.C. § 1404 but must remand the cases to the district courts from which they were transferred. But cf. also Marcus, *Conflicts Among Circuits and Transfers Within the Federal Judicial System*, 93 Yale L. J. 677, 678–79 (1984) (if federal circuits differ on a question of federal law, when a federal claim is transferred, the transferee court should apply the interpretation of the circuit to which it is transferred); Ragazzo, *Transfer and Choice of Federal Law: The Appellate Model*, 93 Mich. L. Rev. 703, 706 (1995) ("transferee federal law should apply after permanent but not [multi-district litigation] transfers").

235. Justice Black concurred in the reversal but believed that the Court should hold that it was error to order these actions transferred. *Van Dusen*, 376 U.S. at 646, 84 S.Ct. at 824, 11 L.Ed.2d at 967.

state "would simply have dismissed the action on the ground of *forum non conveniens.*"[236]

A bizarre consequence of *Van Dusen* is that when actions based on the same event are brought in different states, but then are consolidated in the same federal district, claimants residing in the same state may have different laws applied to them depending on the state in which their case was filed.[237]

The clearest case for freeing the transferee court from the choice-of-law rules of the transferor state is one in which the transferor court did not have jurisdiction over the defendant or over the subject matter. 28 U.S.C. § 1631 accomplishes this by providing:

> Whenever a civil action is filed in a court as defined in section 610[238] of this title or an appeal, including a petition for review of administrative action, is noticed for or filed with such a court and that court finds that there is a want of jurisdiction, the court shall, if it is in the interest of justice, transfer such action or appeal to any other such court in which the action or appeal could have been brought at the time it was filed or noticed, and the action or appeal shall proceed as if it had been filed in or noticed for the court to which it is transferred on the date upon which it was actually filed in or noticed for the court from which it is transferred.

There is a split of authority as to whether 1631 applies only to lack of subject matter, but even courts that limit 1631 to subject matter jurisdiction agree that in a case transferred for lack of personal jurisdiction the law of the transferee state applies.[239]

---

236. Id. at 640, 84 S.Ct. at 821, 11 L.Ed.2d at 963. See Note, 53 Va. L. Rev. 380 (1967). But see In re Air Crash Disaster at Boston, 399 F.Supp. 1106 (D.Mass.1975) (apply law of transferor state even though courts of that state would have dismissed under doctrine of forum non conveniens); D. Currie, *The Federal Courts and the American Law Institute*, Part II, 36 U. Chi. L. Rev. 268, 310 (1969): "*Klaxon* policy tells us that the critical question should be whether the case could have been brought in the courts of the transferor state."

The Court also left open the question of whether the law of the transferor state would apply "if a plaintiff sought transfer under § 1404(a)...." Id. Ferens v. John Deere Co., 494 U.S. 516, 110 S.Ct. 1274, 108 L.Ed.2d 443 (1990), held that the law of the transferor state applies when the plaintiff moves for transfer.

237. Cf. In re Air Crash Disaster at Boston, Mass. on July 31, 1973, 399 F.Supp. 1106 (D.Mass. 1975) (when suits consolidated in Massachusetts federal court under 28 U.S.C. 1407, wrongful death suits for New Hampshire victims first filed in New Hampshire are not subject to Massachusetts limit on recovery, but suits for New Hampshire victims first filed in Massachusetts are subject to the Massachusetts limit); Amer.L.Inst., Complex Litigation: Statutory Recommendations and Analysis §§ 6.01–6.03 (1994) (choice-of-law rules for federal courts when multi-district cases consolidated); Miller & Crump, *Jurisdiction and Choice of Law in Multistate Class Actions After Phillips Petroleum Co. v. Shutts*, 90 Yale L. J. 1, 78 (1986) (federal legislation should provide for "multiparty, multistate federal jurisdiction" and also determine choice of law in such cases).

238. 28 U.S.C. § 610: "Courts defined

"As used in this chapter the word 'courts' includes the courts of appeals and district courts of the United States, the United States District Court for the District of the Canal Zone, the District Court of Guam, the District Court of the Virgin Islands, the United States Court of Federal Claims, and the Court of International Trade."

239. See Johnson v. Woodcock, 444 F.3d 953, 954 n.2 (8th Cir. 2006), cert. denied, 549 U.S. 883, 127 S.Ct. 217, 166 L.Ed.2d 145 (2006) (affirm dismissal for lack of personal

Courts agree that after transfer of a case for improper venue under 28 U.S.C § 1406(a) the statute of limitations of the transferee state applies. There is a split of authority as to whether the date of filing is that in the original forum or is the date of transfer.[240]

§ 10.7D Pendent Jurisdiction

Pendent jurisdiction is another area in which there is danger of interstate forum-shopping because of the extended reach of federal process. Under the doctrine of pendent jurisdiction, a federal court exercising federal question jurisdiction may, when the federal question averred is not plainly wanting in substance, even though the federal ground for relief is not established, retain jurisdiction and dispose of the case upon a non-federal ground that has also been pleaded.[241] In disposing of the non-federal ground on the merits, the federal court must comply with the requirements of the *Erie* doctrine.[242] Under a number of federal statutes that may result in federal claims with pendent state claims, service of process may run across state lines to reach where state process could not reach.[243] There is a split of authority over whether extra-territorial service under such federal statutes confers in personam jurisdiction as to "pendent" non-federal claims.[244]

---

jurisdiction "even though the court was empowered by 28 U.S.C. § 1631 to transfer the action to another court"); SongByrd, Inc. v. Estate of Grossman, 206 F.3d 172 (2d Cir. 2000) (after transfer for lack of personal jurisdiction, law of transferee state applies); Ross v. Colorado Outward Bound School, Inc., 822 F.2d 1524 (10th Cir. 1987) (§ 1631 makes *Van Dusen* inapplicable to cases transferred for lack of personal jurisdiction); cf. Eggleton v. Plasser & Theurer Export Von Bahnbaumaschinen Gesellschaft, MBH, 495 F.3d 582 (8th Cir. 2007) (after transfer under 28 U.S.C § 1406(a) for lack of personal jurisdiction, statute of limitations of transferee state applies); Levy v. Pyramid Co. of Ithaca, 687 F.Supp. 48, 51 (N.D.N.Y.1988), aff'd, 871 F.2d 9 (2d Cir. 1989) (§ 1631 applies to lack of subject matter, not personal, jurisdiction, but though transfer for lack of personal jurisdiction is under §§ 1404 or 1406, the law of the transferee state applies).

For cases decided before 1631 was enacted and applying the law of the transferee state after transfer for lack of personal jurisdiction, see Nelson v. International Paint Co., 716 F.2d 640 (9th Cir.1983); Ellis v. Great Southwestern Corp., 646 F.2d 1099 (5th Cir.1981); cf. LaVay Corporation v. Dominion Federal Sav. & Loan Ass'n, 830 F.2d 522 (4th Cir.1987), cert. denied, 484 U.S. 1065, 108 S.Ct. 1027, 98 L.Ed.2d 991 (1988) (federal question jurisdiction—apply law of transferee state after 1406(a) transfer for improper venue); Martin v. Stokes, 623 F.2d 469 (6th Cir.1980) (if no jurisdiction, transfer is proper only under 1406(a) and the law of the transferee state should be applied).

240. See Lafferty v. St. Riel, 495 F.3d 72, 80–81 (3d Cir. 2007) (applying date of original filing, but noting split of authority).

Goldlawr, Inc. v. Heiman, 369 U.S. 463, 82 S.Ct. 913, 8 L.Ed.2d 39 (1962), held that a court may transfer under § 1406 even if it does not have personal jurisdiction over the defendant.

241. Hurn v. Oursler, 289 U.S. 238, 53 S.Ct. 586, 77 L.Ed. 1148 (1933).

242. United Mine Workers of America v. Gibbs, 383 U.S. 715, 726, 86 S.Ct. 1130, 1139, 16 L.Ed.2d 218, 228 (1966); Systems Operations, Inc. v. Scientific Games Development Corp., 555 F.2d 1131 (3d Cir.1977) (*Klaxon* applicable); Mintz v. Allen, 254 F.Supp. 1012 (S.D.N.Y.1966).

243. See, e.g., Securities Exchange Act of 1934, 15 U.S.C. § 78aa; Public Utility Holding Co. Act of 1935, 15 U.S.C. § 79y; Investment Co. Act, 15 U.S.C. § 80a–43.

244. Yes: Schwartz v. Eaton, 264 F.2d 195 (2d Cir.1959) (dictum); Emerson v. Falcon Mfg., Inc., 333 F.Supp. 888 (S.D.Tex.1971) (in accordance with "the preponderance of the modern authority"); Cooper v. North Jersey Trust Co., 226 F.Supp. 972 (S.D.N.Y.1964);

If federal extra-territorial service does confer in personam jurisdiction as to pendent non-federal claims in a forum where, but for such federal service, jurisdiction over the defendant could not have been acquired, the federal court should not automatically apply the conflicts rules of the state in which it is sitting, but should act as a responsible neutral forum[245] and decide for itself which state law is applicable to the non-federal claims.[246]

§ 10.8   The Proper Scope of Klaxon

What is needed now is not major surgery, not an overruling of *Erie* or even of *Klaxon*, if, in regard to *Klaxon*, one puts aside the suggestion that application of Delaware law to affect the result on the merits, although under a "procedural" label, should be a violation of due process. It is desirable that advantage be taken of the "countervailing considerations" concept articulated in *Byrd* to avoid blind adherence to the outcome-determinative test when the harm caused thereby far exceeds any ill effects stemming from state and federal courts sitting in the same state reaching different results . The following stand out as the situations in which, when jurisdiction in personam over a party is available in a federal court and not available in a state court in the state where the federal court is sitting, a federal district court should not be required to follow state conflicts rules: cases under the Federal Interpleader Act; cases in which a party utilizes federal process beyond the boundaries of the forum state under Rule 4(k) of the Federal Rules of Civil Procedure; actions transferred on motion of the defendant under 28 U.S.C. § 1404(a) when a state court in the transferor state would have dismissed on the basis of *forum non conveniens*; actions transferred by a federal district court that does not have jurisdiction over the defendant, or over the subject matter, or for improper venue; decision of non-federal claims under the doctrine of pendent jurisdiction.

These and other problems flowing from *Klaxon* are eliminated to the extent to which state courts are made to conform to a federal conflicts rule. There are several devices available for requiring such conformity.

First, there might be an expansion of constitutional limitations on a state's choice of law. It would be undesirable, in the present state of development of conflicts rules, to limit a state's application of its own law to advance its own legitimate interests, except when this would result in fundamental unfairness to one of the litigants, or in those few instances when the state's legitimate interests are overshadowed by the need for a nationally uniform result under the public act, record, or

---

Townsend Corp. of America v. Davidson, 222 F.Supp. 1 (D.N.J.1963). No: Trussell v. United Underwriters, Ltd., 236 F.Supp. 801 (D.Colo.1964); International Ladies' Garment Workers' Union v. Shields & Co., 209 F.Supp. 145 (S.D.N.Y.1962). See ALI Study of the Division of Jurisdiction between State and Federal Courts 86, 87 (Tent.Draft #4, 1966) (permitting jurisdiction over non-federal claims).

245. See supra text accompanying notes 215–216.

246. See D. Currie, supra note 236, at 284; Note, *Pendent Jurisdiction*, 51 Iowa L. Rev. 151 (1965); ALI Study of the Division of Jurisdiction between State and Federal Courts 120 (Tent.Draft #6, 1968).

judicial proceeding of a sister state. An example of this latter proposition is compelling a forum state to enforce a judgment of a sister state although a contrary judgment might constitutionally have been obtained at the forum. There is room, though, for making it clearer that a state that does not have sufficient contact with the parties or with the transaction to have a legitimate interest in affecting the result on the merits may not do so under the guise of applying its "procedure." Ironically, *Klaxon* itself might be the first to fall under such a modest expansion of due process standards. Further, the time is ripe for cautious use of the "equal protection" clause of the Fourteenth Amendment to eliminate some of the irrational classifications that still pervade conflicts dogma.[247]

Beyond this, state conformity to federal conflicts rules must await the day, should it ever come, when objective, informed and intelligent appraisal of the situation leads to the conclusion that an overwhelming need for a nationally uniform conflicts doctrine requires that choice of law in interstate transactions is federal law. Even now, as good a case can be made for federal standards for choice of law as for a ship-owner's liability to one not a member of the crew who, while calling on a seaman friend, trips on a boat docked in New York harbor.[248] Perhaps competition from "common markets" abroad will cause this day to arrive or will hasten its arrival.[249] But if and when such a day should come, it would be well to arrange the relevant statutory and decisional framework so that this "federal question" does not provide an independent basis for federal jurisdiction,[250] just as today a claim that a state's conflicts rule is unconstitutional does not provide such a basis. Federal courts would be flooded by such a "federal question" cloudburst.

§ 10.9   Does Federal Law Displace State Law?

Even more basic than the *Erie* problem is whether a particular issue not expressly covered by federal legislation is governed by a federal rule

---

247. Extension of constitutional limits on choice of law may be less likely in the light of Allstate Ins. Co. v. Hague, 449 U.S. 302, 101 S.Ct. 633, 66 L.Ed.2d 521 (1981), discussed in § 9.2A.

248. See Kermarec v. Compagnie Generale Transatlantique, 358 U.S. 625, 79 S.Ct. 406, 3 L.Ed.2d 550 (1959); cf. Stolz, *Pleasure Boating and Admiralty: Erie at Sea*, 51 Calif. L. Rev. 661, 663, 665 (1963) (no federal interest apparent in personal injury cases arising from pleasure boating); ALI Study of the Division of Jurisdiction Between State and Federal Courts § 1316(a) at 19 (Tent.Draft #6, 1968): "Unless otherwise provided by Act of Congress, the admiralty and maritime jurisdiction does not include a claim merely because it arose on navigable waters."

249. Cf. Hancher, *The Commerce Clause and A Common Market*, 8 S.D. L. Rev. 1, 2, 22 (1963).

250. Cf. Romero v. International Terminal Operating Co., 358 U.S. 354, 79 S.Ct. 468, 3 L.Ed.2d 368 (1959) (admiralty not an independent basis for jurisdiction on the law side of a federal court); Robert Lawrence Co. v. Devonshire Fabrics, Inc., 271 F.2d 402, 408 (2d Cir.1959), cert. granted, 362 U.S. 909, 80 S.Ct. 682, 4 L.Ed.2d 618 (1960), writ of cert. dism'd, 364 U.S. 801, 81 S.Ct. 27, 5 L.Ed.2d 37 (1960) (suits involving application of the federal Arbitration Act do not furnish an independent basis for federal jurisdiction); Boner, *Erie v. Tompkins: A Study in Judicial Precedent*, 40 Texas L. Rev. 509, 520 (1962) ("laws of the United States" include only statutes).

that is applicable in all courts, state and federal. To suggest that, in a federal court, the answer to this question turns on whether the basis for federal jurisdiction is diversity of citizenship, in which event state law will apply to all issues, otherwise not, is to suggest a rule of thumb that is so simplistic that it clearly does not adequately describe the results of decided cases, much less provide a desirable guide for future developments. Whether state law or federal law should govern turns on the much more complex determination of whether the "federal interest" in achieving a uniform national result under a federal rule is so great that the issue should be controlled by "federal common law."[251]

In *Kamen v. KemperFinancial Services, Inc.*,[252] a shareholder in a mutual fund brought a derivative action on behalf of the fund against an investment adviser for allegedly issuing a materially misleading proxy statement in violation of the federal Invest Company Act. There was an issue as to whether a uniform federal rule or the law of the state of incorporation of the fund governed the necessity of a pre-complaint demand of the fund's board of director to bring the suit. The Supreme Court held that state law applied and stated this standard for choosing between state and federal law:

> [W]here a gap in the federal securities laws must be bridged by a rule that bears on the allocation of governing powers within the corporation, federal courts should incorporate state law into federal common law unless the particular state law in question is inconsistent with the policies underlying the federal statute. The scope of the demand requirement under state law clearly regulates the allocation of corporate governing powers between the directors and individual shareholders. Because a futility exception to demand does not impede the regulatory objectives of the ICA, a court that is entertaining a derivative action under that statute must apply the demand futility exception as it is defined by the law of the State of incorporation. The Court of Appeals thus erred by fashioning a uniform federal common law rule abolishing the futility exception in derivative actions founded on the ICA.[253]

Bank of America National Trust & Savings Association v. Parnell[254] illustrates the inadequacy of a diversity test to determine whether state or federal law applies. The plaintiff, Bank of America National Trust & Savings Association, on the basis of diversity jurisdiction, brought suit in

---

251. See Ivy Broadcasting Co. v. American Tel. & Tel. Co., 391 F.2d 486, 490 (2d Cir.1968) (holding that, in the absence of diversity of citizenship, a federal court has jurisdiction over a claim for negligence and breach of contract in the rendition of interstate telephone service): "In the absence of any statutory provisions relating to a carrier's liability for negligence or breach of contract, the courts must determine whether these questions should be left to state law or whether the federal interest in the result of such cases is so great that they should be controlled by federal common law." See also Weinberg, *Federal Common Law*, 83 Nw. U. L. Rev. 805 (1989); Note, *The Federal Common Law*, 82 Harv. L. Rev. 1512 (1969) (urging a presumption in favor of the application of state law).

252. 500 U.S. 90, 111 S.Ct. 1711, 114 L.Ed.2d 152 (1991).

253. Id. at 108–09, 111 S.Ct. at 1722–23.

254. 352 U.S. 29, 77 S.Ct. 119, 1 L.Ed.2d 93 (1956).

the Federal District Court for the Western District of Pennsylvania to recover for the conversion of bearer bonds of the Home Owners' Loan Corporation, payment of which was guaranteed by the United States. The bonds were due to mature in 1952, but were called for redemption in 1944. The bonds disappeared from plaintiff's possession while it was preparing to present them to the Federal Reserve Bank for payment. The bonds turned up in 1948 when Parnell, acting for one Rocco, presented them to a Pennsylvania bank. The bank collected the proceeds and paid them to Parnell who subtracted his fee and remitted the rest to Rocco. The principal issue at trial was whether the Pennsylvania bank and Parnell had taken the bonds in good faith, without knowledge or notice of the defect in title. The District Court, thinking Pennsylvania law applicable, charged that the defendants had the burden of proving good faith. The Court of Appeals reversed, holding federal law controlled and that under federal law plaintiff had the burden of showing defendants' notice and lack of good faith.

The Supreme Court reversed, holding that the District Court was correct in finding that Pennsylvania law applied, and remanded to the Court of Appeals to decide what the state law on burden of proof was. The Supreme Court found that the Court of Appeals had erred in relying on *Clearfield Trust Co. v. United States*[255] as indicating that federal law controlled the burden-of-proof issue in *Parnell*. *Clearfield* involved a check drawn on the Treasurer of the United States to the order of an employee of the Federal Works Progress Administration. The check was stolen and cashed by forged endorsement, Clearfield Trust Company acting as agent for collection. The United States delayed several months before informing the bank that the endorsement had been forged and demanding reimbursement. In the suit for reimbursement, the Supreme Court held that because a uniform rule was desirable to govern commercial paper issued by the United States, federal, not state law, applied. Under the federal rule articulated by the Court, mere delay in giving notice of the forgery, without a showing that the delay had caused harm, did not prevent recovery by the United States.

In *Parnell*, the Court distinguished *Clearfield*:

> The present litigation is purely between private parties and does not touch the rights and duties of the United States. The only possible interest of the United States in a situation like the one here, exclusively involving the transfer of Government paper between private persons, is that the floating of securities of the United States might somehow or other be adversely affected by the local rule of a particular State regarding the liability of a converter. This is far too speculative, far too remote a possibility to justify the application of federal law to transactions essentially of local concern.[256]

But even in *Parnell*, some issues were governed by a federal rule:

---

255.   318 U.S. 363, 63 S.Ct. 573, 87 L.Ed. 838 (1943).

256.   *Parnell*, 352 U.S. at 33–34, 77 S.Ct. at 121–122, 1 L.Ed.2d at 96–97.

Federal law of course governs the interpretation of the nature of the rights and obligations created by the Government bonds themselves. A decision with respect to the "overdueness" of the bonds is therefore a matter of federal law, which, in view of our holding, we need not elucidate.[257]

Thus in the same case, in which federal jurisdiction had been invoked on the basis of diversity of citizenship, some issues were held governed by state law and some were of sufficient federal concern, even though the United States was not a party, to be governed by federal law.[258]

---

257. Id. at 34, 77 S.Ct. at 122, 1 L.Ed.2d at 97.

258. Examples of application of state law notwithstanding a contention that federal law should control: CTS Corp. v. Dynamics Corp. of Amer., 481 U.S. 69, 107 S.Ct. 1637, 95 L.Ed.2d 67 (1987) (Indiana legislation governing attempts to take over certain Indiana corporations is not preempted by the federal Williams Act and does not violate the Commerce Clause); Board of Regents v. Tomanio, 446 U.S. 478, 100 S.Ct. 1790, 64 L.Ed.2d 440 (1980) (in action under 42 U.S.C. § 1983, state tolling rule applies as well as state statute of limitations); Miree v. DeKalb County, 433 U.S. 25, 97 S.Ct. 2490, 53 L.Ed.2d 557 (1977) (right to sue as third party beneficiary of contract between county and Federal Aviation Administration); Merrill Lynch, Pierce, Fenner & Smith, Inc. v. Ware, 414 U.S. 117, 94 S.Ct. 383, 38 L.Ed.2d 348 (1973) (validity of arbitration agreement drafted under New York Stock Exchange rule); Crane v. Cedar Rapids & I.C. Ry., 395 U.S. 164, 89 S.Ct. 1706, 23 L.Ed.2d 176 (1969) (whether contributory negligence a defense when nonemployee sues railroad for injury resulting from violation of Federal Safety Appliance Act); United States v. Yazell, 382 U.S. 341, 86 S.Ct. 500, 15 L.Ed.2d 404 (1966) (state law incapacitating wife applies to prevent recovery against the wife in an action by the United States on a note that husband and wife had executed to obtain a loan from the Small Business Administration); Wallis v. Pan American Petroleum Corp., 384 U.S. 63, 86 S.Ct. 1301, 16 L.Ed.2d 369 (1966) (conflicting private claims to federal oil lands leased under Mineral Leasing Act of 1920, "no significant threat to any identifiable federal policy" if state law applied); Commissioner v. Stern, 357 U.S. 39, 78 S.Ct. 1047, 2 L.Ed.2d 1126 (1958) (recovery of estate's tax deficiencies from beneficiary of life insurance policy depends upon law of decedent's domicile); Helvering v. Fuller, 310 U.S. 69, 60 S.Ct. 784, 84 L.Ed. 1082 (1940) (whether husband taxable on income from alimony trust depends on whether, under appropriate state law, the husband can be compelled to make additional payments in the future); Bell v. Tug Shrike, 332 F.2d 330 (4th Cir.1964), cert. denied, 379 U.S. 844, 85 S.Ct. 84, 13 L.Ed.2d 49 (whether woman "surviving widow" under Jones Act).

Cf. United States v. Kimbell Foods, Inc., 440 U.S. 715, 99 S.Ct. 1448, 59 L.Ed.2d 711 (1979) (although the priority of liens resulting from federal lending programs is determined under federal law, that law incorporates state law and customary commercial practices); Oil, Chemical and Atomic Workers Int'l Union v. Mobil Oil Corp., 426 U.S. 407, 96 S.Ct. 2140, 48 L.Ed.2d 736 (1976) (although states may enact right-to-work laws as exemptions from union and agency shop provisions of National Labor Relations Act, if the predominant job situs is outside the boundary of any state, no state's right-to-work laws apply); Chevron Oil Co. v. Huson, 404 U.S. 97, 92 S.Ct. 349, 30 L.Ed.2d 296 (1971) (to the extent that they are applicable and not inconsistent with other federal laws, state laws apply to the portion of the outer continental shelf which would be within the state if its boundaries were extended); Seidelson & Bowler, Determination of Family Status in the Administration of Federal Acts: A Choice of Law Problem for Federal Agencies and Courts, 33 Geo. Wash. L. Rev. 863 (1965); Comment, Choice of Law under Section 1983, 37 U. Chi. L. Rev. 494 (1970) (application of state law to issues in civil rights litigation).

Examples of application of federal law notwithstanding a contention that state law should control: Chambers v. Nasco, Inc., 501 U.S. 32, 111 S.Ct. 2123, 115 L.Ed.2d 27 (1991) (federal courts sitting in diversity can use their inherent power to assess attorney fees as sanction for bad-faith conduct even if applicable state law does not permit such assessment); Offshore Logistics, Inc. v. Tallentire, 477 U.S. 207, 106 S.Ct. 2485, 91 L.Ed.2d 174 (1986) (state wrongful death statutes are pre-empted by the Death on the High Seas Act); California ex rel. State Lands Commission v. United States, 457 U.S. 273, 102 S.Ct. 2432, 73 L.Ed.2d 1 (1982) (federal law determines title to accretions to oceanfront land the title to which derived from the Federal Government); United States v. Little Lake Misere Land

Co., 412 U.S. 580, 93 S.Ct. 2389, 37 L.Ed.2d 187 (1973) (invalidate state statute purporting to affect United States' interest in land); United States v. Mitchell, 403 U.S. 190, 91 S.Ct. 1763, 29 L.Ed.2d 406 (1971) (liability of wife for federal income tax on community income); Kermarec v. Compagnie Generale Transatlantique, 358 U.S. 625, 79 S.Ct. 406, 3 L.Ed.2d 550 (1959) (maritime law determines duty of ship owner to guest of crewmen while ship docked); Vanston Bondholders Protective Committee v. Green, 329 U.S. 156, 67 S.Ct. 237, 91 L.Ed. 162 (1946) (enforceability in bankruptcy proceedings of a claim of interest on interest).

See also Kohr v. Allegheny Airlines, Inc., 504 F.2d 400 (7th Cir.1974), cert. denied, 421 U.S. 978, 95 S.Ct. 1980, 44 L.Ed.2d 470 (1975) (a federal law of contribution and indemnity governs midair collisions). But cf. Bowen v. United States, 570 F.2d 1311 (7th Cir.1978) (in suit by pilot, state law determines whether contributory negligence bars recovery under Federal Tort Claims Act); Smith v. Cessna Aircraft Corp., 428 F.Supp. 1285 (N.D.Ill.1977) (*Kohr* not applicable in case involving single, non-commercial aircraft on intrastate flight).

Robertson, *Admiralty Procedure and Jurisdiction After the 1966 Unification*, 74 Mich. L. Rev. 1628, 1683 (1976): "If the case is totally maritime, it is to be governed by the substantive federal maritime law, whether it has been brought in admiralty, in state court, or in federal court on diversity grounds. If the case is maritime but local in its nature, it may be governed by settled features of the maritime law and borrowed features of state law, but the federal-state blend is to remain the same regardless of whether the matter is litigated in admiralty, in state court, or in federal court on grounds of diversity."

For a split of authority on whether state or federal law governs the conversion liability of auctioneers who sell livestock mortgaged to a federal agency, see United States v. Carson, 372 F.2d 429 (6th Cir.1967) (federal); United States v. Union Livestock Sales Co., 298 F.2d 755, 96 A.L.R.2d 199 (4th Cir.1962) (state); United States v. Matthews, 244 F.2d 626 (9th Cir.1957) (federal); United States v. Kramel, 234 F.2d 577 (8th Cir.1956) (state).

Chapter 11

JUDGMENTS

§ 11.1 Previous Discussion of Full Faith and Credit to Judgments

Previous sections have dealt with full faith and credit to judgments. Section 9.3A[1] concludes that a state must give full faith and credit to the judgment of a sister state unless the second state's interest in giving effect to its own policies outweighs the very great national interest in a uniform result under the judgment of a sister state. Contrary to what one might surmise from Restatement (Second) of Conflict of Laws section 103,[2] this standard would rarely if ever permit denial of full faith and credit to a sister-state judgment. As stated by the Supreme Court in *Baker v. General Motors Corporation*,[3] "our decisions support no roving 'public policy exception' to the full faith and credit due judgments."[4] *Baker* did state that sister states need not enforce injunctions issued in another state: "Full faith and credit, however, does not mean that States must adopt the practices of other States regarding the time, manner and mechanisms for enforcing judgments. Enforcement measures do not travel with the sister state judgment as preclusive effects do; such measures remain subject to evenhanded control of forum law."[5]

Reading & Bates Construction Co. v. Baker Energy Resources Corp.[6] held that a Texas court need not give full faith and credit to a Louisiana judgment that recognized a Canadian judgment because this would have the effect of giving full faith and credit to the judgment of a foreign country "through the back door." The court stated that the proper method of enforcing the Canadian judgment in Texas was under the Uniform Foreign Money–Judgments Recognition Act.[7]

The United Kingdom Foreign Judgments (Reciprocal Enforcement) Act excludes from foreign judgments that may be registered under the

---

1. Section 9.3A text accompanying notes 229–241.

2. Restatement (Second) of Conflict of Laws § 103 (1971) [hereinafter, Restatement, Second]: "A judgment rendered in one State of the United States need not be recognized or enforced in a sister State if such recognition or enforcement is not required by the national policy of full faith and credit because it would involve an improper interference with important interests of the sister State."

3. 522 U.S. 222, 118 S.Ct. 657, 139 L.Ed.2d 580 (1998).

4. Id. at 233, 118 S.Ct. at 664, 139 L.Ed.2d at 592.

5. Id. at 235, 118 S.Ct. at 665, 139 L.Ed.2d at 593. But see 18 U.S.C. § 2265(a) (states must enforce an order issued by another state protecting against domestic violence and stalking "as if it were the order of the enforcing State").

6. 976 S.W.2d 702 (Tex. App.—Houston [1st Dist.] 1998, rev. denied).

7. See infra § 11.6 text accompanying notes 77–87.

Act, a judgment enforcing the judgment of another country.[8]

The Court of Justice of the European Communities reached a similar result under the Brussels Convention (now Regulation). In *Owens Bank Ltd. v. Bracco*[9] the Court held that the judgment recognition and enforcement provisions of the Convention did not apply to a judgment of another European Union country that recognized a judgment of a non-European Union country.

A plurality in *Thomas v. Washington Gas Light Company*[10] held that one exception to full faith and credit to judgments exists with regard to workers' compensation awards. If the state where the worker is injured while on temporary assignment purports by its award to bar the worker's and employer's home state from providing additional compensation, the home state may disregard this limitation.[11]

There are also extensive discussions of full faith and credit to judgments in Chapters 5[12] and 8.[13] This chapter rounds out the picture by analyzing the basic requirements of full faith and credit to sister-state judgments. There also is discussion of comity to judgments of foreign countries and recognition abroad of United States judgments.

§ 11.2 Full Faith and Credit: The Constitution and Implementing Statute

The Full Faith and Credit Clause of the United States Constitution provides: "Full Faith and Credit shall be given in each State to the public Acts, Records, and judicial Proceedings of every other State. And the Congress may by general Laws prescribe the Manner in which such Acts, Records and Proceedings shall be proved, and the Effect thereof."[14] The Clause does not refer to the effect of state judgments in federal courts. The implementing statute, passed under authority of the Clause itself, plugs this hole by requiring federal courts to give full faith and credit to state judgments: "Such Acts, records and judicial proceedings or copies thereof, so authenticated, shall have the same full faith and credit in every court within the United States and its Territories and Possessions as they have by law or usage in the courts of such State, Territory or Possession from which they are taken."[15]

---

8. U.K. stat. 1933 c.13 pt. 1 § 1(2A)(b) (1991 amendment).

9. Case C–129/92 [1994] ECR I–117.

10. 448 U.S. 261, 100 S.Ct. 2647, 65 L.Ed.2d 757 (1980).

11. Id. at 263–86, 100 S.Ct. at 2652–63, 65 L.Ed.2d at 762–76. For the rationale supporting this possible exception, see § 9.3A text accompanying notes 229–241.

12. See §§ 5.2B, 5.2C, and 5.2E2 (full faith and credit to ex parte divorces); § 5.2D (full faith and credit to bilateral divorces); § 5.2E3 (full faith and credit to alimony and support decrees); § 5.3C (full faith and credit to custody decrees).

13. See §§ 8.3, 8.4, 8.5 (full faith and credit to judgments affecting interests in land).

14. U.S. Const. Art. IV, § 1.

15. 28 U.S.C. § 1738. See Migra v. Warren City School District Board of Education, 465 U.S. 75, 104 S.Ct. 892, 79 L.Ed.2d 56 (1984) (holding that a state judgment has the same preclusive effect in federal court as it had in the state where rendered).

In *Holder v. Holder*[16] the Ninth Circuit denied full faith and credit to the custody judgment of a California state court. Mr. Holder had been stationed in Germany with his family for eight months. He and his wife agreed that the wife should take the couple's two boys for a round-trip visit with the wife's parents in the U.S. When his wife refused to return, he sued in a California state court for divorce and custody, but did not assert a right to the return of the children to Germany under the Hague Convention on the Civil Aspects of International Child Abduction.[17] The California court entered an order for joint legal custody with the children remaining with the wife in Washington State. The California Court of Appeal ruled that the trial court had jurisdiction to adjudicate custody and that the Hague Convention did not obligate the court to stay custody proceedings.

Mr. Holder then sued in federal district court in Washington for return to the children to Germany pursuant to the Convention. The district court held that because Mr. Holder had not raised the Convention at trial in California, the California final judgment barred him from making the Convention claim in federal court. The Ninth Circuit reversed and remanded for determination of Mr. Holder's rights under the Convention. The court found no waiver of Convention rights holding that the California appellate decision to the contrary did not preclude relitigation of that issue and that the federal court did not have to give full faith and credit to the California custody determination. The court noted that 42 U.S.C. § 11603(g), enacted to facilitate Convention proceedings in U.S. courts, provides:

> Full faith and credit shall be accorded by the courts of the States and the courts of the United States to the judgment of any other such court ordering or denying the return of a child, pursuant to the Convention, in an action brought under this chapter.

The court then stated:

> [A]lthough 28 U.S.C. § 1738 requires that federal courts generally give state court judgments the same issue preclusive effect that they would be given by the rendering court, because we apply [the] more particularized full faith and credit provision of 42 U.S.C. § 11603(g), we do not give preclusive effect to state court adjudication of issues in a situation in which that court did not have a Hague Petition before it and did not order the return of the children pursuant to the Convention.[18]

Holder is correct if 42 U.S.C. § 11603(g) displaces the general full faith and credit obligation of 28 U.S.C. § 1738 or if the ratification of the Convention and the enactment of implementing federal legislation worked "an implied partial repeal of § 1738."[19] I do not think so.

---

16.   305 F.3d 854 (9th Cir. 2002).

17.   See supra § 5.3B(5).

18.   *Holder*, 305 F.3d at 866.

19.   Marrese v. American Academy of Ortho. Surgeons, 470 U.S. 373, 386, 105 S.Ct. 1327, 1335, 84 L.Ed.2d 274, 285 (1985) (whether the grant of exclusive Sherman Act antitrust jurisdiction to federal courts had this effect).

In *San Remo Hotel v. City and County of San Francisco*[20] the Supreme Court refused to create an exception to § 1738 for claims that a state entity had taken property in violation of the Fifth Amendment mandate: "nor shall private property be taken for public use, without just compensation." The City of San Francisco had charged the hotel a fee of $567,000 as a condition of changing residential rooms into tourist accommodations. The California Supreme Court rejected the claim and "interpreted the relevant substantive state takings law coextensively with federal law."[21] The hotel did not seek a writ of certiorari from the U.S. Supreme Court but instead returned to federal district court, which had abstained from adjudicating the hotel's claims under the U.S. Constitution until the conclusion of the proceedings in state court. The Supreme Court affirmed the district and Ninth Circuit holdings that the state judgment precluded litigating the Fifth Amendment claim in federal court. The Court refused to "create an exception to the full faith and credit statute, and the ancient rule on which it is based, in order to provide a federal forum for litigants who seek to advance federal takings claims that are not ripe until the entry of a final state judgment denying just compensation."[22]

Semtek International Inc. v. Lockheed Martin Corp.[23] discussed the claim-preclusive effect of a federal judgment in state court. The Court first noted, that neither the Constitution nor 28 U.S.C. § 1738, quoted in the first paragraph of this section, provided the applicable rule:

> Neither the Full Faith and Credit Clause, U.S. Const., Art. IV, § 1, nor the full faith and credit statute, § 28 U.S.C. 1738, addresses the question. By their terms they govern the effects to be given only to state-court judgments (and, in the case of the statute, to judgments by courts of territories and possessions). And no other federal textual provision, neither of the Constitution nor of any statute, addresses the claim-preclusive effect of a judgment in a federal diversity action.[24]

The Court then stated that "federal common law governs the claim-preclusive effect of a dismissal by a federal court sitting in diversity."[25] Nevertheless, the Court concluded that when state, not federal, substantive law was at issue and there was no need for a uniform federal rule of preclusion, the federal common law rule governing preclusion incorpo-

---

20. 545 U.S. 323, 125 S.Ct. 2491, 162 L.Ed.2d 315 (2005).

21. Id. at 335, 125 S.Ct. at 2500.

22. Id. at 337, 125 S.Ct. at 2501. The Court distinguished England v. Louisiana Bd. of Medical Examiners, 375 U.S. 411, 84 S.Ct. 461, 11 L.Ed.2d 440 (1964), in which a federal court had abstained from deciding a U.S. constitutional issue until a state court construed the state statute but the state court on its own went on to decide the constitutional issue. In *San Remo Hotel* the hotel raised the constitutional issue in state court. *San Remo Hotel*, 125 S.Ct. at 2502–03.

23. 531 U.S. 497, 121 S.Ct. 1021, 149 L.Ed.2d 32 (2001).

24. Id. at 508, 121 S.Ct. at 1027 (footnotes omitted).

25. Id. at 506–07, 121 S.Ct. at 1028

rated "the law that would be applied by state courts in the State in which the federal diversity court sits."[26]

The Court did not, however, indicate the source of its authority for imposing on state courts the federal common law rule concerning the preclusive effect of federal judgments. It may be that if not the Full Faith and Credit Clause, then the Supremacy Clause,[27] although it does not mention "judgments," provides a constitutional mandate that state courts enforce federal judgments.[28] Perhaps it would be neater if Congress amended the full faith and credit implementing statute to expressly require state courts to honor federal judgments, but there is no pressing need. Rarely has a state court acted in a manner that raises the issue. If necessary, a federal judgment can be enforced in another state by registering it there under the federal registration statute.[29] Moreover, a federal court may enjoin parties from relitigating claims in state court that have been adjudicated in a federal proceeding.[30]

In re Bridgestone/Firestone, Inc.[31] extended to draconian limits the rule that federal law determines the preclusive effect of federal judgments. As indicated in section 6.33,[32] the Seventh Circuit determined that a national class action was not manageable because the trial court would have to apply the laws of all the jurisdictions in which injuries occurred.[33] The following year the court held that its determination was binding on the parties and ordered the trial judge to enjoin all members of the class and their lawyers "from again attempting [in any court, state or federal] to have nationwide classes certified over defendants' opposition with respect to the same claims."[34] The court did, however, hold that its previous statement that statewide class actions were also

---

26. Id. at 508, 121 S.Ct. at 1028.

27. U.S. Const. Art. VI cl. 2: "This Constitution, and the Laws of the United States which shall be made in Pursuance thereof; and all Treaties made, or which shall be made, under the Authority of the United States, shall be the supreme Law of the Land; and the Judges in every State shall be bound thereby, any Thing in the Constitution or Laws of any State to the Contrary notwithstanding."

28. See Loveridge v. Fred Meyer, Inc., 72 Wash.App. 720, 864 P.2d 417, 419 (1993), aff'd, 125 Wash.2d 759, 887 P.2d 898 (1995) (dictum): "Under principles of federal supremacy, a federal judgment must be given full faith and credit in the state courts, which includes recognition of the res judicata effect of the federal judgment."

For discussion of state court recognition of federal judgments see Burbank, *Interjurisdictional Preclusion, Full Faith and Credit and Federal Common Law: A General* Approach, 71 Cornell L. Rev. 733, 829 (1986); Degnan, *Federalized Res Judicata*, 85 Yale L. J. 741 (1976).

29. 28 U.S.C. § 1963 ("[a] judgment so registered shall have the same effect as a judgment of the district court of the district where registered and may be enforced in like manner").

30. Chick Kam Choo v. Exxon Corp., 486 U.S. 140, 108 S.Ct. 1684, 100 L.Ed.2d 127 (1988).

31. 333 F.3d 763 (7th Cir. 2003).

32. See § 6.33 text accompanying notes 396–400.

33. 288 F.3d 1012 (7th Cir. 2002), cert. denied, 537 U.S. 1105, 123 S.Ct. 870, 154 L.Ed.2d 774 (2003).

34. 333 F.3d at 769 (7th Cir. 2003).

not manageable was not binding on plaintiffs in other jurisdiction because that issue was not before the court.[35]

11.3 The Effect of Full Faith and Credit

The effect of the Full Faith and Credit Clause[36] is to require sister states[37] to give a judgment the same claim and issue preclusion effect that it has in the state that rendered it.[38] If a plaintiff obtains a money judgment in one state and wishes to enforce it in another state, the plaintiff must first make the judgment a judgment of the second state. The plaintiff can accomplish this by suing with the first judgment as the cause of action or, if the second state has a registration statute,[39] registering the first judgment. If a judgment is appealed, the law of the state that rendered the judgment determines whether the judgment is final and entitled to full faith and credit.[40]

Within the state in which a judgment is rendered, a valid, final, personal judgment usually affects the parties to the litigation in the following ways. If the judgment is in favor of the plaintiff, the claim on which suit was brought is merged in the judgment and a new claim arises on the judgment.[41] A judgment in favor of the defendant extinguishes the claim and bars further suit on it.[42] These merger and bar effects of a judgment on a subsequent suit between the same parties on the same claim are sometimes referred to as "claim preclusion." In a subsequent action between the parties on a different claim, the prior

---

35. Id. at 766.

36. See supra note 14 and accompanying text.

37. See supra § 11.2 for discussion of federal full faith and to state judgments and state full faith and credit to federal judgments.

38. See Restatement, Second § 93, cmt. *b.*

39. See Unif. Enforcement of Foreign Judgments Act 13 pt. I U.L.A. Despite its title, the Act covers only judgments "of a court of the United States or of any other court which is entitled to full faith and credit in this state." Id. § 1. On January 1, 2006, the Act had been adopted in 46 states plus the District of Columbia, Puerto Rico, and the Virgin Islands. Cf. Potomac Leasing Co. v. Dasco Technology Corp., 10 P.3d 972 (Utah 2000) (noting a split of authority as to whether a forum's statute of limitations for enforcing sister-state judgments applies to judgments registered under the Uniform Act and agreeing with states that applied the same limitations to suit on and registration of a sister-state judgment).

40. See Fehr v. McHugh, 413 A.2d 1285 (D.C.App.1980); Aetna Life Ins. Co. v. McElvain, 221 Mont. 138, 717 P.2d 1081 (1986) (judgment on appeal in a sister state that has issue preclusion effect there must be given the same effect in the forum).

41. See Restatement, Second, Judgments § 17(1) (1982).

42. Id. § 17(2). A judgment for the defendant will also bar a subsequent suit on the same claim by persons not party to the suit if there is privity between those persons and the losing plaintiff. For non-parties to be bound by privity the prior litigation must have given full and fair consideration to the interests of the non-parties. See Richards v. Jefferson County, Ala., 517 U.S. 793, 116 S.Ct. 1761, 135 L.Ed.2d 76 (1996); cf. In re Trust Created by Agreement Dated December 20, 1961, 166 N.J. 340, 765 A.2d 746, cert. denied, 534 U.S. 889, 122 S.Ct. 203, 151 L.Ed.2d 143 (2001) (applying Uniform Parentage Act, bars cousins from questioning paternity of child adjudicated in divorce between child's parents and stating (166 N.J. at 358, 765 A.2d at 756) "courts in other jurisdictions appear to agree that third-party challenges to paternity and legitimacy should be barred once those questions have been resolved by acknowledgement or agreement of the putative parents or by judicial decree").

judgment is conclusive on any issue actually litigated and decided if the determination of that issue was essential to the judgment.[43] This effect of a judgment on a subsequent suit between the same parties on a different claim is sometimes referred to as "issue preclusion" or "collateral estoppel."

The same preclusive effect on litigated issues results when the merger and bar rules do not prevent a subsequent action between the same parties on the same claim. This would be true, for example, if the first judgment dismisses the suit for lack of jurisdiction.[44] This form of issue preclusion is sometimes referred to as "direct estoppel."

If two states render inconsistent judgments between the same parties on the same issues, *Treines v. Sunshine Mining Co.*[45] holds that is the last judgment in time that is entitled to full faith and credit. This makes sense if the winner of the first suit sleeps on their rights and does not demand full faith and credit to the first judgment. It makes less sense if the party who won in the first state unsuccessfully argues at trial and on appeal in the second state that the sister state judgment bars relitigation and the U.S. Supreme Court denies a petition for certiorari.[46]

---

43. Restatement, Second, Judgments § 17(3).

44. See Swan v. Sargent Indus., 620 P.2d 473 (Okl.App.1980) (prior dismissal for lack of personal jurisdiction precludes relitigation of that issue in subsequent proceedings based on the same jurisdictional facts); cf. Kendall v. Overseas Development Corp., 700 F.2d 536 (9th Cir.1983) (prior state court dismissal for lack of personal jurisdiction bars relitigation of that issue in the absence of new circumstances). But cf. Compagnie Des Bauxites de Guinee v. L'Union Atlantique S.A. d'Assurances, 723 F.2d 357 (3d Cir.1983) (plaintiff is not barred from relitigating the issue of personal jurisdiction because in the prior suit the court had terminated discovery concerning jurisdiction and the plaintiff did not have an opportunity to fully contest this issue).

That full faith and credit must be given even to determinations of subject matter jurisdiction when the deciding court had jurisdiction over the parties, see Underwriters National Assurance Co. v. North Carolina Life & Accident & Health Ins. Guaranty Ass'n, 455 U.S. 691, 102 S.Ct. 1357, 71 L.Ed.2d 558 (1982); Durfee v. Duke, 375 U.S. 106, 84 S.Ct. 242, 11 L.Ed.2d 186 (1963); cf. Kelleran v. Andrijevic, 825 F.2d 692 (2d Cir.1987), cert. denied, 484 U.S. 1007, 108 S.Ct. 701, 98 L.Ed.2d 652 (1988) (bankruptcy court must give preclusive effect to state default judgment against debtor despite finding that the creditor's claims are without merit); Equitable Trust Co. v. Commodity Futures Trading Comm'n, 669 F.2d 269 (5th Cir.1982) (dismissal for lack of subject matter jurisdiction forecloses litigation of whether Commission action is subject to judicial review). But cf. Kalb v. Feuerstein, 308 U.S. 433, 60 S.Ct. 343, 84 L.Ed. 370 (1940) (foreclosure proceedings in state court proceedings while petition in federal bankruptcy proceedings was pending may be collaterally attacked by mortgagors who were parties to the state proceedings—the filing in bankruptcy had deprived the state court of all jurisdiction); Morris v. Garmon, 285 Ark. 259, 686 S.W.2d 396 (1985) (Texas finding of domicile of decedent may be collaterally attacked in Arkansas probate proceeding because it goes to subject matter jurisdiction).

45. 308 U.S. 66, 60 S.Ct. 44, 84 L.Ed. 85 (1939). But cf. Gabbanelli Accordions & Imports, L.L.C. v. Ditta Gabbanelli Ubaldo Di Elio Gabbanelli, 575 F.3d 693, 697 (7th Cir. 2009) ("Because the Italian judgment postdates the American one, it cannot be pleaded as res judicata").

46. See Ginsburg, *Judgments in Search of Full Faith and Credit: The Last-in-Time Rule for Conflicting Judgments*, 82 Harv. L. Rev. 798, 803 (1969). Cf. Byblos Bank Europe, S.A. v. Sekerbank Turk Anonym Syrketi, 10 N.Y.3d 243 248, 855 N.Y.S.2d 427, 885 N.E.2d 191, 194 (2008), refused to enforce a Belgium judgment that denied comity to an earlier Turkish judgment and stated: "The last-in-time rule, applicable in resolving conflicting sister state judgments under the Full Faith and Credit Clause of the Constitution need not

The Brussels Regulation, on the contrary, directs the third forum not to enforce a judgment that is "irreconcilable with an earlier judgment given in another Member State or in a third State involving the same cause of action and between the same parties."[47] Under the Regulation, however, a European Union country does not recognize a judgment that "irreconcilable with a judgment [whether earlier or later] given in a dispute between the same parties in the Member State in which recognition is sought."[48]

In *Byblos Bank Europe, S.A. v. Sekerbank Turk Anonym Syrketi*,[49] the Court of Appeals of New York refused to apply the last-in-time rule to judgments of foreign countries. A Belgium bank loaned money to a Turkish bank. When the Turkish failed to repay, the Belgium bank brought attachment actions in Turkey, Germany, and Belgium. The Turkish court rendered judgment for the Turkish bank, dismissing the Belgium bank's claim on the merits. The Turkish bank then sought recognition of the Turkish judgment in the German and Belgium proceedings. The German courts granted recognition. The Belgium courts, under a law since repealed, stated that the Turkish judgment was reviewable on the merits; that the Turkish judgment was wrong. The Belgium court awarded the Belgium bank $5 million plus interest.

The Belgium bank asked for enforcement of the Belgium money-judgment under the New York Uniform Foreign Money–Judgments Recognition Act. The Act provided a discretionary ground for non-recognition when the foreign judgment "conflicts with another final and conclusive judgment."[50] The Court pointed out that the Act does not state whether the conflicting judgment is earlier or later than the judgment that a party is attempting to get recognized under the Act and held that the trial judge had not abused his discretion in denying recognition to the Belgium judgment. The opinion stated that "the last-in-time rule should not be applied where, as here, the last-in-time court departed from normal res judicata principles by permitting a party to relitigate the merits of an earlier judgment."[51]

11.4 Defensive and Offensive Non–Mutual Collateral Estoppel

Sometimes the claim or issue preclusion effects of a judgment apply in favor of someone who was not a party to the suit in which the

---

be mechanically applied when inconsistent foreign country judgments exist. Rigid application of the rule would conflict with the plain language of [§ 4(b)(4) of the Uniform Foreign Money–Judgments Recognition Act] vesting New York courts with discretion to decide whether a foreign judgment that conflicts with another judgment is entitled to recognition."

47. Council Regulation on Jurisdiction and the Recognition and Enforcement of Judgments in Civil and Commercial Matters No. 44/2001, adopted by the Council of the European Union on 22 December 2000, entered into force 1 March 2002, art. 34(4) [Brussels Regulation].

48. Id. art. 34(3).

49. 10 N.Y.3d 243, 855 N.Y.S.2d 427, 885 N.E.2d 191 (2008).

50. N.Y. CPLR 5304(b)(5).

51. 10 N.Y.3d at 248, 855 N.Y.S.2d 427, 885 N.E.2d at 194.

judgment was rendered. This extended effect of a judgment is referred to as "non-mutual collateral estoppel" or sometimes simply as "collateral estoppel." There are two forms of collateral estoppel—defensive and offensive.

Defensive collateral estoppel is more widely accepted and more justifiable than offensive collateral estoppel. Defensive use occurs when the defendant seeks to prevent a plaintiff from asserting a claim that the plaintiff has previously litigated and lost against another defendant. A classic example is *Bernhard v. Bank of America National Trust & Savings Association.*[52] Beneficiaries under a will objected to the account of the estate's executor on the ground that the executor had improperly withdrawn money from the decedent's bank account. The court approved the account finding that during her life the decedent had given the money to the executor as a gift. Then the estate's administatrix sued the bank for improperly permitting the withdrawal. The court held that the administratrix was barred by res judicata from claiming that the withdrawal was improper because she represented the same persons who had lost in the suit against the executor.

Defensive collateral estoppel is usually desirable because it encourages the plaintiff to join all parties against whom the plaintiff asserts a claim arising from the same event. Moreover, the plaintiff can choose the forum and the defendants in the first suit.

Offensive collateral estoppel forecloses the defendant from litigating an issue that defendant has previously litigated unsuccessfully in an action with another party. The classic example is *Parklane Hosiery Co., Inc. v. Shore.*[53] The Securities and Exchange Commission (SEC) obtained a judgment that defendants had issued a materially false proxy statement. *Parklane* held that in a stockholders' class action the defendants were collaterally estopped from relitigating the issues resolved against them in the SEC suit. The court held offensive estoppel proper in this case because the plaintiffs could not have joined in the SEC suit and, because of the seriousness of the charges, the defendants had every incentive to defend that suit "fully and vigorously."[54]

---

52. 19 Cal.2d 807, 122 P.2d 892 (1942). See also Blonder–Tongue Labs., Inc. v. University of Illinois Found., 402 U.S. 313, 91 S.Ct. 1434, 28 L.Ed.2d 788 (1971) (patentee may not relitigate the validity of a patent after a federal court in a previous suit by the patentee has declared it invalid if in the previous suit the patentee had a full and fair opportunity to litigate the validity of its patent); cf. Texas Department of Public Safety v. Petta, 44 S.W.3d 575 (Tex. 2001) (plaintiff collaterally estopped from suing policemen for assault after plaintiff found guilty of fleeing the officer because jury in criminal case determined that plaintiff did not reasonably believe that she was in danger of imminent harm when she fled).

53. 439 U.S. 322, 99 S.Ct. 645, 58 L.Ed.2d 552 (1979).

54. Id. at 332, 99 S.Ct. at 652, 58 L.Ed.2d at 563. See also Koch v. Consolidated Edison Co. of New York, Inc., 62 N.Y.2d 548, 479 N.Y.S.2d 163, 468 N.E.2d 1 (1984), cert. denied, 469 U.S. 1210, 105 S.Ct. 1177, 84 L.Ed.2d 326 (1985) (offensive collateral estoppel approved; finding in prior suit that defendant was grossly negligent is binding on defendant in subsequent suit when defendant did not bear burden of showing the preclusion was unfair); Flanagan, *Offensive Collateral Estoppel: Inefficiency and Foolish Consistency*, 1982 Ariz.St.L. J. 45 (1982).

In cases in which the plaintiff could have joined in the first suit, however, the Court cautioned against the use of offensive estoppel. The Court noted that rather than promoting judicial economy, as is the case with defensive estoppel, offensive estoppel provides an incentive for a plaintiff to stay out of the first suit in order to ride on the coattails of a verdict for the first plaintiff, but remain free to sue even if the first plaintiff loses. In addition, offensive estoppel may be unfair to the defendant if the first suit was for a small amount and the defendant could not foresee the subsequent suit for a large amount. Another possibility for unfairness to the defendant would occur in a mass tort if the defendant wins the first twenty suits but loses the twenty-first and is estopped to relitigate liability against subsequent plaintiffs.[55]

§ 11.4A Virtual Representation

In *Taylor v. Sturgell*,[56] the Supreme Court disapproved of the doctrine of virtual representation, under which some courts have expanded the preclusive effect of judgments on non-parties. The court listed six situations in which non-parties can be bound by the claim and issue preclusive effects of a judgment: (1) the non-party agrees to be bound by the judgment; (2) the preclusive effect of the judgment is based on a pre-existing legal relationship between the non-party and a party to the judgment, such as succeeding owners of property, bailee and bailor, and assignee and assignor; (3) the non-party was adequately represented by a party with the same interests as the non-party, such in class actions, and suits brought by fiduciaries; (4) the non-party assumed control over the litigation; (5) the non-party is proxy for a party, such as when a designated representative or an agent of a party brings the later suit; (6) a statutory scheme that is consistent with due process bars successive litigation by the non-party, such as bankruptcy and probate proceedings and suits on behalf of the public at large.[57]

Then court stated:

> Reaching beyond these six established categories, some lower courts have recognized a "virtual representation" exception to the rule against nonparty preclusion. Decisions of these courts, however, have been far from consistent Some Circuits use the label, but define "virtual representation" so that it is no broader than the recognized exception for adequate representation. But other courts, including the Eighth, Ninth, and D.C. Circuits, apply multifactor tests for virtual representation that permit nonparty preclusion in cases that do not fit within any of the established exceptions.[58]

The court rejected this wider use of "virtual representation." The narrow holding related to a "federal-question case decided by a federal

---

55. *Parklane*, 439 U.S. at 329–31, 99 S.Ct. at 655–51, 58 L.Ed.2d at 561–62.

56. ___ U.S. ___, 128 S.Ct. 2161, 171 L.Ed.2d 155 (2008).

57. Id. at 2172–73.

58. Id. at 2173 (citations omitted).

court,"[59] but the opinion made it clear that due process required this rejection.[60] In *Taylor* a friend of the plaintiff had brought a suit against the Federal Aviation Administration to enforce a request for documents under the federal Freedom of Information Act. The court refused to enforce the request. When the plaintiff later brought suit to enforce a request for the same documents, the D.C. Circuit held that, under the doctrine of virtual representation, he was adequately represented by the party to the prior suit and was precluded by the earlier judgment. The Supreme Court vacated the judgment and remanded for further proceedings in which the Federal Aviation Administration would have the burden of proving that plaintiff is acting as the agent of the prior unsuccessful party.

§ 11.5   Full Faith and Credit to the Collateral Estoppel Effects of Sister State Judgments

There is doubt concerning the extent to which full faith and credit must be given to a sister state's rules on non-mutual collateral estoppel. The second state should be required to give the first judgment at least as much collateral estoppel effect as it has in the courts of the first state if the intrastate effect in the first state is consistent with due process.[61] As a matter of giving effect to its own policies of judicial economy, the second state should be permitted to give a sister state judgment greater defensive collateral estoppel effect than it would have in the state that rendered it if this results in dismissal with the plaintiff free to sue in some other forum. This would not be inconsistent with *Marrese v. American Academy of Orthopaedic Surgeons*.[62] *Marrese* held that if a state court would not hold its judgment barred subsequent federal antitrust claims, it was a violation of full faith and credit for a federal court to give the state judgment such a preclusive effect. In *Marrese* there was no other forum in which plaintiff could pursue his federal antitrust claim.

---

59. Id. at 2178.

60. Id. at 2176: "These protections, grounded in due process, could be circumvented were we to approve a virtual representation doctrine that allowed courts to 'create *de facto* class actions at will.'"

61. See Richards v. Jefferson County, Alabama, 517 U.S. 793, 116 S.Ct. 1761, 135 L.Ed.2d 76 (1996) (holding Alabama res judicata principles violate due process when applied to bar claims because of a prior litigation in which claimants were not sufficiently represented and of which they were not notified); Pielemeier, *Due Process Limitations on the Application of Collateral Estoppel Against Nonparties to Prior Litigation*, 63 Boston U. L. Rev. 383, 385 (1983) (only necessity and "the provision of added protections to nonparties" justifies depriving them of the opportunity "to participate meaningfully in the litigation of claims affecting their interests").

62. 470 U.S. 373, 105 S.Ct. 1327, 84 L.Ed.2d 274 (1985). See also Matsushita Elec. Indus. Co. v. Epstein, 516 U.S. 367, 116 S.Ct. 873, 134 L.Ed.2d 6 (1996) (holding that a state judgment releasing claims under federal securities law bars a subsequent suit on the securities law actions in federal court and finding no reason to create an exception to 28 U.S.C. § 1738, which requires federal courts to give full faith and credit to state judgments); Evans v. Ottimo, 469 F.3d 278 (2d Cir. 2006) (when burden of proof in state court exceeds that in bankruptcy court, finding of fraud in state court precludes relitigation in federal bankruptcy court of whether debt was nondischargeable because fraudulently incurred).

In *Hart v. American Airlines, Inc.,*[63] a New York Court gave more offensive collateral estoppel effect to a Texas judgment than would a Texas court. The Texas case found the defendant's negligence caused the crash of one of defendant's airplanes. In the New York suit to recover for the death of a passenger killed in the crash, the court estopped defendant from relitigating the negligence issue. *Hart* combines the worst aspects of offensive collateral estoppel with refusal to give the Texas judgment the same res judicata effect that it had in Texas. Other cases have ignored or disagreed with *Hart*.[64]

Note should also be taken of the somewhat analogous doctrine of judicial estoppel under which a party to one proceeding is barred in subsequent proceedings, whether or not involving the same claims or same parties, from asserting a fact contrary to a fact successfully asserted by that party in the prior proceeding.[65] *Finley v. Kesling*[66] holds that judicial estoppel bars a father from claiming beneficial ownership of stock that, in an Indiana divorce, he successfully contended belonged to his children. The court had "difficulty believing" that Indiana would not impose judicial estoppel under these circumstances[67] but stated that even if Indiana would not, full faith and credit does not preclude Illinois from doing so.[68] The court distinguished collateral and judicial estoppel stating that it can give the Indiana judgment more judicial estoppel effect than would Indiana even though full faith and credit might preclude the court from giving the Indiana judgment more collateral estoppel effect.[69]

§ 11.6 Recognition of the Judgments of Other Countries

The Full Faith and Credit Clause of the United States Constitution does not apply to judgments of other countries.[70] The law of each state

---

63. 61 Misc.2d 41, 304 N.Y.S.2d 810 (1969).

64. See Columbia Cas. Co. v. Playtex FP, Inc., 584 A.2d 1214 (Del. 1991) (comity prevents Delaware from giving a Kansas federal judgment, to which the insurer was not a party, the effect of precluding the insured from relitigating facts found against the insured in the Kansas diversity case; Delaware law but not Kansas law would collaterally estop the insured); Harvey v. Amateur Hockey Ass'n, 171 A.D.2d 464, 567 N.Y.S.2d 44 (1991) (holding that plaintiffs' action was not barred by prior Michigan judgment in which plaintiffs and defendant in the New York suit were defendants and which resulted in verdict against plaintiffs and in favor of defendant; court reaches this result because Michigan law would not bar plaintiffs' suit; the opinion does not cite *Hart*). See also Scoles, *Interstate Preclusion by Prior Litigation,* 74 Nw. L. Rev. 742, 750–51 (1979); Shreve, *Judgments From a Choice-of-Law Perspective,* 40 Am. J. Comp. L. 985, 988 n.13 (1992) (stating that *Marrese* raises "some doubt about the continuing authority of ... *Hart*").

65. See New Hampshire v. Maine, 532 U.S. 742, 121 S.Ct. 1808, 149 L.Ed.2d 968 (2001) (in boundary dispute with Maine, bar New Hampshire from asserting facts contrary to New Hampshire's position in earlier litigation between the same states over lobster fishing, and discussing circumstances under which judicial estoppel applies).

66. 105 Ill.App.3d 1, 433 N.E.2d 1112, 60 Ill.Dec. 874 (1982).

67. Id. at 6, 433 N.E.2d at 1116, 60 Ill.Dec. at 878.

68. Id. at 8, 433 N.E.2d at 1118, 60 Ill.Dec. at 880.

69. Id.

70. *See* Aetna Life Ins. Co. v. Tremblay, 223 U.S. 185, 190, 32 S.Ct. 309, 56 L.Ed. 398 (1912) (stating that the U.S. Constitution does not require full faith and credit "to the judgments of foreign states or nations").

controls recognition of foreign judgments in that state.[71] Federal courts in diversity[72] and alienage[73] cases apply the law of the state in which they sit[74] concerning recognition of foreign judgments, but apply federal law in federal-question cases.[75]

With the possible exception of Connecticut,[76] United States courts recognize and enforce foreign money judgments. As of October 1, 2009,

---

71. See Restatement, Second § 98 cmt. c (Rev.) (1989).

72. "Diversity cases" are those in which U.S. Const. art. III, § 2 confers judicial power on federal courts over cases "between citizens of different states."

73. "Alienage cases" are those in which U.S. Const. art. III, § 2 confers judicial power on federal courts over cases "between a state, or the citizens thereof, and foreign States, citizens or subjects."

74. See 18 C. Wright et al., Federal Practice and Procedure § 4473 at 742–744 (1981) (stating that recent federal decisions unanimously apply the law of the state in which the federal court sits, but questioning the wisdom of applying state standards to recognition of foreign judgments, especially in alienage cases); cf. Burbank, *Federal Judgments Law: Sources of Authority and Sources of Rules*, 70 Tex. L. Rev. 1551, 1579 (1992) (stating that "[a]ssuming that the Constitution's foreign relations or foreign trade powers, without more, could ground uniform judge-made rules of recognition and enforcement, a showing could not be made, at least under most of the [United States Supreme] Court's recent federal common-law decisions, to support uniform rules as opposed to state law borrowed as federal law except where hostile to or inconsistent with federal interests"). But cf. Casad, *Issue Preclusion and Foreign Country Judgments: Whose Law?*, 70 Iowa L. Rev. 53, 79 (1984) (stating that "[a]lthough the Republic can survive without federalizing the law of foreign judgment recognition, the arguments in favor of that position are strong and the principal argument against it amounts to little more than inertia"); Brand, *Enforcement of Foreign Money–Judgments in the United States: In Search of Uniformity and International Acceptance*, 67 Notre Dame L. Rev. 253, 300 (1991) (stating that "[f]ederal legislation would seem appropriate in the recognition of foreign judgments").

75. See Gordon & Breach Science Publishers S.A. v. American Inst. of Physics, 905 F.Supp. 169, 178–79 (S.D.N.Y. 1995) (rejecting claim that Swiss and German judgments preclude Lanham Act claim and applying federal collateral-estoppel standards); Wright, supra note 74, at 741 (stating that "[i]n deciding federal question cases, there is no apparent reason to consult state law and federal courts routinely determine the res judicata effect of foreign judgments without any reference to state law"). "Federal-question cases" are those in which U.S. Const. art. III, § 2 confers judicial power on federal courts over cases "arising under this constitution, the laws of the United States, and treaties made . . . under their authority."

76. In an attempt to prevent parallel litigation in the United States and abroad, Connecticut has enacted a Conflict of Jurisdictions Model Law. Conn. G. Stat. Ann. §§ 50a–201—50a–203. The Act directs local courts to refuse recognition of a foreign judgment rendered in a parallel proceeding unless a local court has declared the foreign court the proper "adjudicating forum." Id. § 50a–201(a). The Act requires courts to make this declaration within six months of the time of notice that duplicate suits have been filed, or, in the absence of such early decision, when recognition is sought. Id. § 50a–201(b), (d). The criteria for determining the proper adjudicating forum focus on the convenience of the parties and the interest of the forum. Id. § 50a–202 (listing as criteria "interest of the affected courts in having proceedings take place in their respective forums," "law likely to be applicable," "the forum likely to render the most complete relief," location of "witnesses . . . documents and other evidence," "[w]hether designation of an adjudicating forum is a superior method to parallel proceedings in adjudicating the dispute"). This refusal to recognize foreign judgments goes far beyond the Uniform Foreign Money–Judgments Recognition Act's discretionary basis for non-recognition: "in the case of jurisdiction based only on personal service, the foreign court was a seriously inconvenient forum for the trial of the action." § 4(b)(6), 13 pt. II U.L.A. It will be interesting to see what effect the Conflict of Jurisdictions statute has when a litigant seeks recognition of a Connecticut judgment in a country that requires reciprocity as a condition of that recognition. See Brand, supra note 74, at 255 (stating that "enforcement of United States

fifteen states plus the District of Columbia and the Virgin Islands have adopted the Uniform Foreign Money–Judgments Recognition Act and twelve states have adopted a 2005 amendment of the Act.[77] With only a few exceptions to protect due process rights[78] and otherwise assure the fairness of the proceedings,[79] the Act provides that "any foreign judgment that is final and conclusive and enforceable where rendered"[80] is "conclusive between the parties to the extent that it grants or denies recovery of a sum of money."[81] There is a "public policy" exception,[82] but courts have seldom used it.[83]

Several states have already added "libel tourism" protection provi-

---

judgments overseas is often possible only if the United States court rendering the judgment would enforce a similar decision of the foreign enforcing court").

77. 13 U.L.A. pt. II. In 2005 the National Conference of Commissioners on Uniform State Laws approved of a revision of the Uniform Foreign Money–Judgments Act—the Uniform Foreign–Country Money Judgments Recognition Act, 13 U.L.A. pt. II pocket part. The revision clarifies the earlier act, adds to the discretionary grounds for not recognizing a foreign judgment, establishes a procedure for recognizing foreign judgments, and contains a statute of limitations for recognizing foreign judgments.

78. Unif. Foreign Money–Judgments Recognition Act § 4(a)(1), (2), 13 pt. II U.L.A. [hereinafter Unif. Money–Judgments Act] (precluding recognition of foreign judgments when the foreign court did not have personal jurisdiction over the defendant or when "rendered under a system which does not provide impartial tribunals or procedures compatible with the requirements of due process").

79. Id. § 4(b) (permitting non-recognition if the defendant did not receive timely notice, the judgment was obtained by fraud, the judgment conflicts with another judgment, the proceeding violated a forum-selection agreement between the parties, or jurisdiction was based on personal service in a seriously inconvenient forum).

80. Id. § 2.

81. Id. § 3.

82. Id. § 4(b)(3) (permitting non-recognition if the claim "on which the judgment is based is repugnant to the public policy of this state").

83. For cases invoking the public policy exception of the Act to refuse recognition of a foreign judgment, see Transportes Aereos Pegaso, S.A. v. Bell Helicopter Textron, Inc., 623 F.Supp.2d 518 (D. Del. 2009) (applying Delaware law, refuse to enforce Mexican judgment because the court is not satisfied that the judgment was not obtained by the fraud of the judge and an expert appointed by the judge); Matusevitch v. Telnikoff, 877 F.Supp. 1, 4 (D.D.C. 1995) (refusing to recognize an English libel judgment); Jaffe v. Snow, 610 So.2d 482 (Fla. Ct. App., 5th Dist., 1993), review denied, 621 So.2d 432 (Fla. 1993), (refusing to recognize a wife's Canadian judgment against a Florida bail bond company for loss of consortium when the acts of company agents who captured and returned her husband to face criminal charges were privileged under Florida law but not under Canadian law); Bachchan v. India Abroad Publications Inc., 154 Misc.2d 228, 585 N.Y.S.2d 661 (S. Ct. 1992) (refusing to recognize an English libel judgment and noting the constitutional limits that the Supreme Court of the United States has placed on libel recoveries in the U.S.); cf. Bank Melli Iran v. Pahlavi, 58 F.3d 1406 (9th Cir.), cert. denied, 516 U.S. 989, 116 S.Ct. 519, 133 L.Ed.2d 427 (1995), (refusing to enforce Iranian default judgments against the sister of the former Shah because defendant could not have obtained due process in an Iranian court). But see Tonga Air Service, Ltd. v. Fowler, 118 Wash.2d 718, 826 P.2d 204, 208 (1992) (reversing a trial-court opinion that, because Tonga procedure did not provide a verbatim transcript for appeal, had refused to recognize a Tonga judgment; the court holds that review of a trial court's refusal to recognize a foreign judgment under § 4 of the Act is de novo and not for abuse of discretion). But cf. Banque Libanaise Pour Le Commerce v. Khreich, 915 F.2d 1000, 1004 (5th Cir. 1990) (holding that trial judge's refusal to recognize Abu Dhabi judgment because of failure to meet reciprocity requirement of Texas act "can only be set aside upon a clear showing of abuse" of the discretion conferred on the judge by the act and refusing to adopt exception from dictum in Hilton v. Guyot, 159 U.S. 113, 170, 16 S.Ct. 139, 146, 40 L.Ed. 95, 110 (1895), that the American should be bound by the Abu Dhabi judgment because she was the party who brought the suit there).

sions to their Uniform Acts.[84] These amendments give the state's courts discretion to refuse recognition of a foreign judgment applying law that did not provide at least as much protection of free speech and press as would be provided by the United States and state constitutions.

These provisions were triggered by the fact that under the European Union Regulation on Jurisdiction, a libel plaintiff can sue in any jurisdiction where the libel is published.[85] London courts have attracted "libel tourists." For example, an American historian writes a book that contains a statement accusing a foreign official of corruption. Only 20 books are sold in England. The official sues the historian in the High Court in London. If the historian wishes to defend, it will cost over a million dollars. If the historian does not defend, the official will win by default. His judgment will include attorneys' fees.

There is no reciprocity requirement in the Act, but six states have added one to their versions.[86] Colorado, Idaho, and North Carolina formerly had reciprocity provisions, but when they adopted the 2005 amended Act, they did not insert those sections.[87]

The states that have not enacted the Uniform Act recognize and enforce foreign money judgments in much the same generous manner as

---

84. Cal. CCP § 1716(c)(9); Fla. St. § 55.605(2)(h); Ill. Comp. St. ch. 735 § 12–621(b)(7); N.Y. CPLR § 5304. Also see N.Y. CPLR § 302(d) (asserting personal jurisdiction over any person who obtains a judgment in a defamation proceeding in a foreign country against a New York resident or a person subject to personal jurisdiction in New York who has assets in New York).

85. See Shevill v. Presse Alliance S.A., 1995 E.C.R. 1–415 (Ct.J.E.C., Case C–68/93) (holding that a victim of libel may sue at the publisher's domicile and recover for all harm suffered anywhere, or may sue anyplace the libel was published, but may recover only for harm caused there).

86. See Fla.Stat. Ann. § 55.605(2)(g) (providing for discretionary nonrecognition if foreign country "would not give recognition to a similar judgment rendered in this state"); Ga. Code Ann. § 9–12–114(10) (stating that a foreign judgment "shall not be recognized if . . . the party seeking to enforce the judgment fails to demonstrate that judgments of courts of the United States and of states thereof of the same type and based on substantially similar jurisdictional grounds are recognized and enforced in the courts of the foreign state"); Me. Rev. Stat. Ann. tit. 14 § 8505(2)(G) (providing for discretionary non-recognition if "the foreign court rendering the judgment would not recognize a comparable judgment of this State"); Mass. Gen. Laws Ann. ch. 235, § 23A (stating that a foreign judgment "shall not be recognized if . . . judgments of this state are not recognized in the courts of the foreign state"); Ohio Rev. Code Ann. § 2329.92(B) (stating that if the foreign country does not have a procedure for recognizing judgments of other countries "substantially similar" to the Uniform Foreign Money–Judgments Act, its judgments "may be recognized and enforced . . . in the discretion of the court"); Tex. Civ. Prac. & Rem. Code Ann. § 36.005(b)(7) (stating that "[a] foreign country judgment need not be recognized if . . . it is established that the foreign country in which the judgment was rendered does not recognize judgments rendered in this state").

New Hampshire has not enacted the Uniform Act but has a reciprocity provision for Canadian judgments. N.H. Stat. Ann. § 524:11: "In suits on judgments rendered in the courts of the Dominion of Canada or any province thereof, said judgments shall be give such faith and credit as is given in the courts of the Dominion of Canada or any province thereof to the judgments rendered in the courts of New Hampshire."

87. Colorado: repealed Col. Rev. Stat. § 13–63–102(1); enacted Laws 2008 ch. 42. Idaho: repealed Id. Code § 10–1404(2)(g); enacted 2007 Id. S.B. 1012 (NS). North Carolina: repealed N.C. Gen. Stat. § 1C–1804(b)(7); enacted § 1C–1853.

the enacting states.[88] Section 481 of the Restatement (Third) of Foreign Relations Law states:

> Except as provided in § 482,[89] a final judgment of a court of a foreign state granting or denying recovery of a sum of money, establishing or confirming the status of a person, or determining interests in property, is conclusive between the parties, and is entitled to recognition in courts in the United States.[90]

A comment declares that the section "sets forth the prevailing common and statutory law of States of the United States."[91] *Hilton v. Guyot*[92] based recognition of foreign judgments on "the comity of nations."[93] This is hardly an explanation as to why "comity" should be granted. Perhaps the best explanation is the purely practical one underlying the doctrine of res judicata—"promoting certainty and . . . avoiding duplication of litigation, harassing both to the courts and the individual litigants."[94]

---

88. See Phillips USA, Inc. v. Allflex USA, Inc., 77 F.3d 354, 359 (10th Cir. 1996) (applying Kansas law to recognize an Australian judgment and noting that although Kansas has not passed the Unif. Money–Judgments Act, it applies "traditional principles of comity"); Van Den Biggelaar v. Wagner, 978 F.Supp. 848, 853, 857–61 (N.D. Ind. 1997) (applying Indiana law, enforcing Dutch judgment under doctrine of comity, and stating, at 859, that the Unif. Money–Judgments Act codified "State rules that had long been applied by the majority of courts in the United States"); In re Estate of Steffke, 65 Wis.2d 199, 222 N.W.2d 628, 631 (1974) (refusing to accord comity to Mexican divorce when the parties were not domiciled in Mexico, but stating that "comity results in recognition of a decree of a different state not entitled to full faith and credit").

89. Restatement (Third) of the Foreign Relations Law of the United States § 482 (1987) [hereinafter Restatement of Foreign Relations] (providing the same requirements for recognition as the Unif. Money–Judgments Act except for moving lack of subject-matter jurisdiction from mandatory to discretionary grounds for non-recognition and omitting as a reason for non-recognition the basing of jurisdiction on service in an inconvenient forum).

90. Id. § 481(1).

91. Id. cmt. *a*.

92. 159 U.S. 113, 16 S.Ct. 139, 40 L.Ed. 95 (1895).

93. Id. at 163–64, 16 S.Ct. at 143, 40 L.Ed. at 108. See also id. at 202, 16 S.Ct. at 158, 40 L.Ed. at 122 (stating that a foreign judgment should be recognized if there is no "special reason why the comity of this nation should not allow it full effect"). The Court defined comity as follows:

> "Comity," in the legal sense, is neither a matter of absolute obligation, on the one hand, nor of mere courtesy and good will, upon the other. But it is the recognition which one nation allows within its territory to the legislative, executive, or judicial acts of another nation, having due regard both to international duty and convenience, and to the rights of its own citizens, or of other persons who are under the protection of its laws.

Id. at 163–64, 16 S.Ct. at 143, 40 L.Ed. at 108.

Although in *Hilton* the basis for the New York federal court's subject-matter jurisdiction was diversity of citizenship, the case was decided forty-three years before Erie R.R. v. Tompkins, 304 U.S. 64, 58 S.Ct. 817, 82 L.Ed. 1188 (1938), held that in diversity cases federal courts must apply the common-law rules of the state in which they sit. The Court did not shape its rule to conform with New York law on recognition of foreign judgments.

94. Smit, *International Res Judicata and Collateral Estoppel in the United States*, 9 UCLA L. Rev. 44, 58 (1962). See Dart v. Dart, 460 Mich. 573, 587, 597 N.W.2d 82, 88 (1999), cert. denied, 529 U.S. 1018, 120 S.Ct. 1418, 146 L.Ed.2d 311 (2000): "It was evident from the judgment rendered in England that plaintiff had a fair hearing on the merits, that she was present, represented by counsel, and actively participated. Thus, the present action is barred by res judicata."

In federal-question cases, as noted above,[95] federal courts apply a federal standard to recognition of foreign judgments. *Hilton v. Guyot* established a generous recognition standard that is followed today:

> [W]e are satisfied that where there has been opportunity for a full and fair trial abroad before a court of competent jurisdiction, conducting the trial upon regular proceedings, after due citation or voluntary appearance of the defendant, and under a system of jurisprudence likely to secure an impartial administration of justice between the citizens of its own country and those of other countries, and there is nothing to show either prejudice in the court, or in the system of laws under which it was sitting, or fraud in procuring the judgment, or any other special reason why the comity of this nation should not allow it full effect, the merits of the case should not, in an action brought in this country upon the judgment, be tried afresh, as on a new trial or an appeal, upon the mere assertion of the party that the judgment was erroneous in law or in fact.[96]

A bare majority of the Justices in *Hilton v. Guyot* did establish reciprocity as a requirement for recognition of a foreign judgment.[97] It is unlikely, however, that reciprocity is any longer part of the federal recognition standard, just as it is not part of the standard in most states.[98]

The traditional United States rule has been that, unlike the case with sister-state judgments,[99] a cause of action does not merge with a foreign judgment in favor of the plaintiff.[100] Although the res judicata effects of the foreign judgment on fact issues minimize the consequences of this non-merger rule,[101] one important practical consequence is that

---

95. See supra note 75 and accompanying text.

96. *Hilton*, 159 U.S. at 202–03, 16 S.Ct. at 158, 40 L.Ed. at 122.

97. Id. at 228, 16 S.Ct. at 168, 40 L.Ed. at 130.

98. *See* Tahan v. Hodgson, 662 F.2d 862, 867–68 (D.C. Cir. 1981) (stating, in diversity case, that "[i]t is unlikely that reciprocity is any longer a federally mandated requirement for enforcement of foreign judgments or that the District of Columbia itself has such a requirement that this court is obliged to follow"); McCord v. Jet Spray Int'l Corp., 874 F.Supp. 436, 437 (D. Mass. 1994) (stating, in diversity case, that "[t]he reciprocity requirement first announced by the Supreme Court in Hilton v. Guyot is no longer an element of the federal law of enforcement of foreign judgments"); Restatement of Foreign Relations, supra note 89, § 481 cmt. *d* (stating that "[t]hough [*Hilton*'s reciprocity requirement] has not been formally overruled, it is no longer followed in the great majority of State and federal courts"). But see Gordon and Breach Science Publishers S.A. v. American Inst. of Physics, 905 F.Supp. 169, 179 (S.D.N.Y. 1995) (refusing in Lanham Act suit to give collateral estoppel effect to Swiss and German judgments against the plaintiffs and stating "lack of reciprocity" as one reason).

99. See § 11.3 note 41 and accompanying text.

100. See Juenger, *An International Transaction in the American Conflict of Laws*, 7 FLA. J. INT'L L. 383, 388 (1992) (stating that "foreign judgments do not merge the cause of action"); Reese, *The Status in this Country of Judgments Rendered Abroad*, 50 COLUM. L. REV. 783, 788 (1950) (stating that "[i]n contrast to the well-settled rule concerning judgments of American origin, the prevailing view in this country is that the original cause of action is not merged in a judgment or decree rendered in a foreign nation").

101. See Reese, supra note 100, at 788 (stating that "since the judgment will normally be held conclusive of the issues involved, even though there is no technical merger, the question seems of no practical importance").

the plaintiff can seek recalculation of damages hoping to recover a larger amount.[102]

The non-merger rule for foreign judgments makes little sense, and it is doubtful that it now represents the prevailing U.S. view.[103] One argument for the non-merger rule is that the foreign country might not give its judgments the effect of merger. The response is to give the foreign judgment the same issue and claim preclusion effect that it has where rendered.

§ 11.7   Nonrecognition of Foreign Tax Judgments

It is difficult to overcome the rule "long accepted both in international and in United States practice"[104] that one country does not recognize another country's judgments for taxes. In *Her Majesty v. Gilbertson*,[105] the Ninth Circuit noted that British Columbia courts refuse to enforce United States tax judgments and returned the favor by dismissing a suit to enforce a British Columbia certificate of tax assessment on income that the defendants, Oregon citizens, had received from logging in British Columbia.

Gilbertson applies the "revenue rule" under which courts of one country do not enforce judgments of another country for taxes or assist in the recovery of taxes owed to a foreign sovereign. *Attorney General of Canada v. R.J. Reynolds Tobacco Holdings, Inc.*[106] carried the revenue rule to the extent of refusing to permit Canada to bring an action under the Racketeer Influenced and Corrupt Organizations Act (RICO) against a cigarette manufacturer and others to recover tax revenue lost and law enforcement costs incurred as the result of an alleged conspiracy to smuggle cigarettes into Canada. The dissent noted that the holding prevents RICO remedies for conduct in the U.S.

Pasquantino v. United States,[107] however, held that defendants could be prosecuted under the federal wire fraud statute for actions in the U.S.

---

102.   Restatement (Second) of Judgments § 18 cmt. *b* (1982) (stating that if it were not for the merger rule, "if the claim was unliquidated, the plaintiff might [sue again on the original cause of action and] hope to recover a larger sum than that awarded him by the judgment").

103.   See Unif. Money–Judgments Act, supra note 69, § 3 (stating that a foreign judgment "is conclusive between the parties to the extent that it grants or denies recovery of a sum of money [and] is enforceable in the same manner as the judgment of a sister state which is entitled to full faith and credit"); Restatement of Foreign Relations, supra note 89, cmt. *c* (stating that "[a] foreign judgment is generally entitled to recognition by courts in the United States to the same extent as a judgment of a court of one State in the courts of another State"); Scoles et al., Conflict of Laws 1147 (3rd ed. 2000) (stating that "[t]he non-merger rule has been subject to criticism and indeed makes little sense today"). But see Restatement (Second) of Conflict of Laws § 95 cmt. *c*, illust. 1 (Rev.) (1989) (stating that "[n]o merger results, however, in the case of a judgment for money damages rendered in a foreign nation").

104.   Restatement of Foreign Relations, supra note 89, § 483 cmt. *a*.

105.   597 F.2d 1161 (9th Cir. 1979).

106.   268 F.3d 103 (2d Cir. 2001), cert. denied, 537 U.S. 1000, 123 S.Ct. 513, 154 L.Ed.2d 394 (2002).

107.   544 U.S. 349, 125 S.Ct. 1766, 161 L.Ed.2d 619 (2005).

that were part of a scheme to defraud Canada and the Province of Ontario of excise duties and tax revenues applicable to the importation and sale of liquor. The U.S. Supreme Court stated: "The present prosecution is unlike these classic examples of actions traditionally barred by the revenue rule. It is not a suit that recovers a foreign tax liability, like a suit to enforce a judgment. This is a criminal prosecution brought by the United States in its sovereign capacity to punish domestic criminal conduct."[108] The Court further noted that "this prosecution poses little risk of causing the principal evil against which the revenue rule was traditionally thought to guard: judicial evaluation of the policy-laden enactments of other sovereigns.... True, a prosecution like this one requires a court to recognize foreign law to determine whether the defendant violated U.S. law. But we may assume that by electing to bring this prosecution, the Executive has assessed this prosecution's impact on this Nation's relationship with Canada, and concluded that it poses little danger of causing international friction. We know of no common-law court that has applied the revenue rule to bar an action accompanied by such a safeguard...."[109]

With regard to the cases like *Attorney General of Canada v. R.J. Reynolds Tobacco Holdings*, discussed above, the Court stated: "We express no view on the related question whether a foreign government, based on wire or mail fraud predicate offenses, may bring a civil action under the Racketeer Influenced and Corrupt Organizations Act for a scheme to defraud it of taxes."[110] A case that the Court remanded for reconsideration in the light of *Pasquantino, European Community v. RJR Nabisco, Inc.*,[111] reaffirmed its earlier ruling that various foreign sovereigns could not recover under RICO against cigarette companies that allegedly directed and facilitated the smuggling of contraband cigarettes depriving the plaintiffs of duties and taxes not paid on the cigarettes. The Second Circuit stated: "The present civil lawsuit [unlike *Pasquantino*] is brought by foreign governments, not by the United States. Moreover, the executive branch has given us no signal that it consents to this litigation. * * * In short, the factors that led the *Pasquantino* Court to hold the revenue rule inapplicable to [wire fraud] smuggling prosecutions are missing here."[112]

Courts should abolish the rule regarding non-recognition of tax judgments. As stated in the Restatement (Third) of Foreign Relations law, "[i]n an age when virtually all states impose and collect taxes and when instantaneous transfer of assets can be easily arranged, the rationale for not recognizing or enforcing tax judgments is largely obsolete."[113]

---

108. 125 S.Ct. at 1775.

109. Id. at 1779.

110. Id. at 1771 n.1.

111. 424 F.3d 175 (2d Cir. 2005), cert. denied, 546 U.S. 1092, 126 S.Ct. 1045, 163 L.Ed.2d 858 (2006).

112. Id. at 181.

113. Restatement of Foreign Relations, supra note 89, § 483 Reporters' Notes 2. See William S. Dodge, Breaking the Public Law Taboo, 43 Harv. Int'l L. J. 161 (2002) (urging

§ 11.8   Recognition Abroad of United States Judgments

Although many countries impose a reciprocity requirement,[114] recognition of foreign money judgments is common[115] and recent changes have accelerated the trend toward recognition.[116] In 1990, the Supreme Court of Canada held that, as between Canadian provinces, judgments of one province must be recognized and enforced in another if the basis for personal jurisdiction over the defendant was sufficient for domestic judgments in the recognizing province.[117] Previously in Canada, judg-

---

that courts enforce private public law claims for damages and that treaties provide for enforcement of governmental public law claims). But see Hannah L. Buxbaum, *Transnational Regulatory Litigation*, 46 Va. J. Int'l L. 251, 284 (2006) (rule barring enforcement of foreign tax judgments makes sense because court would have to inspect judgment "to ensure that its enforcement will not contravene U.S. public policy" and that "might embarrass the foreign sovereign, or lead to uncomfortable distinctions among the tax policies of different countries").

114. See Restatement of Foreign Relations, supra note 89, § 481 Reporters' Notes 6(d) (stating that in Germany "foreign judgments will be recognized, but only on the basis of reciprocity"); Brand, supra note 74, at 255 (stating that "enforcement of United States judgments overseas is often possible only if the United States court rendering the judgment would enforce a similar decision of the foreign enforcing court"); Kulzer, *Some Aspects of Enforceability of Foreign Judgments: A Comparative Summary*, 16 Buff. L. Rev. 84, 88 (1966) (stating that "[r]eciprocity is an important concept on the Continent"); Rodriguez Ossa, *Recognition and Enforcement of Foreign Judgments*, 4 Latin Am. L. & Bus. Rep. (No. 9, ISSN: 1065–7428 1996) (stating that Colombian courts require reciprocity in order to recognize foreign judgments); Reyes, Jr., *The Enforcement of Foreign Court Judgments in the People's Republic of China: What the American Lawyer Needs to Know*, 23 Brook. J. Int'l L. 241, 260 (1997) (stating that "[w]hen there is no treaty between [China and the other nation], the principle of mutual reciprocity must be used"); Takeshita, *The Recognition of Foreign Judgments by the Japanese Courts*, 39 Japanese Ann. Int'l L. 55, 72–73 (1996) (discussing Japan's reciprocity requirement); Japanese Code of Civil Procedure Article 118(iv) (listing "reciprocity is assured" as a condition to giving effect to the judgment of another country).

115. See Tahan v. Hodgson, 662 F.2d 862, 868 (D.C. Cir. 1981) (stating that even if reciprocity were required for enforcement "we would still enforce the Israeli judgment since Israel in all probability would enforce a similar American judgment"); McCord v. Jet Spray Int'l Corp., 874 F.Supp. 436, 439–40 (D. Mass. 1994) (holding that Belgium meets the reciprocity requirement imposed under Massachusetts law for recognition of a foreign money judgment); Restatement of Foreign Relations, supra note 89, § 481 Reporters' Notes 6 (discussing enforcement of foreign judgments in Great Britain, Canada, France, and Germany); Bombau, *Enforcement of Foreign Awards*, 49 Int'l Com. Litig. 41 (1995) (discussing enforcement in Argentina); Dörig, *The Finality of U.S. Judgments in Civil Matters as a Prerequisite for Recognition and Enforcement in Switzerland*, 32 Texas Int'l L. J. 271, 275 (1997) (stating that Switzerland recognizes foreign decisions and does not review the judgment on the merits); Rodriguez Ossa, supra note 114 (stating that "[f]oreign judgments may be recognized and accepted by Colombian courts without re-trial or examination of the merits"); Takeshita, supra note 114, at 57–58 (stating that in Japan re-examination of the merits is prohibited at the recognition stage by case precedent and at the execution stage by statute), at 74 (stating that "most non-recognition cases are concerned with judgments emanating from the United States" and that "[t]his seems to reflect the differences in thinking between the two countries with regard to matters such as jurisdictional basis, service abroad, damages, and custody"); Romeu, *Litigation Under the Shadow of an Exequatur: The Spanish Recognition of U.S. Judgments*, 38 Int'l Law. 945 (2004).

116. See J. Lookofsky & K. Hertz, Transnational Litigation and Commercial Arbitration 675–82 (2d ed. 2004) (reviewing judgment-recognition practices in European countries) and notes 119–123 infra and accompanying text.

117. Morguard Investments Ltd. v. De Savoye, 76 D.L.R. 4th 256 (Can. S. Ct. 1990); cf. T.D.I. Hospitality Management Consultants, Inc. v. Browne, 117 D.L.R.4th 289 (Manitoba C.A. 1994) (holding that under *Morguard*, suit can be brought on an Alberta judgment

ments, even from another Canadian province, were recognized only if the basis for personal jurisdiction had been one of the narrow grounds that preceded modern long-arm statutes: citizenship, residence, voluntary appearance, or prior agreement.[118]

In 2003 the Supreme Court of Canada extended its 1990 decision to require recognition and enforcement of the judgments of foreign countries if the judgments meet reasonable standards of fairness. *Saldanha v. Beals*[119] requires an Ontario court to enforce a Florida default judgment against Ontario residents including both treble and punitive damages. The majority held that the Florida judgment must be enforced even if it will bankrupt the defendants. The basis for liability was the sale of Florida land to a developer for $8,000. With interest the judgment is over $1 million Canadian.[120]

The decision not to defend in Florida was based on the advice of an Ontario solicitor that a Canadian court would not enforce the Florida judgment because the Florida court would not have jurisdiction over the defendants unless they appeared. The defendants were not aware of the risk of a large judgment because Florida, like many states, only requires pleading that the case is in excess of the stated jurisdictional amount.

The Uniform Law Conference of Canada has adopted the Canadian Uniform Enforcement of Foreign Judgments Act, which contains the following provision:

Limit of damages

6(1) Where the enforcing court, on application by a judgment debtor, determines that a foreign judgment includes an amount added to compensatory damages as punitive or multiple damages or for other non-compensatory purposes, it shall limit enforcement of the damages awarded by the foreign judgment to the amount of similar or comparable damages that could have been awarded in [*the enacting province or territory.*]

Excessive damages

(2) Where the enforcing court, on application by the judgment debtor, determines that a foreign judgment includes an amount of compensatory damages that is excessive in the circumstances, it may limit enforcement of the award, but the amount awarded may not be less than that which the enforcing court could have awarded in the circumstances.

Costs and Expenses

---

even though the judgment could not be registered because of the restrictive jurisdictional requirements of the Manitoba registration act); Sims v. Bower, 108 D.L.R.4th 677 (New Brunswick C.A. 1993) (holding *Morguard* inapplicable to overturn restrictive jurisdictional requirements of New Brunswick foreign-judgment registration act).

118. See Morguard Investments Ltd. v. De Savoye, 76 D.L.R. 4th 256 (Can. S. Ct. 1990). See also infra notes 127–130 and accompanying text discussing the current United Kingdom rule that is the same as the former Canadian practice.

119. [2003] 3 S.C.R. 416.

120. The solicitor's malpractice insurer paid the judgment.

(3) In this section, a reference to damages includes the costs and expenses of the civil proceeding in the State of origin.[121]

Saskatchewan has enacted the statute.[122] The statute repudiates the generous comity to foreign, and particularly U.S. judgments, that the Supreme Court of Canada favored in *Saldanha*. Section 6(1), which mandatorily restricts recognition of punitive damages, is partially mitigated by 6(3). The latter subsection recognizes that punitive damages in the U.S. may in part compensate the plaintiff for attorney's fees. Section 6(2), which at least is discretionary, imposes on a Canadian court the burden of re-computing compensatory damages. The statute is unfortunate backward step.

Recent legislation in Italy and China facilitates recognition of foreign judgments.[123] Perhaps the best known change in favor of recognition of foreign judgments is the French Cour de Cassation's disapproval of *revision au fond*, under which there was re-examination of the merits.[124]

There are dark spots that could be eliminated by a judgment-recognition treaty, such as the one that the United States and other members of the Hague Conference on Private International Law unsuccessfully attempted to negotiate.[125] The failure resulted from disagreements between U.S. and European Union representatives and from opposition by human rights litigators, trial lawyers, and e-commerce businesses. Instead on 30 June 2005 the Conference completed a Convention on Choice of Court Agreements.[126] The Convention will enter

---

121. http://www.ulcc.ca.

122. S.S. 2005, c. E–9.121 (took effect April 19, 2006).

123. See Legge 31 Maggio 1995, N. 218, Riforma del sistema Italiano di diritto internazionale privato, Gazetta Ufficiale, supp. n.68 al n.128 del 3 giugno 1995; Marini, *Recognition of Foreign Judgments*, 49 INT'L COM. LITIG. 25 (1996) (reporting on change in Italian law making it "easier to have a foreign judgment recognized and enforced in Italy"); Reyes, *supra* note 114, at 256–58, 266 (reporting on Chinese legislation that took effect on April 9, 1991, although also stating that there may be difficulties in enforcement that affect all judgments, including Chinese judgments).

124. Munzer v. Munzer–Jacoby, Cass. Jan 7, 1964, [1964] J.C.P.II, No. 13,590. See Restatement of Foreign Relations, supra note 89, § 481 Reporters' Notes 6 (discussing enforcement of foreign judgments in France); von Mehren & Trautman, *Recognition of Foreign Adjudications: A Survey and A Suggested Approach*, 81 HARV. L. REV. 1601, 1666 (1968) (stating that "although there is no formal rule of stare decisis operative in French law, the issue is probably settled by *Munzer*").

125. See Lau, *Update on the Hague Convention on the Recognition and Enforcement of Foreign Judgments*, 6 Ann. Surv. Int'l & Comp. L. 1 (2000).

126. Convention on Choice of Court Agreements, 30 June 2005, available on Hague Conference web site, convention number 37. The Convention applies to exclusive choice of court agreements (derogation agreements) in international cases. The Convention does not apply to consumer or employment contracts. Nor does it apply to sixteen matters excluded in art. 2(2) including "the carriage of passengers and goods", anti-trust, and "claims for personal injury brought by or on behalf of natural persons." The derogation agreement must select a court of a Contracting State. Art. 3(a). A choice-of-court agreement is "deemed to be exclusive unless the parties have expressly provided otherwise." Art. 3(b). The validity of the choice of court agreement is independent of the other terms of the contract. Art. 3(d). [Cf. Scherk v. Alberto–Culver Co., 417 U.S. 506, 519 n.14, 94 S.Ct. 2449, 2456 n.14, 41 L.Ed.2d 270 (1974), stating this doctrine for derogation and arbitration agreements]. A court that has jurisdiction under the agreement may not grant a forum non

into force after the second ratification, but as of 1 October 2009 only Mexico has ratified and the European Community and the United States have signed the Convention.

The United Kingdom still clings to a double standard for personal jurisdiction and, absent a treaty, will not recognize foreign default judgments unless based on the nineteenth century bases[127]—service while present, appearance, or prior consent.[128] Yet, for its own courts, the U.K. maintains a modern long-arm regime exercising specific jurisdiction[129] in contract, maintenance, tort, and other matters.[130]

---

conveniens dismissal. Art. 5(2). A court not chosen must suspend or dismiss proceedings to which the agreement applies unless one of five exceptions applies including "the agreement is null and void under the law of the State of the chosen court" or "giving effect to the agreement would lead to a manifest injustice or would be manifestly contrary to the public policy of the state of the courts seised." Art. 6. Courts of contracting states must recognize and enforce the judgment of a court chosen in the agreement unless one of Convention's seven grounds for refusal applies. Arts. 8, 9. These grounds include failure to notify the defendant in sufficient time for defense and recognition would violate the public policy of the requested state. Art. 9(c), (e). A court may refuse enforcement "to the extent that the judgment awards damages, including exemplary or punitive damages, that do not compensate for actual loss or harm suffered" but in doing so must "take into account whether and to what extent the damages awarded by the court of origin serve to cover costs and expenses relating to the proceedings." Art. 11. "A State may declare that its courts may refuse to determine disputes to which an exclusive choice of court agreement applies if, except for the location of the chosen court, there is no connection between that State and the parties or the dispute." Art. 19.

127. *See* Pennoyer v. Neff, 95 U.S. 714, 733, 24 L.Ed. 565 (1878) (stating that a valid judgment may be rendered against a nonresident only if the nonresident is "brought within its jurisdiction by service or process within the State, or his voluntary appearance").

128. See Restatement of Foreign Relations, supra note 89, § 481 Reporters' Notes 6 (stating that "in respect of foreign default judgments, Great Britain does not recognize many of the bases on which its courts would exercise jurisdiction over absent defendants"); 1 A.V. Dicey & J.H.C. Morris, Conflict of Laws 472–73 (12th ed. 1993, Lawrence Collins, ed.) (stating that the U.K. will recognize foreign judgments only if required by treaty or the basis for jurisdiction was service on the defendant while present, appearance, or consent). See also Civil Jurisdiction and Judgments Act 1982, ch. 27, § 33(1):

> For the purposes of determining whether a judgment given by a court of an overseas country should be recognised or enforced in England and Wales or Northern Ireland, the person against whom the judgment was given shall not be regarded as having submitted to the jurisdiction of the court by reason only of the fact that he appeared (conditionally or otherwise) in the proceedings for all or any one or more of the following purposes, namely (a) to contest the jurisdiction of the court; (b) to ask the court to dismiss or stay the proceedings on the ground that the dispute in question should be submitted to arbitration or to the determination of the courts of another country; (c) to protect, or obtain the release of, property seized or threatened with seizure in the proceedings.

The Swiss Private International Law Statute art. 149 does not recognize some long-arm bases for personal jurisdiction over Swiss domiciliaries in foreign courts even though the same bases for jurisdiction are used by Swiss courts

129. "Specific jurisdiction" refers to "jurisdiction over a defendant in a suit arising out of or related to the defendant's contacts with the forum." Helicopteros Nacionales de Colombia, S.A. v. Hall, 466 U.S. 408, 414 n.8, 104 S.Ct. 1868, 1872 n.8, 80 L.Ed.2d 404, 411 n.8 (1984). "General jurisdiction" refers to jurisdiction "over a defendant in a suit not arising out of or related to the defendant's contacts with the forum." Id. at 414 n.9, 104 S.Ct. at 1872 n.9, 80 L.Ed.2d at 411 n.9.

130. Civil Jurisdiction and Judgments Act, 1982, ch. 27, pt. I, § 2, which declares that the Convention on Jurisdiction and Enforcement of Judgments in Civil and Commercial Matters, Sept. 27, 1968, 1972 O.J. (L 299) 32 "shall have the force of law in the United Kingdom"; id. sched. 1 § 2 (reprinting the "special jurisdiction" provisions of the Conven-

The German Supreme Court rejected on public policy grounds the punitive damages portion of a United States judgment for sexual abuse of a child, but enforced the rest of the judgment.[131] Subsequent German legislation mandates nonrecognition of tort judgments that "go substan-

---

tion). The Convention has since been converted to a Regulation, Brussels Regulation supra note 47.

The English double jurisdictional standard for recognition of judgments might be explained by the fact that even if English courts considered an English statutory basis for jurisdiction to be exorbitant, the courts have no power to invalidate an act of Parliament. See Schibsby v. Westenholz, L.R. 6 Q.B. 155, 160 (1870) (stating that if a foreigner is sued in an English court, the court must recognize the jurisdictional bases enacted by Parliament but if the judgment had to be enforced in the U.S. "a further question would be open, viz., not only whether the British legislature had given the English courts jurisdiction over the defendant, but whether he was under any obligation which the American courts could recognize to submit to the jurisdiction thus created"). See also Nygh, *The Common Law Approach*, in Transnational Tort Litigation: Jurisdictional Principles 21, 29–30 (McLachlan & Nygh eds., 1996) (explaining current use of the British double jurisdictional standard as caused by the courts' continued distrust of statutory enlargement of common law bases).

English Courts acquired a limited power to provide remedies against acts of Parliament when the Human Rights Act 1998, U.K. St. 1998 c. 42, took full effect in October 2000. The Act codifies the provisions of the European Convention for the Protection of Human Rights and Fundamental Freedoms, opened for signature Nov. 4, 1950, 213 U.N.T.S. 222 (Council of Europe) (entered into force Sept. 3, 1953). Under the Act, if a court finds that an act of parliament is incompatible with a Convention right, the court "may make a declaration of that incompatibility." (§ 4(2)). The declaration "does not affect the validity, continuing operation or enforcement of the provision in respect of which it is given" (§ 4(6)(a)). Nevertheless, the Act forbids public authorities from acting "in a way which is incompatible with a Convention right" (§ 6(1)) and courts may provide judicial remedies for such unlawful acts (§ 8). Article 6(1) of the Convention provides: "In the determination of his civil rights and obligations or of any criminal charge against him everyone is entitled to a fair and public hearing within a reasonable time by an independent and impartial tribunal established by law."

131. Judgment of the Bundesgerichtshof, IXth Civil Senate, of June 4, 1992, Docket No. IX ZR 149/91 [1992] Wertpapiermitteilungen 1451. The plaintiff, a fourteen-year old male and an American citizen, sued the defendant, who had dual United States and German citizenship, for sexual abuse. Although the defendant was represented by counsel in the preliminary stages of the litigation, neither the defendant nor his counsel appeared at trial. The plaintiff was awarded $750,260, which included $400,000 in punitive damages. The German Supreme Court held that, notwithstanding the 40% contingent fee to plaintiff's lawyer, the judgment would be enforced in Germany except for the punitive damages. The court stated that it was against German public policy to recognize "a lump-sum award of punitive damages in a not insubstantial amount." [1992] WM at 1460. For comment on the decision, see Hay, *The Recognition and Enforcement of American Money–Judgments in Germany—The 1992 Decision of the German Supreme Court*, 40 AMER. J. COMP. L. 729 (1992); Zekoll, *The Enforceability of American Money Judgments Abroad: A Landmark Decision by the German Federal Court of Justice*, 30 COLUM. J. TRANSNAT'L L. 641 (1992). But cf. Princess Caroline of Monaco v. Publisher of the Magazines "B" and "G", Bundesgerichtshof 1995 Neue Juristische Wochenschrift 861, in which the German Supreme Court held that damages for violation of the right of privacy should be awarded in an amount sufficient to provide satisfaction to the victim and to deter repetition of the conduct. The court held that the damages awarded by the Court of Appeals were not sufficient to have an impact on the defendant or present a genuine disincentive to such conduct. The case was remanded for a new determination of damages. Does this judgment authorize a form of punitive damages? See Behr, *Myth and Reality of Punitive Damages in Germany*, 24 J. L. & Commerce 197, 221–22 (2005): "[A]t least in some areas of law, German courts award damages similar to U.S. punitive damages awards.... But the German judgment will not openly address the awarded damages as being punitive damages.... Anyhow, courts will award damages beyond pure compensation and based on punitive considerations. Such an award may happen by applying a method of damage calculation that not only focuses on the actual damages but additionally on the profit the tortfeasor received from his wrongful behavior. Or it may happen because the German court will take into consideration that damages must have a real deterrent effect."

tially beyond that which is required for appropriate compensation for the injured person."[132] This is not surprising. Although some countries may recognize judgments for punitive damages,[133] many do not.[134] The United Kingdom has gone so far as to pass a "claw-back" statute that not only refuses to recognize foreign judgments for punitive and multiple damages, but also authorizes suits to recover any amount of the judgment already paid that was not purely compensatory.[135] Australia goes further and permits recovery of the entire judgment paid in an antitrust action if the country's Attorney General finds that the foreign court's assumption of jurisdiction is "contrary to international law or inconsistent with international comity or international practice."[136]

There are other trouble spots for recognition of U.S. judgments, including Austria, the Netherlands, Norway,[137] and Brazil.[138] A practitioner, frustrated with the exequatur[139] procedure necessary to obtain recognition for a U.S. judgment in Mexico, has declared U.S. judgments "worthless" south of the border.[140]

---

132. Germany, Bundesgesetzblatt 1999, I, 1026, sec. 5 art. 40(3)(1) (as translated in Hay, *From Rule–Orientation to "Approach" in German Conflicts Law. The Effect of the 1986 and 1999 Codifications*, 47 Am. J. Comp. L. 633, 651 (1999)).

133. *Cf.* Brand, *Punitive Damages and the Recognition of Judgments*, 43 Netherlands Int'l L. Rev. 143, 169 (1996) (discussing a Swiss decision); *cf. id.* at 147–48 (discussing decisions from Australia, Canada, and New Zealand awarding punitive damages in domestic cases); Jablonski, *Translation and Comment: Enforcing U.S. Punitive Damages Award in Foreign Courts—A Recent Case in the Supreme Court of Spain*,.24 J. L. & Commerce 225 (2005) (enforcing U.S. judgment awarding damages for violations of plaintiffs' intellectual and industrial property rights).

134. See Brand, supra note 133, at 163, 167 (discussing decisions from Germany and Japan); cf. id. at 146–47 (discussing the limits that the House of Lords has imposed on domestic judgments for punitive damages); Ostoni, *Italian Rejection of Punitive Damages in a U.S. Judgment*, 24 J. L. & Commerce 245 (2005); Takeshita, supra note 114, at 67 (discussing refusal of Japanese courts to recognize a California judgment awarding "absolutely enormous" punitive damages).

135. Protection of Trading Interests Act 1980, § 6.

136. Foreign Proceedings (Excess of Jurisdiction) Act, 1984, §§ 9(1)(b)(ii), 10 (Austl.)

137. *See* A. Lowenfeld, International Litigation and the Quest for Reasonableness 109 (stating that absent a treaty, those countries do not regard a foreign judgment as having effect outside the rendering state, but pointing out that Netherlands courts often recognize foreign judgments even though not required to do so). But see Juenger, *The Recognition of Money Judgments in Civil and Commercial Matters*, 36 Am. J. Comp. L. 1, 38 (1988) (stating that the Netherlands has "advanced from a narrow, ethnocentric position to one of considerable liberality toward judgments rendered outside the Common Market").

138. See Kim & Cowen, *The Recognition and Enforcement of Foreign Judgments under Brazilian Law and the Uniform Foreign Money–Judgments Recognition Act*. 5 Transnat'l L. 725, 735 (1992) (stating that Brazil will recognize a foreign judgment only if "the Brazilian domiciliary expressly submits to the foreign court's jurisdiction").

139. The exequatur procedure results in issuance of a writ that renders a foreign judgment subject to execution in the same manner as a domestic judgment. The formalities required for the procedure differ from country to country and can be onerous. *See* Kulzer, supra note 114 at 89 n.29 (describing exequatur in France); Vargas, *Enforcement of Judgments and Arbitral Awards in Mexico*, 5 U.S.–Mexico L. J. 137, 147 (!997) (stating that exequatur is also known as homologacíon in Mexico).

140. Kash, 31 Ariz. Att'y 11, 13 (July 1995) (stating that a U.S. judgment is "worthless except in limited circumstances"). See also Adler, *Enforcement in a New Age: Judgments in the United States and Mexico*, 5 U.S.–Mexico L. J. 149, 152 (1997) (stating that a litigant can block enforcement of a U.S. judgment by bringing parallel litigation in Mexico); Vargas,

The decision of the German Supreme Court[141] is a red flag warning that foreign countries are not likely to recognize United States judgments for punitive or multiple damages. Moreover, United States judgments for non-monetary compensatory damages, such as pain and suffering, are widely regarded as excessive. Lord Denning stated that U.S. juries award damages in "fabulous" amounts.[142] Defense of punitive damages will not be helped by the facts that most states have, by statute or decision, placed limits on punitive awards[143] and that the United States Supreme Court has held that a "grossly excessive" award of punitive damages violates due process.[144]

In addition to the difficulty of obtaining recognition abroad for United States judgments that award punitive and multiple damages, no court will recognize a judgment based on a principal of personal jurisdiction that the court regards as exorbitant. The United States employs two bases for general[145] personal jurisdiction that are widely regarded as exorbitant—service on a defendant temporarily present in the jurisdiction ("tag" jurisdiction) and doing business. The Brussels Regulation prohibits the use of tag jurisdiction against defendants domiciled in signatory countries.[146] Domicile is the Regulation's only basis for general jurisdiction.[147]

---

supra note 139, at 147 (stating that even though all conditions for exequatur or homologación "are fully complied with, there is no guarantee the foreign judgment will be enforced").

The Survey on Recognition of U.S. Money Judgments by the Committee on Foreign and Comparative Law of the Association of the Bar of the City of New York, July 31, 2001, makes inconsistent statements on recognition of United States Money Judgments (USMJ) in Mexico. For example the Survey states on page 7: "Mexico will recognize and enforce a USMJ so long as the US court had jurisdiction over the defendant and the USMJ was rendered in accordance with rules of jurisdiction compatible with Mexican law." Then on page 24 appears: "In Mexico, appeal is by way of a proceeding known as the *amparo*. This is apparently a time-tested way for a losing party to avoid paying a judgment for years, and to take the opportunity, if it has already done so, to remove or otherwise shelter assets. Thus, in Mexico, the appeal process is often a significant practical obstacle to the recognition of a USMJ."

141. See supra notes 131–132 and accompanying text.

142. Smith Kline & French Lab. Ltd. v. Bloch, [1983] 1 W.L.R. 730, 734 (C.A. 1982) (Denning, M.R.).

After years of "tort reform" at state and federal levels, U.S. courts are no longer the best venues for plaintiffs in every case. See § 4.33A, note 177 and accompanying text.

143. See Brand, supra note 133, at 163 (stating that "at least 40 of the 50 states have imposed some kind of restriction on punitive damages awards, with a majority of those restrictions being enacted within the past 10 years").

144. BMW of North America, Inc. v. Gore, 517 U.S. 559, 585, 116 S.Ct. 1589, 1604, 134 L.Ed.2d 809, 833 (1996). See also O'Gilvie v. United States, 519 U.S. 79, 84, 117 S.Ct. 452, 455, 136 L.Ed.2d 454, 461 (1996) (holding that an award of punitive damages in a tort suit is taxable because not within an Internal Revenue Code provision excluding from income damages received "on account of personal injuries or sickness" and stating that punitive damages are not designed to compensate victims).

145. For the meaning of general jurisdiction see supra note 129.

146. See Brussels Regulation, supra note 47, Annex I.

147. Id. art 2. The domicile of a company is "the place where it has its: (a) statutory seat or (b) central administration, or (c) principal place of business." Id. art. 60.

Chapter 12

INTERNATIONAL PROBLEMS

§ 12.1 Extraterritorial Application of Antitrust Law

When there is the most blatant form of conspiracy in restraint of trade, a price-fixing agreement between competitors, the antitrust regimes of the world are united in the view that it does not matter that the smoke-filled rooms where the plots are hatched are abroad. The reasoning may differ, the "effects doctrine" in the United States,[1] "the place where [the conspiracy] is implemented,"[2] in the European Union, but the result is extraterritorial application of antitrust law to protect the nation's consumers.

The current debate concerning extraterritoriality is over comity, the degree to which a nation should refrain from applying its antitrust law to activities abroad that are legal where the actions occur. In the United States there is a spectrum of positions on comity, both in the scholarly community and in the courts, ranging from no extraterritorial application in the absence of express statutory language, to no comity when acts abroad cause substantial and foreseeable effects that violate Sherman Act policies. In the middle of this spectrum are various comity positions, the best known of which is section 403 of the Restatement (Third) of Foreign Relations Law. Under section 403, a nation may not exercise jurisdiction to prescribe penalties for acts abroad that cause substantial effects within it if the exercise is "unreasonable."[3] The section then provides a non-exclusive list of eight factors for a court to apply when deciding whether extraterritoriality is reasonable.[4]

The opinion of the Supreme Court of the United States in *Hartford Fire Insurance Co. v. California*[5] should have resolved the comity debate in the United States, but the Court split five to four and flaws in both the majority and dissenting opinions prevent drawing confident conclusions from that case. *Hartford Fire* was a suit by nineteen states and many private plaintiffs against insurance companies including some London-based reinsurance companies. Plaintiffs alleged that the insurers violated the Sherman Act by conspiring to control the form of commercial general liability insurance available in the United States. The

---

1. See RESTATEMENT (THIRD) OF THE FOREIGN RELATIONS LAW OF THE UNITED STATES §§ 402(1)(c), 403(2)(a) (1986) [hereinafter RESTATEMENT (THIRD) FOREIGN RELATIONS LAW].

2. A. Ahlstrom Osakeyhtio v. Commission of the European Communities, [1988] E.C.R. 5193, 5243 [hereinafter *Wood Pulp Case*].

3. RESTATEMENT (THIRD) FOREIGN RELATIONS LAW, supra note 1, § 403(1).

4. Id. § 403(2).

5. 509 U.S. 764, 113 S.Ct. 2891, 125 L.Ed.2d 612 (1993).

London reinsurers claimed that their actions were legal under English law and the British government, appearing as amicus curiae, concurred.

Justice Souter, writing for the bare majority, held that the Sherman Act applied. His opinion has been interpreted by many commentators as holding that there is no room for comity when actions abroad cause foreseeable violations of United States law and the only defense is sovereign compulsion.[6] What makes this interpretation doubtful is that Justice Souter cited as authority section 403 of the Restatement (Third) of Foreign Relations Law.[7] If his opinion rejects comity, Souter cannot rely on the Restatement, which champions comity. It is more likely that Justice Souter is saying that it would be a waste of time in such an egregious case, a conspiracy abroad solely intended to cause anticompetitive effects in the United States, to wade through the comity analysis of the Restatement. Only if the British Government compelled the English defendants to act as they did would they have a possible defense, and there was no such compulsion. The key passage creating this ambiguity reads:

> We need not decide that question [comity] here, however, for even assuming that in a proper case a court may decline to exercise Sherman Act jurisdiction over foreign conduct ..., international comity would not counsel against exercising jurisdiction *in the circumstances alleged here.*

> The only substantial question in this litigation is whether [the English reinsurers could comply with both British and United States law].[8]

There is a similar passage in the famous *Wood Pulp* decision of the Court of Justice of the European Communities, which also is ambiguous with regard to comity:

> As regards the argument relating to disregard of international comity, it suffices to observe that it amounts to calling in question the Community's jurisdiction to apply its competition rules to conduct *such as that found to exist in this case* and that, as such, that argument has already been rejected.[9]

In any event, it is clear that the Ninth Circuit, in which *Hartford* arose, does not read Justice Souter's opinion as eliminating comity concerns. A Ninth Circuit decision has declared: "*Hartford* ... did not question the propriety of the jurisdictional rule of reason or the seven comity factors

---

6. See, e.g., Guzman, *Is International Antitrust Possible?*, 73 N.Y.U. L. Rev. 1501, 1508 (1998); Snyder, *Mergers and Acquisitions in the European Community and the United States: A Movement Toward a Uniform Enforcement Body?*, 29 Law & Pol'y Int'l Bus. 115, 118 (1997).

7. *Hartford*, 509 U.S. at 799, 113 S.Ct. at 2910, 125 L.Ed.2d at 641.

8. Id. at 798–99, 113 S.Ct. at 2910, 125 L.Ed.2d at 640 (emphasis added).

9. *Wood Pulp Case*, supra note 2, [1988] E.C.R. at 5244 (emphasis added) (referring to a conspiracy abroad to fix the price of wood pulp sold in the European Union).

set forth in [*Timberlane Lumber Co. v. Bank of America*, 549 F.2d 597 (9th Cir. 1976)]."[10]

Justice Scalia's dissent in *Hartford Fire* runs through the Restatement of Foreign Relations' section 403 factors for determining when extraterritorial application of law is reasonable. He concludes, "[r]arely would these factors point more clearly against application of United States law."[11] When quoting the very first factor, however, he omits the phrase referring to activity abroad that "has substantial, direct, and foreseeable effect upon or in the territory."[12] This is the language most relevant to *Hartford*.

At least with regard to enforcement actions by antitrust officials, this comity debate is moot. Article VI of the 1991 Agreement on the Application of Their Competition Laws between the European Communities and the United States expressly requires comity and sets out five non-exclusive factors for consideration, similar to the factors in the Restatement (Third) of Foreign Relations Law.[13] The 1995 Antitrust Enforcement Guidelines for International Operations, issued by the Department of Justice and the Federal Trade Commission, states that those agencies "have agreed with respect to member countries of the [Organization for Economic Co–Operation and Development (OECD)] to consider the legitimate interests of other nations in accordance with relevant OECD recommendations."[14] The preamble to the 1995 revised OECD recommendations recognizes "the need for Member countries to give effect to the principles of international law and comity and to use moderation and self-restraint in the interest of co-operation on the field of anticompetitive practices."[15]

With regard to antitrust suits by private parties, such as *Hartford*, the role of comity is less clear. One can sympathize with those courts that feel unable and unwilling "to conduct a neutral balancing of the competing interests" and find a comity approach "unsuitable."[16] I suggest as a feasible comity standard for private litigation a presumption

---

10. Metro Indus., Inc. v. Sammi Corp., 82 F.3d 839, 846 n.5 (9th Cir.), cert. denied, 519 U.S. 868, 117 S.Ct. 181, 136 L.Ed.2d 120 (1996).

11. *Hartford*, 509 U.S. at 819, 113 S.Ct. at 2921, 125 L.Ed.2d at 653 (Scalia, J., dissenting).

12. Id. at 818, 113 S.Ct. at 2921, 125 L.Ed.2d at 653 (Scalia, J., dissenting) (omitting language from Restatement (Third) Foreign Relations Law, supra note 1, § 403(2)(a)).

13. European Communities–United States: Agreement on the Application of Their Competition Laws, September 23, 1991, 30 I.L.M. 1487, 1497–98 (1991) [hereinafter 1991 Competition Laws Agreement]. The 1998 agreement between the same parties does not supersede the 1991 agreement. Agreement between the European Communities and the Government of the United States of America on the Application of Positive Comity Principles in the Enforcement of Their Competition Laws, art. VI, June 4, 1998, 37 I.L.M. 1070, 1075 (1998) [hereinafter 1998 Competition Laws Agreement].

14. Antitrust Enforcement Guidelines for International Operations–1995, § 2.92, reprinted in 4 CCH Trade Regulation Reporter ¶ 13,107 [hereinafter 1995 Guidelines].

15. Revised Recommendation of the Council concerning Co–Operation Between Member Countries on Anticompetitive Practices Affecting International Trade, 28 July 1995, 35 I.L.M. 1313, 1314 (1996).

16. Laker Airways Ltd. v. Sabena, 731 F.2d 909, 948 (D.C. Cir. 1984).

that United States law applies if conduct abroad "has a direct, substantial, and reasonably foreseeable effect"[17] in the United States that is contrary to United States competition policies. The presumption is rebutted when the effects in the United States, though "substantial," pale when compared with the policies of foreign governments that application of United States law will thwart. To take an example from extraterritorial application of both antitrust and securities law, I believe that the Second Circuit violated this minimal comity standard when it enjoined worldwide the tender offer of one foreign corporation for the shares of another foreign corporation even though only 2.5 percent of the shares were held by Americans and the offer did not violate foreign law.[18]

The Foreign Trade Antitrust Improvements Act of 1982 (FTAIA), 15 U.S.C. § 6a, which was intended to assist in clarifying the intended extraterritorial reach of the Sherman Act, provides:

> Sections 1 to 7 of this title shall not apply to conduct involving trade or commerce (other than import trade or import commerce) with foreign nations unless—
>
> (1) such conduct has a direct, substantial, and reasonably foreseeable effect—
>
> (A) on trade or commerce which is not trade or commerce with foreign nations, or on import trade or import commerce with foreign nations; or
>
> (B) on export trade or export commerce with foreign nations, of a person engaged in such trade or commerce in the United States; and
>
> (2) such effect gives rise to a claim under the provisions of sections 1 to 7 of this title, other than this section.
>
> If sections 1 to 7 of this title apply to such conduct only because of the operation of paragraph (1)(B), then sections 1 to 7 of this title shall apply to such conduct only for injury to export business in the United States.

The Act has a limited scope. It excludes cases that are most likely to raise the question of the proper extraterritorial reach of the Sherman Act—conspiracies to fix the price or terms of sale of goods or services exported to the U.S. from abroad.[19] Subsection 1(A) poses the problem of how conduct that does not involve import commerce can affect import commerce. The only likely example is one in which the foreign conspirators, instead of themselves exporting price-fixed goods to the U.S., sell

---

17.   15 U.S.C. § 6a(1). This language appears in the Foreign Trade Antitrust Improvements Act of 1982, which, although not applicable to "import trade or import commerce," provides a desirable standard for all extraterritorial application of United States antitrust law.

18.   Consolidated Gold Fields PLC v. Minorco, S.A., 871 F.2d 252, modified, 890 F.2d 569 (2d Cir.), cert. dism'd, 492 U.S. 939, 110 S.Ct. 29, 106 L.Ed.2d 639 (1989).

19.   See Dee–K Enterprises, Inc. v. Heveafil Sdn. Bhd., 299 F.3d 281, 287 (4th Cir. 2002), cert. denied, 539 U.S. 969, 123 S.Ct. 2638, 156 L.Ed.2d 675 (2003).

the goods to an exporter who is not part of the conspiracy, knowing that the exporter will sell the goods to U.S. users.[20]

An issue on which Federal circuits differed is whether a plaintiff can meet § 6a(2)'s requirement that there is "a" Sherman Act claim by showing that someone other than the plaintiff has such a claim. *F. Hoffmann–La Roche Ltd. v. Empagran S.A.*[21] resolved the disagreement holding that 15 U.S.C. § 6a(2)'s requirement that there be "a" Sherman Act claim refers "to the 'plaintiff's claim' or 'the claim at issue.' "[22] Therefore if the foreign injury was independent of domestic effects, a purchaser in Ecuador could not bring a Sherman Act claim based on foreign harm even though a purchaser in the U.S. had a claim under the Act.

U.S. and foreign manufacturers and distributors of vitamins allegedly engaged in a price-fixing conspiracy that inflated the price of vitamins in the U.S. and abroad. The court stated:

> We have assumed that the anticompetitive conduct here independently caused foreign injury; that is, the conduct's domestic effects did not help to bring about that foreign injury. Respondents argue, in the alternative, that the foreign injury was not independent. Rather, they say, the anticompetitive conduct's domestic effects were linked to that foreign harm. Respondents contend that, because vitamins are fungible and readily transportable, without an adverse domestic effect (i.e., higher prices in the United States), the sellers could not have maintained their international price-fixing arrangement and respondents would not have suffered their foreign injury. They add that this "but for" condition is sufficient to bring the price-fixing conduct within the scope of the FTAIA's exception.

> The Court of Appeals, however, did not address this argument, and, for that reason, neither shall we. Respondents remain free to ask the Court of Appeals to consider the claim. The Court of Appeals may determine whether respondents properly preserved the argument, and, if so, it may consider it and decide the related claim.[23]

On remand the D.C. Circuit affirmed the judgment of the District Court dismissing the case. The court held that there must be "a direct causal relationship" between the domestic effects of defendants' conduct and the foreign injury. The "but for" causation asserted by the plaintiffs is not sufficient.[24]

---

20. See 1995 Guidelines, supra note 14, § 3.121.

21. 542 U.S. 155, 124 S.Ct. 2359, 159 L.Ed.2d 226 (2004).

22. Id. at 174, 124 S.Ct. at 2372.

23. Id. at 175, 124 S.Ct. at 2372.

24. Empagran S.A. v. F. Hoffmann–LaRoche, Ltd., 417 F.3d 1267, 1271 (D.C. Cir. 2005), cert. denied, 546 U.S. 1092, 126 S.Ct. 1043, 163 L.Ed.2d 857 (2006). See also In re Dynamic Radom Access Memory (DRAM) Antitrust Litigation, 546 F.3d 981 (9th Cir. 2008) (affirming dismissal of a class action antitrust suit by a British computer manufacturer that purchased memory chips outside the U.S., the price of which defendants allegedly conspired to fix; holding that proximate causation, which is required under FTAIA domestic injury exception, is not met by the domestic effects of the alleged conspiracy).

§ 12.2   Protecting United States Exporters

There has been much debate over whether the United States should use the Sherman Act and other means, such as threat of trade sanctions, to protect United States companies' access to foreign markets. The Foreign Trade Antitrust Improvements Act of 1982 asserted jurisdiction over conduct abroad that affects "export trade."[25] The Department of Justice and the Federal Trade Commission created a political firestorm when footnote 159 of their 1988 Antitrust Enforcement Guidelines disclaimed an interest in prosecuting acts abroad that did not harm United States consumers. The 1995 Guidelines prudently retreat from this disclaimer and assert that the Department and Commission "may, in appropriate cases, take enforcement action against anticompetitive conduct, wherever occurring, that restrains U.S. exports...."[26] The Agencies mitigate this boldness by then stating that if they "believe that they may encounter difficulties in establishing personal jurisdiction or in obtaining effective relief, the case may be one in which the Agencies would seek to resolve their concerns by working with other authorities who are examining the transaction."[27]

United States efforts to protect exporters' access to foreign markets have created hostility abroad and have had limited success. Beginning in 1986, the United States and Japan participated in a series of bilateral agreements on semiconductor trade to open the Japanese market for foreign-produced computer chips and to prevent dumping.[28] These agreements may have contributed to United States companies gaining a larger share of the Japanese chip market. The European Union, however, protested that the bilateral agreements were a device to gain "privileged access of American firms to the Japanese market" and to cause "the arbitrary increase of semiconductor prices on Community markets."[29] Thus whatever the United States achieved in opening the Japanese market for American semiconductor manufacturers, came at the price of angering our friends.

Forcing access to foreign markets is likely to cause ill will abroad. The 1998 European Communities–United States Agreement on antitrust enforcement reflects the sensitivity of this topic. The Agreement stirs memories of footnote 159 of the 1988 United States Antitrust Enforcement Guidelines. Article IV provides that if anticompetitive activities in one of the signatories "do not have a direct, substantial and reasonably foreseeable impact on consumers in the [other signatory's] territory,"

---

25.   15 U.S.C. § 6a(1)(B). The Act also prevents application of the Sherman Act if acts in the United States have effects only abroad. See Eurim–Pharm GmbH v. Pfizer Inc., 593 F.Supp. 1102 (S.D.N.Y.1984). In 1918 the Webb–Pomerene Act, 15 U.S.C. §§ 61–65, accomplished much of the same objective of not applying the Sherman Act to conduct in the United States that affects only foreign consumers.

26.   1995 Guidelines, supra note 14, § 3.122.

27.   Id. illustrative example D.

28.   Japan–United States: Agreement on Semiconductor Trade, 25 I.L.M. 1408 (1986).

29.   European Community Declaration Concerning Japanese–United States Agreement on Semiconductor Trade, 25 I.L.M. 1621 (1986).

the country whose consumers are not affected will request the other country to remedy the anticompetitive activities on its territory. The "Requesting Party" will then suspend its own enforcement activities "in favor of enforcement activities by the competition authorities of the Requested Party."[30]

Some attempts at prying open foreign markets are not successful. An example is the debacle when, on March 31, 1998, a World Trade Organization (WTO) panel rejected all United States contentions that Japanese governmental measures contributed to Kodak's inability to penetrate the Japanese market.[31] The United States has announced that it will not appeal this loss but will monitor Japanese conduct for compliance with various representations that Japan made during the WTO proceedings.[32]

Trade globalization has important implications for attempts to open foreign markets for domestic producers. When the administration of President George H.W. Bush used threats of trade sanctions to open the Japanese market for Motorola, almost all of Motorola's production activities were in Malaysia. Malaysian workers and Motorola stockholders enjoyed whatever benefits these threats produced.[33] In a global economy a nation is wise to expend its resources on giving its population competitive skills rather than on protecting its exporters.[34]

§ 12.3 Globalization Increases Effects Abroad

Globalization of the economy has also made it more likely that activities abroad will affect a nation's competition policies. An example is the merger of two United States airplane manufacturers, Boeing and McDonnell Douglas. The United States Federal Trade Commission (FTC) approved the merger, finding that there would be little or no anticompetitive effect on the sales of civil aircraft because McDonnell Douglas was swiftly losing the fight to remain a player on that field. The Commission of the European Communities (EC) viewed the merger differently. A European Union antitrust official accused the FTC of distorting its antitrust guidelines to strengthen Boeing as "national champion" to compete with Europe's Airbus. The EC Commission found that "the proposed concentration would lead to the strengthening of a dominant position through which effective competition would be significantly impeded in the common market. . . . "[35] The Commission approved

---

30. 1998 Competition Laws Agreement, supra note 13, art. IV(2)(a)(i).

31. See World Trade Organization, Report of the Panel, Japan—Measures Affecting Consumer Photographic Film and Paper, WT/DS44/R (Mar 31, 1998); World Trade Organization, Report of the Panel, United States—Section 301–310 of the Trade Act of 1974, WT/DS152/R (Dec 22, 1999).

32. See Goldman, *Bad Lawyering or Ulterior Motive? Why the United States Lost the Film Case Before the WTO Dispute Settlement Panel*, 30 Law & Pol'y Int'l Bus. 417, 434 (1999).

33. See Cao, *Toward a Sensibility for International Economic Development*, 32 Tex. Int'l L. J. 209, 261 (1997).

34. See Id. at 213.

35. 97/816/EC: Commission Decision of 30 July 1997, 1997 OJ L 336, ¶ 113.

the merger but imposed conditions that would make it easier for Airbus to compete with Boeing. Boeing promised not to enforce exclusive dealing contracts it had with three major airlines and not to enter into any additional exclusive agreements until August 2007. Boeing also made several other commitments including licensing its patents for use by competitors, maintaining McDonnell Douglas (MD) as a separate legal entity for ten years to increase the likelihood that MD would become an attractive acquisition for a Boeing competitor, and granting the Commission access to Boeing's internal data to monitor compliance with the commitments.[36]

There is another example of the effect of globalization on antitrust enforcement. Some United States companies have found that they can get a remedy for harmful conduct of other U.S. companies from the European Commission more cheaply and faster than they can get help from the FTC. Santa Cruz Operation (SCO), a California software company, took over AT & T's UNIX business and thereby inherited a contractual obligation to pay Microsoft fifteen dollars for each program SCO sold whether or not SCO used Microsoft's technology. SCO no longer used the obsolete Microsoft technology and the payments were threatening to sink SCO. SCO complained to both the United States Justice Department and the European Commission and got a favorable preliminary ruling from the Commission before the Justice Department sent out subpoenas. To avoid the threat of heavy fines that the Commission could impose, Microsoft cancelled SCO's obligation.[37]

§ 12.4 Extraterritorial Application of Securities and Other Laws

United States courts have applied our federal securities laws to actions abroad that have substantial and foreseeable effects in the United States.[38] Sometimes, as demonstrated by *Consolidated Gold Fields PLC v. Minorco, S.A.*,[39] this extraterritorial enforcement is excessive.

Unlike United States antitrust law,[40] our federal securities laws may apply although conduct in the United States affects only foreign investors. There is, however, a circuit split as to how substantial the conduct

---

36. Id. ¶¶ 115–124.

37. See Clark, *Microsoft to Alter Contract To End Dispute With EU*, The Wall Street Journal Europe, Nov. 24, 1997, 1997 WL–WSJE 12216018.

38. See, e.g., Schoenbaum v. Firstbrook 405 F.2d 200, modified en banc, 405 F.2d 215 (2d Cir. 1968), cert. denied, 395 U.S. 906, 89 S.Ct. 1747, 23 L.Ed.2d 219 (1969) (finding sufficient effect in reduction in equity of U.S. holders of stock in Canadian corporation that was sold to foreign corporations at too low a price); Bersch v. Drexel Firestone, Inc., 519 F.2d 974, 997 (2d Cir.), cert. denied, 423 U.S. 1018, 96 S.Ct. 453, 46 L.Ed.2d 389 (1975) (in suit for fraud committed abroad in sale of stock of a Canadian corporation, court orders district court to "eliminate from the class action all purchasers other than persons who were residents or citizens of the United States").

39. 871 F.2d 252, modified, 890 F.2d 569 (2d Cir.), cert. dism'd, 492 U.S. 939, 110 S.Ct. 29, 106 L.Ed.2d 639 (1989) (discussed supra, text accompanying note 18).

40. See supra note 25.

in the United States must be. The D.C. and Second Circuits require that the conduct in the United States be sufficient in itself to violate our securities law.[41] Other circuits impose less strict requirements so long as the conduct in the United States is a cause of the losses in other countries.[42] With regard to purely domestic securities cases, *Central Bank of Denver v. First Interstate Bank of Denver*[43] held that a private plaintiff may not maintain an action under § 10(b) of the Securities Exchange Act of 1934 against a defendant alleged to be "secondarily liable under § 10(b) for its conduct in aiding and abetting the [other defendant's] fraud."[44] *Central Bank of Denver* supports the stricter D.C. and Second Circuit tests for extraterritorial jurisdiction.

Thus courts can base jurisdiction to apply United States securities law either on effects in the United States caused by acts abroad or by conduct in the United States that causes harm abroad. *Itoba, Ltd. v. Lep Group PLC*[45] analyzed jurisdiction to apply United States securities law under both the "conduct" and "effects" tests, stating: "an admixture or combination of the two often gives a better picture of whether there is sufficient United States involvement to justify exercise of jurisdiction by an American court."[46] *Leasco Data Processing Equipment Corp. v. Maxwell*[47] is an example of this "admixture." Leasco and its United Kingdom subsidiary alleged that the subsidiary was fraudulently induced to buy shares in a British company on the London Stock Exchange. Judge Friendly found that "it tips the scales in favor of applicability when substantial misrepresentations were made in the United States,"[48] although he expressed doubt that there would be jurisdiction based solely on the effects on the United States parent company "[i]f all the misrepresentations here alleged had occurred in England."[49]

Equal Employment Opportunity Commission v. Arabian American Oil Co.,[50] held that Title VII of the Civil Rights Act of 1964 does not apply extraterritorially to prohibit discrimination in Saudi Arabia against a United States citizen by a Delaware corporation. The majority

---

41. See Zoelsch v. Arthur Andersen & Co., 824 F.2d 27 (D.C. Cir. 1987); IIT v. Cornfeld, 619 F.2d 909 (2d Cir. 1980).

42. See Securities and Exchange Comm'n v. Kasser, 548 F.2d 109, 114 (3d Cir.), cert. denied, 431 U.S. 938, 97 S.Ct. 2649, 53 L.Ed.2d 255 (1977) ("at least some activity designed to further a fraudulent scheme occurs within this country"); Continental Grain (Australia) Pty. Ltd. v. Pacific Oilseeds, Inc., 592 F.2d 409, 421 (8th Cir. 1979) (conduct in U.S. "was in furtherance of a fraudulent scheme and was significant with respect to its accomplishment"); Grunenthal GmbH v. Hotz, 712 F.2d 421, 424 (9th Cir. 1983) (adopting "the tests used by the Third and Eighth Circuits").

43. 511 U.S. 164, 114 S.Ct. 1439, 128 L.Ed.2d 119 (1994).

44. Id. at 191, 114 S.Ct. at 1455, 128 L.Ed.2d at 141.

45. 54 F.3d 118 (2d Cir. 1995), cert. denied, 516 U.S. 1044, 116 S.Ct. 702, 133 L.Ed.2d 659 (1996)

46. Id. at 122.

47. 468 F.2d 1326 (2d Cir. 1972).

48. Id. at 1337.

49. Id. at 1334.

50. 499 U.S. 244, 111 S.Ct. 1227, 113 L.Ed.2d 274 (1991).

relied upon a canon of construction that "legislation of Congress, unless a contrary intent appears, is meant to apply only within the territorial jurisdiction of the United States." This is the same canon that Justice Holmes used in *American Banana Co. v. United Fruit Co.*[51] to deny extraterritorial application to U.S. antitrust laws. As the materials in section 12.1 indicate, this view with regard to antitrust has been long superseded under the "effects" basis for prescriptive jurisdiction. As *EEOC v. Aramco* indicates, the canon against extraterritorial statutory construction has been revived by the Supreme Court. Congress has already abrogated *EEOC v. Aramco* in the Civil Rights Act of 1991 by including in the definition of "employee," a U.S. citizen employed abroad.[52]

Smith v. United States[53] held that the Federal Tort Claims Act (FTCA) does not apply to tortious acts or omissions occurring in Antarctica. The Court construed several provisions of that Act to reach this result and also stated: "Lastly, the presumption against extraterritorial application of United States statutes requires that any lingering doubt regarding the reach of the FTCA be resolved against its encompassing torts committed in Antarctica."[54] *Sosa v. Alvarez–Machain*[55] held that the FTCA does not apply to injury abroad even though U.S. government agents in the U.S. ordered the injurious conduct, rejecting the so-called "headquarters doctrine" that lower courts had applied in numerous cases.

Several cases have refused to give extraterritorial effect to the Racketeer Influenced and Corrupt Organizations Act (RICO).[56] *Subafilms Ltd. v. MGM–Pathe Communications Co.*[57] held that the Copyright Act[58] does not apply extraterritorially. *Itar–Tass Russian News Agency v. Russian Kurier, Inc.*[59] developed a federal choice-of-law rule to determine what law applied to a claim by Russian plaintiffs that the defendant, a

51. 213 U.S. 347, 29 S.Ct. 511, 53 L.Ed. 826 (1909).

52. S. 1745, 102nd Cong., 1st Sess. § 109(a) (1991). See Michael Starr, *Who's the Boss? The Globalization of U.S. Employment Law*, 51 Bus. Law. 635 (1996).

53. 507 U.S. 197, 113 S.Ct. 1178, 122 L.Ed.2d 548 (1993).

54. Id. at 203–04, 113 S.Ct. at 1183, 122 L.Ed.2d at 555–56.

55. 542 U.S. 692, 124 S.Ct. 2739, 159 L.Ed.2d 718 (2004).

56. See North South Finance Corporation v. Al–Turki, 100 F.3d 1046 (2d Cir. 1996) (finding that the conduct alleged in the United States is insufficient to support subject matter jurisdiction under the civil penalties provisions of RICO); Butte Mining PLC v. Smith, 76 F.3d 287, 291 (9th Cir. 1996) (holding that under either conduct or effects tests there was no basis for a civil action under United States securities laws and "[o]nce the securities fraud claim was dismissed the ... RICO claims that related to this fraud had to be dismissed as well"); United States v. Vasquez–Velasco, 15 F.3d 833 (9th Cir. 1994) (holding that 18 U.S.C.A § 1959, which punishes violent crimes in aid of racketeering activity, as defined in § 1961, did not apply to the murders of two U.S. tourists in Mexico who were killed to maintain and increase defendant's position in a drug trafficking cartel). RICO is codified at 18 U.S.C. §§ 1961–68.

57. 24 F.3d 1088 (9th Cir.) (en banc), cert. denied, 513 U.S. 1001, 115 S.Ct. 512, 130 L.Ed.2d 419 (1994) (refusing to apply the Copyright Act to authorization within the United States of acts abroad and stating that the Act does not apply extraterritorially).

58. 17 U.S.C. §§ 106–120.

59. 153 F.3d 82 (2d Cir. 1998).

newspaper published in the U.S., had violated copyrights by copying articles that the plaintiffs had published in Russia. For the issue of copyright ownership, the court adopted a "most significant relationship" analysis modeled on the Restatement (Second) of Conflict of Laws. The court held that "[s]ince the works at issue were created by Russian nationals and first published in Russia, Russian law is the appropriate source of law to determine issues of ownership rights."[60] U.S. law, which "permits suit only by owners of 'an exclusive right under a copyright,' "[61] then controlled whether plaintiffs had standing to sue after their ownership rights were determined under Russian law. The court then held that the law of the U.S., as the place of the tort and the place of incorporation of the defendant publication governed whether the defendants infringed plaintiffs' copyrights in the U.S. and, if so, what remedies are available.[62]

35 U.S.C. § 271(f) states:

(1) Whoever without authority supplies or causes to be supplied in or from the United States all or a substantial portion of the components of a patented invention, where such components are uncombined in whole or in part, in such manner as to actively induce the combination of such components outside of the United States in a manner that would infringe the patent if such combination occurred within the United States, shall be liable as an infringer.

(2) Whoever without authority supplies or causes to be supplied in or from the United States any component of a patented invention that is especially made or especially adapted for use in the invention and not a staple article or commodity of commerce suitable for substantial noninfringing use, where such component is uncombined in whole or in part, knowing that such component is so made or adapt and intending that such component will be combined outside of the United States in a manner that would infringe the patent if such combination occurred within the United States, shall be liable as an infringer.

Congress passed this legislation in reaction to *Deepsouth Packing Co. v. Laitram.*[63] *Deepsouth* held that a defendant who shipped abroad an unassembled machine patented by the plaintiff was not liable for patent infringement because "it is not an infringement to make or use a patented product outside of the United States."[64]

In *Microsoft Corp. v. AT & T Corp.*[65] the Supreme Court held 271(f) does not apply when the defendant sent the plaintiff's patented comput-

---

60. Id. at 90.

61. Id. at 92 (quoting 17 U.S.C. § 501(b)).

62. Id. at 91. For criticism of *Itar–Tass* see Dinwoodie, *International Intellectual Property Litigation: A Vehicle for Resurgent Comparativist Thought?*, 49 Am. J. Comp. L. 429, 439–40 (2001).

63. 406 U.S. 518, 92 S.Ct. 1700, 32 L.Ed.2d 273 (1972).

64. Id. at 527, 92 S.Ct. at 1706.

65. 550 U.S. 437, 127 S.Ct. 1746, 167 L.Ed.2d 737 (2007).

er software from the United States to a foreign computer manufacturer on a master disk, or by electronic transmission, and then the foreign manufacturer copied the software for installation on computers made and sold abroad:

> The master disk or electronic transmission Microsoft sends from the United States is never installed on any of the foreign-made computers in question. Instead, copies made abroad are used for installation. Because Microsoft does not export from the United States the copies actually installed, it does not "suppl[y] ... from the United States" "components" of the relevant computers, and therefore is not liable under § 271(f) as currently written.[66]

In *Cardiac Pacemakers, Inc. v. St. Jude Medical, Inc.,*[67] the Federal Circuit, en banc, held that 271(f) does not apply to method patents. A method patent protects a process, or series of steps or acts, for performing a function or accomplishing a result.

Contrasted with refusal to apply the Copyright Act extraterritorially, except for narrowly construed 35 U.S.C. § 271(f), courts have applied the Lanham Trademark Act to events abroad that have a substantial effect on U.S. commerce.[68]

Kollias v. D & G Marine Maintenance[69] held that the Longshore and Harbor Workers' Compensation Act applied to longshore workers injured while working on vessels on the high seas because "the LHWCA contains a sufficiently clear indication of Congressional intent to apply the statute extraterritorially."[70]

Spector v. Norwegian Cruise Line Ltd.[71] held that Title III of the Americans with Disabilities Act applies to foreign-flag cruise ships departing from and returning to U.S. ports. The Act prohibits discrimination based on disability in places of public accommodation and in public transportation services. It further requires covered entities to make reasonable modifications in practices to accommodate disabled persons

---

66. Id. at 442, 127 S.Ct. 1751.

67. 576 F.3d 1348 (Fed. Cir. 2009).

68. See Totalplan Corp. of America v. Colborne, 14 F.3d 824 (2d Cir. 1994) (refusing to apply the Lanham Act extraterritorially, finding that affixing trademarks to cameras in the United States for sale in Japan by alien defendants had no substantial effect on U.S. commerce); Sterling Drug, Inc. v. Bayer AG, 14 F.3d 733, 745–46 (2d Cir. 1994) (vacating the extraterritorial provisions of the district court's injunction of defendant's activities and remanding for reconsideration under the following factors: "(1) whether the defendant's conduct has a substantial effect on United States Commerce; (2)whether the defendant is a citizen of the United States; and (3) whether there exists a conflict between defendant's trademark rights established under foreign law, and plaintiff's trademark rights established under domestic law"). See Dabney, *On The Territorial Reach of the Lanham Act*, 83 Trademark Rep. 465 (1993).

69. 29 F.3d 67 (2d Cir. 1994), cert. denied, 513 U.S. 1146, 115 S.Ct. 1092, 130 L.Ed.2d 1061 (1995).

70. Id. at 73.

71. 545 U.S. 119, 125 S.Ct. 2169, 162 L.Ed.2d 97 (2005). See Symeonides, *Cruising in American Waters: Spector, Maritime Conflicts, and Choice of Law*, 37 J. Mar. L. & Com. 491 (2006).

and to remove structural barriers when such removal is readily achievable.

Another basis for jurisdiction to prescribe is "universal jurisdiction." This jurisdiction extends to punishment of offenses internationally recognized as concerning all states. The classic example is piracy.[72]

§ 12.5   The Act of State Doctrine

In *Banco Nacional de Cuba v. Sabbatino*,[73] Justice Harlan states: "The act of state doctrine in its traditional formulation precludes the courts of this country from inquiring into the validity of the public acts of a recognized foreign sovereign power committed within its own territory."[74] *Sabbatino* adjudicated the conflicting claims of the original owners of a Cuban sugar factory and the Cuban government to the sale proceeds of sugar that had been produced at the factory. The Cuban government had expropriated the factory without meaningful compensation along with other enterprises in which American nationals had an interest. *Sabbatino* held that the act of state doctrine prevented United States courts from questioning the legality of the Cuban expropriation, reversed lower court judgments for the former owners, and remanded the case.

The Court noted two variables that affected application of the doctrine—the extent to which the action of the foreign government clearly violates international law and the importance of foreign relations between the United States and the foreign sovereign whose acts are in question.[75] Applying these two variables, the Court held that the doctrine applied. There was no consensus that expropriation without compensation violated international law.[76] The State Department did not give the Court the green light to pass on the validity of Cuba's actions but indicated the delicacy of the situation by stating that it did not wish "to make any statement bearing on this litigation."[77]

Previously the Court had justified the act of state doctrine as necessary so that a court decision would not "imperil the amicable relations between governments and vex the peace of nations."[78] Justice Harlan gave pragmatic reasons for the doctrine. Courts would only rarely have an opportunity to adjudicate the validity of the acts within its own territory of a foreign sovereign. In *Sabbatino* itself, the only

---

72. See United States v. Shi, 525 F.3d 709 (9th Cir. 2008) (affirming conviction of Chinese defendant who forcibly seized control of a Taiwanese vessel registered in the Seychelles and killed crew members); United States v. Yunis, 924 F.2d 1086 (D.C. Cir. 1991) (affirming conviction of person who hijacked a Jordanian airplane in Beirut on which two Americans were passengers).

73. 376 U.S. 398, 84 S.Ct. 923, 11 L.Ed.2d 804 (1964).

74. Id. at 401, 84 S.Ct. at 926, 11 L.Ed.2d at 808.

75. Id. at 428, 84 S.Ct. at 940, 11 L.Ed.2d at 823.

76. Id. at 428–30, 84 S.Ct. at 940–41, 11 L.Ed.2d at 824–25.

77. Id. at 420, 84 S.Ct. at 936, 11 L.Ed.2d at 819.

78. Oetjen v. Central Leather Co., 246 U.S. 297, 304, 38 S.Ct. 309, 311, 62 L.Ed. 726, 736 (1918).

reason the proceeds of the sugar sale were within the Court's jurisdiction
was because Cuba's agent in the United States had blundered and
allowed a United States commodity broker to obtain possession of the
title documents to the sugar before making full payment, as the broker
had contracted to do. The executive and Congress are far better able
than the courts to obtain a remedy against the acts of foreign sovereigns.
The executive can negotiate at the highest diplomatic level. The executive and Congress can impose trade sanctions and wage war. Moreover,
not only is court action likely to be ineffective, it may make diplomatic
negotiations more difficult. If the court rules that the foreign country
acted legally, the judgment will undermine our bargaining position. If a
United States court finds that the act was illegal, the decision is likely to
be read as a parochial advancing of American interests and make the
foreign country more reluctant to negotiate.[79]

In view of the State Department's position that it did not wish to
comment on the case, the Court found it unnecessary to pass upon the
validity of the *"Bernstein* exception" to the act of state doctrine.[80] Under
this exception, the act of state doctrine does not apply if the executive
states that the court is free to adjudicate the validity of the acts of the
foreign sovereign. The Court did reject a reverse *Bernstein* exception
under which a court is free to proceed unless the executive requests the
court to desist.[81]

Justice Harlan stated that neither international law nor the Constitution required the act of state doctrine,[82] although the doctrine did have
" 'constitutional' underpinnings."[83] Thus, in the light of Harlan's pragmatic justification of the doctrine,[84] it is best understood as a judge-made
rule of abstention in matters better left to other departments of government. Moreover, although New York, where the suit in *Sabbatino* was
brought, had an "act of state doctrine in terms that echo those of federal
decisions,"[85] Harlan felt "constrained to make it clear" that state courts
were not free to apply a less restrictive act of state doctrine than that set
out in *Sabbatino*.[86]

When the Court announced the opinion in *Sabbatino* it appeared
that Cuba had won and would receive the proceeds of the sale of sugar.
Then the political animal reared its head. In 1964 the "Hickenlooper"

---

79. *Sabbatino,* 376 U.S. at 427–37, 84 S.Ct. at 940–45, 11 L.Ed.2d at 823–28.

80. Id. at 420, 84 S.Ct. at 936, 11 L.Ed.2d at 819. The doctrine is named for Bernstein
v. N. V. Nederlandsche–Amerikaansche Stoomvaart–Maatschappij, 173 F.2d 71 (2d Cir.
1949), amended, 210 F.2d 375 (2d Cir. 1954), which permitted evidence of the invalidity of
the acts of the Nazi government after the court received a letter from the Acting Legal
Adviser to the State Department, relieving the court of any constraint on its jurisdiction to
determine the matter.

81. *Sabbatino,* 376 U.S. at 436, 84 S.Ct. at 944, 11 L.Ed.2d at 828.

82. Id. at 421–23, 84 S.Ct. at 937–38, 11 L.Ed.2d at 820–21.

83. Id. at 421–23, 84 S.Ct. at 938, 11 L.Ed.2d at 821.

84. See supra text accompanying notes 78–79.

85. *Sabbatino,* 376 U.S. at 424, 84 S.Ct. at 938, 11 L.Ed.2d at 821.

86. Id. at 425, 84 S.Ct. at 939, 11 L.Ed.2d at 822.

amendment[87] to the Foreign Relations Act declared expropriation without compensation a violation of international law and stated: "no court in the United States shall decline on the ground of the federal act of state doctrine to make a determination on the merits giving effect to the principles of international law in a case in which a claim of title or other right to property is asserted by a party including a foreign state (or a party claiming through such state) based upon (or traced through) a confiscation or other taking after January 1, 1959, by an act of that state in violation of the principles of international law ..."[88] On remand of *Sabbatino*, the Second Circuit found the Hickenlooper amendment retroactive and constitutional and dismissed Cuba's complaint.[89]

Other acts of Congress enable any United States national who owned property confiscated by Cuba to sue anyone who "traffics" in the property, which includes purchasing the property.[90] The legislation forbids any United States court from using the act of state doctrine as a reason for declining to entertain such an action. As authorized by the legislation, the President has suspended the right to sue. As a result of this legislation, the European Union has brought a complaint against the United States before the World Trade Organization and Canada has enacted legislation punishing Canadian companies, including subsidiaries of U.S. companies, that refuse to trade with Cuba in compliance with the act.

When a controversy involves intangible property, some courts, when applying the act of state doctrine, have made their decision turn on whether the situs of the property was in the foreign country so that it could be said that the sovereign acted within its own territory. *Allied Bank International v. Banco Credito Agricola de Cartago*[91] held that the doctrine did not prevent a United States bank from recovering from banks wholly owned by Costa Rica despite the fact that Costa Rica had issued regulations suspending all external debt payments. The court held that the doctrine did not apply because the situs of the debt was in the United States. The situs was in the United States because Costa Rica could not effectively complete the taking within its own borders and because of the United States interest in having the rights of the parties determined under recognized principles of contract law.[92]

---

87. Sometimes referred to as the "second Hickenlooper amendment" to distinguish it from a previous amendment sponsored by Senator Hickenlooper suspending assistance to any country that expropriates property of United States citizens and does not make speedy compensation.

88. 22 U.S.C. § 2370(e)(2).

89. Banco Nacional de Cuba v. Farr, 383 F.2d 166 (2d Cir. 1967), cert. denied, 390 U.S. 956, 88 S.Ct. 1038, 19 L.Ed.2d 1151 (1968).

90. The Cuban Liberty and Democratic Solidarity (Libertad) Act of 1996 (Helms–Burton Act), PL 104–114, 110 Stat 785, reprinted in Note following 22 U.S.C. § 6021, amends the Cuban Democracy Act of 1992. PL 202–484, reprinted in Note following 22 U.S.C. § 6001.

91. 757 F.2d 516 (2d Cir.), cert. dismissed, 473 U.S. 934, 106 S.Ct. 30, 87 L.Ed.2d 706 (1985).

92. Id. at 521–22.

The Seventh Circuit took a less metaphysical approach in *F. & H.R. Farman–Farmaian Consulting Engineers Firm v. Harza Engineering Co.*[93] A United States company performed work in Iran before the revolution. The Iran–United States Claims Tribunal ordered the successor regime to pay the company for this work. The owners of an expropriated Iranian company sued the United States company claiming that the expropriated company had not been paid for consulting work done for the United States company and that the Tribunal award included payment for this consulting work. The court held that the act of state doctrine bars the claim, stating:

> [T]o describe the Consulting Firm's claim for payment of [the United States company's] debt to it as an asset located in Iran, as we have done, may be thought to beg the question. A debt (like a word, a number, an idea) has no space-time location; it is not a physical object, and efforts to treat it as such ... seem bound to fail.... What is at issue in this case is not the rights or interests of an American company ... but the propriety of dealings between the Iranian government and an Iranian corporation. With the American interest so attenuated, considerations of comity ... come to the fore; and it is those considerations and the resulting concern with the judiciary's stepping on the State Department's toes, that inform the modern understanding of the act of state doctrine.[94]

§ 12.6   Protection of Investments in Foreign Countries

An abrogation of the act of state doctrine that is less controversial than the Hickenlooper Amendment[95] is a provision of the Federal Arbitration Act (FAA): "Enforcement of arbitration agreements, confirmation of arbitral awards, and execution upon judgments based on orders confirming such awards shall not be refused on the basis of the Act of State Doctrine."[96] When a company invests in a foreign country, that company needs a fair and effective means of resolving disputes with the foreign country. For example, suppose a U.S. company builds a factory in country X. There is a regime change in X and the new X government expropriates the factory and terminates the agreement that the preceding government had made with the U.S. company. The FAA provision quoted above lessens the need for using the conciliation and arbitration procedures of the Convention on the Settlement of Investment Disputes between States and Nationals of Other States.[97] One of the problems with these procedures is that if either party appeals an arbitration award, the Chairman of the Administrative Council of the International Center for Settlement of Investment Disputes (ICSID), established by

93.   882 F.2d 281 (7th Cir. 1989), cert. denied, 497 U.S. 1038, 110 S.Ct. 3301, 111 L.Ed.2d 809 (1990).

94.   Id. at 286–87.

95.   See supra text accompanying notes 87–88.

96.   9 U.S.C. § 15.

97.   Opened for signature Aug. 27, 1965, 17 UST 1270, TIAS 6090, 575 U.N.T.S. 159, reprinted in 4 I.L.M 532 (1965).

the Convention, appoints a committee of three persons, which has the power to annul the award in whole or in part.[98] The parties have no control over the membership of the review committee.

There are countervailing factors that make ICSID arbitration attractive. ICSID is a division of the World Bank and the Convention establishing ICSID requires signatories to enforce ICSID arbitral awards. "Consequently there is a certain coercive effect against governments that [is] not necessarily there with the UNCITRAL [United Nations Commission on International Trade Law] ad hoc arbitration [under the UNCITRAL Arbitration Rules]."[99] Moreover, investors may take out insurance against political risks such as expropriation. "There is typically an arbitration clause in a political risk insurance policy, so that even if you cannot get to an arbitration with the foreign government, you can often get to an arbitration with your political risk insurance company."[100] Perhaps "the principal advantage of ICSID arbitration [is that] the ICSID Convention provides a self-contained process for the resolution of investment disputes, exclusive of other remedies and without a right to appeal the award to a national court."[101]

Another increasingly used method of resolving investment disputes with a foreign country is the procedure included in a bilateral investment treaty. Many developing countries are entering into bilateral investment treaties with countries from which they wish to attract foreign direct investment. These treaties typically protect the investor against government actions such as expropriation and provide a method of resolving investment disputes.[102]

In addition to insurance provided by some private insurance companies, one of the primary functions of the Overseas Private Investment Corporation (OPIC), a U.S. government agency, is to provide political risk insurance for U.S. companies and foreign companies beneficially

---

98. Id. art. 52(3). Art 52(1) limits the grounds on which the Committee may annul the award to "that the Tribunal was not properly constituted; that the Tribunal has manifestly exceeded it powers; that there was corruption on the part of a member of the Tribunal; that there has been a serious departure from a fundamental rule of procedure; or that the award has failed to state the reasons on which it is based."

99. Doak Bishop, *Energy and International Law: Development, Litigation, and Regulation*, 36 Texas Int'l L. J. 1, 3 (2001).

100. Id. at 5.

101. Bowman, *Dispute Resolution Planning for the Oil and Gas Industry*, 17 ICSID Rev.—Foreign Investment L. J. 332, 367 (2002). See also 22 U.S.C. § 1650a:

(a) Treaty rights; enforcement; full faith and credit; nonapplication of Federal Arbitration Act: An award of an arbitral tribunal rendered pursuant to chapter IV of the [ICSID] convention shall create a right arising under a treaty of the United States. The pecuniary obligations imposed by such an award shall be enforced and shall be given the same full faith and credit as if the award were a final judgment of a court of general jurisdiction of one of the several States. The Federal Arbitration Act (9 U.S.C. 1 et seq.) shall not apply to enforcement of awards rendered pursuant to the convention.

(b) Jurisdiction; amount in controversy: The district courts of the United States . . . shall have exclusive jurisdiction over actions and proceedings under subsection (a) of this section, regardless of the amount in controversy.

102. See Lee, *Bilateralism under the World Trade Organization*, 26 Nw. J. Int'l L. & Bus. 357, 368 (2006).

owned by U.S. citizens. OPIC insurance covers the risks that a company doing business abroad (1) will not be able to transfer money out of the foreign country; (2) will have its property abroad expropriated; (3) will suffer losses because of revolution or other political violence abroad.[103]

§ 12.7   State Legislation Interfering with Foreign Relations

The Supreme Court has held that some state legislation unconstitutionally interferes with the foreign relations power of the executive and Congress. *Zschernig v. Miller*[104] struck down an Oregon reciprocity statute as it was applied to block the inheritance of an East German citizen. The court assumed that Oregon could properly condition a foreign citizen's right to inherit Oregon property on a reciprocal right of a United States citizen to take property in the foreign country.[105] The court, however, found unconstitutional as applied Oregon's requirement that the foreign heirs receive the proceeds of Oregon estates "without confiscation," which resulted in Oregon courts undertaking a detailed criticism of the authoritarian nature of the East German government.[106] The opinion concludes:

> Where [state] laws conflict with a treaty, they must bow to the superior federal policy. Yet, even in absence of a treaty, a State's policy may disturb foreign relations. . . . Certainly a State could not deny admission to a traveler from East Germany nor bar its citizens from going there. If there are to be such restraints, they must be provided by the Federal Government. The present Oregon law is not as gross an intrusion in the federal domain as those others might be. Yet, as we have said, it has a direct impact upon foreign relations and may well adversely affect the power of the central government to deal with those problems.[107]

American Insurance Assoc. v. Garamendi[108] struck down a California statute that required any insurer doing business in the state to disclose information concerning all policies sold in Europe between 1920 and 1945 by the company or by any company "related" to it. The Supreme Court held, 5–4, that the statute interfered "with the National Government's conduct of foreign relations" and was therefore "preempted."[109] The President had made executive agreements that when a plaintiff sued a German company in a U.S. court on a Holocaust-era claim, the U.S.

---

103.   For legislation establishing and regulating OPIC see 22 U.S.C. §§ 2191–2200b.

104.   389 U.S. 429, 88 S.Ct. 664, 19 L.Ed.2d 683 (1968).

105.   Id. at 432, 88 S.Ct. at 666, 19 L.Ed.2d at 687–88 (stating that "a general reciprocity clause [does] not on its face intrude on the federal domain") (citing Clark v. Allen, 331 U.S. 503, 67 S.Ct. 1431, 91 L.Ed. 1633 (1947)).

106.   *Zschernig*, 389 U.S. at 435, 88 S.Ct. at 668, 19 L.Ed.2d at 689.

107.   Id. at 441, 88 S.Ct. at 671, 19 L.Ed.2d at 692 (citations omitted). See also Movsesian v. Victoria Versicherung AG, 578 F.3d 1052 (9th Cir. 2009) (a California statute giving California courts jurisdiction over claims arising out of insurance policies issued to "Armenian Genocide" victims and extending the statute of limitations is preempted by the presidential foreign policy against recognition of Armenian Genocide).

108.   539 U.S. 396, 123 S.Ct. 2374, 156 L.Ed.2d 376 (2003).

109.   539 U.S. at 401, 123 S.Ct. at 2379.

would submit a statement that it is in the foreign policy interests of the U.S. that a German Foundation be the exclusive forum and remedy for such claims. The Foundation is funded with 10 billion Deutsch marks contributed equally by the German Government and German companies.

The majority opinion, by Justice Souter, commented on *Zschernig v. Miller*.[110] Souter noted that the *Zschernig* majority held that "state action with more than incidental effect on foreign affairs is preempted, even absent any affirmative federal activity in the subject area of the state law, and hence without any showing of conflict."[111] Justice Harlan, however, concurring in the result in *Zschernig*, stated that in the absence of federal action "the States may legislate in areas of their traditional competence even though their statutes may have an incidental effect on foreign relations."[112] Justice Souter found it unnecessary to choose between the *Zschernig* majority's "field" and Justice Harlan's "conflict" views because "even on Justice Harlan's view" it was likely that the California statute "will produce something more than incidental effect in conflict with express foreign policy of the National Government."[113]

Crosby v. National Foreign Trade Council[114] struck down under the Supremacy Clause[115] a Massachusetts statute barring state entities from buying goods or services from companies doing business with Myanmar (formerly Burma). After the Massachusetts legislature had acted, the federal Congress passed legislation imposing sanctions on Myanmar but authorizing the President to terminate the sanctions or to impose new sanctions in the light of events in Myanmar affecting human rights and democracy. The Court found that the Massachusetts statute improperly conflicted with Congress' delegation to the President of discretion to control economic sanctions against Myanmar and with the President's authority to work with other nations to develop a multilateral strategy concerning that country. Moreover, the Massachusetts act imposed sanctions on acts and persons, including foreign companies, that are not affected by the federal legislation.

Article 36 of the Vienna Convention on Consular Relations[116] provides that that when a foreign national is arrested, the arrested person shall be informed "without delay" of the prisoner's right to communicate with consular officials of his or her home country. The U.S. and Mexico are parties to this Convention. In *Case Concerning Avena and*

---

110. See supra notes 104–107 and accompanying text.

111. *Garamendi*, 539 U.S. at 418, 123 S.Ct. at 2388.

112. *Zschernig*, 389 U.S. at 459, 88 S.Ct. at 664.

113. *Garamendi*, 539 U.S. at 420, 123 S.Ct. at 2389.

114. 530 U.S. 363, 120 S.Ct. 2288, 147 L.Ed.2d 352 (2000).

115. U.S. Const. Art. VI, cl. 2: "This Constitution, and the Laws of the United States which shall be made in Pursuance thereof; and all Treaties made, or which shall be made, under the Authority of the United States, shall be the supreme Law of the Land; and the Judges in every State shall be bound thereby, any Thing in the Constitution or Laws of any State to the Contrary notwithstanding."

116. April 24, 1963, 21 U.S.T. 77, 596 U.N.T.S. 261 (ratified by the U.S. Nov. 24, 1969).

other Mexican Nationals (Mexico v. U.S.),[117] the International Court of Justice held that the U.S. had violated article 36 when Mexican nationals were arrested and convicted without being informed of their right to communicate with Mexican consular officials. The I.C.J. further ruled that the U.S. "shall allow the review and reconsideration of the conviction and sentence by taking account of the violation." U.S. President George W. Bush then issued a Memorandum to the U.S. Attorney General stating that state courts would give effect to the *Avena* decision. Previously *Sanchez–Llamas v. Oregon*[118] had held that (1) violation of the Convention does not require excluding evidence obtained after the violation;[119] (2) claims for violation of the Convention were subject to the same procedural default rules that apply to other federal law claims.[120]

Jose Ernesto Medellin, a Mexican national, was arrested by Texas police, tried, convicted, and sentenced to death without being informed of his right to contact Mexican consular officials. After affirmance of his conviction and sentence and denial of his applications for writs of habeas corpus, Medellin again filed an application for the writ in a Texas court. A Texas rule permits granting such an application only if the factual or legal basis for the review was previously unavailable. In *Ex Parte Medellin*[121] the Texas Court of Criminal Appeals held that (1) *Avena* is not binding federal law and does not preempt the Texas rule that precludes review in this case; (2) "the President has exceeded his constitutional power by intruding into the independent power of the judiciary."[122]

The Supreme Court affirmed on the grounds that neither the *Avena* decision of the I.C.J nor the President's memorandum was enforceable to pre-empt state limitations on the filing of habeas petitions.[123] On July 16, 2008, the I.C.J. ordered the U.S. to "take all measures necessary to ensure that [Medellin and 4 other Mexican nationals on death row in Texas] are not executed pending judgment on the Request for interpretation [of the *Avena* decision] submitted by the United Mexican States, unless and until these five Mexican nationals receive review and reconsideration consistent with [the *Avena* decision]."[124] President George W. Bush stated that the I.C.J. did not have jurisdiction. He had previously announced that the United States withdrew from the Optional Protocol to the Vienna Convention on Consular Relations, in which the U.S. had agreed to the compulsory jurisdiction of the I.C.J. to resolve disputes

---

117.   2004 I.C.J. No. 128 (Judgment of March 31, 2004).

118.   548 U.S. 331, 126 S.Ct. 2669, 165 L.Ed.2d 557 (2006).

119.   Id. at 350, 126 S.Ct. at 2682.

120.   Id. at 358, 126 S.Ct. at 2687.

121.   223 S.W.3d 315 (Tex.Crim.App. 2006).

122.   Id. at 335.

123.   Medellin v. Texas, 552 U.S. 491, 128 S.Ct. 1346, 170 L.Ed.2d 190 (2008).

124.   Request for Interpretation of the Judgment of 31 March 2004 in the Case Concerning *Avena and other Mexican Nations*, 16 July 2008 (available at the web site of the International Court of Justice (www.icj.cij.org)).

arising out of the interpretation or application of the Vienna Convention. On August 5, 2008, Texas executed Medellin.

In contrast to U.S. courts, the Federal Constitutional Court of Germany held that failure to give the notice required by the Vienna Convention on Consular Relations violates the right to a fair trial guaranteed by the German Constitution. The court ordered the Federal Court of Justice to treat the Convention violation as relevant to criminal proceedings and to reconsider the legal consequences of the violation.[125]

There is disagreement among the federal circuits as to whether an alien may sue the officials who failed to inform him or her of their Vienna Convention rights. *Gandara v. Bennett*[126], *Cornejo v. County of San Diego*,[127] and *Mora v. People of the State of New York*[128] held that an alien who is not given the notice required by the Vienna Convention on Consular Relations cannot sue the officials who violated the Convention for violation of the alien's civil rights.

Jogi v. Voges,[129] however, held than an Indian citizen, who was prosecuted and imprisoned in the U.S., may sue Illinois law enforcement officials under 42 U.S.C. § 1983 for failing to inform him of his Convention right to notify his consulate of his arrest. The plaintiff is suing for compensatory and punitive damages. 42 U.S.C § 1983 provides: "Every person who, under color of any statute, ordinance, regulation, custom, or usage, of any State or Territory or the District of Columbia, subjects, or causes to be subjected, any citizen of the United States or other person within the jurisdiction thereof to the deprivation of any rights, privileges, or immunities secured by the Constitution and laws, shall be liable to the party injured in an action at law, suit in equity, or other proper proceeding for redress * * *." *Osagiede v. United States*[130] held that an a Nigerian national, who pleaded guilty after he was not informed of his Vienna Convention rights, was entitled to an evidentiary hearing as to whether he was deprived of effective assistance of counsel in violation of the Sixth Amendment of the U.S. Constitution because that failure prejudiced him.

125. Case No. 2BvR2115/01, 60 Neue Juristische Wochenschrift 499 (2007).

126. 528 F.3d 823 (11th Cir. 2008).

127. 504 F.3d 853 (9th Cir. 2007).

128. 524 F.3d 183 (2d Cir. 2008).

129. 480 F.3d 822 (7th Cir. 2007).

130. 543 F.3d 399 (7th Cir. 2008).

TABLE OF CASES

References are to Pages.

First Sav. and Loan Ass'n of Central Indiana v. Furnish, 174 Ind.App. 265, 367 N.E.2d 596 (Ind.App. 2 Dist.1977), 146

Firth v. State, 98 N.Y.2d 365, 747 N.Y.S.2d 69, 775 N.E.2d 463 (N.Y.2002), 484, 487

Fischl v. Chubb, 30 Pa. D. & C. 40 (Pa.Com. Pl.1937), 424, 679

Fiser v. Dell Computer Corporation, 144 N.M. 464, 188 P.3d 1215 (N.M.2008), 518

Fisher v. Albany Mach. & Supply Co., 261 La. 747, 260 So.2d 691 (La.1972), 250

Fisher v. Fielding, 67 Conn. 91, 34 A. 714 (Conn.1895), 224

Fisher v. Huck, 50 Or.App. 635, 624 P.2d 177 (Or.App.1981), 464

Fisher Governor Co. v. Superior Court of City and County of San Francisco, 53 Cal.2d 222, 1 Cal.Rptr. 1, 347 P.2d 1 (Cal.1959), 238

Fisk v. Royal Caribbean Cruises, Ltd., 141 Idaho 290, 108 P.3d 990 (Idaho 2005), 319

Fitch v. Huntington, 125 Wis. 204, 102 N.W. 1066 (Wis.1905), 272

Fitzpatrick v. International Ry. Co., 252 N.Y. 127, 169 N.E. 112 (N.Y.1929), 63

Fitzsimmons v. Barton, 589 F.2d 330 (7th Cir.1979), 158

Fitzsimmons v. Johnson, 90 Tenn. 416, 17 S.W. 100 (Tenn.1891), 154

Flagg Bros., Inc. v. Brooks, 436 U.S. 149, 98 S.Ct. 1729, 56 L.Ed.2d 185 (1978), 141

Fleet Leasing, Inc. v. District Court In and For City and County of Denver, 649 P.2d 1074 (Colo.1982), 252

Fleet Messenger Service, Inc. v. Life Ins. Co. of North America, 315 F.2d 593 (2nd Cir.1963), 530

Fleet Transport Co. v. Insurance Co. of North America, 340 F.Supp. 158 (M.D.Ala.1972), 702

Fleury v. Harper & Row, Publishers, Inc., 698 F.2d 1022 (9th Cir.1983), 485

Flexner v. Farson, 248 U.S. 289, 39 S.Ct. 97, 63 L.Ed. 250 (1919), 233

Flieger, People ex rel. Mangold v., 106 Ill.2d 546, 88 Ill.Dec. 640, 478 N.E.2d 1366 (Ill.1985), 166

Flogel v. Flogel, 257 Iowa 547, 133 N.W.2d 907 (Iowa 1965), 408

Florance's Will, In re, 27 N.Y.St.Rep. 312, 7 N.Y.S. 578 (N.Y.Sup.Gen.Term 1889), 24

Florida Bd. of Regents of Dept. of Ed., Division of Universities v. Harris, 338 So.2d 215 (Fla.App. 1 Dist.1976), 18, 28

Flowers v. Carville, 310 F.3d 1118 (9th Cir. 2002), 70

Fluke Corp. v. Hartford Acc. & Indem. Co., 145 Wash.2d 137, 34 P.3d 809 (Wash. 2001), 547

Flynn, In re, [1968] 1 All E.R. 49, [1968] 1 W.L.R. 108 (Ch.Div.1967), 33

Folk v. York–Shipley, Inc., 239 A.2d 236 (Del.Supr.1968), 51, 106, 402, 410

Follenfant v. Rogers, 359 F.2d 30 (5th Cir. 1966), 739

Follette v. Vitanza, 658 F.Supp. 492 (N.D.N.Y.1987), 156

Fontanetta v. American Bd. of Internal Medicine, 303 F.Supp. 427 (E.D.N.Y. 1969), 234

Ford v. Ford, 80 Mich. 42, 44 N.W. 1057 (Mich.1890), 602

Ford v. Newman, 77 Ill.2d 335, 33 Ill.Dec. 150, 396 N.E.2d 539 (Ill.1979), 613

Ford Motor Co. v. Atwood Vacuum Mach. Co., 392 So.2d 1305 (Fla.1981), 250

Ford Motor Co. v. Leggat, 904 S.W.2d 643 (Tex.1995), 84

Ford Motor Co. v. National Bond & Investment Co., 294 Ill.App. 585, 14 N.E.2d 306 (Ill.App. 1 Dist.1938), 644

Ford Motor Credit Co. v. Partee, 514 So.2d 640 (La.App. 2 Cir.1987), 645

Foreman v. George Foreman Associates, Ltd., 517 F.2d 354 (9th Cir.1975), 522

Forgan v. Bainbridge, 34 Ariz. 408, 274 P. 155 (Ariz.1928), 644, 645, 646

Forlenza, In re, 140 S.W.3d 373 (Tex.2004), 382

Forsman v. Forsman, 779 P.2d 218 (Utah 1989), 439

Foster v. Leggett, 484 S.W.2d 827 (Ky. 1972), 454

Foster v. Maldonado, 315 F.Supp. 1179 (D.N.J.1970), 466

Foster v. United States, 768 F.2d 1278 (11th Cir.1985), 473

Fourie v. Minister of Home Affairs, Case no. 232/2003 ¶ 49 (S.A. Const. Ct. 2005), 342

Fourth Northwestern Nat. Bank of Minneapolis v. Hilson Industries, Inc., 264 Minn. 110, 117 N.W.2d 732 (Minn.1962), 231, 261

Fowler v. Fowler, 191 Mich.App. 318, 477 N.W.2d 112 (Mich.App.1991), 20

Fox v. Board of Sup'rs of Louisiana State University and Agr. and Mechanical College, 576 So.2d 978 (La.1991), 304

Fox v. Fox, 103 N.M. 155, 703 P.2d 932 (N.M.App.1985), 166

Fox v. Fox, 526 S.W.2d 180 (Tex.Civ.App.-Dallas 1975), 364

Fox v. Morrison Motor Freight, Inc., 25 Ohio St.2d 193, 267 N.E.2d 405 (Ohio 1971), 121, 439, 660

Foye v. Consolidated Baling Mach. Co., 229 A.2d 196 (Me.1967), 247, 248, 250

Frame v. Merrill Lynch, Pierce, Fenner & Smith, Inc., 20 Cal.App.3d 668, 97 Cal. Rptr. 811 (Cal.App. 1 Dist.1971), 118, 518

Frances Hosiery Mills, Inc. v. Burlington Industries, Inc., 285 N.C. 344, 204 S.E.2d 834 (N.C.1974), 229

INDEX

References are to Pages

†